THE CAMBRIDGE HISTORY OF AFRICA

Volume 4
from *c.* 1600 to *c.* 1790

edited by
RICHARD GRAY

CAMBRIDGE UNIVERSITY PRESS
CAMBRIDGE
LONDON · NEW YORK · MELBOURNE

Published by the Syndics of the Cambridge University Press
The Pitt Building, Trumpington Street, Cambridge CB2 1RP
Bentley House, 200 Euston Road, London NW1 2DB
32 East 57th Street, New York, NY10022, USA
296 Beaconsfield Parade, Middle Park, Melbourne 3206, Australia

Library of Congress catalogue card number: 75-13638

ISBN: 0 521 20413 5

First published 1975

Printed in Great Britain
at the
University Printing House, Cambridge
(Euan Phillips, University Printer)

THE CAMBRIDGE HISTORY OF AFRICA

General Editors: J. D. FAGE and ROLAND OLIVER

Volume 4

from *c.* 1600 to *c.* 1790

[illegible]

CAS 9-30-76

CONTENTS

List of maps *page* ix

Preface xi

Acknowledgements xiv

Introduction 1
by Richard Gray, *Professor of the History of Africa, School of Oriental and African Studies, University of London*

1 Egypt, the Funj and Darfur 14
by P. M. Holt, *Professor of Arabic History, School of Oriental and African Studies, University of London*
Ottoman Egypt 14
The Funj sultanate 40
Darfur 50
The expansion of Islam 52

2 The central Sahara and Sudan 58
by H. J. Fisher, *Reader in the History of Africa, School of Oriental and African Studies, University of London*
The process of consolidation 58
The stage in 1600 65
Military considerations 68
Finance and government 80
The role of commerce 84
The Islamic factor 92
The contribution of slavery 97
The impact of the nomads 105
Bornu and Hausaland 114
The *Maghrib al-Adnā* 118
Tuareg, Tubu and the Fezzan 123
Mandara, Bagirmi and the Kwararafa 129
Wadai 136

3 North-West Africa: from the Maghrib to the fringes of the forest *page* 142
by NEHEMIA LEVTZION, *Professor of History, Institute of African and Asian Studies, Hebrew University of Jerusalem*
The Maghrib 145
The pashalik of Timbuktu 152
Timbuktu, Jenne and Massina under the *arma* 158
The *arma*, Songhay and Tuareg 165
The Bambara states 171
Trade and politics among the Dyula and Mossi-Dagomba 181
Islam in the states of the savanna 192
The early jihad movements 199
Africans and Europeans in the trade of Senegambia 216

4 The Guinea coast 223
by WALTER RODNEY, *Lately Associate Professor, Department of History, University of Dar es Salaam*
Yoruba, Aja, Bini 223
Iboland, the delta states and the Cross river 252
The upper Guinea coast 276
The Gold Coast 296

5 Central Africa from Cameroun to the Zambezi 325
by DAVID BIRMINGHAM, *Lecturer in the History of Africa, School of Oriental and African Studies, University of London*
The northern savanna and forest 325
The Kongo kingdom 329
Loango 344
The Kimbundu and Luanda 350
The Ovimbundu and Benguela 359
The lower Kasai 363
The Lunda empire 369
The eastern plains and the upper Zambezi 377

6 Southern Africa and Madagascar *page* 384
by Shula Marks, *Lecturer in the History of Africa, School of Oriental and African Studies, University of London*
and Richard Gray
The kingdom of the *Mwene Mutapa* 385
Butua 393
Butua's neighbours 405
Delagoa Bay and its hinterland 408
The Sotho-Tswana 410
Kalahari and South-West Africa 419
The Nguni 425
Khoisan and Dutch at the Cape 439
The Xhosa frontier 454
Madagascar 458

7 Eastern Africa 469
by Edward A. Alpers, *Associate Professor, Department of History, University of California, Los Angeles*
and Christopher Ehret, *Associate Professor, Department of History, University of California, Los Angeles*
The interlacustrine states 470
Luo interactions east and north of Lake Victoria 482
The Masai and their neighbours 491
The central interior 499
Between Unyamwezi and the coast 507
Between Lakes Tanganyika and Malawi 511
North of the Zambezi 515
The East African coast 527

8 Ethiopia and the Horn of Africa 537
by M. Abir, *Professor of History, Institute of African and Asian Studies, Hebrew University of Jerusalem*
The Muslim threat and the Galla expansion 537
Serse-Dingil and Susenyos 545
The Red Sea trade 550
The Muslim principalities 552
Fasiladas and Yohannes 555
Iyasu I and the Galla 558
The rising power of the Galla 564
The era of the princes 571

9 Africa in Europe and the Americas *page* 578
by Walter Rodney
Europe's image of Africa 578
Africans in Europe 581
The slave trade, racism and capitalism 589
Towards abolition 597
The African contribution in the Americas 602
The cost of survival in the New World 606
The Afro-American cultural heritage 611

Bibliographical essays 623

Bibliography 652

Index 695

MAPS

1	Egypt and the Nilotic Sudan	*page* 16
2	The central Sahara and Sudan	60
3	The Lake Chad area	61
4	North Africa and the Sahara	153
5	The western Sudan	172
6	The lower Guinea coast in the seventeenth century	224
7	The lower Guinea coast in the eighteenth century	225
8	The upper Guinea coast, *c.* 1600	277
9	The upper Guinea coast, *c.* 1800	288
10	Central Africa	326
11	West-Central Africa	330
12	South of the Zambezi	387
13	South-West Africa and the Cape of Good Hope	421
14	South-east Africa	426
15	Madagascar	459
16	Northern East Africa	471
17	Southern East Africa	502
18	Northern Ethiopia	539
19	The Horn of Africa	542

PREFACE

In the English-speaking world, the Cambridge histories have since the beginning of the century set the pattern for multi-volume works of history, with chapters written by experts on a particular topic, and unified by the guiding hand of volume editors of senior standing. *The Cambridge Modern History*, planned by Lord Acton, appeared in sixteen volumes between 1902 and 1912. It was followed by *The Cambridge Ancient History*, *The Cambridge Medieval History*, *The Cambridge History of English Literature*, and Cambridge Histories of India, of Poland, and of the British Empire. The original *Modern History* has now been replaced by *The New Cambridge Modern History* in twelve volumes, and *The Cambridge Economic History of Europe* is now being completed. Other Cambridge Histories recently undertaken include a history of Islam, of Arabic literature, of the Bible treated as a central document of and influence on Western civilization, and of Iran and China.

It was during the later 1950s that the Syndics of the Cambridge University Press first began to explore the possibility of embarking on a Cambridge History of Africa. But they were then advised that the time was not yet ripe. The serious appraisal of the past of Africa by historians and archaeologists had hardly been undertaken before 1948, the year when universities first began to appear in increasing numbers in the vast reach of the African continent south of the Sahara and north of the Limpopo, and the time too when universities outside Africa first began to take some notice of its history. It was impressed upon the Syndics that the most urgent need of such a young, but also very rapidly advancing branch of historical studies, was a journal of international standing through which the results of ongoing research might be disseminated. In 1960, therefore, the Cambridge University Press launched *The Journal of African History*, which gradually demonstrated the amount of work being undertaken to establish the past of Africa as an integrated whole rather than – as it had usually been viewed before – as the story of a series of incursions into the continent by peoples coming from outside, from the Mediterranean basin, the Near East or western Europe. This movement will of course continue and develop further, but the increasing facilities available for its publication soon began to demonstrate a need to assess both what had been done, and what still needed to be done, in the light of some general historical perspective for the continent.

The Syndics therefore returned to their original charge, and in 1966 the founding editors of *The Journal of African History* accepted a commission to become the general editors of a *Cambridge History of Africa*. They found it a daunting task to draw up a plan for a co-operative work covering a history which was in active process of exploration by scholars of many nations, scattered over a fair part of the globe, and of many disciplines – linguists, anthropologists, geographers and botanists, for example, as well as historians and archaeologists.

It was thought that the greatest problems were likely to arise with the earliest and latest periods: the earliest, because so much would depend on the results of long-term archaeological investigation, and the latest, because of the rapid changes in historical perspective that were occurring as a consequence of the ending of colonial rule in Africa. Initially, therefore, only five volumes were planned, of which the first, Africa before *c* 500 BC, based entirely upon archaeological sources (and edited by an archaeologist), would be the last to appear, while of the others – dealing with the periods of approximately 500 BC to AD 1050, 1050–1600, 1600–1790, and 1790–1875 – it was thought that the first to be published would probably be the last. (In the event, of course, it has turned out to be Professor Richard Gray's volume 4, though Professor John E. Flint's volume 5 should not be far behind it.) Only after these volumes were well under way would an attempt be made to plan for the period after *c*. 1875. Eight years later, it can be said that three further volumes have been planned, and that it is hoped that these will appear at regular intervals following the publication of volume 1.

When they started their work, the general editors quickly came to the conclusion that the most practicable plan for getting out the first five volumes within a reasonable period of time was likely to be the simplest and most straightforward. The direction of each volume was therefore entrusted to a volume editor who, in addition to having made a substantial contribution to the understanding of the period in question, was a man with whom the general editors were in close touch. Within a volume, the aim was to keep the number of contributors to a minimum. Each of them was asked to essay a broad survey of a particular area or theme with which he was familiar for the whole of the period covered by the volume. In this survey, his purpose should be to take account not only of all relevant research done, or still in progress, but also of the gaps in knowledge. These he should try to fill by new thinking of his own, whether based on new work on the available sources or on interpolations from congruent research.

It should be remembered that the plan for these first five volumes was drawn up nearly a decade ago, when little or no research had been done on many important topics, and before many of today's younger scholars – not least those who now fill posts in the departments of history and archaeology in the universities and research institutes in Africa itself – had made their own deep penetrations into such areas of ignorance. Two things follow from this. If the general editors had drawn up their plan in the 1970s rather than the 1960s, the shape might well have been very different, perhaps with a larger number of more specialized, shorter chapters, each centred on a smaller area, period or theme, to the understanding of which the contributor would have made his own individual contribution. Indeed, the last three volumes seem likely to be composed more on such lines. Secondly, the sheer volume of new research that has been published since the contributors for the first five volumes accepted their commissions has often led them to undertake very substantial revisions in their work as it progressed from draft to draft, thus protracting the length of time originally envisaged for the preparation of these volumes.

But histories are meant to be read, and not simply to be continually rewritten and modified by their authors and editors. Volume 4 of *The Cambridge History of Africa* is therefore now launched for public use and appraisal, together with a promise that seven further volumes should follow it at more or less regular intervals.

J. D. FAGE
ROLAND OLIVER

January 1974

ACKNOWLEDGEMENTS

The editor gratefully acknowledges the work of Mrs Marion Johnson in compiling the index, of Mr Malcolm McKee in collating the bibliography, of Mr Reginald Piggott in preparing the maps, and of Mrs Penny Carter and Mr Robert Seal as sub-editors.

INTRODUCTION

Two great divides have marked the last seven millennia in Africa: the transition to food production and the modern revolution in the means of communication. The impact of these innovations was by no means felt simultaneously throughout the continent. A few people living in the most inhospitable areas have yet to participate in the first, but the vast majority of Africans were already pastoralists or agriculturalists long before the end of the first millennium AD. The impact of the second, nineteenth-century revolution was more immediate, though certain aspects of communications were already being influenced by much earlier developments. In successive millennia, trade-links within Africa had been profoundly affected by the Phoenician, Arab and Portuguese explorations of, respectively, the North African, Indian Ocean and Atlantic coasts of Africa. North of the equatorial forests, the camel and the horse had increased man's mobility, and Islam had brought literacy to a restricted few. But until the transformation which began, not with colonial rule, but with the steamers, railways, telegraph, vernacular bibles and newspapers of the nineteenth century, communications throughout most of sub-Saharan Africa had remained largely dependent on oral messages and human porterage. Until the nineteenth century, the pace of change was not dependent on an alien technology. The main lines of communication lay not with the outside world, but within the continent itself.

Compared with these watersheds, the year 1600 marked no noticeable break in continuity; yet in some important respects the seventeenth and eighteenth centuries in Africa do constitute a period of transition, distinct from both the sixteenth and the nineteenth centuries. During this period, the import of firearms and the export of slaves foretold, and partly laid the foundations for, the subsequent massive European intrusion. But for most of the continent external forces were still of merely marginal significance. Africa even confined and controlled the immediate impact of the slave trade, and, in the meanwhile, Africans continued to pursue their own inventions, initiatives and interests.

For most of the sixteenth century, black Africa, behind its filter of desert and coastline, could still confront the forces of the outer world on equal terms. Unlike the Americas, it had not succumbed. For nearly a thousand years, Muslims from north of the Sahara had been by far the most important of these outsiders, and for much of Africa they were to remain the predominant external influence at least until the mid-nineteenth century. Egypt became part of the Ottoman world and was apparently only marginally affected by her contacts with the rest of Africa. Relations with the wider world were of great importance for Morocco, and to a lesser extent Ethiopia, though both were far more deeply influenced by events in the African interior. South of the Sahara, from the Atlantic to the Red Sea, Islam had lost much of its alien nature by acquiring and assimilating African characteristics, or by co-existing alongside local rites and customs. But in 1591, with the Moroccan musketeers at the battle of Tondibi, the heart of this great stretch of Muslim Africa experienced a direct intervention of momentarily overwhelming force.

Subsequent events showed that these early firearms by no means immediately rendered obsolete the cavalries and armies of the medieval Sudan, nor indeed the spearmen and archers of the rest of Africa. For most areas the importance of firearms during these two centuries was primarily symbolic. On the field of battle, save for the comparatively rare occasions when they were used by a practised corps of musketeers, their function remained largely psychological, and they were seldom of permanent, decisive importance. In terms of industrial capacity, however, the increasing imports of firearms into Africa represented a profound shift in the balance of power. Here was a military technology which pre-colonial Africa could not adopt on a scale which matched production in the Ottoman empire; still less could it keep pace with the soaring momentum of western Europe.

Shortly before the Moroccan intervention at Tondibi, another assault was launched on black Africa. The expeditions of Dias to Angola (1575) and Barreto to the Zambezi (1569) changed the cautious, coastal reconnaissance of sub-Saharan Africa, which had been carried out by Portugal for more than a century, into an attempt to penetrate the interior by force. The first dream of conquering a trans-continental stretch of Africa was soon born. The kingdoms of the *ngola* and the *mwene mutapa* became therefore the first of the great sub-Saharan states to face the challenge of European invasion. But the conflict remained confined to those relatively restricted arenas, and in the seventeenth and eighteenth centuries, the other European invasion directly affected merely the remote, southernmost tip of the continent. On the Guinea coast, Europeans were kept to the coastal fringe where they rented the land for their forts as part of a contractual relationship with the local African rulers.

The encounter of ideas and ideologies between Africa and Europe remained similarly marginal throughout this period. The two great initiatives of the sixteenth century, the contacts with the kingdoms of Kongo and Ethiopia, had been checked decisively by the second half of the seventeenth century. Africa therefore had virtually no opportunity of participating in the intellectual discoveries which were challenging the mind of Europe during the seventeenth and eighteenth centuries.

Only in the field of trade did contact with Europe affect Africa at all deeply. Already in the fifteenth century the search for labour added slaves to the gold and other products sought by Europeans along the African coast. At first the numbers involved remained small, but with the development of the Brazilian sugar plantations in the latter part of the sixteenth century the forced emigration of Africans to the New World increased rapidly. The plantation system soon spread to the Caribbean and North America, and it is estimated that during the seventeenth century an average of some 13,000 slaves were being shipped every year across the Atlantic. By the mid-eighteenth century the Atlantic trade had reached a plateau estimated at over 60,000 slaves a year, and the plantation system was also established in the Indian Ocean, taking slaves from eastern Africa to the French Mascarene islands.[1]

The consequences for Africa of this massive demand for slaves have still to be investigated in detail. The demographic impact is by no means clear, for there are virtually no reliable data on the size of Africa's population at either the beginning or the end of our period, and there is relatively little evidence of population growth or decline in even those areas about which most is known. We cannot therefore ascertain whether the natural growth was sufficient to replace the thousands taken often in the prime of life, nor, on a continental reckoning, is it possible to balance this factor against the recurrence of epidemics, famines and other causes of mortality. It would, however, seem probable that the rate of growth of some of the African communities most involved was at least halted during the eighteenth century, while that of Europe forged ahead. Certainly the demographic impact of the slave trade varied immensely from area to area. The thinly populated hinterland of Luanda may well have been stunted and spoilt,

[1] P. D. Curtin, *The Atlantic slave trade: a census* (Madison, 1969), ch. 9.

but in the other major area of slave exports, from the Gold Coast to the Cameroun, the effect on population growth appears to have been far less serious, this vast region continuing to be one of the most densely populated areas in Africa.

The fact that in the Atlantic hinterland as a whole the direct, demographic impact of the slave trade was confined to less than disastrous proportions can in some respects be considered as the most important of African achievements during this period. Although external demand could drastically distort the pattern of African trade and lead increasingly to the exchange of guns and even baubles against human beings, Africa still retained a large measure of control over the pace and extent of this development. In part this was because the full weight of technological advance, and hence of European and Arab rapacity, had yet to be unleashed against the continent. Latin America and southern Asia attracted far more European attention, and in Africa outsiders remained almost completely dependent on the co-operation of African rulers and middlemen. Even in Angola the proportion of slaves directly taken by Portuguese armies remained modest, while these armies themselves largely consisted of African auxiliaries and allies, whose response to Portuguese demands remained unpredictable. But it was not merely the mosquito or the balance of technology which controlled external demand in these centuries: African resistance was also responsible. For fairly long periods some of the foremost states refused to sell slaves: until the end of the seventeenth century the *oba* of Benin prohibited the export of male slaves; for several decades Loango was able to maintain a flourishing trade in ivory and copper, and to ignore the Dutch and Portuguese requests for slaves; originally the rulers of Dahomey may well have been opponents rather than protagonists of the slave trade. States, however, depended on power rather than family or humanitarian considerations, and, faced with the increasing necessity of acquiring firearms, the rulers' opposition to insistent European demands gradually changed into a measure of compliance. More fundamental, and sometimes more successful, was the resistance of some acephalous societies. Here the traditional ties of kinship and mutual human obligations sometimes retained a vitality sufficient to preserve an indifference to the slave trade and a fierce ability to retaliate when raided.

Temporary refusals and intractable, small-scale resistance could not, however, by themselves protect the majority of Africans from the destructive inroads of the slave trade. In the long run, the fact that those African rulers and middlemen who co-operated with the Europeans or Arabs did so largely at a pace determined by African conditions was far more effective. The power of the rulers and nobility was seldom, if ever, absolute. The constraints of kinship, the need to retain the allegiance of as many people as possible, and the concepts of traditional justice, albeit becoming diluted and twisted by the trade, continued to operate in most societies. Economic calculations were also relevant. Despite the apparent attractions of alien imports, it was often still manifestly more profitable to retain the productive capacities of captives or 'criminals' rather than to export them. Even when a slave passed into the hands of middlemen, these were ever increasingly conscious of his economic value. The sharp bargaining and substantial profits of African traders were yet another effective brake, forcing up the price of slaves. It is impossible to generalize for the whole area and period. As Dr Rodney argues in chapter 4, 'the capture of African institutions and initiative' by alien demands was, by the eighteenth century, already far advanced in some of the worst-affected areas. Here, in the Bight of Benin, the obstacles posed by African resistance and restraints had become but feebly operative. Yet even here the disaster was kept within bounds, and the bounds were set by Africans.

The direct, demographic impact was not, therefore, the most important consequence of the slave trade. For all participants, the psychological consequences were by contrast immeasurable. The experience of suffering is still a keynote in negritude and black consciousness, and, although slavery and the slave trade were by no means the sole occasions of pain and deprivation, they have provided a major component. Again, although the slave ship and plantation were not the sole sources of white racism, they contributed powerfully to the ethos of arrogance and exploitation, the final nemesis of which has yet perhaps to be seen.

More tangibly, though perhaps with less far-reaching implications, the slave trade of the seventeenth and eighteenth centuries was a potent, and peculiarly vicious, means of increasing the integration of black Africa into the evolving Western economy. Vicious, not merely because Africa was robbed of productive potential, but also because her internal economies were distorted. Whereas the major sixteenth-century exports of gold, cloth, timber, pepper and even ivory had stimulated indigenous skills, the subsequent export of slaves and import of firearms diverted these energies into violence and set a premium on military power and force. The exact incidence of this distortion has yet to be investigated, but several instances can be adduced of these first steps towards a dependent colonial economy. Some of the roots of contemporary underdevelopment can thus be traced to these centuries. And the distortion was not of course confined to local economies. Social, judicial and religious institutions were twisted to provide victims for export.

So long, however, as the response to external demands was controlled by Africans, the rate of distortion was gradual and even reversible. Nor in these centuries should its extent be exaggerated. Development opportunities were occasioned even by the slave trade. Any commercial link could sometimes help to liberate small-scale societies from the severe limitations which exposed them to the treacheries, not perhaps of man, but of nature. Against the dangers of an increasing dependence on external trade must be set the advantages brought by the inroads into isolation, though, as will be seen, isolation was being eroded by internal trade as much as by the more dangerous and uncertain stimulus of foreign contacts. The glaring examples of distortion were limited to those areas most deeply affected and for Africa as a whole these constituted but the fringe. African vitality, seen here in the resistance to, and large-scale control of, the slave trade, was often manifest elsewhere in continued, ordered, constructive innovations. Politically these centuries were marked by many instances of consolidation, by the expansion and centralization of political institutions, by firmer, closer-knit areas of order and security. Again it is impossible to generalize for the continent as a whole. The period of this volume, which began with Tondibi and the collapse of the last great empire in the western Sudan, also witnessed the decline or temporary eclipse of most of the major states first encountered by the Portuguese: Benin, Kongo, Ndongo, Mutapa and Ethiopia. But against these, as the chapters in this volume show, there were many other examples of growth.

In part this political expansion can be traced to the wider commercial horizons resulting from the increase in overseas trade. Yet the overseas market was only a part, and generally only a marginal part, of total African exchanges. The internal lines of communication were still of overwhelming importance. Even the new states of Dahomey and Asante, closely associated with the Atlantic trade, had important links with the northern interior. Asante, which established an effective control over Dagomba in the course of the eighteenth century, has indeed been described as 'essentially a northward-looking power' for the greater part of its history.[1] The rise of Oyo to power and greatness

[1] Ivor Wilks, in J. F. Ade Ajayi and Michael Crowder, eds., *History of West Africa*, I (London, 1971), 381.

was based on its cavalry might, and the supply of horses from the north was always of supreme significance. The export of the kola nut from the forests to the Sudanic area remained of far greater significance than the increasing imports of cheap Dutch gin on the coast. Even slaves, almost everywhere in West Africa and the Sudan, were more important for their internal, domestic roles than as items for export. The internal circulation and consumption of African mineral products continued to have a wide economic significance, sometimes supporting exchanges over enormous distances. Copper from Hofrat en Nahas south of Darfur was carried at least as far as Hausaland, and copper from the Katanga probably reached Buganda. In southern Africa copper again was exchanged over hundreds of miles, and the goldsmiths of the Rozvi empire may well have used as much gold as was exported to the Portuguese. And even if the creations of African goldsmiths were destined to adorn a restricted nobility, salt and iron were essential commodities in the meanest agricultural household. Probably the most widespread indication of the continuing vitality of indigenous skills was the flourishing cloth industries of seventeenth- and eighteenth-century Africa. Although some luxury cloths were imported from overseas, the bulk of the cotton, raffia and bark-cloth worn by Africans was still produced, woven and dyed by African craftsmen.

The profits from, and the needs of, trade, whether overseas or internal, often had obvious political implications. Rulers could benefit in many different ways. They could impose a monopoly over the more profitable sectors of trade; they could levy taxes on markets and traders; by turning their capitals into redistributive centres, they could strengthen centripetal forces; and as the economy became more market-oriented an increasing range of people would value the security provided by the state. It is not surprising that by the eighteenth century many of the stateless societies in Africa were situated far from the main lines of trade.

Yet before too close a correlation is drawn between trade and political centralization during this period in Africa, one should remember that the opportunities for investing these profits were limited. Over much of the continent, wealth was still thought of in terms of women and cattle. And there were many ways of mobilizing these resources other than those of trade. Pastoralism seldom formed the economic basis for a state; but when allied with a reliable production of crops, the mobile, royal herds could bind the subjects closely to the rulers, as in some interlacustrine kingdoms, and among the Fulani in Futa Toro, the

Rozvi and many Sotho and Nguni groups in southern Africa, and the Sakalava in Madagascar. In a favourable environment, a single lineage rich in cattle, exploiting polygyny and the broad network of kinship obligations, could rapidly establish ascendancy over very large numbers of people. Again, a favourable set of crops could substantially increase the surplus to support a complex ruling and military institution. Its relatively carefree cultivation of the banana was perhaps one of the advantages which Buganda enjoyed over its rivals. In the seventeenth and eighteenth centuries much of sub-Saharan Africa benefited from the introduction of American crops, especially cassava and maize, so that by the end of the eighteenth century, even in the farthest north-eastern reaches of the Congo basin, American crops were assisting the expansion of the Azande and were probably already adding to the power of the neighbouring Mangbetu kingdom. The high fertility and dense population of the hill country of Akwapim were as important a factor in the seventeenth-century expansion of the Akwamu state as its acquisition of firearms, and its strategic exploitation of the forest environment gave this new state a decisive advantage over the peoples of the surrounding savanna.[1]

In analysing the factors of political change in these centuries, however, one is not inevitably tied to the realm of economic or environmental determinism by the lack of other evidence. Increasingly one can discern the impact of individual personalities, technological advances, and intellectual or ideological innovations. Occasionally from the lands where there were royal chronicles or from those areas in intimate contact with the outside world, there is sufficient contemporary evidence to provide a sharp delineation of character and motive. Iyasu I of Ethiopia, Mai Aloma of Bornu, Garcia II of Kongo and Queen Nzinga of Matamba, or Herry from the Cape, are all clearly recognizable. Elsewhere individuals are known through their exploits and achievements recorded in tradition, or through the second-hand reports of foreigners; but by these centuries these figures are clearly no longer legendary heroes, even if to contemporaries – European or African – they sometimes seemed to be invested with supernatural powers, as in the case of Frei Antonio's description of the sorcery of Changamire Dombo on the southern Zambezian escarpment.

Thus some of the decisive innovations in political structure and ideology during these centuries can confidently be ascribed to individual rulers and their advisers. On opposite flanks of the continent, in

[1] I. Wilks, 'The rise of the Akwamu empire, 1650–1710', *Transactions Historical Society of Ghana*, 1957, 3, 2, 130.

Buganda and Asante, Kabaka Kateregga and Osei Kwadwo took decisive steps towards the establishment of appointive bureaucracies, a radical and highly significant addition to the traditional structure of hereditary offices. The construction of a state which embraced many different ethnic and lineage groups, was achieved in Darfur during these centuries by its rulers, notably Muḥammad Tayrāb and his successor 'Abd al-Raḥmān al-Rashīd. By their strict control over the import of horses, by their use of slaves as soldiers and officials, and by enlisting Islamic sanctions against local loyalties, these rulers reduced the power of hereditary title-holders and lineage-heads.[1] In Dahomey, Agaja's military and diplomatic skill, and his creation of an original and highly-organized intelligence service and system of military apprenticeship, enabled the state to survive the crises of his reign and to emerge as a tightly centralized unit. But the fundamental ideological innovation had been initiated by Wegbaja, the seventeenth-century founder of the kingdom. It was he who re-oriented the ancestral cults and reformed religious practices to centre on the kingship, so that the conceptual image of Dahomey, while remaining thoroughly indigenous in character, represented a definite break with traditional political ideas.

Even where it is impossible to place an individual signature on political innovations, there is abundant evidence during these centuries of institutional engineering and intellectual creativity. The Sakalava development of ancestral rites, the Rozvi *mambos*' evolving relationships with the cult of Mwari, Rwanda royal manipulation of Ryangombe, the growth of the *ekpe* secret society among the Efik, the widespread and ancient process of combining Islamic and traditional sanctions of political power, all testify to a creative syncretism, a tolerant understanding among rulers, religious leaders and populace of the value of a constructive intellectual response to changing circumstances.

The major, continuing importance of interior lines of communication and of indigenous invention and initiative is, of course, by no means confined to this theme of political centralization. The transmission of language and ideas by the movements of people, sometimes over great distances, with the consequent creation of wider areas of a common culture, is one of the main themes of earlier African history, even if its importance, compared with developments *in situ*, has sometimes been overstressed. The seventeenth and eighteenth centuries witnessed few

[1] See below, chapter 1, pp. 51–2, and also R. S. O'Fahey, 'The growth and development of the Keira sultanate of Dār Fūr', Ph.D. thesis (London, 1972).

large-scale upheavals. One, however, dominated the history of Ethiopia and the Horn throughout this period. The expansion of the Galla and their infiltrations into semitized Ethiopia did not merely bring the disruption and the decline, albeit temporary, of the central institutions of this long-established kingdom; more positively this series of migrations was also marked by creative interaction and assimilation between Galla and Amhara. Indeed, especially where the Galla settled among the Sidama peoples, it sometimes involved a revolutionary restructuring of the traditional egalitarian organization of these powerful invaders. During this period, the irruptions also of the Masai and Kalenjin deeply affected many peoples over a large sector of eastern Africa, and the expansion of the Azande and related peoples involved wide-scale cultural and political changes across the Mbomu basin in North-Central Africa.

Together with these examples of major displacements, the local history of many African peoples during these centuries largely consists of a series of small-scale movements – the expansion, flight or division of individual homesteads, families and lineages. Often this process assumed a more than purely local significance, especially if this cultural diffusion was associated, as in the case of the Lunda or the Akan, with the expansion of a major political power: the present homogeneity of northern and southern Akan-speaking peoples is probably largely the result of the diffusion of southern influences under the aegis of Asante from as late as the eighteenth century onwards. Even where political links were weak or non-existent, the cumulative, small-scale movements of people who retained social and cultural ties with the areas from which they came, could contribute, as in the case of the Ibo, to the massive peaceful expansion of a people's language and culture; while across the great savanna belt of West Africa the slow movements of the Fulani had for long been building up to a point where they were to dominate the immediate subsequent history of a large part of this area. If the day-to-day horizons of most African peoples were extremely limited, the areas in which an individual could find himself at home were far wider than is often envisaged.

In those areas where the long-distance migrations had already occurred, these centuries were often marked by consolidation and the integration of diverse segments into a wider unity. Sometimes, as in the case of Bornu or the interlacustrine kingdoms, this process was directed and encouraged by a central political power. But integration is a theme which embraced far more than mere political initiatives. African societies with their extended kinship systems and their pragmatic, open religious traditions possessed a wide variety of devices for forging and preserving a co-operative unity. Consolidation also comprised not only social integration but, sometimes, a new and revolutionary relationship with a strange environment, which involved considerable technological experimentation and adaptation. The Kenya Luo, at the end of their great migration, proved themselves resourceful and inventive agriculturalists during these centuries, while at the northernmost thrust of the Luo-speaking peoples, the Shilluk turned themselves into a riverain power, took to papyrus canoes, and dominated the whole stretch of the White Nile until the Egyptian conquest in the nineteenth century. Equally remarkable, though as yet less well-documented and recorded, must have been the agricultural revolution attendant upon the reception of American crops. Although it is now easy to see that maize, cassava and groundnuts brought a much-needed enrichment to African agriculture, the successful adoption of these crops meant for many communities an anxious, even dangerous period of experimentation, for the failure of a crop or the neglect of well-proven methods and staples could all too easily spell disaster in a precarious subsistence economy. Yet the success was such that the 9,000 metric tons of maize, which it is estimated were needed annually to victual the Atlantic slave trade at its peak, were provided by African farmers.

Internal communications and the role of market-oriented trade in the development of centralized states during these centuries have already been discussed, but the significance of African trading initiatives was not restricted to this political role. Indeed throughout much of the hinterland of the Indian Ocean, the pioneer traders of this period – the Yao, Bisa, Tsonga and, at the end of the eighteenth century, the Kamba and Nyamwezi – owed and contributed little or nothing to the process of political centralization. The success of these entrepreneurs was partly developed from the experience and profits gained from a much older, internal exchange of the necessities and luxuries of their traditional economies. Then, like the Dyula of West Africa, by utilizing and extending the networks of language and kinship links, and by selecting and changing their coastal outlets with an acute awareness of profit-margins, these explorers began to construct great commercial arteries during this period. In the nineteenth century, these were to be utilized first by Arabs and then by Europeans, but again the vital initiative had come in this earlier period not from outside Africa but from within.

The importance of internal lines of communication can be seen, finally, in the great religious and intellectual tradition which, north of the equator, had become indigenous to Africa. The Muslim Pilgrimage, rather than trade or any other nexus, provided a link, however tenuous, across the expanse of the Sudan from the Senegal to the Red Sea, bringing to the peoples of this area the vision, however faint, of a unity which transcended the limits of kinsfolk, tribe, or state. But it was not merely in this obvious sense that Islam depended on and contributed to African movement and interaction. In North Africa, intellectual and religious development tended to be focussed on the great cities and centres of learning. In the Sudan and on the African frontiers of Islam, the faith had adopted a far greater degree of mobility. Here, too, the towns, especially in Hausaland, were important centres of Islamic learning and jurisprudence, but the points of growth and often of crucial intellectual development were also scattered and highly mobile. They were to be found in the farthest fringes among the dispersed Dyula, or in the Nilotic Sudan among the followers and disciples of itinerant holy men, or among the Zawāyā nomads of the Senegalese hinterland, or among the Kunta, along and north of the Niger bend, with their adoption of the *ṭarīqa*, an institution which proved, with revolutionary consequences, to be superbly attuned to their shifting environment. As much as in the learned circles of the towns, it was at these points that Islam was grappling with the fundamental problems of African syncretism, and it was from the cross-fertilization between these centres and outposts that the call to reform came, a call which owed little to direct external influences, but which derived its force from an indigenous African comprehension of the faith.

It would be wrong to exaggerate the extent of change and the thrust of African innovation during the seventeenth and eighteenth centuries. The basic values and outlook of most African societies were profoundly conservative. Armed with the scantiest of technological equipment with which to face a dangerous and disease-ridden environment, Africans did not lightly lay aside well-proven customs, beliefs and institutions. The present and the past, rather than progress and the future, dominated most African cosmologies. Yet in these last two centuries, while Europe and the outer world were still beyond the horizon of most of the continent, untouched Africa offers abundant instances of invention. For the most part, Africa was still arbiter of her destiny. African initiative was still supreme in most areas, and it exhibited its force in a variety of experiments, adaptations and innovations. Yet these initiatives do not constitute a unilineal pattern of progress. Some horizons contracted, while others expanded; a Great Zimbabwe could be virtually abandoned. Disease and famine often eliminated any growth in population. A restricted communications technology continued to limit advance; intellectual legacies and economic investment remained relatively small. The seventeenth and eighteenth centuries did not witness a monolithic movement towards the market-economy and the supra-tribal state. Rather, in their contrasting, sometimes contradictory and even cyclical variety, the examples of innovation testified to an ever-renewing tradition of intelligent adaptation and social invention. The first faint signs of the challenge of Europe and the outer world were already to be seen, and in the following century this challenge would suddenly mount to a scale and intensity seldom if ever before witnessed in the history of European overseas contacts. The eventual outcome of this encounter has yet to unfold, but already it can be seen that Africa's preservation of its own values and identity has largely depended on that strength and adaptability of her societies so notably manifest in the seventeenth and eighteenth centuries.

CHAPTER 1

EGYPT, THE FUNJ AND DARFUR

OTTOMAN EGYPT

Egypt, although geographically situated in Africa, was at the beginning of the sixteenth century essentially a part of the Near East by virtue of its recent history, its culture and its closest political connections. One of the earliest of Muslim conquests, Egypt had grown in importance as a centre of Islam when, in the thirteenth century, its rulers halted the Mongol advance which had overwhelmed the eastern Islamic territories and extinguished the caliphate in Baghdad. The same episode had confirmed the links between Egypt and Syria, and the Mamluk sultans succeeded the Ayyubids and the Fatimid caliphs as the rulers of an empire situated at the crossroads of western Asia and northern Africa. With the Maghrib, the upper valley of the Nile, and the trans-Saharan Sudan, there were trading connections, while Muslims came from these regions to study at the university mosque al-Azhar or to travel as pilgrims to the holy cities of the Hejaz. But the political bond between Egypt and the adjacent parts of North Africa, which had briefly existed under the Fatimids, was never renewed, while not until the nineteenth century did a ruler of Egypt effectively govern the Nile beyond Aswan. The Ottoman conquest, which ended the Mamluk sultanate, and converted Egypt into an outlying province of an empire with its centre at Istanbul, continued the historic detachment of the country from Africa and its association with the Islamic Near East.

The Mamluk sultanate, as it existed on the eve of the Ottoman conquest, rested on a corps of Circassians recruited in youth as slaves (Arabic singular, *mamlūk*), who were converted to Islam, trained as cavalrymen, and then enfranchised. They formed the *corps d'élite* in the army, and occupied the high military and civil commands. At the head of the pyramid was the sultan, who owed his position to no hereditary principle, but to his own military prowess and political dexterity. As a group, the Mamluks were violent, treacherous and faction-ridden. As rulers they were luxurious, grasping and short-sighted. As soldiers, at the time when gunpowder and firearms were coming to dominate the battlefield, they were gorgeous and archaic survivals of a medieval chivalry.

The reasons which induced Selīm I, the Ottoman sultan, to set his more efficient and up-to-date military machine in action against the Mamluks were complex. Initially the campaign against the Mamluk sultanate seems to have been a by-product of the conflict between the Ottomans and Shāh Ismā'īl, the founder of the Safavid dynasty in Persia. When Selīm defeated Ismā'īl in 1514, Qānṣawh al-Ghawrī, the octogenarian Mamluk sultan, was seriously alarmed at the changed balance of power on the northern frontier of Syria. In 1516, when Ottoman troops began again to move eastwards, he advanced with a Mamluk army to Aleppo. Ostensibly his intention was to demonstrate in support of the shah; privately he seems to have realized that, whatever the result of Ottoman-Safavid hostilities, the Mamluk sultanate was threatened.

Selīm, warned of Qānṣawh's advance, turned his forces against the Mamluks. These were defeated, and Qānṣawh himself died on the field of Marj Dabiq near Aleppo (24 August 1516). The whole of Syria was quickly occupied, and in October Selīm entered Damascus. He had ended the possibility of any military intervention by the Mamluks in his operations against Shāh Ismā'īl, and had interposed a buffer-territory between them and the heartlands of the Ottoman state. A further campaign against Egypt would necessarily be hazardous, since it would involve a further extension of the Ottoman lines of communications, the crossing of the Sinai Desert, and an attack on the Mamluk army entrenched in Cairo or its vicinity. Nevertheless, the campaign was undertaken. Selīm may well have been influenced by a desire to establish Ottoman control over the Red Sea, which, since 1507, the Portuguese had attempted to close to Muslim shipping. There had been a Mamluk naval expedition to India in 1508–9, while another (in which there was Ottoman participation) was establishing a base in the coastlands of the Yemen on the eve of Qānṣawh's conflict with Selīm. The maintenance of an open trading-route through the Red Sea with India, South-East Asia and the Far East was essential at this time to the Ottomans, since the traditional land-routes had been blocked by the rise of Safavid power.

Apart from these considerations of high policy, Selīm was undoubtedly influenced by the advice of a Mamluk collaborator, Khā'ir Bey, the former governor of Aleppo, whose defection during the fighting at Marj Dabiq had contributed to the Ottoman victory. He and some other Mamluk grandees saw in collaboration with the Ottomans the surest way to maintaining their ascendancy in Egypt, and did not hesitate to incite Selīm against their rivals, who had installed a new sultan, Ṭūmān Bāy, in Cairo, and were preparing to continue resistance.

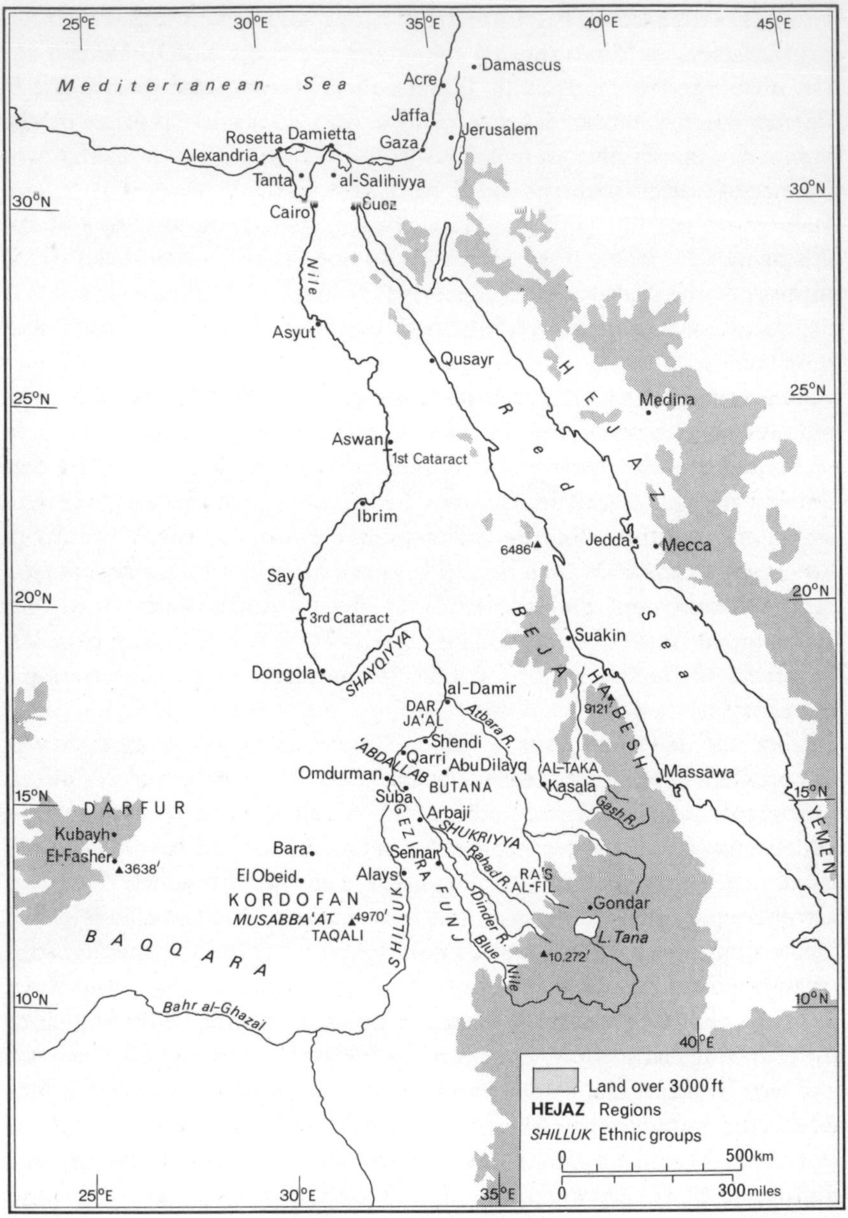

1 Egypt and the Nilotic Sudan

The campaign against Egypt met with rapid success. The Mamluks were overwhelmed in a brief battle at the fortified camp of al-Raydaniyya outside Cairo (23 January 1517); Selīm was proclaimed in the mosques, and, after various adventures, Ṭūmān Bāy was captured and hanged. Selīm thereby became the master of Egypt, but he had not, it should be noted, carried out a detailed territorial conquest: there was indeed a resurgence of tribal power in Upper Egypt, where the chiefs of the great tribe of Hawwāra were for about sixty years recognized as administrators of the region as well as shaykhs of the nomads. Still further south lay Lower Nubia, known to the Turks as Berberistan, the land of the Barābra. Extending from the First to the Third Cataract, this eventually became technically Ottoman territory. It was subdued some time after the Ottoman conquest of Egypt, probably as a reaction to the expansion of Funj power in Nubia. The conquest of Berberistan is associated with Özdemir Pasha, a Mamluk who had governed the Yemen and who, about the middle of the sixteenth century, established Ottoman rule on the Red Sea coast in the region of Suakin and Massawa, thus creating the province of Ḥabesh (Abyssinia). Özdemir seems also to have invaded Lower Nubia, where garrisons of Bosniak troops were settled at Aswan, Ibrim and Say. The Ottoman governor of Berberistan bore the old Mamluk title of *kāshif*, and his office became hereditary.

From the Mamluk point of view, Selīm secured the ascendancy of one faction at the expense of another. Hence, although Mamluk resistance was severely repressed after the Ottoman victory at al-Raydaniyya, there was no attempt to extirpate the Mamluks as an élite, or to end the system of Mamluk recruitment and training. Thus, a tenacious and self-perpetuating group continued to exist in Egypt and largely recovered in the seventeenth and eighteenth centuries the autonomy which their predecessors had lost in the sixteenth. These neo-Mamluks saw in Selīm the ally and preserver, rather than the destroyer, of their race, and gave him an honoured place in legend. The implied compact between the Ottomans and the Mamluk collaborators was manifested very clearly when, on Selīm's departure from Egypt in September 1517, he appointed Khā'ir Bey as his viceroy. Retaining his old Mamluk title of *malik al-umarā'* (king of the commanders), residing in the Citadel of Cairo like the former sultans, Khā'ir Bey retained as long as he lived something of the aura of the defunct sultanate.

It was a fairly regular practice of the Ottomans to incorporate conquered territories into their empire in two stages. In the first, they limited themselves to establishing suzerainty over native dynasties; while in the second, these were eliminated, and direct control was established. Mamluk Egypt had, of course, no native dynasty in the usual sense, but Selīm's appointment of Khā'ir Bey as viceroy may be seen as a local modification of the usual practice. Certainly, with Khā'ir Bey's death in 1522 a period of more direct Ottoman control began. His successor as viceroy was an Ottoman, not a Mamluk, and the Mamluks were henceforward excluded from this highest position in Egypt – although in course of time they circumvented the exclusion, and seized supremacy by other means.

The assertion of Ottoman domination after Khā'ir Bey's death was not accomplished without difficulty. Sultan Selīm had been succeeded in 1520 by his son, Süleymān, known to Western writers as 'the Magnificent'. Two Mamluk grandees, Jānim and Īnāl, governors of sub-provinces of Egypt, thought that the time was ripe for revolt. The rebels moved their forces to the east of the delta, where they could cut communications between Egypt and Syria. They hoped to receive support from other Mamluk malcontents, but were disappointed. The new Ottoman viceroy defeated them, killing Jānim and putting Īnāl to flight.

Shortly afterwards, in 1523, a certain Aḥmad Pasha was sent to Egypt as viceroy. He was a disappointed man, having failed to receive the appointment of grand vizier which had been conferred on his rival, Ibrāhīm Pasha. Like the Mamluks, he was of Caucasian origin. When Ibrāhīm Pasha sought to bring about his death, Aḥmad rebelled, proclaimed himself sultan of Egypt, and, in January 1524, he succeeded in capturing the Citadel of Cairo from its Ottoman garrison. It is not clear how much support Aḥmad could call upon: he intimidated the high officers in Cairo, confiscated the wealth of notables and practised extortion on Jews and Christians – perhaps because the peasants refused to pay taxes. There is a possibility that he was in touch with Shāh Ismā'īl. However this may be, a counter-coup was carried out by Ottomans and Mamluk loyalists in February 1524, and Aḥmad fled from Cairo. In the following month he was captured and put to death. Egypt remained in a very disturbed state, and in 1525 the grand vizier Ibrāhīm Pasha was himself sent to restore order. This he did and (again following regular Ottoman practice) promulgated an edict, the *Qānūn-nāme* of Egypt, to regulate the military and civil organization. This document shows Ottoman, Mamluk and Arab tribal elements playing a part in the administration.

During the sixty or so years which followed the viceroyalty of

Ibrāhīm Pasha, the political structure became firmly established. At its head was the Ottoman viceroy, the *beylerbeyi*, or the pasha, as he was more informally called. His residence was the Citadel, where four times weekly he held the Divan, a council of state, which as a permanent and regular institution has no parallel in other Ottoman provinces in this period. Cairo was garrisoned by seven corps of soldiery. The most important of these were two infantry corps, the Janissaries and the ʻAzebān, both of which had their headquarters in the Citadel. There were, further, three corps of cavalry, one of which was originally recruited from Circassian Mamluks, as well as the viceroy's bodyguard and a corps of pursuivants. As time went on, the ethnic composition of these corps became extremely diversified, including as they did descendants of Ottoman Turks, immigrants from Anatolia and elsewhere, Mamluks, and local people. Quite distinct from the regular officers of the seven corps were the beys, who first began to emerge into prominence in the second half of the sixteenth century. These were salaried military officers, usually of Mamluk origin, who stood outside the corps-system, but were available for special or *ad hoc* commands. As *serdārs*, they commanded expeditionary forces requisitioned by the sultans for service outside Egypt. They became the effective governors of the sub-provinces of Egypt – probably originally by virtue of military commands in operations against the nomad Arabs. They established a prescriptive right to certain great offices of state: the command of the annual pilgrimage caravan to the Hejaz, that of the annual tribute-convoy to Istanbul, the treasurership of Egypt, and, above all, the position of acting viceroy on the death or deprivation of the Ottoman office-holder. It was through the institution of the beylicate, and through the close connection between the beylicate and these great offices, that the Mamluks reasserted their control over Egypt by the gradual extension of their privileges and rights.

The revival of Mamluk power was connected with changes in the fiscal system of Ottoman Egypt. In this, as in earlier periods, the agricultural land of Egypt was the chief source of wealth. Under the Mamluk sultanate, there had been four principal categories of land. First of these was the crown domain, administered by a group of central financial departments. Secondly, there were grants of land (sing., *iqṭāʻ*, often loosely translated 'fief') allotted to the Mamluk *amīrs* and other members of the military and governing élites. Thirdly, certain estates (sing., *waqf*) were devoted in perpetuity to pious foundations. Fourthly, some estates provided income for members or dependants of the military élite, or for pious foundations; these were known respectively as *rizaq* (sing., *rizqa*) *jayshiyya* and *rizaq aḥbāsiyya*.

After the overthrow of the Mamluk sultanate in 1516–17, in order, no doubt, to eliminate the independent financial basis of the former military and ruling élite, extensive changes were made. Although the *iqṭāʿ* was virtually identical with the *timar*, the land-grant which maintained the Ottoman cavalryman in other parts of the empire, it was in practice abolished, and estates so granted were resumed as crown domain. *Waqf* in theory, if not always in practice, was sacrosanct. The two types of *rizaq* were a problem to the Ottoman administrators who reorganized the financial system of Egypt. The *Qānūn-nāme* of 1525 assimilated the *rizqa jayshiyya* to the *iqṭāʿ*, and the *rizqa aḥbāsiyya* to *waqf*, but there remained the difficulty of establishing the precise legal nature of a particular estate. In 1553 and again in 1609–10, inquisitions were held to verify the titledeeds of holders of *rizaq*. Although the *rizaq jayshiyya* were abolished in 1553, the *rizaq aḥbāsiyya* survived until the time of Muḥammad ʿAlī Pasha in the early nineteenth century.

Although the Ottoman conquest was followed by the reversion of almost all the agricultural land of Egypt to the crown, there remained the problem of administering and taxing the domain. At the outset, an attempt was made to withdraw these functions from the Mamluks, and they were confided to salaried officials, known as *amīns*. A few of these were Copts or Jews, but most were Ottomans from the older parts of the empire. Their limited numbers and, no doubt, the difficulties of the peculiar Egyptian system of cultivation and taxation, led them to have recourse to agents (sing., *ʿāmil*), who recompensed themselves by farming the taxes of the districts they administered. The *ʿāmil* thus became a *multazim*, or holder of a tax-farm (*iltizām*). Unlike the *amīns*, the *ʿāmils* were recruited largely from the Mamluks, who as a group thereby regained the control over the revenues of Egypt that they had lost at the conquest. Although *iltizāms* were held by others (e.g. officers of the Ottoman garrison-corps, *ʿulamāʾ*, bureaucrats, merchants and tribal chiefs), by the eighteenth century the Mamluk beys and their clients, especially the great households of the Faqāriyya, Qāsimiyya and Qāzdughliyya, were the principal beneficiaries of the system.

The total revenue from the land was divided into three parts. One portion (*māl al-kharāj*) went to the state treasury. The second (*mukhrijāt*) was used to recompense local officials for the expenses of collection. The third (*fāʾiḍ*, pronounced *fāʾiẓ*) formed the profit of the *multazim*. Although the basic rate of taxation remained formally unchanged throughout the period, and although no new cadastral survey was made after the early seventeenth century, the amount of revenue increased in money terms by about 800 per cent between the end of the sixteenth century and the French occupation. This, however, was a time of prolonged inflation, aggravated by the debasement of the Ottoman currency. At the end of the period, only about 21 per cent of the revenue was assigned to *māl al-kharāj*, while the *mukhrijāt* amounted to 12 per cent, thus leaving about two-thirds in the hands of the *multazims*. In so far as there was a real augmentation in the total amount of land revenue, it resulted partly from an extension of cultivation, but largely from increases in taxation, both in the form of legal additions to the basic rate, and in extra-legal supplements to the *mukhrijāt* and *fā'iḍ* portions.

The most important crops were cereals of various kinds. Wheat was grown chiefly in Upper Egypt, whence large quantities, levied in tax, were shipped to the state granaries in Old Cairo. A substantial portion of this grain was sent to the holy cities in the Hejaz, while of the rest, some was distributed to the '*ulamā*' and other men of religion in Egypt, some to the viceroy and employees of the government. Until about the middle of the seventeenth century, the Egyptian treasury had a surplus of grain, which was sold on the open market – partly to European merchants. During the eighteenth century, as the power of the beys and other notables in Egypt increased, and as political stability diminished, the grain revenues of the Egyptian treasury were seriously reduced. Among the other crops grown in the country, mention should be made of sugar for the sultan's kitchen, and cotton, grown only on a small scale for local manufacture.

The wealth of Egypt was not only derived from agriculture but also from trade, and especially from transit trade. Although the discovery of the Cape route, and the aggressive presence of the Portuguese in the Indian Ocean, posed a threat to sea-borne trade between Egypt and the East, the Ottoman conquest restored Muslim control of the Red Sea, and it was not until the end of the seventeenth century that the commerce of this area seriously declined. During the first 200 years of Ottoman rule, practically the whole of the Red Sea trade passed through Suez, although Qusayr formed a channel for the commerce of Upper Egypt. The eighteenth century saw the decline of Suez and the rise of Qusayr. The principal imports from the East were coffee, spices, and textiles of silk and cotton.

An important vehicle of this trade within the Muslim world was provided by the annual Pilgrimage to the holy cities of Mecca and

Medina. Cairo was the rallying-point, not only for the Egyptian pilgrims, but also for caravans from Morocco, Algiers, Tunis and Tripoli. Other pilgrims from North Africa and from the trans-Saharan Sudan travelled as individuals or in small groups across the desert and from the ports of the Maghrib. The pilgrims would pass some time in Cairo before the great convoy set out, commanded by the *amīr al-Ḥājj* and accompanied by the new covering of the Ka'ba (*kiswa*) and the *maḥmal*, the empty camel-litter, which the rulers of Egypt had sent since the thirteenth century as a symbol of their authority. In Egypt, as at other stages of their journey, the pilgrims would engage in trade, exchanging North African cloth, tarbushes and coral for the fine cottons of India, the coffee of the Yemen, and the pearls of the Persian Gulf. There was also a substantial trade between Egypt and the Barbary states apart from the Pilgrimage. Cairo had its quarters of Maghribī settlement, one of them in the vicinity of the university-mosque of al-Azhar, where the North African *'ulamā'* and students formed an important group. The Maghribī community of Cairo was as a whole a distinctive and turbulent element of the urban population.

Upper Egypt was the area of arrival of trading caravans from the Nilotic Sudan and Darfur. The Sennar caravans had certainly been operating since the emergence of the Funj sultanate early in the sixteenth century, but by the end of the eighteenth century they were less important than the Darfur caravans. At that time the Sennar caravans, of which there were several annually, assembled at Ibrim and then went on to Isna, where they found their principal market. From Darfur an annual caravan went by the desert route called *Darb al-Arba'īn* (the Forty Days' Road) from Kubayh to Asyut and thence to Cairo. This caravan was a principal vehicle of the slave trade, and also carried local products, such as ivory, ostrich feathers and hides. Camels were also imported into Egypt. The Darfur merchants (*jallāba*) were chiefly emigrants from the Nilotic Sudan. The Sennar caravans contributed to a lesser extent to the slave trade, but brought important quantities of gum-arabic, as well as senna, camels and other goods. The slaves brought to Egypt from Sennar and Darfur were not drawn from the Muslim inhabitants of those territories, but were obtained by raiding the pagan tribes on the periphery of the sultanates. The *jallāba* returned with cotton fabrics of Egyptian and Indian manufacture, swords and firearms,[1] coffee and writing-paper.

[1] Firearms were little used in the Nilotic Sudan and Darfur. Burckhardt commented on their rarity in 1814, and remarked, 'To the country people, who seldom visit the towns where traders make any stay, a musquet is an object of the greatest terror, and will frighten

The Mediterranean trade of Egypt passed through the ports of Alexandria and Damietta. Rosetta was less important as a port than as the place of transhipment for goods and passengers going to and from Cairo. Alexandria, although very much decayed by the eighteenth century, traded with Venice, Tuscany, France and England, importing particularly woollen and linen cloth, metal goods, arms and ammunition. Among Egyptian exports were sal-ammoniac, natron and saltpetre, cereals and the products of the Sudan, such as ivory, gum-arabic and senna. Damietta was the port for trade with Istanbul and Syria, exporting (amongst other goods) cereals and black slaves, and importing both the local products of Syria and goods in transit from farther East.

Cairo was the nodal point of Egyptian commerce. It was the rendezvous of caravans arriving from Syria, Upper Egypt and North Africa, as well as for river transport. The Nile was indeed the principal highway of Egypt. Boats carrying the grain of Upper Egypt berthed at Old Cairo, those coming from Rosetta and Damietta at Bulaq. In both these places, as well as at the ports of entry, customs duties were levied. Like other sources of revenue, the customs came to be administered as *iltizāms*, which (with the exception of those of Suez) were from 1671 held by the Janissaries.

Throughout the Ottoman empire, the last quarter of the sixteenth century was a time of social and political crisis. A prolonged inflation played havoc with the fixed salaries of Ottoman officials and soldiers, whose difficulties were reflected in a growth of corruption and indiscipline. Landless peasants from Anatolia swelled the ranks of the imperial army and the private forces of grandees, or turned to rebellion and banditry in time of peace. Egypt shared in these calamities. The last years of the sixteenth century, and the early years of the seventeenth century witnessed a series of revolts by the garrison-soldiers against the viceroys.

Financial and economic grievances were the motives of these risings. The first of them, in 1586, was provoked by an inquiry, conducted by the viceroy, Sinān Pasha, into a deficiency in the tribute due to Istanbul. This was only the first of numerous occasions when a tumult of the soldiery was to end in the suspension of the viceroy. An attempt by the next viceroy, Uways Pasha, to control the soldiery produced another rising in 1589. He was attacked, and his residence in the Citadel

away dozens of them.' (*Travels in Nubia* (London, 1819), 287.) The firearms and artillery of the Turco-Egyptian invaders assured them easy victories over the Shāyqiyya and the Fur in Kordofan in 1820–1.

pillaged, but after a week of disorder the troops were pacified through the intervention of the chief judge and other notables. Uways Pasha was not deprived of office, but he saved himself only by abject capitulation to the mutineers. It is perhaps significant that both this viceroy and his predecessor had formerly served as treasury officials, and may have been appointed to Egypt in order to exercise stricter financial control. The troops who rose against Uways Pasha were *sipāhīs*, members of the cavalry regiments, who served principally as a kind of gendarmerie in the sub-provinces of Egypt. They were ill-paid, and, unlike the Janissaries and 'Azebān who were stationed in the Citadel, were remote from the centre of power. It is not surprising that they played a leading part in this and succeeding military revolts. At the beginning of the seventeenth century, a great dearth in Egypt was followed by a serious epidemic. These troubles no doubt contributed to the misfortunes of the next viceroy, Ibrāhīm Pasha, called ominously by the chroniclers *al-Maqtūl*, 'the Slain'. In 1605, he was trapped outside Cairo by a tumultuous mob of mutinous soldiery, who killed him. His head was paraded around Cairo and then exhibited on one of the city gates. The Ottoman sultan and his representative in Egypt could not be more shamefully treated, and the next two viceroys took strong measures against the troops. The persons implicated in the murder of Ibrāhīm Pasha were identified, arrested and put to death in the audience-hall of the Citadel. An order by the viceroy Muḥammad Pasha forbidding an illegal tax (the *ṭulba*) levied by the *sipāhīs* in the sub-provinces of Egypt produced the most dangerous revolt of the soldiery so far seen. In 1609, the *sipāhīs* gathered at the shrine of Sayyid Aḥmad al-Badawī at Tanta, one of the holiest places in Egypt, and swore not to give up the *ṭulba*. This was not so much a mutiny as a separatist movement, since the troops appointed a sultan and ministers. As they advanced on Cairo, their numbers grew. At al-Khanqa, north of the capital, however, they encountered a motley force, hastily recruited by the viceroy. The rebels' courage rapidly ebbed, they agreed to parley and were put to death or disarmed. Three hundred of them were exiled to the Yemen.

Muḥammad Pasha had won his victory because he had the support of the beys and high military officers, and with their aid was able to suppress a movement of the common soldiery. During the ensuing decades, however, these grandees began to act on their own behalf, and left the viceroys without the means of enforcing their authority. The first symptom of this change in the balance of political power inside

Egypt appeared in 1623, when the viceroy, Muṣṭafā Pasha, was recalled by the sultan, who appointed a certain ʿAlī Pasha as his successor. The troops demanded a rise in pay. The bey who was acting as viceroy complained that this demand recurred every three months. They replied that the frequent changes of viceroy caused hardship and ruin to the Egyptians, and they persisted with their claim. The point of the troops' comment was that each new viceroy paid a sum to the imperial treasury, which thus gained from frequent new appointments, while each viceroy sought to recoup his outlay while he held office. The soldiers tried to protect themselves from the resulting inflation by demanding frequent increases in pay. On this occasion, backed by the beys, the troops refused to accept the new viceroy and petitioned the sultan for the retention of Muṣṭafā Pasha in office. This was conceded. For the first time the holders of power in Egypt had succeeded in imposing their will on the imperial government.

It was not long before the beys emerged as the effective masters of Egypt. In 1631, the viceroy, Mūsā Pasha, procured the assassination of a bey with whom he had a private quarrel. The beys, the corps officers and the troops reacted with complete solidarity. The chief judge was instructed to go to the viceroy, and ask his reason for the assassination. Mūsā Pasha declared that he had acted by the sultan's command, but refused either to produce the order, or to disclaim responsibility by handing over the actual assassins. When he persisted in this attitude, the grandees invested one of the beys as acting viceroy, and sent reports of the affair to Istanbul. Mūsā Pasha was in effect suspended from office. The sultan's government accepted the accusations made against him, and some weeks later sent another to take his place. The grandees of Cairo thereby established a precedent, which in the next century became a prescriptive right, to depose an obnoxious viceroy, and appoint a more complaisant substitute from among themselves, pending a new appointment by the sultan.

The rapid rise of the beylicate to political dominance in seventeenth-century Egypt is mirrored in the career of Riḍwān Bey al-Faqārī, its most outstanding member. He was a Circassian by origin, and belonged to the great Faqāriyya Mamluk household which first begins to appear in the chronicles about this time. At the time of the clash with Mūsā Pasha, he was absent from Egypt as commander of the Pilgrimage caravan. He had, indeed, virtually a life-tenure of this great office of state, which, combined with his headship of the Faqāriyya household, gave him enormous influence in Egypt. Early in his career, he seems to have had the idea of reviving the Mamluk sultanate; in 1632 a genealogy was produced tracing Riḍwān's ancestry back to Sultan Barsbāy (1422–38), and further deriving the Circassians themselves from the Prophet's own tribe, Quraysh of Mecca. The clear implication of this document was that Riḍwān had an hereditary right to rule over Egypt, and a better claim than the Ottoman sultan to assume the protectorate over the holy cities of Islam.

Inevitably, Riḍwān Bey had enemies, both inside and outside Egypt. The early part of his career coincided with the reign of Murād IV (1623–40), the one vigorous sultan of the seventeenth century. This may explain why Riḍwān did not openly put forward the claim to sovereignty adumbrated in the genealogy. The sultan mistrusted Riḍwān, whom he appointed (in 1639) governor of Ḥabesh – the Ottoman province linking Suakin and Massawa. This was equivalent to a sentence of exile. Riḍwān evaded the appointment, and went to plead his cause at Istanbul, where he was placed under house arrest. He was released a few days before Murād's death. The new sultan, Ibrāhīm (1640–9), favoured Riḍwān, who returned to Egypt, and regained his position as commander of the Pilgrimage.

On various occasions, the viceroys sought to deprive Riḍwān Bey of his authority and prestige by obtaining his appointment to a position which would take him out of Egypt. In 1635 and again in 1638, he was nominated as commander of an expeditionary force against the Safavids. In 1639, as we have seen, he was appointed governor of Ḥabesh. These attempts all failed. The viceroys had more success in utilizing the factional spirit, which remained strong among the Mamluks, to discomfit Riḍwān. In rivalry with the Faqāriyya was another great Mamluk household, that of the Qāsimiyya, whose leaders at that time were Māmāy Bey and Qānṣawh Bey. In 1647 the then viceroy (Ḥaydarzāde Muḥammad Pasha) tried to deprive Riḍwān and his comrade, 'Alī Bey al-Faqārī, the governor of Upper Egypt, of their appointments, and confer them on Qānṣawh and Māmāy respectively. Riḍwān had, however, the ear of Sultan Ibrāhīm, and with the support of an imperial order he and 'Alī Bey were able to enforce their will on the viceroy. A proscription of the Qāsimiyya followed, in which Qānṣawh and Māmāy died. This was the first of several armed clashes between the two households, and the seed of a vendetta that lasted for almost a century.

Riḍwān's power was threatened when, in the following year, Sultan Ibrāhīm was deposed and was succeeded by a child, Meḥmed IV

(1648–87). With this change at Istanbul, another viceroy (Aḥmad Pasha the Albanian) endeavoured to break Riḍwān's hold over the command of the Pilgrimage. On this occasion, in 1651, he was replaced by 'Alī Bey al-Faqārī, and was himself given 'Alī's governorship of Upper Egypt. This was clearly an attempt to set the two veteran leaders of the Faqāriyya against each other. But within a fortnight the viceroy had been recalled, the transfers lapsed, and Riḍwān was reconciled to 'Alī. He died in his bed in 1656, 'Alī having predeceased him by three years.

Although Riḍwān and 'Alī were gone, the Faqāriyya sought to maintain their ascendancy under a new generation of leaders. They were confronted, however, not only with the hostility of the viceroys, but with the ambitions of the Qāsimiyya, resurgent after the proscription of 1647. The Qāsimiyya were now led by an able and ruthless Bosniak, named Aḥmad Bey. On Ridwān's death, the viceroy (Abu'l-Nūr Muḥammad Pasha) appointed Aḥmad as commander of the Pilgrimage. The reaction of the Faqāriyya to this infringement of what they regarded as their prescriptive right was instantaneous. They made a tumultuous assembly, and compelled the viceroy to come down from the Citadel. Having appointed a bey as acting viceroy, they procured the exile of Aḥmad Bey the Bosniak, and the appointment of their own nominee, Ḥasan Bey al-Faqārī, to the command of the Pilgrimage. The *fait accompli* was duly reported to Istanbul.

Although Aḥmad Bey was shortly afterwards recalled to Cairo, and the two households were formally reconciled, the schism between Faqāriyya and Qāsimiyya remained as deep as ever. Aḥmad Bey, sent on a mission to Istanbul, returned with an imperial order appointing him treasurer of Egypt. Another crisis soon developed. 'Alī Bey had been succeeded as governor of Upper Egypt by his *mamlūk*, Muḥammad Bey al-Faqārī, who, at the beginning of 1659, received the ominous and unpopular appointment of governor of Ḥabesh, while Aḥmad Bey was nominated to take his place in Upper Egypt. Muḥammad Bey refused to accept the transfer, and prepared to resist. This open disobedience to the sultan, as well as Muḥammad Bey's arrogant bearing towards his colleagues in the beylicate, enabled the viceroy (Shāhsuwāroghlū Ghāzī Muḥammad Pasha) to constitute an expeditionary force against him. The viceroy himself took command. Muḥammad Bey was driven from the Nile valley to one of the oases of the western desert, where he was captured and put to death.

In the following year, 1660, the Faqāriyya were imprudent enough to give their opponents the opportunity to break their ascendancy. A rural affray between the peasants of two tax-farmers had repercussions in Cairo, since one of the tax-farmers was a Janissary officer, while the other had the support of the 'Azebān. The rivalry between these two infantry corps had an economic basis. The artisans and traders of Cairo had been brought under the 'protection' of the garrison, and paid the corps what were in origin illegal levies. The most profitable of these *ḥimāyāt*, as they were called, were held by the Janissaries, and thus excited the jealousy of the other six corps, headed by the 'Azebān. The rivalry between the Janissaries and the 'Azebān was made more serious by the close identification existing between the Janissaries and the Faqāriyya on the one hand, the 'Azebān and the Qāsimiyya on the other. For half a century this system of factional alliances between the corps and the Mamluk households was to be a basic cause of instability in Egypt. It was to provoke three major crises, in 1660, 1692 and 1711, as well as numerous smaller troubles.

The crisis of 1660 developed from the support which the Faqāriyya gave to the Janissary tax-farmer, although he had been incriminated by an investigating commission, and condemned by the chief judge for contumacy towards the viceroy, Muṣṭafā Pasha. The Faqāriyya unwisely decided to resist the viceroy: they intended to reinstate his predecessor, Shāhsuwāroghlū Muḥammad (who had been deprived and imprisoned), and they relied on Janissary support. At the critical moment, however, the Janissaries turned against their Faqārī officers, while the 'Azebān organized a united front of the other corps. Taken at a disadvantage, the Faqāriyya withdrew from Cairo, where the Qāsimiyya established their ascendancy with the viceroy's support. In October 1660, the viceroy left Cairo to command military operations against the fugitive Faqārī beys. These, however, were already splitting up. One made his way to the remote Sudan, where he disappeared from history. Another fled to Upper Egypt, where he was captured. Three others, after a long journey through the western desert, surrendered to Aḥmad Bey the Bosniak, the chief of their opponents, who slew them and rode to Cairo with their heads in his saddle-bag. The Faqāriyya were almost exterminated, and the ascendancy passed to the Qāsimiyya.

But the triumph of Aḥmad the Bosniak and his faction was to be of short duration. His very success rendered him an object of suspicion to the Ottomans. So, although the next viceroy, Shayṭān Ibrāhīm Pasha, entered Cairo accompanied by Aḥmad Bey, he soon plotted his destruction, and in July 1662 the Bosniak was assassinated. More fortunate than Mūsā Pasha thirty-two years before, Shayṭān Ibrāhīm met with no opposition from the diminished and demoralized beylicate. It is probably not a mere coincidence that this late reassertion of viceregal authority, and the period of quiescence which ensued, synchronized with the vigorous rule of the grand viziers Meḥmed and Aḥmed Köprülü (1656–76).

For about thirty years the beys, while retaining their hold on the great offices of state and fulfilling their military functions, ceased to challenge the authority of the viceroys. During this period, the Faqāriyya household was reconstituted, and in 1692 its leader, Ibrāhīm Bey, felt strong enough to bid for political supremacy in Egypt. To achieve this, however, he needed to restore the old link with the Janissaries. This he sought to achieve through the agency of an ambitious Janissary subaltern, named Küchük Muḥammad, who had already for over fifteen years played a leading part in the troubled politics of his corps. Although Küchük Muḥammad never held any of the higher commands in the Janissaries, he was the effective master of the corps, and in 1692 he brought it over to the side of Ibrāhīm Bey. During the next two and a half years, Küchük Muḥammad played a popular role in Cairo. He induced the senior officers of the Janissaries to abolish their *ḥimāyāt*, and, after an abnormally poor harvest, he enforced low corn prices on the middlemen in Cairo. While these measures won him the applause of the artisans, they would inevitably offend profiteers, both within and outside the Janissary corps. The circumstances in which he had obtained power also created him enemies, chief among them a senior officer, Muṣṭafā Kâhya al-Qāzdughlī, who was also an ally of the Faqāriyya. In September 1694, Küchük Muḥammad was shot while riding through Cairo, almost certainly at the instigation of al-Qāzdughlī. The influence of his faction in the Janissaries collapsed at once. His ally, Ibrāhīm Bey, died of plague in the following year. Muṣṭafā al-Qāzdughlī himself founded a Mamluk household, the Qāzdughliyya, which, outlasting its Faqāriyya allies, was to dominate Egypt in the second half of the eighteenth century.

The pattern of troubles within the corps of the garrison repeated itself in the years following the death of Küchük Muḥammad, and produced in 1711 the crisis known to the chroniclers as the Great Sedition. At the centre of events was, once again, an ambitious Janissary subaltern, Afranj Aḥmad, i.e. Aḥmad the European, who, after various vicissitudes in the immediately preceding years, made himself the master of the corps, and ousted eight officers who were opposed to him. These men inevitably obtained the support of the ʻAzebān and the other five corps, and fighting broke out around the Citadel. The beylicate next became involved. The Qāsimiyya under their chief, Īwāẓ Bey, supported the ʻAzebān and opposed Afranj Aḥmad. The Faqāriyya were divided, because of rivalry between two of their leaders, one of whom, Qayṭās Bey, joined forces with the Qāsimiyya. In the fighting, which lasted from April to June, Īwāẓ Bey was killed – an incident which turned the struggle between the two groups into a relentless vendetta. The final outcome was a complete victory for the Qāsimiyya. Afranj Aḥmad was put to death, the Faqārī beys who had supported him fled to Istanbul, while the viceroy, Khalīl Pasha, who had legitimated their acts was deprived of office.

For about twenty years after the Great Sedition, the Qāsimiyya dominated Egypt. Their ascendancy was not, however, unquestioned. The killing of their leader, Īwāẓ Bey, had weakened them, and although Īwāẓ's Mamluk household held together, its nominal head, Ismāʻīl Bey (the son of Īwāẓ) was at the time only sixteen years old. It was in fact Qayṭās Bey who drew most immediate profit from the revolution of 1711. In 1715, Ismāʻīl Bey procured his assassination, and the Qāsimiyya obtained the sole mastery. The Qāsimiyya however, like the Faqāriyya earlier, now split into rival factions. Another group emerged under Muḥammad Bey the Circassian, and in 1723 Ismāʻīl Bey was killed, and his household proscribed.

Since the time of Ibrāhīm Bey al-Faqārī in the last decade of the seventeenth century, the object of ambitious military grandees in Cairo had been to obtain the *ri'āsa*, the *de facto* supremacy amongst the holders of power in Egypt. In the early eighteenth century, certain titles came to be applied to the holder of the *ri'āsa*. Ismāʻīl Bey is called *amīr Miṣr*, ʻthe commander of Cairo'. His successful rival, Muḥammad Bey the Circassian, was apparently the first to be known as *shaykh al-balad* (a term used also for village headmen, and signifying seniority in a town or settlement), and this was henceforward the normal usage when the *ri'āsa* was held by a member of the beylicate. On occasion, however, as we shall see, the *ri'āsa* might be held by officers of the garrison corps.

Muḥammad Bey the Circassian had obtained the *ri'āsa* through alliance with the Faqāriyya, a member of which, Dhu'l-Faqār Bey, had been the actual assassin of Ismāʻīl Bey. The understanding between the two factions was short-lived, and a struggle for domination developed. Both leaders perished in 1730; the Circassian being drowned while fleeing from his enemies, while Dhu'l-Faqār Bey was assassinated.

After 1730 the Qāsimiyya were never again powerful as a faction, although small groups and individuals survived for many years. The political ascendancy passed to their opponents, the Faqāriyya, in alliance with another Mamluk household, that of the Qāzdughliyya. Unlike the Faqāriyya and Qāsimiyya, the early history of which groups is unknown, the Qāzdughliyya had, as we have seen, an identifiable founder: the Janissary officer, Muṣṭafā Kâhya al-Qāzdughlī, who had been Küchük Muḥammad's opponent, and who died in 1703. Unlike the earlier great Mamluk households, which from the outset were closely associated with (and virtually monopolized) the beylicate, the Qāzdughliyya until the middle of the eighteenth century contented themselves with high office in the garrison-corps. This may have been a prudential measure, since members of a corps (and especially of the Janissaries and 'Azebān) enjoyed the protection of the privileged organization to which they belonged, whereas the beys were, in theory at least, creatures of the viceroys and dependent upon them. In the time of Küchük Muḥammad, elevation to the beylicate had been a device for disposing of officers obnoxious to the dominant group.

It was not long before a schism appeared in the victorious faction, with the development of hostility between 'Uthmān Bey, Dhu'l-Faqār's *mamlūk*, and Ibrāhīm Kâhya, the head of the Qāzdughliyya. 'Uthmān fled from Cairo to Upper Egypt and then to Istanbul, where he died over thirty-four years later. By 1748, Ibrāhīm Kâhya had overcome all his opponents. He had as a nominal associate another officer of the corps, Riḍwān Kâhya al-Julfī, the head of a small Mamluk household. The duumvirate lasted until the death of Ibrāhīm, late in 1754. In the meantime, he built up a great Mamluk household, and both he and Riḍwān Kâhya placed their followers in the beylicate. After Ibrāhīm's death, Riḍwān, who had shown no interest in affairs of state, proved incapable of maintaining himself in power, and was assassinated. The ascendancy of the Qāzdughliyya was henceforward assured. For nearly half a century, until the coming of Bonaparte, they filled the beylicate and monopolized the great offices of state, while their successive leaders, with the title of *shaykh al-balad*, were virtually sovereigns in Egypt. The viceroy had become a figurehead, confined to the Citadel, and serving only to legitimize the decisions of the *shaykh al-balad* and the dominant faction.

In the second half of the eighteenth century, some changes in the pattern of political development in Egypt became apparent. With the disappearance from the scene of the Faqāriyya and Qāsimiyya, the old rivalry between the Janissaries and 'Azebān came to an end. With the installation of the Qāzdughliyya in the beylicate, even the high commands in the corps of the garrison were reduced to secondary importance: Ibrāhīm Kâhya was the last corps-officer to play a major political role. The ascendancy of the Qāzdughliyya did not, however, bring to an end the inveterate factionalism of Mamluk society. The Qāzdughlī beys were rivals amongst themselves for power; the households which they established soon displayed as much hostility towards one another as ever the Faqāriyya had shown to the Qāsimiyya. In a sequence repeated with monotonous regularity in this period, factional conflict in Cairo would be followed by the flight of the defeated group to Upper Egypt. There they would build up their strength, attracting the malcontent victims of previous struggles as well as tribal warriors, and would move down the Nile, to evict their opponents, who would flee southwards to repeat the process.

The most outstanding among the Qāzdughlī leaders was a certain 'Alī Bey, known to his contemporaries by the Turkish nickname of *Bulut kapan*, 'the Cloud-catcher', but more usually called 'Alī Bey the Great. As a boy from the Caucasus, he entered the Mamluk household of Ibrāhīm Kâhya, and he was raised to the beylicate shortly after his master's death. He was thus still quite junior in standing when, in 1760, he joined in a plot against the *shaykh al-balad* (another 'Alī Bey), set on foot by 'Abd al-Raḥmān Kâhya al-Qāzdughlī, the hereditary head of the household. At 'Abd al-Raḥmān's request, the Qāzdughliyya recognized *Bulut kapan* 'Alī Bey as *shaykh al-balad*, and his namesake, who was at that time absent in the Hejaz as commander of the Pilgrimage, fled to Gaza.

'Abd al-Raḥmān may have thought that the young 'Alī Bey would be a compliant agent. If so, he was sadly mistaken. 'I will take command', he said on one occasion, 'by my sword alone, and not by the support of anyone.'[1] Once formally installed as *shaykh al-balad*, he proceeded to establish and extend his power with a ruthlessness, not least towards his comrades, that astonished even the hardbitten observers of the Egyptian political scene. In the words of al-Jabartī, the great Egyptian chronicler of the eighteenth and early nineteenth centuries,

> He killed rebels, and cut off opponents, and dispersed those who feigned loyalty. He infringed established principles, shattered customs, ruined the ancient houses, and annulled the rules which had been deemed right.[2]

[1] 'Abd al-Raḥmān b. Ḥasan al-Jabartī, *'Ajā'ib al-āthār fi'l-tarājim wa'l-akhbār* (Būlāq, [1879–80]), I, 380.
[2] al-Jabartī, *'Ajā'ib*, I, 258.

'Alī also sought to impress beholders with his magnificence. In 1761 he secured the marriage of one of his followers, Ismā'īl Bey, to the daughter of Ibrāhīm Kâhya. The marriage was the occasion of a sumptuous festival for the whole of Cairo. The Nile flood had formed lakes in the open spaces within the city, and upon one of these a great floating platform was constructed, where people could watch the performances of jugglers and other entertainers. Around the lake, the houses of the Qāzdughlī grandees shone at night with illuminations, and resounded with banqueting and music. These festivities lasted for a full month, and at its end the bride was taken to her husband in a great procession. Jugglers, cymbal-players and drummers were followed by the grandees. Then came the bride in a coach, beside which walked 'Alī Bey's domestic treasurer, holding a staff of office. Other Mamluks followed, clad in mail, armed with bows and spears, while a Turkish military band brought up the rear.

The next few years saw the further growth of 'Alī Bey's power. In 1764 he himself commanded the pilgrimage caravan from Egypt, and, while in Mecca, had an ominous quarrel with the governor of Damascus, 'Uthmān Pasha al-Ṣādiq, the commander of the Syrian pilgrimage caravan. On his return he raised to the beylicate his treasurer and favourite *mamlūk*, Muḥammad. It was customary for a bey, on appointment, to be invested with a robe of honour by the viceroy, and, as he rode down from the Citadel, to throw silver coins among the crowd. Muḥammad Bey, however, scattered a largesse of gold, and this won him the nickname of Abu'l-Dhahab, 'the Father of Gold'. Other followers of 'Alī Bey were promoted to the beylicate at this time, and now he felt strong enough to strike at his potential opponents. 'Abd al-Raḥmān Kâhya was arrested, and exiled to the Hejaz in 1765. He returned to Cairo only in 1776, after 'Alī's death. While 'Alī was planning the defeat of his former associate, Ṣāliḥ Bey, the last Qāsimī grandee, who had fled to Upper Egypt, he suddenly found that his party in Cairo had turned against him. He yielded to a show of force, and in March 1766 was sent into exile. About a year later, he himself made his way to Upper Egypt, while two of his opponents, Khalīl Bey and Ḥusayn Bey Kishkish, held the *ri'āsa* in Cairo.

At this time, the most powerful person in Upper Egypt was Shaykh Humām b. Yūsuf, the chief of the Hawwāra tribe, whose members held much of Upper Egypt in hereditary *iltizām*. Shaykh Humām overshadowed the transient governors of Upper Egypt, who were distracted by factional politics. He and his tribe belonged to Niṣf Ḥarām, a factional group of Egyptian townspeople and tribesmen which was traditionally associated with the Qāsimiyya, as its counterpart and rival, Niṣf Sa'd, was with the Faqāriyya. Hence he gave asylum to the remnants of the Qāsimiyya after their overthrow, and had particularly close relations with Ṣāliḥ Bey, who served as his agent in Cairo. When 'Alī Bey fled to Upper Egypt, Humām mediated between him and Ṣāliḥ, and the two beys swore an alliance on the Koran and the sword. They agreed to march on Cairo, 'Alī undertaking in the event of success to confer on Ṣāliḥ the life-governorship of Upper Egypt, while Humām assisted the new allies with money and men. An expedition commanded by Kishkish was defeated, and, in October 1767, 'Alī and Ṣāliḥ entered Cairo as victors. A few months later, Khalīl and Kishkish, who were holding out at Tanta, were captured and killed. 'Alī followed up his success with a relentless proscription of his opponents, both actual and potential. Among the victims was Ṣāliḥ Bey. Shaykh Humām, who had assisted the followers of the dead grandee, was hunted down, and died in December 1769. With his downfall, the political supremacy of Hawwāra in Upper Egypt came to an end.

The great power which 'Alī Bey had acquired in Egypt could not fail to alarm the Ottoman authorities. In the winter of 1768, the viceroy attempted to instigate a rising in Cairo, and was promptly removed from office by 'Alī, who became acting viceroy. In the following summer, he repeated the procedure. To his contemporaries, 'Alī seemed about to declare himself the independent ruler of Egypt. Like Riḍwān Bey in the previous century, he was haunted by the dream of a new Mamluk sultanate. Nevertheless, he remained outwardly loyal to the Ottoman sultan, who in 1770 commissioned him to intervene in a conflict between two members of the Hashimite family, which ruled in Mecca. An expedition, commanded by Muḥammad Bey Abu'l-Dhahab, captured Mecca, invested 'Alī's protégé as ruler, and appointed a Mamluk as governor of Jedda, with which port ships of the English East India Company had been trading since the end of the seventeenth century. This successful campaign spurred 'Alī Bey on to a military adventure in Syria. With this region under his control, he would in effect have reconstituted the former empire of the Mamluk sultans. Circumstances were particularly favourable to him. An Arab chief, Shaykh Ẓāhir al-'Umar, had built up an autonomous principality in Galilee, with his capital at Acre, and was in rebellion against the Ottomans. The Ottoman empire was at war with Russia. In July 1770 a Russian fleet had annihilated that of the Ottomans at Cheshme, and thereafter remained in the eastern Mediterranean to assist local opponents of the sultan. ʿAlī's plans, however, miscarried. After an expeditionary force under Abu'l-Dhahab had taken Damascus in June 1771, it suddenly withdrew from Syria, abandoning its conquests and Shaykh Ẓāhir al-ʿUmar.

On Abu'l-Dhahab's return to Egypt, a clash was inevitable. In January 1772, he took the now well-trodden path of the malcontents to Upper Egypt, where he recruited supporters, including remnants of the Qāsimiyya and Hawwāra tribesmen. Abandoned and defeated as Abu'l-Dhahab advanced down the Nile, ʿAlī loaded up his treasures, and, with his personal retinue of 800 cavalrymen, fled in April 1772 to Shaykh Ẓāhir in Acre. The day after his departure, Abu'l-Dhahab entered Cairo, and assumed the position of *amīr Miṣr*. ʿAlī spent nearly a year operating against the Ottomans in Syria, in combination with Shaykh Ẓāhir and the Russians. Early in 1773, he decided to return to Egypt, optimistically believing that he would be supported and welcomed by his former *mamlūks* and associates. The reality was very different. At al-Salihiyya, where the route from Sinai approached the Delta, he was intercepted by a force under Abu'l-Dhahab's command. In the ensuing battle, ʿAlī was wounded and made a prisoner. The victor came out to greet his former master and kissed his hand with all respect. ʿAlī was lodged in a palace in Cairo, and doctors were sent to treat his wounds. A week later he died, and Abu'l-Dhahab (who was inevitably suspected of foul play) gave his corpse honourable burial.

The death of ʿAlī Bey left Muḥammad Abu'l-Dhahab without any competitor for the supremacy in Egypt. In place of the arrogant attitude which his predecessor had assumed towards the Ottoman sultanate, he himself evinced a demonstrative loyalty, although his aims were perhaps not very different from those of ʿAlī Bey – namely the securing of his own position in Egypt, and the extension of his rule into Syria. In 1775, with the sanction of the Ottoman authorities, he led an expeditionary force against Shaykh Ẓāhir al-ʿUmar. Jaffa was captured after a siege, and Abu'l-Dhahab arrived outside the gates of Acre, Ẓāhir's capital. There, quite suddenly, he died on 8 June 1775, and the Egyptian forces, headed by Murād Bey, one of Abu'l-Dhahab's *mamlūks*, forthwith abandoned the expedition, and returned to Cairo, where a contest for power amongst the grandees was inevitable.

The possible claimants were three: Murād himself; his comrade, Ibrāhīm Bey, another *mamlūk* of Abu'l-Dhahab; and Ismāʿīl Bey, the *mamlūk* of Ibrāhīm Kâhya and client of ʿAlī Bey, an older man. In fact,

Ismā'īl Bey held aloof from competition, and the grandees chose Ibrāhīm Bey as *shaykh al-balad*. This was probably because he was of a milder and less decisive character than the ruthless and headstrong Murād, who, however, remained so closely associated with him in the exercise of power and dispensing of patronage that we may properly speak of a duumvirate. Murād was determined to eliminate Ismā'īl Bey, who in 1777 fled, fearing assassination and complaining of the treatment he had received from his colleagues. Faction-fighting ensued, in which the party of Ismā'īl was victorious. Ibrāhīm and Murād left Cairo, and Ismā'īl Bey was in his turn invested as *shaykh al-balad* (July 1777).

He did not long remain in office. Ibrāhīm and Murād, who had fled to Upper Egypt, were able to exert pressure by cutting off the corn supplies of Cairo. The combination of forces which supported Ismā'īl Bey broke up, and in February 1778 he left Cairo. Murād and Ibrāhīm returned, and the latter resumed the position of *shaykh al-balad*. Late in 1783, relations between the duumvirs degenerated to the point of open conflict, and in the following year Ibrāhīm Bey was driven out of Cairo, while Murād assumed sole power. They were, however, reconciled, and Ibrāhīm once again became *shaykh al-balad* in February 1785.

The affairs of Egypt were in the last stage of confusion and debility. Although the duumvirs held Cairo and the Delta, they had no authority in Upper Egypt, where Ismā'īl Bey and a number of other grandees, former *mamlūks* of 'Alī Bey, were in control. An attempt by Murād to dislodge them failed, and in 1781 he negotiated terms which conceded them much of the south. In 1783 and 1784, Egypt was in an appalling condition, as al-Jabartī describes:

This year passed like the previous one, with hardship, dearth, a poor Nile and continued disturbances. Expropriations and oppressions by the grandees went on and on. Their retainers swarmed in the countryside, levying money from the villages and settlements, and devising new kinds of oppressions... so that they destroyed the cultivators. [The peasants]... fled from their villages, so they transferred the demands to the tax-farmers, and sent appointed officers to their houses, so the less well-off were forced to sell their belongings, homes and cattle... Anyone who had a smell of wealth was tracked down: he was arrested and detained, and was burdened with a double tax-assessment. There were endless demands for loans from the coffee and spice-merchants, besides dues levied in advance; and when the merchants realized that they would get nothing back, they compensated their losses by putting up prices. Then [the authorities] put their hands out to legacies. When anyone died, they detained his possessions, whether he had an heir or not... People's wills were corrupted, their hearts changed, and their natures altered...until the country was ruined, the roads became the prey of highwaymen, evil-doers caused disturbances, security was lost, and one could only travel in a convoy.[1]

These anarchic conditions seemed to offer the Ottoman authorities an opportunity for intervention to end the ascendancy of the beylicate, and to bring Egypt back under the control of the sultan's officials. More particularly, the Ottoman government wished to obtain payment of the revenues of Egypt, which had fallen seriously into arrears during the duumvirate. The actual pretext chosen for intervention was the failure of the grandees to fulfil the obligations of Egypt towards the Pilgrimage and the holy cities. Both in 1784 and 1785, the Egyptian pilgrimage caravan failed to visit Medina as the commander would not, or could not, pay the traditional dues. Information about this was sent to Istanbul. The commander of the Syrian pilgrimage caravan, Aḥmad Pasha al-Jazzār, a former retainer of ʿAlī Bey, who, after the overthrow of Shaykh Ẓāhir, had become governor of Acre and (at this time) of Damascus, was involved in the affair. A report from him to the Ottoman government, in the summer of 1785, suggested military and political steps for re-establishing the sultan's authority in Egypt.

Al-Jazzār hoped that he himself would be appointed as viceroy of Egypt to carry out the reconquest. However, he was disappointed, and the command went to a distinguished Ottoman admiral, Jeza'irli Ghāzī Ḥasan Pasha, who arrived at Alexandria with his fleet and expeditionary force in July 1786. The duumvirs, who had sought to avert his coming by negotiations with the viceroy, as well as by attempts to procrastinate, at last determined on resistance. Characteristically, Murād Bey took command of the force which set out from Cairo in the direction of Rosetta, while Ibrāhīm Pasha remained in the capital to watch events. It was significant, too, that Murād confiscated the provisions and finance of the Pilgrimage to supply his force. Ḥasan Pasha, in the mean-time, was trying to win hearts in Egypt. He distributed proclamations promising reduced taxes and an administration adhering to the long-obsolete *Qānūn-nāme* of Sultan Süleymān. He treated kindly a deputation of garrison-officers and *ʿulamāʾ* who had been sent from Cairo to negotiate with him. When he defeated Murād's troops at al-Rahmaniyya on the Nile, the viceroy was encouraged to assert himself, and produced an imperial order granting an amnesty to all but Ibrāhīm and Murād, who were outlawed. Ibrāhīm fled from Cairo, and in company with

[1] al-Jabartī, *ʿAjāʾib*, II, 83.

Murād ultimately made his way to Upper Egypt. In early August 1786, Ḥasan Pasha entered Cairo.

During the first few days of restored Ottoman rule, Ḥasan Pasha put into force a number of measures to characterize the new administration. Attempts were made to define and regularize the status of various groups in Egyptian society. The *Ashrāf*, or reputed descendants of the Prophet, who formed a kind of hereditary aristocracy in the Ottoman empire, were to refer their complaints to the head of their order, the *naqīb al-Ashrāf*; the garrison-troops were to have recourse similarly to the corps authorities, and the native Egyptians to the *Sharī'a* courts, administering the holy law of Islam. The Islamic character of the new regime was emphasized by the enforcement of sumptuary laws against Christians (who were also not allowed to employ Muslims or keep slaves), and by restricting the public activities and appearance of women.

Ḥasan Pasha vindicated the authority of the sultan in Cairo and Lower Egypt, but he could achieve little more. Like Sultan Selīm I at the time of the original conquest, he could not annihilate the strongly entrenched local powers; at most he could dispossess those who opposed him, and build up a pro-Ottoman party in opposition to Ibrāhīm and Murād. New appointments were made to the beylicate and to garrison commands, the new office-holders being selected from different Mamluk households to prevent their combination. Finally, in November, the exiled Ismā'īl Bey entered Cairo, and was appointed *shaykh al-balad* by Ḥasan Pasha.

The Ottoman admiral equally found himself at a loss in dealing with the unbroken power of Ibrāhīm and Murād. Following what were now the traditional tactics of a defeated faction, they had withdrawn to Upper Egypt, and in so doing clashed with Ismā'īl Bey as he returned from exile. Having received a reinforcement of troops, Ḥasan Pasha in September 1786 sent out an expedition against the rebels. But neither by military force nor by negotiation could Ḥasan Pasha impose a settlement, although at one time his army occupied Egypt as far as Aswan. By the summer of 1787, war between the Ottoman empire and Russia was imminent: Ḥasan Pasha, urgently needed in Istanbul, was driven to make terms with Ibrāhīm and Murād, in whose favour events had now begun to turn. On the eve of his departure, late in September 1787, the death sentences which had been pronounced on Ibrāhīm and Murād were reversed, but the two beys were to reside in Upper Egypt (where they had extensive estates), and not to enter

Cairo. A force of 500 Ottoman troops was left to support Ismāʿīl Bey, who, on Ḥasan Pasha's return to Istanbul, assumed supreme power in Cairo.

The situation in Egypt was now substantially what it had been before Ḥasan Pasha's intervention but with the roles of Ismāʿīl Bey on the one hand, and Ibrāhīm and Murād on the other, reversed. The country was virtually divided between the two rival and autonomous regimes. Extortionate and oppressive taxation, and lack of public security, again appeared as the two factions struggled in the valley of the Nile. Then in March 1791, Ismāʿīl Bey died in an epidemic of plague. Four months later, Ibrāhīm and Murād were back in Cairo, and the duumvirate was restored, to last until the arrival of Bonaparte, seven years later.

The people of Cairo were not wholly passive under their oppressors. It is at this time that the chronicler, al-Jabartī, gives information on the first indisputably popular risings in the capital. Unlike the revolts of the seventeenth and early eighteenth centuries, in which the actors were members of the garrison-corps or of Mamluk households, these were risings of sections of the civilians of Cairo. At the same time, the *ʿulamāʾ* appeared in close association with these revolts, even as leaders. This again is something very different from the role of the *ʿulamāʾ* in the previous century, when their authority was invoked by victorious factions to legitimize the acts of the military grandees.

One such rising took place in 1786, shortly before Ḥasan Pasha's expedition, when the exactions and depredations of Murād Bey's henchmen in the Ḥusayniyya suburb (a butchers' quarter) produced a threatening demonstration. It made its way to al-Azhar, where one of the leading *ʿulamāʾ* put himself at its head. Another, in 1787, shortly after Ḥasan Pasha's departure, was caused by a forced loan which Ismāʿīl Bey imposed on the merchants. Again, the demonstrators went to al-Azhar, and secured the support of a member of the *ʿulamāʾ*. A third revolt, in 1790, originated like that of 1786 in the Ḥusayniyya quarter. It was due to the injudicious attempt of the chief of police to arrest a butcher, who was also *shaykh* of the Bayyūmiyya religious order – a dervish organization centred in that quarter. Once again, one of the *ʿulamāʾ* intervened. Finally, in 1795, the exactions of the Mamluk grandees stirred up another popular rising, at the head of which were *ʿulamāʾ* of al-Azhar. Thus, on the eve of the French occupation two new political factors were emerging in Cairo.

THE FUNJ SULTANATE

The early sixteenth century, which witnessed in Egypt the fall of the Mamluk sultanate and the imposition of Ottoman rule, was a time of even more far-reaching changes in the Nilotic Sudan. The penetration of Arab tribal immigrants to the confluence of the Blue and White Niles and the northern Gezira, and the emergence of a non-Arab power on the upper Blue Nile in the Funj sultanate, created conditions in which Islam and Arab culture expanded to limits they did not pass until the middle of the nineteenth century.

The penetration of the Arabs into the Nilotic Sudan began very shortly after the Muslim conquest of Egypt in the seventh century. Tribal migration increased in the ninth century, beginning the erosion of the Christian Nubian kingdoms of al-Muqurra and 'Alwa. The intermarriage of Arabs with Nubians (and with Beja) in the eastern desert led to the establishment of arabized Muslim dynasties in the north, the first of these being Banu'l-Kanz in the neighbourhood of Aswan during the tenth century. From 1317 the rulers of Dongola were Muslims, al-Muqurra was submerged under the immigration of Arab nomads, chiefly belonging to the tribe of Juhayna, and pressure on the southern kingdom of 'Alwa increased. The last two centuries of its history are a dark age, but Sudanese tradition indicates that its final overthrow came with the fall of Suba, the capital, about the beginning of the sixteenth century.

The consequence of these developments was to create, beside the nomadic Arabs of Juhayna, an arabized sedentary or semi-sedentary population in the cultivable lands on the main Nile and in the northern Gezira, the plain between the Blue and White Niles. The name of Ja'aliyyūn was applied generically to many of these arabized groups: more specifically it designated the riverain people dwelling on the main Nile between the Sabaluqa gorge and the confluence of the Atbara. As a token of arabization, the Ja'aliyyūn acquired a genealogy linking their diverse clans with al-'Abbās, the uncle of the Prophet and the ancestor of the 'Abbasid caliphs. Hence in Sudanese usage, *al-'Abbāsī* is a dignified alternative to *al-Ja'alī*.

About the time when 'Alwa was finally crumbling under Arab pressure, another ethnic group entered upon the stage of the Nilotic Sudan. These were the Funj, a group of cattle-herdsmen, who moved into the Gezira from the south. Three hypotheses have been advanced concerning the origin of the Funj. The earliest, propounded by James

Bruce, the eighteenth-century Scottish traveller, derives them from a Shilluk war-band migrating in canoes from the While Nile. This seems to reflect an opinion held at Sennar at the time of Bruce's visit in 1772: it lacks confirmatory evidence in Shilluk traditions and elsewhere. The second hypothesis, which traces the Funj dynasty to 'Uthmān b. Kaday, a fifteenth-century refugee prince from Bornu, seems to the present writer to be highly speculative, and to rest essentially upon the doubtful identification of a place name in a nineteenth-century chronicle. The third hypothesis would bring the Funj to the Blue Nile from Ethiopia (or more specifically from Eritrea), but here again the conclusions reached are largely based on conjecture.

It is perhaps best to admit that, in the present state of our knowledge, nothing can be said with certainty about the origins of the Funj. Some traditions in one early recension of the Funj Chronicle suggest that their early homeland was on the upper Blue Nile, and that they were nomadic cattle-herdsmen, who gradually extended the range of their migrations downstream until they established a settlement in a forest clearing at Sennar. The founder of Sennar and of the dynasty was named 'Amāra Dūnqas. David Reubeni, the Jewish adventurer, who claimed to have passed through the Nilotic Sudan in 1522–3, depicts 'Amāra as a black potentate with a barbaric court, and describes him as ruling 'over black people and white'. The 'white people' were presumably the lighter-skinned Arabs. He mentions Sennar as a place of importance, but the king's headquarters, which is named Lam'ul or La'ul, was farther south.

Bruce and the Funj Chronicle give variant (but not necessarily contradictory) traditions concerning the early relations of the Arabs and the Funj. According to Bruce, in 1504 the Funj invaded the Arab provinces, and in a battle near Arbaji in the Gezira defeated an Arab chief whom he calls Wed Ageeb [Wad 'Ajīb], 'and forced him to a capitulation...and he thus became as it were their lieutenant'.[1] The earliest extant recensions of the Funj Chronicle represent 'Amāra as joining an Arab chief, called 'Abdallāh al-Quraynātī al-Qāsimī, to fight the indigenous people of the region, the 'Anaj, and as appointing 'Abdallāh as shaykh in Qarri, a settlement on the main Nile, not far from Suba. Later recensions of the Funj Chronicle add further details, which are sophistications and may be disregarded.

The impression given by these traditions is of two pastoral peoples

[1] James Bruce, *Travels to discover the source of the Nile*, 2nd ed. (Edinburgh, 1805), VI, 370–1.

competing for the grazing grounds of the Gezira in the political vacuum following the collapse of ʿAlwa. Although the Funj Chronicle does not mention the clash of the Funj and Arabs at Arbaji, it emphasizes, as does Bruce, the superior status of the Funj ruler. Bruce's date of 1504 corresponds with that (910/1504–5) traditionally given for the Funj conquest of the land of the Nubians and the foundation of Sennar by ʿAmāra Dūnqas. Bruce's naming of the Arab chief as 'Wed Ageeb', i.e. Wad, or Walad, ʿAjīb, is anachronistic. ʿAjīb, the son of ʿAbdallāh, was the second shaykh of Qarri, and his successors were commonly known by the patronymic Wad ʿAjīb, i.e. 'son of ʿAjīb'. This ruling clan was also called the ʿAbdallāb.

ʿAbdallāh himself is a semi-legendary personage. He is often called ʿAbdallāh *Jammāʿ*, i.e. 'Gatherer' – a reference to the tribal host he assembled for his campaigns. The traditions of the ʿAbdallāb, in spite of discrepancies, suggest that his ancestor was an immigrant from Arabia and a Sharif (implying in this context a claim to be a holy man) who married into Juhayna. Abdallāh himself is shown as a warrior for the faith of Islam, who defeated the Christians of ʿAlwa (the ʿAnaj) and captured Suba itself. Thus ʿAjīb and his successors were a holy family as well as a chiefly dynasty.

Although both Funj and Arabs were nomads by origin, the ruling families soon settled in permanent towns. The Funj capital was at Sennar, perhaps from the time of Rubāṭ, who reigned from 1616–17 to 1644–5 and founded the mosque there. The ʿAbdallāb royal residence was transferred from Qarri to Halfaya, probably about the middle of the eighteenth century. From these small urban centres they exercised control over the cultivators of the irrigated river banks and islands and of the rain lands, and also over the nomads of the Gezira and of the Butana to the east of the Nile. The horsemen of the ʿAbdallāb and Funj intercepted the nomads on their annual transhumance, and levied a tribute of camels, cattle, gold and slaves.

Of the ten Funj kings who succeeded ʿAmāra Dūnqas, little has been preserved beyond their names (sometimes in varying forms) and regnal dates. In contrast, there is a strong tradition concerning the great ʿAbdallābī ruler, Shaykh ʿAjīb al-Kāfūta, known also by his Funj title as *al-Mānjilak*, the son of ʿAbdallāh Jammāʿ. He was appointed viceroy of the north on his father's death by ʿAmāra II Abū Ṣikaykīn, who ruled from 1557–8 to 1568–9. ʿAjīb is described as a great islamizing ruler, who appointed *Sharīʿa* judges in his territory, made grants of land to holy men, and fought in the jihad. Early in the seventeenth century, a complex crisis developed, which involved the Funj and 'Abdallābī rulers, and the emperor of Ethiopia, Susenyos. Gondar, where Susenyos had his capital, lay not far from the Funj–Ethiopian frontier, which ran among the foothills separating the upper waters of the Blue Nile, Dinder, Rahad, Atbara, Gash and their tributaries. A caravan route linked Gondar with Sennar and Egypt.

In November 1606, the Funj king, 'Abd al-Qādir II, was driven from his throne after a reign of less than three years. According to 'Abdallābī tradition, he was expelled by 'Ajīb because of his religious innovations, i.e. his Islamic unorthodoxy. He had already, it seems, accepted the suzerainty of the Ethiopian emperor, and on his dethronement he found asylum at Chelga, an enclave on the caravan route from Sennar to Gondar where the Funj had a customs post. Funj power revived under 'Adlān I, the brother and successor of 'Abd al-Qādir, who defeated and killed 'Ajīb at the battle of Karkuj, probably in 1611–12. 'Ajīb's sons fled to Dongola. A reconciliation was effected by a holy man, Shaykh Idrīs Muḥammad al-Arbāb, the maternal cousin of the 'Abdallābī princes, one of whom was then appointed as viceroy of the north.

At the end of his victorious campaign, however, 'Adlān was in his turn deposed by the son of 'Abd al-Qādir. The new king, Bādī I Sīd al-Qūm, appears to have resented the protection given by Susenyos to his father; at any rate, he repudiated Ethiopian suzerainty, and stirred up the 'Abdallābī shaykh to raid across the frontier. The relations between the two rulers deteriorated. Susenyos succeeded in detaching the 'Abdallāb from their dependence on the Funj, while Bādī received a fugitive Muslim governor at Sennar and refused to give Susenyos satisfaction in the matter. Bādī died in 1616–17, before the outbreak of hostilities, which began early in the reign of his successor, Rubāṭ. From the summer of 1618 to that of 1619, the Ethiopians in alliance with the 'Abdallābī shaykh raided along the frontier from Fazughli, west of the Blue Nile, to al-Taka, the region of the present-day Kasala, between the Atbara and the Gash. Then fighting seems to have petered out, leaving the frontier-line much as it had been before. It may well be that, as has been asserted, 'What was at stake was not an increase of area but control of an important trade-route and the customs-posts along it.'[1]

The river line of the Blue and main Niles from the marches of Ethiopia to the vicinity of the Third Cataract formed the geographical

[1] O. G. S. Crawford, *The Fung kingdom of Sennar* (Gloucester, 1951), 187.

axis of the Funj state, and the suzerainty of the Funj king over the 'Abdallābī viceroy was its administrative and political basis. Expansion westwards began under 'Abd al-Qādir I, who reigned from 1550–1 to 1557–8, and conquered the pagan rulers of Jebel Moya and Jebel Saqadi, two hills lying in the Gezira west of Sennar. Bādī II Abū Daqan, who reigned from 1644–5 to 1680, fought the Shilluk, who dominated the White Nile. Alays (the modern al-Kawwa) on the eastern bank of the river became the centre of Funj power in the area. Bādī then advanced through the plain of Kordofan on Taqali, a small Muslim state in the Nuba Mountains, ruled by an arabized dynasty, where he imposed a tribute of slaves. These were established in villages around Sennar to protect the capital. Bruce passed through these villages of slave warriors, who, from his account, were constantly being freshly recruited. While the first generation of Nuba remained pagan, their children were usually Muslim.

Essentially, the Funj sultanate was a species of high kingship over subordinate rulers. The territory directly controlled by the Funj king seems to have been limited to the vicinity of Sennar in the southern Gezira and up the Blue Nile, where his officers gathered taxes. Alays was, in Bruce's time, governed by a member of the royal clan; elsewhere local rulers seem to have belonged to established families. The 'Abdallābī shaykh, as viceroy of the north, occupied a similar position in regard to the nomads and sedentaries of the northern Gezira and the main Nile. Some further degree of Funj control in this area is indicated by the presence of members of the royal clan at Dongola and in other northern courts. Nevertheless, neither the Funj king nor his viceroy was able to prevent the secession of the powerful Shāyqiyya tribe in the seventeenth century. The Beja of the Red Sea Hills were never effectively dominated by the riverain rulers, although some kind of connection, possibly a marriage tie, between the Amarar Beja and the 'Abdallāb is implied by a genealogical legend of a marriage between 'Ajīb al-Kāfūta (or his brother) and a girl of the Amarar.

A potential threat to the kings came from the Funj warriors themselves. Bādī II's expedition to Taqali may have been deliberately planned in order to recruit slave troops, to form a personal bodyguard for the king, and an alternative military basis for the Funj dynasty. On at least two occasions the free Funj warriors rose against the reigning king. A revolt against Bādī III al-Aḥmar (1692–1716), led by the Funj commander, the Amīn Irdāb, was supported by the 'Abdallābī shaykh of the time and by the governor of Alays. The rebels appointed a shadow king, and reduced Bādī to desperate straits. Through his sister, however, he succeeded in winning the support of two eminent holy men; and with a small force of cavalry he routed his opponents and killed the *amīn*. His son, Ūnsa III, was deposed in 1720 by 'his people, the Funj, and the troops of Lūlū'.[1] Lūlū (which may be the Lam'ul/La'ul of Reubeni's account) appears to mean the southern part of the kingdom, on the upper Blue Nile, and hence the original homeland of the Funj. The new king, Nūl, who had been a high officer of the royal household, did not belong to the Ūnsāb, the former ruling clan, to which he was related through his mother.

After a short reign, Nūl was succeeded by his son, Bādī IV Abū Shulūkh (1724–62), who was a minor. For some years the kingdom was ruled by a good minister, but on his death Bādī assumed the reins of government. The Funj Chronicle paints him in dark colours:

> He killed the rest of the Ūnsāb, and took their estates from the great families. He gained for himself the support of the Nūba, and gave them the estates of the great families. Likewise he appointed as provincial governors the Fūr, the people of Shaykh Khamīs walad [i.e. son of] Janqal, and gained their support against the Funj and the family of the previous kings.[2]

These phrases of the chronicler suggest a deliberate policy on the part of a parvenu ruler to extirpate the family of his predecessors and to enfeeble the established aristocracy, while seeking the support of alien groups – the Nuba slave-soldiers and the people of Khamīs. These last were refugee members of the Musabbaʿat clan of the Fur, who had been expelled from their former homes in Kordofan. Khamīs and his men played an important part in defeating an Ethiopian army in the vicinity of Sennar (1744). It may have been at Khamīs's instigation that Bādī shortly afterwards (1747) sent an expeditionary force into Kordofan against the Musabbaʿat. The Funj warriors suffered two defeats, several of their leaders being killed, but they were rallied by a certain Muḥammad Abū Likaylik, on whom Bādī conferred the command. Abū Likaylik expelled the Musabbaʿat from central Kordofan, which he governed as a dependency of the Funj kingdom.

In sending an expedition into Kordofan, Bādī may have had the object of removing from Sennar and its vicinity the leaders of Funj opposition to his rule. The news of his actions which filtered through to Kordofan was disquieting. In 1756–7 the king put to death a respected *ʿālim*, the preacher in the royal mosque at Sennar, on a false

[1] al-Shāṭir Buṣaylī ʿAbd al-Jalīl, ed. *Makhṭūṭat Kātib al-Shūna* (n.p., n.d. [? Cairo, ? 1961]), 19.
[2] Ibid. 20–1.

accusation. He was unable to restrain the licence of his sons. Persons who fell into disfavour were sent to work with slaves on the royal estate. Finally he laid exactions on the families of the officers serving in Kordofan. A conspiracy was thereupon hatched. Under Abū Likaylik's leadership the army of Kordofan marched on the Gezira. At Alays they were joined by Bādī's son Nāṣir, to whom Abū Likaylik promised the kingdom. Bādī put up no resistance, and was allowed to leave Sennar under an amnesty (1762). He made his way to Ethiopia where the ruler installed him as governor of the frontier-province of Ra's al-Fīl (the modern Qallabat), but was subsequently induced to enter Funj territory, where he was murdered.

Although the revolt of 1762 had been fomented by the irritation and anxiety of the Funj notables, its outcome profited them nothing. The new king, Nāṣir (1752–69), was a puppet of Abū Likaylik, and Abū Likaylik was neither Funj nor Arab, but belonged to the Hamaj, a term which seems to mean the survivors of the indigenous population of the Nilotic Sudan. Although Abū Likaylik had only the titles of shaykh and vizier, he was effectively regent, and governed both the old Funj dominions and the new province of Kordofan. In 1769, Abū Likaylik deposed Nāṣir, and shortly afterwards had him put to death. He was succeeded by his brother Ismā'īl (1769–?77), equally a *roi fainéant*, in whose time Bruce visited Sennar.

Abū Likaylik died in 1776–7, as did his colleague and friend, Shaykh 'Adlān walad Ṣubāḥī, whom Bruce found acting as minister in Sennar during Abū Likaylik's absence in Kordofan. The new regent Bādī, Abū Likaylik's nephew, was confronted with a conspiracy of the Funj to restore the power of the monarchy. After two months of warfare, the conspiracy was overcome. The regent deposed Ismā'īl, and appointed his son, 'Adlān, as king. 'Adlān II (?1777–89) was the last Funj king to play an effective political role. In 1780 he headed an opposition group against Bādī organized by the sons of Abū Likaylik who had been disappointed of the succession to the regency. They were joined by two important malcontents, Shaykh al-Amīn walad Musmārr, an 'Abdallābī prince, and Shaykh Aḥmad walad 'Alī, who had been the provincial governor of Khashm al-Bahr (the upper Blue Nile). Both of them had been deposed by Bādī. The conspirators first sought out and killed Bādī's colleagues, the governors of Khashm al-Bahr and Arbaji, who had gone out to levy tribute from the nomads. Bādī himself, who had been on campaign in the Butana, returned to fight the rebels outside Sennar where he too was killed.

The sons of Abū Likaylik thus entered into their inheritance, and one of them, Rajab, became regent. King ʿAdlān, however, was still determined to rid himself of the Hamaj, and organized a new conspiracy. Rajab was away in Kordofan, and had left his brother as his deputy in Sennar. This time the king's partners in conspiracy were Shaykh al-Amīn walad Musmārr and a branch of the royal clan of the Jaʿaliyyūn who wished to gain the kingship. In 1784–5, ʿAdlān arrested the regent's brother and other persons, and put them to death in the open place before the royal palace. The daughters of Abū Likaylik were given as concubines to the conspirators. Hearing of these events, Rajab returned from Kordofan accompanied by King Saʿd, the Jaʿalī ruler. He was defeated and killed in November 1785 at the battle of al-Taras while advancing on Sennar from Khartoum, and the Hamaj were dispersed in complete disarray. Rajab's brother and successor, Nāṣir, held out for two years in the Gezira until morale was restored by a holy man, who promised the Hamaj victory. Another battle took place at Intarahna, in the vicinity of Sennar. ʿAdlān's forces were decisively beaten, and the king, already a sick man, died a few days later.

Thus in 1788–9 Nāṣir became regent in fact as well as name. But the events of the previous years had undermined the whole structure of the Funj kingdom. Two of the principal towns had been devastated: Arbaji by a raid of the Shukriyya nomads, incited by Shaykh al-Amīn walad Musmārr in 1783–4, and Sennar itself by Nāṣir, when he captured the town in 1788–9. These were the oldest towns of the Gezira: a well-known tradition told how Arbaji had been founded thirty years before Sennar itself – and indeed they had probably begun as frontier settlements of the Arabs and the Funj respectively. The rise of the Shukriyya to prominence in these years is itself an indication of the breakdown of administration and sedentary control over nomads. In 1779 the regent Bādī walad Rajab suppressed a revolt of the Shukriyya, and killed their chief, but the sacking of Arbaji ensued only five years later. In 1791 a charter in the name of the Funj puppet-king, Bādī VI, witnessed by the regent Nāṣir, granted a considerable block of cultivable land between the Blue Nile and the River Rahad to Shaykh ʿAwaḍ al-Karīm Abū Sinn, the grandson of the Shukrī chief killed by Bādī. Kordofan could no longer be held, and the power of the Musabbaʿat revived.

The troubled history of the later Hamaj regency can be briefly summarized. The descendants of Abū Likaylik were never free from internal faction. A revolt against Nāṣir by his brothers, Idrīs and ʿAdlān, ended in the regent's capture in 1798. He was put to death in a formal act of revenge by a son of the regent Bādī. Idrīs, who succeeded him in the regency, died while levying tribute on the nomads in 1803. ʻAdlān, the next regent, was faced with a conspiracy of two of his nephews, and was killed in an affray after ruling less than three months. The generation of Abū Likaylik's sons was now passing from the scene, and the next regent was his grandson, Muḥammad, a son of the regent Rajab. During his five years' rule, Muḥammad (1803–8) was dominated by his cousin and rival, a son of the regent Nāṣir. The period ended in anarchy: he was finally put to death by another cousin, Muḥammad, the son of the regent ʻAdlān, who thus avenged his father. The regency of Muḥammad walad ʻAdlān lasted from 1808 to 1821. A serious epidemic in 1809–10 aggravated the depopulation and devastation brought about by political instability. In 1813 an embassy arrived from Muḥammad ʻAlī Pasha, the Ottoman sultan's viceroy in Egypt.[1] The chronicler speaks of the emissary as 'the first spy from the Ottomans who appeared in our country', but the incident seems to have made little impression, and the diminished Funj state continued its slide into anarchy. In 1821 when the troops of Muḥammad ʻAlī Pasha were already advancing southwards, Muḥammad walad ʻAdlān was killed in a rising headed by his cousin.

In June 1821, Bādī VI and his notables made their submission to Ismāʻīl Kāmil Pasha, Muḥammad ʻAlī's son and the commander of the invading army. To their surprise, the Turco-Egyptian soldiers found the fabled capital of the Funj to be little more than a heap of ruins.

The ʻAbdallābī shaykhdom and the kingdom of the Jaʻaliyyūn were involved in the stormy and confused politics of the later Funj period. The ʻAbdallābī viceroy, ʻAbdallāh III, was killed with his brother in the campaign against the Musabbaʻat of Kordofan in 1747. His third successor was his son ʻAjīb IV (*c.* 1760–80). Near the end of ʻAjīb's long reign, his nephew, al-Amīn walad Musmārr, a noted warrior, joined in the conspiracy of King ʻAdlān II against the regent Bādī walad Rajab. After ʻAjīb's death, al-Amīn made himself ruler of the ʻAbdallāb. The revival of Hamaj power and the death of ʻAdlān II were fatal to al-Amin's hopes. There was fighting between the ʻAbdallāb and the regent Nāṣir, and in 1790–1 Shaykh al-Amīn was assassinated. His cousin and successor, ʻAbdallāh IV, ruled for ten years until he was defeated and killed in another clash with the Hamaj. The regent Idrīs appointed as his successor Nāṣir, a son of Shaykh al-Amīn. Nāṣir was

[1] The history of Egypt following the French occupation is dealt with in *Cambridge History of Africa*, vol. 5, ch. 3.

the last of the ʿAbdallābī viceroys: he died in 1821 during the Turco-Egyptian invasion.

Apart from a passing mention by Reubeni, we have no documentary information about the tribal kingdom of Dār Jaʿal or the Jaʿaliyyūn before the eighteenth century. The rulers of Jaʿal were vassals of the Funj kings through the ʿAbdallābī viceroys, with whom they had marriage connections. The chronology and relationships of the royal clan, the Saʿdāb, are obscure. Bruce in 1772 spent some time at Shendi, the Jaʿalī capital, and met the ʿAbdallābī princess who was its *de facto* regent on behalf of her son, Idrīs. The Funj Chronicle, however, speaks of an expedition to El Obeid in Kordofan by King Saʿd in 1772–3, and Saʿd appears to have been a son of Idrīs. Further notices in the Funj Chronicle indicate (as is known from other sources) that there was a rift in the royal clan between the immediate family of Saʿd and another branch known as the Nimrāb, who made use of the contending factions around the Funj king to forward their own ambitions. Thus the Nimrāb joined the conspiracy of King ʿAdlān II against the regent Rajab in 1783–4. Their hopes were, for the time being, disappointed, but on the death of King Saʿd in 1800–1, the pretender, Muḥammad walad Nimr, seems to have succeeded him. He did not hold office long. The regent Idrīs, who had defeated and killed the ʿAbdallābī Shaykh ʿAbdallāh IV, sent his brother ʿAdlān to deal with the Jaʿaliyyūn. Muḥammad walad Nimr came to ʿAdlān to treat with him, and was put to death in revenge for the humiliation of Abū Likaylik's daughters in 1784–5. Saʿd's son, Musāʿid, was appointed king of Dār Jaʿal, but once the Hamaj forces were withdrawn, he could not maintain himself in power. In the following year (1801–2), he was defeated in battle by Nimr, the son of Muḥammad by an ʿAbdallābī princess, and fled from Shendi. Nimr became king, and was to maintain his position until after the Turco-Egyptian conquest, when the slaying of Ismāʿīl Kāmil Pasha, the son of Muḥammad ʿAlī, led to the devastation of his country and his own flight to the frontier of Ethiopia.

In 1814, seven years before the Turco-Egyptian conquest, Shendi was visited by the Swiss traveller, John Lewis Burckhardt, who has left a full and careful description of the town. He emphasizes its importance as a trading centre, an importance which may have increased as anarchy grew in the Gezira, with the sack of Arbaji and the long decline of Sennar itself. Shendi was the meeting place of caravans coming from four principal directions. As in past centuries, an important route ran between Egypt and Sennar. Merchants from both Upper

Egypt and the Funj territories took part in this trade, the former generally operating on a very small capital, the latter being chiefly agents of the Funj sultan or the Hamaj regent. The caravan brought Egyptian and European goods; Burckhardt mentions particularly *sunbul* and *maḥlab* (aromatics used as perfumes, condiments and drugs). Slaves and (in 1814) camels for Egyptian military transport were exported in return. From Sennar itself, caravans came to Shendi every six or eight weeks, bringing *dammūr* (the locally woven cotton cloth), gold, slaves, at times large consignments of millet, and other goods. Caravans arriving at irregular intervals from Kordofan linked the trade of the Nilotic Sudan with that of Darfur. They brought large numbers of slaves and also gum-arabic from Kordofan. This was of better quality than the Sennar product, the export of which had declined. Frequent caravans travelled between Suakin and Shendi, bringing Indian textiles and spices, and taking gold and slaves, as well as Dongola horses for sale in the Yemen.

North of Shendi were other tribal groups, among which the most notable was the confederacy of the Shāyqiyya. Since breaking away from Funj overlordship, the Shāyqiyya had dominated their neighbours, and the unrest they caused was a factor in promoting the diaspora of Danāqla and other riverain sedentaries to Darfur and elsewhere. Their territory was an early centre of Islamic learning in the Nilotic Sudan, and this cultural tradition still survived at the time of Burckhardt's travels. In the early nineteenth century, the Shāyqiyya met their masters – first the Mamluk refugees from Muḥammad ʿAlī Pasha, then the Turco-Egyptian forces themselves. Their courage and traditional arms were no match for the soldiery of Ismāʿīl Kāmil, equipped with firearms and supported by artillery. Heavily defeated in two battles, the Shāyqiyya promptly made their submission to the conqueror, whom thereafter they served with great loyalty until the Mahdia.

DARFUR

For the history of Darfur before the nineteenth century there is virtually no contemporary source-material, and in the absence of a local chronicle we are largely dependent on traditions collected by foreigners. The dynasty which created the Muslim sultanate of Darfur came from the Kayra clan of the Kunjara, one of the three tribes of the Fur, a negroid people inhabiting Jebel Marra. Another Kunjara clan, the Musabbaʿat, established a sultanate in Kordofan during the eighteenth century.

While Jebel Marra was always the stronghold of the Fur, the Kayra sultans succeeded in imposing their hegemony to a greater or less extent on the nomadic Arabs of the plains – camel-Arabs in the north and cattle-herdsmen (Baqqāra) in the south. At the same time they were open to Islamic influence, not so much from the nomads as from the old-established Muslim territories in North Africa, the Nilotic Sudan and the western *Bilād al-Sūdān*. Historically, the first two of these had the earlier influence: the traditional genealogies of the Kayra give them a Hilālī or an ʻAbbāsī origin – the former implying links with North Africa, the latter with the Jaʻaliyyūn. Western Sudanese influence, of some cultural and political importance, no doubt developed with the coming of pilgrims through Wadai and Darfur to the Nile valley and Suakin.

Although the traditions speak of earlier folk-heroes, the first historical Kayra ruler was perhaps Sulaymān Solong (i.e. 'the Arab'), reputedly the son of an Arab woman, who appears to have lived about the middle of the seventeenth century. He may have been the first Muslim ruler, but the islamization of the region was a slow process, and even the monarchy retained non-Islamic features throughout its existence. Sulaymān's immediate successors are shadowy figures: several of them were engaged in warfare with Wadai, the ruling dynasty of which, like the Musabbaʻat, claimed kinship with the Kayra. The advantage in warfare seems generally to have lain with Wadai, and from the time of Sultan Muḥammad Tayrāb (*c.* 1756–87), the rulers seem to have sought expansion in the east rather than the west.

The end of the brief period of Funj domination in Kordofan was followed by a prolonged struggle between the revived power of the Musabbaʻat and the Kayra sultans, who sought to annex the province. With the return of the regent Rajab from Kordofan in 1784–5, the stage was set for war between Sultan Hāshim al-Musabbaʻāwī and Sultan Muḥammad Tayrāb, who occupied Kordofan, and drove out Hāshim as a fugitive to Sennar. Tayrāb died at Bara in Kordofan, and his successor, Sultan ʻAbd al-Raḥmān al-Rashīd (1787–1801), had difficulty in holding the province. Hāshim was not only strong enough to re-establish himself in Kordofan, but also in 1797, with an army of nomad warriors and ʻAbdallābī allies, he raided the Gezira and entered Sennar itself. Finally, however, he was defeated by an army commanded by ʻAbd al-Raḥmān's chief minister, the eunuch Muḥammad Kurra, who ruled as viceroy in Kordofan.

ʻAbd al-Raḥmān's election as sultan, to the exclusion of Tayrāb's son and heir-apparent, Isḥāq, had been due to Muḥammad Kurra.

Although ʿAbd al-Raḥmān was pious and scholarly by inclination, he proved an effective ruler. In his reign the royal residence, El Fasher[1] (the site of which had previously varied from reign to reign), was finally fixed to the east of Jebel Marra and became the centre of a permanent capital. Nubians from the Dongola region at this time played an important part in developing the Islamic culture of Darfur: their role as merchants has already been mentioned. Increased contact with Egypt and the outside world is indicated by an exchange of presents with the Ottoman sultan, by the visit of the first European traveller to Darfur, W. G. Browne, and by correspondence with Bonaparte, who asked ʿAbd al-Raḥmān to send him 2,000 strong black slaves.

Muḥammad Kurra acted again as king-maker on the death of ʿAbd al-Raḥmān (1800–1), and installed his young son, Muḥammad Faḍl. He continued to serve the new sultan, but hostility developed between them, and Kurra was killed in 1804. Then in 1821, Muḥammad ʿAlī Pasha sent an expedition under his son-in-law, the *Defterdār* Muḥammad Bey Khusraw, to invade the sultanate of Darfur concurrently with the conquest of the Nilotic Sudan. The viceroy of Kordofan, the *Maqdūm* Musallim, was defeated and killed at Bara, but revolt on the Nile after the murder of Ismāʿīl Kāmil Pasha deflected the *Defterdār* from invading Darfur itself, and the Kayra sultanate survived until 1874.

THE EXPANSION OF ISLAM

It was not until the Funj period that Islam became effectively established in the northern Nilotic Sudan. Although Lower Nubia had been exposed to Islamic influences since the Arab conquest of Egypt in the seventh century, and there had been Muslim rulers in Dongola in the early fourteenth century, the islamization of much of the region was still very superficial even 200 years later. Some traditions tell of Muslim teachers coming to the main Nile at the end of the Middle Ages. Such was Ghulāmallāh b. ʿĀ'id, whose ancestors had lived in the Yemen, and who (probably early in the fifteenth century) settled and taught Islam in the region of Dongola. Another immigrant was the Sufi, Ḥamad Abū Dunāna, who came, it seems, from the Hejaz about the middle of the fifteenth century, and whose tomb is at Abu Dilayq in the Butana. One of his daughters married ʿAbdallāh Jammāʿ, and was the mother of ʿAjīb al-Kāfūta, while another was the mother of the

[1] *Al-fāshir* was, strictly speaking, the open place before the royal residence. The term was also used in Sennar.

holy man, Idrīs Muḥammad al-Arbāb. As in other peripheral regions of Islam, the claims of such immigrants to be Sharifs (i.e. descendants of the Prophet) were uncritically accepted. Even the Jewish adventurer, David Reubeni, posed as a Sharif to ʻAmāra Dūnqas, and spoke of the honour which the Funj king paid to the Sharifs in his territory.

The establishment of the Funj high-kingship, and of the supremacy of the Funj and ʻAbdallāb over the Gezira and the main Nile, created more settled conditions than had been known since the crumbling of the Christian kingdoms in the region. This was a factor in the development of centres of Muslim learning in the Nilotic territories. Another factor was the encouragement of the rulers. In this respect, although the evidence is scanty, the ʻAbdallāb, as an established holy family, were probably more important than the Funj – latecomers to Islam, whose quality as parvenus was concealed by a spurious Umayyad pedigree. It is significant that the *Ṭabaqāt* of Wad Ḍayfallāh, a biographical dictionary of holy men, was compiled by an *ʻālim* of Halfaya, and in geographical range is restricted almost entirely to the ʻAbdallābī territories.

The reign of Shaykh ʻAjīb al-Kāfūta saw the coming of more holy men from the older Islamic lands. The first of these, a Sufi of Baghdād named Tāj al-Dīn Muḥammad al-Bahārī, came by way of Mecca and lived for seven years in the Gezira, where he propagated the Qādiriyya order. It is perhaps worth remarking that his name, al-Bahārī, means 'the spice-merchant'. Another teacher of the Qādiriyya Sufi doctrine is remembered only as al-Tilimsānī al-Maghribī, 'the man of Tlemcen in the Maghrib'. The grandfather of Ḥasan walad Ḥassūna, another holy man, also came from the Maghrib, perhaps even from Spain. A Maghribī influence on Sudanese Islam could perhaps be inferred from its 'maraboutist' features, i.e. the importance attached in popular religion to living and dead holy men, and also from the almost universal adherence of the Sudanese to the Maliki school of jurisprudence. The Shafiʻi school, characteristic of Lower Egypt, had few followers, although an Egyptian jurist who came to the Nilotic Sudan in ʻAjīb's time was a Shafiʻi.

Islamization had two aspects: the propagation of Muslim learning, especially the Koran and *Sharīʻa*, and initiation into the Sufi orders. Native-born Sudanese very soon took up the work of islamization. In the first half of the sixteenth century, Maḥmūd al-ʻArakī returned from studying in Egypt and taught the *Sharīʻa* in a fortified residence on the White Nile – a frontier region between the nominally Muslim Arabs and the pagan Shilluk. At the beginning of the reign of Shaykh ʿAjīb al-Kāfūta, Ibrāhīm al-Būlād b. Jābir (who claimed to be a descendant of Ghulāmallāh), after studying at al-Azhar, established in the territory of the Shāyqiyya the most successful of the early schools. On the whole, however, few Sudanese before the nineteenth century were students at al-Azhar, and most of the immigrant holy men were Sufis rather than teachers of the Islamic sciences. Sufism made an immediate appeal to the Sudanese, who rapidly produced their own teachers and ascetics. One of the most famous of these was Idrīs Muḥammad al-Arbāb, who is said to have lived from 1507–8 to 1650.

While the holy men of the Nilotic Sudan fall for the most part into one or other of the categories of religious teachers or Sufi leaders, Islamic learning and Sufism were by no means mutually exclusive, and some holy men were proficient in both fields. A holy man, whether a scholar or a Sufi, was regarded as a possessor of *baraka*, spiritual power which manifested itself in miracles (*karāmāt*), both during his life and after his death, and was transmissible through physical objects or inheritance. Thus there came into existence families of hereditary holy men, in which the knowledge imparted to successive generations was reinforced by the transmission of *baraka*. In the development and spread of these families, the daughters of holy men played an important part. An early example is provided by the daughters of Ḥamad Abū Dunāna: two were the mothers respectively of ʿAjīb al-Kāfūta and Idrīs Muḥammad al-Arbāb, while a third was the mother of another holy man, Ḥāmid b. ʿUmar. The tradition of Islamic learning established by Ibrāhīm al-Būlād was continued by his brothers and a nephew. His sister, Fāṭima, married one of the students at the family school, and her son, Ṣughayyirūn, migrated about 1611–12 to Jaʿalī territory, where his descendants continued as a holy family. A daughter of Fāṭima was the ancestress of other branches of the family, which established themselves near Shendi and on the Blue Nile.

In the later part of the Funj-ʿAbdallābī period, one of the most important of these holy families was the Majādhīb of al-Damir, near the confluence of the Atbara and Nile. The family, of Jaʿalī origin, emerged into prominence in the early eighteenth century with a Sufi leader named Muḥammad al-Majdhūb (known as *al-Kabīr*, 'the Elder'). His son, Ḥamad, who died in 1776–7 at the age of eighty-five, made the Pilgrimage to Mecca, where he was initiated into the Shādhiliyya order. At al-Damir he combined the functions of a Sufi leader, a teacher of Muslim learning, a jurist and an arbitrator. Burckhardt, who visited al-Damir in 1814, speaks in glowing terms of 'this little hierarchical state', which had become an important centre of education with

several schools, to which young men repair from Darfour, Sennaar, Kordofan and other parts of Soudan, in order to acquire a proficiency in the law, sufficient to enable them to figure as great Fakys in their own countries.[1]

The school of al-Damir came to an end when the region was devastated in 1822 in revenge for the death of Ismā'īl Kāmil Pasha, but the prestige of the family and the Sufi order (Majdhūbiyya) which they propagated still survives.

The holy men played an important part in the politics and society of the Funj period. They served as intercessors and mediators, and were valuable allies of the rulers they sponsored – we have already seen how, for example, they helped to save the sons of 'Ajīb, Bādī III and the regent Nāṣir. At times however they dissociated themselves from the rulers, or were opposed to them. Thus, Ismā'īl b. Jābir, the brother and second successor of Ibrāhīm al-Būlād, refused to use water supplied from the irrigation channels of the Shāyqiyya, because the oxen which turned the water wheels were taken by force. Still more dramatic was the attitude of the Sufi ascetic, Ḥamad al-Naḥlān (d. 1704–5) whose home was in the western Gezira. He laid a heavy and effective curse on an expedition sent by Bādī III to gather taxes, and bade the officers say to the king,

You have caused strife among the Muslims...You have been placed among the drinkers of *marīsa* and the smokers of tobacco: if again you cause strife among the Muslims, I will break your head with the mysteries of God.[2]

The prestige of the holy men amongst the nomadic tribes enabled them to act as protectors of trading caravans, and themselves to participate in commerce. Burckhardt notes that the Majādhīb in this way helped to keep open communications between the Nile and Suakin. However, perhaps the best example of religious prestige in association with commercial activities and even political power is provided by Shaykh Ḥasan walad Ḥassūna (d. 1664–5). The centre of his activities was the Butana, east of the Blue Nile, where he lived as a pastoralist and horse-trader, exporting his horses not only to the Funj and 'Abdallābī territories, but to Taqali, Darfur and even farther west. He had villages of slaves, and a slave bodyguard, carrying silver-mounted swords: his household was modelled on that of the Funj and 'Abdallābī

[1] Burckhardt, *Travels in Nubia*, 266, 268. 'Faky' (*fakī*, from classical Arabic, *faqīh* a jurist) is used in the Sudan of teachers of Islam and Sufism, and of holy men generally.
[2] S. Hillelson, *Sudan Arabic texts* (Cambridge, 1935), 193.

courts. He was killed by the explosion of his musket – one of the very rare mentions of firearms in the Funj period.

The importance which the rulers attached to the holy families is indicated by the extensive grants of land which were made to them. Although there are earlier mentions of such grants, for example by King Bādī I Sīd al-Qūm to Ṣughayyirūn (*c.* 1611–12), the first formal charters now extant are dated 1729 and 1733, in the reign of Bādī IV Abū Shulūkh, and may perhaps be connected with this king's policy of seeking allies and supporters against his rivals from the old royal line. The earliest charters from ʻAbdallābī viceroys are rather later: the first so far published having been granted by Shaykh ʻAjīb IV, not earlier than 1758–9. It may be noted that, although the charters apparently occur without any local precedents, they are highly sophisticated in their construction and terminology. The land is granted in freehold (*milk*), not in *waqf*, as would be usual in Muslim pious foundations, and the charters concede extensive immunities from dues and taxes.

The Qādiriyya order was the most widespread and popular in the Nilotic Sudan. Lacking in centralized organization and direction, it offered much scope for the local leadership of holy men, but on the other hand it was ill adapted to resist popular and unislamic beliefs and practices. Towards the end of the Funj period, its predominance was challenged by the introduction into the Sudan of two new orders, which, although linked with traditional Sufism, bore witness to a revivalist and reforming spirit in the Islamic world.

The first of these was the Sammāniyya, founded in the Hejaz by Muḥammad b. ʻAbd al-Karīm al-Sammānī (1718–75). It was introduced into the Funj territories by a Sudanese disciple, Aḥmad al-Ṭayyib b. al-Bashīr, who was initiated in Medina by al-Sammānī himself about the year 1757–8. After much travelling, he returned to the Sudan, visiting on the way Shaykh Ḥamad b. Muḥammad al-Majdhūb at al-Damir. He settled at his birthplace in ʻAbdallābī territory north of Omdurman, and acquired a great reputation as a holy man. During the regency of Nāṣir, i.e. between 1788–9 and 1798, he was invited to Sennar to cure the regent's brother, and was granted an estate. After dwelling in the south for seven years, however, he returned to his ancestral home, where he died in 1824. He won many adherents for the new order, and his descendants succeeded him as its local heads.

During the last few years of the Funj kingdom, another itinerant holy man arrived from the Hejaz. This was Muḥammad ʻUthmān al-Mīrghanī, descended from a family probably of Central Asian origin but more recently resident in Arabia. Muḥammad 'Uthmān was an adherent of Aḥmad b. Idrīs al-Fāsī, a leading revivalist reformer of Islam in the late eighteenth and early nineteenth centuries. On his master's behalf, Muḥammad 'Uthmān made a missionary tour in 1816–17 through Dongola, Kordofan and the Gezira. In Sennar he was not well received by the ministers of the Regent Muḥammad walad 'Adlān, and popular superstition attributed to this the calamity of the Turco-Egyptian conquest, which ensued a few years later. Nevertheless, he gained some followers for what became (after Aḥmad b. Idrīs's death in 1837) an independent order known as the Khatmiyya, the headship of which in the Sudan passed to his son by a local woman. From it developed an autonomous and rival local order, centred in Kordofan, the Ismā'īliyya, the founder of which, Ismā'īl b. 'Abdallāh, was a holy man of El Obeid.

One Islamic institution was of increasing importance during this period – the Pilgrimage to the holy cities of Mecca and Medina. In the sixteenth century, pilgrims from the Nilotic Sudan were probably few. Shaykh 'Ajīb al-Kāfūta himself made the Pilgrimage, and is said to have opened the route across the Red Sea Hills to Suakin, whereas pilgrims had formerly travelled by way of Upper Egypt and Qusayr. Over a century later, in 1736, one of his descendants established a *waqf* in Medina to provide for the maintenance of people from the Funj, 'Abdallābī and adjoining territories. With the islamization of Darfur, that region became, as Burckhardt observed, an assembly point for pilgrims from the western Sudanic lands, who were known as Takārīr or Takārna (sing., Takrūrī). While some of these westerners went on by Asyut, and others by Sennar, the majority by this time struck the Nile at Shendi, whence they proceeded to the Red Sea by way of Egypt or Suakin.

At the time of the Turco-Egyptian invasion, then, the Nilotic Sudan and Darfur were genuinely part of the Islamic world. The vestiges of Christianity in Nubia had long since been effaced; the frontier of islamization had been pushed forward to the foothills of Ethiopia and to a line, at approximately the twelfth parallel of north latitude, running across the Gezira, Kordofan and Darfur. The establishment of the Muslim Kayra Sultanate in Darfur completed the chain of Islamic states running across the Sudanic belt. The opening of the Sudanic pilgrimage route, and the population movement from the west which it facilitated, were to have important social and political consequences in the nineteenth and twentieth centuries.

CHAPTER 2

THE CENTRAL SAHARA AND SUDAN*

THE PROCESS OF CONSOLIDATION

The primary problem of the central Sudan during the seventeenth and eighteenth centuries was that of consolidation, of state and of society. The main stages of penetration and expansion occurred in earlier centuries: the arrival of outstanding individuals or groups; the more general encroachment of nomads upon settled realms; the transmission of Islam across the Sahara and its planting in the Sudan; the extension of a corresponding framework of trade; the crucial exodus of the court of the Saifawa from Kanem to Bornu towards the end of the fourteenth century. The same patterns may, indeed, be traced in the seventeenth and eighteenth centuries. In Wadai, with the coming of 'Abd al-Karīm in the early seventeenth century, there is an unusually late instance of the *héros civilisateur* theme. Nomad incursions continued, and, as records become fuller in later years, it is possible to analyse the contribution, probably overrated, of such people to state formation; and also, perhaps, by analogy to suggest the process which may have taken place in earlier times. The expansion of Islam was also repeated again and again, on the smaller stages of outlying states, such as Mandara, Bagirmi and Wadai. Even the exodus to Bornu was a continuing affair, often closely associated with nomad groups.

The persistence of these patterns of mobility is one major qualification to be attached to the fundamental theme of consolidation. Another arises from the fact that the same event may be seen either as illustrative of mobility, even of the dissolution of society, or of consolidation, depending upon one's point of view. For example, 'Abd al-Karīm's arrival in Wadai, just mentioned, marks on the Wadai stage the opening of the drama of Islamic state formation there, while from another angle it is, according to some traditions, a far flung ramification of the final dispersal of the 'Abbasids. Again, the same slave raid which contributed to the peopling of the Kano principality might destroy or dislodge some southern chieftancy – at the least, such culling out of people weakened the enemy as it strengthened the raider. Nevertheless, significant as these qualifications may be in themselves, they do not undermine the basic

* The author is grateful to Dr John Lavers, of Ahmadu Bello University in Nigeria, in particular among others, for help and advice at many points of this chapter.

appropriateness of insisting, for the central Sudan in this period, upon the processes of consolidation.

Consolidation – whether consciously pursued, as it seems to have been by several rulers and governments, or unconsciously arising from the requirements of local statecraft – meant in the central Sudan two main things. One was the reception into society of new elements which were constantly arriving. Some may have come almost unnoticed, the peaceful arrival of peaceful folk. The Kano Chronicle says of one eighteenth-century ruler, Muḥammad Yaji, a just and good man of gentle disposition: 'In his time there was no trouble...Many men came and settled in Kano land in his reign.' Such unobtrusive immigration may well be one of the most profound currents in Sudanic history, underlying whether as a primary or a contributory cause the rise and decline of states, but like most currents somewhat submerged and concealed beneath the surface. The unusually well-documented case of the Koyam clerics, whose mild rule resembled that of Muḥammad Yaji, is examined below (pp. 112–13; see also p. 124). Their territory developed, through immigration, into a miniature state, perhaps in some respects a prototype for state formation in the central Sudan. For the most part, however, we must rely upon historical sources whose fascination with more turbulent or harassed groups – nomad invaders, refugees, slaves, all of whom were also immensely important – may distort the overall perspective. More than land, people were the foundation of power: they colonized new lands, provided occasional military and other services, and were taxed. It is significant that grants of land – the traditional Muslim *waqf* and *hubūs*, or more individual gifts – are almost unknown in the central Sudan, unlike the eastern Sudan: instead, favoured groups were often awarded exemption from services and taxes. In Murzuq there was little *hubūs* land, but in Ghadames, which is clearly outside the Sudanic area, this form of holding was recently estimated at 88 per cent of the total.

The overriding need for at least a steady, and if possible an expanding, population may lie behind the widespread interest in the central Sudan in slaves and slaving, epitomized in miniature by the character Son Bawa, the Desirer of a Slave, who in the *bori* or possession cult of the Hausa walks about weeping, calling upon the other spirits to help him in his search for slaves. So diverse was the slave contribution, touching society at every level, that, without the slave, civilization in any recognizably central Sudanic form could scarcely have emerged. The constant demand for new recruits may have arisen in part from severe

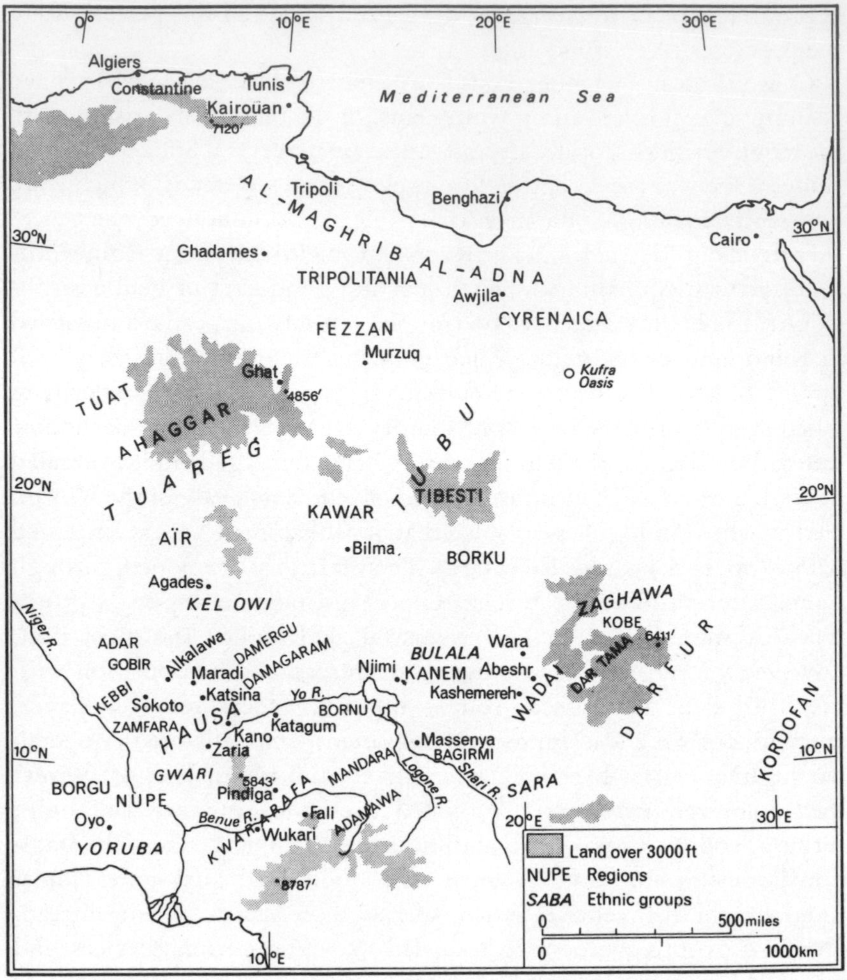

2 The central Sahara and Sudan

infant mortality, handicapping natural reproduction. Demographic information for the central Sudan is scanty in the extreme; yet with more recent estimates as a starting point, careful study of earlier sources might yield some clues. Even today the Kanuri call a newborn child 'little kitten' in the first week of its life, for the chance of its dying is so great that it can hardly be regarded as at once fully a member of the family.

The importance of its citizenry to a government was also shown by the anxiety of the authorities about emigration. Here Islam presented

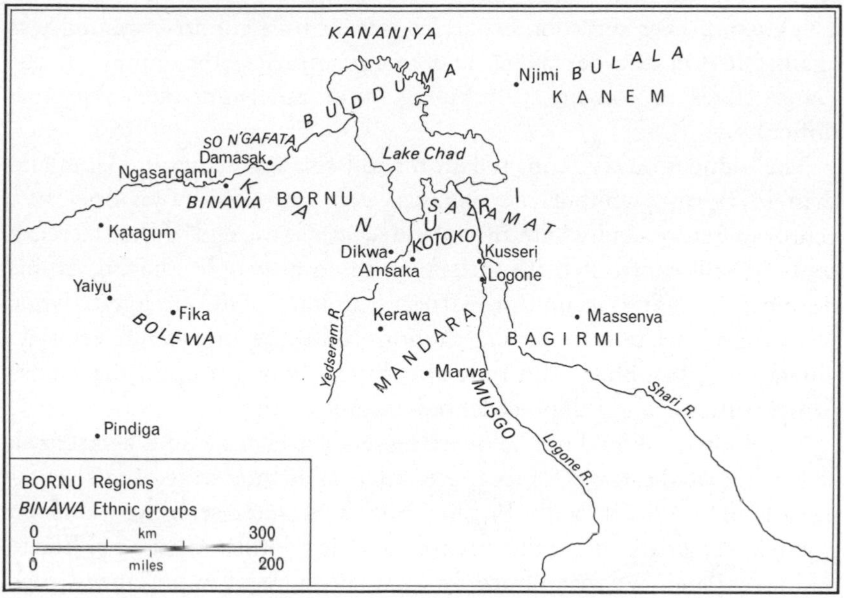

3 The Lake Chad area

a special problem, for that same mobility which brought into the Sudan countries so much of value might also draw people away. The Pilgrimage was one example. *Hijra*, the symbolic re-enactment of the Prophet's withdrawal from an unresponsive Mecca, was another. When the cleric al-Jarmiyu, in the seventeenth century, assured the *mai* of Bornu that he did not wish to encourage the *mai*'s subjects to stray, it is probable that he disclaimed not only a shift in loyalty but also a physical migration (see below, p. 108). The *mai*, his suspicions unresolved, executed him. Towards the very end of the period, when men began leaving the princes of Hausa to follow Usuman dan Fodio, the princes felt they could no longer compromise. In the nineteenth century, various states, Bagirmi and Sokoto among them, intervened actively on occasion in the attempt to stop mass emigration even for such pious purposes as the Pilgrimage or to meet the Mahdi. It is probably not a coincidence that all the instances of emigration just cited are Islamic in character.

The other strand of consolidation was the construction, mainly from these human resources, of relatively settled, centralized states, strongly Muslim at least in the upper ranks. Immigrants who resisted such consolidation were a danger, not an increment of strength: in the mid-eighteenth century, immigrants into Zamfara, from Gobir, grew quickly in power and soon broke from their host country, waging war against it. On a wider stage, and over centuries, the failure of the Hausa states to contain their Fulani immigrants illustrates the same difficulty.

The foundations for consolidation had been laid earlier in Hausaland than in Bornu, whither the Saifawa *mais* had withdrawn only two centuries before, and where Idrīs Aloma, *mai* at the end of the sixteenth century, still confronted the resistance of local people, the So, on his doorstep. Yet it was in Bornu that a unitary state emerged, while Hausaland was rent by jarring factions until the nineteenth century, when the Fulani jihad with rude abruptness imposed upon the Hausa principalities a unity unprecedented among them.

The contrast should not be overstressed, for Hausaland is a vast area, and some of the larger units there, such as Kano, were almost comparable individually with Bornu. But it is interesting to consider possible explanations for the difference in development between Bornu and Hausaland. We may notice, in view of the great importance which some scholars attach to foreign trade as a stimulus to state formation in the Sudan, that even after Hausaland began to take a substantial part in such trade – as was the case particularly after the fall of the Songhay empire in 1591, when the preferred routes shifted east of the Niger bend – a united polity failed to emerge. On the contrary, such trade may perhaps have increased internal tensions, for example between Kano and Katsina. Kano was known even some years before 1591 as one of the three cities in Africa in which, so it was said, there was nothing in all the world that could not be found, the other two being Cairo and Fez. It may be that the nature of economic activity in Hausaland, being in many respects more diffuse, made it difficult for a single political authority to gain control. In each town, leather-working, weaving, dyeing, and other crafts provided the foundation for some independent commercial life. This argument, however, should not be carried too far, for there were also certain principal highways of commerce, south and west to Nupe and Gonja, east to Bornu, north through the Sahara, political control of which would have given great power.

Another line of approach might be to compare the role of Islam in Bornu, where from the earliest settlements, before 1400, it was associated intimately with the ruling, immigrant group, and in Hausaland, where the pioneer Muslims, also immigrants, were commoners and dependent strangers. Their influence varied substantially from principality to principality: in Kano, for example, Islam seems to have been adopted by the ruling class, helping them to consolidate their authority over the ordinary people, and in Katsina Islam was perhaps a rallying point for commoners against rulers. If this argument, of the different impact of Islam in Bornu and Hausaland, can be sustained, and the Pilgrimage provides some confirmation for it (see p. 94), then the contribution of Islam to state formation in the Sudan becomes still clearer.

An adequate policy within the central Sudan implied also the successful cultivation of foreign relations. Such relations with the forest lands to the south are the least well documented, but were clearly of great importance in the supply of slaves and, from the forests farther west, of kola. There are also a few – but perhaps important despite their rarity – references to trade, in which the southern lands helped in the food supply of the Sudan. Within the Sudanic belt itself, east-west relations developed in various ways. The Fulani, expanding slowly and over centuries from the lower Senegal, were a marked feature of the central Sudan during this period. They were well established in Bagirmi and in the early eighteenth century they even reached Darfur. Spreading in somewhat the same way, but in the opposite direction, were the Shuwa Arabs. Other contacts included east-west trade and religious exchange. It is possible to trace a gradual reorientation in these east-west connections of the central Sudan. The move from Kanem to Bornu about 1400 directed attention westwards for much of the two succeeding centuries, and the fall of Songhay in 1591 seemed to leave Hausaland as an undisputed sphere of influence for Bornu. However, the dream of regaining Kanem never disappeared, and Mai Idrīs Aloma made perhaps the most determined of several attempts to bring Kanem under the control of Bornu. Permanent authority over Kanem eluded him, and throughout the seventeenth and eighteenth centuries that region preserved considerable *de facto*, albeit chaotic, independence. About the end of the sixteenth century, important political and religious changes were taking place in Bagirmi, where ʻAbdallāh established a despotic monarchy and introduced some Islamic institutions, and in Wadai, where ʻAbd al-Karīm overthrew the Tunjur. These and other changes, despite the failure of Bornu to incorporate Kanem, meant that events to the eastward were becoming as important for Bornu-Kanem as those in the west had been. Finally, in 1806, Sabun's conquest of Bagirmi brought Wadai and Bornu nearly face to face.

This development of Bornu's involvement to the east marked the third stage of her external relations, following the establishment of links northwards about the end of the first millennium, and westwards after 1400. The sequence illustrates again the enigma of the late, and relatively unimportant, emergence of the Sudan belt as a trans-continental thoroughfare. And, however important east-west movement within the Sudan was, it seems to have been of secondary significance to, as well as of later origin than, the associations across the desert with North Africa, despite the hazard and hardship of the desert journey at even the best of times. The general pattern of historical development has not followed the lines of least geographical resistance: evidently other factors, among them trade and religion, have guided the basic outlines of human movement in the area, rather than simple ease of access.

In the process of consolidation at home, and in the foreign relations associated with it, various principal themes emerge, four of which were of central consequence – the military, the governmental, the commercial, and the religious. The military influence of horses and guns – the former partly, the latter almost exclusively, imported from the north – needs to be weighed carefully. The governmental institutions, both in North Africa and in the central Sudan, were kingships (though the ruler's title might vary) of Muslim appearance; only farther south, in Nupe and among the Kwararafa, did the divine kingship survive, while in the Sahara, both Tuareg and Tubu rejected any effective centralization. In commerce, several rulers in the central Sudan combined an interest in the better implementation of Islam with a concern for the proper organization of trade – weights and measures, regulation of markets, and policing of roads. In every sphere, slaves were of critical importance: they appeared often in the ranks of the armed forces; in individual cases, they wielded substantial authority as government officials; and they were the foremost export from the central Sudan.

It is the religious theme, however, which is in many respects the most interesting. In contrast to the western Sudan, where Muslims had lost their imperial patrons with the decline of the Mali and Songhay empires, and were thus able to assume more independent social and political roles, in Bornu Islam never lost its ideological and institutional integration within the empire, and in Hausaland never quite achieved it. The integration was never, in any case, absolute: for, while the authorities might find Islam a very useful prop to the state – on the domestic front, for example, in the various functions of prayer, and abroad in the Pilgrimage, principal of many strands binding the distant central Sudanic frontiers of the Islamic world to the heartlands – the religion also introduced the concept of a loyalty overriding the ordinary duties of a citizen towards his state. The Fulani jihad was to prove the outstanding instance of the way in which the sword of faith might turn in the hands of those traditional rulers who had sought to brandish it to their own advantage.

To distinguish amongst these activities is to some extent an artificial exercise. The interrelationship, in practice, of commerce and religion is well illustrated, for instance, by the pious foundations established by the bey of Tunis, Ḥusayn b. ʻAlī, early in the eighteenth century, among them a school in Kairouan, with two nearby markets as part of its endowment. In the central Sudan, religion helped to sanction the military slave raids, which provided the export potential of trade, duties upon which were a major source of state revenue.

THE STAGE IN 1600

At the beginning of the seventeenth century, much of the area seemed poised for imperial adventure, and confrontation, on a grand scale. To the north, the *Maghrib al-Adnā*, the near west, roughly Tunisia and Libya of today, had been drawn into the Ottoman empire, pledged to defend North Africa against the Christians. The Christian victories by sea at Lepanto (1571) and on land in the Spanish capture of Tunis (1573) lent urgency to this task. In 1574 Tunis was recaptured, and in 1581 Philip II of Spain abandoned his hopes of an African empire, and agreed to a truce with the Ottomans. Morocco, its ambitions partly deflected by the somewhat uncomfortable proximity of the Ottoman Turks to the east, had overthrown the might of Songhay, so that for the first time since the Almoravids an empire controlled territory on both sides of the Sahara. Should Morocco succeed in maintaining its trans-Saharan dream, the same dream which 300 years later would haunt the French, a state of quite unique dimensions would confront Hausaland on its north-west frontier. And there seemed little to prevent the Moroccans from accomplishing this, armed as they were with the all-conquering musket. East of Hausaland, the armies of Aloma of Bornu, sharing the advantages bestowed by firearms, marched to the gates of Kano, and the gradual subsidence of most of the Hausa kingdoms into tributary status promised Bornu a vast sphere of influence, if not an empire. On the Saharan routes linking Bornu and the Chad region with the *Maghrib al-Adnā*, no power able to master those roads solely for its own benefit was in sight: Tripoli was tampering with the affairs of a weak dynasty in Fezzan; Aloma visited Kawar himself, and influenced the course of events in Aïr. In Wadai, far to the east, a new state was being born, but it would continue in relative isolation for much of the period, since the trans-continental Sudan highway, which it straddled, was so underdeveloped compared to the trans-Saharan routes, from which it was cut off.

In the event, none of these ambitions was realized. In North Africa, the Ottomans gradually brought their possessions within the framework of normal imperial organization, making them into three regencies, Tripolitania, Tunisia and Algeria. These ceased to be the frontier of holy war with the Christians, and became instead rather remote provinces of a mighty empire. Effective centralized Ottoman authority, never strong, waned further during the seventeenth century, and in the eighteenth the *Maghrib al-Adnā* came under two independent dynasties, acknowledging only loosely the suzerainty of the Porte. The Moroccan thrust spent itself in fighting a tenacious Songhay resistance which effectively barred the gates to Hausaland. Bornu's influence over Hausaland declined, though the formalities of tribute were apparently observed by some principalities throughout the period, and it was to Bornu that some of the princes appealed at the time of the jihad of Usuman dan Fodio. It is hard to tell how strong a link such an appeal reflects: Timbuktu appealed to Morocco for help against the French at the end of the nineteenth century, when not even tribute had passed between the two for three centuries. None of the promises of 1600 came true; and in 1800 the basic political outlines were still much the same as they had been. Compared with the Moroccan invasion just before, or the Fulani jihad just after, the period seems in essence rather a static one, of consolidation, not of large-scale innovation. No radical change occurred in a major political centre of gravity, as had happened when the *mai* fled from Kanem to Bornu about 1400. No revolution of ideals overthrew the existing order, as was to happen in the jihad. No major new trade route was opened up, save at the very end when Sabun's merchants broke through the desert north of Wadai. No new technical device transformed patterns of production or the balance of power. Firearms might have done this; yet, after their double introduction in the closing years of the sixteenth century, they gradually faded away. Other technological devices which might have profoundly affected economic life – wheeled transport, for example, facilitating the movement of bulky goods, particularly foodstuffs, or the plough, or water- and wind-mills – were not even attempted. All must have been known to visitors to (or from) North Africa. That they were not introduced reminds us that the Sahara, for all the brave pageantry of the caravans which crossed it, was fundamentally a barrier, a broad isolating belt. That Islam and Muslim culture crossed the desert as early as they did, and maintained themselves so well thereafter, is a measure of the remarkable mobility of that faith. Nothing else of even partially comparable importance survived the crossing, or, having done that, lasted long in the central Sudan.

The dominating figure in the central Sudan about the beginning of the seventeenth century was Idrīs Aloma, *mai* of Bornu. His reign, which according to the most recent calculations may be dated from 1569 to about 1600, is uniquely well documented. Not until the very end of the eighteenth century, when source material becomes more abundant for Sultan Sabun of Wadai, for Shaykh Muḥammad al-Amīn al-Kānamī of Bornu, and for the champions of the Fulani jihad, is there another ruler in the central Sudan who may be known in such detail. Aloma was fortunate in his indefatigable chronicler, the *imām* Aḥmad b. Fartuwa, whose history of the earlier part of the *mai*'s reign – it is not, therefore, a complete biography – has happily survived. This survival is partly historical accident: the written history of a preceding *mai*, to which Ibn Fartuwa himself refers, has been lost. Simply because more is known about Aloma than about any other *mai*, it should not too easily be assumed that he was himself an extraordinary figure. There is reason to believe, for example, that Mai ʿAlī b. ʿUmar, Aloma's grandson, was equally remarkable. In this respect, Ibn Fartuwa's portrait of Aloma is a representative sample of standard patterns of behaviour and achievement in the central Sudan. It may be Ibn Fartuwa, the Thucydides of the central Sudan, who should command, even more than his patron, our surprise and admiration. On the other hand, however, there were clearly exceptional qualities about Aloma, which appear in the chronicle, and which may have been in part responsible for calling forth Ibn Fartuwa's excellently constructive eulogies. Whether we concentrate on those points which Aloma had in common with his successors, or upon his unusual acts and characteristics, it is evident that he contributed substantially to the two main tasks of consolidation: constructive statecraft within the Sudan, and a positive foreign policy. At the opposite extreme in time, Sabun of Wadai

(1803–13) emerges as a figure comparable with Aloma, both in some of the difficulties which he faced and in the achievements which were his. He too illustrates the theme of consolidation.

MILITARY CONSIDERATIONS

It is as a fighter that Aloma has been most remembered locally: 'Idrishi of the fair skin...who waged three hundred and thirty wars; who, when he sent forth his warriors, followed himself; he who made a thousand raids.'[1] His fighting was both domestic and foreign. Indeed, the fact that expeditions were launched against distant places such as Kano or Kanem, and equally against recalcitrant So groups well within any tentative boundaries of Bornu, points again to the primary importance to a state of the loyalty of people, and to the difficulty of defining a state territorially.

Within Bornu itself, some of his earliest clashes were with the So, in the regions of the Yo and Yedseram rivers. These people were among the original inhabitants of the country, the owners of the land, and although some of them had agreed to submit to the Bornu government to the extent of paying the *jizya*, or tribute, others were still quite independent, protected by thick forest and surface water. To subdue these people, or (less usefully) drive them out, was an essential preliminary for the consolidation of the state in Bornu, and of its people the Kanuri, brought together out of many nations including the So.

Of Kanem, another vital sphere of Aloma's military concern, it is difficult to say whether this was a domestic matter, or essentially one of foreign policy. Aloma's mother was a Bulala princess, from the royal house of Kanem, and he apparently spent part of his youth there, particularly when it seemed doubtful whether he would ever succeed to the throne of Bornu. His personal connections with the Bulala royal house facilitated the policy, which he employed here as elsewhere, of championing one claimant to the local throne. The reconquest of at least the old capital of Kanem, Njimi, had been accomplished by Idrīs Katagarmabe early in the sixteenth century, well before Aloma, and Aloma was in a sense trying merely to further the return of Bornu power to that region from which, in the fourteenth century, it had originally sprung. In these respects, the fighting between the Bulala and Bornu, to which Aloma made a notable contribution but which also preceded and followed him, resembled rather a civil war, within the

[1] H. R. Palmer, 'The Bornu girgam', *Journal of the African Society*, 1912–13, **12**, 79.

same nation, divided between its Kanembu and Kanuri branches. The immediate, ostensible reason for hostilities in Aloma's time was the allegiance of three villages north of Lake Chad, villages lying in the border area between Bornu and Kanem. The official result of Aloma's campaigns against Kanem, in so far as these are described to us, was a written agreement delimiting the boundary – perhaps the first written border agreement in the history of the central Sudan.

On the other hand, the agreement seems to have had little lasting effect, and Kanem was never effectively subdued by Bornu, under Aloma or later. Ibn Fartuwa tells of seven campaigns in Kanem, six of them against recalcitrant elements among the Bulala, who were warmly seconded by the Tubu. Here, as at some other points, it is difficult to escape the suspicion that the dedicated chronicler has somewhat magnified the military implications of the events which he describes. In his first famous victory over the Bulala, Aloma lost one man dead and four wounded, while it was impossible to count the number of the enemy dead. That it was thus impossible might, of course, have been true for more than one reason; but this was not, it seems, an intentional subtlety on Ibn Fartuwa's part. In these respects, Kanem was just another field of foreign policy. Yet the exodus from Kanem into Bornu continued, and was clearly not a single event centred upon the flight of the *mai*, shortly before 1400, from Kanem to the south-west. Among those who followed Aloma back into Bornu were some of the Tubu, who had been his opponents perhaps even more than had the Bulala. Other groups went of their own accord as well, while yet others were taken by force, or were encouraged, so to speak, by the devastation of their localities which Aloma's troops wrought, and by the fear which he inspired.

Aloma's fighting shared many of the features of traditional warfare in the central Sudan, with an emphasis on pillage and booty rather than direct confrontation. War was a profit-making enterprise. On Aloma's expeditions against the Tuareg, there was much spoil, including camels, slaves and weapons, and evidently some attempt was made to divide this among the victors according to the requirements of Islamic law. Most of the evidence from the central Sudan suggests, however, that these rules were often disregarded. Usuman dan Fodio threatened with hell-fire those who carried off booty secretly; at the same time, rumours of his largesse towards his troops, keeping nothing for himself, had spread as far as Wadai even in his own lifetime. When Sabun of Wadai marched against Bagirmi, in the dry season of 1805–6, his army was as usual followed by clerics, Sharifs, and the poor, all of whom later received rich presents from the booty which the sultan himself collected. Among the items which Sabun reserved for himself, supplies of war material figured prominently. An additional advantage of slave troops was that they were not legally entitled to any share in booty. Among the pagan Kwararafa, a confederacy centred south of the Benue, all spoil was theoretically the property of the king, but in practice he restored a third, or a half, to encourage his warriors to perform equally well next time.

Yet Aloma did introduce a number of new devices and methods, notable among which were firearms. In the words of Ibn Fartuwa: 'Among the benefits which God (Most High) of His bounty and beneficence, generosity and constancy conferred upon the Sultan was the acquisition of Turkish musketeers and numerous household slaves who became skilled in firing muskets.'[1] Perhaps because Ibn Fartuwa mentions the guns just after referring to Aloma's pilgrimage, it has been generally assumed that Aloma acquired them on the Pilgrimage, or that he came to appreciate their value then and acquired them later. It is, however, fairly clear that Aloma was using gunmen even before his pilgrimage. On his second campaign against Kanem, which may have been as early as the second year of his reign, gunmen, shield-bearers and bowmen are mentioned, the two former groups, at least, each having its own chief. Other explanations for Aloma's acquisition of firearms are possible. One comes from an anonymous Spaniard, a contemporary of Aloma, in Morocco, who described the departure of the Moroccan force against Songhay in 1590. By way of preface, he mentioned that a Turkish army had earlier attempted to attack Bornu. This army, overwhelmed by thirst in the desert, perished, save for some musketeers, who fell prisoner into the hands of the ruler of Bornu. He treated them so handsomely that they chose to stay and serve him of their own will.[2] Less dramatic, though perhaps more likely, is the possibility that Aloma acquired guns and gunmen through normal diplomatic exchanges with Tripoli, or even through adventurers and mercenaries coming to him. If any of these explanations is correct, then Aloma's pilgrimage, important as it may have been in other respects, had little or none of the military significance hitherto attributed to it.

It is not easy to assess exactly the impact of the introduction of

[1] Ahmed Ibn Fartuwa, *History of the first twelve years of the reign of Mai Idris Alooma of Bornu*, tr. H. R. Palmer (Lagos, 1926; reprinted London, 1970), 11.

[2] H. de Castries, 'La conquête du Soudan par El-Mansour, 1591', *Hespéris*, 1923, 3, 475–6.

firearms. Some scholars have thought that Aloma's guns 'altered the whole character' of his campaigns.[1] The change was probably not as significant as this. In Ibn Fartuwa's account of the Kanem wars, there is no mention of guns playing a decisive role, despite the fact that the Bulala forces opposing Aloma may have had none themselves. On one of the three occasions on which the gunmen are mentioned, Aloma is described setting out on a sortie, and leaving his gunmen, shield-bearers and bowmen at the base camp, there being no transport for their food. Still more humiliating, on a campaign within Bornu the gunmen were once set to work with everyone else to cut down trees (see p. 75). Against the pagans of the south, and of the still unsubdued portions of Bornu, guns may have been more effective: Ibn Fartuwa himself says that Aloma owed the conquest of the walled village of Amsaka to firearms. Yet it is quite evident from the detailed account of the siege of Amsaka that other stratagems had to be employed – the defensive moat was filled first with straw, later with earth, and the palisade of the village had to be thrown down – to help the gunmen, for whom the attackers built special platforms. Even so the siege was a long drawn out affair. And the fact that the Bornu casualties amounted to no more than one man killed suggests that even the least lethal resistance still involved gunmen in considerable delays. In general, the importance which Ibn Fartuwa attaches to other tactics, and units, of Aloma's army indicates that firearms gave no overwhelming advantage.

Linguistic evidence suggests that the Hausa word for gun, *bíndígà*, derived ultimately from the Arabic via Libya, was borrowed immediately from the Kanuri. Perhaps this dates back to Aloma's time, but the first substantial introduction of firearms in Hausaland, or at least in Kano, seems to have been only in the second quarter of the eighteenth century, under Sarki Kumbari. This addition to Kano's power may explain renewed military action by Bornu against Kano about this period (see p. 80). But Sarki Kumbari is remembered also as bringing shields from Nupe for the first time – a strange commentary on firearms as a revolutionary new device.

The presence of Turkish gunmen – Turks almost certainly 'by profession', and not strictly by national origin – with Aloma presumably alleviated, though it could not in the long run cure, the difficulties of training soldiers in the use of firearms, the maintenance of the weapons themselves, and the supply of the necessary materials. Hazards are indicated by Shaykh Ḥasan, killed in 1664–5, when his own musket

[1] J. S. Trimingham, *A history of Islam in West Africa* (London 1962), 122.

exploded (see p. 56); by the Sarkin Gobir whose gun, so the story runs, backfired when he attempted to assassinate Usuman dan Fodio; and by innumerable other instances. Such factors suggest that the underlying pattern in the central Sudan was not the introduction of firearms, at some specific time in history, leading thereafter to a new situation, but rather the introduction of firearms, perhaps with considerable immediate impact (though even this is far from clear), followed by a gradual decline in usefulness, to be followed eventually by a reintroduction.

Sabun's experience of guns, resembling Aloma's in several respects, illustrates this cycle. At first, Sabun did not understand guns, but learnt about them from North African merchants. His interest whetted, he then bought all he could get, at whatever price; he also collected horses, and other arms of all kinds. He brought together a considerable number of slaves, whom he had trained to firearms by the North Africans who had sold him the guns. All this was done before his accession to the throne, and made the government suspicious of his intentions. His father, the sultan, sent a deputation of major clerics to intercede with Sabun. He repulsed their overtures. But when Sabun eventually did seize power, the only mention of guns in the act of revolution is of one which set some thatched roofs alight during a night attack, enabling Sabun's supporters to distinguish, and kill by other means, his opponents. Later, attacking a mountain stronghold in Tama, a recalcitrant vassal state, Sabun asked the twenty-two North Africans accompanying his forces to help with their guns. The defenders replied with a hail of stones, wounding fifteen of the marksmen, who were compelled then to fire one by one, hiding with little dignity behind a tree. The mountain was taken, but only after a secret path up it had been betrayed.

Artillery might have been more useful, as in the Turco-Egyptian forces which twice heavily defeated the Shāyqiyya in the eastern Sudan, forcing them to submit (see chapter 1, p. 50), but virtually no large guns were in service in the central Sudan before 1800.

Aloma had several specialist army groups: the shield-bearers are more frequently mentioned than the gunmen. There were also archers, and, especially useful for campaigns in Kanem and northwards, auxiliary camelry from the Berbers of the Koyam. He enlisted Kotoko allies when boats were needed.[1]

Cavalry were probably more important than firearms. Horses were

[1] J. C. Zeltner, 'Le May Idris Alaoma et les Kotoko', *Revue camerounaise d'histoire*, 1971, 1, 36–40.

apparently bred in the central Sudan long before the beginning of our period, but the importance of new stock from the north remained. The control of the more northerly Bulala over the Saharan routes and markets may have been a powerful factor in their initial triumph over the central court in the fourteenth century. A story about the murder of 900 Bulala horsemen with coats of mail, on a friendly visit to Bornu, indicates at least that the Bulala were known for their cavalry, and may also point to special measures taken by Bornu to cancel this advantage: the episode is attributed to Aloma, but more probably belongs to the time of Idrīs Katagarmabe, his grandfather. Returning from his sixth Kanem campaign, Aloma halted in the midst of forced marches to treat with some merchants from Bilma and Kawar, from whom he bought a large number of horses, presumably paying for them with women and children captured on the expedition. Although the balance may have tipped somewhat in favour of Bornu, the Bulala in Aloma's time were still a cavalry power, and the Bulala Sultan 'Abd al-Jalīl prevailed in battle with one of his neighbours partly by using larger horses.

Horses were particularly significant, in a military sense, because of the mobility which they conferred. Again and again in the Kanem wars, horses were used in pursuit, and it was the exhaustion of the horses, together with their need for water, which perhaps more than any other single factor determined the range of operations. Horses were equally useful in retreat. The camel, however sturdy on the march, was no match for the horse in combat or flight, moving much less rapidly. 'Among the retreating Bulala,' runs the description of an incident in the second Kanem war, 'of those who were on foot or mounted on camels, many were killed. Only those mounted on horses escaped.'[1]

In Hausaland likewise, the records suggest the greater importance of horses than of guns. Horses, and armour, are mentioned throughout the seventeenth and eighteenth centuries; in a successful attack on Katsina, possibly during Aloma's reign, the Kano forces under Muḥammad Zaki captured 400 horses and 60 suits of armour. Such references recur. The first Sarkin Kano to have a guard of musketeers, Babba Zaki, probably in the third quarter of the eighteenth century, also amassed horses, and had a strong cavalry force with protective quilting. Some of the early victories of the Fulani jihad were achieved without guns against musketeers, and the theocrats were drawn only reluctantly, during the nineteenth century, into a large employment of firearms.

[1] H. R. Palmer, *Sudanese memoirs* (Lagos, 1928; reprinted London, 1967), I, 32.

Camels, although as we have seen less valuable in battle than horses, were nevertheless extremely important in the more desert regions, and for transport. Aloma's astute tactical sense showed again in his appreciation of camelry, and in this respect his Koyam auxiliaries were particularly useful. Camels were also deployed against him: the Tubu, some of whom were dedicated partners of the Bulala in the struggle with Bornu, were primarily a camel-owning people – later there was at least one major battle between the erstwhile allies, Bulala and Tubu, at which the latter are said to have mustered 1,900 camels (see below, p. 127). And when Sabun prepared his terrible expedition against Bagirmi, saddling his own horses, he demanded from his local Arab allies as many camels as possible.

Although camels are not mentioned specifically in the following episode, it is very likely that they were involved. Aloma, troubled by the way in which the Bulala took refuge in 'the far desert' and 'the most inaccessible wilderness', hit upon the device of enlisting the aid of various nomad tribes. He summoned them to a conference, addressed them with flattery and blandishment, and succeeded in attaching them to the cause of his candidate for the Bulala throne, Muḥammad 'Abdullāh. Ibn Fartuwa thought this a plan such as would have occurred to no one else save Aloma, on account of its ingenuity. But the scheme sounds very much like the policy of Bornu in the nineteenth century, using the Awlād Sulaymān, also Arab nomads, to hold Kanem against inroads from Wadai, a policy which then amounted to little more than granting general licence to the wanderers to plunder.

Aloma broke away from the traditional pattern of seasonal, purely itinerant, raiding. Against the So N'gafata, near the Yo river, with their fortified centre at Damasak, he established two nearby permanent bases. At one, the Great Camp, all his powerful chiefs were ordered to help maintain the garrison, building houses and keeping horses, quilted armour and coats of chain-mail there. Slaves formed a large part of the garrison. In other cases, as on the campaigns in Kanem, the fortification was simply a hedge of thorn trees cut to protect the army's camping place. Even this simple concept is said to have been first introduced by Aloma; among its many advantages, listed by Ibn Fartuwa, was that slaves could not so easily run away from such an enclosure. At the same time the idea of stockading, or walling, villages was spreading in Hausaland, having apparently originated earlier in Zaria (see volume 3, chapter 5). This helped to frustrate Aloma's own attack on Kano. Later in the seventeenth century the walls of Kano were further extended, the completion of the work being sanctified by gifts of 1,000 robes to the workmen, the sacrifice of 300 cattle, and many presents to the clerics. Early in the next century, another Sarkin Kano, Muḥammad Sharīf, is remembered for having walled many towns.

A fixed post, like the Great Camp, allowed more consistent interference with forest cover and agricultural work, a policy employed with undoubted relish and probable efficacy by Aloma. Against the So, he cut down the trees which formed their natural defence. Everyone was called to this task, even herdsmen, merchants and clerics. The cutters worked to the encouraging accompaniment of musicians and dancers, and under the protection of picked shield-bearers and horsemen with both themselves and their mounts in armour. To the destruction of the trees was added that of the crops, as they ripened in the rainy season. Despite the strenuous resistance of the So to this encroachment, and their occasional successes, they were eventually forced to submit. The action of the Muslim cavalry and archers in battle is particularly noted. Similarly, one of Aloma's wars in Kanem took place during the time of the ripening of the dates, specifically to destroy the fruit before the harvest. The districts which he visited suffered heavily: ripe dates were eaten, the unripe destroyed, 'until there was no fruit left in all the country. It was as if a mighty storm of wind had come from the heavens.'[1] Another aspect of Aloma's policy of ecological dislocation was to keep nomads from their normal grazing grounds until they submitted. In this way certain Tuareg groups, who had offended by raiding Fulani pastoralists under Bornu protection, were compelled to renounce their allegiance to Aïr and to accept the suzerainty of Bornu.

A ruler keeping his troops too long in the field faced difficulties, as appears from a Wadai chronicle: the sultan insisted that he would not interrupt his campaign until his pregnant mare had let down her offspring, and this in turn had become large enough to ride. When the discontent of his own followers over this became too great, the sultan died of chagrin. The chronicle attributes this episode to Sabun; this is wrong, but we do know of an earlier sultan of Wadai who was killed while on campaign against Tama, most of his men having deserted to return to their farms (see below, p. 140). Sabun's own tactics did sometimes resemble Aloma's: in his campaigns against Tama, already mentioned in connection with guns, Sabun began with three months' intensive tree cutting, and later sent men to destroy the crops just before harvest. It is possible that, throughout the central Sudan, the

[1] Palmer, *Sudanese memoirs*, I, 44; see also 40, 42.

mere fact of a standing army – and even at the best (or worst) of times these were neither large nor very regular – did not automatically enhance a ruler's power: the important thing was so to deploy one's forces and efforts as to interrupt an enemy's agriculture, a difficult task since one's own men usually had to do their farming on the same seasonal timetable.

The Islamic element in military activity in the central Sudan took various forms. The discipline of the prayer sometimes provided a foundation for military discipline generally. To perform the prayer, at the set times and in the set manner, even while in the field, showed that the commander was in control of the situation. There are recurrent references to Aloma observing the daily prayers, even the festival prayers at the end of Ramadan, in proper fashion despite being actually on campaign in enemy territory. Ibn Fartuwa, wishing to describe the extreme straits of exhaustion to which forced marches had once reduced the army, said, 'So greatly were we taxed, that some of us did not know in which direction to turn when praying unless guided by our camels in that direction.'[1] Prayer, in the sense of divination, might help determine the time and direction of an expedition; it might assist the army along the way, especially through the miraculous discovery of water; it undermined enemy morale by threatening supernatural sanctions, and correspondingly kindled the spirit of those in whose favour it was offered. In prayer of this kind, and in the preparation of amulets and charms of military import, clerics were involved, and often profited accordingly. Muḥammad Zaki, the Sarkin Kano about Aloma's time whose successful raid against Katsina captured 400 horses, had consulted the clerics before setting out. One, a North African, said that he could give the *sarki* supernatural assistance, but that he would then never return. Muḥammad Zaki agreed; he gave the North African great wealth, and the other clerics many gifts; he defeated Katsina, but died on the way home. Pagan devices were also still in use: holy objects, for example, were prominent in the partially successful defence of Kano against a Kwararafa attack later in the seventeenth century. In the 1760s, after a raid by Agades on Gobir had failed, the ruler of Agades summoned his clerics for consultation. One advised him that defeat was a punishment for parsimony; so the sultan gave him a horse and, so it is said, a million cowries, with presents to the other clerics, and returned to Gobir where he cut off the head of the *sarki*, Dan Guddi. Dan Guddi was succeeded by his brother, Bawa, for whose

[1] Palmer, *Sudanese memoirs*, I, 62.

success against Maradi Usuman dan Fodio himself prayed. Bawa overcame Maradi, without trouble, but when he then disobeyed Usuman's instruction and advanced further, trusting to his own strength, he was defeated and killed, in 1789–90.

Religion was sometimes called upon to provide, in various ways, setting and sanction for military activity. The religious flavour of campaigns falling within Ramadan, as did Muḥammad Zaki's attack on Katsina, was naturally heightened. This happened several times with Aloma, whose chronicler, Ibn Fartuwa, particularly remarks the suitability of such a time for raiding. In fact, however, expeditions were determined mainly by the seasons of the solar calendar, and it was only coincidence if these corresponded with the lunar calendar of the faith. Sabun's attack on Bagirmi, that catastrophe which together with the Fulani jihad in the west closes the period, had received the prior approval of the clerics of Wadai, and was justified by the marital irregularities of the ruler of Bagirmi, who had married his own sister, violating religious law. Sabun, as he invaded, was careful at each place along the way to summon the local clerics and leading men, treating them kindly, while he also performed devotional acts at each holy spot he passed, thus further emphasizing the religious propriety of his action.

The dramatic sense of being on jihad may well have stirred the enthusiasm of the troops. Yet the proper procedures of jihad were rarely if ever followed: there is almost no mention of the preliminary triple invitation to one's opponents to convert or submit, and little to suggest that after conquest conversion was imposed. Tribute was usually the more desired end. This is clear in the Bagirmi chronicle of the ruler ʻAbd al-Qādir's jihads; having been on pilgrimage, ʻAbd al-Qādir seized the throne from his father in the mid-eighteenth century, and then raided many peoples, converting them to Islam *and* imposing upon them the *jizya*, that tax specially reserved for non-Muslims living under the protection of a Muslim state.[1] Regulations concerning the correct treatment of Muslim prisoners of war also seem to have been of relatively little effect. There is a celebrated passage in Ibn Fartuwa, telling how Aloma, returning from his second expedition against Kanem, ordered all his followers to bring all their captives, slave or free, to him. Aloma then divided the free from the slave, irrespective of sex; the slaves he set apart to be distributed as booty, but the free he sent back to their homes. Ibn Fartuwa contrasted this with the

[1] Thus the account in *Sudanese memoirs*, II, 108–9; other traditions give the name of almost certainly the same ruler as Muḥammad – cf. below, p. 134.

practice of the Bulala who, on their raids into Bornu, had never released a free prisoner, man or woman.

This, however, is the only such episode which Ibn Fartuwa describes. It may have derived as much from Aloma's personal affiliations with the Bulala, who were in any case kinsmen of the Kanuri, as from religious scruples. It does not seem to have been duplicated in the treatment of enemies other than the Bulala, and may not even have been standard practice towards the Bulala. Aḥmad Bābā, the distinguished Timbuktu scholar, and contemporary of Aloma, included Kano and Katsina, and even part of Zaria, along with Bornu and Songhay as the Muslim states of the Sudan in his time. But this did not win Kano preferential treatment from Aloma. A traditional, and quite disrespectful, explanation of the origin of the name Afuno, by which the Kanuri know the Hausa, tells how Aloma was scornful of the nakedness of the Hausa, whom he accordingly plundered each year, despite the fact that his victims prayed and fasted as Muslims. Similarly, al-Kānamī reports of his expedition against Kano more than two centuries later: 'Our horses reached Kano, and I took as slaves those who were coming out of the gate of the city for firewood or other things.'[1] Similarly many of the Tubu and Tuareg against whom Aloma, and most of his successors throughout the period, repeatedly warred, were almost certainly professing Muslims.

When describing the period after Aloma's death, it is not uncommon for scholars to speak of decline in the affairs of Bornu. The evidence for such decline is not very clear – unless, as seems regrettably to be sometimes the case, success in statecraft is confused with military activity. One historian went so far as to regard it as a bad sign when a ruler or prince died at home in the capital, and he dismissed any praise of a ruler for justice or learning as meaning that he was totally dominated by clerics. History may properly reserve a more honoured place than this for rich men furnished with ability, living peaceably in their habitations. The tradition of royal pilgrimage continued strong, usually though not invariably an indication of stability and security in the state. Three sons of Aloma succeeded him; the third of these, ʻUmar, was a pilgrim. ʻUmar was succeeded by his son, ʻAlī, who was noted for his pilgrimages (see pp. 94–6). Two of his sons succeeded him; the son of one of these became another pilgrim *mai*.

Beneath the shelter of such relatively quiet government, a remarkable

[1] L. Brenner, *The Shehus of Kukawa: a history of the al-Kanemi dynasty of Bornu* (Oxford, 1973), 56.

transformation was taking place in Bornu. In 1400, when the harassed and anxious *mai* fled from Kanem to Bornu, neither the Kanuri language nor the Kanuri people existed; and for much of the fifteenth century it was far from certain that the tender transplants from Kanem would survive. In 1600, under Aloma, the Kanuri nation was still by no means clearly defined; as has been seen, centres of local resistance still demanded elaborate military action to be taken even in the heartlands of Bornu. By 1800, the process of Kanurization had so far proceeded that the Kanuri formed a distinct nation, their language one of the major tongues of the central Sudan, widely employed in trade and travel. Individual Kanuri speakers might be found as far apart as Cairo and Freetown, 5,500 kilometres as the crow flies (see p. 95).

A similar process of the consolidation of society was going on in Hausaland, but it was there less perilous, since the base upon which the Hausa language and people were to evolve was already in place; in Bornu, that base could be constructed only through the amalgamation of an immigrant minority with firmly established local people. Displacement, as of the American Indians or Australian aborigines, was beyond the bounds of the possible: the pattern was closer to that of Normans and Saxons in England after 1066. To trace exactly the outlines of the emergence of Kanuri society is difficult; but we may clearly see in the nineteenth century the measure of success achieved, as traveller after traveller was courteously received in Bornu, both at the capital and in outlying districts, while in Wadai at the same time, amid a welter of petty languages and dialects, and recalcitrant political and social factions, the crown struggled with but indifferent success to impose national unity, and European travellers went in danger of their lives – as most indeed found to their cost. The first full accounts of Wadai, those of al-Tūnusī and Nachtigal, help to interpret Ibn Fartuwa's chronicle, and also reveal the great changes which had occurred by the time of al-Kānamī.

In the slow creation of a new society, many forces, in addition to the military action already described, were at work, governmental, commercial and religious. But, before considering these, it is important to realize that the seventeenth and eighteenth centuries were by no means a time of consistent military decline. By the eighteenth century, firearms had disappeared from the poetry and praise songs of Bornu, and were not mentioned even in the wars against the Fulani in the early nineteenth century; it is likely, however, that the decline and fall of the gun in the central Sudan was more a comment on the marginal utility of that instrument in so distant a region, than a sign of timorous government. ʿAlī b. ʿUmar, grandson of Aloma, *mai* of many pilgrimages, had to wrestle with the continuing problem of the Tuareg, and his long reign of over thirty years, in the later part of the seventeenth century, coincided with the heyday of the Kwararafa (see pp. 134–5), a direr military challenge than any Aloma ever faced. Indeed, it may well be that Bornu's ability to help to defend the frontiers of Hausaland partly reconciled the Hausa principalities to the humiliation and expense of tributary status. Muḥammad b. al-Ḥājj Ḥamdūn, great-grandson of ʿAlī b. ʿUmar, led the expedition already mentioned (see p. 71) against Kano, just as Aloma had done. Perhaps Muḥammad's action was designed to neutralize the acquisition of firearms by Kano, although it is difficult to understand why, if Bornu was so concerned about guns in Kano, it did not take more care to acquire some for itself. The last three *mais* before the Fulani inrush early in the nineteenth century were more given to the exercises of piety than to those of the battlefield, though an attack was mounted against Mandara, south of Bornu, which failed with heavy losses to Bornu.

FINANCE AND GOVERNMENT

Government, as at all times and in all places, had to be paid for. Those governments in the central Sudan, to the defence of which the military activities just outlined were dedicated, were largely occupied with problems of finance, endeavouring to ensure that those who bore the responsibilities of government – and enjoyed its privileges – should not have to bear its cost also. Booty was a main source of revenue. According to the *Sharīʿa* – the strict rules of which, however, seem rarely to have been enforced – one-fifth of the total went to the central authorities, and the rest was divided regularly, a horseman, for example, getting twice the share of a foot soldier. Like many devices of economic policy even today, booty was more attractive in the short term than beneficial in the long. While its prospect might stimulate morale among the troops, in the harsh devastation of looting there was always the danger that the goose laying the golden eggs might be killed. It was therefore better for both parties if some form of tribute could be arranged, either once and for all, or as a recurrent commitment. The dividing line between booty and tribute was often tenuous. Many military expeditions in search of booty were directed against defaulting tributaries: in 1609–10, Ramaḍān Bey of Tunis, having solicited tribute from Ghadames of five handsome young eunuchs for palace service, eight pretty black girls, and 200 skins, and receiving only a courteous answer, marched against the city and besieged it. Contrariwise, agreement to pay tribute might buy off the attackers: Ghadames and the Tunisian column struck a compromise; or, to quote a nineteenth-century example, Shaykh 'Umar of Bornu recalled his son, just about to attack Kusseri, when Kusseri at the last moment submitted tribute of 300 slaves. Sometimes conquest and looting were the necessary preliminary to tribute: Aloma imposed a tributary obligation of 1,000 cattle upon the Kananiya, a major tribe of Kanem, in this way, and it was Sabun's rape of Bagirmi at the very end of the period which permanently established Bagirmi's tributary dependence upon Wadai. Ironically, Bornu had encouraged Wadai's intervention, hoping thus with Wadaian help to restore its own title to tribute from Bagirmi.

The implications of tribute varied enormously. It might be little more than a token of esteem, as when Wadai sent tribute to the Ottoman sultans – indeed, one late and probably spurious explanation of the name Wadai derives it from a word for tribute. It might be the acknowledgment by one virtually sovereign power that its neighbour was more powerful: thus Wadai paid tribute to Darfur, and most of the Hausa states did the same to Bornu, throughout most of the period. According to one report, the dread Kwararafa had so much fallen from their former power that, about 1800, they were paying Bornu an annual tribute of 1,000 slaves; at the same period an officer came every year from Tripoli to Murzuq to collect the tribute of Fezzan in gold, senna, or slaves. Territories or peoples in exposed positions might pay tribute at the same time to two different powers, a situation which well illustrates the fluid and uncertain nature of political boundaries in the area. Within imperial structures, tribute was sometimes among the last vestiges of such structures to survive: when in 1711 the founder of the Karamanli house, and hence of the virtual independence of Tripoli, murdered most of his rivals, he placated Istanbul by payment of large tribute – the property, it was said, of his deceased enemies. Closer to the centres of power, tributary obligations increased: not only had wealth to be surrendered, but the tributary was also expected to give military support, and to guarantee safety and hospitality for expeditions and caravans passing to and from the dominant power. Here tribute merged into taxation; in the central areas of the various states of the central Sudan, revenue-bearing districts or populations were regularly assigned, as a kind of fief, to high officials, to members of the ruling families, even to distinguished visitors.

Duties on commerce were another main source of government income. The fixed Saharan routes made such control easier. Hornemann, just before 1800, encountered agents of the bey of Benghazi in Awjila collecting a tax on each camel in the passing caravans; the measures of Tunis against Ghadames, and of Tripoli in Murzuq (see pp. 128–9), are evidence of North African involvement in Saharan taxation. In Murzuq, Hornemann found the local sultan levying a duty of six or eight dollars on each camel load coming from Cairo, while slaves for sale from Bornu and Hausa paid two mithqals each. A late fifteenth-century source, probably from the Agades region, speaks of market dues on livestock, slaves, clothes and food, and of similar dues at the city gates on entering and leaving – even firewood was taxed. City walls facilitated such controls, though not always effectively, as this passage from Hornemann suggests:

> ... the officers of the Sultan met us to take account of the bales and merchandize, which had not been usually done till arrival at the gates of Mourzouk; and the merchants had been in the habit of previously disposing of at least a third of their goods, in order to evade the duties. Some however had contrived to intermingle their baggage with that of the pilgrims, who pay no duties.[1]

Hornemann added that the government of the Fezzan drew its revenues from taxes on all cultivated land, from arbitrary fines and requisitions, from duties on camels and slaves in caravans, from royal domains, gardens and woods, and from salt pools and natron lakes.

Islamic regulations concerning taxation were known: even in the fifteenth century, al-Maghīlī, for example, had spelt them out for Rimfa, the ruler of Kano. In many respects there was correspondence between traditional and Islamic patterns, making it difficult to assess how far the new religion was making an independent impact. The *Sharī'a* might influence the distribution of booty. Tribute resembled *jizya*, the tax levied upon protected non-Muslims, though Muslims in the central Sudan were also sometimes liable. Grain and livestock taxes on peoples within the central state areas might be calculated according to *zakāt* rules; it is interesting to note that, in al-Maghīlī's advices, the ruler has less discretion in his disbursement of income from this source than from any other. Land taxes resembled *kharāj*. An impor-

[1] The 'Journal of Friedrich Hornemann', in *Proceedings of the Association for promoting the discovery of the interior parts of Africa* (London, 1810; reprinted London, 1967), II, 128.

tant addition to traditional payments on special occasions was the *zakāt al-fiṭr*, or tax levied at the end of Ramadan. In Mandara, for example, each Fulani or Arab village sent a cow to the sultan at this time, and in addition every village chief gave a ram for the pilgrimage festival. The advice of Muslim scholars might be sought about various tolls: the sultan of Agades did this, over caravan duties. Scrupulous observance of the *Sharīʿa* was likely to mean a diminution of the ruler's income: this was particularly clear in punishment by fines, a common feature of traditional justice. Al-Maghīlī complained of such fines as oppressive, and so three centuries later did Usuman dan Fodio.

Taxation affected the movement of population, which in turn determined the basic patterns of social and political consolidation. When the Koyam returned to Bornu early in the eighteenth century, they were, as a religious group, granted exemption from taxes; this privilege, coupled with their generally moderate government, meant that their district rapidly filled with people. Heavy taxation had the opposite effect, driving people away. Kumbari, ruler of Kano in the second quarter of the eighteenth century, taxed the market so severely that it was nearly killed. 'The next year he collected *Jizia* in Kano and made even the mallams pay. There was so much disturbance that the Arabs left the town and went back to Katsina, and most of the poorer people in the town fled to the country. Turaki Kuka Tunku said to Kumbari, "Sarki, if you do not let this *Jizia* alone, there will be no one left in the town but yourself and your servants." The Sarki listened to him.'[1] For many peasants, oppressed on their farms, migration was not easy, and the song of a Bornu tax collector may have been all too often realized:

> The poor are grass,
> They are fodder for horses;
> Work, poor man, so that we may eat.[2]

Forms of government supported by these finances do not seem to have changed radically during our period. The head of state was generally advised by some kind of grand council, called the *nokena* in Kanuri. Membership of this varied, probably deriving in origin from the principal lineage heads, and from the family of the ruler, but supplemented with new additions, important among whom were slave notables more closely dependent upon the ruler. The most recent study of government in Bornu suggests, however, that the council before the

[1] Palmer, *Sudanese memoirs*, III, 124.

[2] R. Prietze, 'Bornulieder', *Mitteilungen des Seminars für Orientalische Sprachen zu Berlin*, 1914, 251.

nineteenth century may have been more amorphously defined than has sometimes been thought, being perhaps even synonymous with the court itself.[1] Individuals exercised influence more by virtue of the trust reposed in them by the ruler, than through hereditary and traditional titles, which might increase or decline in power. Major fief-holders were expected to live at the capital: this allowed the central authority to keep them under surveillance and gave the people living on the fiefs some kind of representation at court, but the natural disadvantages of absentee landlordism often occurred. The fief arrangement was satisfactory for settled populations; in Bornu, nomadic groups came under a general division of the kingdom into four quadrants, the officials of which provided an alternative hierarchy. The concentration of leading men at the court was reinforced by marriage alliances, particularly between princesses of the royal house and leading dignitaries, trusted followers, as well as neighbouring rulers. Fief and tributary arrangements catered for the widest possible variety of local institutions: the presence of the great lords at court, on the contrary, ensured some overall uniformity and control.

THE ROLE OF COMMERCE

Policy concerning commerce involved, in Aloma's case, as with his military activities, both the internal development of Bornu and its foreign relations. Ibn Fartuwa, introducing his subject, promised to give equal prominence to war and trade: he proposed, he said, to tell what Aloma did at war and in camp – that is, on military expeditions away from the capital – and how he cleared roads for merchants, although in fact little of the chronicle is devoted to the latter. It is likely that many of Aloma's expeditions, particularly those to the northern sector, were designed to keep trade routes open. Aloma's initiative in devising better boats, especially for river ferries, also contributed to trade and communication. A passing reference to the introduction, by Aloma, of units of measure for corn among certain peoples, including the warlike Binawa, seems to suggest a new attention to agriculture and exchange; Aloma further commanded some Binawa to settle and farm. Another instance of compulsory relocation occurred in the case of the Ngouma, a hill people whom Aloma had defeated, and whom he then settled in villages where he could keep a closer eye on them.

The episode of the Binawa is informative in various respects. These

[1] Brenner, *The Shehus of Kukawa*, 18.

people, lying to the west of Ngasargamu, along the way to Katagum, had been notorious in the reign of Aloma's predecessor for their harrying of the Fulani, which, incidentally, is the earliest firm indication of large-scale Fulani entry into Bornu. Bornu officials were posted along the way, 'but the Binawa, the inhabitants of those parts, took no heed of them and set themselves to stop the roads, and cut off Bornu from the land of Fali, so that none could go by night from East to West or even from West to East'.[1] At the height of the Binawa troubles, merchants and others had to make long detours. When Aloma came to power, Bultu, one of the Binawa, with a few of his people came to the principal vizier of Bornu, and remained with him, becoming a good Muslim. When Bultu was established as a regular counsellor of the vizier, the latter asked his advice about overcoming the still recalcitrant majority of the Binawa. Bultu and the vizier went together to Binawa country, and persuaded them to submit; this was apparently not a military expedition. Those swore on the Koran who recognized its binding power; others were guided gently. Thus all were reformed, even the worst, and some became Muslim soldiers, some merchants. 'God made safe the road between East and West...' Even allowing for the fact that becoming Muslim in such cases may, particularly in the initial stages, have meant little more than submitting to the central government, it is clear that the progress of the religion was closely intertwined with the extension of commerce and stable rule.

The fact that Sabun confronted similar problems in Wadai 200 years later, shows again that these were basic features of central Sudanic society. In Wadai, roads were unsafe because of highwaymen, sometimes called *'afrīts*, devils; Sabun cleared the roads of these, so that a lone woman clad in gold might walk with none to fear but God.[2] Sabun failed in his attempt to change the *kayl*, the traditional measure of grain in the country, even though he proposed to substitute for it the *mudd* of the Prophet. Similarly he failed in an attempt to introduce minted silver money, on the North African model; conservative opinion feared lest this should cause the Wadawa to become avaricious.

Foreign commerce, particularly across the Sahara, was in every period of great importance. Not all merchants made the full journey: it was possible, for example, for those North Africans who wished to

[1] Ibn Fartuwa, *History of Mai Idris Alooma*, 38.

[2] This is a common ideal, or popular legend, of Muslim states: sometimes the traveller, having met and spoken with such a woman journeying in a particularly wild region, and who later compliments the ruler on the security of his realm, is taken away and beaten for the effrontery of even talking to the woman.

do so to exchange their cloth for slaves at Agades, without going on to the Sudan proper. Nor did all goods traverse the full route, for some were of Saharan provenance or destination. From the Fezzan, corn and dates supplied Ghadames and the mountains beyond on the way to Tripoli; dates from Kawar went south. Raiding supplemented trade: some Tubu suffered yearly depredations at the hands of the Arabs of Benghazi and Awjila, who sallied forth stealing dates and men. Some, perhaps much, of the credit for this agricultural produce in the North African hinterland belonged to slaves, freedmen, and other Sudanic immigrants. Among the various agricultural, and even stockkeeping, duties which were often the special responsibility of Sudanese, the care of date palms was notable. Even in Arabia this vital work was sometimes reserved for blacks. Falls, and the spikes on the trees, made it dangerous: to fall out of the palm tree down a well is a Saharan equivalent to the English proverb, out of the frying-pan into the fire. But it would be wrong to regard nomads as in every case entirely aloof from such work. Nomads came regularly each year, for example, to the plain near Tripoli, planted and raised a crop there if rain were sufficient, and then departed again, and in Tunis nomads often tilled lands belonging to town dwellers.

Salt was the Saharan product most in demand. The salt of the desert near Ghadames was carried north, and was more highly esteemed than that manufactured on the shores of the Mediterranean. Salt from Bilma, in Kawar, was taken to Bornu and Hausaland, perhaps more to the latter since alternative sources of supply particularly around Lake Chad may have reduced Bornu's dependence upon imports. Nevertheless Kawar was of great significance to Bornu, both for its salt production and its position athwart the Fezzan road. Aloma raided into this area, and stayed for some time at Bilma, presumably trying to keep the road open. Bilma salt was not of high quality, but was a major import of Hausaland. The Tuareg of Aïr organized the annual caravans, sometimes 10,000 camels or more and carrying only salt; they also handled some of the distribution within Hausaland, and spent the dry season there. This carrying trade was the principal support of Aïr: the nineteenth-century traveller, Barth, regretted the insipid food there, unsalted in a land whose entire trade was in salt. In exchange for salt and dates, Kawar received millet, cotton cloth, and other products of the central Sudan.

As a stimulus to political and military development in the central Sudan, the most influential material imports from beyond the Sahara were horses, guns and other weapons. Aloma, returning from his sixth campaign in Kanem, met merchants from Bornu, Kawar, Fezzan and the north, and from them bought many horses. The import of horses was evidently a difficult undertaking, and there are several references – one, for example, in the time of Aloma, another apparently in the later eighteenth century – to people refusing to go north for this duty. In both these instances, it was evidently the case that, if horses could not be brought from the north, then local ones were available. The implication seems to be that, while horses from North Africa were highly valued, they were not essential, since local breeding had become established, perhaps centuries before. As has been seen, guns first reached the central Sudan in the time of Aloma.

From North Africa, and sometimes from still farther afield, came a variety of more or less luxury goods: silks and other fine cloths, glassware – a Kanuri proverb, on receiving a useless gift, is, 'The blind man doesn't care if someone brings him a looking-glass from Tripoli' – and other such things. Perfumes and aromatics of all kinds, some exported, some imported, were important luxury items, their use being one of the few indulgences allowed even to the strictest Muslims. They were variously employed: in Tripoli, the well-to-do prepared a body for burial with aromatic substances; and to use perfume again might be a sign that the period of mourning was over.

Among the exports northwards from the central Sudan were cottons, ivory, perfume, wax, hides and skins, ostrich feathers, gold and slaves. Slaves were the most important. An account in 1787 reports that caravans from Ghadames to Tunis brought nothing but slaves; these caravans at that time rarely came more than three times a year, compared with eight or ten journeys that might be made from Constantine to Tunis – caravans on both roads were exempt from direct imposts. Diplomatic exchanges in the seventeenth century provide a more detailed record than do general commercial transactions: Mai 'Umar, Aloma's son, sent gifts to Tripoli including 100 young Negroes and 100 girls; the gifts given in exchange were 200 horses, fifteen young European renegades (presumably slave soldiers), and several muskets and swords. Mai 'Alī b. 'Umar in his turn once sent 100 slaves, with five dwarfs and twenty eunuchs, and another time 200 young slaves and some eunuchs. He requested some more Europeans, who were sent, together with fifty horses. Mai 'Alī acknowledged with gold and slaves the return of his nephew, enslaved and sold in a local war. The intimate relationship between the trade in slaves and that in arms is clear, and this continued until the slave trade was abolished: when Barth, in the mid-nineteenth century, reproached the vizier of Bornu for an intended slave raid towards Mandara, the dignitary replied that such raids were essential in order to obtain guns.

The trans-Saharan trade in Negroes was but one side of a double slave-trading policy in North Africa. Both Tripolitania and Tunisia traded actively in white slaves, as did the states farther west. The black slave, traditionally bound to the prow of a new cruiser when launched at Tripoli, symbolized the joining of the two trades in the Maghrib. White slaves were recruited through corsairs' raids on the shipping of the Christian nations of Europe, sometimes through coastal attacks as well, and by overland commerce through the Near East. Both the state and private enterprise participated. The bey of Tunis, for example, sent out some corsairs of his own; in addition, he was entitled to half the value of the cargo of any ship captured, and a tenth part of the slaves; he might further buy the others for one-third of the usual ransom. Ransom for the bey's slaves was fixed, so much for a seaman, double for a captain or a woman. Ransom profits and prize money constituted an important part of state revenue, which, however, drew also upon customs, export licences, payments by government officials on appointment, the sale of monopolies (in Tunis, such monopolies sold annually included wax, soda, and the tunny and coral fisheries), land and produce taxes, and other sources. In the case of nations which signed treaties with the North African powers to protect their shipping against corsairs, payment for this treaty privilege replaced ransom moneys as an item of revenue. Ransom was also part of the slaving pattern in the central Sudan, though a less important one. Particularly if the children of chiefs were among the captives after raids, conscientious relatives might pawn themselves – another form of servitude – in order to redeem these unfortunates.

The pattern of black and white slaving was already under pressure towards the end of the eighteenth century. Principal sources for the land trade, for example in Georgia, whence the Ottomans had recruited white slaves through tribute, trade, and warfare, shrank with the advance of effective Russian authority. European agitation against the slave trade in general increased, culminating in the abolition of that trade in British dominions from 1807; European supremacy in the Mediterranean, leading ultimately to the French occupation of Algiers in 1830, discommoded corsairing. These winds of recession scarcely affected the trade in black slaves, within the Sudan and across the

Sahara. On the contrary, the dwindling supply of whites in the Ottoman world may have increased the demand for blacks. About 1811, Sabun of Wadai succeeded in sending a caravan through directly to Benghazi, and despite heavy losses on the road merchants were much interested to find that slaves costing seven or eight thalers in Wadai sold in Benghazi for forty or more. Yūsuf Karamanli, who had seized power in Tripolitania in 1795, after a most damaging period of civil strife and war with Tunis, was attracted by the advantages of trade for the restoration of the fortunes of the state. He appointed as receiver of customs his own son-in-law, originally a Georgian slave bought in Istanbul. When the ruler of the Fezzan tried to interfere with Sabun's slaves in transit from Wadai, Yūsuf deposed him.

Trade was also taking place along the other axis of Sudanic development, east and west along the Sudan belt, though available evidence is fragmentary. A principal trade route linking Hausaland with regions farther west and south was the kola road to Gonja. Developed for the first time in the fifteenth century, this trade became of the utmost importance for Hausaland, an importance reflected in many proverbs and legends. The traveller making for Gonja who grows tired at the Waterri crossing (near Kano), is the Hausa equivalent of looking back after putting your hand to the plough. Some Tuareg believed that the Hausa originated in Gonja, and had spread thence through the kola trade: this is pure fantasy as far as Hausa origins are concerned, but quite an apt assessment of the significance of the kola trade to the Hausa. By the nineteenth century, kola was being carried even to Wadai, though it was there a royal luxury. It was sought after in the Fezzan and Tripoli, and among other virtues was thought to cure impotence.

Nupe was an important stage on the Gonja route; the road from Katsina to Nupe was practicable even for camels. In the early nineteenth century, and probably throughout this period also, Bornu caravans did not go farther than Nupe, though individual merchants from Bornu might join Hausa traders travelling on towards Gonja. Nupe was also the gateway for many goods entering the central Sudan: we have already mentioned guns and shields coming to Kano from Nupe in the first half of the eighteenth century. Nupe was a leading slave supplier: the first eunuchs in Hausaland, introduced about the same time as kola, came apparently from Nupe; horses were sometimes sent from Hausaland in exchange for eunuchs. The continent-wide reputation of Nupe appears from an anecdote told by al-Tūnusī, a North African traveller in Wadai and Darfur in the nineteenth century. According to this, a Moroccan merchant went to Nupe with 1,000 slaves, presumably acquired south of the Sahara, to sell, hoping to impress the local people. The chief merchant of the place sent one of his own slaves to buy the whole consignment, and great was the Moroccan's astonishment when he went to collect payment, and found that he had been selling to a slave, and that the chief merchant even professed total ignorance of such minor transactions by his agents. This traveller's tale indicates that slaves were also imported into Nupe, whether for use there or for re-export. This is confirmed by an exchange reported between Bawa, the Sarkin Gobir late in the eighteenth century, who refused to pay tribute to Bornu: he received from Sarkin Nupe 500 female slaves, and 500 boy slaves, each boy carrying 20,000 cowries; in return he sent 100 horses, and female slaves 'which in beauty outshone the sun, beautiful, in form and character, and resplendent with ambergris and silk'.[1] Barth thought that more slaves were exported from Kano in small caravans to Nupe, and to Bornu, than went directly across the desert. The export of slaves from Oyo, through Porto Novo, for the Atlantic trade was growing, particularly in the last quarter of the eighteenth century, and some of these may have come from, or through, Nupe. Parts of Nupe, south of the Niger, may have been under some peripheral hegemony of Oyo, and perhaps the demands for tribute increased. There is, however, no support in Nupe traditions for the view that Nupe as a whole was a vassal of Oyo.[2] An Oyo army sent against Nupe was heavily defeated in 1790 or 1791. Among exports from, or through, the central Sudan to Nupe were horses, swords, silk, cloth, mirrors, leather goods, kohl, perfumes and scents (from as great a distance as Mecca), and, perhaps most important of all, natron from Bornu. Barth estimated that at the very least 20,000 loads of natron, on horses, oxen and asses, passed through Kano each year, on their way from Bornu to Nupe. Natron was also carried on to Gonja and to Yorubaland. Clapperton's interpreter in Nupe, early in the nineteenth century, was a Sharif from Murzuq, married to a daughter of the Nupe ruler.

Cowries, just mentioned in Nupe trade, first came to Hausaland early in the eighteenth century, during the reign of Muḥammad Sharif, 'because he was zealous in raiding'.[3] Perhaps he secured cowries as

[1] H. R. Palmer, 'Western Sudan history: the Raudthât' ul Afkâri', *Journal of the African Society*, 1915–16, **15**, 269.

[2] M. Mason, 'The Nupe kingdom in the nineteenth century', Ph.D. thesis (Birmingham, 1970), 62–3; but I. A. Akinjogbin, in J. F. A. Ajayi and M. Crowder, eds. *History of West Africa*, 1 (London, 1971), 340–2, reaffirms the idea of Oyo overlordship.

[3] M. Hiskett, 'Materials relating to the cowry currency of the Western Sudan', *Bulletin of the School of Oriental and African Studies*, 1966, **29**, 2, 355.

spoils of war, or had sufficient other booty to trade for them. Opinion varies as to whether cowries came into Hausaland mainly from the coast through Nupe, as seems more likely, or across the Sahara perhaps via Timbuktu. They moved slowly east, becoming an important element in the currency of Bornu in the mid-nineteenth century. By the end of the eighteenth century, copper came from the mines south of Darfur right across to Kano, and cloth (perhaps originally from Kano) passed from Bornu to Wadai.

Trade became a vital necessity for many of the peoples in the central Sudan, particularly in urban areas. A passage in Ibn Fartuwa tells how the Bulala, Tubu, and others in Kanem, threatened by Aloma's advance, gathered into a large fortified town. Such a congregation of people could not exist without trade, and this, Ibn Fartuwa tells us, was on a large scale. The newly gathered people

> took their stores and grain supply as food. Between them and the people of the south there was made a pact of friendship and alliance and concord. Traders in foodstuffs were constant in coming and going between this region and the south to buy and sell. They sold food in exchange for cattle and clothes and other articles.[1]

This commentary on the dependence of any large, settled community upon trade is unusually explicit for our early records.

Commerce contributed to the consolidation of states and societies in various ways. On the whole, goods imported from North Africa were in the luxury class, and in themselves affected more the quality of life for the fortunate few in the Sudan than contributing materially to the power of the state. More important was trade, often over quite short distances, in cheaper commodities, such as foodstuffs, salt, natron, and others, which helped provide the necessities of life in areas of increasing population concentration. Such trade also provided market outlets for peasant farmers and local craftsmen, and with the increase of trade came increasing diversification of economic roles within society. The increase of population, and of population density, in certain favoured areas, to which trade thus contributed, was the foundation of state power in the central Sudan, standing in marked contrast to the general under-population of the region. Also of great benefit to the authorities were the customs duties levied on trade, whether in luxuries from abroad, or on such humble items as firewood from just outside the city walls. Less tangible, but perhaps in the long run no less important, were the exchanges in techniques, ideas, and ideals, flowing along the channels maintained by trade.

[1] Palmer, *Sudanese memoirs*, I, 51.

THE ISLAMIC FACTOR

Islam, by the beginning of the seventeenth century, was powerfully rooted in the central Sudan. In domestic affairs, Aloma appealed to Islamic standards in several respects. For example, he sought to reconcile the Koyam and Kuburi, two nomadic groups and traditional rivals: both were Muslim, and Aloma forbade them, as believers, to quarrel with one another. There are many cases of the power of Islam thus exerted for reconciliation, though usually mediators were clerics rather than kings. About the time of Aloma, when the Katsinawa were pressing very hard upon Kano, it is said that they would have destroyed the city had it not been for clerical intervention. After Sabun's conquest of the capital of Bagirmi, clerics and other notables there interceded with him, pleading for a stop to rape and looting in the city.

The encouragement of permanent mosques also strengthened Islam. Aloma destroyed all the old mosques in Ngasargamu, the capital, replacing thatch with brick. These mosques are perhaps remembered in a document which calls Aloma 'the mighty builder'. In the seventeenth century, the *mai* sent burnt bricks to the immigrant Koyam for them to use in building their mosque. In 1658, it is said that there were four Friday-mosques in Ngasargamu, each with an *imām* and 12,000 worshippers, in addition to a small palace mosque where 'Umar b. 'Uthmān, a Fulani cleric officiated, with a congregation of seventy-six. The round figure, no doubt, is exaggerated, but it does seem to indicate a considerable extension of regular religious practice among the common people.

One of Aloma's most surprising characteristics, in Ibn Fartuwa's estimation, was his vigorous repression of obscenity and adultery, 'so that no such thing took place openly in his time'. Ibn Fartuwa seems to have had some reservations about the efficacy of a policy of repression, for he concludes his discussion here saying, 'To God belong the secret sins, and in His hands is direction, and prevention, and prohibition and sanction.' In order to gain a strict observance of the Koran and the Sunna, Aloma stopped giving judgements himself, turning these over to *qāḍīs*; previously, most disputes had been settled by chiefs, not by clerics, but now people generally began having recourse to the *Sharī'a*. At the end of the eighteenth century, however, it was still the custom for oppressed people to appeal to the *mai* – one crying for help, particularly to the king, was *burgama*, and *burguram* was the place where such appeals were heard. This clearly indicates that Aloma's attempt to separate the judicial and executive powers had not been sustained. There is little evidence, either, of any widespread application of the *Sharī'a*, but at the same time Islamic elements were being incorporated at every stage of the life cycle, from naming to burial, and this amongst the common people as well as among townsmen and notables.

Several references, during the Kanem wars, to Aloma's visiting the tombs of former sultans, and hearing the Koran recited there, suggest that he was a man of some personal piety, as well as applying his religion more strictly at the level of statecraft. Ibn Fartuwa summed up all this side of Aloma's activity, saying, 'Most excellent is the fame of just deeds, and justice on the part of a king for one day is equal to service of God for sixty years.' He does not indicate whether the royal day of justice was valued so highly because of its effectiveness, or its rarity. Aloma's son and successor, Ibrāhīm, although he avoided serious oppression, was given to dissolute ways, and neglected prayer, religion and righteousness. There was famine in his time, and when an old lady found her goat taken by a hyena, she complained that this was God's judgement upon the errant sultan. Ibrāhīm repented, returning to prayer, and harvests became abundant. The episode, or perhaps more accurately the story, is interesting, suggesting the gradual and fluctuating advance of Islam, the practical implications of religion, and, perhaps, the small scale of affairs in Bornu. That a woman owning one goat should be concerned with Islamic proprieties seems to indicate that the religion was not strictly confined to the upper classes.

These specifically Islamic details of Aloma's policy illustrate one of the principal themes in the history of the Sudan – the role of Islam in the formation and development of states. In some ways, the contribution of Islam is self-evident: an educational system was introduced, literacy was placed at the service of the state, and liaison with important nations across the Sahara was facilitated. Yet there are other aspects of the action of Islam, more strictly religious, less immediately evident when viewed from a distance, which may none the less have done much to strengthen the state. The Muslim prayer is an example (see volume III, chapter 5); the Pilgrimage is another.

The importance of the Pilgrimage in maintaining the proper standards of the faith, even on the remote Sudanic frontiers of the Muslim world, can scarcely be exaggerated: it may well be that the greater educational impact upon the black pilgrim often came not during the brief period of exaltation at Mecca, but with the opportunity to visit at length many and various Muslim communities on the way to and from the Holy Land.

His pilgrimage was one of Aloma's finest hours. But, as a ruler who was also a pilgrim, he was not an unusual figure, standing rather in a tradition of Kanem-Bornu which is remarkable for its continuity from the days of the first Muslim *mais* in the eleventh and twelfth centuries, and which was actively sustained by Aloma's successors. Even his establishment, in Medina, of a hostel, endowed with a date grove and some slaves, recalls the Kanemi hostel in Cairo in the thirteenth century. Muḥammad Bello, son of Usuman dan Fodio and a sharp critic of Bornu in the early nineteenth century, nevertheless admitted that the ancients of the ruling Saifawa dynasty had been good and devout Muslims, including many pilgrims. Hausaland is in striking contrast: while many of the pious there went on pilgrimage, practically no rulers did so. This may be related to the difference earlier mentioned, between Islam introduced into Bornu, and in a sense into Kanem too at an earlier stage, by the ruling immigrant group, and that brought to Hausaland by groups subordinate to, though often much appreciated by, the traditional rulers.

The next recorded pilgrimage from Bornu after Aloma is that of Mai 'Umar, son and third successor of Aloma, in 1642. 'Umar was accompanied by his son 'Alī, who succeeded him as *mai* in 1647 and thereafter went three more times on pilgrimage, in 1648, 1656 and 1667. The experience of Mai 'Alī illustrates a number of the difficulties which might arise in conjunction with the Pilgrimage – though some of the following details may derive from other *mais*, having been transferred in tradition to 'Alī himself as the most famous pilgrim. Before a pilgrimage, preparations had to be made to carry on the government in the *mai*'s absence: Mai 'Alī wrote to all the kings and deputies who were under him, instructing them to care well for their subjects and to avoid injustice. Such precautions were not always effective: during Mai 'Alī's fourth pilgrimage, his subjects rebelled in diverse provinces. The sultan of Aïr intervened to support the revolt, but an attempt to surprise the capital of Bornu failed. Mai 'Alī, on his return, took vengeance on the rebels, and expelled the Aïr troops. It was in this disorder that his own nephew had been enslaved (see above, p. 87). The *mai* had collected slaves and riding animals before his departure, and ultimately set out with 15,000 slaves, riding and on foot. Of these, he settled 5,000 in Bagirmi, and 4,000 more in each of two places in Wadai. Their descendants might still be seen there in the nineteenth century. Perhaps such slaves were intended, by farming and in other undertakings, to prepare supplies against their master's return. Perhaps they were simply dropped, the burdens which they had carried having been consumed, rather as the booster stages of a lunar rocket are jettisoned. Perhaps they had some political purpose.

It was not uncommon for pilgrims to stop for long periods, even permanently, along the way, and this sometimes had far-reaching religious or political consequences. The original planting of Islam in Bagirmi, at Bidderi, was the direct result of the Pilgrimage. The Awlād Muḥammad, rulers of the Fezzan from the sixteenth century, claimed descent from a pilgrim Sharif. The Feroge people, living between the river Boro and the Bahr al-'Arab, accepted a Bornu pilgrim as their ruler, he having been recognized by Darfur, the suzerain power. Pilgrims stopped also for study, particularly in Cairo. If the pilgrim tarried too long, and finally died abroad, then the Pilgrimage acted as a kind of 'brain drain': Muḥammad b. Muḥammad, for example, a Fulani from Katsina, expert in astrology, numerology, and related subjects, settled and taught in Cairo, and died there in 1741. The fact that the first studies of the Kanuri language published in the west came from Freetown in Sierra Leone, where the informants were freed slaves, and that these studies were then checked in Cairo, where the informants were students at al-Azhar, is an outstanding instance of the way in which slaving and the Pilgrimage served to link the central Sudan with the wider world.[1]

Dangers along the pilgrim's way were real enough. The pasha of Tripoli sent cavalry to try to intercept Mai 'Alī as he returned from his second pilgrimage, but the *mai* escaped. This unfriendly act by the pasha arose from some disrespect which the *mai* had shown to his ambassador, and resulted in an interruption of relations and commerce between the two states for some four years. Aggression against pilgrims was not unknown, particularly on the Saharan passage. Pilgrims, even the most prominent among them, could not be sure of returning safely: apparently one *mai* in the seventeenth century died while on pilgrimage, just as had happened in earlier centuries. There is some evidence, indeed, that the unfortunate was none other than 'Alī b. 'Umar himself, though it is more likely to have been his son.

Mai 'Alī's pilgrimages remain justly celebrated. Dan Marina, a cleric of Katsina, celebrating in verse Mai 'Alī's victory over the Kwararafa, spoke of him as the pious pilgrim to the holy cities, who in this world and the next has earned the pilgrim's highest reward. A Bornu

[1] S. W. Koelle, *Polyglotta Africana* (London, 1854; reprinted Graz, 1963), 8*–12*; Prietze, 'Bornulieder', 134.

document says, still more enthusiastically: 'the journey to Mecca was to him as a night ride'.

Three *mais* of the eighteenth century are remembered as pilgrims. One was Dunama b. 'Alī, perhaps one of the four sons whom 'Alī b. 'Umar is said to have taken with him on his fourth pilgrimage; another was Ḥamdūn b. Dunama, and the third Muḥammad b. Ḥamdūn. In the second half of the eighteenth century the ruler of Bagirmi, Mbang Muḥammad al-Amīn, had returned from pilgrimage to take the throne. Other dignitaries also went: the shaykh, Muḥammad al-Amīn al-Kānamī, who was to rescue Bornu from the hands of the Fulani invaders early in the nineteenth century, had been on pilgrimage with his father, who died in Medina.

Across North Africa, the pilgrims, whether in the great annual *ḥajj* caravans, or in separate parties perhaps associated with a particular prince or dignitary, moved east and west. This route too had its perils, both human and natural. A poet of Tlemcen, in the eighteenth century, spoke thus of the road between Tunis and Tripoli:

> take care, pay attention...
> have confidence in no one;
> everywhere that you see the wandering Arab tribes,
> pass by and leave them behind.[1]

And at the very end of the eighteenth century, the way on from Tripoli to Cairo was described as

> a journey more dreadful than can be conceived, and which would often not be completed, but by the help of the compass, and a knowledge of astronomy.[2]

The desert here claimed victims even amongst the wealthy and well-equipped. Nevertheless the route from Tripoli to Cairo continued to be of great importance.

When Ḥusayn Bey ascended the throne of Tunis in 1705, launching the Husaynid dynasty upon a quarter-millennium of rule, a dissident notable, Muḥammad b. Muṣṭafā, fled to Egypt, and there began lobbying all Tunisian pilgrims, particularly government officials and other men of consequence. When the bey heard of this, he took one returning official who had been influenced by the refugee Muḥammad, and executed him, sequestrating his property. Thereafter Tunisian pilgrims sensibly refrained from any further contact with Muḥammad,

[1] Ben Messaib, 'Itinéraire de Tlemçen à la Mekke', *Revue africaine*, 1900, 269.
[2] R. Tully, *Narrative of a ten years' residence at Tripoli*... (London, 1816), 11–12.

whose pretensions petered out, unlike those of Muḥammad al-Amīn of Bagirmi, whose subversive plotting while on pilgrimage led eventually to his installation as *mbang* (see below, p. 134). Sharīf, sultan of Wadai in the mid-nineteenth century, was believed by some to have earlier fled the country, going on to Mecca, and later returning, with the help of Darfur, to take power. Such implications raise the interesting possibility of a comparison between the fostering and spread of early nationalism, in the twentieth century, among African students at universities abroad, especially in London and Paris, and the centuries-old spread of religious and political ideas, sometimes equally revolutionary, through like contacts among pilgrims. Pilgrimage links were usually of a gentler kind. The ruler of Morocco was so moved by the kind reception paid him when he passed through Tripoli as a pilgrim, that when in the 1780s Tripoli was afflicted by famine he sent several shiploads of grain.

Thus religion, like the military and commercial factors, contributed to the consolidation of states and societies within the central Sudan, binding people more closely together, and extending the bonds of common citizenship far further than would have been possible on any purely kinship basis. And each at the same time provided contacts with other areas, which helped to bring commodities, ideas, and people into the central Sudan.

THE CONTRIBUTION OF SLAVERY

In the process of the consolidation of society, two groups stand out as more easily distinguished and described than the unobtrusive inflow of ordinary people in good times: these are the nomads and slaves. More people were probably incorporated into the new society through enslavement than in any other way, and that not only at the lowest levels, but among people of real authority in the higher ranks.

The domestic demand for slaves, within the central Sahara and Sudan, may well have been even more of a stimulus to slave raiding than was the trans-Saharan trade. The number of slaves in the central Sahara and Sudan was considerable. In the nineteenth century, when fairly accurate estimates first become available, very wealthy individuals in Bornu might own thousands of slaves, while people of modest means normally owned two or three. At the capital, even a wandering scholar might hope to acquire several. Hausa folk tales illustrate the same range: one frugal housewife saved enough – by giving up smoking – to buy a slave girl; while another slave girl was rewarded with two cloths by her owner, flattered by her surprise at finding someone with so many slaves that he could not recognize them all. Turning to less favoured regions, we find that here too slaves were common: among the Budduma of Lake Chad, the average man had two or three; in the still harsher regions of the Kanem desert, and in Tibesti, there were also slaves. Richardson, visiting the desert mountains midway between Tripoli and Ghadames in the 1840s, and hearing from a local shaykh that there were thirty slaves in his district, wondered 'how the people could keep slaves when they can scarcely keep themselves'.[1]

There were many varieties of domestic demand. A majority of the population, certainly in the Sudan, was engaged in agriculture, and slaves contributed largely to this. A Kanuri song, mocking the Hausa, describes the Hausa slave sent to work in the fields, who sleeps instead and must be beaten. Other groups, such as the Gwari, were better esteemed: among the Hausa, 'Gwari's hoe' is the equivalent of the English Jack-of-all-trades. In the Sahara, where free men generally preferred a nomadic life, slaves supplied an essential agricultural complement. Good years were too few, and the good times too short, for pastoralism alone to supply a livelihood: additional resources, from the caravan trade and from cultivation, were essential. Slaves contributed to both. Their presence was an important factor in maintaining many oases for caravans. Slaves were the main farmers, and, as we have seen, were principally responsible for the date palms. Even in pastoral work, the Tuareg of the Ahaggar mountains, for example, might have their camels grazing 500 kilometres or more away from their sheep and goats, and slaves were needed to look after these. Indeed, a slave herdsman might be more knowledgeable than his Tuareg master about certain forms of stock.

Slaves served as artisans; there are many references to them as builders and clothworkers. Slaves from Massenya, capital of Bagirmi, were reputed good weavers. A skilled cook – usually female – was highly prized. Slaves were often employed in salt working. As caravan workers, both porters and guards, slaves made possible a quite elaborate system of transport and communications. Leo Africanus spoke of large bodies of slaves protecting the Agades merchants on the dangerous road from Kano to Bornu, who were set quickly to work as soon as the caravan halted each day. Slaves sometimes held responsible posi-

[1] J. Richardson, *Travels in the great desert of Sahara, in the years of 1845 and 1846* (London, 1848), I, 63.

tions in caravans, or might even be sent by their masters to act almost as free merchants. Caravan slaves had a special part to play in the Pilgrimage. They were porters for their pilgrim masters. They might be established at fixed points along the way. Slaves were part, as we have seen, of the endowment of the pilgrim hostel which Aloma founded in Arabia. Slaves might be sold on the way to help meet pilgrimage expenses, although, sometimes, the temptation to buy slaves in the Near East was a financial danger: one eighteenth-century *mai*, having spent too largely in alms, was unable to pay for certain slaves offered him in the Hejaz until his clerics, through prayer, had miraculously replenished his store of gold.

There were also luxury slaves, such as dwarfs; and the very large numbers of concubines possessed by some notables must be regarded as supernumerary. Slave women were not judged exclusively as concubines: those of Musgo, south-east of Mandara, for instance, were especially disagreeable in appearance, but valued for their trustworthiness and their great capacity for labour. But concubines were one of the major single categories of slaves, both for domestic use and for trans-Saharan export; it has been estimated that a majority of the slaves crossing the Sahara were women and children, in contrast to the Atlantic pattern, and this may in turn partly explain the different subsequent assimilation of the slave population, in North America and North Africa.

Slaves likewise served the state. They might be colonists, put down at essential points abroad – such as the slave settlements on a pilgrimage route, just mentioned – or in territory newly incorporated by the state, much as the Funj established slave villages around Sennar to protect the capital (see chapter 1, p. 44). Slaves were often soldiers. Armed slaves used to accompany their Tuareg masters on raids. In Bornu, where there was little attempt to maintain a centralized armed force, the ruler tended to rely on the contingents which his courtiers and officials maintained. Most of these soldiers in Bornu, and in Bagirmi too, were slaves. The army of Sabun, advancing on Bagirmi, was preceded by two corps of 4,000 slaves each, whose task it was to clear the road: this was the regular practice of Sabun. The army was sometimes, as in the Napoleonic ideal, a *carrière ouverte aux talents*, even for a slave. When a rhinoceros disputed the path with Sabun's army, until killed by a slave, Sabun executed several officers for cowardice, including the commander of an Arab tribe, in whose place he appointed the deserving slave. One of the commanders-in-chief of the Bornu army in the 1820s had, when a lad aged only nine, passed as a slave to Shaykh al-Kānamī. Nearly all the military commanders in Bornu were slaves of the head of state, and the most important of them sat in the *nokena*, or state council. Military officers in Logon, likewise, were of slave origin.

Slaves might also be valued as civil servants by a government aiming at centralization, even despotism. In Hausaland, the increasing reliance of rulers upon eunuchs and slaves freed them somewhat from cultivating the allegiance of their subjects, in much the same way as some of the Funj relied on slaves against the established aristocracy and free warriors. Another variant of the basic scheme of slaves used as a counterweight comes from Tripoli, where it was customary for the pasha's daughters to marry renegades, that is converted Christian captives, who might hold high office, rather than local dignitaries. There were dangers, for excessive haughtiness by slave officials might eventually arouse popular reprisals, or the slaves might come too much to dominate their royal master. In Bornu, Logon, Bagirmi and Wadai, the heads of state had huge slave establishments, civil and military; there was no clear distinction between those slaves who were the ruler's personal property, and those who belonged to the state. The court of Wadai observed the practice, quite common in many parts of Africa, of a large group of pages, including twenty slave boys who carried important messages – such service often leading later to high political office. Some offices were reserved, in Bornu for instance, for free men – though a majority of the court officials there, in the nineteenth century, were slaves or of slave origin – or, in various places, for eunuchs.

Eunuchs had unusual recommendations, in lower appointments caring for the harem, at higher levels as officials free from the temptation to establish their own rival dynasty. Eunuch officials were prominent in Bornu, Bagirmi, Mandara and Wadai, but apparently not in Logon. The rulers of Bagirmi took up eunuchs with enthusiasm during the reign of Mbang al-Ḥājj Muḥammad al-Amīn, in the second half of the eighteenth century. According to one account, the *mbang* first learnt to appreciate eunuchs while on pilgrimage, either in Mecca or at the courts which he visited along the way. Returning home, he purchased one from Mandara for fifty slaves; then, as this was rather expensive, he experimented with domestic production, and despite an initial mortality of 70 per cent Bagirmi soon became an important exporter. In Wadai, castration was a judicial punishment, but most eunuchs at the court there came from Bagirmi. Eunuchs were rarely found in the possession of private citizens. They were significant in the trans-Saharan exchange, for service at the Ottoman court, or at the shrines in the Hejaz. Mbang al-Ḥājj Muḥammad is reported every three years to have sent to Mecca via Wadai 100 garments, 100 slaves, and twelve eunuchs. The ruler of Wadai himself would sometimes, on his accession, send some eunuchs to Istanbul.

With such a diversity of domestic employments prompting the circulation of slaves, it is not surprising that these came to be regarded as almost another form of currency. Slaves were frequently a part of tribute. In the seventeenth century, for example, the ruler of the Fezzan was compelled to agree to pay an annual tribute to Tripoli, the equivalent of 4,000 gold mithqals, and half of this might be paid in slaves. Bornu received slave tribute from several sources: from about the mid-fifteenth century, each ruler of Katsina, partly subject to Bornu, had sent on his accession 100 slaves to Bornu; Bagirmi sent an annual gift of slaves to Bornu, although there was no obligation to do so; at the end of the eighteenth century it was reported that the Kwararafa, who may themselves have been receiving some slave tribute from their own vassals, had, as has been seen, to send 1,000 slaves each year to Bornu; an attack by Wadai against Darfur, late in the eighteenth century, was heralded by Wadai's refusal to pay the customary yearly gift of one girl of royal blood for the Darfur harem. Slaves served as alms and presents, and in this way, when given to clerics, teachers and students, helped to maintain the leisured scholarly group so important for the development of Islam in the area. Slaves were often given as wedding presents, in Bornu, in Wadai, among the Budduma, among the Tuareg and elsewhere. Mai 'Alī b. 'Umar once divorced his wife, she having interfered with his riding out to war; but he was later reconciled with her, giving her 1,000 slaves. A praise song says of her: 'You distribute slave children as you would food.'

Slaves came into the main markets of the central Sudan in three principal ways: through raids and kidnapping; as tribute; and in trade – in the case of Bornu, trade with Hausaland and more particularly Bagirmi. The three styles are in origin not much different, since the tributary or trader in most cases had to resort to force in order to acquire the slaves with which to fulfil his more peaceful transactions. Other methods of slave recruitment – voluntary sale, for example by parents of their children, which is sometimes mentioned in times of famine, or enslavement as judicial punishment – provided no more than a small fraction of the total supply. For people already slaves, sale abroad was sometimes a punishment: incorrigible thieves among the slaves of Ghadames, for instance, were sent to Tripoli. Slaves were sometimes employed as slave raiders: Aloma did this, and also used his slaves on occasion to massacre prisoners. Some captives passed more or less directly to individual raiders, as their share of the booty; others went to the state.

Since the *Sharī'a*, strictly speaking, forbids the enslavement of Muslims, yet encourages jihad against pagans, it was natural that slave raiding took on some features of religious war between Muslim and pagan. Several incidents show that policy was actually influenced by an unwillingness to enslave Muslims. Aloma, as we have seen, after one of his Kanem wars which he did not regard as jihad, released Muslim prisoners of free status. But tribal factors may have been equally, or more, important. There was also the possibility of raiding Muslims, whom one did not in any case intend to enslave, in order to confiscate their slaves. There were many occasions on which the proper restraints were not observed, and free Muslims were, albeit illegally, enslaved. In 1667, for example, as we have seen, even a prince of Bornu was captured and sold across the Sahara.

The cruelties of slave raiding were paralleled by conditions while on the march. Laggards might be killed, in order to discourage others from feigning incapacity. In desert country, a choked well which required some time to clear might mean death for slaves too thirsty to wait. Slave caravans sometimes carried contagious diseases: the Fezzan suffered from smallpox brought in this way, but desert nomads, encountering such caravans less frequently, were better protected.

Treatment of the slave, once more or less permanently settled, varied greatly in individual cases, but tended to be fairly moderate. Certain areas, such as the Fezzan and Tripoli, were reputed for their gentleness; in others, like Tibesti, suicide among slaves from Bornu was known, perhaps chiefly because of the harshness of the environment. Even in such uncomfortable country and among people as brutal as the Awlād Sulaymān, a slave might be accepted almost as a member of the family. With the passing of generations there was still further amelioration of slave status, and it was widely held that a slave born in the house could not be sold: though the stigma of slave origin was hard to wash out utterly, as the hyena's outburst in a Hausa animal fable suggests:

> Well!!! there is no God save Allah! Why – she's been a slave since the days of our grandfather's grandfather! And...he's one of our slaves born in slavery of slave parents.

It has even been suggested that, in Hausaland, the lot of an ordinary slave was sometimes better than that of a peasant, since the position of the slave was more clearly defined. Yet in all this gentle analysis, perhaps there is a trace of the Uncle Tom philosophy, surviving in descriptions of black Africa to an extent which, applied to America, would long since have been intolerable. Al-Tūnusī, a North African resident in Darfur and Wadai in the first half of the nineteenth century, has recorded his general impression of both slave and commoner in those countries: the poor, he said, were in the most sad destitution and frightful misery, suffering ceaselessly under tyranny, forced labour and war – all their life was only the life of slaves.[1]

Recurrent references to runaway slaves – even though many of these may have been among the newly captured – indicate that some did find their condition unacceptable. Slave caravans coming to Ghadames occasionally lost fugitives in the desert, who must almost inevitably have perished. In Bagirmi, the right of one dignitary to retain all fugitive slaves not claimed by their masters was a valuable perquisite of his office. In the nineteenth century, Shaykh Muḥammad al-Amīn al-Kānamī, when ruler of Bornu, wrote to his sister that, were it not for his legal obligations there, he would scurry out of the country like a runaway slave. Slave revolts seem to have been uncommon, though the possibility was recognized – the Yoruba regarded the extension of the Fulani jihad to their country as a revolt by Hausa slaves. Individual acts of violence sometimes occurred.

Slaves tended to become Muslim, through a natural tendency to adopt the religion of their masters. There were also practical reasons for conversion – an unconverted slave could not, for example, prepare his master's food. A slave might be a full Muslim, although his religious obligations in certain respects, such as the Friday prayer, the Pilgrimage, and jihad, were somewhat less rigorous than those of a free man. There was no requirement, in local custom or in Muslim law, to free a slave on his conversion. Emancipation, *'itq*, did occur: as an act of piety, perhaps on a religious festival; in the hope of furthering the owner's recovery from illness; as legal expiation – *kaffāra* – for certain offences; through contract between slave and owner; by the provisions of the owner's will (provisions, it might sometimes be, designed to frustrate grasping heirs). To give two specific illustrations of circumstances in which emancipation was felt appropriate: in the late 1650s the pasha of Tripoli declined to invite Mai 'Alī b. 'Umar to visit Tripoli, partly because of the many Negro slaves, former subjects of the *mai* or his allies, who would have to be freed in honour of the

[1] Muḥammad ibn 'Umar al-Tūnusī, tr. Perron, *Voyage au Ouadây* (Paris, 1851), 360.

occasion. And in 1785, when the widow of a previous pasha of Tripoli died of the plague, the reigning pasha freed four slaves in her honour, and they attended her funeral as free men.

Many, probably most, freed slaves did not try to return home, but stayed near their former masters in some sort of patronage relationship. Yet some did return, and may thus have contributed still further to the expansion of Islam. The faith might also be extended when Muslims were enslaved by non-Muslims: for example, Muslim Hausa slaves in Borgu, in the northern part of modern Dahomey and the adjoining region of Nigeria, were allowed freedom of worship. Religious transference through slaves was not all one way and in favour of the dissemination of Islam: slaves also carried northwards their own traditional beliefs and practices. The slaves at Ghadames, for example, held special dances at their cemetery, and there are references to *bori*, or spirit possession, among slaves in various parts of North Africa. In some towns, just as in Mecca itself, Sudanese slaves had their own communal organizations and officials.

There was, perhaps, no point at which the situation of the white slaves in North Africa differed more sharply from that of the blacks than in conversion. This was generally discouraged among the white slaves. Christian religious orders were allowed to keep hospitals and chapels, attending to the Christian slaves, for in such matters Muslim tolerance reinforced the consideration that such care reduced slave wastage and kept open useful channels of ransom. In the 1640s, Lazarists, inspired in their work among slaves by St Vincent de Paul, were appointed to the French consulates at Algiers and Tunis, though they did not hold these positions for long. Some special groups, such as small children, or women who gave satisfaction in the harem, might be encouraged to convert sincerely to Islam and to adopt the Maghrib as their home: such a convert was the captive Genoese, a favourite of the founder of the Husaynid dynasty in Tunis, whose eldest son by her ascended the throne. Other individuals also, among the white slaves, were able to rise to positions of importance and authority. Conversion, when it did occur among white slaves, led more directly to emancipation than was usually the case in the Sudan or among black slaves in North Africa. This general policy against conversion fitted well with the intention that most of the white slaves should be ransomed, although in the meantime they might be put to useful work, the conditions for which were more comfortable in Tunisia and Tripolitania than in Algiers, where dangerous quarrying and harbour repairs were often involved.

Black slaves, on the contrary, unless destined for further dispersal to still more distant markets, gradually settled into circumstances not unlike those of slaves absorbed directly into central Sudanese society. Particularly in Tripolitania, they were numerous, often engaged in the army or in domestic service, and many had been freed and had settled of their own choosing in various parts of the territory, sometimes in separate villages under the leadership of their own clerics. On the whole, the white slaves in North Africa, while sharing the commercial aspects of the treatment of black slaves, presented a strong contrast to their pattern of social incorporation.

Slavery and the slave trade were obviously institutions of immense importance in the area as a whole: probably the major stimulus to trans-Saharan trade; an important diplomatic lubricant in relations with North Africa and the Near East; essential for transport and communication within the interior, and for many other practical tasks; a main strength of government; a principal form of currency; an avenue of extending the faith; and a means for the incorporation of large numbers of people into initially small ruling or conquering societies. Central Sudanic statecraft was almost unimaginable without the slave.

THE IMPACT OF THE NOMADS

Among nomads, four groups demand attention: the Fulani, most important of all; the Shuwa, coming from the east; the Koyam, a small group but of the highest Muslim prestige; and finally the Budduma, aquatic nomads. Both the Fulani, on whose behalf Aloma warred against the Tuareg, and the Koyam, whose camelry helped him on those and other campaigns, are specifically mentioned in Aloma's time.

These peoples, together with the Tubu and the Tuareg, nomads of the Sahara, may throw some light on the general impact of nomads upon a settled area. Urvoy has vividly set forth the concept of the nomads as a valuable stimulus to state formation in the Sudan, comparing them with Belot's dualist theory of the solar system, according to which a small star, dense, rapidly rotating, is hurled with great speed into a diffuse, immobile and inert nebula.[1] Yet, if the role of the Tubu and Tuareg during our period is considered, the impact of the nomads seems often to have been far more purely destructive.

By contrast, the contribution of the three peoples, Fulani, Shuwa and Koyam, has sometimes been of a positive and constructive kind. Several factors, particularly when combined with one another, seem – not

[1] Y. Urvoy, *Histoire de l'empire du Bornou* (Paris, 1949; reprinted Amsterdam, 1968), 21.

invariably, but in some cases – to have facilitated a constructive nomadic contribution. If the nomads were Muslim, this often recommended them to their hosts in the settled area at a much higher level than if the newcomers had nothing but milk and manure to offer. The Muslim Fulani had much more influence than the pagan or near-pagan Fulani; the Koyam compensated for their small numbers by their religious importance. Again, if the nomads had no base to which they could conveniently withdraw, they became much more amenable to constructive compromises with the local people. This was the case with all three, Fulani, Shuwa and Koyam: they had moved so far afield that return had become impracticable. The Tubu and Tuareg, raiding from impregnable Saharan wildernesses, were under no such compulsion to compromise – while those who moved farther into the Sudan proper did often temper their warlike habits. Again, nomads were more amenable when they depended upon the local state for protection: indeed, it was part of the definition of a state, that it should be able to protect those who sought refuge within its borders. Again, if the nomads were few, they were more obliged to co-operate with their hosts. It is in this light that we should perhaps view the legends of the earliest nomadic arrivals in the Sudan, few in number, rather than thinking that the remembered individuals represent a much larger unremembered influx. Again, wherever there already existed some form of government in the settled area, nomads could often make their contribution felt by taking part in it. Finally, the nomads had to cease to be nomads, if anything new and lasting were to come of the union: whatever the militant flurry of their arrival – and there was often not even that – it was the settled life which eventually overcame and absorbed the nomad.

The gradual infiltration of Fulani from the west had begun well before 1600, and was by the end of the eighteenth century strong enough to overthrow most of the established states of Hausaland, and almost Mandara, Bagirmi and Bornu as well. Fulani legends of origin, which attach their descent to ʻUqbah b. Nāfi of Arabia, say that this movement arose from a desire to return to Mecca, and that the Fulani accordingly travelled slowly east, though groups were constantly breaking away to follow their own purposes.

Despite the orthodoxy of such legends, many of these immigrants were pagan nomads, their lives absorbed by the care of their cattle; and the local people tended to scorn somewhat such homeless wanderers. A Kanuri riddle runs, ʻWho is he that carries all his worldly goods on his head even at daybreak?'; the answer is, 'A Fulani'. Yet at the same time even the humblest cattle nomad had something to offer the society into which he came, and the Fulani were often granted the protection of the local authorities. The first notice of extensive Fulani settlement in Bornu comes about the third quarter of the sixteenth century. Aloma's campaigns, shortly afterwards, against the Tuareg, three of which he conducted himself, arose from Tuareg misdeeds against Fulani. The Binawa had been guilty of the same. By the early seventeenth century, there were several Fulani clans in Kano, numerous enough for the *sarki* there to initiate a new policy of charging them a cattle tax, the *jangali*. This makes it likely that Fulani were also numerous in Bornu by this time, both because the two areas are likely to have developed in somewhat the same way, and because some Fulani may have sought a tax haven in Bornu. Further confirmation of Fulani in Bornu comes later in the seventeenth century, in the time of Mai 'Alī b. 'Umar the pilgrim, when a poem tells of measures to be taken to avenge another Tuareg raid upon the cattle of Fulani who had been under special protection from Bornu. Fulani groups of this sort had sometimes to heed the wishes of their patrons. When Shaykh 'Umar of the Koyam returned to Bornu in the first half of the eighteenth century, he agreed to establish himself in the Gaskeru region, and the *mai* moved the Fulani pastoralists who were already there to new grounds farther south. In sixteenth-century Bagirmi there seems to have been rather more of an alliance between Fulani and the Kenga tribes, also immigrants. The Fulani had at least one important bargaining point, for amongst them were a number of Muslim clerics, whose friendship the local rulers often valued highly, and whose wrath was sometimes feared. The clerics may have preceded the nomads in some cases.

A somewhat uninhibited account of the practical value which it was believed by some attached to the prayers of clerics is preserved in a document describing Ngasargamu in 1658. The career of a Fulani cleric, 'Umar b. 'Uthmān, born in Bornu probably about 1600, is given. He was a great scholar, knowledgeable in many orthodox religious sciences and also in the secret arts. The people flocked to him for the resolution of problems, doubts and disputes. Later he went on the pilgrimage, visiting al-Azhar, Mecca and Medina, and Baghdad. On his return to Bornu, a leading concubine of the *mai* sent him a slave girl to ask him for his prayers. His intercession having proved effective, the *gumsu* or queen sent him another slave girl, that he might pray on her behalf likewise. Again 'Umar b. 'Uthmān was able to intercede effectively; we are not told what the specific requests were. News of this came to the *mai*, who told 'Umar that he was in serious need of a thousand slaves. The cleric prayed, and soon afterwards the *mai*'s mother died leaving her son an inheritance of 10,000 slaves. The *mai*, perceiving the power of 'Umar's prayers, and his other virtues such as abstention from bickering and slander, made him *imām* of the palace mosque.[1]

Incidents illustrating the importance of Fulani clerics continued throughout the period. Ibrāhīm Zaki, one of the champions of Usuman dan Fodio's jihad against Bornu in the early nineteenth century, came from the town of Yaiyu in southern Katagum, whither his father had emigrated from Bagirmi. His father had won some local importance as *imām* to the chief in Yaiyu, whose daughter Ibrāhīm Zaki himself married.

These possibilities for co-operation between rulers and clerics – whether Fulani or other – included also the provision of clerical sanction for a ruler's actions. Sometimes this was given regardless of the propriety of his behaviour: when the ruler of Bagirmi in Sabun's time, for example, wished to marry his own sister, at least one cleric was found, so the traditions of Wadai allege, who approved this, arguing that the ruler's father had more than four wives, that the daughter was in consequence illegitimate, and that she was thus not properly his sister at all. Such specious argument was condemned by reforming Muslims as the work of venal clerics, the *'ulamā' al-sū'*. For, despite the frequent collaboration between religious and political leaders, the introduction of Islam did mean a higher standard, against which local conditions, even local rulers themselves, might be judged and found wanting. In this respect, the fact that the Fulani did not mingle very much with the local population, and were regarded, as we have seen, in local proverbs and sayings as inferior aliens, may have helped preserve the distance necessary for detached criticism when need and opportunity offered. The situation resembled that of the Funj clerics, who also found themselves drawn into opposition, refusing water from wheels turned by wrongly taken oxen, or cursing a ruler's attempts at unjust taxation (see chapter 1, p. 55). The possibility of such criticism, leading to a clash with the established order, is excellently exemplified in the central Sudan in the career of the cleric Waldid, probably a Fulani. He and a Tuareg colleague, al-Jarmiyu, began preaching in Bornu, and found many to follow them, even certain repentant chiefs of the *mai*. The *mai* made inquiries, and the anxiety which he felt may be deduced from al-Jarmiyu's attempt to reassure him, saying, 'We

[1] H. R. Palmer, *The Bornu Sahara and Sudan* (London, 1936), 33–5.

have no desire to cause your subjects to stray from you. Our desire is to lead men into the way of truth.'[1] The *mai* was not satisfied. He killed al-Jarmiyu, and Waldid fled into Bagirmi, where he stayed until he died a little after the year 1000 AH, i.e. a little after 1591. This rather vague presentation of the date suggests that the *mai* may have been Aloma, who ruled till about 1600, but the sources name the *mai* as 'Umar, presumably Aloma's son and successor. It is tempting to identify Waldid with Muḥammad Ould Dede, a Fulani cleric who appears in other traditions as the ancestor of Bagirmi Islam, and founder of Bidderi, but Ould Dede appears to have flourished at the beginning of the sixteenth century (see volume 3, chapter 5).

Among other Fulani clerics at odds with accepted practices were two from Hausaland who were working in Bagirmi, Sulaymān and his son Muḥammad al-Wālī. Sulaymān wrote verses against the sciences of divination, magic and astrology, to which the scholars of Bagirmi were much addicted, including this condemnation:

> They call their knowledge the secret knowledge.
> They lie.
> It is not secret.
> It is the knowledge of evil things.[2]

Another critical Fulani cleric, this time active in Bornu, was al-Ṭāhir b. Ibrāhīm, who died about 1776. The *mai* had evidently entertained al-Ṭāhir with considerable respect, bringing him to the capital and having a house built for him there. The cleric wrote several books, poems and commentaries for the king; but the townspeople resented al-Ṭāhir's criticisms, and so far poisoned the mind of the *mai* that one day he shut the door against him whom he had formerly honoured. Both Waldid and al-Ṭāhir were amongst those who prophesied the coming of a still more vigorous man of faith, prophecies which found their fulfilment at the end of the period, in the rise of Usuman dan Fodio.

In the second half of the eighteenth century, whether for religious or other reasons, certain Fulani groups began to adopt a more aggressive posture, and fighting occurred between them and local people in various areas. Some verses written in 1799 reveal the mood in Ngasargamu on the eve of the full-scale and repeated Fulani assault:

> Verily a cloud has settled upon God's earth,
> A cloud so dense that escape from it is impossible.

[1] Palmer, *The Bornu Sahara*, 245–6.
[2] E. J. Arnett, *The rise of the Sokoto Fulani: being a paraphrase and in some parts a translation of the Infaku'l Maisuri of Sultan Mohammed Bello* (Lagos, 1922), 4–5.

Everywhere between Kordofan and Gobir
And the cities of the Tuareg
Are settlements of the dogs of Fellata
Serving God in all their dwelling places
(I swear by the life of the Prophet and his overflowing grace)
In reforming all districts and provinces
Ready for future bliss.
So in this year they are following their beneficent theories
As though it were a time to set the world in order by preaching.
Alas! that I know all about the tongue of the fox.[1]

The Adamawan proverb was being fulfilled: the Fulani are like a drop of oil on a cloth – if not washed out at once, it spreads into a broad stain.

The antecedents of the Fulani jihad, which was to engulf most of Hausaland early in the nineteenth century, and to extend further, even imperilling for a time the independence of Bornu, are twofold (see volume 5, chapter 6). Within the Sudan, the local tradition of reform and prophecy, just described, was strengthened by the example of the eighteenth-century jihads in the Senegambia far to the west (see below, chapter 3), and by continuing interchange between Sahara and Sudan, epitomized by the Tuareg Jibrīl b. 'Umar's tutelage of Shehu Usuman dan Fodio, creator of the Fulani jihad. And outside, currents of reform in the Islamic heartlands stirred the Sudan, not so much the Wahhābī movement of Arabia itself, but the Sufi revival, generated partly as a reaction against the Wahhabis, which centred upon al-Azhar. The strand of social reform in the Fulani jihad, sometimes exaggerated in contemporary analysis but strong nonetheless, may have drawn upon the new radicalism of al-Azhar clerics, some of whom were involved in popular risings in Cairo in the 1780s and 90s (see above, chapter 1, p. 39). The Pilgrimage was the vital channel transmitting these influences. Along this channel too, at the very end of the eighteenth century, the first warning notes were sounded of that European and infidel advance which late in the nineteenth century was to become a major challenge to the Muslims of the central and western Sudan: in 1798, Hornemann accompanied the first Sudan-bound caravan from Cairo after the Napoleonic occupation, and commented, 'it is incredible how deep and strong an impression the expedition of the French has made on the minds of pilgrims...'[2]

[1] Palmer, *The Bornu Sahara*, 52.

[2] Letter of 31 August 1798, printed together with Hornemann's *Journal*, in *Proceedings of the Africa Association*, II, 10.

As the Fulani moved east, they met Shuwa and Koyam coming west. The time of the first arrival of the Shuwa in the Central Sudan is uncertain: it has been suggested that certain groups were present at the time of the exodus from Kanem to Bornu in the late fourteenth century, or even a little earlier. There was apparently a further move of Shuwa into Bornu in the time of Aloma. They were present already in Bagirmi as that nation took shape during the seventeenth century. The Shuwa came, in the main, through Darfur and Wadai from the east, only a small number having travelled via North Africa. Except for the earliest arrivals, many of whom adopted the Kanuri language, they preserved their Arabic, but were at the same time quite distinct from North African Arabs travelling across the Sahara. Another substantial impetus was given to the Shuwa immigration at the time of Shaykh al-Kānamī, early in the nineteenth century, who summoned the Shuwa to help him against the Fulani. The Shuwa seem not to have passed west of Bornu, and only small numbers moved south into the Mandara and Adamawa regions. Some Shuwa remained pure camel nomads; others, in particular the Salāmāt, converted successfully to cattle pastoralism, and some, deprived of even their cattle by disease, became diligent agriculturalists. Despite these transitions, and the existence of many Shuwa villages, for example on the southern shores of Lake Chad and along the road from Bornu towards Mandara, the Shuwa seem never to have peopled a town, nor to have established for themselves a permanent home. Perhaps partly because of this, they were almost always found in some kind of dependent or tributary relationship with the local authorities. A Bornu court song, from about the middle of the eighteenth century, speaks of the Kurata Shuwa in Kanem as 'slaves' of the *mai*, an indicative attitude although the precise choice of words is vaunting. There are many references in the nineteenth century to the assistance rendered by the Shuwa to the Bornu government, where under al-Kānamī and his successors most major title-holders were immigrant Shuwa or Kanembu, rather than local Kanuri; Shuwa women might marry into the highest ranks – the principal wife of the ruler of Logon, for example, was a Shuwa. At the same time other Shuwa were regarded as dangerous rebels, or unruly frontier elements. It seems likely that a comparable situation, though without so much influence at the highest levels, obtained during at least the eighteenth century.

As has been seen, the Koyam performed valuable service for Aloma as camelry in the Kanem area, and this traditional interest of theirs seems to survive throughout the period. In the late eighteenth century, when the *mai* of Bornu, ʻAlī, returned from his unsuccessful expedition against Mandara, he was visited by the Koyam shaykh and a thousand of his disciples, each mounted on his own horse or camel.

But the Koyam, like some of the nomadic Fulani, combined a nomadic life with an intense religious devotion, and it was a small group of such people, under the shaykh, ʻAbdullāh b. ʻAbd al-Jalīl, which was of unique importance for the growth of Islam in Bornu. They are thought to have arrived in Bornu in the second half of the seventeenth century, during the reign of ʻAlī b. ʻUmar, and they came primarily as clerics. They established the village of Belbelec, and attracted many students. The Bornu clerics jealously tried to influence the *mai* against them; but he, having interrogated Shaykh ʻAbdullāh, was entirely satisfied, even supplying baked bricks and workers to put up a mosque and houses for the Koyam. The *mai* allowed the Koyam to receive all pupils who came to them, without hindrance, and exempted the district from taxation. Unlike the corresponding patronage of clerical immigrants in the eastern Sudan, land itself does not seem often, if ever, to have been given, whether in *milk* or *waqf* (see above, chapter 1, p. 56).

About 1689, the end of the eleventh century of the Islamic calendar, this Koyam settlement broke up, having been frayed by Tuareg raids (in the course of which Shaykh ʻAbdullāh was martyred) and by famine. Some students went south, and, abandoning the life of study to become herdsmen, became also rich. Others moved into Hausaland and by their dispersal gave rise to a number of clerical lineages there. Sometime during the first half of the eighteenth century the shaykh of the Koyam, ʻUmar b. ʻAbdullāh, returned to Bornu, having been with a few disciples as far afield as Nupe, and a new settlement was made at Gaskeru. Again the *mai* provided building workers for mosque and houses, and again he exempted the district from taxation. Gradually, for the first time, a political structure began to emerge from the religious organization of the Koyam. Shaykh ʻUmar's successor, his younger brother Muṣṭafā, placed in each village of the district – there were said to be a thousand, so many people had been attracted by the justice and security there – one of his own disciples, to act as *imām* and village chief. He also appointed a nephew as chief of the warriors, with responsibility for defence. Such a development may have been particularly gratifying to the Bornu authorities, as helping to strengthen one of the country's most exposed frontiers at a time of Tuareg expansion from Aïr, which had led to the loss of Kawar in the second half of the seventeenth century. Continued Tuareg pressure proved too great however: Gaskeru declined beneath their raids, and at last broke up. The Fulani invasions early in the nineteenth century further dispersed the Koyam clerics. Yet their educational and religious influence had been considerable: among their pupils, for example, was Shaykh al-Kānamī. The Koyam settlements were the largest and most successful, but by no means the only clerics', or mallams', settlements – *mallamari* – in Bornu.

The history of the Koyam immigrants in Bornu, so briefly sketched above, is in some respects a miniature representation of the pattern of development throughout the central Sudan. The arrival of camel-owning nomads, adherents of Islam; the gradual transition to a more settled life in co-operation with the already established local authorities, particularly when nomad numbers were small; the services of the newcomers to their hosts – as a camel corps with Aloma, and as spiritual supports for the *mais*; the gradual evolution of institutions of government, arising partly from religious practice and partly from the needs of defence (in this case against other nomads); the attraction of many other people into the haven of security thus created; the ultimately destructive impact of other, more powerful, nomadic groups; and the further diffusion of influence through refugees – all these are themes often repeated in the central Sudan.

The Budduma, the reed people of Lake Chad, are neither nomads nor immigrants, but in their elusive style of life they presented a similar problem if they were to be absorbed into a unified central Sudanese society. In the midst of the lake, they remained almost inaccessible. Aloma, though he enlisted Kotoko canoe forces against the So, and introduced a new form of boat to facilitate river crossings, apparently did not presume to attempt mastery of the Budduma; even the terrible Rābiḥ, in the nineteenth century, did no more. They are divided between fishermen and pastoralists, the latter spending part of their time with their cattle on the islands of the lake. Other economic activities included the production of salt, by burning *Capparis sodada* roots; a carrying trade across the lake, for example in potash from the eastern shore; and the preparation of hippopotamus hide whips for the Bornu market. The Budduma were also involved in the slave trade, often with the Tuareg as accomplices. They are said to have observed the general rule that no Kotoko, Arab, or Fulani might be enslaved. This was not a religious privilege for Muslims, as the Kanuri, themselves Muslim, were among the chief victims of Budduma raids, and were handicapped in their defence by being able to retaliate only on land. Among the Kanuri, the Budduma seemed very much like the warlike Tubu or Tuareg of the desert. However, regular markets provided times and places of mutually agreed truce, and the Budduma themselves were gradually adopting Islam.

Besides the considerable military contribution of camel-owning nomads, and the imposing religious prestige of some nomadic Muslims, nomads were an integral part of the economy. Their livestock grazed the stubble of the past harvest, and manured the ground for the next; milk, butter and cheese were a valuable supplement to the local diet; hides supplied the raw material for local craftsmen, and were also an export item. But most of all, nomads by their mobility allowed the maximum exploitation of the scarce water resources of the Sudan countries, moving according to the availability of pasture and water. This generally harmonious economic interchange depended upon firm government: should disagreement and conflict break out between nomads and settled farmers, the delicate ecological balance might be disturbed, and through overgrazing, or neglect of springs and wells, or in some other way, the desert would encroach upon the sown. This was a recurrent danger particularly in the Sahel.

BORNU AND HAUSALAND

The many facets of consolidation have been illustrated mainly as they affected Bornu, which was the major power of the region, and the territory in which the consolidation process had advanced furthest. But the process was not pursued in isolation. Bornu interacted, at times vigorously, with its neighbours, and some of these were themselves slowly developing their own bases of power. By the nineteenth century, the region was no longer dominated by a single colossus: indeed, the balance of power had rather shifted in favour of Hausaland, and against Bornu.

To the west, the ties of Bornu with Hausaland had been developing ever since the exodus from Kanem to Bornu shortly before 1400. Songhay had intermittently challenged Bornu for the foremost influence over Hausaland, but this challenge had never been strong after the break between Kebbi and Songhay in the early sixteenth century. It was in this century particularly that the deep military penetration of the Kanuri westwards, to Kano and even as far as Kebbi, probably influenced the evolution of political institutions within Hausaland, though it did not create these. A system of tribute to Bornu became widespread, Kano being the first to pay, apparently in the mid-fifteenth century; sometimes the tribute passed through the ruler of Daura, one of the original Hausa states, as intermediary between his colleagues and Bornu (see volume 3, chapter 5).

The Songhay threat at last disintegrated soon after the Moroccan conquest in 1591, though there are indications that the sultan of Morocco, al-Manṣūr, envisaged extending his own influence eastwards. In 1582 he had managed to negotiate with Aloma a declaration of homage, *bay'a*, to Morocco; and a decade later al-Manṣūr wrote reproachfully to Dāwūd, ruler of Kebbi, implying that it was only Kebbi's refusal to submit to Morocco that prevented Kano and Katsina doing the same. These documents were, as far as the success or failure of Morocco's Sudan policy was concerned, no more than scraps of paper; but it is possible that the religious authority which al-Manṣūr, particularly as a Sharif, claimed over the rulers of the Sudan may have encouraged the clerical party to challenge their political overlords. This may have been part of the background to the story of Waldid and to the rise of new rulers in Wadai (see below, p. 137).

Aloma was ruling in Bornu at the time of the Moroccan invasion of Songhay, and had been active in maintaining Bornu's sphere of influence over Hausaland. He had raided, probably early in his reign, to the very gates of Kano citadel, even though the people of the region had begun stockading their villages; but, although he ravaged many such villages, he failed to take the city. Various opportunities for co-operative endeavour between Bornu and Hausaland seem also to have existed at this time. Mohamma Kisoki, the Sarkin Kano against whom it seems likely that Aloma warred, also received clerics from Bornu reverently, making one the *qāḍī* of Kano. Again, about 1600, within Aloma's reign or just after, an aspirant to the office of ruler of Aïr fled south to Kano and Katsina, and later returned supported by both Bornu and Hausa troops, who installed him in power albeit very temporarily. In the area of present-day Katagum, several towns or principalities came under Bornu suzerainty, and their chiefs used to go every year to Ngasargamu: these may have served as buffer states between Bornu and Hausaland proper.

The principal features of Aloma's involvement in Hausaland continued throughout this period. Raiding and co-operation, with the success of the former and acknowledgement of the latter both alike expressed in the payment of tribute, went on alternating. Katsina, the major city of Hausaland was, for most of this period, almost always in some dependence on Bornu, each ruler sending 100 slaves to Ngasargamu on his accession – or even, according to some reports, sending that number annually. But the sovereign rights of the Hausa rulers do not seem otherwise to have been much curtailed. About the second quarter of the eighteenth century there was war again. An expedition led by the *mai* of Bornu marched against Kano, but again without conquering the city. In the Bornu records, a siege of seven months, which failed to reduce Kano, is mentioned. The Kano Chronicle speaks of an expedition at this time, but says that the *mai* did not in fact attack Kano city, merely remaining nearby for three nights and then returning home, apparently after the intervention of some Kano clerics as mediators. The two accounts do not agree as to the *mai*'s name, but almost certainly the same episode is represented in both. This expedition seems to have had wider implications, for in the chronicles of Zaria it is remembered as a war upon all the Hausa, and from this time Zaria joined the ranks of those paying tribute to Bornu.

Other peoples to the west of Bornu were also being influenced, among them the Bolewa – again they served as a buffer state which became a client of its more powerful neighbour. Bolewa records recall that Muḥammad Kai was the first Bolewa chief to adopt Islam, and that he went to Bornu, presumably to do homage there. The dating is very uncertain, perhaps about 1700, or perhaps a little later, in conjunction with the campaigns of the second quarter of the eighteenth century. Among the Azna, Hausa-speaking people in the extreme north-west of Hausaland, strangers from Bornu are said to have been the first to establish a state government, apparently in the seventeenth century.

Hausaland, like Bornu, experienced the pressure of Tuareg from the north and Kwararafa from the south. In the mid-seventeenth century, when Mai ʿAlī b. ʿUmar of Bornu repelled the Kwararafa, at that time pressing hard on the Hausa, a celebrated cleric of Katsina, Dan Marina, wrote a poem in praise of the *mai*, whom he addressed as *amīr al-mu'minīn*, commander of the faithful. Dan Marina had been the pupil of Dan Masanih, who though born in Katsina was of Bornu parentage: Dan Masanih is said himself to have taken a prominent part in the defence of Katsina against the Kwararafa. One author has suggested that also the Bolewa, who were neighbours to the Kwararafa, might have submitted to Bornu about the time of Mai ʿAlī's victory. To the north, the organized state of Damagaram emerged in the first half of the eighteenth century, as Kanuri leadership marshalled a mixed Hausa and

Kanuri population to resist Tuareg encroachment. The capital of Gobir, the principality upon which the chief responsibility fell for defending the northern marches of Hausaland, twice moved during the period, to Tsibiri about the end of the seventeenth century, and to Alkalawa in the middle of the eighteenth, but this may have been more a function of the southern and western expansion of the Gobirawa, than a falling back before Tuareg pressure.

Such was the style of Bornu's western policy during this period: raids and co-operation, submission and tribute, which however rarely if ever meant more than the most informal protectorate – and in the late eighteenth century, when Usuman dan Fodio was already active, Bawa Sarkin Gobir threw off the tributary obligation entirely. Bornu's influence, as a relatively benign overlord, was insufficient to weld Hausaland into a unity. Nor did the Kwararafa, whose raids began about 1600, have this effect, although at times they served that most useful of reconciling and uniting roles, the role of a common enemy.

The underlying pattern of developments among the Hausa during our period was not determined by outside influences, but derived rather from rivalries amongst the Hausa themselves. About 1600, Kebbi, lying on the north-western marches of Hausaland, and peopled by a mixture of Hausa and Songhay, was probably the foremost principality of the Hausa region. Its position enabled it to play an important strategic role in blocking Songhay penetration early in the sixteenth century. Kebbi's role as a major power came to an end about the middle of the period, as a result of successful attacks by Zamfara, Gobir and Aïr. Zamfara's star was briefly in the ascendant in western Hausaland; but in the 1730s Gobirawa immigration began, reluctantly allowed by the Sarkin Zamfara. Before long the immigrants had grown to be a threat to their host country, resulting in a heavy defeat of Zamfara about 1762. Gobir fought with other neighbours as well as with Zamfara—Kebbi, Kano and Katsina among them. The legacy of mutual distrust and dislike which such violence left was an important factor in preparing the way for the military success of the Fulani jihad: the Hausa princes were in general divided, and in particular the jihad forces, during the critical earliest period, were allowed an undisturbed base in Zamfara, while they devoted their main energies to the danger from Gobir. In eastern Hausaland, the rivalry between Kano and Katsina, which had begun as early as the fifteenth century, continued, perhaps for the lion's share of trans-Saharan commerce. Early in the seventeenth century, two Kano *sarkis* died on campaign against Katsina.

The gradual extension of Islam went on, reaching right across Hausaland to Nupe, which, as has already been noticed (see above, pp. 89–91), had become part of the trading network of the central Sudan. The first Muslim *etsu*, or ruler of Nupe, came only in the mid-eighteenth century, but there is evidence that Islam had taken root in the country much earlier. About the 1580s, a cleric from Nupe may have played an important part in reconciling the *alafin* with his estranged nobles at the Yoruba court. Towards the end of the seventeenth century, as has been seen (p. 112), the fugitive shaykh of the Koyam, with some disciples, came to Nupe and spent some time there before returning to Bornu.

Clerical condemnation of royal wrongdoing, such as we have discussed above among the Fulani, might also be observed. According to some accounts, the ruler of Katsina in the mid-seventeenth century was a notorious backslider, against whom both Dan Marina and Dan Masanih preached to no avail – while other clerics, evidently, collaborated with him, for one prepared for him an elixir of everlasting life, for which the too trusting *sarki* paid him handsomely, 100 slave boys, 100 slave girls, 100 horses, 100 mares, and so on. Clerical condemnation in the seventeenth century was a cloud no bigger than a man's hand: but by the beginning of the nineteenth it had become a hurricane. It was only then that the scales of power, between Bornu and Hausaland, dramatically tilted in the opposite direction, as Fulani from the west repeatedly sacked the capital of Bornu.

THE *MAGHRIB AL-ADNĀ*

The *Maghrib al-Adnā*, was, with Hausaland, the other main unit beside Bornu in this area. Unlike Hausaland, it is clear that events here in North Africa were moulded far more by the circumstances of the Mediterranean world than by those of continental Africa. The Sahara, though by no means impenetrable, was essentially a barrier to be overcome; the Mediterranean, though storms and corsairs were perilous enough, was essentially an avenue of approach. As an example of this, somewhat curious yet apt, we may take the plague, which periodically ravaged North Africa. In the 1780s, it came from Tunis to Tripoli, perhaps carried by cruel irony in ships bearing corn for famine relief, and continued there for more than twelve months. In 1783 the plague visited Cairo from Istanbul, the severity of it so often occasioning 'the people to drop while walking in the streets, that an order was issued, that neither man, woman, nor child, should attempt to go out of their houses, without having their name and place of residence written on paper and sewed to their caps'.[1] The central Sudan, cut off though it was from many advantages of conversation with the Mediterranean world, was spared also the plague.

During the sixteenth century, the rising tide of Christian imperialism, particularly Spanish, had thrust the Maghrib, except Morocco, into the arms of the Ottomans. Ottoman naval commanders, although unable to sweep the coasts altogether clear of Christian powers, did secure Algiers, Tunis and Tripoli for the world of Islam. Three regencies were established, their frontiers more or less the same from that day to this, although the geographical division in Libya – Tripoli and Cyrenaica lying apart like two halves of a kola thrown by a diviner – helped delay effective occupation there. In 1551 the Turks took Tripoli from the Knights of St John, but only in 1640 was Ottoman authority acknowledged in Cyrenaica.

At first these newly acquired provinces of the empire remained more or less under the direct control of the Porte, often with viceroys succeeding each other at short intervals. But it was not long before effective political links between the Porte and the regencies had been whittled down to the payment of tribute, or sometimes the award of gifts from the Porte, and some collaboration in military affairs. Another sign of weakened central authority was the way in which the regencies, throughout the period, recurrently plotted against each other, received each other's exiles, and from time to time fought. Throughout the seventeenth century, Tunis and Tripoli were ruled by a variety of soldiers and adventurers. Early in the eighteenth century, however, hereditary dynasties emerged in both territories. In Tunis, a Turkish Janissary of Cretan origin, Ḥusayn b. 'Alī, founded the Husaynid house, which was to rule until Tunisia was declared a republic in 1957. Ḥusayn himself was beheaded in a struggle with his nephew 'Alī, who refused to allow Ḥusayn's sons by a Genoese captive to displace him in the succession; Algerian troops in turn killed 'Alī, and placed Ḥusayn's eldest son upon the throne. In Tripoli, Aḥmad Karamanli, himself of the *kuloglu* class – descendants of intermarriage between the Turkish troops and local people – seized power, massacring most of the Turkish garrison, but averting the Porte's retribution by massive gifts. Despite the virtual independence of these two dynasties, both of which became increasingly acclimatized to their local settings, just as did

[1] Tully, *Narrative of residence at Tripoli*, 101.

immigrants to the Sudan, the theory of Ottoman sovereignty survived, together with many trappings of Ottoman pageantry. It is interesting to speculate how far this shadowy Ottoman authority was thought to extend: in Tripoli, at the end of the eighteenth century, both Bornu and the Fezzan were regarded as equally tributaries of Tripoli;[1] and in correspondence from Tripoli half a century later, the title *ḥākim*, in Ottoman usage a governor, was applied to the shaykh of Bornu. Perhaps there is some comparison to be made here with the way in which Morocco regarded Songhay as *bilād al-sibā* even after any trace of control from Morocco had vanished during the seventeenth century (see chapter 3, p. 148).

The power of the bey of Tunis, or of the pasha of Tripoli, over his hinterland fluctuated widely. Under a powerful ruler like the first Karamanli, a governor of the Fezzan who refused to pay tribute might be carried captive to Tripoli. Under a weak ruler, such as his grandson towards the end of the eighteenth century, bands of nomads threatened the safety of the city of Tripoli itself, and the pasha had to rely on pitting one group against another. An observer commented on such an incident in 1786: 'The hostile Arabs have been driven off, and the next desirable circumstance is to see the auxiliary Arabs depart in peace. As avarice is their passion, their demands are endless, and it often costs the Bashaw as much trouble to disperse them as to call them together.'[2] Even in Tunis, where everything in the interior was on a much smaller scale, with much less serious problems of communication and transport, the bey was often content to make two trips a year through the countryside, with his troops, collecting taxes and administering justice. These tides of advance and recession in the power of the central authorities are reminiscent of similar changes in the states of the central Sudan.

Armed co-existence characterized relations with the Christian powers across the Mediterranean. Having been called in to meet the Christian challenge, the Ottomans continued to regard their North African possessions in part as naval bases, and the tradition of corsairing flourished throughout the period. This variant of the slave trade has already been discussed. Counter-measures included similar action, reprisal raids, and treaties which usually involved the payment of substantial sums to the North Africans. Malta was a prominent centre for preying upon the shipping of Tunis and Tripoli: in 1720 there were

[1] Tully, *Narrative of residence at Tripoli*, 13.
[2] Ibid. 120.

estimated to be 10,000 Muslim slaves in the island, and in 1749 many were executed following an alleged plot.

But at the same time there was trade: marble came from Genoa for sumptuous building, tiles from Malta together with Maltese craftsmen to lay them, wood for graves and coffins from Venice – such supplies came to Tripoli, stricken with plague, even while Venice was at war with neighbouring Tunis – and many other commodities. Maltese sword blades were remounted in Kano for use in many parts of the central Sudan. The British occupation of Malta in 1799 led to a considerable increase in trade with Tripoli, to help supply the British military establishment. European consuls were increasingly involved in the affairs of both Tunis and Tripoli: the absence of such figures farther south is again evidence of the much more sheltered position of the central Sudan until nearly the end of the nineteenth century.

Trans-Saharan connections, between the *Maghrib al-Adnā* and the central Sudan, were maintained primarily for purposes of trade and pilgrimage. They also involved diplomatic relations. The main contact, in this period, was between Bornu and Tripoli, continuing a tradition already well established. Diplomatic links did not overlap entirely with the Pilgrimage, for the major *ḥajj* routes met in the Fezzan, and joined the North African caravan at Awjila: when Mai 'Alī b. 'Umar, who had already been to the holy places, proposed a state visit to Tripoli, the pasha there politely dissuaded him.

Aloma, apparently soon after his accession, sent an embassy to Tripoli; and he may later have received ambassadors from Istanbul (though the text is corrupt and difficult to read). Ibn Fartuwa's exclamation well shows the prestige value of such diplomatic associations: 'Have you ever seen a king equal to our Sultan or like him at the time when the Lord of Stambul, Sultan of Turkey, sent messengers to him from his country, with favourable proposals, indicating his desire to gain his affection and his eagerness for his society and friendship?'[1] Sabun, after opening the desert route north from Wadai, sent an embassy and gifts to Muḥammad 'Alī in Egypt.

For the period up to 1677, at which time the account of a French doctor captive in Tripoli closes, diplomatic exchanges with Bornu continued fairly frequently, and it is reasonable to assume that the same was true after 1677. In the 1630s the pasha wrote twice to the *mai*, and the *mai* responded by sending an ambassador with rich gifts, who was received in magnificent style and sent home with equally remarkable

[1] Palmer, *Sudanese memoirs*, I, 69, 76.

presents. Slaves – black and white, weapons – guns and swords, horses and gold, were among the items exchanged, so that diplomacy cannot be easily disentangled from trade in general, and the slave and arms trades in particular. There was also an element of luxury and conspicuous consumption, as in 1674 when a giraffe was sent north. Tripoli had requested the animal, which was intended as a present for the Grand Duke of Tuscany. Alas, it died in the desert, and only its skin, stuffed with straw, was carried to Tripoli.

An attempt by Tripoli to kidnap Mai ʿAlī b. ʿUmar, on his way back from pilgrimage, led to a break in relations for a few years. But in 1652, a new pasha having come to office in Tripoli, Mai ʿAlī was invited to renew both commerce and alliance, and he accepted joyfully. In 1655 he sent a relative as ambassador to Tripoli, and another splendid exchange of gifts took place. It was this new pasha, ʿUthmān, who later rescued Mai ʿAlī's nephew, enslaved during the civil wars and Tuareg raids in Bornu and sold to North Africa. The pasha redeemed him, honoured him, and sent him home with fine presents. It seems to have been customary, and this was perhaps true both in Bornu and in Tripoli, for a new ruler on taking office to renew the contact. Thus, after the death of Pasha ʿUthmān, new letters were sent from Tripoli to Bornu, in 1672. Such renewal of obligations was fairly common: a new *mai*, for example, might confirm the *maḥrams* – written grants of privilege – of his predecessors.

States in the central Sudan other than Bornu do not seem to have developed such links at this time, save perhaps when Bagirmi, in the later eighteenth century, is said to have begun sending presents, or informal tribute, to Istanbul every third year, part of which was to be forwarded to Mecca. During the nineteenth century, Wadai also sent such tokens, to Istanbul or to the Hejaz.

Such gifts were not the marks of a piety peculiar to the Sudan: Ḥusayn b. ʿAlī of Tunis, for example, sent alms regularly to Mecca, with clothing for the clerics there, oil for the lamps of certain holy tombs in Rosetta and Alexandria, mats and oil to the mosques in infidel lands, and shrouds for Muslims who might die there. Sometimes shrouds were sent to Mecca for blessing, and then returned to North Africa. Gifts, often substantial enough to be of material significance in themselves, were also the outward signs of political entente and religious brotherhood among the faithful.

TUAREG, TUBU AND THE FEZZAN

All trans-Saharan links depended at least on the passive acquiescence, and in very many important respects also on the active assistance, of the Saharan peoples. Two of these, both nomadic, the Tuareg to the west and the Tubu to the east, were frequently involved in disturbances towards the south, and with both Aloma did a good deal of fighting.

Of the several major confederations into which the Tuareg were divided, that which centred upon the Aïr region, with its capital at Agades, was the most significant for the central Sudan. Here, from the fifteenth century, a sultan of sorts ruled, lacking power but endowed with a vague prestige. His chief policy opportunities lay in playing off one Tuareg tribe against another; although, if such internal quarrels became too rancid, as happened in the 1690s, roads were shut, trade halted, and famine was the result, until the sultan succeeded in arbitrating. The sultan's chief income was from caravan tolls, but the tribes apparently had the right to receive some part, especially in horses, of his caravan receipts.

According to Ibn Fartuwa's chronicle, Aloma made three expeditions against the Tuareg, two under his own leadership and the third under a vizier, all in the same year, and in addition to these sorties other officials and allies frequently attacked the Tuareg. The military significance of these exercises is seen through the powerful magnifying glass of Ibn Fartuwa's admiration for his lord. On the first expedition none of Aloma's men was killed; on the second and third, despite innumerable Tuareg casualties, Aloma lost only one man each time, once a Turk and once a slave. It is difficult to imagine such results coming from anything more than rather glancing raids.

Other features of the campaigning are of more interest. The first offence of the Tuareg had been to molest Fulani, who were evidently under Bornu protection; and among the most useful allies of Aloma were the Koyam. Apparently more effective than the three main expeditions, was the constant harassment of Tuareg grazing grounds in Bornu, which Aloma ordered the Koyam to undertake. This policy – and such persistent interference with natural ecology, as we have seen, was a recurrent resort of Aloma's, often to powerful effect – led to the submission of the Tuareg, who were then allowed to return to Bornu. Some exchanged altogether their allegiance to the ruler of Aïr, to become Aloma's vassals.

Trouble between the Tuareg and Bornu continued throughout this period. Mai 'Alī b. 'Umar, in the middle of the seventeenth century, was apparently at war with them more than once. Returning from his third pilgrimage, he found the ruler of Aïr leagued with rebels within Bornu, and waging civil war. This may have been the same occasion on which Ngasargamu, according at least to later reports, was besieged by Tuareg and Kwararafa at once, or the two crises may have been separate. An account, written in 1658, tells of an expedition by Mai 'Alī, which resulted in the capture of the ruler of Aïr. Mai 'Alī said that he would not kill his prisoner, if he would convert to Islam. The emir asked, 'What is Islam?' The *mai* explained that it was to say, 'There is no god but God, and Muḥammad is His Prophet.' The emir said this, so Mai 'Alī released him and went back to Bornu, leaving behind with the emir one slave and four clerics. The *mai* gave 1,000 horses to the people whom he left in Aïr.

That the Tuareg ruler of Aïr should still have been a non-Muslim in the seventeenth century is highly improbable. We know, indeed, from Agades chronicles, that Muḥammad al-Mubārak, a staunch Muslim who went twice on pilgrimage, took power in Agades in 1654. It is possible that his installation owed something to Bornu intervention, or perhaps that Bornu wished to reaffirm its sphere of influence over a newly emergent ruler. The episode is a reminder that the profession of Islam was often a political matter, in which a subordinate state acknowledged the suzerainty, or tribute rights, of another. Sometimes such acknowledgement led to the title of Muslim being applied to people otherwise little or not at all affected by Islam, but in other cases, as apparently in Aïr, the same acknowledgment might lead observers to speak of 'conversion' even among people who had been Muslim for generations. The act of the *mai* in leaving a slave, presumably a fairly high-ranking official, behind to look after his interests is typical. And many of the clerics in the southern central Sahara did come from the Sudan countries.

Whatever does in fact lie behind the 1658 Bornu account, it is clear that Bornu's influence over Aïr was precarious. Barth was of the opinion that the fighting between Aïr and Mai 'Alī b. 'Umar might have been of such severity as to cause permanent depopulation of the border districts. In 1679, according to one Agades chronicle, al-Mubārak sent an army against Bornu, which destroyed the country, capturing children and flocks – but once again, little more than a kidnapping expedition seems to have been involved.[1]

The Koyam, who had helped Aloma against the Tuareg, were them-

[1] Y. Urvoy, 'Chroniques d'Agadès', *Journal de la Société des Africanistes*, 1934, **4**, 170.

selves repeatedly victims of Tuareg raids into Bornu. The first permanent settlement of the Koyam shaykhs in Bornu itself, at Belbelec, was abandoned late in the seventeenth century partly because of successive Tuareg raids; and the second, at Gaskeru, was given up after the Tuareg had overrun it late in the eighteenth century – without, however, their harming the shaykh or those who had taken refuge with him, or in the mosque, or near the tombs of holy men. One shaykh of the Koyam was killed, when Koyam and Bornu forces combined to throw back a Tuareg raid and then pursued the raiders too deeply into their own country.

Relations between Aïr and Hausaland seem to have been still more troubled, with raids and counter-raids involving primarily Gobir, Zamfara and Kebbi. In some cases Aïr acted in reprisal against the oppression of nomadic Tuareg in Hausa country, and it is easy to see how in this way the wide ranging movements of nomads might lead to the escalation of conflict. In one case, Tuareg military expansion led to a major new political development. In 1674 al-Mubārak sent an army, under his eldest son Agabba, which overran the territory of Adar, a buffer state laying between Aïr and Kebbi, and at that time a vassal of the latter. The Tuareg needed time to consolidate their hold on Adar: once they were driven out by Gobir forces, and in retaliation Agabba invaded Gobir, leaving, so the Agades chronicler claims, not one woman or child, sending some to Tuat, some to the Fezzan, keeping some for his own use, until Gobir sued for peace. Finally a new state emerged in Adar, ruled by a Tuareg dynasty, supported from Aïr, and financed by a tax, of one-third of production, on the Hausa-speaking peasantry. Later, in the northern Hausa territory of Damergu, a similar arrangement evolved under the Kel Owi Tuareg. Intermittent fighting continued to the end of the period: the war between Aïr and Gobir in 1767, when the Sarkin Gobir, brother of Bawa, was killed, has already been mentioned.

The Tuareg of Aïr were vital for the Saharan trade of the central Sudan, and despite the fighting, exacerbated as it surely was by racial antagonism, and by the natural chafing between nomad and settled, the ancient awareness of the need for co-operation was time and again renewed. In one sense, the Tubu and Tuareg divided the routes between them: south of the Fezzan, the Tubu were stronger on the road to Bornu, the Tuareg on that to Hausaland. But the Tuareg were generally accepted as more effective and more responsible partners in the network of Saharan commerce. 'Their caravans', Hornemann observed at the very end of the eighteenth century, 'give life to Mourzouk, which without them, is a desert.' He was perhaps thinking of music and conviviality, but his words may equally well bear a much more profound interpretation. The Tuareg were the principal carrying agents: they would, for example, carry goods for merchants of Ghadames and Tuat wishing to trade in Katsina, for so much per camel load, the merchants themselves sometimes having no camels; and the Tuareg would also move slaves across the desert, for so much per head. With this income, and the profits of the salt trade, they were able to buy grain and other necessities from the Sudan. The *zāwiya* of Sīdī Aḥmad, at Aghrezeur in Aïr, reveals some facets of the interaction of trade and religion. At this shrine, to which pilgrims were attracted from afar, and where the pious might enter to read the sacred books, there was sanctuary, and caravans camped there. It was the custom for a caravan bound south to leave some of its possessions at the *zāwiya*, to be called for on the return journey, and also for gifts to be given to the shaykhs of the shrine.

The Tubu, living to the east of the Tuareg, like them lacked any strong sense of national identity. Tubu had been traditionally closely associated with the developing state of Kanem-Bornu, the ruling house of which, the Magumi, had intermarried a good deal with the Tubu nobility. It is possible that the inauguration of a very flimsy form of central government in Tibesti, around the *dardai* or chief, sprang from the return of certain Tubu, particularly the Tomagra, from Bornu to Tibesti about the time of Aloma. But Tubu were also, by Aloma's time, associated with the Bulala resistance movement. Ibn Fartuwa observed that if it had not been for the Tubu, it would not have been necessary for Aloma to go to Kanem more than once. Aloma wrought the fiercest vengeance he was able upon those Tubu who crossed him in war. On the date-destroying expedition (see above, p. 75), the army defeated some Tubu, and Aloma gave orders that all the captives should be killed. 'Not one that we saw with our eyes escaped. Death that day smote them like a plague and that day became fatal to them like the day of destruction of the people of 'Ad in the wind of sickness as our Lord has told us in His Book which explains all.'[1] This was in Kanem; Aloma also sent camel columns to intimidate the Tubu in their own country farther north. Other groups of Tubu actually joined the emigration, or exodus, to Bornu.

[1] Palmer, *Sudanese memoirs*, I, 42–3; the story of 'Ād in the Koran is popular as a prototype of disaster, rather as Sodom and Gomorrah in the Bible.

The relations of the Tubu with their settled neighbours were usually uncertain, and liable to periodic souring. At some stage, probably in the eighteenth century, fighting broke out between the Tubu and their ancient allies the Bulala; in a celebrated battle at Takaté, although the Tubu marshalled 1,900 camels, the Bulala were victorious, killing many and capturing nearly 100 warriors (see above, p. 74). In Wadai, Tubu youths captured on raids were among the relatively small number of people castrated in that country during the nineteenth century. Incidents, for example a Tubu raid upon a caravan of pilgrims, continued into this century; in some sense the fighting in the Republic of Tchad since independence is a continuation of a pattern familiar enough to Aloma.

Particularly important was the influence of the Tubu over the desert routes to North Africa. Much of the highway from the Fezzan to Lake Chad was dependent upon the Tubu. Denham, in the early nineteenth century, described the skill of Tubu guides, navigating by fixed points in sandstone ridges amid wind-driven sand. It may be that the relatively accommodating attitude of the Tubu along this route owed something to the influence of strong powers, when such existed, to north or south, and also to the presence of settled immigrants at oases – in Bilma for example, the settled Kanuri (or Kanuri-ized) population outnumbered the Tubu there. Farther to the east the Tubu were less co-operative. The easternmost route from the Lake Chad area, running through Borku to Tibesti and on to Kufra, although a fairly direct way to Egypt, was never much used, partly because the Tubu troubled it greatly. In Aloma's time, the Tura – apparently immigrants to Bornu from the Fezzan region – refused any longer to bring horses from Egypt, because of the seven perils of the road, one of which was the Tubu. Even when new trade and transit possibilities were available, the Tubu seem to have shown little interest. For example, from about the middle of the seventeenth century, when the tribes of Wadai were united into a single political system, and trade developed between that new state and the Fezzan, the route passing by the Tubu centre of Tibesti, the Tubu there did not lose their reputation as rock-dwelling freebooters. Towards the end of the eighteenth century the rulers of the Fezzan attempted to bring Tibesti under some sort of tributary obligation, but with only temporary success.

The religious history of the Tubu is particularly difficult to glimpse, owing to the remoteness of this elusive people, and to the fact that when, in the nineteenth century, observers did begin to penetrate among them, the Sanūsīya brotherhood was influencing them in a way perhaps entirely new. The religious situation is further complicated because the Saharan Tubu share with other nomads those adjustments to religious life which wandering requires: they have no mosque buildings, for example, and Koran schools are rare among them. At the same time, settled immigrants, a majority in Bilma as has already been mentioned, present a more orthodox appearance. On the whole, there has perhaps been a tendency to underestimate the degree of islamization among the Tubu. According to some traditions, the first missionaries, from the north, arrived not direct via the Fezzan, but in a roundabout fashion through Ghadames, Ghat and Agades. Islam may also have spread into Tubu country from Muslim Bornu, perhaps carried by the Tomagra; and later the arrival of Tripolitanian Arabs, some Sharifs among them, from Murzuk is remembered.

The Tubu remained essentially camel nomads, living ideally in the desert on little else than camel's milk and dates. Even their horses were sometimes fed only on camel's milk.

In contrast, the Fezzan, a little farther north, was relatively a settled, not a nomadic, community, though many nomads continued to move in and out, attracted by the oases. Almost all traces of Bornu's dominion over the Fezzan had disappeared before the seventeenth century. During the sixteenth century, the Awlād Muḥammad dynasty ruled there, founded it is said by a Moroccan Sharif who stopped in the Fezzan on his way back from pilgrimage. Towards the end of the century, Tripolitanian forces began interfering, and not until the eighteenth century was the country spared the succession of Tripolitanian invasions, imposing tribute and often a garrison as well, and Fezzani revolts (mingled with rivalries amongst the Fezzanis themselves) which, temporarily effective, called forth renewed Tripolitanian effort. On several occasions, rebellious Fezzani leaders took refuge in the Sudan, often being summoned back to champion their country's resistance against Tripoli; such episodes suggest the continuation of significant links between the Fezzan and the Sudan. One leader, al-Ṭāhir b. al-Nāsir, early in the seventeenth century, imprudently withdrew to Bornu, whose ruler at that time, 'Umar the son of Aloma – the killer, perhaps, of the cleric al-Jarmiyu – he had formerly insulted, and at whose hands he now suffered a violent death. Another of the Awlād Muḥammad, Muḥammad al-Nāsir, towards the end of the seventeenth century, retired to Agades, where he acquired a Tuareg force sufficient to restore him to power.

Muḥammad al-Nāsir's son and successor, Aḥmad, began his reign early in the eighteenth century with an attempt to refuse tribute to Tripoli; he was captured by the Tripolitanians, now perhaps stronger under Karamanli rule, and was fortunate to escape execution. Restored by the Karamanlis as shaykh of the Fezzan, he then lived out his long reign in peace, and died at last on pilgrimage – the journey to Mecca being often the act of a ruler who felt himself and his country secure. Perhaps this tranquillity is part of the background to an episode in Bornu in 1752, when the *mai* wished to draft some of the Tura in his domains for military service. These people, originally from the Fezzan, refused this duty, and threatened to return again to their first homes. The *mai* thereupon dropped his proposal. The incident is interesting also in that it illustrates how the flow of the exodus, generally towards Bornu, might possibly be reversed if circumstances changed sufficiently. Early in the nineteenth century the last of the Awlād Muḥammad was murdered by a usurper, who took absolute power within the Fezzan for himself, though he was still a tributary of Tripoli.

The economic importance of the Fezzan was twofold. Firstly, it was a junction of many trade routes across the Sahara, for here the easternmost of the routes from Hausaland and the westernmost from Wadai joined with the principal Chad-Tripoli artery. Fezzan traders ranged even farther than this: the Fezzani community in Timbuktu, for example, was among the first to swear loyalty to the Moroccans in 1593, after the conquest of Songhay. In addition to serving as a junction, the Fezzan was also a granary for parts of the barren hinterland of the *Maghrib al-Adnā*: the mountains between Tripoli and Ghadames were chiefly supplied by dates from Fezzan, and Ghadames itself sometimes depended on corn and dates from the Fezzani oases.

MANDARA, BAGIRMI AND THE KWARARAFA

Southwards from Bornu lay three important powers: Mandara, Bagirmi, and the Kwararafa or Jukun. With the first two, Aloma himself had to deal. He intervened in Mandara, adopting two recurrent policies – backing a rival, local candidate for the throne, just as he did in Kanem and Agades, and establishing a base in the field so as to wear down the enemy. He seems to have succeeded without fighting. The ruler of Mandara had nominated his son to succeed him, and then died. The son, deposed by his uncle, fled to Aloma for help. Aloma gave the deposed son a robe of honour, and led an army on his behalf to the capital of Mandara, Kerawa. The people of Kerawa retired to the hills, whence they could not be dislodged, and Aloma had to return home without accomplishing his purpose. In the following year, however, when the Mandarans adopted the same tactic, Aloma blockaded them, until hunger and want forced them to come down from the hills and to submit. Thus the deposed king was restored.

Ibn Fartuwa says explicitly that the king, whose wish for his son's succession Aloma so generously fulfilled, was an unbeliever. Whether his son was also an unbeliever is not stated, but it seems unlikely that Aloma would not have required at least a formal acceptance of Islam. Thus we can perhaps trace the first conversion of Mandara back to the late sixteenth century.

In the early eighteenth century another conversion is recorded in two circumstantial accounts. According to the shorter account, Islam was first revealed to Abū Bakr, ruler of Mandara, who returned from the Pilgrimage in 1723. He ruled for twenty-three years, and was on his death succeeded by his son Muḥammad al-Makkīyī, the Meccan, so-called, as some said, because he was born at Mecca during his father's pilgrimage, or, according to others, because Makia was the name of his mother, a Kanuri woman.

The second account tells how two clerics, father and son, originally from Fez, were returning from pilgrimage through Bagirmi in 1715. The heir apparent of Mandara, Bukar, having heard of the two men, summoned them, and asked them to stay with him. They agreed, on condition that he converted, which he did. When he succeeded as ruler of Mandara, there was some opposition to his Muslim innovations, circumcision, prayer, fasting and alms-giving, and he was apparently threatened with deposition, but was supported with supernatural resource by the clerics. He continued in office until his death in 1737, and was succeeded by his son Madi Makia, who ruled for twenty years. An agreement between Bukar and his North African visitors, that as long as the family of the former should remain in power, so long should that of the latter serve as their respected clerics, was still in effect in the middle of the present century.

Although the two accounts differ substantially in some respects, there is considerable agreement. Abū Bakr and his son Muḥammad al-Makkīyī, and Bukar and Madi Makia, are evidently identical, and the dates given are reasonably alike. Both stories stress the importance of the Pilgrimage in planting Islam in Mandara; it is worth noticing that the second account says that the visiting clerics gave Bukar the title *al-ḥājj*, not because he had been to Mecca, but because he had converted many unbelievers amongst his own people.

A recently published Arab manuscript on Mandara partially confirms these reports. It speaks of the brother of one ruler of Mandara succeeding to the throne, only to be deposed and replaced by his nephew – perhaps this was Aloma's doing. Of Mai Boukar Adji, as he is here called, the manuscript says that he had studied as a youth at Ngasargamu, and that he brought back with him thence one Shaykh 'Abd al-Qādir, who taught the Koran to the Mandaran people.[1]

Such recurrent episodes – Denham recorded another early in the nineteenth century – of conversion and re-conversion, whether they reflect a total relapse into paganism during the intervals, or derive merely from an increasing awareness which makes previously accepted versions of the faith no longer tolerable, are not without parallel. This may well have been what was happening in Kanem during the opening centuries of the second millennium AD. Such a pattern underlines the importance of communications and mobility within Muslim Africa, lest the frontiers fall completely out of touch with the heartlands of Islam; it also illustrates the spontaneously generated passion for reform which seems again and again to have arisen.

Mandara continued to attract the attentions, sometimes unwelcome, of Bornu. Particularly under Mai 'Alī b. al-Ḥājj Dunama, ruling in the second half of the eighteenth century, a number of expeditions, generally unsuccessful, were launched against Mandara. On one, the *mai* was himself wounded and many of his army perished. This, it appears, seriously weakened Bornu in the impending confrontation with the Fulani, and indeed it was partly through the help of the increasing numbers of Fulani entering the plains around the Mandara massif that Mandara had been able to repulse Bornu.

Mandara was attractive as a slave-supplying area, whether from that principality itself or, as seems more probable, from the thickly populated pagan districts surrounding it. According to one account, it was from Mandara that al-Ḥājj Muḥammad al-Amīn, *mbang* of Bagirmi in the later eighteenth century, bought the very expensive eunuch, in the transaction which led him to experiment profitably with home production (see above, p. 100). Mandara was important also because, with the neighbouring Marwa district, it was famous horse country. Denham, early in the nineteenth century, commented several times on the

[1] M. Abbo and E. Mohammadou, 'Un nouveau manuscrit arabe sur l'histoire du Mandara', *Revue camerounaise d'histoire*, 1971, no. 1, 130–69.

excellent horses of Mandara, on one of which even the Shaykh al-Kānamī rode; and it is said that, later in the century, Mandara paid tribute in horses to Adamawa. It is not clear at how early a date horses became a prominent feature in Mandara. Iron also came to Bornu from the Mandara region; in Mandara itself, the smiths were one of the few distinct caste groups.

Bagirmi, to the south-east of Bornu, lies below Kanem, somewhat as Mandara is below Bornu. It was while campaigning in this area that Aloma met his death. During a battle in Bagirmi, Aloma, standing under a tree, was seriously wounded by a knife thrown by someone hidden in the tree. The army withdrew slowly, via Dikwa, towards Ngasargamu; but by the lake known as Alo, Aloma died and was buried – the name by which he is commonly remembered is thus that of his grave.

Notices of fighting in Bagirmi appear in early songs from the Kanem court, in the eleventh and thirteenth centuries, unless these are later interpolations; and the area was apparently from the beginning a slave reservoir. A legend among one group of the Sara, a numerous people living to the south of Bagirmi proper, although it seems improbable as historical fact, is nonetheless an accurate reflection of attitude: according to this legend, there were two brothers, who came from the east fleeing from the Muslims. When they came to Bagirmi, the elder brother decided to stop and convert; he is the ancestor of the Bagirmi. The younger brother would not submit, and continued on his way, southwards; from him derive the Sara-Majingai.

Aloma may have succeeded in bringing Bagirmi under tribute to Bornu during his lifetime. Subsequently, such sway as Bornu may have been able to exercise over Bagirmi was fragile, for the rulers of Bagirmi behaved with the utmost independence, and were sometimes at war with Bornu or, more frequently, with the peoples of Kanem. Yet some sort of authority was evidently fairly widely known, for Usuman dan Fodio, discussing the rise and fall of Sudanic states, was later to say that Bornu had power over Bagirmi.

The first planting of Islam in the region seems to have been about the beginning of the sixteenth century, and to have come as a result of Fulani rather than of Kanuri or Kanembu action. Towards the end of the century, ʻAbdullāh, roughly Aloma's contemporary, was the first committed Muslim ruler, though his predecessors may have been Muslim in form.[1] He had disputed his brother's right to the throne, partly

[1] A thorough study of Bagirmi history remains to be made; unable to resolve the conflicts of the various sources, the author has made G. Nachtigal (*Sahara und Sudan*, reprinted Graz, 1967, II, 698 ff.) his foundation.

on religious grounds; and, after successfully usurping power, introduced new rituals of kingship, new offices of government copied in part perhaps from Bornu, and many features, hitherto unknown in Bagirmi, of Muslim practice. He built a wall around his palace, Fulani clerics tracing the foundations and providing talismans to be buried at each corner. These particular clerics, richly rewarded, served as teachers in various villages. 'Abdullāh appointed a *qāḍī* and an *imām*, established praying places, enforced regular prayer, circumcision and fasting, and invited foreign clerics. Other sources confirm Muslim inter-communication between Bagirmi and other Sudanic states even at this early stage: 'Abd al-Karīm, founder of the first fully-fledged Muslim dynasty in Wadai, early in the seventeenth century, had studied in Bagirmi; and even in distant Kano there is a possible reference to clerics coming from Bagirmi in the third quarter of the sixteenth century. Fulani clerics continued to visit Bagirmi throughout our period. Particularly interesting is the case of Waldid, the cleric who, after the *mai* of Bornu had slain his reforming Tuareg colleague, fled to Bagirmi and there prophesied the coming of a *mujaddid*, a restorer of the Islamic faith, who would drive the *mai* from his home just as the *mai* had expelled Waldid. The dates are uncertain (see above, pp. 108–9), but there is a slight possibility that the *mai* concerned was Aloma. It would be ironical if Aloma, at the end of the sixteenth century the leading Muslim champion of the central Sudan, were to be regarded, as in this story, as the cause of the near collapse of the central Sudan at the hands of the *mujaddid* Usuman dan Fodio, leading champion of the early nineteenth century. But the offender is more likely to have been Aloma's son 'Umar.

Bagirmi's position on the southern pilgrimage route may have contributed to such Muslim links. The first Fulani Muslim settlement in Bagirmi was established by an intending pilgrim. The clerics who, in one account, first brought Islam to Mandara, are said to have been returning through Bagirmi from their pilgrimage. A *mai* of Bornu, on pilgrimage probably in the eighteenth century, is reported, as has been noticed, to have established 5,000 slaves in Bagirmi on his way to Mecca, and to have confirmed them there on his return. A Fulani scholar from Katsina, who died in Cairo in 1741, numbered a Bagirmi cleric among his teachers.

During the seventeenth and eighteenth centuries, rulers who are remembered chiefly for their military exploits alternated with others of more religious bent, at least two of whom were called *al-wālī* or saint, one of these, 'Abd al-Qādir al-Wālī, early in the eighteenth century going so far as to abdicate in order to give himself wholly to meditation and religious exercises. Al-Ḥājj Muḥammad al-Amīn, *mbang* in the later eighteenth century, carried further the islamization of Bagirmi. Muḥammad had hesitated to return from pilgrimage, until an apparently leading individual in Bagirmi, discontented with the government of the time under Mbang Lawal, went likewise on pilgrimage, and established an alliance with al-Ḥājj Muḥammad. Al-Ḥājj Muḥammad fought his way to power, and ruled for much of the second half of the eighteenth century. It was perhaps only during his time that the common people of the area were required to profess Islam. The reign of his son and successor, Gwaranga, came to an abrupt and bloody end early in the nineteenth century, when Wadai forces under Sultan Sabun sacked the capital and killed the *mbang*. From this disaster Bagirmi never fully recovered.

Barth's judgement upon Islam in Bagirmi, in the mid-nineteenth century – that it was of recent establishment there, that the country was still more pagan than Muslim, that there was little learning of any kind and no wide learning save among the Fulani there and foreigners from Wadai – seems to reflect the decline of the nineteenth century, which was so unfortunate for Bagirmi, and does not adequately take into account the progress of earlier times.

The Kwararafa, the third of the southern powers, were based on the valley of the Benue. Wukari, still a walled town today, is the centre of their now tiny remnant: the outlines of a former capital, immense in size, may be traced between Wurrio and Bantaji towns. The Kwararafa, in the days of their strength, appear not to have been a single people, but a loose confederacy of groups, amongst whom the Jukun formed a ruling caste, receiving tribute from allies and vassals.

The Wukari Jukun have no traditions of warlike activity during this period, but certain groups, such as the Pindiga, do, and documentary references to the Kwararafa look back well before the seventeenth century. Usually the theme is relations with Hausaland, although Leo Africanus perhaps speaks of an invasion of Kwararafa territory by a *mai* of Bornu, maybe 'Alī Gaji, towards the end of the fifteenth century, seeking slaves who might be exchanged for horses from North Africa. The Kwararafa were themselves interested in cavalry; some of the tribute they received was in horses. About the time of Aloma, the Kwararafa raided Kano, apparently overrunning the city and eating up the whole country. Another Kwararafa attack on Kano is mentioned about the middle of the seventeenth century, and another about 1671. Kwararafa activity appears to have been particularly intense just at this period, for Katsina escaped only most narrowly from being altogether overrun by these invaders from the south, and Zaria also fell into their hands. It was also some time in the 1670s that the Kwararafa mounted their major offensive against Ngasargamu. This was in the time of Mai 'Alī b. 'Umar, of many pilgrimages, when traditions relate that the Bornu capital managed to escape conquest by playing off the Tuareg against the Kwararafa. It is perhaps this victory that the Katsina cleric, Dan Marina, mentioned above, celebrated in verse; and it may also have been the occasion on which, according to Bornu records, Mai 'Alī killed 1,000 of the Kwararafa, wounded another 1,000, and took 1,000 prisoners, three of whom he sent back to their king with their ears cut off and hung round their necks.[1] This fighting may have led to closer relations, and to a feeling of mutual respect between the Kwararafa and Bornu. Bornu was the only state which the Kwararafa regarded as their equal, and it is said that an almost autonomous colony of Jukun lived in Ngasargamu, while people from Bornu lived among the Kwararafa. The 'foreign minister' of the Kwararafa was always a Muslim. Muslims seem always to have been tolerated within Kwararafa territory, but to have lived there without, during our period at least, influencing local people towards Islam – on the contrary, some Hausa were so fully absorbed by their new surroundings as to lose both the faith and the language of their former home. Apparently one *mai*, probably in the eighteenth century, died fighting against the Kwararafa; by the end of that century the Kwararafa were paying an annual tribute in slaves to Bornu.

The Kwararafa declined in power. It was they who particularly bore the brunt of rising Fulani strength during the second half of the eighteenth century, although their last stronghold did not fall into Fulani hands until late in the nineteenth century, when the French supplied the Fulani with help and guns.

Among the Kwararafa, an elaborate divine kingship centred upon Wukari. They themselves believe that much of their old power sprang from the supernatural resources on which they could draw, and their wars with Muslims to the north often involved a supernatural or religious element. The attack on Katsina is said to have been repulsed owing to the sanctity of one citizen of that city, Dan Masanih, teacher of Dan Marina. But in the attack on Kano, about 1671, the *sarki*'s

[1] Palmer, *Sudanese memoirs*, II, 115.

device of placing about him his most powerful charm together with ninety-nine Muslim clerics came to no good, and few of the clerics escaped alive. In the tales of Bornu-Kwararafa relations, there are many incidents of the pagan command of supernatural power ranged against the Muslim, with the honours always equally divided.

Doubtless many factors helped to explain the decline of the Kwararafa in the latter part of the eighteenth century and later, while the Muslim states of which they had been masters or at least equals increased in authority; but one significant element may have been the consistent transfusion and replenishment of men, ideas and inspiration which the Muslim world of the central Sudan received from the Muslim heartlands, through trade, the pilgrimage and other contacts.

WADAI

With Wadai, which was to emerge during the seventeenth century as the principal power to the east of Bornu, Aloma appears to have had no direct contact; and, despite the reorientation of foreign relations, which was by the nineteenth century to involve Bornu deeply in the affairs of Wadai as well as of Bagirmi, Wadai throughout our period did not much affect the course of events in Bornu. There were, however, developments in Wadai quite closely resembling those elsewhere in the central Sudan.

In the area of Darfur and Wadai, at the beginning of the seventeenth century, the Tunjur were the dominant group. Locally accepted as Arabs, the Tunjur, whose origins are uncertain, are perhaps more properly regarded as Nubians, who adopted the Arabic language through contact with Arabs. Some Tunjur rulers had Arabic names, and professed Islam, but they made no attempt to extend the religion among the heterogeneous population of their tribute-paying subjects.

Perhaps about 1600, a new departure occurred, as an attempt was made to preach Islam locally. There are various traditions telling of this. According to one, the man responsible was Mahamat el-Kap or el-Kab, taking his name from his former post as guardian of the *Ka'ba* in Mecca. The Quraysh, the tribe of the Prophet, there asked him to write on a tablet, and then to take the tablet and bury it wherever he wished to be sultan. He set off, alone and on foot, to spread Islam. Coming to the country of the Tunjur, he buried the tablet there; the people rallied round him, and he became the greatest cleric of Wadai. Later, another cleric, 'Abd al-Karīm, secured the tablet for himself, in exchange for a copper drum – an exchange perhaps reflecting the inherent tension between kingship and Islam. He took the tablet to Wara, and re-buried it there. The people soon left Mahamat el-Kap, and turned to ʿAbd al-Karīm instead.

Other traditions trace an ʿAbbasid descent for ʿAbd al-Karīm (also sometimes called Sāliḥ), probably through the Jaʿaliyyūn of the Shendi district on the Nile, who claim this honourable derivation for themselves. It is interesting that, in these traditions, the role of the refugee figures prominently: according to one, ʿAbd al-Karīm's father had fled to the Hejaz from the Ottoman conquest of Egypt in 1517; according to another, his father had gone to Mecca on pilgrimage, and ʿAbd al-Karīm had later to desert the holy city because of the vindictive jealousy of the authorities there, coming either direct or via Fez (whence he was a second time a refugee from the agents of the Meccan authorities) to Wadai.

ʿAbd al-Karīm apparently had religious links to the west as well as to the east. Some traditions say that he had studied at Bidderi, the Muslim centre associated with the Fulani in Bagirmi. Others again suggest that he was a student with al-Jarmiyu, the reforming cleric put to death by the *mai* of Bornu about 1000 AH (1591 AD). Al-Jarmiyu's colleague, Waldid, fled then to Bidderi, and it is conceivable that, rather than ʿAbd al-Karīm having visited Bornu himself, a posthumous link with al-Jarmiyu may thus have been established at Bidderi. According to one report, ʿAbd al-Karīm after his return from Bidderi to Wadai cherished more and more the notion of a theocratic revolution; according to another, when he left al-Jarmiyu, ʿAbd al-Karīm was accompanied by several companions.

Although there are many uncertainties, unresolved and some probably unresolvable, about names and dates, it is possible at least to suggest a contagion of Islamic unrest, spreading across the Sudan rather as similar revolutions swept from the Senegal to Lake Chad in the eighteenth and nineteenth centuries. The events we have just been discussing are apparently placed in the period immediately following the Moroccan conquest of Songhay in 1591, a conquest partly justified by the claim of the Sharif, sultan of Morocco, to authority in the Muslim world over the secular ruler, the *askiya* of Songhay. It is possible that the repercussions of this traumatic event, coupled with apocalyptic expectancy naturally linked with the turn of the millennium, stirred men's minds in countries to the east, a stirring which was suppressed in Bornu, spilt over to Bagirmi, and culminated in successful revolution in Wadai. The house of 'Abd al-Karīm, like that of the Moroccan sultans, claimed the status of Sharifs.

The details of the revolution which was to place 'Abd al-Karīm upon the throne of Wadai are unclear, but it is likely that the usurper's success depended upon a combination of popular support, strategic marriages, religious power and military action. One tradition with brief perspicacity sums up both the attraction of Islam for traditional rulers, and the possible dangers:

> Then the Sultan of the Tunjur gave him his daughter to wed, and said 'pray God for me'.
>
> But he prayed on his own behalf, and so the Sultan died, but the 'Sherifs' rule Wadai till now...[1]

It seems that, in fact, 'Abd al-Karīm had not married the daughter of Dāwūd, the Tunjur king in Wadai, though he may have wished to do so. According to one account, when Dāwūd attempted to arrest 'Abd al-Karīm for this, 'Abd al-Karīm summoned his Arab allies, bound to him by marriages between their chiefs and the daughters of his family, and his friends among the local black population. He deceived Dāwūd about the size of his army by having the Arabs tie branches to their camels' tails, to increase the dust, and defeated him.

These developments in the centre of Wadai were paralleled by corresponding events nearby. Abdullay Boru, founder of the ruling dynasty of the Kobe Zaghawa, also introduced Islam about the beginning of the seventeenth century. He came from the east – his father is said to have been a cleric, but he had died on the way – and took the supreme authority from the Mira, the previous ruling group. He did not however altogether displace these, reserving for their chief the highest official appointment under the ruler in the new state, and giving his own daughter to one of the Mira – a reversal of the usual pattern in which the newcomer marries, or tries to marry, a local princess.

Abdullay Boru among the Kobe Zaghawa is not remembered as a converter, nor as a builder; on the contrary, it may have been his prowess as a hunter that first won him acceptance. 'Abd al-Karīm, on the other hand, seems to have stood at the turning point between nomadic and settled. Various incidents point to continuing pastoralism: the device of the camels' tails, for many of his Arab allies were nomads, and the fact that the site of Wara, which was to become his capital, was discovered in the search for calves which had strayed while grazing.

[1] Palmer, *Sudanese memoirs*, II, 32.

Yet Wara, where ʿAbd al-Karīm assembled his Muslim community, speedily became a substantial town, and the transfer of the capital to Abeche occurred only in the mid-nineteenth century. Imposing ruins of the brick-built royal palace and mosque at Wara still remain, but the age of these is uncertain, some attributing them mainly to ʿAbd al-Karīm's son, others dating them much later. There is also at Wara a cemetery with the tombs of eleven sultans. The guardians of the tombs still live nearby, and each year the ruler must go there to sacrifice animals just before the rainy season. Nearby is the sacred mount Tireya, or Thurayya, where the enthronement ceremonies for a new sultan took place, mingling pagan traditions with newer Muslim procedures – the last such installation at the mountain was in 1901.

Thus, early in the seventeenth century – 1611 and 1635 are both given as dates for ʿAbd al-Karīm's accession – the state of Wadai was born, as new immigrants and a more vigorous expression of Islam combined with the local heritage. The contribution of the foreign invader, or visitor, in the process of state formation is discussed elsewhere (see volume 3, chapter 5). But, in view of the sharp criticism to which 'the Hamitic hypothesis' in various forms has been recently exposed, it is worth underlining the obvious importance attached, in the Wadai context, to Arab and Islamic origins, as foundations for the legitimacy of government, long before anthropologists perceived, or invented, the necessity of an Hamitic intervention, or European colonialists fancied themselves as the modern embodiment of the *héros civilisateur* – and still longer, of course, before modern historians began to chafe at all such foreign derivations.

The process of consolidation was complex, both because of disputed successions, and because of the diversity of the local people: two informants, in the mid-nineteenth century, trying to number the languages of Wadai on a rosary, came near to forty, a large number even if some were related dialects. The history of Wadai during the period is dominated by the desire to escape from the suzerainty, nominal though it often was, of Darfur, where with the success of Sulaymān Solong a similar state had emerged at about the same time. About the end of the seventeenth century, an attack on Darfur by the sultan of Wadai, who wished to deny the right of Darfur to levy tribute upon Wadai, was thrown back. One report says that the sultan of Darfur, Aḥmad Bukar, had spent two years in training his army and equipping it with firearms from Egypt. Another attributes no such resolution to him, saying on the contrary that when the sultan of Wadai insolently pretended that his invasion was part of his pilgrimage, Aḥmad Bukar sent him one of his own daughters as wife for the long road: but when it finally came to fighting Wadai was defeated nonetheless. Muḥammad Joda, ruler of Wadai in the second half of the eighteenth century, was more successful, the people of Darfur taking the opportunity of an expedition against Wadai to abandon an unpopular ruler to defeat and, it seems, death. Joda's influence extended as far as Kanem, supplanting Bornu's authority there. Sometimes Wadai paid tribute both to Bornu and to Darfur. The sixth ruler of Kobe, the Zaghawa chieftaincy already mentioned, in the line of Abdullay Boru was the first to take the title sultan, conferred on him by the ruler of Darfur, who gave him a drum of red copper to replace the older wooden drum in his regalia. Darfur continued to nominate the Kobe sultans throughout the period.

The unfortunate fate of Sultan Kharīf of Wadai, in the later seventeenth century, illustrates the survival of pre-Islamic attitudes towards the king. Deserted by his troops, whom he had sought to keep on campaign when agricultural duties called them home, he was killed by the forces of Dar Tama, east of Wadai, and was buried far from home (see above, p. 75). His brother succeeded, but for seven years Wadai was stricken with drought and famine, until at last the father and grandfather of the hapless successor appeared to him in a dream, advising him to send for his brother's body and to bring it home. The corpse was found, perfectly preserved, and was carried back with respect: as it crossed the border, the wind began, and when it was reburied with full honours, rain fell. Not even seed corn was left in Wadai, but an ant miraculously carried sufficient from Tama – perhaps another reflection of the seldom remarked, but possibly often important, function of the southern lands as breadbasket of the Sudan countries.

Foreign links were developing in other directions. There is evidence of clerics from the Funj kingdom of Sennar teaching in Wadai – one ill-fated man was murdered there by his own concubines – and of pupils going from Wadai to study on the Nile. Some clerics were also involved in trade with Wadai. Religious links westwards continued, although, with the striking exception of 'Abd al-Karīm's own experience at the very beginning, they do not seem to have become of much significance until the nineteenth century. A missionary in far-away Freetown glimpsed something of this mobility, talking with the only Wadai ex-slave in the city – his very presence there a remarkable instance of mobility of another kind. This man, Yakuba, or John Davis, had been born in Wadai; he then went to school in Darfur for three years, spent a month in Kordofan, and finally went on to Zayla in the Fezzan for nine years. Contacts directly northwards seem also to be chiefly a feature of the nineteenth century, although it appears that Bagirmi, still more isolated than Wadai as far as an outlet to the Sahara was concerned, had been sending presents – cloth, slaves, and eunuchs – every three years, to Mecca via Wadai, from the third quarter of the eighteenth century. One desert route swung west to join the great Fezzan-Tripoli road; attempts to open an alternative road were made vigorously in the nineteenth century, and were eventually successful, though at considerable cost.

There were certainly commercial elements interwoven with the development of Wadai's foreign links, and copper may well have played an important part. The Kano market, in the mid-nineteenth century, was partly supplied by copper from mines south of Darfur, carried west by traders from Wadai. The references, already made, to copper drums may also point to the significance of this trade.

'Abd al-Karīm Sabun, whose brief but memorable reign fell within the first two decades of the nineteenth century, was introduced early in this chapter as a figure comparable to Aloma. Both were intensely interested in trans-Saharan links: it was Sabun's own tenacity which led to the opening of a direct, independent road to Benghazi – his first exploratory caravan, which some say included his mother as an intending pilgrim, perished utterly. Both welcomed immigrant clerics: Sabun assigned, for instance, the revenues of five Kashemereh villages – a docile people in well-watered land – to the father of al-Tūnusī, whose account has been cited several times. Both followed similar tactics in war. Sabun justified his attack on Bagirmi in the name of religion: he tried to establish his influence over Bagirmi by installing a puppet ruler (though of the royal house), and he imposed tribute, according to one account 500 slaves, 30 young girl slaves, 30 horses and 1,000 robes, to be paid every third year. Religious justification, puppet or client rulers, and tribute were all features of Aloma's reign. Both men may have been builders, for some believe that Sabun built the great mosque at Wara. Both were concerned with the regulation of commerce, weights and measures, and so forth. Both met violent deaths, Aloma on campaign, Sabun, so it is supposed, alone in pursuit of two thieves on the highway. Both were certainly men of bloodshed and war, but perhaps Sabun died a martyr for that second, more peaceful, cause which Ibn Fartuwa said was, equally with fighting, a main endeavour of Aloma – to make the roads safe.

CHAPTER 3

NORTH-WEST AFRICA: FROM THE MAGHRIB TO THE FRINGES OF THE FOREST*

The seventeenth and eighteenth centuries in the northern belt of West Africa may be viewed as a period of transition between the collapse of Songhay, the last of the great western Sudanic empires, and the rise of the revivalist militant Islamic movements which shaped the western Sudan in the nineteenth century, prior to the colonial occupation.

The period under survey opened with the Moroccan conquest of Timbuktu, and relations between Morocco and the Sudan remained a principal theme throughout. The history of the middle Niger valley evolved around the unsuccessful attempt of the *arma*, heirs to the Moroccan conquerors, to build an effective government in place of the political structure of the Sudanic empires. All the great empires in the Sudan achieved political supremacy through military conquest, and each had its own ethnic group – Soninke, Malinke or Songhay – as its nucleus. In these cases, however, conquest and domination were mitigated by social and cultural values common to all peoples of the western Sudan. People moved quite freely across ethnic boundaries to be integrated into parallel strata of society. The pashalik of Timbuktu, on the other hand, was based on an unmitigated conquest by an alien group, imbued with a sense of superiority of the white over the black. In the Sudanic empires there was much in common between the local forms of socio-political organization and the administration of the central government. There was also a continuity from one empire to its successor. There was little in common between the organization of the military ruling caste of the *arma* and that of the conquered population, and there was little continuity from the former imperial structures. Only Islam was common to the *arma* and some sectors of the local population, and the *'ulamā'* were important in mediating between the authorities and local rulers.

* Grants from the Central Research Fund and the Research Committee of the Faculty of Humanities at the Hebrew University of Jerusalem helped in meeting expenses incurred at different stages of the research and writing of this chapter. The last draft has been written at St John's College, Cambridge. The author is grateful to the Master and Fellows of the College for electing him to an Overseas Fellowship in 1972–3.

Still, there was a strong element of alienation, which resulted in an almost permanent state of unrest, of revolt and subsequent brutal subjugation. Indeed, even under the Sudanic empires one could detect the persistence of ethnic self-assertion, which became evident whenever the central government weakened, as centrifugal forces accelerated the process of disintegration. Violent rebellions and their suppression seem to have been rare in the Sudanic empires, perhaps because imperial rule was bearable and acquired a certain legitimacy. The *arma*, on the other hand, faced revolts and resistance even when they had an unqualified military superiority and revolts were doomed to fail. Except for some *'ulamā'*, who acknowledged the caliphate of the Moroccan sultan, there was no basis for the legitimacy of the *arma*'s rule.

In modern African historiography the emergence of empires and the enlargement of the scale of political organization are regarded as among the greatest achievements of African history. The seventeenth and eighteenth centuries in the western Sudan, between the collapse of Songhay and the rise of the Islamic states, are viewed as an unfortunate period of political fragmentation. Yet, the disintegration of the empires brought independence to small nations, to the previously subjugated ethnic groups. New identities emerged, and the historical traditions of many peoples in the western Sudan go back to the seventeenth century. Their traditions about previous periods merge into the history of the successive empires, whose ruling dynasties dominated the traditional literature.

Travellers, both Africans and Europeans, found more security in territories under some effective central authority. The disintegration of imperial authority reduced the size of such secure territories in the western Sudan, as the successor states were smaller and their peripheries were the scene of wars and raids. Yet, farther to the south in the savanna, beyond the limits of the old empires, the process of state building added security to new lands. Still, wars and destruction accompanied the emergence of states and their expansion.

Warriors dominated the society, and they lived on booty which consisted mainly of slaves. Slaves were recruited to join the ranks of the warriors, others were employed in agricultural production. With the growing demand for slaves by the Europeans on the coast, the eighteenth century saw caravans of slaves directed towards the Atlantic. Wars became an economic enterprise. Slaves were exchanged in part for firearms, but throughout the period under survey these weapons were rather restricted in the savanna. The metallurgical technology was not yet developed enough for producing firearms or even for repairs. Africans closer to the coast did not encourage the passing of firearms to the interior, and even the Muslim Dyula traders, who handled much of the trade, did not distribute firearms freely. Indeed, it seems that in the eighteenth century Muslims had an advantage over other peoples of the northern interior by having access to firearms.

Recourse to arms by Muslims and the growth of Islamic militancy with the religious revolutions in the Futas, marked a significant departure from the previous dichotomy between warriors who held political authority and Muslims who were associated with the peaceful pursuit of trade. The old pattern, however, survived throughout the seventeenth and eighteenth centuries over most of the interior. The Muslims who had lost the patronage of the emperors of the great empires lived under the auspices of lesser chiefs. But, what Islam had lost in intensity it gained in extension. By the seventeenth century Muslim traders reached the fringes of the forest in growing numbers, and contributed to the integration of the whole open country of the Sahel and the savanna into one system. The interplay of trade, state-building, and Islam, which in the preceding period had shaped the history of the northern belt of the Sudan, now extended as far as the forest.

The trans-Saharan trade declined but did not stop. Saharan salt continued to attract much of the gold of the upper Niger and the upper Senegal. It seems that only a fraction of the gold from these regions reached the Europeans in the Senegambia, who were more successful in obtaining slaves. But, from the Akan forest of the south much of the gold ceased to flow north and reached the Europeans on the Gold Coast. This change was associated with the rise of Asante, which used its economic resources and military prowess to dominate the immediate savanna hinterland. On the upper Guinea coast, on the other hand, the European factories stimulated a vigorous trade, and with no comparable power to the Akan separating them from the coast, the Dyula and other Mande traders, reached the seaboard, widened their commercial system and diversified their trade. From Algeria and Morocco, along the Atlantic coast of Africa, the European presence encouraged the beginning of a reorientation of North-West Africa, but the main developments in these centuries depended on internal interactions across the vast area from Morocco to the forest.

THE MAGHRIB

For centuries the central Maghrib, the modern Algeria, had been disputed and divided between the more powerful centres of Ifrīqiya (Tunisia) and Morocco. In the sixteenth century Algeria, together with Tunisia, became part of the Ottoman empire, and thus was separated from Morocco, which remained an independent sultanate. Algeria, however, was a remote province of the Ottomans. The Porte was unable to exert direct influence, and by the seventeenth century its representative, the pasha, was only a figurehead. Real power was contested between the *ojaq*, the Ottoman militia or Janissaries originally dispatched from Turkey, and the *taifa*, the guild of corsair captains, many of whom were Christian renegades. The city of Algiers throve on privateering, a sequel to the holy war in the Mediterranean. Christian captives were sold as slaves or held for ransom; goods from the booty were re-exported to Europe along with some agricultural products of the land. In the seventeenth century, Algiers was a prosperous city with a heterogeneous population of about 100,000 inhabitants.

In the eighteenth century the corsairs' fleet declined. Instead of seeking protection for their merchant ships by treaties, the major European powers sent marine expeditions. Ships were escorted and European navies bombarded Algiers. The corsairs became severely confined and, as this source of income was gradually drying up, trade also declined. In the second half of the century the city of Algiers was poverty stricken and lost the greater part of its population.

From 1587 onwards pashas were sent from Istanbul as governors for a period of three years. They therefore had no local basis of power and yielded to the pressure of the *ojaq* and the *taifa*. The administration was conducted by the council (Divan) of the *ojaq* under the leadership of the *agha*. In 1659 the *agha* became the governor, leaving the pasha a few ceremonial functions only. But in 1671 the corsairs, the *ojaq*'s rivals, appointed a governor of their own choice with the title of dey. Installed, deposed, and assassinated by corsairs and the militia, the deys ruled over Algiers until the French conquest in 1830. Autocrats living under a constant threat of death, nearly all of them displayed much ferocity. They remained aliens to the country and exploited it as long as they held power.

Under the dey were the beys, as governors of the three provinces. Provided they delivered the tax to Algiers, the beys were independent rulers. But in the government of the hinterland they had to collaborate with the shaykhs, leaders of the local population, many of whom were marabouts, holy men who combined religious prestige with economic and political power. The authority of the Turks was effective over no more than one sixth of present-day Algeria. The rest of the country was virtually independent. By the second half of the eighteenth century, the military power of the Turks in Algeria had declined, and whatever semblance of authority they maintained was achieved by diplomacy rather than by force. As the dey could not rely on the economic resources of the country, he was driven to continue privateering in spite of the growing power of the European navies in the Mediterranean, thus precipitating the fatal collision with Europe and the French conquest of 1830.

For years the Europeans had to compromise in consenting to trade with Algeria and Morocco while their ships were being threatened by the corsairs. The Muslim authorities, and in particular the sultan of Morocco, had also to compromise in consenting to maintain any commercial relations at all with the infidels. Relations with the Europeans, who still occupied some strategic ports, was an important issue in Moroccan politics. Marabouts in opposition to the sultan could denounce a sultan as a traitor for cultivating relations with Europeans. On the other hand, the sultan's power was weakened because local rulers, including marabouts, often traded on their own with the Europeans in order to obtain firearms. Moroccan sultans could also exploit conflicts among the Europeans to reach agreements with certain powers on better terms.

By the beginning of the seventeenth century, English merchants were predominant on the Moroccan coast. The principal staple exchange was English cloth for Moroccan sugar, but English firearms were also exchanged for Moroccan saltpetre, which was necessary for the production of gunpowder. The sultan Mawlāy Aḥmad al-Manṣūr (1578–1603) made the trade in sugar and saltpetre a state monopoly. During the period of anarchy which followed his death, the supply of these commodities diminished considerably. Sale, the centre of Moroccan piracy, developed as an important centre in the first half of the seventeenth century, Dutch traders playing a significant role.

With the consolidation of the central authority under Mawlāy Ismāʿīl (1672–1727), the sultan took firm control over piracy, which he turned into a state enterprise, and over trade, which he endeavoured to confine to a few ports only. Though the sultan himself derived great benefits from piracy, he decided to reduce the corsairs' activities in view of the growth of European maritime power. Mawlāy Ismā'īl's grandson, Sīdī Muḥammad (1757–90), developed Mogador in southern Morocco as the principal port for external trade, where foreign consuls and commercial representatives stayed. In this way he secured a regular levy of customs and limited the intervention of Europeans in Moroccan affairs. Like other great sultans – Mawlāy Aḥmad al-Manṣūr and Mawlāy Ismā'īl – Sīdī Muḥammad employed external trade with Europeans not only as a source of income but also as a tool to strengthen central authority.

During the seventeenth and eighteenth centuries Morocco consisted of two realms: the *bilād al-makhzin*, the land effectively controlled by the central authority and, under the influence of the towns, integrated into the social and economic texture of the sultanate, and, secondly, the *bilād al-sibā*, the lands which were in practice independent, but in theory part of the sultan's dominions temporarily in secession. There were no fixed boundaries between the two; a stronger ruler extended the frontiers of the *bilād al-makhzin*, while at other periods the *bilād al-sibā* covered large parts of Morocco and reached the outskirts of the principal towns.

Even the more successful sultans were unable to solve some of the basic structural problems of Morocco, such as integrating the Arab tribes of the plains and the Berber tribes of the mountains into the imperial system. Another perennial problem was the control of the *zawāyā* (centres of Sufi brotherhoods), whose power under the leadership of marabouts had increased in the course of the holy wars against European aggression on the Moroccan coast in the fifteenth and sixteenth centuries. Through their religious prestige, the marabouts channelled discontent among the Berbers to achieve popular leadership and political power. The decline of the central authority was both the cause and the result of the periodical eruption of these centrifugal forces.

Mawlāy Aḥmad al-Manṣūr ascended the throne in 1578, the day after the Moroccans had scored a decisive victory over the Portuguese at the battle of Alcazar (al-Qaṣar al-Kabīr), which relieved Morocco of the Christian pressure. Ottoman pressure was also eased from 1587 onwards after the ambitious *beylerbeyi* had been replaced, as rulers of Ottoman Algeria, by pashas dispatched from Istanbul for a period of three years each. Al-Manṣūr inherited an army, which had already adopted firearms and was modelled after the Ottoman army. He strengthened this army and employed it to overcome opposition to his rule in Morocco. But this was an expensive undertaking, as was the lavish maintenance of a court modelled after that of the ʿAbbasid caliphs in Baghdad. Al-Manṣūr needed a new source of income, which he hoped to procure in the south. In 1591 he overruled a reluctant council and embarked upon the conquest of the Sudan.

At first large quantities of gold from the Sudan reached the royal treasury, and the Moroccan dinars, made of pure gold and of proper weight, were highly valued in Europe. The new wealth, the victory over the Portuguese, and grand receptions held for European embassies created the impression that the Sharifian sultan was among the greatest of Muslim monarchs.

At home, Mawlāy Aḥmad spent some of this wealth in constructing forts, and in organizing an army equipped with modern European arms. His reign was exceptional in its relative peace, security and prosperity. He divided Morocco into administrative provinces and appointed his sons as governors. This, however, gave them a local basis of power in disputing the succession after Mawlāy Aḥmad's death in 1603. The kingdom split into two, with Marrakesh and Fez as rival capitals, in alliance with Morocco's traditional enemies, the Ottomans and the Spaniards. Continuous warfare introduced a period of anarchy, one of the darkest in Moroccan history. Because of anarchy in Morocco and insecurity on the Saharan routes, the flow of gold from the Sudan diminished. The pashas in Timbuktu became virtually independent, or in the terms of the Moroccan imperial system, became part of the *bilād al-sibā*. As members of the Saʿdid dynasty were fighting each other, other centrifugal forces were released. There was a new upsurge of maraboutism, inspired by holy men, leaders of religious brotherhoods, who mobilized the insurgency of the Berbers in the Atlas and of the Arab nomads. The Saʿdids, who were reduced to rulers of local importance around Marrakesh, forfeited their right to rule as they had failed to provide effective authority and security. They were challenged by regional and factional leaders, whose basis of power was, however, too narrow to succeed in the reunification of Morocco. This was only achieved in the 1660s by Mawlāy al-Rashīd, the real founder of the ʿAlawid dynasty, the second Sharifian dynasty of Morocco.

The ʿAlawids began their struggle for hegemony as yet another regional faction, based on the oases of Tafilelt. There they had at first little military success against the Dala'iyya, the Berber marabouts of the Atlas. Driven away from Tafilelt, al-Rashīd, a descendant of the Prophet, won the allegiance of the Arabs in north-eastern Morocco in 1664. Backed by Arab military power, al-Rashīd entered Fez in 1666, where he contracted an alliance with the *'ulamā'*, representatives of Islamic orthodoxy. The latter became identified with the cause of the *makhzin* (central authority) against local marabouts, who remained in latent or overt opposition. In 1668, Mawlāy al-Rashīd defeated the Dala'iyya of the Atlas and took over Marrakesh. For the rest of his reign, Mawlāy al-Rashīd was busy in the reconquest of different regions in Morocco. His brother and successor Mawlāy Ismā'īl (1672–1727) still had to spend the early part of his reign in suppressing revolts. In a rather brutal way he enforced law and order, and so provided his country with peace, security and some economic prosperity.

Mawlāy Ismā'īl depended on the Arab tribes who had brought the dynasty to power. He was, therefore, exposed to the pressure of their factional interests and risked the alienation of other groups of the population. He turned to the formation of an élite corps, whose members had no roots in the local population. He initiated a large-scale operation to reassemble black slaves, men and women, scattered all over the country. He bought slaves from their masters, and even reduced to bondage black residents in Morocco who had already been freed. They were all confirmed as the sultan's slaves. The sultan wanted these slaves to be personally attached to him by religious ties, and made them swear allegiance on al-Bukhārī's *Ṣaḥīḥ*, a collection of the Prophet's traditions, hence their name *'abīd al-Bukhārī*.

Black slaves had been in the service of the rulers of the Maghrib for centuries. Mawlāy Ismā'īl's originality lay in the elaborate organization of a distinct corps of black slaves. The *'abīd* were assembled in a new town of their own, Mashra' al-Raml, where they had to be ready at the sultan's call. Their children, boys and girls, were taken to the king's palace in Meknes at the age of ten. The boys entered a five-year period of training, and moved from apprenticeship as artisans to the art of horsemanship, and then to the use of spears and firearms. The girls were taught domestic work in the palace. After five years, the boys were assigned to regiments and were given wives from among the girl slaves. These marriages were registered and the children born were taken at the age of ten into the sultan's service. The first intake of children born to *'abīd* were brought from Mashra' al-Raml to the sultan's palace in Meknes in 1688/9.

This was not, however, the only source of black slaves: Ismā'īl also obtained slaves directly from the Sahara and the Sudan. In 1678 he raided as far as Shinqit, and brought back 2,000 black slaves, whom he sent to Mashra' al-Raml. There are other reports of raids to the Sahara and the Sudan at that time. The need to maintain a supply of black slaves for his army may well explain Mawlāy Ismāʿīl's interest in the affairs of the southern Sahara and the Sudan.

Towards the end of Mawlāy Ismāʿīl's reign, according to a register seen by al-Zayyānī (1734/5–1833), there were 150,000 *ʿabīd* (including women and children); 70,000 lived in Mashraʿ al-Raml, 25,000 in Meknes and the rest in forts (*qaṣabas*) that the sultan had built close to rebellious regions, along the main routes and near the principal towns.[1] After the death of Mawlāy Ismāʿīl in 1727, many of the *ʿabīd* left the *qaṣabas* and concentrated in Meknes to become the undisputed masters of the capital. As 'Pretorian guards', the *ʿabīd* contributed to political instability, and supported a candidate who had promised them large salaries, only to abandon him when another candidate offered a higher prize. Mawlāy ʿAbdallāh, son of Mawlāy Ismāʿīl, was installed and deposed by the *ʿabīd* four times.

Peace and stability were restored with the accession of Sīdī Muḥammad (1759–90), son of Mawlāy ʿAbdallāh and grandson of Mawlāy Ismāʿīl. Aware of the destructive role of the *ʿabīd*, he restored the Arab *jish*, troops who were exempted from the payment of tax in return for military service. He also came to terms with the Berbers who had invaded the plains during the preceding anarchy. The power of the *ʿabīd* declined, they abandoned their warlike vocation to become farmers and labourers. Mashraʿ al-Raml was deserted, and pillaged by neighbouring tribes. At the end of the eighteenth century a British resident noted 'the ruins of a town built by Muley Ismael for his black troops'.[2]

Significantly, the two great rulers of the Sharifian dynasties, Mawlāy Aḥmad al-Manṣūr the Saʿdī and Mawlāy Ismāʿīl the ʿAlawī, were both passionately interested in the Sahara and the Sudan. Both imported gold and slaves from the Sudan. But, whereas Mawlāy Aḥmad was closely associated with the quest for gold, Mawlāy Ismāʿīl was concerned mainly with slaves. Their exploits illustrate the economic and political significance of trans-Saharan contacts for Morocco.

Following the conquest of the kingdoms of the Sudan, Mawlāy Aḥmad received so much gold dust that envious men were all troubled and observers absolutely stupefied. So from then on al-Manṣūr paid his officials in pure gold and in dinars of proper weight only. At the gate of his palace 1700 smiths

[1] al-Zayyānī, *al-Turjmān al-muʿrib ʿan duwal al-mashriq waʾl-maghrib*, pp. 15–17, 22. French tr. by O. Houdas, *Le Maroc de 1631 à 1812* (Paris, 1886), 29–32, 42.

[2] J. G. Jackson, *An account of the empire of Marocco* (London, 1814), 36.

were daily engaged in striking dinars... This superabundance of gold earned him the honorific al-Dhahabī, 'the Golden'.[1]

This account by al-Ifrānī, written over a century after Mawlāy Aḥmad's reign, is broadly confirmed by contemporary European eyewitnesses. Moroccan officials who returned from the Sudan brought many camel loads of gold with them. An English merchant, resident in Marrakesh, commented on the arrival of thirty mules laden with gold in 1594: 'The king of Morocco is like to be the greatest prince in the world for money, if he keeps this country [the Sudan].'[2] Yet, in 1638 another English observer remarked: 'The ancient supply [of gold] from Gago [Gao] which was brought in by cafells [caravans] in Ahmad's days, grandfather of this king, is now lost by the troubles of the state.'[3]

Anarchy in Morocco contributed to the decline in the supply of gold. The trade with the Sudan was then controlled by rivals of the Sa'dids who ruled over the Sus and Tafilelt. Indeed, once order had been restored under Mawlāy Ismā'īl, who regained authority over the gates to the Saharan trade routes, the supply of gold was renewed:

It is reported that Muley Ismael was so rich in gold that the bolts of the gates of his palaces and his kitchen utensils were of pure gold... Caravans were going continually from Timbuctoo... travelling across the desert was then as safe as it is now [1820] in the plains of Morocco or on the roads in England.[4]

The expansion of the Arab nomads, the Ḥassān, from southern Morocco into the western Sahara, and as far as the Senegal river, created another link between Morocco and the Sudan. The Moroccan sultan may have claimed sovereignty over these Arab nomads, and when, in 1678, Mawlāy Ismā'īl led an expedition across the Sus into the Sahara, he was extending the frontiers of the *bilād al-makhzin*: 'missions of Arabs of the *qiblah* [South] came to offer him their submission'.[5] In 1719–20 'Alī Shandora, *amīr* of the Trarza Moors, renewed allegiance to Mawlāy Ismā'īl and was supported with Moroccan troops in the war against his rivals the Brakna (see p. 222).

The presence of Moroccan troops, known as 'Ormans', in the

[1] al-Ifrānī, *Nuzhat al-hādī bi-akhbār mulūk al-qarn al-ḥādī* (Paris, 1888), p. 95/tr. 167.

[2] H. de Castries, *Les sources inédites de l'histoire du Maroc* (Paris, 1905–36), 1st ser., pt. III, bk. 2, p. 84. Laurence Madoc to Anthony Dassel, Marrakesh, 1 August 1594.

[3] H. de Castries, *Les sources inédites*, 1st ser., pt. III, bk. 32, 452. Journal of G. Carteret, 30 April–9 November 1638.

[4] J. G. Jackson, *An account of Timbuctoo and Hausa* (London, 1820), 482.

[5] al-Zayyānī, *al-Turjmān*, p. 17/tr. 31.

southern Sahara and in the Senegal valley was attested by French contemporary sources after 1718. They intervened in the internal affairs of the Futa Toro, by installing and deposing rival *satigis*. They raided along the Senegal river from Walo to Galam, disturbed traffic on the river, and clashed with the French. Contemporary French records mention as many as twelve or fifteen thousand 'Ormans'. They were under the command of *qā'ids*, some of whom were renegades, like the one called Françoine.

These Moroccan troops may also have moved from Galam eastwards, because in 1741–2 it was recorded in *Tadhkirat al-Nisyān* that '*al-rumāt* of Mawlāy Ismā'īl's expedition' were involved in fighting with Arabs and Tuareg west of Timbuktu.[1] In Morocco, these operations of the 'Ormans' were regarded as an extension of the empire:

> Mawlāy Ismā'īl conquered the fringes of the Sudan, and reached beyond the Nile [the Senegal]. His authority extended over Sudanese peoples. In this respect he achieved even more than the sultan Abu'l-'Abbās Aḥmad al-Dhahabī al-Manṣūr or any one before him.[2]

Indeed, while Mawlāy Aḥmad conquered a section of the Niger bend only, troops of Mawlāy Ismā'īl were held to have added territories on the lower and middle Senegal river. It was also assumed that at the beginning of the eighteenth century the sovereignty of the Moroccan sultan was still recognized on the Niger bend. The history of the pashalik of Timbuktu, based on the contemporary *ta'rīkhs*, offers, however, a southern view of these trans-Saharan contacts.

THE PASHALIK OF TIMBUKTU

In 1591 Mawlāy Aḥmad al-Manṣūr ordered an élite force, about 5,000 strong, composed mainly of Andalusians (Muslim refugees from Spain) and renegades (Christians who had converted to Islam in captivity) to cross the desert. Only about half of them reached the Niger in March 1591, but these were enough to defeat the Songhay army at Tondibi because of their superiority in firearms.

The pasha Jūdār (or Jawdār), commander of the Moroccan force, believed that the occupation was merely temporary, saying: 'We will stay here until we get the order of the sultan to come back to him.'[3]

[1] *Tadhkirat al-Nisyān fī akhbār mulūk al-Sūdān*, ed. and tr. by O. Houdas (Paris, 1913–14), p. 74/tr. 119.

[2] al-Ifrānī, *Nuzhat al-hādī*, p. 305/tr. 505.

[3] *Ta'rīkh al-Fattāsh*, ed. and tr. by O. Houdas and M. Delafosse (Paris, 1913–14), p. 156/tr. 278.

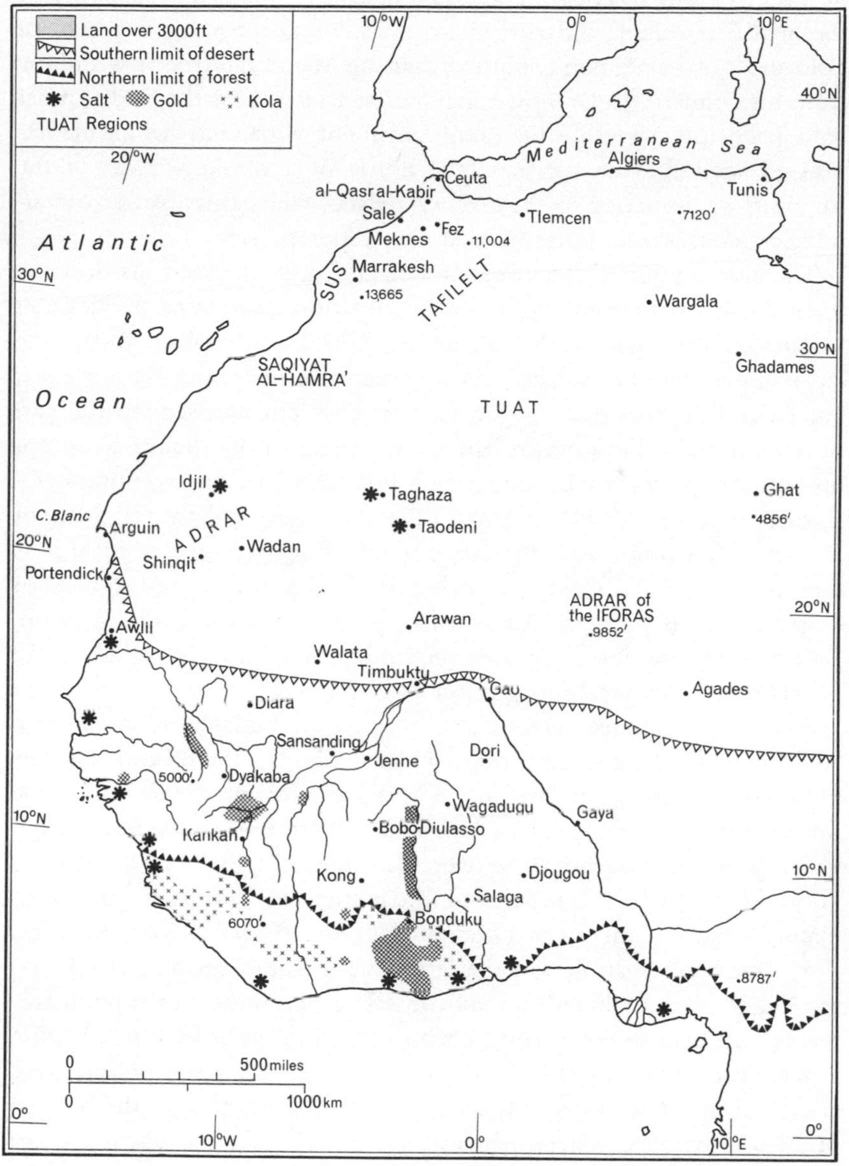

4 North Africa and the Sahara

Jūdār was then waiting for the sultan's reply to a message he had dispatched with the terms of peace which the defeated Askiya Isḥāq of Songhay had accepted. The *askiya* acknowledged the suzerainty of the Sharifian sultan, and agreed to pay a tribute of 100,000 pieces of gold and 1,000 slaves on condition that the Moroccan troops withdrew from his country. Jūdār's own inclination to evacuate the Sudan must have been influenced by his disappointment with Gao, which he expressed with the remark that 'the home of a donkey-driver in the Maghrib was superior to the *askiya*'s palace'.[1] His army had also contracted diseases and Jūdār himself was reported sick.

The sultan rejected the *askiya*'s offer and demonstrated his decision to establish a permanent rule over the Sudan by dismissing the hesitant Jūdār. To the pasha Maḥmūd, whom he sent to replace Jūdār, the sultan gave definite instructions to crush the resistance of Songhay, and his political designs may be seen from a letter he sent to the *qādī* of Timbuktu 'calling him to urge the people of Timbuktu to accept his authority and to be integrated into the Muslim community'.[2] Earlier, in 1582, Mawlāy Aḥmad offered military aid to Mai Idrīs of Bornu on condition that the latter would swear allegiance to him as *amīr al-mu'minin*.[3] In 1588 he based his claim to the salt mines of Taghaza on his prerogatives as *imām*, guardian of the lands of Islam. By extending his authority over the Sudan, Mawlāy Aḥmad advanced his claim for universal recognition as caliph.

So, the Moroccans were there to stay in the Sudan, and during the last decade of the sixteenth century, according to the official register, 23,000 men – among the best of the Moroccan troops – were sent to the Sudan. Only 500 returned to Morocco.[4] In the first expedition renegades were prominent; these were Europeans who became Muslim voluntarily or under compulsion. Jūdār himself, four of the ten commanders (*qā'ids*) and over 1,000 of the élite troops were renegades. For some time Spanish was the language of the Moroccan troops on the Niger. The auxiliary forces of the first expedition and the reinforcements sent later to the Sudan were mostly Moroccans by birth. Within a generation the renegades had lost their separate identity and were absorbed in the factions of the army divided according to the regions of Morocco: Fez, Marrakesh and Haha. The Arabic chronicles of

[1] al-Sa'dī, *Ta'rīkh al-Sūdān*, ed. and tr. by O. Houdas (Paris, 1898–1900), p. 141/tr. 221.

[2] al-Ifrānī, *Nuzhat al-hādī*, p. 93/tr. 164.

[3] al-Fishtālī, *Manāhil al-ṣafā*, ed. A. Ganun (Rabat, 1964), 61–3.

[4] *T. al-Sūdān*, p. 191/tr. 291.

Timbuktu refer to the Moroccans in the Sudan as *rumāt*, that is fusiliers. They became known as *arma* by their African neighbours.

The Moroccan expedition imposed a military government over the occupied country. The pasha, commander of the army, was also the governor, but the treasury was entrusted to the *amīn*, who was responsible in person to the sultan. The pasha was instructed not to interfere with the treasury. When a pasha in 1606 made one of his lieutenants *amīn*, this appointment was overruled by the sultan, who immediately dispatched a new *amīn* from Marrakesh. By keeping the pasha and the *amīn* independent of each other, the sultan hoped to secure better control over his possessions. It was, indeed the *amīn* who in 1595 sent a report to the sultan about the misconduct of the pasha, his violence and his interference with gold which was due to the sovereign. The sultan sent a new pasha and ordered the execution of the former.

Pashas sent from Morocco, however, faced growing opposition from the troops who had already been in the Sudan for several years. Local military commanders (*qā'ids*) had built up such power that no pasha could wield effective authority. In 1600 the pasha Sulaymān preferred to stay away from the fort (*qaṣaba*), as he suspected the loyalty of the army. A new pasha, sent four years later in 1604, found Timbuktu terrorized by one of the *qā'ids*. Unable to deal with the situation himself, he invited another *qā'id*, 'Alī al-Tlimsānī, who had already won distinction as a strong man, to restore order. At the pasha's request, the *qā'id* 'Alī al-Tlimsānī stayed in Timbuktu, to rule on behalf of the pasha. This diarchy continued until October 1612, when 'Alī deposed the pasha. As he made himself pasha, this *qā'id* established a precedent that pashas were no longer sent from Marrakesh, but were elected by the army in the Sudan.

The decline of remote control from Morocco was precipitated by the civil war following the death of Mawlāy Aḥmad in 1603. The army in the Sudan paid allegiance to the prince who was in possession of Marrakesh. Between 1608 and 1613, Marrakesh changed hands three times; the pasha, the army and the population could hardly keep pace with these changes in transferring their allegiance from one prince to the other. An attempt by the new pasha, 'Alī al-Tlimsānī, to assert his independence from Morocco by demanding allegiance (*bay'a*) to himself was rejected by the army. The pashas continued therefore to recognize the sultan as their sovereign and to seek official confirmation.

There was, however, a process of gradual disengagement; while the pashas became practically independent, *amīns* were still appointed by the sultan. In 1618, the sultan's envoy who came to confirm a pasha elected by the army was accompanied by a new *amīn*, Maḥmūd b. Abī Bakr, sent from Marrakesh to replace the former incumbent who had completed thirteen years in this office and had retired honourably. In 1629 the *amīn*, who had by then been eleven years in office, was accused of corruption and killed on the orders of Mawlāy 'Abd al-Malik b. Zaydān. The sultan confirmed his replacement by a local *qā'id*, who had been instrumental in bringing down the former *amīn*. This was the first *amīn* appointed from among the local *qā'ids*, for before they had all been sent from Marrakesh. He was also the last *amīn* appointed by the sultan. After his death in 1631, the next one was appointed by the pasha. Instead of acting as a check on the pasha, the *amīn* became his second in command in the administration. Finally, in 1638, the *amīn* was elected pasha by the army and no one was appointed to fill his office.

Though he lost all temporal power over the Sudan, the Moroccan sultan was still regarded in Timbuktu as the caliph, a remote source of legitimacy. Then 'in 1070 [1660 AD] the *khuṭba* [Friday Sermon] ceased to be pronounced in Takrūr [the Sudan] in the name of the descendants of Mawlāy Aḥmad al-Manṣūr'.[1] This has generally been accepted by modern historians as the final break between Morocco and the Sudan. But in fact it was the inevitable result of the total eclipse of the Sa'did dynasty, whose last sultan – Mawlāy al-'Abbās – had been killed a year earlier in 1659. An attempt to establish an independent sultanate in Timbuktu by one of the army officers failed because of opposition in the army. The *khuṭba* was pronounced in the name of the pasha, but probably for no more than a decade.

In 1666 Mawlāy al-Rashīd was proclaimed sultan in Fez as the first ruler of the new 'Alawī dynasty. In 1669 he conquered Marrakesh and two years later, in 1671, his envoy came to Timbuktu and 'the army pledged allegiance to Mawlāy al-Rashīd'.[2] In other words, as soon as a new Sharifian dynasty assumed authority in Morocco, the *arma* in Timbuktu renewed nominal and symbolic allegiance. It is very likely that once again the *khuṭba* was pronounced in the name of the Moroccan sultans. This indeed is what Matras, the English consul, reported in 1789:

> The Inhabitants [of Timbuktu] though they do not acknowledge the Sovereignty of the Emperor of Morocco, yet publicly pray for the Prosperity

[1] *Tadhkirat al-Nisyān*, p. 90/tr. 146.
[2] Ibid. p. 158/tr. 257–8.

of his reign, a Ceremony, which in this country as strongly ratifies Empire on the one Hand and Subjection on the other, as a Coronation in Europe.[1]

During the seventeenth and the first half of the eighteenth centuries the *arma* constituted a military society, of foreign origin, who ruled over the local population. Structurally, therefore, the *arma* in the western Sudan resembled the *mamlūks* in Egypt. But whereas the sons born to Mamluks by Egyptian women were excluded from the ruling military society, descendants of the Moroccan soldiers from Sudanese women succeeded their fathers into positions in the military élite; hence the development of factional interests among the *arma* in competition over power, authority and wealth.

As long as pashas were nominated by the sultan, some stability had been maintained. Between 1591 and 1617 there were eight pashas, or an average of over three years to a pasha. Between 1617 and 1660, nineteen pashas ruled, an average of over two years. Between 1660 and 1750, there were eighty-six pashas, or an average of only just over a year for each one. Among the latter, two pashas held office four times, eight ruled three times and sixteen were re-elected. As the years passed, internal rivalry increased and pashas were deposed more frequently. Only thirteen pashas died in office, the others were deposed. Eighteen sons and thirteen grandsons of pashas ruled, which indicates the emergence of an hereditary élite.

Pashas were deposed and elected by the soldiers, who expected benefits in return. A newly elected pasha often began his rule by exacting contributions of several thousand mithqals from the merchants of Timbuktu, part of which he distributed among the officers and soldiers, each according to his rank. When a pasha kept for himself the whole or even half of the gold collected, he was immediately deposed by the soldiers. After he had been elected and deposed three times, the pasha Manṣūr (1716–19) tried to free himself from dependence on the soldiers. He started by cutting off all their independent sources of income and reduced them to economic dependency. He promoted Sudanese slaves to high positions as provincial governors at the expense of the *arma*. He cultivated close relations with the Arab nomads in the vicinity of Timbuktu and preferred the society of the *'ulamā'* to that of the *arma*. Yet, his slaves who held authority became tyrants; they oppressed the people of Timbuktu, molested them in the markets and broke into their houses. No one was safe; even Sharifs (who claim descent from the Prophet) and *'ulamā'* were attacked. The *'ulamā'* as

[1] Quoted in R. Hallett (ed.), *Records of the African Association* (London, 1964), 81.

leaders of the civil population opposed the tyranny of the pasha's slaves, and joined hands with the *arma*. A jihad against the pasha and his slaves was proclaimed in the mosques and the *qā'id* led the troops on the pasha's residence. Once again the pashas became dependent on the *arma* troops. The people of Timbuktu gained little.

TIMBUKTU, JENNE AND MASSINA UNDER THE *ARMA*

The whole period of Moroccan rule was one of hardship for the people of Timbuktu. Following the defeat of the Songhay army in 1591, only the governor of Timbuktu and the *askiya*'s servants left the city. The people of Timbuktu, under the leadership of the *qāḍī* 'Umar b. Maḥmūd Aqīt, adopted a policy of passive submission and non-co-operation with the conquering army. When the pasha Jūdār came to Timbuktu towards the end of April 1591, he was given a cool reception. The pasha entered the city and decided to establish a fort (*qaṣaba*) in the quarter of the Ghadāmasī merchants, which was the most prosperous section of Timbuktu. People were forced out of their houses, which were pulled down. The *'ulamā'* and the merchants were called on to provide slaves for the construction of the fort, which was finished in August 1591, shortly before the arrival of Pasha Maḥmūd b. Zarqūn, to replace Jūdār.

In October 1591, when Maḥmūd and the bulk of his troops were fighting against Askiya Isḥāq down the Niger river in Dendi, the former Songhay governor of Timbuktu entered the city. Though he was immediately killed, his arrival caused great excitement, and the Moroccan garrison went about beating people. This harsh treatment ignited a mutiny. The Sharifs called on the *qāḍī* to lead the resistance; others advocated restraint. A message of the *qāḍī* calling for moderation was distorted as a call for a jihad and the fighting began. Seventy-seven Moroccan soldiers were killed and the *qā'id* was besieged in the fort until December 1591. The *qā'id* Mami was sent by the pasha to restore order and tactfully conciliated the population, who renewed their allegiance to the sultan.

The presence of the occupying force continued, however, to disturb life in that city of commerce and scholarship. The Moroccans failed to secure the support of the Sharifs, who led the popular discontent and dissension; two of them, descendants of the Sharif al-Ṣaqlī, were executed in public by the governor of Timbuktu in October 1592. If the Sharifs were the popular leaders, the *qāḍī* held moral authority over the inhabitants of Timbuktu. Under the *askiyas* of Songhay, the Muslim commercial and cosmopolitan city had been almost autonomous. After the Moroccan conquest, Timbuktu became the seat of a military government, and a conflict between the foreign oppressors and the independent proud *fuqahā'* became inevitable.

Towards the end of 1592, the *qāḍī* 'Umar sent a delegation of three '*ulamā'* to Marrakesh. Through the intercession of a local '*ālim*, they pleaded before the sultan. The latter sent two sets of contradictory instructions to the Sudan, which in practice left the crucial decisions to the man on the spot, the pasha Maḥmūd. In October 1593, when he returned to Timbuktu from an expedition to Dendi, Maḥmūd resorted to harsh disciplinarian measures. People had deposited their valuables in the houses of the *fuqahā'* under the illusion that these were immune and safe from the Moroccans' cupidity, but the pasha arrested the leading *fuqahā'* and let his soldiers pillage their houses. After five or six months in custody in the fort of Timbuktu, seventy *fuqahā'* were deported in chains to Marrakesh. Prominent among the exiles were members of the Aqīt family, among them the *qāḍī* 'Umar and the famous Aḥmad Bābā. The latter was a great scholar and a prolific writer whose fame reached the Maghrib. During his residence in Marrakesh, his lectures attracted many students. For two years the *fuqahā'* were under arrest and the old *qāḍī* 'Umar died in prison. After their release in May 1596, the *fuqahā'* were not allowed to return to Timbuktu. Aḥmad Bābā alone among them returned to his native town after almost twenty years in exile.

Following the exile of its leaders, 'Timbuktu became a body without a soul; its affairs were inverted...the lowest became masters of the nobles; faith was exchanged for material benefits...Islamic law and tradition passed away'.[1] The chronicler contrasts this with the prosperity of Timbuktu before the Moroccan conquest, when the town had been animated by learning and justice and was administered by the *qāḍī*. Timbuktu, however, recovered for a short period under such pashas as Manṣūr (1595–6) and Sulaymān (1600–4), who restored peace and security by punishing criminals and by keeping the Moroccan soldiers in their barracks after sunset. Scholarship flourished, provisions reached Timbuktu from all directions and prices were low. 'People almost forgot the [good old days of the] Songhay state.'[2]

The people of Timbuktu began to suffer again when the struggle for power among the *arma* intensified. Pashas succeeded each other rapidly,

[1] *T. al-Fattāsh*, p. 175/tr. 308. [2] Ibid. p. 181/tr. 316–17.

exacting heavy contributions in gold from the merchants. The people of Timbuktu became divided among the opposing factions of the *arma*. Some lost life and property during the hostilities, while others were punished after the victory of the rival faction. Feuds among the *arma* became more devastating in the eighteenth century when the Tuareg were invited in by the warring factions. The '*ulamā*' of Timbuktu sometimes acted as moderators in attempts to make peace among the contenders.

Timbuktu maintained its role as an important commercial centre, though even the few indications of the volume of the trade are contemporary records of disruptions and exactions. In 1694 as many as seventeen boats carrying 37,000 mithqals were intercepted on the river between Jenne and Timbuktu. The merchants of Timbuktu possessed enough gold for successive pashas to exact contributions to the tune of 1,000, 2,500 and 6,000 mithqals. Within the three years of his reign (1716–19), one pasha accumulated as much as 12,000 mithqals.[1]

Timbuktu depended on the agricultural production of the regions of Massina, Jenne and Segu. Peace and security under the rule of Mali and Songhay had encouraged this production and the flow of provisions. Following the collapse of the Songhay empire, peaceful agricultural settlements were subject to raids by nomads, Tuareg and Fulani. Agricultural production decreased, routes were intercepted and the supply of provisions to Timbuktu became more difficult. Conditions became even worse at periods of natural calamities, such as drought or excessive flooding of the Niger. Crops failed, and people were reluctant to store provisions from one year to the other because of insecurity. Famines followed and bred epidemics. During these periodic cycles of famines and epidemics, which occurred at least once every decade, Timbuktu lost thousands of its inhabitants. The situation was aggravated by the irresponsible conduct of many pashas who, in order to feed their troops, did not hesitate to oppress the population even during periods of distress.

Linked by the Niger waterway, Timbuktu and Jenne had developed simultaneously as important centres of trade and Islam. Since the fifteenth century Jenne had been a flourishing town with a densely populated agricultural hinterland. Gold was worked by its famous jewellers, and artisans also processed local products such as skins, hides and cotton. In this urban setting the artisans were part of the bourgeois class, and not, as in most western Sudanic societies, members of debased occupa-

[1] *Tadhkirat al-Nisyān*, pp. 93–4/tr. 149–50; p. 20/tr. 33, and *passim*.

tional castes. Jenne was the hub of an extensive network of trade routes. The Sudanese traders, Dyula and Marka, operated the long distance trade to procure gold and kola from the south and, on a more limited scale, to provide agricultural foodstuffs. Yet, 'Moors' from North Africa and the Sahara were the more prosperous and influential merchants in Jenne, and they controlled the trans-Saharan trade, with the help of correspondents in Timbuktu.

The commercial interdependence of Timbuktu and Jenne made it imperative that the two cities should be included in the same political system. Shortly after the conquest of Timbuktu a Moroccan officer, escorted by a few soldiers only, was sent to Jenne to accept the allegiance of its notables, *'ulamā'* and merchants. A new chief, the *Jenne-were*, was appointed to succeed the former ruler, who had died earlier. Soon after the Moroccan expedition had returned to Timbuktu, Jenne was visited by the son of a former *askiya*. With the support of one faction of the population, he repudiated the authority of the Moroccan sultan and reinstated allegiance to the *askiya*, though in the confusion following the defeat at Tondibi it was not clear who he was. The *Jenne-were*, his officers, and the merchants remained loyal to the Moroccans, and a force of 300 musketeers defeated the rebels. A *ḥākim* (governor) was then appointed to represent the pasha in Jenne. A garrison, under the command of a *qā'id*, was stationed in the city and in posts along the Niger waterway to Timbuktu.

Jenne was ruled by its chief, the *Jenne-were*, under the supervision of the *ḥākim*. Under the Songhay, it had been the *mondyo* who had represented the *askiya* in Jenne. But the Moroccan authorities seem to have intervened more often in deposing and installing or reinstating chiefs. There were nine *Jenne-weres* between 1592 and 1663; two of them ruled twice and one even three times. *Ḥākims* changed even more rapidly, as twenty-three officers held this office; four of them twice and two even three times. The history of Jenne under *arma* rule is a series of tensions and conflicts between the *Jenne-were* and the Moroccan authorities, as well as between the pasha and his representatives in Jenne.

In 1609 a revolt of the *Jenne-were* spread from the city of Jenne to the countryside, and people deserted their villages along the river to seek refuge in the mountains. The Moroccans had to subdue the rebellious villages by force, but Jenne itself surrendered without a battle. The Moroccans left the *Jenne-were* in office, though they imposed a heavy tribute on him, which his subjects hastened to bring forward to aid their chief. The *Jenne-were* then called on the people to return to their villages in peace.

In 1632 the army stationed in Jenne, led by its *qā'id*, revolted against the pasha. The *Jenne-were* was brought into the conspiracy by the army officers, but the latter soon alleged that the *Jenne-were* had broken his pledge by sending secret information to the pasha. The *Jenne-were*, arrested by the *qā'id*, was killed in the fort and his head was exhibited in the market. This act of cruelty provoked the indigenous population, led by dignitaries of the *Jenne-were*'s court, to revolt against the *qā'id* and the army. In this way, a revolt of the Moroccan troops in Jenne against their pasha turned into an uprising of the people of Jenne against the Moroccan authorities. The rebels left the city and, with the support of the chiefs of the rural hinterland, laid siege to Jenne for four months. With no reinforcements from Timbuktu, the army in Jenne was unable to quell a total revolt. In order to appease the local population, a new pasha deposed the *qā'id* of Jenne, who was held responsible for the murder of the *Jenne-were*. The new *qā'id* gave presents to the people of Jenne and spoke soft words to win them back, but the incident left scars of animosity between the *arma* and the city.

The failure of the *arma* to subdue the revolt by force compromised their authority. As soon as the pasha felt sufficiently secure in Timbuktu, he led an expedition to Jenne in May 1634. Chiefs who had participated in the rebellion were forced to renew their allegiance. The people of Jenne were oppressed in order to avenge the Moroccans' humiliation two years before. As the pressure increased, all the merchants left to settle in the nearby town of Bina in 1637. In February 1643 the *arma* troops in Jenne again revolted against the pasha. They were joined by the troops in Timbuktu and the pasha was deposed. In this way, the soldiers stationed in the remote city of Jenne could take part in the struggle for power in Timbuktu.

In 1656, when the account of al-Sa'dī comes to an end, the *Jenne-were* had already been in open revolt for almost three years. He had left the city and had been joined by the whole Sudanic population. No information is available about the outcome of this revolt, because the next detailed account, that of *Tadhkirat al-Nisyān*, begins only in the early eighteenth century. The pattern of politics in Jenne seems, however, not to have changed. In 1713 and 1748 the troops in Jenne again challenged the pasha's authority, while in 1732 the *Jenne-were* quarrelled with the *arma* troops in Jenne and besieged the city. Peace was restored when reinforcements came from Timbuktu. In the second half of the eighteenth century, Jenne, as we shall see, came under the domination of the Bambara.

North of Jenne, the Fulani of Massina dominated the Niger waterway, which for centuries had been of vital importance for trade and for the transportation of troops and supplies. The Fulani pastoralists, who had reached the Niger at the beginning of the fifteenth century, had found the inundated delta of the middle Niger ideal for grazing their herds. Neither the arid area to the north nor the country infested by the tse-tse fly to the south attracted the Fulani, but they had to defend their country against invasion from both directions, the Tuareg from the north and the Bambara from the south. The basic social unit of the Fulani was the sub-clan, but against outside pressure the Fulani developed a class of warriors, known as *dikko*, who also assumed some political authority over the sub-clans. The *dikko* were led by the *ardo*, who was regarded as the supreme authority over the Fulani in Massina. The imperial authorities, the *askiyas* of Songhay, the Moroccan *pashas*, and then the Diara dynasty of Segu, employed the *dikko* and the *ardo* to levy tribute.

Yet, the Fulani were reluctant subjects, and the *askiyas* had used both diplomacy and force to maintain a limited authority over them. Soon after the Moroccan conquest cordial relations were established, as the *ardo* Ḥammadi Amina hastened to accept the new authority. In 1593 he even tried to intervene with the pasha in favour of the imprisoned '*ulamā*' of Timbuktu. The pasha rejected this intercession and threatened to arrest the Fulani *ardo* himself. This sign of the increasingly tyrannical character of the pasha's rule strained relations between the *ardo* and the pasha. In 1598 Ḥammadi Amina refused to come to Timbuktu when called by the pasha, who then dispatched the first in a long series of punitive expeditions against Massina. As the Moroccan force entered Massina, the *ardo* avoided open battle, fearing the firearms of the invader. He retreated to Diara in the Sahel, out of reach of the Moroccans, who were careful not to advance too far from the Niger waterway. The Moroccans severely punished the animist sedentary allies of the *ardo*, took his family as captives, and appointed a new *ardo* as their protégé.

Ḥammadi Amina's family was kept in custody in Jenne. This may have induced the exiled *ardo* to join the king of Mali in an abortive attempt to conquer Jenne in April 1599. The Moroccans put to rout the Malinke and the Fulani who had laid siege to Jenne, but a Moroccan force in pursuit of Ḥammadi Amina was annihilated. Peace was then concluded between Ḥammadi Amina and the Moroccans, and the former was given back his family and his chieftancy.

For almost thirty years, between 1599 and 1628, successive *ardos* lived in peace with the Moroccans and refused to join their neighbours in revolt. 'I am a herdsman', said the *ardo* in 1609, 'and, whoever rules the country, I am his servant.'[1] Relations, however, were strained again in 1628, when the new *ardo*, Ḥammadi Amina II (grandson of Ḥammadi Amina I), refused to come to Timbuktu for his official investiture by the pasha. This almost led to a new series of hostilities, but the *ardo* agreed to renew the payment of the cattle tax (*jangali*). Although he was careful to deliver the tax every year, Ḥammadi Amina maintained sufficient political independence to irritate the pasha. In May 1644 the pasha defeated him and appointed a new *ardo*. The routed Fulani were attacked by the animist sedentary population, who now took revenge for the depredations they themselves had suffered from the pastoralists. Ḥammadi Amina had to keep clear not only of the Moroccans but also of his neighbours who collaborated with the pasha. As soon as the pasha's force evacuated Massina, however, Ḥammadi Amina overcame the new *ardo* and regained authority in September 1644. A year later the *qāḍī* of Massina, together with envoys from the *qāḍī* of Jenne, in the traditional role of Muslims as peace-makers, went to Timbuktu to plead for Ḥammadi Amina before the pasha, and peaceful relations were restored.

In the eighteenth century, the pashas, harassed by the Tuareg, were unable to assert their authority over the Fulani and expeditions went to Massina mainly for booty. The first half of the eighteenth century was characterized by raids and counter raids of *arma*, Tuareg and Fulani on each other. In between the raids there were also periods of peace, when the Fulani joined the pashas in their expeditions.

In the second half of the eighteenth century Massina came within the orbit of the Bambara empire of Segu. Bambara and Fulani, as agriculturalists and pastoralists, lived side by side for a long period. Indeed, it appears as if the Fulani aristocracy of warriors, the *dikko*, and the *ardo* adjusted themselves more successfully to Bambara rule than to former imperial powers, Songhay and the *arma*. *Ardos* spent time in Segu, married daughters of the ruling Diara dynasty, campaigned along with the Bambara troops, and even adopted some Bambara customs. Indeed, the *dikko* seem to have joined hands with the Bambara in the harsh regime, of which some Fulani traditions bitterly complain, mentioning in particular the annual tribute in cattle and slaves.

[1] *T. al-Sūdān*, p. 196/tr. 299.

THE *ARMA*, SONGHAY AND TUAREG

The bravest opposition to the Moroccans was exhibited by the independent *askiyas* of Songhay. Following his defeat at Tondibi in March 1591, the last ruler of the Songhay empire, Askiya Isḥāq, retreated across the Niger river. The peace negotiations with Jūdār allowed him some respite, which lasted until the rejection of any compromise by the Moroccan sultan and the arrival of the new pasha, Maḥmūd b. Zarqūn, who was determined to crush Songhay completely. In October 1591, Askiyā Isḥāq was defeated by the pasha Maḥmūd, and retreated to Dendi, the area of the Niger valley south of Kukiya and Tillabery.

Internal disputes within the Songhay royal family, which had undermined the empire before the invasion, now made it easier for the conqueror to break the Songhay resistance. Askiya Isḥāq had arrested his brothers and ordered them to be castrated. The brothers escaped this fate by seeking refuge in the Moroccan camp. Askiya Isḥāq himself was deposed by his brother Muḥammad Gao, son of Askiya Dāwūd the Great. The new *askiya* suspected that his brothers might intrigue with the Moroccans against him, and he approached the pasha to offer his submission. Maḥmūd invited Muḥammad Gao to come in person to negotiate the terms of his submission. In a dramatic meeting of the *askiya*'s council, opinions split. The *hi-koi*, one of the senior commanders of the Songhay army, warned against the pasha's treachery, but Alfa Bukar, the Muslim councillor of the *askiya*, maintained that the pasha was sincere. According to the *Ta'rīkh al-Fattāsh*, Alfa Bukar had been admitted by the pasha into the conspiracy, and was later favoured by the Moroccans. The *askiya* accepted the Muslim's advice and was led to his own destruction. In Timbuktu, he was treacherously arrested and killed, together with many of his followers. His brother Sulaymān was appointed *askiya* by the Moroccans.

Songhay now became divided into two. Northern Songhay, on the Niger between Gao, Timbuktu and Jenne, submitted to Moroccan rule. But south of Tillabery the spirit of independence among the Songhay was not lost. Over a century earlier, following the seizure of the throne by Askiya Muḥammad, the descendants of Sonni ʿAlī had retreated to this part of the Niger, carrying with them the Songhay traditions, uncontaminated by Islam. These southern Songhay resisted the Moroccans. They were led by Askiya Nūḥ, son of Askiya Dāwūd, who became the independent *askiya*, as distinguished from the puppet *askiya* in Timbuktu. Although Askiya Nūḥ had fewer troops than Askiya Isḥāq, he was more successful in his encounters with the Moroccans. For two years the pasha Maḥmūd pursued Askiya Nūḥ in Dendi. The latter suffered defeats, but also scored victories, mainly through guerrilla warfare. The Moroccans were exhausted by the humid climate and, facing troubles in other parts of the country, Maḥmūd withdrew from Dendi in 1594. The same year this pasha was killed in battle against the animists of Hombori. The latter cut off the pasha's head and sent it to Askiya Nūḥ, who let the king of Kebbi hang it on a pole in the market of his capital. The Kanta of Kebbi, the Songhay of Dendi and the Tombo of Hombori seem to have formed an alliance which extended inside the Niger bend to Bandiagara and Jenne.

In June 1595, the new pasha, Manṣūr, defeated Askiya Nūḥ in Hombori. Nūḥ retreated with his army, but his civilian followers were captured. They were taken to Timbuktu to Askiya Sulaymān, the collaborator, to form his entourage. For seven years, Askiya Nūḥ led the Songhay in fighting the Moroccans. He did not stay in one place, but harassed the enemy from many directions. His followers, however, became tired of the hardship of guerilla warfare, deposed him in 1599, and swore allegiance to his brother Askiya Hārūn. In 1608 Hārūn led his warriors from Dendi across Hombori to the Niger opposite Massina. The pasha at that time had difficulties with the Fulani of Massina, while the Songhay followers of the puppet *askiya* refused to fight against their own kith and kin. For a time, the Moroccan troops did not challenge the Songhay of Dendi. This only increased their audacity and induced other peoples to seek their aid in opposing the Moroccans. Indeed, a year later in 1609, a Songhay army advanced to Jenne in response to the call of the rebellious *Jenne-were*. The Songhay scored a victory over a Moroccan army and departed with many prisoners and much booty, whereupon the Moroccans had to subdue a revolt which by then encompassed the whole region of Jenne.

Askiya Hārūn was succeeded by his brother, Askiya al-Amīn (1612–18). He is remembered as a worthy ruler, who cared for his subjects and helped them during periods of famine and shortage. By then, it seems, the Songhay in Dendi had established a more stable political organization. He was the first *askiya* since the Moroccan invasion to die a natural death. His successor, Askiya Dāwūd, reigned for twenty-two years, another indication of greater stability. There were no hostilities with the Moroccans during that period, and in 1629 Askiya Dāwūd made a formal peace with the pasha. It is likely that the *askiya* of Dendi attempted to recreate the *askiya*s' court of Gao. Yet, in their southern retreat they had lost the urban ethos of the Niger bend and stressed more the animist traditions of Songhay.

Askiya Dāwūd is described as a blood-thirsty ruler who killed many of his subjects, including his relatives and the commanders of his army. His brother Ismāʿīl escaped murder by fleeing to Timbuktu. There he secured the support of the pasha, and returned in 1639 with a force of *arma* to depose his brother Askiya Dāwūd. However, Ismāʿīl did not want to compromise the independence of Songhay, and immediately sent the *arma* back. The pasha retaliated by invading Lulami, the capital of Dendi. Askiya Ismāʿīl was deposed, and another *askiya* was appointed by the *arma*, only to be rejected by the independent Songhay of Dendi as soon as the invaders left Lulami. Dendi regained its independence, but not its stability.

The *Taʾrīkh al-Sūdān*, our source for the history of independent Songhay in Dendi, ends in the middle of the seventeenth century. Songhay traditions recount how competition within the royal family resulted in the fragmentation of the Songhay state of Dendi into several petty states under the rule of the *askiya*s' descendants. Towards the end of the eighteenth century they came under the domination of the Tuareg Iwillimidden, who had invaded the Niger valley. It is significant, however, that the Songhay-speaking Jerma, who in the sixteenth and seventeenth centuries migrated from the lacustrine area to the country around present-day Niamey, did not succumb to the Tuareg invasion, and successfully maintained their independence.

The Tuareg invasion was but the latest phase of a cyclical process in the relations between the nomads of the southern Sahara and the sedentaries of the Sahel. The constant pressure of the nomads was arrested whenever a centralized power dominated the Sahel; but whenever this power declined, the nomads pushed into the country of the agriculturalists. Ghana had checked the Sanhaja, but its conquest by the Almoravids marked the ascendancy of the nomads. Mali had forced the latter to pay tribute, but its decline had opened the way for the Tuareg to gain control of Timbuktu. The *askiyas* of Songhay extended their authority as far as Taghaza, but, following the collapse of Songhay, the Moroccan conquerors were unable to hold back the Tuareg.

The Tuareg lived in loosely organized confederations, but rigidly stratified, divided into nobles and vassals. The nobles, camel-owners and warriors, had to defend their vassals, who paid tribute. Both nobles and vassals had slaves, of Sudanese origin, who did the menial work.

Trade was an important stabilizing factor in the economy of the pastoral Tuareg, and it mainly involved the exchange of Saharan salt for the agricultural products of the Sudan. The Tuareg also levied tolls on the trans-Saharan caravans in return for abstaining from attacking them. Politics were conducted in the council of nobles, which also elected the chief, or *amenukal*, whose responsibility was mainly in foreign affairs and as a leader in war.

The limited resources of the desert oases split the Tuareg into rival units and caused their migration southward to the Sahel. If they encountered a strong authority in the Sahel, the Tuareg usually submitted to it, waiting for a propitious moment. So, by the end of the sixteenth century, the Tuareg in the region of Timbuktu, the Imagsharen, had recognized the sovereignty of the *askiyas*. The Moroccan conquerors deposed Ag-Madol, the Tuareg chief, perhaps because of his loyalty to the *askiya*, and appointed Awsenba in his place. The latter soon had the opportunity to prove his loyalty to the new rulers. In October 1591 he came to the aid of the *qā'id*, who had been besieged by the people of Timbuktu. The Tuareg set fire to Timbuktu and did not spare even the houses of the Aqīt family. This was an act of ingratitude because Awsenba had grown up with the Aqīt, following the custom of the Tuareg chiefs to have their children educated by the *'ulamā'* of Timbuktu.

About the middle of the seventeenth century, the Tuareg of Adrar of the Iforas split into two opposing factions, the Iwillimidden and the Tadmekket, and migrated southward. In 1654, according to al-Sa'dī, the Tadmekket came to seek the protection of the pasha from the pressure of the Iwillimidden. Their appearance in the region dominated by the Moroccans soon caused troubles, and the pashas had to undertake periodical punitive expeditions against the Tuareg. Throughout the second half of the seventeenth century, these expeditions were successful, and the *arma* were in control of the Niger bend. But, as the power of the pashas declined, the Tadmekket became more aggressive. In the first half of the eighteenth century, the Tuareg became involved in the disputes among the *arma* officers. In 1716, when one *qā'id* relied on the support of the local population of the lacustrine area, his rival called in the Tadmekket. The latter entered Timbuktu and pitched their tents in the city. They left the city only after their ally had secured his position as pasha. Once they had been introduced into the city, the Tuareg did not hesitate to enter it again, uninvited, to commit robberies.

In 1729 the Tuareg raided Timbuktu day and night. Those people of

Timbuktu who lived in hovels deposited their property in walled buildings for safety. The impudence of the Tuareg increased as they raided a nearby town and sold the booty in the markets of Timbuktu. The menace of the Tuareg lay heavy upon the city. In November 1736, they intercepted the road between Timbuktu and the port of Kabara on the Niger, the vital link of Timbuktu with its Sudanic hinterland, from where provisions and merchandise reached the city. For eight weeks the donkey drivers travelled under the escort of armed soldiers and the Tuareg were held back. But when under a false sense of security the military escort became irregular, the Tuareg resumed their brigandage.

In February 1737, following an attack on the donkey drivers, an *arma* force was rushed to the scene, but the Tuareg had already melted into the desert with their booty. A small party of the *arma* was ambushed and four were killed. The *arma* deposed the pasha and appointed a new one, who came under pressure to drive the Tuareg away from the river. The pasha organized a large-scale military expedition, in which the *arma* were joined by their Arab and Fulani allies. By that time the *arma* could not have fought on their own and were dependent on the support of local troops. One of the pashas said that no expedition should be sent against the Tuareg unless the *arma* made up no more than one tenth of the troops and the allies added the rest.

Ag-Moru, chief of the Tadmekket, assembled his own people and allies. The *arma* were totally defeated in a fierce battle when two or three hundred of them and many of their allies were killed. The *arma* retreated to an island on the Niger, where they stayed for three or four months until September 1737. In the meantime, Ag-Moru concluded peace with the *'ulamā'* and the merchants of Timbuktu. He imposed tribute on the town and retired eastwards. The decisive victory of 1737 confirmed the Tuareg as the dominant power on the Niger bend. 'The Tuareg became masters of the whole land of Takrūr, from Hausa to Gurma [i.e., on both sides of the Niger river]...They put an end to the rule of the *arma* and even forced them to pay tribute.'[1]

While the Tadmekket, who had moved from Adrar south-west to the Niger bend, were in constant conflict with the *arma*, the Iwillimidden at first maintained cordial relations with the *arma*, because their line of expansion took them from Adrar to the south-east.

In 1741, when the *arma* were in almost complete subjection to the Tadmekket, the chief of the Iwillimidden came to Timbuktu to accept his investiture from the pasha. According to the *Tadhkirat al-Nisyān*,

[1] *Tadhkirat al-Nisyān*, p. 75/tr. 120.

it was their custom since 1700 to be ceremonially enrobed by the pasha. This followed an older tradition whereby the Tuareg chiefs were officially installed by the representative of the imperial government, for in the mid-fourteenth century Ibn Baṭṭūṭa was eye-witness to such a ceremony when the Malian governor of Timbuktu enrobed the Tuareg chief.

In the second half of the eighteenth century, the pashalik of Timbuktu was in total eclipse. In 1770–1, according to the records of the Arabic Chronicle of Walata, a chief of the Tadmekket was murdered by the instigation of a *qā'id* of the *arma*. The Tuareg retaliated by laying siege to Timbuktu, and famine and death were the result. About the same time, the Iwillimidden began their expansion into the former dominions of the pashas by taking possession of Gao. In 1787 the *amenukal* of the Iwillimidden entered Timbuktu, abolished the office of the pasha, but allowed the *arma* to elect a *qā'id* as their representative.

After the middle of the seventeenth century, scholarship in Timbuktu declined. At a time when military and political domination passed into the hands of the nomad Tuareg, spiritual leadership also departed from the city to the nomads' camp. The harshness of the nomads was moderated by the marabouts, whose religious prestige carried political influence. By the end of the eighteenth century, there was a new wave of Islamic revivalism which was closely associated with the Kunta, a clan of Arab and Berber descent, and their leader Sīdī al-Mukhtār al-Kabīr (1729–1811).

For six generations, from the mid-sixteenth to the end of the seventeenth century, leadership of the Bakkā'iyya, a branch of the Kunta, had passed among the descendants of Sīdī 'Umar, who, according to traditions, had been initiated into the Qādiriyya brotherhood by Muḥammad al-Maghīlī of Tuat. In the mid-seventeenth century, the *zāwiya* (a centre for mystical devotion) of the Bakkā'iyya was re-established in Tuat, where religious sanctity was combined with commercial activities in the salt trade of Taodeni. The available evidence suggests that the Bakkā'iyya became influential in the southern Sahara only when their junior branch, which had lived in Tagant, moved to the Hodh and then to Azawad in the late seventeenth or early eighteenth century.

In the southern Sahara, the Kunta immediately enjoyed a special position on account of their religious prestige. In 1720 the people of Timbuktu called in Sīdī Ṣiddīq al-Kuntawī to help in burying *arma* who had been killed outside the city, because none of its residents could venture out for fear of a deposed pasha and his Tuareg allies, who terrorized the countryside. Sīdī al-Mukhtār became *muqaddam*, leader of the Qādiriyya in the western Sudan about 1757. He used this religious authority to extend his political influence by mediating among warring tribes and factions of Arabs and Tuareg. He called loyal groups to fight turbulent ones in an effort to restore some security. The near anarchy, described by the *Tadhkirat al-Nisyān* in the middle of the eighteenth century, was thus somewhat rectified by 'Allāh's truce', imposed by Sīdī al-Mukhtār.

One of the first achievements of Sīdī al-Mukhtār was his treaty with the Berabish, a tribe of Berber origin, who had been arabized through the infiltration of Arab lineages. From the seventeenth century onwards, the Berabish had imposed their protection over the Saharan routes from Timbuktu to Morocco via Arawan and Taodeni; only those caravans which paid tolls or tribute to the Berabish could cross the desert. During much of this period, the Kunta played an important role in the organization of the salt trade under the protection of the Berabish. Once the latter accepted the spiritual leadership of Sīdī al-Mukhtār, the flow of trade grew and the wealth of the Kunta increased.

Sīdī al-Mukhtār's most important political asset was, however, his alliance with the Iwillimidden, by then masters of the Niger bend and the confines of the desert. He was venerated by the Tuareg, whose chiefs sought his advice in political matters. Through his influence over the Tuareg, Sīdī al-Mukhtār extended his patronage over the city of Timbuktu. His religious authority expanded even farther through his numerous disciples, who spread his brand of the Qādiriyya brotherhood into the savanna.

THE BAMBARA STATES

The authority of the Songhay in the sixteenth century had not extended much farther south than Jenne. Kala and Bindugu, the former provinces of Mali between the Niger and the Bani rivers, maintained a precarious independence between the aggressive Songhay and the declining Mali empires. It was in this region that the nucleus of the Bambara state later developed. For Muslims, and therefore also for the authors of the *ta'rīkhs*, Bambara was a general term for animists. On the middle Niger, pastoralists sometimes still call dark-skinned agriculturalists by the term Bambara. The Bambara who gained hegemony over the middle Niger in the eighteenth century were those who called

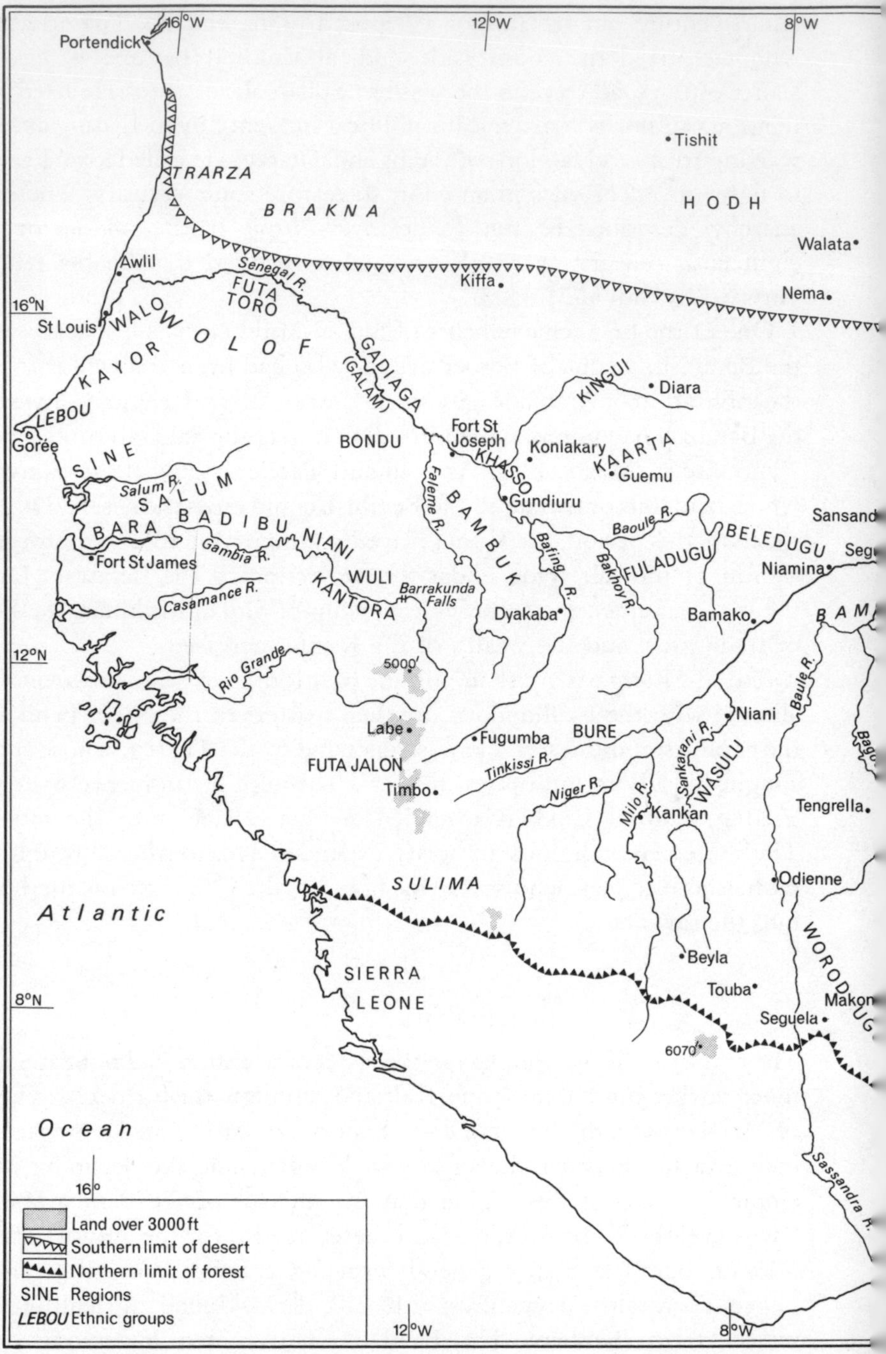

5 The western Sudan

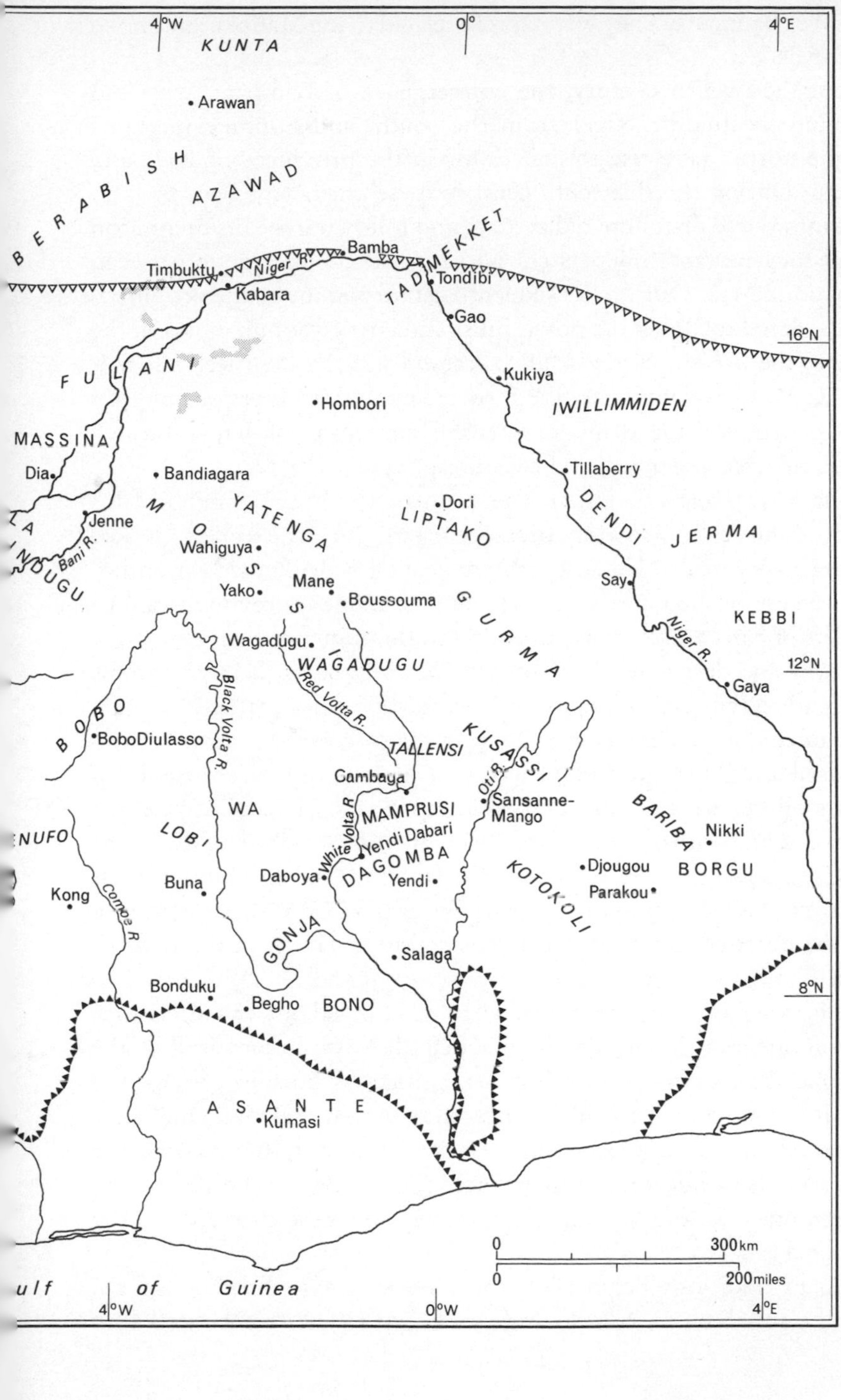
4°W
0°
4°E
KUNTA
Arawan
BERABISH
AZAWAD
Bamba
Timbuktu
Niger R.
Kabara
TADMEKKET
Tondibi
Gao
16°N
FULANI
Kukiya
Hombori
IWILLIMMIDEN
MASSINA
Dia
Bandiagara
Tillaberry
YATENGA
Dori
LIPTAKO
DENDI
JERMA
Jenne
Bani R.
MOSSI
Wahiguya
Yako
Mane
Boussouma
Say
GURMA
KEBBI
Wagadugu
WAGADUGU
Niger R.
12°N
Gaya
Black Volta R.
Red Volta R.
BOBO
BoboDiulasso
TALLENSI
KUSASSI
Cambaga
Oti R.
Sansanne-Mango
BARIBA
WA
MAMPRUSI
White Volta R.
Yendi Dabari
Nikki
LOBI
DAGOMBA
Djougou
BORGU
Daboya
Yendi
KOTOKOLI
Parakou
Kong
Comoe R.
Buna
GONJA
Salaga
8°N
Bonduku
Begho
BONO
ASANTE
Kumasi
0
300 km
0
200 miles
of
Guinea
4°W
0°W
4°E

themselves Banmana. They were closely related to the Malinke and spoke a similar dialect.

About the twelfth century, the convergence of Bambara, who had penetrated the middle Niger from the south, and Soninke migrants from the north, gave rise to chiefdoms in the provinces of Kala and Bindugu. During the thirteenth century these chiefdoms became integrated into the Malian imperial system, and following the disintegration of Mali they became independent and formed a buffer zone between Songhay and Mali. During the sixteenth century 'none of the provincial chiefs...dared to attack the powerful sovereigns of Songhay...On the contrary, the *askiyas* carried out successful attacks on these chiefs.'[1] After the Moroccan conquest the former imperial frontiers of Songhay were violated, and the Bambara attacked the region of Jenne, burned villages, pillaged property, and seized captives.

In the 1640s, al-Sa'dī visited the country south of Jenne, and his account indicates a growing pressure from those he called 'infidel Bambara', very probably bands of Banmana who challenged the authority of the established chiefs. In 1645 animist Bambara revolted against the chiefs of Sana and Fadoku, in Kala and Bindugu respectively, drove them away and destroyed their towns. The collapse of these chiefdoms put an end to the territorial political organization bequeathed by Mali. The Bambara, as the emerging new power, introduced a different system based on the authority of war-chiefs who organized bands of warriors. References in the chronicles to Shā'a Maka illustrate the career of one Bambara war-chief. Born in the province of Kala, he entered the service of the Moroccans in Jenne at the beginning of their rule. After he had learned their war tactics (probably the use of firearms), he deserted and returned to his country. There, at the head of animist Bambara, he ravaged the country of Jenne.

Among the Bambara, communal work was carried out by associations based on age-sets. Each age-set included all boys circumcised at the same time. The association, called *ton*, cut across kinship groups and castes. It was governed by rules which were binding on all its members and carried disciplinary sanctions. Under its leader, the *ton-tigi*, the association also undertook military activities, raids, or the defence of the community, so the *ton* played a decisive role in the evolution of the Bambara states.

Bambara traditions begin with the careers of two brothers of the Kulibali clan – Barama N'golo and Nia N'golo. The former settled in

[1] *T. al-Sūdān*, p. 144/tr. 224.

the region of Segu, and the latter in Beledugu, west of the Niger. Kaladian Kulibali, a descendant of Barama N'golo, who was a hunter and warrior, established an extensive but ephemeral Bambara state, probably in the middle of the seventeenth century, during the period of anarchy depicted by al-Sa'dī at the end of the *Ta'rīkh al-Sūdān*. Kaladian's state collapsed because it lacked an elaborate political organization, and depended solely on feats of arms.

A more durable state was established by Biton Kulibali, sometimes referred to as a great-grandson of Kaladian. Traditions say that Biton excelled among his age mates and was elected *ton-tigi*. His *ton* included young Bambara and some sons of the more wealthy Soninke. Aware of the need for a more homogeneous and cohesive *ton*, Biton provoked a split into two rival *tons*; one was led by a son of the Soninke chief, the other by Biton Kulibali. The Soninke feared the growing power of the Bambara *ton* and conflict became inevitable. In the fighting that broke out, Biton, aided by Fulani allies, emerged victorious.

Biton then consolidated his own position as the undisputed leader of the *ton*. According to some traditions, he killed all the elders of the surrounding villages, so that the young men, left without their natural leaders, were dependent on Biton as their sole authority. The young men were ordered to have their heads shaved as *ton-dyon*, 'slaves of the *ton*', subject to its strict regulations. Biton thus eliminated the voluntary aspects of the association by introducing coercion. He also broke the egalitarian character of the *ton* by building up his autocratic rule. He restructured Bambara society, based on kinship groups and village communities, by subjecting it to the *ton*. The *ton*, which had previously rendered services to the community, now dominated it.

Local chiefs, whose position was menaced by the growing power of Biton and his *ton*, are said to have called in the aid of Kong, the young southern Dyula state, whose troops were then, in 1739, at the gates of Jenne. Segu, Biton's capital, was saved by the intervention of the Fulani of Fuladugu, who chased the Dyula army away from the middle Niger. An alliance with the Fulani is a recurring theme in the Bambara traditions. In their dispersion, Fulani came to live symbiotically with Mande (Malinke or Bambara) peasants and they gradually adopted aspects of Mande culture. About the beginning of the eighteenth century, some Fulani, who had thus assimilated with Mande, established states in Fuladugu (west of the Niger), in Khasso (on the Senegal) and in Wasulu (south-east of the upper Niger).

By 1726, 'Bambara Cana' was reputed on the Senegambia coast to be 'a very large kingdom, well populated and very fertile. All the peoples there [were] slaves of the king and of the nobility. It [was] situated between Tombut [Timbuktu] and Cassou [Khasso].'[1] This probably included both states of the Bambara, that of Biton in Segu, and that of the Massasi in Beledugu, so called after Massa, grandson of Nia N'golo, the brother of Barama N'golo. Massa had assembled armed young Bambara – slaves, clients and associates – and created the nucleus of another Bambara state. This also was based on an association of devoted young men who had been uprooted from their kinship groups and village communities. With this force at his disposal, Massa raided his surroundings, defeated neighbouring chiefs, amassed booty and attracted more warriors to his camp at Sunsan. Massa's sons and successors, Benefali and Fulakoro, contemporaries of Biton, continued their father's exploits.

Biton's state of Segu expanded over the fertile delta of the middle Niger, close to important trade routes and commercial centres. Its economic resources were far superior to those of the Massasi in the sparsely populated country of Beledugu. Both states were aggressive and expansionist, and became involved in constant tension and conflicts. In 1753–4, according to the Arabic Chronicle of Walata and Nema, 'the army of Tekto [*ton-tigi*, i.e. Biton Kulibali] laid siege to Sansa [Sunsan], and killed its chief Fulakoro, son of Massa'.[2] The victory of Biton over Fulakoro is recorded also in Bambara traditions. The defeated Massasi retreated from Beledugu to Kingui in the north-west, where they established the Bambara state of Kaarta, away from their more powerful kinsmen.

According to the same Arabic chronicle, Tekto al-Bambari (that is, Biton) died in 1755 and was succeeded by his son Dekuru. Lacking the statemanship of his father, Dekuru fell victim to the precariously balanced system the latter had established. Dekuru ruled as a despot and cared little for the inherent incompatibility between the power monopolized by the *ton-tigi* and the ideal egalitarian system of the *ton*; he entered into conflict with its members, the *ton-dyon*, and was killed in 1756–7. He was succeeded by his brother Bakary, who had already come under Islamic influence and was suspected of wishing to introduce Islam into the very centre of the state. As he failed to maintain the balance between traditionalism and Islam, the *ton-dyon* revolted, deposed and killed him.

1 P. Labat, *Nouvelle relation de l'Afrique occidentale* (Paris, 1728), III, 334.

2 'Les chroniques de Oualata et de Nema', tr. P. Marty, *Revue des Études Islamiques*, 1927, 568.

The *ton-dyon* reached the conclusion that this conflict was due not to the failure of two individual rulers, but to the system introduced by Biton Kulibali. In this coup d'état the military deposed the hereditary dynasty. They killed all the members of Biton's family together with Bakary, and restored the egalitarian system of the *ton*, which had been violated by Biton. One of them was to be elected as leader through a contract that could be revoked if violated. Indeed, each of the three *ton-tigis* who held authority during the period of transition between 1757 (Bakary's removal) and 1765 (N'golo Diara's accession) were deposed. Ton-Mansa, the first ruler during that period of transition, insisted on staying in his town instead of moving to Segu. He was deposed by the *ton-dyon* who feared the emergence of a new centre of power. Kanuba Gnuma, who succeeded him in 1758–9, was a Fulani, and the *ton-dyon* viewed him with suspicion lest the leadership should be taken away from the more cohesive nucleus of the *ton-dyon* in which the Fulani allies had not been fully integrated. His successful military exploits made Kanuba Gnuma even more dangerous for the *ton-dyon*. The next ruler, Kafa-Diugu, was one of the senior slave chiefs of Biton Kulibali. Bloodshed during the rapid succession of rulers (five in ten years) and the rivalry between different factions undermined the power and unity of the *ton*. It was saved by N'golo Diara.

A slave of Biton Kulibali, N'golo Diara had already been distinguished in war, in administration, and in politics. Throughout the transitory period, N'golo Diara bided his time; then, when called to the chieftaincy, he refused to rule under the collective leadership introduced by the *ton-dyon*. By a show of force, N'golo compelled the *ton-dyon* to pledge fealty to himself. He refused, however, to take the customary counter-pledge of the chief, saying 'slaves only must take the oath'. Once again power was monopolized, and the Bambara of Segu were given strong personal leadership. N'golo decreed that he would be succeeded by his own sons, and established the new Diara dynasty. He appointed his sons as provincial governors, deposed chiefs suspected of disloyalty and created a strong personal guard. Under him the state of Segu entered a new stage of territorial expansion.

The *Tadhkirat al-Nisyān*, which recorded the principal events in the pashalik of Timbuktu until 1750, did not report any intervention of the Bambara in Jenne, which implies that during the lifetime of Biton Kulibali (d. 1755) the Bambara state had not yet extended into the sphere of the pasha's authority. The traditions of Massina record intermittent warfare between Fulani and Bambara in the second half of the eighteenth century, which resulted in the defeat of the Fulani and the conquest of Massina by the Bambara. This was probably accomplished by N'golo Diara, who also extended his rule over Jenne.

In 1796 Mungo Park, the Scottish explorer, observed that Jenne 'was nominally a part of the king of Bambara's dominions'. The governor was appointed by Mansong, son of N'golo Diara; but, Park added, 'it was in fact a city of the Moors'. The people of Massina also paid 'an annual tribute to the king of Bambara, for the lands which they occupy'. Timbuktu was said to be independent under a Moorish king.[1] A few years later (*c.* 1800) 'The king of Bambara...proceeded from Sego to Timbuktu with a numerous army, and took the government entirely into his own hands, permitting the Moors to remain under his protection, and for purposes of trade.'[2] It is likely, therefore, that Timbuktu was conquered by Mansong, the king of Segu (1790–1808) at the very end of the eighteenth century.

With Mansong, the Bambara state of Segu reached its greatest territorial expansion. In September 1805 Mansong sent the following message to Mungo Park:

> Mansong says that he will protect you, that a road is open for you everywhere, as far as his hand extends. If you wish to go east, no man shall harm you from Sego till you pass Timbuctoo. If you wish to go to the west, you may travel through Fooladoo [Fuladugu] and Manding, through Kasson [Khasso] and Bondou...[3]

Under Mansong's successors, however, the fortunes of the state of Segu declined. By 1810 Timbuktu was dominated by the Kunta, and after 1818 Jenne and Massina were lost to Shekhu Aḥmadu. The Bambara ceased to be the dominant power on the Niger.

The territorial expansion of the Bambara state of Segu was not accompanied by administrative reorganization. It did not, therefore, develop along the pattern evolved by the earlier Sudanic empires of Mali and Songhay, which integrated conquered lands into an imperial system. Biton and his successors adopted the military title *faama*, rather than the imperial title of *mansa*. The Bambara rulers remained war-chiefs, whose authority was imposed and maintained by force of arms. Their power was based on the effective organization of the *ton*.

[1] Mungo Park, *Travels in the interior districts of Africa*, 2nd ed. (London, 1799), 202, 214, 215.

[2] 'Information given by l'hagi Mohammed Sheriff, residing at, or near the well of Araouan . . . transmitted to Mr. Cahill at Rabat, April 1803', in *Proceedings of the Association for Promoting the Discovery of the Interior Parts of Africa* (London, 1810), II, 322.

[3] Mungo Park, *Travels in Africa* (London, Everyman's Library, 1957), 359.

Significantly, the tribute paid by conquered people was called *di-songo*; originally this was, according to traditions, the payments by the members of the *ton* to Biton Kulibali's mother for the alcoholic beverage which she used to prepare for them. The Bambara state was, in a way, viewed as an extension of the original *ton*. Yet, in spite of its loose administrative structure, the Bambara state of Segu had a firm territorial basis in the delta of the middle Niger with its complementary economic resources – agriculture, fishing and trade. Their kin and rivals, the Massasi, lacked even territorial stability. Their state may rightly be regarded as a war-camp which, following their defeat by Biton Kulibali in 1754, moved from Beledugu to Kaarta.

Having conquered Kaarta, the Massasi intervened in a civil war between two factions of the ruling clan of the Diawara, a Soninke people whose capital, Diara, lay north of Kaarta. Reduced in territory, the weak Diawara survived as a buffer state between the Massasi of Kaarta to their south and the Moorish Awlād 'Umar (of the Brakna) in the north, and were raided by both their neighbours.

To the west, the Massasi harassed the Khassonke, a Fulani people who had assimilated aspects of Malinke culture. At the beginning of the eighteenth century, when the French established a fort on the upper Senegal to stimulate trade, Khasso was the most powerful state on that part of the Senegal river. By the second half of the eighteenth century, however, the hitherto aggressive Khassonke were forced to defend their country against the Bambara, who tried to obtain access to the Senegal river and its remunerative trade. Khasso was supported by troops from the Futa Toro in an alliance of the riverain kingdoms against the Bambara.

It is said that in the villages he raided, the Bambara ruler reduced the population to slavery, save for the young men, whom he incorporated into his army. Sira Bo (*c.* 1761–*c.* 1788), the third ruler after the migration to Kaarta, was able with this accrued strength to impose a more permanent authority over those territories – as far as Beledugu – which had merely been plundered by his predecessors, and he established his capital in Guemu.

The growing power and territorial expansion of the Massasi brought them again into conflict with Segu, whose new dynasty, founded by N'golo Diara, the Kulibali Massasi of Kaarta regarded as slaves and treated with contempt. Daisy Kulibali, who had succeeded Sira Bo about 1788, felt strong enough to intervene in a civil war among N'golo Diara's sons, and in 1792 he raided Niamina on the Niger. Four years later Mungo Park observed that the city 'had not resumed its former prosperity; nearly half of the town being nothing but a heap of ruins...'[1] Mansong, son of N'golo Diara, eventually defeated the Massasi, and four years later he carried the war over into Kaarta. This invasion of 1796 occurred while Park was visiting the region, and his contemporary account helps to bring to life the wars and raids that are repeatedly mentioned in the chronicles and the traditions of this period.

On 12 February 1796, while Park was at audience with Daisy, one of the scouts came in to bring the news that 'the Bambara army had left Fooladoo [Fuladugu], and was on its march towards Kaarta'.[2] Ten days later, when Park was already safe in Diara, Mansong advanced towards the capital Guemu, and Daisy, without risking a battle, retreated north-west to the fortified town of 'Gedingooma' (probably Guidioume), where he had stored provisions and was determined to make his final stand. His sons engaged the enemy in a few skirmishes, but were totally defeated and joined their father in the fort. Mansong placed a strong force to watch Daisy's movements. He divided the remainder of his army into small detachments, and 'ordered them to overrun the country, and seize the inhabitants before they had time to escape. These orders were executed with such promptitude that in a few days the whole kingdom of Kaarta became a scene of desolation.'[3] He then sent all the prisoners to Bambara, collected a considerable quantity of provisions and besieged Daisy for two months. During this time, Mansong was harassed by sallies from the besieged, and his stock of provisions was almost exhausted. He sent for 200 horsemen from 'Alī chief of the Awlād 'Umar, who had entered into alliance with Mansong against Daisy, but 'Alī refused to help him. In his rage, Mansong marched north against 'Alī, but the latter retreated into the desert. At the end of April, Mansong returned to Segu: the invasion had lasted just over two months, but was enough to 'destroy the happiness of thousands'. Kaarta was laid waste, but Daisy was determined to restore his power and to take his revenge against his neighbours and subjects who had turned against him in time of distress.

The Diawara and other peoples of the Sahel, who had for years been prey to the raids of the Massasi, had thrown in their lot with Mansong. Once the ruler of Segu had left, they became apprehensive of Daisy's vindictiveness. They resolved to attack first with the support of 'Alī

[1] Park, *Travels* (1799), 229–30. [2] Ibid. 95.
[3] Ibid. 107.

of the Awlād 'Umar. But the nomad chief again broke his pledge and refused to send the horsemen he had promised.

> The Negroes thus deserted by the Moors, and fully apprized that the king of Kaarta would show them little clemency...set out making the necessary preparations for quitting the town as soon as possible...Early in the morning, nearly one half of the town's people took the road for Bambara [Segu].[1]

The king of Khasso, who also took advantage of Mansong's invasion, joined with some disaffected fugitive Kaartans in a plundering expedition against Daisy. They fell upon some of Daisy's people, caught and carried them to Koniakary, capital of Khasso. The captives were sent in caravans to be sold to the French at St Louis in Senegal. This attack was soon returned; Daisy led 800 of his best warriors to raid three Khassonke villages near Koniakary. 'All the able men that fell into Daisy's hands were immediately put to death!'[2]

There was little or no territorial gain in this war, but much destruction of the land, and misery for the population. Warriors, however, had their dividends in slaves. Part of the slaves were recruited to the army or employed in agricultural production, and slaves represented an ever growing proportion of the population. The rise of the Bambara states, with their wars and raids, increased the supply of slaves from the interior to the European factories in the Senegambia. The slave trade brought a new prosperity to Muslim trading communities under Bambara rule. Mungo Park's account corroborates oral traditions that regard the reign of Mansong as a 'golden era' for the Muslim traders, and in particular those of Sansanding.

Insecurity along the Niger waterway between Timbuktu and Jenne favoured the development of an overland route from the Sahel to Sansanding, the river port close to the centre of the Bambara state. The Marka traders of Sansanding served as hosts and brokers (*diatigi*) to Moors who frequented Sansanding, bringing salt, tobacco, beads and Moroccan manufactures to exchange for gold, slaves, local cloth and foodstuffs. Sansanding also traded to the west, mainly in slaves, to the Senegal and the Gambia, and to the south, mainly in gold to Bure.

TRADE AND POLITICS AMONG THE DYULA AND MOSSI-DAGOMBA

In the markets of the middle Niger, the trans-Saharan trade of the Moors converged with the Dyula trade system. Since the fifteenth century the

[1] Park, *Travels* (1799), 165–7. [2] Ibid. 109.

Dyula, Malinke-speaking traders, had opened routes to the south to the sources of kola and gold in the forest. Operating beyond the pale of imperial Mali, they played a leading role in opening up the southern savanna to influences from the north. In the maze of the Dyula trading system one may discern three main directions of advance. Two led from the middle Niger towards the Akan forest, with the Black Volta river separating the routes across the Mossi-Dagomba states to the east from the routes across the stateless Bobo and Senufo to the west. The third, farther to the west, led from the upper Niger to Worodugu, 'the land of the kola'. There, the Dyula were soon to be followed by a migration of Malinke peasants and warriors, heirs to the empire of Mali.

The Moroccan conquest of 1591 relieved the old and declining empire of Mali from the pressure of Songhay on its northern frontier. The pashas, we have seen, did not establish a strong military presence in Jenne, let alone south of the delta. In a final attempt to recover the power of Mali, its king, Maḥmūd, attacked Jenne in 1599. But with his defeat at its gates by the Moroccan musketeers, Mali ceased to be a political factor on the middle Niger, and is not mentioned any more in the Arabic records of that region. According to traditions, Niani, the capital of Mali, was destroyed by the Bambara and Fulani, who invaded the Niger valley early in the seventeenth century. The royal Keita dynasty split, and the disintegration of the empire of Mali was complete.

Since the fifteenth and sixteenth centuries, Malinke peasants and warriors had migrated south of the upper Niger in search of new lands. This migration was intensified as the pressure on Mali increased. Mali had never ruled over the new territories acquired by the Malinke, but the latter, and especially the royal Keita clan, carried with them the imperial traditions of Mali's greatness. Politically, however, they were fragmented into numerous *kafus* of several villages each, which resembled the pre-imperial setting before the small Malinke chiefdoms were united by Sundiata (see volume 3, chapter 6). This fragmented political order was occasionally disturbed with the rise of war-chiefs, who extended their military domination over wider areas. Such conquest states were, however, ephemeral and hardly survived the death of the founder.

By the seventeenth century kola nuts had become the main export staple in the north-bound trade of the Dyula. Malinke peasants and warriors as well as Dyula traders did not penetrate into the kola-producing area, but stopped at the fringes of the forest. Along the new ethnic frontiers, where the representatives of the Sudanic civilization encountered the peoples of the forest, the Dyula established trading centres, such as Beyla, Touba, Seguela and Makono. These Dyula, who lived under the authority of non-Muslim Malinke chiefs, acted as brokers between the itinerant traders who came from the north and the local producers of the kola. Along the routes other centres developed, such as Tengrella, Odienne and Kankan.

Kankan had started as a small village at the end of the sixteenth century, and developed as a trading town on the kola route. The later prosperity of Kankan as a centre of trade and Islam was due to the impact of the Europeans' presence on the upper Guinea coast. The Dyula trade routes were extended to the seaboard, across the Futa Jalon westward to the Rivières du Sud, and from the upper Milo river southward to the Liberian coast. At the junction of these two routes to the west and to the south, Kankan was also connected with Bamako by the Milo and Niger waterways. Trade across the Futa Jalon, we shall see later in this chapter, was among the factors which produced the Fulani revolution in the eighteenth century. The success of the jihad created in turn more favourable conditions for trade: relative peace and security under Muslim control. Trade between Kankan and the upper Guinea coast intensified, and the growth of the Dyula population in the town and in the surrounding villages gave rise to the Muslim chiefdom of Bate. About the middle of the eighteenth century, however, Bate was conquered by Konde Birama, the ruler of Wasulu, in his wars against the Fulani of Futa Jalon (see p. 209). In 1778, following the defeat of Konde Birama by the Fulani, Kankan was freed from pagan rule and prospered under the authority of Alfa Kaabine, a Muslim *'ālim*, who died in 1810.

The Dyula state of Kankan was an exception in the area of Malinke expansion, where the Dyula traders generally operated within the existing system of *kafus*. But in the north-eastern section of the modern Ivory Coast, among the loosely organized Senufo, the wealth of the Dyula and their religious prestige was transformed into political power when joined by the Wattara warriors. The latter offered protection to the Dyula traders, and imposed their authority over the non-Muslim population. Kong, an important centre of trade and Islamic scholarship, was the most important of several states established by the Wattara. Yves Person suggests that Kong was the first state of the Mande to base its power on firearms. Through their trade with the Europeans on the upper Guinea coast, the Dyula obtained firearms which the Wattara warriors employed to further the trading interests of the Dyula. This process had its own dynamism, as the consolidation of authority over one trading centre called for its extension over the feeder routes, to secure the flow of trade. Some time after Seku Wattara had gained power over Kong at the beginning of the eighteenth century, his brother Famaghan led an ambitious expedition to dominate the trade system as far as Jenne, which he was reported (by the contemporary chronicler of the *Tadhkirat al-Nisyān*) to have reached in 1739. The march across the country of stateless people was easy enough for the troops of Kong, but on the middle Niger they were defeated by the combined forces of Biton Kulibali of Segu and his Fulani allies from Fuladugu (see p. 175). Subsequently, Famaghan retreated to establish a Dyula state among the Bobo, where he died in 1750.

The Wattara warriors were only the nucleus and the commanders of Kong's army. Seku Wattara recruited many Senufo to his army, and these formed a caste of warriors, with a distinctly animist ethos. The Wattara left the town of Kong to the Muslims, and settled in surrounding villages, and along the trade routes, among their warriors. When he died in 1745, Seku Wattara left one of the largest states of the southern savanna, whose influence was felt – in various degrees – from the fringes of the forest in the south to the Bani river in the north. Yet this empire lacked cohesiveness, and by the end of the eighteenth century it was fragmented into many principalities.

From Kong the route to the Akan forest passed through Buna and Bonduku. The Dyula communities in Bonduku, Buna and Kong claim to have come from Begho, which had been established as an advanced post of the Dyula for the gold trade in the fifteenth century. By the seventeenth century, however, a growing volume of the Akan gold had been diverted to the European factories on the Gold Coast. This change in the pattern of the trade was associated with the rise of Asante, which began to press northwards about 1670. Begho was thus deprived of its commercial function, and was conquered by Asante at the beginning of the eighteenth century. In 1722–3, in the same northward thrust, Asante conquered Bono-Mansu, the northern state of the Akan on the fringes of the forest.

The emergence of Bono-Mansu in the fifteenth century had been associated with its control of the gold and kola sources of the forest. Some of the routes from Jenne to Bono-Mansu crossed the country of the Voltaic-speaking peoples, among whom warlike horsemen, who had come from the north-east, established the several states of the Mossi-Dagomba group. These states offered greater security for trade, and the benefits their rulers derived from controlling the routes helped them in consolidating their authority.

The history of Yatenga, the northernmost of the Mossi states, was closely associated with events on the Niger. Successive expeditions against the Mossi – in 1549, 1562, and 1575 – indicate the continuous pressure of Songhay, which had begun with the defeat of the Mossi by Sonni 'Alī in 1483. But in the seventeenth century, following the collapse of the Songhay empire, the Yatenga *nabas* pursued an expansionist policy to the north. By the end of the century, Yatenga reached the peak of its power. In their northward expansion, the Mossi of Yatenga forced the Dogon to seek refuge in the Bandiagara mountains, though some groups stayed to co-operate with the Mossi chiefs as priests of fertility cults. The Yatenga *nabas* encountered fiercer resistance from the Samo, excellent warriors, who fought furiously for their independence.

In the Mossi states there was constant antagonism between the *naba*'s supreme authority and the territorial chiefs, who were mostly *nakomse*, descendants of former rulers, possessors of the *nam* (political authority). Their courts were a faithful reflection of the king's palace and they endeavoured to secure a greater measure of autonomy. In the first half of the eighteenth century, the power of the *nakomse* nobility in Yatenga increased at the expense of the *naba*'s authority. A rapid succession of some dozen rulers in half a century came to an end with Naba Kango (1757–87), the greatest of the Yatenga *nabas*. Forced into exile by his cousin, Naba Kango stayed for some time in Segu and came back in 1757 with Bambara troops armed with flintlocks, the first ever seen in Yatenga. The Bambara firearms gave Naba Kango the victory. Aided by Bambara, Bobo and Dyula mercenaries, he launched his reforms to strengthen the central authority.

Naba Kango established the new capital, Wahiguya, where he settled his foreign mercenaries as well as royal slaves. Around the capital, he planted villages which were royal fiefs or 'people of the king's house'. The court officials, aided by the royal slaves, were given control over the territorial chiefs, who were of the *nakomse* nobility. He also gave more power to the war-chiefs who did not hold hereditary positions but were nominated by the king. The court officials (*ne-somba*) and the war-chiefs (*ta-soba*) were recruited from lineages which had lost territorial command. The king, therefore, skilfully manipulated their opposition to the *nakomse*. But after Naba Kango's death, the *nakomse* exploited a series of succession disputes to undermine the central authority.

Naba Kango also pursued an aggressive foreign policy and was engaged in many wars, the most famous of which were those against N'golo Diara, the Bambara king of Segu. The first war, some time after 1770, is said to have followed a massacre of the Bambara mercenaries in Yatenga by Naba Kango. He may have been aware of the potential danger of keeping Bambara troops in the heart of his kingdom, and so, as soon as he felt secure enough, he rid himself of them in a treacherous mass massacre. N'golo Diara of Segu retaliated and invaded Yatenga. He was repulsed, but not before his troops had pillaged parts of Yatenga's territory. The second encounter is vaguely reported by Mungo Park. The Mossi chief attacked Jenne, then under Segu, and conquered this commercial city. He retreated after the king of Segu had promised to pay tribute and reparations for the depredations caused by the Bambara army in Yatenga. It was now the turn of the king of Segu to take the offensive. Naba Kango refused to extradite some Dyula who had sought refuge in Yatenga, following a civil war in Segu. N'golo Diara (or according to another version, his son and successor, Mansong) sent an expedition to Yatenga, which was repulsed. The war between Segu and Yatenga was thus drawn out.

The division of the Mossi into two states, between Naba Kumdumye, *mogho-naba* ('king of the world'), and Naba Yadega, founder of Yatenga, occurred about the middle of the sixteenth century. Naba Kumdumye sent his own sons to govern vassal principalities as a *cordon sanitaire* between his dominions and Yatenga. But, in the following centuries, the chiefs of these peripheral principalities, such as Yako, Boussouma and Mane, became practically independent of the *mogho-naba* of Wagadugu, though they continued to pay him nominal allegiance. By the end of the sixteenth century, the formative phase in the political history of the Mossi state of Wagadugu was over. The traditions say very little about the seventeenth century, when a line of undistinguished *mogho-nabas* succeeded each other. More is known of Naba Warga, who reigned in the second half of the eighteenth century. Like Naba Kango of Yatenga, he strengthened the authority of the central government by increasing the number of royal slaves, and by adding to the power of the court's attendants. He also created slave-villages loyal to the *mogho-naba* to balance the independent tendencies of the *nakomse* of the royal family. His son, Naba Zombre, made Wagadugu the permanent capital, whereas earlier the capital had moved with each *mogho-naba* to his own village. The increasing power of the *mogho-naba* in the eighteenth century was marked also by a filial succession (from father to son) instead of a collateral succession (in which brothers and cousins had precedence over sons). Significantly, the greater stability of the political centre was followed by a growing Islamic influence in the *mogho-naba*'s court (see p. 196).

Mossi royals claim an origin from Mamprusi, regarded in the traditions as the senior state in that group. From the centre of their kingdom on the Gambaga scarp, the Mamprusi chiefs extended an uncertain suzerainty over their northern neighbours, such as the Tallensi and the Kusassi. The authority of Mamprusi over these peoples was seldom effective, and although they were drawn into the orbit of its political system, they added more to its complexity than to its strength. Mamprusi was always weaker than Mossi to the north, and Dagomba in the south.

The first king of Dagomba, Na Sitobu, left Mamprusi following a dispute over the paramountcy. Na Nyaghse, Sitobu's son, was the real founder of the Dagomba state in the fifteenth century. He is said to have killed all the earth-priests to accelerate the integration of his warriors with the local population. He established his capital, now known as Yendi-Dabari ('Ruined Yendi'), close to the White Volta river, on a trade route which ran from Jenne to the sources of gold and kola in the Akan forest. Dagomba influence extended southward along this route to the point where the Black Volta river, flowing from west to east, marked the border between the woodland savanna and the fringes of the forest. As early as the sixteenth century, commercial centres had developed on the northern bank of the Black Volta.

The Dagomba expanded also to the west, probably attracted by the prospects of the Lobi gold fields, which lay across the Black Volta river in its flow from north to south (marking the present border between Ghana and the Ivory Coast). During the seventeenth century, two kingdoms were founded on both banks of the river – Buna and Wa – whose rulers claim Dagomba origin. Soon after the foundation of their kingdom, the Buna chiefs organized the exploitation of the goldfields. Assimilated into the local Kulango, the Buna chiefs lost all affinity to Dagomba. The chiefs of Wa, on the other hand, remained, historically as well as culturally, part of the Mossi-Dagomba group of states.

The hegemony of Dagomba in the middle Volta basin was seriously challenged in the second half of the sixteenth century, with the arrival of the Gbanya, warriors of Mande origin, who founded the Gonja state. They may have come along the route from the Niger to the forest, and they seem to have attempted to gain control over the important commercial centre of Begho. But in the fringes of the forest the superiority of their cavalry was lost and they were defeated by the Brong, the northernmost Akan.

The Gbanya turned north, crossed the Black Volta and conquered the country just north of this river. They imposed their authority over the local population. Though they adopted the Guan language of the conquered, the Gbanya warriors remained a closed ruling estate, clearly distinct from the commoners. The consolidation of the new state was achieved in the middle of the seventeenth century. Actual power was vested with the divisional chiefs, who owed ceremonial and ritual allegiance to the paramount. All the chiefs were united in claiming descent from Jakpa, regarded in tradition as the founder of the Gonja state.

During the first half of the seventeenth century, the Dagomba lost to Gonja whatever political influence they had held over the northern bank of the Black Volta. In the second half of the seventeenth century, one of the divisional chiefs of Gonja, probably supported by troops from other divisions, advanced northward and conquered Daboya from the Dagomba. Daboya was an important centre for the alluvial salt which was extracted on the banks of the White Volta in its vicinity, and then distributed over the whole Volta basin. The threat to Dagomba was all the more serious because its capital lay only a few miles across the river from Daboya. The younger vigorous state of Gonja pressed on the kingdom of Dagomba, which had already existed for two centuries, and about 1700, following a series of battles near the White Volta, the Dagomba were forced to abandon their capital. They retreated to the east and conquered part of the Konkomba country on the Oti river. The Gonja continued their pressure, but with their defeat in 1713 the Dagomba finally checked Gonja expansion and liberated the territories they had lost as far as the White Volta. After the Gonja threat had been removed, the Dagomba established their new capital, the present Yendi.

Yendi, the new Dagomba capital, was established on the Hausa route to Katsina, because the Dagomba retreat to the east at the beginning of the eighteenth century coincided with the growth of the trade between Hausaland and the Akan forest. It was part of a significant change in the inter-regional trade patterns of West Africa, with the shift of the commercial centre of gravity from the middle Niger (Timbuktu and Gao) to Hausaland (Katsina and Kano). Though some trade continued across the western Sahara to Morocco, traffic over the trans-Saharan trails between Tripoli and the central Sudan became more intensive. The growing opulence of Hausaland, through its trans-Saharan trade, increased the consumption of kola nuts. Kola is chewed, and its liquid, acting as stimulant, helps to overcome thirst. Kola comprised a most appropriate present, and was given by a host to his guests and by subjects to their chiefs. The rising demand for kola stimulated the lucrative caravan trade between Hausaland and the Akan forest.

The expansion of Asante followed the direction of the trade. In 1732 Gonja became tributary to Asante, and over a decade later Dagomba acknowledged the supremacy of Asante. The musketeers of the forest demonstrated their superiority over the horsemen of the savanna. Asante imposed a form of 'indirect rule' over Dagomba and Gonja, whose rulers were closely supervised by commissioners sent from Kumasi. Both states had to pay an annual tribute, part of it in slaves.

The development of trade between Hausaland and the Akan forest stimulated far-reaching political developments along the alternative itineraries taken by the caravans. In the middle of the eighteenth century, Mande warriors of the Wattara clan, in command of Twi-speaking troops, were invited as mercenaries from Mango (Grumania), in the Ivory Coast, into the Volta basin. After they had been employed by the Gonja in internal conflicts, they were called by the Mamprusi king to help him in warding off the pressure of the aggressive Gurma. Instead of returning home, these Mande-Twi warriors, who came to be known by the Dagomba and Mamprusi as Chakossi, settled in the country they had conquered, making Sansanne-Mango ('the camp of the Mango' in the Hausa language) the centre of their state. The place was well chosen on the way to Hausaland, after the route had left the territories protected by Dagomba or Mamprusi, and before it entered the sparsely populated and hazardous territory of petty Gurma chiefdoms.

South of Sansanne-Mango but still in northern Togo, among stateless peoples, the confederated chiefdoms of the Kotokoli were founded by the Mola clan – of Gurma origin – at the beginning of the eighteenth century. The more important Kotokoli centres developed on the trade routes from Hausaland. Indeed, the foundation of the chiefdoms seems to have been favoured by the growth of the trade on these routes at that time. East of Kotokoli, Djougou (in present-day Dahomey) developed as a major commercial centre on the trade route. The chieftaincy of Djougou was established about the middle of the eighteenth century by a Gurma weaver. According to one tradition, this Gurma stranger was appointed to supervise the toll-post, which the local ruler, an earth-priest, had levied on the busy trade route. From this strategic position, the Gurma's son made himself chief of the region. Djougou assumed its Islamic character when Hausa and Dendi Muslims settled there.

These local histories of kingdoms along the trade routes to Hausaland indicate the role of the Gurma in the process of state-building. The Gurma, or Gurmantche, whose territory extended east of the Mossi, were divided into autonomous chiefdoms. In the eighteenth century they expanded in different directions; they exerted pressure on Mamprusi and provided the ruling dynasties of the Kotokoli and Djougou. Liptako, north of the Mossi, also came under Gurma domination in the eighteenth century. The dynamism of the Gurma at this period may be explained by the influence of the trade routes across their country, from Gaya or Say on the Niger to Sansanne-Mango or to Kupela (an important trading centre in Mossi) and then to Salaga.

Crossing the territory of the Gurma was regarded as dangerous for traders' caravans. On the other trade route, through Djougou and Kotokoli to Salaga, the Bariba of Borgu were notorious for their raids on passing caravans. The Bariba chiefdoms, astride the present Dahomey-Nigerian border, were founded not later than the fifteenth century by the Wasangarani warriors. They imposed their authority through military conquest and sanctioned it by contractual alliance with earth-priests as representatives of the local population. In the seventeenth and eighteenth centuries, the Wasangarani extended their dominions along the trade routes, and the capitals of new chiefdoms were often established in, or near, caravanserais. The dynamism of the Bariba expansion brought them into conflict with the Gurma who had experienced a comparable process of expansion.

In the second half of the seventeenth century, when the Songhay state of Dendi disintegrated, a group of Songhay, led by two members of the royal family, moved down the Niger river. Passing the country already occupied by their Jerma (or Zaberma) kin (see p. 167), they reached that part of the Niger valley where the present frontiers of Nigeria, Niger and Dahomey converge, on the fringes of the Hausa-speaking cultural zone. The Songhay subjugated and assimilated the Tiengas who had lived there in small independent communities. This eastern extension of the Songhay became known as Dendi, taking over the name of the earlier Dendi, which had been farther to the north. Attempts to establish a stable state in this new Dendi failed, and the country was divided among members of the royal family (the descendants of the *askiya*). Because of their political and military weakness, the Dendi came into the orbit of Borgu.

The Songhay migrants to the new Dendi carried with them some of the Islamic heritage of the *askiyas*. Later, Islam was reinforced among them through contacts with the Hausa. During the eighteenth and nineteenth centuries, the Songhay-speaking Dendi spread south to settle in trading centres along the caravan routes leading from Hausaland to Gonja. In Djougou, Parakou and Nikki the cultural influences of the Dendi exceeded their proportion even among the Muslim population. Their language became the *lingua franca* of the Muslims in northern Dahomey, marking the last stage in the expansion of Songhay.

ISLAM IN THE STATES OF THE SAVANNA

It was in the seventeenth and eighteenth centuries that the influence of Islam reached the fringes of the forest in the south. Islam thus became one of the unifying themes of that vast part of West Africa north of the forest, from the savanna to the Sahel, and across the Sahara to North Africa. The influence of Islam, however, was not uniform, and one may discern different shades of Islamic civilization, from its exclusiveness in the cities of North Africa to its rudimentary features in the southern savanna close to the forest. Nevertheless, the constant flow of ideological communication, of books and scholarship, of pilgrims and marabouts along the trade routes, secured the vitality of Islam as far as the remotest commercial outposts in the south.

These two centuries have been described as a period of 'Islamic stagnation and pagan reaction',[1] but one can trace a great measure of continuity in the development of Islam from the preceding period of the great empires. Songhay and Mali had been Islamic empires to the extent that Islam had become integrated into the imperial texture both ideologically and institutionally. Yet even the great *mansas* and *askiyas*, who had been exposed to strong Islamic influence through the trans-Saharan contacts with the wider Muslim world, remained attached to the pre-Islamic heritage as the source for the legitimacy of their kingship. Almost all their subjects – peasants, herdsmen and fishermen – were animists, and Islam was confined to the towns among the traders and the '*ulamā*'. The same pattern continued into the seventeenth and eighteenth centuries, except that the rulers of the smaller states, which had emerged from the ruins of the great empires, had hardly any

[1] J. S. Trimingham, *A history of Islam in West Africa* (London, 1962), 141.

contacts with Islamic centres north of the Sahara, and were more strongly influenced by the traditional particularist spirit of their peoples.

The history of Songhay is explicable in terms of the tension between the Muslim *'ulamā'* and the custodians of traditionalism. The more powerful *askiyas* of the sixteenth century followed the policy, initiated by the founder of the dynasty, Askiya al-Ḥājj Muḥammad, of an alliance with the *'ulamā'*, though some *askiyas*, as well as some pretenders, turned to recruit the support of traditionalists. After 1591, the resistance of the Songhay to the Moroccans was sustained, as we have seen, by the Sohantye, descendants of Sonni 'Alī, who had retreated south to Dendi a century before. The Sohantye came to be regarded as custodians of the Songhay national heritage and as masters of magic. Among the independent Songhay of Dendi, there was a greater adherence to the ancestral traditions, and a movement away from Islam, which was then represented by the aggressive Moroccan conquerors.

Before the rise of the Bambara states, local chiefs on the middle Niger had come under Islamic influence. Chiefs had Muslim names like Mansa 'Alī, Mansa Muḥammad, or Mansa 'Uthmān and they cultivated close relations with *'ulamā'*, among them al-Sa'dī, the author of the *Ta'rīkh al-Sūdān*. These relations brought about conversion in the chiefly families. One *qāḍī* of Jenne, Modibo Bakr Traore, was 'from among the sons of the chiefs of Kala, who withdrew from authority and occupied himself with learning'.[1] These islamized, rather than Muslim, chiefs contrasted with the animist Bambara. Yet, the Bambara themselves were exposed to Islamic influence, and Biton Kulibali, founder of the state of Segu, was known also by his Muslim name Mamari (a Sudanic version of the Arabic Muḥammad). In his efforts to restructure Bambara society, Biton relied largely on traditional Bambara customs and values. Yet, in forcing greater centralization and autocracy, he disrupted the old order of Bambara communal life. In pursuing this policy he may well have clashed with the custodians of Bambara traditionalism, but could have found support from Muslims, both *'ulamā'* and traders. The latter always fared better under the auspices of strong chiefs than in a country of loose political organization. He consulted the *'ulamā'* and sought their blessings. In the process of state-building, Biton/Mamari had to maintain a balance between traditional and Islamic elements.

Following a custom which prevailed among chiefs in the Sudan, Biton Kulibali sent his son Bakary to study the Koran. Though he was not supposed to convert, Bakary became a Muslim in Jenne and on his

[1] *T. al-Sūdān*, p. 19/tr. 34.

accession he attempted to introduce Islam into the very centre of the state. He failed to keep the balance between traditionalism and Islam, and was deposed. The restoration of the egalitarian system of the *ton*, which followed, was also a reassertion of traditionalism. Shortly afterwards, power was again monopolized by N'golo Diara, founder of the second dynasty in Segu.

During the lifetime of Biton Kulibali, the adventures attributed by traditions to N'golo Diara had brought him on several occasions under the influence of '*ulamā*' in Jenne and Timbuktu, and he is said to have learnt the Koran. But N'golo Diara did not become a Muslim. He returned to Segu to be appointed 'grand priest of the idols', and it was on these idols that the *ton-dyon* were forced to take their oath. N'golo skilfully maintained the balance between traditionalism and Islam. In the Bambara state, Muslim clerics were called to intervene as arbiters when traditional mechanisms failed. They had the reputation of integrity and impartiality as well as knowledge of the sacred texts. N'golo Diara extended his protection over the Muslim trading communities, who enjoyed security but were allowed to maintain their autonomy.

Traditions say that Mansong, son of N'golo Diara, was aided by Muslims in the succession dispute against his brothers. He is said to have had four marabouts, whom he consulted on all affairs of the state. Mungo Park was aware of the influence of Muslims in Segu, alleging that Mansong 'would willingly have admitted me into his presence at Sego; but was apprehensive he might not be able to protect me against the blind and inveterate malice of the Moorish inhabitants'.[1] In Segu, Park reported, 'Moorish mosques are seen in every quarter.'[2] In Guemu, capital of the rival Bambara state, he observed 'that the disciples of Mahomet composed nearly one half of the army of Kaarta'. When the whole army concentrated in the capital, 'the mosques were very crowded', but Park was careful enough to note that these were 'of those Negroes who, together with the ceremonial part of the Mahomedan religion, retain all their ancient superstitions and even drink strong Liquors'.[3]

Exposed as they were to Islamic influence, the newly created nobility of the Bambara became culturally differentiated from the animist peasants. The Bambara sometimes distinguish among themselves between 'believers' and 'unbelievers'; the former were the Kulibali, the Diara and other aristocratic clans. Thus as long as the Bambara

[1] Park, *Travels* (1799), 200. [2] Ibid. 195.
[3] Ibid. 195.

were submerged in Muslim states they had hardly been influenced by Islam, and even manifested resistance to Islam as well as to other aspects of imperial authority. But in their own process of state-building, with Bambara clans in political authority, their dealings with Muslims within the state and outside resulted in acculturation. Islam became part of the religious practices to which clan chiefs were initiated. The Kulibali and the Diara rulers practised rudimentary Islam without abandoning their idols, which they shared with the Bambara commoners.

The role of Muslims as advisers to rulers and as masters of supernatural powers through prayer and amulets was carried from the middle Niger down to the Volta basin in the south by the Gbanya, founders of the Gonja state. These warriors were accompanied by Muslims when they entered the Volta basin. Muslims shared the conquest of the land with the chiefs, and became an integral part of the socio-political system of the Gonja state from its foundation. The descendants of Fati-Morukpe, the Muslim companion of the founder, were appointed *imāms* of the principal divisional chiefs. Chiefs had Muslim names, they were circumcised, and used to call Muslims to officiate in the major rituals of the life cycle. Muslim festivals became the official feasts, though celebrated in a way which retained little of their Islamic origin. The Gonja chiefs absorbed Islamic influence, but did not become Muslims themselves; like the Bambara, they adopted a position midway between Islam and traditionalism. Chiefs referred both to shrine-priests and to their *imāms*; they required the ritual ceremonies of the earth-priests as well as the prayers of the Muslims. The participation of Muslims in the conquest brought them into intimate relations with the chiefs, but the differentiation into distinct social estates – chiefs, Muslims and commoners – which had been crystallized soon after the conquest, hardly allowed any mobility, and inhibited the spread of Islam from the Muslim to the other estates. Significantly, a similar pattern prevailed in the Chakossi state of Sansanne-Mango, where Muslims had also participated in the conquest and the same rigid division into social estates occurred.

Gonja traditions ascribed their success in wars to the prayers and charms of their Muslim followers. The Dagomba, who had been defeated by the Gonja towards the end of the seventeenth century, may have responded to this challenge when they turned at that time to Muslims, who had already resided in their country for some generations. Dagomba history was later to provide another example of their ability to adopt their adversaries' advantages; responding to the challenge of firearms, after they had been defeated by the Asante, the Dagomba created units of musketeers on the Asante model. From the beginning of the eighteenth century, Muslims from Hausaland, who frequented the routes to the kola markets, found their way to the courts of the Dagomba rulers. There they soon replaced the earlier Mande Muslims in rendering religious services to the chiefs. The vitality of the Hausa accelerated the progress of Islam in Dagomba. Chiefs, as in Gonja, adopted a middle position between Muslims and commoners, but because the lines of demarcation among the social estates in Dagomba were not so boldly engraved as in Gonja, individuals often moved from the chiefly to the commoners' or to the Muslims' estate. There are documented cases of chiefs' sons and grandsons who became practising Muslims. The cohesive political system of Dagomba, in which chiefs were sent from the centre to rule over villages, and then moved up the hierarchy towards the paramountcy, contributed to the spread of Islam from the capital to the divisions.

A survey of the spread of Islam in the Volta basin clearly indicates that Islam gained ground only in centralized states; stateless peoples remained uninfluenced, even though their country was traversed by caravan routes. The small kingdom of Wa (west of Dagomba, near the Black Volta river) is a good illustration of the close association of chiefs and Muslims. Both represented ideas and institutions alien to the local acephalous population, and found mutual support in each other. Wa emerged during the eighteenth century as a citadel of Islam amid pagan stateless peoples.

Islam was introduced to Mamprusi at the same time as to Dagomba, but there was tension between the Muslims, led by the *imām* of Gambaga, and the *nayiri*, the Mamprusi paramount. In the first half of the eighteenth century, with the development of the Hausa trade route and the growth of the Muslim community in Gambaga, the *nayiri* moved his residence to the secluded and walled village of Nalerigu. Set apart from the cosmopolitan Gambaga, it was yet close enough to control this important centre of trade and Islam. In two of the other three divisions of Mamprusi, the chiefs' villages were also separated from the Muslims' towns, which may indicate reserved relations between chiefs and Muslims in Mamprusi compared with the intimate relations in Gonja and the close association in Dagomba.

The Mossi are often referred to as 'the successful champions of paganism'. Though by the nineteenth century Islam had gained much ground among the Mossi, they had resisted Islamic influence for two centuries. The first Muslim traders, the Yarse, had settled among the Mossi in the sixteenth century. They adopted the language of the Mossi and many of their customs. But it was only about the end of the eighteenth century that Naba Dulugu appointed the first *imām* and that the first mosque was built in Wagadugu. Traditions also suggest that in introducing an *imām* into his court, the *mogho-naba* followed the example of the Mamprusi king, to whom Mossi chiefs give the title of 'father'. The Mossi had faced the brutal challenge of the islamized empire of Songhay, and may have been suspicious of Islamic influence coming from the north. But once Islam had been accommodated in the sister states of Dagomba and Mamprusi to the south, without undermining their political structure, it was presented in a way acceptable to the Mossi. It is significant also that the growth of Islamic influence in the *mogho-naba*'s court occurred in the second half of the eighteenth century, after Wagadugu had been established as the permanent capital and the power of the central authority had increased.

Naba Dulugu, reckoned by the traditions as the first islamized king, is said to have been sent by his father to study the Koran with the Muslims. But he himself later sent away his son for having been too favourable to Islam. The more conservative elements in the court, the custodians of traditional religion, attempted to arrest Islamic influence, and even islamized chiefs in Wagadugu were anxious to avoid the interference of Islam with those traditional rites which supported the political system.

The traditions of Borgu, in northern Dahomey, also reflect ambivalent attitudes towards Islam. On the one hand, chiefs came under a certain Islamic influence from Muslims who had settled along the trade routes, in a way typical of other West African states. On the other hand, there is a strong tradition about resistance to Islamic pressure, for which there is historical evidence in at least two cases, namely the Songhay invasion in the sixteenth century and the Fulani jihad in the nineteenth century. External aggression might have conditioned the impact of Islam, for Islamic influence was reluctantly accepted. In Gonja and Dagomba, chiefs willingly celebrate the Islamic festivals and they pray occasionally, whereas in Borgu the tradition insists that the chiefs pray twice a year only. The name Bariba, by which the people of Borgu are known, has the connotation of 'unbelievers'. It is therefore impossible to speak of a 'Muslim Bariba'; a Bariba who becomes Muslim is referred to as a 'Dendi', which in that part of West Africa became generic for Muslims.

In the eighteenth century, therefore, Islam was integrated into the socio-political system of the savanna states, a process which can hardly be called stagnation. Islam was the most dynamic cultural factor north of the forest, where it was carried by Muslim traders. In the context of general insecurity, when peasants refrained from travelling away from their homes, the Muslims were still engaged in long distance trade. They were protected by reverence for their supernatural power, and found hospitality among their brethren in the Muslim communities which developed along the trade routes. In the context of general political fragmentation and particularism, the Muslims created a vast network of alliances based on kinship, trade and religion.

One can distinguish three patterns of relations between the Dyula and the non-Muslim local peoples. In the Mossi-Dagomba group of states, east of the Black Volta river, Muslims lived under the auspices of the chiefs, adopted their language and became integrated into the socio-political system. West of the Black Volta river, among stateless non-Mande peoples, such as the Senufo, the Dyula preserved their separate ethnic and linguistic identity. They formed autonomous Muslim communities, and participated in a process of state-building. Farther to the west, on the modern frontiers of the Ivory Coast and Guinea, the Dyula differed from their Malinke neighbours only by their commercial occupation and Islamic religion. Indeed, they were commonly known as Maninka-Mori, or Muslim Malinke. Isolated Dyula who had ceased to move about as traders and had turned agriculturalists, gradually shed Islamic practices and became assimilated into the Malinke. The process developed in the other direction also, where Malinke who turned to trade moved closer to Islam and became Dyula.

Most Dyula acquired only a very elementary knowledge of reading and writing in Arabic, but a few attained a higher level of Islamic education to become teachers and religious functionaries and formed a professional class of '*ulamā*' or *karamokho*. The '*ulamā*', like the traders, communicated along the trade routes with the large centres of trade and Islam, such as Jenne. The leading '*ulamā*' of Jenne were Marka of Soninke origin, and Islam there was Sudanic in its character, with greater emphasis on the ritual rather than the legal aspects of Islam. It was in Jenne that a man who 'was ignorant and knew nothing about legal questions was appointed *qāḍī*'.[1] In the seventeenth century, according to al-Sa'dī, Muslims in Jenne did not refer to the *qāḍī*, but preferred to litigate before the preacher, who used to settle affairs by

[1] *T. al-Sūdān*, p. 302/tr. 457.

conciliation, and very likely with reference to customary law as well as to the *Sharīʿa*. Jenne produced some eminent scholars, such as the Baghayogho brothers, but even these moved to Timbuktu, the recognized seat of learning. Muslim education in Jenne was widespread but not of the highest level. These Islamic standards of Jenne later irritated Shekhu Aḥmadu Lobo, and led him to protest against the established ways of Islam. But, it was also in Jenne that he was inspired by a mystic of the Qādiriyya brotherhood, which became influential in the Sudan from the second half of the eighteenth century.

Shekhu Aḥmadu's milieu was the society of the pastoral Fulani, who were closely attached to magico-religious rites and observances to secure the prosperity of their cattle herds. Relations between men and their cattle were both economic and religious. Before the religious revolutions of the eighteenth (Futa Toro and Futa Jalon) and the nineteenth (Hausaland and Massina) centuries, the pastoral Fulani had hardly been influenced by Islam. In the historiography of Massina, the period before the jihad of Shekhu Aḥmadu is known as *dyahilaaku*, equivalent to the *jāhiliyya* of pre-Islamic Arabia.

The Fulani of Massina, however, lived along the islamized axis between Timbuktu and Jenne and in the vicinity of the old centres of Islam like Dia and Diafarabe. Individual Fulani converted to Islam, and al-Saʿdī mentioned names of Fulani *ʿulamāʾ*, one of whom became the *imām* of the Great Friday mosque in Timbuktu. As a result, quasi-clans of *ʿulamāʾ* developed among the Fulani, known as Diaobe, or 'people of Dia', because of the importance of Dia as a centre for the diffusion of Islamic influence. People could join the ranks of the *ʿulamāʾ* by learning, but most of the *ʿulamāʾ* were concerned with the fabrication of amulets, and few were really scholars. In Massina itself, there was a *qāḍī* and other *ʿulamāʾ* closely associated with the *ardo*. In this respect the position of Islam in Massina was similar to that in other Sudanic states, where Muslims rendered religious services to chiefs. Under their influence, the *ardos* adopted Muslim names and practised some Islamic rites. Ḥammadi Amina II (1628–63) is said to have prayed. In fact, for a pious Muslim like al-Saʿdī, the Bambara were animists, but the Fulani were not, or at least they were not described as such. When the *ardo* Ḥammadi Amina accepted the pasha's authority through the intercession of the *qāḍīs* of Jenne and Massina, it was said that 'he entered the sacrosanctity (*ḥurma*) of Islam and the *fuqahāʾ*'.[1]

A radical change in the role of Islam among the Fulani and in the

[1] *T. al-Sūdān*, p. 251/tr. 385.

role of the Fulani in the history of Africa came about during and after the eighteenth century. The jihad movements engulfed the whole breadth of the northern belt of the western Sudan, but did not reach the states of the southern savanna until the second half of the nineteenth century. Not only was Islam in the Sahel and the northern savanna of longer duration and therefore ripe for the religious revolution, but it was also closer to the desert, from where Islamic militancy expanded to the south.

THE EARLY JIHAD MOVEMENTS

The Islamic revivalism which culminated in the jihad movements of the nineteenth century was by no means a new phenomenon in the western Sudan. The nineteenth century merely experienced the expansion and intensification of a revival which had been developing in the south-western Sahara and the Senegal valley since the seventeenth century. One may even seek the origins of this process in the Almoravid movement and in the Islamic militancy of Takrur in the eleventh century. The disintegration of the Almoravid movement left the Sanhaja of the south-western Sahara weak and divided. The more aggressive and warlike clans imposed their protection upon weaker groups. Some of the latter, whose arms had failed, adhered to the religious heritage of the Almoravids; they gave up fighting and became devoted to Islamic learning and piety, being known as Zawāyā or maraboutic tribes. This pattern of relations between warriors, who cared little for Islam, and the Zawāyā, had probably preceded the arrival of the Ḥassān, Arab nomads who had been penetrating into the south-western Sahara since the fifteenth century. Under Arab domination a Moorish society evolved, comprising Ḥassān, Zawāyā, and the tributary *laḥma*.

Successive Ḥassānī rulers of the Sahara, north of the Senegal, exerted pressure on the Zawāyā, who had to pay *gharama*, a form of collective tribute, in return for protection. Yet, their protectors were often incapable of defending them. Insecurity disrupted the commercial and pastoral pursuits of the Zawāyā. Under these conditions the Ḥassān were regarded as a legitimate target for a jihad. According to the eighteenth-century historian Muḥammad al-Yadālī, the worst enemies of Islam were the 'godless' Ḥassān, 'Arabs' who were 'cutters of the road', and who refused to accept the obligations of Islam, although nominally Muslims.[1]

[1] H. T. Norris, 'Znaga Islam during the seventeenth and eighteenth centuries', *Bulletin of the School of Oriental and African Studies* (1969), **32**, 3, 508.

The leader of the Zawāyā in their war against the Ḥassān was Awbek b. Ashfaga, known to posterity by his title Nāṣir al-Dīn. An ascetic scholar, punctilious in religious observances, he was a healer of body and mind, whose *baraka* was widely acknowledged. He began his preaching by calling for repentance (*tawba*), but as soon as he attracted followers from among his own people, the Banū Daymān and other Zawāyā, he proclaimed his political orientations. He aimed at creating a community that would transcend tribal and ethnic divisions and would resemble the ideal society of the early caliphs. He styled himself *Sayyidunā* (our master), *Imāmunā* (our *imām*), then *Mushī' al-Dīn* (he who spreads the Faith), and finally *Nāṣir al-Dīn* (protector of the Faith). All the Zawāyā were to be united in loyalty to their *imām* and every Zawāyā leader had to swear allegiance (*bay'a*) to him. He appointed a vizier and four *qāḍīs*, and was determined to establish order and political stability in the *Qibla* (the southern Sahara). Fighting against warriors who 'cut roads', neglected Islam and oppressed the believers; creating a supra-tribal community to overcome fragmentation; establishing a new divinely guided order: these goals of Nāṣir al-Dīn were also to be prominent in the jihad movements of the eighteenth and nineteenth centuries, and he stands in the line of Muslim leaders and revivalists from 'Abdallāh b. Yāsīn to al-ḥājj 'Umar.

Nāṣir al-Dīn started his jihad in 1673 by invading Futa Toro and the Wolof states across the Senegal river. In attacking to the south, Nāṣir al-Dīn may have sought to avoid a premature confrontation with the more powerful Ḥassān. There were probably also economic considerations, associated with the growth of French trade on the Senegal since the first half of the seventeenth century. By controlling the entrepôts for the gum trade on the Senegal he could offset the control of the Ḥassān over the trade to the ports of the Saharan coast.

Nāṣir al-Dīn then turned to build up his Islamic state and imposed the *zakāt*, the Islamic legal tax, on the tributary tribes (*laḥma*) north of the Senegal. Bubba, one of the tributaries, is said to have called in the aid of Hādī, the chief of the Trarza, one of the Ḥassānī groups. Traditions maintain that Bubba was responsible for the outbreak of the war between the Zawāyā and the Ḥassān, which became known as Shurbubba or 'the war of Bubba'. In his attempt to exercise political authority in the Sahara, Nāṣir al-Dīn challenged the political and military supremacy of the Ḥassān.

The Ḥassān were united, and although the main burden fell upon the Trarza, their Brakna kinsmen sent contingents as reinforcements and immobilized the Zawāyā in their region so that they could not join Nāṣir al-Dīn. Most of the Zawāyā of the southern Sahara rallied around Nāṣir al-Dīn, but some remained neutral, or even rendered support to the Ḥassān. A scholar of the Idaw Balhasan, a Zawāyā from Shinqit, issued a *fatwa* (legal opinion) that Nāṣir al-Dīn was not a caliph and had no right to impose the *zakāt*. This was in defiance of Nāṣir al-Dīn's political claims, which were couched in religious terms. Hādī, the Trarza chief, sent troops to seize animals that had already been collected as *zakāt*.

Three battles between Nāṣir al-Dīn and Hādī are on record. Two of them – the first near the port of Portendick and the second near the salt mines of Awlil – may indicate that they were also fighting over the economic assets of the south-western Sahara. The Zawāyā were victorious in all three battles, but in the third and most crucial one Nāṣir al-Dīn was killed, together with many of his close companions, probably in August 1674.

As their second *imām* and successor to Nāṣir al-Dīn, the Zawāyā elected *al-faqīh* al-Amīn b. Sīdī al-Fāḍil, whose ancestors had employed their *baraka* in the service of the Ḥassānī chiefs. He was, therefore, better disposed to conciliate the Ḥassān, while the latter, who had been defeated three times, were ready to come to terms. They seem to have accepted the spiritual authority of the Zawāyā *imām*, provided the latter would give up political claims, including the levying of the *zakāt*. The majority of the Zawāyā, however, remained loyal to the militant heritage of Nāṣir al-Dīn, and the compromising *al-faqīh* al-Amīn was deposed. He was succeeded by the *qāḍī* 'Uthmān, Nāṣir al-Dīn's vizier and one of his closest companions.

The *qāḍī* 'Uthmān revived a militant policy of unmitigated confrontation with the Ḥassān. He reintroduced the levy of *zakāt* from weaker tribes and factions. But even they resisted, joined together and sought the support of Hādī, the Trarza chief, whose troops annihilated the Zawāyā's tax-collecting expedition. The *qāḍī* 'Uthmān was killed in fighting the Wolof, while the three *imāms* who succeeded him (among them Munīr al-Dīn, brother of Nāṣir al-Dīn) were defeated when they faced a concerted effort of the Ḥassān.

The unconditional defeat of the Zawāyā is interpreted in the traditions as a justification for the rigid stratification in Moorish society. The Zawāyā renounced all pretensions to temporal authority, both military and political, and paid tribute in return for protection. Ḥassānī warriors had the right to drink the milk of the Zawāyā's herds and had access to a third of the water of the Zawāyā's wells. Zawāyā were obliged to accommodate passing warriors for three days. The Zawāyā became divided among the warriors, so that every Ḥassānī group had its own Zawāyā or *ṭulabā'*. It seems, however, that conditions of the Zawāyā after the war differed little from what they had experienced before. Their subjugation by the Ḥassān was a longer process, and the war was merely a convenient historiographical landmark.

The Shurbubba war was an attempt to rectify existing relations between the believers and the warriors. Its goal was therefore similar to that of the Torodbe jihad against the Denianke in the Futa Toro a century later. The Zawāyā jihad, however, failed, and the embryonic Islamic state of Nāṣir al-Dīn was destroyed. The *'ulamā'* remained politically subjected to the warriors, but the defeat deepened the spiritual experience of the Zawāyā and added militancy to their religious teaching in the neighbouring Sudanic countries. The position of Islam in the Sudanic kingdoms on the Senegal was, eventually, decided by the outcome of internal tensions and competition between Islam and traditionalism. By the end of the eighteenth century, the former had triumphed in the Futa Toro, whereas the latter was still predominant in the Wolof states.

By the seventeenth century, Kayor had emerged as the most powerful state of the Wolof, mainly due to its favourable position on the coast for trade with the Europeans. Kayor traded in gum and indigo, in slaves and in ivory; salt was also carried into the interior to be exchanged for gold. In order to secure a growing share of the profits from the trade, the *damel*, or king of Kayor, pursued a policy of centralization at the expense of the *lamanes*, local chiefs and earth-priests. The latter lost their autonomy as they became functionaries of the central authority. The *damel* increased the number of royal slaves, on whom he relied in his policy to reduce the power and the freedom of local chiefs. He recruited among them the *tyeddo*, professional warriors who were always at his disposal.

Intensive commercial activities and political centralization enhanced the position of Muslims in Kayor. Muslims were already serving in the courts of Wolof chiefs as secretaries, counsellors and divines in the middle of the fifteenth century, according to the earliest Portuguese observers. Islamic influence over the Wolof chiefs followed the pattern known from other kingdoms of west Africa. The growing influence of the Muslims in the *damel*'s court was counter-balanced by the *tyeddo*, who formed the core of the *damel*'s military power, and by the *griots*, the custodians of the traditional heritage. Islam in Kayor remained marginal, and the Muslims were waiting for the opportunity to gain authority with the help of an outside Muslim power.

In 1673, when the Zawāyā under Nāṣir al-Dīn invaded the Wolof states, they were aided by the Muslim elements there, who in their turn exploited internal tensions among the royal clans. In Kayor the ruling *damel* was deposed and a new *damel* from a rival branch was installed. He converted, and was expected to rule under the spiritual direction of N'Diaye Sall, a Muslim cleric. The *griots*, whom he was forced to chase away, later came to him and recited the glory of his ancestors. Moved by national pride, he brought the *griots* back into his service, and under their influence neglected his prayers. This apostate was deposed and the cleric N'Diaye Sall was made *damel*, only to be rejected by the assembly of Kayor's freemen as trespassing on the national traditions. N'Diaye Sall was overthrown after his Zawāyā supporters had lost power.

Walo, on the lower Senegal river, more than the other Wolof states, was subjected to constant raiding by the Moors, who also intervened occasionally in internal disputes over succession. The Moors supported one dynasty while the Tukolor supported another. The French in St Louis also became involved in the politics of Walo. In Walo, the invading Zawāyā encountered fierce resistance, but having overcome this the Zawāyā appointed a new *brak* (ruler), who had accepted their way of life and agreed to rule under their authority. In 1674, after Nāṣir al-Dīn had been killed in battle against Hādī, the Trarza chief, the French urged the *brak* to renounce allegiance to the Zawāyā, and promised their support. Fighting in the Senegal valley had disrupted the trade, and the French were reluctant to deal with the arrogant Muslims 'who despise us [the French] because of the difference between our religion and their superstitions'.[1] The *brak* revolted, defeated the Zawāyā's army and killed the *qāḍī* 'Uthmān, their third *imām*. Harassed from all sides by the Moors, the Fulani, the Wolof and the French, the Zawāyā were weakened. Early in 1679 the *brak* began a full-scale offensive to drive the Zawāyā away from the whole Wolof country.

Among the Wolof, according to contemporary European sources, the movement of the Zawāyā – also known as the *tubenan* or 'the penitents' – had some millennial overtones. People believed that if they

[1] A report by Louis Moreau de Chamboneau to the director of the Compagnie du Sénégal, in Carson I. A. Ritchie, 'Deux textes sur le Sénégal (1673–7)', *Bulletin de l'IFAN* (1968), **30**, 1, 352.

repented, the land would yield its harvest without labour. They therefore abandoned their fields and overthrew their king. But the promise failed and the country was devastated by famine. The people turned against the marabouts, restored their king, and vowed not to let any marabout enter their country.[1] Diminished harvests precipitated the collapse of the Zawāyā in the Senegal valley, and this experience stiffened opposition to Islam among the Wolof.

Over a century later, *c.* 1790, inspired by the successful Islamic revolution in the Futa Toro (see p. 213), the Muslims of Kayor revolted against the *damel*, but were defeated. Many were sold into slavery, while others escaped to the Cape Verde peninsula, where they joined the Lebou in seceding from the *damel*'s domination. Dial Diop, a Muslim divine's son by the daughter of a Lebou chief, organized the resistance of the Lebou. The peninsula was fortified, and the *damel*'s attack was repelled. Dial Diop, known as Serin Ndakaru, became the first ruler of the Lebou 'republic'. The Lebou's particularism, however, negated the Islamic zeal of the militants, and Islam did not win over the Lebou until the second half of the nineteenth century.

In 1796 the *almamy* of Futa Toro invaded the Wolof country. He forced the *burba* of Djolof and the *brak* of Walo to accept Islam, but was heavily defeated and taken prisoner by the *damel* of Kayor, Amari Ngone Couba, who had already quelled the internal rebellion, and who now repulsed a direct external Muslim assault. The *almamy*'s defeat in Kayor allowed the *burba* and the *brak* to renounce their forced conversion. Though they failed to take over the political centre of Kayor, which was defended by the *tyeddo*, the Muslims continued to foment opposition to the court. As the court and the *tyeddo* became more oppressive, Islam attracted the commoners. This was one of the very few cases in West Africa where islamization was more advanced among the commoners. By the end of the eighteenth century, the undermining of Kayor's political system through islamization was already under way, though it did not finally collapse until the end of the nineteenth century.

Unlike the Wolof, the Tukolor, people of ancient Takrur, were among the earliest Muslims in the western Sudan, and remained attached to Islam even after authority over the Futa Toro had passed to rulers with little Islamic inclination. Their Denianke dynasty of Fulani origin was founded by Koli Tenguella at the beginning of the sixteenth century. For the author of the *Ta'rīkh al-Sūdān*, Koli's second

[1] J. Barbot, in A. Churchill, *A Collection of Voyages and Travels* (London, 1732), v, 62.

son, Galadyo Tabāra, was the equal in justice of Mansa Mūsā of Mali. Al-Saʿdī would have said this only of a ruler whom he regarded as Muslim. The same applies to Koli's grandson, Samba Lām, in the first half of the seventeenth century, who 'pursued justice and prohibited iniquity'.[1] But there was another opinion about those chiefs who oscillated between Islam and traditionalism. This was the viewpoint of the Torodbe – the Muslim clerical clan of the Tukolor – for whom the Denianke were non-Muslim rulers.

In 1673 Nāṣir al-Dīn, the Zawāyā reformer, sent emissaries to the *satigi* (or *silatigi*, the title of the Denianke rulers of the Futa Toro), urging him to change his way of life and to observe the precepts of Islam. Otherwise the king would be declared an enemy of God, and be expelled from his kingdom. Following the *satigi*'s refusal, emissaries were sent for the second and third time (according to the law of the jihad), but were again rejected. Nāṣir al-Dīn then entered the Futa with his followers, passing from one village to the other. People who had been captured by his preaching tore off their clothes, shaved their heads and doubled their praying. They declared their king a tyrant and took up arms against him. Abandoned by his own people, the king was forced to escape with his family and a few followers to Galam. Nāṣir al-Dīn deposed village chiefs and appointed Muslims in their stead. Some of the Futa – led by Torodbe – co-operated with the Zawāyā against their oppressive rulers, while the *satigi* entered into an alliance with the Ḥassānī warriors. Alignments, therefore, cut across ethnic boundaries, ruling warriors united against Muslims, Ḥassān and Denianke opposed Zawāyā and Torodbe. By 1677 the warriors emerged victorious, both in the southern Sahara and in the Futa Toro.

It was about that period, in the last quarter of the seventeenth century, that some Torodbe migrated southwards from Futa Toro to the sparsely populated Bondu. This migration may well have been caused by the suppression of the Torodbe who had co-operated with the Zawāyā against the Denianke. The Torodbe migrants accepted the leadership of Mālik Sī, an *ʿālim* from Futa Toro, who had settled in Bondu about the 1680s with the permission of the *tunka* (king) of Gadiaga, the Soninke state in Galam on the Senegal river. By then Mālik Sī had accumulated wealth during visits to royal courts in neighbouring states, through his religious prestige and thaumaturgy. He transformed this wealth into military power to establish political authority over clusters of semi-autonomous villages of diverse ethnic

[1] *T. al-Sūdān*, p. 77/tr. 128.

origins in Bondu. In assuming the politico-religious title of *elimani* (*al-imām*) he may have been influenced by Nāṣir al-Dīn's unsuccessful jihad and the attempt to establish an *imam*ate. Mālik Sī thus created the first religiously oriented state of the Halpularen (Fulani and Tukolor). He did so not by taking over an existing state, but by carving out a new polity in a region recently settled by the Tukolor, and only loosely dependent on the *tunka* of Gadiaga.

In his attempts to extend his domains, Mālik Sī clashed with the *tunka*, who was defeated and killed at the very end of the seventeenth century. His son, Būbū Mālik Sī, defeated the *tunka* with the aid of Fulani warriors from the Futa Jalon, and Bondu's secession from Gadiaga became final. Būbū Mālik Sī then invaded Bambuk, across the Faleme river, but was killed. In a counter-attack, the Malinke of Bambuk invaded Bondu and forced the Sisibe, descendants of Mālik Sī, to seek refuge in the Futa Toro. For some time, in the early 1730s, Bondu disintegrated, but the Sisibe restored their authority with the aid of troops from the Futa Toro. For the second time in their short history, the Sisibe were back in power through the support of Fulani warriors, first from the Futa Jalon and then from the Futa Toro.

Maka Jiba, son of Būbū Mālik Sī, consolidated his rule over the people of Bondu and turned to fight the Malinke of Bambuk, who remained the avowed enemies of Bondu. His successful raids brought him much booty, which he used to buy horses and ammunition. His increased power, however, raised the apprehension of the *satigi* Sule Ndyaye of Futa Toro. The *satigi* addressed a letter to 'his humble and loyal servant Maka-Guiba, who dared to style himself *elimani*. His family came from the Torodbe, who were destined to remain miserable and to live off charity.'[1] As '*ulamā*', the Torodbe, according to the *satigi*'s view, should not have aspired to political authority, and the Sisibe should remain his subjects, though they had established themselves outside his territorial jurisdiction. In the 1740s the *satigi*'s army invaded Bondu, but was defeated. A peace treaty was then signed in which the *satigi* recognized the independence of Bondu. Indeed, it was high time for the established dynasties of non-Muslim warriors to recognize the rise of Islamic militancy and the political aspirations of the hitherto docile '*ulamā*'.

In the aftermath of the Zawāyā jihad, militant Torodbe migrated from Futa Toro not only to Bondu, but also to the Futa Jalon. Oral

[1] A. Rançon, *Le Bondou: étude de géographie et d'histoire soudanaise de 1861 à nos jours* (Bordeaux, 1894), 53.

traditions refer to 'Fulani fugitives from the Futa Toro who had fought against the animists, were defeated and sought refuge with their brothers in the Futa Jalon'.[1] Other circumstantial and traditional pieces of evidence also indicate that the Muslim Fulani, who contributed to the militancy of the Fulani herdsmen in the Futa Jalon, had not come from Massina, as has generally been accepted, but from the Futa Toro by way of the upper Senegal valley. Dyakaba on the Bafing river, the city of the Dyakanke and a centre of Islamic scholarship (see p. 217), also radiated its influence to the Futa Jalon. This increased the impact of Malinke-speaking Muslims in the Futa. During the seventeenth century, a further stimulus to change came with the considerable growth of trade over the routes across the Futa Jalon to the European factories on the upper Guinea coast (see chapter 4, p. 285). The Futa Jalon, which had previously been peripheral to the core area of the western Sudan, now became more closely integrated into its trading system and was exposed to political innovations and the process of islamization.

From the fifteenth century onwards, the Fulani pastoralists had filtered into the Futa Jalon and had lived in peace among the local agriculturists. Whereas Susu and Dyalonke had settled in the valleys of the Futa Jalon, the Fulani were attracted to the plateaux. These dispersed Fulani groups had at first accepted subordinate positions in the Futa Jalon, as they still do among the Mossi and the Bariba, but new economic and religious developments brought about a radical change in these relations. Hides were in great demand by Europeans on the coast, and the Fulani increased their herds. The growing numbers of Fulani and their cattle caused pressure on the available pasturelands and increased tension with the peasants, whose lands the pastoralists coveted. As slaves were the principal staple of the trade at that time, the Fulani were tempted to take part in this trade as well. The growing supply of slaves from the Futa Jalon during the eighteenth century was thus perhaps not only a by-product of the jihad waged by the Fulani, but also an incitement to it.

Closer contacts in commercial transactions between Malinke-speaking Muslims and the Fulani brought the latter under stronger Islamic influence at a time when militant Torodbe joined their ranks. The new Muslim arrivals challenged the existing order, and offered new leadership to their Fulani kinsmen. Wealth, accumulated by Muslims through trade, was used for political purposes. The prestige and sanctity of the '*ulamā*' increased the number of their followers. Islam also helped to

[1] P. Marty, *L'Islam en Guinée: Fouta Djallon* (Paris, 1921), 36–7.

overcome geographical divisions: a meeting of nine *'ulamā'*, who represented different regions of the Futa, is said to have marked the beginning of the jihad. Non-Muslim Fulani were drawn into the Islamic community, as Islam became the *raison d'être* of a Fulani national rising; an ideological expression of a protest movement among the Fulani to free themselves from political and economic subordination.

The Fulani encountered resistance from local non-Fulani chiefs who had ruled over small chiefdoms. The most important pre-jihad kingdom in the Futa was that of the Solima Dyalonke. It was founded towards the end of the seventeenth century, perhaps in response to the increasing pressure of the Fulani. The jihad, however, was not directed against this king who, having been partly islamized, was for some time an ally of the Fulani. In the Futa Toro, and later in Hausaland, the leader of the jihad became the sovereign of an already existing state. In the Futa Jalon there was no state to take over, and the leaders of the jihad had to carry out a process of state-building along with their jihad. This goes a long way to explain why the jihad extended over half a century, from 1725–6 to 1776, until a state was consolidated.

The nine *'ulamā'* who had initiated the jihad elected one of their number, Ibrāhīma Sambeghu, better known as Karamokho Alfa, from Timbo, as their leader. Traditions indicate that Karamokho Alfa was not an undisputed charismatic leader; his authority, and that of his successors, was compromised by the other eight *'ulamā'* who had created their own provinces (*diwal*, pl. *diwe*). Some of them had more extensive territory and more temporal power than the paramount, who was also chief of the *diwal* of Timbo. The political capital at Timbo was counterbalanced by Fugumba, the holy city and the seat of the council of the *'ulamā'*, where the *almamy* was officially invested. According to traditions, the *'ulamā'* of Fugumba were descendants of Seri, brother of Sedi, the ancestor of the *almamy* of Timbo. Relations and tensions between the political (Timbo) and the religious (Fugumba) poles are therefore stated as between two branches of the same family. This family, which had come to Futa Jalon by the way of Dyakaba, is credited with having sown the first seeds of Islamic militancy some two or three decades before the eruption of the jihad. These traditions explain the central role of Timbo and Fugumba in the direction of the jihad. Later, when chiefs of the other *diwe* were almost exclusively concerned with their own provinces, competition over the office of the *almamy* was restricted to Timbo and Fugumba.

The chronology of the jihad in Futa Jalon is uncertain, but it is likely that Karamokho Alfa, its first leader, died in 1751. He was succeeded by his cousin Ibrāhīm Sori, also known as Sori Maudo ('the great'). He was the admired commander of the army, hero of the young warriors, and his accession marked the end of the first stage of the jihad, the pious and learned Karamokho Alfa having given way to the military commander. In the 1750s, under Ibrāhīm Sori, a more aggressive policy was pursued, which brought more wars and more slaves. Reports from Sierra Leone in 1751 indicated a prodigious trade in slaves, due to an increasing supply from the Futa Jalon.

Ibrāhīm Sori carried his wars outside the Futa Jalon and was aided by the king of the Solima Dyalonke. The latter had retreated south of the Futa under the pressure of the Fulani, but soon joined the Fulani in raiding their neighbours for slaves and booty. In 1762 the combined forces of the Fulani and the Solima were defeated by Konde Birama, the ruler of Wasulu, whose territory they had invaded. The Wasulunke people were a fusion of Fulani migrants with the Bambara beyond the Sankarani river. Konde Birama led the animists of the upper Niger in reaction to the rising tide of Islamic militancy. The alliance between Fulani and Solima, which had been cemented in successful raids, did not survive a defeat. Alignments changed as the Solima, whose half-hearted islamization had been due to expediency, joined the Wasulunke against the Fulani. The latter were then forced to defend their own territory in face of repeated raids. In 1767 the Solima and the Wasulunke advanced deeper into the Futa, conquered Timbo, but were checked at the gates of Fugumba. Annual raids into the Futa continued until 1776, when the Solima and the Wasulunke were severely defeated. The scales had turned again; the Fulani – under Ibrāhīm Sori – resumed an aggressive policy, and forced the Solima to accept Fulani predominance.

It was only after the victory of 1776 that the success of the jihad was secured, and it was marked by the adoption of the title *almamy*, with its politico-religious connotation, by Ibrāhīm Sori. Significantly, it was in that same year that 'Abd al-Qādir, the leader of another jihad, in Futa Toro, assumed the title of *almamy*. Ibrāhīm was granted the title of *almamy* on the condition that he always recognized the right of the council of elders to give their advice on all matters of internal or external policy, and that his successors would be confirmed by a vote of the assembly. Provincial assemblies throughout the Futa each elected two or three representatives for the council of '*ulamā*' in Fugumba. The council was in charge of the tithes collected and the booty seized to defray the expenses of the jihad. It was responsible for the administration of the *Sharī'a*, and used its prerogatives to try and punish chiefs suspected of laxity. The *'ulamā'* were apprehensive of the growing power and prestige of Ibrāhīm Sori, and waited for an opportunity to employ their religious and judicial sanctions against him. Sori, however, was determined to keep his authoritarian rule. He entered Fugumba and beheaded those councillors who had led the opposition against him. He then convened a general assembly, with the participation of his warriors, to pass a vote of confidence in him. He filled the council with his partisans and transferred it to Timbo. In the conflict between the religious and the military factions, the latter emerged victorious, at least until Sori's death in 1791–2.

Ibrāhīm Sori was succeeded by his son Sa'īd, who was killed in 1797–8 by those who supported the claim of Karamokho Alfa's descendants to the office. 'Abdulai Bademba of the Alfaya (Karomokho Alfa's family) was appointed to be the next *almamy*, and the pattern was laid for institutionalized competition between the two branches – Alfaya and Soriya (Ibrāhīm Sori's descendants). This division was extended into the ruling families of the *diwe*, where the chieftaincy is said to have rotated between Alfaya and Soriya according to the rhythm of changes in Timbo.

Rivalry between Alfaya and Soriya, conflicts between the *almamy* and the council of *'ulamā'*, and the tensions between the *almamy* and the provincial chiefs, suggest an inherent instability in the political system of Futa Jalon. Yet the political struggle, fierce as it was, took place within the ruling aristocracy which had come to power after the jihad. No matter how divided this aristocracy was internally, it proved very cohesive vis-à-vis other social groups within the state. Fulani who did not belong to the aristocracy were passive participants in the political system. Most of them became Muslims only after the jihad and they remained herders, but their status was higher than that of the non-Fulani Muslims.

The non-Fulani inhabitants of the Futa Jalon – Dyalonke, Tenda and Landouma – were subjugated, and their conquered villages turned into *rundes*, villages of serfs or slaves. These servile subjects, the *rimaibe*, formed the majority of the population of the Futa. Under the supervision of their own chiefs, who in turn were responsible to their Fulani masters, the *rimaibe* cultivated the land. The surplus of their agricultural products was taken over by the Fulani aristocracy, for their own consumption and for trade with the Europeans. The latter needed these products, mainly rice, for feeding slaves on the ships across the Atlantic.

Many of the slaves purchased by the Europeans on the upper Guinea coast in the latter part of the eighteenth century were produced by the raids of the Fulani on their neighbours. The jihad, in fact, gave them licence to destroy the animists, or all their neighbours. The Fulani, however, did not raid peoples under their authority; these they used as a labour force.

Following the jihad, all Fulani became identified as Muslims, but the tributaries were only slightly affected. Islam provided the ideological basis for the political system and the Islamic law was to be applied, at least in theory. Many Koranic schools were established, and the towns of the Futa Jalon became important centres of Islamic education. Islam extended from the Futa Jalon to the coast, mainly among local chiefs. To the north, influence from the Futa Jalon caused greater Islamic commitment in Bondu and rekindled Islamic militancy in the Futa Toro.

One of those who came to study in the Futa Jalon was the shaykh Sulaymān Bal of the Futa Toro. He was inspired by the successful jihad there, and he returned to the Futa Toro with the blessing of the '*ulamā*' of Futa Jalon. By then a century had elapsed since the defeat of the Zawāyā and their Torodbe allies in the 1670s. Though the Zawāyā had lost political freedom, they increased their religious influence over their masters, and Moorish influence in the Futa also had religious overtones. The *satigi* Sire Sawa Lamu (d. 1702) employed Moors in his army, and introduced a marabout into his court under whose influence the *satigi* became a devoted Muslim. He spent his days studying the Koran, and left the affairs of his kingdom in the hands of his son, whom he designated as heir presumptive. His brother Sabbaboye, the legitimate heir, deprived of his rights, went into exile in Galam, followed by many of the Futa dignitaries. The death of the *satigi* Sire in 1702 brought Sabbaboye back to power. He chased the Moors away from the Futa and reversed the pro-Islamic policy of his predecessor. The Futa Toro became involved in a series of succession disputes which were aggravated by Moorish influence. For over thirty years after 1718, the 'Ormans', the Moroccan troops who roamed over the Senegal valley (see p. 152), were called to intervene in disputes among Denianke rivals, installing and deposing *satigis* at will.

Politics in the Futa Toro were disturbed also by the growth of French commercial traffic on the Senegal, which stimulated centrifugal tendencies, as local chiefs aspired to greater political independence from the *satigi* in order to derive larger profits from customs paid along the river. The most serious challenge to the *satigi*'s authority came from the chief of Dekle, on the northern bank of the Senegal, who assumed the title of *satigi* and sought to become independent. In the 1760s, during the reign of Sule Ndyaye II, the Futa became divided between two rival *satigis*. The *satigi* of Dekle, who ruled over the upper Futa, was supported by the Moors when he raided his rival's territory every summer. When the river was in flood and Dekle was deprived of the Moorish support, the *satigi* of the Futa retaliated in raiding Dekle.

It was during this disturbed period that Sulaymān Bal returned to the Futa Toro. He combined his religious mission with the determination to restore unity and order in the Futa and to put an end to Moorish aggression. By turning against the Moors, who constantly raided the Futa and oppressed its people, he gave the movement a patriotic flavour. In this way he won over the majority of the population, leaving the Denianke ruler with little popular support.

When he had first arrived in Futa Toro, Sulaymān Bal went to consult Tafsiru Boggal, one of the leading *'ulamā'* in the Futa Toro, who had avoided any contact with the Denianke and devoted himself to Islamic teaching. In this behaviour he may well have represented the disenchantment of the Torodbe with their non-Muslim rulers, an initial stage in the development of a jihad. Sulaymān Bal himself was not admitted into the *satigi*'s court, and remained unattached to the existing socio-political system. As an independent *'ālim*, Sulaymān Bal preached throughout the country and soon attracted both commoners and chiefs. After he had fought against the Brakna Moors for several years, Sulaymān Bal called his followers to elect an *imām*, or *almamy*, as their leader. He himself refused to fill this role, and is said by tradition to have mysteriously disappeared, in order to clear the way for a new leader. The charismatic leader, who had instigated the religious revolution, took no part in the establishment of the *imam*ate, the new politico-religious order. This must have weakened the office of the *almamy*, even before it was created.

In 1775–6 'Abd al-Qādir b. Ḥammadi, whose election had been endorsed by Sulaymān Bal, was proclaimed the first *almamy*. He continued the war against the Brakna, defeated these Moors and imposed tribute on them. Only then did he turn against the Denianke, overcoming the *satigi* in a series of battles. In October 1786 the Almamy 'Abd al-Qādir intervened in the internal struggle for supremacy among the Ḥassān; he helped the Brakna, who had already acknowledged his authority, to defeat 'Alī Kawrī, the Trarza chief. The *almamy* became, therefore, the dominant power on the Senegal and felt that he could raise the tolls levied on the passage of French trade on the Senegal. This was in violation of a treaty signed in March 1785 between the French and representatives of the *almamy*, which had stipulated fixed rates for different categories of traders. During the European wars which followed the French Revolution, the trade stopped and the *almamy* complained of losses in income. He insisted that the annual customs should be paid even when no boats were sailing up the river, and this was written into the new treaty signed in May 1804. But the *almamy* was unable to force his sub-chiefs to respect treaties, so that in 1805 French boats were attacked on the river and the French governor sent a punitive expedition. By then the French realized that they had to deal with a more turbulent partner than the *satigi* had been. The *almamy* was more reserved in relations with Europeans and more demanding.

Almamy 'Abd al-Qādir reached the peak of his power in 1796, when he attempted to impose his authority over Khasso and Bondu to the north and the Wolof to the south. On 5 January 1796, Mungo Park witnessed the arrival of an embassy from 'Abd al-Qādir to 'Teesee', a town in Khasso, calling the people there to accept Islam or to face hostilities. 'A message of this nature from so powerful a prince could not fail to create great alarm; and the inhabitants of Teesee, after a long consultation, agreed to conform to his good pleasure, humiliating as it was to them. Accordingly, one and all publicly offered up eleven prayers [*sic*], which were considered a sufficient testimony of their having renounced paganism, and embraced the doctrines of the Prophet.'[1] Several weeks later 'Abd al-Qādir marched against Bondu, deposed the reigning *almamy* of Bondu and appointed a new subordinate *almamy*.

'Abd al-Qādir was less successful in his attempt against Kayor. He sent an embassy to the *damel* calling him to embrace Islam or to prepare for death, but the *damel* rejected the ultimatum. In the dry season, at the end of 1796, the *almamy* invaded Kayor, and for three days encountered no opposition, but his army suffered thirst because the retreating people had filled up their wells and had destroyed all provisions. When his soldiers eventually reached water and quenched their thirst, they carelessly fell into deep sleep. Before daybreak they were attacked by the *damel*; many were killed, others were captured, and among them was Almamy 'Abd al-Qādir himself. The *damel* did not kill 'Abd al-Qādir, but put him to work as a slave for three months, 'at the end of which

[1] Park, *Travels* (1799), 79.

period, Damel listened to the solicitations of the inhabitants of Foota Torra, and restored to them their king'.[1]

The deputy who had governed the Futa during the *almamy*'s absence in captivity, hastened to render homage to the returning *almamy*. Yet opposition to ʿAbd al-Qādir was growing because of his advanced age (he was then about eighty), because he was disgraced by working as the *damel*'s slave, and because people were tired of the uninterrupted wars the *almamy* had carried on. About that time a new *almamy* of Bondu renounced allegiance to the *almamy* of Futa and entered into an alliance with the Bambara of Kaarta. The old Almamy ʿAbd al-Qādir, who had been left with only a few devoted disciples, was defeated and killed in 1806–7. This was the end of the formative phase in the creation of a new order in the Futa Toro.

Following his victory over the Denianke, the *almamy* had confiscated the land of those former rulers who had not converted, and distributed it among the leaders of the Torodbe. They formed the new aristocracy, which took over power and carried on the exploitation of the peasants. The Torodbe emerged as a religious, political and economic élite. The jihad brought about not a strict theocracy, government according to the principles of the *Sharīʿa*, but a religious oligarchy. Unlike the leaders of the jihad movements in the nineteenth century, who created a community of believers out of dispersed Muslim groups in the course of the jihad, in the Futa Toro the leadership of the jihad had to be endorsed by the Torodbe, who were already an established social estate with vested interests. Sulaymān Bal had been carefully tested by the Torodbe leaders before they consented to follow him; ʿAbd al-Qādir had once been rejected as candidate for the office of *almamy* before he was elected. The elective system which prevailed in Futa Toro throughout the nineteenth century put serious limitations on the authority of the *almamy*. His power was further restricted by the independence of the Torodbe provincial chiefs, and by dignitaries both religious and lay. The *imam*ate of Futa Toro, therefore, lost the dynamism generated by the revolution soon after its formative stage; it was later to be exposed to the revolutionary impact of al-ḥājj ʿUmar and the Ṭijāniyya.

The inherent dichotomy in the western Sudan and the southern Sahara between warriors who held political authority and Muslims who

[1] Park, *Travels* (1799), 341–4; significantly, the traditional account of this war in Siré Abbas Soh, *Chroniques du Fouta Sénégalais*, tr. M. Delafosse (Paris, 1913), 49–53, is strikingly similar to the account Mungo Park recorded in May 1797, a few months after the event.

pursued peaceful commercial activities had its impact on the development of Bondu. Though its dynasty had been established by an *'ālim*, his successors dropped their religious calling to become secular rulers. But following the consolidation of the jihad in the Futa Jalon and the successful Torodbe revolution in Futa Toro, Islam in Bondu, lying between the two Futas, was invigorated. Aḥmadi Gaye, the great-grandson of Mālik Sī, followed his neighbours in assuming the title of *almamy* (instead of *elimani* as his predecessors had been styled). He attempted a reform by applying the hitherto neglected Koranic laws, and he is credited by traditions as the first ruler who established a better organized and more permanent administration.

Yet, neither in its foundation by Mālik Sī, nor in the time of Aḥmadi Gaye, had Bondu gone through a profound revolution, and reform in the context of Sudanic Islam was not enough. By 1795 the reforms of the 1770s had been partly wasted, as can be inferred from the account of Mungo Park:

> Their government differs from that of the Mandingues chiefly in this that they are more immediately under the influence of the Mahomedan laws; for all the chief men (*the king excepted*) and a large majority of the inhabitants of Bondu, are Musselmen, and the authority and laws of the Prophet, are everywhere looked upon as sacred and decisive.[1]

The exception of the king is significant. 'This monarch was called Almami; a Muslim name, though I was told that he was not a Mahomedan, but a Kafir, or pagan.'[2] Park's informant in this matter may have been a pious Muslim, who was influenced by the religious revolutions in the Futas, where the *almamy* was then a real *'ālim*. The *almamy* of Bondu in 1795, though he continued to hold a politico-religious Islamic title, reverted to the middle position between Islam and traditionalism, typical of chiefs in the western Sudan. On the other hand, the influence of the religious revolution in Futa Toro probably had a more lasting influence on the Torodbe in Bondu, who were described by Park as observant Muslims.

The tension between the Muslim subjects and the so-called pagan *almamy* in Bondu brought about the military intervention of Almamy 'Abd al-Qādir of Futa Toro in 1796. He was called in by Muslims, who complained that they had been pillaged by troops of Sega Gaye, the *almamy* of Bondu. Sega Gaye was defeated and killed by 'Abd al-Qādir, who appointed a new *almamy*, Aḥmadi Pate, son of the reformer Aḥmadi Gaye. This appointment was challenged by Aḥmadi Issata,

[1] Park, *Travels* (1799), 60 (my italics). [2] Ibid. 53.

brother of Sega Gaye, who defeated Aḥmadi Pate and reasserted Bondu's independence from the Futa's *almamy*. Issata fortified his country and entered into an alliance with the king of Kaarta. Some years later, in 1806–7, the old Almamy 'Abd al-Qādir, after he had been deserted by his own people, was defeated, as we have seen (p. 214), by the armies of Bondu and Kaarta and was killed in cold blood by Almamy Issata of Bondu. What had begun as a religious war between Futa and Bondu was soon to develop into a four-cornered struggle over the control of the upper navigable section of the Senegal river.

In the nineteenth century the jihad movements engulfed the whole breadth of the Sudan. That this process had begun in the Futas a century earlier may be explained by three main factors: first, a higher concentration of Fulani, both sedentary and pastoralists, who also played leading roles in the later jihad movements; second, the direct contact with the Zawāyā of the south-western Sahara, who carried the heritage of Islamic militancy of the Almoravids, and whose impact on the Torodbe we have attempted to demonstrate; third, the exposure of the Futas to the growing commercial activities of the Europeans in the Senegambia.

AFRICANS AND EUROPEANS IN THE TRADE OF SENEGAMBIA

Although trans-Saharan trade lost its monopoly with the opening up of alternative outlets on the coast, it continued to operate successfully during the seventeenth and eighteenth centuries. Two English travellers, at both ends of the period under survey, bear witness to this. In 1620–1 Richard Jobson heard of Moors coming to exchange Saharan salt for gold in a town which was only six days' journey from Barrakunda, the farthest point for European navigation on the Gambia. In 1797 Mungo Park observed in the markets of the upper Niger that 'by far the greater proportion [of the gold of Bure was] annually carried by the Moors in exchange for salt and other merchandise'.[1] This is a significant remark, for it indicates the predominance of gold in the northbound trade to Morocco, and of slaves in the westbound trade to the European factories, which failed to divert the bulk of the gold of Bambuk and Bure from its old established route to the north.

Yet the south–north trade with the Sahara and the east–west trade with the coast were linked by the overlapping and the interconnection between the different sectors of the Sudanic commercial networks.

[1] Park, *Travels* (1799), 305.

Though each sector was dominated by traders from one ethnic group – Soninke, Marka, Dyula, Dyakanke or Bonduka – they all shared common cultural features and were bound together by common economic interests. They were all Muslims, most claimed Soninke origin, and those who lost their Soninke dialect in their dispersion became culturally assimilated into one of the Mande-speaking peoples among whom they operated.

On the upper navigable part of the Senegal river, beyond Futa Toro, the Bathily warriors established the Soninke state of Gadiaga. Under their authority Soninke Muslims traded to Diara in the Sahel to meet the Moors and to the commercial centres of Sansanding and Segu on the middle Niger. In the south–north trade they exchanged gold, millet and kola for salt, livestock and products of the Maghrib. In the east–west trade they exchanged slaves and some gold for European cloth, maritime salt, and some firearms. From their strategic commercial position, much of their trade was carried to the coast by the Senegal river. But if, as often happened, the Senegal waterway was disrupted by warfare or political upheavals, the Soninke traders of Gadiaga channelled their goods overland to the Gambia, using the trading network of their Dyakanke neighbours.

The Dyakanke claim that their ancestors had come from Dia, the famous centre of trade and Islam in Massina, and established their own centre at Dyakaba on the Bafing river. In Bambuk and its surrounding area, the Dyakanke adopted the dialect of the western Malinke, who had expanded from the heartland of the Mande-speaking peoples and colonized the country. The Dyakanke were distinguished from their neighbours in their adherence to Islam and in their commercial vocation. By the seventeenth century, they had established colonies along the routes leading to the Gambia, and on the Gambia itself, to control the trade with the Europeans in this direction.

In 1621, during his expedition up the Gambia river, Jobson met 'many hundreds' of those Muslim traders who, he says, 'have free recourse through all places' even in times of war.[1] In 1698 the director of the French company on the Senegal, André Brüe, wrote of the Dyakanke colonies which extended from Galam to Dyakaba:

> They are numerous, united, and confederated in a way that they formed a republic, and are not afraid of the king... There is a considerable town called Conjour, built of stone where the greatest merchants live. The town serves as the capital of the marabouts' republic.[2]

[1] R. Jobson, *The Golden Trade* (London, 1932), 17–18, 84, 106.

[2] Labat, *Nouvelle relation*, III, 371, 338.

The autonomy of Conjour (or Goundiourou, south-east of Kayes) in the middle of the seventeenth century is confirmed by the contemporary author of the *Ta'rīkh al-Fattāsh*: 'It is under the authority of the *qāḍī* and the *'ulamā'*. No warrior may enter the town, and no tyrant has ever lived there.'[1]

In a period of insecurity, in a country divided among small principalities of Malinke and Soninke, the solidarity of the Muslim merchants was vital, and their towns were defended by walls. The Dyakanke were free to travel safely, and their towns became sanctuaries, not only because they were strong enough to resist the king but also because 'it is well known that whoever dared to cause [them] any harm, would die within three days...'[2] This was the 'republic' created by the Dyakanke, a commercial and religious organization which cut across the boundaries of the existing states.

The Malinke states on the Gambia, which in the sixteenth century had still been nominally under the suzerainty of Mali, were completely independent by 1621, when Jobson sailed up the Gambia river and heard nothing of Mali in the interior. Commercial relations with the Europeans added wealth to the Malinke rulers along the Gambia, who accumulated large herds, slaves and many retainers and clients. On the northern bank of the river were the Malinke states of Bara, Badibu, Niani and Wuli, but by the seventeenth century the rising Serer state of Salum expanded southwards to have its share in the trade of the Gambia. On the southern bank of the Gambia, European travellers mentioned the state of Kantora. It was perhaps part of Kabu, a loose confederation of Malinke principalities.

South of the Gambia, on the upper Guinea coast, were the European factories of the 'Rivières du Sud'. The more important routes to these factories crossed the Futa Jalon, and much of the trade over these routes was carried on by the Bonduka (lit. 'people of Bondu'), who specialized in the slave trade. Though many of them were Fulani-speaking in origin, they soon adopted the Dyakanke dialect, the commercial language of the west.

The growth of trade in the seventeenth and eighteenth centuries along the routes leading from the interior to the coast caused the migration of Muslims, traders and *'ulamā'*, westwards, and the establishment of new Muslim settlements. These Muslims, though they lived under the auspices of local chiefs, increased their power through their wealth and by controlling the supply of firearms. The three regions where the

[1] *T. al-Fattāsh*, pp. 179–80/tr. 314–15.

[2] Labat, *Nouvelle relation*, III, 335.

early jihad movements developed – Futa Toro, Bondu and Futa Jalon – were traversed by trade routes. This combination of Muslim trade and Fulani ethnicity helped in stimulating Islamic militancy.

On the navigable parts of the Gambia and the Senegal rivers, the Europeans had their own commercial agents. On the Gambia these were Afro-Portuguese mulattoes, descendants of early Portuguese traders. By the eighteenth century, however, they were hardly distinguished physically from their African neighbours, though they retained Portuguese names and rudiments of Christianity. In the second half of the eighteenth century they declined, as Europeans became involved more directly in the river trade. Their counterparts on the Senegal, the Afro-French *métis*, held the river trade well into the nineteenth century.

In the seventeenth century, the royal monopoly of the Portuguese over the trade in Senegambia was overthrown by English, Dutch and French commercial companies. They introduced competition, which not only increased the volume of the trade, at more advantageous terms for the Africans, but also injected new ingredients into African politics. In 1618 some London merchants formed a 'Company for the countries of Ginney [Guinea] and Binney [Benin]' with the purpose of 'discovering the golden trade of the Moors in Barbary'. The Gambia river seemed to them the most likely access to the hinterland of the fabulous gold fields, and they established a factory on James Island. The French maintained a factory at Albreda, on the northern bank of the Gambia, opposite James Island. It caused anxiety to their English competitors and involved local rulers in European rivalries, but attracted only a small fraction of the trade, the bulk of which flowed to the English traders. As they had failed to compete on the Gambia, the French hoped to divert the gold and slave trade to the Senegal river, which is navigable (for three months during the year) over 600 miles to the Felou rapids in Bambuk.

The French reached Galam in 1685. In 1689 the ambitious director of the French company, André Brüe, recommended the establishment of a permanent fort at Galam. The fort of Saint Joseph was built in 1700, but the Muslim traders were reluctant to have the Europeans so close to the sources of gold and slaves. In December 1702 the fort was attacked, and its French garrison escaped under cover of the night, the French blaming the English for inciting the Dyakanke traders. The fort of Saint Joseph was abandoned for almost twelve years, during Brüe's absence from the Senegal, but soon after his return in 1714 it was rebuilt.

Between 1716 and 1720 the fort of Saint Joseph was threatened and the trade on the Senegal was disturbed by the 'Ormans', the bands of Moroccan warriors who roamed over the Senegal valley (see p. 152). When the trade was resumed in 1722, the employees of the French company encountered difficulties both with the Dyakanke traders and with the chiefs. Most of the trade was conducted on the boats, and when one employee dared leave the boat he was pillaged. The French, therefore, established a fortified store in Tambounkane, which became an important centre for trade. The commander of the fort of Saint Joseph had to use both diplomacy and force to promote trade and security.

Difficulties in maintaining their position in Galam were matched by commercial disappointments. Brüe advised the French agent in Galam that he should convince the Dyakanke traders that they might profit more from two or three shorter journeys to Galam than from one long and arduous journey to the Gambia. Whereas the English on the Gambia paid forty iron bars for a slave, the French offered twenty bars in Galam, and argued that the Dyakanke would be more than compensated for the difference in price by the shorter and more frequent journeys. The Dyakanke were not convinced, because their whole commercial organization was based on the long distance trade. The French failed to appreciate the logic of the African trade system: what seemed to them a wasteful long and arduous journey was in fact the principal economic role of the Dyakanke. The English, on the other hand, encouraged established patterns of trade, and were not interested in penetrating into the hinterland. They relied on their competitive trade, better and cheaper industrial commodities, to attract African traders to their factories on the lower Gambia. When the English occupied the Senegal in 1758, during the Seven Years' War, the fort of Saint Joseph in Galam was abandoned.

The supply of slaves to the Europeans on the Senegambia increased considerably in the middle decades of the eighteenth century, as a result of wars and raids carried on by the Bambara kingdoms. The prospects of the slave trade intensified the Franco-British commercial rivalry. In response to French efforts to divert the trade from the Gambia to the Senegal, the English sought the friendship of Bondu, employing for this purpose the freed slave Ayūba Sulaymān Dyallo, a son of one of the aristocratic families in Bondu. Between 1735 and 1746, Ayūba maintained irregular contacts with the Royal African Company's agents on the Gambia. Bondu's preference for trade with the English paid off, when regular English supplies of arms from the Gambia helped the *almamy* of Bondu to defeat his enemy the king of Bambuk. The latter complained to Major Houghton in 1791, that the French who formerly had supplied him with arms at the fort of Saint Joseph had ceased for some reason to sail up the Senegal river.[1] The king of Bambuk thus paid dearly for the French Revolution and the consequent disturbance of French trade on the Senegal.

The coast of what is now Mauritania was also the scene of European competition and African involvement. In the middle of the fifteenth century, the Portuguese established a factory at Arguin to divert the gold of the trans-Saharan trade, but only a very little gold reached them. After 1580 the Portuguese possessions passed to the Spanish crown, and in 1638, during the war between Holland and Spain, the Dutch captured Arguin, which by then had become a port for the trade in gum.

Gum was important for various printing and finishing processes of the growing textile industry of Europe, and for pharmaceutical use. The acacia trees, which provided a large part of the world supply of gum, were located about equidistant between the Atlantic coast and the Senegal river. An alternative outlet for the gum trade suggested itself. In 1638, when Arguin was taken by the Dutch, French traders established a factory on the island of Bakosse at the mouth of the Senegal. In 1659 the French established a more permanent base at St Louis. The gum was obtained from the Moors at several calling stations on the lower Senegal, whereas other commodities – slaves, ivory, ostrich feathers, hides and gold – were procured from the region up the Senegal river. Provisions had to be purchased from the peasants along the river to maintain the growing population of St Louis, and to feed the slaves waiting to be carried across the Atlantic. African politics on the Senegal were influenced by the French commercial activities, and by the desire of Moors, Tukolor and Wolof to have a greater share of the income accruing from the trade. The French had to reach agreements with rulers on the payment of 'customs' and, as has been seen, did not hesitate to intervene in African politics when the flow of the trade was affected (see p. 213).

Competition over the supply of gum became more acute because the trade on the Senegal was in the hands of the French, while other European nations traded on the Mauritanian coast. In 1664 the French proclaimed their sovereignty over the African coast from Cape Blanc to Sierra Leone, in order to secure a monopoly over the trade, but they

[1] Hallett, *Records*, 136.

had no means of implementing this unilateral proclamation. In 1665 the English captured Arguin, but a year later the Dutch regained control of the fort. In 1678 Arguin was taken over by the French, who hastened to close it down, and prohibited trade on the coast in order to divert the gum trade to the Senegal. In 1685 the fort came back into the hands of the Dutch and the trade there was resumed.

Both on the coast and on the Senegal, the gum was brought by the Trarza Moors, who tried to take advantage of the European competition. The ambitious Trarza chief, 'Alī Shandora (1703–27), sought to overcome his Brakna rivals, who still controlled part of the gum trade on the Senegal. 'Alī Shandora allowed the Dutch to establish a new fort at Portendick, and encouraged trade with the coast. He did this to embarrass the French, who realized that only through co-operation with 'Alī Shandora could they eliminate European competitors from the Mauritanian coast. The French, therefore, extended support to 'Alī Shandora in his war against the Brakna in 1723–7. Following his victory over the Brakna, 'Alī Shandora controlled the main gum trade on the Senegal, and was more willing to yield to French pressure and to close down the coastal forts of Arguin and Portendick. This French success was later sanctioned by the 1727 treaty of the Hague between France and Holland, in which the latter abandoned the Mauritanian coast.

The withdrawal of the Dutch in 1727 left the French with little rest, since their monopoly was challenged by English interlopers. The Trarza Moors exploited European competition to obtain better prices and to procure arms and gun-powder with less restrictions. The French patrolled the coast; in 1738 French guns fired on the Moors in Portendick to deter them from trading with the English, but could not prevail. The Trarza Moors succeeded in playing off the two European nations to increase their profits from the trade, and to maintain their independence.

In the seventeenth and eighteenth centuries the Europeans were thus present on the African coasts from the Mediterranean to the Atlantic coast of Morocco, and down to Mauritania, the upper Guinea coast and the Gold Coast. But they remained restricted to the periphery. Trade routes were extended to meet the Europeans near their ships, and a more complex African trade system developed. In turn this stimulated a greater measure of economic inter-regional unity and dependence, as the extended trade routes linked together Sahel, savanna, forest and coast. In West Africa, from Morocco to the forests, the internal dynamics of indigenous trade and Islamic expansion, with their manifold cultural and political consequences, were still supreme.

CHAPTER 4

THE GUINEA COAST

The Guinea coast at the start of the seventeenth century was less developed than the western Sudanic hinterland, which had larger territorial states and more differentiated societies and whose peoples displayed a greater capacity to organize production and to defend or expand their spheres of socio-political control. But also on the coast one is dealing with a historical situation which has as its antecedents millennia of slow population growth, enhancement of technology, and spread of specialization. An outstanding consequence of cumulative growth and development was the emergence of distinctive cultures over relatively large zones. Moving from west to east one could distinguish four areas: upper Guinea, with a dominating Mande presence; the Gold Coast, where the Akan were prominent; Yoruba/Aja territory; and eastern Nigeria, comprising mainly the Ibo and Ibibio. Social differentiation and the emergence of state powers were of major significance in all of these areas, and the internal contradictions were invariably affected in some degree by the presence of Europeans.

YORUBA, AJA, BINI

The culture zone which had the deepest roots by 1600 embraced all the Yoruba and included the Bini and the Aja. The family was the most important unit in daily life, and the specific patterns of family organization throughout the region had much in common. The Yoruba word *ebi* is equivalent to 'family' among most of the groups involved – from the Aja to the Itsekiri. Understandably, the *ebi* family principles were extended to the political superstructure. The leading states of this '*Ebi* Commonwealth' (as it has been called) were Oyo, Benin and Dahomey.[1] Traditions in Oyo and Benin mention the same founding dynasty of Oranmiyan, and there were a large number of Yoruba under Benin's authority. Political relations between Oyo and Dahomey were substantial, the former exercising some degree of control over Aja country throughout the eighteenth century. Furthermore, while relatively little has been researched concerning the utilization of the material resources

[1] I. A. Akinjogbin, *Dahomey and its neighbours, 1708–1818* (Cambridge, 1967), 13–17. For a critique, see R. C. C. Law, 'The fall of Allada, 1724 – an ideological revolution?', *Journal of the Historical Society of Nigeria*, December 1969, 4, 4.

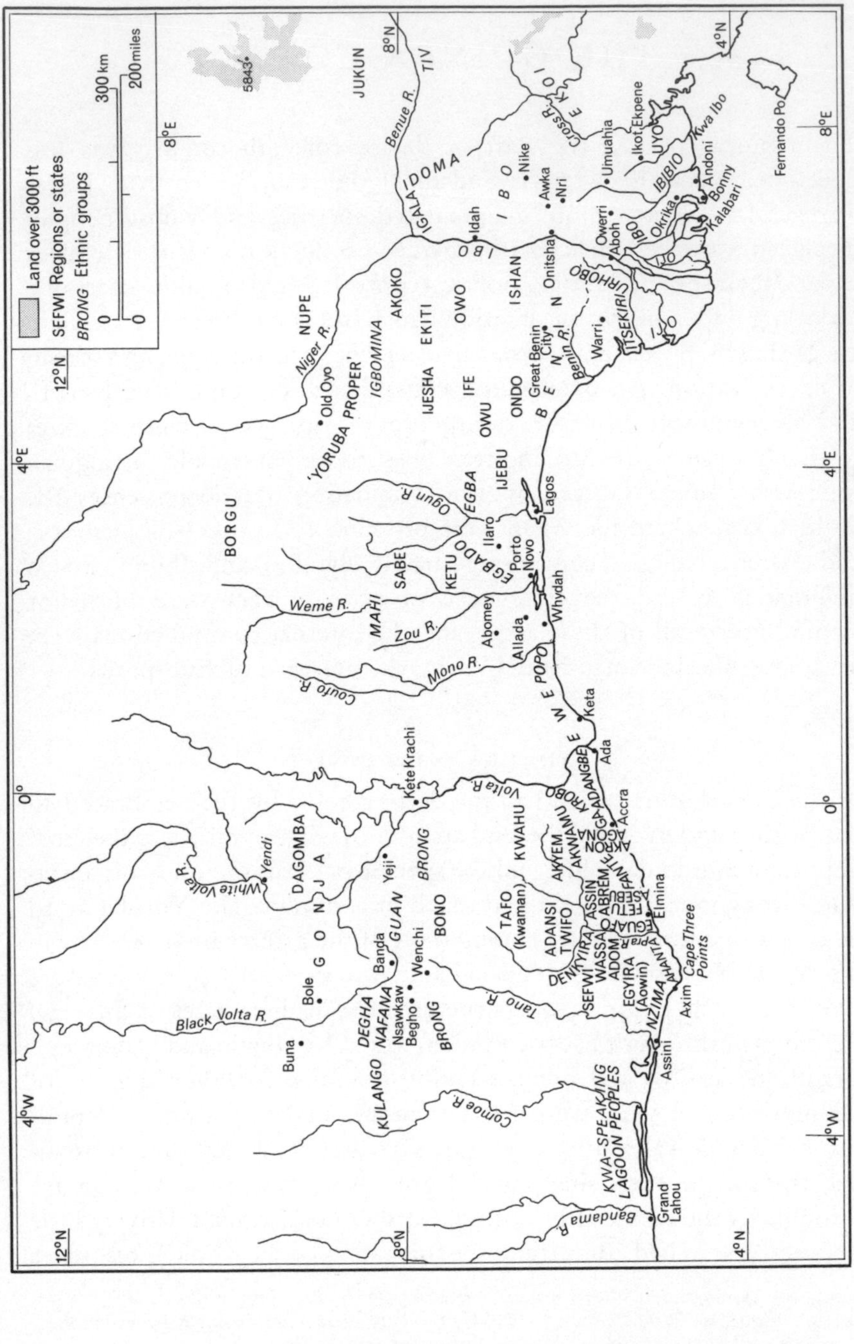

6 The lower Guinea coast in the seventeenth century

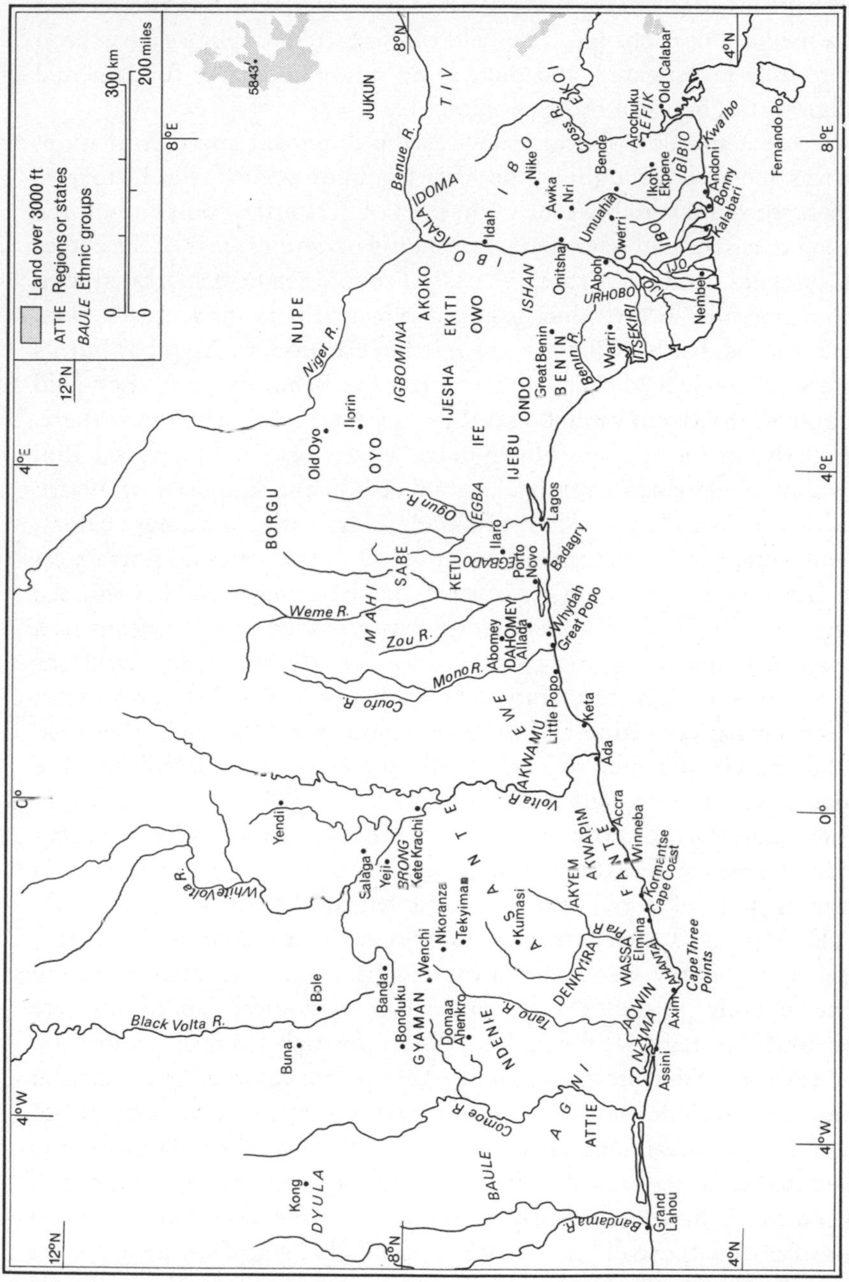

7 The lower Guinea coast in the eighteenth century

of the region, the existence of internal trade and of taxation and tribute mechanisms attests to the integration of resources, with cowries serving as a medium of exchange. The field of comparative religions has been more fully investigated, and there is no doubt about the fundamental religious ties between these peoples.

Where a sizable political state was the dominant social formation, as was the case throughout the '*Ebi* Commonwealth', the history as reconstructed invariably centres on the political macro-unit and on the ruling dynasties. An issue that is constantly in doubt is that of the extent of the states. In Benin's case, the coastal sphere can be demarcated with some precision, as extending from the Niger delta to the Lagos lagoon. The town and state of Lagos was inhabited mainly by Yoruba; but its rulers acknowledged their descent from the Benin dynasty, they paid tribute to the Benin capital, and they had their titles sanctioned there. Similarly, in the western Niger delta, it was originally a vassal Bini dynasty which ruled over Itsekiri subjects in the kingdom of Warri. Further inland, the position is not as clear; but, at its maximum extent, Benin comprised large areas of Yorubaland to the west and north-west of Great Benin city, while eastwards its influence went beyond the Niger into Iboland. The Ijebu ruler was regarded by Europeans as a vassal of Benin in the early seventeenth century, but Ijebu traditions do not mention Bini suzerainty. The likelihood is that Benin could not effectively back its claims in this district. However, Ondo, lying between Ijebu and Great Benin, did not escape some form of control, and the same applies to Owo and most of Ekiti.

The question of territorial extent merges into that of determining what degree of control would justify describing any given area as forming part of a political state. Pre-feudal and early feudal states seldom achieved clear territorial definition on any continent. A great deal of autonomy was retained by regions within the territory of the state, notably on the outskirts and where ecological conditions were favourable to regional resistance. Almost invariably, a distinction arose between the stable areas and the marcher provinces. Such a distinction does not preclude the use of terms such as 'realm' and 'empire' to describe the maximum area in which some degree of authority was exercised even sporadically. It is justifiable to draw the boundaries of Benin much more generously than would be the case if one were to consider only those districts in which the daily lives of the people were immediately affected by the coercive power of the state. Benin should be understood to mean a central nucleus plus a large number of tributary states. In the nucleus of the state, the *oba* alone could inflict the death penalty. Differences in dialects and facial marks were among the clues which provided ready identification concerning both regional origins and position in the social hierarchy.

Areas distant from Great Benin occasionally had resident representatives or military settlements, but the *oba*'s authority was minimal in day-to-day affairs. The test of his claims lay in the ability to collect tribute and exert himself when challenged. For instance, in the reign of Oba Ehengbuda, the town of Akure in Ekiti tried to assert its independence, but its opposition was quelled by a Benin army returning from a campaign farther north. Moreover, force and the threat of force would obviously have been buttressed by other familial, cultural and ideological bonds, especially within the ruling dynasties. Local hereditary rulers had family connections with the *oba*, and his confirmation of their titles was symbolically and politically significant. Tradition reveals the tutelage of the future ruler of Owo at the court of the *oba*, and such an arrangement was probably not exceptional. The obligation to raise troops was also met by regions outside the capital. The *oba* was held to be capable of mobilizing an army of 80,000 to 100,000 men in a short time, but, by the seventeenth century, Benin was not engaged in regular warfare. This implied a high degree of consolidation, since many of the earlier wars were waged to assert superiority in districts such as Ishan and Iyerhiomo which were not far from central Benin. Benin City or Great Benin, as it was called, was surrounded in part by a high earthen embankment and a deep ditch; and on one side there was a marsh serving as a natural barrier. Access to the city centre was controlled by large wooden gates. But, in the seventeenth century, the ditch was dry – with tall trees growing within – and the suburbs had spread far beyond the gates. Defence against armed attack was not the keynote of policy at the *oba*'s court; and Benin's military power was something talked about and displayed ceremonially.

By the end of the eighteenth century, Benin's military power had declined somewhat, and the extent of the kingdom had been reduced by former tributaries opting out. One instance concerns the polity of Warri. According to one version of Warri traditions, the *oba* of Benin was never the overlord of the *olu* of Warri. Presents from the *olu* to the *oba* were wrongly interpreted as tribute, and that is why the Itsekiri had to abolish the practice of sending presents.[1] However, other facts suggest that Benin initially exercised sovereignty which was slowly

[1] W. A. Moore, *History of the Itsekiri* (London, 1970), 24, 25.

whittled away. Sometime before the middle of the seventeenth century, it was already possible to say of Warri that the *olu* was more the ally than a vassal of the *oba* of Benin, and that in most respects the *olu* was absolute in his own domains. By the eighteenth century, Warri is to be considered as an independent Itsekiri political state, comprising also a few Urhobo and Ijo.

Histories of Benin have tended to date its 'decline' from as early as the seventeenth century, or at least to suggest a significant contraction of boundaries. The breakaway of Warri and other coastal cities is cited as evidence to this effect. For instance, on the Benin river, a number of trading towns had become virtually independent of the *oba*. Yet, it has been admitted that around 1690 'the Oba's power could still extend with decisive effect to these river settlements, even if it could not regulate their routine affairs'.[1] Besides, it is not at all certain whether the situation on the coast can be the basis for generalizing with regard to inland districts of Benin. Trading settlements derived most of their rationale from the European presence, and their positions as gateways of trade would have given the respective local élites considerable opportunities to break away from the Benin metropolis. Warri apparently achieved its independence with the aid of Europeans, and this intrusive factor must be reckoned with on other parts of the coast to which Benin laid claim.

Olaudah Equiano provided an African's eye-witness description of Benin in the middle of the eighteenth century, in which he indicated that his own Ibo homeland (probably near the Niger on the east bank) fell within the confines of Benin. He was very conscious of Benin's extent and wealth, although its political power in his homeland was nominal.[2] The main implication of Equiano's observations is that the 'empire' of Benin was still far-flung, and was not necessarily any less effective than it had been before, because extensive local autonomy seemed always to have been a principal feature of the political structure. It was only when a province completely rejected the idea of overlordship that the central government was forced to exert itself. Up to the early nineteenth century, Benin was still capable of asserting itself successfully in the interior. Oba Obanosa (*c.* 1804–16) is credited with the capture of Ute in Owo; and in 1823 Benin again crushed opposition in Akure.

The Benin presence in eastern Yorubaland was not merely military. Important socio-economic ties were established with the residents there

[1] Alan Ryder, *Benin and the Europeans, 1485–1897* (London, 1969), 126.
[2] Paul Edwards (ed.), *Equiano's travels* (London, 1967), 1.

and with the Oyo empire. Benin exerted its influence on folklore, ritual, music, dance and regalia; and it maintained commercial relations. Each branch of its trade with the hinterland was organized under a trading association, having the *oba* as patron and a Benin noble as president. Metropolitan Benin manufactured brass utensils and iron implements; coastal areas produced salt; while cloth was the most valuable commodity originating in the near interior. Other domestic resources which entered into the cycle of local trade included ivory, coral beads, leather, beans and palm products.[1]

In Oyo's sphere, military confrontations persisted throughout the seventeenth and eighteenth centuries. It seems likely that claims to sovereignty were made in the wake of any successful encounter, but it was a lengthy process before anything approaching effective occupation of disputed territory could be brought about. Oyo's military strength was based largely on the possession of cavalry and the consequent manoeuvrability of its armies within the savanna. When Oyo armies ventured into the forests, they initially suffered reverses – particularly at the hands of the Ijesha. The latter strengthened their defences in the early seventeenth century by building Osogbo as an outpost some twenty miles north-west of their capital at Ilesa. However, with experience, Oyo surmounted the problem of fighting in the heavier vegetation; and reduced to vassalage (in whole or in part) regions such as Igbomina, Ijesha, Owu, Ife, Ekiti and Egba.

To the west and south-west, Oyo's military expansion was more readily achieved, for horses could be used on the open plains which gave access to the sea from Sabe via Ketu and Egbado. In the reign of Alafin Ajagbo, around the middle of the seventeenth century, the *alafin*'s armies took over the state of Weme on the lower reaches of the Weme river. Farther west, the Aja states felt the might of Oyo. Allada was conquered in 1698, while in 1730 Dahomey was reduced to vassalage. With this latter achievement, Oyo, by then under Alafin Ojigi, came very close to its maximum territorial extent. Possibly, there was a small amount of expansion under Alafin Onisile and Alafin Abiodun later in the century.

It is said that Alafin Ojigi dispatched a military expedition which made the rounds of the whole empire. It struck out northwards to the Niger, followed this river to the coast, proceeded west to the Weme, and finally swept north and east to the Oyo capital, 'in order to show

[1] S. A. Akintoye, 'The north-eastern districts of the Yoruba Country and the Benin Kingdom', *Journal of the Historical Society of Nigeria*, December 1969, 4, 4.

[Ojigi's] undisputed sovereignty over the whole of the Yoruba country, including Benin'.[1] This is misleading because Benin was not a tributary state, and Benin had a hold on the coast which is sweepingly claimed in this tradition. Furthermore, the inclusion of Ijebu would be questionable. The people of Ijebu seemed to have kept both Benin and Oyo at bay – helped by the forest. Conversely, on the open western savanna, there is no denying the reality of Oyo's claims. Oyo's grip over Sabe and Ketu was seen in the ease with which the *alafin*'s armies crossed these territories to discipline Abomey. Furthermore, Oyo's trade corridor to the sea was initially through Ketu and Allada, and, when Abomey absorbed Allada in 1726, Oyo shifted its hold to Ajase Ipo, or Porto Novo, which remained under the direct tutelage of Oyo for another century.

Relations between the several Yoruba polities within Oyo's sphere constituted a complex political pattern. Not only did the degree of the *alafin*'s control vary from place to place, but between any two adjacent regions local arrangements of domination and subordination often prevailed. As in Benin, a distinction was drawn between the provinces and the central nucleus, the latter being referred to by the Yoruba historian, Samuel Johnson, as 'Yoruba Proper', and comprising four metropolitan districts. Yoruba proper lay in the savanna lands which were drained by the Ogun river. It was bounded on the north-east by the Niger, on the west by the upper Weme, and on the east by Nupe. The population of this nucleus was overwhelmingly Yoruba, and some small penetration of Nupe and Bariba through intermarriage did not interfere with cultural homogeneity. It was the core area which Oyo had held, lost and regained; and it was a sound base for the central government of the extended Oyo empire. Not until the nineteenth century was there to be disintegration in Yoruba proper.

As the southern Yoruba were brought under some measure of control by armies from metropolitan Oyo, local rulers usually remained in office, most of them claiming descent from Ife and kinship with the *alafin* himself. It would seem that real 'power' had passed to Oyo, in the sense of the capacity to make and implement decisions, based ultimately on military strength. Ife had to recognize this military and political power, but it counterposed its 'authority' as father of the Yoruba – the said authority being exercised in the constitutional and ceremonial spheres. The most important ceremony at the investiture of any *alafin* was that of obtaining from the *oni* of Ife the *Ida Oranyan*

[1] Samuel Johnson, *History of the Yorubas* (Lagos, 1921), 174.

(Oranyan's sword), without which the *alafin* elect would have no authority to order an execution and hence no supreme judicial authority. The *igba iwa* or divination calabashes, which were essential to the installation of the *alafin*, also came from Ife. As far as the rest of Oyo was concerned, items brought to the capital attested to the subordinate status of the donors. The much-prized *bere* thatching grass was brought from the savanna provinces by the many crowned heads of Yoruba proper, as a symbol of their attachment and vassalage. This gift was also in effect a form of economic tribute, and the *bere* festival was one of the three public functions held at Oyo which necessitated the presence of the *alafin*. Regions outside the savanna sent tribute in other forms. From Ijesha and Ekiti came kola nuts, mats, Guinea pepper, firewood and other forest products; from slave-raiding districts captives were forthcoming; and European goods were dispatched from sea-coast towns.

Apart from the collection of gifts and tribute, the *alafin* asserted hegemony through the appointment of *ilari*, senior officials recruited originally from the ranks of captives. Their principal function abroad was to act as messengers and envoys of the *alafin*. Crowned rulers in Yoruba proper had the privilege of creating their own *ilari*. This applied for instance to rulers of Igana, Ikoyi, Ede and Iwo. In the provinces, the persons of the *alafin*'s *ilari* were inviolable and they were treated like royalty. An envoy could also be appointed resident agent in a provincial town, in which case he became an *ajele*. The *ajele* supervised the collection of tax and tribute for forwarding to the capital. In Egba country, this mechanism was highly developed. The Egba retained little autonomy because they lacked a military organization capable of defending their territory, and they were extremely fragmented politically. The *alafin* had his *ajele* in each of the Egba towns, and they had become lords of even the kings. Resentment against Oyo's domination eventually promoted Egba national sentiment, and in the late eighteenth century this gave rise to an armed revolt across the country. Over 600 *ajele* were killed, showing the extent of the *alafin*'s administrative network.

Egbado was the province which saw the novel and significant development of an influx of colonists from the metropole. Yoruba was the *lingua franca* of trade in the vicinity of Porto Novo by the 1660s, and it was being adopted in preference to the Aja language. Previously, Oyo must have been sending colonists down to the sea in significant numbers, and they would logically have settled around the Lokwe lagoon for purposes of trade – especially in salt. These Yoruba settlers were divided into several groups, the most important being the Anago and the Ilaro. In the seventeenth century, the Anago were under the jurisdiction of the *elehin-odo* of Ifonyin; and, though this kingdom split later on, the Anago remained subject to the *alafin*. The Ilaro also constituted a long-established Oyo immigrant group in Egbado. Being centrally placed, the settlement of Ilaro was made into a provincial headquarters. Its ruler, the *olu*, was retired and recalled to metropolitan Oyo after a three-year term, so as to keep the settlers on leash. Even so, ties between Oyo and the colonists were loosened during the third quarter of the eighteenth century, and Alafin Abiodun reasserted control by sending a Nupe to become *onisare* at Ijanna, close to Ilaro. This official gradually assumed many of the functions previously carried out by the *olu*, and he was required to commit suicide at the death of the *alafin*, thereby ensuring that a new king at Oyo would not be faced with an experienced *onisare*.[1]

Relations between Oyo and Dahomey provide an example of the difficulties facing Oyo as it extended itself. For several years after the conquest of 1730, Oyo's sovereignty over Dahomey seems to have been based only on the collection of tribute by means of full-scale annual military expeditions. Yet these expeditions are themselves evidence of Oyo's resoluteness and capacity. In 1739, sometime after the death of Alafin Ojigi, the Dahomeans broke the agreement which was forced on them in 1730; but by 1748 they had to succumb once more, with the bitter memory of two disciplinary campaigns waged by Oyo against Dahomey. Subsequently, Oyo officials received from Dahomey a heavy tribute handed over each November at Kana, not far from the town of Abomey. The question of what 'strong names' should be used by Dahomean monarchs was decided at least once by Oyo (in 1774), and this was an important symbol of Oyo's hegemony. Dahomey did not manage to shake off Oyo's overlordship for the duration of the eighteenth century.

Dahomey's history was played out on a much narrower stage than that of Oyo, largely because of the latter's dominance. It was restricted to the southern half of the long corridor that approximates to the modern state of Dahomey, but within that space there was a great deal of growth and expansion. It is useful to maintain a distinction between

[1] Peter Morton-Williams, 'The Oyo Yoruba and the Atlantic trade, 1670–1830', *Journal of the Historical Society of Nigeria*, December 1964, 3, 1; and Kola Folayan, 'Egbado to 1832, the birth of a dilemma', *Journal of the Historical Society of Nigeria*, December 1967, 4, 1.

the kingdom of Dahomey and the original principality of Abomey, because the kingdom of Dahomey represented the sum of developments taking place in Aja country, of which Abomey was only one section. The state of Abomey was probably not in existence in 1600, and at that time state systems were just beginning to emerge in Aja country. The presence of Yoruba offshoots from Ife, the similarity of Yoruba and Aja religious beliefs, and the proximity to Yoruba kingdoms such as Sabe and Ketu were features of the political environment in which Dahomey developed; while the more immediate setting was the early history of the kingdom of Allada.

Most writings on the founding of Allada greatly over-emphasize the role of the immigrant clan from Tado, which became the ruling dynasty round about 1575. Little attention is paid to the population which was already resident *in situ*, and no evaluation is made of the socio-economic activity which provides a base for any political structure. Many visitors to Whydah and Allada thought it necessary to remark on the population factor. Bosman said that the country of Allada 'is so very populous, that in one Village alone, as the King's or any of his Vice-roy's Villages (for Instance) there are as many people as in a common Kingdom on the Gold Coast: And this Land is well furnished with these large Villages, besides innumerable small ones.'[1]

The gap in the forest in which the Aja kingdoms emerged was dryer than Yoruba territory to the east, but grains flourished there, and the oil palm was available. Maize (introduced in the sixteenth century) was harvested twice a year, as a supplement to millet, while beans were inter-planted among other crops. The landscape in Whydah was completely humanized: there were numerous planted trees and the undergrowth had been cleared. The Popo people were dependent upon food exported from Whydah. Besides, there was a great deal of fishing in the coastal lagoons: and poultry, cattle and small livestock were reared. As in Yorubaland, considerable amounts of cotton were grown in Aja territory, and there was a flourishing cloth industry, distinguished by the quality of some of its cotton pieces. It was said that the men in Allada had more wives and kept them more richly clothed than on the Gold Coast. Iron was worked and salt-making near the coastal lagoons was the other major manufacturing activity. Finally, one must not overlook the numerous domestic handicrafts which produced pottery, decorated calabashes, wooden vessels, raffia mats, etc., nor the labour

[1] William Bosman, *A new and accurate description of the coast of Guinea* (London, 1967), 339.

and skills required to build several new towns and palaces in the seventeenth century.

Numerous markets were dotted all over the Aja region. Some four or five miles outside the town of Ba, there was a daily market which attracted residents from all over Allada, who brought a variety of commodities for exchange. Nearby, a major fair was held every four days for dealers in salt, some of which was transferred to Oyo. But it was probably the smaller local markets which accounted for most of the total turnover of trade. These were held in villages or on open plains, and dealt mainly with foodstuffs and simple artefacts. Internal trade implies specialization and integration of the economy. This is one of the reasons why a given clan – the immigrants from Tado – was capable of organizing the household heads into a single state at Allada, while off-shoots could do the same at Whydah and Abomey.

Abomey's expansion in the seventeenth century was connected not only with military success but also with population growth and increased production. The new state always welcomed immigrants and gave them citizenship. Under Wegbaja (*c.* 1650–*c.* 1680) additional territory was conquered, and he is also said to have encouraged agriculture.[1] Spinning and weaving were apparently extended at this period. Contemporary data are lacking, but the level of the arts and crafts in inland Dahomey in the eighteenth and nineteenth centuries is indicative of considerable stimulation at an earlier date. At the time of the secession of Dogbagri from Allada and the founding of Abomey (about 1620), the Aja country was ripe for the extension of state organization. The economic base was there, the examples of Oyo and Benin were known, and the Aja themselves were experimenting with state organization from about the end of the third quarter of the sixteenth century. At Abomey, the Dogbagri kings undoubtedly made innovations with respect to the political superstructure, but the return to Allada and Whydah as conquerors ensured that the state of Dahomey incorporated all previous efforts of the Aja people. Furthermore, the fact that the south was Abomey's primary target for expansion and consolidation suggests that the Dogbagri line was consciously construing rule over Allada and Whydah as its heritage. Therefore, both objectively and at the level of consciousness, Dahomey was the outgrowth of developments not merely in Abomey but throughout the Aja region.

Each of the three nuclei of Dahomey had an independent internal history, with certain differing characteristics. Though united by kinship

[1] M. Quenum, *Au pays des Fons* (Paris, 1938), 24.

ties, they also had a tradition of rivalry, which began in the period when only Allada and Whydah were in existence. Allada insisted on its seniority over Whydah, and tried to dictate policies on trade; but Whydah had easy access to the coast, so that by the second half of the seventeenth century it was concentrating on overseas trade, in competition with Allada. Most of the reigns of the last Whydah kings, Amat (1703–8) and Huffon (1708–27), was taken up by a trade war between Allada and Whydah. This smouldered on in the form of occasional armed clashes, especially in the period 1712–20, when Allada imposed a trade blockade on Whydah. Meanwhile, Whydah's expansionist tendencies were expressed in a westward direction – towards Popo. Great Popo was a large fishing village, whose people came to serve as brokers in the European-generated trade. After Akwamu inflicted its crushing defeat on the Ga of Accra in 1679 (see below, p. 310), Great Popo gave shelter to the Ga refugees. Fante canoe-men and traders from Elmina were also welcomed in this coastal lagoon region, and it was mainly the immigrant Gold Coast community which made up the settlement of Little Popo. Whydah maintained a keen interest in Great Popo and Little Popo, which can be regarded as the westernmost outposts of the Aja community, and a section that was mainly concerned with foreign trade.

Abomey's speciality was far removed from trade: it was the organization of military force. The Dogbagri faction of the Aja dynasty founded their settlements alongside the compounds of Igede people on Abomey plateau. Given their Allada background, the Dogbagri were consciously engaged in state building; and, with a level of political awareness in advance of that of the family heads of the plateau, they sought power for themselves. The Dogbagri were encouraged by the arrival of further Aja adherents from the south; and the accession to power over the Igede was achieved by a blend of persuasion, stratagem and force – the last factor becoming more important as the seventeenth century advanced. The result of a hundred years of slow growth from 1620 to 1720 was that Abomey had intensified its military power to a degree which allowed it to assert itself as the dominant element within Aja country. Dogbagri himself was a tenant of the Igede; but his son and successor, Dukodonu (*c.* 1625–*c.* 1650), wrested power from a number of small rulers in his vicinity. Then came Wegbaja (*c.* 1650–*c.* 1680), who is credited with reorganizing the warrior bands, providing them with training, and introducing new tactics such as surprise night attacks. He was often placed first on the list of kings because of his many victories, one of which was scored over an invading army of the ruler of Tokple on the Mono river. In this instance, Wegbaja was making his presence felt in the district which was the original home of the Aja, who migrated to Allada. To the east, Abomey's expansion under Akaba (*c*. 1680–1708) brought conflict with the Weme people. The kingdom that was inherited by Agaja in 1708 comprised some forty towns and villages, bounded by the Lama marshes to the south, the Mahi mountains to the north, the Weme to the east and the Coufo to the west.

When Agaja made his descent on Allada and Whydah in the 1720s, the defenders had to scrape together mercenary armies from Popo and the Gold Coast, for this is how they had previously been carrying on their own war. Forces levied within Allada and Whydah were disunited, and suffered from serious leadership problems. The most prominent rulers stayed at home and sent individuals of lesser status to command the fighting forces. The contrast with Abomey is sharp, for there two of the highest officers of the land were the military commanders, who fully appreciated that success in war was the requirement for continuation in office. Abomey, like Benin and Oyo, was capable of mobilizing a large number of troops at short notice. When war was announced, clan heads brought their kinsmen and dependants to Abomey, along with their own weapons. The king and his immediate followers and kinsmen were armed and constituted something of a standing army. Already under Agaja there existed both the practice of placing youths as apprentices to adult soldiers (at public expense) as well as arming women to serve as guards. Abomey was specializing in the military art, and was maximizing its supply of able-bodied fighters. A disciplined national army became one of the most outstanding social institutions in the kingdom of Dahomey, as the latter emerged with the political unification of the Aja country.

For the whole of the eighteenth century, Dahomey did not grow to be a match for Oyo's armies, and consequently remained tributary; but this was in no way inconsistent with Abomey's takeover of Aja territory. Oyo delayed and complicated the takeover, but it could not prevent it. Agaja had the requisite military instruments and he showed his ability to use them in campaigns against Weme and in police actions north and south of Abomey town. He had also shown a desire to intervene in Allada's affairs, but was not afforded an opportunity until March 1724 when he moved south under the pretext of supporting a candidate to the throne of Allada. After crushing Allada's army and killing the king, Agaja took over the capital, and the kingdom of Dahomey came into being.

Oyo responded to Agaja's success by a punitive expedition in 1726. Dahomey's army did not fare well against Oyo cavalry. Yet this did not prevent the attack against Whydah in February 1727. Huffon, the king of Whydah, barely escaped with his life, and he and other survivors took up residence at Great Popo. For many years, Huffon cherished the hope of regaining his throne, but not even the *alafin*'s horses and men could achieve this on his behalf. Oyo's successive raids on Dahomey in 1729 and 1730 confirmed that a new political entity had come into existence, and paradoxically strengthened the hold of the Dogbagri line. Oyo was capable of taking command of the Abomey region for several weeks at a time, leaving Agaja and his supporters with no alternative but to withdraw to the north and to the south. Agaja himself headed for the tough bush country north-west of Abomey, while other lieutenants fell back southwards on Allada and Whydah. When Oyo forces were advancing in January 1730, Agaja sent large numbers of his followers into Igelefe, the Whydah port, thus thwarting Huffon's hopes of returning to power while Abomey was hard pressed. Then Agaja retreated to Allada, which remained the capital of Dahomey for the next thirteen years.

Dahomey had to come to terms with Oyo in 1730. The agreement which made Dahomey tributary guaranteed Dahomey's territorial integrity, although it protected the Allada dynasty in their new kingdom of Porto Novo, as well as shielding Weme from Dahomey. Oyo wanted Porto Novo and Weme to be within its own orbit, but by implication it accepted that Allada and Whydah were no longer independent and that Mahi was within Dahomey's sphere. Agaja and his successors were thus able to consolidate their rule within this north–south corridor bounded by the Weme and Mono rivers. Just as Oyo chastised Dahomey regularly over a period of many years to achieve unquestioned obedience, so the central authority of Dahomey had to bring force to bear on different sections of the enlarged kingdom to hammer it into shape. Jakin, Allada's chief port, had submitted without a fight in 1724, but its ruler tried to pursue an independent policy and flouted Agaja's authority. Consequently, Dahomey's troops carried out severe reprimands in April 1732 and again in November 1734. Another rebellious zone was the coastal strip between Whydah and Great Popo. Whydah refugees at Great Popo, who were called 'Old Whydah', were familiar with the marshy environment where the Dahomean army floundered, and they were expert in manipulating their canoes on the creeks. Tegbesu (1740–74) inherited this problem from Agaja. The 'Old Whydah' and the Popo together launched a serious attack on the Dahomean port of Igelefe in 1763, placing Dahomey in the unusual position of needing the aid of the English fort. In 1774, peace was finally concluded with the Popo, after Dahomey had killed the last successor in the line of the exiled Huffon.

Dahomean royal authority encountered its greatest problems in the hill country of the Mahi, especially the territory between the Zou and the Weme rivers. Some residents of the area were driven from the Abomey plateau by the expansion of the Dogbagri dynasty, while others were Yoruba with very tenuous links with Ife. The Mahi emerged as a distinctive Yoruba/Aja amalgam. One of their characteristics was small-scale political organization, but they were no easy prey for their bigger neighbours, Oyo and Dahomey. Combativeness and independence were the most marked features of Mahi history. Dahomey invaded Mahi territory time and time again, especially during the reign of Tegbesu. He was able to conquer the southern clans of the Mahi (the Za), but had to compromise with the Gbouele and Dassa to the north. One could infer that by Kpengla's reign (1774–89) most of Mahi was an integral part of Dahomey, and regular campaigns were no longer required to enforce obedience. The Mahi were providing levies for the Dahomean army, and the province was secure enough for Dahomey to mount a major attack across the Weme on Ketu in 1789. Conflicting claims that Oyo was in control of Mahi can possibly be justified only with regard to the northern portion of the region.

When large kingdoms like Whydah and Allada were conquered, their kings were removed, but lesser rulers were often confirmed in their positions. The local government structure of village heads or *tohusu* was left intact, and perhaps strengthened. Within the Dahomean administration, new offices were created and old ones reinforced to meet new situations. The two most important posts in the government of Dahomey were those of the *migan* and the *mehu*, both of which were given added scope with the expansion of Dahomey. Allada went under the portfolio of the *migan*, who was formerly sacrificial priest at Abomey, and who remained resident at Abomey as a powerful court figure. The *mehu* was responsible for receiving all foreigners who had business with the state and for transferring Whydah customs dues to the Dahomean treasury. Whydah itself was left under the *yevogan* or 'captain of white men', because it was there that Dahomey dealt with European forts and traders.

Dahomey displayed a great deal of administrative resourcefulness, but social policies were more important in holding together the nation. Just as the state had to unite provinces, so too it had to impose unity on various religious cults. Wegbaja laid down common rules for funeral rites, and he appointed a *dokpwegan* to consecrate ancestral shrines, standardizing different cult practices in this regard. Changes introduced by the monarchy in the form and content of ancestral cults emphasized the dependence of these cults on the king. Many provincial bureaucrats were religious figures, and (as would be expected in that stage of social development) religion dominated the consciousness and ideology of Dahomeans. Reference to the Dahomean administration in a purely secular context has led to an exaggerated notion of Dahomey's efficiency as an economic unit. For instance, the conduct of a regular census was not a means of maintaining centralized control of the country's production. The enumeration was not accurate and was not intended to be, since it served symbolic functions connected with the kingship.[1]

There were, however, some centralizing policies with a specific economic rationale. States in the Yoruba/Aja group exercised wide powers over money and trade. Having developed a monetary system based on cowries, the state treasury controlled the inflow and circulation of currency. Foreign trade was exclusively under the administration of the central government, since it brought in cowries and several other items upon which a high value was placed. Local production and distribution also came to some extent under central control. In Agaja's time, efforts were made to induce the return of those who had fled because of wars, and they were encouraged to resume normal agricultural activities. Much later in the century, Kpengla set out to bolster Dahomey's internal trade by improving the road system. In 1779, he ordered his subjects to build roads ten yards in width, placing the responsibility on the clan heads in each district. Communications with the south across the Lama marsh were improved by filling in gullies and widening bridges.

In assessing the degree of central government control over the provinces, one has to deal with the related issue of internal contradictions within the central government. The two principal sets of interests which were reflected in and protected by the state were those of the

[1] W. J. Argyle, *The Fon of Dahomey: a history and ethnography of the Old Kingdom* (Oxford, 1966), 97–103.

royal lineages and the groups which were without the right to produce successors to the throne. The lines were not sharply drawn, being complicated partly by struggles within the ruling dynasty and partly by the fact that many of the nobility had territorial bases of power lying outside the capital. Within Dahomey, royalty was elevated above other clans by having several rules and practices peculiar to itself, such as the rules of succession and the practice of overriding taboos on endogamous marriage. These special rules served to increase the numbers, skills, wealth and power of the royal clan. The relationship of royalty to the nobility was ceremonially portrayed in the various annual 'customs' held in Benin, Oyo and Dahomey. These were (among other things) opportunities for kings to show their wealth and generosity. The ceremonies of the 'customs' glorified royalty, but to the informed local observer they must also have illustrated to what extent the king could be considered powerful and independent in relation to the provinces and the élite at court.

At every level in the hierarchy of the state, controls were exercised over persons in authority. The *olu* of Warri boasted of his independence from the *oba* of Benin, but his own power was limited by that of three nobles. With regard to matters of purely local interest in a village, this system was democratic in nature; but within the central government it meant that an oligarchy operated. The early history of Benin was apparently one of changing fortunes with regard to relative power between the *oba* and the *uzama*, or senior Edo rulers. By the beginning of the sixteenth century, there was in existence a hierarchy of 'palace chiefs' as well as one of 'town chiefs'. The former supposedly served the *oba*, while the latter were more representative of the *uzama*. In practice, there was competition for place and power among the various dignitaries, since their offices were appointive. At the same time, the power of the *oba* was whittled down relative to that of the collective nobility. The titled élite interposed between the *oba* and the rest of his subjects. By the early seventeenth century, the *uzama* ran many aspects of the state while keeping the *oba* in ignorance. They worked hand in hand with the 'town chiefs', who passed on to them much of the revenue derived from sources such as trade, taxation and judicial fines. As one would expect, command over the army was also decisive in determining the political balance. The reputation of early *obas* lay both in the military and religious spheres. But subsequent to certain developments, Benin armies were no longer led by the *oba*. Instead, the task fell on the *iyase*, the leading 'town chief'. Oba

Ehengbuda's death by drowning on a war campaign (*c.* 1600) led to the complete separation of the *oba* from military activity. The *iyase*, as general of the armies, joined the leading palace nobility in deciding many day-to-day affairs of state as well as the question of royal succession. A major civil conflict arose towards the end of the seventeenth century when the *oba* tried to free himself from restrictions. He succeeded in deposing the *iyase* as commander of the army and in promoting the rule of primogeniture to counter the manoeuvres of the senior nobility around the succession issue. However, the principle of primogeniture was not always accepted by members of the ruling dynasty, and besides it was difficult to apply it in a polygamous situation. Support by substantial sections of the nobility was required both for the king's accession and for the success of his reign. Instead of the *iyase*, it was the *ezomo* (one of the *uzama*) who commanded Benin armies in the eighteenth century; and he developed power rivalling that of the *oba*.

Oyo's history is particularly susceptible to analysis in terms of the conflict between the *alafin* and the Yoruba nobility, the most powerful of whom were the seven *Oyo Mesi*, with the *basorun* as their spokesman. Sometimes a king managed to increase his effective power to the point of autocracy, while at other times he was reduced to a mere figurehead. The overall trend was in favour of the nobility, especially since the *Oyo Mesi* were the commanders of the metropolitan Oyo armies as well as the royal electors. They also won the support of the *Ogboni* 'secret society', which was in some respects the religious arm of the state, with constitutional rights to advise and restrain the crown. From about the middle of the eighteenth century onwards, the *Oyo Mesi* regularly deposed *alafins* and forced them to commit suicide. It is not clear whether this was a constitutional innovation or whether they were invoking a right which was reputedly theirs in previous times. The *Oyo Mesi* also decreed that the crown prince should die with his father, and they chose the successor. In effect, the mode of succession had been changed from primogeniture to election by the major non-royal lineages. The path was therefore clear for the nobility to rule with nominal reference to the *alafin*, and this happened during the ascendancy of Basorun Gaha (*c.* 1754–74). Gaha was called a dictator, but he must have been representative of most of the *Oyo Mesi* and other powerful interests. Otherwise he would have had no base on which to stand in opposition to the *alafin*'s lineage.

The context in which the élite found it possible successfully to neutralize the *alafin* was the great territorial expansion of the empire, which strengthened military commanders (the *Oyo Mesi*) and governors at the *alafin*'s expense. As Oyo grew large, so did the power stakes at court. The *Oyo Mesi* accused the *alafin* of insatiable greed, no doubt feeling that they and their kinsmen should have a greater share of the wealth of the expanding state. Oyo's involvement in overseas trade meant 'luxury' goods and prestige, things about which the ruling strata cared a great deal. The metropolitan court nobility of Oyo were no less of a centralizing force than the *alafin* himself. They aided him in his expansionist wars. Ojigi's conquest of Dahomey was the responsibility of the *basorun* Yau Yamba and the *gbonka* (general) Latoyo, so they presumably felt entitled to more of the fruits of conquest. It is also suggested that one of the points of disagreement between Basorun Gaha and the *alafins* in the two decades of his hegemony was that he was in favour of further expansion while they wished to call a halt and carry out a policy of consolidation.

The Oyo dynasty showed its resilience in the re-emergence of the powerful Alafin Abiodun around 1770. In 1774, he organized an uprising which took the life of Basorun Gaha. But the *alafin*'s problems continued. Abiodun placed the administration of coastal trading provinces in the hands of his own palace officials (as in the case of Ijanna), thus fanning the jealousy of titled personages who felt that the monarch gained at their expense. Even more decisive is the fact that the hostility of Nupe was again evident at this period. This meant difficulties in acquiring horses for the Oyo cavalry. Indeed, Abiodun may have deliberately weakened the army – a tactic which is comprehensible, given that the army under the *Oyo Mesi* had previously been a check on his power. The best that Abiodun could do was to set up a personal guard of Popo under the command of his son. This situation implied the weakening of central government power *per se* as well as the continued assertion of oligarchic rather than autocratic principles of rule.

Only the king of Dahomey was exceptional, in so far as the crown defended and enlarged its powers over the course of the sixteenth, seventeenth and eighteenth centuries. Though paying tribute to Oyo, the king of Dahomey was in a stronger position than the *alafin* with regard to his own titled élite. The Dahomean monarch was not subject to the control of any powerful group comparable to the *Oyo Mesi* or the *Ogboni* society; he played a decisive role in the choice of his successor; and he was virtually immune from the threat of being deposed. Adandozan (1797–1818) was the only Dahomean monarch to have been dethroned through a political process – and then it was with the connivance of his brother Gezo. The *mehu* and the *migan* were extremely influential at the Dahomean court. Next to them in importance were the army commanders, the *gau* and *kposu*. However, Dahomean kings dealt with these senior officials in a manner that was not paralleled in Benin or Oyo. When the *mehu* engaged in rebellion against Tegbesu in 1745 he was killed by the *gau*, who was himself executed at a later date on a charge of treason. Yet the collective oligarchic element may have been supreme even in Dahomey. There is great plausibility in a nineteenth-century European comment to the effect that 'The ministers, war captains and fetisheers may be, and often are, individually punished by the King: collectively they are too strong for him and without their cordial co-operation he would soon cease to reign.'[1]

A just assessment of the Dahomey kingship would seem to place it in the same category as that of Oyo or Benin, while admitting that there was a marked difference of degree in the power wielded by the Dahomean kings. The difference is partly attributable to the fact that both Abomey and Dahomey were set up more through conquest than by association of descent groups. Another important set of factors lies in the historical conditions surrounding the birth of Dahomey contemporaneous with the ravages of the slave trade, for the struggle against the slave trade decisively influenced the form of the Dahomean state.

Dahomey fell within that area of West Africa which received the grim toponym of the 'Slave Coast'. Throughout the seventeenth century, the Dutch had obtained some slaves from Allada, especially after 1635 when their Brazilian possessions required African labour. The period of notoriety began when the Dutch were joined by other Europeans in the scramble for slaves from 1670 onwards. The French started trading at Allada in 1670; they built the first European factory at Whydah in the following year; and English slave traders established a factory in Allada in 1674. Meanwhile, Great Popo had been opened up to European trade, and within a few years Whydah was at the centre of a great concourse of slave ships. Up to about 1671, an estimated annual average of only about 3,000 captives were exported from Aja ports. Within a decade, the figure was probably doubled at Allada, and Whydah went to the forefront. Not all or even a majority of captives were Aja, but it was a bleeding process none the less. Coastal societies were fully exposed to the damaging impact of the European slave trade.

[1] Richard Burton, *A mission to Gelele, king of Dahomey* (London, 1966), 159.

This was discernible in the extent of European intervention in the affairs of Allada and Whydah and in the sundering of lineage alliances represented in the state.

Slave trading, with European capitalism behind it, was too strong a force to be contained in Aja society. Up to 1670, Tezifon, the then king of Allada, was still opposing unrestricted European trade in slaves. He told the French that already there were arriving more ships than he could load with captives, and that he wanted neither ships nor merchandise. He was then master in his own house, and he warned the Dutch and the French that if they kept quarrelling he would eject them both. As the trade in slaves developed, Allada lost control of the situation both internally and with respect to Whydah and Great Popo. Soso, the Allada king who died one year before the Abomey invasion, had for many years been helpless in the face of the court nobility, and he also met serious opposition from the provinces. The port of Jakin tried to break away, with the intention of monopolizing trade with Europeans. This rebellion was quelled by the king of Allada, with the aid of Little Popo; but Whydah was able to assert its independence.

Europeans preferred the amenities provided by the ruling class at Whydah. English ships started arriving at Whydah in 1681. Then came the Dutch in 1682 and the Brandenburgers in 1684. Dating from this same period, the presence of Portuguese and Brazilians was of special importance, being linked with the increased demand for slave labour in Brazil. Whydah's slave exports soared to appalling heights in the first quarter of the eighteenth century. Europeans had a real stake to protect, so they bridled their national rivalries. In 1704, they agreed that Whydah should be a free port, and that even in time of European war, ships in and around Whydah should not face hostilities. They also intervened to place their nominee on the Whydah throne. This king, Huffon, came to the throne in 1708 as a thirteen-year-old minor, contrary to the Whydah constitution, but backed by European traders. In spite of attempts to assert himself as he grew older, Huffon was faced with the intransigence of the directors of the European trading 'factories' as well as with opposition from that section of the Whydah élite which offered Europeans the most favourable terms.

So long as it attracted ample trade goods, any African export would have opened up some possibilities for dissensions among the nobility in the division of the imported items. The procurement of captives was particularly disastrous. Internal recruitment was the most damaging aspect as far as any given society was concerned, while raiding beyond the boundaries of a particular political unit was also a very poor way of deploying their labour resources. Like so much of the previous African long distance trade, commerce with Europeans was mainly in the hands of hereditary ruling groups. This was certainly the case with Aja participation in overseas trade, and the social rot set in from above. Once the nobility were trapped in the pursuit of European imports in exchange for captives, the clan-based society was split from top to bottom into dozens of competing entities. In Whydah, the nobles had their own armed encounters, which the central government was powerless to stop. Division then degenerated further into lawlessness. The volume of slave exports from Whydah, Allada and Great Popo was stepped up in the last quarter of the seventeenth century on the basis of extensive man-stealing and raiding, both of which became professional operations sanctioned by rulers.

Contagion spread beyond the states harbouring European forts and factories, and it affected Abomey. In 1687–8, Abomey barred the way to Allada slave traders, and that may not have been the first instance. The *ebi* or family theory was no defence against one group of Aja raiding another. Individuals from Whydah did not scruple to steal their Popo neighbours, in spite of the close ties between the rulers of these two areas. Dahomey built up defences against such practices both militarily and ideologically. A fundamental conception of the Dahomeans was that all subjects of the king were inalienable. Ostensibly, this should have applied in any of the communally oriented African societies, but wherever there was some internal social stratification the principle was flouted. With the rise of Dahomey, the inhabitants of the state were guarded not by lineage heads but by the king himself. The king required of his subjects complete obedience and in return they asked for unqualified protection. This was a considerable departure from the notion of rights and obligations springing solely from birth and family relations.

Some years before the takeover of Whydah, its king realized that traditional relationships were no longer a sufficient foundation for state power and he turned to new men who were called 'king's servants'. In 1712, he formed them into a council from which he excluded all hereditary rulers and in which he vested the final decision on important issues. This expedient did not stop the splitting and weakening of Whydah; and the new enlarged Dahomean state of the 1720s faced the task of dealing with the intrusive European commercial element which was undermining the normal process whereby the state became more cohesive. Agaja Trudo, Dahomey's greatest king, appreciated that the pursuit of slaving in and around Dahomey and the export of such captives represented a policy incompatible with Dahomey's development. He wreaked vengeance on Allada, Whydah and European slavers. Trade 'factories' in Allada and Whydah were looted and burnt, and forts were also besieged in the late 1720s, with no regard to the consequence of diminished trade. Dahomean soldiers blocked routes by which captives were brought down from the interior, and in the years immediately following his conquests, Agaja permitted only a greatly diminished flow of slave exports – releasing mainly females, who were presumably surplus to local requirements. It was at this time that European slave traders began to try Badagry as an alternative, building it into an important slave mart by the 1740s. Meanwhile, they were bitterly opposed to Agaja and wished to revive the power of their former Whydah collaborators. For engaging in such mad schemes, the English fort commander was executed in November 1729. Agaja himself hoped to induce Europeans to sponsor commerce in which Africans engaged in production rather than pillage and self-immolation. For this purpose, Agaja sent a spokesman to England in 1725 to indicate that he wanted Europeans other than those with slave ships. Agaja was prepared to provide labour for Europeans engaged in economic activity inside Dahomey. As one European put it, 'the natives would sell themselves to us on condition of not being carried off, that we might settle plantations'.[1] This may well have meant plantation agriculture with labour being exploited on a semi-capitalist and semi-feudal basis, through an alliance between Dahomean rulers and European investors, because Agaja had already embarked on using captives on royal farms instead of selling them abroad. Their inseparability from the land gave that form of production a feudal flavour. In any event, the decision to ask European capitalists to engage in plantations was aimed at transforming chaos into relative stability.

Agaja saw the need to make the best use of skills which Europeans possessed. In a manner reminiscent of the Kongo kings in the first encounters with Portuguese, Agaja offered invitations to European craftsmen such as tailors, carpenters and blacksmiths. However, these overtures to establish relations with Europe other than those of slave trading evoked no positive response; and by 1730 Agaja was forced to

[1] John Atkins, *A voyage to Guinea, Brazil and the West Indies* (London, 1970), 119, 122, 132. See also, I. A. Akinjogbin, 'Agaja and the conquest of the coastal Aja States', *Journal of the Historical Society of Nigeria*, December 1963, **2**, 4.

come to terms with the European slave buyers. Apparently, his only successful stipulation was that the trade should come under exclusive royal control. There was the experience of Allada and Whydah which could be drawn upon to show that foreign trade tended to multiply competing centres of authority; and this tendency was manifested elsewhere on the Guinea coast. As it was, Dahomean overseas trade after 1730 was concentrated at Igelefe in Whydah, that being the main site of European forts. The slave trade did not climb to its former levels, but the basis was laid for Dahomey's continued participation in slave trading during the rest of the eighteenth century and for many decades into the nineteenth century.

With a strong army, Dahomey became in part a slave-raiding state and in part a middleman for the transfer of slaves brought from farther north. But unlike Allada, Whydah and numerous other African states that had been caught up in slaving, Dahomey did not engage in the internal recruiting of so-called 'criminals', 'debtors' and other citizens by force or fraud. Besides, for most of the rest of the eighteenth century, Dahomey was by no means single-mindedly pursuing the slave trade. It was furthering the process of state consolidation within difficult conditions posed by the presence of Europeans. This can be illustrated with reference to Mahi, which is invariably described as the slave-raiding grounds of Dahomey. In fact Dahomey carried out a great deal of trade with and through Mahi, which was on the route of long distance trade from Hausaland, Nupe and Oyo through Dahomey to the coast. The presence of several Muslims at the court of Dahomey in the second half of the eighteenth century and the popularity of Muslim amulets were visible signs of how far the northern influence had penetrated Dahomey. As already indicated, Tegbesu constantly attacked Mahi and achieved some form of ascendancy over southern Mahi during his reign from 1740 to 1774. Tegbesu explained that his main grievance against the Mahi was that each ruler imposed taxes on traders from Dahomey passing through their territory. Tegbesu wanted to destroy the autonomy of those local governments, so that the area could be merged into a single kingdom ruled by an individual responsible to Dahomey. His son and successor, Kpengla, made no secret of the fact that his mother was a Mahi, regarding this as an added reason for wanting to integrate that region. The rulers of Dahomey, far from regarding Mahi as a human warren, attacked her as part of the process of trying to establish and expand a unitary kingdom and to gain security on this important trade route.

Dahomey managed to maintain a national purpose in spite of the slave trade. The ruling class at any rate sought to make the nation strong and prestigious, and the power of the monarchy allowed sectors of the population to continue developing creatively in certain directions. The glory of armed exploits was the main inspiration for the art that flourished around the royal court. The reliefs modelled in clay on the palace walls depicted memorable military events; while the appliqué cloths were used on umbrellas, caps and banners which carried the colours and emblems of Dahomey's fighting units.

In the final analysis, however, Dahomey could not escape the contradictions posed by slave raiding and slave trading. Since the demand was entirely beyond African control, the lack of European interest in Dahomey at the end of the eighteenth century could not be remedied by local policies. The slaving sector went into a steep decline, one consequence of which was the murder of the king (Agonglo) in 1797. Professional slave raiding and the brutish trade with Europeans cheapened human life to a measure of cowrie shells, tobacco and alcohol. In Dahomey, as in so many other societies of the pre-feudal world, human sacrifice had been a limited and special feature. Man, a priceless living being, was sacrificed solemnly and sparingly in the interests of the society as a whole, as religion indicated. But as the epoch of the slave trade advanced, human beings were sacrificed by the hundreds in the annual Dahomean 'customs' – for, after all, at the international free port of Whydah they were yielded up by the thousands every year to the minions of a white god.

From some accounts, Benin appears to have been the classic case of social deterioration attendant on participation in slave trading. Recent studies have cast valid doubts on the picture of human sacrifice in Benin, both with regard to the extent of the phenomenon and the period of its origin and increase.[1] It is also important to bear in mind that Benin never became a major exporter of captives. On the other hand, there is clear evidence of an unsuccessful struggle to avoid involvement even to the extent which came about, obviously indicating dissatisfaction with the trade in their own kind. The slave trade from Benin in the late eighteenth century was sufficiently important to its ruling class for them to react aggressively against external attempts to stop the traffic. Since this trade had already prejudiced fruitful interactions between Benin and its neighbours, it contributed to the isolation which

[1] James D. Graham, 'The slave trade, depopulation and human sacrifice in Benin history', *Cahiers d'études africaines*, 1965, 5, 18.

deepened when adjacent regions continued their more intimate involvement with Europe. Therefore, Benin's participation in slave trading was an important factor in the crisis which it underwent in the nineteenth century. Benin initially responded creatively to the European presence. Its trade in peppers and cloth was proof of the agricultural, manufacturing and organizational capacity of the people and the state. Between 1644 and 1646, Benin supplied the Dutch with 16,000 cloths, and the British received about the same amount. A small amount of cotton was grown in parts of the kingdom, and the weaving of cotton and raffia was practised at the capital. However, most of the cloth came through stimulating trade with the north-eastern Yoruba, among whom the term *aso-Ado*, meaning 'Benin cloth' or 'cloth for Benin', survives from this early period. Throughout the seventeenth century, Benin dealt more successfully with Europeans than did Allada and Whydah. The latter two preyed on themselves and their neighbours to export captives, while the *oba* kept slave exports to a minimum by imposing a ban on the sale of male captives. Instead of the arrest of African economic integration characteristic of the pursuit of captives, there was some drawing together of economic boundaries on account of the cloth trade, probably extending as far as Nupe. Even so, foreign trade was under the direction of Europeans. They took the initiative that encouraged an undue and ultimately unhealthy preoccupation with overseas commerce.

On the Benin river, centres of authority were created rivalling that of the *oba*, especially after 1644 when the principal place of trade was no longer Ughoton (near Benin City) but Arbo which was farther away and less easily controlled by the *oba*. The fact that the *oba* eventually removed the ban on the export of males may well have been linked to the growing independence of the Niger delta areas, since that effectively ended the *oba*'s trade monopoly. In any event, the Benin river subjects (Ijo and Itsekiri) were much more responsive to European requests for slaves, since to them it meant mainly the acquisition of captives by trade farther up the Niger. Most decisive of all in removing the barriers to slave trading was Benin's dependence upon European and world forces over which it had absolutely no control. For instance, European decisions to promote the pepper trade in the Asian sector of their international commerce left Benin with no option but to cease any significant export of peppers before the middle of the seventeenth century. By the end of that century, Benin cloth was not as crucial within the scheme of European redistribution, owing to increases in

European manufacturing output. Slave labour, however, was constantly and insistently required in the New World. To fulfil their wish for items such as Brazilian tobacco, Indian Ocean cowries, brass pans and brandy, the *oba* and other Benin policy makers opened their ports more fully to slave traders in the second half of the eighteenth century than at any previous period.

It is also noteworthy that tension existed over the sale abroad of Benin subjects who had been brought into the society as captives, but who were at least partially assimilated as new citizens. Members of the Benin nobility affirmed that they would not sell those of their dependants or menials who had been acquired through slaving. Apparently, these affirmations did not constitute unbreakable guarantees. Ambivalence on the issue shows the persistent distaste for the handing over of human beings to the European slave dealers as well as the debasement that ensued when the slave trade did increase. Benin was not destroyed or swept away because of the nature of its contacts with Europeans over the centuries, but the Benin seen by French visitors in the late eighteenth century was not the same clean, dynamic Benin that the Dutch spoke of 200 years earlier.

Lying some 320 kilometres inland, Old Oyo was not open to European comment and inspection like Benin, Whydah or even Dahomey's capital; and trends clearly illustrated in the coastal kingdoms are more faintly outlined in Oyo's history. One parallel is the expansion of contact with European traders during the eighteenth century – in this instance by indirect means. Like Kpengla of Dahomey (1774–89), Abiodun of Oyo (1770–89) turned to trade, and this was the main occupation of his successor, Awole (1789–97). European slavers had shifted eastwards from Dahomey ever since the 1730s, and they concentrated on extracting cargoes from Porto Novo and Badagry. These were outlets for the Oyo empire. In the late eighteenth century, Porto Novo was the most populous town on the coast, with the exception of Benin. It had a significant Muslim sector, whose inhabitants were mainly Yoruba Muslims; and political power was shared between the hereditary (Ajase Ipo) line and the new compradors of the slave trade. By that time, too, more of the Yoruba themselves were finding places in the holds of slave ships. From 1770 onwards, Yoruba were carried in such numbers from Porto Novo and Badagry to Bahia that they were able to transfer intact much of their religion and social practices.

It is held that many Yoruba who reached slave marts came from the eastern and north-eastern sections of the Oyo empire, where settlements had a unique defensive posture suggesting that they were subject to raids. The Egbado to the south were also the victims of man-stealing before the period of the Yoruba civil wars. One of the immediate causes of these wars was the attack by Owu on certain Ife towns in 1821 in an attempt to stop Ife slave raiders, with the (coastal) Ijebu being involved on Ife's side. Slave recruitment in southern Oyo developed in the last decade of the eighteenth century. Alafin Awole's raid on Ife and the separatism which became rampant in the Egbado provinces are features remarkably similar to events in Allada and Whydah when those slaving states were faced by crisis in the years before Agaja took over. Oyo citizens were fleeing from parts of the empire in the interregnum after Awole's death in 1797. This was probably due not only to the absence of an *alafin* from the throne but also to the insecurity engendered by active participation in obtaining more Yoruba as captives for sale and expatriation.

Meanwhile, under Alafin Abiodun and Alafin Awole, the Oyo empire also faced threats from the north. There were unsuccessful Oyo campaigns against Borgu (1783) and Nupe (1791), which deprived Oyo of any remnant sovereignty over non-Yoruba provinces to the north. These setbacks interrupted valuable commerce; they affected military potential; and they apparently had a disruptive influence within the core area of 'Yoruba Proper'. Even so, one must avoid the procedure of using the subsequent break-up of the Oyo empire as the premise for assuming that Oyo was in disarray before the end of the eighteenth century. In the kind of state-building process that was being carried on by Oyo, there always existed a delicate balance between centralizing and centrifugal tendencies – apart from the potential conflict between different state-building nuclei. Although there was undoubtedly an increase in political and social problems for Oyo before the turn of the nineteenth century, no new situations had arisen which had altered that balance in a manner that was irreversible or decisive.

Many scholars have been fascinated by the religious aspect of Oyo's culture. The various cults and deities were the religion of the people and of the state. Religion, there as elsewhere, played a key role in social control and in buttressing the whole political order. In this respect, no major rifts occurred until the significant islamization of parts of metropolitan Oyo in the nineteenth century. Nor is there reason to believe that Oyo as an economic unit grew significantly less viable over the two centuries in question. The Oyo empire was productive.

Cloth manufacture survived vigorously, and these centuries must have formed part of the long period in which specialization and localization emerged with respect to functions such as spinning, weaving and dyeing. Central Oyo exported its cloth to various places, notably to the Porto Novo market in the second half of the eighteenth century. On the eve of the civil wars, the Oyo empire was still a hive of agricultural, manufacturing and commercial activity, extending from the centre to a point as peripheral as Ijanna in Egbaland. Ijebu products were also incorporated into this pattern of exchanges; while for most of the eighteenth century Oyo's commerce with the north was considerable, and it linked Oyo indirectly with the trans-Saharan network.

The dynamism of Oyo as illustrated was not entirely unique within the context of the Guinea coast as a whole, but neither was it the norm. Oyo of course was not a coastal kingdom and did not have the same seawards preoccupation as Allada, Whydah, Dahomey and Benin. Yoruba residents closest to the sea were the 'weeds' or lesser people within the worldview of metropolitan Oyo citizens. But the presence of Europeans was working to upset this scale of values throughout the '*Ebi* Commonwealth', and most sections of the Guinea coast outside of Oyo were to experience a much more profound reorientation towards the sea over the course of the seventeenth and eighteenth centuries.

IBOLAND, THE DELTA STATES AND THE CROSS RIVER

Many of the eastern neighbours of the Yoruba and the Bini had good reason to be preoccupied by the sea long before the arrival of Europeans, and the inland Ibo appropriately named them 'people of the salt water'.[1] The Niger delta was a major geographical feature of this part of the coast, with its numerous waterways, swamps and riverain islands. The Cross river estuary also reproduced some of these conditions, which determined a particular kind of economic activity. Fishing was the basis of subsistence; the extraction of salt from sea water was the major manufacturing activity; and the canoe was the principal means of transport. These factors made the Ijo and the Itsekiri exceptional within the Benin kingdom, while at the same time they imposed a broad cultural unity from the Niger delta to the Cameroun. Important ties were also established between the coast and the immediate hinterland, since the coastal and riverain specializations were complementary to the agricultural endeavours of populations sited on land favourable to

[1] K. Onwuka Dike, *Trade and politics in the Niger delta, 1830–1885* (Oxford, 1956), 30.

farming. Yams in particular were welcome on the coast in exchange for salt and sea foods; and the deep penetration of the rivers allowed the interchange to take place in large canoes. Local specializations in various products such as pottery, canoes and palm oil also enabled a network of African commerce to be set up from east to west along the coast.

The terrain was a major determinant of the size of the political entities on the coast, most of which were fishing villages. Seldom did the political writ of a village extend beyond its own boundaries; and family and clan allegiances led to the division of political power and authority – often expressed in religious terms. Such was the socio-political pattern on the littoral among the Ijo, Ibibio and Efik. Inland, too, segmentary lineages and small-scale political organization were the norm in the region south of the Benue and east of the Niger. The only exceptions were Idah on the Niger and Jukun (or the 'Kwararafa') straddling the Benue to the east. Absence of major territorial states in Africa and elsewhere often went hand in hand with little specialization and division of labour, isolation from other neighbouring societies, and insufficient strength to defend the particular culture from external aggression. However, the Ibo, constituting the majority in eastern Nigeria, were exceptional in all these respects. Their agriculture allowed major trade in surpluses; they were proficient in iron-working; their commercial activity extended throughout this region; and they had devised judicial and religious institutions which partially transcended the boundaries of their village governments. Over a wide area, large numbers of people spoke the various dialects of the Ibo language. Obviously, the fundaments of their way of life had been preserved and extended over a very long period.

Because of the fragmentation of political authority in eastern Nigeria, its history in one sense is the record of what separately transpired in numerous small communities. Yet, certain characteristics were of a general application, and pointed to the direction of historical development. The most indicative in the early seventeenth century were local migration movements, the increase in population, the growth of a few centres of more substantial political power, and the raising of the level of material production. Of course, the arbitrary date of 1600 has no special significance. All the trends were inherited from the sixteenth century and earlier.

Histories which were orally preserved by the peoples of this region allocate considerable attention to migrations. In the seventeenth century, one is not concerned with the problem of ethnic origins as such.

All residents had undoubtedly lived within the area for several centuries; and some (like the Ibibio and the Ijo) were for all practical purposes autochthones. Nevertheless, village histories of the Ibo, Ijo, Ibibio, Efik, and Ekoi do dwell on what were obviously local and short-distance migrations of significance to the communities at the time. The people of the Niger delta are particularly noted for their history of movement – always in very small flows. One factor accounting for this characteristic was that the delta served as a refuge for people escaping from Benin's power, with something of a billiard ball effect. Thus, the Itsekiri moved south, displacing and combining with the Nembe or Brass Ijo. An Itsekiri deity, Ogidiga, became the war-god and supreme deity of the entire Nembe area; and the Itsekiri controlled the dynasty at Nembe until the end of the fourth decade of the seventeenth century. Nembe in turn had close connections with Okrika, confirmed by traditions in both places and by similarities in religious practice. The eastwards spread of the Ijo across the delta was essentially complete by 1600, but small eddies did continue, bringing them into contact with the Ibo and Ibibio, with consequences for their social institutions, dialects, rituals and much else. Even where population displacements did not mean the constant mingling of different ethnic groups, they still had a major historical impact, as can be illustrated with reference to the Ibo in the interior.

Traditions referring to Ibo movement are least frequently encountered in the Owerri-Umuahia region, which forms the physical centre of Iboland. Away from this centre, gradual outwards displacement has been a significant feature. To the south, this meant pressure on and partial assimilation of Ijo and Ibibio. To the east, the Ekoi were placed in a similar situation. To the west, the Ibo were part of the Benin empire on the right bank of the Niger, while on the left bank Benin influence was also strong. The Igala and the Idoma were the immediate northern neighbours of the Ibo, and there is evidence of interpenetration. Movements giving rise to these ethnic and cultural fusions are not precisely datable, but many would have taken place in the seventeenth and eighteenth centuries, while others of an earlier date proved consequential during this period.[1]

The central Ibo have a rather exceptional lineage system in which single genealogies embrace many thousands of people and in which there is little room for principles of social organization outside the

[1] This section benefited from Elizabeth Isichei, *The Ibo people and the Europeans* (London, 1973).

lineage. This uniqueness is attributed to steady population expansion by birth, and peaceful outwards expansion into adjacent territory. Thus, unlike the Yoruba of Oyo, the Ibo expanded in the seventeenth century without recourse to warfare. Their religious oracles can be interpreted as evidence of cultural dynamism, for it was only through steady expansion that some of the local oracles could have acquired nation-wide reputations. The oracles at Awka, Umonoha, Ozuzu and Aro attracted petitioners seeking arbitration far from their home communities. It seems very likely that the Nri-Awka area was a cradle of the Ibo people and their culture in a period no later than the epoch of the food-producing revolution. Until contemporary times, the saying has existed that 'the street of the Nri family is the street of the Gods, through which all who die in other parts of Iboland pass to the land of the spirits'.[1] The Nri kingship also had political and ritual influence beyond its own domains.

A process of slow migration must have been a feature at the beginning of the seventeenth century. It continued without significant interruption until the eve of colonial subjugation; and in certain sectors the movement was quite vigorous, notably in the north-east. Migration on the outskirts of Iboland led to borrowing from non-Ibo cultures. Benin kingship patterns entered Aboh and Onitsha perhaps as early as the fifteenth century, and the Igala kingship had a similar impact on north-western Iboland. Other changes were effected in facets of social life such as recreation. One recorder of Ibo local history has pointed out that for many Ibo the source of popular dances was southern Onitsha, and that the people in this latter district were taught singing and dancing by others living across the Niger. Dancers from areas regarded as having greater expertise in this matter were hired for ceremonies in different villages, and in this way the fast lively dances of Onitsha spread eastwards across the country. The hiring and spread of dance types continued to contemporary times.[2]

It must be reiterated that changes deriving from local African interactions in the seventeenth century were part of a long continuum. What oral historians present as definitive acts were in many instances the summation of a process. For instance, a fishing village was not built overnight. The trend was for sites to be temporarily occupied for some months in a given year, and annual visits were paid several times

[1] For importance of Nri, see F. I. Nzimiro, 'Eastern history research scheme', *African Notes* (Ibadan, 1963), I, I.

[2] R. O. Igwebe, *The original history of the Aro Ndizuogu* (Lagos, 1962), 58, 59.

before permanent occupation ensued. A comparable process probably operated inland, where traditions refer to settlements by hunters.

Another inference which must be drawn from the recollection of population movement is that there was a constant increase in the population of the region as a whole. In the nineteenth century, this section of West Africa was already known for having a relatively dense population, in spite of the experience of the slave trade. The Niger delta and the littoral as a whole were more sparsely peopled than the Ibo and Ibibio hinterland because of environmental factors, but even the delta was experiencing population growth in the sixteenth and seventeenth centuries. Early Portuguese visitors found at least one exceptional settlement of around 2,000 people. When such numbers were involved, the transition was made from fishing village to city-state. It seems that most of the city-states which later became well-known to the outside world were already nuclei of population growth before the start of the seventeenth century. This trend continued, along with interrelated factors such as economic development and increase in political power on the part of certain groups within the state. The communities affected stretched between Nembe (or Brass) on the middle delta of the Niger and the Efik townships on the Cross river.

At Nembe there occurred in the seventeenth century a transformation of the basic Ijo village political structure to a strength beyond all its immediate neighbours. The Nembe ruler, Ogio (*c.* 1639) is regarded as the founder of a new dynasty. He arrived in Nembe from the north as a refugee, but was soon raised in high esteem as a religious leader. The reigns of Ogio, his son Peresuo, and the latter's sons Obia and Basuo covered the remainder of the seventeenth century, and it was an era of many changes. Nembe became a populous centre and the protector of much of the Brass country. There was increased trade with Warri in the western delta, with Bonny in the east and with the Ibo on the Niger. The Brass people, under the aegis of Nembe, were themselves responsible for making the trade-canoes at given spots on the shoreline where timber of a suitable kind replaced the mangrove. Local trade was very likely one of the stimulators of the House institution – the most distinctive socio-political institution in Nembe and the other city-states. In Nembe the oldest House bears the name of Peresuo, who ruled sometime around the mid-seventeenth century.[1]

The two most famous city-states which emerged in the Niger delta

[1] E. J. Alagoa, 'Long distance trade and states in the Niger delta', *Journal of African History*, 1970, 11, 3; and 'Nembe: the city idea in the eastern Niger delta', *Cahiers d'études africaines*, 1971, 11, 41.

were those of Bonny and Kalabari (New Calabar). Their origins go back to the fourteenth century, with many traditions suggesting some link with Benin. In the eastern Niger delta, the changes associated with the rise of the city-states appeared to have come about at an earlier date and in a more complete form than elsewhere. The virtually unstratified descent groups of the Ijo were sufficiently transformed to allow the people of Bonny to boast of having 'kings' for many generations, instead of merely heads of lineages or guardians of particular earth- and water-spirits. Kalabari and Bonny apparently advanced further than Nembe as foci for local and long-distance trade, judging from the first European accounts of the considerable exchange of yams, livestock and other foods for salt and fish along the trade axis that ran in a north south direction.

Reports originating on the coast in the sixteenth century implied that the Ijo were proceeding 'up the river', but it should not be assumed that the initiative was one-sided; and developments in the delta must be seen partly as expressions of the expanded capacity of the Ibo and the Ibibio in their more congenial environment. Tradition and geographical deductions suggest that most parts of Ogoja were producing an agricultural surplus in the seventeenth century, while Ekoi groups on the upper Cross river were also producers of substantial agricultural surpluses for sale towards the coast. In return, the salted fish moving north might have been destined mainly for the belt of Ibo country that stretches from Owerri to Onitsha and for that portion of Ibibio territory which lay beyond the mangrove swamps, for both of these zones appear to have been heavily settled.

Iboland was dotted with four-day and eight-day markets. Exchange was based on surplus and specialization. Certain towns were noted for specific skills such as iron-working, wood-carving and pottery-making. River ports such as Aboh and Onitsha gained their reputations in the period when they served as staging points for a commerce that was externally oriented. However, their first stages of growth pre-dated their massive involvement in European trade. In the first decades of the seventeenth century, their trade would still have been part of the African exchange pattern linking hinterland and coast. Aboh and Onitsha were the Ibo response to the development of the Niger as a commercial highway. Aboh in particular, being at the apex of the delta, was likely to have been part of the earliest trade of this region. It was badly sited for human habitation, given the flooding at that point on the river; and only trade could have provided a rationale for its settlement.

The hinterland initiative is also illustrated by the large and long-established Ibo segment in all layers of the society of the eastern delta city-states, especially Bonny. Marriage and trade ties were established between the Ijo ruling families of Bonny and the Ndokki (Ibo) of the River Imo before the period under discussion. Kamalu appears on the king-lists of Bonny as a child of this alliance, and the name also features in Kalabari genealogies. 'Kamalu' was not a typical Ndokki or southern Ibo name. It is the Cross river Ibo name for the spirit of lightning and the sky – a very common personal name among the Aro and other Cross river Ibo, and one that suggests an early connection between the delta and the south-east section of Iboland. One would expect Ibo producers and traders to have been at least co-responsible with the Ijo for fostering these ties.

The large Ibibio population seemed to have played a rather more marginal role in the integration of this region, as compared to the Ibo and Ijo. Only at Andoni was there a notable Ibibio presence in the delta, and foreign visitors did not report much activity on the coast between the Niger delta and the Cross river estuary. However, north of the mangrove shoreline, Ibibio country was fertile and abounding in palms. There is no reason to believe that the present high density in Ikot Ekpene and Uyo is a phenomenon of recent origin. On the contrary, oral traditions once more suggest this as a dispersal centre. Displacement of Ibibio groups eastwards to the confluence of the Cross and Calabar rivers created the Efik communities of the city-state that Europeans called 'Old Calabar'. Apart from one dubious tradition, the Ijo of 'New Calabar' (Kalabari) and the Efik of 'Old Calabar' do not claim any relationship. The Efik identify their origins as being in Uruan, west of the Cross river. In the sixteenth century, land shortage and conflict in Uruan forced a number of lineages to break off. After reaching the far side of the Cross river, some proceeded southwards into sparsely settled terrain which was nominally that of the Kwa (an Ekoi segment). The first major Efik settlement was at Ikot Etunko (now Creek Town).[1]

As the seventeenth century opened, the Efik were consolidating their hold on their new environment. Some small amount of farming was conducted; but, having broken off from a group that earned its livelihood by fishing in the creeks of the region, the Efik also continued with that specialization, thereby engendering the exchanges typical of

[1] Nigerian National Archives, Intelligence Report 31382, Enyong Clan, Aro District, Calabar.

coastal fishing villages. Salt was manufactured and canoes constructed so that the rivers could be used as highways for exchanging salted fish for agricultural produce from other Ibibio and presumably from the Ekoi and Ibo on the upper reaches of the Cross river and its tributaries. Local production among the Efik also included pottery and raffia cloth, while itinerant Ibo wood-carvers and blacksmiths from Abiriba were attracted south to render their services. Simultaneously, political structures were being erected on a social base characteristic of the Ibibio and (more broadly speaking) of all the segmentary lineage societies of this section of the Guinea coast. The compound or House (*ufok*) was a pivotal unit, and there were seven houses within the two founding lineages of Creek Town. From among these, there was chosen a village head, a village council and the guardian of the Efik water deity. Age-grades and 'secret societies' were other social elements which were destined to play decisive roles in the evolution of the city-state among the Efik and elsewhere within eastern Nigeria. These different strands were brought together in a complex and changing manner. Their evolution towards producing a particular kind of state was under way by the turn of the seventeenth century and in the decades that followed.

The outstanding new factor in the history of this part of the Guinea coast after 1600 is not the extension of political scale or the rise of a more differentiated society, or even the increase in trade as such. Rather it was the momentum gathered through the export trade with Europeans. Previous historical tendencies continued to manifest themselves, but they were profoundly altered within the new situation of foreign trade orientation. Europe's first ingress into eastern Nigeria was made via Benin. From the outset, part of Benin's trade with the Portuguese and the Dutch was based on control of the western Niger delta and the lower parts of the main channel. The Itsekiri, Sobo, Ijo and Ibo, who were already involved in exchanging local products, became the purveyors of a few slaves. This continued during the seventeenth and eighteenth centuries. Apart from Benin, there was initially no African state capable of providing Europeans with captives from the forests and swamps of eastern Nigeria. It was in relationship to Angola and Brazil that the Portuguese and Dutch prized and fought for São Tomé; and they would have used São Tomé to tap the eastern Nigerian and Cameroun hinterland, if those places had had captives to offer on any significant scale. Instead, São Tomé both used and re-exported slaves from Angola and Allada in the sixteenth century.

European traders had to find African rulers who could be persuaded or bamboozled into acting as agents. This was possible with the kings of Allada and Ndongo (Angola), but there were no authorities of similar stature in the Bight of Biafra. Two centuries later, there were in existence on the coast the political units with the requisite capacity to secure regularly large numbers of victims from their neighbourhood and the hinterland. Their size, social composition and politico-religious institutions had departed considerably from models found in the small fishing villages. During the same period, this section of the coast was also heavily supporting the Atlantic slave trade. The evolution of the city-states and the escalation of slave trading were mutually reinforcing.

The parameters of the slave trade were set in Europe and the Americas rather than Africa. Thus, the rapid increase of Africa's exports of its own population in the seventeenth and eighteenth centuries was determined essentially by external forces. Nevertheless, the response in given African regions was affected by local circumstances. In eastern Nigeria, the onset of protracted and extensive slaving came in the wake of a degree of maturation of the city-states. This is a salient factor accounting for the delay between the moment when the delta first came into contact with Europeans and the time when African effort went into procuring captives on a massive scale. The changed conditions are clearly revealed on the Cross river, which had little attraction for Europeans until the mid-seventeenth century. The rise of the Efik city-state and its concomitant inland trade contacts provided instruments competent to organize the disorder that went under the name of 'trade' with Europeans. In turn, the city-states grew in size much faster while carrying on the trade in slaves than they would otherwise have done. By the end of the eighteenth century, Bonny had 3,000 residents on its tiny island site, with many more on plantations and trading colonies (some of which were larger than Bonny itself). Kalabari and the Efik towns were in much the same position. As in earlier days, the population build-up came from the hinterland; however, most of the movement was now involuntary, the new members of the society being some of the captives secured in slave raiding and slave trading.

This large population influx, profoundly modified the character of social relations within the city-states. Not surprisingly, the Ijo and Efik of the city-states tried to assimilate the new influx of residents within the context of prevailing social institutions. Since the House was the basic family unit, purchased captives were introduced as members of particular Houses. This radically transformed the old descent-based Houses, especially in the delta. The House, as it developed in the eighteenth and nineteenth centuries, was as much a commercial firm as an extended family. It owned assets such as trading canoes; it controlled the labour and property of its members; it conducted credit operations and it organized agricultural plantations. The man power that became available as part of the slaving operations also contributed to the rise of 'Canoe Houses' in Bonny and Kalabari during the latter part of the eighteenth century. It became possible to start new Houses, whose leaders were qualified in terms of trade skills, fighting ability and wealth – the two latter qualifications stemming from the number of dependants acquired by purchase. Anyone able and willing to equip a war-canoe was permitted to establish a new House, and hence the term 'Canoe House'. Such an individual remained politically subordinate to, though commercially independent of, his House of origin. The head of a Canoe House had powers of taxation which built up the revenues of his new House, and permitted him to gather a larger number of retainers as he pursued the trade in slaves.

Man power made possible the more rapid development of the House as a trading institution, and it simultaneously made it imperative that the House should serve as a mechanism of social control. The original populations of the city-states were outnumbered and constituted an élite of freemen. The House became hierarchical in structure with the original descent groups controlling the power. Those at the apex were very few in number, and there were many among the freeborn who were not eligible for high office. Nevertheless, the latter were socially superior to the vast majority of those who entered the society as purchased slaves or as 'strangers'. A few slaves, or the children of such, achieved great distinction within the city-states, especially during the late eighteenth century and subsequently. But, apart from the occasional 'success story', the non-freeborn remained the most dis-privileged section of the commonalty, some being very close to the status of chattel slaves. Their labour went into accumulating profits for the House, and it took a generation or two before one who was purchased as a slave acquired rights equivalent to those of earlier inhabitants. Exploitation and oppression had come upon the scene in a manner and with an intensity previously inconceivable in what were communal and egalitarian societies. Therefore, forms of social control had to be devised to keep the structure viable.

The task of a House head and the élite freemen was to make the House a new focus of loyalty for the heterogeneous elements which it incorporated. This could be achieved because, firstly, there were no major cultural barriers between the ruling stratum and the immigrants; secondly, the rulers did not elect to establish any rigid racial or caste differences; and, thirdly, the type of exploitation practised was not impersonal. Bonds of solidarity were forged from top to bottom within the society. By according the maximum social mobility to a few of those who were originally slaves, the Houses were providing achievement models which presumably helped to strengthen the identification between the House and those of its members in the more servile categories. Besides, rivalry between Houses was fierce and often violent, so that, for the incoming captive, defence of his House may well have been a means of self-defence and survival.

There were certain predispositions within the communal Ijo and Efik societies which allowed for the rapid integration of a dispossessed majority. They shared the general African world-view that an individual's family was his immediate badge of identification. Therefore, purchased slaves were immediately the 'sons' or 'daughters' of the buyer, who was usually a House head. Many of the slaves who were fortunate not to be exported were very young. This facilitated their being allocated to 'mothers' and their being adopted by many 'sisters', 'brothers', etc. At Kalabari, the movement into a new family was accompanied by a poignant ceremony in which the head of the young slave child was shaved by the new mother. Severe penalties were attached to making allusion to the fictional nature of these relations. Where children grew up domiciled with their (House) mothers, they increased House membership. Females were encouraged to marry outside the House at Nembe and apparently among the Efik also. In the eastern delta, the House heads sponsored the *egwa* marriage form which required a small dowry and permitted their poor male servants to obtain wives who were looked after by their natal family while husbands were away on House business. In fact, many marriages were permitted within the House, which would have been impossible in regular exogamous family or clan. This sort of flexibility lends credence to the suggestion that the early fishing communities were never as firmly and exclusively tied to the descent principle as some of the people inland.[1] The migrations which established the coastal fishing villages were more disruptive than the spread of the Ibo. As such, the delta settlements and those on the Cross river valued initiative highly;

[1] Robin Horton, 'From fishing village to city-state: a social history of New Calabar', in Mary Douglas and Phyllis Kaberry, eds., *Man in Africa* (London, 1969).

and, prior to trade with Europeans, they were already adopting open criteria for citizenship, along lines of residential and cultural identification.

Secret societies were also among the major social institutions which were diverted to facilitate the objective of trade with Europeans as well as to strengthen the position of the élite in an increasingly differentiated context. This has been discerned in the case of the *ekine* or *sekiapu* masked dancing societies found throughout the delta. Their principal purpose was the performance of masquerades representing the water-spirits and they were open to anyone capable of doing the dances. *Ekine* became a major acculturative agency, because in order to move from the lower to the higher of its two grades members had to become steeped in the language, history, ritual and world-view of the particular Ijo groups concerned. There was great social pressure on individuals to join *ekine*. As far as the rich were concerned, it bestowed the kind of prestige that was not gained by the mere possession of wealth; while those strangers who entered on the lowest rungs of the social ladder had even greater incentive to grasp an opportunity for individual progress. Successful accomplishment of the masquerades was a public seal of full acceptance; and the stranger or purchased slave who advanced in this respect was likely to find political openings. The lower grade of *ekine* comprised young people, while the senior grade was further subdivided into a decision-making minority and their executives. The most accomplished (and usually semi-retired) dancers who governed *ekine* also had certain judicial functions within the state. Unlike the Houses, *ekine* functioned to integrate the society as a whole at the cultural level.

Ekine operated alongside a more violent association, the *peri ogbo*, which comprised notable warriors. This too offered a means of upward mobility for the outsider willing to be totally committed to his new situation; and it went a step farther by disciplining those who were slow to identify. Among the Kalabari Ijo, coercion was carried out by the *koronogbo*, which is described as an inner group of *peri ogbo*. Both *ekine* and *koronogbo* were promoted much more vigorously in the city-state of Kalabari than in the surrounding fishing villages which shared the same cultural sub-stratum. It is clear that the conditions of trading in slaves and accumulating some for domestic use provided the rationale for the new developments. The Ijo language continued to be used in Kalabari, in spite of the large influx of non-Ijo. Bonny had no *ekine*, or at least only a very weak dancing society; and Bonny's population turned increasingly to the Ibo language, both among rulers and ruled. What the two had in common was the achievement of cultural homogeneity to counterbalance the stratified and plural nature of the fast-growing settlements in the era of slaving and foreign trade. If the embryonic ruling class had been minded to distinguish sharply between themselves and the majority, they would probably have been too weak to utilize effectively that alternative technique of social control. As it was, when the secret society acquired a political role, it came close to representing the potential and overt power of a ruling class, while clinging to the concept of cultural unity within the city-state. This development also took place among the Efik.

The best known of the secret societies of lower Guinea and one of the best known on the African continent is the *ekpe* society of the Efik. Like *ekine*, it existed prior to any external contacts made by the local African community concerned, and it may have derived from the Ekoi. The latter were forest-dwellers, and *ekpe* was dedicated to a forest spirit, rather than a deity connected with water, which was the primary orientation of the Efik. *Ekpe* could not therefore have been important from the date of the founding of Creek Town late in the sixteenth century. Indeed, it was probably not until the second quarter of the eighteenth century that an earlier secret society was transformed and given the name '*ekpe*'. Major innovations were carried out under Esien Ekpe Oku, grandson of one of the founders of Creek Town. He became Eyamba I, the first president of *ekpe*. The reconstituted *ekpe* proved itself a useful commercial tool in Efik dealings both with Africans in the hinterland and with Europeans. One of its principal functions was to regulate credit and to provide sanctions for the recovery of debts. This was very effectively carried out. The Cross river and its hinterland were partially integrated into the enlarged sphere of European capitalism, and an institution like *ekpe* was ideal for servicing the African sector to permit the accumulation of capital in Old Calabar, in Europe and to some extent in the Americas.

Viewed from another perspective, foreign trade helped build up *ekpe*, and its tremendous political power was used to hold together the village segments. The Houses or Wards among the Efik had complete authority over their own people in local matters, but *ekpe* made laws for the community as a whole and settled disputes between Houses. In this respect, the Efik were better organized than the Kalabari Ijo, where inter-House rivalry was very pronounced. However, it seems as though the Efik allowed their purchased slaves less mobility than was possible in the delta. The Canoe House did not emerge on the Cross river, and the founding Efik lineages maintained a near monopoly on political power vis-à-vis the lower strata of former slaves. An institution such as *ekpe* must have been particularly valuable to the Efik rulers, since secret societies are formidable instruments of social control. They invariably combine a hierarchy, discipline, commitment and fear; and *ekpe* was an extreme case. It had nine grades, entry to each one requiring a fee and the pre-condition that the applicant had reached the grade immediately below. But purchased slaves seldom ever rose from the bottom rungs, and the top grade comprised exclusively the immediate descendants of Efik founders.

A sharper delineation of political authority within the city-states was another major socio-political transformation which was partially related to the great involvement with Europeans. The direction of change was away from the loose and light authority of village councils and village heads towards the emergence of monarchies or republican regimes. The dynasty of Perekule in Bonny and that of Amakiri in Kalabari were both firmly in the saddle by the latter part of the eighteenth century; while among the Efik the *ekpe* society amassed the decisive political power. The several Efik towns were considered small republics, each with its own chief and council, united only by the *ekpe* confraternity. Even within a limited area such as the eastern Niger delta, careful scrutiny has revealed differences in each type of authority that grew up in the respective city-states. These variations are attributable to small differences in the social institutions of groups of Ijo and also to the degree of influence of other African neighbours. At Bonny in particular the creation of a monarchy was under way at an early date, with a marked Ibo influence. The strong Ibo intrusion into Ijo ruling families of Bonny and Kalabari was noted by European visitors in the eighteenth century; and the Ibibio must also be taken into account. In the eastern delta, Andoni remained closest to the Ibibio in language and culture; and very important totems and religious symbols were borrowed by Bonny from Andoni as late as the eighteenth century. At one level, therefore, there is no doubt that the city-state formations encountered at the end of the eighteenth century were the end-products of an indigenous process which pre-dated significant foreign involvement and which persisted in the era of foreign trade. Yet, forces unleashed by trade with Europeans affected a range of variables such as the rate of political centralization, the location where polities survived, the mechanics by which given institutions attained political ascendancy, and the actual life-style of the ruling class.

The House institution allowed power to be concentrated in the hands of the few. The increasing importance of foreign trade meant the increasing importance of the House head, who bargained with Europeans on behalf of his House, who decided which House members could trade, and who benefited financially when he made that decision. With the new wealth, the House head could purchase females, who became his wives or were distributed as patronage. It followed that the House heads grew collectively more powerful relative to the rest of the population in the city-states. In an early period, Ijo villages were administered by popular assemblies in which youths as well as elders participated. A vital change took place at Kalabari in that the assembly ceased to be open to all adult males, and was restricted instead to House heads. At the same time, it was subdivided not according to age, but in two divisions of 'big chiefs' and 'small chiefs', the former being personages with control over a number of Houses.

Bonny and Kalabari were the first of the city-states to produce strong monarchies. Before any foreign influences were operative, the village chairmanship was located within the senior lineage. This was different from, and probably a development away from, the situation in the western delta where the chairman was merely the oldest man in the village. From Nembe to Bonny, the chairman was known as the *amanyanabo* or 'owner of the town'. The potential of the office was further and more speedily manifested when the *amanyanabo* became representative of all the Houses in their dealings with Europeans. The latter called him 'king', and in due course the advantages accruing from being the go-between enabled him to amass wealth and power over the citizenry. The *amanyanabo* was the principal recipient of 'comey', or customs dues, from European traders and the principal recipient of 'gifts' of different sorts. At the same time, he had a hold over other House heads in so far as he introduced them to the European traders. This meant that one House head was eclipsing the others, and they were persuaded to accept this because of the undivided command needed in wars and trade rivalry with other city-states. Religious beliefs current among the Ijo were put to the service of centralization more than ever before. Traditions link the definition of political authority with developments in the worship of the supreme deity in the respective towns. In addition, each of the major lineages had its own religious cult. For example, the Perekule dynasty in Bonny had its own cult of the Iguana (which was borrowed from Andoni). Not surprisingly, this became the dominant ancestral cult in Bonny, thereby reinforcing the authority of the king.

In the era of foreign trade and slaving, the House heads supervised a far larger number of subjects and the movement of a greater volume of material goods. Competition ensued to determine who among the House heads would benefit most from these expanded opportunities. Thus the emergence of centres of authority was intimately bound up with struggles between the Houses that comprised the respective city-states.

On the Cross river, this took a dramatic turn, because the competition was accompanied by settlement changes. Efiom Ekpo and Ema were the two lineages that founded Creek Town. A dispute led to the departure of two of the four descent groups which comprised the Ema lineage. They settled at Obutong, which was later called Old Town. Afterwards, there was another split from Creek Town to Atakpa, which has been called New Town and Duke Town at different times. In spite of some uncertainties about dating, the move to New Town was probably effected in the first half of the seventeenth century. Trade with Europeans may already have been assuming significance, because the site chosen makes most sense in relation to an external trade orientation.

Once occupied, Old Town became the Efik town closest to the sea. It could cut Creek Town off from any overseas ships, while it still maintained access to the Cross river via creeks. The second movement away from Creek Town by-passed Old Town, and chose a spot which commanded the portion of the river which European ships selected for anchorage. Oral histories suggest that the breaking of a taboo concerning twins forced the departure of twin brothers who were products of the marriage between a woman of the Efiom Ekpo line and an Efut man. But it could hardly be a coincidence that on both occasions the relocation put the respective communities in a better position to conduct export trade. Besides, the founding of New Town was apparently more in the nature of a Creek Town colonization (by the Efiom Ekpo lineage) rather than an antagonistic break, as was the case of Old Town. New Town subsequently attracted many families from Creek Town and outstripped the latter in growth; but, in terms of inter-town rivalry, Creek Town and New Town were allied against Old Town. Another House was established at Henshaw Town, about a mile south of New Town. But Henshaw Town derived from the same Efiom Ekpo lineage, and it was no threat to New Town in commercial terms because the best anchorage remained on the frontage of New Town.[1]

At the time of the relocations and for many years subsequently, changes also took place in the locus of institutional power. The most outstanding personage at the founding of Creek Town was the chief priest (*oku ndem*). He was guardian of the water-god that was paramount when fishing was the major occupation. Since the office was handed down within a particular family, it is conceivable that had the Efik continued along their own uninterrupted path it might have provided a royal dynasty. As it was, the chief priest was still referred to by Europeans as 'king of Old Calabar' right into the nineteenth century; but his cult was far less important because of the switch to export trade. The priest himself was barred from trading and the office lost its political dynamism. Meanwhile, the village headship was enhanced. The Efik counterpart of the *amanyanabo* of the Ijo was the *obong*. The office of *obong* came to be monopolized by the Houses within the principal Efik trading centre, namely New Town. The formerly dominant branch of the Efiom Ekpo lineage accepted a subordinate role at Henshaw Town and Creek Town, while the Houses at Old Town were badly outdistanced. The fact that all the Efik Houses and towns retained a certain unity of purpose is largely attributable to *ekpe* and a few other integrative mechanisms. *Ekpe* as an association was far more important than any single individual, but its top positions were also the objects of competition. The Houses that were most attuned to trade captured the most important political posts, because these were the Houses that built up the greatest material resources and the largest population by retaining slaves for domestic use.

Trade with Europeans also left a deep mark on the character of the kingships of the city-states. Rulers and the upper class in general displayed a pattern of consumption which accorded the highest priority to European goods, regardless of quality or utility. European manufactures were part of their regalia; trade goods were buried underground to be stored for prestige; European houses were built for ostentation; and the dress to which city-state rulers were attached was invariably that cast off by Europeans. The king of Bonny in 1699 was described as wearing an old-fashioned scarlet coat, laced with gold and silver, very rusty, and a fine hat on his head. When the records provided a description of the Efik ruler in 1762, it was virtually identical with that given

[1] R. K. Udo, 'The growth and decline of Calabar', *The Nigerian Geographical Journal*, December 1967, 10, 2; A. J. H. Latham, *Old Calabar 1600–1891* (Oxford, 1973), chapter 1.

for the Bonny king. All the rulers in the Bight of Biafra had a partiality for gold-laced caps and stained European finery. Besides, the very names of the monarchs and other dignitaries were rendered as European – being either translations or more usually approximations to Ijo and Efik names. Often the choice was mundane to the point of 'Tom' 'Dick', and 'Harry'; and it was always incongruous, being no different from the slave names imposed on those Africans that the worthy House heads were helping to dispatch to the Americas. Elsewhere in Guinea, rulers who actively participated in the slave trade maintained their own life-styles and a measure of dignity. They were from states that had deeper roots. The difference between the city-states and the older Guinea coast polities is that the city-states were going through their formative years contemporaneously with the export trade. The whole ambience of their society was therefore far more conditioned by this overwhelming experience than was the case in Benin, Dahomey or even any of the smaller kingdoms which were already in existence in upper Guinea when the Portuguese arrived in the fifteenth century.

The redirecting of the coastal society of eastern Nigeria began in the latter part of the seventeenth century, intensified towards the middle of the eighteenth century, and produced its major results within a few decades thereafter. This period of nearly 150 years coincides with the heavy export of captives; and, at the end of the eighteenth century, the Bight of Biafra was a slaving zone second to none in Guinea. A considerable amount of violence erupted within the city-state environment, caused indirectly by the slave trade and having its more immediate rationale in the struggle for political power within and among the city-states. In the delta, Kalabari was able to assert itself over Okrika, while Bonny eclipsed first Andoni and later Kalabari. There was also fighting between the towns of 'Old Calabar', resulting in the supremacy of New Town after the latter received direct European support. Internal developments accompanied and reflected these inter-state struggles. Socio-political changes at Bonny and Kalabari centred around the persons of Perekule and Amakiri, respectively. Both introduced major innovations by allowing persons of slave origin to advance socially and by permitting the formation of Canoe Houses. They also had the support of the priests, who played an important integrative political rôle. Meanwhile, on the Cross river, the movement of important positions from one lineage to another was probably the most decisive change brought about by the local hostilities.

The city-states have often been extolled for the ingenuity of their social mechanisms. Yet, they illustrate most clearly the paradox whereby the creativity that went into survival and adaptation in the epoch of the slave trade was antithetical to the best interests of the community involved and of Africa as a whole. There is no lack of evidence of the personal qualities of many of the individual African traders of the city-states. At Bonny in 1700, 'Captain Pepple' was described as a sharp blade and a mighty talking Black who drove hard bargains. A century later, 'John Africa' of Bonny was capable of maintaining with exactitude open running accounts with fourteen or fifteen European ships at the same time, although he could neither read nor write. There must have been many a sharp blade among the Efik traders also, because they succeeded in extracting high customs dues from European ships, and they also took pains to become literate in the trading *lingua franca* of 'Pidgin English'. These talents, along with institutions such as the Houses and *ekpe*, went into securing Africans from near and far to fill the holds of European slave vessels.

Meanwhile, the history of the interior was also characterized by the same capture of African institutions and initiative, to greater or lesser extent; and the consequences beyond the littoral were even more negative, since the hinterland was the principal arena for slave recruitment. In this context, the rise of Arochuku is the outstanding phenomenon. With the exception of precise dating, most of the facts concerning the Arochuku oracle and the Aro traders have been reasonably well established. The cave of the Arochuku oracle was located in a frontier zone of Ibo expansion to the south-east, and it was taken over from the Ibibio, many of whom continued to reside in the area. The oracle was one to which pilgrimages were made from considerable distances, and the Aro themselves were traders who moved widely in Iboland. The Ibo of Aro town were established before the effects of European trade were felt, but to some extent the oracle was co-opted for use by slave traders. Cause and effect were intertwined. On the one hand, the Aro traders capitalized on their oracle to get captives; and, on the other hand, Arochuku grew more widely feared and respected than ever before, emerging as a powerful religious, judicial and political force. By the nineteenth century, Aro Town had grown from nine wards to nineteen, including some of Akpa and Efik derivation. Throughout eastern Nigeria, Aro citizens spread into dozens of colonies. They retained links with the wards in Aro Town and their persons were considered inviolable because of the oracle. Each ward had its sphere of influence in a co-ordinated trade network, which was built in part around the pre-existing village group markets, but which also had its own unique features. For instance, a major trade fair was made to rotate between Bende and Uzuakoli in the south, and it was co-ordinated with a similar fair rotating between Uburu and Okposi in the north. These fairs and the Aro colonies were connected by well-trodden trade paths.[1]

One of the main routes ran through central Iboland to Awka in the north-west. Awka was itself a district noted for markets and trading expertise. From there, traders travelled to Nike in the north-east, where they joined others who came directly from Arochuku. The southern part of the country was covered by trade paths that branched off the main Arochuku/Awka route. Aro Ndizuogu turned out to be the most important colony, having the advantage of being situated in the middle of Iboland, with easy access to the coastal plains, the uplands to the west and north, and the Cross river basin to the east. Most of the Aro settlements have been assigned seventeenth-century dates, and Aro Ndizuogu was one of the earlier ones. At the same period, Aro Town strengthened its ties with the coast. Kalabari traditions attribute the introduction of Arochuku to Owerri Daba, the *amanyanabo* who founded the 'Monmouth' House that was known to Europeans at the end of the seventeenth century. Bonny people claim that their ruler, Asimini, got the secrets of the European trade from Owerri Daba. The likelihood is that the Aro traders, who stuck to the inland cross-country routes, recognized the necessity for more co-ordination with the Ijo and Efik who conducted the canoe trade.

Arochuku was popular with litigants from all over eastern Nigeria, and the oracle 'ate' those who were judged guilty by Arochuku functioning as a tribunal. This meant that they entered the cave of Arochuku and disappeared, only to reappear in the slave marts of the city-states. Other oracles were used for the same purpose. The Agballa oracle at Awka had a wide audience among the northern Ibo, since its keepers were the famous Awka blacksmiths. Then there was Igweke Ala at Umunoha in Owerri district, Onyili-ora near Nri, Ogba at Ogbanika in Onitsha district, and a witch-finding cult at Usere which catered for Ijo, Sobo and Isoko. Emphasis must be placed on those who manipulated oracles, rather than on the oracles themselves. Only Aro colonists could conduct clients and ritual offenders to Arochuku and bring back pronouncements and medicines to local people. The 'Aro abroad' (as they called themselves) kept in close touch with the Aro

[1] Ukwu I. Ukwu, 'The development of trade and marketing in Iboland', *Journal of the Historical Society of Nigeria*, June 1967, 3, 4.

at home, and funnelled victims to the cave. Even so, only an infinitesimal part of the Bight of Biafra exports could have passed through Arochuku's cave. It was the widespread Aro community which carried on slave trading, by exploiting the authority of the oracle but not necessarily carrying each captive or purchase to Aro Town. The cosmopolitan origins of the Aro helped in this respect, because while the Ibo Aro moved north, the Akpa penetrated eastwards and the Ibibio operated within their own homelands to the south. The Mkpokk and Ikot Akpa-Atakk dominated Ibibio country west of the Kwa Ibo stream, and their raids on surrounding villages dove-tailed with Aro activity. Aro traders organized armed cohorts from among the Abam, Abiriba and Ada groups of Ibo north of Aro Town. These allies protected the oracle from attack, while they went out to seize debtors and raid villages which did not bow before the Aro. They were also deployed in inter-village conflicts to secure captives, and many areas of Iboland recalled wars promoted by the Aro and other slave dealers. An African purchased at a city-state for local use or export was of course always in the first instance subjected to violent deprivation of freedom. The greater percentage of those who reached the coast has passed from hand to hand as 'purchases', but were initially taken in slave wars or raids. Small children were frequently included among the victims, as in the case of Olaudah Equiano.

Efik Houses at 'Old Calabar' received captives through several intermediaries. On the upper Cross river, the Akunakuna (Ekoi) were very responsive to the requests of the Efik, and *ekpe* was promoted in that area to integrate it with the trading patterns of the Atlantic coast. Possibly, the chain reached right into the Jukun of Kwararafa kingdom, which was at its strongest in the seventeenth century and for some time afterwards (see chapter 2, pp. 134–6). Warfare north of the Benue would have been a source of captives. The Kwararafa were on the southern fringe of the more ancient though far less prolific slave trade which led northwards across the Sahara, so that for them the sale of human beings antedated the arrival of Europeans on the Guinea coast. In 1824, when Sultan Bello of Sokoto mentioned Jukun and Igala to a European traveller, he said that near to these two were the anchorages for European ships.[1] Igala was certainly part of the Niger trade complex, and Igala subjects mixed together with Ibo from Onitsha in a

[1] *Narrative of travels and discoveries in northern and central Africa by Denham, Clapperton and Oudney* (London, 1826), vol. II, see map following p. 330; Igala (Atagara) is designated as the place where Christians come to trade.

large market close to their mutual boundary. The fact that Jukun was linked to the sea or to a large river in Bello's mind might suggest that, like Igala, Jukun sent captives to the coast and received European goods and some coastal products in return.

Nevertheless, the deep hinterland (comprising Igala, Jukun and beyond) was a marginal source of supply for the European slave trade across the Atlantic. The same can be said for the coast itself. There was some slaving within the Niger delta, but more often than not a reference to slaves as being (say) 'Brass country negroes' meant simply that they were acquired through intermediaries in the western delta. It must have been Iboland and to a lesser extent Ibibio country and the Cameroun highlands which supplied the vast majority of the many thousands per annum that were consistently shipped from the Bight of Biafra. This is suggested by evidence such as the random sample of recaptives in the Sierra Leone colony in the early nineteenth century and by the coverage of the Aro network.[1] Close scrutiny reveals that the impact varied from place to place within this major supply zone. Some localities maintained large populations in spite of the experience of slaving, while others suffered visibly in numerical terms.

One of the most striking features of the population distribution in the eastern part of Nigeria is a high-density belt which runs north-west to south-east from Onitsha through Owerri, Ikot Ekpene and Uyo to just north of the mangrove swamps. It comprises both Ibo and Ibibio. Soil characteristics and crop preferences do not explain why the above belt of country is densely settled and the surrounding areas sparsely settled. Nor do the physical factors explain a low-density break between the Ibo and Ibibio sectors of this high-density zone. Significantly, this was the slave route from Aro Town to Bonny via the Aro trade fairs at Bende and Uzuakoli. It was also a frontier zone between the Ibo and Ibibio, who were both expanding. There was potential for conflict as well as greater exposure to the sort of predatory activity surrounding slave recruitment. The very sparse population of the Cross river basin also requires some historical explanation, given the very favourable environmental setting. This forest area was never heavily peopled, so slaving reduced an already small population to the point where the scattered groups that survived were incapable of keeping tse-tse and other pests in check. In turn, this led to further population reduction. Slaving also induced changes in settlement location. Villages had to be

[1] Philip Curtin and Jan Vansina, 'Sources of the nineteenth century Atlantic slave trade', *Journal of African History*, 1964, 5, 2.

sited because of considerations of defence rather than economic rationality. There is still a marked tendency for farmers in the region to live on ridges away from the rivers and valleys which were used as means of penetration by slave traders.[1]

Evidence of population loss and physical relocation is not matched by equally clear data about social changes in the particular communities most involved. Given the nature of slaving, one can only posit some general lines of social distortion. A large proportion of eastern Nigerian captives were extracted from their society by so-called legal and religious devices. Under such circumstances, one could expect that disputes were fomented to trap the convicted and that there took place a fundamental revision of the customary law so as to recruit more slaves. Field research in Onitsha province in the present century revealed that 'the whole of the criminal judicial system was built up on the possibility of being able to sell the accused'.[2] To whom were they to be sold and when was the system built up in that form? The answers to these questions indicate the great and sordid changes which took place during the slave trade epoch and probably most of all during the eighteenth century.

There is a tendency to describe twentieth-century eastern Nigerian societies as 'traditional', to the extent that they display features not attributable to contact with Europeans in the colonial period. Thus, 'slaves', 'cult slaves' and other exploited categories are treated ahistorically, as though they must always have existed in pre-colonial Ibo society. On the coast, it is readily seen that the expansion of servitude was based on the opportunity presented by participation in slaving for European ships and probably on the necessity to maintain food supplies in conditions that were otherwise chaotic; and by the end of the eighteenth century, purchased slaves were working on the large agricultural plantations set up by the Houses. Among many of the delta peoples like the Nembe Brass and the Itsekiri, agriculture was low-prestige work entirely handled by a servant class recruited from outside the ethnic group in question. Some of the same tendencies were manifested in the up-country regions. For instance, the Aro required servants both for load-carrying and for agricultural work. An internal slave trade went on during the nineteenth century after exports had ceased. There had to be substantial changes in the communal society before it could accommodate such a number of vendible persons.

[1] R. K. Udo, 'Patterns of population distribution and settlement in eastern Nigeria', *The Nigerian Geographical Journal*, December 1963, 6, 2.

[2] Nigerian National Archives, Intelligence Report 29001, Onitsha.

Some theoretical constructs are also necessary to gain insight into the economic consequences of protracted large-scale slaving as in eastern Nigeria. Economic development implies the maximization of local natural and labour resources, the enhancement of technology and skills, and the growth of multifaceted and self-supporting economies by the integration of different districts into a composite whole.[1] This process was already well advanced in the sixteenth century among the peoples east of the Niger, and it was the very existence of the canoe trade that permitted European ships to have their wants easily met. Thereafter, it may superficially appear that the same canoe trade was being plied on the main rivers and that regional cross-country trade persisted and even expanded through Aro activities. However, mutual African interchange was no longer the leading commercial force, having been superseded by a prototype of the import/export sector of the dependent colonial economy.

The Guinea coast imported a significant proportion of shoddy goods from Europe in the seventeenth and eighteenth centuries, and the Bight of Biafra was no exception. Even when utilitarian, these imports served only to replace African manufactures or to block the emergence of local industry and technique. The Ibo at one time made iron to send to the coast, but in the slave trade era the city-state communities looked outwards for their supplies. At best, African craftsmen contented themselves with working the imported iron, which meant the demise of iron extraction. Since the Cameroun was a main source of this basic mineral, the export trade closed off the possibility of more valuable links between the Efik and the hinterland beyond the Cross river, which was the most logical direction in which economic boundaries could have been extended. Agricultural productivity, too, was necessarily adversely affected, although in specific localities the trade in slaves permitted or even protected agricultural endeavour. For one thing, the Aro professionals encouraged some of their neighbours to grow yams in peace; and in addition the captive Africans on the Atlantic passage were fed mainly on yams, in the case of those picked up from the shores of eastern Nigeria. In effect, it was always the import/export enclave that was registering growth – to the benefit of the international capitalist economy and to the detriment of indigenous development. The consequences of what took place in the seventeenth and eighteenth centuries are incorporated in the present political

[1] Walter Rodney, *How Europe underdeveloped Africa* (London and Dar es Salaam, 1972). For an elaboration of this argument, see chapter 1 and chapter 4, section 1.

economy of underdevelopment and dependency. This is generally true on the Guinea coast, and very markedly so in this eastern portion of Nigeria, where the city-states survived only in so far as they could serve as entrepôts of export trade in palm products. Otherwise, they plunged into obscurity, having no viable independent economic links with their own hinterland.

THE UPPER GUINEA COAST

Processes of social differentiation revealed themselves with considerable clarity on the upper Guinea coast during the seventeenth and eighteenth centuries, going hand in hand with the process of state formation. One type of society which persisted throughout this period was that which was organized communally without a coercive state superstructure. Examples were to be found among the Diola, Balante and Tenda. At the other extreme, there were conquest states, incorporating quasi-feudal social and labour relations. Malinke, Susu and Serer states were prominent in this respect. A third category was the most common, comprising polities that were both small and stratified. They proliferated among the Gola, Kissi, Bullom, Temne, Loko, Nalu, Baga, Limba and Kokoli (all of the Mel language cluster), among the Kwa-speaking De, Bassa, Belle and Kru, and also among the remaining members of the West Atlantic linguistic group to the north: namely the Bijago, Pepel, Biafada, Bainuk and Kassanga. No doubt, developments internal to each of these types of society led to the gradual emergence of individuals with greater control over their fellows, over the allocation and usufruct of land, and over the distribution of seeds, tools, labour and wives. However, such changes were brought about more decisively through the interplay of the many ethnic groups, social formations and cultures within a framework of state building and foreign trade.

A considerable stretch of territory from the Gambia to Cape Palmas could be regarded as the upper Guinea coast. It was an area of great diversity and flux, and present knowledge with respect to its constituent parts is very uneven. Nevertheless, the concept of a culture zone is still viable, given the role played by the Mande. Irrespective of their own significant linguistic sub-divisions, the Mande invariably forged powerful ties between the savanna hinterland and the forest zone. The Malinke (northern Mande) played the leading role on the Gambia; the Dan and Gouro (eastern Mande) were the intrusive elements in the hinterland

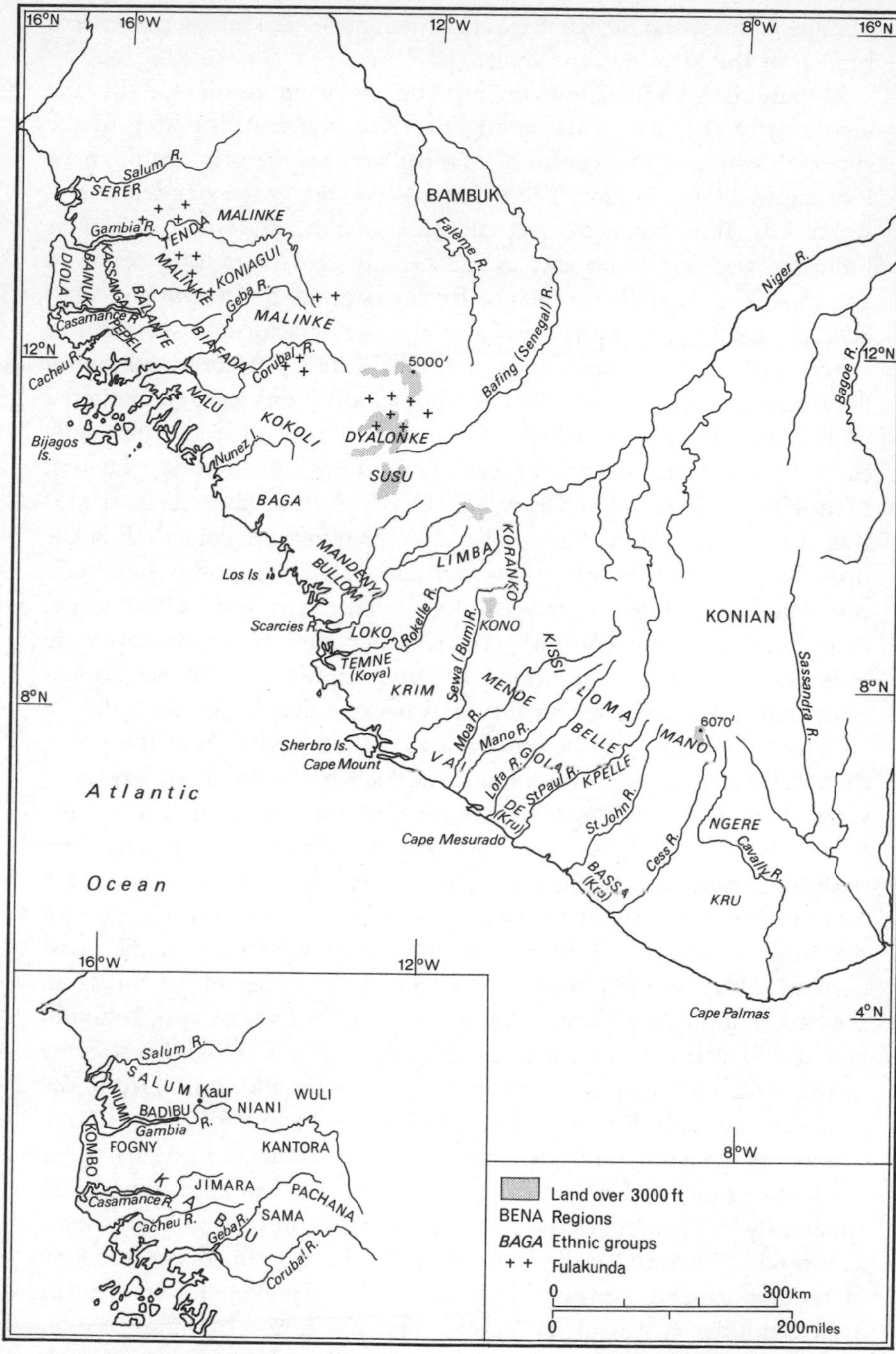

8 The upper Guinea coast, *c.* 1600. Inset map: Gambia – the Mande states

of Cape Palmas; and the Kpelle and Loma represented the south-western branch of the Mande in the centre.

Monarchical and aristocratic institutions were reinforced by the intrusion of the Mani élite among the Kru and Sapi, or Mel, in the sixteenth century. The centre of Mani power on the coast came to be located near Cape Mount. Their claims to sovereignty extended north-westwards along the coast to the Los islands, and indirectly their influence was felt as far east as the Grand Cess river, as a result of accompanying Kru displacements. By the beginning of the seventeenth century, the Mani 'empire' was already merely a loose association of states, with a few strong kings at Cape Mount, Sherbro, the Sierra Leone peninsula and Port Loko. Further subdivisions were encountered within the jurisdictions of the important rulers, and these gradually came to constitute dozens of petty kingdoms. Bai Farma, the first Mani king of Port Loko, was called 'emperor'; and his successors held this title because they were rather like 'paramount chiefs'. But the underlings made themselves big men, and took the power into their own hands. Similarly, there was a king of the northern Bullom at the beginning of the seventeenth century, but later on his vassals were independent. Yet the Mani political structure did not entirely disintegrate, and the entities which survived became deeply entrenched.

Before the generation of actual invaders had passed from the scene, the integration of the Mani among the Sapi had reached an advanced stage. Ultimately, only one group on the upper Scarcies retained the name Mani (or Mandenyi), but in composition it was basically Sapi with Mani and perhaps Susu intermingling. The true élite among the Mani traced their origins to the Kamara clan of the Konyan region of the western Sudan, but in practice the Mani who reached the coast derived not from the distant hinterland of the upper Niger but from the basins of the rivers which flow to the coast between Cape Mesurado and the Sherbro. Some Mani came along the sea coast. These were mainly Vai and Quoja (Koya), while an overland route from the south-east brought Kpelle and Loma (Gbande included).

Some of the ethnic tensions caused by the invasions did not disappear for a long time, and new conflicts emerged. For instance, the Limba apparently lost ground to the Loko, the latter representing Loma interaction with the local Temne. However, the Limba retook the initiative in the seventeenth century. Hostilities also developed between the Loko and the Koya-ruled Temne. The south-eastern hinterland of Sierra Leone and most of the interior of modern Liberia continued to be politically disturbed right into the nineteenth century. Unsettled conditions encouraged the existence of war captains and of loose confederacies of small chiefdoms, serving partly as a defence against the pressure exerted from the Mande heartlands. Nevertheless, there was growing cultural homogeneity, with the Mande as the leading force. Both the Mel and the Kwa-speaking groups were heavily influenced by the Mani, and among the De and the Gola there was a tendency to claim to be Vai. The Mende and Loko advanced as ethnicities through penetration of the Gola, Kissi, Bullom, Krim and Temne. Occasionally, multiple influences were discernible, as in the case of the Belle who are Kru-speaking but who also display Gola and Mande traits. Cultural fusion helped to reformulate the contradictions between natives and aliens into one between contending strata inside the same society, with ethnic and family origins retaining pride of place in determining positions within the socio-political hierarchy.

Modern field studies reveal Mande traits within the ruling class and a cultural cleavage between rulers and the masses in polities such as those of the Mende. As far as the coastal Mani/Sapi societies were concerned, European observers noted the existence of hierarchical layers in the early seventeenth century. The Vai, Koya and Kwia were the cream of the aristocracy in Cape Mount, Sherbro and Sierra Leone. They claimed to be authentic Mani, although they were really dependants of the original Kamara. The Vai and the Vai-speaking Koya continued to rule in an unbroken line in the Gallinas and Cape Mount. The Kwia were of Kru origins, and they appear to be the same as the Kwiate – a small caste providing poets, historians, heralds, politicians and diplomats. Like the Vai and Koya, they were fond of displaying their pedigree, and stressed their connections with Filamanka, an early Kru and Mani hero. Next on the social ladder were the 'Aperme', described as 'half-slave and half-free', because they descended on one side through conquered peoples. By the same token, the bulk of the conquered people were 'slaves' or commoners whom the hereditary ruling class regarded as being entirely at its disposal.

With their military reputation and skill at building fortifications, it is not surprising that Mani war 'medicines' and their other 'fetishes' were held in awe, but the dominance which they acquired over the indigenous inhabitants in key aspects of metaphysical belief must have been subsequently more important than their military prowess.

An institution which was very effective in the hands of the ruling strata was that of the secret society. Some secret societies were probably introduced by the Mani and their cohorts. Highly organized and powerful secret societies survive among the Loma, Kpele, Gola and Vai; and their strength wanes farther north and west. The Temne say that the *poro* society was borrowed from the Bullom, who are to the south-east on the route whence the Mani came, and its female counterpart (the *bundu*) is derived from the Sande of the Mende. Furthermore, Portuguese contemporaries stated that the *poro* was brought by the Mani. Secret societies were clearly part of the mechanism of Mani rule. They were more stratified than those already noted in eastern Nigeria. Members of the highest grades had the Mande title *solategi*, and when they donned their masks they enjoyed politico-religious power extending across the boundaries of many political units.[1]

As with the *ekpe*, it is also essential to stress that the upper Guinea secret societies were integrative in social function. They constituted forums for resolving conflicts which arose within the ruling class or at least within the ruling class of a broad ethnic community; they set values for all citizens through educational programmes; and they regulated economic activities. New situations called forth responses, and their reaction to European trade was particularly important. A great deal of the trade oriented towards the Atlantic had its origins in the deep hinterland, sometimes passing along well-established trade routes and at other times percolating slowly through the many intervening societies. In any event, this trade meant in effect a meeting of the two powerful forces of the Europeans and the Mande, respectively, often at the expense of the other residents of the upper Guinea coast. Coastal trade was itself probably one of the factors drawing the Mande closer to the sea.

The strongest representation of the Mande was in the north-west, where the Malinke, Susu and Dyalonke were all prominent in the history of the region since the extension of the Mali empire to the Atlantic in the fourteenth century. With the decline of Mali, its western outposts became independent states, dozens of which were to be found in the basins of the rivers Gambia, Casamance, Cacheu and Geba/Corubal. A few reached as far south as the upper Scarcies, where the Susu of Bena were strong enough to repulse the Mani. An outstanding feature of the states derived from Mali was their territorial stability. Niumi, Badibu, Niani and Wuli, which were on the right bank of the Gambia, maintained the same frontiers for centuries; and so too did Salum,

1 For the most recent historiographical review on this subject, see Yves Person, 'Ethnic movements and acculturation in upper Guinea since the fifteenth century', *African Historical Studies*, 1971, 4, 3.

having detached itself from the Wolof empire in the sixteenth century. The Susu kingdom of Bena and the adjacent Susu and Dyalonke also retained the same narrow boundaries until new pressures arose in the eighteenth century in the form of the Futa Jalon jihad.

The most important of the former vassals of Mali in the west was Kabu, lying between the Gambia and the upper Corubal. Kabu was itself a small imperial system. The metropolitan area comprised Jimara, Sama and Pachana; and these three in rotation filled the supreme office of *faring* (or *mansa*) *Kabu*. There were about forty other states in a dependent position, although their rulers enjoyed considerable autonomy. The *faring Kabu* had no direct jurisdiction within the many villages over which a client king exercised authority. The client kings were obliged to supply a yearly tribute and to levy troops for Kabu when called upon to do so. Most of the taxes which were collected never left their domains; and, inevitably, there were instances of refusal on the part of the client kings to give the *faring Kabu* his due in material and political terms. Besides, there were no direct bonds between the client kings other than family ties, and their alignments in wars were based on self-interest. There was no apparent expansion of territory or even intensification of control over the constituent units. Instead, it was in the relations between the ruling élite and the rest of the population that the critical dynamic was perceptible.

Wherever the ruling dynasty was of Mande origin, many aspects of cultural life reflected Mande hegemony, with the exception of Salum, where indigenous Serer and external Wolof influences were decisive. Along the Gambia river, more and more people came to designate themselves as Malinke during the seventeenth and eighteenth centuries. The Tenda and Bassari were the ones affected; while varying numbers of Koniagui, Bainuk, Kassanga, Diola, Balante, Pepel, Biafada and Kokoli were similarly acculturated in the neighbouring areas to the south. Self-identification with the Mande ruling class on the part of the masses meant that political authority was strengthened, and it gave greater homogeneity to the societies, especially since acculturation in the reverse direction was also taking place.

There was no need initially to distinguish between the Susu and Dyalonke, the latter term being merely an indication that the particular Susu lived in Futa Jalon. However, by the middle of the eighteenth century, local usage identified Dyalonke (Yalunka) and Susu separately. The minor differences of language and custom which warranted this must have arisen as the Susu interacted with the local population. The

Susu seemed to have been more affected culturally by the West Atlantic peoples than were the Malinke. Observers on the coast tended to include the Susu or at least part of the Susu in their concept of Sapi; and the small Susu/Dyalonke states were not far removed from those prevailing among most of the non-Mande on the upper Guinea coast. The Malinke maintained more of the political stature of Mali, but specific practices were undoubtedly influenced by the cultures encountered. The Malinke of Kabu gave up their own prestigious clan names in favour of local titles such as Mane, Sane and Sonko; and the matrilineal element in royal succession was also determined by coastal usage. As would be expected, intermarriage between the conquerors and the conquered was not unusual.

Certain Houses remained in undisturbed possession of power in respective Malinke states. For instance, the Wali were supreme in Wuli; Diamme, Sonko and Mane rotated in Niumi; while Sane and Mane held sway in metropolitan Kabu. The latter two were known as *nyancho* or royal princes. They traced their origins back to Tiramang Traore and Balaba – the former being a famous general of Sundiata Keita, while the latter was supposedly a Dyakanke woman. Only the sons of *nyancho* women were eligible for the title of *faring Kabu*. The remaining princes born to *nyancho* men and commoner women were *koringo*, and did not enjoy the same high status. A comparable situation existed in Salum, where the ruling *guelwar* established their title through the female line, and the offspring of the *guelwar* and non-noble women constituted a junior section of the nobility. It is commonly admitted in oral traditions that the *guelwar* are derived from Kabu Malinke, and the respective dynasties maintained friendly contacts through reciprocal visits into the nineteenth century.

The Mande nobility lived by an aristocratic militaristic ethic, which of course precluded direct participation in production. It is said that,

> When the emperor [of Kabu] ate at night, it was the property of others he ate; when he ate in the morning, it was likewise the property of others which he ate; for the nyanchos and koringos lived on the toils of their subjects. It was unbefitting that a nyancho's hand should touch a hoe or that he should take up trade; and there was no other way for him to live except by taxes and plunder. Although a nyancho did not accumulate wealth for himself, his appetite was inexhaustible, for his family and retinue were large.[1]

[1] B. K. Sidibe, 'The story of Kaabu: its extent', paper presented to the Conference on Manding Studies (London, 1972). See also Sekéné Mody Cissoko, 'Introduction à l'histoire des Mandigues de l'ouest: l'empire de Kabou (XVIe–XIX siècle)', Conference on Manding Studies (London, 1972).

There were many layers within the large sections of the population which laboured for the benefit of the nobility. Cultivators provided the bulk of the economic product, mainly in the form of rice, pennisetum and *fonio*. Some of the producers were freemen and some were not, and both of these were broad categories with many subdivisions. Craftsmen were organized in castes, the principal ones being the cloth workers, leather workers and iron workers. The Dyula were in effect a caste of a special kind, fulfilling important commercial and political functions. The *griots* or entertainers were held in relatively low social esteem, in spite of a few exceptional privileges with regard to freedom of speech before the rulers. And, finally, the lowest ranks comprised the farming population and the intrusive Fulani herdsmen. The seventeenth and eighteenth centuries were an important part of a continuum in which more surplus was extracted from the producers, and there was a marked increase in the servile and caste sectors of Mande-dominated societies as well as other parts of the upper Guinea coast.

Many of the crafts reached the coast by way of the Mande. With respect to cotton weaving, it was the Malinke loom which prevailed in the north-west, while the peoples of Sierra Leone obtained their models via the Susu and Koranko. To the east, the Gouro were also well known for their workmanship in cloth and leather. The Dyalonke were mining iron and trading it to the coast, so this was another major material technique which was diffused. The Mani were not distinguished over a wide range of industrial skills. They probably brought a new ceramic tradition inferior to that which had previously prevailed, but in iron working they were undoubtedly superior.[1] This is not surprising, since the Kpelle conducted extensive mining and forging in their home region between the St John and St Paul rivers. The degree of specialization appeared to have been greatest in the north and the west. The Serer and Malinke had separate specialists for iron and wood, while the two seemed to have been combined in most parts of Sierra Leone. The formation of classes or castes of such workmen also proceeded apace in the north, along with a more elaborate development of the minstrel class which invariably accompanied any immigrant Mande group.

It has been noted that the caste institutions of Salum and Serer were introduced by the Wolof and Tukolor.[2] South of the Gambia, the

[1] For some tentative archaeological confirmation of these points, see T. M. Newman, 'Archaeological survey of Sierra Leone', *West African Archaeological Newsletter*, 1966, no. 4 and Paul Ozanne, 'A preliminary archaeological survey of Sierra Leone', 1966, *ibid.* no. 5.

[2] Pathé Diagné, 'Pouvoir politique traditionel en Afrique Occidentale', *Présence africaine*, 1967, 71, 72.

Malinke were the principal agents for this change, and the process by which they influenced the Diola was still evident in recent times. The arts and crafts among the Diola were professions open to all rather than closed castes. Even those Malinke who practised among the Diola of Kombo were not organized into castes until recently. One can infer that the transition first took place in areas such as central Kabu, and it continued to spread outwards slowly until it touched peripheral zones like Kombo. The heightened demand for certain products on the part of the nobility provided the need for bringing together artisans. For instance, constant recourse to wars and raids on the part of the *guelwar* and *nyancho* dictated the need for concentrations of regular iron workers, rather than relying on the sporadic output of families whose main activity was on the land. The nobility also dressed differently from the commoners, and they dressed well. The *nyancho* usually wore quality material dyed orange, while special occasions required better garments. Being very keen horsemen, the Malinke ruling class also needed saddles, stirrups and other accoutrements for their horses. These provided regular work for blacksmiths and leather workers. The latter were also responsible for the manufacture of sandals.

Most of the items produced were for local consumption and for trade within a fairly circumscribed radius. A few were important enough to fulfil the function of currency: notably, cloths and iron in the form of a bar about nine inches long. The arrival of Europeans expanded the market for these principal commodities. Iron occupied a significant proportion of the cargo space of European ships bound for upper Guinea, thereby undoubtedly weakening the indigenous extractive iron industry, while stimulating the transformation of the semi-manufactured product into articles for consumption. Hand-woven cloth was in a favoured position. In the Gambia/Geba region, as in Benin, Europeans avidly sought African cloth for resale elsewhere. According to their reports, the best cottons on the Gambia were the bleached white *sake*, the blue *barrafula* and the blue and white *bontan*. The Portuguese set up an industry in the Cape Verde islands to manufacture such cloths, using labour and techniques imported from the mainland; while the English and Dutch made imitation prints in Europe. However, it was not until the colonial period that the initial pattern was completely reversed, forcing the inhabitants of the Gambia to export raw cotton fibre and import finished cloth. In the period under review, cloth exports from parts of upper Guinea constitute an index to certain economic and social developments.

The cotton was woven on a narrow frame, requiring at least six strips to be sewn together to produce one cloth. The *bontan* had six, the *sake* had eight and the *barrafula* was the widest. Technological limitations meant a considerable expenditure of labour merely in weaving, which itself was the outcome of cultivation, spinning, a complicated dyeing industry and the assembly of the raw material at given points. Given that caste relations were favoured by the nobility, the addition of an export sector probably increased the numbers of workers in the cloth-making caste and intensified the exploitation of their labour. A similar inference can be drawn with respect to leather workers, judging from the export of hides. A report in 1606 claimed that 40,000 hides were purchased annually by Europeans in Senegambia. The figure covers a wide area, including Tukolor and Futa Jalon, and it may be exaggerated, but the general impression was created on the coast that the export of hides was a lucrative business. Another report in 1669, based on twenty years' experience of trade in upper Guinea, suggested that the quickest way in which a middleman could enrich himself was by buying and selling hides.[1] This aspect of European-oriented trade had serious implications for the Fulani cattle owners.

The growth of trade stimulated more trading specialists. Here, as in many other parts of West Africa, the Mande-speaking Dyula traders constituted the professional trading class. The Dyula helped integrate the production of upper Guinea with that of Futa Jalon and the western Sudan; and they seized additional opportunities offered by European demand for slaves, gold, ivory, hides, etc. The Dyakanke of Bambuk were the principal western Malinke traders. They reached the coast both singly as peddlers as well as in large caravans, although their area of concentration was the near hinterland close to the limit of the tides on the rivers. In Wuli, Kantora and Niani on the Gambia, the Dyula were within reach of the gold mines of Bambuk and Bure; and it was the gold trade with which they were initially most closely associated. The most valuable commodity obtained from the coastal people was salt. African rulers who tapped this trade strengthened their economic and political bases. For instance, the people of Salum were in the forefront of salt manufacture, and the *bur* of Salum established fortified towns along the river to ensure that salt was safely ferried up river. The main riverain ports such as Kaur (Salum), Niani Maron (Niani) and Sutoko (Wuli) attracted large numbers of Dyula, and

[1] Damião Peres (ed.), *Duas descrições seiscentistas da Guiné de Lemos Azevedo Coelho* (Lisbon, 1953), 11.

Malinke rulers undoubtedly welcomed them. The ruling élite saw to the protection of trade, and the Dyula were free to come and go without molestation.

Besides, the Dyula presence was virtually inseparable from the expansion of Islam. The marabouts or *mori* men were often the same persons as the Dyula, and at all times they were closely associated. Some Muslim Malinke were settled in upper Guinea before the fourteenth century, but the rulers were all Soninke. Each state had its own 'fetish' or totem around which their religion centred. Sacrifices and offerings made as part of local worship were crucial to the performance of government. However, rulers of the Mande states considered Islam and its agents as adjuncts reinforcing the existing political authority. When a Soninke consulted the ancestral totem, he consulted a marabout as well. Gradually, individual marabouts came to acquire special reputations. Their respective patron kings placed more confidence in their information and advice than in traditional consultations; and Islam came to be regarded as an indispensable 'medicine', which partly complemented and partly supplanted the more widespread African religious beliefs.

Over the seventeenth and eighteenth centuries, the Dyula and Muslims in general also acquired much of the wealth, independence and prestige which ultimately allowed them to seize power from the Soninke in the late nineteenth century. In the 1620s, there lived just beyond Barrakunda on the Gambia one Abubakar Sano, who maintained 300 donkeys in the trade to Bambuk. A century later, the most famous African merchant on the river was named as 'Serin Donso' of Kaur – *serin* or *bisserin* being a title equivalent to *imām*, while Danso was a prominent Dyakanke House in upper Guinea. Kabu tradition also recalls the Dyula, Mamadu Konte, who had so many slaves that they could bring cotton from the field, spin it and weave it all in the same day. Cotton cloth being the principal local currency, Mamadu Konte acquired a great deal of wealth. This last example suggests that the Dyula sometimes invested profits from trade in productive enterprises. Many of them were poor itinerant peddlers, but, viewed as a collective, they were better off than the rest of the non-noble population.

Apart from trade and their advisory politico-religious role with respect to the ruling class, there were four main factors accounting for the growth in the influence of Muslims in upper Guinea. Firstly, they enjoyed almost unlimited physical mobility over wide areas. Secondly, they lived in separate communities (known as *morikunda*), and they expanded their settlements by introducing wives and slaves. Thirdly, they kept alive the tradition of Islamic scholarship through Koranic schools and mosques, forming a cultural net which stretched from the Gambia estuary to Futa Jalon. And, fourthly, Muslims used this basic literacy to prepare charms comprising written Koranic verses. These 'greegrees', as they were called, were held in high esteem among the majority of the people, and therefore gave the marabouts a sphere of social influence that was not directly controlled by the hereditary ruling class. In practice, the Muslim dignitaries and the Soninke were two sections of the same ruling class. The contrast in their life-styles was often great, because many Muslims were ascetics, while the secular leaders were given to flamboyance and conspicuous consumption. But both enjoyed privilege and power in the minutely ordered society which had evolved in large parts of upper Guinea.

Within these societies, the Fulani herdsmen were placed towards the lower end of the social scale. No only were they aliens within the coastal region, but they came as clients rather than conquerors. In the early seventeenth century, the Fulani of upper Guinea were still essentially semi-nomadic and transhumant. Seasonal camps slowly gave way to more permanent settlements after the Fulani came to terms with the Malinke and Susu and, to a lesser extent, the Biafada. Permission to build houses and to graze their cattle did not initially cost the Fulani much – usually a token bull per annum out of any given herd. Over the course of the seventeenth century, the Fulani and their animals became more numerous, and Fulani family heads were more exposed to a variety of exactions from their overlords.

Many Fulani crossed the Gambia river and settled in Jimara, Sama and Firdu (later to be called Fuladu, 'country of the Fula'). There they resided in their own *fulakunda*. With the extensive commercialization of hides and milk, Fulani livestock were far from being merely symbols of social prestige. Besides, the Fulani of upper Guinea practised mixed farming, and they were noted for conserving their harvest from one year to another. The Mande nobility sought to appropriate the benefits of increases in Fulani productivity. They demanded a share of every animal slain; the annual tax on a herd was raised to as many as ten bulls by the nineteenth century; and the herds became subject to random depredations. Fulani crops were similarly taxed, and the Kabu *nyancho* were said to have allowed their horses to eat from the stored grain.[1] The Fulani were also potential victims for enslavement, while cruel

[1] B. K. Sidibe, 'The story of Kaabu: the fall of Kaabu', Conference on Manding Studies (London, 1972).

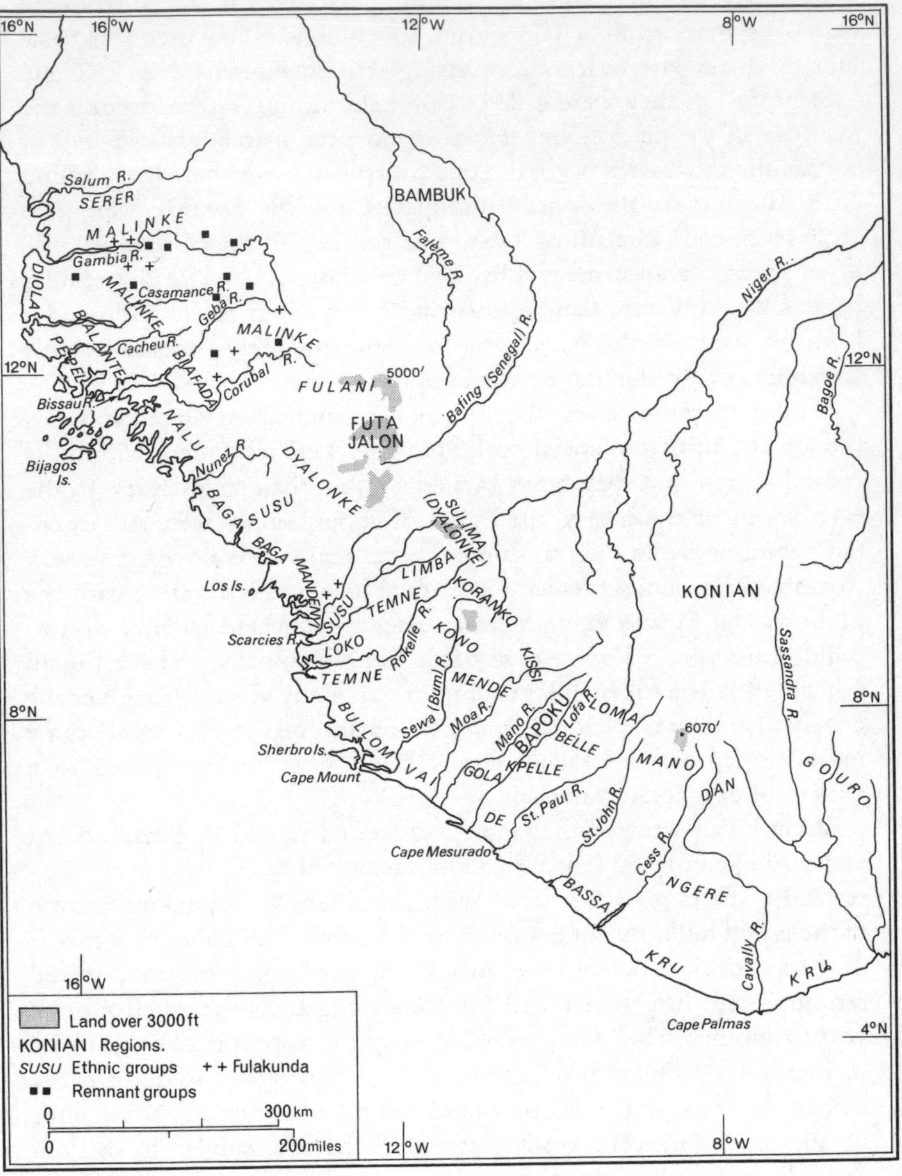

9 The upper Guinea coast, *c.* 1800

punishments meted out to them reflected the superiority complex of the ruling class. Some inter-marriage did take place between the Fulani and their hosts, and there was also differentiation among the Fulani themselves; but their identification with cattle singled them out as a distinct social caste.

In neighbouring Futa Jalon, the contradiction between the increasing wealth of the Fulani and the increasing socio-economic oppression led to a revolution in the second quarter of the eighteenth century. There the Fulani had the advantage of Islam as an alternative ideology, and the few who belonged to this faith provided leadership for the non-Islamic majority. They also gained support from the Malinke, Susu and Dyalonke Muslims and from traders and craftsmen. The jihad which broke out in 1725 led to an up-ending of class relations in Futa Jalon, so that the Fulani became owners of the land and holders of political power. A similar transformation eventually occurred in Kabu in the nineteenth century.

Fulani grievances are well known, because on seizing power they made their own propaganda. However, the individuals most exploited were among those categorized as 'slaves', recruited from the smaller groups of cultivators who could not offer effective defence against the Mande. At the beginning of the seventeenth century, societies in Salum and Kabu were sufficiently differentiated to find room for chattel slaves, acquired from outside by capture or purchase. Children of chattel slaves born locally were protected from sale, and had clearly defined rights with respect to marriage and inheritance. The principal languages of the Senegambia (Wolof, Serer and Malinke) all distinguish between saleable and non-saleable 'slaves'. The latter in effect became serfs on the land or retainers in households or occasionally members of the ruling class. A slave, serf or domestic also had his status determined in accordance with his master's place in the hierarchy. If attached to the royal family, the individual in a supposedly servile position could be more privileged than most free persons. Terms such as 'patron' and 'client' designate these social relations more accurately than 'slave-master' and 'slave'; but during these two centuries there was a marked increase in the numbers of the first-generation slaves and of the field serfs, whose upward mobility was extremely limited. By the end of the eighteenth century, the Mande and Fulani-dominated societies of upper Guinea and Futa Jalon were described as having slaves constituting the majority of the population. These were genuine slaves of recent purchase or capture, and they were highly visible since for the most part they lived together in large 'slave-villages'. This was closely tied up with previous evolution towards social classes (on the basis of ethnic subjugation) and with the European slave trade.

Malinke expansion into the Casamance region had taken place at the expense of the Kassanga, Bainuk and Diola. The Kassa *mansa* or 'king of Casanga' originally ruled the Kassanga and related Bainuk, as part of the extended Mali empire. Early Portuguese reports spoke of an important Diola king called Mansa Felupe – a figure so at odds with Diola social structure that he must have been Malinke-imposed if not actually a Malinke.[1] Similarly, in the Malinke state of Fogny, it was the Diola who formed the majority of the population. The process by which they were subjugated was slow, and it involved their capture for sale to Europeans. Malinke slave procurers sailed out of the Gambia in their large canoes and fell upon the Diola as they gathered sea-food on the coast. From Bintang Creek, the Malinke also moved overland to discipline Diola whom they regarded as recalcitrant subjects; and, while establishing their claims to sovereignty, they took captives.

The Diola put up a fierce resistance to external aggression and slave raiding. They repulsed attacks along the coast and in the near interior. In October 1722, visitors met the king of Fogny organizing a funeral lament for some of his relatives killed in an attack on the Diola; and physical resistance was matched by the maintenance of an independent culture. The Malinke overlay on their culture is lighter and more recent than in the case of the Kassanga and Bainuk who were further inland. The Balante to the south and east of the Diola and Bainuk also carried out protracted and successful resistance, in response both to the Malinke and to the Portuguese who were operating from Cacheu and Bissau. Direct raids on Africans did not constitute a major method of slave acquisition on the part of Europeans, but they did resort to this technique from time to time. After one or two attempts, the Portuguese knew that incursions into Balante territory were most ill advised. Both physically and economically, the Diola and Balante survived and thrived in spite of external pressures. They were skilled at irrigated rice farming, devising techniques for drainage, desalination and flooding. They continued to open up new areas of rice production, using the communal unit; and by the colonial era the Balante were the largest ethnic group in Guinea Bissau. Portuguese accounts in the early sixteenth century did not suggest this, so a considerable population increase can be inferred.

[1] On Diola political authority, see L. V. Thomas, 'Les "Rois" Diola hier, aujourd'hui, demain', *Bulletin de l'Institut Fondamental d'Afrique Noire*, January 1972, sér. B, 34, 1.

The Bijago islanders were also resistant to European enslavement, but their behaviour was very ambivalent. European traders were successful in harnessing the considerable qualities of seamanship and the fighting ability which the islanders possessed. By plying them with alcohol and other trade goods, slave buyers induced the Bijago rulers to launch their war-canoes on regular expeditions against the mainland, using the many waterways to penetrate the territory of the Pepel, Biafada and Nalu. A small but steady source of captives derived from this activity. On the other hand, the Bijago were seldom enslaved, because their military prowess intimidated both European visitors and African neighbours, and the islands were not raided from the mainland. Besides, on the occasions when Bijago men were captured, they were said to resort to suicide at the earliest opportunity, and their reputation in this respect warned off European buyers.

Some other groups did not fare as well as the Diola, Balante or Bijago. On the middle Gambia and the upper reaches of the rivers running east–west to the coast, many ethnicities organized communally and on a small scale were almost wiped out. In part, this was due to loss of identity within the Malinke fold, but it was also a form of genocide based on the mass exportation of the Tenda, Bassari, Koniagui and others that are today mere fragments. Tenda country was originally a vast tract of land along the Gambia river; and the name was retained throughout this period, even when the population was being called Malinke. Close observers noted the victimization of 'those belonging to a subject race', and specified that the Bassari were among the principal captives from the northern part of upper Guinea.[1] In the latter part of the eighteenth century, the Kissi were also badly hit. Furthermore, the same peoples who were exported in large numbers came to populate the slave villages that abounded by the late eighteenth century. The nobility were the ones who supervised slaving for export and they also accumulated slaves for domestic use.

Within Diola and Balante society, no slave institution came into being. Two inter-related factors plausibly explain the difference between themselves and the Malinke in this respect. Firstly, at the time of contact with Europeans, the Diola and Balante were as near to egalitarianism as made no difference; and, secondly, they did not participate as agents of the European slave trade. European contact with African society was via the ruling class. It presupposed some prior degree of

[1] See, e.g., P. Cultru, *Premier voyage de Sieur de la Courbe fait à la coste d'Afrique en 1685* (Paris, 1906), 194.

stratification before regular trade was established. Finding their presence rejected by the Diola and Balante, European traders described them as 'wild' and 'unsociable'; and it is no coincidence that Balante 'kings' were said to have worked in the field like any common citizen.[1] In fact, there were no kings – only elders who won respect in their own lifetime. Rulers of other ethnic groups who did have state structures were able to utilize slaves locally after becoming active participants in the slave trade, indicating that embryonic class differentiation was sufficiently advanced to allow the incorporation of captives into the society as the property of élite families. Senegambian society had its castes, a small slave sector and an external (trans-Saharan) slave-trading connection before the advent of Europeans. The European slave trade offered great scope for the Malinke nobility to strengthen their control of the society by vastly increasing their hold over production and over the number of 'domestic' slaves.

The *faring Kabu* was noted both as a faithful supplier of captives to Europeans and as a potentate who kept slaves for his own use. The dividing line between the two was thin, since captives destined for export were put to work if no European buyer was immediately available or if the exchange was held up for one reason or another. In the Sierra Leone hinterland, it was found profitable to engage a proportion of those captured on the production of rice for victualling slave ships; and, when the price of a slave fell below a certain level, the rulers judged it better to retain the labour on rice cultivation. This was the situation by the late eighteenth century, after such developments had been greatly intensified by the Futa Jalon jihad. The impact of the jihad on differentiation in upper Guinea societies was pronounced, and this was inter-related with the other major themes of population movement, state-building, the slave trade and the spread of Islam.

The Futa Jalon jihad displaced some of the Susu and Dyalonke and pushed them towards the coast. They in turn sometimes attacked the coastal peoples and took over power in many localities, initiating a complex pattern of diplomacy and conflict. The Dyalonke fought several long rearguard battles against the Fulani well into the second half of the eighteenth century, until most of their numbers were stabilized within the state of Sulima with its fortified capital at Falaba. Sulima resisted and counter-attacked the Fulani with Koranko support. Meanwhile the Koranko clans reached down to the centre of Sierra Leone among the

[1] Th. Monod, A. T. da Mota and R. Mauny (eds.), *Description de la côte occidentale d'Afrique par Valentim Fernandes, 1505–1510* (Bissau, 1951), 60.

Temne, in a process that was part peaceful and part militaristic. The same applies to the Susu thrust, which was carried out at the expense of the Kokoli, Nalu, Baga, Bullom and Temne, and which actually brought the Susu on to the littoral for the first time in the mid-eighteenth century. New ruling families such as the Sankong and Bangura in the Scarcies and Melakori date from this period, bringing about the first dynastic changes since the era of the Mani invasions. The Malinke entrenched themselves as far east as the Lofa river, where the important state of Kondo at Bopolu dominated the Loma people in the second half of the eighteenth century. Significantly enough, its ruling class incorporated Muslims and traders who controlled the route from Cape Mount to the deep hinterland, via Kissi country.

The new ruling class were either Muslims or under heavy Muslim influence, because the Futa Jalon jihad vastly increased the power and prestige of Muslims. Virtually every ruler in Sierra Leone had a Muslim adviser or 'prime minister', according to European reports in the 1790s, and local traditions confirm this. Marabouts are ubiquitous in the oral histories of Mendeland, being closely associated with the process of state formation in the eighteenth century.[1] State bureaucracies benefited from the modicum of literacy possessed by the Muslims, and coastal rulers began to send their sons to school in Futa Jalon. While it is true that the European pull had caused the coastal peoples to face towards the Atlantic, the Futa Jalon jihad was a political and cultural reference point which countered this trend. It was also a reference point for a society which emphasized social gradations and sanctioned raw oppression in the forms of slavery. The Susu, Temne, Koranko and Sulima countryside was full of slaves, with individual rulers having 200 or 300 each, thereby differing from the Futa Fulani only in so far as the latter were bigger slave owners. European ships were still the principal destination of captives to the end of the eighteenth century, but the internal distribution and use of coerced labour assumed an independent reality – so much so that it was to persist for a century after the European slave trade had ended.

It is necessary to distinguish between New World chattel slaves and African 'domestics'. The latter were juridically semi-privileged and they could be integrated into family structures, a pattern that was possible when small numbers were involved. However, the late eighteenth-century situation on the upper Guinea coast was quantita-

[1] Arthur Abraham, 'Some suggestions on the origins of Mende chiefdoms', *Sierra Leone Studies*, July 1969, new series, no. 25.

tively and qualitatively different. Proof of the exploitative and oppressive nature of the system was provided by the endemic nature of resistance and rebellion. The *rimaibe* or agricultural serfs of Futa Jalon staged one of their most determined revolts in 1785, and many were able to flee to freedom. The Fulani and Susu rulers were all Muslims at this date, but power struggles still continued. The fugitives received sanctuary from the Susu, and they built several independent settlements which attracted further runaways, along lines that were very familiar in the New World. Their example of successful revolt threatened the whole structure of social relations which had been built by the Mande and Fulani and which was receiving powerful rationalization from believers in Islam. Because of growing disaffection among their own slaves, the Susu formed an alliance with the Fulani to crush the runaways, and this was achieved in 1796 after protracted struggle. This extended slave revolt is an outstanding episode in the history of the masses of upper Guinea, and the very fact of their dramatic appearance on the historical stage attests to the sharpness of class contradictions which had arisen out of a complex of internal and external factors. The institution of slavery persisted among the Kpelle, Vai, Mende, Susu, Malinke and Fulani into the present century, its tenacity attesting to its deep roots.

Small coastal societies away from direct Mande or Fulani influence did not all experience the rapid expansion of servile categories, but invariably the trend was towards a greater gulf between commoners and ruling lineages. The rounding up of slaves by raids and warfare was conducted under the auspices of the rulers of the many polities and ethnicities in a manner that guaranteed their own self-preservation. Nobles were not offered for sale even if captured, and if this misfortune befell them strenuous efforts were made to secure their release. Moreover, the ruling authorities also engaged in the direct exploitation of their own subjects by so-called 'legal' means: namely, by making sale into slavery the penalty for a wide range of offences and by framing persons on false charges. The slow process of internal stratification was obviously speeded up by this external involvement, while at the same time the local rulers came into a new relationship of dependence.

The intensity of European impact varied along the coast. Traders did not favour the eastern shores known variously as the 'Malaguetta Coast', the 'Grain Coast', the 'Windward Coast' and the 'Qua Qua (Kwa Kwa) Coast'. Trade in malaguetta pepper persisted throughout the period under discussion, but it was unattractive. European disinterest may partly be explained by difficulty of access and partly by the lack of strong kingdoms which would have been viable trading partners. The few ships which landed found that the small villages were independent political entities, with an elder elected chairman by his fellows. These coastal settlers were usually acting as middlemen when they supplied small quantities of ivory, a few slaves and some amount of rice, which was the distinguishing staple as far east as the Bandama river. Only at the very end of the eighteenth century did the coastal Kru intensify their involvement with European ships in the capacity of canoe-men and seamen in ocean-going vessels. Meanwhile, the peoples between Cape Mount and the Gambia were experiencing much more lengthy and profound contacts with European traders, one consequence of which was the rise of a unique social formation in the persons of the mulatto traders.

Extensive personal contact between Europeans and Africans led to the wide dispersal of mulattoes, specializing in the trading professions of their European fathers. The majority were of part-Portuguese descent, while many in the Sherbro and the Sierra Leone peninsula were born of English fathers. The mulattoes served as middlemen, collecting African produce and slaves at convenient points and in convenient quantities for loading on ocean-going ships. As a subsidiary activity, they also engaged in many branches of purely local commerce in items such as kola and indigo. The mulattoes were as dynamic as their Dyula counterparts, and many local trading centres had representatives of both groups. Like the white agents of European trading companies, they retained captives to serve in their establishments, while wealth in the form of trade goods ensured that they could acquire other dependants through patronage and marriages. Their manpower permitted them to operate canoes and boats in a manner similar to the Houses of the Niger delta, and they also moved into the supervision of direct production such as agriculture, the collection of beeswax and the transport of camwood logs. Not only did the mulattoes achieve ascendancy in economic spheres, but they also gained considerable authority. In the districts immediately south of the Sierra Leone peninsula, the Caulkers, Rogers and Clevelands breached the power monopoly of the Mani descendants in the eighteenth century, to the extent that they took control of the *poro* and used it to further their interests as compradors for the trade in slaves and for European trade in general.

Although the commercial nexus drew together Europeans, mulattoes and African rulers, it also created areas of disaffection. This was most evident where European forts were constructed. The Portuguese at Cacheu and Bissau, the English in Sierra Leone and the Courlanders in the Gambia all built forts at one time or another, which raised many contentious issues between the local African population and themselves. At these sites and elsewhere, the African ruling class quarrelled with resident and visiting Europeans over prices, over the quality and the supply of goods, and over taxes and customs which were their due. Mulatto middlemen became involved in these disputes, and also in the struggle over whether trade should be open to all or restricted by and to a particular European nation.

The question of sovereignty was seldom far from the surface in trade disputes, and Europeans tried to intervene in domestic policies to further their objectives. On the whole African rulers did quite well in the direct confrontation with Europeans, and did not stop short of administering a clout or two when the necessity arose; but, on balance, Europeans were bargaining from a position of strength based on the nature and development of the political economy of capitalist Europe.

By the end of the eighteenth century, changes were about to descend upon the African population as a whole – changes about which they had no knowledge and over which they had no control. Botanists like Smeathman were poking around, adventurers like Mungo Park were 'discovering', European powers were debating the possibility of making the trade in slaves illegal for their respective citizens, and schemes were being devised for repatriating black people in England and the Americas to Africa. The establishment of the colony at Freetown and the abolition of the English slave trade did not have an immediate impact on the history of the region, but they marked the beginning of a new phase in which the form of the integration into the European world was to be altered.

THE GOLD COAST

What came to be called the Gold Coast was almost synonymous with Akan country, which was first linked to the European economy through the export of gold. Most Akan lived along a belt about 300 kilometres wide, running parallel to the coast between 80 and 400 kilometres inland from what is now the eastern Ivory Coast to the Volta. Europeans on the coast were able to distinguish Egyira, Sefwi, Aowin, Wassa, Twifo, Akyem, Akwamu and Kwahu – moving from west to east in the southern part of the belt so described. Many later developments hinged on what was taking place in 'Akani', around the confluence of the Pra and the Offin. The majority of the ruling clans traced their origin to this region, which was rich in gold resources and densely populated. 'Akani' has been identified with one or other of the Akan states, Assin and Twifo being the most likely. However, the word was used in virtually the same sense as 'Akan', and it applied to several districts. Oracles were held in common esteem over a wide area; dialects of the Twi language were mutually intelligible; there was an extensive trade network; and political and military institutions readily passed from one state to another. During the seventeenth century, the Twi language and other aspects of Akan culture progressed steadily on the coast itself, largely through the Fante, the Ahanta and Nzima. At that time, there were significant elements of the population which identified themselves as 'Adesi' (Guan) in the territory now considered to be inhabited by Fante, and there were unassimilated Guan among the Akan in the hinterland, but throughout the western and central Gold Coast the Akan culture was in the ascendant.

The state which first led Akan socio-political development was Adansi, lying immediately north of the Pra/Offin confluence. Its power is said to have been based on the knowledge, wisdom and fame of its principal oracle. Adansi remained the senior Akan state throughout the first half of the seventeenth century, and it must obviously have formed the core of 'Akani'. However, Adansi was defeated by Denkyira by 1659, and soon afterwards Denkyira reduced the small states to the immediate north of Adansi. Denkyira also registered victories over Twifo, Assin and Wassa to the south, and over Aowin and Sefwi to the west. As a consequence, Denkyira controlled the western trade routes that led to the coast between Assini and Axim; it played a major role in the commerce conducted at Elmina and Cape Coast; and it must also have taken the greater share of the marketing of southern Akan gold in the northern states of Bono-Mansu and Begho. Denkyira became the Akan state with the richest material possessions by the 1680s. The Denkyira nucleus lay in the gold-producing belt, its capital, Abankeseso, being an ancient gold supply centre serving the north. In the early eighteenth century, Europeans on the Gold Coast were aware of the large number of deep pits which were dug near Abankeseso. All of Denkyira's conquests and tributaries were also gold producers. Adansi was the principal mining area in the subsequent epoch of colonialism, and the areas from which Europeans extracted gold coincided closely with those worked previously by Africans. Gold was valued as a commodity to be consumed within Akan society, especially by royalty and the nobility, in order to buttress their own status and that of their respective nations. The kings of Denkyira made shields and swords adorned with gold, while their linguists acquired gold-headed canes. Denkyirahene Boa Amponsem (*c.* 1677–92) is said to have created ornaments out of freshly mined gold for every ceremonial occasion, and he is credited with the introduction of the golden stool as a symbol of the Denkyira people. Obviously, this affluence was connected with territorial expansion and should be deduced as a factor which consciously motivated the nature and direction of expansion.

To accomplish its takeover of so much of the Akan heartlands, Denkyira had to pay considerable attention to its armies. During the period of its development in the early seventeenth century, military and administrative divisions were combined, so that the principal civilian authorities were responsible for mobilizing forces and assuming command in times of war. The king maintained his position as supreme military commander and representative of the nation as a whole; and a number of things were done to glorify the nation and the office of *Denkyirahene*. Most of the national symbols coincided with the king's regalia, notably the state stool (originally of precious beads), the state sword and the executioner's knife. The Guan population played a part in supplying these, just as their beliefs must have helped in elevating the *akomfo* (priest) into an important central figure in Denkyira.[1] However, rapid expansion outside Denkyira proper raised many practical problems of administration, which were inadequately tackled. Little was done to integrate the conquered Akan states. On the contrary, the maintenance of crude tribute relations soon resulted in a generalized hostility towards Denkyira, and in some population displacements towards the coast in a south-westerly direction.

Another rich Akan area was that controlled by the Akyem. It was referred to as 'Great Akani', largely because of the wealth of its rulers, the Agona clan. Akyem country was rich in gold, and the utilization of imported labour leaves no doubt that this resource was being tapped. Large numbers of captive Africans or purchased slaves were integrated into Akyem society as an exploited class, being used as farm labourers, miners and porters. From them, Akyem rulers derived not merely

[1] R. A. Bravmann, 'The state sword, a pre-Asante tradition', *Ghana Notes and Queries* 1968, no. 10.

material advantages but social prestige. Those in positions of power displayed the arrogance and conspicuous consumption which is not uncharacteristic of ruling classes. Throughout the seventeenth century and up to its eventual conquest by Asante, Akyem country lay under the jurisdiction of two or three powerful chiefs at any one time, each having a territorial sphere in which he was considered 'king'. During the last years of the seventeenth century, the most prominent was Ofusuhene Apenteng in a district near the Pra river, while Kutukrunku was lord of Akyem Abuakwa to the south-east. Political divisions notwithstanding, Akyem country was one of the leading sectors of the Akan. Its size, populousness and wealth made an impact beyond its boundaries to the east and south.

The power of Denkyira and Akyem was reflected in their ascendancy over Assin, which was considered a state of some consequence. In the early seventeenth century, most of the output of gold from Adansi, Denkyira and Akyem probably still went northwards. But, of course, a southern outlet had also come into being. The 'Akani' obtained akori beads, certain cloths and captives from Benin, through the agency of the Portuguese and later the Dutch. The most important paths to and from the coast passed through Assin – itself a small gold producer, with a labouring force similar to Akyem's. Assin was known for its prowess in warfare. It exercised great influence over the Fante and the 'Adesi' states of Fetu, Komenda and Asebu, which were little more than fishing villages, in spite of pronounced internal stratification and the existence of a privileged group of *caboceers*. Around 1619, the Abrem countryside was ravaged by Assin, and the peaceful relations subsequently restored included the element of Assin hegemony. When a son of the king of Assin was killed accompanying Abrem in an attack on Fetu in 1666, Fetu hastened to pay compensation in gold in order to divert the wrath of Assin. European traders helped to bring about conciliation, since they could not afford to alienate a state which handled two-thirds of the gold which reached the coast. By this time, Assin traders were residing in Kabesterra (north of Komenda) and in the coastal towns near the forts. They learnt the trade *lingua franca*; they became as 'deceitful and cunning in trade' as Europeans and coastal Africans; and they took care of their countrymen who spent three or four days travelling along the winding paths from their capital at Great Assin.

Assin was hard put to resist Akyem and Denkyira attempts at overlordship. Its territory came under attack from Denkyira when problems arose over payment of tolls by Assin traders. In 1666, there was a war over this matter with 'Alcance', which is taken to mean Adansi, and the latter had already been conquered by Denkyira. Victory in such a confrontation did not lead to occupation: rather, it stimulated claims to sovereignty and gave rise to subsequent military action if tribute was refused. Thus, in 1697, Denkyira inflicted a severe defeat on King Agyensam of Koshea in Assin, and this could be interpreted as a disciplinary measure against a recalcitrant tributary. Meanwhile, Assin had to endure similar claims made by Akyem rulers.

In the east, the location of the state of Akwamu away from the powers in central Akan territory was an advantage. Its ruling clan was propelled eastwards by tensions in 'Akani', and settled at Nyanaoase near the northern Ga shortly before 1600. Ultimately, Akwamu held sway over some Akyem and Kwahu, but the majority of its new subjects were Ga, Guan, Adangbe and Ewe. These communities – all relative newcomers on the Gold Coast in the seventeenth century – were small and non-militaristic. They concentrated on farming, fishing and pottery-making in extended families, each under the authority of a *wulomo* or priest of the family god. Akwamu took them over peacefully or by the use of force where necessary. The major economic objective of Akwamu's rulers was to control its own trade and that of inland people to the coast. Akwamu traders from Nyanaoase first went to the nearby Abonce market as clients of the Ga. In 1634, the Dutch reported a sharp increase in gold available at Accra. This of course was not supplied by the Ga, but by the Akwamu and Akan peoples farther north. The continuation of this upward trend in gold exports was of special interest to Europeans and to Akwamu. Late in 1645, an official of the Dutch West India Company made two journeys into the interior to settle disputes which had arisen between Akwamu and the Ga traders of Accra. It was confirmed that Akwamu should receive payments in gold to allow merchants to come to Accra through Akwapim. This marked both the greater independence of Akwamu relative to Accra and the starting point of notable territorial advance.

Continuous fighting in the Accra vicinity from 1662 to 1666 had so devastated the countryside that the Danes at Christiansborg could not obtain any provisions locally. This is clearly part of the period spoken of in oral traditions when the branch of the Ga on Ayiwaso Hill were being dispossessed by Akwamu. Misrule on the part of the principal *wulomo*, Okai Koi, contributed to lack of Ga response when he was killed by the Akwamu. These disturbed conditions gave rise to a movement of refugees to Accra. Accra residents were in some measure protected by the three European forts in existence at this point, although they were to prove of little avail. After a crushing defeat in 1680, Accra was brought within the boundaries of the Akwamu state, and the conquerors automatically became landlords of the European forts. From a European standpoint, this turn of events was inconsequential, provided the free flow of import/export trade was maintained. In fact, the English decided to change horses at an early juncture, and helped Akwamu overcome the Ga. Once Akwamu rulers had gained control of the coast, they used the profits from trade and their access to firearms as the basis for an ambitious programme of expansion. To the west, Akwamu had allies in Akron and Agona, whose populations were sources of hired soldiers; but Akwamu also had plans for extending its boundaries in that direction. Agona enjoyed the reputation of tenaciousness in guarding its independence, and for a long time it resisted encroachment by Akwamu, by Fante and by the Europeans who were trading at Winneba. However, Agona was defeated by Akwamu in 1689 and again in 1693, and became a tribute-paying province. On the other side of Accra, Akwamu forces had already overrun Ladoku in 1679. Sporadic resistance was finally crushed in 1702, by which time Akwamu's armies had pursued Accra and Ladoku refugees across the Volta. In fact, Akwamu's sphere of influence included some Ewe groups and reached to the frontiers of Whydah.

Akwamu profoundly influenced military and administrative practices on the Gold Coast. The Ga received most of their military knowledge from Akwamu, and the same applied to the religious ritual surrounding military matters. The most significant innovation was the adoption of the *mantse* stool as a powerful war medicine. In their previous rituals, such as the *kple* harvesting ceremony, the Ga used millet offerings; and the import of yams to carry out the ritual surrounding the *mantse* was double testimony to the Akan influence. On the practical side, Akwamu had devised effective means for mobilizing large numbers of troops. It pressed into service those of its citizens who had themselves become incorporated by conquest. Akwamu conceivably contributed to this practice becoming as widespread as it was in the eighteenth century. Akwamu's weaponry comprised swords, spears and bows. Hunters and soldiers acquired great expertise in the handling of bow and arrow. The sword, which was a principal weapon of the Akan armies of the seventeenth century, was later to fall into disuse, being preserved only in the form of the state sword. On the other hand, some form of the bow was becoming more popular, and Akwamu apparently led in this development. Trade with Europeans also allowed the acquisition of muskets, and Akwamu was undoubtedly a front-runner in the race to acquire firearms and gunpowder.

Akwamu divided the conquered coastal zone into two provinces: Accra and Ladoku. These were directly under the control of Nyanaoase, as distinct from Agona and Little Popo, which merely paid tribute. The provinces were subdivided into districts, each of which was attached to a stool. The *Akwamuhene* had power to appoint and remove stool-holders, and the latter were granted revenue from their districts. With few exceptions, Akwamu rulers and administrators on the coast were either from the king's family or office holders in his household, rather than members of the hereditary nobility of Nyanaoase. This suggests that the expansion of the state strengthened the monarch at the expense of the hereditary nobles.[1] Certainly, the *Akwamuhene*, Ansa Sasraku, who conquered Accra in 1680, is an outstanding figure in Akwamu's history, and he benefited a great deal by being the first king to have authority over the European forts. Conquest also strengthened the capital vis-à-vis the provinces, since most of the important officials resided at Nyanaoase, including those in charge of provinces and forts. At a more fundamental level, the military success of Akwamu enhanced socio-economic stratification and strengthened the ruling class at the expense of other citizens. The king, governors of provinces and stool-holders were in the habit of maintaining armed contingents which protected trade routes, gathered taxes and served as domestic police forces. Class interests were being protected, because, in so far as there were profits from the overseas trade in which Akwamu became deeply involved, they were in terms of consumer goods that went primarily to the king and his officials.

The pre-eminence of Denkyira, Akyem and Akwamu over the western, central and eastern sections of Akan country, respectively, was of short duration. As is well known, Asante came to dominate the whole of Akan territory in the eighteenth century. The groundwork for Asante's ascendancy was laid before the actual state-building process, which began no earlier than the 1670s in the region of Kwaman or central Asante. In the savanna to the north-west lay Bono, which had a great reputation as a gold-trading state, most of its supplies coming from the forest area. The forests were also rich in kola nuts, unexploited

[1] This section has benefited from unpublished work by Mr R. A. Kea, School of Oriental and African Studies, London.

farming land and game. This wealth attracted immigrants such as the Domaa, who moved northwards at the turn of the seventeenth century to settle near Tafo. They came from 'Akani', which was both densely peopled and tightly organized politically. Thus, disputes and over-population were factors propelling the immigrants out of the Pra/Offin country. This applied especially to segments of ruling groups who were eclipsed in succession battles. It was true of the Bretuo clan, who moved from Ahensen in Adansi; and it was true of the Oyoko, whose displacement to the north followed upon civil war in Asantemanso in Adansi. These two clans assumed the dominant roles in building the Asante state. At first, they were merely refugees seeking land, but their objective of settler rights was not always peaceably attained. Frequent clashes stemmed from rapid population increase, for previous Akan immigrants had already done much of the pioneer work of establishing towns, hunters' camps and roads within the forest. Further newcomers from the south strengthened the settlement pattern typical of the Akan: namely, towns and large villages, each with its own political superstructure. The town polities of Kumasi, Juaben, Bekwai, Mampon, Kokofu and Nsuta were founded or expanded by the new wave of immigrants from Adansi in the 1670s. These *amanto* states, as they were known, served as the matrix for the Asante kingdom.

The Asante *amanto* paid tribute and deference to Denkyira. One of the ways in which Akan rulers expressed clientship was by sending young men to the court of the overlord. Such was the case with Osei Tutu. As maternal nephew of the foremost Oyoko chief, Obiri Yeboa, he served as shield-bearer to Denkyirahene Boa Amponsem (1677–92); and, after an escapade, he fled to Akwamu, remaining there as a personal favourite of the *Akwamuhene*. Osei Tutu symbolized in his personal experience the continuity of developments in Akan country, in terms of the political inheritance which passed from Denkyira and Akwamu to Asante. His accession to power in Asante was facilitated by a company of Akwamu troops, who stayed on in Asante. The fact that the second-in-command of the Asante army is called the *Akwamuhene* probably attests to borrowings from Akwamu military organization. The foremost figure in Osei Tutu's retinue, according to tradition, was Okomfo Anokye, a priest of the shrine of the war-god Otutu in Akwapim. Anokye was of Guan descent, but had ample experience with large Akan political formations in both Akwamu and Denkyira. Osei Tutu and Okomfo Anokye possessed a fund of knowledge and a set of motivations which were important in accounting for the rapid rise of Asante as a kingdom and for their own aggrandizement as part of the ruling class. What was required was the correct handling of the Asante *amanto* communities, so as to maximize the advantages of the natural wealth and manpower resources of the region.

Obiri Yeboa was killed while fighting, and Osei Tutu followed up the campaigns waged by his uncle. Diplomacy was judiciously combined with force of arms. Those who allied with Osei Tutu were rewarded with positions that afterwards remained located within their families. Generous marriage alliances were formed with defeated ruling families; and Osei Tutu used considerable restraint after his victory over the forces of Tafo. With the help of Okomfo Anokye, Osei Tutu united the several *amanto* into a confederation and a nation, with Kumasi as the capital and leading element. Symbols of unity were important in this exercise. It is now clear that many of the items of regalia such as the golden stool and the state sword were not new creations, but rather the revival of ritual objects which were widely distributed and which already had socio-political roles. The close kinship ties between the new immigrant Asante communities also offered a basis for political unity. Obiri Yeboa, Osei Tutu and most rulers of the *amanto* belonged to the Oyoko. The Bretuo *Mamponhene* was exceptional, and his importance in the Asante hierarchy shows that his clan must have been deliberately conciliated. The *Mamponhene* possessed a silver stool, he commanded the right wing of the Asante army, and he served as commander-in-chief on the many occasions on which the *Asantehene* himself did not take the field. Intelligent use of national symbols and the unifying potential of kinship were factors that were meaningful in the context of Asante struggles for land and political power vis-à-vis the already settled population. While these struggles were going on, another common enemy was on the scene in the form of Denkyira. Asante national cohesion was undoubtedly intensified in the process of reacting against unwanted Denkyira overlordship.

Kumasi and the protective circle of the other *amanto* must have sufficiently distinguished themselves militarily by the 1690s that they could confidently consider confrontation with Denkyira. It would be an exaggeration to equate Asante's strength with that of Denkyira, even on the eve of the conflict in which Asante proved victorious. But, Denkyira's bullying and intemperate attempts to exploit a huge section of Akan country had created many enemies and potential members of a hostile alliance. Asante's role was precisely to lead such an alliance and to capitalize on the ill-will engendered by

Denkyira. The rise of Akwamu was also relevant to the creation of an effective alliance. Since Akwamu and Denkyira were the inland Akan states with strong coastal interests by the 1680s, they had areas of friction; but the two were not bound to collide, given that Akwamu's sphere of interest was the eastern Gold Coast and Denkyira's was the western Gold Coast. In 1690, Denkyira's relations with Akwamu were sufficiently good for a Denkyira embassy to seek Akwamu's goodwill on behalf of English traders. Akwamu's eventual alliance with Asante against Denkyira was dictated by close friendship with Asante and by fear of Akyem rulers who were making claims on Akwamu. There is a tradition that Osei Tutu was born to a niece of Obiri Yeboa only after medicine had been procured from the oracle Otutu in Akwapim, with the permission of the *Akwamuhene*. This provides one explanation for the close relationship between Asante and Akwamu ruling families, which was consolidated when Osei Tutu was under the protection of Akwamuhene Ansa Sasraku. This *Akwamuhene* and his successors could not but appreciate the value of a strong Asante ally in Akyem's rear. When Asante and Denkyira headed for conflict in 1699, the line-up was Asante and Akwamu versus Denkyira and Akyem. In addition, several of Denkyira's tributaries either failed to render their suzerain any assistance or actively contributed to Asante's cause. The result was that Asante emerged victorious in the fighting which lasted till 1701 and culminated in the battle of Feyiase.

Asante's incursion into the politics of the coast followed upon its defeat of Denkyira. Immediately prior to this, the Dutch were making overtures to Asante, so that an alliance was readily confirmed. At the same time, Africans at Elmina also opted for close ties with Asante. The town of Elmina had grown under the patronage of the Portuguese, and it became independent of its former sovereigns, Fetu and Komenda. When the Dutch triumphed over the Portuguese, the Elmina reconciled themselves to these new trading partners. Throughout the seventeenth century and for most of the eighteenth century, the Elmina maintained their independence in the face of attacks from Komenda and Fetu, and Asante was a welcome ally. However, on the local scene, it was Fante expansionism that was most marked. This in itself was partly a reaction to the rise of centralized Akan states and to that of Asante in particular. The Fante then and subsequently were unique among the Akan with regard to the extent to which their structures were decentralized. Considerable constitutional power was granted to the *braffo*, an elected war leader. It was the *braffo* who signed a military treaty with the

Dutch in 1624, and, from a European standpoint, he was the foremost authority in Fante country. But the Fante lived their lives under the direct control of numerous chiefs, each ruling a village or two; and these petty rulers often disregarded the *braffo*. At the same time, the Fante population was numerous and quite capable in military matters. It was fairly obvious that political unity was necessary if this populous section of the Akan were to become a power. A typical observation of the late seventeenth century was one to the effect that the Fante were a very formidable nation, and were it not for the continual divisions among themselves, they might have proved very troublesome to their neighbours.[1] The rise of a centralized state comparable to Asante and Akwamu was never to be seen among the Fante, but some degree of consolidation and expansion did take place early in the eighteenth century.

The Borbor Fante line established at Mankessim responded to changes in the hinterland balance of power by pursuing a more ambitious policy. A new and effective alliance was entered into with Assin. Assin's rulers had suffered under Denkyira, were continually threatened by Akyem, and were faced by the prospect of further domination by Asante. All the small coastal polities, along with Assin and the 'Etsi' states, recognized the necessity for unity if they were to withstand their powerful hinterland neighbours, given that both Asante and Akyem rulers had expansionist ambitions that directly affected the central Gold Coast. Furthermore, the whole of the southern Gold Coast had by the turn of the seventeenth century been transformed into a single political arena. Fante could and did turn to Akwamu for an alliance, because Akwamu and Akyem were in conflict. Fante's immediate eastern neighbours were also friendly. D'Anville's map of 1729 showed most of Akron 'under the protection of Fantin' – a situation that came about mainly through mutual agreement rather than war.

At no point did the increase in Fante influence appear dramatic, because it was the continuation of a process of acculturation which was already advanced in the seventeenth century. The spread of the Fante dialect of Twi highlighted this process, together with the increase in the number of people offering their devotion to the principal Fante deity. Since, in contrast to the Akan, the Guan were patrilineal, the expansion of Fante matriclans must also have represented an important social change. Some idea of the length and slowness of the cultural transition can be gained from the fact that up to recent times the Fante of Asebu, Winneba and Komenda reverted to the Guan language for

[1] See, e.g., William Bosman, *A new description of the coast of Guinea*, 56.

certain prayers and ceremonies. Yet it remains true that from early in the eighteenth century the Fante presence had manifested itself so decisively that it would have been meaningless to refer to Africans in those areas as Guan. It is against this cultural backcloth that political events must be viewed. The trend in the eighteenth century was towards an association of the increasing number of rulers and communities who identified as Fante. This association took the form of regular consultations at Abora, somewhat inland from Mankessim. At Abora, the Fante chiefs met in conclave from time to time; it was there that they signed treaties. The Fante Confederacy which was constituted in 1868 had behind it at least 150 years of confederal association, embracing the majority of signatories to the latter document. The question arises as to why in all those years political power was not stabilized within some section of the Fante ruling class and within the territorial boundaries of a nation-state, as was happening among the other Akan peoples and their neighbours. Undoubtedly, one factor to be taken into account was the presence of Europeans.

The building of a large number of forts increased the foci of African political power, since African towns grew up in conjunction with each fort. Even where there was no fort, trade with the chartered companies or with interlopers transformed coastal villages into centres of commerce. Towns over which the Fante culture was spreading supported hereditary leaders devoted to trade, along with new *caboceers* created by trade. Old and new elements worked hand in hand, the latter being 'ennobled' by the traditional rulers on application. In effect, the dominant class on the coast was a commercial one. Their wealth and prestige derived from trade and not from productive resources over which they had any control or over which they could conceivably acquire control. The Fante and Ahanta ruling class certainly pursued a vigorous policy of attempting to command the local distributive process, but they were middlemen in relation to the Akan hinterland and to Europeans, and their town polities were little better than retail outlets. Along the Bight of Biafra, topographical conditions were conducive to the emergence of these outlets in a few of the most favoured spots, and no physical European presence militated against the elimination of the weaker ones by Africans themselves – hence the consolidation of power in a very few city-states. On the Gold Coast, the export orientation and middlemen roles must be taken together with the multiplicity of trade paths and the existence of forts to explain the proliferation of towns and mini-states.

Sections of the Fante ruling class and individuals within it struggled to maintain relations with this or that European company or trader, while at the same time being engaged in a prolonged confrontation with their European principals to increase their own share of the profits. Africans coming into close contact with Europeans on the Gold Coast included independent or semi-independent traders as well as craftsmen and labourers who entered into a wage relationship with Europeans. A few wage-earners graduated to become traders; and both of these categories included mulattoes and members of coastal ruling families. Access to European wages became one of the principal aspects of the power base of the local ruling class. In some instances, limitations were imposed on traditional rulers with regard to participation in trade, comparable to the prohibition placed on the *ndem* priest among the Efik. Instances are on record of *caboceers* who were eligible to become kings in Fetu or Asebu, and who refused the honour since it excluded direct participation in trade. However, the king at any given time would usually have had some previous experience as a trader or employee of a European fort, and his relatives continued to fulfil these functions.

As on the upper Guinea coast, numerous contradictions arose between Europeans and Africans of the coastal mercantile community. Europeans were both served and opposed by men like Edward Barter, a mulatto, schooled in England at the expense of the Royal African Company between 1690 and 1693. On his return to the Gold Coast, he was employed by the Royal African Company. Within a few years, Barter was for all practical purposes an independent broker, although he still acted on behalf of the Royal African Company, and gave it preference. John Kabes and John Konny were two African traders who were even more outstanding than Barter in the history of the western Gold Coast. The Ghanaian historian, Kwame Daaku, describes them as 'merchant princes', and they were the most successful exemplars of the phenomenon of the rise of a coastal comprador class.[1] John Kabes spent his active trading life at Komenda from about 1680 to 1716, during which time he acted as broker to the Dutch and the English. He diversified his efforts into farming, salt manufacture and canoe-making; and, through his acquisition of political power, Kabes became deeply involved in the complicated diplomatic games played out by coastal states, inland powers and resident Europeans. Most of these remarks apply equally well to John Konny, who built up a power base at Cape Three Points in Ahanta, and whose heyday was between 1711

[1] K. Y. Daaku, *Trade and politics on the Gold Coast, 1600–1720* (Oxford, 1970), ch. VI.

and 1725. He was the merchant prince who went furthest in asserting his autonomy from the Europeans, and his stronghold fell to the Dutch only when the latter mobilized all the force that they could muster on the Gold Coast. John Konny's long career of jockeying between Europeans, manipulating them, serving them, and ultimately succumbing to their power, clearly illustrates the European fixation of African politics on the western Gold Coast.

Because of the forts, a physical European presence was paramount on the Gold Coast more than anywhere else. Africans living in villages nearest to the walls and guns of the fort were subject to considerable European control. Komenda, Fetu and Asebu experienced the greatest impact on their internal affairs. Asebu was an ally of the Dutch at the beginning of the seventeenth century, but subsequently it was more often than not on the side of the English. Komenda remained a fairly constant friend to Dutch interests until relations deteriorated and gave rise to the Dutch/Komenda wars in 1688 and 1694–9. Europeans managed to intervene in the internal affairs of these states by sponsoring rival claimants to political authority. Power changed hands rapidly, and kings could do little other than choose between a pro-Dutch or a pro-English orientation.

Some of the same trends were observable on the eastern Gold Coast, although there were far fewer forts in this area. The greatest impact of foreign trade orientation was understandably at Accra, and after the construction of forts there in the mid-seventeenth century there were responses approximating to those noted in the west. Accra attracted not only Ga and Adangbe but also residents from Akwamu and from as far afield as Denkyira, especially since politico-military developments in the hinterland were creating a refugee problem. Africans linked up with Europeans inevitably came under European patronage and suffered from European intervention. The European presence generated hostilities involving the Ga of Accra, the Adangbe of the coast and those of Krobo, and the Ewe of the trans-Volta region. One classic instance is that of a so-called civil war which broke out in 1777. It enmeshed Africans between Akwapim and Ada. African belligerents knew nothing of the cause of the war: they were only called on by their respective masters, armed and set to fight each other. Of course, Europeans did not want a state of absolute chaos, since that was prejudicial to trade. Thus, it could and did happen that they intervened to halt conflict. For instance, in the years after the flight of the Akwamu rulers, Akwamu soldiers committed acts of brigandage which interrupted trade, and the Dutch hastened to finance Akyem to conduct a search and destroy campaign. Again, it should be noted that Europeans were regularly called upon to fight in the interests of Africans, as perceived subjectively by the combatants.

Within the Ga communities of Accra, socio-political institutions were shaped by the need to accommodate overseas commerce. In the Sempi ward of Accra, the first *mantse* (probably in the last quarter of the seventeenth century) relegated his priestly duties to an assistant in order to be free to negotiate with Europeans. In that same period, the Ga of Osu deserted their *mantse* and created the post of *mankralo* for another junior priest who was free to attend to business with Europeans. These offices and other innovations associated with warfare were borrowed from Akwamu, as previously indicated; and on this section of the coast it was the Akwamu who provided most reference points for socio-political developments during the latter part of the seventeenth century and until the destruction of the Akwamu kingdom in the early 1730s. So long as Akwamu itself was on a conqueror's path, one of the far-reaching consequences was the flight of large numbers of people. The Ga of Ayiwasu began withdrawing to Accra in the 1660s and 1670s. After the defeat at Accra in 1680, the main escape route turned out to be eastwards. The eastwards movement of population across the Gold Coast was nothing new. Traditions indicate movement from places like Asebu and Komenda to what is now Togo, during the sixteenth century and in the early seventeenth century. Emigration was set off by political squabbles, and the Togo hills had ample land and game to serve as attractions.[1] Of course, the Ga and Adangbe had come from the east, so that their flight from Akwamu's power was forcing them to double back on the path along which they had entered the Gold Coast. The Ga of Accra went principally to Little Popo; the Adangbe of Late moved to Aflao on the Togo coast; the Shai refugees went into the Togo hinterland near the Mono river; while other Adangbe from Ladoku went into the Togo hills about 150 kilometres from the coast into what is now the Adangbe district of Eweland. The Ewe were themselves split into dozens of small polities. The Ga-Adangbe came into contact mainly with the Anlo on the coast immediately beyond the Volta and with the Peki and Ho of the near hinterland. Rivalry ensued between the immigrants and their Ewe hosts and also among different sections of the Ga-Adangbe, adding to the already existing conflicts

[1] M. B. K. Darkoh, 'A note on the peopling of the forest hills of the Volta region', *Ghana Notes and Queries*, 1970, no. 11.

in Eweland. Akwamu rulers deliberately encouraged these confrontations, which were very prominent on the eastern Gold Coast at the turn of the eighteenth century. To further complicate matters, it was also at this time that some Ga-Adangbe refugees started trying to return to their Gold Coast homelands.

Akwapim suffered most from the violence unleashed by Akwamu. The majority of small Guan towns in Kyerepong and Late were destroyed and most social achievements were virtually erased between 1677 and 1681, for the Akwapim population had previously achieved a high level of control over the material environment, especially with regard to agriculture, pottery and the working of iron and brass. Their only major failing, from a practical standpoint, was the lack of political centralization. Subsequently, under the hegemony of Akwamu and Akyem, the Akwapim peoples made the transition from loosely organized and priest-led social formations. Remnants of destroyed towns drew together as a means of survival. Guan political nuclei grew in strength partly under Akwamu tutelage and partly as a reaction to oppression from the Akwamu capital, Nyanaoase. Aburi, an Akwamu settler town, also developed a sense of independence. By 1730, dissident elements within Akwapim felt it possible to throw off Nyanaoase rule. They requested assistance from the Akyem Abuakwa ruler, Ofori Panyin, who sent forces under his brother, Ofori Dua. Hostilities lasted for a few years and ended with Akwamu's destruction and the creation of Akyem Abuakwa hegemony. By 1732 most of the Akwamu ruling line had fled eastwards to the Volta, where they subsequently established another kingdom. At the same time, a unified Akwapim state was consolidated. Akyem settlers led by Ofori Dua controlled the stool of the *Akwamuhene* and took charge of administration and finance. For a while, Aburi was the senior division of the state, apparently because its Akwamu settlers had to be conciliated by the new Akyem dynasty. Another group of Akwamu who were residents of Akwapim since the early seventeenth century fought unreservedly for the new state and were rewarded with high office. The right and left wings went to Guan families.

Political centralization among the Ga-Adangbe, too, should probably be dated to the latter part of the seventeenth century and more particularly to the eighteenth century. As authoritative a figure as Reindorf speaks of the Accra kingdom as the earliest on the Gold Coast, and it is conceivable that it existed and was pulverized by Akwamu. However, it is more likely that the Akwamu attacks caused the Ga to realize that scattered rural homesteads offered inadequate defence. The Ga first fell back on the coastal positions of Accra, Osu and Labadi. They came together for self-defence, and this offered the basis for greater political unity. The *mantse* stool was created as a war mascot for a number of families, grouped together in a given ward in Accra. The ensuing socio-political consolidation represents a survival technique, for long after the conquest of 1680 Akwamu committed depredations on Accra. By the time of the demise of the Akwamu empire, the principal Ga *wulomo* at Accra had acquired sufficient stature that he might loosely be termed a 'king'. Significantly, Reindorf himself attested to 'the great improvement of the Akra kingdom in the time of Ayi Kuma Teiko', who led the struggle against Akwamu around 1730, and also during the rule of his successor, Tete Ahene Akwa. However, the limits of the centralization were quite narrow. Accra was never a single military entity, as shown by the fact that there was no *mantse* with powers over the whole town. Political power resided in the wards, and it was the council of stool-holders from these wards which was supreme. Other coastal towns also developed as part of the regrouping triggered by Akwamu. Nungwa, Tema, Ladoku and Prampram attracted additional extended families of Ga-Adangbe to become significant centres of population. Interrelationships between these towns added a new dimension to the politics of the eastern Gold Coast during the eighteenth century.

Meanwhile, state-building in the hinterland was continuing unabated, with Asante moving towards control of Akan territory, once Denkyira was humbled. Akyem was an obvious target, given its support for Denkyira; and Asante armies turned against the Akyem chiefs on the Pra in 1717. The first encounters were disastrous for Asante, and the *Asantehene* was killed in battle. But, on the accession of Opoku Ware, the situation was immediately reversed. The Akyem Kotoku ruler was killed; part of Akyem was annexed; and several Akyem princes removed to Nsuta as Asante hostages. Akyem maintained a semi-independent tributary status with respect to Asante, especially after another defeat in 1742. Were it not for Asante's presence and their own political disunity, Akyem rulers might well have imposed themselves on Akwamu at an earlier date and in a more permanent manner. As it was, once Asante finally tamed Akyem in 1742, it brought the trans-Volta Akwamu into its fold as a client state.

To the west, Asante expanded into what was then and subsequently called the Ivory Coast. It did so by overwhelming Aowin and Sefwi – the former late in 1715 and the latter two years later. Sefwi attacked Kumasi while Opoku Ware was dealing with Akyem in 1717; and it was a tribute to Asante capacity and flexibility that its military command could afford to leave contingents to oversee Akyem, while swiftly withdrawing enough forces to pursue the Sefwi army and defeat it. From 1701 onwards, refugees from Denkyira, Sefwi and Aowin sought shelter on the coast near Appolonia and Assini. Metropolitan Asante subjects also spread out to the south-west. In 1715, there were several thousand Asante in Aowin, comprising an army that had refused to return to Kumasi. More refugees were created when Asante struck the coastal Nzima in 1721. These further stimulated a westward movement of the Nzima along the coast – a movement which was taking place at the expense of the Kwa fishermen of the Aby lagoon, and one which goes at least as far back as the early seventeenth century. At Assini, each new group of Nzima immigrants intermingled with previous newcomers as well as with the original inhabitants. Sometimes, the newcomers were welcomed as guests and kinsmen, while at other times conflict ensued. As a result, the small Akan groups who fled from the power struggles east of the Tano river carried the Twi language and the yam culture across the Comoe and on to the Bandama.

It was on the northern front that Asante achieved its most spectacular advance. Asante foot-soldiers broke out of the forest and successfully tackled the cavalry-using savanna peoples on their own terrain. The first state to be overrun by Asante in the north-west was Wenchi, whose capital fell in 1715. The queen mother was taken prisoner, and many Wenchi residents were re-settled farther south in Aowin and Asante Akyem. The long-established and prestigious kingdom of Bono-Mansu or Tekyiman fell before Asante armies in 1722–3; and very soon afterwards the famous gold-mining and gold-marketing towns of Begho, Banda and Bole passed under Asante control without much resistance. In the case of Begho, internal dissensions had already weakened the state and led to the partial abandonment of the town. Greater difficulties were faced by Asante in relation to Gyaman. The Domaa had proved stubborn opponents of Asante expansion from the early years of Asante settlement in Kwaman. After their expulsion from the Kwaman area by Osei Tutu, they emigrated north-westwards to Abesim, and were still under pressure from Asante in the reign of Opoku Ware. At this time, the Domaa founded the Gyaman kingdom at Bonduku, possibly at the expense of Bono-Mansu and definitely over Nafana, Kulango and earlier Agni Akan residents. The Gyaman polity had a solid material base in gold production, and it proved quite effective militarily in the face of Asante threats. Eventually, however, Opoku Ware achieved a noteworthy victory over Gyaman at Bonduku around 1740. The *Gyamanhene* was killed and many of his followers fled to Kong. This victory gave Asante control of extensive territory up to the Black Volta; and Buna, which lay to the north of this river, was soon brought within Asante's sphere. Once more, the consequences of wars and state-building extended far beyond the locale in which they were taking place – in this case, the Asante and Gyaman territories. One of the key side-effects was the intensification of a southwards Brong trek from the savanna fringes into the forests, giving rise to the Agni (Anyi) and Baule ethnicities covering the entire south-east of the modern Ivory Coast.[1]

A similar record of achievements was set in the north-east and the east. Campaigns were waged against western Gonja in 1732–3, partly motivated no doubt by the help which this region gave to Bono-Mansu in its resistance to Asante. Successful engagements at Yeji and Salaga led to the subjugation of eastern Gonja; and Asante also expanded into Dagomba, Kwahu, Kete Krachi and the Eweland districts on the other side of the Volta (see chapter 3, p. 189).

Asante displayed tremendous military development, not merely in the tactics of battle and the strategy of single campaigns, but also in the broader strategic and logistic sense. Its armies were constantly called upon to fight on several fronts, in varied terrain and in a total operational theatre that was almost as large as modern Ghana. Military intelligence was also a speciality, while Asante diplomacy was as potent as its armed forces. In fighting Bono-Mansu, for instance, Asante first secured the support of Nkoranza and the neutrality of Nsawkaw and Banda. Hostility from any one of these could easily have turned the balance against Asante. Nsawkaw came within Bono's sphere of influence, and was called upon to help in the defence against Asante. But its rulers were persuaded to withdraw by an Asante emissary. Asante also effectively exploited the presence in Nkoranza of members of the Asere clan, who had migrated from Adansi via Kwaman – and some of whose relatives were still resident in metropolitan Asante. Equally striking was Asante's ability to mobilize recently conquered peoples to participate in the succeeding round of conquests.

Peace did not come immediately with the winning of a major battle. Pockets of resistance often remained for a long time, as was the case

[1] G. Rougerie, 'Les Pays Agni du Sud-Est de la Côte d'Ivoire Forestière', *Études éburnéennes*, no. 6 (1957).

with Denkyira and with Akyem after 1717. Besides, Asante's conquests sparked off further conflicts, notably in the north. Between 1732 and 1750, there was a series of wars in the north-west, following the dislocation caused by Asante invasion. Some of these involved Asante subjects or tributaries, who were independently and unauthorizedly participating. Most significant of all was the fact that sporadic rebellion was endemic in the Asante empire in the eighteenth century. For the most part, rulers of conquered states were allowed to remain in power, and they retained a great deal of independence, provided they paid their tribute and supplied military contingents. Through this semi-independence, Denkyira, Wassa, Assin, Aowin and Akyem all found it possible to engage in hostile alliances against Asante, especially since they could combine with the Fante on the coast and the rebellious Brong of the hinterland. Occasionally, states which felt shackled by Asante could find allies farther afield. In 1763, for instance, Akyem made contact with Dahomey, while planning a rebellion with Kwahu and Brong forces. This caused Asante to move against Dahomey, but its forces were ambushed and badly defeated near Atakpame by an army which included Dahomey's famous female cadres. Possibly, some Oyo levies were also involved, because the news which reached Europeans on the coast was that Oyo had defeated Asante. Asante had its revenge on Dahomey, since a visitor to Dahomey in 1803 discovered that 'Dahomey had been extremely humbled by unsuccessful wars with Oyo and Ashanti', although friendly relations seem to have been more usual.[1] In any event, Asante was quite capable of bringing its own subjects to heel. When Osei Kwadwo succeeded Kusi Obodum as *Asantehene* in 1764, opposition was at its height in the empire, due to military reverses and to the fact that the succession period was always utilized as a favourable opportunity for revolt. However, Osei Kwadwo dealt with his enemies in the north and in the south with despatch; and Asante also pursued a successful offensive against the Fante in 1765.

Asante victories marked the ascendancy of the southern Akan over their northern Akan or Brong kinsmen. The Brong had contributed to the physical stock and ruling clans of Asante, Denkyira and probably Akwamu in their formative years. When southern Akan like the Domaa moved north in the seventeenth century, they were incorporated into the Brong culture. The situation was reversed with Asante's rise. Brong rulers adopted the stools, umbrellas, palanquins, swords and

[1] See Adu Boahen, 'Asante-Dahomey contacts', *Ghana Notes and Queries*, 1965, no. 7.

other paraphernalia of the southern Akan; and these were only the external manifestations of the new pattern of acculturation. At the same time, the scattered Guan population was subject to further integration within the Akan fold. Considerable linguistic and social change took place once the Asante empire was created, and only a few pockets of unassimilated elements persisted.

Cultural unity facilitated the working of the provincial administration. Some conquered polities had to be remodelled, usually by depriving them of some territory. Parts of Denkyira and Akyem were annexed, while the Bono-Mansu dynasty remained in power over a much smaller area. In this instance, the territory seized was granted to Nkoranza, a reliable client state; and the new capital, Tekyiman, was brought closer to Nkoranza. On the whole, however, Asante achieved its objectives simply by appointing a few officials, notably toll collectors and supervisors of oaths. They were strategically located at places like Mamfe in Akwapim, which was the junction of important trade routes to and from the coast. This loose sovereignty worked fairly well. At the same time, Asante did gain administratively through its penetration of the northern areas, in that it was able to draw upon the services of Muslim scribes.

The *amanto* states remained as the core of Asante authority. Each one secured a vested interest in given parts of the provinces or tributary areas. Occasionally, *amanto* rulers clashed over a particular province, and such conflicts required the *Asantehene*'s adjudication. Constitutionally, metropolitan Asante retained the character of a union of equal states, but Kumasi moved into a pre-eminent position among the *amanto*. Firstly, the *Kumasihene* was of course simultaneously the *Asantehene*, and as such had greater stature than the other *amanto* heads. Secondly, Kumasi secured a larger share of the spoils of expansion, starting with Denkyira, the earliest of the major conquests. Thirdly, the *Kumasihene* embarked on successful emancipation from the authority of his own council, and this strengthened his position as ruler of Asante. Contradictions with the Kumasi nobles derived from the fact that conquests were placed under their control, making them much more wealthy than their counterparts in other *amanto*. It is said that Opoku Ware gained some insights from the *Tekyimanhene* with regard to his personal elevation above the Kumasi nobles. Claims were made on the estates of deceased nobles, and fines were levied to the benefit of the *Kumasihene*. During the reign of Kusi Obodum (1750–64), the nobility restored the balance in their own favour; but Osei Kwadwo renewed the offensive.

The variety of politico-administrative innovations attributed to him is such that it has been described as 'the Kwadwoan Revolution'.[1] In brief, Osei Kwadwo's measures undermined the hereditary Kumasi chiefs, and replaced them with his own appointees. During this reign and subsequently, the new councillors became professional administrators. The offices often stabilized within given families, the *Kumasihene* maintained control over the stools, and he used these officials for the government of the provinces. Petitioners to the *Asantehene* from various parts of the empire had to seek access through the Kumasi appointees. One of the most powerful new posts was that of the *Gyaasewahene*, who was responsible for the national treasury. Opoku Ware had had to retreat before the military commanders with respect to some of his reform proposals, and it is significant that Osei Kwadwo carried through sweeping changes after creating a permanent military bodyguard directly responsible to himself.

The politico-military dimensions of Asante expansion were inseparable from the economic dynamic. The empire constantly strengthened its productive base with each conquest. After completing the takeover of the southern gold fields, Asante secured access to the Lobi gold fields through its conquests in the Black Volta area and the acquisition of Buna. Simultaneously, Asante came into possession of the major distributive outlets for the gold trade: namely, the centres of population with the Dyula residents. Gold mining techniques probably received a boost also. The Numu ethnic community of Bono-Mansu was a caste with specialist knowledge of mining, and Bono-Mansu had been consciously 'modernizing' its mining by looking to the Bure and Bambuk gold fields of the Western Sudan in the sixteenth and seventeenth centuries. Asante must have had access to these skills after the conquest of Bono-Mansu. The same applied to other sectors of production such as pottery, cloth-making and the casting of brass and bronze – all being more highly developed in the savanna areas. Besides, there were several other commodities which had local significance. For instance, yams constituted a staple that was obtained not merely by subsistence farming but by trade. Apparently, some varieties were imported by Asante from the north, since traditional accounts give as a *casus belli* for the Asante–Bono confrontation the refusal of the latter to allow the export of

[1] Ivor Wilks, 'Aspects of bureaucratization in Ashanti in the nineteenth century', *Journal of African History*, 1966, 7, 2; and 'Ashanti government', in Daryll Forde and P. M. Kaberry (eds.), *West African kingdoms in the nineteenth century* (London, 1967). For qualifications, see George P. Hagan, 'Ashanti bureaucracy', *Transactions of the Historical Society of Ghana*, 1971, **12**.

seed-yams to Asante. Tribute exaction increased the integration of the economy of the region as a whole, with produce such as cattle, shea butter, iron and salt moving towards the centre during the annual *odwira* festivals and during the *adai* festivals which were held every forty days.

There may have been an increase in the economic surplus within the boundaries of the Asante empire over the eighteenth century, but it would be difficult to ascertain and measure. With respect to distribution and consumption, one can infer that the pattern departed further away from egalitarianism. The *amanto* capitals and Kumasi town in particular appropriated the surplus produced over a large area. Kumasi was described by visitors in the early nineteenth century in terms reminiscent of earlier accounts of Benin: namely, populous, clean, and well-endowed with regard to houses and material wealth. At one level, therefore, the increasing inequality in distribution was regional, being based on the transfer to metropolitan Asante of wealth created in the provinces. Furthermore, within Kumasi and the principal towns, wealth was concentrated in the hands of the hereditary rulers and the new administrative élite. A great deal of the surplus was withheld from re-entry into the productive process, in that it was converted into regalia kept under lock and key by the *Asantehene* and other members of the ruling class. Some of it went into the financing of crafts and into the promotion of trade; while the greater portion was either directly consumed by the rulers or redistributed among the population. The undoubted presence of redistributive mechanisms should not obscure the extent of socio-economic differentiation and especially the increase of exploited servile strata. The latter were introduced into Asante society as captives or purchased slaves or tribute goods, as part of the same process of recruitment for sale to Europeans.

For an understanding of the role of slaving and slave trading within the Gold Coast, it is necessary to return to the rise of Akwamu. Ga traditions recall that several of their towns were founded at a time when 'all the earth was spoiled' – by Akwamu's depredations and slave raiding.[1] On the eastern Gold Coast, slaves rather than gold constituted the nexus between the local rulers and the Europeans. Like the other Akan communities, Akwamu was a heavy user of its own gold resources. Gold ornaments were common, and a debased gold known as *kra kra* was standard currency. Akwamu decided not to export its own limited gold holdings, and obtained European imports by selling captives instead. Its eastern conquests shifted interest farther away from the

[1] M. J. Field, *Social organization of the Gã people* (London and Accra, 1940), 72.

gold-rich regions and deeper into the sphere of the Slave Coast. This trend was a boon to European slave merchants, and so too was the conflict between Akwamu and Akyem, when it erupted into violence. Akwamu behaved more like Allada and Whydah than like the other Akan states. It placed a ban on gold exports in 1707; withdrew *kra kra* gold from circulation; and adopted the cowrie currency from the Aja. Akwamu sold slaves for cowries, for European trade goods, and for tobacco and rum from the New World. In the early eighteenth century, the Portuguese and Brazilians were so anxious to obtain slaves that they purchased with Brazilian gold.

Initially, Akwamu rulers may have been selling captives merely as a by-product of their expansionist wars, but it is clear that cause and effect soon became telescoped, and even the distinction between citizens and outsiders was ignored in the process of slave recruitment. Akwamu kings and their chiefs exploited their own subjects intensively. One stratagem was to locate in provincial villages a number of women who were nominally the wives of particular rulers. Once a year, these wives would be visited and asked to 'eat fetish' and confess who had touched them. The offending males were then sold as slaves, unless they were ransomed. These accusations went under the rubric of 'women palavers' in upper Guinea, and they were a generalized feature of slaving in West Africa. In addition, there was widespread man-stealing in areas subjugated by Akwamu. Akwamuhene Ansa Kwao employed about 1,000 'smart boys' for the purpose of catching Akron residents. Europeans plied him with alcohol, which led one observer to remark that 'every year [Ansa Kwao] and his smart boys drank up the value of a couple of thousand people (and these were his countrymen)'.[1] Similar conditions existed over most of the eastern Gold Coast, and followed the establishment of Akwamu hegemony over the inland Ewe and Kwahu early in the eighteenth century. War and slave raiding affected food production around Accra, farmers fearing to extend cultivation inland. Accra residents were therefore obliged to travel to Nungwa, Krobo and places on the Volta to obtain food, and they were liable to be captured while on that undertaking. At the Volta estuary, one of the principal reasons for the long-standing dispute between the Adangbe of Ada and the Anlo of Keta was the pursuit of kidnapping.

The Accra forts served as entrepôts for the slave trade from the time of their construction in the mid-seventeenth century. The trading posts

[1] R. F. Roemer, *The coast of Guinea*, part IV (translation, Institute of African Studies, Legon, 1964).

and forts which arose to the east also specialized in this branch of exploitation, the Danes being in the forefront among the Europeans. They had considerable dealings with both the first and the second Akwamu kingdoms, as well as with the Adangbe and Ewe peoples. The Anlo for a long time refused the Danes permission to build a fort at Keta. This helped determine a Danish alliance with Ada forces in their clashes with the Anlo, notably in the period 1750–67 and again from 1776 to 1782. Although the Danes were the first of the Europeans to consider the epoch of the slave trade to be closed (in 1802), they had been constructing fortifications throughout the 1780s: at Ada and Keta in 1784 and at Teshi in 1787.

Slave trading began making inroads into the western Gold Coast only at the end of the seventeenth century. This must be correlated externally with the increase in demand in the Caribbean and internally with the growth of Fante influence and the rise of the 'merchant princes'. From the 1670s onwards, Europeans (and Englishmen in particular) collected a few slaves from places such as Sekondi and Kormantse so as to make up the complement of ships whose main cargo was acquired elsewhere. In effect, the Gold Coast was at first allocated the role of gold supplier within the international economy of the seventeenth century. Evidence of the end of this era is seen in the increased prices paid for captives on the coast and the relative decrease in prices paid for gold. For a male slave in 1704, the English were offering merchandise to the value of nearly three ounces gold, so that 'the Negroes seeing this, now pay more attention to the slave trade than to the gold trade, as they do better by it'.[1] Twifo, Aowin and Wassa, which were renowned for gold, began to acquire reputations as slave purveyors while under Denkyira overlordship, and this became more marked when Asante achieved dominance. The search for captives and tribute-slaves constituted an additional motivation for waging war, and warfare disrupted the mining and trading of gold. Ports like Assini and Axim ceased offering worthwhile quantities of gold, and instead rose to notoriety as suppliers of slaves; Anomabo was the haunt of English private traders; and Cape Coast Castle was the centre of slave purchases for the Royal African Company. This English company had decided that its main slave-recruiting ground should be the Aja region, but after Agaja Trudo had intervened, the emphasis was shifted to the Gold Coast.

[1] Legon, Furley Collection, Foolscap MS., bk. 1, General William de la Palma, 31 August 1704.

Most of the long line of forts from Axim to Accra were built to facilitate the trade in gold, but they were available to serve a second purpose as slave barracoons. Thus, 4,239 captives passed through Christiansborg Castle between 1687 and 1700. In 1709, the governor of Cape Coast Castle recommended the building of 'a convenient slave-house' within that fort. Forts constructed in the eighteenth century usually had the protection of the European slave trade as their primary rationale. For instance, the French were relative newcomers to the Gold Coast in the early eighteenth century, and in 1717 they were reportedly anxious to obtain a fort to help in the conduct of the slave trade.

The Dutch, with a string of about one dozen forts and factories, maintained interest in gold for the longest period. An account of 1706 indicated that captives were taken to the English and gold to the Dutch. However, in 1711, the Dutch West India Company also started using Akan country as a slave recruiting ground, subsidiary to Allada and Whydah; and, within another decade, slave exports were more important than gold exports even for the Dutch. Throughout the seventeenth century, the Akan exported gold to the value of £200,000 per annum. An Elmina report of 1720 noted that the gold then received was about half what it was about ten to twelve years previously, and it expressed the fear that if prices for slaves continued to rise, the 'Gold Coast' would be transformed into the 'Slave Coast'. According to the Dutch employees, this prediction was realized by 1726. Their assessment was as follows:

> At present the gold trade is so scarce that we hardly get sufficient gold to pay the subsistence of the servants, so that this coast can more properly be called the slave than the gold coast. Your Honours can easily see this from the quick despatch of slave ships: for we have sent them one after the other with their required cargoes to their destinations within 5 weeks.[1]

From September 1701 to April 1704, some 2,300 slaves were ferried by English ships from this part of Guinea. In 1706, it was said that over the previous two and a half years Cape Coast Castle had handled 10,198 captives, and Anomabo was then another growing outlet. It appears that slave exports ran at between 5,000 to 8,000 per annum until 1790, when they declined rapidly.

With the increase of slaving, residents in Akan country took to highway robbery. This assumed disastrous proportions within a few years, so that by 1714 man-stealing had become so common that no

[1] *Ibid.* Dutch Records, bk. II, Elmina, March 1726.

one dared to take to the road without company; and even members of large trading caravans did not necessarily enjoy security. This probably affected the distribution of gold along paths which led to the coast as well as those which led to northern markets. Some Akan groups neglected the search for gold, and instead made war upon each other to obtain captives, because a single marauding expedition held out more promise of easy fortune than the demanding task of mining gold. Besides, the shift away from gold to slaves had cumulative effects. Captives represented a drain of manpower and skills needed in the gold-mining industry; and, by making insecurity endemic, slaving further jeopardized peaceful evolution of agriculture and industry.

Slave extraction not only varied in intensity over the years but it was also spatially uneven. The Akan shifted a great deal of the burden of slaving on to the less well-organized peoples to the north. The Nafana, the Degha and Guan communities scattered south of the Black Volta and along the Volta to Kete Krachi must have suffered considerably, judging from the pattern of Asante warfare. The conquest of Gonja and Dagomba freed Asante from the necessity of continual raiding north of the Volta, because these two relatively strong states themselves pursued the slave recruitment in order to fulfil tribute quotas or to engage in trade with Asante. States that were principal suppliers of slaves often preyed upon residents within their own boundaries, while a more conserving response was to use some of the externally acquired manpower as local labour. Both of these tendencies were manifest on the Gold Coast, the latter more fully than in some other parts of Guinea. During the sixteenth century, the Gold Coast was in the unique position of *importing* captives through the medium of the Europeans. These captives, who were mainly from Benin, were used by the Akan in gold mining, transport and agriculture, and were assimilated within the prevailing family structures. This practice was sufficiently well entrenched for some areas to continue using captured or purchased labour after the net flow of labour had been oriented towards the Americas.

State-building on the Gold Coast was up to the eighteenth century still essentially a process of agglomerating people rather than territory as such. In Akwapim, some of the new centres that emerged during Akwamu's sway were based on a large sector of coerced labour. For instance, the ruler of Mamfe built up a village of captives taken from the surrounding Guan of Kyerepong and Late. This became the principal settlement of the Akyem dynasty which took over leadership of the liberation of Akwapim from Akwamu rule. Akwamu itself was not averse to utilizing captive labour. This was done by the *Akwamuhene* and other chiefs. Their farms supplied agricultural produce which was exchanged on the coast for salt, fish and European goods. However, the contradiction between internal utilization and the continuous supply for export was resolved decisively in favour of the latter. In contrast, Akyem was primarily a gold-producing zone, whose rulers persisted in reducing captives to the position of an indigenous serf-like class. The different policies pursued by Akyem and Akwamu was one of the reasons advanced to explain Akyem's ascendancy over Akwamu, in spite of the latter's political centralization and the relative political disunity that prevailed in Akyem. Outsiders (including Akwamu) who were taken by Akyem were socially integrated within the existing exploited labouring class and within a few years they were regarded as nationals.

Asante became more involved with the European slave trade as the eighteenth century progressed. Yet, at all times it defended and increased the population of metropolitan Asante at the expense of the provinces and more so at the expense of tributaries and areas on the frontiers of their empire. Asante's strength in the eighteenth century is often erroneously attributed to slave raiding. In 1819, Asantehene Osei Bonsu denied that he made 'war to catch slaves in the bush like a thief. My ancestors never did so.'[1] Osei Bonsu's disclaimer is not entirely acceptable, but it is close to the truth, because Asante made slaving largely derivative from its own wars of expansion. Certainly, man stealing – the catching of slaves in the bush like a thief – must have been rare in Asante, because the ruling class protected its own citizens from sale into slavery. Asantehene Osei Kwame (1777–1801) is said to have forbidden the selling of 'real Asantes' from the country. These included captives and their descendants who were domiciled in Asante.

Its strength and independence also allowed Asante to make effective use of European firearms. Firearms became decisive in inter-African rivalry on the Gold Coast towards the middle of the eighteenth century. For instance, the *Asantehene*, Opoku Ware, is said to have ordered several hundred new muskets before the battle with Akyem in 1742. After assiduous practice, Asante marksmen proved their worth, although archery was just as important to the outcome of this confrontation. On the one hand, Asante conquered the coastal states who were armed with muskets for many decades previously. On the other hand, firearms

[1] Joseph Dupuis, *Journal of a residence in Ashantee* (London, 1966), 163.

in Asante's possession did make a difference when it tackled the savanna states, which had not as yet acquired the new weaponry. What mattered, therefore, was that Asante had the social and political strength to maximize the value of the innovation.

Altogether, Asante's development had a degree of independence lacking in most other parts of the Guinea coast. Asante reinforced its links with the Niger bend and Hausaland, and did not elevate European culture or trade goods to a place of primacy. Its rulers were willing to borrow from outside on their own terms. Opoku Ware tried to get Europeans to build factories and distilleries, but of course the response was negative. He also encouraged the import of satins and silks, such as those available from Hausa and Mande traders. These were unravelled so that the threads could be used with local cotton to weave *kente* cloth. This patient operation, which transformed a consumer good into a raw material for manufacture, is as much a highlight of Asante history as its conquering armies; but already it was too late to evolve independently of Europe, as events in the nineteenth century were soon to prove.

CHAPTER 5

CENTRAL AFRICA FROM CAMEROUN TO THE ZAMBEZI

THE NORTHERN SAVANNA AND FOREST

In the seventeenth and eighteenth centuries the northern fringes of Central Africa[1] presented a totally different picture from that of West Africa. Here there were no great population clusters, no expansive cavalry empires, no walled cities and no markets thronged with caravans from the coast or the Maghrib. There were no kingdoms like Benin and Dahomey and no mines as in Bambuk and Asante. The area had no wealth or minerals sufficient to attract traders across the Sahara. Only in the nineteenth century was its border pierced by Khartoum ivory hunters and Fulani slave raiders. Until that time the occupants of the northern savanna were almost exclusively concerned with subsistence agriculture. Even peoples like the Azande, who expanded the scope of their territory, did not expand the scope of their social institutions. Instead each advance swarm of Zande colonial pioneers cut itself off from its parent society and began a new, independent, political existence. Not until the nineteenth century did the Bandia clan create the Bangassou 'sultanate' in order to resist the encroachments of slavers.[2]

In the west, North-Central Africa had a small opening on to the maritime world of lower Guinea. This was through the Cameroun port of Duala. The small coastal kingdom of the Duala appears to have been founded by Bantu-speaking peoples from the surrounding forest in the early seventeenth century. They moved to the coast when the first Dutch sailors penetrated the Bight of Biafra seeking trade in exotic African curiosities. The Duala sold them local cloth, beads, and probably ivory, and furnished their ships with grain and goat's meat. The

[1] Central Africa has meant different places to different peoples at different times. To Heinrich Barth it meant the Chad basin, to many English-speakers it meant the Zambezi region, and in Belgium the term describes the Congo basin. In this work Central Africa includes the three sub-regions of North-Central Africa (from the Nigeria-Cameroun border eastward to the Central African Republic and southward into the equatorial forest), West-Central Africa (the lower Congo and western Angola), and South-Central Africa (southern Zaïre, eastern Angola and Zambia). The emphasis is on West-Central Africa, which is better documented than either the northern or the southern parts of Central Africa during this period.

[2] Eric de Dampierre, *Un ancien royaume Bandia du Haut-Oubangui* (Paris, 1967).

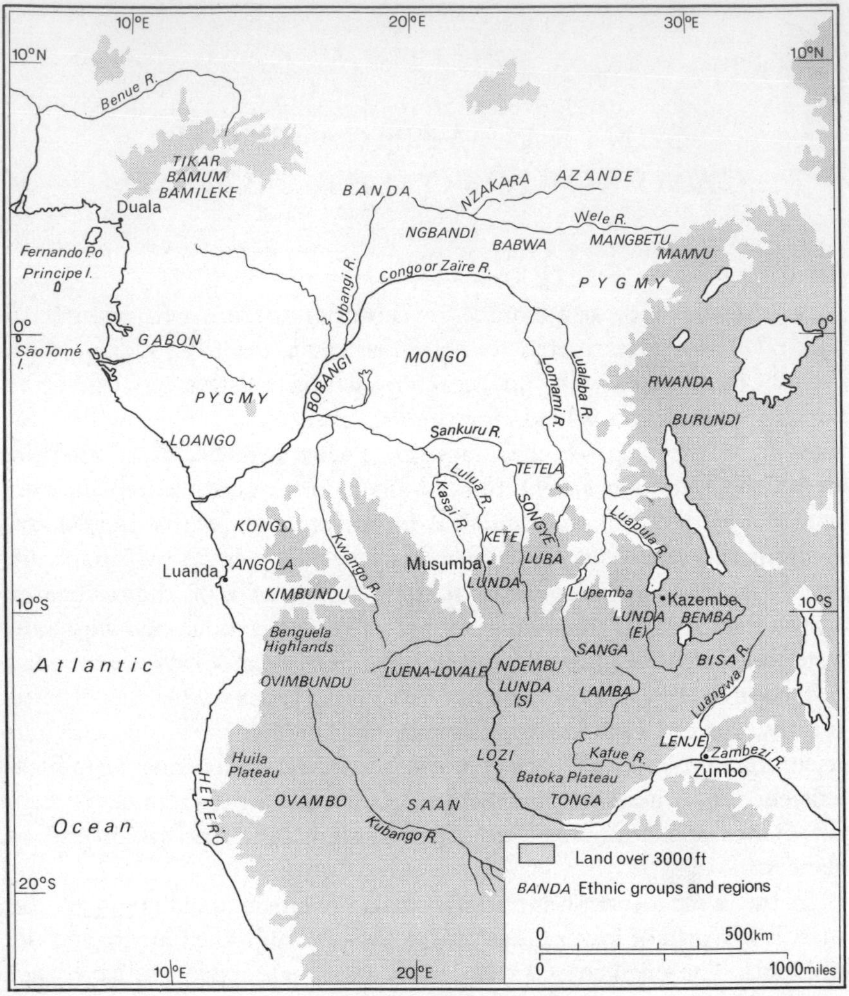

10 Central Africa

Dutch were not especially interested in slaves, but in 1614 a ship's surgeon bought four young men as supplementary crew. He paid one pitcher of Spanish wine for them, and they soon learnt fluent Dutch and became effective sailors. The extent to which Duala trade influenced neighbouring peoples of the equatorial hinterland is quite uncertain. In the Cameroun highlands, small kingdoms such as Tikar and Bamum arose during the eighteenth century, but it is not established that their prosperity was influenced by trade with either the Duala coast, or the Hausa market towns of Nigeria. The most fertile and prosperous part of the Cameroun highlands was occupied by the Bamileke. It was not, however, until the nineteenth century, and later, that population growth began to drive these enterprising peoples from their overcrowded farms, to seek commercial employment along the coast.[1]

External relations – whether with the Atlantic or the Sahara – were of much lesser concern to the peoples of the northern savanna in the seventeenth and eighteenth centuries than were their relations with forest neighbours to the south. Both the Central Sudanic-speaking peoples in the east, and the Eastern Nigritic-speaking peoples, who, at a very remote date, had apparently overflowed into North-Central Africa from the west, made attempts to colonize the forest borders.[2] Most successful, perhaps, were the Mangbetu in the north-eastern corner of modern Zaïre. Their flourishing banana economy was enhanced by an active relationship with their pygmy neighbours. The hunters supplied them with more meat than their own herds of goats could provide, and in return received iron wares and vegetable produce. Less successful than the Mangbetu were a related Central Sudanic-speaking people called the Mamvu. When the Mamvu penetrated the forest they came into contact with the Bantu-speaking Babwa. The Babwa had already adapted their agricultural economy very effectively to forest living, and saw no attraction in entering into a symbiotic relationship with the Mamvu, as the pygmies did with the Mangbetu. Instead many Bantu farmers absorbed Central Sudanic-speaking immigrants into their own societies. In some cases Bantu domination of their neighbours may even have led to temporary Bantu colonization of savanna areas beyond the northern border of the forest.

Along the western sector of the forest boundary, the influence of Eastern Nigritic-speaking peoples seems to have been stronger than that of Bantu speakers. Already in the past Eastern Nigritic-speaking peoples had expanded at the expense of Central Sudanic ones. Now they expanded into Bantu-speaking areas as well, carrying Ngbandi and other savanna languages to the forest peoples, and adopting in return the South-East Asian complex of forest crops. Some of the influence of Eastern Nigritic-speaking peoples may have spread far beyond the forest borderland and brought new cultural attributes to peoples deep in the forest. A more important cultural interaction in these southerly regions of the forest was between Bantu and pygmy. Many pygmies

[1] Edwin Ardener, 'Documentary and linguistic evidence for the rise of trading polities between Rio del Rey and Cameroons 1500–1650', in I. M. Lewis (ed.), *History and social anthropology* (London, 1968).

[2] The speculative ethno-linguistic terminology and its historical implications for North-Central Africa is adapted from Greenberg and Murdock. The classification is subject to caution, but so far only methodological criticisms rather than constructive alternatives have been offered.

were absorbed into Bantu communities, taking with them their forest crafts and influencing the genetic characteristics of their hosts. Other pygmies retained a separate identity, but exchange relationships with the Bantu led to slow acculturation. By the nineteenth century pygmies apparently had no distinct languages but spoke that of their neighbours. A marked case of close interchange of peoples and cultures occurred among the Mongo and their pygmoid clients, at the very heart of the Congo basin. Among these same Mongo, however, there were traits of northern influence which might even be attributable to a southward spread of Eastern Nigritic-speaking peoples. Some amateur ethnographers have even thought to discern northern influences among peoples of the southern forest such as the Tetela. In this area, however, more important cultural changes came from the south. In the seventeenth century, and more dramatically in the eighteenth century, the southern forest began to receive immigrants and refugees from the great southern savannas of Central Africa. These immigrants brought with them not only new political forms, such as the kingship which evolved among the Kuba, but a whole new series of American food-crops, which were almost as well suited to tropical forest conditions as they were to the moist southern savanna.[1]

THE KONGO KINGDOM

The first savanna area to receive the new crops, and to be disturbed by events which caused long-distance migration, was the lower Congo region. The lower Congo was one of the more favoured areas of Central Africa. Several localities, such as Nsundi, south of the river, and Mayombe to the north of it, had fertile soils, reliable water supplies, and prosperous populations of farmers and fishermen. Only in the marginal forests of the north were there peoples who still relied primarily on the gathering of wild plants for their vegetable foods. Elsewhere, even in the eastern forests of the Kwango, agriculture had long since become the primary economic activity. The predominance of agriculture over hunting, fishing and collecting, had further increased in the lower Congo during the sixteenth century by the introduction of maize and cassava from tropical America. Although the new crops did not replace the indigenous millets, their obvious success as staple foods in the neighbourhood of Portuguese trading posts led to their wider adoption. In the less populated areas the economic importance of the

[1] Jan Vansina, *Introduction à l'ethnographie du Congo* (Kinshasa, 1966) contains ethnographic data, historical speculation and bibliographical notes for the forest area.

hunter probably continued to match his social prestige. Where population grew, however, and game became scarce, the major source of meat was small domestic stock. Very few parts of the lower Congo were suitable for cattle-keeping, and great chiefs who wanted large livestock to enhance their status, had to import cattle from highland country in the south.

The basic economic activities of the lower Congo peoples showed a fundamental uniformity, but over and above the subsistence level there was a series of specialized economic pursuits which relied on regional resources. Some areas produced baskets, others dried fish, others pottery. The metal and textile industries were dependent on local materials and local skills.[1] In addition to the local economic differences, there were important political differences between the areas north and south of the Congo river. The main kingdom of the north was Loango. The south was wholly dominated by the single kingdom of Kongo. During the sixteenth century, Kongo had been brought into intimate contact with maritime traders from Portugal, and had been effectively compelled to participate in the Atlantic slave trade. Loango, on the other hand, had a more limited experience of early European contacts, and preserved more of its traditional economic and political customs.

In the seventeenth century each responded in its own way to renewed and increased European influence. Although Kongo had been partly successful in absorbing the early alien influences, it now began to falter and crack under the demoralizing impact of intensified slave trading and intervention in its affairs by the Portuguese colonies of São Tomé island, in the north, and Angola, on the mainland to the south. Loango was more successful in retaining its integrity, and in controlling its economic relations with the Atlantic powers. As the political and economic strength of Loango increased, so its influence spread into the northern interior. At the end of the seventeenth century, when Kongo had virtually disappeared as a commercial kingdom, Loango extended its economic control to dominate a new pattern of southern trade routes as well.

In the early seventeenth century, the Kongo kingdom was still remarkably similar to the state first visited by the Portuguese a century before. Its internal structure was still recognizable, with six major provinces and a machinery of government centred on the king. The limits of the kingdom still stretched to the Congo river in the north, and to Luanda

[1] See *Cambridge history of Africa*, volume 3, chapter 8, for more detailed information about the traditional economy of this area.

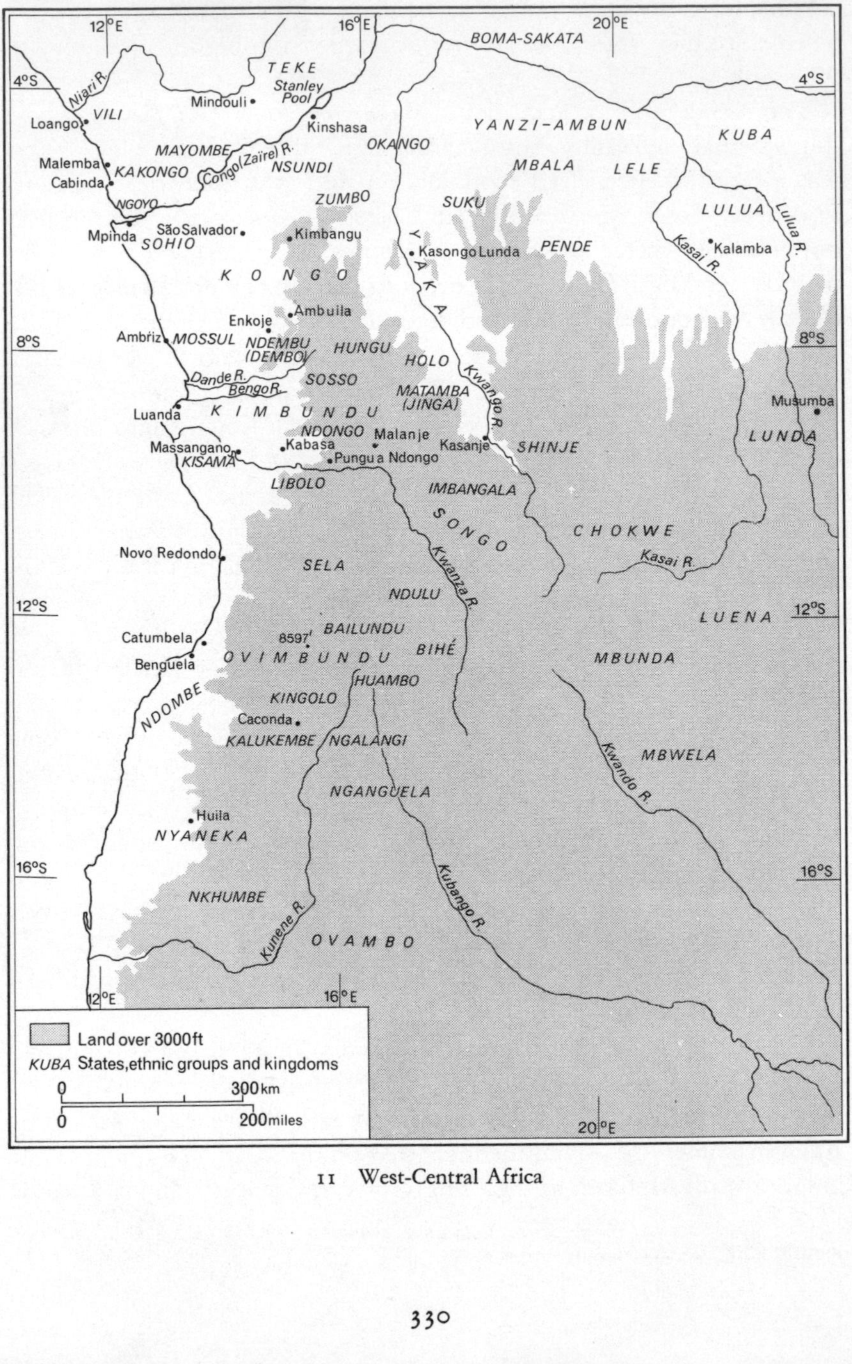

11 West-Central Africa

in the south. The changes which had occurred in Kongo during the first 100 years of Portuguese contact had not undermined its essential unity. In 1600 the king of the Kongo kingdom was Alvaro II. He was a man of vigour and intelligence who ruled from 1587 to 1614. During this long, uninterrupted reign he became an experienced administrator, and under his guidance the Kongo began to look outward on the world with increasing sophistication.

During the sixteenth century a small foreign community of traders, teachers and priests from Portugal had been built up in Kongo. The descendants and successors of these pioneers formed a Luso-African community whose role in the country was useful, if sometimes ambiguous. Their loyalty, in particular, was distinctly volatile, and they tended to maintain their own economic and social status by playing off the interests of Kongo against those of Portugal. Thus the price which Alvaro had to pay for foreign technical assistance was a diminution of sovereignty. Even more irksome to Alvaro than the potential disloyalty of his semi-European middle-class subjects, was Portuguese control of his foreign relations. So long as he was dependent on Portuguese ships for all external communication, whether commercial or diplomatic, he could not create any counterbalance to their influence. His ancestors had sought to resolve the dilemma by acquiring their own ships, but never with any degree of success. Alvaro sought to open diplomatic relations with non-Portuguese foreigners as a means of breaching his isolation.

Alvaro's first opening was in ecclesiastical diplomacy. To demand better Christian facilities for his people could hardly be construed as disloyalty by the most Catholic king of Portugal. On the other hand, domination of the Kongo church by the bishops of São Tomé had been harmful to Kongo's interests. The Tomistas, including their bishops, were primarily concerned to obtain slaves cheaply and plentifully from Kongo. In order to do so they attempted to subvert the Kongo state monopoly of external trade. For such a committedly mercenary bishop to be the ultimate moral and ecclesiastical authority in Kongo caused fierce resentment at São Salvador, the Kongo capital. Alvaro's father had sought to solve the problem by requesting the creation of a separate Kongo bishopric, and in 1596 his son succeeded in obtaining the concession. Although this move weakened the ecclesiastical power granted to Portugal under the *padroado*, Alvaro's success was less than complete. The first titular bishop of São Salvador was still a Portuguese subject, and Alvaro had to begin a new campaign to persuade the pope that

Portuguese bishops were liable to identify themselves with the interests of Portuguese nationals, notably the new settlers then arriving in Angola. To make his point, Alvaro sent an African ambassador, Antonio Manuel ne Vunda, to Pope Paul V. The ambassador, however, was detained three years in Lisbon, thus highlighting Alvaro's crippling dependence on Portuguese communications. He eventually proceeded to Rome under escort, but died before he could expose the ecclesiastical abuses in Kongo. Alvaro thus failed to break his diplomatic isolation. Even his success in getting a bishop nominated to São Salvador was short-lived. Within a few years the bishops transferred their seat informally to Luanda, where they found more comfortable quarters among their compatriots in the colonial capital of Angola.[1]

Despite this setback, Alvaro continued to seek support for his church. The Christian commitment of Kongo kings was in all probability less a matter of personal belief than one of diplomatic status within the Catholic commonwealth of nations. Kongo kings were anxious to show sufficient Christian enthusiasm to maintain the credibility of their Christian status, yet they did not want to damage the hallowed customs of themselves or their subjects. To maintain world recognition, Alvaro therefore requested the dispatch of new missionaries to Kongo. Three Dominicans eventually arrived and were received by the Duke of Bamba who greeted them with drums and royal bells. They were given hens, goats, food and two million small brown *nzimbu* shells to cover the expenses of their journey by hammock-carrier along the sparsely populated road to the capital. They found São Salvador flourishing and fertile, and estimated that the metropolitan region could raise 25,000 fighting men. The power and prestige of King Alvaro was at this time considerable. His immediate subjects worked hard to support the court and cultivate its surroundings. His provincial governors were still heavily dependent on the royal patronage for their positions. The king controlled the rural clergy, and priests were maintained in each provincial capital, as well as in the important 'kingdom' of Okango, on the caravan route to Kinshasa. Since the king remained so very powerful, the Dominicans soon found that the real positions of influence were among his personal servants and retainers at court. The major rival to the court had become the new cathedral. It had attached to it twelve priests paid out of revenue due to the Portuguese crown. This endeavour to maintain an autonomous Portuguese ecclesiastical in-

[1] Sigbert Axelson, *Culture confrontation in the lower Congo* (Uppsala, 1970), contains full references to the extensive literature on the ecclesiastical history of Kongo.

fluence, and to make foreign priests independent of royal Kongo patronage, had some success. The independence of the cathedral priests was a flaw in the royal absolutism, and yet the kings were dependent on the priesthood for the Christian elements of their legitimacy and for the rituals of their enthronement.

The foreign missionaries were not the only Christian factor in the Kongo political situation. There had also emerged a limited number of African and mestizo priests who were able to exercise considerable power over the partially Christianized peoples of the towns. Their influence was frequently considered by foreign observers to be pernicious, but no independent Kongo testimonies shed light on their role. What appeared pernicious and even treasonable to foreigners may well have appeared to Kongo peoples as highly patriotic. This rivalry of indigenous and foreign clerics was accentuated when the mestizo priests in São Salvador, seeing their influence threatened by the better-educated white Dominicans, persuaded Alvaro II to reverse his policy and evict them. Despite this episode, however, mission policy still vacillated in São Salvador, and Alvaro III (1614–22) succeeded in attracting Jesuits into the country in 1619. For a time the power of the mestizo clergy was eclipsed by an influential Portuguese priest, Bras Correia, who became confessor to the king. He played a dominant role in the country's internal politics, and in the succession dispute of 1622 apparently placed his own nominee on the throne. His role, however, was resented not only in Kongo, but also in Luanda where the Portuguese expected him to defend their interests rather than his own.

Alvaro II's search for external openings was not limited to an ecclesiastical foreign policy. He also sought tangible technical aid from the governments of Spain and Portugal. His requests for smiths, masons and craftsmen were all refused lest he build strategic fortifications against Portuguese military interventions. Alvaro also requested that a captain of the Portuguese foreign community in Kongo be appointed who would be independent of São Tomé and Angola. He would receive a public letter of instruction clearly setting out policy on matters of extra-territorial rights. The Portuguese government rejected this request, and expressed concern that Portuguese should be allowed to reside in Kongo at all, since they were liable to impart military skill and firearm technology to potential enemies of Portugal. Since a withdrawal of all Portuguese was impractical, however, the government in Lisbon recommended that a captain should be appointed. His secret terms of reference would require him to group all the

Portuguese settlers and their women and children in a single, well-enclosed quarter of São Salvador, preferably with a fort for its defence. The captain should be quite free of any grace or favour from the king, and should be replaced in the event of a vacancy by a Portuguese officer from São Tomé or Angola, precisely in the manner Alvaro most resented. This attempt to apply to the traders the West African policy of political disengagement, and military autonomy, did not work. It was clearly inappropriate when the main trading centre was not on the coast but 150 kilometres inland. Traders therefore remained dependent on royal recognition before they could obtain the freedom to travel on business expeditions. Alvaro must have been aware of the traders' dependence when he sought to build up the foreign community to his own advantage. Rather curiously, he requested that he be allowed to expel all Jews from his kingdom, and asked that new immigrants be sent in their place, particularly white women who would marry existing settlers and strengthen the settler community. His policy was of course opposed by Portugal. A growing European community at São Salvador would only strengthen the king's position vis-à-vis his undeclared opponents in the new Portuguese colony of Angola.

Angola became the major subject of concern in Alvaro's external policy. The negotiations outlined above show clearly that, beneath the niceties of diplomatic exchange between equal allies, lay the realities of a rivalry which verged on war. The bitterness of this rivalry was emphasized when Alvaro sent a Portuguese subject, who had attempted to assassinate him, to Luanda for punishment. Instead of receiving punishment, the man was rewarded by the governor and set free. One bone of contention between Kongo and Angola was Luanda island. Although only a stone's throw from the Angolan capital, this island belonged to Kongo and was the source of its currency shells. The Kongo right to the island was commonly recognized by Luanda governors, but João Furtado de Mendonça had none the less granted land on the island to a monastery, and had justified his action by saying that the site would only be used for temporary straw huts in which to baptize slaves. Some claimants to island plots said that Alvaro I had granted the island, or part of it, to Angola in return for the great expense incurred on Kongo's behalf by Portugal during the Jaga wars (see volume 3, chapter 8). A further irritant to the growing conflict between Kongo and Angola, was the land along the lower Bengo and Dande rivers. These plains were suitable for cultivation, unlike most of the coastal strip, and Portuguese governors had been granting gardens to settlers. Alvaro II protested at the infringement of his sovereignty, while the settlers denounced Kongo expansionism. Another confrontation between Kongo and Angola occurred over mining. Alvaro had tried to interest the pope in copper mines during his search for ecclesiastical allies. When that failed, he turned to the Portuguese for skilled mining engineers. At the time, the Portuguese were disillusioned with mines after thirty years of fruitless conquest and mineral prospecting in Angola. The offer did, however, slowly rekindle the old popular belief in Kongo's mineral riches. In the imagination of many, the vision was transformed from copper to gold mines.

In 1622 the various tensions which had been developing between Kongo and Angola finally led to war. The attack was launched by João Correia de Souza, then acting governor of Angola. Correia probably hoped to improve the forward defence of the settlers' farms in the frontier valleys, and perhaps to gain intelligence about Kongo's mineral prospects. He may also have hoped to put a weak king of his own choice on the Kongo throne. A more immediate factor, however, was probably a desire to use his temporary governorship to make a quick profit out of the slave trade. The southern provinces of Kongo were by this time better populated than the war-torn hinterland of Angola, and Correia may have hoped to capture large numbers of war prisoners. In this he was probably spurred on by his auxiliary troops. The role of these black mercenaries, known as 'Jagas', in the war of 1622 left a marked impression on the Kongo folk memory. Plunder was an essential ingredient of the economy of these Portuguese auxiliaries, and their desire to raid the fertile provinces of southern Kongo may have required little encouragement from the Portuguese.

Whatever the motive for the war of 1622, its results were decisive and far-reaching. Although the invaders failed to capture any mining regions, the campaign reinforced a belief in the mines, which became the cause or excuse for a series of wars between Angola and Kongo over the next fifty years. The governor and his captains captured numerous slaves, thus demonstrating the profitability of raiding, despite the protests of the traders whose security they endangered. The war marked the end of the uneasy peace which had persisted between Angola and Kongo during the reigns of Alvaro I and Alvaro II, and the beginning of hostilities which eventually would lead to the destruction of the Kongo monarchy in 1665.

The war of 1622 had another effect which was to prove damaging to the very Portuguese who had initiated it. It undermined the basis of the whole trading system they had evolved in West-Central Africa. The basic essential for a flourishing trade was relatively unhindered access to the main sources of supply, many of which were on the northern and eastern fringes of Kongo. Caravans led by *pombeiros* (trading agents of Portuguese, mestizo or African origin) were dispatched from the business houses of Luanda with trade goods from Europe and India. Within Kongo these agents dealt with resident Portuguese-speaking intermediaries, or went through the kingdom to the frontier fairs. It was estimated that in 1622 there may have been as many as 1,000 'Portuguese' trading agents in Kongo with their own villages, farms and extended African families. When the governor of Angola invaded the southern provinces, xenophobic attacks were launched on many of these establishments. Pedro II, the new Kongo king, intervened to protect many individual Portuguese merchants, while at the same time declaring war on Angola. His success was limited, and many 'Portuguese' were killed or driven out. The king rightly saw this as a weakening of his own authority. The former prestige of Europeans, the influence of the Christian religion, and above all the ability of traders to supply foreign consumer goods, made the Portuguese presence in Kongo a valuable tool of the monarchy. The basis of this Portuguese presence, which had contributed to the long stable reign of Alvaro II, was now being eaten away by the predatory ambitions of the governor of Angola.

The war of 1622 marked the collapse of the diplomatic manoeuvres initiated by Alvaro II and Alvaro III. They had been unable to establish an effective alliance with the papacy, and had failed to persuade the Hapsburg rulers of Portugal to modify the semi-hostile attitude which had developed towards Kongo since the establishment of Angola. It was developments in an entirely different, and unexpected, direction which began to alter the situation in Kongo's favour and postpone her day of reckoning with Angola. By the closing years of the sixteenth century, English, French and Dutch corsairs had begun raiding the Portuguese settlements on the coast of West-Central Africa, and on the islands of Principe and São Tomé. After 1600, expeditions culminated in the development of regular trade to Kongo's western province of Sohio, where the Dutch established factories. Alvaro II welcomed this sudden and unexpected commercial break-through, which gave him an alternative outlet for his own goods and a new source of European imports. Competition led to a rise in export prices, a drop in import prices, and a new appreciation of such commodities as ivory and dyewood. The

Portuguese naturally reacted strongly against their loss of monopoly. They threatened in vain to build a fort at Mpinda, the Sohio port, in order to exclude by force the competition which they were unable to defeat by economic advantage. They warned the Kongo of the moral dangers of associating with heretics, and called on the bishop to threaten Alvaro III if he tolerated Dutch traders in his kingdom.

The success of the Dutch soon presented the Kongo kings with a new problem. Their trade was mostly conducted through the province of Sohio, which had previously been in decline after the main caravan route from São Salvador had been diverted southwards to Luanda. Under Dutch influence, Sohio now revived. Mpinda acquired schools and a priest to run the church. The count of Sohio and his advisers wore fine oriental cloaks, and hats, and gold chains of office in which to receive the Dutch merchants.[1] This new affluence enabled Sohio to become increasingly independent of the Kongo central king. The count began effectively to challenge the principle of monopoly state trading which had theoretically been espoused by both Kongo and Portugal throughout the sixteenth century. The count, more even than the king, was immune to Portuguese threats. He was also relatively immune to threats from his suzerain. The advent of a second trading power thus created a major rift in the kingdom. It was to be followed during the seventeenth century by other divisions.

The war of 1622, and the death of Alvaro III in the same year, marked the end of a long period of relative stability during which the centralized nature of Kongo government remained clearly recognizable. Thereafter centrifugal tendencies became paramount and the centre weakened. Over the next nineteen years, six kings succeeded each other to the throne, and factional struggles became severe. Each faction not only claimed a right to the central throne but simultaneously, though inconsistently, claimed independent rights over individual provinces. Newly introduced European titles of nobility proliferated and new provinces were created. To add strength to the factions, provincial courts were able to welcome and protect some of the 'Portuguese' traders who had fled from the capital. The process whereby trade had strengthened the central monarchy was now transferred to the smaller centres of power. Each state attempted to develop its own monopoly trading, to tax the flow of goods through its lands, and to hinder the business of its rivals.

[1] K. Ratelband (ed.), *Reizen naar West-Afrika van Pieter van der Broecke 1605–1614* (The Hague, 1953).

The next turning point in Kongo history occurred in 1641, when the growing fragmentation was temporarily curbed. By that year, the Dutch had become such large-scale slave consumers that their trade with Sohio was insufficient to meet the demands of their American colonies. They therefore sent an armed fleet from Brazil which captured Luanda in August 1641. In the same year, Garcia II came to the throne of Kongo and began to reconsolidate central power. His reign, from 1641 to 1661, marked the last phase of effective Kongo unity. It also re-emphasized many of the old and deep-rooted problems which contact with European culture had brought to his country. Among the foremost of these was the question of conflicting religious practices. In the traditional structure of Kongo, religion obviously played an important role in the never-ending search for security and for protection against famines, disasters and epidemics. When court circles began to adopt alien religious customs, they were in constant danger of cutting off their traditional grass-roots support by neglecting ancestral religious values and rites. However arbitrary and authoritarian Kongo monarchs may have appeared to European observers, they were nevertheless political figures who had to secure some element of acquiescence from the peoples they ruled. A king closely associated with religious achievements became stronger and more acceptable; if he attempted further to increase his influence by adopting the substance or trapping of European religions, he could still not afford to neglect his traditional religious roots. Garcia II was fully conscious of his religious dilemma.

On the Christian side, Garcia sought to attract the Jesuits back to São Salvador in order to foster European education. He also approached the Italian Capuchins, whom the papacy had long been hoping to send to Kongo, and in 1645, while Portugal was preoccupied in a bitter war with Spain, and when Angola was under Dutch occupation, the first Capuchin mission slipped into the country despite Portuguese protests. Although a Capuchin mission had the advantage, from Garcia's point of view, of being non-Portuguese, it soon showed the marked disadvantage that its members were more numerous, and travelled more widely in the rural areas, than their predecessors had done. They came into regular contact with traditional forms of worship which they condemned with vigour. In 1653 Georges de Geel was killed for interfering with local shrines, and Garcia had to protect the Capuchins. Later in his reign the king had to turn more openly to traditional religious practices for support, and became known as *kimpaku*, the sorcerer. The acceptance of Christian monogamy would, if strictly applied, have precluded his consolidation of royal authority by multiple marriage ties. The church might also have interfered in the royal succession, which the missionaries interpreted through European concepts of family legitimacy, rather than as a Kongo custom of political selection among eligible clan members. Worse still the church tended to favour candidates for sectarian interests, rather than national ones, and so in the latter part of his life Garcia was in constant conflict with the missions.

During the first seven years of Garcia's reign, Kongo had a respite from the pressing problem of its relations with Angola. Under Dutch occupation, Angola showed little of the expansionist ambition of the preceding period. Garcia's most aggressive challenger was his own western province of Sohio, fortified by its special relationship with the Dutch. After a series of wars, battles and skirmishes, Garcia was forced to recognize Sohio independence. Peace did not long survive, for in 1648 the Portuguese returned to Luanda determined to press ahead with the subjugation of the Kongo kingdom which had so treacherously supported their Dutch enemies. Garcia tried to forestall war with diplomacy, and proposed a peace treaty. He wanted the Kongo episcopal see to be restored to São Salvador, and the continuance of the Capuchin mission to be safeguarded. He wanted the integrity of his kingdom to be guaranteed against dismemberment and border raids. He asked that a just price be established for all trade goods coming into his kingdom and that judges be appointed to examine all slaves leaving it to ensure that no freemen were captured. Finally, he wanted a stop put to the importation of foreign shells, which were causing inflation to his *nzimbu* currency.

In Luanda, Salvador de Sá, the conquering governor, rejected Garcia's proposals as impertinent and made counter proposals revealing his own basic interests. Territorially he demanded that Ambuila, the Dande valley, and Luanda island, be transferred to Angola as payment for war damages during the Dutch occupation. Commercially his major concern was the free flow of trade across Kongo. He demanded that Portuguese cloth, salt and slaves be given tax-free transit across the whole kingdom without obligation to ferry dues or other levy. A single and unique duty would be levied on the Angola border. Furthermore the charge for porters must be reduced to its pre-war level and porters must be compelled to carry goods to their destination, and not to some half-way point. This concern with porters' fees and local customs dues was critical for the Luanda traders. Only as an afterthought did they seek control of the copper mines (invariably called gold mines) by offering Garcia the option to retain his *nzimbu* fisheries in return for the transfer of the mines to Portugal. One further clause demanded that all Kongo connections with Europe pass through Luanda, thus permitting the Portuguese to restrict any further activities by the Dutch or the Capuchins.[1]

Garcia initially rejected these Portuguese proposals despite the precarious position in which he had been left by the Dutch withdrawal. As the Portuguese and Brazilians rebuilt their military strength in Angola, Garcia recognized his weakness and signed the Luanda terms. He did not, however, accept the offer to exchange Luanda for the copper mines, and these became a new excuse for Portuguese encroachment during the next decade of simmering dispute. The country's troubles were also increased at this time by the introduction of the plague. In 1661 Garcia died and was succeeded by Antonio I, and four years later full-scale war broke out anew between Kongo and Angola. Antonio called up men from every province and reputedly raised 70,000 supporters reinforced by about 200 white and mestizo musketeers. He met the Angolan army at Ambuila on 29 October 1665. The Angolans, with some 360 'Portuguese' and 7,000 Africans won the day, allegedly killing 400 Kongo noblemen, including Antonio himself. The first effect of the battle was a wave of attacks on European settlements throughout Kongo and a mass exodus of traders. The Portuguese did not, or could not, follow up their victory by seeking and exploiting the copper mines. Neither did they attempt to establish a colonial government based on garrisons of small forts as in conquered Angola. They did try to control the coastal province of Sohio, but after a brief moment of success their invading force was decisively routed in 1672. Instead of imposing control over the kingdom, the Portuguese waited, ready to buy slaves from the warring factions which emerged.

The tensions which caused the breakdown of Kongo after the death of Antonio I had been in evidence for some years. The country had been producing or marketing a large share of the 15,000 or so slaves which were taken out of the lower Congo area each year. As exactions grew, villages revolted against their chiefs in protest against slavery, against labour dues, against carrier services and against tribute. The

[1] Garcia's peace proposals were drawn up in São Salvador on 19 February 1649. A copy may be found in the archives of the Vatican's Propaganda Fide, S.R.C.G., vol. 249, fols. 4–4v. and is reproduced in A. Brásio, *Monumenta Missionaria Africana*, x (Lisbon, 1965), 326–8. Salvador de Sá's response was allegedly drafted on 13 April 1649 and is reprinted in Ralph Delgado, *Historia de Angola*, III (Lobito, 1953), 64–9.

chiefs, in their turn, revolted against the impositions of regional governments and the demands of royal factions which pretended to live in royal pomp. At each level, tax had either to be collected by force, thus raising the level of violence and counter-violence, or to be forfeited, thus weakening the power and prestige of authority. The extent to which the government hierarchy had become a chain of greater and lesser oppressors of the people may have been exaggerated by the Capuchin witnesses, but after the death of Garcia II oppression appeared to grow beyond controlled bounds, and after 1665 no central government could effectively limit the powers of increasingly small and fragmented chiefdoms. Three factions claimed the Kongo throne, though none occupied São Salvador. The contenders were not only divided in their territorial hold on different parts of the kingdom, but were split between hostile groups on clan affiliations. The Kimpanzu clan with intermittent Sohio support, attempted to regain power after the long reign of Garcia II and of Antonio I, who belonged to the Kimulaza clan. This western bid to restore the old royal clan was stopped by a series of rival northern kings who established their capital at Lemba, near Matadi. This northern influence was in turn supplanted by an eastern dynasty from Mount Kimbangu. In 1709, after numerous wars, assassinations, and intrigues, the Kimbangu faction regained São Salvador and placed Pedro IV on the throne. His victory, however, was modest, for although the Kongo monarchy retained considerable prestige, the real power of Pedro's successors declined steadily during the eighteenth century. Indeed Pedro himself might never have achieved such wide recognition had it not been for a curious religious revival in the kingdom.[1]

The Italian Capuchin missionaries had been spreading their Christian message through the main provinces of Kongo ever since 1645. Their efforts were greatly impeded by the jealousy of the Portuguese missions, by the catastrophe of Ambuila, where the only Mukongo Capuchin priest was killed, by the civil wars that followed the death of Antonio, and by the burning of São Salvador in 1678. They nevertheless persevered. Much of their teaching was rejected by peoples who could not give up their house-gods, their polygynous families and their traditional safeguards against witchcraft and sorcery. Some of the Catholic rituals and sacred objects found favour among the Kongo, but were incorporated into customary ceremonies and shrines in a way that seemed

[1] François Bontinck (ed.), *Diaire Congolais de Fra Luca da Caltanisetta* (Louvain, 1970) contains information on this confused period of Kongo history.

blasphemous to the provincial Italian Capuchins with no toleration for religious syncretism. Even the movements which tried to give an African form to the spiritual message of Christianity seemed unacceptable to them, but, in spite of mission denunciations, black prophets did occasionally become popular in Kongo.

Few details are known about the early prophets who preached Christianity while rejecting a foreign, white church. In the late seventeenth century, however, when fear and conflict increased in Kongo, and the foreign missions failed to reconcile the political factions, the country was ready to welcome a messianic saviour. This saviour was found around 1700 in the form of a young woman called Beatrix Kimpa Vita. She began to attract attention to herself by claiming to be the voice of Saint Anthony. She travelled the country performing miraculous healings and preaching a religious and national revival. She denounced foreign missionaries and claimed that Christ was a Mukongo born in São Salvador. She attacked traditional fetishes and superstitions, and called on her followers to accept a truly African messianic Christianity. She finally settled in São Salvador and, like Joan of Arc, began to inspire new confidence in the nationalist cause.

The success of the Antonine movement was due to many factors. The extreme fears and uncertainty of the previous thirty years had made people anxious to accept a movement which would offer security and which had an aura of success. The name of Saint Anthony may have revived memories of the last great king, Antonio, destroyed at the battle of Ambuila. Finally, the success of the Capuchins in carrying Christianity to many remote parts of the kingdom may have made people more disposed to accept a movement with Christian manifestations. This successful messianic movement was a threat, however, both to the mission authority and to traditional political authority. Pedro IV and the Capuchins therefore combined to condemn Beatrix as a false saint. In 1706 they had her burnt at the stake. It was shortly after this that Pedro IV was able to move to São Salvador, the capital city which the Antonines had rebuilt.[1]

The recovery of São Salvador did not lead to a large-scale revival of the Kongo monarchy. The country's military power had been permanently broken at Ambuila and was never regained. The peasants suffered from famines and epidemics in the remote areas to which they had been forced to withdraw. The aristocracy no longer possessed the wealth it

[1] Louis Jadin, 'Le Congo et la secte des Antoniens', *Bulletin de l'Institut Historique Belge de Rome*, 1961, **33**, 411–615.

had once derived from agriculture, artisan production, and internal commodity trading. Instead a parasitic class of dukes, earls and princesses lived in a fantasy world where prestige was based on memories, and where kidnapped slaves were the source of wealth. The control of trade, which the central court had once practised, was permanently lost, and the kings no longer enjoyed their monopoly, even in a restricted area. Instead, many separate groups of 'bourgeois' entrepreneurs emerged to take over from the state-controlled system. At the same time, direct Portuguese participation in trade was eliminated. The new class of businessmen did not belong to the old Luso-African community which had mounted the *pombeiro* caravans of the sixteenth and early seventeenth centuries. They were wholly African in their culture and politics. In the west, the most important group were the Mussorongo of Sohio. To some extent they succeeded in maintaining trade relations with the European maritime powers while avoiding their corruptive effects. By the eighteenth century, in order to safeguard their independence, the Mussorongo kept Atlantic shipping out of their own ports and traded through Cabinda and later Boma on the north of the Congo estuary. In eastern Kongo, the most influential trading entrepreneurs were the Zumbo. They initially controlled some of the trade routes to Kinshasa and the north-eastern Kongo hinterland. From there they gradually took over the management of the trade sector between the Kwango river and the lower Congo. In southern Kongo, part of the coast was controlled by the Mossul peoples who attracted English and French traders to their harbour at Ambriz. This port became an important trade outlet for Angola, and a source of supply for all the contraband goods which the Portuguese would not admit through Luanda. The Portuguese tried to limit this traffic on several occasions. They built a fort in the interior of southern Kongo in the hope of blocking the trade paths. When this failed, they tried to capture Cabinda, the French base on the coast north of the Congo from which many trade goods came southwards. When all else failed, the Portuguese even attempted an overland excursion into Mossul from Luanda. None of these assaults was effective. Even in 1855, when Portugal succeeded in garrisoning Ambriz from the sea, the pattern of trade had only to be slightly diverted to avoid Portuguese customs duties and administrative interference.

LOANGO

As the trade routes of Kongo passed from the hands of political princes into the control of trading clans, a new foreign group began to infiltrate the country and seek economic preferment. These were the Vili from the Loango coast. Caravans of Vili ('Mubires') penetrated deep into the old kingdom after the crash of 1665, and by the 1680s they were even tapping the slave markets of Angola. This growth of the economic dynamism of Loango needs to be explained by returning to the early seventeenth century, and examining events in the northern half of the lower Congo region.

The Loango coast, between the Congo estuary and the Gabon forest, had been much less affected by the trading developments of the sixteenth century than the southern areas of the Kongo peoples. It had preserved its traditional political and economic systems more distinctly. The area was divided into the three kingdoms of Loango, Kakongo and Ngoyo, centred on the anchorages of Loango Bay, Malemba and Cabinda. Loango, the largest of the kingdoms, had an important market at its inland capital, and the peoples of the coast appear to have been active traders long before the first Europeans arrived on the scene. Their economy was already partially geared to surplus production for marketing and export. The major manufacture was cloth woven in different qualities and patterns from palm fibres. This cloth was used for clothing and furnishing, and in some areas it became a ready standard of currency. As a token of wealth, cloth had an advantage over agricultural produce, in that it could be more easily stored for long periods. At all levels of society, cloth became a guarantee against financial disaster, or a hoard to be spent on great family occasions. In its role of currency, cloth had the further advantage that it maintained a fairly stable value, owing to the fixed amount of labour which went into its production. Although less durable, and more bulky than shell currencies, it was also less liable to suffer from inflation caused by a flood of new supplies. Loango cloth therefore became a useful yardstick by which many lower Congo peoples measured relative values in the seasonally fluctuating market for foodstuffs and consumer goods.

Another important product of Loango was salt, dried from sea lagoons along the low-rainfall coast. From the seventeenth century onwards, Loango salt was traded to increasingly remote peoples in the interior, and may also have been sent up the coast to the high-rainfall areas of Gabon. A third Loango export was copper from the Mindouli region 150 kilometres inland. In the seventeenth century the mines were under Teke control, but the trade to the coast was conducted by Vili merchants from Loango. Copper ornaments, together with cloth, were among the major forms of material wealth among the savanna peoples. Copper bracelets and necklace wires were particularly prized as heirlooms or personal property. In addition to the three commodities of cloth, salt and copper, Loango supplied the local and coastal traders with elephant tails, needed for charms and bracelets, and with ivory used for ornamental carvings and musical instruments. The level of locally inspired economic exchanges went far beyond the bounds of a 'subsistence-oriented' trading system. Many of the goods produced required a high degree of entrepreneurial specialization. The cloth weaver produced large quantities of cloth and not merely a small, almost incidental, surplus to the requirements of self-sufficiency. The copper traders, and perhaps also the salt merchants, undertook their commercial activities as more than a sideline to agriculture. The presence of a currency was also a sign of Loango's sophisticated economy and its advanced method of evaluating comparability in the market sector of economy. In exchange for its exports, one of the major imports of Loango was alleged by a late sixteenth-century Portuguese trader to be iron. This essential commodity was needed to make tools, weapons and knives. Since the sandy soils of the Loango hinterland were seriously deficient in quality iron ores, the country was forced to produce exportable goods to pay for its iron imports.

In the hundred years from the late sixteenth to the late seventeenth century, Loango's varied economy was stimulated by the growth of exports to Europe. This development was closely associated with the arrival of the Dutch. Holland had many advantages over Portugal as a commercial power, since its control of the Rhine route into Germany provided her with a large market for colonial imports and a ready supply of manufactured commodities in exchange. Holland began her trade with Loango by purchasing copper in some quantity. At that time the copper mines were probably still controlled by the Teke king, the *makoko*. The rising demand for copper seems, however, to have coincided with a challenge to the Teke by Loango traders who managed the distribution of copper. By the 1660s Loango had a well-organized copper producing enterprise. Each September a large caravan of smiths and unskilled labourers travelled up the Niari valley to Mindouli. While the workers extracted the ore, the craftsmen smelted it until, at the onset of the next dry season, they were able to trek back to the coast.

Payment was made to the local peoples, as well as to those along the route, in the form of royalties, tribute and protection money.

The Loango ivory trade also expanded with Dutch demand. As elephants became scarce near the coast, new supplies of ivory had to be sought farther afield. This advance of the ivory-hunting frontier required the development of new transport enterprises to head-load tusks to the coast. In most of West-Central Africa the rising cost of carriage, the extermination of coastal elephants, and the low prices offered by Portuguese traders licensed under a restrictive royal monopoly, curtailed ivory trading in the seventeenth century. In Loango, where there was no competing trade in slaves from which quicker profits could be gained, a long-distance ivory network emerged which apparently tapped supplies as far afield as the Teke plateau and possibly even as far as the upper Ogowe basin.[1] This growth of ivory trading tended to be a stimulant to other forms of commerce and industry. Traders did not buy their ivory direct from hunters. The exchange process was more complex, and benefited several sectors of the economy. The elephant hunters of 'Bukkameale', who may have been pygmies, were particularly in need of salt, so that the ivory trade in that quarter stimulated the coastal salt industries. In other areas it is suggested that palm oil was traded for ivory, thus bringing agricultural produce into the market sphere of activity. It is likely that other local products were marketed with increasing intensity in order that capital goods could be accumulated to buy tusks. When the ivory was delivered to European traders, the goods received in exchange began to percolate back through all the channels which the ivory had followed. The trading thus stimulated the whole economy.

The most striking aspect of the international trade of Loango in the first half of the seventeenth century was the virtual absence of any slave trading. Two reasons may be offered. The first was the reluctance of the Loango peoples to trade in slaves. To some extent, they had a choice open to them. Either they could use their labour to manufacture cloth for export, or they could sell their labour and buy cloth from overseas. In the late sixteenth century the price offered for slave labour on the Portuguese-dominated Atlantic market was not sufficiently attractive to entice Loango businessmen. In contrast to this, the Portuguese were offering good prices for palm cloth, which they could readily sell for slaves in Angola. The Angolans, partly because of their comparative economic deprivation, but more especially because of a strong

[1] Phyllis M. Martin, *The external trade of the Loango coast 1576–1870* (Oxford, 1972).

Portuguese military presence on their territory, had no such choice open to them. Angola, unlike Loango, was compelled by economic and political pressures to trade in slaves. In Loango a second reason for the absence of slave trading in the early seventeenth century was the commercial influence of the Dutch. The Dutch arrived at a time when the European demand for African ivory and dyewood was increasing. Already parts of the upper Guinea coast were changing their trade pattern from slaving to commodity trading.[1] The Dutch, who had as yet no tropical colonies, and no need for slaves, responded to this European demand and sought mainly ivory, copper and dyewood in Loango. Only in the 1630s did Holland begin to acquire colonies in Brazil and the West Indies, and to take a more direct interest in the supply of labour to maintain the sugar and tobacco plantations they had captured.

The change in Dutch demand was not sufficient to reverse immediately the Loango refusal to deal in slaves. Several decades of adaptation were necessary. Loango itself had a sparse population, and if the national policy was to switch to slaving, a whole new economic structure would be needed. Only in the 1660s did this new policy become effective and Loango begin to trade in slaves on an expanding scale. The reasons for the change must be sought in the growth of the commercial economy. The country had become accustomed to a high level of international trading activity. To refuse to trade in slaves, when both the supply of other commodities, and the demand for them, was dwindling, would result in an apparent economic decline, and in a dangerous failure to meet immediate expectations. Loango therefore became caught, as Kongo and Angola had been before her. One influential new factor on the demand side was the growing strength of the Portuguese economy in Brazil. From the mid-seventeenth century onwards the Portuguese were better able to pay competitive prices for slaves, and Brazilian rum and tobacco both became very popular in the trade. Loango thus found both the Dutch and the Luso-Brazilians offering more attractive trade terms for slaves.

Once the trade had begun, Loango rapidly became one of the most important slaving areas of the whole Atlantic seaboard. From the late seventeenth to the late eighteenth century, 10,000 and more slaves a year were shipped to the New World. The Portuguese and Dutch were joined in the business by the British, and above all by the French. In

[1] Walter Rodney, *A history of the upper Guinea coast* (Oxford, 1970); K. G. Davies, *The Royal African Company* (London, 1957).

addition to paying for slaves with the traditional imports of cloth, clothing, beads, iron goods, brass, alcohol and tobacco, the European traders began to develop a substantial business in guns and gunpowder. During this period large numbers of guns, perhaps as many as two per slave, were being sold to West-Central Africa via the Loango coast. The effect of such large-scale imports of guns was important. Powerful broker states such as Kasanje (see below, p. 355) developed large armies of musketeers. The potential military and political consequences of these large gun sales were, however, somewhat reduced by the poor quality and inaccuracy of the weapons. On the economic side, the sale of guns had the attractive advantage for the Europeans of creating a permanent demand for gunpowder and for further muskets to replace defective or broken ones, thus encouraging yet further slave sales as payment.

As the Loango trade expanded, so the extent of its trading connections grew, and the sources of its slaves became more diverse and remote. In the north, Loango was linked to the 'Bobangi' peoples of the middle Congo, who sent slaves from wide areas of the central Congo basin across the north Teke plateau to the coast. The southern Teke had long had important slaving posts which supplied the Portuguese in Kongo and Angola. An even more important dimension was the southern trade which took Vili ('Mubire') caravans across Kongo and into Angola where they posed a severe challenge to the Portuguese at Luanda. The rapid growth of trade to, and beyond, the Teke and Kongo regions meant that during the eighteenth century the slave trade of Loango was probably greater than that of Angola.

The growth and change in the trade of the Loango coast during the seventeenth and eighteenth centuries had important effects on the political and social structures of the coastal societies. In 1600 the *maloango* was a powerful king whose influence extended not only over his own kingdom of Loango, but also along the whole coast from Cape Saint Catherine in the north to the smaller kingdoms of Kakongo and Ngoyo in the south. The advent of foreign traders in the late sixteenth century seems to have stimulated the growth of his power. Internal trade was conducted through the king, whose government collected taxes and used the unconsumed surplus for commercial exchanges. The seventeenth-century *maloango* was surrounded by a class of nobles from whom he chose his royal officers and provincial governors. It was they who levied tribute and exacted export duties in the outlying provinces. It was they who benefited most from the imported luxury goods which enhanced the material culture and prestige of the court and its retainers. Their success was further stimulated by the growth of sharp competition among European buyers. Whereas sixteenth-century Kongo had had to sell to the Portuguese or not at all, seventeenth-century Loango was able to play off rival customers and so improve the terms of trade. Any attempt by one European nation to restrict free competition was severely dealt with by Loango officials.

By the eighteenth century, the position and power of the *maloango* had begun to change. The first cause of this was the rapid rise of the slave trade. Whereas the trade in ivory, timber, elephant tails, cloth and copper had come from within Loango, or from its eastern hinterland, a larger part of the slave trade came from the south, across the Congo estuary. This meant that the southern kingdoms of Ngoyo and Kakongo, with their excellent ports of Cabinda and Malemba, had the advantage over Loango of being 150 kilometres nearer to the main source of supply. They therefore began to assert their independence and to refuse more than token tribute to the *maloango*. They even attempted to close the routes from Kongo to Loango altogether. By the end of the eighteenth century, Loango had shrunk in both territory and trade and was recognized only in name as the premier kingdom of the coast.

A second major change, which came about in Loango during the period of the eighteenth-century slave trade, was a change in the basis of political power. The conduct of the slave trade required many employees with new specializations: brokers, merchants, caravan leaders, interpreters, surfboatmen, water-carriers and house servants. The development of these new forms of employment opened economic opportunities to ordinary Vili who did not necessarily belong to the traditional nobility. Commoners, and even domestic slaves, who showed business skill were able to rise in the ranks of a new 'bourgeoisie'. The most powerful official was the *mafouk*, who collected dues from newly arrived ships. As he, and other trading officials, grew in wealth and authority, they gradually replaced the nobility as the most powerful members of the royal council. They became so influential that by the end of the eighteenth century the *maloango* was almost a captive of his council. When the king died, the council was sometimes reluctant to fill the vacancy and preferred to operate without royal supervision. Whereas in the seventeenth century Loango royal succession was clearly defined, in the eighteenth century there were frequent disputes about succession to the titular leadership of the state.

Between the early seventeenth and late eighteenth century, the internal power structure of Loango, and its economic base, had changed out of all recognition. The kingdom did, nevertheless, remain a whole and recognizable entity. Like some of the coastal states of West Africa, but unlike the Kongo kingdom, it had achieved a stable working relationship with the Atlantic slave traders. Its attempts to gain a monopoly of slave brokerage on the coast north of the Congo were a failure, however, and by the late eighteenth century rival ports such as Cabinda had an independent control over a large share of the traffic.

THE KIMBUNDU AND LUANDA

The highlands of West-Central Africa presented a rather different historical pattern from the coasts of the lower Congo. In this region, more notably even than in the Kongo kingdom, the major feature of the seventeenth and eighteenth centuries was the variety of response to Portuguese activity. The Kimbundu-speaking peoples of the Luanda plateau were at war with colonial invaders throughout the period. As their resistance was ground down, a small white colony was created in Angola. Only in the upper Kwango was a real degree of Kimbundu independence retained. Farther south, the Ovimbundu, on the Benguela plateau, were better able to resist military penetration. By the eighteenth century, however, they became inexorably drawn into the Portuguese commercial system. Thus both the northern and the southern highlands suffered from the steady rise of the Atlantic slave trade, though the Kimbundu[1] of the north were the earlier and more direct victims.

The earliest Portuguese attempt to penetrate the highlands occurred along the Kwanza river. In 1571 the colony of Angola[2] was created by royal charter, and three years later an ambitious colonizing expedition set out to conquer and settle the territory of the western Kimbundu. Despite repeated reinforcements, the whole venture was a fiasco, and by the early seventeenth century much of the original colonizing and proselytizing zeal had been exhausted. The Portuguese campaigns had,

[1] Properly the Kimbundu-speaking peoples should be known as Ambundu, or Mbundu, with no prefix at all, as cited in David Birmingham, *Trade and conflict in Angola* (Oxford, 1966). This usage can lead to confusion as the neighbouring Ovimbundu have the same root when the prefix is dropped. The style Kimbundu has therefore been adopted in lieu of Mbundu.

[2] The name Angola, derived from the Kimbundu title *ngola*, was originally adopted for the Portuguese colony around Luanda, and later applied to the whole Kimbundu-speaking area. In the nineteenth century Angola was joined to the Portuguese colonies of Benguela and Moçâmedes as well as to new territories in Kongo and a large eastern hinterland. The united territories of 'Portuguese West Africa' gradually came to be known by the name Angola.

however, taken on a new momentum of their own. The desire to establish plantations and open mines gave way to a growing thirst for slaves with which to develop Brazil.

The major victim of continued Portuguese aggression was the kingdom of Ndongo. This kingdom had been created in the early sixteenth century by the unification of a series of small Kimbundu lineages. The keeper of the *ngola a kiluanje* shrine became king of the new state, and succeeded in synthesizing the political experiences of several neighbouring peoples. While resisting encroachment by Ovimbundu raiders from the south, the *ngola* successfully adopted some of the invaders' political symbols and institutions. In fighting off attacks by mobile warrior units of Imbangala intruders (see below, p. 355, and volume 3, chapter 8), he gained new ideas about the training of youths in military skills.[1] The challenge presented to him from the west by the Portuguese was, however, of a different order. It involved not only a direct military confrontation, but a much more invidious demographic seepage which drained away the basis of the kingdom's vitality.

Ndongo's demographic response to the Portuguese wars and to the accompanying slave trade is hard to analyze with any degree of confidence. In the early seventeenth century both the Portuguese and Dutch talked in terms of 10,000 or more slaves leaving Angola each year. A recent reassessment of the Atlantic slave trade and in particular of the numbers landed in Latin America suggests, however, that it is unlikely that such a level was consistently maintained at this time. An average of 5,000 slaves per year seems more probable.[2] This still represented a major drain on the Kimbundu whose total population is unlikely to have exceeded half a million. The loss through forced emigration was therefore extremely high, perhaps proportionally higher than in any other zone of the Atlantic slave trade. This loss was, moreover, accentuated by other factors. First, it was concentrated among the younger element of the population, since slave merchants primarily valued men and women under thirty years of age. Secondly, since Portuguese wars of conquest were a direct source of supply, the major drain was from the central Kimbundu area. This was in contrast to normal slave-trade practice in which the capture of slaves occurred on the periphery of strong kingdoms. Thirdly, the Angolan slave trade represented a much more violent and arbitrary exaction of victims

[1] Joseph C. Miller, 'Kings and kinsmen', Ph.D. thesis (Wisconsin, 1971), contains details of sixteenth-century Kimbundu politics.

[2] D. Birmingham, *Trade and conflict in Angola*; Philip D. Curtin, *The Atlantic slave trade: a census* (Madison, 1969).

than did the trade of some other regions. Where African rulers remained masters of their own house, as in Loango, they could make conscious and moderately rational economic decisions about their participation in trade and about the relative values of slave labour and of European goods. In Angola, on the other hand, the system of Portuguese monopoly trading, and the military enforcement of fixed prices, deprived the Ndongo chiefs of any economic initiative. They received only a restricted economic advantage from trading, and none at all from war losses. It may be also that the intensive Portuguese campaigns of the early seventeenth century were particularly destructive of human life, even if reports of cannibalism by auxiliary troops were exaggerated. Finally, as well as failing to stem the internal haemorrhage of the slave trade, Ndongo increasingly lost its self-governing status as the Portuguese forts and garrisons moved up-country towards the royal capital.

The slave trade was not the only demographic drain on Angola. There was also a growing series of refugee migrations. These may have played as large a part as the slave trade in reducing Angola from the rich and populous country witnessed by the sixteenth-century Jesuits, to the sparse, deserted regions described by seventeenth-century Capuchins. The closest region of refuge for escaping Kimbundu was south, across the Kwanza river to Kisama, Libolo and to the Benguela highlands beyond. The north was more thickly wooded and more densely peopled than the south, but the Ndembu peoples of southern Kongo nevertheless absorbed many Kimbundu refugees. The third, and most important refuge area during the Angolan wars was in the east, farthest removed from the military depredations. The eastern migrations were initially connected with the fortunes of the Ndongo royal house.

The thirty-year decline of Ndongo's political and military power reached new depths in the critical campaign of 1617, in which Portuguese encroachment penetrated the woody country dividing the coastal plain from the plateau, and a new fort was added to the chain of Portuguese advance. In 1618 Luis Mendes de Vasconcellos made a break-through on to the plateau itself and invaded the heartland of the kingdom. The royal compound was looted and burnt. Large numbers of land-owning chiefs were executed and the king fled to an island sanctuary in the Kwanza river.[1] The campaign was followed by a long drought which intensified the country's distress and caused widespread famine. The destruction of the old kingdom did, however, bring forth

[1] Details of these wars are retold in Birmingham, *Trade and conflict*, chapter v and the primary documentation is mostly reproduced in Brásio, *Monumenta Missionaria Africana*, vol. VI.

a new military leadership which was more capable of resisting the Portuguese advance than had been the declining dynasty of Ndongo. The symbol of this revival was a royal princess called Nzinga, whose personality dominated the Angolan scene for the next half century.

Nzinga took over the leadership of the Ndongo with three policy objectives. She wanted to stop the war which was still devastating the centre of the Luanda plateau. She wanted to obtain from the Portuguese the diplomatic recognition which they had customarily accorded to Kongo. And she wanted to establish a regular and profitable trading relationship with Luanda. These were to remain the cardinal issues of her policy for forty years. If the Portuguese would recognize the independence of Ndongo, and agree to trade with it, the slave trade could be conducted round the fringes of the kingdom leaving the centre unmolested. The traders in Luanda accepted Nzinga's case, arguing that war was of only temporary benefit to the slave trade and was destructive to long term growth in trade routes and markets. The Luanda government also accepted these arguments in the aftermath to its much criticized Kongo war of 1622. In 1623 Nzinga went personally to Luanda to offer peace and trade. She was received with great ceremony, and returned triumphally to Ndongo bearing the baptismal name of Dona Ana de Souza from her newly acquired godfather, the Portuguese governor. Portuguese recognition of Nzinga's pre-eminence on the plateau did not solve all her problems. She continued to be threatened inside Ndongo by bands of Imbangala warriors who plundered her commercial networks and raided her markets. Portuguese help in driving them out proved worse than the raids themselves. The re-entry of Portuguese troops on to the plateau caused such panic among the Kimbundu, that Nzinga was forced to join them in fleeing to the east. She finally settled in Matamba, beyond the range of Portuguese intervention. There she created a new kingdom and adopted some of the powerful rituals which had enabled the Imbangala to build strong and cohesive armies. She welded camps of Kimbundu refugees into hardened military élites who gained courage and invulnerability by practising such rites as child sacrifice. Her key warriors were adolescent captives who had undergone rigorous military and psychological initiations. Once she was established in Matamba, and had trained her new fighting units, Nzinga was ready to face the Portuguese again and attempt to recover Ndongo.

When Nzinga had been driven out of Ndongo, the Portuguese decided to govern the kingdom by indirect rule. They had conferred the title of *ngola* on a chief called Ari Kiluanji, but their puppet met with considerable resistance. It was not so much his lack of hereditary legitimacy, an essentially Portuguese concept, which bothered Ngola Ari's subjects, as his lack of religious power. A king who had not been installed with full rituals was unlikely to provide effective rain-making or protection from disasters. His Kimbundu subjects therefore rebelled as much against his lack of credible authority, as against his Portuguese promoters. Nzinga naturally fostered their rebellion, and from the mid 1620s to the late 1630s war was pursued in Angola as fiercely as ever. The Portuguese military naturally favoured a war policy and ignored the protest of the traders. So busy were they with their annual raids among the Kimbundu, that they rather neglected the coastal defence of the colony. Nzinga suddenly acquired a new, powerful and unexpected ally when in 1641 the Dutch landed on the Angolan coast and succeeded in capturing Luanda itself. Nzinga immediately signed a treaty with them and moved her headquarters forward into the western Kimbundu region. She hoped, with Dutch support, to be able to destroy the Portuguese in Angola once and for all. Her initial efforts to capture the Portuguese town of Massangano, on the Kwanza, were inadequate, and by the time her forces had been increased it was too late. In 1648 Salvador Correia de Sá was sent from Brazil to drive the Dutch out of Angola. He then forced Nzinga to retreat once again to Matamba. Not until 1656 did she again attempt to negotiate a treaty with the Portuguese.

After 1656, Matamba became an important commercial kingdom. *Pombeiros* arrived with caravans of cloth, rum, tobacco and other luxuries, and went again with coffles of slaves. A Portuguese factor was appointed to control prices and prevent cost-inflating competitions between rival Portuguese agents. A Capuchin mission, headed by Antonio Cavazzi, re-converted the queen and her court to at least the outward forms of the Christian religion.[1] By the time of Nzinga's death in 1663, Matamba had become a major broker in the slave trade. No *pombeiros* travelled beyond Matamba and no inland supplier from Suku, Pende or Yaka was allowed direct access to the Portuguese trading agencies. Nzinga had thus created an effective commercial kingdom. She acted in the ideal manner of the middleman where the distinction was narrow between practising highway robbery and providing an essential economic link in the chain of communication.

[1] G. A. Cavazzi, *Istorica descrizione de tre regni Congo, Matamba et Angola* (Bologna, 1687) is the major source for this period.

While Nzinga was rising to power in Matamba, new political developments took place among the Imbangala settlements in Angola. The role of the Imbangala was seen by contemporary witnesses as entirely predatory.[1] Their only skill was thought to be warfare, either in alliance with the Kimbundu or the Portuguese, or else on their own account. The most important title-holder among the Imbangala of the early seventeenth century was the *kasanje*, a chief who in 1617 actively assisted in the Portuguese irruption on to the Luanda plateau and the defeat of Ndongo. After that, the Imbangala began to settle down. They were particularly attracted to the Kwango valley which had good agricultural soils, and a ready supply of salt. The *kasanje* retired there during the 1630s and began to create a trading empire similar to Nzinga's kingdom of Matamba. His followers were both Imbangala and Kimbundu. As the Kasanje kingdom extended its trade links towards the south and east, so its capital became a major concourse for Portuguese *pombeiros*. A resident factor was installed to supervise the conduct of trade and check the units of cloth measurement. For nearly two centuries, Kasanje made substantial profits as a commercial gateway from the interior. In 1680 Cadornega described a barter system whereby what were apparently Lunda traders came to the river bank, indicated their arrival with smoke signals and waited for the Imbangala to meet them at the market. They principally bought salt for which they paid with palm cloth and occasionally with ivory. There was also a growing trade in slaves at Kasanje. They were bought by *pombeiros*, who led caravans of Kimbundu porters carrying wines and textiles across the fifteen-day waste-land of eastern Ndongo which had been depopulated by the Angolan wars. The main supply of Kasanje slaves seems, during the seventeenth century at least, to have been from the south. Cadornega reported that the kingdom of Kasanje was extremely skilled in warfare and that its raids stretched hundreds of miles into the lands of the Nganguela, the Songo, the Shinje and the Ovimbundu. The king of Kasanje, known proudly to Cadornega as 'Our Jaga', had the bearing of an emperor. He dressed in the finest silks, and was accompanied by a band of xylophones and by the ceremonial double bell of state. He travelled either by horse or in a hammock surrounded by a guard of musketeers. Succession to the office of king or 'Jaga' rotated by election among three founding clans. Cadornega estimated that the kingdom had 300,000 people, of whom 100,000 could bear

[1] Alvaro III of Kongo wrote to Pope Paul V about 'una natione di gente tanto barbara chiamata Giagas et Iagas, che vivono di carne e di corpi humani'. Brásio, *Monumenta Missionaria Africana*, VI, 290, from the Vatican Archives.

arms. Exaggerated though his figures may have been, Kasanje was clearly a major military power.[1]

The relationship between the Portuguese and the Kwango states was not dissimilar to the relationship which other European powers had with coastal kingdoms along the West African stretch of the Atlantic seaboard. It was a relationship of bluff diplomatic threats and hard commercial bargaining. The Kwango states were not accorded the same esteem by the Portuguese as Kongo had been, for although independent, their status was described as 'pagan' and of second rank. Although Kasanje and Matamba were the largest and most powerful brokers, many smaller states also functioned as commercial middlemen. The Holo for instance, who lived a little farther down the Kwango, managed to enter into direct dealings with the Portuguese. The treaty signed with them in 1765 may have been typical of such agreements. In it, the Holo recognized the sovereignty of the Portuguese crown and allowed freedom of worship, and unhindered access to missionaries. The Holo were, moreover, to refrain from war against Matamba, their main enemy and rival, but an important Portuguese trade partner. The Holo were also to ban all Vili traders from their market. This market would come under the care of a Portuguese clerk, the *escrivão*, with privileged extra-territorial rights. In return for all these concessions to Portuguese interests, the Holo received a diplomatic status superior to that of many Kimbundu peoples. They were recognized as a self-governing trading community. The culture of this and other broker kingdoms was a curious mixture of African and European tradition. The treaties were drafted in diplomatic Portuguese, but the language of trade was usually Kimbundu, widely spoken by the white community. Although Christianity was formally introduced to the Kwango states, the traditional religion remained far too strong to be ignored, even by Europeans. Kasanje became a particularly important centre of worship and of healing for both black and white. The two-way exchange of culture operated even in Luanda, where white parents were much criticized because their children did not speak Portuguese and because they practised 'pagan' ceremonies.[2]

While Matamba and Kasanje grew as broker-kingdoms on the Kwango, the Portuguese struggled to maintain their colonial state in Angola. Although their original plan to create a settler colony was subverted

[1] António de Oliveira Cadornega, *História geral das guerras Angolanas* (Lisbon edition, 1940–2), vol III, part 3.

[2] Jean-Luc Vellut, 'Relations internationales du Moyen Kwango et de l'Angola', *Études d'histoire africaine*, 1970, 1.

by slave-trading interests, a small colony did evolve around the city of Luanda. This rise of Luanda was comparable, in African terms, to that of Cape Town, the other European-built city on the Atlantic coast. The population was of exceedingly mixed social and racial origins. The élite community never achieved freedom from racial minorities, and even the earliest settlers probably included Jews, Gypsies and other persecuted groups from Portugal, Madeira and Brazil. In the later seventeenth century, there were probably about 100 households in Luanda whose heads could claim Portuguese citizenship rights. Unlike the Dutch in Cape Town, however, most of these residents (*moradores*), like the convicts and soldiers without civic rights, had African wives, and Cadornega referred to Angola as the country where sons were brown and grandsons black.[1] This mestizo population of Luanda was both socially and economically important and many *pombeiros* were mestizo.

In addition to the city, the Portuguese colony spread out to local farming communities initially along the Kwanza, near the city of Massangano, and later in the north, along the Bengo and Dande rivers. Some of these communities were the country estates of rich city dwellers, but some were permanent farms and ranches managed by their owners. Their produce was largely food for local consumption. Suggestions that sugar and tobacco would thrive, and add diversity to the colony's economy, were discouraged by Brazilian plantation interests opposed to African competition. Angolan Portuguese, therefore, limited themselves to selling labour and to growing food to maintain the exported slaves until they had crossed the Atlantic. The continuing growth of the Portuguese colony meant that pressure was maintained on the remnant kingdom of Ndongo. The puppet ruler, Ngola Ari, had frequent occasion to complain that settlers were kidnapping his subjects on the pretence that they were run-away slaves from the Bengo estates. An even more serious burden was Ndongo's role in manning the trade routes to the interior. The major disadvantage, from the European point of view, of driving Nzinga and the Imbangala into the backlands of Angola was the logistic problem which it created in transporting goods to the inland markets. Elsewhere along the Atlantic coast, the administration of trade routes was an African matter. Caravans were mounted either by the coastal brokers, as in the case of the Vili caravans from Loango, or by inland middlemen such as the Ovimbundu on the Benguela plateau. In Angola, by contrast, the colony had to create its

[1] Cited in C. R. Boxer, *Race relations in the Portuguese colonial empire* (Oxford, 1963).

own land transport system to reach the Kwango ports of trade. It did so by forcibly recruiting conscript carriers among the subjects of Ngola Ari of Ndongo. The recruitment led to frequent disputes over impressment, over under-payment, over the acceptable scale of carrier fees, and over the abuses of local military administrators who were the official recruiting agents. When Ngola Ari II gained power in Ndongo in 1664, he decided to become a private and independent broker between Portuguese Luanda and the Kwango kingdoms. He seized control of several trade routes, defeated a number of subservient chiefs, and created a fortified camp at Pungu a Ndongo from which to tax or waylay rival caravans. In reply the governor at Luanda resolved to destroy the dynasty which his predecessors had created, and impose direct military rule over the whole of Ndongo. In 1671 he launched one of the most successful of the Portuguese campaigns. The Ndongo royal family was captured and sent to a monastery in Portugal and a fort was built on the site of their last capital.

In the century that followed this final collapse of Ndongo, the economy of Angola hardly changed. The most dynamic sector was still the Atlantic trade, and it was into this that most capital continued to be invested, largely through Brazilian banks. In the 1760s one short attempt was made by the governor, Souza Coutinho, to diversify the modern sector of the economy by investing in iron works, cotton production, a soap factory and in extensive new salt pans, but these activities came to nothing.[1] Both the traders and the soldier-administrators remained wedded to the slave trade. Although the slave trade absorbed most of the capital and enterprise vested in Angola, a small plantation economy survived based on local slaves and servile clients, many of them women. These rather feudal land-holdings were mainly grouped round five Portuguese inland forts. Their security was ensured by militia, auxiliaries, some artillery pieces and an occasional cavalry visit. The captain of each fort had a right to exploit allegedly vacant lands, and to control the operation of the long-distance trade fairs. A few private estates called *arimos* survived and were worked partly by slaves and partly through labour service, but they were not even as economically or socially important as the Mozambique *prazos*. In addition to plantation work, subject peoples in the Angolan domains were expected to perform carrier duties, military service, road and dyke repairs, as well as to pay tithes.

[1] Ralph Delgado, 'O Governo de Souza Coutinho em Angola', *Studia*, 1960–2, nos. 6–10.

During the course of the eighteenth century, the Portuguese slave trade from Luanda normally fluctuated between 5,000 and 10,000 slaves per year. The Portuguese suffered increasingly, however, from the competition of France, Holland and England. Throughout the century they sought to impose barriers to the free movement of trade, and thus compensate for their lack of economic competitiveness. They continued to persuade themselves that they alone had the legal right to trade in Angolan slaves. Their interventions on the coast at Novo Redondo in 1769, at Ambriz in 1790 and at Cabinda in 1787, all failed. So too, as was seen above, did their attempt to control the trade routes in the Kongo–Angola borderland, through which slaves were siphoned from Luanda's natural catchment area both to the English at Ambriz and to the French at Loango. In 1759 a fort was built at Enkoje, but the trade routes were soon diverted to by-pass it. A final factor which weakened Portugal vis-à-vis her European rivals was the growing trade in guns. Portugal, as a semi-colonial power with territorial interests, had always feared the gun trade lest it increase her opponents' military power. Her trade rivals had no such compunction about selling guns, and the French included up to two pieces in every slave lot. In the eighteenth century Portugal could no longer hold out against such competition, but as a non-industrial power she had difficulty in establishing a gun trade of her own. Only the disruption caused to British and French trade by the American war of independence allowed the Portuguese to recover some ground.

THE OVIMBUNDU AND BENGUELA

In the southern part of the Atlantic highlands, Portuguese influence began to be felt in the sixteenth century when preliminary attempts were made to explore the commercial potential of the Benguela plateau. Open boats ran up and down the coast buying small quantities of salt, ivory, dried fish, beef, beans, copper and occasionally slaves. Overland expeditions tried, though with little success, to penetrate the harsh scrubland which separated the Kwanza valley from the southern uplands. In the seventeenth century, these efforts were renewed as awareness of the populous Ovimbundu kingdoms increased. The coastal colony of Benguela was founded as a small off-shoot of Angola in 1617, and in time acquired an outpost in the plateau foothills. It was not, however, until the eighteenth century that a deeper Portuguese penetration caused commercial responses among the plateau peoples which were similar to those seen farther north on the Kwango.

In recent times the population of the Benguela plateau has grown rapidly from one million towards two million. In the seventeenth century the region was already well peopled by crop farmers who held the highlands against the herding, hunting and gathering communities which flourished in the lower regions along the rather arid coast. The Ovimbundu had probably been long subject to political and demographic influences from the north and north-east. Already by the sixteenth century the Ovimbundu had influenced, and been influenced by, the military traditions of the Imbangala. In the seventeenth century they absorbed Kimbundu refugees from the war zones of Angola. These refugees probably stimulated population growth and an effective extension of agriculture. The history of these Kimbundu refugees will only be convincingly written when the traditions of the Ovimbundu states have been recorded. On tentative evidence, however, it would seem that they introduced novel concepts of state formation to the Ovimbundu. The traditions of Huambo, for instance, refer reverentially to the Ngola Kiluanji, the king of Ndongo. They recorded in particular his conflicts with the 'Jaga', conflicts which presumably took place not in Huambo itself, as the tradition implies, but farther north during the Angolan wars. The old peoples of Huambo belonged, according to tradition, to the Ndombe pastoralists who now occupy the western edge of the highlands. The kingdom probably began to emerge near the middle of the seventeenth century, and, according to some very tentative calculations, may have been the first of the modern Ovimbundu kingdoms.[1] Another link between the Ovimbundu and their northern neighbours may have been forged by the Imbangala. The early roving bands were followed by a more purposeful advance of the Kasanje kingdom conducting slave-trading wars in the eastern highlands. These raids may have led to organized resistance and the emergence of new Ovimbundu kingdoms. Several other late Ovimbundu states, such as Ndulu and Kingolo, have traditions which refer to founders who escaped from the north after the dramatic fall of Pungu a Ndongo in 1671.

Although many Ovimbundu kingdoms may have been founded by, or in response to, Kimbundu and Imbangala fugitives or raiders, two states have different traditions. In the far south, Ngalangi has traditions linked to the pre-dynastic history of the plateau and therefore claims a rather dubious historical seniority. In the east, the kingdom of Bihé

[1] G. M. Childs, 'The kingdom of Wambu (Huambo): a tentative chronology', *Journal of African History*, 1964, 5, 367–79.

claims that the ruling dynasty was founded early in the eighteenth century by a Songo princess, who brought to Bihé political influences from the new Lunda state system. Another factor in the late rise of the Bihé may have been the eastward expansion of trade routes from the western side of the plateau.

Once the Ovimbundu kingdoms were created, they slowly came into contact with Portuguese Benguela. The colony had survived precariously on its local trade despite Ndombe enmity, an arid countryside, a frequently rebellious garrison, and a hostile governor in Angola, who resented the diminution of his sovereignty. The most valuable assets were the local salt pans, which were used to supply Luanda, and to buy ivory and skins brought by peoples from the far southern interior. Despite the vicissitudes of its early years, Benguela did eventually become the outlet for plateau trade, and its fortunes rose. The first Portuguese traders to visit the courts of the Ovimbundu kings travelled as private individuals unprotected by the force of Portuguese arms, and dependent for their safety on the goodwill of their customers. The expansion of these *sertanejo* (backwoodsmen) had begun early in the seventeenth century among the mobile coastal pastoralists. By 1680 they were travelling so far that the Portuguese decided to build a fort at the foot of the plateau which could be used as a strong-room for their trade goods. The creation of this fort in the Benguela hinterland marked the beginning of a second phase of the Portuguese activity. The advance was now on two fronts. In the van were the *sertanejo*, who adapted themselves to the culture of their African customers, married into chiefly families, and peacefully created their own compounds near the Ovimbundu capitals. Their situation was comparable to that of the Portuguese trading houses in Kongo before 1665. Behind the *sertanejo* came the military frontier, which advanced in a disruptive manner as it had done in Angola after 1575. This military penetration reached the fringes of the Ovimbundu country in the early eighteenth century when campaigns were fought against Kalukembe in the south-west. As the Portuguese-led armies reached the richer, more populous regions, the slave trade grew rapidly. Benguela began to ship slaves direct to the New World without sending them to Luanda. The volume of Benguela trade rose to match, or even surpass that of Luanda. The two ports became rivals rather than the twin pillars of a mercantilist monopoly.

By about 1770 the growth of trading networks across the Ovimbundu plateau had reached a new peak. The military advance enabled the governor-general of Angola and Benguela to move the fort of Caconda from the lowlands to the plateau, where it became the nucleus of a new Luso-African 'kingdom'. On the advanced frontier of the *sertanejo*, a Portuguese resident was installed at the Bihé court with functions similar to those of the Kasanje resident. Also in the 1770s the Portuguese began to realize that a large part of the Ovimbundu trade was not going north to Luanda or south to Benguela, but along a new route to the coast through the north-western kingdom of Sela. Once on the coast, slaves were being sold both to unauthorized Portuguese ships and to English and French vessels on their way to Loango.[1] In order to cut down 'smuggling', a fort was built at Novo Redondo. The Ovimbundu suppliers reacted violently against this interference with their 'free' route, and the Sela army descended on Novo Redondo and captured its Portuguese garrison. This coup led the Portuguese to attempt the outright conquest of the Ovimbundu kingdoms, a feat comparable to the invasion of Ndongo a century before. By advancing their military front into the central kingdoms of Huambo and Bailundu, they hoped to gain control over all the trade routes. Two columns set out, the first from Angola and the second from Benguela. They were to join forces at a central cross-roads on the plateau. The war was arduous, and spread over the three campaigning seasons of 1774, 1775 and 1776. In such a drawn-out action the Ovimbundu ceased to rely on guerilla tactics, and began to use stone forts like the Portuguese. To counter this new development, the Portuguese hauled in field guns for siege warfare. These engines were finally successful, but some fortifications were so elaborate that they took months to dismantle. During the war the Portuguese defeated Bailundu, the largest kingdom, but the achievement had few lasting consequences, and Caconda remained the most advanced Portuguese military outpost.[2] Traders reverted to their former methods, with Portuguese, mestizo, and African agents all operating under Ovimbundu political protection.

Effective Portuguese domination over the Ovimbundu was not achieved until more than a century after the campaign of 1774–6. Trade, however, continued to grow, and by the end of the eighteenth century Ovimbundu caravaneers, known as 'Mambari', were exploring the upper Zambezi. This southern caravan system matched the central and northern systems of Luanda and Loango. By the nineteenth century,

[1] Birmingham, *Trade and conflict in Angola*, 156.

[2] G. M. Childs, *Umbundu kinship and character* (London, 1949), ch. 12. This is still the only accessible survey of Ovimbundu history, although a wealth of published and unpublished Portuguese data are ready to be tapped.

the network had branches which spread out to cut across some of the older routes. One route reached the Kuba in the heart of Zaïre, and met the Nyamwezi advancing from East Africa. In the south, the Ovimbundu kingdoms used their new-found military skills to conduct large-scale cattle and slave raids on the peoples as far away as Huila, the most southerly plateau of West-Central Africa (see volume 5, chapter 9). Thus the Ovimbundu, who in the seventeenth century had been the victims of Kasanje slave raiding, themselves became the raiders of peoples less fortunate.

THE LOWER KASAI

The middle savanna of Central Africa is divided into two rather sharply contrasted regions. The lower Kasai region is fertile and densely occupied by an extreme variety of ethnic and linguistic groups broken up into small political fragments. The upper Kasai, on the other hand, is dry, sandy, and thinly populated by peoples who mostly bear some kind of ethnic, historic, linguistic or political relationship to the Lunda peoples.

The lower Kasai is currently divided between the Bandundu and Kasai provinces of Zaïre, and the Lunda province of modern Angola. During the seventeenth and eighteenth centuries the whole of the lower Kasai was in growing contact with its western neighbours. Indirect ripples of influence were beginning to be felt from the Atlantic. In the north, along the lower Kasai river itself, the influences came through the Teke, and the people most affected were the Boma-Sakata, the Yanzi-Ambun and the Kuba-Lele. In the south, between the middle Kwango and the middle Kasai, change derived from Kongo, and three more groups were affected, the Yaka-Suku, the Mbala, and the Pende. In addition to the new influences from the west, these peoples were in contact with two other important groups. In the north-east they abutted the great forest cultures of the Mongo. In the south-east they began to be influenced by the even greater savanna cultures of the Lunda of the upper Kasai.

Many of the lower Kasai peoples were closely associated with the rivers in their culture and economy. Fishing was important, both as a local activity and as a large-scale business enterprise involving long-distance expeditions of several months and leading to communication with such far-away peoples as the Bobangi of the middle Congo river. Migrant fishermen also used their canoes to carry such heavy items as pottery, iron and copper, which were difficult to trade far by head porterage. The traditional agriculture of the lower Kasai was founded on sorghum and bananas, but these were gradually being supplemented or replaced by maize, and later by cassava, which became the staple food by the nineteenth century. Other crops, new and old, included groundnuts, beans, sugar cane, colocasia, yams, millet, oil palms, kola nuts and tobacco. This diverse agriculture led parts of the Kasai to become heavily populated by Central African standards. Regional artisan production also led to specialization. At the western and eastern fringes of the region, the Teke and the Lele made up for their sparse agricultural resources by producing fine raffia textiles. The peoples of the lower river, and the Kuba of the Sankuru, were noted for their pottery. The peoples who organized markets usually conducted them on a four-day cycle. The major currency of the region came to be the Kongo *nzimbu* shells, but copper manillas, Indian cowries and various beads also commonly served as currency. Although it is clear that crops, agricultural techniques, currencies and material goods spread from the west into the lower Kasai area, it is not clear by what means these influences spread, or at what periods. There is also much uncertainty about the social, political, linguistic and demographic changes which may be ascribed to the influence of western neighbours.

The traditions of the lower Kasai peoples tend to suggest that they 'came from the west', from the Teke lands or from the region at the confluence of the Kasai and Congo rivers.[1] What these traditions mean is debatable. They might imply that the bulk of the population expanded from the west as new agricultural lands were needed by peoples of the rather barren Teke plateau. If so, they might have filled out the area with its present population of farmers. The relative linguistic homogeneity of the region, despite its cultural diversity, might favour such a literal interpretation of the traditions, though over a long time-scale. Alternatively, the traditions might relate to limited prestige groups which spread eastwards. Fishermen, for instance, may have evolved their skill in contacts with the great fishing peoples of the Congo river, and then introduced them gradually up the Kasai. On another level, the traditions might relate mainly to the political systems of the lower Kasai. Although the pattern of settlement was almost everywhere one of small villages and hamlets, most peoples were governed by chiefs, or even by hierarchies of chiefs culminating in a king, like the great

[1] Jan Vansina, *Kingdoms of the savanna* (Madison, 1966), ch. 4, especially 110–18, and Jan Vansina, *Ethnographie*, 129–30, cautiously synthesize the amateur ethno-historical observations of early Belgian officials in this area.

makoko of the Teke. Another possible vehicle for the transmission of culture and tradition from the west into the lower Kasai basin was trade. The Teke had early contact with the growing Atlantic trade systems, and by the seventeenth century coastal merchants were familiar with the titles of chiefs in the lower Kasai region. It seems likely that pioneers from the west had begun to penetrate the Kasai and bring slaves to the Teke markets. This penetration may have been responsible for introducing regular markets, American food crops, widely circulating currencies, and chiefs with new traditions of foreign origin. Traditions of the lower Kasai also refer to connections with the lower Kwango. This too could be consistent with trade penetrations, since important land routes from Teke led into the interior by way of the Kwango river crossings.

Hypotheses about the growth of trade and the spread of cultural links still need much research in the lower Kasai region. At the same time attention must be given to the importance of this area as a zone of refuge. It is quite possible that the purposeful and organized penetration of traders was less significant than the hasty retreat of peoples who found themselves in the raiding zone of the Atlantic hinterland. The Kasai might have gained its western cultural features from refugees rather than from traders or conquerors. Only very detailed historical, ethnographic and linguistic researches will be able to shed a more certain light on the assorted components of the Kasai cultures.

Of the peoples of the lower Kasai, three have particularly interesting political histories. The least known are those north of the river who have contacts with their Mongo neighbours. The interaction between the western Mongo and the eastern Teke apparently led to the creation of a new system of kingship with a strong religious core and hereditary court of secular administrators. This pattern of 'socialized kingship' seems to have influenced the Boma-Sakata peoples and led to the evolution of a more complex political hierarchy than existed south of the Kasai.

The second interesting group of lower Kasai peoples are the Ambun (Bambun, Mbuun). They are divided into some twenty-eight clans, each of which has its own history and has brought its own contribution to Ambun tradition and culture. The language of the group is related to that of their north-western neighbours, and the majority of clans claim a north-western origin. There is also, however, an important strand of tradition which refers to a western line of influence from Kongo which affects the dialect and leadership of three clans. A third strand of Ambun tradition claims that one influential stratum of the society came across the Kwango from the south-west. This might have been led by Kimbundu migrants who spread far to the east of Matamba to reach the Ambun, and possibly to give them their name. The link with Angola might equally well have been a refugee one or a trading one. The political system which evolved among the Ambun drew not only on the western streams of cultural influence, but also on the growing experience of the Lunda in the east. Lunda emblems of chiefship appear to have been acquired from such Lunda-influenced peoples as the Shinje or the Pende to the south of the Ambun territories. The political culture which evolved among the Ambun does not appear to have resulted in the creation of a centralized kingship. It did, however, influence the Kuba, an important neighbouring people to the east, who went on to create the most interesting and sophisticated political system of the whole Kwango-Kasai area, if not of the whole of Central Africa.

The earliest traditions of the Kuba refer to the drift from the west, be it a drift of peoples or of clan leaders or of ideas and institutions.[1] Reference is made in these traditions to the western Mongo, to the lower Kasai, and even to the region of the Congo cataracts. The origins of the drift probably go back into the sixteenth century, and stimulus may have been given to the movement by the turbulence associated with the Jaga wars or rebellions in Kongo (see volume 3, chapter 8). More interesting, however, than these early legends are the changes which occurred among the Kuba and their Lele brethren after about 1600, when their societies began to take recognizable shape on either side of the middle Kasai. Although the Lele and the Kuba are similar in origin and language, they occupy very dissimilar terrain, and have evolved sharply contrasted levels of economic wealth and very different systems of government.

The Lele occupied the poorer, western half of the region, which has inadequate soils, little forest and limited supplies of game. This ecological disadvantage resulted in a low density of population, small villages, greater mobility of population and, it has been argued,[2] less powerful incentives to economic development. This meant that strong political structures did not emerge and the country was constantly

[1] Vansina's main work on Kuba history is his *Geschiedenis van de Kuba* (Tervuren, 1963), but summaries have appeared in his English and French publications, e.g. *Ethnographie*, 130.

[2] Mary Douglas, 'Lele economy compared with the Bushong: a study in "economic backwardness"', in Paul Bohannan and George Dalton (eds.), *Markets in Africa* (Evanston, 1962), ch. 8.

weakened by insecurity and strife. Much of the young men's energy went into defence, thus further hindering economic growth, and causing the economically productive working life of a Lele man to be comparatively short. The improvement of techniques in agriculture, hunting and fishing was discouraged by low yields. This failure of technological evolution affected the design and finish of houses, utensils, ornaments, embroidery, wine tapping and all artisan production except raffia weaving. The lack of variety and specialization in both agricultural and industrial production meant that the Lele developed no markets and no currencies. The most important form of accumulation was not in investment wealth such as canoes, nets and granaries, but in prestige wealth stored in the form of raffia cloths. There existed among the Lele no form of economic incentive whereby an individual could gather riches and wives by inventiveness and initiative. Wealth was reserved for middle-aged and elderly men, who alone were permitted to amass raffia cloths for bride wealth, and thereby achieve a married status. Craftsmanship was limited to the elderly and competition from the young was restricted.

The Kuba, although similar in origin to the Lele, developed along very different lines from the early seventeenth century. Their country was ecologically more rewarding. They were able to build up hunting, fishing and agriculture to a much higher level of skill, efficiency and variety than the Lele. They also grew much faster demographically and created larger villages and communities. The large-scale polygyny which restricted incentive among the Lele was among the Kuba limited to chiefs, while the rest of the population remained virtually monogamous. Technology in house building, food storing, tool manufacture and artisan production soon far outstripped that of the Lele as success bred success. Prestige was gained not just with old age, but by the accumulation of wealth and the production of goods for the important internal market system. Trade in its turn led to increasing specialization among individuals and groups. Exchanges and valuations were carried out in organized markets by means of different currencies, firstly raffia squares, later cowries, and later still beads and copper bars. One of the most important factors, however, which facilitated the growth of the Kuba market economy and which in turn led to its striking development, was the Kuba political structure. This structure was capable of protecting the markets and trade routes and ensuring the smooth redistribution of an increasingly large section of Kuba production which was surplus to the needs of subsistence survival.

The Kuba kingdom or empire was a federation of some eighteen different 'tribes'. The dominant group were the central Bushong, who conquered their related Kuba neighbours and then spread farther afield to incorporate some Mongo and Lulua into the kingdom. The formation of the Kuba kingdom probably began in the late sixteenth century. The Bushong kings appear to have acquired their initial wealth and prestige from their skill as fishermen. Agriculture seems to have been less important in the early period, when populations were more sparse and mobile, but in the reign of the great seventeenth-century innovator, Shyaam, agricultural prosperity was stimulated by the introduction of maize, tobacco, cassava and beans. There followed a growth in population. Shyaam also strengthened the kingship by creating a capital and attracting notable traders to it. He established a guard of young men and created new offices of state to reward and strengthen his relatives and supporters. Some prisoners of war were incorporated into the king's army, to further Bushong domination, and others were settled in new villages to strengthen the Kuba economy. The king safeguarded his position by giving preferment to his children, while keeping a severe check on his nephews, from whom his successor would be chosen. In each reign these two factions maintained a balance of power. By the eighteenth century the Kuba empire was at its height and had developed indirect trading relations with distant peoples of the Kwango in the west and the Lualaba in the east. The Kuba are particularly important in Central African history because they show the degree of originality and adaptability which the peoples of the Kasai could demonstrate when creating institutions best suited to the control and exploitation of their own environment. The Bushong kingship permitted the Kuba to develop a thriving empire and drive back or conquer rival peoples who coveted their fertile land. Strong kingship also facilitated the establishment of a rich and varied economy based on a high level of both internal and external commercial exchanges.[1]

South of the lower Kasai, in the region between the Kwango and the middle Kasai similar developments took place to those on the lower Kasai. But whereas the lower Kasai traditions of an eastward cultural drift are mainly connected with the Teke people, the Kwango region is more closely connected with the Kongo. Most peoples in the area, except the recently arrived Lunda and Chokwe in the south-east, speak languages related to Kikongo. Once again it is impossible

[1] Jan Vansina, 'Trade and markets among the Kuba', in Bohannan and Dalton, *Markets in Africa*, ch. 7.

to say how old this affinity is. The fragmentation of ethnic groups is, if anything, even greater than in the north. In recent centuries peoples have moved long distances, either in flight or following more purposeful lines of migration. The Pende, for instance, have two traditions.[1] One relates to a flight from the seventeenth-century break-up of the kingdom of Ndongo, of which they formed part, and whose traditions they accurately remember. The other refers to the emergence of trading relations between the Pende and Angola, and the growth of new prosperity brought by the traders. Each of these traditions may have a level of truth in it. Since the Pende are the easternmost of the Kwango peoples, it is likely that all the others were to a greater or lesser degree influenced by these two strands of influence from the Atlantic zone. The Suku and the Mbala both have traditions which bring peoples or influences from the Kwango valley, and the Yaka claim convincingly that some of their ancestors once lived in Kongo. The traditions concerning the seventeenth century therefore clearly relate to an eastward drift. In the eighteenth century, however, a new spread of ideas, influences and peoples reached the Kwango area, from precisely the opposite direction. This new diffusion was connected with the rise of the Lunda empire.

THE LUNDA EMPIRE

The story of the Lunda empire, and of the many savanna peoples who lived on its periphery in Zaïre, Angola and Zambia, is potentially one of the most interesting, if neglected, themes in the whole history of pre-colonial Central Africa.[2] The basic research data are oral evidence, but although some traditions have been collected over the past hundred years, many are known only to the local sages. A beginning has, however, been made in analysing central Lunda traditions. These speak of the rivalry between clans and clan leaders in the scattered agricultural societies of the upper Kasai. These rivalries often led to armed conflict and one faction or other was forced to flee to new land. In the process several Lunda leadership titles became known among the Luena and Chokwe of the south and west; Lunda epic poems were incorporated into the literary culture of many neighbouring societies; Lunda social and political customs became widely distributed; material symbols of the Lunda were adopted for prestige by peoples as far west as Angola.

[1] G. L. Haveaux, *La tradition historique des Bapende orientaux* (Brussels, 1954).

[2] Jean-Luc Vellut, 'Notes sur le Lunda et la frontière luso-africaine (1700–1900)', in *Études d'histoire africaine*, 1972, 3, 61–166, is the most recent and most competent account.

While this dispersion of refugees, of symbolic artefacts, of legendary hero-worship, and of social customs was going on, fundamental changes began to occur among the Lunda themselves.

During the sixteenth century a new form of centralized leadership began to emerge among the Lunda. A legendary warrior-hero, Kibinda Ilunga, gained domination over the minds of several Lunda clan leaders. His prestige was enhanced by alien rituals and charms connected with the skills of the hunter. Gradually the three strands of religious leadership, of traditional clan leadership, and of practical political leadership began to coalesce round an embryonic royal court. The emergence of a new kingdom out of the old web of kinship ties was extremely slow. Although the process began before 1600, political experimentation and consolidation continued throughout the seventeenth century. As the central government matured it had to accommodate old customs and absorb once-powerful lineage titles. The symbol of political office was the *lukano* bracelet of human (or elephant) sinews. Inheritance among the new political office-holders tended to be through brothers and sons, rather than through maternal nephews of the old matrilineal clans. To compensate for this, many of the supporting titles which ensured lineage loyalty were female titles. They were either deemed to be married to the male royal titles, or were held by female rulers. The offices of *swana mulunda*, mother of the people, and of *lukonkeshia*, mother of the king, were held by women. By the end of the seventeenth century the process of political innovation had culminated in the creation of the kingly title of *mwata yamvo* (or *mwant yav*). A Lunda dynasty was inaugurated which has survived until the present time.[1]

The initial stimulants to the growth of a centralized system of Lunda government have been interpreted as primarily internal factors. During the course of the seventeenth century, however, the Lunda and their neighbours gradually became aware of changes emanating from the commercial economy of the Atlantic. It has already been suggested above that new trading opportunities and new forms of exotic prestige wealth were introduced into the lower Kasai by merchants and refugees in the early years of the seventeenth century. In the dry, and more sparsely peopled regions of the upper Kasai such a process probably occurred more slowly. Communication over land was probably more difficult than the river communication of the north. Even in the eighteenth century, long distance caravans suffered from the unreliability of

[1] Miller, 'Kings and kinsmen' contains a new interpretation of early Lunda history. See also *Cambridge history of Africa*, vol. 3, ch. 8.

food supplies and the hazards of river crossing by canoe or pedestrian ford. On the other hand a sparse population offered less resistance to organized parties of foreign travellers than did richly occupied farmland. Although no details are yet available for the opening of the southern trade systems, one can reasonably suppose that by the latter half of the seventeenth century the long distance trade paths were beginning to carry such foreign merchandise as European hardware, Brazilian alcohol and tobacco, and Asian textiles. Many of these paths were not newly created for the purpose of foreign trade but pre-dated the arrival of European and Indian manufactures from Luanda. They had been used to carry indigenous salt bars and raffia strip cloth. They may also have served in the exchange of local metal goods, possibly even copper crosses from the mines of the Lualaba. As this local trade was supplemented and increased, during the late seventeenth century, by the inflow of foreign goods, so the 500 kilometre route-sector between the middle Kwango and the upper Kasai became strategically important. One end of this sector was controlled by the king of Kasanje. The other end was firmly grasped by the new *mwata yamvo* of the Lunda.

The Lunda established their capital in open woodland about 100 kilometres east of the Kasai. The metropolitan region lay between two small rivers, about 15 kilometres apart, and was surrounded by a fortified earth rampart and dry moat of 30 or more kilometres in length. Within this royal zone each new *mwata yamvo* built his official *musumba* compound. The king's personal *musumba* consisted of a large fortified enclosure with a double fence of live trees, or stakes, and numerous inner courtyards, each with well defined practical or ceremonial functions. One part of this large domain was laid aside for royal burials and was watched over by special religious guardians. European visitors who saw several *musumbas* during the nineteenth century were invariably impressed with the straight roads, the open public squares, the cleanliness and the hygiene. By comparison with this 'city', Portuguese Luanda was described by some travellers as small and rather squalid.[1]

During the eighteenth century, eight kings, belonging to the first two generations of the dynasty, governed the Lunda empire. The history of these early kings has been so inextricably telescoped with the early legends of the Lunda, that a detailed account of the period is difficult to reconstruct. Four themes seem, however, to have been

[1] The most observant visitors were Paul Pogge, *Im Reiche des Muata Jamvo* (Berlin, 1880) and Henrique Dias de Carvalho, *Expedição Portugueza ao Muatiânvua* (Lisbon, 1890).

important. The first was the strengthening of the home base of the Lunda domestic economy. The second was the colonial expansion of Lunda and the incorporation into its political system of chiefs from many neighbouring societies. Thirdly the Lunda created an administrative bureaucracy capable of managing the affairs of a growing society. Lastly control of the country's external commerce became a central function of royal authority.

The domestic economy of the Lunda was of course based on agriculture. By the eighteenth century this agriculture was probably undergoing transformation as maize, and more especially cassava, began to supplant millet and bananas as the primary staples. The difficulty which the Lunda faced when trying to expand their prosperity was not that they lacked land – there were still wide open spaces on every side. What they lacked was people. The new state therefore soon developed a military character, and began raiding its neighbours. The objective was not territorial aggrandizement, but the capture of men and women who were brought to the lands round the *musumba* in a large programme of 'internal colonization'. The king, and other members of the Lunda oligarchy, staked out cassava plots where they put their new serfs to work. Population was thereby funnelled from the fringes of Lunda towards the centre, and royal prosperity increased. The status of farm serfs, and household slaves acquired in this way, was distinctly more favourable than that of plantation slaves under European ownership. In this African society, captives rapidly absorbed the culture of their captors and became integrated into their host community.

The expansion of Lunda soon reached beyond the immediate neighbourhood from which captive slaves could be easily brought to the capital. A new policy was devised whereby Lunda kings founded satellite colonies among their more remote neighbours. These satellites were created partly by conquest, partly by settling Lunda colonists, and partly by absorbing local chiefs into the prestigious Lunda political hierarchy. A chief who accepted Lunda overlordship was initiated into the Lunda and became the representative of the *mwata yamvo* among his own tribe. He was granted a cow-hide belt or other symbol of political office and became responsible for dispatching tribute from his own people to the Lunda capital. The obligation to pay periodic tribute was the primary consequence of Lunda domination. Regular tribute caravans provided the essential, if not the only, link between the royal capital and the satellite chiefdoms. Some tribute was in the form of young wives for the Lunda courtiers, or field-hands for their plantations. Other contributions consisted of cassava flour or other farm produce, game, dried fish, household furnishings and agricultural implements. In exchange for their offerings loyal subjects received counter-gifts from the *mwata yamvo*. These rewards might be small luxuries like beads or more practical assets such as livestock.

The growing Lunda empire needed an expanding system of administration. Initially court functions were probably filled by elders called *ṭubungu* who represented the Lunda ancestors. These elders continued to be influential members of the royal council, maintaining the balance between the old and the new, together with the great lineage office-holders. The most powerful of the old offices was that of the *lukonkeshia*. She ruled over an almost independent court of her own, where she received tribute independently from that sent to the *mwata yamvo*. She had no husband to limit her autonomy, but governed as a great chief. Her counsel was particularly influential in determining succession to the throne, for which reason she was symbolically known as the mother of the king. In addition to traditional leaders, selected according to their quasi-religious status, the new state required administrators appointed by virtue of their political skills. It is possible that new positions at court, and seating arrangements at royal councils, were influenced by the position which officers held in the field during military campaigns. The royal council, like the army, had members designated as 'eyes', as 'wings', and as the 'tail'. Both the *swana mulopwe* and the *kanapumba* combined military rank with political authority.[1] Beside the military captains and courtiers there was a series of great political chiefs called the *kilolo*. In the mid-nineteenth century, thirty-six great chiefs were reputed to pay tribute to the *mwata yamvo*.[2] Imperial stewardship of the outer domains was supervised by numerous royal messengers, called *tukwata*. These, more than any one else, were the personal bureaucratic agents of the monarch and they actually ran the business of state. They travelled up and down the empire, checking on each satellite, and ensuring that adequate tribute was paid at the proper time. When external trade became important to the Lunda, it was the *tukwata* who supervised caravans, escorted foreign travellers, safeguarded royal

[1] There is some lack of correspondence between the two most detailed recent descriptions of the Lunda power structure by Léon Duysters, 'Histoire des Aluunda', in *Problèmes de l'Afrique Centrale*, 1958, **12** and Daniel Biebuyck, 'Fondements de l'organisation politique des Lunda du Mwaantayaav en territoire de Kapanga', in *Zaïre*, 1957, **11**, 8. See also Vansina, *Kingdoms of the savanna*, ch. 3.

[2] J. R. Graça, 'Viagem feita de Loanda ...', in *Annaes do Conselho Ultramarino*, 1855; republished as 'Expedição ao Muatayanvua' in *Boletim da Sociedade de Geografia de Lisboa*, 1890.

monopolies, and punished subjects who evaded tolls and tariffs. From the court's point of view they formed an efficient administrative cadre. For the people, their activities were often burdensome and even violent.

The earliest long distance trade of the Lunda was an extension of the tribute system. As Lunda domination spread, new subjects brought in goods such as copper and salt which were scarce in the original Lunda homeland. They also brought an increased range of raffia textiles. Both copper and palm cloth were marketable on the Kwango, and in exchange the Lunda bought tobacco and Angolan salt. It was through this trade that the Lunda first came into contact with the Luso-African economy of the Atlantic seaboard. During the eighteenth century, neither Africans nor Portuguese from the Atlantic regions succeeded in gaining direct access to the Lunda sphere of influence. Their trade, however, spread far and fast, carried either by Lunda subjects or by intermediate middlemen such as the Imbangala of Kasanje. It was suggested above (p. 355) that peoples tentatively identified as the Lunda were selling palm cloth on the Kwango in the late seventeenth century. In the opposite direction, the first Imbangala caravan is alleged to have reached the Lunda *musumba* in the reign of Naweji I, the second *mwata yamvo* title-holder.[1] This was approximately in the second quarter of the eighteenth century. The nineteenth-century data do not suggest that the Lunda themselves were great caravaneers. On the other hand their state-wide administration was extremely competent at supervising the movements of foreign caravans. The *tukwata* led them directly to a specially appointed camp near the royal capital, and there the *mwata yamvo* was given first choice of all their wares.

As the external trade of Lunda grew, a new factor became important. This was the role of the slave trade in the country's foreign policy. There is no evidence as to when the *mwata yamvo* was first seduced by the attractions of this form of commerce. It is likely, however, that slaves were used to buy foreign imports from quite early in the eighteenth century. A substantial proportion of the slaves sold were war victims. Raiding campaigns were launched, notably among the Luba Kalundwe, Luba Kaniok and middle Kasai peoples of the north-east and north. These raids can be distinguished from strategic campaigns aimed at securing control of the great commercial routes to the west. A second source of slaves was internal. Criminal convicts of all kinds found their sentences being commuted to slavery with increasing readiness. When in 1843 Rodrigues Graça told Lunda chiefs of the

[1] Vellut, 'Notes sur le Lunda', 92.

abolition of the Portuguese slave trade, they warned him that this would lead to a most unchristian revival of the death penalty among the Lunda. It seems likely, however, that the internal production of slaves, whether by taxation, by judicial penalties, or by feuds between villages, was only a secondary source of supply. Intensive internal slaving would have had serious weakening effects on the social and political structure of the nation. No such weakening was apparent in Lunda until the second half of the nineteenth century, by which time many of the country's foreign raiding grounds had been lost to rival powers.

It is difficult to understand why the Lunda empire throve economically on a commerce so disruptive, and so demoralizing, as the slave trade. The first answer may be that the scale of the trade was small, at least when compared to the wholesale extractions practised in Angola. The profits, on the other hand, were high by Lunda standards. The Lunda empire probably governed a million or more subjects, but it is unlikely that the external trade ever rose to 3,000 slaves per annum most of whom were foreign captives. The hardships, fears, and uncertainties of the trade, which had destroyed the Kongo kingdom during the late-seventeenth century, only began to be felt widely in Lunda in the nineteenth century. The profits, on the other hand, amounted to very tangible benefits. Goods obtained in exchange for slaves played an important role in strengthening political authority. Imported cloth and *missanga* currency-beads increased the wealth and prestige of a chief, and enabled him to reward his most faithful supporters. The redistribution of exotic imports was carefully restricted, however, and only the Lunda oligarchy and its retainers acquired the extensive rewards of the trade. The spread of trade-wealth to the Lunda subject states created some conflict between the centre and the periphery of the empire, but at least until the end of the eighteenth century the *mwata yamvo* seems to have remained a fairly effective monopolist. This was possible because the main centres of population from which slaves were captured lay in the north and east, whereas the markets to which they were sold were in the west and south-west. Whether by accident or design, the site of the king's *musumba* was therefore strategically placed to control a slave-exporting economy.

During the course of the eighteenth century, the territorial authority of the Lunda kings expanded in three geographical stages. The first stage was towards the west and north-west. One of the first peoples to be affected were the Pende, some 300 kilometres down the Kasai from the Lunda capital. The Lunda began to impose their form of subtle political domination by intruding into the Pende region and creating a Lundaized ruling group which would pay tribute to the *mwata yamvo*. This intrusion probably occurred quite early in the eighteenth century. Soon afterwards the Lunda created another dynasty, even farther west, among the Yaka on the Kwango. The town of Kasongo Lunda became an important outpost of the empire. The Lunda also gained influence among such other peoples of the Kwango valley as the Suku, Shinje and Holo. Their main concern was presumably to improve access to the western markets of Angola and Kongo. In the 1760s, Lunda attacks on the area caused Hungu refugees to flee westwards and settle under Portuguese protection along the Kongo-Angola border. At the same time a coup d'état occurred in Matamba, and the new king was alleged to have been helped to power by 'Molua' soldiers from Lunda. In 1768 the Portuguese feared that the Lunda might even capture Kasanje town and confiscate its large stocks of trade goods.[1] This fear was not realized, however, and the Lunda later eased their pressure on the upper and middle Kwango. Nothing is known about the history of the lower Kwango at this period, but it is likely that Kasongo provided another gateway to the west. The Zumbo traders of northern Kongo seem to have been rising in influence, and may have been the agents of Lunda trade.

The second area of Lunda expansion was in the south and south-east, towards the upper regions of the Lualaba and Zambezi rivers. One of the peoples affected was the Ndembu, whose chief, Kanongesha, was drawn into the Lunda empire. He then became a powerful agent for the spread of Lunda influence among his neighbours and sent slaves north as tribute. Another attraction which drew the Lunda southwards was the copper and salt of the Lualaba. Copper became an important item of trade in the empire, and a new currency of copper-wire bracelets began to circulate among the wealthy. The exploitation of this new mineral wealth caused acrimonious disputes between Lunda factions on the imperial frontier. Disaffected groups began to move away and spread widely and thinly over the featureless woodland of north-western Zambia. For the most part these wanderers remembered their ancestral or acquired allegiance to the *mwata yamvo*, and sent him occasional tributary payments. Towards the end of the eighteenth century the remote backwaters to which they spread suddenly gained a new importance within the empire. Ovimbundu traders from the south-west succeeded in crossing the inhospitable Chokwe forest and reaching

[1] Birmingham, *Trade and conflict in Angola*, ch. VII.

the Luena-Lovale peoples of the upper Zambezi. This rapidly led to the opening of a major new high road from the Atlantic to the Lualaba. Copper crosses began to make their appearance at Benguela. In the opposite direction, a whole new branch of the Atlantic slave trade was opened up, and the southern Lunda became dangerously exposed to its demands. Meanwhile, however, the primary attention of the Lunda kings had been diverted from the south to the east.[1]

THE EASTERN PLAINS AND THE UPPER ZAMBEZI

The wide eastern plains of Central Africa stretch across to the Great Lakes and down to the middle Zambezi. They were sparsely inhabited by small clusters of scattered peoples, some farmers or fishermen, others pastoralists or gatherers. The most numerous and influential of them were the Luba, who were spread across the Lualaba and away towards Lake Tanganyika. The history of the Luba has yet to be written, but their traditions reveal an interesting pattern of domination by chiefs of royal blood known as *balopwe*. These chiefs claim to be strangers who invaded the Lualaba and won domination by feat of arms. Their emergence may, in truth, have owed rather more to local political initiatives, for instance among the important Kalundwe group, who seem to have had a seminal influence over other Luba peoples. These royal chiefs acquired a strong religious aura around them. Like many other Central African kings, they were never seen to eat or drink, but were presumed to subsist like gods. When a new chief was invested, he lit a fire from which his subjects were required to kindle their own fires in sign of loyalty. The snake and the rainbow were adopted as royal symbols. More personal chiefly paraphernalia included a *lukano* bracelet, and a basket of dried bones from former kings. Luba chiefs, like the king of the Lunda, received material tribute from their subjects. Goods flowed towards the centre of the chiefdom and power flowed out from it. The Luba systems, like the Lunda ones, were operated by a hierarchy of officials. The *kilolo* were village and district chiefs, the *mwine ntanda* were land chiefs, and the *mfumu* were court councillors.[2] Although the Luba had a very clear concept of royalty, there was no single Luba state. By the seventeenth century, four kingdoms had

[1] New research on southern Lunda history is being carried out by Robert Schecter of the University of Zambia.

[2] The most recent collation of the ethnographic data on the Luba was undertaken in the mid-1960s by Stephen A. Lucas and presented together with his own field work in 'Baluba et Aruund: étude comparative des structures socio-politiques', unpublished doctoral dissertation (Paris, 1968).

gained a degree of unitary strength, but many Luba chiefs remained independent of them. At this time, in fact, many Luba were migrating out of their traditional homelands and colonizing the more fertile country of the Lulua and eastern Kasai. They took with them their language and their clans, and some features of their culture, but they did not create kingdoms such as those which developed south-east of them in the eighteenth century.

Some oral tradition suggests that the growth of Luba kingship preceded the growth of Lunda kingship. It may well be true that the concept of a royal authority transmitted through the male line was known earlier among the Luba than among the Lunda. The application of that principle to imperial expansion seems, however, to have taken root rather more quickly among the Lunda. The development of the small Luba kingdoms of Kikonja, Kaniok, Kalundwe and Kasongo may have paralleled the Lunda genesis, but the emergence of a dominant Luba empire probably only occurred rather later. Before the late eighteenth century, the Luba had only limited commercial relations with their neighbours. Kaniok and Kalundwe were heavily preoccupied with western defence against Lunda raids. The Kikonja had a prosperous internal economy based on lake fish and oil palms. The major copper mines were exploited by Sanga and Lamba chiefs, whose culture was similar to that of the Luba, but who remained independent of them. The wider economic opportunities of the eastern savanna were not, therefore, grasped by the Luba at all, but by Lunda immigrants from the west.

The Lunda expansion into the eastern part of Central Africa came only very shortly after its western drive towards the Atlantic. The first Lunda action on the eastern front took the form of raiding wars against the Luba. Although these wars yielded captives, the Luba frontier states succeeded in mounting such resistance that no permanent Lunda penetration or conquest of the lands of the Lomami and middle Lualaba occurred. Instead the Lunda turned southwards to the upper Lualaba, where people were more thinly scattered and less well organized. Long-distance Lunda expeditions not only reached the Lualaba copper mines, more than 300 kilometres from home, but pressed on eastwards into the plains, to reach the Luapula. The *kazembe*, the chief who led these advance excursions, sent back salt and copper and slaves to his sovereign. Gradually, however, he discovered a new and potentially greater source of wealth. This was the East African ivory trade.

The ivory trade of East Africa was about 2,000 years old, but only in the seventeenth century had an increasing demand made itself felt beyond the lands of the lower Zambezi. The agents who carried the search for ivory from the river ports out into the plains of Central Africa were probably the Bisa, whose territory lay mid-way between the Luapula and the Zambezi. They hunted ivory over a wide area and carried it to the Portuguese markets at Tete, and perhaps Zumbo, farther up the Zambezi. Another outlet for Bisa ivory was by a more easterly route across, or around, Lake Malawi. Here the Bisa sold their tusks to Yao traders who became the great ivory caravaneers of the eighteenth century (see below, chapter 7).

The Lunda role in this growing commerce was a largely political one. As in the west, the Lunda were not themselves great mercantile entrepreneurs. They were, however, adept at the administration of trade, and so built an eastern wing to their empire through which to concentrate the collection of ivory. A convenient central point was found at the Luapula crossing. The Lunda explorer of the region became a colonial king and took the title *mwata kazembe*. He created a court similar to the *musumba*, though he remained a fairly loyal vassal of the *mwata yamvo*. The initial growth of the *mwata kazembe* state was based on less prestigious, though perhaps more fundamental, economic bases than the external trade in ivory. The Luapula valley had a stable and flourishing economy of its own. The indigenous people had both an important fishing industry and a successful agriculture. The latter was enhanced by the Lunda introduction of cassava, which rapidly replaced older crops as a more reliable staple food. On to the local social system, the *mwata kazembe* grafted the prestige of belonging to the Lunda. Chiefs who supported the new court were given a seal of approval and became Lunda by virtue of their function. Many, if not most, of the chiefs and courtiers were Lunda by appointment, rather than migrants who had settled on the Luapula. Once the Lunda system was established, it began to collect tribute from newly subjected peoples. At first this came from domestic subsistence activities, but soon the court was able to profit from regional trade. Lualaba copper was channelled through the *mwata kazembe* to the peoples of northern Zambia, and later Tanzania. The salt trade provided royal revenue. When longer range trade became important, it was managed through the traditional tribute system. Bisa traders came to the *mwata kazembe* and offered him gifts of Asian textiles, which they had brought from the *va-shambadzi* agents of Portuguese trading houses (see below, chapter 6), or from Yao caravan leaders in Malawi. In return Kazembe gave them gifts of tusks which had been brought to him by his tributaries. During the eighteenth century, the Bisa changed their role of ivory hunters for that of trading intermediaries between Lunda and the eastern markets. The Lunda, at the same time, found a major new source of foreign earnings which they succeeded in guarding as closely, and jealously, as they did their western monopoly in slaves. Only towards the end of the eighteenth century did Kazembe's control of the ivory trade become weakened. Elephants became so scarce, and ivory so dear, that the Bisa sought means to by-pass the Luapula and move farther north. They carried their trade to the Lomami river, where the Luba Kasongo state was able to build the same kind of ivory-based power that the *mwata kazembe* had gained a generation earlier. From this base Luba Kasongo defeated Luba Kalundwe and began a rapid wave of expansion to the north and east. This created the unified Luba empire which became familiar to the first foreign travellers who visited eastern Zaïre in the nineteenth century.[1]

Kazembe was the only major kingdom of the eastern plains in the eighteenth century. Its territorial expansion was, however, limited by the Bemba, a strong warrior people who occupied the plateau due east of the Luapula. From their inhospitable retreat, the Bemba conducted raids on more fortunate farming and cattle-rearing peoples. By the end of the eighteenth century, these raids were beginning to take on a systematic quality which led to the creation of Bemba chiefs among conquered peoples. Later in the nineteenth century, these chiefs formed the foundation of a strong military kingdom which attempted to disrupt the orderly pattern of trade which the Lunda had fostered. Meanwhile, however, the *mwata kazembe* had enjoyed his undisputed hegemony over the area for nearly a century before the rise of the Luba Kasongo and Bemba empires to the west and east.

The southern half of Zambia was beyond the range of the Bisa trade routes, or even of Lunda raiding activity. Of the many peoples in the area, two are particularly worthy of mention. These were the Lozi, in the Zambezi valley, and the Tonga on the neighbouring plateau. The Lozi, although a small and isolated people, present an interesting example of political evolution in South-Central Africa. The upper Zambezi flood plain provided environmental opportunities of a kind which did not exist along other stretches of the great rivers. This flood

[1] This interpretation of the chronology of Luba history follows Anne Wilson, 'Long-distance trade and the Luba Lomami empire', *Journal of African History*, 1972, 13, 575–89.

plain provided a long, narrow oasis in the southern woodland. The recurrent fertility of the soil and natural pattern of irrigation may long have been recognized, and may well have attracted gatherers or farmers from as far afield as Zaïre or eastern Angola. By the seventeenth century, intensive occupation appears to have begun, and large settlement mounds were built above the flood level to permit year-round occupation. Cattle were skilfully moved from the mainland to the mounds in large canoes. By about the late seventeenth century, a political system began to emerge in the north of the valley. Later a secondary centre was created in the south, and by the nineteenth century the Lozi state had succeeded in dominating the whole area, though tension still arose between north and south. One role of its government was to co-ordinate the labour force necessary to build mounds and dams and drainage canals. A system of labour regiments was created on a kinship model. The Lozi kings, like the Kongo kings, maintained an economic balance between the various parts of their empire. The woodland peoples surrounding the valley supplied game, hides, iron, woodwork, cloth and honey as their tribute. The valley people supplied fish, grain, baskets, and pastoral produce. The court, after consuming many of these goods, acted as the centre of exchange for the remainder. This economic role of the king was further enhanced by the distribution among his followers of captured cattle and slaves. The cattle were held on trust from him. The slaves were attached to the land as serfs and were rarely, if ever, sold outside.[1]

The Tonga have sometimes been presented as the epitome of the stateless, self-sufficient, subsistence peasant, living in total isolation from his neighbours and caring only for his crops and his cattle. His situation contrasts quite sharply with a powerful Lunda chief commanding a wide range of African or foreign luxury goods, and selling his ivory and slaves on the world market, albeit through the hands of rapacious middlemen. The contrast, however, is not quite complete. The Lunda chief still had his feet firmly planted in the soil, and even at the *musumba* the rotation of the seasons and the bounty of the harvest were important. Furthermore the Tonga peasant was not altogether devoid of material aspirations. He traded with his neighbours to obtain essential materials like hut poles and iron ore and arrow shafts, or to gratify a luxury taste for honey, shea butter and dried fish. Some of his possessions, such as beads and wire bangles, were relayed by many peoples before they reached him. Even when a Tonga had a narrow

[1] Mutumba Mainga, *Bulozi under the Luyana kings* (London, 1973).

range of material wealth, his cattle provided him with a form of prosperity which was never available to the Lunda or other peoples of the Zaïre woodland.

During the seventeenth and eighteenth centuries, three innovations had affected the predominantly small-scale farming societies of Central Africa. The first, and perhaps most pervasive, was the agricultural change brought about by the introduction of American maize and cassava from the west. A change of staple crop must have been seen as beneficial by local peasants since the new crops had spread rapidly, if selectively, to reach such far-off regions as the Kuba kingdom in the north and the Luapula valley in the east by the eighteenth century. Higher yields, greater drought resistance, better storage qualities and reduced labour requirements made the American foods popular. In good years there may have been some decline in the quality of diet as people moved a step farther from the mixed and varied eating habits of the hunter-gatherer to increased dependence on low-grade starch crops, but in bad years famine was more readily staved off.

The second change to be seen during this period was commercial. The local societies had never been totally isolated and self-reliant. Exchanges of material goods always occurred at two levels. One concerned the production and supply of essential raw materials and tools. The large majority of Central African peoples were now dependent on iron. Even when hoes were made of wood, iron adzes and chisels were needed to fashion them. Game may have been caught in nets and pits, but iron knives were used to clean the skins and share the meat. Other important items of early trade were various kinds of cooking salt and domestic pottery. A second important kind of exchange was based on luxury objects, often connected with the circulation of bride-wealth. Here items were governed as much by cultural preference and tastes in fashion as by basic necessity. Raffia textiles, copper beads, ostrich shell pendants, livestock and grain beer were forms of wealth which could be consumed or exchanged during marriage negotiations. It was into this group of prized possessions that external trade made important new contributions. Glass beads and sea shells were bought, metal objects of iron and brass were introduced, new stimulants like rum, brandy, and tobacco came into use, and cotton textiles or European-cut clothing acquired prestige value. This new range of material wants gradually drew more and more peoples of the lower Congo, the western plateaux, and the woodland middle-belt into the sphere of influence of the Atlantic slave trade. Only a small minority succeeded in gaining the new riches. Others lost everything and were carried away as destitute slaves. To the majority, the growth of trading meant a rise in the daily level of fear, insecurity and violence, while only rare samples of the new material wealth filtered down to the villages.

The third set of changes to affect Central Africa in this period was political. The old kingdoms were profoundly modified, like Loango, or even dismembered, like Kongo, and new states emerged in positions of growing strategic importance. The first of the new states was the intrusive Portuguese colony of Angola which established the pattern for small, aggressive, trader-states equipped with firearms. The African rivals of the colonial state drew on older customary political skills in the political management of small societies, as their growth was stimulated by new commercial opportunity. Even the greatest of the broker kingdoms, Kasanje, did not, however, rely on commercial acumen alone for its acquisition of wealth, but built up a raiding empire in which slaves replaced cattle as the pre-eminent prize, and soldiers could be alternately used to loot enemies or to protect trade routes and markets. State-formation, however, had only a minimal effect on most Central African peoples, who continued to live in small isolated villages, rather than in kingdoms. Their isolation may even have increased rather than diminished when elders were forced to lead their people into hidden and remote woodland areas. Yet the Central African kingdoms, even though only affecting a minority, do enable interesting parallels to be drawn with the more familiar field of West African history. Loango, Kasanje, Bihé and Lunda bear some resemblance to the merchant kingdoms of West Africa in seeking to defend their autonomy while at the same time acting as the indirect agents of the Atlantic trade. This similarity between the broker kingdoms of Central Africa and those of Guinea did not outlive the eighteenth century. In this ill-fated southern region the nineteenth century was possibly even more destructive than the eighteenth. It left a legacy of violence, cruelty and despair which has been the burden of the area until the present day. Neither colonial tutelage nor nationalist idealism has succeeded in restoring the freedom from fear which was so rudely shattered two centuries ago.

CHAPTER 6

SOUTHERN AFRICA AND MADAGASCAR

Throughout the subcontinent south of the Zambezi, population densities, political power and many social developments were largely determined by agricultural production. Other economic activities could add comfort, magnificence and even relative luxury to life in some places. The foundations, however, rested firmly on agriculture, and rainfall, more than any human factor, influenced this basic activity. On the fringes of the Kalahari and in other arid areas, hunting or a meagre herding remained the key to bare survival. Elsewhere, over much of the cultivable area, population growth was severely limited by uncertain rainfall, and man's conquest of the harsh environment was still precarious. Yet in the more favoured areas, on the eastern plateaux and the plains flanking the Indian Ocean, a mixed agricultural economy maintained relatively dense and active populations. Here economic specialization and political centralization had developed many varied and resilient cultures. Here were the real centres of power in southern Africa, and before the end of the eighteenth century new crops, principally maize, had begun to increase – perhaps dramatically – the agricultural potential of some of these more favoured areas.

For more than a millennium, the mining and working of gold, copper and iron had provided a subsidiary source of wealth. In a few areas other industrial skills – fine pottery and cloth-weaving – were well established. These indigenous goods, together with salt and agricultural products, formed the basis of the internal trading networks. The export of gold from north of the Limpopo had also long attracted a flow of exotic imports, while in the seventeenth and eighteenth centuries the products of the hunt – ivory, skins and furs – became an increasingly important export from south of the Limpopo. This market-oriented trade for export and internal consumption was in itself a powerful avenue of social change. African traders operated over routes extending up to 1,200 kilometres. In the states that are best known – the Mutapa and Changamire kingdoms – the profits from trade were a fairly important source of political power. South of the Limpopo, the expansion of trade seems to have been a factor, perhaps a major factor, in the growth of centralized organization. Yet wealth and economic power south of the Zambezi were predominantly identified with cattle. Desert and tse-tse fly restricted herding, but on the plateau and on parts of the coastal plains cattle constituted the principal, and often the sole, investment of most rulers and families. Even Butua, source of much of the gold north of the Limpopo, was primarily renowned for its herds. Cattle and other material riches were used primarily to attract and maintain dependants. In Butua, among the Nguni and Tswana, and in the Sakalava kingdoms of Madagascar, this wealth mobilized the energies of loyal subjects on a relatively large scale. The social virtues of co-operation, intimately appreciated by the hunting band or kinship homestead, were magnified. The gods and spirits who dispensed rainfall and intervened in misfortune were seen to sanction royal power. Profits, production and people were bound together in strong concentrations which enabled southern Africa in these centuries rigorously to confine the initial impact of European settlement to its fringe.

Disease, dissensions and ineptitude, although appealed to by the contemporary chroniclers, do not by themselves explain the Portuguese failure to conquer south-east Africa. African strength, together with the lack of Portuguese resources, was far more fundamental. Francisco Barreto's force, which left Lisbon in April 1569 to take over the riches of the Zambezian interior, consisted of no more than 1,000 men, and although, three years later, firearms enabled them to defeat a large army near Sena, the fruits of victory amounted to fifty cows and as many sheep. The expedition retired exhausted to Sena, and Portugal was unable to mount a comparable force for 300 years. Meanwhile, confined to marginal encounters, the Portuguese failed to perceive the basic disparity between European and African power throughout this period. In numbers, economic resources and organizational ability, Africans possessed far greater strength and resilience. Arrogantly relying on the arquebus, and only dimly conscious of the more powerful African kingdoms on the plateau or to the north of the Zambezi, the Portuguese continued to nourish dreams of continental conquest, unaware that even on the lands which they acquired in the valley, the African way of life was stronger than their own.

THE KINGDOM OF THE *MWENE MUTAPA*

Ironically, the Portuguese at first overestimated the power of the African ruler of whom they were most conscious, believing that the *mwene mutapa* controlled the export of gold from the whole of southern Africa. In fact his monopoly was never absolute, for rival and richer kingdoms had alternative outlets. Yet the products and profits of external trade were of considerable significance to the Mutapa dynasty, which claimed an overlordship of the valley and escarpment south of the Zambezi from the area of Dande to the sea. Besides the regular taxes paid by the traders, the indirect benefits to the king were numerous. Many of the luxury imports – silks, carpets, ceramics, glassware – were used by the court and high officials to augment the ruler's prestige or increase his patronage. Beads and imported cotton cloths, which had a much wider circulation, strengthened the court as the redistributive centre. Muslim traders had therefore an established role along the Zambezi and in the *mwene mutapa*'s kingdom, and possibly the most significant action of Barreto's expedition was his sudden attack on the Muslim settlement at Sena, which, together with the subsequent agreement with the *mwene mutapa*, enabled the Portuguese traders to supplant the Muslims.

This intimate link with alien traders by no means involved dependence upon them. They came as suppliants, and by the late sixteenth century each new captain of the Portuguese fort at Mozambique island had to pay the *mwene mutapa* a *curva* of 1,000 crusados (*c.* £200) per annum to open the land to the traders. The Captain of the Gates, who resided at Masapa, the principal entrepôt in the kingdom for merchants from Sena and Tete, then collected for the *mwene mutapa* a further 50 per cent tax on the cloth imported. Elected by the traders, this official symbolized the Portuguese position of subordinate symbiosis, for his appointment had to be confirmed by the *mwene mutapa*, whose insignia he carried and without whose permission he could not leave his post on pain of death. Similar taxes were paid to the ruler of Uteve, the state which dominated the immediate hinterland of Sofala, and the Dominican Dos Santos describes how at the *sachiteve*'s court the Portuguese 'throw themselves upon the ground sideways...and so speak without looking at him, clapping their hands after every four words', while in 1620 Mwene Mutapa Gatsi Rusere still insisted that even distinguished European visitors should enter his presence unshod and squat before his throne.[1]

External trade, however, was merely one of the bases of the *mwene mutapa*'s power. Even in the acquisition of luxury, prestige items, the

[1] Jesuit archives, Rome. Goa series, vol. 9, I, fols. 47, 56–7. Letters of Julio Cesare Vertua, 23 April 1621 and 3 October 1623. Dos Santos in G. M. Theal, *Records of south-eastern Africa* (Cape Town, 1898–1903), VII, 195.

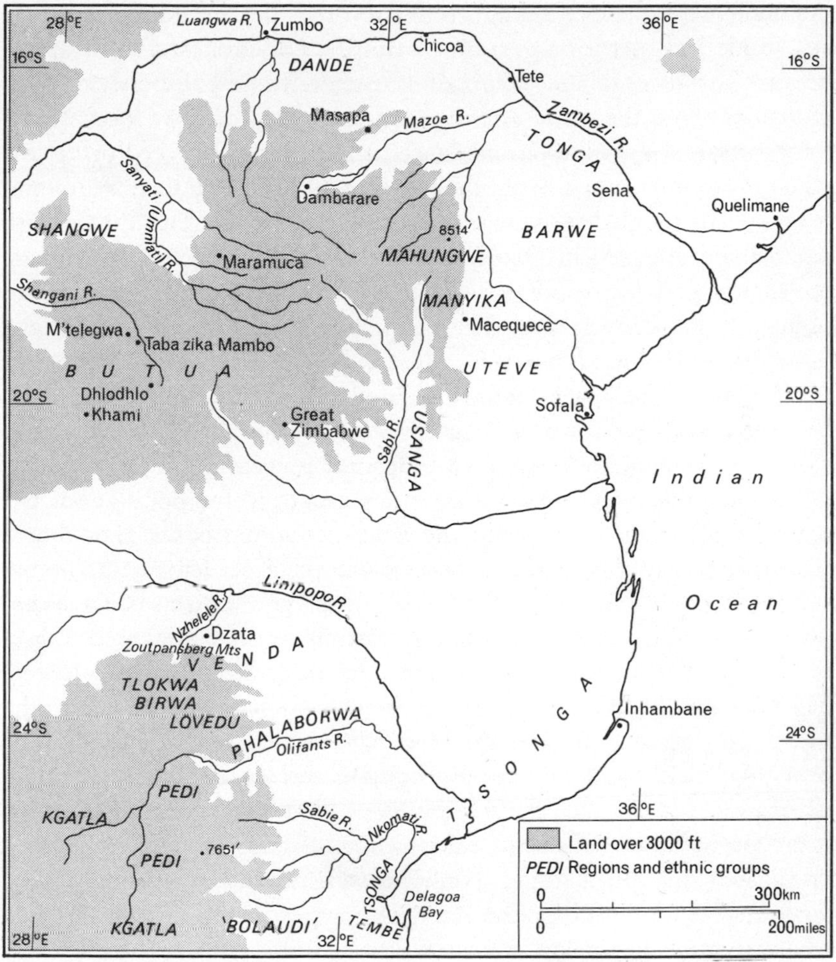

12 South of the Zambezi

products of local craftsmen were probably still of greater significance than imports. Gold, finely drawn and intricately worked into bracelets or plated on furniture and insignia, was supplemented by silver ornaments, also made from local ore, the use of which was restricted to the royal family and the highest officers of the state. When the court was sacked in 1629, the Portuguese were confronted by the sacred *ngoma*, 'an immense copper drum, covered with rich silk cloths and lion skins, and inside full of various vermin'.[1] But the commonest and most impressive instances of the continued importance and prosperity of local industries were the *machira* cloths woven slowly on low looms from local cotton. In 1573 the Jesuit Monclaro considered that the Portuguese could make more profit from the local trade in *machira* than by mining for gold. Although dressed in silk, Gatsi Rusere covered his throne with *machira* and adorned his walls with them; while even the Portuguese merchants at Dambarare were buried throughout the seventeenth century in *machira* shrouds. The peoples of the northern bank of the Zambezi were specialists in this industry, but the production and use of *machira* penetrated deep into the southern plateau and across the Limpopo, and *machira* held their own until submerged by the cotton cloths of the nineteenth-century industrial revolution.

Yet craftsmen were merely a minute segment of the population, and agricultural produce provided the solid economic base for a ruler's power. In Uteve in the late sixteenth century each settlement and homestead cultivated a crop of millet for the ruler. The subjects of the *mwene mutapa* annually sent livestock and foodstuffs to the court, receiving in return a gift of cloth or other goods. In an economy still so largely dependent on small-scale agriculture, rainfall played a crucial part in the prosperity of the state, and the ruler participated in the rituals which brought fertility and rain. In Portuguese references to the monthly, new moon dance which the *mwene mutapa* held for his ancestors, to his great annual feast of *chuano*, and to his *marombe* or musicians who 'awakened' the spirits to the people's need for rain, can be glimpsed the sanctions which provided the ruler with supernatural power precisely where it was most relevant materially. The dynasty had successfully assimilated the powerful Dzivaguru rain-making cult, so in both economics and religion the *mwene mutapa* stood at the centre and his ritual united these spheres.

This economic and religious strength was not, however, expressed

[1] E. A. Axelson, ed. 'Viagem que fez o Padre Antonio Gomes, da Companhia de Jesus, ao Imperio de de (sic) Manomotapa; e assistencia que fez nas ditas terras de Alg'us annos', *Studia*, 1959, 3, 191.

in a rigid, all-embracing political structure. The ruler could mobilize vast numbers for war. Mwene Mutapa Nogomo offered Barreto a force of 100,000 men, and even minor campaigns involved tens of thousands. But, apart from a small bodyguard, there was no permanent disciplined standing army. At the court there were a number of well-established offices and positions of leadership, many of them often held by members of the royal family. Legal cases were heard regularly on the six holidays in every thirty days, and the ruler's judicial function was of considerable importance. But with communications difficult and at times non-existent, the huge kingdom was loosely organized. Some of the subordinate chiefs maintained their *chuanga* or procurators and representatives at court. Beyond this inner circle there were the vassal or tributary rulers whose annual embassies constituted their main contact with the centre. There were few fixed boundaries; exclusive, monolithic allegiance was rare, for men identified themselves with different groups – village, kinship, ritual and kingdom – in varying degrees of intensity. The diffused nature of this rule was to give the kingdom a flexible resilience; but its fluctuating power, partly dependent on the personal energy and abilities of its rulers, was vulnerable both to incursions from without and dissensions from within. And it was this which gave the Portuguese their opportunity.

The dangers became apparent soon after Gatsi Rusere succeeded Nogomo as *mwene mutapa* in *c.* 1589. The kingdom's territories in the Zambezi valley were attacked by the Zimba in 1592, and then, five years later, the gold-producing lands south of the escarpment were invaded by a neighbouring chief. During this crisis the *mwene mutapa* quarrelled with an influential relative whom he put to death. Many of his other relatives and subordinate chieftains then rose against him in a rebellion led by Matuzianhe, one of the guardians of the king's cattle on the high veld. Instead of relying on a mobilization of his traditional resources, Gatsi Rusere appealed to the Portuguese traders at Masapa, Tete and Sena, who successfully came to his assistance in a series of minor campaigns. The payment was exacted in instalments, almost imperceptibly. After 1599 the king allowed the Portuguese to enter the kingdom with guns, a thing, according to Bocarro, 'strictly forbidden by him before'.[1] The interventions on his behalf continued, and on 1 August 1607 Gatsi Rusere publicly ceded the mineral wealth of his kingdom through the trader, Diogo Simões Madeira, to his 'brother-in-arms' the king of Portugal.

[1] Bocarro in Theal, *Records*, III, 364.

Alliance and infiltration had proved more profitable for the Portuguese than a frontal assault, but even so their success was more apparent than real. They lacked the resources to exploit their opportunity, and the African kingdom showed unsuspected powers of recovery. The location of the silver mines was not disclosed, and once Matuzianhe had been decisively defeated, Gatsi Rusere successfully asserted his independence. When, in 1610, a new Portuguese commander refused to pay the *curva*, the *mwene mutapa* imposed the traditional sanction: a *mupeto*, or forcible confiscation throughout his kingdom. Portuguese traders were raided, several were killed, and their goods were seized, including those of Madeira. Five years later Gatsi Rusere sent a combined Karanga and Tonga army against a Portuguese force which, prospecting for silver near Chicoa, had shot the son of a local chief; in 1616 the Portuguese in Tete itself only escaped attack from his forces by hurriedly paying a ransom of cloth; and right through his later years the *mwene mutapa* negotiated with the Portuguese from a position of independent superiority, only on his death bed in 1622 sending a messenger to request Christian baptism.

The pressures experienced during Gatsi Rusere's reign, nevertheless, soon produced a crisis which involved all the major contestants for power in the Zambezi valley. The uncertainty following his death, during which four of his seventy sons disputed the succession, facilitated a further incursion from north of the Zambezi. Led by Muzura, ruler of the Maravi (see below, chapter 7, p. 517), this invasion was however more than an extensive raid. It was specifically directed against the developing Portuguese possessions. For Muzura was assisted by Chombe, ruler of a chieftaincy which had co-operated with Barreto, but who had subsequently amassed firearms through trade with the Portuguese and who in 1613 had with difficulty been expelled from his lands by Madeira after refusing to pay an annual tribute to Sena. Muzura's campaign provoked a vigorous Portuguese response. Chombe was wounded and forced north of the Zambezi, and the lands of several chiefs, some of whom had not been implicated originally, were put to the sword.[1] But in November 1628 the new *mwene mutapa*, Nyambo Kapararidze, joined in the active hostility to the Portuguese by killing an ambassador and declaring a *mupeto* on the Portuguese trade. Kapararidze seems to have been acting in alliance with Muslim traders operating from their base in the coastal sheikdom of Angoche, south of

[1] Jesuit archives, Rome. Goa series, vol. 33, II, fols. 767–9. Letter of Barreto, 15 December 1624.

Mozambique island, where in 1627 a Portuguese priest had been killed, and in 1629, when Kapararidze was defeated, the Portuguese once again insisted that all 'Arab' traders should be expelled from the kingdom.

Internal conflict within the Mutapa dynasty was, however, a prime factor in the Portuguese victory. Since the early sixteenth century the dynasty had been divided into two separate Houses or lines of descent. Gatsi Rusere and his son Kapararidze belonged to one, while Nogomo, the *mwene mutapa* before them, had belonged to the other. For Mavura, Nogomo's son, the accession of Kapararidze presented a major challenge, for it seemed as if he and his House were being excluded from the succession.[1] In order to protect the interests of his House, Mavura allied himself with the Portuguese and ascended to the throne with their help. On 24 May 1629 he signed a treaty which purported to make him a vassal of the king of Portugal, and spelled out in detail the respect which henceforth he should show to Portuguese officials, traders and missionaries. Yet, despite its appearance of finality, the treaty in fact decided nothing. As soon as the Portuguese force withdrew, Mavura demanded payment of the *curva*, the Portuguese continued to consider plans to 'conquer' his kingdom, and in 1631 Kapararidze placed himself at the head of an uprising against the Portuguese, which swept through the kingdom and that of Manyika, reaching as far as Quelimane at the mouth of the Zambezi, and killing, according to one account, 400 Portuguese.

For a moment it seemed as if the *mwene mutapa* dynasty might reassert its dominance throughout its former lands, but its internal divisions were now too great, and its central authority too weak, to overthrow the Portuguese hold on the Zambezi commerce. By sending payments of cloth, Mavura was able to recruit a large army from north of the Zambezi, while a reinforcement of 200 Portuguese musketeers, under Sousa de Meneses, captain of Mozambique, was sufficient to relieve Quelimane and to rally the Africans on Portuguese lands in the valley. As the viceroy's secretary observed: 'conditions are now very different from what they were in former times, for we fight them with the same Kaffirs with whom they formerly fought us'.[2] Meneses stormed into

[1] This division of the dynasty is mentioned in traditions collected by D. P. Abraham, 'The early political history of the Kingdom of Mwene-Mutapa (850–1589)', in *Historians in Tropical Africa* (Salisbury, 1962). Its implications for the seventeenth century have been discussed by D. Beach in an unpublished seminar paper, 'Historians and the Shona Empires', 1972.

[2] Rezende in Theal, *Records*, II, 418.

Manyika, captured the *chikanga*, and, placing a vassal on his throne, pressed on to defeat Kaparaidze in battle on 24 June 1633. Mavura was re-established on the throne, but now his status as a vassal was no longer in doubt. The initiative in the Zambezi valley had passed to the Portuguese: yet not to the imperial authorities, but to the local traders, settlers and adventurers, who by the 1630s were already carving out for themselves vast estates, or *prazos*.

The assimilation of the Portuguese by Africans is perhaps nowhere better illustrated than in the development and functioning of the Zambezi *prazos*. As an estate leased by the crown for a limited period in return for military and fiscal services rendered by the holder or tenant, the *prazo* could be viewed in Portuguese legal theory as an overseas extension of a Portuguese feudal institution. In practice, the residents exhibited not merely a blatant disregard of their obligations towards the Portuguese crown but also, and more subtly, an intimate dependence on local African institutions. The first land rights had been granted in the sixteenth century by still powerful African rulers. Even in the mid-seventeenth century when the balance of power had shifted, the establishment of the *prazos* often still involved the initiative and co-operation of traditional African authorities. Sisnando Dias Bayão, a forceful, acquisitive warrior and *prazo*-holder, was regarded by contemporaries as a supreme example of a *conquistador*. Yet his greatest estate was given him by the ruler of Uteve after he had intervened to quell a revolt at the latter's request. And upon the *prazos* themselves, the tenant, as we shall see, remained dependent on traditional African institutions.

By the mid-seventeenth century these Portuguese had begun to penetrate deep into the plateau of Mashonaland, establishing trading posts as far as Maramuca in the neighbourhood of the upper Sanyati river. A fairly level-headed Jesuit, Manuel Barreto, could even maintain in 1667 that 'a hundred able musketeers' would suffice to impose Portuguese authority throughout the whole area south of the Zambezi. This boast, however, overlooked the fundamental weaknesses of the Portuguese position and seriously underestimated African resources and powers of recovery. The Portuguese were never sufficiently numerous to hold so vast an area, and while African divisions had provided the invaders with their opportunity, the Portuguese were even more disorganized and disunited. The *prazo* owners threatened the crown's authority and were bitterly divided amongst themselves – Bayão, for instance, was poisoned by jealous rivals at the height of his power.

African divisions, on the other hand, tended to mask the resilience of their flexible, loosely organized political allegiance. The different levels of social identification, and the customary fluctuations in a ruler's personal prestige, rendered it difficult if not impossible for the Portuguese to weld a conquered kingdom into anything like a monolithic obedience. Although Kapararidze had been overwhelmingly defeated in 1633, ten years later he was still feared by the Portuguese, and, on the death of Mavura in 1652, the Dominicans hastened to install and baptize Mavura's son 'fearing some disturbance on the part of Caprasine'.[1]

Even over the 'puppet' kings, Portuguese control was by no means absolute. Manuel Barreto regarded the *mwene mutapa* as 'still a very powerful king', receiving the homage of Barwe, Manyika and a great part of the Zambezi Tonga, though he considered that the Portuguese at Dambarare with their private armies were more powerful than the king himself. Yet by 1682 the captain at Sena reported that the *mwene mutapa* was constantly threatening to rise in rebellion and there were then only two or three Portuguese residents at Dambarare, still the 'chief town' of the rivers. Shortly afterwards the fragility of the whole Portuguese position in the interior and the unsuspected resources of their adversaries were dramatically exposed by a sudden onslaught of Changamire Dombo from Butua.

BUTUA

Although the existence of Butua, lying to the south-west of the *mwene mutapa*'s kingdom, had been known to the Portuguese since the early sixteenth century, they still had but the vaguest concept of it. It was famous for its wealth in cattle and gold. Fernandes had reported that much gold was extracted alongside its rivers. Barreto's expedition was supplied with draught oxen from Butua, and Dos Santos stated that its people were 'much occupied with the breeding of cattle'.[2] It was variously reputed to stretch towards the Cape and to be in tenuous commercial contact with Angola. Only once is a Portuguese force known to have penetrated its territories, when in 1644 Sisnando Dias Bayão marched there to intervene in a succession dispute; but after the murder of Bayão during his return journey, the small garrisons he

[1] 'Autentica testimonianza del Battesimo...', in Theal, *Records*, II, 445.

[2] Veloso's description of Fernandes's journey in *Documents on the Portuguese in Mozambique and Central Africa* (Lisbon, 1962 in progress), III, 185. Dos Santos in Theal, *Records*, VII, 274.

had left in the interior were hastily withdrawn, and Butua remained virtually a *terra incognita*.

Yet this area of Guruhuswa, or Gunuvutwa as pronounced by the Tavara informants of the Portuguese, who then transformed the name to Butua, lies at the centre of Shona traditions. Stretching from Shangwe in the north-west across to the Sabi and Limpopo rivers, Guruhuswa was the realm of the ancient Togwa dynasty, which is linked in Shona traditions with Great Zimbabwe. Primarily this centre is remembered as 'a holy place', but it is also known as the capital where chiefs came to pay homage and from where the messengers of the Togwa *mambo* or ruler were sent out to install chiefs.[1]

To the Togwa dynasty is ascribed the period of greatest construction, but by 1600 the glory and importance of Great Zimbabwe seems already to have been eclipsed: for the absence of imported ceramics from this site of a date later than the fifteenth century forcibly suggests that during the Portuguese period it was no longer the centre of a powerful kingdom, though it retained some ritual significance well into the nineteenth century. At so disturbed a site the archaeological evidence is notoriously difficult to interpret, but this supposition of a relatively early decline is perhaps strengthened by a hearsay Jesuit report of 1649 that only the ruins of a once famous building in Butua were still to be seen.[2]

Yet even if the most impressive site linked with the Togwa dynasty was no longer an important political capital, the royal dynasty itself continued to flourish well into the seventeenth century. In 1633 a Dominican in charge of the Manyika missions was told by African traders, who came annually to trade in Manyika from Butua, six days journey to the west, that the treasure of Togwa, their king, was bars of gold, while a Portuguese document of 1683 refers to Togwa as still being the ruler of Butua.

The process by which the upstart line of Changamire seized control of this ancient kingdom of Butua is by no means clear. Writing in 1696, within a year of the death of Changamire Dombo, Fr. Antonio da Conceição stated that originally the *changamire* had been the herdsman of the *mwene mutapa* who had given him land adjoining Togwa's Butua. Having taken possession of this land, the *changamire* began to conquer the lands of Butua and finally became master of nearly all of it, 'aided only by his reputation of being a most able sorcerer'. Fr. Antonio writes

[1] Tradition mentioned in E. M. Lloyd, 'Mbava', *NADA*, 1925, 3, 62–3.

[2] Jesuit archives, Rome. Goa series, vol. 34, I, fol. 210. Report by G. Maracci based on information from Fr. A. Gomes.

as if all this had been achieved by Changamire Dombo, and much later, in an account of the 1760s, it was specifically stated that the *changamire* had been a herdsman sent to the lands of the Rozvi by Mwene Mutapa Mukombwe, who ruled from *c.* 1667 to *c.* 1694. The description, in Diogo de Alcáçova's letter of 1506, of how '*changamir*' had risen against and killed a *mwene mutapa* at the end of the fifteenth century, shows, however, that both the title and the rivalry have a far greater antiquity.[1] Although, therefore, Fr. Antonio's informants may well have accurately identified the secrets of the *changamires*' success, and in particular those of Changamire Dombo, they seem to have overlooked a genealogy and its chronological implications.

Yet if the rise of the Changamire dynasty remains somewhat obscure, the consequences were dramatically plain, both for the Shona and the Portuguese. Most obvious and immediate was their military impact. In 1684, at a battle in Mahungwe, 'this proud enemy', in Fr. Antonio's words, 'dared to measure his bows against our muskets'. Changamire Dombo's own weapons were by no means despicable: besides bows and arrows, his troops were armed with spears, a special club called *goromondo* (which is also the Shona term for an outsize cob of maize), and battle-axes, which much later were envied and respected even by the Ndebele. But the outcome was decided by martial qualities other than armaments, and the battle of Mahungwe should have destroyed the Portuguese myth of the invincibility of their firearms. Fr. Antonio attributed the *changamire*'s victory to his cunning and subtlety, and in particular to a ruse by which, during the night, after the battle had raged undecided throughout the day, the Portuguese army and their auxiliaries suddenly found themselves encircled by the fires of their enemy, 'and like the Midianites on seeing the torches of Gideon' fled panic stricken, leaving Dombo to take unopposed possession of the Portuguese position and booty. Undoubtedly ambushes, stratagems and 'war-medicine' were an important component in the *changamires*' military successes: Shona traditions contain several accounts of the skilful duplicity of royal Rozvi women who successfully murdered or immobilized enemy leaders; there are numerous examples of the Rozvi ability to enlist swarms of bees and supernatural agencies to their assistance; and one of the functions of the *tumbare*, a military commander,

[1] Antonio de Conceição, 'Tratado dos Rios de Cuama', in J. H. da Cunha Rivara, ed., *O Chronista de Tissuary* (Goa, 1867), 105. L. F. de Carvalho Dias, ed. *Fontes para a história, geografia e comércio de Moçambique (sec xviii)* in *Anais*, 9, i (Lisbon, Junta de Investigações do Ultramar, 1954), 133, for account dated 20 January 1763. Letter from Diogo de Alcáçova, 20 November 1506, in *Documents on the Portuguese*, I, 393.

was to supply the requisite medicines. Essentially, however, both medicines and stratagems merely strengthened, and reflected, a reputation and prestige which enabled the *changamires*, alone among their adversaries, whether African or European, repeatedly to rely in battle on the basic military virtue of disciplined obedience: as Fr. Antonio confessed, 'in being so well obeyed by his people he enjoyed a great advantage over us'.

Although it is difficult to discern the course of Changamire Dombo's foreign policy, the Portuguese were under no misconceptions as to the basic causes of his hostility. 'Judging from what everyone from the Rivers uniformly writes to me', the viceroy reported from Goa, 'the insolence of our people was the cause of these wars, for those who hold power and own African servants commit such excesses that from the scandalized Kings and Princes break forth these disasters'.[1] After his victory at Mahungwe, Dombo did not immediately proceed to press home his advantage. Then in November 1693, at the request of Nyakumbiru, a usurper who had seized the throne on the death of Mwene Mutapa Mukombwe, Dombo suddenly swept down on the principal Portuguese fair of Dambarare. Once more his success was total, and not one Portuguese or Indian trader escaped from Dambarare. Those at the neighbouring fairs fled to Tete, together with the Portuguese garrison from the *mwene mutapa*'s capital, and thus, as the Jesuit Francisco de Sousa moralized,

> came to an end all the fairs of gold in consequence of the injuries and injustices, which from our side were committed against the Emperors of Mwene Mutapa, who always received and treated us as if we were their sons, or, as they put it to show us greater good-will, their wives.[2]

Eighteen months later Dombo's military power was felt in Manyika and the Portuguese fair at Macequece was destroyed. Much later, towards the end of the eighteenth century, a Portuguese visitor to Manyika, Manuel Galvão, picked up the story that the *changamire*'s conquest of Manyika had been inspired by the fact that the Portuguese commander there twice flogged one of his sons or vassals – a tradition that at least tends to support the contemporary verdict of Jesuit and viceroy.

Yet it is unlikely that vengeance, however justifiable, was Dombo's sole or even principal motivation. Almost certainly his policy was

[1] Letter from the viceroy, 16 November 1694, in S. R. Welch, *Some unpublished manuscripts relating to the history of South and East Africa* (Pretoria, 1933), 35.

[2] Francisco de Sousa, *Oriente Conquistado a Jesus Christo pelos Padres da Companhia de Jesus da provincia de Goa* (Lisbon, 1710), 1, 835.

influenced by the quest for security. Previous Portuguese activities on the plateau – the settlement at Maramuca, the expedition of Dias Bayão – must have alarmed any ruler of Butua. It is also possible that an economic motive entered into his considerations. By expelling the Portuguese from the fairs in the Mazoe area and by conquering Manyika, the ruler of Butua, by common repute itself the richest area of gold mining, was able to assert a virtual monopoly over the supply of gold to the Portuguese. No longer would the Portuguese be able to penetrate to the richest sources of gold south of the Zambezi. Certainly for more than a century, while the Changamire dynasty constituted the dominant power in the area, it remained a cardinal point of policy with Dombo's successors never to permit a Portuguese trader from the Zambezi to set foot in Butua.

Cut off, as Fr. Antonio reported, with 'not a grain of gold' to maintain themselves, the remaining Portuguese feebly barricaded the streets of Sena and awaited Dombo's final onslaught. Once more, as in 1631, it seemed as if the Portuguese would be expelled from the Zambezi, but in January 1696 news reached them of Dombo's death, a succession dispute and the withdrawal of his army. Yet the impact of Dombo's conquests was permanent. Excluded from the plateau, the Portuguese were unable to establish any direct contact with the major sources of gold production and were denied the climatic advantages which the highlands offered for European settlement. Expulsion from the plateau led to a minor extension of the Zambezi river route and the founding of the trading centre of Zumbo at the confluence with the Luangwa. But essentially, after their encounter with Dombo, the Portuguese remained confined to, and increasingly dependent upon, the *prazo* system in the valley.

On the *prazos*, the chiefs and village headmen seem to have retained many of their traditional functions over the *colonos* or customary inhabitants, while rendering an annual tribute (*misonkho*) and other services to the holder as their overlord. In addition to this network of traditional authorities, the holder's power depended on his slaves or clients, who were organized into bands of armed warriors (*chikunda*). Some particularly trusted slaves acted as traders (*va-shambadzi*, sing. *mu-shambadzi*) and as *chuanga* or spies on the traditional authorities. It was a complex, fluctuating, unstable relationship punctuated by protests, occasional revolts and mass disruptions when *colonos* or *chikunda* transferred their allegiance to other overlords or withdrew to independent rulers beyond the confines of the *prazo* system. Politically the Portuguese overlords lacked the supports of traditional legitimacy, and both *colonos* and clients retained considerable areas of initiative. Economically, the *prazo* rested on an inefficient exploitation of the subsistence agriculture, supplemented, until the growth of the export slave trade in the last decades of the eighteenth century, by some traditional gold mining and the trade of the *va-shambadzi* with neighbouring African polities. This dependence on African institutions, skill and techniques extended also to the realm of religion, with some Portuguese adopting traditional modes of divination and practising African rites. The dilution of Portuguese culture on the *prazos* was paralleled by the failure of the Catholic missions to make an impact on Africans in the valley or beyond. Even on the *prazos* owned by the Jesuits until their expulsion in 1759, the number of baptized Christians was pitifully small. Confined to the valley by Dombo's conquests, Portugal found that even when metropolitan energies were mobilized under Pombal, she lacked any real base for development in south-central Africa.

For the Shona-speaking peoples, the internal consequences of Dombo's career were no less far-reaching than his external triumph. Yet it would seem that the successful establishment of the Changamire dynasty by no means involved a complete break in Shona political and social organization. Nor, apparently, did it represent the intrusion of a new ruling people. Rather, it would seem that the *changamire*s' success merely strengthened the centralizing forces within Butua. But they achieved this at a moment and in a manner which left an indelible imprint on Shona memories.

The first Portuguese references to the Rozvi or 'borobzes' occur in the eighteenth century, identifying them as the people of the *changamire*, and Shona traditions collected from the end of the nineteenth century refer to the Rozvi, with the totem and praise *moyo ndizvo*, as constituting the ruling clan before the Ndebele conquest in the 1830s. Some of these Rozvi also have traditions of a relatively recent migration from the south, and it has sometimes been assumed therefore that the *changamires* came into power as the leaders of a small yet powerful group of alien invaders. One line of recent research indicates, however, that the term originally referred to a much more ancient stratum of Shona society, identifying the Rozvi as the people of the fish eagle, probably connected with some of the earliest building at Great Zimbabwe.[1] On this reckoning both the Mutapa and Togwa dynasties were Rozvi dynasties, and the rise of the *changamires* merely represented the successful emergence of

[1] Personal communication from Mr D. P. Abraham, March 1969.

a family of war-leaders. The documentary evidence, however, links the Rozvi clearly with Dombo and his successors, and in common usage the term refers to the close adherents of this upstart dynasty.

Since relatively little is as yet known of the previous Togwa dynasty, the innovations introduced by the *changamires* cannot be assessed in detail, but it is possible to identify some of the changes which helped to consolidate their power and influence. Although military strength lay at the root of at least their earlier successes, they do not appear to have made any fundamental alterations in this sphere. They did not create a standing army; mobilization was on an *ad hoc* basis, warriors assembling at the cry of 'fill your bag with food', although an eighteenth-century Portuguese report that the army was divided into two squadrons may suggest that its organization was rather more developed than that of the *mwene mutapa*. During the eighteenth century, the *changamires* began to add firearms to the Butuan armoury: muskets and ammunition were presented to their embassies and despatched to them by traders at Zumbo and Sena; a document of 1831 reported that the *changamire* had armed one of his palaces with four 'large' pieces of artillery, and in 1897 when James Bryce visited Dhlodhlo, site of a Rozvi centre, he reported that bullets, fragments of muskets and a small cannon had been found there. In the nineteenth century, after the Ndebele invasion, the purchase and use of guns by the Shona played an appreciable part in their resistance to Ndebele raids, but in the *changamire* period the relatively small numbers of firearms reaching the plateau could have had little effect on military tactics, their significance probably being more psychological than practical. Throughout the eighteenth century, as at the battle of Mahungwe, the *changamire*s' military power seems to have depended on strict discipline linked to a formidable prestige: 'very powerful and well obeyed', wrote Luis Figuerido, who had been governor of Zumbo in 1754, the *changamire* 'is the terror of this hinterland'.[1] Such was their reputation that relatively small armies of 2,000 men were sufficient to punish distant chiefs for interfering with trade routes or for refusing to pay tribute. Warfare remained confined to limited objectives, battles and fighting were still of a conventional nature with few casualties; it was a far cry from those areas affected by the slave trade and very different from the total warfare which was to follow the Shakan revolution (see volume 5, chapter 11).

If in the military field the *changamires* rested on their early laurels, economically and politically they strengthened their position by several

[1] Carvalho Dias, ed., *Fontes*, 260.

fundamental innovations. Their vigorous exclusion of Portuguese traders, in successful contrast to the situation under the Togwa dynasty when aliens had been allowed to penetrate and establish themselves deep into the interior, was but one aspect of their attempt to control the sources of economic power. The trade in gold was by far the most important means of obtaining overseas trade-goods, which, as in the case of the *mwene mutapa*, may have been a significant support for royal power. The *changamire*'s trade with Zumbo began very soon after its foundation early in the eighteenth century, and in 1769, after a brief interruption, the *changamire* sent an embassy there with a pressing request for armaments and cloth 'with which to clothe himself', while fifteen years later another embassy to Zumbo testified to their concern over this trade. Beads and alcohol were also regularly imported, and gifts of Oriental and European porcelain and metal ware augmented the ruler's prestige. The *changamires* appear to have been successful in controlling both the production and the exchange of gold, the key to these imports. In 1750 a well informed governor of Sena reported that the *changamire*'s subjects were forbidden on pain of death to mine gold on their own account, and the 1769 embassy recounted how three detachments of his troops had been sent to punish some miners for not having reported the discovery of new mines. Their control over major transactions in gold is also revealed by the fact that, besides excluding the Portuguese from their kingdom, the *changamires* prevented their subjects from gaining direct access to the Portuguese. The Rozvi expeditions to Zumbo were embassies not trading caravans, and the only permitted intermediaries in the gold trade were the *va-shambadzi*, the influential indigenous agents, even if technically termed slaves, of the traders and Dominicans at Zumbo. Although these men amassed wealth of their own in Butua, one of them being fined some 800 head of cattle by the *changamire*, they remained dependent both on their links with Zumbo and on royal favours. They were therefore far easier to control than either the Portuguese or independent Rozvi traders would have been, although in 1784 the *changamire* complained that they were trading independently with a chief flanking the Zumbo route.

Zumbo was the most important outlet for Butuan gold during the first half of the eighteenth century, and in a good year Butua provided nearly half a million crusados worth of gold (*c.* £100,000), but the fair in Manyika, re-established with the *changamire*'s approval in the first quarter of the eighteenth century, also traded in products from Butua. Here the *changamire*'s control was much less absolute than in the

Zumbo hinterland. Butuan traders took to Manyika a variety of products including gold, ivory and ostrich eggs. Portuguese trade there was dependent on an annual payment of cloth, beads and liquor, which was divided between the local potentates and the ruler of Butua, and the *changamire*s' profit from the Manyika trade seems to have been mainly confined to this tribute. Ivory from tributary areas on the eastern marches of Butua was also traded at ports on the coast, probably with little or no centralized control, but Portuguese accounts leave no doubt that external trade was dominated by the supply of Butuan gold, and over this export the eighteenth century *changamires* exercised a far more effective control than either the Mutapa or Togwa dynasties.

The *changamires* were also the masters of an important sector of the internal economy: they were the principal patrons of indigenous industrial skills and dominated the production and consumption of luxury items. Gold was not only the most important export; as an ornament it was used to embellish the courts and royal burials. At Dhlodhlo, one of the royal residences, 700 ounces of gold were found in the form of beads, finely engraved with chevron patterns, gold tacks, chainwork, wire made into filigree baskets and threaded into cloth, and gold-plate beaten into what Hall described as 'a marvellous thinness' to be used as a covering for headrests and household furniture.[1] Much of this splendour was produced on the site by goldsmiths, and this royal concentration of skill and ostentation was matched in other materials. The beautiful and famous band and panel, black and red pottery, found almost exclusively in association with the highly decorated stone buildings in the heart of Butua, was made, according to one tradition, by Lilima and Humbe women at the rulers' courts; at Dhlodhlo there is also evidence of ivory and soapstone carving and of much iron and copper work, while weaving was carried on at Khami probably during this period. But while, in terms of prestige and power, this patronage of specialized skills must have been of considerable political significance, economically this palace control and centralization may well have shackled further development. Despite its prosperity and potential, Butua under the *changamires* did not develop a flourishing market-oriented commerce. The stimulus of commercial expansion and widening opportunities was excluded. Instead, its long-distance trade and its industrial skills seem to have been largely confined to serving the relatively limited demands of the royal courts, and the wealth of

[1] R. N. Hall and W. G. Neal, *The ancient ruins of Rhodesia* (London, 1902), 95. J. F. Schofield, *Primitive pottery* (Cape Town, 1948), 84.

Butua as a whole continued to be predominantly that of a subsistence agriculture, whose products together with those of the hunt still provided a very substantial part even of the ruler's riches.

The collection of this tribute, largely consisting of foodstuffs, tobacco, cattle, skins and game, involved what was probably the most significant political innovation effected by the *changamires* or Rozvi *mambos*. Whereas in the *mwene mutapa*'s kingdom, and possibly therefore also in Togwa's Butua, tribute was brought to the capital by embassies from provincial rulers, its collection being organized in a hierarchical pyramid and largely dependent on the loyalty of the principal vassals, in the *mambo*'s realm there was a centralized corps of tribute collectors, the *banyamai*. These men, commanded by specially selected headmen, relatives of the ruler being excluded from this office, were sent out from the centre by the *mambo* himself, and their activities were supervised by the *tumbare*, who was a principal official of the royal court as well as being a commander of the army. If necessary the *banyamai* were supported by military expeditions, several instances of punishment for non-payment being well remembered in Shona traditions. Apart from this important issue of tribute-collection, the influence of the *changamire mambo* over much of the area of Butua was seen mainly in his right of ratifying the succession to subordinate chieftaincies. In a wide arc from Shangwe to Usanga, and inwards to the central Karanga area, a number of traditions testify to the importance attached to this right. The installation ceremonies appear to have differed slightly, but they all involved the participation of representatives from the Rozvi ruler, who generally presented a handful of soil to the new chief, symbolic perhaps of an ancient 'Rozvi' ownership of the soil now reinforced by the power and prestige of the *changamires*. In at least one case, that of the frontier kingdom of Mahungwe, the Rozvi appear to have maintained a permanent representative at the vassal's court, and here the right of ratification was often effectively used to influence the choice of succession. Elsewhere newcomers were given permission by the Rozvi ruler to settle, and their relationship was sealed by marriage, the client chief becoming a son-in-law. This political influence was, however, never cemented into a close-knit hegemony. Communications remained tenuous, for although the Rozvi, like Tswana groups, used oxen for riding, they had no horses. At the local level, the politics of this period are indeed remembered as a process of fluctuating alliances rather than of rigid centralization, new lineages being founded easily and continually by the dissatisfied, unsuccessful claimants to office. Only in the far south-east, in the districts towards the Limpopo, do some traditions indicate that a different state of affairs might have existed, for here apparently 'there were no chiefs' and only the sovereign rule of the *mambo* is said to be remembered.[1]

In one other sphere, that of religion, great changes have been attributed to the Changamire dynasty. It has been suggested that the Rozvi cult of Mwari, the oracular deity whose shrine during the nineteenth and twentieth centuries was situated in the Matopos, differs radically from those of the *mhondoro* spirits of the northern and eastern Shona groups.[2] In contrast to the numerous ancestral spirits, the religion of Mwari has also been seen as monotheistic, and this far-reaching 'reformation' has been linked with the *changamire* 'revolution'.[3] The evidence for such an abrupt dichotomy between the Mwari and *mhondoro* cults is, however, slender; yet while there is little evidence to isolate the Mwari cult from the main stream of Shona religious beliefs, the rise of the *changamires* may possibly have caused a slight shift in the relationship between secular and religious power. The Mwari oracle was served by three principal officials – the Mouth, the Ear, and the Eye – who through their subordinates controlled an efficient information service throughout the wide area covered by the cult. With communications always a prominent problem, the political utility of this organization was considerable, and under the earlier Togwa rulers, when the cult's centre was probably at Great Zimbabwe, it may well have been a major source of the dynasty's political influence. It is almost inconceivable that the *changamires* did not in turn closely ally themselves with the Mwari cult and utilize its influence and information. Indeed religious officials, such as the *mabvudzi*, *riropenga* and *nerwande*, are clearly remembered as being important councillors at the *changamire mambo*'s court. Yet there are persistent accounts of quarrels and disputes between at least some *changamires* and the Mwari oracle, and, although these traditions may in part reflect later attempts to explain the overthrow of the Changamire dynasty, it is possible that, strong in their grasp of military and economic power, the *changamires* were content to give rein to a certain secular scepticism. Their co-operation with and dependence upon the Mwari cult may therefore have been rather less close than had been that of the Togwa dynasty.

[1] H. von Sicard, 'The origin of some of the tribes in the Belingwe Reserve', *NADA*, 1950, **27**, 12.

[2] T. O. Ranger, *Revolt in Southern Rhodesia 1896–7* (London, 1967), 17–18.

[3] H. von Sicard, 'Reiche und Königtum der Rozwi vom Ende des 17. bis zum Anfang des 19. Jahrhunderts', in E. Haberland, M. Schuster and H. Straube, eds., *Festschrift für Ad. E. Jensen* (Munich, 1964), II, 649.

Although the *changamires* rose to power as military commanders, life under their rule was by no means dominated by naked military force. They lived in a milieu of peace and prosperity, maintaining and expanding the cultural achievements of their predecessors. The stone buildings of this period, which include Dhlodhlo, Matendere and Khami, served little or no defensive purpose. Grain-storage huts at Khami were built in the open, not concealed among the rocks, and Caton-Thompson pointed out that 'one can imagine nothing more helpful to enemies swarming over the girdle wall (at Dhlodhlo) than the excellent footholds provided by the chequer pattern'.[1] Walls were built for ostentation and privacy, rather than protection. Twenty-three different patterns, 'far superior to and more interesting than those at Zimbabwe', were, Hall reported, still visible on the walls at Dhlodhlo at the end of the nineteenth century, this lavish decoration proudly proclaiming the royal presence with a splendour matched inside the enclosure by a profusion of exotic and local luxuries. The royal residences attracted relatively dense populations. At Khami the great number of huts, 'not only within the stone enclosures but outside all over the plain', indicated to MacIver 'a very considerable population', and at Dhlodhlo Caton-Thompson was 'struck by the extensive former occupation of the surrounding ground'. Taba zika Mambo, where the last *changamire mambo* was killed by the Swazi, was surrounded, according to Hall, by traces of 'a very great population', and it lay at the centre of a whole cluster of massive stone buildings, one of which, M'telegwa, a gold-mining centre, yielded three pounds of gold jewellery found in what tradition asserted to be a ruler's grave.[2] Careful investigation of this and other sites will undoubtedly add much to our knowledge of the *changamire* period, but this impression of wealth and order is strengthened by the remarks of Portuguese contemporaries. Francisco de Melo e Castro, governor of Sena, praised the peace and security of the *changamire*'s rule in 1750, and Baltasar Pereira do Lago, governor of Mozambique from 1765 to 1779, referred to the 'most civilized justice' with which the *changamire* in 1768 treated the inhabitants of Zumbo, later describing, in a revealing phrase, the *changamire* as being 'a man without defect, save that of colour and paganism'.[3]

[1] K. R. Robinson, *Khami ruins* (Cambridge, 1959), 16. G. Caton-Thompson, *The Zimbabwe culture* (Oxford, 1931), 166.

[2] Hall and Neal, *Ancient ruins*, 275, 313–13. D. R. MacIver, *Mediaeval Rhodesia* (London, 1906), 58. Caton-Thompson, *Zimbabwe culture*, 166.

[3] Francisco de Melo e Castro, *Descripção dos Rios de Senna anno de 1750* (Goa, 1861), paras 62–70. Baltasar Manuel Pereira do Lago, 'Instrucção . . .', 20 August 1768, in A. A. de Andrade, ed. *Relações de Moçambique Setecentista* (Lisbon, Agência Geral do Ultremar,

BUTUA'S NEIGHBOURS

Yet although the *changamires*' renown spread far beyond their territories, the impact of this kingdom on its neighbours seems to have been relatively slight. After Dombo's wars of conquest and expansion, the *changamires* had but little contact with the *mwene mutapas*, whose activities in the eighteenth century were mainly confined to the riverain area of Dande. Here, in symbiosis with the few Portuguese at Tete, who provided a small garrison for their court, the *mwene mutapas* preserved a surprisingly large measure of independence, relative prosperity and local influence. As late as the 1760s Antonio Pinto de Miranda reported that the *changamire* still sent embassies to the *mwene mutapa*, but, even if this report was correct, this must have been a tribute more to the *mwene mutapa*'s former glory than to his contemporary importance, and there is little to suggest that the two rulers maintained close contact with each other after the end of the seventeenth century. To the east, after Dombo's destruction of the fair of Macequece in 1695, the *changamires* established, at least in Portuguese eyes, a claim to suzerainty in Manyika. The fair there was re-opened only with the *changamire*'s approval, and the rulers of Butua continued to demonstrate their interest in maintaining this commercial outlet. After being accidentally burnt down in 1780, the fair was rebuilt following the intervention of an army sent by the *changamire* to prevent any interference from the ruler of Manyika. But beyond this concern for a trade route, Rozvi intervention in Manyika internal affairs seems to have been minimal.

In the Zambezi valley above Zumbo, trade does not seem to have been oriented in any significant way towards Butua. It is even doubtful whether the *changamires* obtained regular tribute from the Rozvi who settled in the Wankie area, and they had but slender contacts, if any, with the region beyond the Zambezi and the Victoria Falls. In the direction of the Kalahari and the northern Tswana, their influence may have been greater and may well be reflected in the widespread distribution of the Shona-speaking Kalanga, but the evidence so far recorded deals mainly with the nineteenth century.

Far to the south-east, among the Venda-speaking peoples south of the Limpopo, the kingdom of Butua seems to have exerted a strong, indirect influence, though this has yet to be adequately investigated. The history of this area is dominated by the tradition of an invasion

1955), 334. Letter of Pereira do Lago, 15 August 1773, in Arquivo Historico Ultramarino, Lisbon, Caixa Moçambique 14.

from the north led by a heroic figure, Dimbanyika, who settled at Dzata, in the Nzhelele valley towards the heart of the fertile Zoutpansberg mountains, and whose descendants, the Singo, subsequently established themselves as the ruling lineage in most of the Venda chiefdoms. Dimbanyika is said to have moved southwards as a result of succession disputes with the *mambo* or ruler of the Rozvi to whom he was related, and on the basis of Singo genealogies this event has been dated to 'about the end of the seventeenth, or the beginning of the eighteenth century'.[1] The reliability of the published genealogies would, however, seem to be assured only as far back as Ramabulana, who was ruling in the first quarter of the nineteenth century. Before that date there are serious discrepancies, and the possibility of the omission of even several generations cannot be discounted. It is, therefore, at present impossible to date the arrival of the Singo with any certainty, though a seventeenth-century dispersal from Butua might accord well with the supplanting of the Togwa dynasty by the *changamires*. Yet, whatever the exact date of Dimbanyika's invasion, its significance should not be over-estimated. Certainly this event did not mark the arrival of the original Venda nucleus. Venda culture owes much of its distinctiveness to the earlier inhabitants of the Zoutpansberg, whose contacts with the north long predated the Singo migration and who, at least in the case of the Dau of the Ngona, probably had extensive links also with early Sotho groupings to the south. Culturally the Singo conquerors seem to have been assimilated into a distinctive Venda amalgam which had already long been in process of formation, and the Singo impact was principally felt in the political sphere. Yet even here, in the absence of further information concerning the Tavhatsindi dynasty and the other predecessors of the Singo, it is impossible to judge the extent to which they were innovators; all that is clear is that none of the Singo paramountcies achieved anything like the ascendancy of the *changamires*, nor did they control external trade: Dimbanyika's polity seems to have had little in common with that of Dombo.

One other southern monarchy looks back in its tradition to the Shona kingdoms for the origin of its ruling lineage. The Lovedu tell how the daughter of a *mambo*, himself the son of a *mwene mutapa*, had to flee southwards from her father's court with her infant son. He and his successors subsequently ruled a small kingdom with its capital on the foothills of the Drakensberg about 100 kilometres south of Dim-

[1] G. P. Lestrade, 'Some notes on the ethnic history of the Vhavenda and their Rhodesian affinities', *South African Journal of Science*, 1927, **24**, 490.

banyika's Dzata. The evidence at present available is insufficient to identify the *mwene mutapa*, or even the period to which this tradition refers; complete king lists have not been published, though several names are mentioned before that of Mugodo, the last king, who reigned at the end of the eighteenth century. Early in Lovedu history, the ruling lineage had been assimilated by Sotho-speaking aboriginals, and the Lovedu received additional strong Sotho influences from the area of Phalaborwa to the south-east. In the eighteenth century, contacts with Venda-speaking peoples to the north were also strong: Mashau, the chief of a Venda section, intervened on behalf of Mugodo in a civil war which devastated the Lovedu. The turmoil of Mugodo's reign led to a dramatic dynastic change, and Mugodo was succeeded by a daughter, Mujaji, the first of the rain-making queens who were to preserve their domain relatively intact during the tumults of the nineteenth century. South of the Limpopo, then, the *changamires* seem to have exercised no direct impact, and, although the fame of the Rozvi *mambos* remains enshrined in Venda and Lovedu tradition, the development of these southern kingdoms owes at least as much to local culture and initiative as to any extraneous influence from the north.

The relations of Butua and these other inland kingdoms with the hinterland of the coast are still largely uninvestigated. Yet it is apparent that, as in the area north of the Zambezi (see below, chapter 7, p. 525), far-ranging developments were occurring in this southern coastal hinterland during the seventeenth and eighteenth centuries with African entrepreneurs responding to new openings in the Indian Ocean trade. By the end of the seventeenth century only a handful of poverty-stricken Portuguese still remained at Sofala, and trade was mainly restricted to the port's immediate neighbourhood. But farther south commerce was rapidly expanding. At Inhambane, where the Portuguese had begun to trade in the sixteenth century, a small Portuguese force was permanently established after 1731 – a testimony to the fact that this trade provided one of the few exceptions to the general decline in Portuguese fortunes. By the mid-eighteenth century Inhambane exported a considerable amount of ivory, second only to that of the Zambezi, and the port had acquired the ugly reputation of being by far the best source of slaves, who were exported to the Mascarenes and even across the Atlantic. These slaves were probably obtained from the immediate hinterland, but the ivory was drawn through African intermediaries from a far larger area. Much of it came from, and possibly through, Usanga, the mountainous area west of Uteve and contiguous with the Sabi river, which separated it from the *changamire*s' kingdom. An unpublished Portuguese report for the eighteenth century gives an itinerary from Inhambane inland to the Rozvi, and the *changamires* are reputed to have intervened in succession disputes in Usanga: these hints suggest that here, as in the older market of Manyika, an important economic interest for the rulers of Butua was beginning to develop.

DELAGOA BAY AND ITS HINTERLAND

Still farther to the south, at Delagoa Bay, Portuguese trade was challenged by other Europeans, and African middlemen quickly seized the opportunities opened up by this rivalry. In the seventeenth century, English ships trading with India regularly visited the Bay, and changed the terms of trade to African advantage by introducing a richer range of trade-goods and raising the price of ivory. English and Indian ships, especially from Bombay and Surat, continued to carry on a flourishing trade in the eighteenth century, and they were joined by Dutch and French shipping. A trading factory was briefly established in the Bay by the Dutch from the Cape (1719–30), and a similar attempt by an Austrian trading company (1777–82) stimulated a Portuguese occupation of the site, which in turn was destroyed by the French in 1796. This keen European competition for the Bay's exports brought considerable changes to the Tsonga-speaking peoples of its hinterland. Around the Bay all the kingdoms found there by the Portuguese in the sixteenth century still existed at the end of the eighteenth century, but some, for instance the southernmost kingdom of Tembe which lay athwart the trade routes to Natal, were greatly strengthened by commercial profits, and new kingdoms sprang up from fragmented segments. But much the most dramatic change occurred in the interior, where the Tsonga were developing sophisticated entrepreneurial skills and were reaching out to exploit the trading opportunities of an immense arc, stretching from Uteve in the north to the Venda in the Zoutpansberg and the Pedi on the high veld, and southwards, through the length of Natal, as far away as the Xhosa. Through much of this vast area an incipient migration, similar in many respects to that of the Yao north of the Zambezi, was developing by the end of the eighteenth century, with professional Tsonga traders settling in Uteve, among the Venda and on the high veld.

During their brief stay at Delagoa Bay, the Dutch raised prices sufficiently to attract exports of copper and tin and a small trickle of gold. In their anxiety to discover the sources of mineral wealth in the interior, the Dutch cross-examined all comers to the Bay. They learnt that the copper and gold came from the closely associated kingdoms of Paraotte, Chiremandelle, Bvesha and Tsangamena. Though Chiremandelle has not been satisfactorily identified, the other three are fairly certainly the Phalaborwa, the Venda and Changamire. Despite the difficulty of deciphering Dutch versions of Sotho names transmitted by Tsonga informants, and the probably deliberately conflicting accounts given by African informants concerned to protect their trade routes, it is clear that by this time there was a complex network of trade involving most peoples of the eastern Transvaal, and possibly many of the central and western groups as well.[1] This is corroborated by the archaeological evidence of metal working in the Transvaal in pre-European times. Ancient iron, tin and copper mines extend through the whole of the northern Transvaal down to the edge of the high veld near present-day Pretoria. Their beginnings go back to the first millennium, but in the absence of more than a handful of excavated sites and carbon dates, it is impossible to know when they reached their heyday. The apparent dearth of imports apart from beads suggests that most of the metal was circulated internally, although by the time of the Dutch settlement at Delagoa Bay, Inhambane and Sofala were important outlets.

Much of the copper traded at Delagoa Bay came, through intermediaries, from the Venda. Equally important as a source of copper was Paraotte or Phalaborwa in the eastern Transvaal. The Paraotte were frequent visitors to the Bay, some of them wearing cloth acquired at Inhambane and probably also Sofala. The entire economy at Phalaborwa appears to have been based on mining. Situated in an area of tse-tse fly and malaria and with poor soil, it was able to support only a sparse population that subsisted by trading copper ingots and iron hoes for grain and cattle. Its ruling dynasty was relatively new. Like the Venda and Lovedu, the population trace their remote origin to the Shona-speaking area, though the chiefly line appears to have come to Phalaborwa from 'Bolaudi' in the south, probably in present-day Swaziland, in the course of the sixteenth or seventeenth centuries; this may have been part of a rather widespread dispersal of peoples from that area who made their way northwards through the eastern Transvaal

[1] This is based on the original documents on the Dutch settlement at the Bay between 1721 and 1730 in the Cape archives, C120–9, *Bylagen* (Annexures), C291–2, Resolutions of the Council of Policy and C438–43, Incoming letters. See also A. Smith, 'Delagoa Bay and the trade of South-Eastern Africa', in R. Gray and D. Birmingham, eds., *Precolonial African trade* (London, 1970), 265–89.

at roughly the same time (see below, pp. 431–2). At Phalaborwa they absorbed the earlier population, and for a period in the mid-eighteenth century even challenged the hegemony of the Lovedu on the low veld. They expanded as far west as Gravelotte, taking advantage of internal dissensions amongst the Lovedu, and also perhaps of the increased trading opportunities at Delagoa Bay which they were in a better position to exploit. Their triumph however was temporary. They lacked the essential agricultural resources for the establishment of any larger-scale political organization, and during the eighteenth century sections broke away in search of food and a more hospitable environment.

THE SOTHO-TSWANA

The predominance of the Venda and Lovedu chiefdoms in the north-east Transvaal was more seriously challenged by the eastward movement of offshoots from the Kgatla lineage cluster of the western-central Transvaal, such as the Tlokwa and the Pedi. The Tlokwa, generally regarded as a subgroup of the Kgatla, spread over a wide area of Botswana, the Transvaal and Natal. One group, known as the Thokwa, moved into the north-east Transvaal, where they established their hegemony over north Sotho groups like the Birwa. Their expansion, which reached its height towards the end of the eighteenth or beginning of the nineteenth century, led to warfare with the Lovedu, who at that time were in the process of changing to female rulers.

In the long run, however, the Pedi were to prove the more formidable threat to Venda-Lovedu influence. An early offshoot of the Kgatla, who were renowned iron workers, they moved from the area near present-day Pretoria to the Lulu mountains, probably in the mid-seventeenth century. There, partly through superior military organization, partly through diplomatic marriages, they conquered and absorbed the earlier Sotho, Koni and Roka inhabitants, during the reigns of Mohube and Morwamotse I. This process reached its height under Chief Thulare in the late eighteenth and early nineteenth centuries, and may have been partly stimulated by the expanding ivory trade at Delagoa Bay at this time. Tsonga traders, especially the Hlengwe, made their way in increasing numbers to the Pedi to exchange European beads, brass and cloth for the ivory, cattle and skins from the interior, and by the beginning of the nineteenth century the Pedi were occasionally even sending their own caravans to the coast. The Pedi were well placed to take advantage of this trade, straddling as they did one of the main routes to the Bay from the Kgatla of the central Transvaal and the Kwena farther west.

Documentary evidence of the route linking the western Tswana peoples to the trade outlets on the east coast comes only with the reports of the first European explorers and missionaries to the area in the early nineteenth century. Nevertheless, the extensive iron and tin mines as far west as the Middleburg and Rustenburg/Marico districts, and the profusion of beads on sites in the western, central and southern Transvaal, suggests very considerable local trade in earlier times. In this region, according to the archaeologist, Dr Revill Mason, the Iron Age remains are so abundant 'that we may presume a population increase from a few hundred at the height of the Stone Age, to many hundreds of thousands in communities that broke up and moved elsewhere to merge again', leaving the evidence of their passing in the thousands of stone-walled villages whose remains can still be discerned by aerial photography.[1] The southern section of this area in particular, from Lydenburg to Zeerust and Klerksdorp, must have been one of the most densely populated in southern Africa in this period.

It was from this area that, according to tradition, the dominant Sotho-Tswana lineage clusters which have populated most of the Transvaal, Botswana, Lesotho and the Orange Free State, proliferated and dispersed. Until the eighteenth century, the predominant pattern of political development in the area appears to have been one of segmentation and fission, with new chiefdoms being formed relatively easily from two or three main lineage clusters which perhaps owed their dominance to their being patrilineal and polygamous cattle keepers, thus enabling them to expand at the expense of cattle-less peoples and lineages.[2] In the well-watered and healthy south-western Transvaal, population and cattle increased, while the availablity of land and water enabled dissatisfied contestants in disputed successions to the chieftaincy to strike off on their own and colonize new areas with their followers, conquering and absorbing the earlier inhabitants.

On the whole we know so much of the process of segmentation because the oral histories of the Sotho-Tswana consist, in the main, of royal genealogies which record the links between chiefs (some of which

[1] R. J. Mason, *The prehistory of the Transvaal* (Johannesburg, 1962), 375. See also R. J. Mason, 'Transvaal and Natal iron age settlement revealed by aerial photography and excavation', *African Studies*, 1968, **27**, 4, 167–79.

[2] M. Wilson, 'Changes in social structure in Southern Africa: the relevance of kinship studies to the historian', in L. Thompson, ed., *African societies in southern Africa* (London, 1969).

may be spurious) and the point of departure of new chiefdoms. They place far less emphasis on the complementary process of the absorption and assimilation of new entities into existing chiefdoms. It is only from the end of the seventeenth century that these chiefly histories consist of much more than a mere recital of chiefs' names, and there is not always agreement on these. The difficulties of interpretation are increased in that even the relationships between lineage clusters may be distorted by their contemporary territorial association and relative political power.[1]

From this time, however, two apparently contradictory processes seem to be at work. On the one hand, the subdivision of major lineage clusters continued and may possibly even have accelerated, giving rise to a number of important new chiefdoms; on the other, a number of the major chiefdoms were asserting a wider hegemony over their neighbours through conquest and perhaps through their control of natural resources. It must however be borne in mind that, though we are only able to discern this latter process clearly from the end of the seventeenth century, this may be a function of the more easily recollected oral tradition rather than a peculiarity of the time. State formation may have far earlier precedents amongst the Sotho-Tswana, which could only be revealed by detailed archaeological excavation and a far more sophisticated analysis of the oral tradition than we have at present.

By the late seventeenth, early eighteenth century, the Kgatla, Hurutshe, Kwena and Rolong had established relatively large states in the south and western Transvaal, while by the end of the eighteenth century, their offshoots had formed similar chiefdoms as far east as the Pedi in the Lulu mountains, the Ngwaketse and Ngwato in Botswana to the west and north-west, and the Tlhaping at Dithakong in the south. It is impossible to state which, if any, of the parent groups held dominance over the others, though the Hurutshe were regarded by many as having ritual seniority.

The Hurutshe lineage, which had, in earlier times, given rise to at least five other important chiefdom clusters, including such major groups as the Kwena and probably the Kgatla, divided further at the end of the seventeenth and beginning of the eighteenth centuries during the reigns of Chiefs Menwe and Thekiso. Under Menwe, the capitals of the Hurutshe were at Kaditshwena and Tshwenyane. Although by the beginning of the nineteenth century, Kaditshwena was

[1] M. Legassick, 'The Sotho-Tswana peoples before 1800', in Thompson, ed., *African societies*, 103.

ruled by the representatives of a junior Hurutshe lineage, it was described by the missionary, John Campbell, as a large stone walled settlement containing well over 15,000 people, divided into some fifty wards, each governed by their own headman. The settlement was surrounded on all sides by cultivated lands, several miles in extent. At the cattle outposts some distance from the centre, were large herds of sleek cattle, many the personal possession of the chief, on whose behalf they were being tended. The ruler also held a monopoly of all trading activity.[1] Under Menwe's successor, Thekiso, the territory of the Hurutshe stretched from Tlhabane and the Rustenburg area to the Pilansberg and Saulspoort. It is in his reign that we hear of conflict with other groups for the first time, and the amalgamation of smaller communities into the Hurutshe chiefdom. In part the increased conflict with other groups, especially the Kwena, which is evident in the second half of the eighteenth century and which reached its height during the reign of Pheto (died *c.* 1810), may have been the result of attempts to control the rich iron deposits at Thabazimbi and in the Waterberg.

Next to the Hurutshe, the Kwena were genealogically the most senior and probably the most powerful and prolific of the Tswana chiefdoms in the seventeenth and eighteenth centuries. Even at the beginning of the nineteenth century, after considerable fragmentation, they had the reputation of being the most populous and skilled of the groups across the Vaal, while their offshoots in Lesotho and the Orange Free State became predominant in the south Sotho area. According to tradition, their nuclear homeland was in the south-western Transvaal. From there at least one group crossed the Vaal southwards, where they intermarried extensively with the earlier Fokeng inhabitants and probably also with Khoisan hunter-gatherers and pastoralists, giving rise to new amalgams of peoples. According to the traditions collected by Ellenberger, some time in the seventeenth century some of this mixed Fokeng-Kwena group recrossed the Vaal and settled in the Middleburg district, whence there was a considerable secondary dispersal over a large area of the southern Transvaal, northern Orange Free State and Lesotho. So widespread were the Kwena chiefdoms to the south of the Vaal, that 'Kwena' became virtually a generic term amongst the coastal peoples for the people of the interior. A recent analysis of the distinctive Iron Age settlements in the north-eastern Orange Free State, neighbouring south-eastern Transvaal and Lesotho

[1] J. Campbell, *Travels in South Africa undertaken at the request of the Mission Society, 1813* (London, 1815), 255.

suggests that the first move south of the Vaal took place no later than the mid-fifteenth century, although this may not be associated with the Kwena-Fokeng dispersal.[1]

North and west of the Vaal, the Kwena were also divided into several groups by the end of the eighteenth century. During the reign of Mogopa (probably late seventeenth century), both the chief's brother, Motsele, and half brother, Kgabo, moved off with their own followers, and though the ostensible causes were rooted in royal rivalries and local disputes, the breaks may have had their more general roots in population pressure and famine. Certainly during this period, the Kwena appear to have moved around over a considerable area, presumably in search of better grazing, perhaps also in search of fresh timber resources for fuel and building, with sections hiving off and returning to older sites. In the course of time, Motsele's section, which had settled in the Magaliesberg-Pilansberg district, divided into a further four sections, though it is not clear whether they all considered themselves completely independent entities.

The splits from Kgabo's Kwena who had settled at Molepolole were of greater moment. Through the eighteenth and early nineteenth century Kwena dominated the area west of the Notwane river, as first Kgabo's Kwena and later the powerful Ngwaketse and Ngwato sections, which separated from Kwena jurisdiction, expanded and ousted the earlier inhabitants of the area, known collectively as the Kgalagadi. The Kgalagadi, a group of people of diverse origin, were situated along the fringes of the Kalahari desert. Forced westward into the desert by Kwena expansion, they lost their cattle and took to a hunter-gatherer mode of existence or became clients of the new intruders, herding their cattle or paying them a tribute of the skins and ivory they hunted on their behalf.

There is considerable conflict in the traditions as to when and how the break between the Kwena at Molepolole and the Ngwaketse occurred. It has been suggested most convincingly that at the time of their separation the Ngwaketse were a relatively large section or ward of the Kwena, to whom they were subject. Like the Ngwato, the Ngwaketse claim descent from the son or brother of Kwena, the founding father of the lineage cluster, though this may be one of the instances where a genealogical link is claimed to legitimize later political eminence. Although they appear to have lived at a succession of different

[1] T. M. O'C. Maggs, 'The Iron Age of the Orange Free State', in H. J. Hugot, ed., *Actes du VIe Congrès Panafricain de Préhistoire* (Chambery, 1973), 179.

villages through the late seventeenth and eighteenth centuries, the final assertion of their independence probably only came during the reign of Mongala in the mid-eighteenth century. By that time, however, they must have been a large and wealthy group, for their subsequent rise was swift. Mongala, who lived at Seoke, married into the royal family of the Kgatleng people, who were subordinated to the Ngwaketse, and the process of conquering and absorbing alien groups was continued by his successors, Moleta and Makaba II, as they moved southwards along the Molopo river. Makaba II was one of the strongest and most feared chiefs on the western high veld before the *Difaqane*.[1]

A little later than the Ngwaketse, the Ngwato also broke away from the Kwena at Molepolole, establishing themselves in the Shoshong hills to the north. They too conquered and absorbed the local peoples in a variety of clientship roles, so that today both the Ngwaketse and Ngwato are the most heterogeneous of the Tswana groups, though in the case of the latter this was a nineteenth-century development.

South of the Kwena at Molepolole, towards the end of the seventeenth century and beginning of the eighteenth, the Rolong were the dominant chiefdom. Under Tau, an able but ruthless ruler, whom the Rolong compare to Shaka Zulu, they held sway over a large area bounded by the Molopo and Setlagole rivers in the north-west, and stretching to Molemane and Klerksdorp in the south-west, and Taungs and Khunwana in the south. Tau ruled over a mixed group of people including the Kgalagadi, the hunter-gatherer Sarwa, the Taung and the Tlhaping. The Rolong empire reached its greatest extent under Tau's son, Rratlou, who died between 1775 and 1780, perhaps of smallpox which spread from the epidemic raging amongst the Khoisan in the Cape Colony, perhaps in battle against the Hurutshe. On his death it broke into four sections, allegedly through a dispute between his brothers over his widow, though the minority of his rightful heir, over-extended communications and population increase may all have played a part.

Even before this fragmentation, however, the Tlhaping, under Mokgosi, had asserted their independence. During Tau's reign, they defied the chief's demands for tribute, and, forming an alliance with the pastoral Korana people, were able to resist his attacks. Though their traditions are contradictory, many, if not all the Korana appear to have entered the south Tswana area at the beginning of the eighteenth

[1] The wars associated with the rise of the Zulu in the second and third decade of the nineteenth century (see volume 5, chapter 11).

century as fragments of the original Khoi tribes of the Cape peninsula (see below, p. 451). Dispossessed of their cattle and grazing lands by the expansion of the Dutch settlers at the Cape, they were the first of a number of such groups to find refuge along the Orange river. Like their late eighteenth century successors, the Griqua and the Oorlams of South-West Africa, they introduced a new element into the area, upsetting the local political balance and bringing some knowledge of European weapons and warfare. Though their impact was perhaps not as disruptive as that of the later groups, there is a tradition that they defeated Tau on four occasions, driving him north from Taungs to Setlagodi, and helping the Tlhaping to defect.

After their defeat of Tau, Korana prestige was high, and they established close connections with the Tlhaping. Both Mokgosi's son and grandson married Korana women as their chief wives, and by the last quarter of the eighteenth century mixed groups of Tlhaping and Korana were found along the Orange river. Though it was unusual for the Tswana chiefs to take Khoi wives, the Tlhaping may have been more willing than most to intermarry with the newcomers. Their traditions tell of a period of extreme poverty, when they eked out a subsistence by hunting and fishing along the tributaries of the Vaal river, subject to constant harrying by other groups. Though their chiefs claim descent from the Rolong royal lineage and their settlements were architecturally similar, it seems probable that they included earlier inhabitants conquered by the Rolong: this seems to be implied by their tributary status, their dependence on hunting and even fishing – a practice generally avoided by most of the Sotho-Tswana peoples – and their relative ignorance of iron-smelting.

Even under Mashwe, Mokgosi's successor, the Tlhaping's existence was at first troubled. Mashwe took refuge in the Langeberg until driven out by drought and famine, but later in his reign the Tlhaping established themselves at Nokaneng and later at Dithakong, and their fortunes began to improve. Here, they were able to take advantage of their position to mediate in the trade between the main Tswana groups farther north, with their skilled metallurgy and craftsmanship, and the purely pastoral Khoi peoples along the Orange river and in South West Africa. By 1779, when we have the first published eye-witness account of the Orange River of any length,[1] the Tlhaping, or Briqua,[2]

[1] *The journals of H. J. Wikar*, ed. E. E. Mossop (Van Riebeeck Society, 15, Cape Town, 1935).

[2] Briqua/Brijkje/Bliqua/Brikwa/Blip/Brigoudys people are mentioned in the Dutch records of the seventeenth century, and according to Nama informants they traded with them in

as the Khoi then called them, came to trade along the river annually, bringing copper and ivory ornaments and spoons, copper, iron and glass beads, iron axes, knives and barbed assegais and soft well-tanned hartebeest skins, as well as tobacco and dagga (Indian hemp), to exchange for cattle. By the end of the century, the Tlhaping, despite raids from the Korana and other marauding bands of mixed origin, were relatively affluent. Thus Truter and Somerville, who were sent in 1801 by the Cape government to explore the prospects of expanding the colonial cattle trade to peoples north of the Orange river, estimated that Dithakong, which was to fragment shortly thereafter, contained some 15–20,000 inhabitants, and that it was as 'large in circumference as Cape Town with all the gardens situated in Table valley'.[1]

Most of the other European observers of the early nineteenth century who were able to witness the Tswana settlements before the destruction wrought by the *Difaqane* were equally impressed by their size, their outward appearance and internal law and order. They noted their extensive agriculture, large herds of cattle, their skilled metallurgy and craftsmanship and flourishing trade in skins, ivory, horns, corn, cattle and iron and copper artefacts. As elsewhere in southern Africa, the chief held supreme religious, judicial, legislative and executive power over his people, and controlled trade. In carrying out these functions, he was aided by a small council of his close relations and trusted advisers, which was enlarged when necessary into a council or *pitso* of the whole nation, a feature shared also by other Sotho groups. In other ways, however, these strikingly large settlements with their organization into wards and their relatively complex social stratification were quite unlike the far more scattered and smaller scale societies established even by the related southern Sotho peoples or the neighbouring Transvaal Ndebele. South of the Vaal, for example, the dominant Kwena lineages did not, in pre-*Difaqane* times, create states or settlements of any size, with one or two notable exceptions. In so

gold (probably copper) and silver (probably tin or mica). They have generally been identified with the Tlhaping, and for the late eighteenth century the identification appears correct. The term, however, simply means the 'goat people', and was a general term for the Bantu-speaking peoples with whom the Khoi were in contact across the Orange. In 1661 the Nama claimed to be at war with the Brigoudys for their failure to deliver tribute in 'gold' and here the term may even have been referring to the Bergdama copper miners of south-west Africa. As from their own traditions, the Tlhaping only achieved a separate existence in the eighteenth century, and ousted earlier Bantu-speakers – probably Fokeng – from Dithakong, the unqualified identification of the Briqua and the Tlhaping seems unwarranted, at least before the mid-eighteenth century.

[1] In J. Barrow, *A voyage to Cochinchina . . . to which is annexed an account of a journey made in the years 1801 and 1802 to the residence of the chief of the Booshuana nation* . . . (London, 1806), 391–2.

far as they conquered and absorbed groups like the Fokeng, they appear to have created fairly homogeneous new societies, rather than stratified ones. Similarly, as we shall see, in the eastern Cape, where the pastoral Khoi were absorbed by the expanding Xhosa chiefdoms, the social stratification was far less complex than that of the Tswana chiefdoms of the eighteenth and nineteenth centuries.

Although we have no documentary evidence of the administration of these large settlements in the south-western Transvaal, north-western Orange Free State and Botswana before the beginning of the nineteenth century, archaeological investigation in this area suggests that the basic division of Tswana settlements into wards existed relatively unchanged from the sixteenth or seventeenth century,[1] and that the organizational features described in the nineteenth and twentieth centuries can legitimately be extrapolated back in time. Thus, the smallest social grouping amongst the Tswana, as amongst the other southern Bantu, was the household, consisting of a man, his wives and children, living in a compound of their own huts and granaries. Households descended from a common male ancestor tended to live side by side, and formed the sub-divisions of wards: distinct social and administrative units under hereditary headmen, who could be commoners as well as chiefs or members of the royal family. Wards varied in size from a mere hundred to more than one thousand strong. The number of wards also varied from settlement to settlement and within the same settlement over time: in 1812, Burchell described thirty or forty for Dithakong,[2] while Campbell enumerated fifty, eight years later.[3] The administrative system may well have facilitated the absorption of new groups into the polity: wards sometimes consisted entirely of immigrant or subject communities, ruled by their own hereditary headmen.

In view of the absence of documentary evidence before the nineteenth century, the uneven and limited nature of oral tradition and the paucity of archaeological excavation and carbon dates, it is impossible to postulate with any certainty the reasons for the development of these large, well organized and stratified settlements. It seems probable that this stratification was intensified as the Kwena lineage clusters and the Rolong-Tlhaping chiefdoms pressed up against the desert fringes and conquered peoples who had lost their cattle by being forced into the

[1] T. M. O'C. Maggs, 'Bilobial dwellings: a persistent feature of southern Tswana settlement', The South African Archeological Society, Goodwin Series, 1, *The Interpretation of Evidence* (June 1972), 54–64.

[2] W. J. Burchell, *Travels in the interior of Southern Africa*, ed. I. Schapera, 2 vols. (London, 1953), II, 362. This was in 1812, six or eight years after it had divided in two and moved site.

[3] *Travels in South Africa*, 255.

Kalahari. Nor could agriculturalists move farther south: by the seventeenth century if not earlier, it seems, the Tswana had probably already reached the ecological limits for effective cultivation, given their technology and their dependence on rainfall.[1] Chiefs who controlled large herds of cattle could attract clients more readily in these circumstances than farther east, where the expansion was through the conquest of people who retained their hold over the cattle and over mineral resources. Moreover, in an area of limited water supplies, the monopoly of springs may also have enabled chiefs to establish their control over clients. It has also been suggested that the increasing significance in the eighteenth century of trade, especially in skins and ivory, with new outlets south along the Orange river westward into South-West Africa, and along new routes north-eastwards to Inhambane and Delagoa Bay may explain the pre-industrial towns of the Tswana. With the increase in the importance of trade, patron-client relationships became both more feasible and more attractive to both sides. Chiefs who monopolized this trade wanted not only herders, who could be absorbed relatively easily into their polities, but the less assimilable hunters to bring in skins and ivory; clients could be attracted not only by cattle, milk and agricultural produce, but also by the imported goods which the chiefs now used as patronage. Whether the cattle and trade monopolies in themselves led to the dense concentrations of population is far less clear however. Trade may have flourished and chiefs may have been able to exercise their control more successfully once their people were settled in a single centre, but this does not necessarily mean that the large concentrations were the direct consequence of the increased trade.

KALAHARI AND SOUTH-WEST AFRICA

To the south and west of the Tswana, population was far sparser. In the dry lands of the Kalahari, Karroo and South-West Africa, the expanding Iron Age farmers found their ecological frontier. Here specialized pastoralism or hunting and gathering remained man's most effective way of exploiting his environment. Although pockets of racially and linguistically diverse Stone Age peoples co-existed with their Bantu-speaking neighbours in a wide variety of relationships all over southern Africa in this period, in the western half of the subcontinent their way of life probably remained least affected by contact with new ideas and a new technology.

[1] T. M. O'C. Maggs, 'Pastoral settlements on the Riet River', *South African Archaeological Bulletin*, 1971, **26**, nos. 101 and 102, 58–9.

For the historian, purely hunter-gatherer communities pose peculiar problems. Each small, isolated patriclan, often not more than ten or twenty strong, has its own generally unrecorded history, dominated but by no means totally determined by the rhythms of nature; but on a large scale it is impossible to chart its inner life except in generalities. We lack both the sources and the methodology to trace the developments within these small groups with the precision demanded of the historian, except perhaps in so far as they were in contact with other communities – very often only at the point at which they were changing their way of life, and thus, by definition, disappearing as hunter-gatherers.

In the seventeenth and eighteenth centuries, this process of change can still be glimpsed in the documentary record in the relationships of San hunter-gatherers and Khoi[1] pastoralists encountered by the Dutch in the south-western Cape, Little Namaqualand, and later on along the Orange river. Thus wherever whites encountered Khoi pastoralists in these centuries, they found hunter-gatherers, whom the Khoi generally called San, living in some form of symbiotic relationship with them; in many areas they acted as herders, hunters or client soldiers for the Khoi, could speak the Khoi language and were in the process of acquiring their own sheep and cattle on a permanent basis, sometimes through the theft and raiding which the Khoi complained of through the years. Even in the desert area, however, where the contact was less intimate, San groups traded with both their Khoi and Bantu-speaking neighbours, exchanging honey, ostrich egg-shell beads and the products of the chase for pottery and grain, and even at times metals.

If the dry western half of southern Africa has remained the home of Late Stone Age hunter-gatherers until the present, the central zone of South-West Africa, between the Namib desert and the Kalahari has

[1] The terminology for the Late Stone Age pastoral and hunter-gatherer peoples of South Africa is immensely complex and confusing. Generally termed 'Hottentot' and 'Bushmen' in the older texts, they are now usually called 'Khoi' and 'San'. While Khoi is probably satisfactory for the largely pastoral communities (although there were always some cattle-less Khoi) speaking the Khoi language, San is increasingly unsatisfactory as a term for the wide range of Late Stone Age people in South Africa who were not 'Khoi'. At the Cape and elsewhere the Khoi included both purely hunter-gatherer groups and poor hunters who had some cattle, or hunters who spoke Khoi in the San group. As used in the text, San generally means non-Khoi. Where it is not clear whether a Khoi or San group is being referred to, the composite term Khoisan has been used. For the problems involved in the terminology see E. O. J. Westphal, 'A re-classification of southern African non-Bantu languages', *Journal of African Languages*, 1962, **1**, 1–8; A. Traill, 'N4 or S7? Another bushman language', *African Studies*, 1973, **32**, 1; S. Marks, 'Khoisan resistance to the Dutch in the seventeenth and eighteenth centuries', *Journal of African History*, 1972, **13**, 1; and R. H. Elphick, 'The Cape Khoi and the first phase of South African race relations', unpubl. Ph.D. (Yale, 1972).

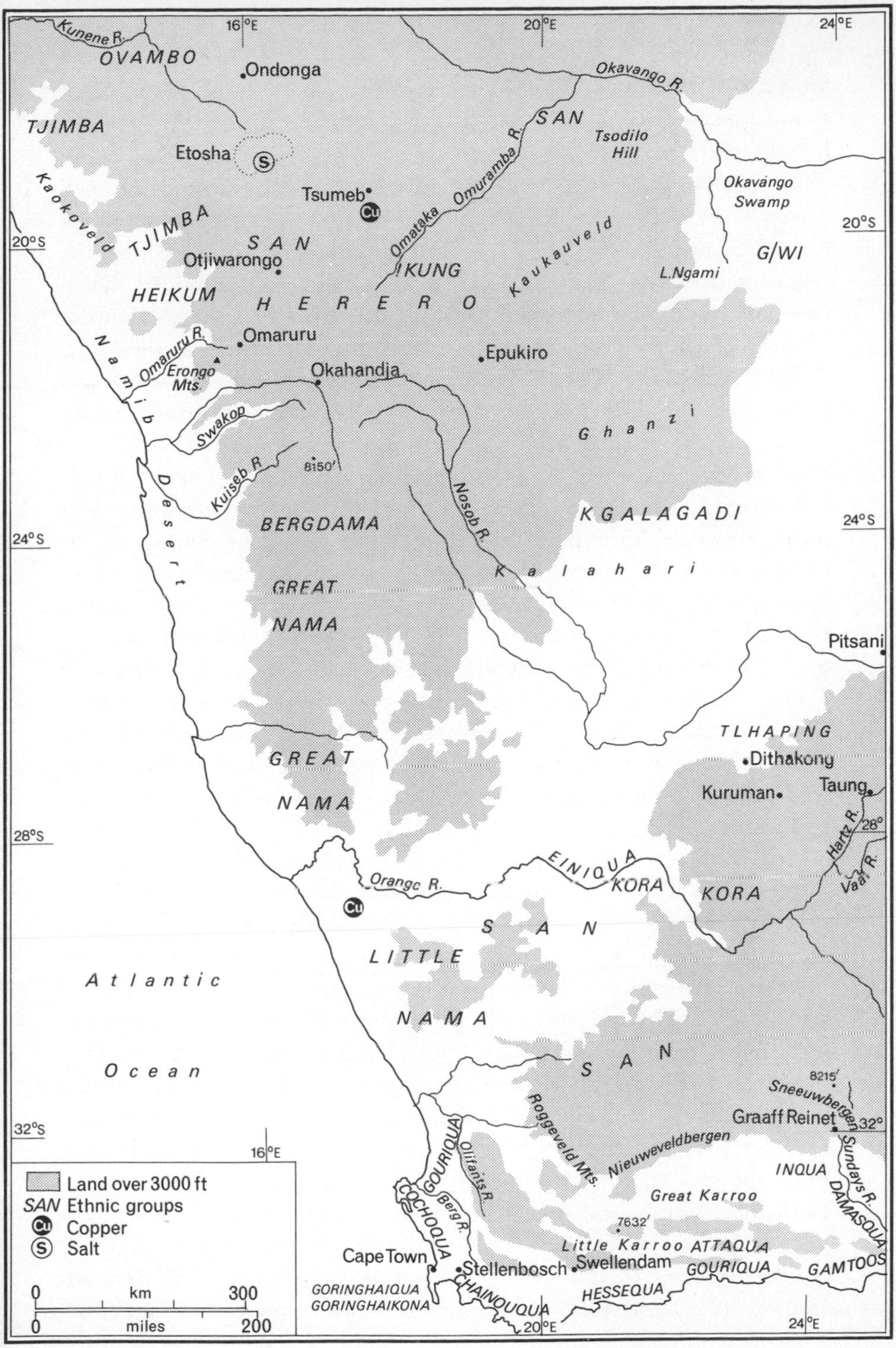

13 South-West Africa and the Cape of Good Hope

also lent itself to specialized pastoral pursuits. To the north of the Swakop and Kuiseb rivers live the only example of a purely pastoral Bantu-speaking people, the Herero, with their sacred herds of long-horned cattle, while to their south are the Khoi-speaking Nama tribes with their flocks of fat-tailed sheep. Evidence for the history of both these groups in the seventeenth and eighteenth century is scanty. When possible, European mariners rounding the coasts of Africa avoided the 'skeleton coast' of South-West Africa, as it is still ominously called from the number of shipwrecks, while after an initial spate of enthusiasm in the 1660s, explorers from the Dutch settlement at the Cape, disappointed in their hopes of reaching the fabled wealth of the Mutapa kingdom in this direction, found little to attract them in the arid scrub-lands of Namaqualand. Though Nama informants, encountered in the seventeenth century as far south as the Berg and Olifants rivers, volunteered a certain amount of information about the peoples to their north, this does little more than to establish that the forebears of the contemporary inhabitants of the area were already there in the seventeenth century. It was only after the middle of the eighteenth century that literate observers penetrated as far as the Orange river, and not until the nineteenth that they reached the Bantu-speaking Herero, or Damara, as they were called. Archaeology in this area is in its infancy, and, as is common amongst purely pastoral, decentralized and relatively unstratified societies, genealogies have little time depth, while traditions tend to dwell on the seasonal migrations of herders in search of grazing and water.

According to tradition, the Herero migrated into South-West Africa in two streams, one, the Mbanderu, remaining behind in the east, the other, the Herero mainstream, taking a northerly route into the hilly, westward-sloping Kaokaoveld, where many of the sacred grave-sites of their clan-heads of the seventeenth and eighteenth centuries are still remembered. That they arrived in this area relatively late is borne out by both oral tradition and archaeology, although 1550, the date generally given for their arrival, may well be too late. Nor should one be misled by the precision of this date into thinking of this process as a once and for all arrival of large numbers of pastoral Herero, sweeping into an uninhabited area, and carrying with them a ready-formed way of life. Both their Nama and their Ovambo neighbours identify the Herero with earlier, probably Stone Age peoples; the Nama use the same term, 'Dama' to refer to the Herero (or 'cattle Dama'), and the Berg (or 'mountain') Dama, a negroid hunter-gatherer people, who today speak

Nama and are generally found as 'servants' of the Nama and cattle-rich Herero. The Ovambo call the Herero 'Tjimba', 'ant-diggers', though the name is usually used today to refer only to 'poor' Herero, in contrast to the Himba, who are the aristocratic cattle-keepers *par excellence*. Recent field work in the mountains of the Kaokaoveld, however, has shown that isolated pockets of Tjimba still exist who have never had cattle, who differ physically, culturally and linguistically from the Herero, and who still make and employ Stone Age tools in their everyday lives.[1]

A clue to the relationship of the Tjimba and Herero in the late sixteenth century is perhaps to be found in the somewhat vague references in Portuguese and Dutch sources to the coastline below Angola as 'Cimbeba'. This was reputedly ruled by the kingdom of 'Mataman', which was said to stretch to the Mutapa kingdom, and it has been very tentatively suggested that Cimbeba was the land of the Tjimba, and that the Mataman could perhaps be the Dama, or Herero.[2] The reports would suggest that at this time the Tjimba were dominated by the incoming Herero, but had not yet been absorbed into Herero society as a subordinate class of a single society. Once so absorbed, aboriginal Herero who lost their cattle became 'Tjimba', while Tjimba who acquired the requisite cattle were transformed into 'Himba', in much the same way as the upward or downward swing of fortune partially determined 'Khoi' and 'San' identity (see below). It may well have been their close interaction with these small, loosely organized and patrilineal Tjimba, together with the exigencies of their environment, which led to the differentiation of the Herero from their northern neighbours, the agricultural, matrilineal Ovambo, to whom they are closely related linguistically.

The Ovambo kingdoms which straddle the frontiers of present-day Angola and South-West Africa appear in general to have been isolated from developments farther south in this period: culturally and economically, their ties were to the north. They constituted a complex of kingdoms, the strongest of which at the end of the period were Ondonga and Kwanyama, which may have owed their dominance not only to the higher agricultural potential of their lands, watered by the Kunene river, and the fine grazing to the north of the river, but also to their ability to monopolize key resources like copper, iron and salt. Even in the seventeenth century there are hints of a complex trading network,

[1] H. R. MacCalman and B. J. Grobbelaar, 'Preliminary report on two stone-working Ovatjimba groups in the northern Kaokaoveld of South West Africa', *Cimbebasia*, 1965, 13, 5–28. [2] *Ibid.*

linked to the Portuguese settlements in Angola to the north and to the Nama in the south, which were to be confirmed when the first British and German traders, explorers and missionaries penetrated this area in the mid-nineteenth century.

The first recorded conflict between Herero and Ovambo came towards the end of the eighteenth century, after the Herero pastoralists, following in the wake of renowned hunters like Tjiponda and Hembapu, made their way south-eastwards from the Kaokaoveld into the north-central region, ousting the earlier San and Bergdama inhabitants. Significantly enough, the conflict with the Ovambo was not however over grazing lands and water, but over the copper mines at Tsumeb. The sides were unevenly drawn in this instance, as the Herero, with their decentralized clan organization and apparently very limited iron technology, were confronting highly organized kingdoms, whose soldiers fought with superior iron weapons, and who were able to defend themselves behind the high stockades of their villages.

If the late eighteenth century saw the Herero expanding against the Ovambo outposts, it was also the period in which we hear for the first time of the conflicts between the Herero and the Nama to their south which were to dominate the history of this area in the nineteenth century. Like the Herero, the Nama had been expanding through the eighteenth century in search of fresh water and grazing, their vanguard probably reaching the Swakop and Kuiseb rivers at about the same time.

At this time, it would appear that five of the seven Nama tribes of South-West Africa were loosely allied under the leadership of the so-called Red Nation, which was said to have been formed of several clans welded together under their first chief, Hab. This unification may well have occurred in the course of Nama conflict with the San and Bergdama, as the Nama groups expanded north of the Orange river. In their conflicts in the eighteenth century, Nama and Herero were relatively evenly matched, though the balance was to shift dramatically in the nineteenth century when the former acquired horses and guns, as well as fresh leadership, from Cape Khoi groups fleeing northwards from the Cape Colony.

By the time this happened, the Nama of South-West Africa had become very considerably differentiated from the related Khoi communities of the Cape, and this differentiation was already well in evidence when the Dutch arrived at the Cape in the mid-seventeenth century. Indeed, although most previous authorities have maintained that the

Cape Khoi were simply an extension of Khoi expansion southwards through South-West Africa, it has recently been cogently argued that the separation of the Nama and the Cape Khoi took place farther back in time, and from a dispersal point on the middle Orange river.[1] Although we have no way of dating this migration at present, it was reflected in the seventeenth century by the relationship of the various Khoi groups to one another, and the pattern of their settlement along the south-east coast, along the Orange river and to the north and south of it. This suggests that from the middle Orange, the Khoi moved in two directions: one westward along the Orange to the sea, whence they spread north and south to form the Nama tribes; the other, south-eastwards, following the gaps in the mountains, perhaps through the Sneeuwbergen and then into the valleys of the Sundays or Great Fish rivers, and perhaps even farther east, until they came up against Bantu-speakers. From here they spread west along the coast, to form the cluster of Khoi chiefdoms encountered by the Dutch at the Cape. In the mid-seventeenth century, they all still explicitly acknowledged the suzerainty of the powerful Inqua or Hancumqua people in the east, who appear to have owed their paramountcy to their genealogical superiority.

THE NGUNI

In some sources, the Hancumqua appear themselves to have been subject to an even more powerful chiefdom, that of the Chobona, who may either have been the Xhosa, or perhaps a group of mixed Xhosa and Khoi people, who are at times described in the sources as 'Hottentots, but a little darker than they', and at others as being cultivators, who lived in permanent dwellings and who had metals. Though the evidence is confused and contradictory, there is little doubt that in this period the easternmost Khoi were being absorbed by the closely related people living between the Drakensberg and the sea, from the Pongola river in the north to the Kei in the south, who are generally classified as Nguni. Speaking variants of the same language and practising a relatively uniform culture, they lived in scattered homesteads which clustered along the valleys and hillsides near running water, avoiding the sour veld along the coast. Unlike the Khoi, they were both cattle-keepers and cultivators. The central feature of each homestead was the cattle enclosure, round which were grouped their beehive shaped huts, belonging to the male agnates and their families. At the head of each

[1] R. H. Elphick, 'The Cape Khoi and the first phase of South African race relations', unpublished Ph.D. (Yale, 1972), fols. 41–50.

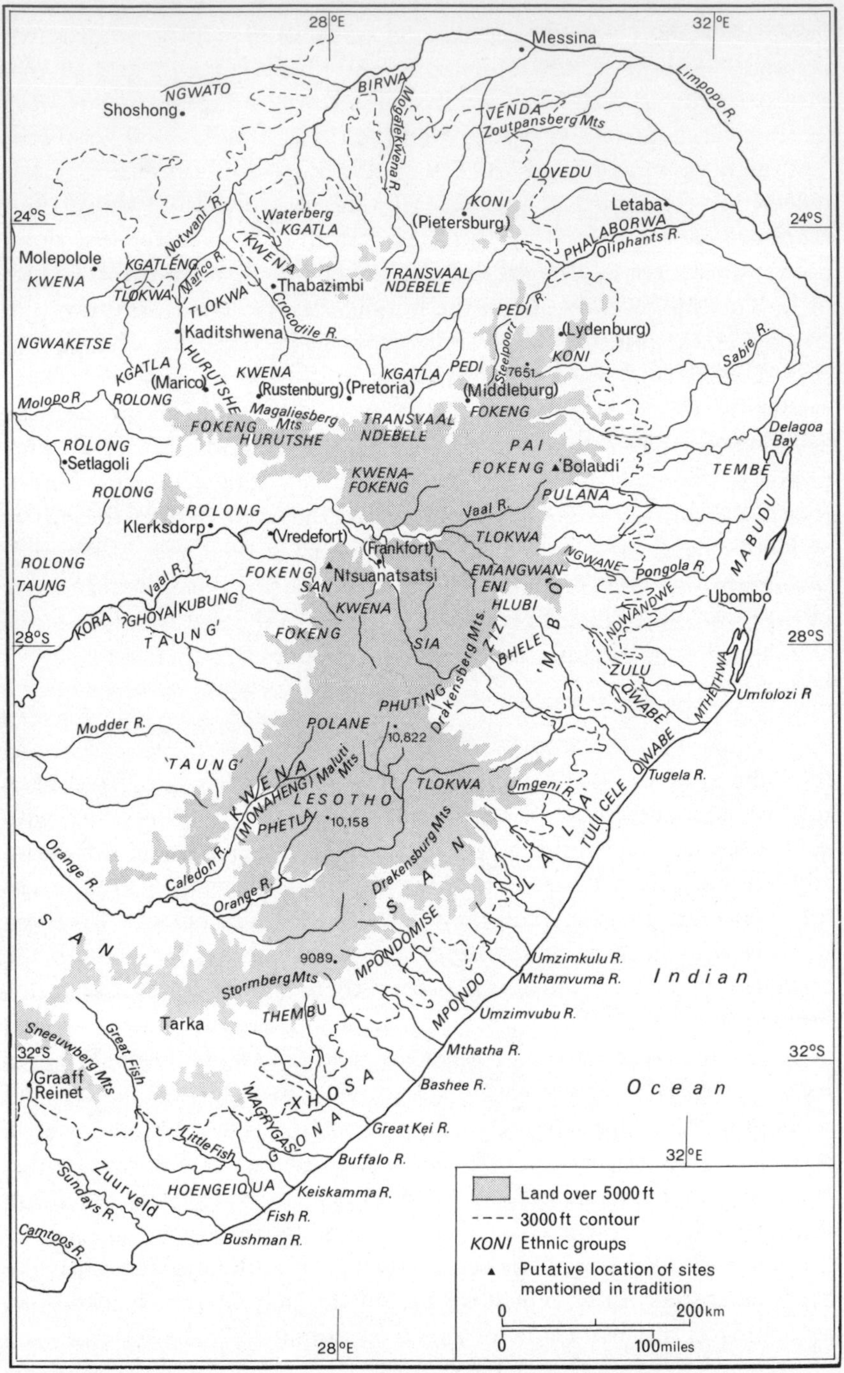

14 South-east Africa

homestead was the senior male by descent, the *umnumzane*, whose role, like that of ward headman amongst the Tswana, was probably of great importance at the local level in settling disputes, adjudicating land claims and controlling the movement of cattle and people. Several homesteads were united under chiefs who were the male heirs in the senior lineage. On the whole these chiefdoms tended to be rather small-scale, and the Portuguese drew a distinction between the chiefs of the south – *inkosis* – and the more powerful Tsonga rulers around Delagoa Bay. Nevertheless the chiefdom was a political and territorial unit, not a purely kinship grouping, and each chiefdom included people of different clans and origin. Between each different chiefdom was a stretch of uninhabited territory marking its boundaries – areas which ship-wrecked whites making their way along the coast towards Delagoa Bay referred to as 'deserts'.

As amongst the Sotho-Tswana, the chief held supreme judicial, administrative and legislative authority over his people, controlling both internal and external relations. Moreover in a society in which there does not appear to have been a separate class of priests, he mediated between the people and their ancestors, the *amadlozi*, who were believed to look after the welfare of their descendants. He performed religious ceremonies, and, as the greatest medicine man and rainmaker, he was responsible for the fertility of the soil and the success of his people's crops. In performing his duties, the chief was aided by an *induna* or minister of state and by a council of elders. They were generally of royal birth, as were the subordinate officials in different parts of the kingdom. As long as chiefdoms remained small-scale, however, the administrative machinery does not appear to have been as developed as amongst the Tswana.

The pattern of settlement and the *mores* of the people as described both by the Portuguese in the fifteenth and sixteenth centuries, and the Dutch in the seventeenth and eighteenth, do not reveal much in the way of change. Nevertheless, although it is apparent that already in the seventeenth and eighteenth century there was a strong common culture which could be differentiated from that on the high veld or to the north around Delagoa Bay, one should not exaggerate the static quality of life along the coast, nor the homogeneity of the population.

Both north and south of the Umzimvubu, the dividing line between the present-day Nguni of the Cape and of Natal, there were differences between peoples of different culture and tradition, perhaps originating in and being reinforced by enviromental variations. Portuguese sources show that in the late fifteenth and sixteenth centuries, there were still non-Bantu click-speaking peoples as well as various hybrid groups, all along the coast between latitudes 28° and 33° south. As late as 1686, the survivors of the shipwrecked *Stavenisse* found people they called 'Mygrygas', probably Khoi pastoralists, east of the Xhosa on the Buffalo river, though in the course of the next century they had been totally absorbed by Bantu-speakers. In Natal, it would appear there were non-Nguni Bantu-speakers who did not yet share the common culture: thus in 1635, Portuguese sailors were able to purchase fish from people who also planted millet and herded cattle, although today the Nguni peoples are generally described as having an aversion to fish.

Moreover, although all the peoples who today make up the Nguni culture complex were present along the south-east coast by this period, and south of the Umzimvubu were already settled in their present-day relation to one another by 1686, the picture to the north of the river presents no such tidy pattern. While the traditions of the Cape Nguni chiefdoms south of the Umzimvubu are relatively well preserved, the Shakan wars of the early nineteenth century which shattered and scattered the northern Nguni chiefdoms, gravely disrupted and distorted their oral traditions and blurred previous ethnic and linguistic divisions. Although the remaining oral traditions were devotedly and conscientiously collected by the missionary A. T. Bryant in the early twentieth century, his cumbersome style and flights of fantasy have, unfortunately, on occasion served only to make confusion worse confounded.[1] In addition, apart from the pioneering work of J. F. Schofield on the pottery of Natal's coastal middens, and one or two more recent excavations on Iron Age settlements such as that at Blackburn Ridge at Umhlanga Rocks,[2] archaeological evidence is conspicuous by its absence, while the records of shipwrecked sailors are uneven and for the most part confined to the few groups encountered on the immediate coast. Thus, though some of the history of the northern Nguni before the last quarter of the eighteenth century can be salvaged, it must of necessity remain limited and tentative.[3]

[1] A. T. Bryant, *Olden times in Zululand and Natal* (London, 1929) and *A history of the Zulu and neighbouring tribes* (Cape Town, 1964).

[2] J. F. Schofield, 'Natal coastal pottery from the Durban district, a preliminary survey', *S.A.J.Sc.*, 1935, **32**, 508–27, and 1937, **33**, 993–1009. O. Davies, 'Excavations at Blackburn', *S.A. Arch. Bull.* 1971, **26**, 103 and 104, 164–78.

[3] This section is based on S. Marks and A. Atmore, 'The problem of the Nguni: an examination of the ethnic and linguistic situation in South Africa before the Mfecane', in D. Dalby, ed., *Language and history in Africa* (London, 1970), 120–32, and S. Marks, 'The traditions of the Natal "Nguni": a second look at the work of A. T. Bryant', in Thompson, ed., *African societies*, 126–44.

If, however, one looks at the pattern of warfare which evolved during the *Difaqane*, or as it was termed by the Nguni, the *Mfecane* (or 'crushing'), it is clear that the area north of the Tugela river must have experienced very considerable population growth during the seventeenth and eighteenth centuries. Traditional evidence shows the proliferation of literally hundreds of chiefdoms and sub-chiefdoms from the seventeenth century onward, which spilt over into Natal and even into the less hospitable areas along and over the Drakensberg. We can do no more than speculate on the reasons for this. In part, it may have been no more than the natural build up of population in a well favoured but highly complex environment. The Nguni were pastoralists who practised shifting cultivation. As the human and cattle population grew apace, so chiefdoms split and colonized new areas. From linguistic and traditional evidence, moreover, it would seem that the northern Nguni acquired maize from the Portuguese on the east coast at an earlier date than either the Cape Nguni or the Sotho-Tswana of the interior. Natal-Zululand, with its high rainfall and fertile soil, was particularly well suited to the production of maize, which yielded two crops a year. By reducing the periodic famines which cut down most subsistence-level communities, the cultivation of maize may well have accelerated this natural process of population increase.

By 1600 there were three dominant lineage clusters proliferating and expanding in the northern Nguni area: the 'Lala', the Mbo-Dlamini and the Ntungwa Nguni. As their alternative names, 'Tsonga-Nguni', 'Sotho-Nguni' and 'pure' Nguni, suggest, by the nineteenth century the chiefdoms they dominated already represented a certain mingling of different population layers, Sotho, Nguni and Tsonga. The Ntungwa Nguni appear to have been the cattle-keepers *par excellence*, the 'Lala' were more closely associated with agriculture and metal-working, and the Mbo, who trace their origin to the Lebombo Mountains and the hinterland of Delagoa Bay, while continuing their agrarian pursuits, also maintained their contacts with the Bay and became the key traders and state builders of the eighteenth century, though these distinctions are more likely to reflect environmental factors and specific historical developments than any genetic differences. Through the seventeenth and eighteenth centuries these lineages expanded and sent offshoots in different directions, changing their geographical relationship to one another, diffusing their separate cultural traits and creating a new cultural amalgam, today labelled 'Nguni'.

Although Bryant frequently writes of the 'sweeping movements' of 'clans' and of 'tribal Moses' who led their people into the 'promised land', implying the large-scale migration of family groups, it is far more probable that this movement of peoples in the seventeenth and eighteenth centuries represents simply a trickle of new lineages over relatively short distances into new areas where they absorbed or were absorbed by already existing polities.

Thus the 'Lala', who were probably responsible for the NC3 pottery found in abundance north of the Tugela and at scattered points along the coast, and who are generally regarded as amongst the earliest 'Nguni' inhabitants of present-day Zululand, appear to have sent their Cele and Tuli offshoots southwards in the late seventeenth or early eighteenth century. In 1686, the mariners from the *Stavenisse*, for example, recorded the presence of pipe-smoking peoples at Port Natal and the relative paucity of iron amongst the inhabitants. The Tuli, who inhabited the Bay by the early nineteenth century, possessed iron, but not clay pipes, which have been associated with the makers of NC2 and not NC3 pottery, and with the Mpondo farther south. This southward movement of the Cele and Tuli, who headed large chiefdoms in pre-*Mfecane* times, may have been the result of the population pressure along the Tugela or of pressure from the expanding Qwabe chiefdom in their rear. The Qwabe appear to have moved from their heartlands near the Babanango mountains in the seventeenth century, together with the closely related Zulu chiefdom, which established itself on the Mhlatuze river at approximately the same time. By the time of the rise of the Zulu empire-builder, Shaka, both the Cele and Qwabe chiefdoms were of considerable size and had split into numerous sub-chiefdoms.

To the east of the expanding Cele and Tuli chiefdoms, at a distance of some fifteen to thirty kilometres from the coast of Natal, an apparently earlier population layer, classified by Bryant as the Debe sub-group of the Tsonga-Nguni, stretched in a broken column from the Umvoti river to the Umzimkulu. Unfortunately representatives of this group were so dispersed during the *Mfecane* that virtually no traditions of migration or even genealogies appear to have been retained. Unlike the Lala, Ntungwa and Mbo Nguni, they practised facial scarification, a habit they shared with the Tsonga people of Delagoa Bay. Whether they were also the fish-eaters[1] encountered by the Portuguese or not, they seem to represent the earlier, less organized inhabitants of the Natal area who were partially absorbed by the newcomers, partially pushed inland.

[1] The Tsonga are also fish-eaters.

Farther north, in a half circle, the Mbo-Dlamini lineages were expanding and consolidating their hold over a considerable area along the Pongola in Swaziland and in northern Zululand, and in the uplands of Zululand and Natal. According to Manuel de Faria e Sousa's *Portuguese Asia*, in the late sixteenth century the 'Vambe' inhabited a great part of 'Terra de Natal', to the south of the Tsonga of Nyaka who pressed down as far as St Lucia Bay and to the north of the smaller scale societies, governed by 'ankoses', which he maintained stretched to the Cape of Good Hope. These 'Vambe' are almost unmistakably the 'Mbo' with the Tsonga plural prefix, Va. This evidence is confirmed by the genealogies and traditions of the Mbo. The vanguard of the Mbo lineages, all of whom trace their origins to the Komati river and the Lebombo mountains in the hinterland of Delagoa Bay, had already made its way south to the Umzimvubu river by the sixteenth century to form the Mpondo chiefdom. By the same period, the Zizi-Bhele and Hlubi of the same Mbo-Dlamini lineage cluster had made their way south-westwards, to colonize the uplands of Natal and Zululand, probably conquering and absorbing the earlier peoples, both hunter-gatherers and ancient Sotho stock related to the Pai and Pulana of Swaziland. Thus, although both the Zizi and Hlubi are generally classified with the Nguni of the south-east coast, they appear to have shared characteristics of both Sotho and Nguni culture complexes, holding an intermediate position between the two.

According to G. W. Stow, in an unpublished manuscript written in the late nineteenth century,

> not only the Amazizi themselves but native authorities belonging to other tribes, assert that the Amizizi are the direct descendants of the main or original stem from which both branches of the great Bantu family [i.e. Nguni and Sotho] have descended. For many generations it is said that their chiefs and people...[represented] the paramount tribe, whose precedency and supremacy were acknowledged by all others.[1]

By the early nineteenth century, both the Zizi and Hlubi chiefdoms had splintered into several sub-chiefdoms; while the Zizi were noted as iron-workers and traders across the Drakensberg, the Hlubi were involved in the ivory trade with Delagoa Bay.

The settlement of the Zizi and Hlubi chiefdoms on the edge of the escarpment must have very considerable time-depth, for many of the smaller 'Koni' and Ndebele chiefdoms of the Transvaal who trace

[1] G. W. Stow, 'The Intrusion of the Stronger Races', unpublished MSS (South African Public Library, n.d.), fols. 178–9.

their origins to the south-east, appear to have some connection with either the Hlubi or the Zizi, and the earliest Bantu-speakers to cross the Drakensberg to Lesotho, the Phuti, Polane and Pehla, trace their origins to the Zizi chiefdom. This spill-over must have occurred during the seventeenth century at latest, though it is impossible to determine whether it was the result of a search for new grazing lands or internal political pressures.

By the late eighteenth century, however, two further offshoots of the Mbo-Dlamini lineage cluster were beginning to dominate the scene in northern Nguniland: the Ngwane of Swaziland and the Ndwandwe of north-eastern Zululand, both of whom were closely associated with the Tembe kingdom of Delagoa Bay. In both cases their movement from the lower Lebombo hills and along the Pongola river appears to have been rather later than that of the other members of the cluster. Although the traditions of the Ndwandwe are extremely confused – as Shaka's chief rivals, they were more devastated than any other of the larger groups during the *Mfecane* – the pattern of trade and politics at Delagoa Bay may have been responsible for the rise and migration from the coast of both groups.

Throughout the seventeenth and eighteenth centuries, ivory was consistently the most important export from the Bay, and an important part of it was obtained from the south. Already by the end of the sixteenth century, the Portuguese noted Africans from Natal bearing ivory northwards to the Tembe and Inyaka. With the great increase in the demands for ivory from the second half of the eighteenth century and the increasing pressures of the traders at the Bay, conflict and competition amongst chiefs anxious to monopolize the trade increased. Until the eighteenth century, the Tembe were able to maintain their monopoly, but increasingly in this century their position was challenged by the rising power of Mabudu to their south: Mabudu had the advantage of being closer to the Natal sources of ivory and of having a more secure agricultural and pastoral base to its economy. It may well be that it was in the course of the conflict between Tembe and Mabudu that the Dlamini-Ngwane, who claim close links with the Tembe royal family, decided to strike out on their own, and to move south-westward along the Pongola.[1]

It has been suggested that the rise of strong and militant kingdoms in the northern Nguni area at the very end of the eighteenth century

[1] Personal communication from David Hedges, who is currently working on the rise of state systems in northern Zululand/south Mozambique from the mid-eighteenth century.

was the result of the attempts of chiefs to monopolize the ivory trade to Delagoa Bay.[1] The ability of chiefs to monopolize external trade and thus to increase the patronage at their disposal to attract followers may well have been significant in this period. Essentially, however, the Nguni were cultivators and cattle-keepers. As chiefs acquired additional followers – and their cattle – through their distribution of beads and copper, new sources of tension may well have arisen. According to tradition, the portentous battle between the Ngwane-Dlamini and the Ndwandwe which heralded the *Mfecane* was over 'gardens', not ivory. Subsequent strife was occasioned by cattle raiding and disputes over grazing in an area where local variations of soil type and rainfall can mean that one district may be suffering from drought, while its neighbour has lush pasturage. The attempts of chiefs to rationalize the use of grazing land and the mobility of their herds is as plausible a reason for the increasing conflict at the century's close as the desire for trading monopolies, and could equally well account for the warfare, conquest and consolidation of new, larger-scale kingdoms of the time.[2] This consolidation dramatically distinguishes the history of the northern Nguni from that of the Cape Nguni. The centralized organization and the military innovations occurred on a scale and with a speed that was unique. While however the very different external pressures at the southern and northern periphery of the Nguni peoples were to set in motion quite contrary developments in each area by the end of the eighteenth century, the area south of the Umzimvubu was also characterized by the gradual movement of dominant lineages and their offshoots southward and westward, conquering and absorbing the earlier peoples in their path.

Thus traditions – perhaps incorrectly – speak of the movement of the Xhosa, Mpondo and Mpondomise royal clans from a tributary of the Umzimvubu in the foothills of the Drakensberg, during the reign of the Xhosa chief Sikhomo, father of Togu, whose reign should probably be placed at the beginning of the seventeenth century.[3] By

[1] A. Smith, 'The trade of Delagoa Bay in Nguni politics, 1750–1835', in Thompson, *African societies*, 171–89.

[2] J. Guy, 'Cattle-keeping in Zululand', unpublished paper presented to the Research group on cattle-keeping in Africa, School of Oriental and African Studies, London, 1970. This ecological emphasis has been corroborated by the research of Professor Colin Webb of the University of Natal, on eighteenth- and nineteenth-century royal and military sites in Zululand. (Report presented to the Conference on the History of the Transkei and Ciskei, Rhodes University, Grahamstown, 1973, to be published).

[3] The common origin of the Xhosa, Mpondomise and other clans from the Dedesi is being increasingly questioned; preliminary archaeological survey in the general area indicated by tradition has so far proved negative. (Robin Derricourt, introduction to 'Settle-

1622 there were Xhosa on the Bashee river. Togu himself moved to the Kei river, while his sons Ntinde and Ketshe moved to the area between the Chalumna and Buffalo rivers in the mid-seventeenth century. By the beginning of the eighteenth century, outliers of the Xhosa encountered white hunter-traders as far south as the Little Fish river, while by the last quarter of the eighteenth century, a number of offshoots of the Tshawe royal lineage, the Ntinde, Mbalu, and Gwali together with the mixed Xhosa-Khoi Gqunukwebe, lived in the area between the Bushman and Sundays rivers known as the Zuurveld. This small area was to be the scene of contest between black and white for the next fifty years. Behind the Xhosa block east of the Kei, the Mpondo, Mpondomise and Thembu peoples appear to have expanded in an uneven movement south and west in similar fashion.

The way in which new areas were colonized, and the purely pastoral but culturally compatible Khoi people absorbed, has been best illustrated for the Xhosa.[1] In part this must be traced back to the fissiparous nature of the Nguni political structure. The tendency was especially marked when the heir to the chieftaincy was a minor, a not infrequent occurrence amongst the Nguni, because the general rule of succession was that the oldest son of the 'great wife' of the chief succeeded his father. The 'great wife' was generally married late in a chief's life, after he had acquired wealth and prestige. The division of chiefs' families for the purposes of the distribution of property into a great house and a right-hand house, increased this predisposition to fission. The wife of the right-hand house was the first to marry the chief – and her firstborn son was often appointed regent for the political heir. In this position he was able to build up his following – and make a bid for his independence. So much was this the case that the right-hand house had almost a pre-emptive right to establish its independence and was recognized as having almost equal status with the royal house. These structural arrangements played a key role in the politics of the period, primarily the politics of the segmentation and fission of the Xhosa royal Tshawe lineage.

Thus from the beginning of the seventeenth to the end of the eighteenth century, the Tshawe royal lineage divided in almost every generation, giving rise to several new chiefdoms. Though on occasion

ment in the Early Transkei and Ciskei', paper presented to the Conference on the History of the Transkei and Ciskei, 1973). The date 1686 for Togu's reign, hitherto the foundation stone of Xhosa chronology, has been shown to be invalid by G. Harinck, 'Interaction between Xhosa and Khoi: emphasis on the period 1620–1750' in Thompson, *African societies*, 154–5 n. 30.

[1] Harinck, 147.

the splits were peaceful, more often than not warfare ensued, and in the struggles several groups fled westwards, some of them seeking refuge or lands from the Khoi they encountered across the Kei river. The strife for example between Gandowentshaba, Togu's right-hand son, and Tshiwo, his grandson and heir in the royal line, left a large number of the Xhosa dissidents, followers of Gandowentshaba, embedded in Khoi society. The Khoi chief, Hintsati, himself received a daughter in marriage from the incoming Gandowentshaba, and their son, Cwama, headed a mixed Khoi-Xhosa group known as the Gona. During the first half of the eighteenth century, the Gona were in turn partially absorbed by other breakaway Xhosa chiefdoms settled between the Keiskamma and the Kei rivers. By the time Ensign Beutler visited the Transkei, on behalf of the Dutch government at the Cape, he found Gona herders, soldiers and messengers serving Mbange, chief of the Ntinde.[1] Mbange was described as being second only in power to Palo, chief of the royal Tshawe lineage, although the Ntinde themselves owed their origin to the marriage of Togu to a Khoi wife in a minor house in the first half of the seventeenth century.

Not all these mixed groups were the result of quarrels in the royal family. The Gqunukwebe, another mixed Khoi-Xhosa group, traced their origin to a group of Xhosa covertly rescued by Tshiwo's counsellor, Kwane, from accusations of witchcraft. As Kwane's secret following grew, Tshiwo, appreciating the increase in his counsellor's power, granted him separate jurisdiction over these people. In the course of the eighteenth century, however, they were forced still farther westward to the Hoengeiqua, a mixed group of people situated between the Bushman and the Fish rivers. There they were to obtain land in exchange for cattle, a transaction they were to cite in defence of their position when their territory was claimed by white settlers in the last quarter of the eighteenth century. They further legitimized their position by considerable intermarriage with the local Khoi.

Though the segmentation and westerly movement of the Xhosa during Tshiwo's reign resulted in conflict and intermixture with Khoi groups, during the long reign of his successor, Palo (*c.* 1702–*c.* 1775),[2] both the newly created Xhosa-Khoi groups and the breakaway chiefdoms came up against the expanding white settlers from the Cape for

[1] C. A. Haupt, 'Journal gehouden . . . op de togt door den Vaandrig August Frederick Beutler (1752)', in E. C. Godée-Molsbergen, *Reizen in Zuid-Afrika* (The Hague, 1916–32), III, 297–8.

[2] This inordinately long reign is well authenticated in written records; Palo was a posthumous heir, which may account for it.

the first time. Another minor heir, the early years of his reign saw the separation of the followers of Gwali, his brother in the right-hand house, and of his uncles, Ntinde and Mdange, and their movement across the Kei river as far as the Fish. Later in his reign, Palo, apparently rather a weak ruler, was faced with the intrigues of his heir, Gcaleka, who tried to usurp his father's position during his lifetime. This led to the deepest split in the Xhosa paramountcy. Rarabe, Palo's son in the right-hand house, supported his father against the rebel; after being defeated in battle, Rarabe and Palo moved across the Kei, where they conquered the local Khoi chief, Hoho, and received permission to settle in return for cattle. The majority of the chiefdom, however, remained with Gcaleka, who became paramount chief of the Xhosa on Palo's death. Rarabe's heirs, who remained between the Kei and the Fish rivers, were further divided in the 1790s when the regent, Ndlambe, refused to give way to the rightful heir, his nephew and Rarabe's grandson, Ngqika. The Ngqika and Ndlambe groups were the most powerful to confront the settlers in the late eighteenth and early nineteenth century, while the rivalry between them was to affect deeply the nature of their relationship with the white man.

Throughout the seventeenth and eighteenth centuries the Xhosa had been involved in an extensive trading network, which mounted in importance as the eighteenth century wore on. Even at the end of the sixteenth century, Portuguese sources record the copper ornaments worn by chiefs along the coast, and red beads from the Indian Ocean trading network had reached as far south from Delagoa Bay as the Umzimvubu. It is not clear where the copper came from, though by the mid-seventeenth century there was a long distance trade route linking the Xhosa with the Nama on the Orange river and possibly with the Tswana mining cultures beyond. All these networks would appear to have converged on the powerful Khoi chiefdom of the Inqua or Hancumqua, which was recognized as politically superior by all the Cape Khoi in the seventeenth century. The route may well have extended to Cape Town, where from the end of the sixteenth century Dutch, British and French ships called in increasing numbers. Situated in the middle distance between the Cape and the Xhosa on the Kariega river, the Inqua passed copper, iron and beads, from the interior and from the Cape, to the Xhosa, in exchange for cattle and sheep and dagga, which was always in demand at the Cape. Throughout the seventeenth century, however, copper and iron remained sufficiently rare along the coast for Africans to barter eight cows for two crusados of copper, and even on occasion to murder shipwrecked Europeans to possess the metal they carried. Though the Cape Nguni knew the art of smelting and working ores, and were smelting iron round the Buffalo mouth in 1686, mineral deposits along the coast were relatively meagre and difficult to mine, and even at the end of the seventeenth century metals were in great demand. The 'Lala' peoples farther up the coast were renowned as skilled metal-workers, however, and as they moved south along the coast and into Natal from Zululand, metal tools and ornaments were probably more easily obtainable from the north-east as well as the more westerly trade routes.

The great expansion of the cattle trade from the Cape after the settlement of the Dutch in 1652 was probably even more significant in the wider diffusion of beads, iron and copper amongst the coastal peoples, both Khoi and Nguni. By the time Ensign Beutler visited the Xhosa and Thembu in the mid-eighteenth century, he found the price of cattle so inflated that he was unable to purchase any. Although the Africans maintained that their reluctance was the result of drought and poverty, he observed that the abundance of beads and the surplus of iron was the more likely reason. Though traditional trade to the north-west and east continued, the trade with the Dutch diminished its importance. Alberti, writing in 1806, noted 'the enthusiastic propensity for business' amongst the Xhosa, and remarked that, before the arrival of Europeans, spearheads were used as currency, and this was still the case, though 'copper, brass and glass beads command equal respect'.[1]

It is tempting to ascribe the segmentation and westerly movement of the Xhosa to the attractions of the new trade routes. There is however far too little evidence as yet to support fully such a view. Nevertheless, once the Xhosa offshoots had settled across the Kei river, the possibilities of trade may, together with other factors, have drawn some groups farther towards the colonial frontier.

Avid as they were to trade, commerce had very different results for the Xhosa to those already observed amongst the northern Nguni. Although Xhosa chiefs strove to maintain a monopoly of the cattle trade and to use the benefits of the trade to increase their power in the same fashion as Tswana or northern Nguni chiefs, there were major differences in their historical situation which undermined their ability to do so. Unlike the situation to their north, where most intercourse between black and white took place at clearly defined sea ports, the

[1] L. Alberti, *The Kaffirs of the south coast of Africa*, tr. W. Fehr as *Ludwig Alberti's account of the tribal life and customs of the Xhosa in 1807* (Cape Town, 1968), 71.

existence of a land frontier between the Xhosa and the whites made it far more difficult for chiefs to maintain a monopoly over trade routes, especially in view of the scattered nature of Nguni settlement. Moreover, although ivory was an important article of commerce, in the main it was the cattle trade which interested both the settlers and officials of the Dutch East India Company. While the ivory trade demanded increased social organization for the hunting of elephants and trading of the tusks, which was best organized by chiefs, the cattle trade was far more open to individual exchange. It was also far more open to abuse. In the long run, therefore, this trade was to have a disintegrating rather than a consolidating effect on Xhosa society, though never to the same extent as it had had on the more loosely organized Khoi peoples.

While ivory was never in demand amongst Africans, except as an article for export, cattle were a vital part of their economy and social organization. Not infrequently Africans were loath to part with the numbers demanded by whites. Though the Xhosa never lost their cattle through white raiding to the same extent as did the Khoi people of the western Cape, the temptation for unscrupulous whites simply to take by force what they could not obtain through fair exchange was always strong.

The first skirmish in the cattle trade between the Xhosa and white settlers occurred as early as 1702, when a gang of marauding hunter-traders from the Cape penetrated as far as the Great Fish river, and had to be driven off by force. By this time, the country eastwards of the Cape must have been fairly well known to the Dutch, as parties of hunters were sometimes absent from the colony eight or nine months and more at a time. In 1736 a similar expedition was driven off by Palo, and the leaders killed. Despite the most drastic punishments threatened by the government at the Cape against anyone participating in the illegal barter of cattle with the indigenous population, by the 1730s more than one annual party was hunting and trading amongst the Xhosa. By the mid-century there was a well-worn route into the eastern Cape, and in 1768 a Commission appointed to fix the eastern frontier of the colony found a wagon-road leading from the district of Swellendam to the 'abode of the Kafirs'. Between the Gamtoos and the Fish rivers, colonists were found carrying on the illicit trade, or employing Khoi servants to do so on their behalf.

As the trading frontier between the Dutch and the Xhosa changed into a settlers' frontier, this skirmishing entered a new phase. It was almost inevitable that once the colonists and the Xhosa were face to face along a land frontier, conflict would ensue. By this time the needs of both groups for land, water and cattle were basically similar. A boom in the demand for fresh meat at the Cape in the 1770s led, in addition, to new irregularities in the cattle trade, as whites became even more impatient with African reluctance to part with more than a limited number of their cattle, and looked longingly at the area of high rainfall across the Fish river, with its excellent grazing. Africans reacted to the whites' abuse of the cattle trade by stealing their cattle in exchange, and before the century was out, minor incidents had escalated into three frontier 'wars'.

KHOISAN AND DUTCH AT THE CAPE

To understand this phase of the contact and conflict between black and white on the eastern frontier, however, it is necessary to turn to the beginnings of Dutch settlement at the Cape and its evolution, as well as to the relationships of the Dutch with the first groups of population they encountered, the pastoral Khoi and hunter-gatherer San.

Though, until well into the eighteenth century, for the vast majority of black peoples in South Africa the whites at the Cape were little more than a rumour and an alternative source of beads and brass, their impact on the Khoisan was far more dramatic and ultimately far more destructive.[1] From the beginning of the seventeenth century, ships of Dutch and English companies, formed from the 1590s to tap the wealth of the East, began to call regularly at the Cape to stock up with the fresh meat and greens necessary to ward off that scourge of European mariners to the East, scurvy. The earlier Portuguese sailors had tended to avoid the Cape on their eastward journey on account of its capricious storms and apparently equally capricious inhabitants (in 1510 they had murdered no less a person than the Portuguese viceroy for the East, Francisco d'Almeida, and sixty of his companions); with their sturdier vessels and different sea routes, the Dutch, British and to some extent the French, found the Cape a useful half-way house. The Khoi pastoralists they encountered at the Cape were initially quite willing to exchange their cattle for the iron, copper, tobacco, brandy and beads of the Europeans. These, as we have seen, they exchanged for more cattle, tobacco and dagga in the interior. Though the Khoi fiercely resisted unfair attempts to take their cattle, and were reluctant to part with

[1] This section is largely based on S. Marks, 'Khoisan resistance to the Dutch in the seventeenth and eighteenth centuries', *J. Afr. Hist.*, 1972, 13, 1, 55–80, and Elphick, 'Cape Khoi . . .'.

more than a certain number of their surplus stock, they were quick to respond to the newly created market.

From about 1610, the price of fresh meat, however, was subject to fairly constant price inflation, perhaps because the Cape market became glutted with iron. This was especially marked in 1614 after the return to the Cape of one 'Goree', whom the British had taken to London in an effort to teach him English and use him as mediator in the trade. On his return, Goree reputedly spoilt the market by informing the Khoi of the low value of the goods they were being offered in exchange, so that as one Englishman bitterly remarked: 'itt were better hee hadde been hanged in Englande or drowned homewarde'[1] than returned to his people.

If Goree proved a recalcitrant intermediary, the Dutch and British were able to find more willing collaborators at the Cape from quite early on, to negotiate in the trade, to look after the mail they left behind for the return fleets and even, on occasion, when ships were stranded at the Cape, to help fetch wood and carry water. Already by 1639, Europeans noted the existence of a small mixed class of Khoisan whom they termed 'Beachrangers', who lived at the Bay and who had lost their cattle, either in the course of the trade, through the internecine warfare which may have been its result, or through a variety of natural disasters. By the 1650s their leader was one 'Herry', a man of many parts. Herry spoke broken English, having been taken to Bantam on a ship of the English East India Company, and on the strength of this acted as interpreter to British and Dutch visitors to the Cape. The Khoi were already relatively sophisticated traders, refusing to take thin copper or notched and rough copper wire, and insisting on only fresh and strong Caribbean tobacco, which had rapidly become an essential element in any trading transaction. The variety of relationships established in this half-century of trading profoundly influenced the nature of the contact between the Khoi and the Dutch when, in the mid-century, the latter decided to establish a more permanent outpost at the Cape.

Originally the aim of the directors of the Dutch East India Company, which had been granted a monopoly of the trade to the East by the States General in Holland in 1602, was simply to establish a refreshment station, where fresh fruit and vegetables could be grown by its servants, and meat bartered from the local inhabitants. In 1652 they dispatched

[1] VC 58 no. 7 (verbatim copies of documents in the India Office, London, made by G. M. Theal in the late nineteenth century), Cape archives, letter from E. Bletterman to Sir Thomas Smythe from Bantam, 20 February 1614.

three ships of company servants – some 125 men – under the command of Jan van Riebeeck, to effect this. It soon became apparent, however, that in the short term, it would be easier to release some of the men as free burghers and allow them to cultivate and raise cattle on the company's behalf. Almost imperceptibly, and despite the reluctance of the company's directors, the refreshment station began to change into a colony of settlement, though one governed by, and in every way subordinated to, the interests of a commercial company, anxious to maintain its trading monopolies and maximize its profits.

In 1657 the first handful of free burghers were granted lands along the Liesbeck river, behind Table mountain. Their immediate demand was for labour. The local Khoi people were not regarded as suitable for this purpose. Although the Dutch had found it possible to employ individuals on a temporary basis, while the Khoi still had an abundance of cattle and sufficient grazing, and their social system was intact, there was little reason why more than those few who were already dispossessed of their cattle should take regular employment with the white intruders. The company had, moreover, from the first forbidden the enslavement of the local population. In any case, the Khoi were a purely pastoral people, who did not take easily to the idea of cultivating for others, and could easily escape into the interior if enslaved. To answer the demand from the freemen as well as from the company servants for an additional labour supply, the first batch of slaves was landed at the Cape, also in 1657.

As the first freemen took up their lands, tensions between them and the Khoi inhabitants of the Cape peninsula – whom they called Capemen – increased. These had been present as soon as the Khoi realized that, unlike their previous visitors, the Dutch had come to stay. They asked longingly when the more generous English would reappear, and their petty pilfering infuriated the Dutch. At the same time, the white presence at the Cape disturbed the normal pattern of transhumance, as Herry and his 'Beachrangers', or Goringhaikona, tried to build up their own herds again by monopolizing the cattle trade and preventing other Khoi groups from coming to the Company's fort. Within seven years the cost of sheep and cattle had trebled. While handling the Khoi with the utmost tact, Van Riebeeck gave vent to his fantasies of revenge in bloodcurdling letters to the Directors, who, fully aware of the weakness of the settlement, failed to sanction his punitive proposals; the freemen and lesser company servants were more prone to act out their frustrations on the local inhabitants in this strange and trying new environment. The introduction of slaves exacerbated the situation; as they immediately tried to escape, the Khoi were accused of harbouring them, and Khoi hostages were seized against their return. At the same time the inland Cochoqua were beginning to break the blockade of the peninsular Khoi and to intrude into their pastures. In 1659, the first of the two Khoi wars in the seventeenth century broke out.

All the Khoi groups of the peninsula, or Capemen, were involved: Herry's Goringhaikona (though Herry himself had been banished before the outbreak of war); the more powerful Goringhaiqua under Gogosa and one Doman, who had been to the East and had acquired a useful knowledge of the limitations of European firearms; and the Gorachouqua, who had already received the revealing epithet, the 'Tobacco Thieves'. For the following year, the Capemen, by stealing the plough oxen and conducting elusive guerrilla warfare, brought agricultural work in the small colony virtually to a standstill. In April 1660, however, after Doman had been injured, the peninsula alliance crumbled, and, perhaps in response to pressure from other groups for a resumption of the trade, the Capemen sought peace, though they had by no means been conquered. They complained that the Dutch were

> taking every day...land which had belonged to them from all ages and on which they were accustomed to depasture their cattle. They also asked whether if they were to come into Holland they would be permitted to act in the same manner,[1]

and their complaint was to be echoed by Khoi groups through the next century and more, as they came up against the expanding Dutch settlement.

Though the number of actual settlers was extremely small, the constant demand for meat for company ships led to considerable expansion from the Cape in search of new cattle supplies, and fresh Khoi groups were brought into the company's orbit. Though initially most of the trade took place at the Fort, by 1663 cattle traders had crossed the Hottentots Holland to the populous and cattle-rich Chainouqua people in the Caledon river–Danger Point area and were bartering with their allies, the Hessequa, beyond the Storms river area as far east as Riversdale and the Rivier Zonder End. In the next two decades, trade expeditions reached the Nama in the north and the

[1] D. Moodie, ed., *The record or a series of official papers relating to the condition and treatment of native tribes of South Africa* (Amsterdam and Cape Town, 1960, photographic reproduction of the original imprint of 1835). Van Riebeeck's Journal, 4 April 1660.

Attaqua in the east. Thousands of cattle were bartered for iron, copper, beads, arrack and tobacco. As one group became impoverished or reluctant to trade, another would take its place. This in turn set up rivalries between the Khoi chiefdoms, and may partly explain some of the internecine fighting observed amongst them in this period, though undoubtedly older rivalries and disputes also played their part.

Increasing tension over the trade and fear of the gradual encroachment of whites in their preserves may have been behind the restlessness which led to the second conflict between the Dutch and the Cochoqua, under chief Gonnema, which broke out in the early 1670s. By this time the Cochoqua, who had probably been the most powerful of the groups near the Cape, and had remained neutral during the war of 1659–60, had been considerably weakened by a decade of warfare with the Chainouqua. Gonnema, unlike his co-chief, Oedasoa, in 1659, had been suspicious of white intentions from the outset, and had already moved towards the middle distance between the Berg river and the Fort to escape their demands. At the end of 1670, the Cochoqua and their client soldiers, the Ubiqua, a mixed San and Khoi group, were alleged to be committing 'in a spiteful manner various acts of mischief',[1] breaking into farmhouses, stealing provisions and assaulting freemen hunters and soldiers. By the end of 1672, at a time when the government was taking a less conciliatory line with the Khoi and was planning to open the Hottentots Holland to white settlement, hostilities broke out in more serious fashion, and continued over the next four years. Though the Dutch captured large numbers of Cochoqua cattle and sheep, they were unable to track down the chief and his people, perhaps through the double dealing of their San spies. It was not until 1677 that Gonnema, still unsubdued, sued for peace.

Resistance was only one of the Khoi responses to the Dutch presence, and perhaps not the dominant one even in the seventeenth century. In both these Khoi wars, the Dutch were heavily dependent on 'loyal' Khoi levies and outnumbered by them. In 1670, when there were rumours of a French invasion, the Dutch defences were augmented by Khoi soldiers, while throughout the eighteenth century, they formed the backbone of the colonial defences against both internal and external enemies. During the war with Gonnema, the Dutch were joined by a large number of Khoi allies, the most prominent of whom was one Dorha, or 'Klaas', who was the key intermediary in diplomacy and

[1] H. C. V. Leibbrandt, *Précis of the archives of the Cape of Good Hope, journals 1662–1670* (Cape Town, 1901), 343. Journal, 22 December 1670.

trade, from this time to his death in 1701. Though it was illegal to sell arms to the Khoi after 1674, by this time a number were skilled musketeers. The custom was soon adopted of recognizing 'loyal' Khoi chiefs, or, as the Dutch called them, captains, who were granted copper staffs of office and official white recognition in exchange for their services. Though at the beginning it would appear that the Company were simply acknowledging the already legitimate heads of Khoi chiefdoms, by the end of the eighteenth century, and probably a good deal earlier, the effect was to separate chiefs from their people in the manner familiar to nineteenth- and twentieth-century colonial Africa. Thus one Khoi informant remarked to the Swedish traveller, Sparrmann, in 1775:

> Captain...is merely an empty title, formerly bestowed by the regency at Cape Town on some princes and patriarches of the Hottentots, and particularly on such as had distinguished themselves by their fidelity to their allies by betraying their countrymen or by some remarkable service...it is required of the captain that he shall be a spy on the other Hottentots.[1]

Already by the 1670s some six or eight of these staffs of office had been granted to Khoi captains, and by the end of the century chiefs as far off as the Nama had come to seek company recognition at the Cape.

In Cape Town itself, there was considerable acculturation. In the early days of the colony, middlemen, mediators and interpreters were essential to the Dutch, and they took great pains to establish a class of collaborators, like the interpreters, Doman and Herry, even though at times the attempts appeared to backfire. By the end of the century, peninsular Khoi were turning to the whites for employment, and supplemented the slave labour force, especially in inland areas. Increasing numbers of Khoi spoke Dutch, which was heard in their mouths fifty miles from the Fort; many also spoke Portuguese or Malay, the *linguae francae* amongst the Indian Ocean slaves. It has been cogently argued that it was the need for communication in the multi-racial, multilinguistic society at the Cape which led to the rapid divergence of the local patois from Dutch – a process already noted in little more than a generation after the first settlement.[2] There was also intermarriage

[1] A. Sparrman, *A voyage to the Cape of Good Hope, 1772–6* (Dublin, 1785), I, 240.

[2] The reasons for the rapid evolution of Afrikaans have been hotly debated by linguists and linguistic historians. For the opposing points of view see M. Valkhoff, *Studies in Portuguese and Creole, with special reference to South Africa* (Johannesburg, 1966), and his collected essays, *New light on Afrikaans and Malayo-Portuguese* (Louvain, 1972) in which the debate is summarized. For the other side, J. du P. Scholtz, *'n Voorstudie tot 'n Geskiedenis van Afrikaans* (Pretoria, 1963).

between the white men and slave or Khoi women – the most famous, but not the only, case being the marriage of Eva, who had been brought up in the Commander's home, to the ship's surgeon and explorer, Pieter van Meerhoff. Concubinage also undoubtedly continued in both town and country, to give rise in the course of the eighteenth century to a considerable half-caste population, known today as the Cape Coloureds: this was hardly surprising given the heavy preponderance of males in the white population.[1] For some Khoi the strain of acculturation proved too great: Eva herself ended her days in squalor and drunken disgrace, while the records contain other examples, like the young Khoi girl, who was 'respectably educated by burghers' but eventually hanged herself in a sheep-pen. Others took refuge in the apathy, alcoholism and addiction to dagga, already noted by Peter Kolbe at the beginning of the eighteenth century.[2] Nevertheless by the end of that century, though they were not by then granted full burgher status, there were fairly substantial numbers of baptized 'Basters' (half-castes) on the tax rolls of the colony and participating in the commandos against Khoisan raiders as well as against European invaders.

After 1677, white expansion was rapid, both to the north and the east. In part, this was the result of the increase in the white population at the turn of the century, during the dynamic governorships of Simon van der Stel (1679–99) and his son, Willem Adriaan (1699–1707). As late as 1679, when van der Stel arrived, there were only about 600 whites at the Cape, of whom eighty-seven were free burghers. Although by this time they were able to provision the passing ships with sufficient fresh meat and vegetables, they were still heavily dependent on the Batavian empire for grain and rice. The Cape was regarded as a costly and burdensome, if useful and strategically necessary, appendage of Batavia. Van der Stel, however, was determined to increase both its importance and its prosperity. Almost immediately, he established the new district of Stellenbosch, with its own full-time *landdrost*, or magistrate, and initiated agricultural reforms. In 1685, the Company decided cautiously to increase the number of settlers, in order to strengthen the colony's defences against external enemies – this was a time of political uncertainty in Europe – and to increase its agricultural yield.

[1] This point has been clearly shown in an unpublished paper by R. Ross 'Speculations on the origins of Cape society' (Cambridge, 1972), and is based on the genealogies in C. C. de Villiers and C. Pama, *Geslags registers van die Ou Kaapse families* (Cape Town, 1966).

[2] *The present state of the Cape of Good Hope, containing a particular account of the several nations of the Hottentots*, tr. G. Medley, 2nd ed. (London, 1738), I, 76.

For a short period, then, the Cape enjoyed state-aided immigration. A number of orphaned girls were sent out to redress the balance between the sexes, and in 1688 refuge was granted to some 160 French Huguenots fleeing from religious persecution in France. By 1694 the number of whites had risen to nearly 1,000, and by 1707 it had almost doubled. Of these, about two-thirds were German and Dutch and nearly one-third French; the rest were Swedes, Danes and Walloons. Despite their heterogeneous origins, their common vicissitudes and the insistence of the company that they all speak Dutch and that only the Calvinist Dutch Reformed Church be officially recognized (though a considerable proportion were probably Catholic) went far towards moulding them into a distinctive new entity: by 1707 one at least was already calling himself an Afrikaner.

By the end of the seventeenth century, there were perceptible differences within the white population, between company officials, town burghers and free agriculturalists, and tensions between them. Almost all the company employees were concentrated in Cape Town, which remained the only city and the centre of administration throughout the Dutch period. In the higher echelons, they were conscious of their rank and remained somewhat aloof from the burgher population, though never to the extent that obtained in the East. The town burghers were mainly innkeepers and were almost entirely dependent on the trade with the passing ships. Many indulged in trading on the side, and smuggling was the natural outcome of the monopoly system and the low prices imposed by the Company. In the immediate hinterland of Cape Town lived the wine and wheat farmers of Stellenbosch, Drakenstein and Roodezand. They were legally bound to dispose of their produce to the Company at fixed prices, a source of considerable grievance. The grievance was the greater, in that at the turn of the century they were in direct competition with a number of senior officials, from the governors, Simon and Willem Adriaan van der Stel downwards. The officials farmed on a far larger scale, with the most advanced methods, and had, in addition, privileged access to the limited market. At this time, less than a dozen efficient, capital-intensive farms supplied almost the entire needs of the calling fleets, rendering the free-burgher scheme virtually redundant. In the event, and with considerable consequence for the history of South Africa as a colony of white settlement, it was the governor and his clique who were recalled to the Netherlands, after burgher discontent erupted into a major crisis in 1707. The company, ever anxious to avoid trouble and expense, came down on the side of the burghers and once again forbade official farming. They also took care, however, to end subsidized immigration. Thereafter, apart from a steady trickle of single male immigrants, the Cape became virtually dependent on its own high birth rate for its population increase. By the mid-eighteenth century, the white population numbered four or five thousand; by the century's end, approximately sixteen thousand – a very substantial increase.

Differences in wealth between the burghers were also in evidence by 1707; one of the leading opponents of the governor was Henning Huising, who had been granted a monopoly to supply meat for the Company's ships in 1684, and who by this time vied with the governor himself in wealth and ostentation. By the eighteenth century, a slave-owning burgher aristocracy had emerged, and in many ways set the social and racial standards for the rest of the community. Lichtenstein describes the patriarchal household of one of the richest colonists a century later: '...the family included masters, servants, Hottentots and slaves and consisted of one hundred and five persons...' He aptly calls it 'a state in miniature, in which the wants and means of supplying them are reciprocal and where all are dependent on one another'.[1]

By the mid-eighteenth century, a class of burgher capitalist entrepreneurs, with diverse interests extending well into the interior, was also emerging, though its numbers remained very small. Though in many ways it was associated with the bureaucratic élite, it also provided the leadership for the opposition to the Company's policies of low prices and monopolies. Crises between the Company and the colonists erupted again in 1743, at the time of the visit of Commissioner van Imhoff, and in more organized fashion in the 1780s, when, inspired by news of the American War of Independence and the contemporary Patriot movement in Holland, they formed the Cape Patriot movement to demand constitutional reform and free trade. Neither of these was to be achieved in any substantial sense until after the end of Company rule at the Cape at the end of the century.

Although the Cape burghers undoubtedly suffered from the fact that they were governed by the Dutch East India Company, a company moreover that was in steady decline for much of the century, their problems were compounded in that they were in direct competition with European wine and wheat farmers. There was little demand for Cape wine, which, apart from the governor's own, was poor in quality,

[1] H. Lichtenstein, *Travels in southern African in the years 1803, 1804, 1805 and 1806*, tr. Anne Plumptre (Van Riebeeck Society, 10, 11, Cape Town, 1928–30), 1, 57.

while the low price of wheat, which dropped still further in 1717, rendered it barely profitable.

Once the burghers had expanded more than fifty or sixty miles from the Cape, the absence of roads across the mountain ranges made it difficult to transport grain to their only market, while the carriage of fresh fruit and vegetables was almost impossible. Cattle and sheep obligingly walked themselves to market. Moreover, in a country where capital was scarce, labour inadequate and land seemed inexhaustible, pastoral farming was the most feasible economic activity. Thus, though the Company tried to encourage arable farming, the constant demand for fresh meat on the long journey to the East made cattle farming a far more attractive proposition.

Apart from farming, there were few alternatives open to free burghers. Slaves, together with an increasing number of Khoi and half-castes, not only provided the labour for the wine and wheat farms, they also constituted the skilled and unskilled artisan class of Cape Town. Until the opening of the slave trade with Madagascar on a firm footing in the 1680s, there had been relatively few slaves in the colony, most of them in the service of the company. With the expansion of the colony under the van der Stels, the slave population also greatly increased and was drawn from a wide arc around the Indian Ocean – Madagascar, Mozambique and Indonesia. Many of the latter slaves, in particular, were highly skilled craftsmen who left their stamp on Cape architecture, furniture and cuisine. Burghers were accustomed to hiring these slaves out by the day or month, to perform a wide range of tasks in the town and countryside. Some of the more fortunate were ultimately able to buy their freedom, or were emancipated by their masters. They then joined the ranks of the 'free blacks', emancipated slaves and political exiles from the Dutch possessions in the East, who performed many of the same economic functions as the slaves, though they had the status of free men. On the farms, the unskilled labour was performed by African slaves for the most part, though never on the scale of the plantations in the Americas: the average wine farm employed fifteen slaves, the average wheat farm six. Both groups became mixed with the Khoi and whites, though those Indonesian slaves who were Muslims retained their own identity within the Cape Coloured group and became known as the Cape Malays. From under 1,000 at the beginning of the eighteenth century, the slaves had risen in number to over 25,000 by its end, out-numbering the white population.

In the early days of the colony an experiment of using white labour had been made. This however had proved unsatisfactory – as visitors to the Cape through the eighteenth century remarked, the presence of a large non-white servile class and the availability of land made the white man loath to undertake work for another in a subservient capacity, and tended to identify manual labour with the status of slave. Most of the white labourers or 'knechts' found it more attractive to strike off on their own in the interior than to work on the wine and wheat farms, or to compete with the skilled slave artisans. In 1717 the governing Council of Policy at the Cape debated whether white could be substituted for slave labour; they decided overwhelmingly against it. Despite the frequent attempts at escape by the slaves and the inevitable violence beneath the surface engendered by the system, they argued that white labour would prove too expensive. They also opposed any further increase in the white population of the Cape from Europe, on the ground that already the burghers were finding it difficult to make a living, other than by making their way into the interior as pastoral farmers and hunters. This view was to be repeated through the century.

Thus it was that, already by the end of the seventeenth century, Simon van der Stel noted with concern the existence of a class of cattle farmers beyond the confines of the settlement, where they supported themselves by combining hunting with the illegal cattle trade with the Khoi. At times it was difficult to distinguish their trading and raiding operations.

For the eighteenth-century cattle farmers, or trekboers as they were called, the greatest hurdle was crossing the first mountain barrier behind the Cape. Once this was overcome, they moved on to the great inland plateau of South Africa, thousands of square miles of dry scrubland, where movement was easy and population sparse. If rainfall was scant and the soil, except in isolated patches around the mountain ranges, poor, these defects could be compensated for by the appropriation of vast farms: in a region where it required an acre of land to support a sheep and five to support a cow, 6,000-acre farms rapidly became the norm. Many farmers indeed moved between two such farms, following the rainfall in the way of the earlier Khoi herders. The 'loan farm' system of land tenure formalized in 1714 further facilitated the expansion of the trekboer. With minor reforms, this system, whereby farmers could lease land indefinitely in exchange for a nominal rent, remained the basic form of land tenure until the nineteenth century. Despite the leasehold nature of the tenure, the Company rarely, if ever, took back land, even when the colonists defaulted on their payments, and many farms were not even registered. It was a system well-suited to the needs of cattle farmers with little capital and of necessity with a roving disposition.

In this harsh interior of the Cape, in the Little Karroo with its extremes of temperature and monotonous landscape, the cattle farmer was thrown very largely on to his own resources. Despite one or two sporadic attempts, the Dutch East India Company made little effort to follow him. Though the new districts of Stellenbosch (1685), Swellendam (1745) and Graaff Reinet (1785) were formed, they were large and unwieldy, and their centres remained far from the expanding trekboers. The authority of the full-time magistrate, or *landdrost*, and his burgher assistants, the *heemraden* and *veldkornets*, was not supported by an adequate police force, and could hardly control the trekboer, who became accustomed to handling emergencies on his own and taking the law into his own hands.

The trekboer was not wholly self-sufficient. He depended on the Cape market to dispose of his cattle, butter, soap, ivory and other animal products, in exchange for the essential arms and ammunition, and luxuries like clothing, sugar, tea, coffee and brandy. New market towns did not however spring up in his wake. Instead he relied on the butchers' agents, both white and Khoi, who made their way into the interior in increasing numbers in response to the demands of calling ships for meat. South African historiography has generally stressed the isolation, factionalism and exaggerated individualism of the trekboer, following the views of eighteenth-century European visitors, who saw signs of degeneration in this. Of necessity, the trekboer became Africanized; nevertheless he also retained considerable contact with the more settled and prosperous community in the south-west, with which he was linked by kinship and interest. At least twice in a man's life, at his baptism and marriage, he had to make the long journey to the Cape; at the great gathering of the church, the Nagmaal, the ties were further consolidated: as late as the 1790s, the furthest church was only 100 miles from Cape Town. For many, the burgher community of the west was still the chief reference group. Nor can it be simply assumed that it was on the 'frontier' that racial antagonism was at its sharpest: recent research suggests that in the eighteenth century, racial antagonisms were sharper in the slave-owning south-western Cape than in the interior.[1]

1 J. A. Heese, *Die herkoms van die Afrikaner* (Cape Town, 1971), 19–20. I am grateful to Dr Robert Ross for this reference.

Nevertheless, for the majority of the Khoisan peoples of the interior, the expansion of the trekboer ultimately spelt the destruction of their social system and their independent existence, although the process took longer and was more complex than is generally realized. Nor should the disintegration of Khoi society be attributed solely to white intervention: the socio-economic institutions of the Khoisan were fragile, and even before the advent of whites, warfare, drought and weak leadership could lead to the decline of particular communities.[1] The presence of armed whites, however, who were able to take advantage of the weaknesses and cleavages within Khoisan society became increasingly important as the Dutch settlement established itself, and prevented the normal cyclical recovery of pastoral groups. Thus, already by the end of the seventeenth century, the groups in the western Cape had become impoverished. Although increasingly dire penalties were proclaimed against anyone indulging in the illegal cattle trade with the Khoi, this injunction was being disregarded even during the first Khoi war. After 1680, as the colony expanded, Company servants began to grow tobacco on their outstations for cattle trading on their own behalf, and burghers built up their stock in similar fashion. By 1699 the Chainouqua and Hessequa, amongst the wealthiest of the Khoi groups fifteen years earlier, had lost their cattle, and though the Hessequa apparently recouped their losses for a while in the early eighteenth century, they did this in part by working for the colonists for payment in cattle.

Some Khoi found an escape route northwards or eastwards. Thus fragments of the Goringhaiqua, Gorachouqua and, possibly, the Cochoqua fled to the Orange river, where they formed the Korana people or mingled with the Tlhaping. In the second half of the eighteenth century, they were joined by other mixed groups, like that of the half-caste Adam Kok, who fled to the Khamiesberg and built up a following of Grigriqua and other groups before moving on to the Orange river. Those who fled eastward mingled with still independent Khoi groups or the mixed Xhosa-Khoi on the frontiers of Xhosa settlement. On the peripheries of the Bantu-speaking world, they constituted a kind of Voor-Voortrekker class, bringing the first intimations of the destructive implications of the white man's presence and an increased policial awareness.

The majority, however, were converted into the menials of the white man, depressed socially, economically and politically. Though in the

[1] Elphick, 'Cape Khoi', 52–85.

more settled areas, they remained the transport riders, guides, messengers and, on occasion, trusted emissaries, and some in the interior were even able to retain considerable independence as skilled ivory hunters, their position on the farms in the remoter districts may well have been considerably worse than that of the slaves at the Cape. Although even here, in the course of the eighteenth century, punishment became harsher and emancipation more rare, at the very least a slave was regarded as valuable property; at best, he could earn money through plying his trade, and so buy his freedom. In the near subsistence economy of the interior, Khoi servants earned little more than their keep, plus the occasional head of cattle or sheep and some cast-off clothing. Though legally entitled to redress, the primitive administrative and judicial machinery left servants at the mercy of their masters, and there is little doubt that the relationship was not infrequently violent. Many could and did desert: Jager Afrikaner, who murdered his master after years of ill treatment, and formed his own raiding chiefdom along the Orange river, is a case in point. Some indulged in millenarian fantasies; in Swellendam, for instance, in 1788, about 200 servants burnt their Dutch clothes, and killed their white animals, prophesying the end of the world and threatening to kill all whites, after which they would inherit their goods;[1] while at the century's end, Khoi servants deserted en masse and joined the Xhosa in open warfare against the whites, their absence cansing almost as much consternation as their arms. The alternative for many, however, was listlessness and despair, at least before the permanent work of the missionaries which began in the 1790s brought some kind of refuge and hope.

Before this happened, however, there was yet another form of resistance. From the first decade of the eighteenth century, farmers in the northern part of Stellenbosch began complaining of the robbery of their cattle, and there is little doubt that these were raids by Nama and Grigriqua peoples,[2] accompanied by their San client-soldiers, in retaliation for earlier plundering by the white man. The raiders, who are generally described as 'Bosjesmans-Hottentotten', have been identified by most previous writers with the San or 'Bushmen'; there is strong evidence, however, to suggest that while the San were undoubtedly involved in the raids, both on this occasion and throughout the eighteenth century – and even Gonnema had his San spies and mercenaries – these

[1] C471 *Ink. Brieven*, Cape archives, 1121–1256. Reports of *landdrost* of Swellendam and evidence of witnesses, October 1788.

[2] They are, in fact, named in some of the relevant documents.

so-called 'Bosjesmans-Hottentotten' were Khoi who had lost their cattle and had reverted to a 'Bushman' way of life. There was after all little to distinguish the two groups, once the Khoi had lost their cattle and grazing lands. The process whereby a herder-Khoi became a 'Bushman' was well delineated by the *landdrost* of Stellenbosch when commenting on the results of the temporary lifting of the ban on the cattle trade between 1699 and 1707; not only had this led to retaliatory raids of revenge, but it had turned kraal against kraal, 'so that from a contented people peacefully supporting themselves with their cattle, they have mostly all been changed into *bushmen*, hunters and robbers, scattering everywhere and among the mountains'.[1]

The pattern of violence and counter-violence, raid and counter-raid, punctuated every decade in the eighteenth century. In 1715 'Bosjesmans-Hottentotten', or Khoisan, raids led to the first settler commando being called out, without a complement of company soldiers from the Cape, a precedent which established itself thereafter as the norm. Under their own elected officers, and subject only to the overall direction of the *landdrost*, the burghers were left to their own defence. In 1739, when the burghers in the Piquetberg, the Bokkeveld and the Lange valley were robbed by Khoisan in search not only of cattle but also guns and horses, burgher service became compulsory for anyone with interests in the outlying districts, though many who were not in the direct line of Khoisan raiding sought to evade their responsibilities or sent Khoi servants as their substitutes.

The power of the Khoi to resist white expansion was gravely undermined by the outbreak of smallpox in 1713, the most disastrous of the epidemics to strike at this relatively non-immune group. This was followed, as was the 1755 outbreak, by cattle disease, which further added to their impoverishment. It may be partly for this reason that it was only in the 1770s, when the trekboers were up against the last refuge of the Khoisan in the mountains, that Khoisan resistance reached anything like formidable proportions. Nevertheless, even in the earlier period, it is clear that the Khoisan, regarded by the colonists as a 'predatory people with whom no communication can be held', and who should therefore be extirpated,[2] saw their raiding as attempts to drive the white man back from their lands and cattle.

The snowball effect of cattle marauding was felt beyond the confines

[1] Leibbrandt, *Précis . . . the defence of Willem Adriaan van der Stel* (Cape Town, 1898), Ann. N2, 161. Report of *landdrost*, W. A. Starrenburg. October 1705. Author's italics.

[2] C459 *Ink. Brieven*, Cape archives, 81–3. Report of *landdrost* of Stellenbosch on Daniel Koekemoer's Commando, 13 March 1764.

of the colony, as groups of Khoi sought to retain their stock by raiding their weaker fellows. Thus in 1752 Beutler found the Khoi on the Gamtoos poor and starving, having been robbed by 'Bushmen', while the Attaqua had moved from Attaqua's Kloof, to the sources of the Gouritz and Olifants rivers, or had taken service with the farmers, in order to escape. Between the Lange and Cromme rivers, the Khoi had become so impoverished through wars with the 'Bushmen', between themselves and with the Xhosa, that 'now they lived like the Bushmen on theft, hunting and veldkos [food of the field]'[1] – added confirmation, if any is needed, of the way in which herders were turned into hunter-gatherers.

The level of Khoisan attacks on the colonists reached a new pitch in the 1770s, when the entire northern frontier erupted in violence, with escaped slaves, white deserters and Khoi servants joining the Khoisan ranks. It would be tedious to relate the details of their incursions, though the records of Stellenbosch, Swellendam, and, after 1786, Graaff Reinet, consist very largely of the numbers of sheep and cattle stolen and herders murdered, together with the reports of the bloodthirsty reprisals by the burghers. Unfortunately the records give very little indication of the nature of Khoisan organization, leadership or objectives; the bands, however, were sometimes several hundred strong – in 1790 one band was reported of 1,000 – while hundreds of head of cattle and thousands of head of sheep were stolen annually. Though the commandos were out constantly during the last thirty years of the century, they were unable to subdue the raiders, though thousands of Khoisan were reported to have been killed. By 1785, the Khoisan had taken over the land behind the Hex river to the Swarteberg, from the Roggeveld, Koup, Sneeuwbergen and Camdebo, and the commandant of the north, appointed specifically to deal with the threat, prophesied that before long they would penetrate to the wine and wheat farms of the land of Waveren. Those farmers who were not ruined by the robberies were being exhausted by constant military service. Though farmers began to wear the Khoisan down by pure bloodletting, further colonial expansion northwards was prevented for some thirty years.

THE XHOSA FRONTIER

This was the more serious for the trekboers in that it coincided, as we have seen, with their coming up against the far more numerous and

[1] Haupt in Godée-Molsbergen, *Reizen*, III, 279–80, 291–3.

better organized Xhosa chiefdoms. Their expansion was thus blocked on both fronts, while they were facing two enemies simultaneously. In the eighteenth century, contrary to popular belief, the Khoisan were the more formidable foe. By comparison with the robberies committed on the northern frontier, the cattle thefts complained about by farmers through Xhosa depredations were paltry. Nevertheless the wars which broke out between the colonists and the Xhosa in 1779–81 and 1793 were the prelude to a struggle that was to last well nigh a hundred years, and ultimately the trekboers were only able to expand again, in the nineteenth century, by outflanking the Xhosa.

The underlying causes of the first two frontier clashes were rooted in the nature of the societies which had evolved on both sides by the last quarter of the eighteenth century, though the precipitating causes and the personalities involved differed in each individual struggle. During the 1770s, trekboers drifted across the official frontiers, which had been moved from the Great Brak river, fixed in 1743, to the Gamtoos in 1770, and came increasingly into contact with the Xhosa chiefdoms settled between the Great Fish and Bushman rivers. By and large, they were left to handle the situation as they saw fit, though in 1775 the frontier of the colony was moved yet again to the Bushman river in the south-east and the Upper Fish to its north. In 1778, the governor himself, van Plettenberg, made his way eastwards to try and separate trekboers and tribesmen. He met a number of the breakaway Xhosa chiefs in an attempt to persuade them to leave the area, and believed he had done so, though they almost certainly did not understand the significance of his decree establishing the new frontier and had little power to make any binding agreement to move if they did. Frontiersmen on the white side were no more disposed to take the new frontiers any more seriously than they had the old. Within less than a year, tension between the two had led to open warfare.

After two unauthorized commandos across the Fish river had killed several Xhosa and captured thousands of head of cattle, the government appointed Adriaan van Jaarsveld commandant of the East, to try yet again to get the Xhosa to leave the Zuurveld, whether by force or persuasion. By this time, the Council of Policy at the Cape had decreed that the frontier should lie along the indeterminate course of the Fish river to the south as well as to the north. Van Jaarsveld conducted an unscrupulous but only semi-successful campaign against the Xhosa in 1781, which was followed by an uneasy peace. Neither he, nor any of the subsequent Boer commandos were able to dislodge the Xhosa from the Zuurveld, until they were joined by professional British soldiers in the nineteenth century.

Though van Jaarsveld's orders were to prevent the intercourse of black and white along the frontier, his task, like that of his successors, was made impossible by the increasing number of Boers who came to settle in the frontier zone amongst the Xhosa and Gqunukwebe. In response to his appeals, in 1785 the new district of Graaff Reinet was delimited – though with new and unrealistic boundaries along the Great Fish river to the south-east, and the Tarka and Baviaans river to the north-east. In the absence of adequate military support, neither the first *landdrost*, M. H. O. Woeke, nor his successor, the humane and much-maligned H. C. Maynier, were able to control the movements of the frontiersmen, who had already openly defied van Jaarsveld's authority.

As in 1779, the provocations of frontier farmers, irregularities in the cattle trade, and the retaliation taken by the Xhosa lay behind the outbreak of war in 1793. The friction was increased by severe and prolonged drought on the frontier, and the fresh movement of trekkers across the Fish river in search of grazing. A complicating factor was introduced by the number of Xhosa who had taken service with the Boers as a result of the cattle trade, drought, and warfare between the Gqunukwebe and Ndlambe's followers in 1790. On this occasion, neither the unauthorized burgher commando under Barend Lindeque, nor the joint commando organized by Maynier and the *landdrost* of Swellendam, was able to achieve much success, though the former was afforded some assistance by Ndlambe, apparently in pursuit of his own political objectives. By this time, some of the Boers' Xhosa opponents possessed firearms, and had been joined by a number of runaway slaves and Khoi servants, some of whom were also armed with guns. Dissensions amongst the Boers weakened their campaign, however, and ultimately Maynier was forced to make peace with the Xhosa and acknowledge the impossibility yet again of driving them from the Zuurveld with the inadequate and ill-disciplined commandos, which were collected with difficulty, and tended to disband as soon as sufficient cattle had been looted.

Dissensions among the Boers were taken a stage farther in 1795, when Maynier's refusal to allow commandos to sally forth yet again against the Xhosa, and his attempts to regulate master-servant relationships and to bring law and order to the unruly and turbulent frontier, led to open rebellion. The insurgents stormed the *drosdty*, forced Maynier out and declared Graaff Reinet an independent republic; though its independence was shortlived, the populism and millenarianism, which were in some measure derived from revolutionary movements in Europe, as well as the attitudes to authority moulded on the frontier and which the Republic of Graaff Reinet embodied, were to be carried forward into the nineteenth century.

Confronted with the violence on the frontier, historians of South Africa have tended to attribute contemporary racial attitudes to a 'frontier tradition'. Paradoxically, however, the frontier zone, an area of overlapping jurisdiction and ineffective government, was also an area where black and white men, often on the fringes of their own society, met and mixed on the most intimate terms.[1] A Coenraad de Buys, responsible for the abduction, perhaps even murder, of African women, and who certainly raided and robbed African homes, was not only a leading rebel against Cape governmental authority: he was one of Ngqika's closest advisers and legally married an African wife. The community of sons and clients he established can best be compared to those of the Africanized *prazo*-holders of the Zambezi valley. A social bandit, his way of life nevertheless points to an alternative and not insignificant tradition at the Cape in the eighteenth century.

From the vantage point of the late eighteenth century, the societies of the Africans and the trekboer were still more or less evenly matched, and in somc ways were more remarkable for their similarities than their differences. Despite their origin from and links with the more cosmopolitan and technologically more advanced Afrikaners of the west, the frontiersmen lived like the Africans in a small-scale, closely knit society prone to fragment along lines of kin. Both economies were based on pastoralism and subsistence agriculture, and wealth and prestige depended very largely on the size of a man's flocks and herds. Both were becoming increasingly, if differentially, linked to the metropolitan market. Both Bantu-speaker and Afrikaner had subordinated the earlier Khoisan peoples in a variety of clientship roles, had intermingled with them to produce new, mixed groups, culturally almost indistinguishable from the dominant stem, or were waging a bitter and relentless struggle against dispossessed, but still independent Khoisan fragments. Though the trekboer had the wheel, the gun and a fragile literacy, Africans had the advantage of numbers, probably a more complex social organiza-

[1] M. Legassick, 'The frontier tradition in South African history' in *Collected seminar papers on the societies of southern Africa in the nineteenth and twentieth centuries*, **2**, 12 (Institute of Commonwealth Studies, London, 1970–1), 1–33, critically re-examines this issue.

tion, and in some respects a more highly developed system of law and order. The Tswana chiefdoms and some of the Nguni polities were larger scale and better organized than the society of the cattle farmers of Graaff Reinet, who even to the Xhosa must have appeared little more of a threat than their traditional African neighbours.

The stratified, plural society of the western Cape, with its townsmen and Company officials, its wine and wheat farmers and their slaves and labourers, was, of course, more complex. Though with the decline of the Dutch East India Company and its enormous indebtedness in the last years of the century, administration was inefficient and finances were chaotic, white settlers in the western Cape still formed part of a more sophisticated and articulate community, recognizably European in its origins, though greatly influenced by the East. Ultimately it was the Cape's links with both Europe and the East which were to tilt the balance in favour of the white man, an event presaged by the coming of the British in 1795.

By the time the British took over the Cape from the Dutch East India Company in 1795, some of the diverse strands of South African history were beginning to be drawn together and many of its future developments were being hinted at. On the south-east coast, whites were now confronting the great block of Bantu-speaking peoples, and the century-long struggle over land, cattle and water had begun. While to the north their advance was still being resisted by the Khoisan, a trickle of white hunters and traders was making its way to the Orange river, in the wake of the Korana and Griqua, and individuals were bringing back reports – though still largely hearsay – of the populous Tswana chiefdoms in the interior. At Delagoa Bay, trade routes were extending west onto the high veld and southwards to Natal, where the first rumblings of what were to be the most dramatic changes of all were beginning to be heard.

MADAGASCAR

Across the Mozambique channel, the western shore of Madagascar still bore at the beginning of the seventeenth century unmistakable signs of African settlement and influence. The island had long participated in the commerce of the Indian Ocean, and Arab traders continued to visit the north-western coast, where they had established flourishing settlements on small islands in Mahajamba and Boina Bays. In 1613 Luigi Mariano, the Italian Jesuit who made four visits to Madagascar and who also worked on the Zambezi and among the Maravi, described

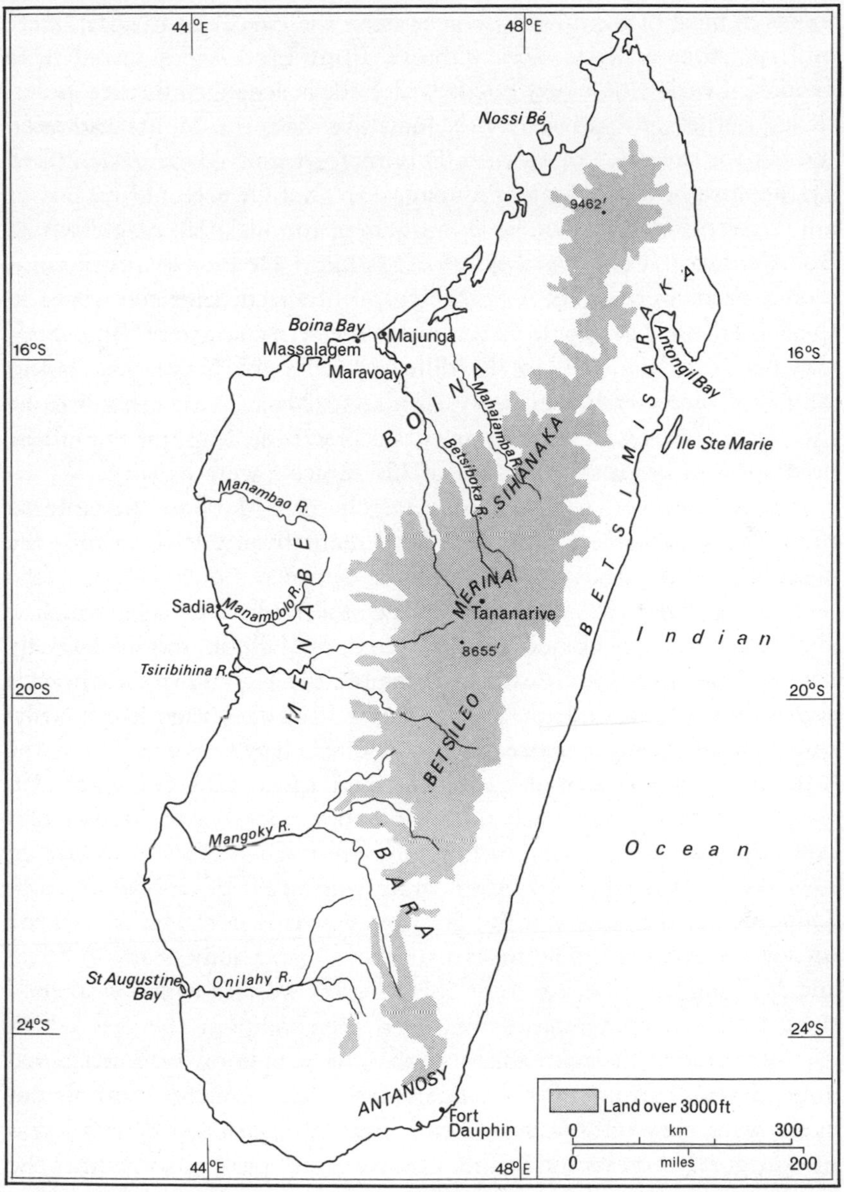

15 Madagascar

Massalagem in Boina Bay as a Moorish town of six to seven thousand inhabitants, the centre of a vigorous cloth industry with three to four looms in most of the houses, which, as on the East African coast, were built in stone with terraces. Dhows from East Africa and Arabia brought a variety of luxury goods which they exchanged for rice, poles, slaves, cattle and beeswax. At Mahajamba Bay, the Moors had been trading for several decades with Tingimaro, whom Mariano described as 'the most powerful king of Madagascar', but the extent of his power and influence should not be exaggerated, for his near neighbour at Boina showed 'great hostility' towards him.[1] Despite an active commerce, there were as yet no powerful, centralized, extensive states in this hinterland. The people on this north-western coast were 'Bouques'; they spoke a language 'totally different from the Kaffir [i.e. Bantu] language' but which was 'very similar to Malay'.[2] In other words, they spoke Malagasy. Tingimaro was a practising Muslim, though he used 'poison ordeals' and some of his subjects were pagan.

It was, however, south of Massalagem that Mariano encountered the most remarkable evidence of settlement from Africa. Along the coast known to Mariano as Bambala, between Boina Bay and the Tsiribihina river, the inhabitants spoke 'the Kaffir language, which is almost that of Mozambique and of the coast of Malindi', they had woolly hair and in 'colour and features resemble the Kaffirs, from whom it seems they are descended'.[3] Each coastal town or village had its own ruler, and the people practised fishing and mixed agriculture. There was little or no direct external trade, but the small communities kept 'in constant contact' with each other and they traded with Massalagem both by sea and overland. In 1614 a shortage of food supplies in Massalagem was remedied by the arrival of a fleet of ten canoes from Sadia, one of the largest of the Bambala towns, where Mariano stayed on several occasions. The town had about 1,000 homesteads in 1613, and Mariano described not only the constant warfare which weakened these Bambala communities, but also their religious beliefs, which forcibly recalled their African origins. The people of Sadia attributed good or evil fortune to the influence of their ancestors, and almost every week they offered 'sacrifices' of cattle or rice to obtain success in war, good harvests and health. An important person, sometimes the king or a member of the royal family, known as a *maganga* (cf. Bantu

[1] Letter of L. Mariano, 24 August 1619, in A. and G. Grandidier, eds., *Collection des ouvrages anciens concernant Madagascar* (Paris, 1903–20), II, 317–18.

[2] L. Mariano, 'Relation, 1613–14', in Grandidier, *Collection*, II, 21–2.

[3] Ibid.

nganga), interpreted dreams and used other means of divination for the purposes of government. In particular, Mariano noted two aspects of the Bambala ancestral cults which were soon to assume considerable political significance: he described how a person could become possessed by an ancestral spirit, and he reported that the nobility preserved the hairs and nails of their dead, either wearing these ancestral relics or depositing them in wooden statues.[1] Here then, along 300 miles of coastland, the linguistic and cultural testimony to an earlier, profound and massive impact from Africa was still obvious.

South of the Bambala coast the people again spoke Malagasy, but instead of mixed agriculture, pastoral activities were dominant, and visitors to the coast caught scattered references to developments in the interior of great political significance which were about to change the whole of western Madagascar. By the end of the sixteenth century, several related ruling dynasties had established themselves among the pastoral peoples of south-western Madagascar. Certain elements in their traditions suggest that in part they may have derived from a group of royal adventurers or exiles from the Zimbabwe area. Having crossed the Mozambique Channel to Madagascar, they established, through alliance and inter-marriage with local lineages, close links with Malagasy who had probably been already exposed to earlier influences and settlement from Africa. From these contacts the indigenous Maroserana dynasties eventually developed.

Rabaratavokoka, who founded the early Bara state probably during the first half of the sixteenth century, is also remembered in the traditions of other Maroserana dynasties as a founding ancestor. Three generations later, early in the seventeenth century, the ruler of the Bara state dominated southern Madagascar. Known as the 'master of a hundred thousand [cattle] parks', his reign was remembered as one of peace and prosperity, but on his death his sons quarrelled, enabling a rival, a related Maroserana ruler, Andriamanely, to intervene.[2] This newcomer destroyed the early Bara state, captured its cattle riches, and before his death in 1653 had established his family as rulers over many of the conquered peoples. While these developments were taking place in the southern interior, however, to the west a new and far stronger power was emerging.

During the second half of the seventeenth century, the political

[1] Letters of L. Mariano, 22 October 1616 and 24 May 1617, in Grandidier, *Collection*, II, 228–33.

[2] E. de Flacourt, *Histoire de la grande île de Madagascar*, 2nd ed. (Paris 1661) in Grandidier, *Collection*, VIII, 44.

structure of western Madagascar was completely transformed. The petty kingdoms and confined horizons were replaced by two powerful Sakalava states, Menabe and Boina, which were to dominate the vast area north of the Onilahy river until well into the nineteenth century. Once again it was a Maroserana dynasty which initiated and controlled this development, and this phenomenal political achievement rested on a complex interaction of indigenous and external factors.

The rise of this new power can be traced in contemporary documents. Étienne de Flacourt, who from 1648 to 1658 governed a small French force established from 1642 at Fort Dauphin on the south-eastern coast, made no direct mention in his writings of Andriandahifotsy, the Maroserana ruler who during these very years was creating the future state of Menabe. Yet his kingdom was shown on Flacourt's map, extending northwards through the western pastoral plains, and in the following decade European observers became increasingly aware of the growth of his power and influence. In 1663 his warriors were attacking St Augustine Bay, soon afterwards defeating and killing the three principal chiefs there. By 1666 Andriandahifotsy's army was in action as far north as Sadia, and in 1671, in response to an earlier embassy sent by him to Fort Dauphin, a Frenchman, Desbrosses, visited his kingdom, bringing back an account of his lavish hospitality, his 120,000 head of cattle, and his well-disciplined fighting force of more than 12,000 warriors.[1] The impression is of an inland state whose power was based at least originally not on any external contact, but on the capture and exploitation of pastoral riches, in the same tradition of other Maroserana rulers, such as Andriamanely and the founders of the Bara state. On Andriandahifotsy's death, which probably occurred in the 1680s, his kingdom of Menabe passed to his son Tsimanongarivo. Another younger son, Tsimanatona, assisted by royal ritual experts and a force of Sakalava warriors, continued his father's career of conquest northwards, overrunning the north-western shore and founding the extensive Sakalava kingdom of Boina before the end of the century.

As in the case of the Rozvi *mambos*, traditions attribute Andriandahifotsy's military success primarily to ruse and magic: a hostile chief and his men were assassinated at a feast, the roars of a hidden bull terrified his opponents, and the conqueror was assisted by ritual specialists. Traditions also assign a significant role to firearms. Tradi-

[1] These figures from Desbrosses's account are found in Du Bois, *Les voyages faits par le Sieur D.B. aux Illes Dauphine ou Madagascar, et Bourbon, ou Mascarene, és années 1669–1672* (Paris, 1674), 107. Cf. R. K. Kent, *Early kingdoms in Madagascar 1500–1700* (New York, 1970), 200, where 'six vingts milles' has been rendered as 26,000.

tions collected in the 1920s recounted how a wife of Andriandahifotsy dispatched firearms to him at a crucial battle, and two centuries earlier Robert Drury, a shipwrecked Englishman, was given similar information. He was told by a grandson of Andriandahifotsy that before the Sakalava obtained firearms they 'were insulted by all (their) neighbours' but were then made 'too strong for them'.[1]

By the eighteenth century, firearms were undoubtedly a significant element in the strength of both Menabe and Boina. In 1719 the king of Menabe was seen with 4,000 to 5,000 men armed with muskets, and the crew of the Dutch ship *Barneveld* were astonished at the skill with which they were handled. Three years later Bucquoy, another Dutchman, noted that the men of Boina were able marksmen; by mid-century the king of Boina had constructed a fort armed with thirty to forty large cannon, and right down the west coast European traders found that large quantities of firearms and ammunition were the normal means of purchasing slaves, who were shipped in fairly large numbers as far as Brazil, the Caribbean, and North America. By the eighteenth century, then, regular imports of firearms and ammunition were readily available on a scale which, in this period, was paralleled in Africa only on the Atlantic coast. The rulers of Menabe and Boina maintained a strict control over the imports of firearms. In Menabe, Drury was told by visiting Hova from the interior that they had been prevented from acquiring firearms and hence had been defeated by the western kingdoms. It is also possible that Andriandahifotsy's attacks on St Augustine Bay and his desire to maintain amicable relations with the French, whose marksmen had successfully raided several Malagasy rulers including his neighbour, Rahesaf, from whom the French had captured 40,000 cattle in 1668, are evidence of his concern over these new weapons. It has even been suggested that it was principally firearms which facilitated the creation of these large-scale kingdoms, but this seems most unlikely.[2] Certainly the intensification of international trade through the Mozambique Channel had transformed the commercial geography of Madagascar. Whereas in the pre-Portuguese period, external trading contacts had been focussed on the north and north-eastern tip of the island lying nearest to the main Indian Ocean trade, during the seventeenth century increasing numbers of Dutch, French and English ships passing through the Mozambique Channel robbed

[1] R. Drury, *Madagascar or Robert Drury's journal during fifteen years captivity on that island*, 7th ed. (London, 1890), 282–5. Kent, *Early kingdoms*, 200–1, for references to the traditions.

[2] H. Deschamps, *Histoire de Madagascar*, 2nd ed. (Paris, 1961), 91.

the northern ports of their earlier advantage. When linked with the introduction of large numbers of strategic trade-goods, it would have been surprising if this commercial reorientation had not provoked far-reaching changes in the southern and western areas of the island. But the ability of the Sakalava rulers to exploit and control these opportunities depended, as with the Rozvi *mambos*, on their dynastic and indigenous sources of strength.

The mobilization of warriors and the accumulation of pastoral wealth were the two aspects of Andriandahifotsy's rule which most forcibly impressed Desbrosses, who does not mention firearms. Andriandahifotsy's successors continued to depend on the incorporation of peoples and the centralized redistribution of vast herds of cattle, which flourished on the mild western plains where the river valleys provided adequate dry season pasturage, and where, unlike the central highlands, there was no night frost to bring disease. If the sudden onset of an overwhelming military power was of decisive significance in establishing Sakalava predominance over this vast area, it seems that royal cattle riches were subsequently the main bond uniting an extensive clientage. Drury was taken to see the area where Tsimanongarivo's cattle were kept; he reported that there were 'so many thousands of them it is not known to two or three thousand how many he has'; the king's principal herdsman, a very old man who had also held this post under Andriandahifotsy, lived in princely style with 8,000 head of cattle of his own and 300 slaves. Drury also observed how Tsimanongarivo had used this wealth to reward his own subjects and 'to entice people to come from other countries' to live under his rule.[1] By the early eighteenth century the wide range of varied peoples who had been brought under the sway of this Maroserana dynasty were known as the Sakalava, the name also of a small tributary of the Mangoky river in the south of Menabe, where according to one tradition the father of Andriandahifotsy had established his capital. Little is known concerning this process of absorption into the Sakalava kingdoms. In the course of it, the Bambala place names and language disappeared, save among a few isolated groups such as some of the Vazimba fishermen on the River Tsiribihina, whom Drury noted as speaking a distinct language.

Economically the political transformation of western Madagascar probably brought few benefits. The earlier mixed agriculture seems to have declined with the new emphasis on pastoral activities, and the vigorous coastal interchange of commodities noted by Mariano was

[1] Drury, *Madagascar*, 271–4.

increasingly overshadowed by the slave trade. But some of the older culture survived in the new way of life. As Andriandahifotsy and his successors advanced northwards, they rapidly assimilated for their dynastic purposes some of the fundamental institutions of the conquered peoples, which may indeed have reawakened echoes for the Maroserana of their African progenitors. The Bambala practice of possession by an ancestral spirit and the veneration accorded to ancestral relics, observed by Mariano at Sadia, were soon developed into the *tromba* (spirit-possession) and the *dady* (relics) to become the principal religious supports of the Sakalava monarchies. As early as 1741 Hemmy, a Dutch slave trader from the Cape of Good Hope, was shown the royal relics or *dady* by the king of Boina. Hemmy described them as consisting of four gold and silver shields, each one representing a royal ancestor going back to the father of Andriandahifotsy. Hung on poles, with bowls of incense placed below them, they were covered, like the *mwene mutapa*'s drum, with a square of indigenous cloth, and were kept secluded by themselves in a separate enclosure.

The same Dutch visitor was forcibly impressed by the material prosperity of the ruler of this northern Sakalava kingdom. The capital at Marovoay consisted of 'thousands of houses and contain[ed] an enormous crowd of inhabitants'. Inside the royal palace, which was 'larger than the castle of the Governor of the Cape', were several store houses where 'hundreds of chests and cupboards were piled up full of all sorts of wares'. There were also fortified houses containing firearms, jewellery, silver ornaments, precious vases and a carved lacquered throne, which French traders had brought specially for the king from China.[1] Even though the spoils of external trade were not the foundations of Sakalava power, evidently they provided a powerful reinforcement for royal prestige. It is not clear whether this wealth was mainly hoarded at the capital, or exchanged for slaves in an extensive redistributive system. With their capitals close to the coast and with governors called *mason-drano* (eyes-of-water) placed in the ports, the kings kept a strict surveillance over all foreign shipping. An official of the short-lived Dutch settlement at Delagoa Bay, who was captured there in 1721 by some of the European pirates frequenting Madagascar and the Indian Ocean in the eighteenth century, has left a vivid account of how the king of Boina was informed of a ship's arrival by means of smoke-signals. Without royal permission, he reports, 'no one could set foot even on the beach and no Malagasy had the right to approach the

[1] Report by O. L. Hemmy in Grandidier, *Collection*, VI, 114–17.

strangers nor to sell them anything'.[1] Even if this account is somewhat exaggerated, the royal control was sufficient throughout the eighteenth century to prevent any Europeans from obtaining a foothold on the western coast and to contain the potentially disruptive forces generated by trading rivalries. Nor was this control effective merely along the coast: in 1774, when the first European attempted to open an overland route to the west from the east coast, he found himself frustrated as soon as he reached the farthest Sakalava outposts deep in the interior, for no stranger could proceed without messengers first being sent to inform the king and obtain his permission to enter the kingdom. Indeed Sakalava power was not limited to the island. As early as 1719 the crew of the *Barneveld* reported that the Sakalava were expert navigators, and were raiding neighbouring countries with outrigger canoes capable of carrying up to fifty men. By the end of the century, these raids were carrying the Sakalava, together with the Betsimisaraka of the east coast, far beyond the Comoro islands to the mainland of northern Mozambique and Mafia island, where combined fleets of as many as 500 canoes ransacked the coastal ports and carried away African slaves.

Of the administrative and political organization which lay behind this power and efficiency, the contemporary European records reveal but little. Like the Rozvi, the Sakalava rulers maintained no permanent, standing army, but they could quickly mobilize large forces. In 1741 the king of Boina readily marshalled a force, estimated at 15,000 men, to raid and punish the Sihanaka peoples in the interior. Andriandahifotsy appointed his sons and close relatives as governors and tribute collectors in the provinces, and his successors seem to have followed this practice, but it is not clear how, and to what extent, centrifugal forces were neutralized. There is confusion even over the rules of succession, one source asserting that the king nominated one of his sons as successor, while another states that succession was by election involving 'all the country's elders'. Relatively little is known of the political significance of the *dady* and *tromba* symbols and cult. Until far more research has been carried out on Sakalava traditions – both those already collected and those still to be recorded – our understanding of the organization and achievements of these remarkable kingdoms will remain seriously incomplete.

Not much is known concerning the causes of the decline of Sakalava power, the first signs of which began to appear in the last quarter of

[1] Bucquoy in Grandidier, *Collection*, v, 104–5.

the eighteenth century. In the kingdom of Boina, the succession passed to a line of queens from about 1780, and this seems to have coincided with increased alien influence centred on the Arab and Indian Muslim traders at the recently founded port of Majunga. One of the sons of Queen Ravahiny, who reigned at the end of the eighteenth century, converted to Islam, and the growing Muslim influence may have weakened the traditional religious supports of Sakalava kingship.

Dissensions within Boina were matched by the growing power of its rivals. On the east coast, strong trading links developed during the eighteenth century with the French settlements on the Mascarene islands, which, in return for provisions and slaves, provided a source of firearms beyond the reach of the Sakalava monopoly. The first ruler to exploit this opportunity was Ratsimilaho, son of an English pirate and a Malagasy princess, who briefly united the coastal peoples in the Betsimisaraka kingdom, which extended over 300 kilometres of coastline from the Ivondro to the north of Antongil. Marrying a daughter of the king of Boina, he successfully resisted Sakalava raids, and, although his kingdom disintegrated on his death in 1750, the Betsimisaraka continued into the nineteenth century to share with the Sakalava, and even to lead, the maritime raids to the Comoros and the African coast.

It was however in the interior, on the plateau behind the southern Betsimisaraka coast, that the most serious rival to Sakalava power was gathering its resources. As with the rise of the Sakalava, this development resulted from the gradual accumulation of internal indigenous strength, with ultimately an accession of an additional source of power through external trade. Here, in the neighbourhood of what was to become Tananarive, the Vazimba, who were the earliest remembered inhabitants of this part of the plateau, had probably for several centuries been intermixing with and confronted by the Hova. Some of the Hova may have moved into the area from the south, bringing with them cultural influences some of which emanated from the Antanosy in the south-east corner of the island. At some point, probably in the sixteenth century, the Andriana dynasty established itself as arbitrator in the conflicts between Vazimba and Hova. The new dynasty was itself the product of an intermixture between the Vazimba and immigrant ritual experts, who here, as elsewhere in the island, brought to the service of the royal courts the prestige associated with the earlier Anteimoro culture with its religious texts and writings (see volume 3, chapter 4). During the seventeenth and eighteenth centuries, the Hova gradually assimilated or expelled the Vazimba to become, under the Andriana, the commoners or freemen of the new Merina kingdom. Traditions, set down in the *Tantara* a hundred years ago, attribute to Ralambo, a seventeenth-century Andriana king, many of the secular and ritual institutions connected with Merina kingship. It was he who is remembered as having created the castes of the nobility, instituted a head-tax to maintain a bodyguard, and adopted the institution of *fandroana* (the royal bath) as a focal, annual ceremony for the nation. Ralambo is therefore said to have 'defined Merina',[1] organizing the kingdom and interpreting ancestral wishes, and in the process he assimilated many of the pre-existing features of the Vazimba. As an economic basis, he and his successors encouraged an intensive cultivation of rice by irrigation which made use of the swampy valleys of the interior plateau, and which maintained a numerous and highly industrious population. The first European to visit the area reported in 1777 that the king of Tananarive could send 20,000 warriors into battle. But the size of eighteenth-century Imerina was minute, and it was weakened by internal divisions: when Andrianampoinimerina ascended the throne in *c.* 1787, Imerina was still confined to a tiny radius of thirty kilometres surrounding Tananarive, and it was only in about 1796 that Andrianampoinimerina took possession of this capital, having already begun to exploit the east coast trade by purchasing large numbers of firearms in return for slaves. Under him and his successors, the Merina kingdom was to expand over most of the island and in the process to eclipse completely the Sakalava states. This development of the Merina kingdom still lay in the future, but during the seventeenth and eighteenth centuries the Sakalava dynasties had already demonstrated how indigenous resources and external contacts could be mobilized, controlled and moulded to maintain powerful and extensive kingdoms.

[1] G. S. Chapus and E. Ratsimba trs. and eds., *Histoire des rois* (Tananarive, 1953), I, 284.

CHAPTER 7

EASTERN AFRICA

Variety of experience is perhaps the most striking feature of the history of eastern Africa during the seventeenth and eighteenth centuries. Along the coast this vast region stretches southwards from Mogadishu to the mouth of the Zambezi river. Inland it extends from the southern Ethiopian escarpment and the southern Sudan down along the western edge of the great lakes region, across the corridor between Lakes Tanganyika and Malawi, and then follows the Luangwa river until its confluence with the Zambezi. In the northern interior – including most of modern Kenya, Uganda, Rwanda, and Burundi – both Nilotic-speaking and Bantu-speaking peoples were still isolated from the coast, still able to resolve their problems without having to confront the economic and allied challenges that would emanate from the coast in the nineteenth century. In the central interior – encompassing most of the Tanzanian mainland – it is possible to see a gradual transition by the end of the eighteenth century from the northern pattern of historical development to that of the southern interior – comprising what is today southern Tanzania, northern Mozambique, Malawi, and the easternmost region of Zambia – where the main challenge to the Bantu-speaking peoples was the growth and impact of international trade. On the coast, the various Swahili-speaking communities were already concerned to preserve what they could of their ancient political and economic independence from two successive sets of overlords, the Portuguese and the Omani Arabs. Yet throughout these two centuries it is also possible to discern common processes at work in these four regions of eastern Africa. The principal theme tying together developments through the northern interior – the varying responses of different societies to the problems of the social and political integration of immigrant groups – can also be seen as a persistent theme elsewhere in eastern Africa.

Unevenness of documentation makes it particularly important to grasp these common processes, since the nature of the sources for each region distinctly reinforces, and in some situations largely determines, our perceptions of the regional themes. For the northern and central interior internal sources, including oral tradition and linguistic evidence, provide the only data from which the historian can build his interpretations. With respect to the coast and the southern interior, however, our principal sources are still primarily external and written. This is not to say that internal evidence is always more revealing and less biased than external documentation, in this case mostly Portuguese, but rather that little internal evidence has so far been recorded for these two regions. The gap is slowly being filled, but there remains a severe imbalance in the sources for the history of these regions for this period. What we can legitimately assert, then, must be tempered by the realization that much was taking place that remains unknown to us, and that these themes yet to be recovered might well be of equal or greater significance than the dominant economic interpretation that emerges from the existing source materials.

THE INTERLACUSTRINE STATES

For the areas westward of Lake Victoria, the greatest problems of social integration had been created in the period preceding the seventeenth century. There had been an interval of instability and shifting political allegiances among local populations, which had come under pressure from immigrant groups. North and north-west of the lake, these immigrants had tended to be of Luo background; to the south-west, the dislodged groups often derived from elements of earlier lacustrine societies. By the seventeenth century, a process of consolidation had started. The official dynastic histories portray this development as one of conquest and the establishment of new kingdoms by the immigrants. From the viewpoint of social history, on the other hand, the local populations can be seen as gradually neutralizing the immigrant, disruptive forces by offering them tradition-sanctioned roles of leadership and responsibility as kings and chiefs.

By the seventeenth and eighteenth centuries, if immigration remained a factor, it no longer disrupted the political context. Established state structures became the avenues of assimilation: immigrants attained indigenous status by becoming clients of kings and chiefs. The central role of the king also held some plural societies together; the roles of Hima and non-Hima in Nkore, for example, were integrated by the common subordination to the central authority of the kingdom. Interlacustrine history came thus to centre not on changing local allegiances within a situation of great political and demographic flux; rather, in this socially more settled period, it focussed on the larger polities defining themselves in relation to the smaller states and to each other.

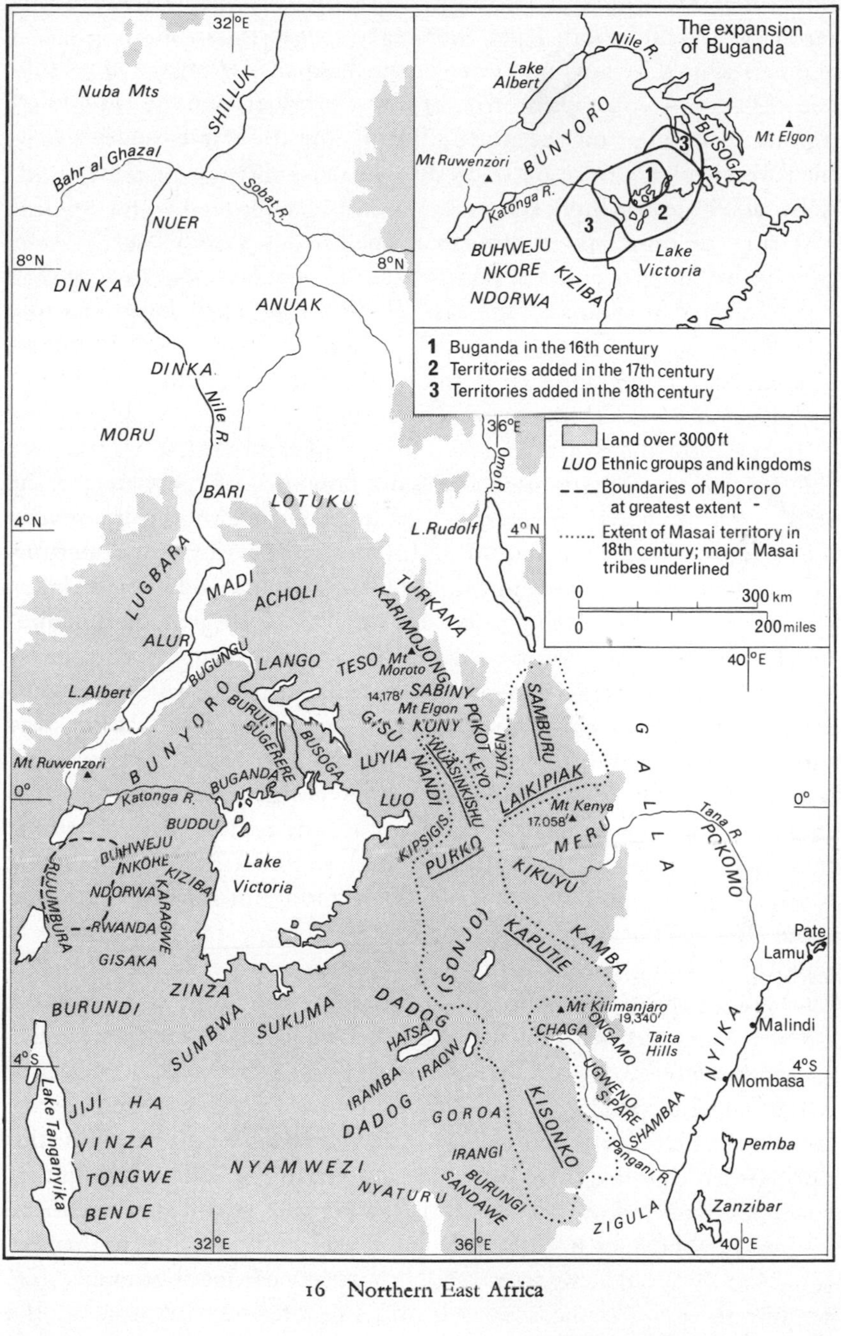

16 Northern East Africa

At the beginning of the seventeenth century, one great kingdom, Bunyoro, predominated through most of the region; its central territory stretched from Lake Albert southward to the Katonga river and was ringed by a whole series of much smaller tributary kingdoms and chiefdoms. Areas thus brought into the wider Bunyoro dominion included Bugungu on the north; Buruli and Bugerere on the east; the several small chiefdoms of Buddu on the south-east; and the kingdoms of Nkore and Buhweju, among others, on the south. Beyond this first ring of tributary lands, other small states stayed usually independent of Nyoro political control though not outside the reach of Nyoro armies: Buganda on the east, along the shore of Lake Victoria, and Rwanda, to the south of Nkore and Buhweju, are examples. One medium-sized kingdom in the south, Karagwe, behind Buddu as its buffer, also remained free of Nyoro rule.

Though not the equivalent of Bunyoro in the north, Karagwe was able to remain as the largest and most powerful of the states to the south-west of Lake Victoria from the early seventeenth century on into the eighteenth. It was far enough south no longer to draw the attentions of Bunyoro, and it was bounded on the east, south, and west by kingdoms smaller than itself, such as Kiziba, Kyamutwara, Buzinza, Gisaka and Rwanda. Among all these states, the seventeenth century appears, from the evidence available, to have been a relatively uneventful period. Conversely, the eighteenth century was an increasingly turbulent era, marked both by greater internal strife and greater interstate conflict and, in the second half of the century, by increasing penetration of the eastern part of the region by the political and economic influence of Buganda. Toward the end of the eighteenth century, Karagwe gained added significance as an important stage on the trade route north to Buganda. But by then Karagwe's pre-eminence, too, was rapidly becoming undermined by the growth of other states – Rwanda on the west and, more important, Buganda to the north.

On its northern margins, on the other hand, Bunyoro had to deal not with centrally organized, smaller kingdoms, but with a multitude of mutually independent clan territories, each presided over by a hereditary clan head. Perhaps because of this lack of suitable central authorities through which to maintain 'indirect rule', the imperial control of Bunyoro was extended only as far as the Paluo, the most southerly of the congeries of peoples bordering Bunyoro on the north. But the region could hardly avoid being influenced in a variety of ways by its powerful neighbour, and the most notable instance of such influence in the seventeenth and eighteenth centuries had both political and ethnic repercussions. Two Paluo groups had supported the losing side in a Bunyoro succession dispute in the later seventeenth century. Forced in the aftermath to emigrate, both were able to establish themselves to the north as ruling clans over several previously independent clan territories in the area of what is today eastern Acholi. As former participants in the interlacustrine world dominated by Bunyoro, they shared in the ideas and paraphernalia of interlacustrine chiefship, such as royal drums and payment of tribute. Their success in establishing states stimulated others to follow their political example, and by the late eighteenth century the numerous tiny units of Acholi, which previously encompassed one or occasionally two clans, had become centrally organized chiefdoms controlling an average of eight to ten clans.[1] At the same time the former linguistic diversity of the region, with Madi-speakers predominating in the west, Luo in the centre, and Karimojong-Teso-speakers more numerous in the east, was giving way to the spread of Luo speech. As the different groups joined into single chiefdoms, Luo speech prevailed, presumably because of its association with the Paluo innovators.

Nyoro had thus an indirect, yet important, influence on its northern neighbours compared with the stronger and more directly imperial impact on its southern and eastern peripheries. During the seventeenth and eighteenth centuries, an emerging challenge to this initial Nyoro pre-eminence developed on a variety of fronts, so that by the last decades of the eighteenth century Bunyoro had become just one, though still the strongest, of several states which divided among themselves the interlacustrine territories.

Even by the beginning of the seventeenth century some rolling back of the farthest extent of the Bunyoro sphere was occurring, particularly in the aftermath of the war of succession which secured Winyi II as the king of Bunyoro. It is from this time that Nyoro traditions recognize the ending of Bunyoro's direct influence on events in Karagwe on the far south and in the Busoga region to the east. The new dispensation is evident in any case, from that point on, in a zone of developing Nyoro conflict with tributary states on the southern edges of its domain, where the Nkore and Rwanda kingdoms were later to obtain pre-eminence. It is apparent also in Bunyoro's continuing inability to reduce the then small, formerly tributary kingdom of Buganda, which

[1] These ideas are drawn largely from an unpublished paper by Ronald Atkinson, entitled 'State formation and development in Western Acholi', presented to the Department of History, Makerere University, 11 August 1971.

nestled between Bunyoro and Lake Victoria. In the long run it might perhaps have been to Bunyoro's advantage to have concentrated on holding a more restricted empire. But its rulers seem unlikely to have considered such a solution, and its history in the seventeenth and eighteenth centuries is characterized by recurrent efforts, with varying degrees of success, to hold its southern tributaries and to diminish Buganda.

That these efforts can be seen in the end to have been insufficient to hold together the old Bunyoro hegemony creates the impression that the period was one of decline for Bunyoro and inclines the historian to look for causes of weakness within the kingdom. To be sure, internal political developments did lessen Bunyoro's ability to deal effectively with the problems of empire. The coincidence of wars of succession in seventeenth- and eighteenth-century Bunyoro with the rebellions of tributary states is too close to avoid the conclusion that succession disputes provided major opportunities to disaffected tributaries to throw off Nyoro overrule. It can also be argued that the king's authority and ability to wage war was too dependent on the concurrence of the hereditary chiefs of the kingdom to allow him to act with the despatch and decisiveness necessary to undercut the attractiveness of rebellion. Yet it might be an equally fruitful approach to consider this history to represent not so much a decline of Bunyoro as the rise of other states, whilst Bunyoro carried on much as it had before. From this point of view, Bunyoro can be seen from the start to have been over-extended in terms of the great breadth of tributary territory it claimed over people whose primary political allegiance was not likely in the long run to devolve on Bunyoro. The growing stabilization of local allegiances created the potential bases for eventual resistance to Nyoro dominion, and the development of active opposition by these small states in the seventeenth and eighteenth centuries simply made manifest Bunyoro's over-extension.

An examination of the events surrounding a serious Nyoro military setback, dating to the second half of the seventeenth century and often considered to mark the downturn of Nyoro fortunes, shows how intertwined all these factors were. A Nyoro army campaigning in Rwanda and the areas west of it met with a sharp check when the Nyoro king, Chwa I, was killed in battle. Returning in some disarray to its base of operations in the very small kingdom of Nkore, the army was routed in a surprise attack led by the Nkore ruler, Ntare IV. What compounded the disaster for Bunyoro, and perhaps in the first place contributed to it, was the coincidence of the defeat with internal strife. Campaigning in the southern tributary areas had already been under way when Chwa had seized power by killing his predecessor in office, Nyarwa. Then, before Chwa had time to resettle the Bunyoro political situation, he himself became a war casualty. His death was followed by an attempted usurpation of the kingship by Masamba, husband of the princess regent, before the rightful succession could be re-established in the person of Winyi III. For perhaps a generation thereafter, Nyoro attentions appear to have been turned inward, and the southern sections of its claimed empire were left free of effective Nyoro presence.

In the vacuum thus created, the first major attempt in the south to build a viable political alternative to Nyoro overrule took shape in the creation of the short-lived kingdom of Mpororo. Under its first king, Kahaya ka Murari, Mpororo had weathered the great Nyoro campaign which resulted in Chwa's death. Then, taking advantage of the ensuing Nyoro retreat, Kahaya and his son, Kahaya Rutindangyezi, after him, rapidly expanded the kingdom through their conquest of a number of small states. At its height under Rutindangyezi in the first half of the eighteenth century, Mpororo stretched from parts of present-day Rwanda northwards to the edges of Bunyoro proper. But its second king, Rutindangyezi, was also its last. The local administration of the kingdom had been apportioned among the royal princes, and with Rutindangyezi's death, the administrative units became independent chiefdoms ruled by his sons. Some of these successor states, in particular Igara, in the north of the former Mpororo domains, and Rujumbura on the west, remained strong independent forces through the rest of the eighteenth century. Others, smaller and weaker, found it increasingly useful to seek the protection of one or the other of their stronger neighbours, Nkore and Rwanda.

Nkore and its north-western neighbour Buhweju, two states not swallowed up by Mpororo, took advantage in their own ways of the Nyoro débâcle to strengthen themselves against possible future assertions of Nyoro suzerainty. The Nkore king, Ntare IV, in order to tie the various clans of the kingdom closer to the kingship, greatly extended the established technique of creating royal offices or tasks which were to be fulfilled only by members of a particular clan. At the same time, he set about establishing a formal, though very simple, regimental organization, together with military training, particularly in archery, for the men liable to be called up in event of war. Ntare seems to have copied these innovations from Buhweju, which successfully used similar techniques under its king Kabundami III, a contemporary of Ntare IV, to fend off Nyoro attacks and claim independence from the former overlord. In the mid-eighteenth century, Buhweju still appeared militarily the stronger of the two states. But the growth of Nkore population through the incorporation of immigrants fleeing from unstable conditions in the former territories of Mpororo, together with the expansion of Nkore regimental organization under Rwebishengye at the end of the century, eventually tipped the balance in favour of Nkore.

The return of Bunyoro to an active role in the south during the first half of the eighteenth century suggests that the bases of Nyoro strength remained largely undissipated. Yet that kingdom now faced a very different kind of opposition. Nyoro traditions claim that both Kyebambe II, whose rule followed that of Winyi III, and his successor Olimi III, waged successful wars against Nkore and other states on their southern borderlands. Their success must have been mixed; the very fact that Olimi repeated the efforts of Kyebambe certifies the resilience of the opposition to Bunyoro. Nkore seems, in any case, to have been largely unaffected, and both it and Buhweju maintained their effective independence. On the other hand, the small states of Buzimba and Kitagwenda, immediate northern neighbours of Buhweju and Nkore, remained Nyoro tributaries throughout the rest of the century. In the reign of Duhaga I, in the last third of the century, Bunyoro could still muster raids against the south, even as far as Rwanda, but hopes of wider empire had dissolved away.

While the collapse of Mpororo had earlier given Nkore an opening for expansion westward, the opportunity was not to be acted on until the nineteenth century. On the most recent evidence, Nkore, largely preoccupied with internal concerns, grew relatively little during the last fifty years of the eighteenth century.[1]

Unlike Nkore, the nearby Rwanda kingdom very soon took advantage of Mpororo's disintegration. In the early seventeenth century, the inception of a new Rwanda dynasty under Ndoori, a usurper of apparent Karagwe antecedents, had set off a period of moderate expansion which continued through the reigns of the next two kings; but Rwanda still remained a relatively small state. Only in the reigns of Rugujira and his son Ndabarasa, coincident with increasing turmoil in the former lands of Mpororo, can the expansionist drive of Rwanda be said to have begun. In a period of five or six decades, the kingdom doubled the area under its direct control and brought a still wider region within

[1] S. R. Karugire, *A history of the kingdom of Nkore* (Oxford, 1972).

its sphere of influence. The beginnings of this process involved the acceptance of Rwanda protection by some chiefdoms as an escape from the chronic raiding and counter-raiding which had developed among the successor chiefdoms of Mpororo and, at the same time, the spread of Tutsi colonists, members of the Rwanda ruling class, into southern parts of that region. While these policies effectively undermined the independence of its north-western neighbours during the second half of the eighteenth century, Rwanda was taking more direct measures on its north-eastern and south-eastern frontiers, where it faced the strong opposition of Ndorwa, located between Rwanda and Nkore, and the Gisaka state. Gisaka itself had attained a brief eminence under Ruregeya in the early eighteenth century, almost equal to that of contemporary Mpororo; but repeated Rwanda invasions in the second half of the century finally broke its power and divested it of a large proportion of its territories.

Rwanda dealt with the resultant problems of integrating different populations by trying to give a rigid definition to all social and political roles. This policy had its origins in the practice of incorporating other states by giving the former independent kings an integral part in the fate of Rwanda: they were converted into *abiiru*, hereditary guardians of the principles, rituals, and emblems of Rwanda royal power. By the end of the eighteenth century, this tactic would seem to have evolved increasingly toward the complex definition of all aspects of social existence, even to the point of creating a rigid class structure, a process which could only have been reinforced by the rapid growth of Rwanda during the later eighteenth century.

The history of Burundi to the south of Rwanc [illegible] understood. Like Rwanda, Burundi grew into [illegible] through the incorporation of small states all ab [illegible] and timing of the growth of Burundi and the vi [illegible] history remain to be deciphered. A theme in the hi [illegible] ing Nkore, Rwanda and Burundi kingdoms which [illegible] investigation is the role of social inequalities in c [illegible] political stress and change. The majority of the po [illegible] (as in Nkore) or Hutu (as in Rwanda and Burundi), came eventually to be looked down upon as mere tillers of the soil, while the minority of pastoral people, known variously as Huma, Hima, or Tutsi, held a prestigious and superior position. This view was not universally accepted then or later: there were kingdoms in the region ruled by non-Hima or non-Tutsi kings even into much later times. But because rulers of the expanding Nkore, Rwanda and Burundi states claimed Hima or Tutsi descent, this social distinction became increasingly important.

Rwanda provides the extreme example of how this idea of inequality between the two population elements could later become enshrined in institutions and ideology. While the distinction in Nkore was primarily one of wealth in cattle, in Rwanda it was elaborated into rigid class difference, with all political power and social worth belonging to Tutsi, and the Hutu becoming little more than serfs. The Rwanda situation also illustrates the depth of the individual human repercussions of social oppression. To the extent that the kingdom established an oppressive system, it created also a condition of covert, but endemic, social and psychological tension in its population. At the same time, the development of a caste system undermined the older clan basis of social loyalties and thus destroyed the underpinnings of traditional, clan-tied religion. When the cult of the hero-king, Ryangombe, began to develop in the western and southern lacustrine regions in the seventeenth and eighteenth centuries as a cult of affliction, it found therefore a receptive audience among the people of Rwanda. The tensions it ministered to affected both sides of the social line, for both Tutsi and Hutu could be numbered among its devotees. It provided as well an alternative to the no longer functional clan-based religion.

Faced with the rapid growth of a religion which was, by implication at least, anti-royal, and in the Rwanda social context also anti-caste, the central authorities of Rwanda responded characteristically to the threat to their position and power, by institutionalizing Ryangombe as a royal cult.[1] But though the Rwanda state held together, continued to grow, and gave an outward impression of great strength, it could never attain the cultural cohesion and sense of nationhood already developing in eighteenth-century Buganda.

At the start of the seventeenth century, Buganda still remained a tiny kingdom clinging to the shores of Lake Victoria, able to maintain some degree of autonomy by avoiding offence to Bunyoro. The beginning of Buganda's rise came during a period of three successive reigns of strong kings, Kimbugwe, Kateregga and Mutebi. By far the most important of the three was Kateregga, who was able to double the size of his kingdom by extending his rule north and north-eastwards into areas previously dominated by Bunyoro. It was a small gain in territory in

[1] Catherine Robbins, 'Rwanda: a case study in religious assimilation', paper delivered at the Dar es Salaam–UCLA Conference on the historical study of African religious systems (University of Dar es Salaam, June 1970).

absolute terms, but from that point Buganda was no longer just another small bordering, sometimes tributary, state of Bunyoro.

Several striking advantages favoured the continuing growth of Buganda. For one, Buganda was more homogeneous. It had none of the problems engendered by the existence of separate, sometimes endogamous, classes allied in one polity through their common allegiance to the kingship, as had several interlacustrine kingdoms. And Buganda deliberately sought to foster and maintain that homogeneity even as it grew. A concomitant of ethnic homogeneity, and perhaps of small original size, was the commitment of Ganda rulers to political centralization, a commitment which simultaneously strengthened the cohesion of the kingdom and built up the king's personal authority. The most significant steps in this direction were taken by Kateregga, when he installed his important war leaders as chiefs over the territories newly gained from Bunyoro. Kateregga thus established the principle that conquered territories should be fully incorporated where possible, rather than left tributary and liable to revolt under their traditional rulers – a great departure from the practices then common through the region. At the same time he set the precedent of creating entirely new offices for loyal followers.

Under Kateregga, these new positions, once established, became hereditary, like the older chiefships of the kingdom; but Kateregga's successor, Mutebi, sought to carry the idea one step farther by attacking the hereditary principle itself. While able to create more new chiefships, his attempts to dismiss some of the established chiefs were frustrated by their concerted opposition. Nevertheless, the size of the new class of chiefs, king's men dependent on the king for their tenure, continued to grow. Increasingly, young men who aspired to political or social importance had to find a place for themselves in the service of the king, and not at the homesteads of the old aristocracy. Tebandeke, who ruled Buganda near the end of the seventeenth century, only two generations after Kateregga, was already beginning to act without reference to the traditional hereditary chiefs.

It was Buganda's territorial expansion over these two centuries which allowed these political developments. The reigns of Kateregga and, later, of Mawanda, both characterized by important conquests, were consequently marked by the proliferation of new chiefships; during Mawanda's reign, in the first half of the eighteenth century, these had become appointive positions. The older hereditary chiefships were not abolished; rather they became greatly outnumbered by chiefships established in newly incorporated areas, and thereby demoted in importance and influence. Probably as early as the reign of Mawanda, all non-royal offices in Buganda had become for all intents and purposes appointive. The positions still hereditary were so in the sense that succession was limited to a particular family line, but the choice of successor from among the eligible candidates had to have royal approval, and the king also often had the effective power to dismiss the incumbent.

The final step in the centralizing of power in the hands of the Ganda king was accomplished only at the very end of the eighteenth century, and its origins lie in the peculiarities of the reign of the last king of the century, Semakokiro. Having himself seized the kingship by killing Junju, his predecessor and brother, Semakokiro was especially sensitive to the dangers posed by royal relatives who were eligible to rule. Faced with rebellion by one of his sons, he defeated and executed that son and then proceeded to kill or put in custody the rest of his sons, systematically removing men of recent royal descent from all positions of authority. That Semakokiro thereafter had a peaceful reign and died of natural causes was a lesson not lost on his successors, and both protective custody of royal princes and exclusion of royal persons from positions of authority became established practices in later eras. The king of Buganda, therefore, entered the nineteenth century holding a power in his kingdom unparalleled in interlacustrine history.

Buganda had also strategic, as well as social and political, advantages over its neighbours. Long and narrow in shape in the later seventeenth and eighteenth centuries, Buganda would have been difficult to defend had it been landlocked. But backing as it did on the shore of Lake Victoria and bordering east and south on smaller states than itself, the kingdom faced serious defence problems only on its north-western and western borders with Bunyoro. Moreover, the lake gave Buganda what amounted to exceptionally good internal lines of communication, and this advantage in turn encouraged the development of Buganda 'sea-power'. In the nineteenth century, Lake Victoria was to become almost a Ganda sea.

The growth of Buganda eventually brought the kingdom into touch with developing trade networks in Tanzania. Already by the third quarter of the eighteenth century, plates, cups, saucers and glass imports were reaching the court of the Ganda king of that period, Kyabaggu; and his second son to rule after him, Semakokiro, seems to have moved wholeheartedly to exploit and expand this trade. The trade was a royal monopoly, and Semakokiro himself employed hunters to obtain ivory and then had the ivory transported to the south of Lake Victoria to be exchanged for imported manufactures, among which cotton cloth gained increasing favour. The kings of Buganda thereby still further enhanced their roles as central distributors of wealth and power in the kingdom. At the same time, the growth in trade would lead increasingly to direct conflict between Buganda and Bunyoro for control of the trade routes: a new era was appearing out of the events of the close of the eighteenth century.

The continuing strength of Bunyoro should not be underestimated. Despite Buganda's growth in size, Bunyoro must have remained potentially the strongest power of the region, even up to the end of the eighteenth century. The pattern of Ganda expansion is itself sufficient indication of this fact: Buganda extended its hegemony along the north shores of Lake Victoria, but avoided encroaching upon Bunyoro proper; the Buganda sphere of influence reached well into southern Busoga in the eighteenth century. The kingdom also expanded along the western shores of the lake, but again away from the centres of Nyoro power. When Buganda incorporated a territory previously claimed by Bunyoro, it was a peripheral and only tributary area, such as Buddu, conquered by Junju in the second half of the eighteenth century.

That Buganda was no match for Bunyoro is evident also in specific instances of conflict. Kyebambe II's cession of lands to Buganda, in return for help in gaining the Bunyoro kingship over rival princes in the early eighteenth century, reveals continuing Bunyoro problems with succession strife; on the other hand, the incident simultaneously bears witness to a continuing Nyoro confidence in its own predominant strength, for Kyebambe, after establishing himself, reconquered the lands he had ceded. In the following reign of Olimi III, Buganda made incursions into Bunyoro proper while Nyoro forces were occupied with fighting in the south of its claimed domains; but, after gaining victory in the south, Bunyoro then turned its attentions to Buganda and quickly reclaimed the lands temporarily seized by its eastern neighbour. Even during the rest of the eighteenth century, Ganda control was not pushed to any great extent north-westwards, towards Bunyoro itself. What developments of the seventeenth and eighteenth centuries did create was a Buganda which would be able finally in the nineteenth century directly to challenge Bunyoro.

LUO INTERACTIONS EAST AND NORTH OF LAKE VICTORIA

If immigration had a declining importance in the seventeenth and eighteenth centuries in lands around the westward sides of Lake Victoria, it remained still the predominant factor in the area to the east of the lake. Bantu-speaking groups spread eastward, reshaping societies of the country south of Mount Elgon and absorbing the former inhabitants; Luo immigrants moved into country about the Kavirondo Gulf, absorbing earlier Bantu inhabitants of the region into new Luo-speaking communities; while other Bantu movements affected the regions south from the gulf.

As an integrating factor, kingship was generally lacking among peoples on the eastern shores of Lake Victoria. The importance of this difference is illustrated by the Luo role in different parts of the lake region. In the western lacustrine area, Luo immigrants had seized the positions of leadership in the fifteenth and sixteenth centuries, but were nevertheless culturally and linguistically assimilated by the Bantu-speaking peoples already inhabiting the area; whereas, along the eastern shores of Lake Victoria, Bantu peoples in large numbers acculturated to the styles and speech of incoming Luo. Political and social units among the Bantu of Central Nyanza in modern Kenya, where the Luo settled, were not in the seventeenth century of a size sufficient to absorb large bodies of immigrants. There were no kingships capable of solving the conflicting jurisdictions of immigrants and locals, or of adjudicating the possession of lands, settled by immigrants but traditionally claimed by locals. The resultant communal insecurities tended to be overcome by a levelling of ethnic distinctions within local areas, a levelling usually favouring Luo language and cultural ideas.

By 1600 a scattering of Luo communities had already settled through Central Nyanza, among Bantu communities speaking dialects closely related to the modern Bantu dialects of North Nyanza. During the two centuries that followed, partly from the expansion of these nuclear settlements and partly from continuing Luo migration from the north, these scattered communities developed into a solid block of Luo-speakers spread all along the north side of the Kavirondo Gulf. Then, in the second half of the eighteenth century, Luo communities began to settle south of the gulf. Expansion north of the gulf did not entirely cease, but southward migrations marked the opening of a new era of accelerated Luo expansion which carried Luo language and culture to the borders of Tanzania by the twentieth century.

Reasons for the 'success' of the Luo are difficult to determine. Impetus was given, in part, by continuing new Luo immigration into Central Nyanza from outside the region. Perhaps also the very situation of the Luo-speakers as intruders and, initially, as minority people in Central Nyanza engendered attitudes, such as military preparedness or social aggressiveness, which gave them the advantage in social and other encounters with already established, and therefore less insecure, peoples. Another factor may have been patterns of subsistence in the early period of Luo immigration into Nyanza. Tradition and other evidence of original Luo subsistence practices suggest a greater emphasis on grazing by Luo in the seventeenth century than by their Bantu-speaking neighbours.[1] Stock-raising requires much more land than cultivation, and thus the Luo perforce would have exerted a greater pressure on resources and had a greater tendency toward expansion than the surrounding Bantu.

A broader question is raised by the possible interrelation between the Luo movements and contemporaneous population movements among Bantu-speaking peoples of the eastern Lake Victoria shore. It is far too simplistic a solution merely to suggest that one people moved because another people drove them out of their old country. A people too weak or broken to defend their own country are not often strong enough then to march out and take away somcone else's. Still, in some instances, Luo pressure had a direct effect on Bantu movements in the seventeenth and eighteenth centuries. Several Bantu communities, disturbed by Luo expansion north of the Kavirondo Gulf, but unwilling to adopt the course of acculturation to the Luo, re-established themselves south of the gulf in South Nyanza. They gained only temporary respite from Luo pressure, which was renewed with the beginning of Luo migration across the gulf in the later eighteenth century.

Some elements among the Bantu communities who make up the so-called Luyia also derive from groups dislodged by Luo expansion, but many of the migrations of Bantu-speakers which were to rearrange social groupings of people in North Nyanza came, on the other hand, from the near west, on the modern border of Kenya and Uganda. For these migrants, indirect connections with Luo movements can be suggested. Luo immigration had to pass through the regions of the Kenya–Uganda borders in order to reach Central Nyanza and was thus one, albeit important, element in an interplay of peoples which made the region a place of rapidly shifting and reforming cultural settings and political

[1] B. A. Ogot, *History of the southern Luo* (Nairobi, 1967).

allegiances in the sixteenth century. But during the seventeenth and eighteenth centuries, Bantu population movements in North Nyanza seem to have been often independent of, though parallel with, Luo movements in Central Nyanza.

Bantu migrations, like those of the Luo, meant the growth of new communities, formed by the immigrants through assimilation of the local people; in the instance of North Nyanza, these were usually former speakers of languages closely related to modern Kalenjin, now spoken east and north-east of Mount Elgon. Their contribution to the new Bantu-speaking societies was strongest along the east and north of the Nyanza region, where they presumably formed the numerically more important element in the new societies. It was less notable westward towards the border areas with Uganda, from which many of the Bantu immigrants had originally stemmed. New Bantu-speaking communities along the east and north of the region took up, among other traits, a Kalenjin type of age organization, whereas none of the westerly communities made so great a shift.

Immigration into North Nyanza in the seventeenth and eighteenth centuries was not entirely a Bantu affair. Several peoples from the Kalenjin-speaking regions to the east also pressed into Nyanza during the period, but, moving against the tide of change, were acculturated to the Bantu and came to adopt Bantu speech.

The basic unit of the individual's allegiance – and thus the medium for the assimilation of diverse elements – through much of the Nyanza region during this period was the local, territorially based clan. The right to hold land, and to live on and work it, depended on membership of a recognized clan. Individuals were assimilated by gradually gaining community acceptance as clan members, and communities were naturalized by gaining acceptance as putative clans belonging to larger clusters of clans which claimed descent from a common eponymous ancestor. Both Luo and Bantu settlers used the clan as a device for social integration. One of the cultural effects of Bantu assimilation of former Kalenjin-related peoples was that in the new communities the clan came to supersede the Kalenjin type of age-set organization as the basic organizing principle of society,[1] although age-sets were retained in some cases as a subsidiary element. Through Bantu influence, even some of the Kalenjin of Mount Elgon adopted the territorial clan principle, though retaining their Kalenjin language.

[1] Christopher Ehret, 'Aspects of social and economic change in Western Kenya, *c.* 500–1800 A.D.', in B. A. Ogot, ed., *Aspects of the pre-colonial history of Kenya* (Nairobi, forthcoming).

Despite the general predominance of clan-based polities, a few chiefdoms had minor roles in seventeenth- and eighteenth-century Nyanza, especially in a limited region about the lower Nzoia and Yala rivers. Only one of these chiefdoms, Wanga, was primarily Bantu-speaking. The important early Luo-ruled chiefdom in those centuries was nearby Alego. It has been suggested that the intensity of social interaction in this region over a long period between a variety of both Bantu and Luo communities created pressures and conflicts which could best be resolved by the integrative factor of chiefship. Though a larger territorial unit of peoples was thus included within a common peace, these chiefdoms still remained very small through the eighteenth century. Wanga towards the end of the century did enter into a period of expansion under its sixth ruler, Netia. A particular factor in this process was the arrival of a group of immigrants, apparently Wuasinkishu Masai, who were allowed by Netia to settle in Wanga in return for placing their military skills at the call of the Wanga ruler. But while Netia's efforts secured a somewhat larger territory for Wanga and a closer-knit polity, his kingdom still remained very small compared to some of the contemporary states on the west of Lake Victoria.

The Busoga region, lying to the north of Lake Victoria, seems to have marked a historical as well as geographical transition between the developments affecting the eastern Lake Victoria region and those affecting the states to the west. Organized after the interlacustrine pattern into kingdoms, albeit very tiny kingdoms, Busoga nonetheless faced in part the same sort of pressures of migration as the Nyanza region to the east. The north-east of Busoga lay along the line of Luo movements into central Nyanza, and the establishment of the Luo-speaking Padhola society in that north-eastern area paralleled the establishment of the large Luo-speaking populations of Central Nyanza in the seventeenth and eighteenth centuries. But over most of northern Busoga, the assimilation of Luo elements by the Bantu-speakers proceeded in accordance with the interlacustrine pattern of the immediately preceding centuries – immigrants acculturating to local language and customs, but often being able to move into positions of chiefly authority – while only a few of the southern Busoga states were directly affected. The growing power of neighbouring Buganda seems in the long run to have extended a vaguely defined Ganda hegemony over parts of Busoga. The willingness of the Musuubo rulers in central Busoga to seek Ganda assistance against the pressure of Luo settlers can be seen as a step in this development, but it also indicates that local concerns remained pre-eminent in eighteenth-century Soga political considerations and that the power of Buganda constituted no immediate threat to local rights and privileges.[1]

Northward of the area adjacent to Lake Victoria and the western highlands of Kenya, lay another large area in which population movements had some importance in developments of the seventeenth and eighteenth centuries. For the fifteenth and sixteenth centuries, the history of most of the area could be tied together in the theme of Luo expansion, which in those centuries had affected all the country from the Bahr al-Ghazal in the far north to Lake Victoria. But by the beginning of the sixteenth century the several centres of Luo settlement were already established: the Kenya Luo, as already discussed, along the north of the Kavirondo Gulf; the ancestors of the Acholi and Alur in northern Uganda; and the Shilluk and Anuak in southern parts of the modern republic of Sudan. Continued slow extension of these settlement areas, as well as the movement of Luo groups from one such area to another, did occur; but the most extensive population movements of the period belonged to Karimojong-Teso groups in eastern Uganda and north-western Kenya. North of the borders of present-day Uganda, the Bari and Lotuko communities were taking shape. Little can yet be said about the seventeenth- or eighteenth-century history of the Dinka and Nuer, who lived northward of the Bari along the Nile river; but for the rest of the groups, some aspects of their interactions with other peoples and of their internal developments can be discerned.

The most prominent instance in the northern parts of East Africa where population movement can be identified as the major factor in social reorganization in the seventeenth and eighteenth centuries is that of the Karimojong-Teso peoples. The centre for these population movements lay in the regions along the modern borders of Uganda and Kenya near Mount Moroto. Probably beginning in the seventeenth century, and certainly under way in the eighteenth, these developments spread the ancestors of the Turkana to the dry hot lands on the west and south-west of Lake Rudolf, the Karimojong southward from an area north of Mount Moroto, and the Teso apparently from an area south-west of Mount Moroto westward toward Lake Bisina. Other Karimojong-Teso communities, the Jie and Dodoth, were beginning to take shape to the north, between the Karimojong and the Lotuko.

[1] D. W. Cohen, *The historical tradition of Busoga: Mukama and Kintu* (Oxford, 1972), 150.

But it would be wrong to interpret this history as a simple expansion of once small Karimojong-Teso groups over territories previously not Karimojong-Teso in speech. Karimojong tradition explicitly admits the incorporation of related peoples during this expansion. Evidence of contact with other peoples also indicate that the Karimojong-Teso had been for long a major factor in eastern Uganda and adjoining areas. The Pokot were so strongly influenced by them that, alone among the Kalenjin, the Pokot have assimilated in many outward respects to the norms of Karimojong-Teso societies.[1] Some of this Karimojong-Teso influence on the Pokot is attributable to recent Pokot contacts with Turkana and Karimojong; but other aspects of it date probably even earlier than the eighteenth century, and thus antedate the later Karimojong-Teso expansions and imply the existence of earlier Karimojong-Teso populations as far south as the edges of the western highlands in Kenya. Indeed in some areas in the north and east of their present-day territories – in Topotha country and parts of Turkana, for instance – Karimojong-Teso population movement probably reached into country where their language was not before spoken. Yet, for the most part, seventeenth- and eighteenth-century Karimojong-Teso migrations began a restructuring of social and political units and allegiances rather than a shift of cultural values and habits of speech. And if the area of Karimojong-Teso speech was expanded to the north and east, in the south-east it retreated before the beginnings of Pokot expansion northward out of the western highlands.

Although considerable historical data are available on the various Luo groups of Uganda and the southern Sudan, they have been little analyzed for what they can reveal about internal social and political history. The most northerly Luo-speaking people, the Shilluk, evolved in the sixteenth century as a string of independent communities, formed around a core of Luo-speaking immigrants and located along the White Nile below the Bahr al-Ghazal confluence. The development of a common Shilluk allegiance to one primary king, called the *reth*, appears to have arisen out of a crisis in Shilluk relations with the Dinka in the latter seventeenth century. One Shilluk chief, Tokot, took the lead in defeating the Dinka in battle. Through this victory, and through a series of other victories over neighbouring Nuer, Anuak, and Nuba peoples during the course of his career, Tokot appears to have so established his pre-eminent position among the leaders of the Shilluk

[1] See especially G. W. B. Huntingford, *The Northern Nilo-Hamites* (London, International African Institute, 1953), charts on pp. 18 and 19.

that it passed to his son, Tugo. Under Tugo, the formal apparatus of kingship began to take shape, and from that point the *reth*-ship was clearly established as the central symbol of Shilluk society. The various Shilluk communities continued, however, to retain much of their old independence of action throughout the eighteenth century. This autonomy was to the benefit of the northern Shilluk, who carried on an older pattern of successful canoe raiding against populations northward down the Nile. This was to the detriment of the southernmost Shilluk, who had usually to see to their own defence against the expansive pressure of the neighbouring Nuer.

One aspect of Anuak history has also received notice. In general, the Anuak, who lived along the modern border of Ethiopia with the south-eastern Sudan, were organized into autonomous villages under hereditary headmen. But in the eastern part of Anuak country in the seventeenth and eighteenth centuries, there developed a sort of 'kingship' based on the possession of certain sacred emblems. The position did not so much confer political power as enormous social prestige; rather, it coexisted with, generally without dislodging, the autonomous local governance of the individual villages. Before the late eighteenth century, this kingship seems to have been a fairly stable institution and evidently was recognized by only a few eastern Anuak villages. Then a sudden exacerbation of competition for the position in the late eighteenth century – when nine persons in rapid succession seized the kingship by killing their predecessors and taking forcible possession of the emblems – turned the institution into a potential force for instability, and marked the beginning of the spread of the competition for the 'kingship' to wider and wider areas of Anuak country.

Although the major Luo population movements in northern Uganda date to earlier than the seventeenth century, two later extensions of Luo speech areas are nonetheless interesting for the processes of assimilation involved. The settlement of the Alur to the west of Lake Albert from the late seventeenth century on, was in essence no more than the spread of scions of a Luo chiefly clan among formerly chiefless Central Sudanic-speaking peoples. But the gradual shift by subjects of the chiefs from their Central Sudanic language to Luo frequently followed. The rule of Alur chiefs usually spread not by conquest, but by invitation. Chiefs were valued because it was believed that they were able to control rain, and they had also the important secular function of maintaining order through adjudication of inter-clan and inter-lineage disputes which, in the absence of chiefs, would have led to fighting. But because the quality of chiefliness was believed to be hereditary, chiefs could not simply be created to fill the need. A community instead received its chief by inviting a recognized Alur chief to send one of his sons to rule them. This new chief, or his son or grandson, would eventually assert his independence of the senior chiefdom by ceasing to send back tribute and by beginning to perform rain ceremonies on his own. In turn, he might then send his own sons out as chiefs and so continue the process of the spread of Alur chiefships and eventually Alur speech.

The spread of the Lango dialect of Luo accompanied very different social circumstances. Diverse groups of both Luo immigrants and Karimojong-Teso settlers from the east interacted in the Lango area.[1] Luo speech eventually predominated, but the social practices of the developing Lango communities blended both the Luo and the Karimojong-Teso experience. Just how basic the Karimojong-Teso element was in shaping the culture is evident in the detailed Lango adoption of features of Karimojong-Teso age organization and in the strong component of Karimojong-Teso loan-words in modern Lango vocabulary. Moreover, hereditary chiefship was not present among the Karimojong-Teso contributors to Lango society, and it does not appear, in contradistinction to the Alur situation, as a factor in Lango history. Many of the modern clans of the Lango region identify themselves historically with the Luo-speakers, but the strength of the linguistic and comparative cultural evidence makes it difficult to avoid the conclusion that former Karimojong-Teso speakers formed a considerable, in all likelihood the major, element in the interaction of peoples which, by the nineteenth century, had given rise to Lango society.

The examples of Alur and Lango history raise the question of the historical significance of chiefship among Luo-speaking peoples. The ancestral Luo language possessed a word indicating a position of leadership in early Luo society. In a majority of later Luo societies, this position turned out to be a chiefly one and, where it is found, it often can be shown to have had that role at least back to the seventeenth century or earlier. On the other hand, the Lango, notably, and many of the Kenya Luo lack chiefship. A perhaps unwarranted evolutionary assumption has often been applied to this problem, whereby non-chiefly organization was presumed to be primary and chiefship secondary in the evolution of Luo societies. The balance of evidence rather supports the idea of an original, though probably simple and small-scale, Luo institution of chiefship. The correlation of the non-chiefly

[1] Personal communication from Professor B. A. Ogot.

Luo settlements with areas that lacked chiefship before Luo immigration favours the solution that, in political matters, Luo settlers may often have been deeply influenced by local ideas. In the example of the Kenya Luo, the new societies can be seen as sometimes maintaining chiefship, when it had practical value in subsuming ethnic plurality under a wider unity, but elsewhere losing the institution because it did not fit the ideas of the earlier, though otherwise acculturated, populations.

Much less information has been collected on Bari or Lotuko history than on Luo. Still, a few processes and trends seem discernible, especially for the Bari peoples in the seventeenth and eighteenth centuries. From the end of the sixteenth century into the seventeenth, the still extant Bari-speaking societies were beginning to take shape. Very often these communities defined themselves by the line of rain-chiefs – ritual experts who wielded great personal and official influence – which they recognized. The Bari proper began the seventeenth century as that group of people which supported the rain-chiefs whose shrine was at Shinduru. By the second half of the eighteenth century, their self-identification as the Bari was strong enough to withstand a split within the community between those who continued to recognize the rain-chief at Shinduru, and those who supported a new line of ritual experts.

The development of the new Bari-speaking societies during these centuries was not simply a reformulation of social relationships among people already speaking Bari dialects, but often involved also the incorporation by these expanding communities of other peoples not previously Bari in language. The peoples thus drawn into Bari societies had generally spoken languages closely related to those of the Central Sudanic Madi and Lugbara, who still adjoin the Bari-speaking peoples on the west. This incorporation of Central Sudanic elements was prominent not so much among the Bari proper as among two other Bari-speaking communities, the Mondari and the Kuku, who continued to grow by adopting Madi- and Lugbara-related people into their societies, even during the nineteenth century.

To the east of the Bari peoples, the Lotuko communities stabilized out of a series of small local population movements of the later seventeenth and early eighteenth centuries. Like the Bari, different Lotuko groups defined their allegiances according to which rain-chief they recognized. It should be possible eventually to place Bari and Lotuko events in this period in the more satisfying context of an areal history of social interaction and change. Late extensive influence of Bari, Lotuko and the neighbouring Acholi on each other is apparent in nearly every aspect of the cultures of these peoples.[1] Central Sudanic-speaking peoples to their west must also have played some part in shaping these developments. But too little is as yet known of internal Lotuko, as also of Bari or Acholi, history to discern either patterns or specifics of social and cultural change in the seventeenth and eighteenth centuries.

THE MASAI AND THEIR NE

For the variety of polities and societies whi
eighteenth centuries inhabited the lands betv
coastal region of northern East Africa, one
all in varying degree, and that element wa
non-Masai people of those areas bordered
territory; the dealings between the Masai ar
from chronic warfare to peaceful market cc
The Masai-speakers formed no unified nation, but consisted of a number of independent, though often loosely allied, confederations or tribes, who, during these two centuries, achieved a continuing territorial expansion. Especially far-reaching advances were those of the Samburu Masai, who established themselves in the central part of northern Kenya; the Wuasinkishu, who wrested control of the plateau named after them in western Kenya from its former Kalenjin inhabitants; and the Kisonko, who, before the end of the eighteenth century, spread across the Masai steppe in Tanzania as far south as modern Gogo country.

The key to Masai military strength was their age-set organization. Each boy in the society was initiated along with his fellows into an age-set to which he would belong for the rest of his life. With the other members of his set, he passed through successive age-grades. The significant grade for military purposes was the warrior grade; typically the age-set to which a Masai man belonged would occupy the warrior grade from the time he was in his teens to the time he was in his thirties. As a corporate, named group, the age-set occupying the warrior age-grade formed in effect a regiment permanently ready to defend or attack.

An interesting cultural change, which probably occurred during the seventeenth and eighteenth centuries, was the development by some of

[1] Vocabulary evidence for these contacts can be adduced from C. Muratori, *English-Bari-Lotuxo-Acoli vocabulary* (Okaru, 1948).

the southern Masai tribes of a prohibition against consuming anything but the products of livestock raising. The trait did not spread to northern tribes such as the Laikipiak, Samburu and Wuasinkishu, who continued to cultivate as well as to herd; and although many southern Masai adopted this new idea, not all did. Historically, this prohibition of all but a limited range of foods appears as an extension, induced by the Masai preference for herding over cultivation, of a much older Masai prohibition against the eating of wild game, fowl, or fish, such that the avoidance came to be applied to cultivated foods as well.

The Masai tribes reached the height of their power and influence towards the end of this period, around the time of the birth of their greatest ritual expert, the *ol-oiboni* Supet, in the last quarter of the eighteenth century. Masai territories approached their greatest extent, from Lake Rudolf to central Tanzania, and the military strength of the different tribes was unchallenged. Until the end of the eighteenth century, Masai attentions seem to have been turned outward towards other peoples, and the Masai tribes remained generally at peace with each other. In the nineteenth century, however, the Masai began to fight among themselves and so eventually to undercut their own predominant position.

The most potent Masai pressures were felt by separate communities which maintained a precarious existence within Masai-inhabited territory. Yet a number of such communities maintained their identity for centuries. The root of their ability to survive lay in the sharp differences between their economies and those of the surrounding Masai. Most of the separate groups were hunter-gatherers living among a people who abstained from the flesh of wild animals; one group, the Bantu-speaking Sonjo of the rift valley country of far northern Tanzania and far southern Kenya, were intensive irrigation agriculturists scattered among purely pastoral Masai who avoided consuming the products of cultivation. These communities coexisted with the dominant Masai because they pursued subsistence activities which did not conflict, or compete for resources, with those of the Masai. In Masai political and military considerations, these peoples can rarely have been important. The Masai did obtain some products, primarily hides, from hunting groups, but the major Masai trading relations were with surrounding agricultural peoples.

Masai relations with their neighbours on the west in the seventeenth and eighteenth centuries seem, from the meagre evidence yet available, to have been generally warlike. The clearest example is provided by the

Wuasinkishu Masai and the Kalenjin. The Wuasinkishu, in gaining control of their plateau in western Kenya, split Kalenjin territory down the middle. The Nandian group of Kalenjin were separated into the ancestors of the Tuken, Keyo and Marakwet to the east of the Wuasinkishu territory, and the ancestors of the Nandi proper, the Kipsigis, and Terik (Nyang'ori) to the west. Farther north in the western highlands, the Wuasinkishu pushed a wedge between the Pokot and the Kalenjin of Mount Elgon.

The histories of all these peoples in the period between 1600 and 1800 have received entirely inadequate study, but what is known of Nandi history suggests that the Wuasinkishu penetration may have had extensive repercussions even outside its immediate compass. The Nandi developed from a small group of people located along the southern Nandi escarpment in the early seventeenth century. Incorporating other small Kalenjin groups, they expanded north and eastwards during the seventeenth and eighteenth centuries, coming thus into direct conflict with the Wuasinkishu. The military threat posed by this Masai tribe became, certainly by the eighteenth century, the dominant concern of the Nandi in their external relations. Indeed, it can plausibly be suggested that the crucial factor leading the Kalenjin groups of the hill country along the west of the plains to develop a view of themselves as one, Nandi, people, was their common experience of the Wuasinkishu threat.

The integrative institution among the formative Nandi, as among other Kalenjin and among the Masai, was age organization. Age-sets cut across considerations of clan or family origin in favour of a territorial grouping larger than that usually allowed by clan loyalties. In addition to allowing the gathering of a larger war party than might be possible in a society organized territorially around clans, the Kalenjin systems, like those of the Masai, provided for a warrior age-grade permanently ready for battle. Though usually unable to defeat the Wuasinkishu in the seventeenth and eighteenth centuries, the Nandi were enabled by this social system to survive within their more defensible hill country and even to expand within those limits during this period.

While the relations of the Masai with their eastern neighbours in the seventeenth and eighteenth centuries could be equally bellicose, the importance of more pacific relations comes out in the available evidence here with greater clarity than it does for Masai-Kalenjin interactions. The Kikuyu, for example, traded and intermarried with Masai in the eighteenth century at the same time as they were subjected to Masai raiding. This duality could persist because both sides valued their mutual trade. The Kikuyu needed the hides that the Masai, with their abundance of cattle, could provide; the Masai in return obtained iron goods, tobacco and ochre from the Kikuyu. Judging from later practices in the nineteenth century, trade may have continued even in times of particular hostility; women of the two groups seem to have been allowed to go on trading with each other even when their men were at war. Local trade appears in other areas also to have been quite important to the Masai tribes, and the example of the Pare of northern Tanzania suggests that the acquisition of iron tools and weapons was in general the primary Masai objective in this trade. The Pare used the iron trade to obtain livestock in return from the Masai.

Yet if contact with neighbouring Masai-speakers was the common factor in the history of many of the peoples of the north-eastern quarter of East Africa, still it was not the only factor in the history of most groups, nor even the major factor in the history of some. For instance, relations with neighbouring peoples to the west were of quite obvious importance in Kalenjin history. A significant constant in Nandi affairs was trade with the Bantu and Luo communities of Nyanza. The contrast between the eastern and western relations of the Nandi is apparent in the kinds of words borrowed in the period. Nandi *kapsiro*, 'market', was a borrowing from their western neighbours, while *olpul*, the word for the place where warriors meet to slaughter an ox before going to war, was borrowed from Masai. For the Kalenjin of Mount Elgon, Bantu contacts had far greater effects on their development than contacts with Wuasinkishu Masai, which were generally unfriendly and probably did not become important until after the eighteenth century. In aspects of social structure and in their reliance on cultivation, especially of the banana, peoples such as the Kony and Sebei (Sabiny) came eventually to resemble their Bantu neighbours more than their Kalenjin congeners.

Kalenjin groups in general maintained through the eighteenth century the much older practice of adopting new ideas in agriculture from the peoples to their west. Both maize and tobacco were introduced into the Kalenjin-speaking parts of the western highlands from the Bantu and Luo to the west during this period. The limit of this western influence on cultivation seems to have been the Rift Valley: the Tuken, the easternmost people of the Nandian group of Kalenjin, have two words for maize, one borrowed from the west and the other from agricultural Masai who bordered them on the east.[1] The Pokot alone

[1] Borrowed from the west is the Tuken form *ipantia*; from Masai, the word *alpai*.

among the Kalenjin of Kenya do not seem to have been significantly influenced by either Masai or the Bantu. Some Pokot did on occasion engage in fighting with the Samburu, but their major contacts were rather with their northern Karimojong-Teso-speaking neighbours.

Similar limitations of the impact of the Masai can be noted on the east side of Masai-influenced country. The Kikuyu, for example, were deeply influenced socially and economically by the Masai, but the course of their expansion was directed southward away from the early area of Masai contact, which can be placed along the stretch of country between Mount Kenya and the northern Nyandarua (Aberdare) range. The Masai pressure may possibly first have shunted Kikuyu expansion southward, but, once turned in that direction, the Kikuyu faced no immediate threat like that of the Masai. Spreading through the then forested lands along the east of the Nyandarua range, they had only to deal with less numerous hunting peoples who posed no military threat. In any case, only the peripheries of Kikuyu country in the eighteenth century had anything like daily contacts with Masai, and even in war Masai raids may only occasionally have penetrated deeply into Kikuyu farmlands.

In respect of Masai contacts, the situation of the Chaga around Mount Kilimanjaro probably resembled that of the Kikuyu. Though apparently growing in numbers and territory, the Chaga remained organized in the seventeenth and eighteenth centuries in a great many very small and very local social and political units, whose histories are still largely unstudied. But if the Masai, settled in the open plains around much of the Chaga country, cannot presently be credited with great influence on Chaga affairs during this period, another people, the Ongamo or Ngassa, who were closely related in language to the Masai, did have a major part in Chaga history. The beginnings of Chaga interaction with the Ongamo date to well before 1600, and at some point in time the Ongamo had even been the dominant people through much of the Kilimanjaro area.[1] By the seventeenth and eighteenth centuries, the Ongamo were probably becoming increasingly restricted, by Chaga expansion, to eastern Kilimanjaro. Yet within that region they must have remained an important and still independent society, since even as late as the second half of the nineteenth century and in the face of massive acculturation to the Chaga about them, Ongamo society retained sufficient cohesion to keep its age-set system functioning to some extent.[2]

[1] Ehret, *Ethiopians and East Africans* (Nairobi, 1974), table 8–2.
[2] Testimony of Petre Mutui of Reha, Rombo, Tanzania, 4 October 1967.

The peripheral nature of the Masai presence is most obvious, however, in the case of the Pare. The long-established Ugweno kingdom in the North Pare mountains maintained a loose unity based on payment by constituent communities of a nominal tribute, and on their participation in the Ugweno initiation rite. In the early seventeenth century, the main problems which the kingdom had to face revolved around the assimilation of a number of immigrant groups. The Sangi, who came to Pare from the Taita hills to the east, were for a while tied to the Ugweno state by their acceptance of the initiation rite and payment of tribute. But they were never as satisfactorily integrated into Ugweno society as earlier communities had been and, towards the end of the eighteenth century, were able to establish their complete political independence from Ugweno. Southern Cushitic-speaking Mbugu immigrants from the south were more satisfactorily neutralized as a threat to the kingdom. Cattle herders by inclination, the Mbugu gained an accepted economic role as providers of cattle, a valued item in internal Pare trade.

The South Pare mountains, on the other hand, were occupied in the seventeenth and eighteenth centuries by a number of small independent chiefdoms. Though politically separate from the north, the people of South Pare had a culture largely identical with that of the northerners and spoke the same language as at least some of the North Pare communities. And in the seventeenth century they, like the northerners, were affected by Mbugu settlement from the south and more important migrations from the east. Unlike North Pare, they were not united in one kingdom, and the South Pare communities had greater difficulties in dealing with these immigrants. The leaders of several immigrant groups from the east were able to gain acceptance as chiefs by already established Pare clans; according to tradition, this was because of their special ritual powers. But an obvious contributing factor was the role which these leaders and their followers took in Pare conflicts with an enemy people settled about the South Pare mountains, remembered only as 'Wagalla'.[1] Under the leadership of the immigrants, the Pare had effectively removed the 'Wagalla' threat by the eighteenth century.

Masai appear to have had no contact with the Pare till some time in the eighteenth century. Even the extent to which the Masai traded for Pare iron amounted to only one aspect of Pare trade relations. Ugweno was an important producer of iron long before the seventeenth century,

[1] These people do not seem identifiable, however, with the Cushitic-speaking Galla of northern and eastern Kenya in the seventeenth and eighteenth centuries.

and from later evidence it would appear that the Chaga to the immediate north of Ugweno were the major market for Pare iron. The Masai merely entered into the existing trade arrangements.

In Ukambani, too, little if any Masai influence is apparent in events of the seventeenth and eighteenth centuries. Though near neighbours, neither people had a demonstrable impact on the other's social existence. The original Kamba society was only beginning to take shape in the seventeenth century in the central parts of what is today the Machakos district. The role of immigrant groups from the south in this development is apparent in the traditional records, which view the formation of Kamba society entirely in terms of immigrant settlement.[1] But, in fact, these southerners were catalysts who reshaped the self-perceptions of a population which was perhaps largely of northern, i.e. Mount Kenya, origin; for, despite the southern immigrants' social impact, the language of the developing Kamba society remained one of unquestionably recent northern derivation, closely interrelated with the Kikuyu, Meru and other Bantu dialects of Mount Kenya.

The early stages of Kamba history seem to have been marked by a rapidly growing population, and eventually by overpopulation in the regions of original Kamba emergence – overpopulation probably not in absolute terms, but in terms of traditional expectations of the human and livestock densities that should obtain. By the eighteenth century, especially its second half, this interpretation of their situation was impelling many Kamba to settle in the drier, less favourable, but also little populated, country to the east of Machakos, in modern Kitui district. Thus by the latter part of the eighteenth century, Kamba were beginning to occupy most of the areas they inhabit today, and the stage was set for the beginning of Kamba long distance trade to the coast, a development in which ambitious Kamba of the agriculturally marginal Kitui region were, understandably, to take the lead.

In the combined light of Kamba and Pare history, the present lack of knowledge of the history of the region about the Taita hills in the seventeenth century becomes a severe handicap to our overall understanding of events in the intermediate region between the interior and the coast of northern East Africa. Immigrant groups, as was noted, had importance both in the Pare mountains and in Ukambani around about the seventeenth century, in Ukambani perhaps earlier than in Pare, and in both cases the immigrants came from the general direction

[1] This discussion of Kamba history is indebted to Kennell A. Jackson, 'An ethnohistorical study of the oral traditions of the Akamba of Kenya', unpublished Ph.D. thesis, (University of California, Los Angeles, 1971).

of the Taita hills. What could have been taking place at that time that could have made such a small region take on a wider importance? A minor Masai impact on the Taita people is evident, but hardly great enough nor early enough to explain major emigrations from the Taita hills. On the other hand, the encounter of Bantu and Southern Cushitic societies, strikingly attested in the linguistic evidence for Taita social history, might possibly have created the kind of turmoil and pressure for cultural readjustment in which many groups might have chosen to seek new homes.[1] But this encounter as yet lacks a clear chronological context, a lack which study of archaeology and oral tradition should eventually remedy.

Another such zone of merely peripheral Masai influences lay diagonally across Masai territory from the Ukambani, Taita and Pare region, in the areas of modern Singida, Mbulu and Kondoa in Tanzania. At least by the eighteenth century, Masai inhabited all the country to the east, and around as far as the north-west, of this region. Large Masai raiding ventures may have taken place here, but direct Masai social impact, like that which was exerted on nearby Gogo, where intermarriage and other peaceful levels of interaction seem to have occurred, is not supported in the evidence as it relates to the era before 1800. Some settlement of Masai-speaking Baraguyu may have touched parts of Kondoa, as it did other areas bordering on the southern bulge of the expansion of the Masai proper, but if so it was a slight and scattered settlement. Through most of Kondoa, Mbulu and Singida, it was the shifting relations among long established population groupings which were most characteristic of seventeenth- and eighteenth-century history.

The most common tendency in these relations was the expansion of Bantu-speaking societies. In Kondoa, the Irangi incorporated former Southern Cushitic-speaking peoples. On the west, in Singida, on the other hand, what happened has broad similarity to contemporary developments in the adjoining Nyamwezi-speaking regions (see below, pp. 503 ff.). Some similar and perhaps even related political developments may have been taking place, particularly in Iramba, although specific determination of this has still to be confirmed. On a wider economic level, Bantu expansion in Singida was probably coterminous in a few cases with the spread of the knowledge and practice of agriculture. This is also the situation recorded, for instance, in the traditions of Ukimbu, and for the same reason: that both regions had much agricul-

[1] Ehret, *Ethiopians*, tables 8–2 and 4–6.

turally marginal land where hunter-gathers were long left in possession. One such hunter-gatherer people, the Hatsa, located on the north of the Iramba, maintained their old economic ways, though no doubt on a shrinking territorial base, down to the present century. A second people, the Sandawe of south-eastern Kondoa, staved off the pressure of agricultural peoples on their land by themselves becoming agriculturists. This development may have taken place during the seventeenth and eighteenth centuries; such a dating, though plausible, remains to be confirmed, however. In any case, Bantu influence is not evident in the Sandawe adoption of food-production: Southern Cushites seem from linguistic evidence to have provided the model for Sandawe ideas of cultivation; Dadog (Tatoga) influence seems important, on the other hand, in the development of Sandawe herding pursuits.[1]

Like the Sandawe, other non-Bantu peoples in this Singida, Kondoa and Mbulu region seem mostly to have held their own during the seventeenth and eighteenth centuries. The Dadog, as well as influencing Sandawe history, were the dominant people through a large part of Singida and in southern and central Mbulu. They had perhaps already lost some ground to the Mbugwe and the Southern Cushitic-speaking Gorowa in northern Kondoa, but their decline, both in Singida before the advance of the Bantu-speaking Nyaturu and in Mbulu in the face of expanding Southern Cushitic Iraqw, was not to become a notable trend until the nineteenth century.

THE CENTRAL INTERIOR

A decade ago, it was believed that the history of the central interior of eastern Africa during this period was dominated by the extension of a diluted form of interlacustrine political organization throughout the entire region. Recent research has since demonstrated that although the form and content of chiefship here is remarkably similar, the derivation and spread of these ideas is a much more complex problem than was previously recognized. During the seventeenth century, the principal themes in the central interior, as in the north, were the steady occupation of the land by successive and overlapping small-scale migrations and the closely related establishment of chiefly dynasties. These dynasties to a very large extent became the foci of those social and political units that persisted throughout the remainder of the precolonial era. As the eighteenth century progressed, however, there are

[1] Ibid. ch. 2 and table 4–1.

very clear indications in the traditions of some of the peoples involved that they were inexorably drawn into a more intimate relationship with the non-African world. In some respects, then, the central interior can be viewed as thematically transitional, in terms of its history, between the northern and the southern regions of East Africa, and not simply as lying midway between them on the map.

The history of western Tanzania embodies both these processes. In the extreme north-west, this region is linked directly to the interlacustrine area by the migration southwards of Hima/Tutsi ruling houses. Among the Haya, Ha and Zinza, these were associated with the earlier invasion of Ruhinda from southern Uganda (see volume 3, chapter 9). By the seventeenth century, however, both Buha and Buzinza were independent states, although they seem to have recognized the seniority of the Haya kingdom of Karagwe. Towards the end of the eighteenth century, Buha seems to have increased its power considerably, dominating some of the northern Nyamwezi chiefdoms and providing invaluable assistance to Mukama Ntare VI of Karagwe against a powerful invading army from Bunyoro. Less can be said about the smaller chiefdoms which took root among the western Nyamwezi and neighbouring peoples, except to note that some of them apparently derived from states which had earlier been established by Hima/Tutsi invaders. Thus certain ruling houses among the Galagansa (western Nyamwezi), Sumbwa, Vinza, Tongwe, Bende and Jiji claim origins in Rwanda, Burundi, Buha or Rusuubi. But although their chiefly regalia clearly reveals interlacustrine influence, there is no agreement as to whether or not these dynasties were themselves the work of Hima/Tutsi immigrants.

An exception to this generally obscure situation is Ufipa, situated in the western end of the corridor between Lakes Tanganyika and Rukwa. Here research has brought to light a rich history in the eighteenth century which, among other things, reveals a unique interaction between two of the greatest extended systems of state formation in Bantu-speaking Africa, those of the Luba-Lunda and the East African interlacustrine complexes.[1] A leader called Ntatatkwa ascended the fertile Fipa plateau after migrating from Buluba. In a typical charter myth, he and his people are said to have introduced the cultivation of millet, with its need for co-operative labour, and iron working. Together these two developments, it is said, made it possible to support a larger and

[1] R. G. Willis, 'The Fipa', in A. D. Roberts (ed.), *Tanzania before 1900: seven area histories* (Nairobi, 1968), 82–95.

more highly concentrated population in Ufipa. Perhaps more credibly, it is also asserted that Ntatatkwa introduced the form of territorial chiefship which was one of the hallmarks of the Luba-Lunda system of government. Ntatatkwa established his chiefdom at Milansi, and from there he established subordinate chiefs – fictitious 'sons' of the Milansi paramount – across the plateau. In comparing the impact of these Luban immigrants to others who established a much more limited rule among the nearby Nyiha, the difference in the scale of political organization would appear to have been primarily a function of geography, with the broken mountainous corridor area being much less susceptible to any sort of unified rule than the uninterrupted tableland of Ufipa.

In the middle of the eighteenth century, however, during the reign of Milansi III Ntaseka, a second period of political restructuring was brought to Ufipa by the arrival of Tutsi immigrants from the north. Although their exact provenance remains unknown, these immigrants introduced the Tutsi system of political organization, stressing the personal bond between the ruler and his loyal followers, who governed on his behalf. As the result of a process intermittently peaceful and bellicose, the Tutsi succeeded in replacing the Milansi dynasty with their own Twa dynasty. The chief of Milansi was able to maintain supreme ritual authority over Ufipa, but practical political power was transferred to the Twa. Ufipa had been transformed from a country which appears previously to have been only sparsely populated by wandering hunters, into a stratified kingdom of the Tutsi type. But the final success of the Twa could not have been achieved without the intervening agricultural revolution that is linked in tradition to the Milansi chiefs and their followers. In this the political development of Ufipa was typical of earlier examples of state-building in the interlacustrine region.

Ufipa remained just beyond the reach of influences emanating from the coast throughout the remainder of the eighteenth century. After the Twa had firmly established their hegemony, Ufipa suffered a temporarily disruptive invasion by the Nyiha (although it is not known which Nyiha chiefdoms were involved in this conflict). But the end of the century was marked in particular by the emergence of civil strife between disputing claimants to the Twa chiefship. The result of this internecine struggle was the division of the kingdom into the two rival chiefdoms of Nkansi and Lyangalile, whose continuing struggle for supremacy on the plateau persisted unabated into the first half of the nineteenth century.

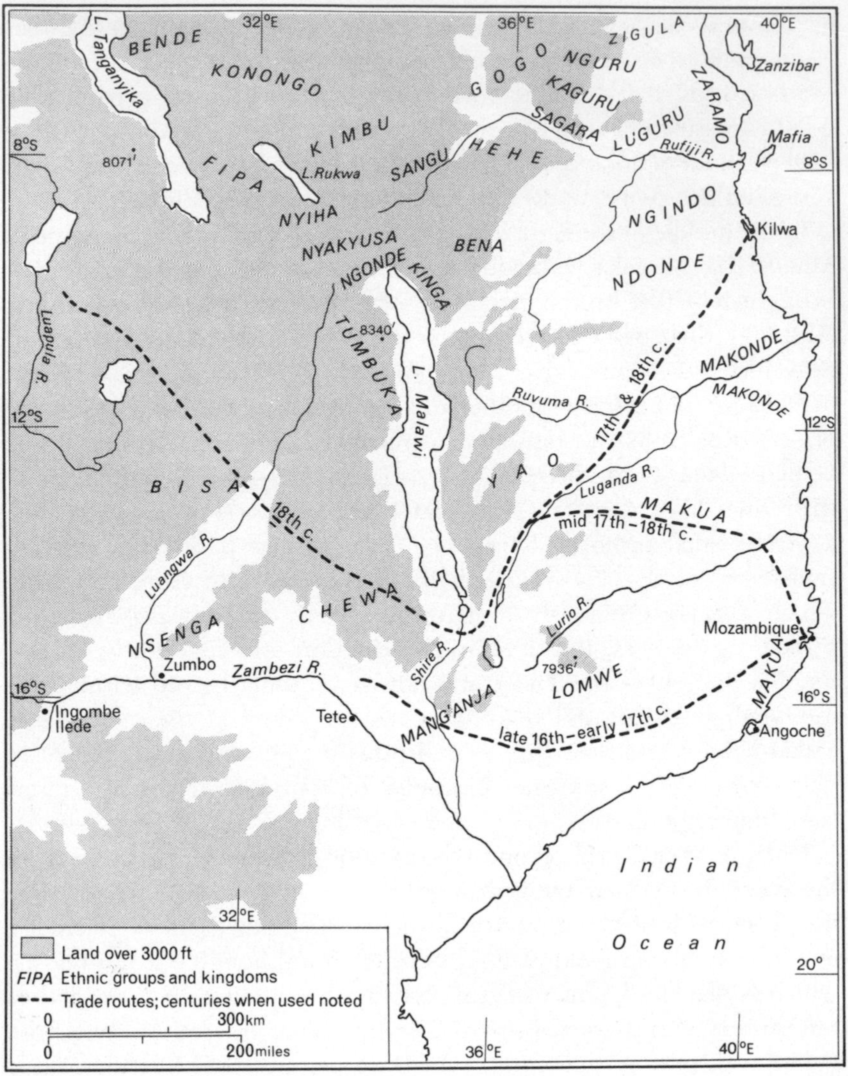

17 Southern East Africa

The history of greater Unyamwezi – including the Nyamwezi, Sukuma, Sumbwa, Kimbu, Galla[1] and Konongo – exhibits the familiar pattern of successive clusters of chiefdoms being established in overlapping sequence by diverse groups of immigrants. This region has also been called the *ntemi* region, since most of the chiefs of greater Unyamwezi bear a variation of this title. More significantly, in the second half of the eighteenth century, this vast area reveals the growth of coastal influences on the history of the interior, including some which are apparently unrelated to the development of the ivory trade to the central Tanzanian coast. That so much detailed knowledge of this area exists is largely due to recent research among the Kimbu,[2] whose country extends from Lake Rukwa northwards into that of the Nyamwezi, to whom the history of the Kimbu during this period and on into the nineteenth century is closely linked. Ukimbu is divided into some thirty-eight distinct chiefdoms, which are associated in clusters according to their place of origin and time of arrival in the land. Ukimbu, an exceedingly dry area, was initially occupied by scattered bands of hunters and gatherers. The first group of immigrants who began to develop the agriculture and political structure of Ukimbu were the Nyisamba, a group combining mixed millet cultivation with hunting and gathering. They claim origins in Usumbwa, which they probably left not long after the Sumbwa chiefdom was founded by its immigrant ruler. This migration then occurred at least no later than the last quarter of the seventeenth century. The Nyisamba established their central chiefdom at Wikangulu, north-east of Lake Rukwa. Before long a number of associated chiefdoms proliferated to the north and west, where their expansion was halted by the arrival of people from Ukonongo, who established the four Nyazina chiefdoms.

The chiefdoms created by the Nyisamba were characterized by a division of power between a ritually important chiefship, to which succession was always matrilineal, and a patrilineal hereditary nobility who exercised political authority. In practice, matrilineal succession to chiefship enabled a commoner to become the father of a chief by marrying the sister of a chief, or her daughter. Thus the people of a chiefdom were bound more closely to their chief. Furthermore, the children of royal women who were married in alliance to the sons of neighbouring chiefs remained within the chiefly family, while potentially ambitious sons-in-law were denied access to the succession. This

[1] The Nyamwezi-speaking Galla are not to be confused with the Cushitic-speaking Galla.

[2] A. Shorter, *Chiefship in western Tanzania* (Oxford, 1972).

system still reserved the important positions of government for the chief's male descendants, who also were responsible for selecting a new chief, but they and their heirs were excluded from succeeding to the chiefship in their own right. Finally, this arrangement kept the office of chief within a single family, and reinforced the special ritual position of the chief within Kimbu society.

A similar constitutional pattern of matrilineal chiefship and patrilineal headmanship was also found during this period among many Nyamwezi and Sukuma chiefdoms. Succession to chiefship among the Kamba chiefdoms of northern Unyamwezi reveals very much the same procedure as occurred among the Kimbu, with ritual officers and headmen, who were themselves ineligible to succeed, selecting and installing the *ntemi*. The investment of the chief was presided over by a special officer, the *kitunga*, who was banished permanently from the chiefdom as soon as the chief was installed. Among the Kimbu this person was called *itéma 'míse*. Similarly, the first councillor of a chiefdom among each of these people – *ngabe* or *mugabe* among the Nyamwezi, *ngabe* or *ntemi ngh̲oja* among the Sukuma, and *mugave* or *umwàantándi* among the Kimbu – was responsible for organizing the installation ceremonies.

Another political device which the Nyisamba introduced into Ukimbu was their symbol of chiefly authority, the wooden ghost-horns. These are large, elaborately carved ceremonial horns which are blown only in honour of the incumbent chief or his ancestors. Their use as a symbol of chiefship has not been reported for any other part of the East African interior, and it separates the Nyisamba group of chiefdoms from those deriving from the interlacustrine region, where the comparable emblem of political office was the royal drum.

Shortly after the Nyisamba were well established in Ukimbu, during the first quarter of the eighteenth century, a new group of chiefly immigrants arrived as part of the widely influential, but little understood, expansion of the Sagara in central Tanzania. In Ukimbu, where they established eight chiefdoms, these people were called Nyitumba. In Unyamwezi they were responsible for the foundation of the eleven important Sagali chiefdoms. At the south end of Lake Rukwa, they established a chiefdom in Ubungu. In Ukimbu the Nyitumba contributed to the agricultural development of this harsh land by bringing a variety of squashes with them, together with a better knowledge of iron smelting and smithing than was possessed by the Nyisamba. They also introduced yet another new symbol of chiefship into western Tanzania, the conus-shell (*conus litteratus*) disc emblem, which is produced by sawing off the base of the shell. Because of the wide dispersal of the various Sagara groups, the conus-shell gained a much wider distribution than the ghost-horn of the Nyisamba, who naturally regarded their own chiefly standard as superior to that of the Nyitumba, although in time each group utilized both symbols. Even before 1800, however, when closer contact with the coast made conus-shells more readily available for distribution and adoption in the interior, the Sagara immigrants seem to have succeeded in spreading the idea of its validity as a new symbol of political authority. At the end of the eighteenth century, the conus-shell disc emblem was introduced into Usumbwa on the return of a trading expedition to the coast which had been led by Kafuku, the son of Chief Imaliza. This manner of introduction soon became common in many of the non-Sagali chiefdoms of western Tanzania, as chief's sons were typically the first to venture to the coast to investigate the trading possibilities in ivory. Among the Sukuma, however, it was the Arabs who introduced the conus-shell itself; but the symbol of the disc emblem had preceded the introduction of the actual article, and the Sukuma fashioned imitations out of vegetable fibres before the shells were made available by the opening of Usukuma to the coastal trade. Even in the secondary Nyitumba chiefdoms of Iswangala Kamanga and Iswangala Mwanisenga, sections of duiker horn and leaden discs were used in place of the conus-shell before its actual introduction.

There are many important questions that need to be asked about the Sagara dispersal during the eighteenth century, but until eastern Tanzania receives the attention of historians that western Tanzania has enjoyed, it is possible only to speculate in the most tentative fashion. Like the chiefly head-dress which was introduced into Tumbukaland by the Balowoka in the later eighteenth century (see below, p. 513), the coastal provenance of the conus-shell disc emblem is quite obvious. But whereas the Balowoka head-dress very clearly derives its symbolic content from its place within the Swahili political cultural tradition, the same automatic link cannot be made for the conus-shell disc emblem, which is a symbol of the sun. Throughout central and western Tanzania, the introduction of both sun symbolism and the disc emblems is generally associated with the Sagara. It is therefore likely that the origin of sun symbolism ought to be looked for in conjunction with the origin of the conus-shell disc emblem at the coast. Sun symbolism in association with royal status has been identified in Pemba island, and may also be represented on at least one example of a more familiar Swahili emblem of political authority, the *siwa* horn.[1] In view of the slowly growing links between the interior and the revitalized *mrima* coast (the stretch between the Pangani and Rufiji rivers) in the eighteenth century; the coastal provenance of the conus-shell itself and its early eighteenth-century introduction into Ukimbu by the Nyitumba; and the likelihood that the links between coast and interior were the product of intersecting and overlapping regional trading networks, it seems reasonable to suggest the possibility that the sun symbol may also trace its origins to coastal, Swahili culture.

While the coming of the Nyisamba and Nyitumba to Ukimbu may possibly have reflected the gradual infiltration of certain coastal symbolic notions of chiefship into the interior by way of Usagara and Ugogo, the beginning of the ivory trade in Ukimbu is traced specifically to the arrival of the third major group of chiefly immigrants, the Igulwibi. The middle decades of the eighteenth century witnessed only minor readjustments in the political structure of Ukimbu. Two Mya chiefdoms were established in Isanga and Isenga by immigrants – probably Baraguyu – from Uhehe; these were later to be early staging points for the vanguard of the Arab and Swahili penetration of the interior. In the south a number of client chiefdoms were established under the hegemony of the Nyisamba by refugees from across Lake Rukwa, possibly fleeing in the wake of the Twa-Milansi contention for political supremacy in Ufipa. But the Igulwibi state unequivocally that they came to Ukimbu from Mount Hanang, near Iramba, in search of elephants. The migration of the Igulwibi is even more complex than those of their forerunners in Ukimbu, but they may ultimately have had links with the Ngulu mountains and possibly even the Pangani valley. When they finally settled in the northern reaches of Ukimbu at the end of the eighteenth century, they established a cluster of six chiefdoms that were known collectively as Nyangwila. Like the Nyitumba before them, their chiefly emblem was the conus-shell disc. The two most important of these Nyangwila chiefdoms were Ngulu and Unyanyembe, extending from Ukimbu into Unyamwezi, the latter of which was shortly to become the focus of Arab activity in central Tanzania.

Here again it is important to recognize that the political organization of the Nyamwezi, although much less well known during this period,

[1] F. B. Pearce, *Zanzibar, the island metropolis of eastern Africa* (London, 1920), 391–3; the *siwa* horn referred to comes from Lamu and is in the personal collection of Edward A. Alpers. Also see Shorter, *Chiefship in western Tanzania*, plate 1, facing p. 20, for a photograph of the ghost-horn of Ilamba chiefdom (Nyisamba group) with a sun symbol carved near the foot.

was similarly composed of several associations of chiefdoms. In Nzega, the Kanga dominated a grouping of twenty-one small chiefdoms; in Tabora, the Sagali ruled nineteen and the Songo fourteen; in Kahama, the Kamba gave rise to a cluster of seven chiefdoms. Within these associations, relationships of seniority were often recognized, although the evidence is much less clear than among the Kimbu. Finally, before the nineteenth century, western Unyamwezi was apparently dominated by the larger chiefdom of Ugalla, much as Buha seems to have been predominant in northern Unyamwezi (see above, p. 500). In Sukumaland, however, although there is evidence that the leadership of many chiefdoms was derived from several important clans, there is no indication that the idea of associations of chiefdoms was ever an important factor in Sukuma history.

As for Unyanyembe, initially it was just another small chiefdom bordering on the Sagali chiefdom of Uyui. Significantly, though, its origin lies in a dispute over elephant hunting rights. Thus, by the end of the eighteenth century the central interior of East Africa, from the north end of Lake Malawi to western Tanzania, was being penetrated by a variety of elephant hunters and ivory traders whose ways of life had been called into being by the economic revival of the coast that was being engineered by the Busa'idi dynasty of Oman. At the same time it is clear that rumours of the new opportunities which the growing demand for ivory (and, in a little while, slaves) generated in the interior lay at the root of most of the early ventures from the interior to the coast, although it is possible that some of these may have been undertaken in order to procure conus-shells. It also bears mentioning that, although Unyanyembe in the nineteenth century was the chiefdom from which caravans headed north to Buganda via Karagwe, during the late eighteenth century no specific crossroads of trade, such as later arose at Tabora, are known to have existed in the central interior. Yet, in a few years there would be scarcely any corner of the interior which had not been drawn into a significant relationship with the coast and its international market economy.

BETWEEN UNYAMWEZI AND THE COAST

The history of southern and eastern Tanzania is not well known during these two centuries. Political units were very localized and they probably proliferated through a regular process of fission. Here, as in so many other regions of Africa, land was plentiful, but not especially productive. Until the development of international trading in the interior during the nineteenth century and the concomitant challenge posed by the intrusion of the Ngoni, there was little reason for political and social units to have been anything but very small. Indeed, where historical research has taken place in this region, among the Hehe, the results confirm the general picture of small-scale migrations and the establishment of a multitude of small chiefships in the period before the great centralizing developments of the mid-nineteenth century. The generic name Hehe only dates from that period of reorganization, so that the history of the Hehe-speaking peoples before about 1850 must again be conceived of in terms of the various chiefdoms and clans who were eventually amalgamated into the larger political unity. These groups were closely related to the Bena and had links with Usagara, in central Tanzania, which provided the ruling Muyinga dynasty of both Hehe and Bena in the nineteenth century. Some time during this period, probably in the eighteenth century, the founder of the Muyinga dynasty migrated to Uhehe in search of game. Other chiefly immigrants came from Ukimbu, while some emigrated from Uhehe north into Ugogo. The Kaguru and Luguru seem also to have been particularly influenced by a steady penetration of immigrants from Uhehe and Ubena. Thus movement was not unidirectional; small groups of people moved both into and out of Uhehe during the eighteenth century, and by the beginning of the nineteenth century there were at least fifteen small, often inter-related chiefdoms among the Hehe. It also seems likely that the history of the Bena and the Sangu was not dissimilar during this period.

To the east of greater Unyamwezi, the intrusion of northern influences appears to have been at least as important as those emanating from the south and the coast during the seventeenth and eighteenth centuries. The expansion of the Masai extended as far south as Ugogo, and significantly affected Gogo culture. Although they remained essentially agriculturalists and retained a diluted form of *ntemi* political leadership that was limited to the ritual authority of clan heads, particularly in respect to rainmaking, the Gogo adopted many of the personal vestments and adornments of the Masai, much as other peoples of the interior were later to adopt Swahili dress. It is not known, however, if pressures from the Masai were a factor in the dissemination of chiefly emigrants from Usagara, the history of which remains a challenging lacuna in the reconstruction of the East African past.

Elsewhere it is possible only to assume that the general pattern of multiple small chiefdoms or clans prevailed in the same context of ever-shifting population movements. Towards the end of the eighteenth century, however, the formation of the Zaramo people provides a focus for appreciating the links that were already developed between the coastal strip and the interior of eastern Tanzania. The causal factor in bringing the similar, but wholly independent, matrilineal peoples of the Dar es Salaam hinterland into being as the Zaramo was an invasion by a number of Kamba hunting parties from the Kamba homelands in the north (see p. 497). Kamba commercial penetration of eastern Tanzania was accomplished by scattered, initially temporary, all-male vanguard colonies of hunters and traders which remained independent from local political authorities in the Pangani valley and throughout the modern Handeni region. Trading local products of their own manufacture, the single purpose of these Kamba colonies seems to have been to acquire ivory for trading to the Mombasa coast. Their intrusion into eastern Tanzania probably served as an additional stimulus to the penetration of western Tanzania by peoples of the eastern interior. In fact, the existence in northern Unyamwezi of the seven Kamba chiefdoms seems to indicate that at least some Kamba colonies pursued the possibilities of hunting and trading in western Tanzania for themselves.

The Kamba invasion of the *mrima* coastal belt was a particular threat to the recently established small Swahili communities of Bagamoyo and Dar es Salaam. Unable to fend off the Kamba by themselves, the people of these settlements called upon a well known Kutu hunter from Lukelele, well up-country in the Ruvu valley, who was known variously as Pazi Kilama or Kibamanduka. Pazi was offered gifts of salt and other items in exchange for his military assistance. Together with a number of Doe allies from the country north of Uzaramo, Pazi succeeded in defeating the Kamba and in driving them from the *mrima* hinterland. In the aftermath of his triumph, Pazi established a number of Kutu settlements in Uzaramo and exacted a yearly tribute which became known as the *kanda la Pazi* from the two towns that had called upon him for aid. In the nineteenth century, when Busa'idi control over Zanzibar and the coast became more effective under Sayyid Sa'id b. Sulṭān, the payment of this tax became the responsibility of the sultan of Zanzibar. In the late eighteenth century, however, there was no effective recourse to Zanzibar for military or other assistance by the newly established Swahili towns of the *mrima* coast. Faced with a challenge like that of the Kamba invasion, they had to rely upon assistance from the non-Swahili peoples of the mainland in order to maintain their communities intact. As for the Kutu settlements in

Uzaramo, these became the foci for the emergence of a culturally unified, though politically fragmented, Zaramo people. Thereafter all Zaramo chiefs carried the title of *pazi*.

A final example of the potential political significance of famous hunters in late eighteenth-century East Africa links the otherwise unknown history of the Ngulu to the much better appreciated history of the Shambaa. Most of the turmoil in the lower Pangani valley during the eighteenth century was the direct result of Masai expansion (see above, pp. 495–7). The Chaga appear to have been able to protect themselves from these pressures by remaining safely within the confines of the forested middle belt of Mount Kilimanjaro. The Pare were apparently more preoccupied with the changing political situation that was being brought about by the progressive integration of northern and southern Upare, with their different systems of political organization. They seem also to have succeeded in absorbing those Mbugu who settled with their cattle in Upare. The Shambaa, however, were faced with a much more serious challenge from Masai raiders, and especially from the large-scale immigration of cattle-keeping Mbugu and Nango refugees from the Masai steppe. It would appear that the survival of Shambaa culture and society was imperilled by this combination of factors. That the Shambaa did not succumb to them is largely due to the arrival of a famous hunter from Ngulu, named Mbegha, and the foundation of the Kilindi dynasty whose absolute authority over a new Shambaa kingdom was established by his descendants.

In contrast to the official history of the Kilindi dynasty, which was recorded initially by Abdallah bin Hemedi al-Ajjemy at the turn of the nineteenth century, and which represents one of the earliest published examples of East African historiography, a re-examination of Shambaa history indicates that Mbegha never held effective political power himself.[1] His popularity stemmed from his ability as a hunter and a provider of meat, while his main function politically seems to have been that of impartial arbiter of disputes between the various communities vying for control of Usambara. Mbegha eventually solidified his ties with the Shambaa by marrying the daughter of Mbogho, the powerful head of the immigrant Nango community. Effective Kilindi domination over Usambara was finally brought about by the son of this political union, Bughe, who killed his grandfather, Mbogho, and seized the emblems of royal authority for himself and his family line. Usambara

[1] Abdallah bin Hemedi, *Habari za Wakilindi* (Nairobi, 1963); S. Feierman, *The Shambaa Kingdom* (Madison, 1974).

being a very divided community in the eighteenth century, it is not difficult to perceive that there would have been at least as many people who supported this coup as opposed it. In the end, the Kilindi totally reorganized the political structure of Usambara. Vugha became the capital of the *simba mwene*, or lion-king, who ruled his domain with a very authoritarian hand, although the Kilindi made a specific accommodation with the powerful Nango community. Culturally the Kilindi became Shambaa, and the rituals over which they officiated were Shambaa, not Ngulu, rituals. By the end of the eighteenth century the Kilindi kingdom was well established, but the accession of *simba mwene* Kinyashi, an independent-minded and aggressive warrior, caused a split in the kingdom. The disappointed claimant, his full brother, Maghembe, fled to Mshihwi, in the inaccessible north-eastern extremity of the Usambara mountains, where he successfully defended the independence of a second Kilindi kingdom against the repeated punitive attacks of Kinyashi. By about 1800, then, two independent Kilindi kingdoms controlled Usambara. Mshihwi, the smaller, remained an exclusively Shambaa state; Vugha, the major kingdom, embarked on a larger phase of imperial expansion which, although it resulted initially in the death in battle against the Zigua of Kinyashi, was eventually to lead to the inclusion of alien territories and peoples to both the east and west of Usambara under the dynamic leadership of Kimweri ye Nyumbai.

BETWEEN LAKES TANGANYIKA AND MALAWI

The picture of social and political growth is much the same in the corridor area between Lakes Tanganyika and Malawi at this time. Among the Nyiha, who live immediately east of Ufipa and south of Ukimbu, a dozen petty chiefdoms derived from at least three different areas of origin. The Simbeya group of chiefdoms claims Luban origins by way of Ubisa, and asserts its links with the Kyungu dynasty in Bungonde to the south, although this is quite different from what the traditions of the Ngonde have to say. Two other smaller chiefdoms also claim to have come from present-day Zambia, while the Nzowa and Mwamlima dynasties are said to have derived independently from Ugogo. The chronology of these migrations is very uncertain, but they would appear to have taken place over a period of years from possibly as early as 1600 to about the middle of the eighteenth century. Here, too, as in Uhehe and the remainder of the southern highlands-corridor area, detailed knowledge of the past begins no earlier than the middle of the nineteenth century.[1]

The suggestion that the central interior represents a transitional zone between the internal developments of the northern interior and the increasingly externally influenced developments in the southern interior and on the coast is nowhere more clearly demonstrated than in the contrasting histories of the Nyakyusa, Ngonde and Tumbuka peoples who live in the plains and highlands at the extreme north-west corner of Lake Malawi. While they border to the south with Chewa country, the Tumbuka were at no time significantly affected by the important developments taking place there, although the *undi*'s kingdom is known to have included some Tumbuka-speakers in the first half of the nineteenth century (see below, pp. 520–1). Until very recent times, in fact, there was no historical unity among Tumbuka-speakers, their historical experience being focussed instead upon the many family groups and clans that composed the broader, evolving linguistic group. The subdivisions of Tumbuka country into a northern and a southern zone, which is based upon differences in systems of inheritance (patrilineal in the north, matrilineal in the south), religious systems, and early chiefly regalia, do not alter this situation in any way. Rather, together with recent lexical analysis of the Tumbuka language, they indicate the diverse origins of the many groups that came together to form the Tumbuka-speaking peoples during the eighteenth century.

In the north of Tumbuka country, the Phoka group traces its origins to northern immigrants who arrived in the early eighteenth century or earlier, and became intermingled with the sparse, pre-existing Tumbuka-speaking population. At about the same time, the Nkhamanga area was being similarly transformed by immigrants from the west. These were soon followed by small groups from other points of the compass. The immigrants succeeded in imposing their political organization over localized areas of the country, with some clans becoming more important than others, while in the process they adopted the language of the original inhabitants. In the Henga district, the immigrants were predominately from what is now southern Tanzania, with the important Hango clan claiming origins in Ubena. Although there can be no certainty about the reasons for these various migrations, at least some of the northern groups testify that they were seeking new opportunities for trading salt and iron, while those from the west were probably uprooted as part of the final eastward push of peoples from the Luba-

[1] Beverley Brock, 'The Nyiha', in Roberts, ed., *Tanzania before 1900*, 59–81.

Lunda area. In these restricted, scattered communities there was little need for strong central government. Most political power rested with local chiefs and clan heads, although several paramount chiefships with ritual, rather than effective political, authority flourished by the middle of the eighteenth century.

A totally different group of immigrants arrived in Tumbuka country in about 1780. These were the Balowoka, who take their name from the eponymous leader of their migration, Mlowoka, a praise name meaning 'he who crossed over [the lake]'. The Balowoka were ivory hunters who were attracted across the north end of Lake Malawi because they had heard of the extensive supply of ivory in Tumbuka country. Of their origins nothing is known; they may well have been Yao affecting coastal manners, for they are said to have come 'as Arabs'. The rumours of potential wealth proved to be reliable, and the Balowoka found themselves among a people who appeared to have had no conception of the economic value of ivory. Equally important, there was no single source of authority, ritual or political, among the Tumbuka that might have been able to organize a coherent and unified response to the new trading opportunity offered by the Balowoka. Very soon, then, the Balowoka ensured their ability to hunt and trade without impediment among the Tumbuka. Mlowoka established a loose hegemony over the local chiefs by treating them with respect, by marrying their daughters to himself and his cohorts, and by distributing exotic trade goods as gifts to them. How long this process of binding the chiefs to him took is uncertain, but his final ascension to the position of trading overlord of the Tumbuka-speaking area was marked by his distribution of a new symbol of chiefly authority, a dark blue or black turban, which clearly reflects the coastally linked origins of the Balowoka migration.

Despite this, Mlowoka himself seems never to have held political office among the Tumbuka. This role was left to his son, Gonapamuhanya, who established the Chikulamayembe line in the first decade of the nineteenth century. For himself and his followers, Mlowoka was content to protect rich Tumbuka hunting grounds, and to foster the east-west trade route linking the Luangwa watershed and the Bisa ivory trade to the lakeshore and, ultimately, to the coast. The Balowoka came as traders, and their interests and local strategies were defined in this context. The situation obtaining among the Tumbuka did not necessitate direct political intervention, so none was attempted. In this tailoring of their trading interests to the specific political situation of the Tumbuka, the Balowoka were setting a pattern that would be followed by the Arabs, Swahili, and various intrusive African entrepreneurs in the nineteenth century. While the general economic impact of the growing links between coast and interior was to subordinate African trading economies to the world market system, the political impact of immigrant traders who were helping to create those links varied according to the specific pre-existing local situation in the interior.

A vivid contrast to the Tumbuka political situation as it was evolving under the Balowoka at the end of the eighteenth century is provided by their immediate neighbours to the north, the Ngonde. Certain traditions of the ruling Kyungu dynasty and fragmentary remains of glass beads, blue and white porcelain and cowrie shells at Mbande Hill (*c.* 1400) have led to a reconstruction of Ngonde history which sees the early formation of a centralized state based on trade to the coast. None of this conforms to what is known elsewhere in eastern Africa at this time, and it seems more credible to see in the royal traditions a projection of events from the more recent into the more distant past. Instead, it can be argued that the ritually powerful *kyungus* exercised no more secular authority than did the *lwembes* among the geographically isolated, but very closely related Nyakyusa to the north. Here there was never a unified kingdom, but a multiplicity of independent, yet linked small chiefdoms, in which ritually important chiefs remained politically dependent on their headmen, as in greater Unyamwezi.

Among the Ngonde, however, other traditions of the Kyungu dynasty recall an opening up to the coastal ivory trade at about the same time as the country of the Tumbuka, during the reign of the tenth *kyungu*, in the last two decades of the eighteenth century. Unlike the situation to the south, however, the traders who forged a route across the northern tip of the lake here found themselves in contact with a people who recognized a widely acknowledged and ritually powerful authority. The *kyungu* appears to have served as the representative of his people in the initial dealings with the traders and he soon turned the new situation to his advantage. Steadily he increased his economic power through his control of the export trade in ivory and his resultant ability to distribute its proceeds among his followers. No longer constitutionally limited by his dependence upon the hereditary nobles for the provision of tribute, he was able to limit the scope of their authority so that in time they became clearly subordinate to him in secular, as well as religious matters. The transformation of Ngonde political structure which was brought about by the opening of the coastal ivory trade, with its implicit conflict between the authority of a ritually powerful paramount chief and politically powerful hereditary nobles, foreshadows later developments elsewhere in East Africa during the nineteenth century. It also suggests that the coastal traders who had opened up Ngonde to the ivory trade were content to do business with a single, powerful local authority, and that they did not themselves have any reason for superimposing their own commercial hegemony over the Ngonde in direct contrast to the actions at the same time of the Balowoka in Tumbuka. Until the arrival of coastal traders from across the lake in the late eighteenth century, then, it is much more likely that effective political power was no more centralized among the Ngonde than it was among the Tumbuka and Nyakyusa, or indeed among the peoples of greater Unyamwezi, where the Sukuma apparently enjoyed an isolation from most of these developments that allowed them to remain as politically fragmented as the Nyakyusa.*

NORTH OF THE ZAMBEZI

If the northern and central interior of eastern Africa shows that population movements in precolonial Africa were generally piecemeal and gradual, that they involved an intricate interweaving of indigenous and immigrant cultures, rather than a wholesale replacement of earlier populations, then it is in the southern interior that the two most heralded exceptions are generally believed to have occurred. Yet even in these cases the process of interaction was no more one-sided than, for example, was Ruhinda's invasion of the Haya states after 1500. The later and best known of these mass invasions was that of the Ngoni, who forded the Zambezi river in November 1835. The earlier invading horde was the heterogeneous Zimba, whose outburst from the Zambezi valley in the waning years of the sixteenth century so greatly impressed contemporary Portuguese observers, in particular the Dominican chronicler, João dos Santos, that the Zimba have acquired a position, regrettably misunderstood, of mythical proportions that until recently was matched only by the equally notorious Jaga of West-Central Africa. Earlier treatments of this period in the southern interior of East Africa are dominated by the garbled and bowdlerized version of Dos Santos's masterpiece published in 1625 by Samuel Purchas. Since the route of the Zimba is believed to have extended from the middle

* This was written before the completion of the thesis by O. Kalinga which considerably modifies previous interpretations of Ngonde history. [Ed.]

reaches of the Zambezi valley to the East African coast as far north as Malindi, in what is now Kenya, it is appropriate to begin an interpretation of the seventeenth and eighteenth centuries in this part of East Africa with a reconsideration of their origins, the reasons for their movement, and their impact on the societies who lay in their path.

The view that the Zimba were merely a savage horde has always been suspect on both cultural and historical grounds: culturally, because Europeans were ever too willing to accept uncritically, and to perpetuate for their own purposes, the idea that Africans were uncivilized; historically, because earlier interpretations of the phenomenon of the Zimba explosion did not challenge the ahistorical notion that things simply happen for no apparent reason and with no apparent purpose. New attitudes towards the writing of African history and the discovery of new sources now enable us to see that the stirrings of the peoples called Zimba were a direct response to the impact of Portuguese penetration up the Zambezi river after 1530.

As economic motivation dominated Portuguese activities in the Zambezi valley from the very beginning, so they appear to have determined African responses to their intrusion. Although the evidence is not wholly conclusive, it can be argued that African societies to the north of the river had been trading directly with coastal merchants in ivory and other products at various locations along the Zambezi since about AD 1400, when Ingombe Ilede, in Zambia, near Lake Kariba, was in contact with active trading to the coast. During this period a number of important kingdoms were taking shape among the Maravi, who occupied the northern hinterland of the central Zambezian reaches in what is now eastern Zambia, the Tete province of Mozambique, and central and southern Malawi.

By the late sixteenth century, the major Maravi kingdoms were well established under the leadership of the ruling Phiri clan. While recognizing the nominal paramountcy of the *kalonga*, whose authority derived from the leadership which his line had provided during the Phiri migration from Buluba, each chief strove to strengthen and extend his own kingdom. Indeed, the opportunity to trade in ivory at points along the north bank of the Zambezi probably became a major cause of contention between the more important Phiri chiefs, especially during the sixteenth century. Thus, when the Portuguese finally succeeded in driving coastal traders out of middle Zambezia in the 1570s, the Phiri chiefs of the Maravi were suddenly deprived of their access to the Indian Ocean ivory market, which had apparently become an important basis for their [illegible] political authority. Still blinded by the lure of gold, the Portu[illegible]d not discovered that the greatest commercial wealth of north[illegible]mbezia was its ivory. Where they knew of no gold they were n[illegible] willing to turn, and until the discovery of gold in the *undi*'s Chewa kingdom in the eighteenth century, they not only made no effort to cultivate the ivory trade of the north bank of the river, they actually seem to have discouraged it. For the Phiri chiefs, the Portuguese did not offer themselves as substitutes for the coastal traders. They could only have appeared as a most unwelcome and seriously disruptive new factor in the political economy of these competing kingdoms.

It is in this context that the Zimba come to make sense and to take on historical proportions. It can now be asserted with some confidence that the warriors called Zimba were controlled by the *lundu*, chief of the Mang'anja of the lower Shire valley, whose open conflict with the *kalonga* dominates the political history of the region for about half a century until the *lundu* was defeated by the great Kalonga Muzura in 1622.[1] After the Portuguese gained the upper hand along the middle reaches of the Zambezi, it would appear that the *lundu* was in a favourable position to control the Muslim coastal traders who continued to operate through Angoche, located between the Zambezi delta and Mozambique island. The *lundu* would therefore have been able to prohibit their movement beyond his town on the west bank of the lower Shire, which now became the only route available to them into northern Zambezia, and he would have been quick to turn this situation to his own advantage and to use it to build up a position of strength against his nominal overlord. But although the *lundu* was clearly becoming a menace to the *kalonga*'s traditional position of hegemony, he was unable to expand his domain to the west, as the *kalonga* held his ground, presumably on the basis of his pre-existing strength. Ambitious and seeking an outlet for the increasingly impatient energies of his followers, the *lundu* at last, in the mid-1580s, turned loose his forces in a campaign directed locally against the Portuguese and eastwards against the Makua-Lomwe peoples of northern Mozambique. The vanguard of this expansion were known as the Zimba.

How the *lundu*'s warriors acquired this name is not known. For the Portuguese, 'Zimba' seems to have been a generic term that they applied to almost any northern Zambezia marauders. Whether the name 'Zimba' was used in this same context by the Maravi in the late six-

[1] Georg Schurhammer, 'Die Entdeckung des Njassa-Sees', *Stimmen der Zeit*, 1920, 349.

teenth century is a matter for speculation; but it is the only name that has come down to us from that period of great confusion and little Portuguese familiarity with the peoples of the region. To the east of the Shire river, the epithet seems to have lost the universal currency that it enjoyed among the Portuguese of Zambezia. Traditions from the area surrounding Angoche clearly identify these same invaders as 'the men of Lundu'. In the immediate hinterland of Mozambique island and Cape Delgado they carried no specific name. Here, however, it is important to focus upon the significance of the *lundu*'s invading force for the history of the Maravi.

At first sight, the most that can be read into the record, which is wholly deficient on this problem, is the suggestion that the *lundu* was able to draw some immediate benefit from his imperial venture in the form of tribute. It seems less likely, however, that he was ever able to capitalize completely on his control of the eastern marches of his newly created realm by securing any direct, regular trading connections with the coast. Indeed, the tremendous expansion of his influence quite probably dissipated much of his fighting capacity at the centre of his kingdom. Having extended his authority hundreds of miles beyond the Maravi homeland, he found himself once again in a precarious position on his western frontier, where his aggressiveness had perhaps contributed to an alliance between the Portuguese and Kalonga Muzura. The *lundu*'s defeat did not occur at once, to be sure, nearly forty years elapsing from the irruption of his warriors to the defeat in 1622. But so far as the Portuguese were concerned, the early years of the seventeenth century in northern Zambezia were dominated by the rise of Kalonga Muzura to a position of imperial authority. In 1608, Muzura ordered 4,000 troops across the Zambezi to assist the Portuguese in their efforts to preserve the authority of Mwene Mutapa Gatsi Rusere. Although it seems probable that the Portuguese needed Muzura more than he needed them, he maintained the alliance of convenience until the final subjugation of the *lundu* was effected by a joint campaign with the Portuguese and their African levies. Once assured of his complete domination of the Maravi world, Muzura was in a position to exercise his very considerable might against his former allies. Not many months after the defeat of the *lundu*, on the occasion of Gatsi Rusere's death in 1623, his army stormed across the Zambezi, seizing a sizeable haul of booty and very nearly destroying all Portuguese operations on the Zambezi. This demonstration of military vitality and sheer audacity clearly established that the *kalonga* was indeed the master of northern

Zambezia. Nor was Muzura unaware of this fact. As the Portuguese chronicler, António Bocarro, recorded in 1635, 'This Muzura, vainglorious with the victories that he had attained against the other Kaffirs, was no longer content to be addressed as King and wanted all to recognize him as Emperor, threatening already to [assume the position] of Mwene Mutapa, who is addressed by this title of Emperor'.[1]

From 1622 onwards, Portuguese accounts describe the Maravi empire as stretching from Maravi country itself far away eastwards to the coast, where it extended from the mouth of the Zambezi to perhaps some fifty kilometres north of Mozambique island. Kalonga Muzura's creation was essentially an over-kingdom. Effective political authority remained localized in the respective kingdoms and chiefdoms of the Maravi and the Makua-Lomwe who were its subjects. The *kalonga*'s constitutional authority among the Phiri chiefs rested upon his genealogical position as senior chief among all the earlier Phiri invaders, while his effective authority depended upon his proven military superiority and the knowledge that he could bring his army into play in any crucial situation. The final basis of his authority and strength may well have been his consequent ability to control the newly developed overland ivory trade to the coast at Mozambique island. Before the 1630s, trade with the hinterland of the Portuguese stronghold had been expressly prohibited to its colonists by the royal edict that all trade was to be directed to the Zambezi settlements under the monopoly of the governor of the rivers of Sena, as the Portuguese called their Zambezian administration. But as a belated reward for their services in defending the fortress of São Sebastião against the seige that was laid by the Dutch in 1608, this ban was lifted, and the trade of Macuana, as the Portuguese called the coastal hinterland and its farther interior, was granted exclusively to the colonists of Mozambique island. For the next fifty years or so, this trade appears to have been the most tangible evidence of the existence of the extended Maravi empire. Portuguese references to the military strength of the Maravi at Quelimane and near Mossuril, on the mainland opposite Mozambique island, also indicate that the Maravi domination of the Makua-Lomwe peoples remained a significant factor during this half-century.

By the beginning of the eighteenth century, however, the Maravi empire appears to have collapsed. To the east, the *kalonga*'s control of the trade to Macuana was challenged and superseded by the rise of the

[1] A. B. Bragança Pereira, ed., *Arquivo Português Oriental*, nova edição, tomo IV, volume II parte I (Bastorá, 1937), 14, and British Museum, Sloane MS. 197, fol. 100.

Yao, who were never subordinated by the Maravi and who appear to have been able to consolidate their strength by drawing upon the trade of both Kilwa and Mossuril. But the principal cause of its dissipation was more likely the inherent inner weakness of the imperial structure and the fact that Muzura's successors were unable to maintain the military advantage that he had developed. The decentralized nature of the *kalonga*'s political domination made it impossible for him to achieve any social control over the Makua-Lomwe peoples, who had indeed been more significantly influenced by the *lundu*'s sub-system than by the imperial *kalonga* superstructure. By the end of the seventeenth century, neither the *kalonga* nor the *lundu* appears to have exercised any effective political control over the Makua-Lomwe peoples who lived beyond the Shire valley. At the same time there is reason to believe that, in the west, the expansion of the *undi*'s Chewa kingdom may have aggravated the *kalonga*'s decline by posing a direct challenge to the *kalonga*'s more immediate domain to the south-west of Lake Malawi. Finally, the pattern of Phiri state-building suggests that conflict and fragmentation within the ruling Phiri clan of the *kalonga* was another fundamental cause of imperial decline. The *kalonga*, like the *lundu* before and the *undi* afterwards, had overreached the capacity of Phiri political structure and had thereby fatally exposed his political system to both internal and external attack. Thereafter the Phiri chiefship of the *kalonga* was little more than a shadow of its former self.

During the eighteenth century, the dominant political authority among the Maravi was the *undi*. The exclusion of the Portuguese from any direct involvement in the Rozvi empire from the end of the seventeenth century (see p. 400) had forced a reorientation of their commercial activities to the north, where they began to develop their relations with the *undi*, who was able to control the trade and to use it for strengthening his own position by redistributing part of the proceeds that came from it. Indeed, in this period of expansion from the late seventeenth century through the early eighteenth century, the *undi*'s kingdom seems to have dealt more successfully than did those of the *lundu* and the *kalonga* with the persistent problem of political fragmentation. But from the middle of the eighteenth century, the *undi* began to lose control over these external agents of change, and the process of disintegration started.

By 1750, gold had been discovered in his territory. A number of concessions were granted to individual Portuguese holders of crown-estates (*prazos*) who worked the mines with slave labour. Almost immediately the *undi*'s attempts to assert his control over their activities proved ineffectual. When locally established Portuguese and their *chikunda* (armed slave retainers) began to trade directly with subordinate chiefs for ivory and other items, and to hunt elephants themselves, the situation was further aggravated. Moreover, by this time both the Bisa, who were coming to dominate the carrying trade from the Luangwa river to the recently established eastern Lunda state of the *mwata kazembe*, and Yao ivory traders were operating within the *undi*'s kingdom. Consequently, the *undi*'s former trading connection – the source of much of his economic ability to bind his junior chiefs to his side – was effectively severed at its source. But perhaps even more important in this respect was the historical Portuguese fascination with gold. Once the gold rush was on, the official Portuguese establishment virtually lost any interest in acquiring other varieties of wealth from the *undi*'s domain. By the end of the eighteenth century, the *undi*'s once large and unusually well-controlled Chewa kingdom was following its more grandiose if less stable predecessors, the victim of its own internal weakness and, more clearly, of the external intruders.

The gradual decline of the *undi*'s effective hegemony after 1750 was paralleled by the rise of the *prazo*-holder. Unlike the Portuguese officials and the settlers who inhabited the principal Zambezi towns, the *prazo*-holders – Portuguese, Goan, and mestizo alike – were sufficiently Africanized in their outlook to appreciate that there were other forms of wealth to be procured in the *undi*'s lands. Although none were as militarily powerful as those who operated south of the Zambezi during the seventeenth century, at least one *prazo* family, the Caetano Pereiras, had gained sufficient strength to begin to play a comparable role in the context of the declining Maravi political system by the end of the eighteenth century. Almost nothing is known about their earlier activities, but the location of their settlement at the mining centre of Java, five days' march from Tete, and the fact that the progenitor of the line, Gonçalo Caetano Pereira, was at one stage in his career appointed Captain-Major of Mixonga, suggests that they were involved in the campaigns against the *biwi*, a chief under the *undi*, in 1755–63. By 1793 Gonçalo was trading with the Bisa; three years later he was in direct contact with the *mwata kazembe*.[1] His son, Pedro, forged an alliance with the *undi* – an alliance at once military, political, economic, and matrimonial – and in return was granted authority by

[1] Francisco José de Lacerda e Almeida, *Travessia da África* (Lisbon, 1936), 385 and 394.

the *undi* over the outlying region of Makanga. From his base in Makanga, he laid the foundations for the over-kingdom that, in the nineteenth century, came to dominate the western reaches of northern Zambezia and earned him the epithet of *Chamatowa*, 'the conqueror'.

The africanization of the Caetano Pereiras was later duplicated by other *prazo* families. In the context of Afro-European frontier studies, their search for political legitimacy from every available quarter, and their acculturation to the African surroundings in which they found themselves, bears a striking resemblance to the development of Griqua frontier states in Transorangia in South Africa during the late eighteenth and early nineteenth centuries.[1] But they also represent an aspect of the same familiar pattern of interaction between immigrant groups and indigenous populations that characterizes so much of the precolonial history of Africa, including that of the northern and central interior of East Africa during the seventeenth and eighteenth centuries. The only significant difference with the *prazo*-holders in northern Zambezia at this time was that the intrusive element was non-African, rather than African.

Although the eastward invasion of the *lundu*'s Zimba warriors did not permanently affect the development of Maravi society, it had quite the opposite impact on the conquered Makua-Lomwe peoples of northern Mozambique. Contemporary documentation is completely lacking, however, so that the reconstruction of how these lasting influences were established must necessarily be inferred from our knowledge of the invasion in the late sixteenth century and scattered accounts of the situation during the twentieth century. The two major aspects of the *lundu*'s impact in this region were political and religious, the one being intimately linked to the other. In the hinterland of Angoche in the early 1900s, Eduardo do Couto Lupi found that virtually all important chiefs in the district claimed an origin from the *lundu*. How effectively the *lundu* ever controlled their activities after 1600 is a matter for speculation. The account of the Jesuit, Manuel Barreto, however, leaves no doubt that in the 1660s the Maravi occupied a superior social position among the Makua-Lomwe, and the maintenance of identification with the *lundu* after more than three centuries is a testimony to the pervasiveness and durability of his prestige. Even more impressive is the modern vitality of the M'Bona cult, which was and is

[1] This subject is brilliantly explored by Martin Legassick, 'The Griqua, the Sotho-Tswana, and the missionaries, 1780–1840: the politics of a frontier zone', unpublished Ph.D. thesis (University of California, Los Angeles, 1969).

still intimately linked to the *lundu* paramountcy, among the people who inhabit the northern banks of the Zambezi river below the Shire confluence. In the twentieth century, the cult's worship has been observed among the Phodzo, to the south of the Zambezi delta, beyond the boundaries of the *lundu*'s known political control, as well as in Manganja da Costa, just south of Angoche. The M'Bona cult offered the southern Makua-Lomwe, with their highly segmentary political system, access to an unprecedented source of religious strength in times of trouble. By providing for local control of the shrines it could serve as an agency through which to express dissent, but the fact that the M'Bona cult was a Mang'anja institution, implicitly reinforced the cultural prestige of the *lundu* paramountcy and, more generally, of the Maravi, wherever it was accepted by the non-Mang'anja peoples.[1]

Among the northern Makua-Lomwe peoples, the impact of the *lundu*'s invasion is rather more difficult to perceive. If claims of chiefly origins from the *lundu*, and the M'Bona cult, enjoy any currency to the north of Manganja da Costa, they have not been recorded to date. Indeed, in the northern reaches of Makua-Lomwe country, the prevalent focus of reported religious practice in the twentieth century is, at its most centralized level, worship of the High God through the medium of the chiefly 'ancestral' spirits. This in turn may well be related to the fact that political authority, while by no means especially strong, is more centralized among the northern than among the southern Makua-Lomwe. This greater degree of political centralization may also trace its origins to the impact of the *lundu*'s invasion on the northern Makua-Lomwe.

Sometime before 1585, a powerful Makua chief, with the title *maurusa*, moved with his followers from the Macuana interior into the area opposite Mozambique island. For several years his warriors ravaged the coastal hinterland, until in 1585 the Portuguese felt compelled to mount an expedition against him. Almost the entire Portuguese column was obliterated, and the *maurusa* was permanently established in Uticulo (Tugulu) as the most powerful Makua paramount chief on the mainland until the Portuguese conquest of Macuana at the very end of the nineteenth century. The most probable explanation for his sudden appearance in coastal Macuana is that he was pushed from his

[1] Eduardo do Couto Lupi, *Angoche: breve memoria sobre uma das capitanias mores do districto de Moçambique* (Lisbon, 1907); M. Barreto, in G. M. Theal, *Records of South-Eastern Africa* (London, 1898–1903), vol. III; M. Schoffeleers, 'The history and political role of the M'Bona cult among the Manganja', in T. O. Ranger and I. Kimambo, eds., *The historical study of African religion* (London, 1972), 73–94.

homeland farther inland by the repercussions of the *lundu*'s imperial expansion, his polity being forged in response to (and apparently in flight from) the *lundu*'s challenge. Thus, like the *mfecane* some two and a half centuries later, a significant ramification of Maravi empire-building in the sixteenth and seventeenth centuries may well have been the creation of new and stronger political structures among contiguous unconquered peoples.

The *maurusa* paramountcy does not appear in the available seventeenth-century documentation, but it was probably affected by the growth of the long distance trade route that was pioneered between northern Zambezia and Mozambique island by the Maravi (see above, p. 519). More immediately, its formation was certainly influenced by the development of the trade of Macuana by the colonists of the Portuguese administrative capital, although in what manner it is impossible to surmise. As the Maravi were displaced by the Yao during the last half of the seventeenth century, however, and their southern route to Mozambique island was superseded by a more northerly one from Yao territory, the *maurusa* found himself squarely athwart the path of the Yao as they descended from the interior plateau to the coastal plains. Until the end of the eighteenth century, the *maurusa*'s relations with both the Portuguese and the Yao, not to mention those of all the petty Makua chiefs of coastal Macuana, were dominated by the desire to maintain some control over the lucrative ivory trade that the Yao were driving to Mozambique island. For their part, of course, both the Yao and the Portuguese, including the Indian Banian traders who actually financed and handled the trade of both the island and the mainland, wished to avert a situation in which the Makua chiefs succeeded in establishing themselves as effective middlemen.

Almost nothing concrete can be said about Yao history in the seventeenth century. But by 1616, when Bocarro travelled overland from Tete on the Zambezi to Kilwa off the southern coast of Tanzania, right through the heart of what is now Yao territory, it is virtually certain that the Yao were already developing those impressive commercial skills which were to dominate the trade of the southern interior of East Africa until the imposition of colonial rule. During the seventeenth century the Yao appear to have carried most of their ivory to Kilwa, which enjoyed a mild revival under Portuguese tutelage after having been disastrously ravaged by both the Portuguese and the Zimba in the sixteenth century. Eventually they must also have come into contact with the outermost fringes of the comparably growing trade of Macuana. As Yao trading acumen advanced and the far-flung Maravi trading links disintegrated, the Yao also gained the upper hand in the traffic between the Lake Malawi region and the Mozambique coast.

The commercial decline of Kilwa during the first half of the eighteenth century completely changed the trading situation in northern Mozambique. The Yao had no difficulty in perceiving the realities of the market, and very rapidly they made Mozambique their primary outlet on the East African coast. By the middle of the eighteenth century, the Yao ivory trade comprised some 90 per cent of the regional trade of the island capital, and was one of the mainstays of the entire commercial economy of the newly organized Portuguese administration of Mozambique, which until 1752 had been subordinate to the viceroy at Goa. This sudden and overwhelming importance of the trade of the Yao to Mozambique island greatly intensified the competition for control of the carrying trade of Macuana, which undoubtedly traced its origins back into the second half of the seventeenth century. The middle decades of the eighteenth century were dominated by a continuous series of sporadic military conflicts involving the Makua (in every instance), the Portuguese and the Yao. On the Portuguese side there was, in addition, a constant meddling in the monopolistic trading operations of the Banian community of Mozambique island that always worked to the disadvantage of all parties concerned, the Yao included.

While the conditions of trade in Macuana deteriorated, the commercial fortunes of Kilwa revived under the influence of the Busa'idi dynasty of Oman. By the mid-1780s the Yao had therefore redirected the overwhelming bulk of their trade to Kilwa, and their trade to Mozambique island was reduced to a bare fraction of its mid-century proportions. In the space of a single century the Yao had demonstrated the depth of their entrepreneurial commitment by responding immediately and intelligently to the rapidly changing market conditions of the coast, which was at once the source of demand for the raw materials of the continent and the provider of the exotic goods that were desired by Yao and other Africans of the interior.

One further indication of the growing links between the peoples of the southern interior and the expanding world economy, as reflected in the western Indian Ocean, was their response to the expansion of the slave trade. Once they had come to regard the Indian cloths, Venetian beads and other products of wide currency in the interior as essential elements in their own trading economies, East Africans had little practical alternative but to respond positively to the new and insistent demand for slaves. At Mozambique island the demand for slave labour was generated by the French, who had developed a classic colonial plantation economy on the Mascarene islands in the second quarter of the century. Less significantly, but not without importance, the French plantation owners of St Domingue, the most important of the eighteenth-century Caribbean sugar colonies, also sought slaves from East Africa, and French traders conducted the greatest proportion of the slave trade from the Kerimba islands, the most northerly outpost of semi-effective Portuguese control in East Africa in this period, where other Makua, and some Makonde as well, were most intimately affected. Finally, in addition to the more widely known French activities at Kilwa, especially during the 1770s, a rival demand for slaves to the north of Cape Delgado was being created by the gradually expanding economy of Oman (see below, p. 533). The slave trade of the Kilwa coast enmeshed the decentralized peoples who lived in the immediate hinterland: Makonde, Ndonde, and the vanguard of the nineteenth-century Makua immigrants, as well as others not mentioned in the contemporary documentation, such as Ngindo, Mwera and Machinga. But this slave trade also made important inroads on the trade of the market-sensitive Yao, who rapidly assumed the additional role of major slave traders for which they became so notorious in the nineteenth century. The restrictions that the slave trade imposed everywhere on the normal development of African societies highlight the contrast between the histories of the southern and northern interiors of East Africa during the seventeenth and eighteenth centuries.

The history of those African societies lying beyond the ken of Portuguese documentation at this time, or not yet studied by professional scholars in the field, can be perceived in only the barest outline. A case in point is the Yao, who are known exclusively from their activities as traders at the coast and in northern Zambezia. While it is fairly simple to deal with the Yao as a semi-abstract nation of traders, it is all but impossible to gauge the impact of their trading. The effects of the many important shifts of emphasis in terms of routing to the coast, and the extension of trade into the interior and products of the land, on the internal economic, political and social development of the Yao have still to be investigated. The most that now can be asserted about the Yao before the nineteenth century is that they were not a unified trading state of any sort. Political and concomitant economic power was probably focussed in chiefdoms that were similar to those better known after 1800. In any case, when Bocarro made his journey from Tete to Kilwa through the interior in 1616, he encountered a series of co-operative, but apparently independent chiefdoms among people who, in view of the considerable dialectic differentiation within the Yao language family, were in all likelihood already Yao-speaking.

Even less is known about the peoples who inhabited the Kilwa hinterland as far west as the north end of Lake Malawi. At the end of the sixteenth century the 'Zimba' passed behind the coast on their path north, which may possibly account for some of the uninhabited lands through which Bocarro passed between the Rovuma river and the immediate coastal strip, but it surely cannot explain the fact that, although he was travelling along an established trade route, he encountered only one village in eleven days' march from the northern banks of the Rovuma to the immediate hinterland of Kilwa. More probably this region, like much of the agriculturally less productive interior plateau of Tanzania, only came to support a larger settled population during the nineteenth century, when the introduction of new food crops, notably maize, enabled the land to support a more dense population. Those people inhabiting the region in the two preceding centuries were probably scattered about in small homestead settlements, and were as much dependent upon hunting, fishing and gathering as upon their own domestic agriculture. Only in the comparatively less harsh environment of the Makonde plateaux which flank the mouth of the Rovuma river, and in the valleys of the Rovuma and its tributaries, is it possible to think concretely of the ancestors of the peoples who inhabited the region in the nineteenth century. For the rest of the region, the modern populations were provided principally through a series of immigrations – Makua, Yao and Ngoni – that became pronounced only during the first half of the nineteenth century.

THE EAST AFRICAN COAST

By the last decade of the sixteenth century, the peoples on the coast of East Africa had already experienced ninety years of desultory, though violent, Portuguese interference in their established way of life. The coastal city-states had been born of a unique trading situation which had its origins in the pattern of Indian Ocean trade. Their orientation was exclusively seaward, dependent equally upon Asia and the Near East for most of their manufactured goods – and for the markets which had called them into being as entrepôts on the African coast – and upon the seaborne trade with Sofala, to the south of the Zambezi delta, for the great preponderance of their African wealth, in particular gold and ivory (see volume 3, chapter 4). From the beginning, then, they had always been subject to extra-African influences over which they had virtually no control, yet which deeply affected their development as African societies. Within this far-flung oceanic trading system, however, some of them had been able to rise to a position of great economic importance and considerable cultural achievement. This the Portuguese destroyed during the course of the sixteenth century. But until the very end of the century, the Portuguese were not so immediately concerned with the coast north of Cape Delgado that they attempted anything more than a series of raids and occasional displays of maritime might. From their own point of view, not to mention that of the coastal city-states, they attempted nothing constructive during this initial period of contact. The sixteenth century was for coastal society in many respects a transitional period between an independent past and a progressively foreign-dominated future.

The arrival of the Portuguese in East African waters rapidly created a tradition of resistance to the imposition of foreign rule that was to persist among coastal towns for the next four centuries. Coastal society was far too greatly fragmented politically, however, ever to admit of a united front against the Portuguese. Towns were generally separated by great distances, and were always in competition with each other for control of the seaborne trade. On the coast the Portuguese sailed into a situation where there was no real possibility of temporary unity in the face of a common enemy, as, for example, had been the case for a while in Macuana. This situation, as much as Portugal's undoubted superiority in the manoeuvrability and firepower of her fleet, and her possession of a strategic vision that encompassed the entire Indian Ocean, lay at the root of whatever success the Portuguese had on the East African coast.

During the sixteenth century Portugal's principal antagonists had been the Shirazi rulers of Mombasa, while the ambitious, but much weaker rulers of Malindi, farther north along the modern Kenya coast, seized the opportunity to make common cause with the European invaders. In 1591 Mombasa fell to their combined forces, and the ruler of Malindi, Shaykh Aḥmad, was installed by the Portuguese as shaykh of Mombasa. With the building of Fort Jesus at Mombasa at the end of the sixteenth century, the city was transformed from the focal point of Swahili resistance into the principal bastion of Portuguese power on the East African coast to the north of Mozambique island.

For the next century the Portuguese maintained a dominant influence in the political and economic life of the coast. Nevertheless, the Swahili city-states continued to offer regular resistance to their rule, and Portuguese chronicles of the period are replete with accounts of one rebellion after another. Each individual Swahili town, or faction within each town, attempted to protect its independence of action and to maximize its economic and political position within the limitations that were imposed by Portuguese domination. The rebellion of Yūsuf b. Ḥasan, last shaykh of the short-lived Malindi dynasty of Mombasa, best illustrates the motivations of the Swahili communities in their relations with the Portuguese during the seventeenth century.

After the death of Shaykh Aḥmad of Mombasa in 1609, relations between the new Malindi dynasty and the Portuguese deteriorated sharply as a consequence of Portuguese abuses and of the Portuguese attempt to harness the dynasty as their puppets. To that end, Yūsuf b. Ḥasan was sent as a youth to study under Portuguese tutelage in Goa. He returned home to reign as shaykh in 1626, a baptized Christian who had taken the name of Dom Jeronimo Chingulia and had been married to a Christian woman of mixed Portuguese-Eurasian descent. His rebellion in 1631 against Portuguese imperiousness demonstrates that, once the Malindi dynasty had obtained what it wanted from the alliance with the Portuguese – political supremacy on the northern Swahili coast – it fell heir to the tradition of resistance that the Shirazi dynasty of Mombasa had previously maintained. The Portuguese apparently recognized the futility of attempting to maintain a subservient Swahili dynasty as rulers of Mombasa, and after Yūsuf b. Ḥasan was driven away from the coast in 1631, the Portuguese captain of Mombasa ruled the island directly.

Elsewhere along the coast, affairs were little different. Lying far to the south of the centre of the Swahili complex, Kilwa was the seat of a Portuguese customs-house, and appears to have turned in upon itself in an effort to rebuild the economic basis of the town. Yet Kilwa was not spared internal intrigues. Indeed, the assassination in 1614 of the sultan of Kilwa, and the similar fate of its *wali*, Ḥasan b. Aḥmad, about two years later, apparently reflect the tensions between pro- and anti-Portuguese factions within the ruling class.[1] Similarly, although Zanzibar remained a nominally loyal ally and was spared any significant Portuguese presence as a reward for the co-operation of its rulers, in

[1] B. G. Martin, 'Notes on some members of the learned classes of Zanzibar and East Africa in the nineteenth century', *African Historical Studies*, 4, 3, 1971, 529, and letter to E. A. Alpers, Bloomington, 13 April 1972.

1652 the ruling dynasty seized the occasion of the first Omani raid into East Africa to proclaim its independence once again, as did the *mrima* coast town of Utondwe. To the north of Mombasa, the Portuguese also established a customs-house at Pate, but the ambitious Nabahani dynasty was too deeply involved in the politics of the northern Swahili coast to accept their presence passively. Pate responded to the call for rebellion that was raised in 1637 by the exiled shaykh of Mombasa, Yūsuf b. Ḥasan, although without much success. In the second half of the century, however, the Nabahani city-state became the focus for resistance against Portuguese rule, rebelling in 1660, 1678, 1686 and 1687 with increasing effect on the declining Portuguese position. The island of Pemba, which was a prime source of contention between Mombasa and Pate because of its importance as a source of provisions, especially rice, was particularly vexed by random acts of violence by the small Portuguese community that maintained itself there. In the general rising that seems to have swept the off-shore islands and the *mrima* in 1652, Pemba launched an attack on Kilwa, while in 1694 it raised the last independent resistance to the Portuguese before the three-year Omani siege of Mombasa that concluded with the Portuguese withdrawal from the Kenya and Tanzania coasts.

The great siege of Mombasa marks the culmination of a steady deterioration in Portuguese sea power during the seventeenth century. Much has been made of the bravery of the Portuguese defenders of Fort Jesus, but in the context of African history it can be seen that these men represented only the first victims of a dying, yet persistent, colonialism. The Portuguese had been able to hold on for so long to Fort Jesus partly because of their determination and the continued support which some of the peoples on the mainland gave them, and partly as a result of the inability of their enemies to muster enough strength among themselves to evict them forcibly. In the end, however, Portuguese weakness in the Indian Ocean, compounded by the ineptitude of Portuguese leadership and the ravages of disease, enabled the combined forces of the Swahili and their Arab allies to win the day.

On the economic front, the impact of Portuguese imperialism in the seventeenth century was quite different. Earlier interpretations argue that the decline which set in as a result of Portuguese disruption of traditional trading patterns in the sixteenth century continued throughout the next hundred years. On the contrary, after eradicating the Turkish threat, the Portuguese sought to defray some of the expenses of controlling the East African coast by actively encouraging trade. The captain of Mombasa attempted not to interfere with trade, but only to tax it at a rate which would provide revenue for the royal coffers. Furthermore, through his personal agent at Kilwa, he endeavoured to stimulate trade by providing a regular demand for the products of the interior, notably ivory. From a strictly economic perspective, then, the seventeenth century was a period of revival along the coast, especially in the south.

The most tangible demonstration of this interpretation comes from Kilwa. During the sixteenth century the Portuguese seizure of Sofala had forced the merchants of Kilwa to explore new continental sources for the African products current in the western Indian Ocean. By the third quarter of the sixteenth century, a new trade route linking Kilwa to the southern interior of East Africa was already beginning to take shape. The so-called 'Zimba' attack on Kilwa in 1588 would seem to have caused a temporary set-back to the town's slow recovery, but the principal hindrance was more likely the general economic depression that plagued the coast in the sixteenth century. When Gaspar Bocarro reached Kilwa from Tete in 1616, however, he was greeted by the Portuguese factor and a small, but apparently thriving, Portuguese community. For the remainder of the seventeenth century, Kilwa appears to have continued its gradual development.

Trade at Mombasa during this period was apparently less considerable and more erratic than at Kilwa. Political conflicts within Mombasa itself were one source of instability, but events on the mainland were probably the main cause of uncertainty. The Mombasa hinterland was transformed during the seventeenth century by a prolonged series of small-scale migrations of Bantu-speaking peoples retreating southwards from Galla pastoralists who were raiding eastwards into their ancient homeland of Shungwaya. These migrants settled among the Giriama and other peoples behind Mombasa in large defensive strongholds called *kaya*. At the coast they became known collectively as the Nyika, after their harsh new country, or the *Miji Kenda* (Nine Tribes), as they call themselves. During their migration they appear to have intermingled with at least one of the major mainland peoples noted in sixteenth-century Portuguese records, the 'Mozungullos'. During the eighteenth century, the *Miji Kenda* were to become the principal middlemen for the interior trade of Mombasa, but in the seventeenth century their migration and the persistence of Galla raids in the hinterland appear to have adversely affected the former trade of the

'Mozungullos' to Mombasa. Trade with the mainland in ivory continued at Mombasa in the seventeenth century, but increasingly the captain of Mombasa came to rely upon the trade of Kilwa to provide the Portuguese establishment with a steady revenue and himself with an appropriate stipend.[1]

The expulsion of the Portuguese from the coast at the end of the seventeenth century did not, as has often been implied, lead to an immediate revival of the coast under the hegemony of the Arab state of Oman in the Persian Gulf. In fact, the Ya'arubi dynasty, which had built up Omani sea power in the Persian Gulf during the seventeenth century, proved at once to be even more unpopular than the Portuguese with the fiercely independent Swahili city-states. It was also soon embroiled in a fatal round of internecine struggles that culminated in its replacement as the ruling dynasty of Oman in 1741 by the Busa'idi family. The Ya'arubi had been called in by the Nabahani dynasty of Pate, and were no doubt seen as potential liberators by many other Swahili up and down the coast. But the Swahili were no more inclined to accept subservience to co-religionists than they were to the Catholic Portuguese. The tradition of resistance to foreign domination manifested itself immediately in a series of revolts against the abuses of the Omani garrisons which were established during the first decade of the eighteenth century from Pate to Kilwa. For a brief period Kilwa was drawn into the wider political affairs of the coast by carrying on secret negotiations with the Portuguese at Mozambique island on behalf of the entire coast. In 1728 a Portuguese expedition succeeded in retaking Mombasa from the Omani, but the offensive behaviour of the new captain of Mombasa proved sufficiently aggravating to precipitate a final expulsion from Fort Jesus a year later, this time without any outside assistance. Politically, then, the first half of the eighteenth century was marked by a final assertion of the traditional independence of the Swahili towns of the coast in the face of both Portuguese and Omani unpopularity and weakness.

Economically, this half-century was once again one of depression, especially in the south. The Omani garrison at Kilwa pilfered as much wealth as it could locate, and the governor thoroughly mismanaged

1 The fully documented argument behind this interpretation is in E. Alpers, *Ivory and slaves in East Central Africa* (London, 1975), but some of the major sources may be found in G. S. P. Freeman-Grenville, *The East African coast: select documents from the first to the earlier nineteenth century* (Oxford, 1962), 132, 140, 156, 178–9, 184, and 190; see also, National Archives of India, Panjim, Goa, Livro das Monções 75, fols. 174v.–175, Luís Gonçalves da Camara e Coutinho to Viceroy, Moçambique, 10 August 1710.

trade before the Omani were barred from the town by an irate citizenry in the early 1720s. Kilwa lost much of its hold over the ivory trade of the Yao (see above, p. 525), and was reduced to a coasting trade largely directed southwards to Mozambique, the Kerimba and the Comoro islands. Less is known about the trade of Mombasa at this period, but Portuguese intelligence reports for the first three decades of the eighteenth century (most of which were admittedly provided by disgruntled Swahili) suggest that Omani high-handedness with respect to both the Swahili of Mombasa and their *Miji Kenda* trading partners severely disrupted the normal flow of trade. At Pate, too, it appears that Omani domination was not conducive to profitable trade at this time. Even the sultan of Pate, who, less than thirty years previously, had been the most bitter anti-Portuguese leader on the coast, was moved to write in the late 1720s to the Portuguese at Goa. He complained that the Galla were diverting their ivory trade from his town to the more northerly port of Brava, where each year three merchant vessels from Surat came laden with cloth to buy ivory at a price superior to that obtainable at Pate.[1] However biased the Portuguese sources may be on this point, there seems to be little doubt that although this period of limbo between two important imperial orders, Portuguese and Omani, allowed the Swahili greater political independence than they had enjoyed for perhaps two centuries, it also produced a situation in which political jockeying within and between communities, and the absence of a strong economic power, combined to depress market conditions on the coast.

The accession in 1741 of the Busaʿidi as the ruling dynasty of Oman and the selection three years later of Aḥmad b. Saʿīd al-Busaʿidi as *imām* were the first in a series of events which were to revitalize the coastal economy and to lay the foundation for the Zanzibari trading state, which was consolidated by the most famous Busaʿidi ruler of Oman, Sayyid Saʿīd b. Sulṭān (1804–56). From the middle of the eighteenth century, trade in ivory again increased, and the slave trade began to grow slowly in significance as Muscat, the Busaʿidi capital of Oman, developed into a major commercial centre in the western Indian Ocean. Kilwa lost all vestiges of its political autonomy in 1785, in the wake of a fraternal challenge to the authority of the new Busaʿidi *imām*, Saʿīd b. Aḥmad. But its economy flourished under the reinvigorated Busaʿidi overlordship, and Kilwa was the unchallenged port for the Yao and Bisa trade of the southern interior by the end of the eighteenth

[1] National Archives of India, Panjim, Goa, Livro das Monções 95-B, fols. 585 and v., King of Pate to Viceroy, trans. at Goa, 10 October 1728.

century. Zanzibar town was secured, as well, and the commitment made by the new *imām*, much as that made by the Portuguese at the end of the sixteenth century, assured the active presence of an increasingly aggressive economic and political power in East Africa for the next century. The towns of the *mrima*, in particular Bagamoyo, were to a large extent called into being as a by-product of the growth of Zanzibar town as the centre of Busa'idi authority in East Africa. Some of these towns were entirely new settlements, while others were established on or near by the sites of minor pre-Portuguese communities. At the same time, however, it appears that a secondary stimulus to their growth was the steady trickle of northern immigrants from the declining Swahili towns between Mombasa and the Lamu archipelago.

If Busa'idi control was the key to economic revival at Zanzibar and along the *mrima* and Kilwa coasts during the second half of the eighteenth century, then it was the challenge posed to their imperial control which brought prosperity to Mombasa during the same period. How Mombasa came to occupy such a prominent and thriving position in opposition to the Busa'idi after mid-century merits discussion, for the experience of Mombasa, although unique, reveals much that is otherwise obscure about the inner workings of Swahili society during this period. Mombasa was never a completely unified community during the seventeenth and eighteenth centuries. The town had been a major point of refuge and reintegration for a number of Swahili immigrants from the coast north of the island during the sixteenth century, so that by the time that it fell to the Portuguese these newcomers were quite probably numerically superior to the earlier 'Shirazi' settlers whose dynasty had elevated the town to its position of prominence. During the seventeenth century, the various immigrant groups aligned themselves into twelve different tribes, the *Thenashara Taifa*, which in turn divided into two distinct and highly competitive confederations, the more numerous *Thelatha Taifa* (The Three), who settled at Kilindini at the south-west corner of the island, and the *Tisa Taifa* (The Nine), who inhabited the old Shirazi town of Mombasa-Mvita in the east of the island. The development of moieties at Mombasa would appear to have been characteristic of Swahili communities, rather than exceptional, as research at Kilwa Kivinje and Lamu suggests.[1] When the Portuguese were expelled at the end of the century,

[1] P. Lienhardt, *The medicine man: swifa ya nguvumali* (Oxford, 1968), 12–20; idem, 'The mosque college of Lamu and its social background', *Tanganyika Notes and Records*, 1959, **53**, 228–42; A. H. J. Prins, *Didemic Lamu: social stratification and spatial structure in a Muslim maritime town* (Groningen, 1971).

however, there was no internal mechanism available for achieving political unity on the island. The Ya'arubi dynasty installed another Omani family, the Mazrui, as governors of Mombasa; and it was under their mediating leadership, first as representatives of the Ya'arubi and after about 1735 as independent rulers, that the island was successfully moulded into a single polity. The two main roles of this ruling dynasty were to arbitrate between the *Thelatha Taifa* and the *Tisa Taifa*, and to represent and co-ordinate their united efforts in all external affairs, notably in their conflicts with the Busa'idi and the Nabahani of Pate, who were Mombasa's only serious rivals for supremacy over the northern Swahili coast during the eighteenth century. In these roles the Mazrui fit into a pattern of state formation that is familiar to students of African history. But unlike many, if not most, African dynasties who at one time or another fell into this category, for example the Kilindi in Usambara (see above, p. 510), the Mazrui failed to establish effective internal authority over the two competing confederations in Mombasa.

The real strength of Mombasa was certainly not its internal cohesion. Instead, it was the intimate relationships which existed between the *Thelatha Taifa* and the *Tisa Taifa* and their respective *Miji Kenda* clients which gave Mombasa its unique vitality as a Swahili community. The *Thelatha Taifa* had their links with the Digo and Duruma, while the *Tisa Taifa* were associated with the Giriama, Kauma, Kamba, Ribe, Chonyi and Rabai. These relationships, characterized as 'patron-client', were probably developed before the various *taifa* moved from the mainland on to Mombasa island and may trace their origins to the sixteenth century. Individual shaykhs of the appropriate *taifa* were responsible for conducting business between the *Miji Kenda* and the Mombasa Swahili and acted both as patrons for them on the island and as their representatives to the outside world. At the same time, however, it is clear that the *taifa* drew great strength and stability from their links with the peoples of the coastal hinterland, upon whom they depended for trade and in war. Given our present inadequate state of knowledge, it appears that Mombasa was uniquely favoured in its ability to draw upon the full resources of the non-Muslim mainland during the eighteenth century; but it seems reasonable to suggest that the same situation may also have prevailed at Kilwa, which had been trading successfully with the interior since late in the sixteenth century. Indeed, it was not long into the nineteenth century before Kilwa's seat of activity was transferred from the off-shore island of Kilwa Kisiwani, where it had attained its pre-Portuguese greatness on the basis of the seaborne trade to Sofala, to the mainland town of Kilwa Kivinje, which soon gained notoriety as the greatest slaving port in East Africa.

After the Mazrui definitively established their independence from Oman in 1746, they were able to weather all internal conflicts at Mombasa, including dynastic rivalries, for the remainder of the eighteenth century and well into the nineteenth century. Pate, on the other hand, was seriously debilitated by civil strife for the remainder of the century and could do no more than offer occasional resistance to Mombasa's increasingly expansionist attitude. Pemba was snatched from Omani suzerainty, and Zanzibar seriously threatened for a time. In the 1770s, Mombasa succeeded in gaining recognition from Pate that it was, in effect, the major power on the northern Swahili coast, and an alliance was struck between the two that remained in effect until the decline of Pate as the most important town in the Lamu archipelago in the second decade of the nineteenth century. Mombasa also held at least diplomatic sway over the towns lying to its south as far as Tanga.

At the end of the eighteenth century, then, the coast was experiencing a marked economic revival which drew its inspiration from two different and competing sources. From Zanzibar southwards to Kilwa, the prime mover in this rejuvenation was the maturing Busa'idi dynasty of Oman; in the northern Swahili region it was the revitalized Mombasa state, which was rising to new heights under the skilful leadership of its Omani-derived Mazrui dynasty. In each case the prime mover was not indigenous to coastal society. If in the eighteenth century the Mazrui had already put down roots in East Africa, they were soon to be emulated in the nineteenth century by the eventual victors in this struggle for political and economic control of the coast, their Busa'idi rivals. Increasingly the life of the coast was pointing towards a future domination by external powers. The slave trade was already asserting itself as a persistent factor in the economic life of the coastal towns by the century's end. In a few decades the coast would be witnessing the development of a large-scale colonial plantation economy on Zanzibar and Pemba islands and the arrival of increasing numbers of European traders, in search of ivory for the cultural paraphernalia of their recently industrialized societies. For most of the peoples of the interior these ominous developments were as yet only faint glimmerings by the end of the eighteenth entury, but for those of the southern interior and the coast the need to adapt to the increasingly internationalized situation in which they found themselves was all too apparent.

CHAPTER 8

ETHIOPIA AND THE HORN OF AFRICA*

Historians of North-East Africa have been largely concerned with developments in the kingdom of Ethiopia and, to a lesser degree, with the principalities of the coast. These communities were literate, had recorded their history and were occasionally visited by foreigners. The Galla peoples on the other hand, illiterate until modern times and considered hostile to foreign visitors, have been relatively neglected, but the story of their great migrations, the evolution of their society and culture, the growth of their political power and their transformation into the predominant element in the Horn of Africa is in reality the principal theme throughout this period. Even contemporaries in Ethiopia failed to recognize for a time the significance of the Galla invasion, for they remained largely preoccupied with internal rivalries and with the threat still posed to the Christian kingdom in the second half of the sixteenth century by the Muslim elements of the coast.

THE MUSLIM THREAT AND THE GALLA EXPANSION

Imām Aḥmad Gragn, who had conquered Ethiopia at the head of the armies of Adal and dominated the country for more than a decade, was killed in 1543 at the battle of Woina-Dega. Galawdewos, who had succeeded his father Lebna-Dengel in 1540 as king of kings of Ethiopia, quickly reconquered the northern and central plateaux, but it took him several years to overcome the resistance of the rulers of Damot and the Muslim sultanates of the south. By the beginning of the 1550s, Ethiopia was once again united within its old borders. Nevertheless, Galawdewos realized that most of the factors which had contributed to the collapse of the kingdom in the days of his father were still in existence. He had emerged from the battle of Woina-Dega with tremendous prestige, and he did not hesitate to exploit his power in order to strengthen the authority of the monarchy at the expense of the traditional nobility. But because his primary aim was to rebuild the unity of

* A rigorous transcription of Ethiopian names has been discarded in favour of a simple system which should be readily comprehensible to English readers. It has proved almost impossible to eliminate all inconsistencies. [Ed.]

the country, he refrained from introducing revolutionary changes into the traditional structure and institutions of the kingdom. Instead, he gradually extended the control of the monarchy over the subordinate rulers and governors, and dedicated himself to re-establishing the solidarity between his subjects and the national church, which they had previously betrayed. This gifted, scholarly and deeply religious monarch considered the Ethiopian church as the most important pillar of the kingdom and as a major tool for bridging the cultural and ethnic diversities of the population of Ethiopia. Aware of the moral and cultural inferiority of the clergy and of the church's intellectual weakness, he took a personal interest in the task of its spiritual revival and reorganization.

Most of the Portuguese who joined Galawdewos's camp in 1542 insisted that he submit to the See of Rome, as Lebna-Dengel had promised to do when he applied to Portugal for aid. But even before the battle of Woina-Dega, Galawdewos informed the Portuguese that he had no intention of abandoning the faith of his ancestors. When a number of Jesuit priests reached Ethiopia in 1557, Galawdewos made it clear to them that there was no question of him becoming a Catholic. After long but fruitless theological discussions in the court, the disillusioned Jesuits retired in 1559 to Tigre,[1] where they lived under the protection of its provincial governor, the Bahr-Negash Yishaq.

The arrival of the Jesuits in 1557 had not passed unnoticed among the Muslim authorities of the Red Sea basin. The Ottomans, who controlled the Red Sea, were unaware of the fact that Portuguese resources were by this time stretched to their limit, and they suspected that the Jesuit mission might be a prelude to renewed Portuguese intervention in the Red Sea basin. Hence, Uzdamir Pasha invaded Baher-Meder, captured its capital Dibarwa and began to raid Tigre. News of the Turkish invasion reached Galawdewos just when the Galla erupted from Bali, and while the king was encamped near the south-western borders of his kingdom in the expectation of an attack from Adal. Consequently, Bahr-Negash Yishaq was sent to deal with the situation. Between 1557 and 1559 he succeeded in defeating the Turks and drove them back to the coast.

Galawdewos, who feared the revival of Adal's power, repeatedly ordered his armies to penetrate its territories, to burn its towns and villages and harass its pastoral population, with the aim of disrupting

[1] Tigre proper is a small province south of the Mareb. In most cases the term Tigre is understood to mean all the provinces of the Tigrigna-speaking people. In the widest sense the term Tigre is used to denote all the provinces east of the Tekeze.

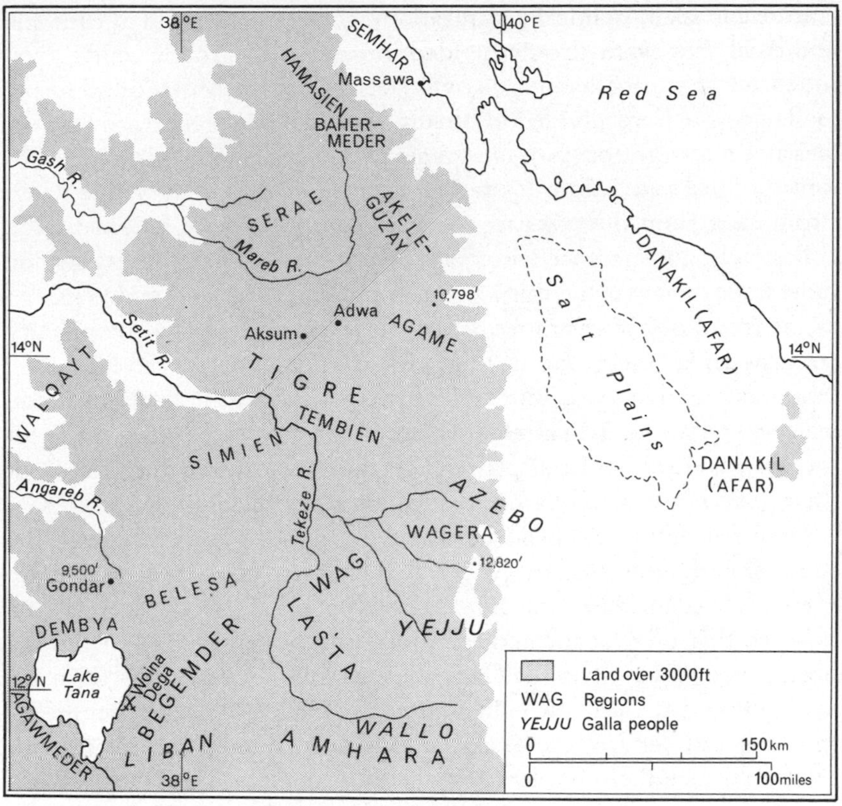

18 Northern Ethiopia

the economy of the sultanate and breaking its military power. Ironically, the resounding Ethiopian victories awakened among the different elements of the sultanate a reaction similar to that which had preceded their great irruption into Ethiopia. Differences and rivalries were forgotten and the population united around Nūr b. Mujāhid, Gragn's nephew, in an effort to defeat the Christians. After taking the title of *imām* about 1551/2, Nūr completely reorganized the administration and the army of the sultanate. In 1559 he advanced towards Shoa and met part of the Ethiopian army commanded by Galawdewos. In the ensuing battle, the Ethiopians were defeated and Galawdewos was killed. However, instead of following up his success, Nūr immediately returned to Harar to drive off the Galla who were attacking the town.

The Galla peoples, who always called themselves Oromo, began their migration into Ethiopia and Adal probably in the first decades of the sixteenth century. Cushitic pastoralists with a common language, culture and socio-political organization, when first reported in Ethiopia and Adal they were already divided into different groups which acted independently, each having its own elected leaders. Most, or all of the Galla groups were divided internally into five *gadas*. The *gada* system was not a straightforward age-grade system, because a son could not join the first *gada* before his father completed the cycle of five *gadas*. Promotion from one *gada* to another then took place automatically, collectively and irrespective of age every eight years.[1] Militarily the most important was the third *gada* commonly called *folle*, which served as the spearhead of each group. Its war-leader was in fact the military commander of the group in time of war. Theoretically the fifth *gada*, *luba*, was the ruling *gada*. But Galla society, like most pastoral societies, was egalitarian in the extreme. Office-holders were elected and, with the *luba*, were considered *primus inter pares*, executing the wishes of their group as a whole rather than themselves making decisions.

Until recently it was believed that the Galla originally inhabited the south-eastern and eastern parts of the Horn of Africa which are presently occupied by the Somali and by the Danakil. It was also believed that the Danakil and even more the Somali, coming from the north, gradually pushed the Galla southwards and westwards from the beginning of the second millennium AD. Hence, it was thought, by the sixteenth century the Galla had come to inhabit the semi-desert areas on the southern borders of the Ethiopian plateau and the northern parts of present-day Kenya, and from there under the pressure of the expanding Somali tribes they began their migration into Ethiopia. However, on the basis of new evidence and the re-evaluation of earlier sources, it now seems more probable that the Galla tribes did not inhabit the south-eastern and eastern parts of the Horn before the turn of the sixteenth century. The existence of Galla enclaves, uncertain archaeological evidence and traditions of Galla presence in parts of present-day Somalia are attributed to the period of Galla expansion in the sixteenth and seventeenth centuries. By this period, it seems, the number of the Galla people and their herds had grown and they began to migrate to new areas. The main Galla drive was directed northwards into the rich plateaux of Ethiopia and Adal, where an opening was created by the devastating wars between the Muslims and the Christians. However, some Galla tribes, mainly the Borana, the Kereyu and lesser branches of the Baraytuma, advanced in north-easterly and

[1] There are indications that there might have existed some variations in the *gada* system.

south-easterly directions, so that at the end of the sixteenth century they reached the Dankali coast near Assab and, in the south, the coast of the Indian Ocean near the Benadir ports and as far south as the area of Malindi.[1]

Nūr b. Mujāhid succeeded in saving Harar from the Galla and from the Ethiopians. However, after his death in 1567, the sultanate began to disintegrate. The emirs ruling the different provinces fought each other for the predominance. The nomads attacked the settled population and the Danakil clashed with the Somali. This situation was exploited by the Galla who raided deeper and deeper into Adal. In 1576 the Adalis tried to invade Ethiopia from the south, but were defeated by the Ethiopians and the sultan of Adal was killed. Following a period of confusion a member of Gragn's family, Muḥammad b. Ibrāhīm Gāssā, came to power and took the title of *imām*. By then the situation in and around Harar was so precarious that in 1577 the new *imām* transferred the seat of his government from Harar to the oasis of Awsa. This move proved to be a fatal mistake. Awsa was too far removed from the centre of the sultanate to control its different provinces. Moreover, the deserts surrounding Awsa were an inadequate barrier against Ethiopian, Somali and above all Galla raids. In the decades following the transfer to Awsa, one *imām* followed another, the governors of Harar became autonomous and Zeila was captured by the Ottomans. The Somali tribes belonging to the Dir, Darod and Isaq groups, living in the vicinity of Harar, ignored the authority of Awsa, and the Danakil raided its territories.

Galla pressure on Adal and on the entire eastern part of the Horn continued to increase, and the links between Adal and the Benadir coast were completely disrupted. By the beginning of the seventeenth century, the Galla advance forced the Hawiya Somali and their kinsmen, who had been living along the Benadir coast and possibly in the Majerteyn since at least the twelfth century, to move northwards, southwards, and even into the interior. The town of Mogadishu, inhabited by Arab mercantile communities, was conquered by the Somali and its ancient Muzafar dynasty was overthrown. The Hawiya, however, were not left in possession of the Majerteyn for long. By the second half of the seventeenth century they were expelled from it

[1] For this interpretation see mainly H. S. Lewis, 'The origins of the Galla and Somali', *Journal of African History*, 1966, 7. See also Ato Asmiye, 'Ye Galla tarik' (an unpublished manuscript, a copy of which is to be found at The Institute of Ethiopian Studies, Addis Ababa), fol. 87; C. Guillain, *Documents sur l'histoire, la géographie*, etc. (Paris, 1856), III, 169–70; H. Salt, *A voyage to Abyssinia etc. in the years 1809 and 1810* (London, 1814), 176; Jerome Lobo, *Voyage historique d'Abissinie*, ed. M. Le Grand (Paris, 1728), 19–22.

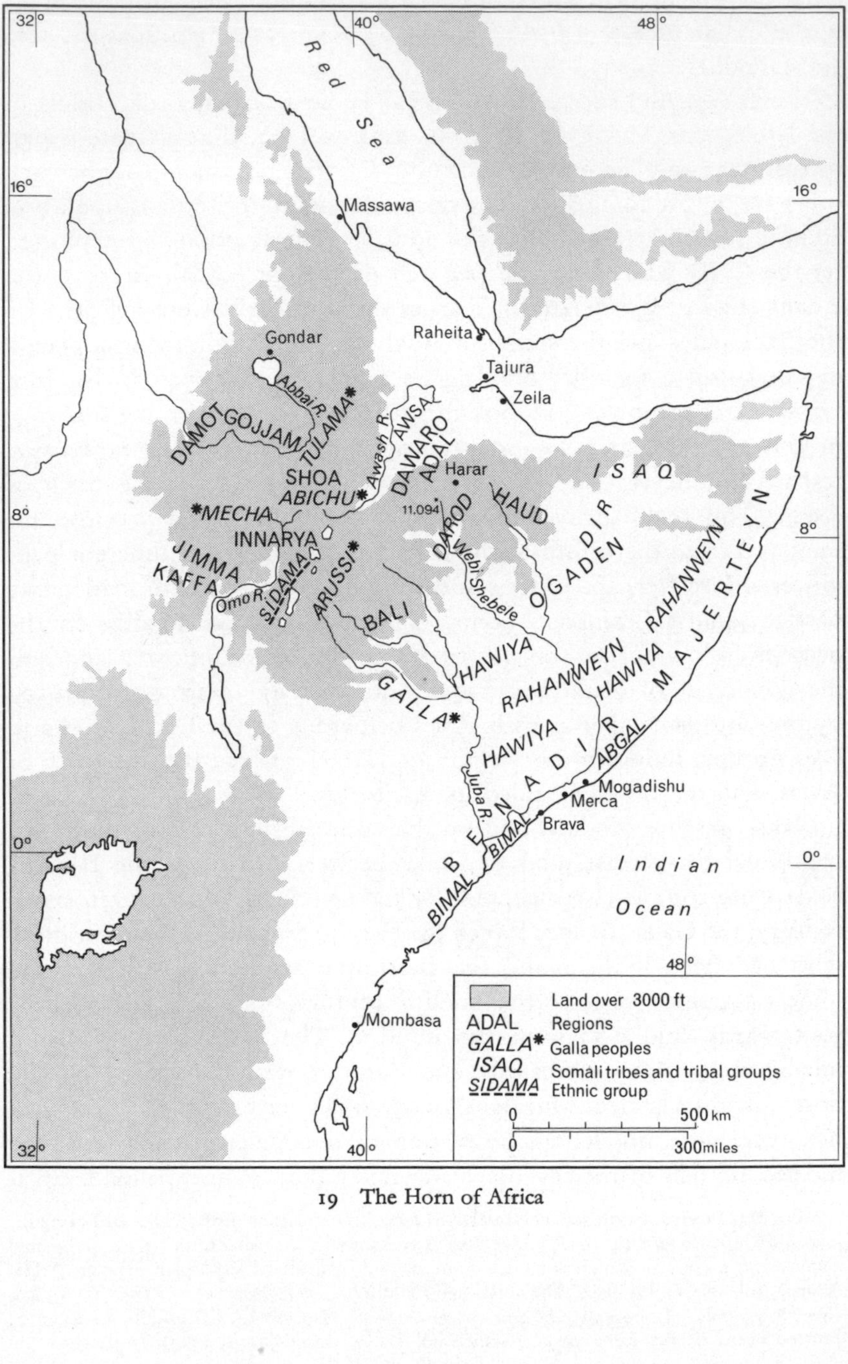

19 The Horn of Africa

by another Somali group, the Rahanweyn. The latter also drove away or annihilated in the last decades of the century the relatively weak Galla tribes between the Shebele and the Juba rivers. The remnants of these Galla crossed the Juba and settled along its right bank.

In the north, a Danakil sultanate had been in existence even before the time of Gragn. Its northern border was the bay of Anfilla and in the south it touched Adal near the bay of Tajura (Tadjoura). In the interior the line separating Adal and the Danakil was very vague. By the end of the sixteenth century a number of independent Danakil sultanates may have already existed, and Raheita was the capital of the strongest and most important of them. The Danakil, like the Galla, were an extremely egalitarian society, and the authority of their sultan was merely nominal. Because of the harsh conditions of the Dankali desert and the fierceness of its population, the minor ports on the Dankali coast were only rarely visited by caravans from the plateau. The greatest asset of Dankali territory was the salt plains of Arho, which supplied the plateau with most of the raw salt consumed by the population and their cattle, and with all the salt blocks (*amole*) used as currency even beyond the borders of Ethiopia. Wishing to profit from the salt trade, the Danakil sultan accepted the overlordship of the king of Ethiopia in the second half of the sixteenth century and, as a result of the continuous raids of the Baraytuma Galla, the Danakil became even more enfeebled and dependent on Ethiopia.

While the power of Adal was declining, Ethiopia faced the far more serious threat of the Galla. Galawdewos had managed to curb most of their irruptions and to contain them within the extreme south western provinces, but on his premature death in 1559, the remnants of the royal army dispersed and southern Ethiopia lay open before the Galla. The *folle* of each Galla group, composed of a few thousand dedicated warriors, moved swiftly into enemy land. The fact that they were disunited might have proved a disadvantage against a numerous enemy, but in most cases their mobility, greatly enhanced after they adopted the use of horses, and their ability to attack simultaneously in different areas, made resistance to their raids almost impossible. Gradually the Galla, meeting little resistance, pushed their camps northwards into the plateau. The other Cushitic peoples in the area which they overran were either absorbed into Galla society or made serfs of the Galla tribes who settled in their areas. Thus, within a relatively short period from the beginning of their migration the number of the Galla and their power were greatly increased.

The deep scars left by the Muslim invasion were still unhealed when Ethiopia was confronted by this Galla migration. The process of reintegrating the badly shaken population of the plateaux into a nation had only just begun. Ethiopia's heterogeneous society and medieval military and administrative system was therefore even less capable of dealing with the new onslaught. Moreover, the gravity of the new threat was not even fully comprehended at first by the rulers of the country. The Galla did not want to establish a new 'ideology' nor did they try, at first, to impose a new superstructure upon the semitized society, as Gragn had attempted. It seemed that the Galla merely sought land for grazing their cattle and for settlement, and there was plenty of open land available in the central and southern plateaux. Consequently, the Ethiopian ruling class and the church did not regard the Galla as a serious threat to their interests. The struggle against the Galla was considered for a time to be of secondary importance and was not treated as a national war of survival.

Galawdewos died without leaving any male descendant, and his brother Minas was elected king of kings, regardless of the fact – or maybe due to the fact – that he was extremely unpopular. It seems that the king's kinsmen and some Amhara nobles who elected Minas hoped to exploit the weakness of the new ruler to strengthen their position and to reduce the power of Galawdewos's favourites, especially the non-Amhara ones. Minas's first act was to lead an expedition against the Falasha of Simien in 1559. This turned out to be a complete failure, but it afforded the king and his advisers an opportunity to detain Bahr-Negash Yishaq, governor of Tigre and Baher-Meder, and to appoint one of the king's favourites as governor of Tigre. Yishaq succeeded in escaping to Tigre, where at the end of 1560 he and his allies declared a nephew of Minas king of kings. Earlier, the Jesuits and the Portuguese in Tigre, who resented Minas's attitude to Catholicism, requested the Portuguese authorities at Goa to help their old friend. Fearing such a development, Minas hurriedly marched against Yishaq, defeating him and capturing his 'king'. At the beginning of 1562, despairing of Portuguese aid, Yishaq allied himself with the Ottomans. He and the Ottoman commander entered Baher-Meder and Tigre and crowned another nephew of Minas as king. Minas's army tried to stop Yishaq's advance, but disintegrated under Turkish artillery fire. Minas, who escaped to Shoa, died of fever at the end of 1562, while marching on Tigre with a new army which he had collected.

SERSE-DINGIL AND SUSENYOS

On the instigation of the queen mother, the commanders of Minas's army, who were mainly Shoans, elected Serse-Dingil, Minas's young son, to succeed his father. This was clearly an attempt to create a new regency and Serse-Dingil was faced with a general rebellion of all the feudatories, including his own kinsmen. Fortunately for the young king, his enemies underestimated his capabilities and were far too divided among themselves to pay him serious attention. Thinking that he could place his candidate on the throne, Yishaq pursued the Turks from the plateau. But the Amhara aristocracy, fearing the revival of Tigrean influence in the court, were not willing to co-operate with Yishaq. While the great lords of the country manoeuvred for power, Serse-Dingil consolidated his position, and by 1567 even Yishaq prudently came to the royal camp to pay allegiance to the king.

In spite of his youth, Serse-Dingil realized that the weakness of the Ethiopian monarchy stemmed mainly from the archaic 'feudal' military and administrative system of the country. The king of kings had only a small bodyguard. He could, however, always call upon the services of the private armies maintained by the traditional rulers and governors of provinces. Recognition of the authority of such rulers or the appointment of governors was conditional on their placing themselves, together with their armies, at the disposal of the king whenever called upon to do so. The king could also mobilize the *chawa* (militia) battalions. These units, recruited from Amhara or Tigrean elements, were settled as garrisons in newly conquered provinces and were entitled to part of the taxes of the areas in which they were settled. In practice these units usually inter-married with the indigenous population, becoming part of the local aristocracy, and the king exercised little or no control over them. Serse-Dingil gradually changed the entire concept of the *chawa*. Although these units still received revenue from the areas allotted to them, they accompanied the king on campaigns all over the plateau. Moreover, he strengthened the *chawa* by incorporating into them several private armies of governors and feudatories who had died or fallen out of favour. In the same manner Serse-Dingil also expanded the guard regiments. The bodyguard was composed mainly of freed slaves and men of foreign origin who had no loyalties other than to the king. It became, therefore, the backbone of his new army. Moreover, he personally led his army and abolished many customs which separated him from his subordinates. While offices of the court connected with the traditional aristocracy declined in importance, the king surrounded himself with officials whom he elevated from the ranks.

Following their success in 'pacifying' the Yemen, the Ottomans reinforced their army on the Ethiopian coast, and were able to renew the offensive against Ethiopia at the beginning of 1572. The Turks were driven back to the coast by Bahr-Negash Yishaq, but nevertheless, in the following years Baher-Meder and Tigre were successively ravaged by them and by the Galla. Yishaq, whose appeals to the king for help remained unheeded, felt that he was deliberately being abandoned to his fate. Embittered, at the end of 1575 he allied himself once more with the Ottomans. Serse-Dingil eliminated the possibility of being attacked simultaneously by Adal and the Turks by defeating the former in 1576. He was prevented, however, from dealing immediately with Yishaq and the Turks by several irruptions of the Galla. But in the last months of 1578 he marched into Tigre and defeated his enemies. Yishaq and the Turkish pasha perished on the battlefield. This victory terminated the last serious Ottoman attempt to conquer Ethiopia: not until the nineteenth century were the Muslim elements of the coast again in a position to threaten the existence of Christian Ethiopia. Serse-Dingil's victory also temporarily put to an end the hopes of some of the Tigrean nobility to achieve the independence, or at least autonomy, of their provinces.

As a result of the Galla expansion, Ethiopian colonization in Serse-Dingil's reign took a northerly and a north-westerly direction. Its main victims were the Falasha of Simien, Wagera and Dembya, whose power was broken in a series of expeditions in the late 1580s. These expeditions accelerated the settlement of semitized elements in the north and paved the way for the transfer of the centre of the kingdom to the provinces adjacent to Lake Tana. Ethiopian expansion to the western parts of the plateau inhabited by Cushitic Agaw and Sidama cultivators was mainly motivated by economic reasons. The agricultural produce of these fertile regions supplied the king's camp and army with all its needs, but even more important was the fact that the west was the main source of Ethiopia's exports, such as ivory, incense and, above all, gold and slaves. Because the Galla were in control of large parts of the country, the king needed new sources of revenue to cover the expenses of the reorganized army and the administration. Hence, after defeating the Turks, Serse-Dingil concentrated his efforts on consolidating his government in Damot and the neighbouring areas. His conquests in the west and the forced evangelization of some of the

Agaw were not, however, accompanied by the settlement of northern semitized elements, and the process of integrating these areas into the kingdom was, therefore, relatively slow. Even less effective were the expeditions which he led to the rich Sidama kingdoms of the Gibe area. Serse-Dingil tried to use evangelization as a means of strengthening their ties with the Ethiopian kingdom. However, his efforts in this direction coincided with the penetration of the area by the Mecha Galla, and he was forced to conduct numerous military expeditions against the Mecha in order to maintain contact between Damot and Innarya.

The continuous employment of the *chawa* by the king in his campaigns against the nobility, the Agaw and the Ottomans enabled the Galla to raid and settle in the unprotected provinces. In fact, while the Baraytuma turned from the eastern escarpments into the fertile plains of Amhara and Begemder, the Borana Galla began to migrate north-westwards through the south and Shoa. The gravity of the Galla threat was not fully grasped by Serse-Dingil, however, until the 1580s. By this time the Galla were already entrenched in the southern and central plateaux. Realizing the futility of trying to drive them out of these areas, Serse-Dingil tried to block their further expansion into the remnants of his empire.

Serse-Dingil died in 1597, and his infant son Ya'qob was appointed king of kings. In the following decades, the new military aristocracy created by Serse-Dingil usurped the power of the king. When Ya'qob reached maturity and tried to assert his authority, he was deposed and replaced by Za-Dingil, a cousin of Serse-Dingil. However, when Za-Dingil tried to introduce radical reforms into the organization of the army and the system of taxation, the nobles rebelled and killed him. Ya'qob was once again appointed king of kings, but he was defeated in 1607 by Susenyos, a grandson of Lebna-Dengel.

When Susenyos became king of kings, the situation in Ethiopia was extremely serious. The inhabitants of several provinces supported pretenders to the throne, thus demonstrating traditional separatist tendencies and the unwillingness of some local rulers to forego their newly gained autonomy. The Galla were attacking the remnants of the empire from the south, while the pastoral tribes subject to the Funj kingdom of Sennar raided Ethiopia's northern provinces. Susenyos, however, was able to suppress the rebellions and to halt the encroachment of the Galla and the other pastoralists. He was careful to avoid Serse-Dingil's mistake of creating a new military aristocracy, and fell back on the old custom of appointing his brothers and closest kinsmen to the command of the army and the governorship of the major provinces. Though there is evidence that Serse-Dingil had already settled friendly Galla tribes on the borders of his kingdom, Susenyos was the first monarch to incorporate large Galla units into the army, and he settled Galla tribes as *chawa* in various provinces of his domains. These innovations were to have a profound influence on the future of the country. The 'loyal' Galla were settled in several important provinces, the kings gradually became more dependent on their support and, on the other hand, more estranged from their semitized nobility and population. In the western and northern provinces, Susenyos vigorously followed Serse-Dingil's policy. During the second and third decades of the seventeenth century his armies raided farther west than ever before. However, while the Agaw were cruelly subjugated and gradually converted, most of the Falasha were annihilated, forced to convert or sold into slavery when they lost their last strongholds in Simien and Walqayt. The colonization of Dembya, Wagera, Simien and Walqayt was accelerated and the remnants of the indigenous inhabitants were soon assimilated.

The expansionist policy of Susenyos in the west and north brought Ethiopia into areas which had been nominally dependent on the Funj kingdom of Sennar since the sixteenth century. Relations between Ethiopia and Sennar were relatively cordial during the first years of Susenyos's reign. Gradually they began to deteriorate with each side raiding the borderland of the other. Finally, between 1617 and 1619 Ethiopian armies penetrated Sennar's territories as far as Fazughli in the west, Dabarki on the route to Sennar, and Taḳa in the north-east.

In the midst of this campaign Susenyos was informed that one of his brothers, some of his kinsmen and closest aids, together with the *abuna* (the head of the Ethiopian church) were conspiring to depose him, believing that he was about to submit to the See of Rome. Catholicism had made little or no progress in Ethiopia until the beginning of the seventeenth century, when, after successive failures, some more Jesuit missionaries managed to reach Tigre. Of these the most outstanding was Pero Paez, who was a gifted scholar and linguist, of modest and congenial personality. Under his influence, the king was already won over to Catholicism in 1612 and Susenyos hoped that the Catholic nations might help him revive the power of Ethiopia. He was prudently prevented by Paez from submitting to Rome in 1612 because the country was still not ready for such a step. Nevertheless, in the following years Susenyos encouraged his relatives and his court officials to follow the teachings of the Jesuits. Moreover, by his impolitic behaviour and the favour shown to some of his kinsmen and especially to his brother Si'ile Kristos, the staunchest supporter of Catholicism in the court, he caused a deep rift among his family and supporters. Many took up the cause of the national church, which they considered the pillar of the Ethiopian polity, and decided to depose Susenyos at the first opportunity. Although the king harshly punished the conspirators, the rebellion of 1617/18 was the first of many rebellions with religious and personal motivations which further destroyed the unity of the kingdom.

Susenyos openly confessed the Catholic faith in 1622. At this crucial moment Pero Paez died. It is most unlikely that even Paez would have brought about the religious and cultural transformation of Ethiopia envisaged by the Jesuits. But Paez's successor, Afonso Mendez, who reached Ethiopia in 1625, was far less suited to advise the king. Even less than Paez did he comprehend the enormity of the revolution which the Jesuits were attempting. Ethiopian Christianity had its roots in age-old traditions which were part of the cultural heritage of the people, and in some cases of the African soil. Susenyos's conversion, the reforms of the church, and his administrative policy aroused the opposition of the ecclesiastics, the population at large and some of the king's relatives who governed huge provinces and commanded large armies. The threat to the monarchy drove the king to extremities, and the large army which Susenyos was forced to maintain brought economic ruin upon the country. Moreover, the king's relations with his officials, and the haughty behaviour of Mendez towards Susenyos, gradually eroded the prestige of the monarchy. Finally, with rebellion and bloodshed becoming more widespread from year to year, Susenyos succumbed to the pleading of his own family. In 1632 the disappointed monarch re-established the Ethiopian church and abdicated in favour of his son, Fasiladas. Although the Jesuits were soon expelled from the country, rebellions with religious motivations were not terminated. The impact of the Jesuits lingered on, as they left behind some loyal adherents and the seeds of doctrinal controversies which were to divide and weaken Christian Ethiopia, while the fear of Portuguese retribution drove Fasiladas to develop stronger relations with his Muslim neighbours and traders in the Red Sea basin.

THE RED SEA TRADE

Before the Portuguese succeeded in diverting much of the Far East trade from the Red Sea to the Cape route, the trade of the Horn of Africa had been a minor branch of the commerce of the Red Sea. It was to be expected that, with this diversion in the sixteenth century, the trade of the Horn of Africa would have grown in importance for the commercial communities of the Red Sea. In spite of the abortive attempts of the Ottomans to obtain a foothold on the plateau as late as the 1590s, caravan trade between the coast and the plateau did indeed develop. Moreover, the trade between the Funj sultanate and Ethiopia also expanded until the beginning of the seventeenth century, and Funj and other merchants travelled by way of Gallabat and Chilga to Ethiopia. Nevertheless, the overall growth of the trade of the Horn was relatively small in the sixteenth and early seventeenth centuries owing to the continuous instability in Adal and in Ethiopia. As for the Benadir coast, Brava was sacked and Mogadishu attacked by a Portuguese fleet as early as 1506, and, because of continuous Portuguese and Turkish maritime activities in the Gulf of Aden and along the Somali coast throughout the sixteenth century, the trade of the Benadir towns greatly diminished.

Ottoman power in the Red Sea basin declined sharply from the beginning of the seventeenth century. The pasha commanding the Ethiopian coast henceforth kept only a token garrison at Massawa and relied mainly on the power of the *nā'ib* of Arkiko to maintain his authority in the area. The *nā'ib* was the chief of the descendants of the Janissaries stationed in Massawa in the sixteenth century, who had married Belew women, and gradually he and his men had gained control over the pastoral tribes of the Semhar plain. Exploiting their position, they exacted heavy payments from merchants who visited Massawa and thus were partly responsible for the stagnation of its trade.

Contemporary Catholic sources claimed that Ethiopia entered a period of isolation during the reigns of Fasiladas and his heir Yohannes (1667–82). Instead the contrary is true. A number of Italian merchants, the Dutchman Peter Heyling, and even a German Jesuit in the guise of a physician were allowed to enter the country. Moreover, already at the turn of the sixteenth century and especially after the conquest of the Tihama coast and Aden by the *imām* of the Yemen in the second quarter of the seventeenth century, trade began to increase on the eastern side of the Red Sea. By this time the coffee trade of Mocha also began to grow in importance. Consequently, Indian merchants renewed their activities in the Red Sea, and they were followed by British and Dutch merchants who also occasionally traded with Ethiopia through Massawa. Even earlier, Greek, Armenian and Italian merchants had 'rediscovered' the trade of the Red Sea and traded with its ports by way of Egypt. Some entered Ethiopia and a few even settled there. Together with Arab and local Muslim merchants, they contributed to the revival of the trade of the plateau. Fasiladas and Yohannes employed Greek, Armenian and Arab merchants as their commercial representatives. These merchants, travelling to many countries, carried friendly messages and presents from the Ethiopian kings to a number of Muslim rulers including the Great Mogul in India, as also to the Dutch governor of Batavia and to the British authorities in India.

Relations between Ethiopia and the Funj sultanate had been normalized as early as the first years of Fasiladas's reign. Relations with the Ottomans were also improved, for they held Suakin and Massawa and their goodwill was essential whenever a new *abuna* was needed from Egypt. Moreover, both Fasiladas and Yohannes wanted the Ottoman governors of the coast to prevent missionaries from entering Ethiopia and to repulse any attempted landing of Portuguese troops on the Ethiopian coast. Relations with the *imām* of Yemen during Fasiladas's reign were motivated, to an even greater extent than those with the Turks, by political considerations as well as by commercial ones. In the second quarter of the seventeenth century the *imām* of the Yemen had become the guardian of the southern approaches of the Red Sea, and Fasiladas, who constantly feared a Portuguese attack, toyed with the idea of a military alliance with him. After two Ethiopian embassies had visited his capital in the 1640s, Imām al-Mutawwakil dispatched the grand *qāḍī* of San'a, Ḥasan al-Khaimī, hoping to convert Fasiladas to Islam. The *qāḍī* reached the Ethiopian court in 1650, but his arrival caused such consternation that riots broke out in the capital and he was hurriedly spirited out of the country.

The volume of the Red Sea trade grew even more rapidly in the last quarter of the seventeenth century. To some extent this was due to the growth of Omani maritime power, which caused a revival of the trade and the Pilgrimage from Muslim communities in the Indian Ocean. But it was also due to the growth in the demand for Yemen's coffee, resulting from the spread of coffee-drinking in Europe. Consequently, British and Dutch factories were set up at Mocha, and by the beginning of the eighteenth century the French appeared in the area as well.

Jedda, too, flourished because of its position as an entrepôt of trade between the southern and northern parts of the Red Sea. However, the Ottoman empire had a highly unfavourable trade-balance with the Far East, and this constant drain on its gold resources could not continue for ever. Thus, towards the last quarter of the eighteenth century, the economy of the Red Sea basin began to stagnate once again. The fluctuations in the Red Sea trade no doubt affected Ethiopia and, to some extent, the policy of its rulers in the seventeenth and eighteenth centuries, but they were even more detrimental to the development of the Muslim principalities, towns and nomads of the Horn who were greatly dependent on trade.

THE MUSLIM PRINCIPALITIES

Founded about the middle of the seventeenth century by ʿAlī b. Dāwūd, the sultanate of Harar, more than any other political unit which grew out of the ruins of Awsa, could be considered as the successor of Adal. Harar had served for a time as Adal's capital. Its rulers were the descendants of Gragn, and the population of the town preserved its ancient Semitic language and culture. Moreover, Harar was the most important centre of Islamic learning in the Horn of Africa, and during the eighteenth century its caravan merchants became an important factor in the revival of Islam in southern Ethiopia. The development of trade in the Red Sea in the last decades of the seventeenth century probably affected the economy of Ḥarar and contributed to some extent to its relative political stability. The sultanate, nonetheless, began to decline at the end of the eighteenth century. The economy of the town was no doubt affected by the stagnation of trade in the Red Sea basin, but it seems that Harar suffered even more from the internal strife in the ruling dynasty, from the unruliness of the Somali and from the continuous attacks of the Galla.

Some Galla tribes began to settle in the vicinity of Harar and became cultivators (*qottu*) as early as the end of the sixteenth century. Gradually they adopted Islam, and towards the end of the seventeenth century they accepted the emir of Harar as their nominal master, but although they gave up some aspects of their original culture and socio-political organization, they still preserved their tribal system and maintained an independent political hierarchy at the side of that of the emir. By the end of the seventeenth century, the emirs had begun to take Galla and Somali wives in order to assure themselves of tribal support. Consequently, a number of emirs rose to power only through the intervention of their tribal kinsmen. The majority of the Galla tribes on the Harari plateau, however, remained pastoralists, recognizing only the authority of their traditional office-holders, and they raided Harari territory and caravans. These continuous Galla attacks, the disregard shown by most of the northern Somali for the authority of the emir and the perpetual struggle for power within the dynasty were the main reasons why Harar remained politically unimportant until its conquest by the Egyptians in the nineteenth century.

Inhabited by Arab, Somali, Dankali and Harari merchants, Zeila served as the main outlet for the trade of Harar. Although the situation in Harar affected Zeila, the town retained its relative importance until the last decades of the eighteenth century. Nearby, the annual fair of Berbera, attended by tens of thousands of Somali tribesmen, attracted caravans from Harar, Shoa and southern Ethiopia and merchants from Arabia and India. The revenues derived from this fair were always a bone of contention between the northern Somali tribes. However, a truce was usually preserved in the area while the fair was in progress. The rest of present-day Somalia was hardly affected by developments in the Red Sea. Here the determining factor was the migration of the Somali tribes, prompted by the very nature of nomadic peoples, the growth of certain tribes or long periods of drought. By the first decades of the eighteenth century, tribes belonging to the Dir group had displaced the Dijil in the hinterland of parts of the Benadir coast. About the same time, tribes of the Darod group began to expand from the Ogaden southwards, pushing before them Somali tribes who had preceded them in the area. However, when they moved up the Juba, they met with fierce Galla resistance. Though the Galla were forced to withdraw farther north-westwards, they not only succeeded in curbing the Somali expansion but by the beginning of the nineteenth century they were even raiding deep into the Somali-held hinterland of the Benadir coast.

The Benadir towns were occupied by the *imām* of Oman, Sayf b. Sulṭān, in the last decades of the seventeenth century during his campaign against the Portuguese strongholds on the East African coast. Under Omani protection the merchant communities of the Benadir coast redeveloped their Indian Ocean and Red Sea trade. But after the Omani forces had evacuated the area at the beginning of the eighteenth century, and with the decline of Omani power towards the middle of the century, the government of the Benadir towns passed into the hands of the Somali tribes of the nearby hinterland. Such was the case with Mogadishu, where the Abgal became the true masters of the town, as also with Merca which was ruled by the Bimal. This transformation, the continuous threat to the towns and their trade with the interior by the unruly Somali, and the importation of cheap cloth from India and Europe which competed with the better quality cloth produced locally, were the main causes of the decline of the Benadir towns. As for the small ports of the coast of the Majerteyn, their traditional trade with Arabia was too insignificant to be affected by commercial fluctuations or to introduce changes into the political or economic life of the Somali tribes thinly spread in the hinterland.

Farther north, the *imam*ate of Awsa passed by the middle of the seventeenth century into the hands of immigrant Sharifs of the Ba-Alawi family of Hadhramaut. This dynasty, however, was unable to protect Awsa from Galla and Dankali raids. Finally, in the first decades of the eighteenth century, Awsa was overrun by the Mudaito tribe of the Asaimara branch of the Danakil, who formed a new Mudaito dynasty of Awsa. The greater peace and stability afforded by a number of strong sultans who ruled Awsa in the eighteenth century, its successful agriculture, and its position between the coast and the plateau turned the sultanate into a relatively flourishing mercantile centre. This development was also connected with the growing power of the new Menzian dynasty in Shoa.[1] However, at the end of the eighteenth century the Mudaito sultanate began to decline. The area was probably affected by the general economic stagnation in the Red Sea basin. Moreover, at the beginning of the nineteenth century, with the accession of an infant sultan, Awsa was plunged into a period of anarchy and instability. Finally, the Adoimara Danakil overran the area and forced the Mudaito sultan to share his revenues with them.

During the course of their expansion in the seventeenth century, branches of the Baraytuma Galla penetrated Dankali country in several areas, thereby perpetuating the division between the southern and the northern Danakil. Thus, in the eighteenth century the Dankali sultanate lost control of the salt plains of Arho, and the northern tribes henceforth obeyed only the elders of each clan. In the south, the Danakil further disintegrated into a number of insignificant sultanates, with centres along the coast. The most important of these in the eighteenth century was probably that of Tajura. Because they controlled Lake Asal, a source of salt, the people of Tajura also became involved in

[1] See below p. 560.

the caravan trade with Shoa and Harar. The sultan of Tajura, however, had little authority, if any, over the Adoimara tribes of the hinterland supposedly belonging to his sultanate. The real authority in the deserts lay, as in the north, in the hands of the elders of each clan.

Though some of the Muslim elements of the coast and Harar benefited from the revival of trade in the Red Sea since the end of the sixteenth century, this did not halt their political disintegration and decline. In the past the Muslim elements had rallied around Adal mainly because of the pressure of the Christian kingdom and the temptation of rich loot on the plateau. However, since the death of Galawdewos, the Muslims and the Christians were separated by Galla who had overrun parts of Adal, Dankali territory and Ethiopia. The Galla pastoralists did not supply an ideological incentive for unity, and the Muslim societies returned to their traditional rivalries.

FASILADAS AND YOHANNES

Fasiladas's new policy of friendship and co-operation had been welcomed by his Muslim neighbours. However, his internal policy, aimed at rebuilding the power of the monarchy by mending the alliance of the ruler with the national church, completely misfired. The fruitless termination of al-Khaimī's mission from the *imām* of Yemen was but an example of the tremendous power which the ecclesiastics exercised in Ethiopia during the reign of Fasiladas, and especially during the reign of Yohannes. The heads of the church and the monastic orders were members of the royal council, and, together with ecclesiastics from all over the country, they participated in councils which were held from time to time to discuss matters of law and belief. These gatherings developed into a battle between the supporters of the two monastic orders of Tekla-Haymanot and Ewostatewos over the interpretation of those aspects of monophysitism which had been challenged by the Jesuits.

In the period of Susenyos, Ethiopian scholars had countered the Jesuits' arguments concerning the two natures of Christ by maintaining that Christ's human nature had become perfect through its union with the divine, and that the two natures became inseparable (*tawahdo*). During the reigns of Fasiladas and Yohannes, the followers of Ewostatewos, mainly from the Gojjam branch of the order, maintained that the union between the two natures was brought about through the unction (*qibat*) of the Holy Ghost, and that Christ became son of God and elevated to divinity by this unction. Later on they claimed that Christ's body was made of material which was not consubstantial with the human. These theories of the 'unctionists' (*qibatoch*) were unacceptable to the followers of Tekla-Haymanot ('unionists'), who considered them a deviation from the original concept of *tawahdo*. The 'unionists' also felt the need for a formula which would explain the references to the human character of Christ in the scriptures and would maintain the principle of 'redemption'. Thus they supported a theory which argued that, although the human and the divine natures of Christ were united, the Grace, or the unction of the Holy Spirit, did not elevate from an inferior state to a superior one and did not bring about the union of divinity and the flesh, though it had restored to his humanity the dignity lost by the sin of Adam. Consequently they also claimed at a later stage that Christ was the son of God by Grace, and that his elevation to the quality of a natural son of God was a result of the union of the human nature with the divine. Henceforth, the 'unionists' were called *Sega Lijoch* (sons of Grace).

Having failed to bridge the early differences between the two opposing camps in a number of councils, Fasiladas gave his sanction in 1654 to the formula of the 'unctionists' (*qibatoch*), hoping to bring to an end the controversy. However, this step only led to a rebellion of the 'unionists' which the king was forced to suppress. The power of the ecclesiastics, especially the *qibatoch*, became even more noticeable during the reign of Yohannes 'the Pious'. At a council held in 1668, some monks even dared to excommunicate Yohannes for marrying a distant relative. Nevertheless, the king convened several councils during the 1670s, in which he actively participated and in which he sided with the *qibatoch*.

The reconciliation of the kings of the Solomonic dynasty with the national church thus failed to reunite Ethiopia and to enhance the power and prestige of the monarchy. While the power of the ecclesiastics grew, their controversies supplied religious ideologies for rebellions which were, in most cases, an expression of regional particularism. Because Fasiladas, in his latter days, and Yohannes, who succeeded him, supported the *qibatoch*, they alienated most of the Amhara nobility, which traditionally supported the order of Tekla-Haymanot. The kings tended to rely, therefore, more and more on their bodyguard regiments composed of Negroid slaves, Turks, Arabs, 'Qayla' (Falasha) and local Muslims loyal only to the king, their master. At the council of 1668 it was decided to expel from Ethiopia the descendants of the Portuguese and to segregate the local Muslims, Turks and 'Qayla' from the Christian community. It is possible that this decision, which was later reaffirmed by another council, was not only a reaction to Fasiladas's attempts to improve his relations with the Muslims, but was also a reaction to the growing power of the foreign elements in the palace and in the army.

The preoccupation of Fasiladas and Yohannes with the suppression of rebellions and with theological controversies left the kingdom at the mercy of the Galla. The main target of Galla expansion in this period was Gojjam, which was attacked from the south by the Mecha and Liban Galla and from the east by the Tulama. At the same time the Tulama continued to expand from Shoa into Amhara, while the Wallo, Yejju and Azebo, who had advanced along the eastern escarpments, overran Angot and parts of Amhara and raided into Wag, Begemder and Tigre. In 1642 the eastern Galla virtually annihilated the royal army in Tigre. Following this catastrophe, Tigre and Baher-Meder were abandoned to their fate and were successively ravaged by the Galla and by the coastal pastoralists. Only in the last years of his reign, failing to re-establish his authority by force, did Yohannes exploit local rivalries and gain the nominal allegiance of most of the nobility of Tigre and Baher-Meder.

Fasiladas and Yohannes concentrated their efforts on preserving their authority in the provinces west of the Tekeze. A symptom of the shift of the kingdom's centre of gravity to the area of Lake Tana was the establishment of Gondar as a permanent capital of Ethiopia in the days of Fasiladas. This step enhanced the importance of the functionaries connected with the palace and that of the nobles and ecclesiastics living in the capital or around it. It also accelerated the colonization of Wagera, Dembya, Begemder and Simien, and the amharization of their Cushitic-Agaw population. The process of integrating the Agaw population of the bend of the Abbai river into the Ethiopian polity was also somehow maintained in spite of the constant raids of the Galla. Nevertheless, the Agaw of Lasta defeated all attempts to subdue them and preserved their independence until the end of the seventeenth century.

The period of Fasiladas and Yohannes was one of prolonged decline. While the Galla continued their expansion nearly unchecked, the centrifugal forces in Ethiopia, enhanced by religious controversies, grew in power. Bruce describes Fasiladas as a strong ruler and a brilliant general, but the truth is that during his reign he did not distinguish himself as a ruler and on the few occasions when he led the Ethiopian army, he was totally defeated. As for Yohannes, all accounts agree that he was not an able ruler and was more concerned with religion than warfare. Hence, by 1680 the prestige of the monarchy was at a low ebb. There was general dissatisfaction among the nobility with Yohannes's government, and even Iyasu, the king's son who succeeded him in 1682, joined the opposition to his father.

IYASU I AND THE GALLA

A gifted, brave and far-sighted ruler, who was also a modernizer and a lover of arts and crafts, Iyasu I, called 'the Great', was the last important king of the Gondarine dynasty. Determined to reunify the kingdom and to reform the foundations of the Ethiopian polity – the church, the administration and the army – he was the first monarch since the days of Serse-Dingil who seriously resumed the offensive against the Galla and tried to re-establish Ethiopian authority in the provinces which they had overrun. Although, in the circumstances, the gigantic task which Iyasu undertook was unrealistic, his vain efforts to revive the power of the Christian kingdom served at least to postpone its disintegration.

Iyasu's first objective was to curb the interference of the ecclesiastics in the affairs of state and to terminate their controversies. He refused to be drawn into endless religious polemics, but he gave his support to the 'unionists'. The order of Tekla-Haymanot had always been considered part of the 'establishment', and more likely to bow to the will of the king. The monarch coerced the *qibatoch* to agree to the 'unionists'' theory and, although it took more than a decade to break their resistance, in the 1690s the Ethiopian church was unified, at least on the surface, behind the 'unionists'' formula. To preserve this unity, Iyasu did not hesitate to censure and even to punish some of the spiritual leaders of the order of Tekla-Haymanot when they evolved new theories which threatened the newly won dogmatic unity. The ecclesiastics, however, resented the loss of their power, and they closely watched the king while awaiting their chance to revenge their humiliation.

The Agaw of Lasta were exhausted by the continuous war with the Amhara and by the pressure of the eastern Galla, and their resistance petered out in the first decade of Iyasu's reign. During the same period, the king soundly defeated the *qibatoch* of Gojjam and Damot, who tried several times to rebel against him. However, new and powerful elements began to resent the king's policy and authoritarian rule in the 1690s. Iyasu closely supervised the administration of the provinces west of the Tekeze and personally commanded the army. Many court officials, provincial administrators and nobles soon realized that they were now subject to dismissal if they failed to please the king or abused their authority. Hence, Gondar was the scene of many intrigues and plots. Matters became even more serious when the traditional semitized *chawa* units, objecting to the king's long and dangerous expeditions against the Galla, joined the opposition.

The *chawa* battalions had been the backbone of the Ethiopian army since the reign of Serse-Dingil. By Iyasu's time, however, they were corrupted by wealth and by the power which they had gained over the weak kings. They had inter-married with the nobility of the areas in which they were stationed and in fact had again become part of the local aristocracy. Iyasu became convinced that they were untrustworthy when, on several occasions, they refused to follow him. He therefore gradually strengthened the power of the bodyguard regiments until by the beginning of the eighteenth century the cavalry, infantry and fusiliers numbered over 12,000. This army was maintained by a special treasury, so that it should not become attached to any part of the country. The *chawa* system was not abandoned by the king, yet, following in the steps of Susenyos, he recruited new *chawa* almost invariably from loyal Galla tribes, whom he settled in newly conquered areas. Moreover, to counter-balance the influence of the traditional *chawa* units, Iyasu even settled Tulama and Liban Galla in northern Gojjam and Begemder. The king encouraged the amharization and the conversion to Christianity of his new Galla soldiers, and appointed some of their chiefs to high offices in the army and in the administration of peripheral provinces, although these Galla elements were still relatively foreign to the heritage of Christian Ethiopia.

The contact with the peoples of the plateau had a profound impact on Galla society and culture. Although this impact varied from one area to another, many Galla gradually came to realize that their traditional organization was not suited to their new environment, and some began to adopt aspects of their neighbours' culture and political institutions. In some cases traditionally elective offices became hereditary. In one instance, several Mecha and Gudru tribes united under the command of one leader in the face of Amhara pressure and even appear to have considered the adoption of a monarchical system.[1] But

[1] I. Guidi, ed., *Annales Iohannis I, Iyāsu I, Bakāffā* (Paris, 1903), 254.

in this period such radical innovations were still the exception rather than the rule. Far more often, the Galla affiliated themselves to the political institutions of their neighbours. This was especially true of the first wave of Galla immigrants, who had ample lands and had been living for some time alongside the Cushitic societies of the plateau. Such was the case, for instance, with the Tulama in Shoa and in parts of Amhara, and of branches of the Baraytuma around Harar. However, this process of settlement and assimilation was constantly disrupted by other Galla tribes who were still seeking land for settlement and for grazing, such as, at the end of the seventeenth century, the Mecha in south-western Ethiopia and the Wallo, Yejju and Azebo in Amhara and on the eastern verges of the Ethiopian escarpments.

Shortly after coming to power, Iyasu tried to take the initiative from the Galla and conquer parts of the kingdom which they had overrun. In a series of campaigns during the 1680s and early 1690s, he systematically reduced the power of the Tulama and the Borana who were settled in Amhara and on the verges of Gojjam. During the 1690s, Iyasu penetrated Shoa several times with the intention of re-establishing his authority in the province and driving the Galla from the parts which they controlled, for, as a result of Serse-Dingil's policy, Shoa had been virtually abandoned to the Galla. Nevertheless, some Amhara principalities continued to exist in different parts of the province and maintained contacts with the king of kings. The Amhara rulers in Shoa, however, were unenthusiastic about Iyasu's plan to attack their Galla neighbours who were partly amharized and with whom they maintained relatively friendly relations. Realizing the true situation, Iyasu left matters in Shoa as they were. Hence the 'reconquest' of Shoa, as most of Iyasu's achievements, was but a temporary affair. Nonetheless, Iyasu's campaigns in Shoa may have been partly responsible for the emergence there of a new dynasty, founded by Niguse, a nobleman from the district of Menz. Traditions connected with this dynasty claim that Niguse co-operated with Iyasu, and on the latter's command left Menz for Ifat in order to help the local Muslim dynasty against the Galla. Ifat served as a base for the descendants of Niguse who gradually conquered most of Shoa in the following centuries, already using firearms with success against the Galla during the reign of Ammehayes in the second quarter of the eighteenth century. Once converted, the Galla were incorporated into the administration and the army. Muslims also enjoyed the rulers' tolerance and increased trading profits. On this basis of military strength and prosperous homogeneity, the Shoan rulers, particularly Asfa-Wasen (1770–1808?), established a centralized administration, and, with the help of judicious matrimonial alliances, effectively prevented the emergence of rival war-lords, in striking contrast to other parts of Ethiopia.

In 1704 Iyasu led a military expedition to re-establish Ethiopian authority in the Sidama[1] plateau of the south-west which was the source of most of the luxuries which Ethiopia exported. Although he had abandoned the south to the Galla, Serse-Dingil had tried to preserve and consolidate Ethiopian authority in the south-west and especially in the kingdom of Innarya. This kingdom was probably the most important in the region. It served as an entrepôt for the trade of all the monarchies and principalities which surrounded it, and was regularly visited by merchants. Its population was employed in cultivation and in cattle breeding. In other aspects Innarya was probably typical of the larger Sidama kingdoms. Although its king was considered by outsiders to be all powerful, Innarya had a decentralized system of government. Innarya proper, where the king's rule was probably absolute, was relatively small in size, and it was surrounded by districts, principalities and tribal areas which, although they recognized the authority of the king, maintained some degree of autonomy. In fact, the king consulted his subordinate rulers and chiefs on every matter of importance. On the other hand, the small neighbouring Sidama kingdom of Janjero was far less influenced by contacts with the outside world and still preserved elements of divine kingship.

Serse-Dingil had led several military expeditions to Innarya and encouraged the conversion of its population to Christianity, hoping to strengthen the ties of this monarchy with the Ethiopian kingdom. The recognition of Ethiopian overlordship by the kings of Innarya and by his neighbours depended, however, on Ethiopian ability to 'show the flag' there. Already in the last decades of the sixteenth century, the Mecha and the Liban Galla had subdued nearly all the area between Damot and the Gibe basin, and had even penetrated into the northern parts of Innarya. In the first decades of the seventeenth century the route between Damot and Innarya was nearly cut off by the Galla, after the latter conquered Bizamo. Ethiopian armies, nevertheless, forced their way from time to time through the multitudes of Galla pastoralists to collect the tribute of Innarya, which amounted to a large sum always paid in gold. Innarya still prospered, precariously maintain-

[1] A general term used for convenience to describe the Cushitic population of southern Ethiopia.

ing its trade relations with the coast and with its neighbours while its army repulsed all the attacks of the Mecha. By this time, however, Christianity, if it had ever penetrated beyond court circles, was nearly extinguished and the majority of the inhabitants of Innarya were animists.

Galla resistance to Ethiopian attempts to reach Innarya increased, and during the third quarter of the seventeenth century the Innarya route was abandoned altogether. The Mecha tribes gradually devastated the peripheral districts of the kingdom and conquered some of the neighbouring principalities. When Iyasu I led the expedition to Innarya in 1704, all the area between Damot and the Gibe basin was already occupied by Galla tribes belonging to the Gudru and the Mecha groups. Although they still preserved their traditional institutions, many of the Galla in this area had become cultivators and were in the process of adopting a more regular and centralized system of government. The entrenchment of the Galla in all the areas which he traversed and their incessant attacks on his army convinced Iyasu of the futility of any attempt to retain control over this area. By the end of 1704 Iyasu returned to Damot, accompanied by a number of dissatisfied Mecha tribes whom he settled as *chawa* along the Abbai. Although Iyasu's expedition failed to re-establish Ethiopian authority in the south-west, it was not a complete failure. The heavy losses which the Gudru and Mecha suffered curbed the northern expansion of these tribes and probably saved Gojjam and Damot.

At the beginning of the eighteenth century the Galla conquered Innarya and its sister Sidama principalities, and they gradually absorbed into their society the Sidama population left in the area. In turn they adopted many Sidama customs and began to copy their social and political organization. Finally, by the first decades of the nineteenth century, the Galla had established in the Gibe basin a number of highly centralized monarchies. This revolutionary transition in Galla society was no doubt influenced by their Sidama neighbours and by the transformation of the Mecha from pastoralism to agriculture. The revival of Islam in Ethiopia during the second part of the eighteenth century and the great development of caravan trade on the plateau during the early nineteenth century probably also contributed to the founding of these Galla monarchies, Islam being welcomed by the Galla rulers as a unifying factor which helped them to consolidate their authority. Their adoption of the monarchical system and Islam may also have been a response to the growing pressure of Christian Shoa from the last decades of the eighteenth century onwards.

Iyasu's attempt to reconquer the south-west was probably connected with the growing demand for Ethiopia's export products resulting from the expansion of the Red Sea trade. His strong rule was conducive to the development of trade in Ethiopia, and trade intensified between the coast, Sennar and the plateau. Nevertheless, the trade of Massawa did not increase to its full potential. As a result of the rapid decline of Ottoman authority in the Red Sea basin, the real power in the area of Massawa was, by the last quarter of the seventeenth century, in the hands of the *nā'ib*. The *nā'ib* frequently attacked Hamasien and Akele-Guzay, stepped up his exactions from merchants visiting Massawa and, probably on the instruction of the pasha of Suakin, prohibited the importation of firearms into Ethiopia. Thus, in many cases Ethiopian merchants preferred the longer and far more difficult route to Arabia by way of Suakin, or to Egypt by way of Sennar.

At this time the Funj sultanate was enfeebled by the long rebellion of the Shāyqiyya, by the struggle for power between the weak sultans and their Hamaj viziers and by the lawlessness of the Arab and other pastoral tribes (see chapter 1, p. 44). Aware of the situation in Sennar, Iyasu pursued the policy initiated by Susenyos of establishing Ethiopian overlordship over the northern marches of the plateau. He wanted to terminate the continuous pressure of the pastoralists and the negroid cultivators on the newly settled northern provinces, and to keep open the caravan routes to Sennar and Suakin. The culmination of Iyasu's policy in this direction was a co-ordinated attack in 1692–3 by the king and several of his governors especially aimed at the Dubayna Arabs and the negroid cultivators of the Mareb water course.

The expedition of 1692–3 also afforded Iyasu an opportunity to re-establish the authority of the monarchy in Baher-Meder and Tigre. Ever since the disastrous defeat of Fasiladas's army in Tigre in 1641–2, these provinces had been only nominally under the control of the king of kings. But although Iyasu had a large army at his disposal, he exercised great caution in his relations with the traditional feudatories of Tigre, preferring not to alienate the Tigrean nobility with their special cultural and historical heritage and their resentment of Amhara predominance. At the same time, the king did not hesitate to use coercion when it became necessary to regulate the crucially important salt trade.

The presence of Iyasu's army in Tigre, and a blockade of the coast ordered by the king, brought the *nā'ib* to submission. He promised to facilitate the trade of Ethiopia, to refrain from attacking the plateau and to share with the king the customs of Massawa, as had been the tradition in the past. Even before 1692–3, Ethiopia's trade by way of Massawa with Arabia, with the Dutch, the British and the rulers of India had continued to develop. However, after 1692–3 the volume of this trade grew considerably. The presence of an Ethiopian 'commercial representative' in Persia was even reported, and in 1700 a British commercial delegation from Bombay tried to enter Ethiopia.

Iyasu's fame and his trade relations with European powers encouraged Catholic missionaries to renew their efforts to enter Ethiopia. Moreover, at the end of the seventeenth century the French were attempting to share in the rich trade of the Red Sea. Consequently, a number of Jesuits, Franciscans and French emissaries reached Sennar. Because Iyasu and his son Tekla-Haymanot were interested in the development of foreign trade, and were misled into believing that the French were of a faith similar to that of the Ethiopians, a few even entered Ethiopia. However, the intensified traffic of Europeans to Ethiopia aroused the suspicion of Ethiopian ecclesiastics and the apprehension of the Muslim authorities. Finally, a French emissary to Ethiopia was murdered in Sennar in 1705. Consequently, the French temporarily lost interest in Ethiopia and the missionaries abandoned the Sennar route.

The nobility and the *chawa* of the semitized provinces had refused to accompany Iyasu to Innarya, and while he was there his overthrow was prepared by them together with the ecclesiastics and Iyasu's wife, whose son Tekla-Haymanot deputized for the king in Gondar. In the second half of 1705, as Iyasu prepared in Gojjam to march upon Gondar, he became desperately ill and recognized Tekla-Haymanot as his regent and heir. Nevertheless, when some of Iyasu's supporters appeared in Gojjam in 1706, Iyasu was assassinated by the queen's kinsmen and Tekla-Haymanot became king of kings.

THE RISING POWER OF THE GALLA

The period following the death of Iyasu up till the death of Dawit III in 1721 was one of rapid decline. In this period the centrifugal forces in Ethiopia were completely triumphant, and the country was governed by courtiers and army commanders. The kings 'reigned' in Gondar and seldom did more than lead small military expeditions to the neighbouring provinces. The guard regiments were now constantly held by the kings in and around Gondar. They were corrupted by inactivity and by the knowledge that the king completely depended on their support. Gradually they grew undisciplined, constituting a threat to the security of the kingdom. As recognition of the central authorities depended to a great extent on their ability to call up and maintain large armies and to enforce the collection of taxes, the area under the effective control of the king continuously shrank in size and many provinces became semi-autonomous. Those who most benefited from the situation were the Galla who, with the exception of the Mecha, attacked Ethiopia from all directions. In Gondar the power of the 'amharized' Galla was constantly on the rise. The weak rulers, needing Galla support, appointed Galla nobles to high positions in the palace and administration, and increasingly depended on the Galla household guard.

The *qibatoch*, who at first supported the king, Tekla-Haymanot, rebelled in 1706. They were defeated and all the spiritual leaders of the movement perished on the battlefield. The turn of the 'unionists' came soon afterwards. Dawit III and his *ras bitweded* (an officer who combined the position of commander of the army and head of the administration) were staunch supporters of the *qibatoch*. When the 'unionists' rioted in Gondar in 1720–1, the Galla household guard massacred hundreds of monks, including some of the most important scholars of the Tekla-Haymanot order. Thus by the second quarter of the eighteenth century, the ecclesiastics' power to influence developments in Ethiopia had been drastically reduced, although the controversy over 'union' and 'unction' persisted.

Less than two years after becoming king of kings, Tekla-Haymanot was assassinated. He was succeeded by Iyasu's brother, Tewoflos, who died in 1711. By this time the nobility thought that they could abolish the Solomonic dynasty, and Yostos, one of their leaders, was proclaimed king of kings. However, Yostos was considered a usurper by the populace, and in 1716 he was deposed and Iyasu's son, Dawit III, was enthroned. Even then, the real power remained in the hands of a group of nobles and guard commanders. In 1721 Dawit was poisoned by a servant of the palace and another of Iyasu's sons, Walde Giyorgis, popularly known as Bekaffa, was enthroned.

The rise of Bekaffa to power ended the government of the court officials. Though exceedingly cruel, he was brave, gifted and just. He hated the nobility intensely and especially the courtiers, whom he considered to be the main cause of the decline of Ethiopia. Hence, every suspicion of a conspiracy served the king as a pretext for mass arrests and executions of the 'culprits'. Even the nobles and officials whom he employed in his administration were mere tools whom he deposed whenever he wished. And because the descendants of the royal family could be used to undermine his power, these too were savagely persecuted. Immediately after coming to power Bekaffa virtually annihilated the troublesome slave regiments of the guard. As other household units, including the *chawa* in the Amhara provinces, had also proved untrustworthy, Bekaffa turned for support to the Galla and especially to the Mecha settled by his father in Damot. He recruited Galla to special bodyguard regiments, and Galla *chawa* units became the backbone of his army. With the growing importance of firearms in Ethiopian warfare, he greatly expanded the fusilier units as well.

Bekaffa was determined to re-establish his authority in the provinces east of the Tekeze. These provinces, though traditionally inclined to particularism, had always been an integral part of the kingdom and they were most important to its economy, especially when Ethiopia's trade was expanding with the relative stability of Bekaffa's reign. Hence, after 1724 his army subjugated Wag and Lasta and brought to submission the nobility of Tigre and Baher-Meder. By 1727, through a regime of terror and by relying even more than his predecessors on Galla military power, Bekaffa had succeeded in re-establishing the authority of the monarchy from Tigre in the east to Damot in the west.

Bekaffa became seriously ill in 1728. It seems that thereafter and until his death, probably in 1730, Ethiopia was actually ruled by Queen Mantuab. During this period the queen carefully prepared for the succession of her infant son, Iyasu II. Her kinsmen from the province of Qwara were given key positions in the administration and the command of the guard. The loyalty of the officials who were close to Bekaffa was assured by promotion and bribery. Consequently, when Bekaffa died, Iyasu II was proclaimed king of kings and Mantuab his regent and co-ruler. In this manner the Amharized elements of the newly settled northern provinces asserted themselves in Gondar.

At first the authority of Iyasu II was recognized only in a handful of provinces around the capital. Between 1730 and 1734, however, with the help of Warena, Bekaffa's loyal Mecha general, and of Wadajo, the governor of Amhara, Mantuab was able to extend her authority to all the provinces which had been ruled by Bekaffa. Following an abortive rebellion of the traditional nobility and military forces in and around Gondar in 1735–6, the appointment of the queen's Qwara kinsmen to key positions in the administration was greatly accelerated. Mantuab's kinsmen were, however, a relatively small group, who needed allies in order to maintain their power. Therefore, the importance of Galla officials, guards and *chawa* constantly increased during the reign of Iyasu II. By this time the Galla expansion appears generally to have ceased, and the process of Galla settlement and assimilation had made noticeable progress. In western Amhara, most of the Tulama had become amharized and were considered an integral part of the local population. In Shoa, Abiye, of the Menzian dynasty, ruled a mixed population of 'Amhara' and amharized Galla, thereby further facilitating the process of integration which had started much earlier. The Mecha, who had been settled in Damot by Iyasu I just a quarter of a century earlier, were rapidly integrating into the kingdom under the governorship of Warena. An outstanding exception were the Yejju and the Wallo. These tribes were still trying to expand their territories in Lasta and Amhara, but their efforts were constantly frustrated by Dejazmach Wadajo and his Tulama allies. Possibly in order to win over the aggressive Wallo, Mantuab arranged the marriage of Iyasu with the daughter of an important Wallo chief.

Mantuab, or more exactly her brother Walde-Li'ul, continued the policy of expansion northwards. Ras Walde-Li'ul, hoped, it seems, to make Sennar a tributary of Ethiopia, and the Ethiopians carried out a number of exploratory raids between 1741 and 1743. In 1744 Walde-Li'ul invaded Sennar at the head of a large army, but when he was only a short distance from the capital, his forces were attacked from the rear and fled in confusion. Nearly 20,000 Ethiopians lost their lives or were taken prisoner in this catastrophe. To add insult to injury, the Funj captured Iyasu's crown and the most sacred religious relics of Ethiopia, which always accompanied the king on a major campaign. In order to avenge the defeat, between 1744 and 1753 Iyasu repeatedly attacked the border provinces of Sennar from Fazughli in the west to the very gates of Suakin in the east. Iyasu might have wanted also to establish Ethiopian overlordship over these areas. Yet although they eased the pressure of the pastoralists on the newly settled areas in the north, these expeditions did not change the status of the borderlands. Instead the trade between Sennar and Ethiopia came to a standstill and Ethiopia became completely dependent on the Massawa trade route.

Taking advantage of the disorder in Ethiopia following the death of Bekaffa, the *nā'ib* of Arkiko had forced the weak *bahr-negash* who ruled some of the provinces north of the Mareb to cede to him a number of districts in Hamasien and Akele-Guzay. Because the *nā'ib* continued to encroach upon his territories, the *bahr-negash* appealed in the early 1730s for help to Mika'el Suhul, the governor of Tigre. The latter defeated the *nā'ib*, but left the contested districts in his hands on the promise of an annual tribute and facilitation of the supply of firearms. Mika'el Suhul is said to have been a descendant of the ancient dynasty of the Tigre Mekwannin. Yet he was an upstart. He had gained control over the province of Tigre only about 1730, after rebelling against its previous governor. In the following years, and especially after defeating the *nā'ib*, Mika'el managed to accumulate a large arsenal of firearms, to build up his military power and to extend his territories. By 1745 Mika'el was probably one of the strongest rulers east of the Tekeze, and his ambitions already stretched far beyond the horizons of Tigre. A symptom of this was the fact that he completely ignored the order of Iyasu to punish the *nā'ib*, his client, when the latter maltreated an embassy sent by the king to Egypt to bring a new *abuna* and once again when it returned with the *abuna*. Later in the year, when the king entered Baher-Meder to accompany the *abuna* to Gondar, Mika'el did not present himself in his camp, though the king passed near his territories. In 1747, after Iyasu penetrated Tigre with a large army in order to establish his authority in the area, Mika'el was the only Tigrean noble who did not submit to the king. For a time he resisted the king's armies which tried to storm his stronghold until finally he was forced to surrender and was sent to the state prison. He was pardoned, however, in 1748 and was given back the government of his old province. This incident mitigated his ambitions. Thereafter, realizing that if he was ever to succeed in establishing his independence, he had first to strengthen his position and military power, he became Iyasu's most loyal subordinate east of the Tekeze.

In 1749 Iyasu tried further to erode the power and autonomy of the nobility of Tigre and Baher-Meder. Consequently, in 1750 most of the provinces east of the Tekeze were in a state of rebellion. Previously the king had alienated his Qwara kinsmen when he tried to assert his authority and to limit their powers. The one who profited most from this turn of events was Mika'el, who constantly demonstrated his loyalty to the king. In 1751 he was appointed viceroy of Tigre and two years later, with tension constantly increasing between the king and his Qwara kinsmen, Mika'el, who had a strong army at his command, was appointed governor of all the provinces east of the Tekeze.

Following the death of Iyasu at the beginning of 1755, Mantuab and her brother Walde-Li'ul enthroned Iyoas, Iyasu's son by his Wallo wife. As Iyoas was still a minor, Mantuab and Walde-Li'ul ruled the country in his name. However, a number of governors, and especially Mika'el, had become so powerful during Iyasu's last years that Mantuab needed their consent to the succession of Iyoas. Consequently, by 1756 Mika'el Suhul became governor of all the provinces east of the Angareb river. Thereby the power and resources of the central authority were further diminished, and Mantuab became even more dependent on the good will of the feudatories and especially of Mika'el. Tigrean particularism, which had been crushed in the sixteenth century, was thus gradually now emerging as a major challenge to the authority of the House of Yekunno-Amlak and to the predominance of the Amhara elements of the kingdom.

Another element which increasingly asserted itself in the kingdom in this period was the Galla. Already in the days of Bekaffa the authority of the monarchy had been greatly dependent on the military support of the western Galla, but the Galla had remained relatively unimportant in the administration of the central government. On the succession of Iyoas to the throne, however, thousands of Wallo warriors led by his Wallo uncles reached the capital. It appears that Mintuab and Walde-Li'ul hoped that by allying themselves with these aggressive eastern Galla they might somehow counter-balance the power of the great feudatories. Wallo chiefs were therefore appointed to offices in the palace and the administration, while the rank and file joined the Yejju and the other Galla soldiers in the service of the king. Consequently, Ethiopia had a king who was half Galla by birth and depended on Galla soldiers and administrators; Galligna even replaced Amharic as the language of the court.

The first to be affected by Mantuab's new policy was Wadajo, the governor of Amhara, who had blocked the Wallo and the Yejju expansion since the days of Bekaffa. Many of the Wallo and Yejju chiefs were Muslims and were therefore especially inimical to the Christian population, Amhara and amharized Galla, in his province. Because of the entrenchment of the Wallo and Yejju in the capital, Wadajo's relations with the Qwara group progressively deteriorated. In 1758–9 he was stripped of his governorship and Amhara was given to Dulo, Iyoas's Wallo uncle. Thus, the Qwara ruling clique lost one of the only true allies they had among the Amhara nobility and became even more dependent on Galla co-operation. And it was not long before Iyoas's Galla kinsmen realized their own power and the weakness of the Qwara group which stood between them and the government of Ethiopia.

During the reign of Iyoas, new religious controversies broke out among the ecclesiastics and divided still further the semitized Christian population of Ethiopia. At the end of the seventeenth century some of the spiritual leaders of the order of Tekla-Haymanot had evolved a theory which was not very far from confessing dyophysitism. Although this 'heresy' was suppressed, it did not disappear. As late as 1763 it caused a bitter controversy in Gondar to the extent that riots broke out in the capital. Peace returned only after the chief instigators of the 'heretical theory' were banished from Gondar and Mantuab and Walde-Li'ul announced that the king adhered to the orthodox belief.

The orthodox majority of the 'unionists' then gave their blessing to a new theory which had its roots in the 'unionist' formula. According to this theory, which came to be known as *Sost Ledet* (lit. three births), Christ was first born in eternity, was born once again and anointed by the Holy Spirit on his incarnation in the womb of Mary, and finally he was born in time free of the sin of Adam. The dyophysitic tendencies of ecclesiastics belonging to the order of Tekla-Haymanot and the theory of the 'three births' aroused a strong reaction among the followers of the order of St Ewostatewos in Tigre. They objected to any formula which could be interpeted as holding that at any moment Christ might have had two natures or was not inherently divine. They believed that he incarnated and anointed himself. Hence, they rejected the three births, because for them the second and the third births were but one. Consequently, they were called *Karra Haymanot* (lit. the belief of the knife) or *Hulet Ledet* (lit. two births).[1] This new controversy quickly developed into a major dispute. It was even more dangerous to the unity of Christian Ethiopia, because the opposing camps came to represent the traditional division between Tigreans and Amhara. This division was yet another factor which helped to pave the way for Galla predominance in Ethiopia.

The death of Ras Walde-Li'ul at the end of 1766 sparked off the unavoidable clash between the Qwara party and Iyoas. Because Mantuab's kinsmen converged upon Gondar, Iyoas called upon Mika'el Suhul for help. This was the moment for which Mika'el had long been waiting, using his vast revenues to acquire firearms and build up the strongest military force in Ethiopia. With an army of 30,000 Tigreans, of whom 8,000 were fusiliers, he reached the capital in December 1767 and was appointed by Iyoas to the office of *ras*

[1] It was also known as *Wald Qib* (lit. son anointing). M. Abir, *Ethiopia: the era of the princes* (London, 1968), 39–40; I. Guidi, 'La Chiesa Abissina', *Oriente Moderno*, 1922, **2**, 5, 188–9; M. Kamil, 'Letters to Ethiopia', *Bulletin de la Société d'Archéologie Copte* (Cairo, 1942), 95–6.

bitweded. In the following year, while the power of Mantuab's kinsmen was broken, Maryam-Barya, her son-in-law, tried to form a coalition of Amhara, Agaw and Yejju chiefs in order to dethrone Iyoas. In October 1768 the king marched against Maryam-Barya with the army of Tigre commanded by Ras Mika'el and with 30,000 Mecha from Damot commanded by Fasil, son of Warena. Maryam-Barya was defeated and the Yejju and Wallo among whom he sought refuge were coerced to surrender him and he was executed. Relations between Iyoas and Mika'el, however, deteriorated during and after this expedition. Fearing Mika'el's ambitions, the king became friendly with Fasil Warena, and, just before entering Gondar, the king ordered Ras Mika'el to return to Tigre. Mika'el, however, ignored the king's command and in January 1769 he marched against Fasil, whose army, encamped at Azezo, had been previously reinforced by Iyoas's guard. The Galla cavalry was decimated by the Tigrean fusiliers, and Fasil escaped to Damot. Immediately after the battle, Iyoas was assassinated on Mika'el's orders. Thus began the *Zamana Mesafent* (lit. the era of the princes, or 'the Judges', in the biblical sense), which lasted until 1855, during which period the kings of Ethiopia were but puppets in the hands of the war-lords who ruled in Gondar.

THE ERA OF THE PRINCES

Following the assassination of Iyoas, Mika'el enthroned Bekaffa's old brother Yohannes Agaw, but soon afterwards replaced him with his son Tekla-Haymanot. In the meantime Fasil and his Wallo and Qwara allies gathered their forces in Gojjam. In October they clashed with Mika'el at Fagitta but were totally defeated. Again the determining factor in the battle was the effectiveness of the Tigrean fusiliers, commanded by Kifle-Iyasu, the governor of Tembien and a kinsman of Mika'el. The Amhara nobility, however, objected to a Tigrean *ras* ruling in Gondar and had not forgotten Mika'el's part in what happened to Maryam-Barya. Moreover, the *Sost Ledet* ecclesiastics incited the Amhara nobility against Ras Mika'el, a murderer of a Solomonic monarch and a supporter of the *Karra Haymanot*. Consequently, in the middle of 1770, Mika'el discovered that his allies had betrayed him and that he was facing an Amhara-Galla coalition. Fearing that the rainy season would swell the Tekeze and cut him off from his sources of supply, he retreated to Tigre taking with him Tekla-Haymanot.

Mika'el was back in Gondar at the end of 1770. In the coming months he cruelly punished all those whom he suspected of betraying him. Among the many who were executed were the most important members of the hierarchy of the church and the heads of the order of Tekla-Haymanot. However, while Mika'el was wasting valuable months in satisfying his wounded pride, Fasil and his allies, Goshu of Amhara and Wand Bewasen of Begemder, prepared for the decisive battle. At the beginning of 1771, the army of Tigre met the joint Galla-Amhara army at Sabarkusa. The battle lasted several days, and the Tigrean army was finally defeated. Mika'el surrendered to his enemies and was exiled to Shoa. Tekla-Haymanot was retained as puppet king by Goshu, who became *ras bitweded*. It was not long, however, before Fasil, the strong chief of the Mecha of Damot, became *de facto* ruler of Ethiopia. But Ethiopia as such no longer existed. It was a collection of principalities, ruled by different war-lords. The centrifugal forces in the country were completely triumphant.

Fasil was defeated and killed by a coalition of Amhara nobles in 1775. But another Mecha chief entered Gondar in 1778, and in the following year he dethroned Tekla-Haymanot and enthroned his brother Tekla-Giyorgis. The Mecha remained the masters of Ethiopia until about 1781. Then the Amhara war lords, allied with the Yejju, broke the power of the Mecha, and the western Galla ceased to be an important element in the struggle for power in the empire. As for the provinces east of the Tekeze, they were once again under the governorship of Ras Mika'el who returned to Tigre in 1772. The *ras* executed Kifle Iyasu, his loyal subordinate, who had been appointed governor of Tigre in his absence, and when Mika'el died in 1780, he left his son Walde-Gabri'el with a strong government and with the best equipped army in Ethiopia.

The preoccupation of the Amhara nobility with the internal struggle for power since 1771 was exploited by the Yejju and Wallo Galla. The Yejju continued their penetration of Lasta and Wag. The Wallo, for their part, at first occupied all the territories between the river Wankit and the river Bashilo. Later, profiting from the rivalries of the Amhara nobility, they penetrated the districts of Dawint and Wadla and raided Begemder. Hence, large Amhara communities were cut off from the main body of the empire, and some of the amharized Tulama Galla gradually reverted to animism. Many of the Wallo chiefs were by this time ardent Muslims, so whenever they erupted into Amhara districts they burned churches, killed the ecclesiastics and sold Christians into slavery.

'King of Kings' Tekla-Giyorgis had no love for the Amhara nobles who oppressed him, and he tried to increase his power with the help of the Yejju. He appointed 'Alī, the son of the most powerful Yejju chief, as the commander of his guard and filled his court with officials of Yejju origin. Consequently, from the early 1780s the eastern Galla gradually entrenched themselves in Gondar. In 1783, after re-establishing for a time the authority of the monarchy, Tekla-Giyorgis, who was a devoted Christian and a supporter of the *Hulet Ledet*, decided to punish the Wallo for the atrocities which they had committed against the Christian communities in Amhara. He also planned to subjugate Shoa, whose ruler Wasen-Seged had crowned a pretender to the throne and had declared for the *Sost Ledet*. The king's army supported by the army of Tigre fought its way through Wallo territories up to the border of Shoa, and Wasen-Seged paid his tribute and surrendered his 'king'. The expedition was nevertheless a failure. The resistance of the Wallo and the insubordination of some nobles forced Tekla-Giyorgis to abandon his plans to subjugate Shoa and break the power of the Wallo. Following this campaign, relations between the king and the Amhara nobility and ecclesiastics further deteriorated. Finally, in the last months of 1784, the disgruntled Amhara nobles allied themselves with 'Alī, the commander of the king's guards, and Tekla-Giyorgis was deposed.

Tekla-Giyorgis was the last king in Gondar to assert some authority, at least in the closing years of his reign. Thereafter, until 1855, the real power in Ethiopia lay in the hands of *dejazmaches*, who ruled the different provinces. The 'kings' of Ethiopia who 'reigned' in Gondar had no authority or power. They depended completely on the war-lords who governed the country in their names. In theory the governor of Begemder and the master of the 'king of kings' in Gondar was the *ras bitweded*, and he was supposed to be the ruler of Ethiopia. But in practice, he was only *primus inter pares*, exercising limited authority beyond the provinces around the capital, and even that only so long as he was able to uphold his position against his many rivals, who in some cases had their own pet 'kings'. The governors of the different provinces were the absolute masters of the lives and property of the population over which they ruled. Yet even the *dejazmaches* were never secure. They were always forced to defend themselves against the avidity of their neighbours or the rebellions of their jealous subordinates. The armies of the different nobles lived off the land. They ravaged not only the territories of their enemies but also the domains of their own masters. Many desperate cultivators left their fields to become soldiers or highwaymen. The provinces west of the Tekeze were depopulated and ruined economically, and the capital, Gondar, was repeatedly looted and burnt. For all that, Gondar remained the goal of every war-lord, because the Christian semitized population were still attached to their historical heritage, and Gondar symbolized the central authority of Ethiopia.

Ras 'Alī, who in deposing the king became the regent of Ethiopia in 1784, was born a Muslim. Although he converted to Christianity, he was detested by the Christian population. By 1787 the Christian nobility east and west of the Tekeze joined forces to rid themselves of the Yejju overlordship and 'Alī's despotism. 'Alī called upon his Yejju kinsmen from Ambasel, Lasta and Wag for help. At Amed Ber, in Belesa, the Christian army was defeated by the Yejju cavalry, in spite of the cannon and the thousands of fusiliers in Walde-Gabri'el's army. Thousands of Amhara and Tigreans, including Walde-Gabri'el, were killed. Notwithstanding this victory, the Yejju were unable to maintain their hold even over the provinces west of the Tekeze. 'Alī died in 1788, and although 'Alī's brother, Aligaz, took the title of *ras*, his position was challenged by his own brothers and nephews and by some Wallo chiefs. Hence, until the last years of the eighteenth century, Gondar and the central provinces were abandoned to the local war-lords who gave no thought to the future of the semitized Christian kingdom. They savagely fought one another for power, ravaged the country and did not shrink from selling the Christian population into slavery. Some even allied themselves with Imam Ahmade, the Muslim leader of the Wallo, who raided Begemder, burnt its churches and ravaged Gondar. Finally at the end of the eighteenth century, the Yejju ended their internal war, and Gugsa, Aligaz's nephew, re-established the Yejju predominance in the provinces west of the Tekeze. Although a nominal Christian, Ras Gugsa had no respect for the Christian heritage of the country. He treated 'his' kings like servants and the population as if they were his slaves.

The Ethiopians who, at first, had thought that the Galla were only interested in land for settlement and had no intention of imposing a new superstructure upon the semitized society of the country, now found to their sorrow how wrong they had been. Moreover, unlike some of the Galla tribes and other Cushitic elements who had been integrated into the Christian kingdom, the eastern Galla were not assimilated by the Ethiopian Christian society. Bewailing the degeneration of the kingdom, the Ethiopian chronicler of the period wrote:

'How is it that the kingdom has become contemptible to striplings and slaves? How is it that the kingdom is a laughing stock of the uncircumcised?'[1]

In the years following the death of Walde-Gabri'el in 1788, Walde-Sellassie, the son of Kifle-Iyasu, succeeded in making himself the master of all the provinces east of the Tekeze. After consolidating his position in Tigre, he broke the power of the Azebo Galla and captured from the Yejju all the mountain passages in Lasta leading to Tigre. He also stemmed the gradual expansion of the *nā'ib* of Arkiko into Baher-Meder, and forced him to renew the payment of the tribute which he had paid in the past. Once the *nā'ib* became his vassal, he assisted Walde-Sellassie's trade with Arabia and the importation of large quantities of firearms for his army. By the first decade of the nineteenth century, Walde-Sellassie was not only considered the strongest ruler in Ethiopia, but also the protector of Ethiopian Christianity and the heritage of the kingdom. In order to terminate Yejju domination, Walde-Sellassie prepared for war and allied himself with other Christian rulers, especially with Gebru of Simien and Walqayt and Wasen-Seged of Shoa. The last was an important ally because the Menzian dynasty had succeeded by the nineteenth century in annexing most of the Amhara principalities and conquering much of the territory of Shoa which had fallen into the hands of the Galla. Asfa-Wasen, who succeeded his father Wasen-Seged at the beginning of the nineteenth century, took for himself the title of *ras* and openly challenged the authority of the Yejju, Gugsa.

Following the death of Abuna Yosab in 1803, a strange coalition emerged between Gugsa and the lords and ecclesiastics supporting the order of Tekla-Haymanot in Gondar. At the head of these ecclesiastics was the *ichege*, the principal Ethiopian monk, who although second to the *abuna* in the hierarchy of the church was, as an Ethiopian, far more powerful. Because of the opposition of the Coptic church in Egypt to the theory of *Sost Ledet*, the *ichege* and the monks in Gondar knew that a new *abuna* would automatically join their adversaries. Gugsa for his part feared that an *abuna* would not only support but also strengthen the anti-Yejju coalition. Hence, for several years he made no move to bring an *abuna* from Egypt. Walde-Sellassie on his own initiative sent for an *abuna*, but several years passed before one arrived. In the meantime Walde-Sellassie's government was shaken by a number of rebellions. When Abuna Qerlos finally arrived in 1816, the aged Walde-Sellassie was unable to open the long-awaited campaign against Gugsa

[1] H. Weld Blondel, ed., *Royal chronicles of Abyssinia* (Cambridge, 1922), 467–9.

and he died shortly afterwards. Thereafter Tigre was far too occupied with the internal struggle for power to present a threat to the Yejju predominance. Dejazmach Gebru, Walde-Sellassie's ally, died in 1815. His son Haile-Maryam was brought over to Gugsa's camp by coercion and matrimonial arrangements. Shoa was involved in a long civil war, following the rise to power of Sahle Sellassie in 1813. Thus, by the 1820s, it seemed that the Yejju under Gugsa had succeeded in establishing themselves as the masters of the Ethiopian kingdom.

The Galla tribes, who had begun their sporadic migration into the different parts of the Horn of Africa in the sixteenth century, thus controlled most of the area by the first quarter of the nineteenth century. In Gondar, the 'king of kings' of Christian Ethiopia was a puppet in the hands of his Yejju Galla regents, and the emirs of Harar had Galla blood in their veins. Galla population had replaced or had submerged the indigenous inhabitants of most or parts of Lasta, Amhara, Shoa, the southern parts of the Ethiopian plateau, the neighbourhood of Harar and the northern Dankali territory.

After the conquest of the Sudan and the Ethiopian coast by Muḥammad 'Alī in the first decades of the nineteenth century, Ethiopia had as her neighbour an aggressive and strong Muslim power. Moreover, the revival of Islam in Arabia and elsewhere during the latter part of the eighteenth century was affecting the Muslim communities in the Horn. From the turn of the nineteenth century the revival of Islam coincided with the expansion of trade in the area, and Muslim caravan merchants, fired by a new zeal to spread their religion, penetrated every corner of the plateau. Earlier, the conversion to Islam of some Galla chiefs and elements had been mainly the result of their contact with Adal and the Muslim communities along the eastern escarpments. It may also have been a manifestation of their animosity to the Christian empire. By the turn of the nineteenth century, however, Islam was spreading among the Galla for the further reason that, while they were undergoing rapid economic, social and political changes, Islam contributed to a greater cohesion and to a more centralized and authoritarian system of government. It appeared as though the Galla had not only become the masters of most of the Horn, but that Christianity would be supplanted by Islam on the plateau. In this crucial period, the centrifugal forces were completely triumphant in Ethiopia, and the Christian semitized nobility were involved in a continuous struggle for power in the different provinces of the kingdom. The Ethiopian church, despite the advantage of its roots in the African soil, was at the end of the eighteenth century completely unconcerned with the animist masses and had itself little appeal for them. Since the end of the sixteenth century it had been stagnating spiritually and had greatly contributed to the division among the Christian population by its endless theological controversies. By furthering the centrifugal forces in the country it had indirectly undermined its own position, because the monarchy and the church were the pillars of the Christian kingdom. However, in spite of the attitude of the church and the nobility and the complete decline of the monarchy at the beginning of the nineteenth century, the heritage of Christian Ethiopia was still alive among the populace, especially in the newly settled and amharized northern provinces, in Tigre and Shoa, and it was from among these elements that the future saviours of the kingdom were to emerge.

CHAPTER 9

AFRICA IN EUROPE AND THE AMERICAS

European sea voyages to Africa and America in the fifteenth century laid the basis for an extensive operation linking up the three continents. From an African viewpoint, there were three sets of relationships which can be isolated for analysis. First, there were direct ties between Africa and Europe; secondly, there was an African presence created in the Americas; and thirdly, there was a tri-continental interaction which was more than just the sum of the other two. This interaction involved commerce, the establishment of settler colonies and the creation of new social relations – amounting to a different international political economy, with its centre in western Europe and with its dynamics supplied by capitalist accumulative tendencies.

EUROPE'S IMAGE OF AFRICA

Portuguese navigational achievements intensified contacts between Europe and the western Sudan – contacts which had until then stretched tenuously across the Mediterranean and the Sahara, and which had been mediated by the Muslims of North Africa. Farther along the western coast and in southern Africa, Europeans made completely new acquaintances. The people of the Kongo kingdom, the Khoisan (Hottentots) and the *mwene mutapa*'s kingdom were all featuring in European literature in the sixteenth century. When the Portuguese sailed up the East African coast, they met not only new African faces, but also their familiar antagonists, the Muslims. Catholic Europe had entertained the hope that the political power of a Christian 'Prester John' somewhere in Africa or Asia might be drawn into the balance against the Muslim world; but this was never to be, although relations were established with the Christian state of Ethiopia, signifying the renewal of cultural links which had been severely attenuated since the rise of Islam. It was still North Africa which continued to manifest a direct political presence in Europe. North African rulers were part of the Mediterranean diplomatic network. Their armies, navies and pirates had to be taken into account by European powers. Nevertheless, the image of Africa which became dominant in the European mind was that of a hot, rainy, forested continent with exotic fauna and black people.

By the turn of the seventeenth century, individuals from every country in western Europe had had an opportunity to gain some authentic information on previously unknown parts of Africa and to view black Africans in person both in Africa and Europe. Already, old Greek legends about Africa had been giving way to first-hand reports from travellers, although this new information was largely restricted to West Africa. Peter Martyr's collection of travels was gathered early in the sixteenth century, and was translated into English by Richard Eden in 1555. The famous work of Leo Africanus was published in 1550 in Italy and shortly afterwards in France; and in 1600 John Pory made the English translation, which was read by Ben Jonson and probably by Shakespeare and John Webster.[1] This period also saw the appearance of the extremely influential travel collections of Richard Hakluyt and Samuel Purchas.

What was known of Africa in Europe was limited to the coasts of the continent and particularly to the west coast, where trade was most intense. The Portuguese accumulated a mass of detail on coastal topography. Some of this remained within the files of the royal administration and was kept out of the hands of commercial rivals, but most of it was published in the form of navigational charts and chronicles of Portuguese expansion. Cartographers of other European nations also relied on Portuguese evidence in dealing with the map of Africa. Of course, Portuguese observations were not restricted to physical features. They wrote about the political structures and customs of the African peoples whom they met. Their records on Kongo, the *mwene mutapa* and Ethiopia are invaluable, and were extremely influential among other Europeans. This had also a negative aspect, however, for where the Portuguese made errors of fact or judgement those misconceptions persisted.

One of the agencies which served to internationalize knowledge on Africa was the Jesuit order. The three volumes of Jesuit missionary reports edited by Fr. Fernão Guerreiro in the first decade of the seventeenth century treated at length upper Guinea, Cape Verde, Angola, Kongo, the *mwene mutapa* and Ethiopia. These reports were specifically requested for publication, indicating the order's awareness

[1] Eldred Jones, *Othello's countrymen: the African in English renaissance drama* (London, 1965), 21.

of the need to reach the literate public. The Jesuit example was later followed by the Capuchins. Giovanni Cavazzi's *Istorica descrizione de Congo, Matamba et Angola* (1687), which derived from Capuchin involvement, was extensively reviewed, quickly reprinted and also translated into German in 1694. Meanwhile, impressions of European traders in West Africa were also more regularly put into print by their authors or more usually by compilers who may or may not have had travel experience. Thus, de Marees produced an excellent first-hand account of the Gold Coast in 1601, arising out of Dutch trade there; and Dapper's influential work on West Africa some sixty years later was based on trading reports and the observations of visitors, such as de Marees and the Jesuits. Europe was then displaying sufficient interest in the non-European world to make travelogues into a significant literary form. Hakluyt and Purchas set a tradition which was followed in the eighteenth century by collections such as those of the Churchills, Astley and Labat. Writers of more and more European nations contributed to their continent's awareness of Africa, because availability of information was related to the pattern of European commerce with Africans. More European nations were becoming caught up in this commerce, as was strikingly illustrated by the many flags flying on the forts of the Gold Coast. By the same token, English and French sources became preponderant, reflecting their achievement of hegemony in the trade to Africa. Publications were prolific in the second half of the eighteenth century, and information presented in monographs was cited with varying degrees of accuracy in universal histories and geographical texts. This literature on Africa obviously had European preoccupations. Thus, most of the accounts of the river Gambia were concerned with the search for gold. In most of the texts there was invariably emphasis on that which Europeans considered unusual, there were occasional flights of fancy, and African social life was often rather incidental. Nevertheless, the dominant element in these accounts was realism, and they remain valid evidence for the portrayal of African life.

The persistent interest in travel literature and the proportion of this which was allocated to Africa have led to the justifiable conclusion that 'relative to their knowledge of the world in general, eighteenth-century Europeans knew more and cared more about Africa than they did at any later period up to the 1950s'.[1] However, the extent to which written

[1] Philip Curtin, *The image of Africa: British ideas and action 1780–1830* (Madison, 1964), 9, 10.

descriptions influenced the average European in the seventeenth and eighteenth centuries was narrowly circumscribed by class barriers, by the illiteracy of the majority of the population, and by a matrix of preconceived ideas. There were only a few individuals with a professional interest in Africa: namely, administrators of overseas affairs, merchants and missionaries. In our own time, detailed knowledge about Africa in the hands of a minority of Europeans is compatible with crass ignorance on the part of the rest of the population. This is so in spite of widespread literacy and the availability of mass communications media. Furthermore, Europeans were unfamiliar with the vast interior of Africa. It was ignorance rather than knowledge which characterized Africa's image within Europe, so that novelists, poets, painters and playwrights catered to the new awareness of Africa mainly at the level of the exotic.

AFRICANS IN EUROPE

Wherever there was a gap in substantive knowledge of any part of Africa, imagination was likely to play a greater role. Writing in 1648, Vincent le Blanc romantically embellished such facts on the *mwene mutapa* as had been presented by the Portuguese chronicler, João de Barros. Vincent le Blanc's description of the *mwene mutapa*'s palace fits into the genre of myths relating to a terrestrial paradise, supposedly evoking the human condition before the Fall. However, because Europeans were unfamiliar with the Zambezi area, Vincent le Blanc's portrayal was taken seriously and was reproduced in many works in the eighteenth century. Above all, it is essential to note that new facts did not necessarily change old myths and fancies. On the contrary, for all sections of the population, genuine data reinforced the conceptualization based on many previous centuries of vague information and speculation. Ultimately, what was written about Africa and Africans either by informed Europeans or by romanticists was far less relevant to the formation of European opinion and far less integral to the history of Afro-European relations than was the role played by Africans as chattel slaves – beginning within Europe itself. Portugal and Spain were the principal importers of African slaves, and the social structure in the Iberian peninsula readily accommodated the introduction of large numbers of slaves. Religious wars with the Muslims had helped to keep alive the institution of slavery in Iberia at a time when it was disappearing from the rest of Europe. Besides, there was a brisk slave trade from the eastern Mediterranean to Iberia, and the Atlantic slave trade was its successor.

Overseas ventures were a serious drain on Portugal's population, and large areas of the south had been laid waste in the previous cycle of wars against the Moors. Consequently, the cultivation of the great estates was done more and more by African labour. In addition, Africans were used extensively as domestics and in various occupations in the towns. By the middle of the reign of John III (1521–57), foreigners were commenting on the number of black slaves in Lisbon. An estimate of 1551 gave Lisbon a population of 100,000, of whom one-tenth were slaves. Imports by then were running at the rate of several thousands per year, and there were sixty to seventy slave marts in Lisbon. In the 1590s, the proportion of blacks was so high that a well-placed observer claimed that Lisbon was more black than white, and the annual black festival was a highlight of social life in the city.[1] By the following century, the importation of African slaves continued at a greatly reduced rate, since the demand for and value of black labour was greater in the Americas; but it was not until 1773 that slavery was formally abolished within Portugal.

Developments in Spain approximated closely to those in Portugal, although the numbers involved were less. Serfdom of a harsh kind, the institution of slavery and the presence of a few African slaves since the thirteenth century made it easy to increase the number of black slaves in Spain. The principal slave-using areas of the country were Catalonia, Aragon, Valencia and Majorca, where feudalism was still prominent and the Moorish serfs were in rebellion at the turn of the sixteenth century. Subsequently, African slaves imported through Lisbon gradually replaced Arabs and Circassians as the most exploited and oppressed sector of the labour force. The first black slaves to reach the Americas were sent from Spain rather than directly from Africa.

Slavery in Iberia had some of the features exhibited by the more notorious slave societies of America. Black slaves in Portugal were frequently refused burial, and in 1515 the king ordered that their bodies be thrown into a separate common ditch, the *poço dos negros*. The fear of revolt hung about the shoulders of slave owners here as elsewhere. Legislators in Spain were much concerned about the allegedly subversive character of free blacks, and the Cortes proposed that persons in this category be prohibited from living outside the region where they

[1] W. C. Atkinson, *A history of Spain and Portugal* (London, 1961), 151; and Vatican Archives, Fondo Confalonieri, vol. 45, fol. 3 (from the Papal collector in Lisbon, *c.* 1593–5).

were known. They were to be punished with lashes if they greeted or fraternized with slaves. Yet, the presence of freedmen attests to frequent manumission. Free blacks in Lisbon, Barcelona and Seville founded religious and welfare associations, displaying a sense of racial consciousness by seeking to include black slaves and by mobilizing to obtain freedom for some. One of their principal functions was to provide for decent burials, and both slave and free blacks participated in the numerous religious celebrations and festivals. The extent of the involvement of blacks in Portuguese society can be judged from the fact that in 1580 the defence against Philip of Spain in favour of Antonio of Crato was carried out by peasants aided by thousands of Lisbon blacks, comprising mainly slaves who fought on the promise of freedom.

Agricultural slavery in Iberia was an aberration within the European context. Both feudalism and capitalism found it necessary to discard the fetters of slavery. Fortuitous circumstances like the religious wars and the backwardness of social development in Portugal allowed field-slavery to burgeon for a while, but the only slavery for which there was scope within the embryo capitalist structure of Europe itself was household slavery. In the 1730s, the demand for young slaves in Cadiz and Lisbon was so great that it erased the considerable difference in price which normally existed between children and adults in the Gambia slave markets. The functions of these juveniles could only have been that of pages and servitors within well-to-do households and certain institutions. This type of household slavery permitted a more humane relationship between master and slave, more frequent manumissions, and a greater possibility of inter-marriage and other forms of social integration. The main historical significance of the African presence in Portugal and Spain is the miscegenation which took place. Africans disappeared as a separate and distinct section of the population, but their large numbers ensured a lasting impact. Throughout the seventeenth and eighteenth centuries, it was common to refer to the Portuguese as dark, swarthy, Negroid, Moorish; and the mulatto element ran throughout all classes of the society.

The European nobility used Africans as domestics, even if slavery was not widespread in the given country. The practice was common at an early date in Italy, which had a tradition of enslaving Africans since the days of the Roman empire. Black children were distributed as gifts in Italian Renaissance courts, and this became fashionable throughout Europe in the seventeenth and eighteenth centuries. In numerous kingdoms and principalities, from the Netherlands to Russia, Africans appeared in a variety of roles, such as mascots, pets, favourites, mistresses, adopted children, pages and footmen. Occasionally, one such African rose into prominence. Ibrahim Hannibal (*c.* 1692–1782) was specially cared for by Peter the Great, and became an artillery officer and a powerful land-owning nobleman in Russia.[1] For the most part, however, Africans were supposed to add distinction to their masters rather than to distinguish themselves: they were evaluated not on the basis of their common humanity but as oddities to be incorporated in a life style that was always ostentatious, often bacchanalian and not infrequently bizarre.

Outside Iberia, it was in England, France and the Netherlands that Africans were most commonly found in enslavement. The voyages of Lok and Wyndham offered the English their first opportunity to acquire Africans directly from West Africa, and they must also have sought slaves from Portugal. In the last years of the sixteenth century, blacks in England were causing concern, and in 1601 Queen Elizabeth issued an order for their deportation. The numbers involved were probably quite small, but a few blacks entering a white country are often portrayed as an invading horde, and they were ready scapegoats in the face of prevailing national difficulties such as food scarcity and vagabondage. Yet, in spite of the deportation order, it became more fashionable for aristocratic and other wealthy English families to hire black servants, and West Indian planters went to reside in England accompanied by considerable numbers of slaves from the islands. English captains and sailors also brought a few captives directly from Africa, catering to the social taste for black menials which had become a veritable fad. Ladies of leisure and courtesans bestowed on their black slaves names like Pompey and Caesar, which were inscribed on pretty dog-collars, obtained from shops like Matthew Dyer of Duck Lane, Liverpool, which made padlocks and collars for dogs and Africans.

The role played by the African slave in England must be evaluated in relation to that of free white servants. Servants constituted one of the largest occupational groups in seventeenth- and eighteenth-century England. Many black slaves managed to escape, and, along with those who were manumitted or deserted by their masters, they were able to pass into the ranks of 'service'. There, they were subject to surviving medieval restrictions, but the stigma of their occupation was mild, and the domineering tendencies of their masters could be, and were,

[1] Albert Parry, 'Abram Hannibal', *Journal of Negro History*, October 1923.

countered by combination on the part of servants. Servants changed place regularly and exercised choice in seeking positions, which set them off from those blacks who were slaves. A handful of blacks reached the top of the hierarchy of domestic service in England, by becoming butlers and valets and by acquiring an education in the process. Among the most famous in this category were Francis Barber, Ignatius Sancho, Soubise and Ottobah Cugoano, all of whom gained their freedom and distinguished themselves within English society. However, below the posts of butler and valet there were dozens of more menial 'liveried offices'. From the viewpoint of owners, blacks were displayed to best advantage in these lowly positions.

The maintenance of untrammelled chattel slavery in England was always difficult. The social framework permitted no more than a qualified form of feudal service, and even this was facing the challenge of the contractual individualism of capitalist relations. Black slaves in England were quick to appreciate the contradiction between their status and the values of the society. The main stratagem used by them was to play upon the widespread belief that English common law did not support slavery on English soil, especially with regard to Christians. This issue was real enough to cause the Virginian planters in 1705 to pass a law that a slave's being in England was not sufficient to discharge him without other proof of manumission; and in 1729 the West Indian interests appealed to the law officers of the crown for a ruling on the question of slavery in England. The opinion favoured the maintenance of slavery and it was reiterated in 1749. The oft-quoted Mansfield decision in the Somerset case supposedly reversed the prevailing legal trend, although this decision in 1772 merely established that the master had no right forcibly to transport a slave from England back to the colonies.[1] Subsequently, slaves continued to be held legally in England, and to the extent that the institution was undermined it was due to wider social forces and to the determined efforts of slaves and their sympathizers.

A report in 1768 by the London magistrate, John Fielding, stated that experience had shown that blacks 'cease to consider themselves slaves in this free country...nor more willingly perform the laborious offices of servitude than our own people, and put to do it are generally sullen, spiteful, treacherous and revengeful'.[2] A large number of slaves

[1] James Walvin, *Black and white: the Negro and English society 1555–1945* (London, 1973). The position is convincingly argued in ch. 7, 'The Somerset Case, 1772'.

[2] David Davis, *The problem of slavery in western culture* (Cornell, 1968), 211.

made themselves sufficiently troublesome and dangerous to their masters that they were got rid of. Having secured their legal or *de facto* freedom, blacks organized to make contact with and liberate others who came to England as bondsmen. A keen sense of organization led to black delegations being present in court during the hearing of cases affecting their interests. Prominent free blacks were also helpful to their kinsmen. Olaudah Equiano made a direct political contribution to the abolitionist movement. He served as a link between the ordinary blacks and white liberals like Granville Sharp, who espoused their cause. Inevitably, the activity of the black masses in fact outran the support which privileged blacks or sympathetic whites were prepared to offer. This was revealed with regard to the so-called problem of the 'Black Poor' in the 1780s. Numerous black loyalists from America were disbanded after the peace of 1783, and on travelling to England they increased the already existing sector of black unemployed. Having a high degree of visibility, blacks were singled out as constituting a major social problem, which comprised destitution, crime and the threat of miscegenation. Not for the first time, and possibly not for the last time, the solution was that they should be transported out of the realm. By 1787, reactionary tendencies had combined with humanitarianism to find blacks a home in Sierra Leone. Blacks correctly perceived that the dominant thrust behind the scheme was to dump them outside Britain without security, and only a tiny minority took up the offer. The distinct black sector remained in England well into the nineteenth century.

Developments with regard to Africans in France were very similar to those in England, because of the similarity of social structure. The laws governing enslaved Africans in the French colonies were brought together in the *Code Noir* of 1685; and at this time the French government pointed out that Africans who came to France as slaves could acquire freedom according to the law and custom of France, and could not be compelled to return to the West Indies. Of course, there were numerous evasions and compromises in applying this principle. A decree of 1716 allowed planters to register their slaves as having been brought to France for education, and such slaves could not claim their liberty. Besides, the remnants of serfdom provided some justification for slavery. The serf was bound to the soil, but the right to his service could be transferred by sale. By analogy, a master could own slaves in France provided they were of his own household. This interpretation had sufficient weight to allow 4,000 slaves to be kept in the country in

1738. Some years later, labour shortage in the colonies caused the government to order slaves to be taken back to the plantations, even though they returned 'imbued with a spirit of independence and indocility', as was the case with Africans moving from England to the West Indies. A royal decree of 1777 closed France to 'Negroes and mulattoes', both slave and free. The French West Indian slave owner was not allowed to send over or bring with him any further slaves, apart from a single personal servant when travelling.[1] The economic well-being of the colonies was the sole ostensible reason for this legislation, but the following year a decree forbade black/white marriages in France, suggesting that important social considerations were also operative.

The serious disproportion of black males to black females led to considerable sexual relations between black men and white women in Iberia, England and France. Opposition to inter-racial sexual ties is one of the perennials of racism, and Shakespeare's *Othello* provides an early and significant treatment of this phenomenon. A great deal of dramatic potential arose from the interplay of skin colour, given that in the European consciousness black was associated with evil and white with purity and beauty. Many vague prejudices such as this must have gone into the evolution of early racial antipathy; notably, aversion towards strangers and towards those of different religious beliefs. The application of the notion of 'pure blood' to classes was also contemporaneous with the enslavement of Africans. Monarchs and nobles found it necessary to identify themselves in terms of their blood and race when faced by the challenge of the aspirant bourgeoisie. New justifications of slavery, including that of racial inferiority, arose at the time when European monarchs were defending their power not merely with the medieval concept of consecration but with the theory of sovereignty transmitted by royal blood. Initially, such ideas could scarcely have had much impact on the working classes. English workers were prepared to aid the individual black who made a bid for freedom, and would gang up to prevent runaways from being re-arrested. Above all, the diminution of the black population is the best testimony that inter-racial sexual relations persisted in spite of caricatures and lampooning sponsored by vested interests like the West Indian planter class.

It appears that, during the seventeenth and eighteenth centuries, various eddies of prejudice flowed into the mainstream provided by the immediately visible differences between Africans and Europeans.

[1] H. A. Wyndham, *The Atlantic and slavery* (Oxford, 1935), 241.

Elements of modern racism were manifested within the literate minority which was dominant in moulding social attitudes, and which was fully conscious of the fact that Africans had been relegated to an inferior position in the world order based on European expansion. Hume, in his essay on 'National Character' (1771), remarked that 'there are Negro slaves dispersed all over Europe, of which none ever discovered any symptoms of ingenuity'.[1] Even if this falsehood was based on ignorance, it is explicable only in terms of the consciousness produced by the exploitation of Africans as slaves. For that matter, racist assumptions were quite capable of discounting examples of African slaves with 'symptoms of ingenuity', and exceptions to the stereotype were not welcome for long.

An interesting example of evolving European attitudes towards Africa and Africans is provided by the case of William Amo, an Nzima from the Gold Coast who was taken to Europe as a boy by the Dutch. In 1707, Amo was given as a present to the (German) Duke of Wolfenbüttel, serving him as a page for many years. In 1727, he was sent to the University of Halle, where he studied philosophy and jurisprudence; and in 1734 he successfully defended a doctoral dissertation at the University of Wittenberg. On that occasion, the rector of the University stated as follows:

> Great once was the dignity of Africa, whether one considers natural talents of mind or the study of letters, or the very institutions for safeguarding religion. For she has given birth to several men of the greatest pre-eminence by whose talents and efforts the whole of human knowledge, no less than divine knowledge has been built up.[2]

He proceeded to cite several names, Augustine being the most outstanding. But of course this older image which derived from northern Africa and Ethiopia had all but disappeared, and the rector added that Africa had become prolific in things other than learning. Therefore, William Amo's career was supposed to prove the mental capacity of African people, a test which indicates an increasingly racist environment. Amo continued to distinguish himself as an academic, but in 1747 he was driven away from Europe because of a racist play which made him the object of attack.

The only possible exceptions to the pressures placed by Europeans on Africans in Europe were the few who went to Europe as diplomats

[1] In *Gentlemen's Magazine*, 1771, cited in Averil McKenzie Grieve, *The last years of the English slave trade* (London, 1968 ed.), 33.

[2] *Anton Gulielmus Amo Afer of Axim in Ghana: translation of his works* (Martin Luther University, Halle, 1968), 77.

or for schooling. Diplomatic missions were infrequent, but they occurred at intervals throughout the period of contact with Europe. The polities involved spread on the one hand mainly from the Senegambia to Kongo and on the other hand from Portugal to Scandinavia in western Europe. Asebu sent two envoys to Holland early in the seventeenth century; Allada dispatched a distinguished ambassador to the French court in 1670; several Gold Coast rulers were entertained by the Elector of Brandenburg in 1683; and the son of the king of Bissau represented his people in Lisbon in 1696. In the eighteenth century, such visits increased, and there were also instances of pretensions on the part of false African 'princes'. Meanwhile, the number of students also increased substantially, with Liverpool as their principal destination. Some of these students were also the sons of rulers, while others were the protégés of the chartered companies and individual African, European or mulatto traders. Little seems to be known about how they fared in an atmosphere where the public auction of Africans was a common occurrence, but presumably they were insulated by their transience, their class origins and the positions of their benefactors.

THE SLAVE TRADE, RACISM AND CAPITALISM

Those Africans about whom Hume purported to know in Europe, and from amongst whom Amo distinguished himself, were but a fractional representation of the millions enslaved by Europeans outside Europe. The act of enslaving Africans on the west and east coasts of Africa was a critical stage in the production of racism. The dehumanization or reification of the African was revealed in the terminology used in the slave trade. To the Portuguese, Dutch and Spanish in the early seventeenth century, an African became a 'piece', measurable in practically the same way as a piece of cloth. English slave traders continued for a while to refer to African slaves as servants, but when the charter was granted to the Royal African Company in 1672, official language for the first time denoted the African as a thing. Thereafter, African men and women were bracketed together with gold, ivory and beeswax as the commodities of Africa. Slavery and slave trading existed long before the Atlantic slave trade, especially in Europe where slavery constituted a distinct socio-historical era. Yet the identification between black African and saleable object became so overwhelming that '*Negrero*' and '*Négrier*' arose as the standard terms for 'slave trader' in Spanish and French, respectively. The dehumanization was taken for granted in many passing references, apart from being propounded in texts specifically devoted to the Atlantic trade. Towards the end of the slave trade, racial attitudes were strongly influenced by the debate on abolition which attracted considerable attention. Generally, the pro-slaving case rested on derogatory remarks about Africans and Africa. These stressed the supposed cruelty and dishonesty of individuals as well as socio-political deformities. Thus two English slave traders, Robert Norris and Archibald Dalzel, were active sponsors of the view that African states like Dahomey were exemplars of despotism and barbarism. However, some slave traders occasionally noted that African societies were orderly, so as to counter the charge that slaves were obtained only because of the corrupt nature of African rulers and the corrupting influence of the trade itself. Altogether, it was the negative view which triumphed. Reports from Europeans visiting Africa in this period reinforced the concept of the African as an inferior being, and even those morally opposed to the trade in slaves accepted this stereotype.[1]

Above all, it was the institution of slavery in the Americas which ultimately conditioned racial attitudes, even when their more immediate derivation was the literature on Africa or contacts within Europe itself. It has been well attested that New World slave-plantation society was the laboratory of modern racism. The owners' contempt for and fear of the black slaves was expressed in religious, scientific and philosophical terms, which became the stock attitudes of Europeans and even Africans in subsequent generations. Although there have been contributions to racist philosophy both before and after the slave trade epoch, the historical experience of whites enslaving blacks for four centuries forged the tie between racist and colour prejudice, and produced not merely individual racists but a society where racism was so all-pervasive that it was not even perceived for what it was. The very concept of human racial variants was never satisfactorily established in biological terms, and the assumptions of scientists and laymen alike were rooted in the perception of a reality in which Europeans had succeeded in reducing Africans to the level of chattel. Racist scholarship did not need to be widely read to be effective. It was sufficient for a few notions to escape and confirm the unstated racist beliefs of the population at large. There still exists a sub-stratum of received ideas about the 'Negro' which finds expression equally among whites of limited educa-

[1] See James Anthony Barker, 'British attitudes to the Negro in the seventeenth and eighteenth centuries', Ph.D. thesis (London, 1972).

tion and among the intelligentsia. When Trevor-Davies asserted that in Portugal during the period of slavery 'intermarriage with negroes produced a hybrid type that lacked vitality of body and mind', he probably did not know that he was echoing writers like Edward Long, the Jamaican slave owner who maligned the mulatto in order to prove that Africans and Europeans were different and incompatible species, the latter of course being superior.[1] Such statements assumed the mantle of self-evident truths in the post-slavery era.

Within Anglo-Saxon slave-owning societies, the initiative in developing racist ideology was taken by the sugar islands like Barbados, from which influences passed to the continental American colonies. The articulate defence of slavery in the ante-bellum South[2] drew heavily on the racist ideas of British West Indian slave owners. Dutch and French plantation societies did not lag far behind their English counterparts in producing the stereotypes and distortions which comprise racism. There was a larger element of 'free coloured' in the French West Indies, and in some respects planters hated and feared these mulattoes even more than the blacks. The multiple fine distinctions based on varying proportions of African and European intermixture were never fully workable, but nothing was more thoroughly racist than the principle of grading individuals in a hierarchy which descended from white to black through dozens of shades. Therein was enshrined the mystique of 'blood', 'purity' and the like.

In some works, Portuguese and Spanish slave possessions are said to constitute a distinct Catholic Mediterranean variant, in which Africans allegedly received much better treatment than in the colonies of the northern Protestant Europeans. But it is impossible to establish a consistent set of differences between the condition of blacks in areas controlled on the one hand by the English and the Dutch and on the other hand by the Portuguese and Spanish. The purported superiority of the latter arises mainly through romanticizing the situation in Brazil and by ignoring the fact that throughout the Americas one found the same racist structures ensuring the low socio-economic status of Africans and their descendants. Legal statutes were perhaps more favourable to slaves in Iberian possessions, but their practical implementation (or non-implementation) was determined by social realities, which therefore acted as the equalizing factor. Ultimately, the critical

[1] R. Trevor-Davies, *The golden century of Spain* (London, 1937), 189; and Edward Long, *The history of Jamaica* (London, 1970 ed.), II, 335, 336.

[2] In this chapter, the term 'South' refers to the southern mainland colonies in North America.

variable was the intensity of capitalist plantation production. Thus, the Dutch had a terrible reputation in Surinam, but not so in Curaçāo which was essentially a trading colony. Slavery in Latin America was occasionally domestic and paternal, but the majority of Africans taken to Latin America worked on plantations or in mines, with northern Brazil as one of the most important plantation centres throughout the centuries of slavery. The Portuguese were no exception to the generalization that one race cannot systematically enslave members of another on a large scale for over three centuries without acquiring a conscious or unconscious feeling of racial superiority.[1] Slavery persisted and racism was inordinately strengthened because Europe was in pursuit of profits. These phenomena were the consequence of the expansion of capitalism, the increasing differential between African and European societies from the point of contact onwards, and the relocation of Africans in a new society where power was monopolized by whites.

Given the context of European capitalist expansion, one measure of the African contribution to Europe and the Americas is in relationship to particular European nation-states. Portugal was first on the scene, and virtually monopolized trade with Africa during most of the fifteenth and sixteenth centuries. Portugal then secured the greatest share of the gold of West Africa and was the only European competitor with the Arabs for the gold, ivory and slaves on the east coast. After 1637, when they lost Elmina to the Dutch, the Portuguese concentrated in West Africa on slaving. Their transatlantic trade pattern was established in collaboration with the Spanish, and the relations were still close after the end of the Hispano-Portuguese monarchy in 1640. Payment for slaves in Spanish America was often made in gold and silver – the same gold and silver which was produced only because of the supply of African labour. The principal areas of Portuguese activity in West Africa were upper Guinea and Angola, and they also secured a significant proportion of captives leaving the Aja states. The Spanish ports of entry on the other side of the Atlantic were Cartagena, Vera Cruz, Porto Bello and Rio de la Plata, with the mines of Antioquia and Potosi as the main capitalist institutions consuming African labour. Although Lisbon had direct contacts with Africa, Seville was the lynch-pin of the Iberian structure. Seville issued the licences to load slaves in Africa for Spanish America. It was a cosmopolitan city, with numerous merchants from England, France, the Dutch Provinces,

[1] C. R. Boxer, *Race relations in the Portuguese colonial empire* (Oxford, 1963), especially section III, 'Brazil and Maranhao'; and H. Hoetinck, *Caribbean race relations* (London, 1971), 4–21.

Portugal and Italy. Through a gateway like Seville, Africans at home and in the Americas made the contribution to the European economy in the sixteenth and seventeenth centuries which caused Marx to observe that 'the discovery of gold and silver in America, the extirpation, enslavement and entombment in mines of the aboriginal population... the turning of Africa into a commercial warren for the hunting of black skins signalised the rosy dawn of the era of capitalist production'.[1]

In addition to servicing Spanish America, Portugal had a special interest in its own Brazilian territory. Angola was seen as the perfect complement to Brazil, and until the early eighteenth century the Lisbon/Luanda/Bahia triangle was one of the best defined of those which criss-crossed the Atlantic. Having beaten off a challenge from the Dutch, the Portuguese were then able to tap the agricultural and forest wealth of north-eastern Brazil. This region alone was productive enough to allow John IV (1640–56) to refer to Brazil as his milch-cow; and by the 1690s the discovery of gold opened up still greater possibilities. The labour requirements of Brazilian mines and plantations were fulfilled by more intensive exploitation of Angola and the 'Slave Coast'; and by the beginning of the eighteenth century, Brazilian gold was a major constituent in the goods offered for slaves between Cape Coast and Whydah. This practice of paying gold for slaves was carried out by Portuguese and Brazilian slavers against the wishes of the Portuguese crown. Similarly, directors of the Royal African Company of England were unhappy when their agents purchased slaves with gold in the eastern sections of what was supposed to be the 'Gold Coast'; but nothing demonstrates more vividly the value of African labour than the fact that buyers and users of this labour were prepared to pay for it in gold.

Portugal failed to benefit substantially from the value created by African labour in Brazil, mainly because Portugal was itself dependent upon the more developed areas of western Europe, and consequently it was to those countries that colonial profits ultimately flowed. Besides, such benefits as accrued to Portuguese citizens from the Atlantic trade tended to accumulate in the hands of those who settled in Brazil. In some respects, Brazil was more akin to the English colonies of settlement in North America than to the plantation colonies of the West Indies. Colonists enriched themselves and sought emancipation from metropolitan control. A major manifestation of their independent spirit

[1] Karl Marx, *Das Kapital* (Moscow, 1961), I, ch. XXXI, 751.

was their attempt to define the terms on which Brazil should trade with Africa. Brazilians insisted on selling rum in Guinea and Angola, although this was damaging to Portuguese wines and brandy. Brazilian rum, tobacco and gold were the only items which the Portuguese had at their disposal as readily saleable goods in West Africa; and by the end of the eighteenth century most of the successful Portuguese-speaking slave traders were Brazilians. Portuguese profits from their African ventures were also limited by direct competition from other European powers and by the extent of Portuguese commitments relative to the nation's social and administrative capacity. Yet sometimes too much is made of the supposed over-extension of small countries like Portugal. The Dutch Provinces were also small in terms of size and population, but the character of their operations was quite different and the profits which accrued were much larger.

Because of conflicts with Spain and Portugal in the 1590s, the Dutch could no longer obtain salt and colonial products from Lisbon. The availability of cheap salt off the coast of Venezuela drew Dutch shipping into the Caribbean, and once in the area they noticed other possibilities. Having secured Pernambuco in 1630, the way was open to the production of cane sugar. This automatically augmented the demand for labour, and placed the Dutch in the same position as their Portuguese forerunners who were trading in and using Africans as slaves. In 1634 a memorandum of the first Dutch West India Company asked members to 'come with ripe advice and deliberation over the point of buying in and selling the blacks, as is the custom of the Portuguese, without which means the sugar mills cannot be kept going'.[1] Within a few years, the Company's advisers were enthusiastic about the slave trade from Allada and the Niger delta. It quickly became obvious to the Dutch West India Company that, in dealing in slaves and sugar, they had committed themselves to a system which was a logical and indivisible whole. In 1644 the agents on the Guinea coast used three ships to return cargoes directly to Europe, because they claimed that the price for slaves was low in Brazil. The directors sharply reproved this action, pointing out that they could not afford to hold up Brazil's labour supplies and that sugar was awaiting shipment in Pernambuco. Their chief agent could only apologize and promise that, unless otherwise instructed, he would load captive Africans and ship them to Brazil. Involvement in slave trading also led the Dutch to break into the profitable Spanish American

[1] Furley Collection, University of Ghana, Dutch Records. Minutes of the Admiralty Blue Book 2, fol. 136.

market. The Dutch supply of African labour to Spanish America was well established by the 1650s, with the island of Curaçāo being a base for transhipment. The Dutch themselves took the initiative in starting a sugar industry in the British-owned islands. They transferred techniques from Pernambuco, capital equipment from the United Provinces and labour from Africa. Eventually, the British ousted the Dutch from this powerful position.

The Dutch were less interested in African labour *per se* than in the financial and commercial aspects of the slave trade and the Atlantic system. During the seventeenth century, the Dutch attached more importance to gold than to African captives. They held the reins of the European monetary and financial system, which was based on gold. Most of the Dutch gold coin was minted from Guinea gold, and from 1637 onwards they had the greatest share of gold exports from the 'Gold Coast'. Dutch representatives on the Guinea coast began concentrating their efforts on the three-cornered slave trade only in the second decade of the eighteenth century. Meanwhile the Dutch invested heavily in northern Europe. The first Swedish company to function on the Guinea coast, after receiving a charter in 1649, was virtually run from Amsterdam. It used Dutch ships and sailors and it employed a former official of the Dutch West India Company as its chief of operations. Even in the era of mercantile competition, some forms of capitalist activity transcended national boundaries. From the seventeenth century onwards, profits made by Europe in Africa, Asia and the Americas were fed into an expanding network of exploitation of the non-European world, which at all stages was stimulating the growth and restructuring of the European economy. Dutch financiers assisted the industrial revolution in England by making capital available (even to the detriment of Dutch industry). Indeed, there was already in existence an international capitalist system, characterized by a subdivision into dominant and subordinate subsystems. The subordinate colonial regions provided labour, for whose production and reproduction the capitalists paid nothing except for the insignificant cost price of a slave and his maintenance at a level of bare subsistence determined by Europeans themselves. The colonial sector also supplied primary products from the soil and sub-soil, for refinement and consumption within Europe. The choice of which colonial resources were to be developed was left in European hands, and this choice was always in relation to European demand. Meanwhile the metropoles accelerated the formation of new productive forces, extended the exploitation and integration of their domestic resources to meet internal needs, and created new linkages within and across national European economies. Given the differences in power, technology and social organization which existed between the two subsystems, it also followed that the exchange relationship was unequal and accentuated inequalities – to the detriment of Africa and in favour of Europe.

Africa's contribution to capitalism as a global system is best illustrated with reference to France and England, the leading capitalist powers in Europe by the end of the eighteenth century. Both countries had independent connections with West Africa. France was active in the gum trade of the Senegal, and French ships also returned directly to France with ivory, hides, beeswax and civet. The same applied to the British, to greater or lesser extent, the trade in camwood being particularly noteworthy. But the most significant fact about Africa's relations with England and France was that these two acquired commanding positions in West African trade while being in possession of productive territories in the Americas. This was the prerequisite to setting up viable 'triangular trade'. The rise of ports like Bristol, Liverpool, Nantes and Bordeaux was perhaps the most spectacular consequence of the triangular trade so far as Europe was concerned. These ports in turn stimulated inland centres whose development gave rise to the concept of industrial revolution. The connection is most obvious in the case of Liverpool and the English industrial heartlands. As Paul Mantoux put it, 'the growth of Lancashire, of all the English counties the one most deserving to be called the cradle of the factory system, depended first of all on the development of Liverpool and her trade'.[1] To towns, docks, ships and capital, one must also add the invaluable experience gained by the young capitalist nations in the spheres of commercial and financial organization. Not all of the companies floated for West African trade were money-spinners, but their value is not to be measured only in terms of their cash-books. West Africa and the West Indies were serving as a laboratory for numerous experiments in associating capital, limiting liability, developing credit institutions and setting up maritime insurance, all of which were vital to subsequent capitalist organization.

Because it was Europe which took the initiative in internationalizing trade, the inputs from various sectors of world trade intermingled within Europe. New World produce grown by African labour was re-exported from England and France to other parts of Europe; and

[1] Paul Mantoux, *The industrial revolution in the eighteenth century* (London, 1961 ed.), 108.

Hamburg, though not directly associated with the slave trade or slave plantations, was the biggest sugar-refining centre in Europe in the first half of the eighteenth century. Germany supplied manufactures to Scandinavia, Holland, England, France and Portugal for resale in Africa. England, France and Holland (though national rivals) found it necessary to exchange various classes of goods the better to deal with Africans for gold, slaves and ivory. In the Americas, there were also subsidiary trades based on the slave trade. The British colonists of New England sent supplies of food, livestock and timber to the West Indies and received in return sugar, molasses, coffee and indigo. This trade contributed to the growth of the eastern sea-board ports, to the formation of capital in North America, and to the strengthening of trade with Europe by giving northern colonists tropical produce which was marketable in Europe.

TOWARDS ABOLITION

The fact that a number of countries ceased participation in the slave trade in the early nineteenth century meant a significant diminution in the scope and relative global value of the slave-based triangular trades; and this partial abolition also reflected important changes in the relationship between Africa, Europe and America in the second half of the eighteenth century. One of the earliest of the major changes was the American War of Independence, through which the white colonists opted out of the Atlantic pattern designed by Britain. Following upon this was the Revolution of St Domingue in 1791, which meant not merely the breakaway of a colony but an abrupt end to the institution of slavery on that part of the island of Hispaniola. St Domingue played in the economy of eighteenth-century France the role played by the whole of black Africa in the twentieth century, accounting for just over ten per cent of the external trade of France. Its value was enhanced by the declining fertility of the British islands, which had been unscientifically exploited for sugar-cane for a much longer period. Consequently, France took over from England the role of re-exporter of plantation produce within Europe. There were about 500,000 slaves in St Domingue in 1790, a large proportion of whom had been born in Africa; and the island was undoubtedly the most profitable slave mart in the Americas. When the Africans of St Domingue liberated themselves by struggle, they were decisively abolishing a major sector of the slave trade, and they were doing so many years before European nations passed abolitionist legislation of varying degrees of effectiveness.

Indirectly, the Revolution of St Domingue also hastened the appreciation of the French and British that slavery in the West Indies was dangerous and ultimately unrewarding. The fear of slave revolts was rooted in the minds of Europeans in the New World and was also a factor in the consciousness of the metropoles. The English and French publics knew of the revolts, the discovered plots and the violence which were part of their overseas slave society. In 1787, Samuel Johnson proposed a toast 'to the next insurrection of the Negroes in the West Indies'; and, in his opening address to the Estates General in 1789, Necker showed himself to be well aware of slave revolts in the Caribbean. Necker was prepared to concede the moral injustice of the slave trade and slavery, but he was not convinced that these institutions had yet lost their profitability, especially in view of competition with England. This juxtaposition of the 'humanitarian' and 'economic' considerations weighing for and against slavery and the slave trade is of course at the centre of the historiographical debate on the topic of abolition.

It is often stated or implied that the abolitionists mobilized humanitarian feelings to triumph over more mundane considerations such as profits to be made from the slave trade. The 'economic interpretation' of the same phenomenon suggests that changes in productivity, technology and patterns of exchange in Europe and the Americas made it necessary for the British to end their participation in the trade in 1807. It is not enough to conclude lamely that the truth lies somewhere between these two approaches. One has to identify priorities, and profit had top priority within the capitalist commerce which linked the three continents. A decline in the profitability of the triangular trades made it possible for certain basic human sentiments to be asserted at the decision-making level in a number of European countries – Britain being the most crucial because it was the greatest carrier of African captives across the Atlantic.

Most books on the abolitionist movement, beginning with Clarkson's, make references to several precursors in the field. Within Catholic countries, the attack against the slave trade usually assumed the form of theological arguments against the 'unjust' means by which slaves were procured. This was strongly advanced by some clerics in Guinea and Spanish America as well as in Europe. They contended that it was rare for an African to be legitimately enslaved according to ecclesiastical canons, and they insisted that European slavers should accept only those Africans who had been justly enslaved, which amounted to a call for the abolition of the slave trade. Among Protestants, Quakers were the most consistent questioners of slavery, and they wrestled with contradictions posed by Quakers owning slaves in the Americas. Quakers in the northern American colonies often made the decision to disassociate themselves from slavery. However, before the latter part of the eighteenth century, neither Catholics nor Protestants could persuade a slave-using community or nation to eschew economic benefits and abolish the trade in captive Africans. On the contrary, church and state rationalized the *status quo*. The humanitarian concern of some individuals was rebuffed by economic considerations, until England found that the pattern of its own Atlantic trade was altering in the second half of the eighteenth century in such a way as to make the slave trade dispensable.

By 1750, slave ships reaching the British West Indies returned virtually empty to England because sugar buyers organized their own direct shipping between England and the West Indies. Bristol became the biggest sugar-manufacturing centre in England and had the greatest proportion of trade with the West Indies in the second half of the eighteenth century, although it had withdrawn almost completely from slave trading. Significantly, Bristol put up no real opposition to the abolition of the British trade in slaves. Liverpool's activities had stocked the islands with a population sufficient to meet production targets which had ceased to be ever expanding, given declining fertility and external competition. The East Indian sugar interests also challenged the West Indian planters and merchants at their own game of political lobbying in parliament. Equally crucial was the fact that, although Europeans in North America had broken the mercantilist colonial bonds, they were even better trading partners of an industrializing Britain by the end of the eighteenth century; and at this time (before the cotton era) the slave economy of the South seemed to have been on its way out. There was also the beginning of a new awareness that the factory system in England would need from Africa raw materials for industry, requiring the exploitation of African labour within Africa. Interest in palm oil, for example, was displayed before the British abolition of the slave trade, and several other items which subsequently constituted 'legitimate' articles of commerce were being investigated or actually traded. By 1807, the complex network of commerce linking the three continents was already being replaced by bilateral arrangements between Europe and the Americas and to a lesser extent between Europe and Africa. These factors made it possible for English abolitionists to receive a favourable hearing within the legislative councils of the nation.

The anti-slavery movement in North America predated the most active period of its European counterpart, so that Clarkson could call upon the writings of Anthony Benezet and French abolitionists invoked the name of William Penn. Furthermore, the American abolitionists could supposedly count upon the support of no less a person than President Jefferson. But Jefferson temporized and compromised with the slave South and with his conscience, hoping that slavery would eventually cease to be economically viable. By the end of the first decade of the nineteenth century, some states in the Union had passed anti-slave trade legislation, but few were prepared to put such legislation into practice if it hurt material interests. When the cotton gin appeared on the scene, the South was already entrenched politically and constitutionally, so that slavery and the slave trade had a further lease. This demonstrated how the abolitionist movement was dependent for its success on prior and continuing economic changes which greatly diminished the profitability of slavery and the slave trade, as far as a particular nation was concerned.

In France, too, anti-slavery tendencies appeared before the abolitionist movement in Britain and yet failed to make an impact locally. Montesquieu, born and bred in the slaving town of Bordeaux, was the first philosopher of international repute to raise his voice in favour of abolition. There are frequent references to French writers of the Enlightenment in the works of early English abolitionists, but the French abolitionists were a minority within the French Revolution. The Abbé Raynal, Brissot, Broglie, Mirabeau, Lafayette, La Rochefoucauld, Condorcet, Pétion and the Abbé Gregoire were the leading lights of the Société des Amis des Noirs. The planter lobby which they confronted in the form of the Club Massaic was not declining like that in England, and it was able to recruit to its side powerful business interests and political spokesmen. All proposals against the slave trade, slavery and racial discrimination in the French colonies were rejected or deferred by the Constituent Assembly of 1789 and the Legislative Assembly of 1792. Only Robespierre had the strength and conviction to carry through an abolitionist measure; and even when France legally abolished slavery in January 1794 this was largely frustrated by events in the colonies.

In the islands of the Indian Ocean, white planters decided that the Declaration of the Rights of Man was not written for black Africans, and the emancipation proclamation remained a dead letter. In subsequent years the slave trade from East Africa to Mauritius, Seychelles and Réunion intensified considerably. In the West Indies, French planters betrayed the French government and joined the British rather than grant freedom to their slaves. In 1794 the British took Martinique, Guadeloupe and St Lucia with the connivance of slave owners. Victor Hughes, the Jacobin Commissioner who was sent out to the Caribbean, realized that emancipation could be achieved only by relying on the efforts of the black population. When assured that they were free under French law, the blacks speedily ousted the British from Guadeloupe and St Lucia. Unfortunately, this freedom did not last long – partly because islands changed hands regularly as pawns in European conflicts, and partly because of the rise of Napoleon. Napoleon had a personal interest in West Indian slavery through his wife, Josephine, whose family had long-standing and extensive investments in Martinique and Guadeloupe. Under Napoleon, slavery was re-established in the Caribbean territories held by France, and the French slave trade in the region persisted until the 1830s, although it was nominally abolished in 1815. France trailed behind England in ending the slave trade because it trailed behind England in moving towards the factory system and in transcending the mercantilist phase in which slave trading was the mainstay. Portugal lagged even further behind. This unevenness of socio-economic development within western Europe, coupled with the profitability of slave production in Cuba, Brazil and the USA allowed the Atlantic slave trade to extend far into the nineteenth century.

Meanwhile, new Afro-European involvements were arising in the scientific and cultural spheres. Europe's interest in more direct trade with Africa was complemented by a scientific, investigatory approach to the continent as a whole. Botanists were particularly active in collecting and classifying African flora in the last years of the eighteenth century, and the fauna also attracted some attention. Naturalists as distinguished as Carl Linnaeus and Joseph Banks sent expeditions to West and South Africa. It was Banks who in 1788 founded the Association for Promoting the Discovery of the Interior Parts of Africa – the sponsorship of Mungo Park being the Association's most successful venture. To the extent that the settlement of Sierra Leone was bolstered by Christian organizations, it was also a new departure in Afro-European relations. Previous Christianizing efforts were few and far between, and were bedevilled by the participation of the same Christians in the slave trade. Priests or missionaries rarely disassociated themselves from the other white residents on the African coasts. In fact they often carried on trade themselves or ministered to white merchants rather than to Africans as such. But by the 1790s, Sierra Leone was already contributing to the European image of Africa as a place to rule, Christianize and civilize.

THE AFRICAN CONTRIBUTION IN THE AMERICAS

By the time that the black people of St Domingue broke violently with the Atlantic slave system, the African presence in the Americas was massive. At a conservative estimate, some seven million Africans were landed alive in the Americas before the end of the eighteenth century. In some areas, particularly in North America, slow natural increase added considerably to the figure of imports. The significance of the black population must be measured in relation to geographical distribution and to the other ethnic components of the population at different times. In the Caribbean islands, the indigenous Indians were rapidly eliminated, and Europeans were usually an insignificant proportion of the population, in spite of many efforts at voluntary and involuntary white immigration. Africans carried similar weight in north-eastern Brazil, in the southern colonies of the British in North America and on the Guyana coastlands. On the Spanish American mainland, their numbers were overwhelming in particular places at particular times. The accepted Mexican image is that of a mixture of indigenous Indian and immigrant European, while in reality the whites were greatly outnumbered by black slaves until the eighteenth century. Argentina's image is even more lily-white, and yet the Rio de la Plata had flourishing slave imports in the sixteenth and seventeenth centuries. Besides, there were heavy concentrations of black people in parts of Panama, Colombia, Venezuela, Bolivia and Peru. Major white immigration drives were necessary before the black population in these countries became a tiny minority, giving place instead to a high proportion of mulattoes.

The children of Africa were dispersed throughout the length and breadth of the Americas from Quebec and Nova Scotia to the southern Andes; and this physical presence meant a fundamental contribution to the economy and culture of the Americas. General histories, because of white bias, consistently fail to recognize this fact, although numerous revealing studies are available on specific aspects of Africans working in and contributing to the growth of the American continent. The essence of the African contribution was the labour which made possible the extensive cultivation of the soil and the eventual transition to an industrial society in North America. It may appear paradoxical that the areas where slavery was most deeply entrenched were left with a legacy of soil exhaustion, technological stagnation and socio-political retardation. But this historically created backwardness was an integral part of capitalism as a system – one of its many inequalities and aberrations, without which its 'achievements' would not have been registered.

Having been carried to the Americas as a slave, the African was ambivalently defined as a part of capital stock and as a worker. The latter, however, was more important, and the range of working occupations in the new environment is worthy of comment. The greatest proportion of African men and women went into the farming sector, growing crops such as cotton, sugar-cane, rice, indigo and tobacco, along with their own 'ground provisions'. Many others were involved in mining, cattle herding, domestic service, porterage, sailing, timber-felling and building. In some cases it appears that given groups of Africans brought with them to the Americas skills which were directly relevant to the tasks which they were forced to perform. The economy of the Spanish islands of Hispaniola and Cuba in the sixteenth and seventeenth centuries relied heavily on cattle raising and on the labour of Senegambians and upper Guineans. These particular Africans (including Fulani, Wolof, Biafada and Mande) were no strangers to cattle raising. Nor were they unfamiliar with mining, which constituted the principal activity on the Spanish mainland. The washing of alluvial gold was well known on much of the Guinea coast, while open-pit mining of gold and iron ore was long practised on the upper Senegal and in Futa Jalon. Similarly, it is a striking fact that in the eighteenth century, when the 'Gold Coast' began exporting considerable numbers of slaves, one of their major destinations was the province of Minas Gerais in Brazil, where gold deposits were being tapped. Another specific instance of the transfer of skills is provided by the intensive connections between Guinea-Bissau and the Brazilian state of Maranhão in the second half of the eighteenth century. On the swampy lowlands between the Casamance and the Nuñez, African peoples like the Diola and the Baga had raised rice-farming to a level which drew the admiration of European visitors, and rice was also a staple grain on more hilly areas of the near interior. It was from this nursery of rice growing that Guineans were uprooted and sent to Maranhão, where they rapidly built up a successful rice industry.

In many instances, the tasks which faced Africans on the other side of the Atlantic required a phenomenal amount of physical energy. This energy cleared forests and built roads, ports and cities. Much has been written about the white American frontiersmen, but the first frontiersmen were blacks working under the lash. Besides, many tasks called for training and skills. There emerged throughout the plantation zone a corps of artisan slaves identified in the first instance with the agrarian economy. Sugar plantations were particularly demanding of skilled labour because of the manufacturing process involved, while cotton also underwent the early stages of processing on the plantation. Irrespective of the crop grown, estates needed coopers, blacksmiths, masons and carpenters. The luxurious mansions and the 'Great Houses' of the slave owners attested to the quality of slave labour.

The evolution of skilled labour illustrates some of the contradictions inherent in the slave system to which Africans were subjected. Forced labour imposes narrow limits on the extent of technological innovation. Crude implements were actually preferred because they were less susceptible to deliberate breakage by slaves; while specialization and the division of labour brought complications which could not be encompassed by sheer coercion. Indeed, the special feature which distinguishes a plantation from other agricultural enterprises is the combination of a few skilled supervisors with as many unskilled labourers as is economically profitable.[1] There were also subjective factors militating against the emergence of a sector of artisan slaves. For instance, owners in the South initially placed a low economic value on manufacturing enterprise, and they also feared that exposure to crafts would enable blacks to make themselves weapons and to contact free white workers. But scarcity of skilled white labour forced the adoption of skilled black labour as a small but important sector within the labouring force of slaves. Therefore, on large plantations, a few young blacks were apprenticed to older craftsmen and kept at their calling irrespective of the need for them in other work. The expertise gained in a specific trade or even as a handyman allowed the slave concerned a degree of mobility. Slave owners with artisan slaves hired them out at great profit. A slave moving from one place to another had greater opportunities for escape and his knowledge probably enhanced his confidence. Skilled slaves were also heavily in demand in the towns. In the North American colonies during the eighteenth century, the

[1] See George L. Beckford, *Persistent poverty: underdevelopment in plantation economies of the Third World* (London, 1971), 6.

largest proportion of black artisans were to be found not in the plantation belt but in New York, Philadelphia, Baltimore and a few New England centres. Some of these workers were freemen, and craft skills were a useful source of employment if a slave managed to gain his freedom. In Brazil, free blacks and especially free mulattoes (who were the ones most likely to be manumitted) virtually monopolized industrial and artistic crafts in the cities of the north-east; while in the South masters who manumitted slaves at times allowed them to take their tools as a means of livelihood.

Although the agricultural field work was essentially manual labour, this too required knowledge which one African was obliged to pass on to another. This largely accounts for the much higher value of a 'seasoned' slave in comparison with a green recruit from Africa. During the process of 'seasoning' on a plantation, Africans fresh from the continent were placed under more experienced slaves so as to learn the routine of work. Black people mastered the processes of New World production partly on the basis of previous African experience and more so through learning on the spot. Europeans provided the organizational and supervisory structures, but their presence was often nominal. It has been said of Brazil that 'the Negro foremen on the plantation, or later in the gold mines, knew more about the technological processes than did many of the Portuguese owners; [and] from the seventeenth to the nineteenth century, agricultural and mining enterprise in Brazil owed a large debt to the Negro labourers and technicians'.[1] This conclusion applied to most parts of America.

Africans transferred to the New World more than just simply their labour power. Discussion of the traumatic nature of capture and the Atlantic passage is meaningful only in so far as it concentrates on the degree of disruption relative to aspects of continuity. Obviously, Africans could not continue without modification their own customs and ceremonies, given the structures of the new societies in which they found themselves. It is also crucial to stress how much needed to be learnt in the new environment. But, from the very beginning, the slave society held together only because Africans came from their mother continent with a heritage of social organization and solidarity at a level which was sufficiently high to allow them to survive collective labour at its most rigorous. The obverse of this truth is that Indians such as those in the Greater Antilles who had barely entered the epoch of settled agriculture were absolutely bewildered when imposed upon

[1] Preston James, *Latin America* (London, 1959), 308.

by the Europeans. For this and other reasons they failed to survive. Africans survived.

THE COST OF SURVIVAL IN THE NEW WORLD

The cost of survival was phenomenal. It has seemingly become unfashionable to dwell upon the sufferings of Africans under slavery, but no assessment of Africans in the Americas (however brief) could justifiably omit mention of the unique African contribution to the history of suffering. Slaves were often the object of perversity and cruelty of the worst kinds. It is not surprising that contemporary disciples of the Marquis de Sade found French West Indian slave society an ideal testing ground. Nor were acts of cruelty merely expressions of individual psychoses; they were embedded in the system of slavery itself. Punishments, for example, were necessarily harsh because they had to discourage pugnacious and runaway slaves. Balancing between the need to keep the slave at full working capacity and effectively disciplined, the master at times considered it logical and justifiable to mutilate and disable the slave. Indeed, the very life of the African was considered dispensable in relation to the all-round maintenance and profitability of the system. Planters debated the issue of whether better treatment and a longer working life was preferable to intensive exploitation which would finish a slave in a few years. They usually opted for the latter, so long as Africa was a source of cheap replenishment. Little wonder that there was a huge excess of deaths over births as far as the African population on the sugar plantations in the Americas was concerned. Africans were being consumed like raw material in an industrial process, and every year fresh consignments arrived from the commercial warrens which had been established mainly in western and central Africa.

The oppression and suffering of slavery was directly proportionate to the level of exploitation of African labour. The plantation slave was given a fixed ration, which represented the minimum requirements for the production of his living labour; and in return he was forced to give up to sixteen or eighteen hours per day. To maintain such exploitation, slave owners went beyond physical oppression and tried to dehumanize the captive people of Africa, following in the wake of the slave traders. For those who survived the Atlantic passage, sale and dispersion on landing was another harrowing experience. Equiano attested that he had often seen his fellow Africans in the West Indies 'put into scales and weighed, and then sold from three pence to six pence or nine pence a pound'.[1] If they were sold by public auction, it was even more horrific, especially since this took place shortly after landing when the captive cargo was weakened and bewildered by the crossing. The slave born in America was spared the sufferings of the Atlantic passage and was more readily socialized within slave society. Paradoxically, however, his chances of being dehumanized were greater, because he never knew any existence other than that of being someone else's property.

Slavery undoubtedly took toll on the personality of its African victims. The slavish stereotype, which goes under the name of 'Sambo' in North American scholarship and 'Quashee' in the Caribbean, refers to a slave who was docile, obsequious and unintelligent, although capable of low cunning and definitely given to lying. This picture was an idealization from the master's viewpoint, in the sense that he could argue that such a person ought 'naturally' to be a slave. It would be futile to deny that there were slaves who approximated to Sambo or Quashee; and, more important still, such elements probably formed one of the two sides of the ambiguous character of most slaves. However, the presence of literally slavish types has been overstated not merely because of racist bias but also because of failure to recognize the degree of conscious role-playing in which slaves engaged. The slave/master situation presented apt conditions for the working out of what has been termed 'self-fulfilling prophecy'.[2] To begin with, owners sought to create circumstances which would actualize the stereotype which they had of Africans. Brutality does tend to transform men into brutes, and deficiencies in the diet of slaves would also have led to sluggishness, whether or not the planters were aware of this. In the second place, the slaves themselves either pretended to confirm to the master's norms or actually internalized them. Difficulty arises in separating what may have been a fixed personality trait from calculated role-playing. By the very nature of things, the evidence is not always forthcoming as to how black people 'ran games' on the slave owners; but those few whites who were privileged to see slaves socializing away from the immediate eyes of authority were always amazed at the transformation from brutish servility to human vitality. Warmth, volubility and precision were the qualities which superseded seeming taciturnity, once the slave squatted before his own fire. In this latter context and even openly in the fields, slaves displayed a special knack

[1] Paul Edwards, ed., *Equiano's travels: his autobiography* (London, 1967), 71.

[2] Orlando Patterson, *The sociology of slavery, an analysis of the origins, development and structure of Negro slave society in Jamaica* (London, 1967), 179–81.

for satirizing, mocking, deflating pretensions and attaching apt nicknames to whites and their fellow blacks.

It is very clear that the goal of dehumanization, whether as an unstated premise of slavery or as a conscious aim of certain slave owners, was seldom if ever achieved. The essential humanity of the slaves broke through the restrictions of the system at numerous points. Small acts of solidarity helped to make daily life tolerable and to frustrate the intentions of the masters, however absolute their power may have appeared in theory. It was essential for masters to employ those Africans who, in order to survive, took the opportunist path of breaking ranks. Such individuals were promoted to become slave drivers and to wield the feared whip. Yet the black slave driver was not always a figure of nemesis, and he co-operated with the rest of the slaves on given plantations. One slave driver testified to having learnt to handle the whip 'with marvelous dexterity and precision, throwing the lash within a hair's breadth of the back, the ear, the nose, without, however, touching either of them'.[1] Individual slaves depended upon their own wit and cleverness to avoid unpleasant tasks, to cut down on their work load, and even occasionally to win their freedom. The theme of the clever slave matching wits with the planter appears with relative frequency in the slim surviving literature produced by slaves and ex-slaves, suggesting that it was an integral part of their reality as well as part of their dreams. African women were particularly vulnerable to the depredations of slavery, since European owners theoretically had unlimited access to their female property. Nevertheless, black women who were forced into sexual relations with white men, or who by choice entered into these relations, found means of transcending the difference of status, and asserted their feminity and humanity in these sexual liaisons. Occasionally, slaves managed to have black mistresses intervene on their behalf; and even the good offices of a neighbouring planter could be invoked.

Probably, the most common and the most significant form of African reaction to enslavement in the Americas was passive resistance. First, there was perpetual recourse to slacking and slowing down of work, so long as strict supervision was relaxed. This was widely acknowledged by planters and other white observers in all areas where the institution of slavery existed. Secondly, there was careless and destructive handling of equipment and livestock – often deliberately, although attributable

[1] Solomon Northrup, *Twelve years a slave* (1853), 226, cited in Raymond and Alice Bauer, 'Day to day resistance to slavery', *Journal of Negro History*, October 1942.

to general indifference. An important consequence of this was the fact that tools had to be crude and heavy to resist breakage. Thirdly, there was widespread malingering, used not only to avoid work but also to avoid passing into the hands of a particular master. Of course, planters knew that there would be malingerers on every day's roll call and there was a constant battle on this issue. But because many genuinely sick slaves were worked to death, this possibility restrained owners in dealing with doubtful cases. Finally, there were extreme instances of recourse to self-mutilation, suicide or infanticide. Each of these many methods of passive resistance amounted to a serious counter-attack against the power of the slave holders, because they each meant considerable financial loss.

Besides many forms of indirect aggression, Africans in the Americas also took positive collective steps to use violence in freeing themselves. Small rebellions are dotted throughout the history of the slave region and interspersed with similar events on a more epic scale. Uprisings started from the earliest years of Spanish slavery in the Greater Antilles, and they continued throughout the sixteenth, seventeenth and eighteenth centuries in the many areas of concentrated slave populations on the Spanish American mainland. The Portuguese sphere in Brazil was also plagued by small and large revolts, flatly contradicting the idealization of the slave/master relationship in this part of the Americas. The territory held by the Dutch in Guyana was no easier to handle. There were slave uprisings in Berbice in 1749 and 1752, which were brutally suppressed by the Dutch; but from 1762 to 1767 there occurred another outbreak, second in ambition and achievement only to the subsequent Revolution of St Domingue. It sought to make at least the Berbice colony of the Dutch into a free black state, and this would have had important repercussions in Surinam, Demerara and Essequibo. This type of slave revolt which was designed to liberate a whole colony can be distinguished from others of more modest aims, such as those which prepared the way for flight. The latter involved the slaves of a given plantation or vicinity, while the former demanded careful planning so as to embrace whole islands or large administrative units. For instance, a revolt in Cartagena in 1599–1600 aimed at uniting most of the 20,000 slaves of the province; a great rebellion in Jamaica, which lasted for several months in 1760, was island-wide in scope; and another on the same island in 1765 broke out prematurely on seventeen plantations. By the end of the third decade of the nineteenth century, a series of revolts in the British West Indies coincided with the debate on emancipation, and slaves consciously used rebellion and the threat of rebellion to hasten the achievement of this objective.

Whatever the size or effectiveness of a given slave revolt, it added to the tradition of violent resistance, a tradition of which the owners were the first to take cognisance. Undoubtedly, rebellions were more frequently planned than executed, many being abortive because the news leaked out prematurely. Yet, these too made their impact, as is evident from the salutary fear inspired throughout the South by the frustrated rebellion of Gabriel Prosser in Virginia in 1800. The fear of revolt hung like a pall on the shoulders of masters, conditioning their response to the suppression of rebellions and to the ethnic or 'tribal' choice and mixture of African slaves, as well as to other seemingly unrelated matters such as whether or not slaves should be exposed to Christian doctrines and, ultimately, whether or not the emancipation legislation should be accepted. In the English colonies in particular, laws sought to guarantee a certain minimum number of whites relative to blacks, precisely so as to have sufficient forces to maintain the Africans in subjection; and these laws were flouted only because of the impossibility of attracting enough whites and the tempting profits of allowing the unrestricted entry of Africans as slave labourers. The fear of revolt co-existed with the stereotype of the docile slave, because exploitation and bigotry will together contain the most palpable illogicalities. But the slave masters (more so than many subsequent scholars) knew well that the same slow shuffling Sambo or Quashee was liable to explode at any time. Even the house-slave, identified as a progenitor of the modern 'Uncle Tom', was a potential revoltee, as convincingly illustrated by Toussaint l'Ouverture, the former coachman and trusted servant who led the liberation forces in St Domingue. African names predominate in the leadership of most New World slave revolts, excepting those in the South in the nineteenth century, suggesting that these leaders were African-born or not far removed generically and culturally. Field-slaves and house-slaves, African-born and local-born helped set the tradition of struggle and resistance.

Escape individually and in groups was another aggressive aspect of the African response to enslavement. The prevalence of such fugitives in Spanish America gave rise to the term 'cimarrones' or 'maroons', by which they are commonly known. Maroons in Panama fought protracted guerrilla wars from about 1540 until 1574 when the Spaniards had to come to terms with them. There were 2,000 maroons estimated to have been at large in Mexico in 1579, amounting to one-tenth of the black population at the time. The best-known examples of the runaway slave phenomenon were provided by the maroons of Jamaica, the 'Bush Negroes' of Guyana, and the residents of the *quilombos* in Brazil; but slaves escaped everywhere else, including the small islands of Barbados, Antigua and Curaçāo. Of course, favourable terrain in regions adjacent to wherever the slaves were being kept was a distinct advantage. The hills of Jamaica, the forests of Surinam and Brazil, and the swamps of the South were ideal for refuge.

Mass escapes were usually the product of rebellions, and gave rise to a free life which was often surprisingly well rounded. Agricultural and craft activities were carried on, and it was even possible in some instances to conduct trade with white communities. However, on the whole, life had to be placed on a militant footing. Maroons defended their separate existence in fortified villages and also attacked European property and lines of communications. Their greatest threat to the whites lay in the fact that maroon settlements were poles of attraction for other runaways, and all self-liberated Africans were potential allies of Africans still in slavery. For example, the long cycle of slave disturbances in Brazil from 1641 to 1697 and again in the eighteenth century was interwoven with wars against the *quilombos*, reaching a high point in the campaigns against the *quilombo* of Palmares in the 1690s. Similarly, planters in Jamaica faced rebellion in their midst coupled with maroon wars from 1655 to 1740. For this reason, the whites were prepared to come to treaty arrangements with the maroons, guaranteeing that the latter would not be harassed provided that they discouraged and returned newcomers who had escaped. This was the sort of arrangement which the Spaniards had made on some parts of the mainland since the sixteenth century. Some fugitives did carry out police activity on behalf of slave owners, thereby placing their own immediate interests above those of the rest of the black population; but the effectiveness of maroon treaties concluded between the sixteenth and eighteenth centuries was very limited. Time and time again, maroons offered refuge to slaves who were minded to rebel or escape, and in the Revolution of St Domingue the co-operation between slaves on the plantations and runaway Africans in the hills was particularly important.

THE AFRO-AMERICAN CULTURAL HERITAGE

Communities of self-liberated blacks in America during the slave epoch are also significant as the purest representations of African culture in the New World. In the 'Cockpit Country' of the Jamaican maroons, isolation ensured the survival of African cultural traits long after slavery ended on the island. They were not homogeneous, and one large section referred to as 'Madagascars' might have also come from Mozambique. But the majority appeared to have been from the Gold Coast, and in the early eighteenth century were said to speak 'the Coromantee language' – presumably Twi. At this time Akan personal names such as Kofi (Cuffee), Kwadjo (Cudjoe) and Acheampong (Accompong) were encountered among the leadership. Their military skills and especially their reliance on scouts, military intelligence and ambushes are reminiscent of the situation on the Gold Coast itself. Mainland territories offered better conditions for total withdrawal from the plantation or mining areas. In the bush of Dutch and French Guyana, groups such as the Djuka, Saramaka and Boni maintained an African way of life, which probably preserved eighteenth-century West African features after these had disappeared in their places of origin. The 'Bush Negroes' numbered over 6,000 by the mid-eighteenth century, and lived in numerous small settlements in the interior. Belief in the power of religion and witchcraft was all-pervasive; and secular authority was weak, although symbols of authority such as the cane and the stool continued to exist. These items and their particular tradition of carving point once again to the Gold Coast and perhaps to the Aja and Ewe. The third famous example of maroon African culture is that of Palmares in Pernambuco, which survived for nearly the whole of the seventeenth century, finally succumbing to Portuguese attacks in 1697. By 1612 Palmares was already known as an unusually powerful *mocambo* (*mukambo* in Kimbundu meaning 'hideout'). Its population was recruited from a wide cross-section of Africans from the Guinea coast, Congo and Angola, and it also came to include many Creoles and racially mixed individuals. Unlike the small Guyana villages, Palmares was not an egalitarian society. The elected king was a powerful secular figure before whom subjects had to prostrate themselves. The royal enclave had its own officials, while the attached settlements were ruled by potentates in the name of the king. Members of the ruling class were usually closely related, and the same dynasty persisted throughout the existence of Palmares. Its political system and the majority of its citizens came from West-Central Africa, and probably from the hinterland of Luanda.[1]

[1] R. K. Kent, 'Palmares: an African state in Brazil', *Journal of African History*, 1965, **6**, 2, 161–75.

Other smaller pockets of maroons scattered in the Americas tended to lose their African identity. In these and in the plantation areas the total social conjuncture was not African, but there were African cultural elements forming part of the heritage of black people as well as serving to distinguish American culture as a whole. Certain aspects of language, religion, music, dance and folk-lore are clearly identifiable as African survivals and as adaptations of African elements.

The failure of African languages to survive for long in the Americas was due to the mixing of different language speakers both by chance and design. However, in parts of the Americas, African languages remained alive for short periods contemporaneous with the trade in slaves. Yoruba was more widely spoken than Portuguese among Brazilian slaves in the first decades of the nineteenth century, and many Yoruba words still survive in the language spoken by the priests of certain cults. In an early period Kimbundu was in common use in Brazil, and one of the reasons for a continued preference for Angolan slaves on the part of the slave holders was the fact that newcomers could be seasoned by older hands in their own language or in a language which they both understood. Yet Brazil was the single plantation area in which the language of the masters eventually spread throughout all strata of the society. In this instance, the Portuguese language was itself transformed to incorporate many 'Africanisms'. What generally developed throughout most parts of the Caribbean and the South was a *lingua franca* which blended European and African words and language concepts. In this Creole language slaves passed scathing satirical comments on their masters and on the society. Its evolving vocabulary and style was both a barrier and a weapon against the whites. One West Indian authority provides the insight that 'it was in language that the slave was most successfully imprisoned by his master; and it was in his (mis-)use of it that he perhaps most effectively rebelled. Within the folk tradition, language was (and is) a creative act in itself'.[1]

African religions were attacked by the white slave owners. Nevertheless, African elements strongly persisted in the religion of slaves and their descendants either in the form of syncretisms with Christianity or as a separate genre. Syncretism was most common in areas colonized by European Catholics; and there was a remarkable consistency in the way in which Africans in Brazil, Cuba and Haiti assimilated Catholic saints to their own African deities. This was accepted by Catholics as a means of co-opting and submerging 'savage' African features.

[1] Edward Braithwaite, *Folk culture of the slaves in Jamaica* (London, 1970), 17.

Anglo-Saxon slave owners tended to try and uproot African religious practices, commonly referred to as 'Obeah' in the British West Indies. Suppression sent African religions underground. Some slave owners admitted the hopelessness of trying to stamp out African religious ideas, because of the rate of introduction of new Africans from the continent. Ritual experts were usually African-born rather than Creoles. The above distinction between the Catholic and Protestant contexts is not rigid, for it was with French Catholic slavemasters that Haitian Voodoo developed as an underground religion, and the early dramatic separation of St Domingue from European society ensured the continued independent evolution of Voodoo. On the other hand, there were several African/Protestant syntheses, resulting in spirit-possession cults, Shango groups and 'shouters'. The African tradition was thereby imposing itself on different varieties of social experience in the Americas.

African music and dances were seldom opposed, except by a few Catholic clergy. Instead, on many plantations slaves were allowed or encouraged to engage in their own dances. These were separated from the African socio-religious experience and tied instead to the calendar of the Christian Church. The *cabildos* of the Catholic territories were confraternities which celebrated feast days and other events with African musical instruments, songs and dances. The West African yam festivals and the public activity of their secret societies found expression in carnival and masquerade. Ethnic communities such as the Ibo and Popo had their own distinctive masks during the 'John Canoe' parades in eighteenth-century Jamaica. The music and dance of these public diversions passed into New World culture, and so too did the private musical manifestations of the slaves, telling of their joys and sorrows and hopes. These latter have understandably remained largely within the black sub-culture, as far as their dynamic is concerned. In many parts of the central and South American mainland, where the black population as such has almost disappeared, folk songs still display African influence in many ways – in their improvisory character, their rhythmic complexities, their communal significance and their reflection on life and topicality. This attests to the vigour of social life among the slaves and the extent of their creativeness up to the early nineteenth century when the institution of slavery ended. In the larger islands of the Caribbean and in the South of the USA, it is possible to outline the evolution of the powerful 'Afro' music out of the original slave renditions of work songs, lullabies and other songs. This development was advanced by Creole slaves who also drew upon the prevailing European forms, as was often the case with Afro-American spirituals. Even so, the purity and longevity of survivals is sometimes striking. Alongside the spirituals and jazz of the USA, there is an older African musical tradition archaically preserved until quite recently in isolated districts like low country South Carolina and the offshore islands.

A similar pattern of retention and adaptation is to be found in story-telling. Animal stories still abound and are easily linked with African prototypes. The hare, the tortoise and the spider remained central figures in the New World context as they were in Africa, and several of the tale types have been correlated with those appearing in published African material. The heroes were transformed to some degree, as was the case with Brer Rabbit, who was presented as an unusually weak and frightened creature. It has been correctly observed that his essential characteristic was his ability to get the better of bigger and stronger animals, and that to the slave this theme of weakness overcoming strength must have been endlessly fascinating.[1] This made such creations more than animal tales, but the hidden dimensions were apparently not recognized by planters in the epoch of slavery, since they considered African animal stories as a harmless way for slaves to pass the time and also to entertain the masters' children.

Many other social features have African characteristics, though the connections are difficult to establish and alternative hypotheses can be sustained. For instance, co-operative work-parties emerged in a number of black peasant societies in the post-slavery epoch, and these are likely African derivatives, with the possibility of European influence being more remote given the emasculation of earlier European collectives under feudalism and capitalism. Of course, African land tenure and property relations could not possibly be implanted while slavery lasted, but the concepts would have been kept alive with each new shipload of African captives. By paying attention to the origins and destinations of particular groups of captives, it is also possible at times to be more specific than the generalizations about 'African' cultural retentions. Given traits can be identified as 'Mande' or 'Yoruba' or (at an intermediate level of precision) 'East African' or 'Central African'. Slave traders and buyers supposedly correlated American slave populations with areas of origin in Africa because of market preferences. Owners created their own stereotypes of which particular African 'tribes'

[1] See Langston Hughes and Arna Bontemps, eds., *Book of Negro folklore* (New York, 1958), introduction, viii, ix.

were lazy, diligent, rebellious, etc.; and they communicated these preferences to slave traders, but it is unlikely that this factor seriously affected the distribution of specific ethnic groups within America.

A glance at the Brazilian scene exposes some of the problems and pitfalls in dealing with the issue of slave provenance in a planter's framework. The terms used to describe Africans in contemporary sources and subsequent scholarship are frequently so general as to be meaningless as a basis for comparison, examples to this effect being 'Guinean' or 'Bantu' or 'Sudanese'. Owners in Brazil used the word 'Mina' to embrace not only the Gold Coast but also the 'Slave Coast' and the Bight of Biafra, though sometimes they added 'Ardra' (Allada) to cover the Aja. The name 'Angolas' is also extremely broad, covering a variety of ethnicities leaving Africa via Luanda or Benguela, and thereby extending over a great deal of West-Central Africa. Planters who were supposedly expert on African groups did not seem to realize that the area tapped for supplies of captives was not necessarily close to the particular port of exit. These difficulties, along with the subjective nature of the assessments, led to many conflicting statements. At one point the 'Angolas' might be referred to as being so robust that no labour tires them, but then one hears that 'Guinea' slaves were preferred for the demanding work of the mines. If another account corroborates that the 'Guinea' slaves were the most robust, yet another would assure us that they were the best for domestic service, which was hardly the most efficient use of the strongest slaves. One could wriggle out of the dilemma by taking a version that the 'Guineans' were lazy, but then so too were the 'Angolas' who were largely employed in agricultural labour and had to be kept at it always with many lashes. Brazilian planters also exerted a great deal of energy determining which Africans were most likely to rebel. The 'Minas' were reputedly 'fierce' while the 'Ardras' were 'fiery'. Yet the same planters took good care not to allow a preponderant number of slaves from any ethnic group to be assembled in a single *capitania* or province, implicitly recognizing as the operative feature not innate 'tribal' characteristics, but the socio-cultural context which could promote unity and rebellion. Three slave conspiracies in Minas Gerais in 1719, 1724 and 1756 were said to have been foiled because of rivalry between different ethnic groups. Conversely, a relaxation of this policy of mixing seems to be one of the factors which permitted an upsurge of revolts among ethnic and religious groups in the first half of the nineteenth century in Bahia. Brazil was supplied most consistently by Angola, and secondly by the

'Slave Coast'. This pattern was determined by considerations other than the verandah gossip of owners in Brazil.[1]

Jamaican planters were also articulate in categorizing Africans. In their estimation, the 'Coromantine' slaves were aggressive and prone to rebel, while the Ibo and Angolans were passive and likely to commit suicide. Neither seems an enticing possibility from a slave holder's viewpoint, and the contrast is not borne out by the evidence of references to actual suicides. Gold Coast Africans were indeed prominent in Jamaican revolts as in everything else, since they were the largest group brought from any one area. Jamaican slave owners, too, would have liked to recruit speakers of different languages, but they were chronically short of labour and took whatever was offered them. English chartered companies controlled several forts on the Gold Coast, and this was decisive in the transfer of so many inhabitants from there to the fastest growing English plantation society in the Caribbean in the late seventeenth century and in the first half of the eighteenth century. These included Akan as well as large numbers of Gã, Adangbe, Ewe, Guan and 'Northerners' raided, purchased or received as tribute by the Akan from peoples of the hinterland.

Only in one instance did planter prejudice have a clearly measurable effect. This took the form of orders from the Royal African Company that ships from Gambia and Sierra Leone were to avoid carrying Africans across to Barbados, where they were held in low esteem and that instead they should be taken to South Carolina where they were prized. The composition of the South Carolina population reflected preference for upper Guinea and aversion to the Bight of Biafra. It could be that there were substantial factors affecting these choices, and that the 'tribal' traits were rationalizations. A case in point is the close relationships between upper Guinea and the Spanish American mainland in the sixteenth and seventeenth centuries. These two regions established early contact via the Cape Verde islands. A few Spanish Americans moved to reside in upper Guinea, and several Portuguese served as agents in Mexico, Cartagena and Panama. Upper Guinea captives were supplied in the required volume, with regularity and in good physical condition. Precedent, familiarity and confidence were established; and this atmosphere survived into the late seventeenth century when the commercial connections were no longer substantial. In the meanwhile,

[1] Elements in the above discussion are taken from two standard texts: namely, Gilberto Freyre, *The masters and the slaves* (New York, 1963), 299–305; and C. R. Boxer, *The golden age of Brazil* (Los Angeles, 1962), 153, 154, 176, 177.

the relationship had been felicitously rationalized by ascribing numerous virtues to upper Guinea Africans, including happiness under slavery – although this was blatantly contradicted by the frequency of escape and rebellion.[1]

Scholarship is on firmer ground when it links areas of provenance of slaves not to character traits but to cultural features. By the end of the Atlantic slave trade, different African cultures had established themselves in various parts of the Americas. Akan, Aja, Yoruba and 'Bantu' are the African cultures identifiable as predominant. Akan survivals were outstanding in Virginia, Jamaica and the Guyanas. For instance, the *Anansi* (Anancy) cycle of folk-tales featuring the spider-hero is distinctively Akan and has a fully developed counterpart only in Jamaica and among the 'Bush Negroes'. Aja is most closely identified with Haiti, where Aja as well as Yoruba and Ewe were responsible for the evolution of the Voodoo cult. The same influences touched parts of northern Brazil, as well as Louisiana, which served as a place of refuge for some St Domingue planters and their slaves. Yoruba elements were in vogue in Cuba, Trinidad, Bahia and Minas Gerais. 'Bantu', a linguistic category, is much vaguer, but embraced mainly Congolese and Angolan peoples, whose cultural influence was most noticeable in Brazil. Finally, even the East Africans added to the labour and cultural life of America. It is in eastern rather than western Africa that the rabbit or hare (Swahili, *sungura*) is the outstanding animal hero, and motifs around the clever rabbit are widespread in the USA.

There was obviously a basic correlation between numbers of Africans brought from a given region and their cultural influence, but the relationship was not entirely straightforward. It has been judiciously observed that a distinction should be drawn between culture and ethnicity.[2] A given Brazilian *candomble* fraternity might call itself Nago (Yoruba), Ewe, Ijesha, Congo, etc., but its membership was not exclusively or even predominantly of the particular ethnic group. It could include other Africans, many Creoles and some mulattoes; and in this way one African people represented within the slave population could spread its cultural influence far beyond its own numbers. Probably, historical priority had a role to play here. The first Africans to arrive in a locality in substantial numbers would establish their African subculture within the total slave culture. Provided they were not over-

[1] Walter Rodney, 'Upper Guinea and the significance of the origins of Africans enslaved in the New World', *Journal of Negro History*, October 1969.

[2] Roger Bastide, *Les Amériques Noires: les civilisations africaines dans le nouveau monde* (Paris, 1967), 16.

whelmed by an influx of Africans from a different part of the continent, their particular norms in religion, language, music and so on would continue to predominate. This point has been raised with regard to Akan influence in Jamaica. A negative example bearing out the same conclusion is that of the Mande in Spanish America, whose impact was very great in the sixteenth century, but they and other Upper Guineans were swamped by new imports during the course of the seventeenth century. It was, therefore, primarily specific New World situations which determined the regional nature of African survivals. At the same time, a knowledge of African historical developments is by no means irrelevant to an understanding of this problem, for it does appear that cultural predominance was sometimes transferred from the African continent.

The Akan, Aja and Yoruba all presided over expanding socio-political formations in West Africa; and something of this dynamic must have been preserved when they crossed the Atlantic. The Akan can serve as the main illustration. Non-Akan Gold Coast groups like the 'Adesi' of Fetu and some Gur-speakers of the northern savannas were becoming absorbed into Akan kingdoms. When such people were picked up by ships along the Koromantse coast, they were identified as Akan, and presumably they went along with this identification in the New World, just as they would have done had they stayed in their homelands – given the trend of events. Therefore what was significant in Jamaica and the Guyanas was the presence not only of original Twi-speakers but also of other peoples familiar with and exposed to acculturation by the Akan in West Africa. Similar arguments can be advanced with regard to the relationship between the Aja and Mahi people from the northern part of the Dahomean kingdom. For that matter, most of the Africans shipped at ports like Whydah as 'Dahomeans' were recruited outside the boundaries of the original kingdom of Dahomey.

In the final analysis, the fundamental similarities between different African cultures allowed black slaves to retain concepts and patterns uniquely African. If there had been lack of mutual intelligibility, the slave masters would have succeeded in forcing Africans to adopt the one thing which would have been common to them all in slave society: namely, bastardized European culture. As it was, a common African element emerged because there was a very wide substratum of basic ideas in the world-view of all black Africans. This or that region in the Americas did adopt some particular variant of regional African culture, but there were more syntheses between respective African cultures than there were between African and European.

The broad clash between Europe and Africa in the Americas was represented in the master/slave relationship. However, other more complex social relations began to develop during the slavery epoch because of the presence of free blacks, mulattoes and poor whites. There were free black servants in the English mainland colonies in the early seventeenth century, but American society tried to identify Africans exclusively with slave status and vice versa, so that within a few decades no more Africans were introduced as free labourers, and the condition of slavery was bequeathed to their offspring, leaving the latter with a very slim option for manumission. Conversely, white indentured labour was withdrawn from the fields in several Caribbean territories when the plantation system was being established; and in Brazil whites preferred destitution to manual labour, which was reserved to Africans and their descendants. Nevertheless, there were always a few exceptions. There were whites in North America who remained enmeshed in some forms of legal bondage throughout the eighteenth century, and in any event the economic status and work of the numerous poor whites did not distinguish them from black slaves. Meanwhile, manumission of individual slaves came to create throughout the region a small minority of free blacks who fitted uneasily into the dominant slave society.

It is estimated that around the end of the eighteenth century there were about 406,000 manumitted ex-slaves in Brazil, while in the USA the comparable figure was about 186,000.[1] Slaves won their freedom through distinguished acts such as meritorious military service in colonial wars. Masters were guided by their own emotions and scruples of conscience and religion in freeing slaves, and understandably showed a greater degree of sympathy towards their own mulatto children. However, the overall rate of manumission depended upon the kind and intensity of exploitation prevailing in the society as a whole. In places such as Puerto Rico and Curaçāo, where the plantation system was not entrenched, manumission was easier to obtain. In the South, laws seriously limiting manumissions were passed from the late seventeenth century onwards, once planters felt that the society was irrevocably slave based. Where the legal possibility existed, manumission was a target which individual slaves set themselves and achieved through tremendous perseverance and sacrifice for the most part, because they

[1] Hoetinck, *Caribbean race relations*, 29.

had to accumulate money to purchase this freedom. The option of retaining possession of part of the product of his labour was often open to the slave if he could manage to work beyond the time necessary to satisfy his master. The situation was precarious, because payment and retention of goods and property earned depended mainly upon the goodwill of the master. In spite of the disadvantages, slaves earned substantial amounts in all the plantation zones, especially in the nineteenth century. In the mining districts of Latin America, slaves apparently developed great expertise in 'liberating' some of the gold and diamonds which they turned up, and thereafter using the funds to liberate themselves. Free blacks and mulattoes participated in the national independence movements in North America and in the Spanish colonies, alongside free whites and enslaved blacks. They were also prominent in the abolition campaigns of the nineteenth century. However, during slavery some were recruited to police the plantations and especially to recover escaped slaves. This was a function which planters delegated to poor whites, free blacks, mulattoes, maroons and, above all, to Indians who remained on the periphery of white settlement.

Rarely did Africans have truly independent contacts with Indians throughout the former's sojourn in the Americas. The possibility came about if a slave vessel was seized near the shore. One incident of this kind was reported on the coast of Ecuador in 1623; while out of the wreck of two Spanish ships off St Vincent in 1635 there developed the unique historical phenomenon of the Black Caribs. Joined by a stream of fugitives from plantations in and around St Vincent, the community of mixed blacks and Carib Indians supplanted the pure Indians after five or six decades. When they were deported to the Honduran mainland at the end of the eighteenth century, the Black Caribs had for the most part the physical features of black Africans and the language and culture of the Caribs. Elsewhere, African/Indian relations were virtually always mediated by whites. Africans were part of the 'discovery' and 'civilizing' of the Americas, as seen from a European standpoint, which means that inevitably they were part of the immense historical aggression against the native American peoples. From Chile to Quebec, blacks served in the white onslaught which sometimes perpetrated genocide and always spelt disaster for the Indians. In turn, Indians were effectively used by whites to keep African slaves in check. 'Mosquito' Indians from the Central American mainland were carried to Jamaica to help cope with the maroons, although the policy of using Indian slave catchers was of course fully operative only on the mainland where strong Indian ethnicities survived – Brazil, the Guyanas and the South of the USA being the key areas.

Some positive results emerged from African/Indian contacts, in spite of conscious efforts by whites to keep them mutually estranged. Many Indians continued to be fellow slaves of Africans, and it was occasionally possible to arrive at a common purpose both on and around the plantations, as was the case with fugitive slaves among the Seminoles of Florida. The Spanish and Portuguese were both very preoccupied with the theme of race mixture, and they found specific terminology for the offspring of African and Indian as well as for the combination which included African, Indian and European ancestry. Such mixtures were reportedly common in Mexico in the seventeenth century, but they were most often found in the ranching areas of Venezuela, Brazil, Argentina and Uruguay. The many ties, sexual and otherwise, allowed Africans to contribute to and benefit from Indian cultures. Material techniques were passed on in both directions; Africans adopted cultivated plants and foods favoured by the Indians; and Indian borrowings of African folk-tales were extensive in parts of Latin America and the South of the USA. Such examples must be added to the many others illustrative of the slaves' capacity to survive and their creativity. Africans were carried to the Americas for the single though multi-faceted purpose of labouring in the interests of European capitalism. But the significance of their presence in this part of the world extended far beyond the aims and dispositions of the masters.

BIBLIOGRAPHICAL ESSAYS

1. EGYPT, THE FUNJ AND DARFUR

In spite of its proximity to our own times, the period of Egyptian history from the conquest by Sultan Selīm to the occupation by Bonaparte is, comparatively speaking, a dark age. Historians have tended to concentrate either upon the Mamluk sultanate which preceded it, or the period of modernization which followed. The documentation, although abundant, has only very partially been exploited. This is particularly true of the vast corpus of archives preserved in the Başbakanlık Arşivi and Topkapı Sarayı Arşivi in Istanbul, and the important collections in the Egyptian state archives in Cairo. A valuable summary account with detailed bibliographical references is provided by Stanford J. Shaw, 'Turkish source-materials for Egyptian history', in P. M. Holt, ed. (1968), 28–48. Shaw's pioneer research into the archives has resulted in his detailed study, *The financial and administrative organization and development of Ottoman Egypt, 1517–1798* (1962), some of his findings in which are summarized in his article, 'Landholding and land-tax revenues in Ottoman Egypt', in Holt, ed. (1968), 91–103.

A second important source of information is provided by the chronicles, both Turkish and Arabic. The Turkish chronicles are discussed by Shaw in his article, 'Turkish source-materials', cited above, and the Arabic chronicles by P. M. Holt, 'Ottoman Egypt (1517–1798): an account of Arabic historical sources', in Holt, ed. (1968), 3–12. The Turkish chronicles of Egypt (as distinct from the general Ottoman chronicles) are extant wholly, and the Arabic chronicles almost entirely, in manuscript. The earliest Arabic chronicle which has been published is Ibn Iyās (1961), which covers the Ottoman conquest and the first few years of Ottoman rule, and has been translated by Gaston Wiet (1960). The early seventeenth-century chronicle of al-Isḥāqī, of which several editions were printed in Cairo in the nineteenth century, is a thin work. The great chronicle of the late seventeenth and eighteenth centuries is al-Jabartī (1880 and later editions), of which there is a poor French translation by Chefik Mansour and others (1888–96). For al-Jabartī and his work, see David Ayalon (1960).

Important data are provided by travellers, whose works must, however, be used with care and circumspection. The very full late seventeenth-century account by the Ottoman traveller, Evliya Çelebi,

Seyahatname, vol. x (Istanbul, 1938), awaits translation and detailed evaluation. The writings of French travellers and residents, the most abundant in this period, are examined in Jean-Marie Carré, *Voyageurs et écrivains français en Égypte*, 2nd ed. (Cairo, 1956), which gives much bibliographical information. One of the most important works is that of Volney [Constantin-François Chassebeuf], *Voyage en Égypte et en Syrie*, ed. Jean Gaulmier (Paris, 1787) (Paris and The Hague, 1959). Volney travelled from 1783 to 1785. Some of the monographs by Bonaparte's savants in the monumental *Description de l'Égypte* (Paris, 1809–22), 2nd ed. (Paris, 1821–9), contain material of value, particularly on the situation in the late eighteenth century.

Among the secondary sources, the accounts of the period by Henri Dehérain, *L'Égypte turque*, vol. v of G. Hanotaux, ed., *Histoire de la nation égyptienne* (Paris, [1931]), and by Étienne Combe in *Précis de l'histoire d'Égypte*, vol. III (Cairo, 1933), have been rendered obsolescent by later research, which, however, has not yet resulted in a detailed authoritative study. A reinterpretation of the political history of Ottoman Egypt is offered by P. M. Holt (1966). The periodical literature is particularly important: readers will find indispensable the guides by J. D. Pearson, *Index Islamicus, 1906–1955* and its *Supplements* (Cambridge, 1958, 1962, 1967), listing articles that have appeared down to 1965. There are also relevant articles in the *Encyclopaedia of Islam*, 2nd ed. (Leiden and London, in progress).

Primary source-materials on the Nilotic Sudan and Darfur before the Turco-Egyptian invasion of 1820–1 are extremely sparse. The archives of the Funj and Kayra sultanates, like those of the smaller tribal kingdoms, no longer exist, although some land-charters and related documents remain in private ownership. A few of these, originating under the Funj sultanate, have been published by Muḥammad Ibrāhīm Abū Salīm, *al-Fūnj wa'l-arḍ* (Khartoum, 1967); and by P. M. Holt (1969), in the latter case with translations.

The region is also singularly poor in chronicles. One, conventionally called the Funj Chronicle, was probably first written before the Turco-Egyptian invasion by a certain Aḥmad b. al-Ḥājj Abū [*sic*] ʻAlī, known as Kātib al-Shūna. It is extant only in post-invasion recensions, of which two have been published. The earlier and (for the Funj period) better text was edited by al-Shāṭir Buṣaylī ʻAbd al-Jalīl (1961), while a later recension was edited by Makkī Shibayka [Mekki Shibeika] (1947). An English translation of a late recension was made by H. A. Mac-

Michael (1922, repr. London, 1967), II, 354–430. A chronicle of the 'Abdallāb, written (from internal evidence) in 1916 or later, is now known from an English translation by A. E. D. Penn (1934). No chronicle of the sultanate of Darfur is known to exist. Much light is shed on conditions under the Funj sultanate by the biographical dictionary of holy men which was compiled in the second half of the eighteenth century by Muḥammad b. Ḍayfallāh, and is known as the *Ṭabaqāt* of Wad Ḍayfallāh. The two printed editions of this work, edited respectively by Ibrāhīm Ṣidayq and Sulaymān Dāwūd Mandīl (both Cairo, 1930), are now superseded by the edition of Yūsuf Faḍl Ḥasan (Khartoum, 1971). Parts of the Arabic text and a summary translation (not always accurate) were published by MacMichael (1922), II, 217–323.

Genealogical works may also be made to yield historical data, even if their ostensible claims are unfounded. A number of these were published in summary translation with notes and commentary by MacMichael (1922), but are susceptible of a more sophisticated analysis. The Arabic originals are now in the Central Records Office, Khartoum.

Some tribal traditional material has been published in *Sudan Notes and Records*, and work in this field is now proceeding under the auspices of the Sudan Research Unit of the University of Khartoum, which has made some publications. Historical traditions relating to the sultanate of Darfur were first recorded by Browne and al-Tūnusī (see below), and in the later nineteenth century by G. Nachtigal, *Sahara und Sudan*, III (Leipzig, 1889); Rudolf C. [von] Slatin, *Fire and sword in the Sudan* (London, 1896); and Na'ūm Shuqayr [1903]. Nachtigal's account is now available in English translation by A. G. B. Fisher and H. J. Fisher, *Sahara and Sudan*, IV (London, 1971).

The accounts of travellers are neither numerous nor, with a few exceptions, detailed. The principal data which they provide on the Nilotic Sudan are summarized in O. G. S. Crawford (1951), which has useful bibliographical notes. Of the two accounts in non-European languages, that in Hebrew by David Reubeni (relating to the year 1521) has been translated by S. Hillelson (1933), while that in Turkish by Evliya Çelebi, *Seyahatname*, vol. x, is available in an Italian summary translation by Maria Teresa Petti Suma, 'Il viaggio in Sudan di Evliyā Čelebī', *Annali dell'Istituto Orientale di Napoli*, N.S. 1964, **14**, 433–52. The most valuable accounts are from late in the period: James Bruce (1805), vol. VI (relating to the year 1772); and John Lewis Burckhardt (1819, repr. London, 1968), relating to the years 1813–14. There are no early travellers' accounts of Darfur. That by W. G. Browne (1799, repr. London, 1971) relates to his visit in 1793–6, much of which he spent in semi-captivity. Of greater value is Muḥammad b. ʻUmar al-Tūnusī (1850, 2nd ed., 1966), the record of a residence in Darfur from 1803 to 1811. There is a French translation by [A.] Perron (1845).

There is no detailed and reliable history of the Nilotic Sudan and Darfur in this period. Although Crawford (1951) offers a wide range of data, his accuracy and interpretation are vitiated by his dependence on translations of Arabic source-materials. The account in P. M. Holt, *A modern history of the Sudan* (1963), is brief and in part out of date. Recourse is constantly necessary to the periodical literature listed in Pearson, *Index Islamicus*, and to the *Encyclopaedia of Islam*. Indispensable guides to the published material on the Sudan are R. L. Hill (1939); Abdel Rahman el Nasri, *A bibliography of the Sudan, 1938–1958* (London, 1962); and Yūsuf As'ad Dāghir, *al-Uṣūl al-ʻarabiyya li'l-dirāsāt al-sūdāniyya* ([Beirut], 1968).

2. THE CENTRAL SAHARA AND SUDAN

Local central Sudanic written records, often official or semi-official, survive, but give very uneven coverage. Outstanding among these is Ibn Fartuwa's incomplete biography of Aloma, which has provided the foundation for this chapter. How far Aloma, distinct from all the other rulers of Bornu, deserved the peculiar encomiums bestowed on him by his faithful *imām* is a matter for prudent speculation; but there is no doubt Ibn Fartuwa's chronicle is of profound importance. We do not find its like, east of Timbuktu, until the nineteenth century. In Hausaland, the Kano Chronicle supplies much more superficial coverage, but over a much wider time span. Both the Kano Chronicle and Ibn Fartuwa, although published in Arabic and in English translation (Palmer, ed., 1928 and 1926), still await detailed critical editions, and important corrections to the published translations continue to appear (for example, Zeltner, 1971). A number of lesser accounts have happily survived, such as that, recently discovered, which describes Mandara (Abbo and Mohammadou, 1971), or the well known Agades Chronicles (Urvoy, 1934). In Bornu, *maḥrams*, official documents bestowing privileges upon certain specified individuals or groups, for example exemption from taxation or customary duties, have been preserved. Their practical value to their beneficiaries meant that they were treasured, recopied, and often revalidated by successive rulers. As with Ibn Fartuwa, we are indebted to Palmer, especially his *Sudanese memoirs*, for the publication in English of many of these documents, but again detailed critical editions are lacking. Religious apologetic writing, which becomes of such crucial significance in the nineteenth century, most of all for Hausaland, is sparser earlier. Hiskett (1962) surveys the field.

Travellers' reports are lamentably few before the nineteenth century. Leo Africanus, early in the sixteenth century, is the invaluable exception, but can provide only background for our period. Evliya Çelebi, the Turkish traveller of the late seventeenth century, supplies a few details (Lange, 'Un vocabulaire kanuri', 1972), but by hearsay only; his main contribution is farther east (see above, p. 623). Among early European geographers, who wrote informatively about the African interior, though without visiting it, Anania (see Lange, 'L'intérieur de l'Afrique', 1972) is of particular interest. In the nineteenth century, a succession of visitors added historical and other information to their contemporary observations. Of special merit is the account of al-Tūnusī (1851), for Wadai, since as a North African Muslim he was able to take a more intimate part in central Sudanic society than was possible for European voyagers. Barth (1857–8) gives the most useful account of all for the central Sudan; Nachtigal (1879–89), however, is also rich in valuable detail, which in the absence of any full translation from the German has been relatively neglected.

Oral tradition in the central Sudan has been explored in two recent books, Low (1972), with particular reference to the marcher emirates, Gombe, Katagum and Hadejia, east of Sokoto, and Salifou (1971) for Zinder. Low especially pays close attention to the methodological problems involved. Both works, however, are in the main confined to the nineteenth century, and it is doubtful how much earlier than that the approach can fruitfully be applied. There is a fairly sharp cut-off at the time of the Fulani jihad in Hausaland, and, slightly less distinct, with the rise of the house of al-Kānamī in Bornu. Koelle (1854) was fortunate in gleaning some oral information before the cut-off had been long in operation. That some earlier material still survives in oral form is clear from the rhymed Hausa king-list recorded and translated by Hiskett (1964, 1965). Patterson (1926) illustrates the useful historical harvest of even quite short courtly songs.

Archaeological evidence for the central Sudan has potentially much more to teach us than we have yet learnt. Bivar and Shinnie (1962) provide a preliminary essay on the Kanuri side, though some of their suggestions have been overtaken by more recent studies. The works of the Lebeufs contain much archaeological material. Connah has carried out detailed and expert work, though primarily for earlier periods; much of this, regrettably, is not easily accessible. Even when all these, and other, contributions are taken together, much remains to be done. The walled towns of Hausaland are one instance of hitherto relatively neglected archaeological opportunity.

Anthropology and linguistics may also contribute to our knowledge of the central Sudan. Several very thorough anthropological studies, for example on the Fulani (Hopen, 1958, and Stenning, 1959), or the Tuareg (Nicolaisen, 1964), help us to reconstruct the life styles of earlier centuries, though providing little hard historical detail. M. G. Smith, on the contrary, has done outstanding work as an anthropologist contributing directly to historical study of the Hausa, and R. Cohen has a similar accomplishment for the Kanuri. Linguistic evidence has been used by earlier scholars – there is a good deal, for instance, in *Sudanese memoirs* – but it is only lately that a strict scientific appraisal has begun. Abdullahi Smith (in Ajayi and Crowder, 1971) points the way most interestingly for the central Sudan, though mainly for an earlier period.

The colonial period led to a considerable accumulation of historical data, as it was part of an officer's duty, particularly in the early years, to take an interest in local history; Marty, Meek, Rattray, Temple, Tilho, Palmer himself, are leading examples. Motives were mixed: the officer might be seeking some utilitarian insight into the background of local politics, and his informants may have been well aware that a certain historical slant might strengthen the authority of one group or another in the present. Comparable problems had arisen in the nineteenth century, as Fulani dynasts viewed earlier Hausa history, or the Shehus of Bornu looked back to Saifawa days. Nevertheless a great deal of the information gathered in the colonial period was free from such bias, or may be with care disentangled from it. Hogben and Kirk-Greene (1966) bring together much material of this nature.

In North Africa, the situation with regard to sources is quite different. Archives, particularly those of the Ottomans, exist in considerable abundance, but have yet to be thoroughly explored. There are local chronicles (for example Mohammed Seghir, 1900). Western European records – consular, commercial, and others, many connected with slavery and ransom – survive; Tully (1816) is an excellent instance. Throughout all this material there are scattered details of Sudanic relevance (see for example Martin, 1962 and 1969, J. Hunwick in

Ajayi and Crowder, 1971, and especially Fresnel, 1849). An elaborate historiographical tradition grew up, fostered primarily by the French, culminating with Julien (1970). Whereas for the central Sudan such an outline, by and large, is only now being constructed, for North Africa it was created some time ago, and has now to be 'decolonized' (Wansbrough, 1968).

3. NORTH-WEST AFRICA: FROM THE MAGHRIB TO THE FRINGES OF THE FOREST

The importance of the European presence along the African coast, from Morocco to the Gulf of Guinea, in the seventeenth and eighteenth centuries, is paralleled by the growing value of European contemporary records as sources for the history of that period. They supplement the Arabic chronicles, which are our basic sources for the history of the Maghrib and parts of the western Sudan. Elsewhere oral traditions are essential to fill in gaps left by the written sources, and more research is needed into these traditions before a comprehensive history of this vast area can be written.

The Arabic historiography of Morocco under the Sharifian dynasties, since the sixteenth century, was brilliantly analysed by Lévi-Provençal (1922). He distinguishes two categories of sources: the biographical literature (*tarjama* pl. *tarājim*) and the chronicles (*ta'rīkh* pl. *tawārīkh*). The former were more respectable among orthodox scholars, and are therefore numerous. The biographies shed light on religious life in Morocco, on the marabouts and their relations with the *makhzin*. History (*ta'rīkh*) was not counted among the religious sciences, and was undertaken only by a few scholars, who were closely associated with the *makhzin*.

'Abd al-'Azīz al-Fishtālī (d. 1621–2) was an official court historian, who is said to have composed an eight-volume history of the Sa'dids. Only an abridgement of this history survived (published in 1964), but al-Fishtālī is extensively quoted by later chroniclers, and in particular by al-Ifrānī (also al-Ufrānī or al-Yafrānī), who wrote his chronicle *Nuzhat al-hādī* in 1738–9. Though he lived under the 'Alawid dynasty, al-Ifrānī sympathized with the Sa'dids. Over a third of the chronicle is dedicated to Mawlāy Aḥmad al-Manṣūr (1578–1603). Its value is enhanced by al-Ifrānī's care in mentioning his sources and in incorporating original documents in the text.

The principal source for the history of the 'Alawid dynasty is al-Zayyānī, who died in 1833. He served successive sultans as a minister, a provincial governor and as an ambassador. His writings reflect his rich experience as a statesman and a traveller. He is exceptional among local chroniclers in referring to the complicated international relations of Morocco both with the Ottomans and with Europe.

European visitors to Morocco were traders or consuls (Chenier and J. G. Jackson), captives (Sieur Mouëtte and Thomas Pellow) or redemptionists sent to ransom captives (Père Dan and John Windus). Some of them, like those mentioned above, produced detailed accounts of their experience in Morocco. Many others left shorter reports or dispatches. The latter were carefully collected and published in the monumental series of H. de Castries (1905–36), based on archives and libraries in France, the Netherlands, England, Spain and Portugal. Most of the Europeans, however, were restricted to the ports, and had few opportunities for better acquaintance with the interior. Their evidence mainly concerns the external trade of Morocco, corsairs' activities and diplomatic relations with Europe. Their accounts of social life and internal politics are rather superficial. In fact the limitations of these sources are reflected in histories of Morocco written during the last three centuries. They tell the story of piracy and human suffering, of the impetuous autocracy of the sultan and the anarchy in the countryside. This view of Moroccan history was partially perpetuated into the twentieth century and has only recently been somewhat rectified.

The fruits of half a century of French scholarship, dedicated to the study of the history of Morocco, were synthesized by H. Terrasse (1950). Julien's *History of North Africa* is now available in an English translation (1970), to which C. C. Stewart added an analytical bibliography. The publication of this translation almost coincided with Abun-Nasr's *History of the Maghrib* (1971). Finally, the history of North Africa, as viewed by a Moroccan professional historian, is presented by A. Laroui (1970).

The principal sources for the study of the pashalik of Timbuktu, or the middle Niger between Jenne and Gao, are contemporary Arabic chronicles written in Timbuktu. Significantly, two of the most important works of Muslim historiography in Africa were written about the same time: *Ta'rīkh al-Sūdān* by al-Sa'dī, shortly after 1655, and *Ta'rīkh al-Fattāsh* by Ibn al-Mukhtār (the grandson of Maḥmūd Ka'ti), sometime after 1664. *T. al-Fattāsh* is concerned mostly with the sixteenth century, and only less than a third of its text (pp. 136–84 of the text and pp. 263–321 of the translation) deals with the aftermath of the Moroccan conquest in the years 1591–9. On the other hand, well over half of the pages of *T. al-Sūdān* (pp. 137–323 of the text and pp. 215–489 of the translation) deal with the period after 1591. In the service of the Moroccan pashas, al-Sa'dī travelled as far as the Bambara country south of Jenne. His first-hand account is indispensable for the study of the first half of the seventeenth century. The reconstruction of the history of the pashalik during the following hundred years is based largely on the anonymous *Tadhkirat al-Nisyān*, written in the middle of the eighteenth century.

At about the same time when *Tadhkirat al-Nisyān* was compiled in Timbuktu, two Muslim scholars in Buipe, near the fringes of the forest, concluded the writing of the Arabic chronicle of Gonja. This chronicle recorded events also among Gonja's neighbours: Asante, Dagomba, Mamprusi, Bonduku, Buna, and Kong. At least in one case – the siege of Jenne by an army from Kong in 1739 – the Gonja Chronicle and *Tadhkirat al-Nisyān* converge to help in co-ordinating dates and events across the width of the savanna. Other local Arabic chronicles are of great value, such as the chronicle of Walata and Nema, written in 1917, that suggests firm dates for Biton Kulibali and the emergence of the Bambara states.

Contemporary evidence on the Bambara states is offered by Mungo Park, who in 1795–7 was the first European traveller to reach the Niger. Before him Europeans had been confined to the coast and to the navigable parts of the Senegal and the Gambia rivers. For these regions one can derive valuable information from the accounts of R. Jobson (1620–1), J. B. Labat (1728), F. Moore (1738) or Xavier de Golbéry (1791). European commercial competition in the Senegambia produced rich archival sources, which had first been used mainly for the study of European activities (see, Delcourt and A. Ly), but have recently been examined in their African context.

Invaluable as both Arabic and European sources are, the history of the period also depends on the collection and interpretation of oral traditions. Such traditions, collated with documentary evidence, are incorporated in works by administrators, anthropologists and historians.

A comprehensive study of the pashalik of Timbuktu has still to be written, though this task has already been initiated by S. M. Cissoko (1968 and 1969). Songhay traditions have been studied by J. Rouch (1953). The pioneering study of Richer (1925) on the Tuareg of the Niger bend can be profitably supplemented by the excellent work of Nicolaisen (1963). Early studies of the Kunta by I. Hamet (1910–11) and P. Marty (1920) served 'Abd al-'Azīz Batrān in his Ph.D. dissertation (1971) on Sīdī al-Mukhtār. W. A. Brown (Ph.D. diss. 1969) has analyzed socio-political developments among the Fulani of Massina in the eighteenth century.

Monteil (1924) and Tauxier (1942) are still the two basic studies of the Bambara states. But more recent works by Pâques (1954), Pageard (1957 and 1961), Meillassoux (1963), Leynaud (1966), Bazin (1972) and others are significant contributions to a better understanding of the socio-political dynamics among the Bambara of the middle Niger. Yves Person skilfully reconstructed the history of the Malinke from the upper Niger to the fringes of the forest. While Person studied the Dyula in the context of the Mande world, Ivor Wilks is concerned with the Dyula as a link between the middle Niger and the Volta basin. N. Levtzion studied the process of islamization in the Volta basin, from Mossi to Asante and as far as Borgu in the east. Some Voltaic peoples had the benefit of anthropological and ethno-historical studies: J. Goody on Gonja, J. C. Boutillier on Buma, P. Alexandre and J. C. Froelich on the Kotokoli and J. Lombard on Borgu. Izard's recent publication (1970) is the first reliable and coherent history of the Mossi kingdoms.

The history of the jihad in the Futa Jalon needs a serious revision, *pace* Arcin (1911), Marty (1921), Saint-Père (1929) and Tauxier (1937). Two Marxist oriented scholars – W. Rodney (1968) and J. Suret-Canale (1971) – have recently emphasized the social and economic undercurrents of the jihad. P. D. Curtin (1970) and N. Levtzion (1971) suggested more direct connections between the jihad in Futa Jalon and the jihad of Nāṣir al-Dīn in 1673–6 in the south-western Sahara and in the Senegal valley. Until recently the only sources for Nāṣir al-Dīn's jihad were the accounts recorded in Basset (1900) and Hamet (1911). Recently two contemporary French documents were published by C. I. A. Ritchie (1968), and H. T. Norris (1969) presented an excellent analysis of 'Znaga Islam during the seventeenth and eighteenth centuries'.

The *Chroniques...Sénégalais* of Siré Abbas Soh are still the major source for the history of Futa Toro. Two independent studies by O. Kane (1970) and by Robinson, Curtin and Johnson (1972) combined oral traditions with French archival documents to establish a tentative chronology of the Futa Toro under the dynasty of the Denianke. Historical traditions of the Wolof states were published by V. Monteil

(1966), Wade (1964), Diop (1966), Leyti (1966) and Barry (1972). Pathé Diagne (1965) studied the history of the Serer kingdom. The most authoritative work on the history of the region is J. Boulègue's Ph.D. dissertation on the Senegambia from the middle of the fifteenth century to the beginning of the seventeenth century. The study of the Malinke states on the Gambia has recently attracted young scholars. Not less than four papers presented to the Conference on Manding Studies (1972) were concerned with the kingdom of Kabu. An anthropological study of the Dyakanke, Muslim traders of the Gambia, was undertaken by P. Smith (1965), and P. D. Curtin's forthcoming book contains a new wealth of source material on the Dyakanke, the organization of their trade, and on the economic history of the Senegambia.

4. THE GUINEA COAST

Carson (1962) and Ryder (1965) point to materials on West African history in European archives. Before their systematic presentations, historians had drawn upon European archival material on the Guinea coast. However, recent studies have been more comprehensive in their use of these records, and the character of the writing has changed since Dike (1956) and especially during the 1960s. African relations with Europeans and with each other replaced European activity as the focus of attention. Akinjogbin (1967), Ryder (1967), Daaku (1970) and Rodney (1970) chose particular states or regions and closely examined their contacts with neighbours and Europeans over extended periods. In such reconstructions, European contemporary descriptions and compilations have been heavily utilized. These latter derive from persons associated with trade or occasionally from missionaries, as in the case of Anguiano (1957). Several western European nationalities were involved in generating this evidence, and their accounts touch on all sections of the Guinea coast with varying intensity. Dutch and English descriptions dominate the seventeenth and eighteenth centuries, respectively, as a reflection of commercial ascendancy. The well-advanced process of publishing new annotated editions further facilitates the use of these descriptions.

European archives and published comments on the Guinea coast in the pre-colonial period are best suited for certain tasks. For instance, Curtin (1969) synthesizes from a wide variety of European and American sources to obtain a statistical overview of the Atlantic slave trade. External sources are indispensable for an understanding of Afro-

European relations, but of course the evidence is produced by only one party to the relationship, with rare exceptions such as Olaudah Equiano (1789). The nature and consequence of European bias has been specifically pointed out with reference to Dalzel (1793), who was markedly pro-slavery and anti-African. However, it is not the anti-African but the non-African character of the European sources which limits scholarship dependent on them. The limitations include the reference to given African ethnicities by European designations, the assumption that European preoccupation with slaves and firearms constituted the principal motivation of Africans, the use of unclear ethno-linguistic categories, and the omission of broad areas of African life where these were ignored by Europeans. The latter is the most serious shortcoming to which even African-born historians are susceptible. 'Trade and Politics' tends to be trade with Europeans and politics deriving therefrom, with little reference to indigenous production and life outside this pattern. One reaction to these weaknesses is to make an *a priori* relegation of the European trade factor to the periphery of West African history – an equally indefensible position.

Historians using European primary material have availed themselves of information deriving from non-written sources, but only in a subsidiary or marginal role. Nevertheless, several outstanding monographs are based on non-written sources. The publications of the African writers Reindorf (1895), Samuel Johnson (1921) and Egharevba (1934) are classics of oral history – modified and endorsed by more recent researchers into oral history such as Goody and Arhin (1965), R. S. Smith (1969) and Bradbury and Lloyd (1957) with regard to the Akan, Yoruba and Bini. Anthropological research sponsored by the colonialists also tapped oral traditions, giving rise to the 'Intelligence Reports' of the National Archives of Nigeria and to published accounts such as those of Partridge (1905), Leonard (1906), Rattray (1923, 1929) and Field (1940). Although utilized to buttress colonial rule, they have been useful to subsequent scholars, and they retain the value which attaches to forerunners in a given field. By the end of the colonial period, the International African Institute had also offered anthropological surveys which covered large parts of lower Guinea but little of upper Guinea. Their preoccupation is with kinship systems and beliefs, their historical sections are brief, and often what they present as 'traditional' features of the society were actually engendered during the previous two or three centuries.

The post-independence period witnessed a number of conferences and schemes on oral history, but they yielded little, with the exception of projects related to the Akan. Continuing individual contributions to oral research tended to produce substantial articles, as seen in Person (1961), Folayan (1967), Cissoko (1969), Alagoa (1970, 1971) and Sidibe (1972). There have been positive developments in the use of such sources, mainly because of the rise of historically-oriented cultural anthropology. G. I. Jones (1963) is a good early example to this effect, while Horton (1969) has revealed a great deal more on the same area by first identifying a present-day social formation comparable to the forerunners of the delta city-states. Oral and written sources have been combined in approximately equal measure by Priestley and Wilks (1960), Wilks (1966), Arhin (1967) and Latham (1973) to provide a more precise chronological framework as well as to explore the evolution of socio-political institutions.

Excavation of coastal sites yielding both European and African artefacts is the archaeological operation most directly relevant to the seventeenth century on the Guinea coast, as seen in the report of Ozanne (1964). The limited number and extent of excavations has led to the tentative nature of the conclusions offered in the *West African Archaeological Newsletter*. Historians have often received advice from archaeologists with respect to the area and period in question, but relevant publications are scanty. The same remark would apply to linguists. They have their own priorities. Linguistic studies specifically addressed to problems of historical reconstruction are found in Hair (1967, 1968). These, together with d'Azevedo (1962) and Dalby (1965), fill what would otherwise be considerable gaps in our knowledge of Sierra Leone and Liberia. On all parts of the Guinea coast contributions by scholars in other disciplines such as geography and botany have been very limited.

Compared to some parts of the continent, the Guinea coast is well provided with historical source-material and scholarly literature. The number and quality of locally produced journals should be noted, along with the proliferation of secondary school and general texts. However, there is also considerable unevenness within the region. In the English-speaking sphere, Ghana and Nigeria have led the way in attracting foreign scholars and in producing indigenous historians. Gambia and Liberia have been most lacking, while Sierra Leone has at least been favoured by many years of amateur and professional inquiry recorded in the pages of *Sierra Leone Studies*. Liberian studies have also recently given rise to a journal. In French-speaking West Africa, most historical research is concentrated outside the Guinea coast (as defined in the text) and/or outside the seventeenth and eighteenth centuries. Dahomey is a clear exception. Local and foreign scholars have long been active in recovering oral traditions and exploring the artistic and political heritage, as with Le Herissé (1911), Hazoumé (1937), Herskovits (1938), Akindélé and Aguessy (1953) and Adandé (1962). Argyle's anthropological monograph (1966) has a substantial historical foundation, while that of Polanyi (1966) focusses attention on economic structures.

The present study has been shaped by published sources and by secondary works. Therefore, the unevenness of the prevailing literature asserts itself – little or no reference to large parts of Liberia and Ivory Coast being an obvious example. The ideological constraints may be less obvious, but virtually all of the scholarship on the Guinea coast is framed from a single ideological perspective. The full significance of this point for purposes of bibliographical and historiographical review will emerge when there is an alternative body of interpretation utilizing the methodology and insights of historical materialism.

5. CENTRAL AFRICA FROM CAMEROUN TO THE ZAMBEZI

So far very little archaeological work has been done on the terminal Iron Age of this area, even in Zambia and surrounding regions of South-Central Africa, and preliminary historical assessment has relied on traditions and documents. In West-Central Africa documentary data are comparatively rich by African standards. The early seventeenth century witnessed the arrival of Dutch traders such as van den Broecke who saw the scene with fresh eyes and wrote perceptive accounts of the coastal and near coastal peoples. The most important Dutch work was that of Dapper, who compiled his mid-seventeenth-century account from many sources. The Dutch were followed a few decades later by Italian Capuchin missionaries who travelled widely and wrote profusely. Several score of their published and unpublished works provide essential evidence on social, political and religious history with which to complement the Dutch economic data. The most famous works are those of Cavazzi, Luca da Caltanisetta and Francesco da Roma, now all available in scholarly editions. Later in the seventeenth century, English and French traders began to frequent the west coast of Central Africa and records of their slaving ventures provide further valuable information.

One of the most informative English sources consists of the published adventures of Andrew Battell who spent twenty years in Angola.

Portuguese activities both on sea and on land continued to create considerable source-material. Throughout the seventeenth and eighteenth centuries detailed evidence was sent to Lisbon concerning trade, wars, diplomatic activity, litigation, church tithes and economic expansion. These archival materials were eventually housed in the Arquivo Histórico Ultramarino. Inside Angola nearly all archival records were destroyed during the Dutch occupation of Luanda from 1641 to 1648, but since then documents have been accumulating though in a slow and haphazard manner, and with many losses due to water seepage and termites. By the end of the eighteenth century preservation was more systematic, and future historians of Central Africa should have access not only to the records of the Angolan Central Government, but also to the correspondence files of several district administrations of the eighteenth century. One extremely valuable published source helps to compensate for the loss of earlier local records; this is Cadornega's history of the Angolan wars written in 1680 and completed by an extensive ethnographic gazetteer of the colony. A similar eye-witness description was published a century later by Silva Correia, a Brazilian merchant. In addition to these contemporary publications, the historian has at his disposal numerous volumes of collected archival documents which have been published at various times over the last hundred years. The most notable are Paiva Manso (Kongo), Felner (Angola), Jadin (about a dozen works), Brásio (includes six volumes relating to the period 1600–50), and *Arquivos de Angola* (the Luanda archive journal published since 1933).

Away from the coastal zone of Central Africa, documentary evidence becomes exceedingly rare. The Arab authors, with the possible exception of Leo Africanus, have only the slightest references to the northern borderland of Central Africa. The Portuguese penetration of the lower Zambezi sheds a little light on the interior of Zambia, especially in the eighteenth century. Elsewhere one is entirely dependent on oral traditions which have, in most cases, only been collected erratically if at all. Modern research which has been undertaken, though not yet published, in the aftermath of Vansina's pioneering study of Kuba, includes Miller (Imbangala and Kimbundu), Vellut and Ndua (Lunda), Roberts (Bemba), Mainga (Lozi), and Vansina himself on Teke. In addition to this new work in progress, there is an older school of amateur scholars who, although primarily concerned with ethnographic research, collected valuable fragments of historical data and in some cases quite detailed histories. Examples include van Wing and Ihle (Kongo), Childs (Ovimbundu), van der Kerken (Mongo), Redinha (Lunda), Estermann (Ovambo), Verhulpen (Luba), Calonne-Beaufaict (North Zaïre). At an even earlier date the best of the European pioneer travellers were able observers and linguists who collected historical evidence which has since become lost in the rapid changes which overcame many Central African societies in the colonial period. A few of the more prominent travellers were Graça and Carvalho (Lunda), Magyar and Silva Porto (Ovimbundu), Lacerda and Gamitto (eastern Zambia), Livingstone and Coillard (western Zambia), Wissmann and Pogge (central Zaïre), Stanley and Cameron (eastern Zaïre).

From this mixed range of data a number of modern scholarly works of history have been written. A few not so far mentioned include R. Delgado (Angola, 4 vols, 1948–55), Bouchaud (Cameroun, 1952), Vansina (*Kingdoms of the savanna*, 1966, and *Ethnographie*, 1965, both with extensive bibliographies), Birmingham (Angola, 1966), Ardener (Cameroun, 1968, article), Randles (Kongo, 1968, includes bibliography), Vellut (Angola, 1970, Lunda, 1972, articles), S. Axelson (Kongo, 1970, includes bibliography), Miller (Imbangala, 1971, thesis), Kalck (Central Sudan, not available at the time of writing), Martin (Loango, 1972, includes bibliography especially on Dutch sources), Wilson (Luba, 1972, article).

6. SOUTHERN AFRICA AND MADAGASCAR

The history of southern Africa and Madagascar in the seventeenth and eighteenth centuries is known primarily, though still most inadequately, from oral tradition. There has as yet been no thorough, systematic collection of Rozvi traditions. F. W. Posselt (1935) conveys an impression of Rozvi central power. This can be supplemented by other writings (Muhlanga, Marodzi, Sebina, von Sicard), by a few valuable textual fragments (Fortune, Robinson) and by material in the Salisbury archives, some of which has been critically assessed by Mudenge. Daneel has added to our knowledge of the Mwari cult, though some of his references to this period must be treated with caution. Abraham's work on the traditions of the Mutapa dynasty is particularly important, though unfortunately he has yet to make fully available his texts and his findings both for this and earlier periods. Interesting accounts of early Venda and Lovedu history based on their traditions have been published (van Warmelo, Stayt, Krige) though, with the exception of some of van Warmelo's material, they represent a secondary synthesis rather than the primary sources.

For the south-east Bantu as a whole, there is a considerable body of published and unpublished tradition recorded from the beginning of the nineteenth century. Of varied time-depth, geographical scope and reliability, much of it still awaits critical assessment. By far the most systematic compilation and analysis has been Schapera's work on the Tswana, which can be supplemented by more fragmentary collections going back to the beginning of the nineteenth century for the southernmost groups. The recent compilations by P. L. Breutz for the Native Affairs Department, Ethnological Publications (nos. 28, 30–2, 37, 46), are useful, if used with caution. The best collection of south Sotho traditions remains that by Ellenberger and MacGregor; the traditions of the northern and north-eastern Sotho-speaking peoples, as well as lesser groups like the Transvaal Ndebele, are far less adequately recorded and have to be pieced together from fragments in the Ethnological Publications of the N.A.D. (van Warmelo, nos. 12–22, Myburgh, no. 25) and journal articles (E. and J. Krige). Martin Legassick (in L. M. Thompson, ed., 1969) provides a valuable introduction to the nature and range of Sotho-Tswana traditions, and attempts a synthesis, as does Monica Wilson in Wilson and Thompson, eds. (1969).

Natal Nguni and Swazi traditions have been collected pre-eminently in the works of A. T. Bryant, though this is not easy to handle. (See S. Marks, in Thompson, ed., 1969 for an assessment.) James Stuart's publications in Zulu, and the forthcoming publication of his hitherto unpublished compilation of Zulu and Swazi oral tradition, add depth and substance to some of Bryant's material, though both his and Bryant's works are most reliable on the period just prior to and during the Shakan wars. J. H. Soga (1930) also deals in part with the Natal Nguni, but is rather more reliable on the Cape Nguni: even here it should be used with caution, and should be weighed against such older authorities as Kropf, Barrow, Alberti, and other compilations. The recent synthesis of Nguni traditions in Wilson and Thompson, eds. (1969) should be supplemented by Harinck in Thompson, ed. (1969).

For the south-western Bantu and Khoisan peoples of South-West Africa, Vedder (1938) remains indispensable, although again for the period before 1800, which is largely based on oral tradition, it needs critical handling. It should be supplemented by late nineteenth-, early twentieth-century German authorities (Irle, Tönjes) and by the historical fragments in the publications of the N.A.D. (van Warmelo no. 26, Kohler nos. 40, 42–4), and other ethnological work (Hahn, Loeb). Taken as a whole, however, the oral evidence for this area before 1800 is unsatisfactory.

Even less adequate are the collections of Khoisan traditions, a reflection of their small-scale, isolated societies. G. W. Stow (1905) has a lengthy and sympathetic account of San traditions, and also deals with Khoi history, but it cannot be relied on too heavily. Linguistic and ethnographic work (Bleek, Hahn, Hoernlé, Thomas, Silberhauer) contain valuable evidence of the past, which can be pieced together with the rather fuller documentary record on the Khoisan peoples of the Cape in the seventeenth and eighteenth century, as has been done by I. Schapera (1930) and Monica Wilson (in Wilson and Thompson, eds. 1969). Most recently, Elphick has reassessed most of the source material on the Cape Khoi.

In Madagascar, Merina traditions were extensively collected by Father Callet and are partially available in a French translation (Chapus and Ratsimba). There has been no comparable collection of Sakalava or other Maroserana traditions; echoes and fragments are found in Birkeli, Flacourt, Guillain and Rusillon. These and other unpublished sources have recently been reassessed by Kent, and our account depends heavily on his analysis and interpretation, which supplements and extends the synthesis of Deschamps.

The records of European contemporaries rarely deal at first hand with the major developments of the southern African interior. Their fragmentary and often inaccurate references are nevertheless sometimes of great value, particularly for chronological purposes. Many of the general descriptions written by the Portuguese have been published, with a rich concentration on trade and on developments in the Zambezi valley (Conceição, F. de Melo e Castro, Axelson, Theal, Andrade, Carvalho Dias). Much of the archival correspondence is concerned with Portuguese policy and administration and relatively little has as yet been published for this period. (See however, C. Montez, 'Inventario'.) It has been used fairly extensively by historians of Portuguese and missionary activities (Axelson, Lobato, Hoppe, Schebesta, A. da Silva) and recent research has exploited this material to open up the history of the *prazos* and of African states and peoples in contact with the Portuguese (Newitt, Isaacman, Mudenge, A. Smith, Bhila).

Dutch archival sources on the Cape of Good Hope are voluminous, and a great deal of material has been published (Moodie, Leibbrandt, Theal, *Suid-Afrikaanse Argiefstukke*, Jeffreys ed. *Kaapse Plakkaatboek*). Though this has been mainly utilized by Afrikaner historians concentrating on their own history (van der Merwe, Boeseken, Beyers, Scholtz, and Nienaber, etc.), there is great scope for work on socio-economic relations at the Cape in this period, and for the history of the Cape Khoi (Elphick, Marks). Many accounts of travels into the interior of the Cape colony have been published (see in particular Godée-Molsbergen and the Van Riebeeck Society series) though until the mid-eighteenth century there is little of substance on the Bantu-speaking peoples beyond the Orange river or, apart from the evidence of shipwrecked sailors (publ. in Theal, Boxer), on the south-eastern Nguni. These fragments have however been put together, most notably by Saunders and Wilson.

The French settlement on the south-east coast of Madagascar in the seventeenth century produced a corpus of documentary evidence and one classic (Flacourt). The published reports of European visitors to the west coast provide glimpses of the area before and after the rise of the Sakalava kingdoms, together with one volume of vivid personal recollections (Drury). Many of these sources can be found in the collection edited by the Grandidiers, but there is also material to be traced in European archives.

Besides this evidence from traditions and documents, other disciplines have made major contributions to our knowledge of this period. The archaeological examination of Zimbabwe has been more intense than any other area in tropical Africa. Although many of the results probably refer to an earlier period (Garlake, 1968), the work on sites more closely connected with the Rozvi (Robinson, MacIver, Caton-Thompson) provide a clear testimony to some of the achievements of this period. Some references in Hall and Neal (especially the finds from 'a Mambo's grave', pp. 107, 313–14) point the need for further examination of sites of this period and for the recording of traditions associated with them. Excavations at Dambarare have also shown the importance and interest of investigating sites of Afro-Portuguese contact (Garlake, 1970).

South of the Limpopo, too, archaeological work, particularly on the

Iron Age in the Transvaal and Orange Free State, is beginning to yield important information on the continuity of population groups and their interaction, as well as their settlement patterns in this period, (Mason, Maggs, van der Merwe). Aerial photography (Mason) has revealed the density of the stone building sites in the southern Transvaal and northern Orange Free State, extending into Natal, and has suggested the enormous scope for archaeological excavation, which is beginning to take place under the Iron Age Project of the University of Witwatersrand. Recent work in the Transkei (R. Derricourt, personal communications) may also add to our understanding of Cape Nguni history. The archaeological exploration of Madagascar in this period has not yet developed, but it may yet throw much light on the Maroserana dynasties and their immediate antecedents.

7. EASTERN AFRICA

Historical knowledge of eastern Africa in the seventeenth and eighteenth centuries, in the absence of adequate archaeological and linguistic study, continues to depend largely upon written and oral sources. The former are almost exclusively Portuguese and are restricted to the coast and the southern interior, but despite their limitations they provide us with an indispensable framework for the history of these regions. The most important collections of unpublished Portuguese documentation are the Arquivo Nacional da Torre do Tombo, the Arquivo Histórico Ultramarino, both located in Lisbon, and the National Archives of India, Panjim, Goa (especially useful for the early eighteenth century). A number of major contemporary accounts were translated into English and published by Theal (1898–1903), but a full translation and scholarly edition of Dos Santos (1609) is very much needed. Strandes wrote an exhaustive history of the coast under Portuguese domination from these sources in 1899, while Axelson (1960) dealt with Portuguese activities throughout eastern Africa in the seventeenth century. Both are not without their limitations. Alpers's forthcoming study of trade in this area is also based upon the Portuguese archives. That much more remains to be learned from oral traditions in these two regions is demonstrated by Berg's research on Mombasa (1968) and by the remarkable work of Schoffeleers on the Mang'anja in Ranger and Kimambo (1972); see also in Pachai (1972).

For the rest of eastern Africa, it is to the oral data that the historian must turn. Long before any professional historians began to work on the history of the peoples of the interior by collecting and interpreting their traditions, a great many amateur students of the past had used this material. Their work is very uneven, but in many cases it is all that exists. Two of the most comprehensive attempts to gather traditional histories were the result of official colonial policy. With the introduction of indirect rule in what was then Tanganyika territory, district officers and their assistants were instructed to collect the histories and chiefly genealogies of the peoples under their administration so that the government could appoint the right individuals as chiefs and headmen. The purpose of this exercise frequently produced spurious genealogies, and many district officers were less than rigorous in their historical methodology. But there is still much to be learned from the District Books, which are now housed in the National Archives of Tanzania, Dar es Salaam. Similarly, the published Reports of the Kenya Land Commission contain a wealth of historical and ethnographic information, although the burning issue of land in colonial Kenya produced its own distortions.

The work of early ethnographers and anthropologists also contains much useful information on pre-colonial history, although the lack of historical conceptualization and the prevalent belief in the unchanging persistence back in time of 'traditional' African society means that the historian must use these sources with a great deal of care. The work of Hans Cory is particularly valuable for the central interior, while that of John Roscoe is important for the interlacustrine zone. For the Nilotic-speaking peoples, the work of G. W. B. Huntingford, Lawrence, Driberg, and Crazzolara is especially useful.

Two final examples of early and much more serious attempts to preserve traditional knowledge of the past are the work of Africans who were themselves intimately involved with the government of their societies. Abdallah bin Hemedi was secretary to the great king of Shambaa, Kimweri ye Nyumbai, and Apolo Kagwa was prime minister of Buganda from the end of the nineteenth century to 1927. Kagwa's history is notable because it is not a partisan piece of history as is Abdallah's.

In the past twenty years the pace of historical research based upon field work and oral traditions has increased noticeably. Much of this work has been produced by social anthropologists. Outstanding work has been done on Buganda by Southwold and on the Fipa by Willis, while Southall's work on the Alur, Lambert's on the Kikuyu, and that of Jacobs on the Masai is also important. Still of great interest, but increasingly disputed by both anthropologists and historians, is the work of Godfrey and Monica Wilson on the Nyakyusa and Ngonde. Charsley's revision of the Nyakyusa implicitly raises a number of critical methodological questions about the political organization of Ngonde, while Vail's important reinterpretation of Tumbuka history (in Pachai) lucidly demonstrates the pitfalls of accepting dynastic history uncritically.

Among those who operate primarily as historians, a regional overview of their work will serve to give some idea of the unevenness of its geographical distribution. The greatest concentration has been in the interlacustrine area, where the existence of older, stable states has predictably attracted historians. Oliver was the first modern scholar to draw attention to this area, and his overview in the first volume of the Oxford *History of East Africa* is still an impressive synthesis. A different interpretation of the history of the interlacustrine region as a whole has been suggested by de Heusch and challenged in a review article by Cohen, a student of Oliver's. Histories of individual kingdoms and sub-regions have been produced recently as dissertations at the School of Oriental and African Studies, University of London, by Kiwanuka on Buganda, Karugire on Nkore, and Cohen on Busoga. Bunyoro still lacks this sort of attention, and Dunbar's history is not particularly helpful for this period. Karagwe has recently been studied by Katoke, but there is a disappointing lack of discussion of the seventeenth and eighteenth centuries. Vansina has published an important short history of the development of Rwanda and a substantial monograph on Burundi.

To the east of Lake Victoria, the most important work published to date has been done by Ogot on the Luo and Kimambo on the Pare. Were and Osogo have both studied the Luyia, neither with the same authority that Ogot and Kimambo bring to their work. Muriuki's history of the Kikuyu also marks a major step forward in the precolonial historiography of Kenya, while the theoretically oriented dissertation by Jackson on the Kamba is also important. Feierman's studies of Shambaa history and society (1974, and in Roberts) are another outstanding example of the blending of historical and anthropological training. Shorter's seminal study of the Kimbu fills an enormous gap in our knowledge of western Tanzania and provides leads for a cluster of studies in the area around Ukimbu. His revision of Oliver's *ntemi* hypothesis has been echoed by Kimambo (in Kimambo and Temu). Nyamwezi history is still fairly obscure before the nineteenth century, but Roberts's essays (in Roberts, and in Gray and Birmingham) are a useful beginning. In the southern interior, there is only Langworthy's work on the Chewa (also in Pachai) and Isaacman's and Newitt's excellent studies of the *prazo*-holders to add to the efforts of Schoffeleers and Vail. [The thesis by Kalinga on the Ngonde was presented after this was written. Ed.]

Nevertheless, many major gaps remain in the oral documentation. Critical areas for future study are those of the Taita, Sagara and Kinga, each of which was a centre of emigration for ruling houses among other peoples of eastern Africa. More studies among the Nilotic-speaking peoples of the northern interior are needed, and very little is known about the history of the Southern Cushitic-speaking Galla. Elsewhere in Tanzania the areas which seem most in need of study are Usukuma, Buzinza, Buha and the Singida and Mbulu areas. A history of the Nyakyusa is also a major priority. Finally, to the east of Lake Malawi, the key priority is for field work among the Makua-Lomwe peoples, although the histories of both the Yao and Makonde also cry out for attention.

Two other potential sources of historical information for this period are archaeology and linguistics. For the most part, however, the priorities of archaeologists in eastern Africa have been on the Early Iron Age and there has not been much serious work directed towards the period after 1500. Nevertheless, a useful beginning has already been made by the work of James Kirkman on Fort Jesus at Mombasa, John Sutton on the western highlands of Kenya, Hamo Sassoon on Engaruka in northern Tanzania, and Peter Schmidt in Buhaya. At the same time, Ehret's pioneering work on Kenyan and northern Tanzanian history has demonstrated the variety of uses to which linguistic evidence can be put, and not only for periods beyond the ken of oral tradition. Here, too, the field is wide open for the historian who seeks to reconstruct the history of eastern Africa during the seventeenth and eighteenth centuries.

8. ETHIOPIA AND THE HORN OF AFRICA, 1543–1820

The history of the Horn between the sixteenth and the nineteenth centuries seems to be amply documented. Unfortunately this extensive material is relevant mainly to the sixteenth century and to the first decades of the seventeenth century and is concerned in most cases with the Ethiopian kingdom which, after the end of the sixteenth century, was greatly reduced in size.

The most important group of sources for the history of Ethiopia in this period are the royal chronicles written by ecclesiastics who held offices in the court. These chronicles have been edited and published by several scholars, notably C. Conti Rossini, I. Guidi, W. E. Conzelman, J. Perruchon, R. Basset and F. M. E. Pereira, and for some reigns they are virtually the only source of our knowledge of what happened in Ethiopia. Unfortunately the chroniclers were interested in most cases only with recording the king's campaigns, his pious deeds and events connected with the palace or the church. They were hardly ever concerned with the social, economic or even the general political history of the country. Moreover, the quality of the chronicles greatly deteriorated with the final decline of the Gondarine kingdom.

A good number of local chronicles, theological works and lives of saints still await 'discovery' in monasteries and elsewhere in Ethiopia. Many, however, have been edited, translated and published. Though important for church history, this material is in most cases of limited importance for other fields. There are, however, a number of exceptions. An outstanding example is the autobiography of the monk, Pawlos (edited and translated by C. Conti Rossini), which is a most valuable source for the political history of the period.

Important contributions to our general knowledge about Ethiopia and the non-Ethiopian population of the Horn come from Catholic missionary sources. However, after the expulsion of the Jesuits from Ethiopia in the 1630s, these sources, depending on news coming occasionally out of Ethiopia, are not only unreliable and incomplete, but in some cases are also intentionally misleading. Even for the sixteenth and early seventeenth centuries this material should be used with reservation, since it was written by foreigners with a cultural, religious and, to a certain degree, political bias. Many of these sources have been published. One of the earliest and most useful is F. Alvarez, *The Prester John of the Indies*, edited and translated by C. F. Beckingham and G. W. B. Huntingford (1961). Important information received from Ethiopians or from Europeans who had been to Ethiopia is also to be found in general works such as João de Barros and Diogo de Couto (1936 ed.) as well as in Gaspar Correa, edited by R. J. de Lima Felner (1858–64). The most outstanding of this group of sources, though it still awaits a thorough and critical editing, is C. Beccari ed. *Rerum Aethiopicarum scriptores occidentales inediti a saeculo XVI ad XIX*. This is a collection of reports, documents and books written by some of the Jesuit fathers who had lived in Ethiopia (including those of

Paez, Barradas, Almeida and Mendez). Unpublished archival material is mainly to be found in the archives of the Society of Jesus in Rome and archives in Portugal. According to Dr Merid Wolde Aregay of the University at Addis Ababa, who consulted these archives while writing his Ph.D. thesis at SOAS, London, in most cases these unpublished sources only enlarge on the material already mentioned.

Accounts of Ethiopia by visitors who entered the country after the 1630s are rare and not very rewarding. Such is the description of Ethiopia about the middle of the seventeenth century by the Yemeni al-Khaimī (F. E. Peiser, 1894). Not less disappointing is C. Poncet. A manuscript of the book called *Itinerarium* by Remedio Prutky, who entered Ethiopia about the middle of the eighteenth century, still awaits publication. However, the parts published by Somigli di S. Detole (1928–48) show how little can be expected from this confused source. With all his shortcomings and his uncritical acceptance of some of the information which he received, James Bruce, who visited Ethiopia just at the time of the final disintegration of the Gondarine kingdom, provides the most comprehensive picture of the Ethiopian kingdom and affords the historian a glimpse into areas completely neglected since the expulsion of the Jesuits.

Surprisingly little has been published on the Muslim principalities and sultanates of the Horn in the period covered by this chapter. Tribute should be paid to Enrico Cerulli, who has painstakenly collected materials concerning the Muslim population of the south-eastern and eastern parts of the Horn. In this connection one should also mention J. S. Trimingham (1965), and the contributions of P. Paulitschke, who left us with a number of important books and articles.

An important contribution to the political and economic history of the Red Sea basin is Albert Kammerer's voluminous work *La Mer Rouge, l'Abissinie et l'Arabie*, which contributes to our meagre knowledge about the Ottoman involvement in the history of the Horn. Another contribution to this subject is C. Conti Rossini's 'La guerra turco-abissina del 1578'. Unfortunately our knowledge in this field will remain incomplete until material from Ottoman archives concerning Ethiopia has been brought to light.

The most important source for the early history of the Galla is the account written by the Ethiopian monk Bahri at the end of the sixteenth century, edited by C. F. Beckingham and G. W. B. Huntingford (1954). C. Conti Rossini, 'I Galla Raia' and I. Guidi, *Historia gentis Galla* are based on the same source. All the important books and reports of the Jesuit fathers (Paez, Almeida, Lobo, Fernandez and others) contain some information about the Galla. In addition to works in various fields concerning the Galla published by modern European scholars, there are a number of relatively modern contributions by Ethiopians which are partly based on oral tradition. Such, for instance, is Ato Asmiye's 'Ye Galla tarik' (an unpublished manuscript in the National Library, Addis Ababa). Unfortunately all the sources concerned with Galla history are inadequate and in many cases inaccurate or subjective. This is so because the informants were never in close contact with the Galla, were biased, or accepted unreliable information. Although Ethiopian studies have attracted a number of outstanding scholars, these have concentrated on editing manuscripts discussing certain aspects of Ethiopian life, and they have been especially interested in linguistic research. Hence, most secondary sources, with a few exceptions such as J. S. Trimingham (1965) or Conti Rossini (1928), are of little value and the scholar is forced to use primary sources in most cases.

9. AFRICA IN EUROPE AND THE AMERICAS

Data on European attitudes to Africa and Africans is scattered and often ephemeral, mainly taking the form of allusions in novels, poems and plays. Analysis often proceeds through literary criticism, as seen in Dykes (1942), McCullough (1962) and Eldred Jones (1965). Travel literature deriving from contact with Africa represents substantial documentation, although the information on attitudes is also oblique. These sources have been tapped by Curtin (1964) and Barker (1972). Literary references, along with surviving social legislation and judicial records, provide the basis for reconstructing the history of Africans in Europe. More primary data may have been generated by and about Africans in Portugal, but presumably loss was sustained in the earthquakes which destroyed Lisbon records.

The subjective racist factor has contributed to the neglect of the topic of 'Africans in Europe', apart from its marginality and difficulties of access to the material. African slave imports into Portugal and Spain have usually been passed over in silence by subsequent historians. Holland had on its own soil appreciable numbers of slaves and free blacks from Africa or the American colonies, but histories covering the period in question overlook the phenomenon. Modern French writers touch on race and slavery in seventeenth- and eighteenth-century

France only in connection with the colonial issue and the French Revolution, as in Jameson (1911), Le Clerc (1933) and Debien (1953). The Afro-American, Joel Rogers (1934, 1940, 1947) was a lone pioneer showing indefatigable energy in tracing the 'Negro' in every nook and cranny of Europe. His concern to 'prove' that the 'Negro' was not inferior now appears trite, but it highlights the fact that some commitment is required before the field is explored. Significantly, the resumption of black immigration to Britain in this century and the resulting tense race relations have provided the spur for historical investigation of the earlier African presence, as illustrated by Little (1948), Mason (1962), Banton (1967), Walvin (1971, 1973) and Scobie (1972).

Themes linking the history of Africa, Europe and America have received greater (though far from adequate) attention. The trans-Atlantic slave trade was a field of research even before it was ended, but basic questions concerning its dimensions have been glossed over until recently when new empirical initiatives were taken by Chaunu (1955) and Curtin (1969). Similarly, the role of trans-Atlantic trade as a factor in European capital accumulation has often been acknowledged and occasionally denied, but texts such as Williams (1944) and Mauro (1960), which explicitly relate to the issue, are rarely produced. Fortunately, a great deal can be gleaned from discussions emanating from the field of European economic expansion – as in the *Cambridge Economic History of Europe*, vol. IV (1964) and Pike (1966) – and particularly from the study of business history, as with Pares (1950) and Cavignac (1967).

In contrast to the above-mentioned subjects, 'Africans in the Americas' is a data-rich research area and one which has produced extensive scholarship. Documentation for the period up to the early nineteenth century is located almost exclusively in Europe, because of the colonial status of New World societies. The English colonies which became the USA provide the only significant exception. Indeed, being a metropolitan sub-centre in its own right, the USA became the locus of some primary material relating to the history of other parts of the Americas. Because of the slave trade, many of the descriptions of West Africa also contained observations on the Americas and particularly on the West Indies. Moreover, the data extend far beyond the descriptions of transients, since resident whites produced journals, memoirs, letters and financial statements in the course of daily life in slave-owning societies. Together with historical writings of the nineteenth century, these contemporary materials are invaluable, notwithstanding their pronounced bias in favour of the white ruling class. Understandably, Africans as slaves hardly ever formally recorded their own sentiments, except for former slaves writing after the events – see, for example, Nichols (1963), Montejo (1968) and Bontemps (1969). The direct expression of the mass of African-born blacks and the early generations of their descendants was in the form of folklore, music, dance, religious manifestations and the various 'creole' dialects. Use of this important supplement to the written European record was pioneered and given greater currency by Ortiz (1916), Herskovits (1941) and Freyre (1956); and developed more recently by Bastide (1967).

Present-day scholarship reflects the wide dispersal of Africans in the Americas, so that there are monographs on relatively peripheral areas like Canada (Winks, 1971) and the Danish possessions (Westergaard, 1917), although the coverage is not even. The Spanish-speaking mainland, the Dutch territories and the French territories other than St Domingue do not show the quantity of research which the proportion of the black population would suggest as necessary. But Brazil, the 'South' of the USA, the British West Indies, Cuba and St Domingue have been given attention on the basis of the large numbers of slaves imported. Emergent nationalism in the British West Indies contributed as it usually does to quantitative and qualitative changes in historical writing. Besides, both there and in the USA and Brazil, the period of slavery is so self-evidently relevant to an understanding of the subsequent political economy that the historical role of black people was never entirely neglected by scholars, whatever their race and ideological perspectives, although the degree of interest has been small until recent times. The unique *Journal of Negro History* makes a rather arbitrary separation of black history from mainstream American history, as much because of prejudiced white writings as because of disinterest on the part of establishment historians.

To appreciate the range of scholarship on Africans in the Americas, one must necessarily have recourse to bibliographical aids: notably, Work (1928), Miller (1970), *Current Caribbean bibliography* (1951 *et seq.*), and *Index to periodical articles by and about Negroes* (1960 *et seq.* and precursor journals). Studies on the black population merge into and often derive from other thematic concerns like the profitability of slavery; but general works addressed to the history of blacks include Johnston (1910), Saco (1938), Franklin (1947) and McCloy (1966). Research areas which have received broad and penetrating study in recent years include comparative slavery (Tannenbaum, 1947; Hoetinck, 1971), slave behaviour (Aptheker, 1943; Genovese, 1961; Patterson, 1967), and the genesis of racism (Davis, 1968; Jordan, 1968). In these instances, historical discussion has not been pursued exclusively or even primarily by historians, but rather by scholars from a wide spectrum of disciplines. This is also a strong point of studies of African cultural survivals; and Caribbean linguists have taken the further step of fostering co-operation with Africanists – for which, see Le Page (1961). More effort in this direction could well stimulate new advances in elucidating the African contribution to black American culture and to the general history of the Americas.

BIBLIOGRAPHY

GENERAL

The following bibliography and reference works are of value to the study of the period covered by this volume as a whole. Space permits only a very selective list, which does not purport to be comprehensive.

The most complete guide to the literature of African studies available is P. Duignan's *Guide to research and reference works on sub-Saharan Africa*, Stanford, 1971. This most valuable work should be consulted for further information.

Ajayi, J. F. Ade and Crowder, M. eds. *History of West Africa*, vol. I. London, 1971.

Brunschwig, H. *L'avènement de l'Afrique noire* (Collection 'Sciences politiques'). Paris, 1963.

Cornevin, R. *Histoire des peuples de l'Afrique noire*. Paris, 1960.

Cox, E. G. *Reference guide to literature of travel*, vol. I, *Old World*. Africa, pp. 354–401. Seattle, 1935.

Curtin, P. D. *African history*. New York, 1964.

Curtin, P. D. *The Atlantic slave trade: a census*. Madison, 1969.

Dapper, O. *Naukeurige Beschrijvinge der Afrikaensche Gewesten*. Amsterdam, 1668.

Deschamps, H. *L'Afrique tropicale aux XVIIe–XVIIIe siècles*. Paris, 1964.

Donnan, E. ed. *Documents illustrative of the history of the slave trade to America*, vols. I, II. Washington D.C., 1930–5.

Duignan, P. ed. *Guide to research and reference works on sub-Saharan Africa*. Stanford, 1971.

Fage, J. D. *An atlas of African history*. London, 1966.

Garling, A. *Bibliography of African bibliographies*. Cambridge, 1968.

Guides to materials for West African history in European archives (series). London, 1962 onwards.

Hallett, R. *The penetration of Africa: European exploration in North and West Africa*, vol. I, *to 1815*. London, 1965.

International Council on Archives. *Guide to the sources of African history outside of Africa* (series). Zug, 1970 onwards.

McEwan, P. J. M. ed. *Readings in African history* (series), vol. I, *Africa from early times to 1800*. London, 1968.

Matep, B. *Heurts et malheurs des rapports Europe-Afrique*. Paris, 1959.

Mauny, R. 'Contribution à la bibliographie de l'histoire de l'Afrique noire des origines à 1850', *Bulletin de l'IFAN*, 1966, **28**, ser. B, 3–4.

Meyer-Heiselberg, R. *Bibliographi over Afrikansk historie: nyere litteratur orn syd for Sahara*. Copenhagen 1963.

Pearson, J. D. ed. *A guide to documents and manuscripts in the British Isles relating to Africa*. London, 1970.

Thomas, D. H. and Case, L. M. eds. *Guide to the diplomatic archives of Western Europe*. Philadelphia, 1959.

I. EGYPT, THE FUNJ AND DARFUR

'Abd al-Maḥmūd Nūr al-Dā'im. *Azāhīr al-riyāḍ fī manāqib al-'ārif bi'llāh ta'ālā al-ustādh al-shaykh Aḥmad al-Ṭayyib*. Cairo, 1954.

Abū Salīm, Muḥammad Ibrāhīm. *Al-Fūnj wa'l-arḍ: wathā'iq tamlīk*. (Sudan Research Unit, Occasional Papers, no. 2.) Khartoum, 1967.

American in the service of the viceroy, An. *See* [English, G. B.].

Ayalon, D. 'The historian al-Jabartī and his background', *Bulletin of the School of Oriental and African Studies*, 1960, **23**, 2, 217–49.

Browne, W. G. *Travels in Africa, Egypt and Syria from the year 1792 to 1798*. London, 1799.

Bruce, James. *Travels to discover the source of the Nile*. 2nd ed. Edinburgh, 1805.

Burckhardt, J. L. *Travels in Nubia*. London, 1819.

Carré, Jean-Marie. *Voyageurs et écrivains français en Égypte*, 2nd ed. Cairo, 1956.

Combe, E., Bainville, J. and Driault, E. *L'Égypte ottomane, l'expédition française en Égypte et le règne de Mohamed Aly (1517–1849)*. (*Précis de l'histoire d'Égypte*, tome III.) Cairo, 1933.

Crawford, O. G. S. *The Fung Kingdom of Sennar*. Gloucester, 1951.

Elles, R. J. 'The kingdom of Tegali', *Sudan Notes and Records*, 1935, **18**, 1, 1–35.

El Nasri, Abdel Rahman. *A bibliography of the Sudan, 1938–1958*. London, 1962.

[English, G. B.] *A narrative of the expedition to Dongola and Sennaar*. London, 1822.

Evliya Çelebi. *See* Petti Suma, Maria Teresa.

Ḥasan, Yūsuf Faḍl. *The Arabs and the Sudan*. Edinburgh, 1967.

Ḥasan, Yūsuf Faḍl, ed. *Kitab al-ṭabaqāt*. Kartoum, 1971.

Herrold, J. C. *Bonaparte in Egypt*. London, 1963.

Hill, Richard L. *A bibliography of the Anglo-Egyptian Sudan from the earliest times to 1937*. London, 1939.

Hill, Richard L. *A biographical dictionary of the Sudan*, 2nd ed. of *A biographical dictionary of the Anglo-Egyptian Sudan*. London, 1967.

Hillelson, S. 'David Reubeni, an early visitor to Sennar', *Sudan Notes and Records*, 1933, **16**, 1, 55–66.

Hillelson, S. *Sudan Arabic texts*, Cambridge, 1935.

Hillelson, S. 'Tabaqât Wad Dayf Allah: studies in the lives of scholars and saints', *Sudan Notes and Records*, 1923, **6**, 191–230.

Holt, P. M. *A modern history of the Sudan*, 2nd ed. London, 1963.

Holt, P. M. *Egypt and the fertile crescent, 1516–1922*. London, 1966.

Holt, P. M. 'Four Funj land-charters', *Sudan Notes and Records*, 1969, **50**, 2–14.

Holt, P. M. 'Funj origins: a critique and new evidence', *Journal of African History*, 1963, **4**, 1, 39–47.

Holt, P. M. *Holy families and Islam in the Sudan*. (Princeton Near East Papers, no. 4.) Princeton N.J., 1967.

Holt, P. M. ed. *Political and social change in modern Egypt*. London, 1968.

Holt, P. M. 'Sultan Selim I and the Sudan', *Journal of African History*, 1967, **8**, 1, 19–23.

Holt, P. M. 'The sons of Jābir and their kin: a clan of Sudanese religious notables', *Bulletin of the School of Oriental and African Studies*, 1967, **30**, 1, 142–57.

Holt, P. M. *Studies in the history of the Near East*. London, 1973.

Ibn Īyās, Muḥammad b. Aḥmad. *Badā'i' al-zuhūr fī waqā'i' al-duhūr*, vol. v. 2nd ed., ed. Mohamed Mostafa. Cairo and Wiesbaden, 1961. *See also* Wiet, Gaston.

al-Isḥāqī, Muḥammad 'Abd al-Mu'ṭī b. Abi'l-Fatḥ. *Kitāb akhbār al-uwal fī man taṣarrafa fī Miṣr min arbāb al-duwal*. Cairo, 1311/1893–4.

al-Jabartī, 'Abd al-Raḥmān b. Ḥasan. *'Ajā'ib al-āthār fi'l-tarājim wa'l-akhbār*. Būlāq, [1879–80]. *See also* Mansour, Chefik.

Kātib al-Shūna [Aḥmad b. al-Ḥājj Abū 'Alī]. *See* al-Shāṭir Buṣayli 'Abd al-Jalīl, ed., and Shibayka, Makkī, ed.

Lane, E. W. *The manners and customs of the modern Egyptians*. London, 1836; many reprints.

MacMichael, H. A. *A history of the Arabs in the Sudan*. Cambridge, 1922. 2 vols.

Mansour, Chefik and others, tr. *Merveilles biographiques et historiques*. Cairo, 1888–96. Translation of al-Jabartī, *'Ajā'ib al-āthār*.

Nur, Sadik. 'Land tenure during the time of the Funj', *Kush*, 1956, **4**, 48–53.

Penn, A. E. D. 'Traditional stories of the 'Abdullab tribe', *Sudan Notes and Records* 1934, **17**, 1, 59–82.

Perron, [A.] *Voyage au Darfour par le Cheykh Mohammed Ebn-Omar el-Tounsy*. Paris, 1845.

Petti Suma, Maria Teresa. 'Il viaggio in Sudan di Evliyā Čelebī', *Annali dell'Istituto Orientale di Napoli*, 1964, n.s., **14**, 433–52.

Poncet, C. J. *A voyage to Aethiopia, made in the year 1698, 1699 and 1700*. Repr. in Foster, W., ed. *The Red Sea and adjacent countries at the close of the seventeenth century*. (Hakluyt Society, Second Series, no. C.) London, 1949.

Raymond, André. *Artisans et commerçants au Caire au XVIIIe siècle*. Damascus, 1973–4.

al-Shāṭir Buṣaylī 'Abd al-Jalīl, ed. *Makhṭūṭat Kātib al-Shūna*. n.p., n.d. [Cairo, 1961].

Shaw, S. J. *Ottoman Egypt in the age of the French Revolution*. (Harvard Middle Eastern Monographs, xi.) Cambridge, Mass., 1964.

Shaw, S. J. *Ottoman Egypt in the eighteenth century*. (Harvard Middle Eastern Monographs, vii.) Cambridge, Mass., 1962.

Shaw, S. J. *The financial and administrative organization and development of Ottoman Egypt, 1517–1798*. (Princeton Oriental Series, no. 19.) Princeton, N.J., 1962.

Shibayka, Makkī. *Ta'rīkh mulūk al-Sūdān*. Khartoum, 1947.

Shuqayr, Na'ūm. *Ta'rīkh al-Sūdān al-qadīm wa'l-ḥadīth wa-jugrhrātiyyatuh*. Cairo, n.d. [1903].

Trimingham, J. S. *Islam in the Sudan*. London, 1949.

al-Tūnusī, Muḥammad b. 'Umar. *Tashḥīdh al-adhhān bi-sīrat bilād al-'Arab wa'l-Sūdān*. Paris, 1850; Cairo, 1966. *See also* Perron, [A.]

Wad Ḍayfallāh [Muḥammad b. Ḍayfallāh b. Muḥammad al-Ja'alī al-Faḍlī]. *See* Ḥasan, Yūsuf Faḍl, ed.

Wiet, Gaston, tr. *Journal d'un bourgeois du Caire. Chronique d'Ibn Iyâs*, tome II. [Paris], 1960. Translation of last part of Ibn Īyās, *Badā'i' al-zuhūr*.

2. THE CENTRAL SAHARA AND SUDAN

Abadie, M. *La Colonie du Niger*. Paris, 1927.

Abbo, H., Lebeuf, J.-P. and Rodinson, M. 'Coutumes du Mandara', *Bulletin de l'IFAN*, 1949, **11**, 471–90.

Abbo, M. and Mohammadou, E., 'Un nouveau manuscrit arabe sur l'histoire du Mandara', *Revue camerounaise d'histoire*, October 1971, no. 1, 130–69.

Ajayi, J. F. A. and Crowder, M. eds. *History of West Africa*, vol. I. London, 1971.

Alexander, B. *From the Niger to the Nile*. London, 1908. 2 vols.

Arnett, E. J. tr. 'A Hausa chronicle', *Journal of the African Society*, 1909–10, **9**, 161–7.

Arnett, E. J. *The rise of the Sokoto Fulani: being a paraphrase and in some parts a translation of the Infaku'l Maisuri of Sultan Mohammed Bello*, n.p., n.d. [1922].

Barbour, N. *A survey of North West Africa*. London, 1959.

Barth, H. *Travels and discoveries in north and central Africa*. London, 1857–8. 5 vols.

Benton, P. A. *The languages and peoples of Bornu: being a collection of the writings of P. A. Benton*, intro. by A. H. M. Kirk-Greene. London, 1968. 2 vols.

Bisson, J. 'Éleveurs, caravaniers et vieux sédentaires de l'Air', *Travaux de l'Inst. de Recherches Sahariennes*, 1964, **23**, 95–110.

Bivar, A. D. H. and Hiskett, M. 'The Arabic literature of Nigeria to 1804: a provisional account', *Bulletin of the School of Oriental and African Studies*, 1962, **25**, 1, 104–48.

Bivar, A. D. H. and Shinnie, P. L. 'Old Kanuri capitals', *Journal of African History*, 1962, **3**, 1, 1–10.

Boulnois, J. 'La migration des Sao du Tchad', *Bulletin de l'IFAN*, 1943, **5**, 80–121.

Bovill, E. W. *The golden trade of the Moors*. London, 1958. 2nd ed. by R. Hallett, 1968.

Bovill, E. W. ed. *Missions to the Niger*. Hakluyt Society, Cambridge, 1964–6. 4 vols.

Briggs, L. C. *Tribes of the Sahara*. Cambridge, Mass. and London, 1960.

Brouin, G. 'Du nouveau au sujet de la question de Takedda', *Notes africaines*, 1950, **47**, 90–1.

Burdon, J. A. *Historical notes on certain emirates and tribes*. London, 1909.

Carbou, H. *La région du Tchad et du Ouadaï*. Paris, 1912. 2 vols.

Castries, H. de. 'La conquête du Soudan par El-Mansour, 1591', *Hespéris*, 1923, **3**, 433–88.

Chapelle, J. *Nomades noires du Sahara*. Paris, 1957.

Clapperton, H. *Journal of a second expedition into the interior of Africa...* London, 1829. Reprinted London, 1966.

Cohen, R. 'The Bornu kinglists', *Boston Papers on Africa*, 1966, **2**, 41–83.

Cohen, R. 'The dynamics of feudalism in Bornu', *Boston Papers on Africa*, 1966, **2**, 87–105.

Cohen, R. *The Kanuri of Bornu*. New York, 1967.

Cohen, R. 'Slavery among the Kanuri', *Trans-action*, January–February 1967, **4**.

Connah, G. E. *First* and *Second interim reports of the Northern History Research Scheme*, Zaria, Ahmadu Bello University and University of Ibadan, 1966 and 1967.

Daumas, E. and Chancel, A. de. *Le grand désert: itinéraire d'une caravane du Sahara au pays des nègres, royaume de Haoussa*. Paris, 1856.

Eldblom, L. *Structure foncière: organisation et structure sociale: une étude comparative sur la vie socio-économique dans les trois oasis libyennes de Ghat, Mourzouk et particulièrement Ghadamès*. Lund, 1968.

Fisher, A. G. B. and Fisher, H. J. *Slavery and Muslim society in Africa*. London, 1970.

Folayan, K. 'Tripoli during the reign of Yūsuf Pāshā Qaramānlī'. Ph.D. thesis, University of London, 1970.

Fortier, J. *Le mythe et les contes de Sou en pays Mbaï-Moïssala*. Bruges, 1967.

Fremantle, J. M. *Gazetteer of Muri Province*. London, 1920.

Fremantle, J. M. 'A history of the region comprising the Katagum division of Kano province', *Journal of the African Society*. April 1911, **10**, 39, 298–319. Subsequent sections of this article concern the nineteenth century.

Fresnel, M. 'Mémoire de M. Fresnel, Consul de France à Djeddah, sur le Waday', *Bulletin de la Société de Géographie*, 1849, pp. 5–75.

Gaden, H. 'États musulmans de l'Afrique centrale et leurs rapports avec la Mecque et Constantinople', *Questions diplomatiques et coloniales*, 1907, **24**, 436–47.

Gaden, H. 'Note sur le dialecte foul parlé par les foulbé du Baguirmi', *Journal asiatique*, 1908, **11**, X série, 5–70.

Gall, F. B. *Gazetteer of Bauchi Province*. London, 1920.

Gowers, W. F. *Gazetteer of Kano Province*. London, 1921.

Greenberg, J. H. *Languages of Africa*, rev. ed. Bloomington, 1966.

Greenberg, J. H. *Studies in African linguistic classification*. New Haven, 1955.

Gwarzo, H. I. 'The life and teachings of al-Maghili, with particular reference to the Saharan Jewish community'. Ph.D. thesis, University of London, 1972.

al-Hajj, Muhammad. 'A seventeenth century chronicle of the origins and missionary activities of the Wangarawa', *Kano Studies*, 1968, **1**, 4, 7–42.

Harris, P. G. 'Notes on Yauri', *Journal of the Royal Anthropological Institute*, 1930, **60**, 283–334.

Heussler, R. 'Research on pre-British northern Nigeria: a note on limitations and potentialities', *The South Atlantic Quarterly*, 1966, **65**, 523–31.

Hill, P. *Rural Hausa: a village and a setting*. Cambridge, 1972.

Hirschberg, H. Z. *A history of the Jews in North Africa*. Forthcoming in an English translation from the Hebrew.

Hiskett, M. 'An Islamic tradition of reform in the Western Sudan from the sixteenth to the eighteenth century', *Bulletin of the School of Oriental and African Studies*, 1962, **25**, 3, 577–96.

Hiskett, M. 'Materials relating to the cowry currency of the Western Sudan', *Bull. SOAS*, 1966, **29**, 1, 122–42 and 2, 339–66.

Hiskett, M. 'The "Song of Bagauda": a Hausa king list and homily in verse', *Bull. SOAS*, 1964, **27**, 3 and 1965, **28**, 1, 2.

Hogben, S. J. and Kirk-Greene, A. H. M. *The emirates of Northern Nigeria*. London, 1966.

Hopen, C. E. *The pastoral Fulbe family in Gwandu*. London, 1958.

Hornemann, F. 'Journal', *Proceedings of the Association for promoting the discovery of the interior parts of Africa*. London, 1810. Reprinted London, 1967.

Hunwick, J. O. 'The dynastic chronologies of the Central Sudan States in the 16th century: some reinterpretations'. Forthcoming article in *Kano Studies*.

Hunwick, J. O. 'A little-known diplomatic episode in the history of Kebbi (*c.* 1594)', *Journal of the Historical Society of Nigeria*, 1971, **5**, 4, 575–81.

Hunwick, J. O. 'Notes on a late fifteenth-century document concerning "al-Takrūr"', in C. Allen and R. W. Johnson, eds., *African perspectives*. Cambridge, 1970.

Hunwick, J. O. 'Source materials for the study of Songhay and the Central Sudan states in the sixteenth century', *Research bulletin of the Centre of Arabic Documentation*, 1971, **6**. Ibadan.

Ibiraa, Sarkin Makada, *Histoire du Dawra*, tr. Issaka Dankoussou. Niamey, 1970.

Julien, C.-A. *History of North Africa: Tunisia, Algeria, Morocco: from the Arab conquest to 1830*, tr. J. Petrie, ed. C. C. Stewart. London, 1970.

Youssouf Kamal, *Monumenta cartographica Africae et Aegypti*. Cairo and Leiden, 1926–51, 16 vols.

King, A. 'A *boorii* liturgy from Katsina: introduction and *Kiraarii* texts', *African Language Studies*, 1968, **7**.

Koelle, S. W. *African native literature, or proverbs, tales, fables and historical fragments in the Kanuri or Bornu language*. London, 1854.

Krieger, K. *Geschichte von Zamfara*. Berlin, 1959.

Kumm, H. K. W. *From Hausaland to Egypt, through the Sudan*. London, 1910.

Landeroin, M. 'Du Tschad au Niger: notes historiques', *Documents scientifiques de la mission Tilho 1905–9*. Paris, 1911, 3 vols.

Lange, D. 'L'intérieur de l'Afrique occidental d'après Giovanni Lorenzo Anania (XVIe siècle)', *Journal of World History*, 1972, **14**, 299–351.

Lange, D. 'Un vocabulaire kanuri de la fin du XVIIe siècle', *Cahiers d'études africaines*, 1972, **12**, 277–90.

Lebeuf, A. M.-D. 'Boum Massénia, capitale de l'ancien royaume du Baguirmi', *Journal de la Société des Africanistes*, 1967, **37**, 1, 215–44.

Lebeuf, A. M.-D. *Les populations du Tchad*. Paris, 1959.

Lebeuf, J. P. 'The site of Wara', *Journal of the Historical Society of Nigeria*, 1962, **2**, 3, 396–9.

Lebeuf, J. P. and Detourbet, A. M. *La civilisation du Tchad*. Paris, 1950.

Le Coeur, Ch. and M. *Grammaire et textes Téda-Daza*, *Mémoires de l'Institut français d'Afrique noire*, 1965, no. 46, IFAN Dakar.

Lembezat, B. *Les populations païennes du Nord Cameroun et de l'Adamaoua*. Paris, 1961.

Le Rouvreur, A. *Sahéliens et Sahariens du Tchad*. Paris, 1962.

Lethem, G. J. *Colloquial Arabic: Shuwa dialect of Bornu, Nigeria, and of the region of Lake Chad*. London, 1920.

Lewicki, T. *Arabic external sources for the history of Africa to the south of Sahara*. Wroclaw, 1969.

Lovejoy, P. E. 'Notes on the Wangara Chronicle', *Kano Studies*, 1969–70, **2**, 1/2.

Low, V. N. *Three Nigerian emirates: a study in oral history*. Northwestern University Press, Evanston, Illinois, 1972.

Lukas, J. *A study of the Kanuri language*. London, 1937.

Lukas, J. *Zentralsudanische Studien: Wörterverzeichnisse der Deutschen Zentral-Afrika-Expedition 1910/11 nachgelassene Aufnahmen von Gustav Nachtigal und eigene Sammlungen*. Hamburg, 1937.

Martin, B. G. 'Five letters from the Tripoli archives', *Journal of the Historical Society of Nigeria*, 1962, **2**, 3, 350–72.

Martin, B. G. 'Kanem, Bornu, and the Fazzān: notes on the political history of a trade route', *Journal of African History*, 1969, **10**, 15–27.

Marty, P. 'L'Islam et les tribus dans la Colonie du Niger', *Revue des études islamiques*, 1931.

Mason, M. 'The Nupe kingdom in the nineteenth century: a political history'. Ph.D. thesis, University of Birmingham, 1970.

Mauny, R. *Tableau géographique de l'ouest africain au moyen âge d'après les sources écrites, la tradition et l'archéologie*. Dakar, 1961.

Meek, C. K. *A Sudanese kingdom: an ethnographical study of the Jukun-speaking peoples of Nigeria*. London, 1931.

Meek, C. K. *Tribal studies in northern Nigeria*. London, 1931. 2 vols.

Migeod, C. O. *Gazetteer of Yola Province*. Lagos, 1927.

Mischlich A. and Lippert, J. 'Beiträge zur Geschichte der Haussastaaten', *Mittheilungen des Seminars für Orientalische Sprachen zu Berlin*, 1903, **6**.

Mohammed Seghir ben Youssef, *Mechra el melki: chronique tunisienne (1705–1771)*, tr. V. Serres and M. Lasram. Tunis, 1900.

Motylinski, A. de C. *Le dialecte berbère de R'edamès*. Paris, 1904.

Mouchet, J. 'Note sur la conversion à l'Islamisme, en 1715, de la tribu Wandala', *Études camerounaises*, September–December 1946, nos. 15–16.

Nachtigal, G. *Sahara und Sudan*. Berlin 1879, 1881; Leipzig, 1889; complete reprint Graz, 1967. 3 vols. English translation of vol. III of the German, *Wadai and Darfur*. London, 1971.

Nicolaisen, J. *The ecology and culture of the pastoral Tuareg*. Copenhagen, 1964.

Palmer, H. R. 'The Bornu girgam', *Journal of the African Society*, 1912–13, **12**, 45, 71–83.

Palmer, H. R. *Bornu, Sahara and Sudan*. London, 1936.

Palmer, H. R. *Gazetteer of Bornu Province*. London, 1929.

Palmer, H. R. 'History of Katsina', *Journal of the African Society*, April 1927, **26**, 103, 216–36.

Palmer, H. R., ed. and tr. *History of the first twelve years of the reign of Mai Idris Alooma of Bornu, by his Imam, Ahmed Ibn Fartua*. Lagos, 1926, reprinted London, 1970.

Palmer, H. R. 'Notes on the Korôrofawa and Jukon', *Journal of the African Society*, July 1912, **11**, 44, 401–15.

Palmer, H. R. 'Notes on some Asben records', *Journal of the African Society*, 1909–10, **9**, 388–400.

Palmer, H. R., ed. and tr. *Sudanese memoirs: being mainly translations of a number of Arabic manuscripts relating to the Central and Western Sudan*. Lagos, 1928, reprinted London, 1967.

Palmer, H. R. 'Western Sudan history: the Raudthât' ul Afkâri', *Journal of the African Society*, 1915–16, **15**, 261–73.

Pâques, V. 'Origine et caractères du pouvoir royal au Baguirmi', *Journal de la Société des Africanistes*, 1967, **37**, 183–214.

Patterson, J. R. *Kanuri songs*. Lagos, 1926.

Pignon, J. *Un document inédit sur la Tunisie au XVIIe siècle* (Publications de l'Université de Tunis). Tunis (?), n.d.

Prietze, R. 'Bornulieder', *Mitteilungen des Seminars für Orientalische Sprachen zu Berlin*, Dritte Abteilung, Afrikanische Studien, 1914, 134–260.

Rattray, R. S. *Hausa folk-lore, customs, proberbs, etc.* Oxford, 1913. 2 vols.

Richardson, J. *Travels in the great desert of Sahara, in the years of 1845 and 1846...* London, 1848. 2 vols.

Robinson, C. H. *Hausaland*. London, 1900.

Robinson, C. H. *Specimens of Hausa literature*. Cambridge, 1896.

Rodd, F. *People of the veil* (Tuareg). London, 1926.

Rohlfs, G. *Kufra: Reise von Tripolis nach der Oase Kufra*. Leipzig, 1881.

Roncière, C. de la. 'Une histoire du Bornou au XIIIe siècle par un chirurgien français captif à Tripoli', *Revue de l'histoire des colonies françaises*, 1919, 2nd sem., 73–88.

Rossi, E. 'Per la storia della penetrazione turca nell'interno della Libia e per la questione dei suoi confini', *Oriente moderno*, 1929, **9**, 4, 153–67.

Roth, A. and Fourcade, J.-F. *Dossiers de la Recherche Coopérative sur Programme no. 45, Populations anciennes et actuelles des confins tchado-soudanais, dossier 1, Études arabes (1966–7)*. Paris, 1968.

Ruxton, F. H. 'Notes on the tribes of the Muri Province', *Journal of the African Society*, April 1908, **7**, 27, 374–86.

Salifou, A. *Le Damagaram: ou sultanat de Zinder au XIXe siècle*. Niamey, 1971.

Schön, J. F. *Magana Hausa: native literature, or proverbs, tales, fables and historical fragments in the Hausa language, to which is added a translation in English*. London, 1885.

Schultze, A. *The sultanate of Bornu*, tr. and ed. P. A. Benton. 1913. Reprinted London, 1968.

Skinner, N. *Hausa tales and traditions: an English translation of Tatsuniyoyi na hausa, originally compiled by Frank Edgar*, vol. 1. London, 1969.

Smith, Abdullahi. 'Some considerations relating to the formation of states in Hausaland', *Journal of the Historical Society of Nigeria*, 1970, **5**, 3, 329–46.

Smith, H. F. C. 'A seventeenth century writer of Katsina', *Supplement to Bulletin of News*, Historical Society of Nigeria, 1961, **6**, 1.

Smith, H. F. C. 'Source material for the history of the Western Sudan', *Journal of the Historical Society of Nigeria*, 1958, **1**, 3, 238–48.

Smith, M. G. *Government in Zazzau, 1800–1950*. London, 1960.

Sölken, H. 'Die Geschichte von Kabi nach Imam Umaru', *Mitt. Inst. für Orientforschung*, 1959, **7**, 1 and 1963, **9**, 1.

Stenning, D. J. *Savannah nomads: a study of the Wodaabe pastoral Fulani of western Bornu Province, Northern Region, Nigeria*. London, 1959.

Talbot, P. A. 'The Buduma of Lake Chad', *Journal of the Royal Anthropological Institute*, 1911, **41**, 245–59.

Tardivet, R. 'Les sultans de l'Air', *Bulletin de la Comité des études historiques et scientifiques de l'AOF*, 1928, **11**, 689–94.

Temple, O. *Notes on the tribes, provinces, emirates and states of the northern provinces of Nigeria*. 2nd ed. 1922. Reprinted London, 1965.

Tilho. *See* Landeroin.

Tremearne, A. J. N. *Hausa superstitions and customs*. London, 1913.

Trenga, G. *Le Bura-Mabang du Ouadaï: notes pour servir à l'étude de la langue Maba*. Paris, 1947.

Trimingham, J. S. *A history of Islam in West Africa*. London, 1962.

Tubiana, M.-J. 'Un document inédit sur les sultans du Waddāy', *Cahiers d'études africaines*, 1960, **1**, 2, 49–112.

Tubiana, M.-J. *Survivances préislamiques en pays zaghawa*. Paris, 1964.

Tully, R. *Narrative of a ten years' residence at Tripoli in Africa: from the original correspondence in the possession of the family of the late Richard Tully, Esq., the British Consul*. London, 1816.

al-Tūnusī, Muḥammad bin 'Umar [Cheykh Mohammed ibn-Omar el-Tounsy], *Voyage au Ouadây*, tr. Dr Perron. Paris, 1851.

'Umar al-Naqar, *The pilgrimage tradition in West Africa*. Khartoum, 1972.

Urvoy, Y. 'Chroniques d'Agadès', *Journal de la Société des Africanistes*, 1934, **4**, 145–77.

Urvoy, Y. 'Chronologie du Bornou', *Journal de la Société des Africanistes*, 1941, **11**, 21–32.

Urvoy, Y. 'Essai de bibliographie des populations du Soudan central', *Bulletin de la Comité des études historiques et scientifiques de l'AOF*, 1936, **19**, 243 ff.

Urvoy, Y. *Histoire de l'Empire du Bornou*. Paris, 1949. Reprinted Amsterdam, 1968.

Urvoy, Y. *Histoire des populations du Soudan central*. Paris, 1936.

Vadala, R. 'Essais sur l'histoire des Karamanlis, pachas de Tripolitanie de 1714 à 1835', *Revue de l'histoire des colonies françaises*, 1919, pp. 177–288.

Vischer, H. *Across the Sahara from Tripoli to Bornu*. London, 1910.

Wansbrough, J. 'The decolonization of North African history', *Journal of African History*, 1968, **9**, 643–50.
Whitting, C. E. J. *Hausa and Fulani proverbs*. Lagos, 1940. Reprinted 1967.
Zeltner, J. C. 'Le May Idris Alaoma et les Kotoko', *Revue camerounaise d'histoire*, October 1971, **1**, 36–40.

3. THE MAGHRIB AND THE WESTERN SUDAN

'Abd al-'Azīz Batrān. 'Sidi al-Mukhtār al-Kuntī and the recrudescence of Islam in the western Sudan and the middle Niger, c. 1750–1811'. Ph.D. thesis, University of Birmingham, 1971.
Abun-Nasr, J. M. *A history of the Maghrib*. Cambridge, 1971, 2nd edn., 1975.
Alexandre, P. and Froelich, J. C. 'Histoire traditionnelle des Kotokoli et des Bi-Tschambi du Nord-Togo', *Bulletin de l'IFAN*, 1960, **22**, 211–75.
Arcin, A. *Histoire de la Guinée française*. Paris, 1911.
Ba, A. H. and Daget, J. *L'Empire Peul du Macina*. Paris, 1962.
Barbot, J. *A description of the coasts of North and South Guinea*, vol. v of Churchill's *Collection of voyages and travels*. London, 1732.
Barry, B. *Le royaume du Waalo; le Sénégal avant la conquête*. Paris, 1972.
Basset, R. 'Recherches historiques sur les Maures', in Basset, R., *Mission au Sénégal*. Paris, 1900.
Bathily, A. 'Notices socio-historiques sur l'ancien royaume Soninke du Gadiaga', *Bulletin de l'IFAN*, 1969, **31**, 31–105.
Bazin, J. 'Commerce et prédation: l'état Bambara de Ségou et ses communautés Marka.' Unpublished paper, Conference on Manding Studies. London 1972.
Bennett, N. R. 'Christian and negro slaves in eighteenth century North Africa', *Journal of African History*, 1960, **1**, 65–82.
Bernus, E. 'Kong et sa région', *Études éburnéennes*, 1960, **8**, 239–324.
Boulègue, J. *La Sénégambie du milieu du XVe siècle au début du XVIIe siècle*. Ph.D. thesis, University of Paris, 1968.
Boutillier, J. L. 'Politique et commerce: l'insertion des communautés mande-diula dans le royaume de Bouna à l'époque précoloniale'. Unpublished paper, Conference on Manding Studies. London, 1972.
Bovill, E. W. *The golden trade of the Moors*. 2nd ed. London, 1968.
Bowdich, T. E. *A mission from Cape Coast Castle to Ashantee*. London, 1819.
Boyer, G. *Un peuple de l'Ouest africain: les Diawara*. Dakar, 1953.
Brett, M. 'Problems in the interpretation of the history of the Maghrib in the light of some recent publications', *Journal of African History*, 1972, **13**, 489–506.
Brigand, F. *Histoire traditionnelle du Sénégal*. St Louis, 1962.
Brown, W. A. 'The caliphate of Hamdullahi ca. 1818–1864: a study in African history and tradition'. Ph.D. thesis, University of Wisconsin, 1969.
Busnot, D. *Histoire du règne de Mouley Ismael, Roy de Maroc, Fès, Tafilet, Souz, etc*. Rouen, 1714.
Castries, H. de. 'La conquête du Soudan par El-Mansour', *Hespéris*, 1923, **3**, 433–88.

Castries, H. de and others. *Les sources inédites de l'histoire du Maroc*. Paris, 1905–36. 18 vols.
Chapelle, F. de la. 'Esquisse d'une histoire du Sahara occidental', *Hespéris*, 1930, **9**, 35–95.
Chenier, M. *The present state of the empire of Morocco*. London, 1788.
Cissoko, S. M. 'Famines et épidémies à Timbouctou et dans la boucle du Niger du 16e au 18e siècle', *Bulletin de l'IFAN*, 1968, **30**, 806–21.
Cissoko, S. M. 'Introduction à l'histoire des Mandigues de l'Ouest: l'empire de Kabou (16e–19e siècle)'. Unpublished paper, Conference on Manding Studies. London, 1972.
Cissoko, S. M. 'La royauté (*mansaya*) chez les Mandingues occidentaux d'après leurs traditions orales', *Bulletin de l'IFAN*, 1969, **31**.
Cissoko, S. M. 'Traits fondamentaux des sociétés du Soudan occidental du 17e au début du 19e siècle', *Bulletin de l'IFAN*, 1969, **31**, 1–30.
Colin, G. S. ed. *Ta'rīkh al-Dawla al-Sa'diyya* (Chronique anonyme de la dynastie Saâdienne). Rabat, 1934.
Cour, A. *L'Établissement des dynasties des Cherifs au Maroc*. Paris, 1904.
Curtin, P. D. 'Ayuba Suleiman Diallo of Bondu', in Curtin, P. D. ed., *Africa Remembered* (Madison, 1967), pp. 17–59.
Curtin, P. D. *The Atlantic slave trade*. Madison, 1969.
Curtin, P. D. 'Jihad in West Africa: early phases and inter-relations in Mauretania and Senegal', *Journal of African History*, 1971, **12**, 11–24.
Curtin, P. D. 'The western Juula in the eighteenth century'. Unpublished paper, Conference on Manding Studies, London, 1972.
Delafosse, M. 'Les débuts des troupes noires au Maroc', *Hespéris*, 1923, 1–12.
Delafosse, M. 'Les relations du Maroc avec le Soudan à travers les âges', *Hespéris*, 1924, 153–74.
Delcourt, A. *La France et les établissements français au Sénégal entre 1713 et 1763*. Dakar, 1952.
Deschamps, H. 'Les Européens sur les côtes atlantiques aux 17e et 18e siècles', in Deschamps, H., ed., *Histoire générale de l'Afrique Noire*, vol. 1. Paris, 1970.
Désiré-Vuillemin, Mme. 'Les grands traits de l'histoire de la Mauritanie', in Deschamps, H., ed., *Histoire générale de l'Afrique Noire*, vol. 1. Paris, 1970.
Deverdun, G. *Marrakech des origines à 1912*. Rabat, 1966.
Diagne, P. 'Le royaumes Sérères', *Présence africaine*, 1965, **54**, 142–72.
Diop, A. B. 'Lat-Dior et le problème musulman', *Bulletin de l'IFAN*, 1966, **28**.
Dupuis, J. *Journal of a residence in Ashantee*. London, 1824.
Fisher, G. *Barbary legend*. Oxford, 1957.
al-Fishtālī, 'Abd al-'Azīz. *Manāhil al-ṣafā'*, ed. A. Ganun. Rabat, 1964.
Genevière, J. 'Les Kountas et leurs activités commerciales', *Bulletin de l'IFAN*, 1960, **12**, 1111–27.
Girard, J. 'Notes sur l'histoire traditionnelle de la Haute Casamance', *Bulletin de l'IFAN*, 1966, **28**, 540–54.
Golbéry, S. M. X. *Fragmens d'un voyage en Afrique*. Paris, 1802.
Goody, J. 'The over-kingdom of Gonja', in Forde, C. D. and Kaberry,

P. M., eds., *West African kingdoms in the nineteenth century* (London, 1967), pp. 179–205.

Gray, J. M. *A history of the Gambia*. London, 1940.

Hallett, R. ed. *Records of the African Association*. London, 1964.

Hamet, I. *Chroniques de la Mauritanie Sénégalaise*. Paris, 1911.

Hamet, I. 'Les Kounta', *Revue du Monde Musulman*, 1911, **15**, 302–18.

Hamet, I. 'Littérature Arabe Saharienne', *R.M.M.*, 1910, **12**, 194–213.

Hecquard. *Voyage sur la côte et dans l'intérieur de l'Afrique occidentale*. Paris, 1853.

Houdas, O. ed. and tr. *Tadhkirat al-nisyān fī akhbār mulūk al-Sūdān*. Paris, 1913–14.

Hunwick, J. O. 'Ahmad Baba and the Moroccan invasion of the Sudan', *Journal of the Historical Society of Nigeria*, 1962, **2**, 3, 311–28.

Ibn al-Mukhtār. *Ta'rīkh al-Fattāsh*, ed. and tr. by O. Houdas and M. Delafosse. Paris, 1913–14.

al-Ifrānī. *Nuzhat al-ḥādī bi-akhbār mulūk al-qaru al-ḥādī*. Paris, 1888. French translation by Houdas, O. *Histoire de la dynastie saadienne au Maroc (1511–1670)*. Paris, 1889.

Izard, M. *Introduction à l'histoire des royaumes Mossi*. Paris–Ouagadougou, 1970.

Jackson, J. G. *An account of the empire of Marocco*. London, 1814.

Jackson, J. G. *An account of Timbuctoo and Hausa*. London, 1820.

Jobson, R. *The golden trade*. London, 1623.

Julien, C. A. *Histoire de l'Afrique du Nord*, vol. II. Paris, 1961. English translation by Petrie, J. *History of North Africa*. London, 1970.

Kaba, L. 'Les Mandinka-Moré de Baté en Guinée: étude préliminaire d'ethnohistoire'. Unpublished paper, Conference on Manding Studies. London, 1972.

Kane, O. 'Essai de chronologie des *satigis* du 18e siècle', *Bulletin de l'IFAN*, 1970, **32**, 755–65.

Kesteloot, L. 'Introduction to an episode in the Bambara epic of Segou'. Unpublished paper, Conference on Manding Studies. London, 1972.

Labat, J. B. *Nouvelle relation de l'Afrique occidentale*. Paris, 1728.

Laing, A. G. *Travels in the Timanee, Kooranko, and Solima countries*. London, 1815.

Laroui, A. *L'histoire du Maghrib*. Paris, 1970.

Lévi-Provençal, E. 'Un document inédit sur l'expédition sa'dide au Soudan', *Arabica*, 1955, **2**, 89–96.

Lévi-Provençal, E. *Les historiens des Chorfe*. Paris, 1922.

Levtzion, N. *Muslims and chiefs in West Africa: a study of Islam in the middle Volta basin in the pre-colonial period*. Oxford, 1968.

Levtzion, N. 'Note sur les états dyula de Kong et de Bobo', *Bulletin de Liaison, Centre universitaire de Recherches de Développement*, 1971, **1**, 61–2.

Levtzion, N. 'Notes sur les origines de l'Islam militant au Fouta Djalon', *Notes africaines*, October 1971, no. 132, 94–6.

Levtzion, N. 'A seventeenth century chronicle by Ibn al-Mukhtār: a critical review of Ta'rikh al-Fattāsh', *Bulletin of the School of Oriental and African Studies*, 1971, **34**, 571–93.

Leynaud, E. 'Fraternités d'âge et sociétés de culture dans la haute-vallée du Niger', *Cahiers d études africaines*, 1966, **6**, 41–68.

Leyti, Oumar N'Diaye. 'Le Djoloff et ses Bourbas', *Bulletin de l'IFAN*, 1966, **28**, 966–1008.

Lombard, J. 'Le Sénégal et la Gambie', in Deschamps, H., ed., *Histoire générale de l'Afrique Noire*, vol. I. Paris, 1970.

Lombard, J. *Structures de type 'féodal' en Afrique Noire: études des dynamismes internes et des relations sociales chez les Bariba du Dahomey*. Paris, 1965.

Ly, Abdoulaye. *La compagnie du Sénégal*. Paris, 1958.

Martin, A. G. P. *Quatre siècles d'histoire marocaine*. Paris, 1923.

Marty, P. *L'Émirat des Trarzas*. Paris, 1919.

Marty, P. *Études sur l'Islam en Guinée*. Paris, 1921.

Marty, P. *Études sur l'Islam et les tribus du Soudan*. Paris, 1920.

Marty, P. ed. and tr. 'Les chroniques de Oualata et de Nema', *Revue des études islamiques*, 1927, **1**, 355–426, 531–575.

Masson, P. *Histoire des établissements et du commerce français dans l'Afrique barbaresque, 1560–1793*. Paris, 1903.

Meillassoux, C. 'Histoire et institutions du *kafo* de Bamako', *Cahiers d'études africaines*, 1963–4, **4**, 186–227.

Mojuetan, B. A. 'The rise of the Alawi dynasty in Morocco, 1631–72'. Ph.D. thesis, University of London, 1969.

Mollien, C. T. *L'Afrique occidentale en 1818*, ed. H. Deschamps. Paris, 1967.

Montagne, R. *Les Berbères et le makhzen dans le sud du Maroc*. Paris, 1930.

Monteil, C. *Les Bambara du Ségou et du Kaarta*. Paris, 1924.

Monteil, C. *Une cité soudanaise: Djenné*. Paris, 1932.

Monteil, C. *Les Khassonké: monographie d'une peuplade du Soudan française*. Paris, 1915.

Monteil, V. 'Contribution à la sociologie des Peuls (Le "Fonds Vieillard" de l'IFAN)', *Bulletin de l'IFAN*, 1963, **25**, 351–414.

Monteil, V. 'Le Dyoloff et Albouri N'Diaye', *Bulletin de l'IFAN*, 1966, **28**, 595–637.

Moore, Francis. *Travels into the inland parts of Africa*. London, 1738.

Mota, A. Teixeira da. *Guiné Portuguesa*. Lisbon, 1954.

Mouëtte, G. *Histoire des conquestes de Mouley Archy, connu sous le nom de Roy de Tafilet; et de Mouley Ismael*. Paris, 1683.

Mouëtte, G. *Relation de la captivité du sieur Mouette dans les royaumes de Fez et de Maroc*. Paris, 1683.

al-Nāṣirī, Aḥmad b. Khālid al-Salāwī. *Kitāb al-Istiqṣā li-akhbār duwal al-Maghrib al-aqṣā*. Cairo, 1894. Tr. in *Archives marocaines*, 1906, vol. IX, 1936, vol. XXXIV.

Nicolaisen, J. *Ecology and culture of the pastoral Tuareg*. Copenhagen, 1964.

Norris, H. T. 'Znaga Islam during the seventeenth and eighteenth centuries', *Bull. SOAS*, 1969, **32**, 496–526.

Pageard, R. *Notes sur l'histoire des Bambara du Ségou*. Paris, 1957.

Pageard, R. 'La marche orientale du Mali (Ségou–Djenné) en 1644 d'après le *Tarikh es-Soudan*', *Journal de la Société des Africanistes*, 1961, **31**, 75–90.

Pâques, V. *Les Bambara*. Paris, 1954.

Park, Mungo. *Travels in Africa*. Everyman's Library, London, 1969.
Park, Mungo. *Travels in the interior districts of Africa*. London, 1799.
Pellow, T. *The adventures of T. P. of Penryn, mariner*, ed. A. Brown. London, 1890.
Person, Y. 'Les ancêtres de Samori', *Cahiers d'études africaines*, 1963, **4**, 125–56.
Person, Y. 'The Dyula and the Manding world'. Unpublished paper, Conference on Manding Studies. London, 1972.
Person, Y. 'En quête d'une chronologie ivoirienne', in Vansina, J., Mauny, R. and Thomas, L. V., eds., *The historian in tropical Africa*. London, 1964.
Person, Y. 'Les Kissi et leurs statuettes de pierre', *Bulletin de l'IFAN*, 1960, **23**, 47–57.
Person, Y. 'Nyani Mansa Mamudu et la fin de l'empire du Mali'. Unpublished paper, Conference on Manding Studies. London, 1972.
Person, Y. 'Samori et la Sierra Leone', *Cahiers d'études africaines*, 1967, **7**, 5–26.
Person, Y. *Samori: une révolution dyula*. Dakar, 1968.
Person, Y. 'Le Soudan nigérien et la Guinée occidentale', in Deschamps, H., ed., *Histoire générale de l'Afrique Noire*, vol. I. Paris, 1970.
Proceedings of the Association for Promoting the Discovery of the Interior Parts of Africa. London, 1810. Repr. London, 1967.
Rançon, A. *Le Bondou: étude de géographie et d'histoire soudanaise de 1861 à nos jours*. Bordeaux, 1894.
Richer, A. *Les Oullimidens*. Paris, 1925.
Ritchie, C. I. A. 'Deux textes sur le Sénégal (1673–1677)', *Bulletin de l'IFAN*, 1968, **30**, 289–353.
Robinson, D., Curtin, P. D. and Johnson, J. 'A tentative chronology of Futa Toro from the sixteenth through the nineteenth centuries', *Cahiers d'études africaines*, 1972, **12**, 4, 555–92.
Rodney, W. *A history of the Upper Guinea coast, 1545 to 1800*. Oxford, 1969.
Rodney, W. 'Jihad and social revolution in Futa Djalon in the eighteenth century', *Journal of the Historical Society of Nigeria*, 1968, **4**, 269–84.
Rouch, J. *Contribution à l'histoire des Songhay*. Dakar, 1953.
al-Sa'dī, 'Abd al-Raḥmān. *Ta'rīkh al-Sūdān*, ed. and tr. O. Houdas. Paris, 1898–1900.
Saint-Père, J. H. B. de. 'Création du royaume du Fouta Djallon', *Bulletin du Comité d'études historiques et scientifiques de l'AOF*, 1929, **12**.
Saki Olal N'Diaye. 'The story of Malik Sy', ed. and tr. A. N. Skinner and P. D. Curtin, in *Cahiers d'études africaines*, 1971, **11**, 467–87.
Sidibe, B. K. 'The story of Kaabu'. Unpublished paper, Conference on Manding Studies. London, 1972.
Smith, P. 'Les Diakhanke: histoire d'une dispersion', *Bull. et Mém. de la Société d'Anthropologie de Paris*, XIe série, 1965, **8**, 231–62.
Soh, Siré Abbas. *Chroniques du Fouta Sénégalais*, tr. M. Delafosse and H. Gaden. Paris, 1913.
Stewart, C. C. *Islam and social order in Mauritania: a case study from the nineteenth century* [*with special reference to Shaikh Sidiyya al-Kabir*]. Oxford, 1973.

Suret-Canale, J. 'The western Atlantic coast, 1600–1800', in Ajayi, J. F. A. and Crowder, M., eds. *History of West Africa* (London, 1971), I, 387–440.

Tauxier, L. *Histoire des Bambara*. Paris, 1942.

Tauxier, L. *Moeurs et histoire des Peuls*. Paris, 1937.

Terrasse, H. *Histoire du Maroc*, vol. II. Casablanca, 1950.

Traoré, D. 'Notes sur le royaume mandingue de Bobo', *Éducation africaine*, 1937, **26**.

Trimingham, J. S. *A history of Islam in West Africa*. London, 1962.

Vieillard, G. 'Notes sur les Peuls du Fouta-Djallon', *Bulletin de l'IFAN*, 1940, **2**, 85–210.

Wade, Ahmadu. 'Chronique du Walo Sénégalais', pub. and annotated V. Monteil, *Bulletin de l'IFAN*, 1964, **26**, 440–98.

Wilks, I. 'Abu Bakr al-Siddiq of Timbuktu', in Curtin, P. D., ed., *Africa remembered*. Madison, 1967.

Wilks, I. 'The Mossi and Akan states 1500–1800', in Ajayi, J. F. A. and Crowder, M., eds. *History of West Africa* (London, 1971), I, 344–86.

Wilks, I. *The northern factor in Ashanti history*. Legon, 1961.

Wilks, I. 'The transmission of Islamic learning in the Western Sudan', in Goody, J., ed. *Literacy in traditional societies* (Cambridge, 1968), 161–97.

Willis, J. R. 'The Western Sudan from the Moroccan invasion (1591) to the death of al-Mukhtār al-Kuntī', in Ajayi, J. F. A. and Crowder, M., eds. *History of West Africa* (London, 1971), I, 441–84.

al-Zayyānī. *al-Turjmān al-mu'rib 'an duwal al-mashriq wa'l-maghrib*. French translation by Houdas, O. *Le Maroc de 1631 à 1812*. Paris, 1886.

4. THE GUINEA COAST

Adams, J. *Remarks on the country extending from Cape Palmas to the River Congo*. London, 1968. Reprint of 1823 ed.

Adandé, A. *Les récades des rois du Dahomey*. Dakar, 1962.

Agyeman, E. A. 'Gyaman – its relations with Ashanti, 1720–1820'. M.A. thesis, University of Ghana, 1965.

Ajayi, J. F. and Crowder, M. eds. *History of West Africa*, vol. I, London, 1971.

Akindélé, A. and Aguessy, C. *Contribution à l'étude de l'ancien royaume de Porto Novo*. Dakar, 1953.

Akinjogbin, I. A. *Dahomey and its neighbours 1708–1818*. Cambridge, 1967.

Akintoye, S. A. 'The north-eastern districts of the Yoruba Country and the Benin Kingdom', *Journal of the Historical Society of Nigeria*, 1969, **4**, 4.

Alagoa, E. J. 'Long distance trade and states in the Niger delta', *Journal of African History*, 1970, **11**, 3.

Alagoa, E. J. 'Nembe: the city idea in the Eastern Niger Delta', *Cahiers d'études africaines*, 1971, **11**, 41.

Alagoa, E. J. *The small brave city state: a history of the Nembe Brass in the Niger Delta*. Ibadan, 1964.

Anguiano, M. de. *Misiones Capuchinas en Africa*, ed. Buenaventura de Carrocera, vol. II. Madrid, 1957.
Arcin, A. *Histoire de la Guinée française*. Paris, 1911.
Argyle, W. J. *The Fon of Dahomey*. Oxford, 1966.
Arhin, K. 'The structure of Greater Ashanti, 1700–1824', *Journal of African History*, 1967, **8**, 1.
Astley, T. *A new collection of voyages and travels*. London, 1968. Reprint of 1743–7 ed. 4 vols.
Atkins, J. *A voyage to Guinea, Brazil and the West Indies*. London, 1970. Reprint of 1735 ed.
Azevedo, W. d'. 'Some historical problems in the delineation of a central West Atlantic region', *Annals of the New York Academy of Sciences*, 1962, **96**.
Barbot, J. *A description of the coasts of North and South Guinea*. London, 1732.
Barcelos, C. J. de Sena. *Subsidios para a história de Cabo Verde e Guiné*. Lisbon 1899–1913.
Barreto, J. *História da Guiné*. Lisbon, 1938.
Bosman, W. *A new and accurate description of the coast of Guinea*. London, 1967. Reprint of 1705 ed.
Bradbury, R. E. and Lloyd, P. C. *The Benin Kingdom and the Edo-speaking peoples of south-western Nigeria, together with a section on the Itsekiri*. International African Institute, London, 1957.
Brásio, A. *Monumenta Missionária Africana: Africa Ocidental*. Lisbon, 1952 onwards.
Carson, P. *Materials for West African History in the archives of Belgium and Holland*. London, 1962.
Cissoko, S. M. 'Introduction à l'histoire des Mandingues de l'Ouest: l'empire de Kabou (XVIe–XIXe siècle)'. Unpublished paper, Conference on Manding Studies, London, 1972.
Cissoko, S. M. 'La royauté (*mansaya*) chez les Mandingues occidentaux, d'après leurs traditions orales', *Bulletin de l'IFAN*, 1969, **31**, ser. B, 2.
Crow, H. *Memoirs of the late Captain Hugh Crow of Liverpool*. London, 1970. Reprint of 1830 ed.
Claridge, W. *A history of the Gold Coast and Ashanti*, 2 vols. London, 1915. Reprint, 1961.
Cornevin, R. *Histoire du Togo*. Paris, 1959.
Cornevin, R. *Histoire du Dahomey*. Paris, 1962.
Cultru, P. *Premier voyage de Sieur de la Courbe fait à la coste d'Afrique en 1685*. Paris, 1906.
Curtin, P. D. ed. *Africa Remembered*. Madison, 1967.
Curtin, P. D. *The Atlantic slave trade: a census*. Madison, 1969.
Daaku, K. Y. *Trade and politics on the Gold Coast, 1600–1720*. Oxford, 1970.
Dalby, D. 'The Mel languages: a reclassification of the southern "West Atlantic"', *African Language Studies*, 1965, **8**.
Dalzel, A. *History of Dahomey*. London, 1967. Reprint of 1793 ed.

Davies, K. G. *The Royal African Company*. London, 1957.
Dike, K. O. *Trade and politics in the Niger delta 1830–1885*. Oxford, 1956.
Egharevba, J. U. *A short history of Benin*. 1934. 3rd ed. Ibadan, 1960.
Equiano, O. *The interesting narrative of the life of Olaudah Equiano*. 1789. Abridged and ed., Paul Edwards, as *Equiano's travels*. London, 1967.
Field, M. J. *Social organisation of the Gã people*. London, Crown Agents, 1940.
Foà, E. *Le Dahomey*. Paris, 1895.
Folayan, K. 'Egbado to 1832, the birth of a dilemma', *Journal of the Historical Society of Nigeria*, 1967, **4**, 1.
Forde, D. ed. *Efik traders of Old Calabar*. London, 1956.
Forde, D. and Kaberry, P. M. eds. *West African kingdoms in the nineteenth century*. Oxford, 1967.
Goody, J. and Arhin, K. eds. *Ashanti and the North-west*. Legon, 1965.
Guerreiro, F. *Relação anual das coisas que fizeram os Padres...nos anos de 1600 a 1609*, ed. A. Viegas. Lisbon, 1930–42. 3 vols.
Hair, P. E. H. 'Ethnolinguistic continuity on the Guinea Coast', *Journal of African History*, 1967, **8**, 2.
Hair, P. E. H. 'An ethnolinguistic inventory of the Lower Guinea coast before 1700: Part 1', *African Language Review*, 1968, **7**.
Hair, P. E. H. 'An ethnolinguistic inventory of the Upper Guinea coast before 1700', *African Language Review*, 1967, **6**.
Hazoumé, P. *Le pact du sang au Dahomey*. Paris, 1937.
Herskovits, M. J. *Dahomey, an ancient West African Kingdom*. New York, 1938.
Hopkins, A. G. *An economic history of West Africa*. London, 1973.
Horton, R. 'From fishing village to city-state: a social history of New Calabar', in M. Douglas and P. Kaberry, eds., *Man in Africa*. London, 1969.
Isichei, E. *The Ibo people and the Europeans*. London, 1973.
Jobson, R. *The golden trade or a discovery of the River Gambra*. London, 1632.
Johnson, S. *History of the Yorubas*, ed. O. Johnson. Lagos, 1921.
Jones, G. I. *The trading states of the Oil Rivers*. London, 1963.
Kumah, J. E. 'Denkyira, 1600–1730 A.D.'. M.A. thesis, Legon, 1965.
Kup, P. *A history of Sierra Leone, 1400–1787*. London, 1961.
Labat, J. B. *Nouvelle relation de l'Afrique Occidentale*. Paris, 1728.
Labouret, H. and Rivet, P. *Le royaume d'Arda et son évangélisation au XVIIe siècle*. Paris, 1929.
Latham, A. J. H. *Old Calabar 1600–1891*. Oxford, 1973.
Law, R. C. C. 'The fall of Allada, 1724 – an ideological revolution?', *Journal of the Historical Society of Nigeria*, 1969, **4**, 4.
Law, R. C. C. 'The Ọyọ Empire: the history of a Yoruba state, principally in the period c. 1600–c. 1836'. Ph.D. thesis, University of Birmingham, 1971.
Le Herissé, A. *L'ancien royaume du Dahomey*. Paris, 1911.
Leonard, A. G. *The Lower Niger and its tribes*. London, 1968. Reprint of 1906 ed.
Little, K. *The Mende of Sierra Leone*. London, 1951.
Machat, J. *Documents sur les établissements français de l'Afrique Occidentale au XVIIIe siècle*. Paris, 1906.
Matthews, J. *A voyage to the River Sierra Leone*. London, 1966. Reprint of 1788 ed.

Mensah, A. A. 'The Guans in Music'. M.A. thesis, Legon, 1966.
Meyerowitz, E. *The Akan of Ghana*. London, 1958.
Moore, W. A. *History of the Itsekiri*. London, 1970. Reprint of 1936 ed.
Mota, A. Teixeira da. *Guiné Portuguesa*. Lisbon, 1954. 2 vols.
Newton, J. *Journal of a slave trader*, ed. B. Martin and M. Spurrell. London, 1957.
Nørregård, G. *Danish settlements in West Africa, 1658–1950*. Boston, 1968.
Ogilby, J. *Africa*. 1670.
Ozanne, P. 'Notes on the later prehistory of Accra', *Journal of the Historical Society of Nigeria*, 1964, **3**, 1.
Parrinder, E. G. *The story of Ketu*. Ibadan, 1956.
Partridge, C. *Cross River natives*. London, 1905.
Person, Y. 'Les Kissi et leurs statuettes de pierre', *Bulletin de l'IFAN*, 1961, **23**, ser B, no. 1.
Polanyi, K. *Dahomey and the slave trade*. Washington, 1966.
Priestley, M. *West African trade and coast society*. Oxford, 1969.
Priestley, M. and Wilks, I. 'The Ashanti kings in the eighteenth century: a revised chronology', *Journal of African History*, 1960, **1**, 1.
Rattray, R. S. *Ashanti*. Oxford, 1923.
Rattray, R. S. *Ashanti law and constitution*. Oxford, 1929.
Reindorf, C. C. *The history of the Gold Coast and Asante*. Accra, 1966. Reprint of 1895 ed.
Rodney, W. *A history of the Upper Guinea coast 1540–1800*. Oxford, 1970.
Roemer, R. F. *The coast of Guinea*, part IV, 'African history, customs and way of life', tr. from Danish ed. of 1760. Legon, 1964.
Ryder, A. F. C. *Benin and the Europeans 1485–1897*. London, 1969.
Ryder, A. F. C. *Materials for West African history in Portuguese archives*. London, 1965.
Sidibe, B. K. 'The story of Kaabu'. Unpublished paper, Conference on Manding Studies, London, 1972.
Smith, R. S. *Kingdoms of the Yoruba*. London, 1969.
Smith, W. *A new voyage to Guinea*. London, 1744.
Talbot, P. A. *The peoples of Southern Nigeria*. London, 1969. Reprint of 1926 ed. 4 vols.
Tenkorang, S. 'British slave trading activities on the Gold and Slave Coasts in the eighteenth century and their effect on African society'. M.A. thesis, University of London, 1964.
Thomas, L. *Les Diola*. Dakar, 1959. 2 vols.
Uchendu, V. C. *The Igbo of Southeast Nigeria*. London, 1965.
Ukwu, U. I. 'The development of trade and marketing in Iboland', *Journal of the Historical Society of Nigeria*, 1967, **3**, 4.
Verger, P. *Bahia and the West Coast trade, 1549–1851*. Ibadan, 1964.
Wilks, I. 'Aspects of bureaucratization in Ashanti in the nineteenth century', *Journal of African History*, 1966, **7**, 2.
Wilks, I. *The northern factor in Ashanti History*. Legon, 1961.
Wilks, I. 'The rise of the Akwamu Empire, 1650–1710', *Transactions of the Historical Society of Ghana*, 1957, **3**, 3.

5. CENTRAL AFRICA FROM THE CAMEROUN TO THE ZAMBEZI

Almeida, F. J. de Lacerda e. *Travessia da África*. Lisbon, 1936.

Angola. *Catalogo dos Governadores do Reino de Angola*. Lisbon, 1825. Reprinted in *Arquivos de Angola*. 1937.

António, M. *See* Oliveira, M. A. F.

Ardener, E. W. 'Trading polities between Rio del Rey and Cameroons 1500–1650', in Lewis, I. M., ed. *History and social anthropology*. London, 1968.

Arquivos de Angola. Review published occasionally since 1933 in Luanda.

Axelson, S. *Culture confrontation in the lower Congo*. Uppsala, 1970.

Bal, W. ed. *Description du Royaume de Congo et des contrées environnantes par Filippo Pigafetta et Duarte Lopes (1591)*. Louvain, 1963.

Balandier, G. *La vie quotidienne au royaume du Congo du XVIe au XVIIIe siècle*. Paris, 1965. English tr. 1968.

Barbot, J. and Casseneuve, J. 'An abstract of a voyage to the Congo River or Zaire and to Cabinda in the year 1700', in Churchill, A., *A collection of voyages and travels*. London, 1732.

Battell, A. *See* Ravenstein, E. G.

Biebuyck, D. 'Fondements de l'organisation politique des Lunda du Mwaantayaav en territoire de Kapanga', *Zaïre*, 1957, **11**, 8, 787–817.

Biographie coloniale Belge. Bruxelles, 1948–56. 5 vols.

Birmingham, D. *Trade and conflict in Angola: the Mbundu and their neighbours under the influence of the Portuguese, 1483–1790*. Oxford, 1966.

Bontinck, F. ed. *Brève relation de la fondation de la mission des Frères Mineurs capucins...au royaume de Congo*. Louvain, 1964.

Bontinck, F. ed. *Diaire Congolais de Fra Luca da Caltanisetta, 1690–1701*. Louvain, 1970.

Bontinck, F. ed. 'Histoire du Royaume de Congo (c. 1624)', *Études d'histoire africaine*, 1972, **4**.

Bohannan, P. and Dalton, G. *Markets in Africa*. Evanston, 1962. Especially ch. 7 by Jan Vansina and ch. 8 by Mary Douglas.

Bouchaud, J. *La côte du Cameroun dans l'histoire et la cartographie*. Douala, 1952.

Bouveignes, O. de and Cuvelier, J. *Jérôme de Montesarchio*. Namur, 1951.

Boxer, C. R. *The Dutch seaborne empire 1600–1800*. London, 1965.

Boxer, C. R. *The Portuguese seaborne empire 1415–1825*. London, 1969.

Boxer, C. R. *Portuguese society in the tropics*. Madison, 1965.

Boxer, C. R. *Race relations in the Portuguese colonial empire*. Oxford, 1963.

Boxer, C. R. 'Uma relação inedita e contemporâea da Batalha de Ambuíla em 1665', *Boletim Cultural do Museu de Angola*, 1960.

Boxer, C. R. *Salvador de Sá and the struggle for Brazil and Angola 1602–1886*. London, 1952.

Brásio, A. *Monumenta Missionária Africana: Africa Ocidental* (1st series). Lisbon, 1952 onwards.

Brito, Domingos de Abreu e. 'Sumário e descripção do reino de Angola...', in Felner, A. A., *Um inquérito à vida administrativa de Angola*... Coimbra, 1931.

Burton, R. F. *The lands of Cazembe*. London, 1873.
Byvang, M. van der. 'Notice historique sur les Balunda', *Congo*, 1937, **1**, 2.
Cadornega, A. de Oliveira de. *História geral das guerras Angolanas*, ed. M. Delgado and A. da Cunha. Lisbon, 1940–2. 3 vols.
Calonne-Beaufaict, A. de. *Azande*. Brussels, 1921.
Carvalho, H. A. Dias de. *Expedição ao muatiânvua: ethnographia e história tradicional dos povos da Lunda*. Lisbon, 1890.
Carvalho, H. A. Dias de. *O Jagado de Cassange na Provincia de Angola*. Lisbon, 1898.
Cavazzi [da Montecuccolo]. *Istorica descrizione de tre regni, Congo, Matamba et Angola*. Bologna, 1687. New annotated Portuguese tr. Lisbon, 1965. 2 vols.
Childs, G. M. *Umbundu kinship and character*. London, 1949. Reprinted as *Kinship and character of the Ovimbundu*.
Coimbra, D. *Livros de oficios para o Reino, 1726–1801*. Luanda, 1959.
Cordeiro, L. *Questóes histórico-coloniais*. Lisbon, 1935–6. 3 vols. Includes six reports originally published separately in 1881 as *Memórias do Ultramar*.
Corrêa, E. A. da S. *História de Angola [1792]*. Lisbon, 1937. 2 vols.
Couto, C. *Os Capitães-Mores em Angola no século XVIII*. Luanda, 1972.
Cunnison, I. *The Luapula peoples of Northern Rhodesia*. Manchester, 1959.
Cunnison, I. ed. and tr. *King Kazembe*. Lisbon, 1962.
Curtin, P. D. *The Atlantic slave trade: a census*. Madison, 1969.
Cuvelier, J. *L'ancien royaume de Congo*. Brussels, 1946.
Cuvelier, J. *Documents sur une mission française au Kakongo, 1766–1776*. Brussels, 1953.
Cuvelier, J. and Jadin, L. *L'Ancien Congo d'après les archives romaines, 1518–1640*. Brussels, 1954.
Dampierre, E. de. *Un ancien royaume Bandia du Haut-Oubangui*. Paris, 1967.
Dartevelle, E. 'Les N'Zimbu, monnaie du royaume du Congo', *Société Royale Belge d'Archéologie et Préhistoire*, 1953, **64**, 1.
Davidson, B. *Black mother*. London, 1961.
Davidson, B. *The Africans*. London, 1970.
Davies, K. G. *The Royal African Company 1672–1713*. London, 1957.
Degrandpré, L. *Voyage à la côte occidentale d'Afrique faits dans les années 1786 et 1787*. Paris, 1801. 2 vols.
Delgado, R. *A famosa e histórica Benguela*. Lisbon, 1940.
Delgado, R. 'O Governo de Souza Continho em Angola', *Studia*, 1960–2.
Delgado, R. *História de Angola*. Benguela and Lobito, 1948–55. 4 vols.
Delgado, R. *O reino de Benguela*. Lisbon, 1945.
Delgado, R. *Ao Sul do Cuanza*. Lisbon, 1944. 2 vols.
Dias, G. S. *A Batalha de Ambuila*. Lisbon, 1942.
Dias, G. S. *Os Portugueses em Angola*. Lisbon, 1959.
Dias, G. S. *Relações de Angola*. Coimbra, 1934.
Dias, G. S. 'Uma Viagem a Cassange nos meados do século XVIII [by Manuel Correia Leitão], *Boletim da Sociedade de Geografia de Lisboa*, 1958, **56**.

Doutreloux, A. *L'Ombre des fétiches: société et cultures Yombe*. Louvain, 1967.

Duysters, L. 'Histoire des Aluunda', *Problèmes de l'Afrique Centrale*, 1958, **12**.

Estermann, C. *Etnografia do sudoeste de Angola*. Lisbon, 1956–61. 3 vols.

Felner, A. de A. *Angola, apontamentos sobre a ocupação e inicio do estabelecimento dos Portugueses no Congo, Angola e Benguela*. Coimbra, 1933.

Graça, J. R. 'Expedição ao Muatayanvua', *Boletim da Sociedade de Geografia de Lisboa*, 1890, **9**.

Gray, R. and Birmingham, D. eds. *Pre-colonial African trade*. London, 1970.

Guerreiro, F. *Relação anual das coisas que fizeram os padres da Companhia de Jesus*... 2nd ed. Coimbra, 1930–42. 3 vols.

Haveaux, G. L. *La tradition historique des Bapende orientaux*. Brussels, 1954.

Hildebrand, P. *Le Martyr Georges de Geel et les débuts de la mission du Congo 1645–1652*. Anvers, 1940.

Ihle, A. *Das Alte Königreich Kongo*. Leipzig, 1929.

Jadin, L. 'Aperçu de la situation du Congo et rites d'élection des rois en 1775', *Bulletin de l'Institut Historique Belge de Rome*, 1963, **35**, 246–419.

Jadin, L. 'Le clergé séculier et les Capucins du Congo et d'Angola...conflicts de jurisdictions 1700–1726', *BIHBR*, 1964, **36**, 185–483.

Jadin, L. 'Le Congo et la secte des Antoniens', *BIHBR*, 1961, **33**, 411–615.

Jadin, L. 'Pero Tavares, missionaire jésuite et ses travaux apostoliques au Congo et en Angola 1629–1635', *BIHBR*, 1967, **38**, 271–402.

Jadin, L. 'Relations sur le Congo et l'Angola tirées des archives de la Compagnie de Jésus 1621–1631', *BIHBR*, 1968, **39**, 333–454.

Jadin, L. 'Rivalités luso-néerlandaises au Sohio, Congo, 1600–1675', *BIHBR*, 1966, **37**, 137–359.

Kalck, P. *Histoire centrafricaine*. Paris, 1973.

Kerken, G. van der. *L'ethnie Mongo*. Brussels, 1944.

Lima, J. J. Lopes de. *Ensaios sobre o statistica das possessões Portuguezas*, vol. III, *Angola e Benguella*. Lisbon, 1846.

Lopes, E. *A Escravatura, subsídios para a sua história*. Lisbon. 1944.

Lucas, S. A. 'Baluba et Aruund: étude comparative des structures sociopolitiques'. Ph.D. thesis, Paris, 1968.

Mainga, M. *Bulozi under the Luyana kings*. London, 1973.

Mannix, D. P. and Cowley, M. *Black cargoes: a history of the Atlantic slave trade 1518–1865*. New York, 1962.

Manso, M. L. J. Visconde de Paiva. *História do Congo* (*Documentos*). Lisbon, 1877.

Martin, P. *The external trade of the Loango coast 1576–1870*. Oxford, 1972.

Miller, J. C. 'Kings and kinsmen: the Imbangala impact on the Mbundu of Angola'. Ph.D. thesis, University of Wisconsin, 1971.

Mota, A. T. da. *A Cartografia antiga da Africa central e a travessia entre Angola e Mozambique, 1500–1860*. Lourenço Marques, 1964.

Neves, A. R. *Memória da Expedição a Cassange*. Lisbon, 1854.

Oliveira, M. A. F. de. *Angolana—Documentação sobre Angola*. Lisbon, 1968 (in progress).

Planquaert, M. *Les Jaga et les Bayaka du Kwango*. Brussels, 1932. Revised ed. 1972.

Randles, W. G. L. *L'ancien royaume du Congo des origines à la fin du XIXe siècle*. Paris, 1968.

Ratelband, K. ed. *Reizen naar West-Afrika van Pieter van den Broecke 1605–1614*. The Hague, 1950.

Ratelband, K. ed. *De West Afrikaansche Reis van Piet Heyn 1624–5*. The Hague, 1959.

Ravenstein, E. G. *The strange adventures of Andrew Battell of Leigh in Angola and the adjoining regions*. London, 1901.

Redinha, J. *Etnossociologia do nordeste de Angola*. Lisbon, 1958.

Rego, A. da Silva. *A dupla restauração de Angola (1641–1648)*. Lisbon, 1948.

Rego, A. da Silva. *O Ultramar Português no século XVIII (1700–1833)*. Lisbon, 1970.

Rinchon, P. D. *Les armements négriers au XVIIIe siècle*. Brussels, 1956.

Rinchon, P. D. *Pierre Ignace-Lievin van Alstein*. Dakar, 1964.

Rinchon, P. D. *La traite et l'esclavage des Congolais par les Européens*. Paris, 1929.

Roberts, A. D. *A history of the Bemba*. London, 1973.

Rodrigues, J. H. *Brazil and Africa*. Berkeley, 1965. Portuguese ed. Rio de Janeiro, 1961.

Souza, L. M. R. de. *Moedas de Angola*. Luanda, 1967.

Torres, J. C. Feo Cardoso de Castello Branco e. *Memórias contendo...a história...de Angola desde 1575 até 1825*. Paris, 1825.

Vansina, J. 'The foundation of the kingdom of Kasanje', *Journal of African History*, 1963, **4**.

Vansina, J. *Geschiedenis van de Kuba*. Tervuren, 1963.

Vansina, J. *Introduction à l'ethnographie du Congo*. Brussels and Kinshasa, 1965.

Vansina, J. *Kingdoms of the savanna*. Madison, 1966.

Vansina, J. *The Tio kingdom of the Middle Congo*. London, 1973.

Vellut, J.-L. 'Notes sur le Lunda et la frontière luso-africaine (1700–1900)'. *Études d'histoire africaine*, 1972, **3**.

Vellut, J.-L. 'Relations internationales du Moyen-Kwango et de l'Angola dans la deuxième moitié du XVIIIe siècle', *Études d'histoire africaine*, 1970, **1**.

Verhulpen, E. *Baluba et Balubaïsés*. Anvers, 1936.

Wilson, A. 'Long-distance trade and the Luba Lomami empire'. M.A. dissertation, University of London, 1970. Summarized in *Journal of African History*, 1972, **13**, 4, 575–589.

Wing, J. van. *Études Bakongo*. 2nd ed. Louvain, 1959.

Zucchelli, A. *Relazione del viaggio e missione di Congo nell Etiopia inferiore Occidentale*. Venice, 1712; Frankfurt, 1715 (in German).

6. SOUTHERN AFRICA AND MADAGASCAR

Southern Zambezia

Abraham, D. P. 'The early political history of the Kingdom of Mwene-Mutapa (850–1589)', in *Historians in Tropical Africa*. Salisbury, 1962.

Abraham, D. P. 'Maramuca: an exercise in the combined use of Portuguese records and oral tradition', *Journal of African History*, 1961, **2**, 2, 211–25.

Abraham, D. P. 'The Monomotapa Dynasty', *NADA*, 1959, **36**, 58–84.

Andrade, A. A. de, ed. *Relações de Moçambique Setecentista*, Lisbon, Agência Geral do Ultramar, 1955.

Andrade, J. J. N. de. 'Descripção do Estado em que ficavão os negocios da Capitania de Mossambique nos fins de Novembro do anno de 1789', *Arquivo das Colónias*, 1917, **1**, 73–96, 115–34, 166–84, 213–35; 1918, **2**, 32–50.

Axelson, E. *Portuguese in South East Africa 1600–1700*. Johannesburg, 1960.

Axelson, E. ed. 'Viagem que fez o Padre Antonio Gomes, da Companhia de Jesus, ao Imperio de de (sic) Manomotapa; e assistencia que fez nas ditas terras de Alg'us annos', *Studia*, 1959, **3**, 155–242.

Bhila, H. K. 'The Manyika and the Portuguese, 1575–1863'. Ph.D. thesis, University of London, 1971.

Blake-Thompson, J. and Summers, R. 'Mlimo and Mwari: notes on a native religion in Southern Rhodesia', *NADA*, 1956, **33**, 53–8.

Botelho, S. X. *Memoria estatistica sobre os Dominios Portuguezes na Africa Oriental*. Lisbon, 1835.

Boxer, C. R. 'A Dominican account of Zambezia in 1744', *Boletim da Sociedade de Estudos de Moçambique*, 1960, **125**, secção E, 5, 1–14.

Boxer, C. R. 'Sisnando Dias Bayão conquistador da "Mae de Ouro"', *Primeiro Congresso da Historia da Expansão Portuguesa no Mundo*, 4a secção, Africa, III, 99–115. Lisbon, 1938.

Bryce, J. *Impressions of South Africa*. London, 1897.

Bullock, C. *The Mashona and the Matebele*. Cape Town, 1950.

Carvalho Dias, L. F. de, ed. *Fontes para a história, geografia e comércio de Moçambique* (*sec XVIII*), in *Anais*, **9**, 1. Lisbon, Junta de Investigações do Ultramar, 1954.

Caton-Thompson, G. *The Zimbabwe culture*. Oxford, 1931.

Conceição, A. de. 'Tratado dos Rios de Cuama', in Cunha Rivara, J. H. da, ed. *O Chronista de Tissuary*, pp. 39–45, 63–9, 84–92, 105–11. Goa, 1867.

Daneel, M. L. *The God of the Matopo hills: an essay on the Mwari cult in Rhodesia*. The Hague, 1970.

Documents on the Portuguese in Mozambique and Central Africa 1497–1840. National Archives of Rhodesia and Centro de Estudos Historicos Ultramarinos, Lisbon, 1962–71 (in progress). 7 vols. (Covering the period 1497 to 1560 so far.)

Fortune, G. 'A Rozvi Text with translation and notes', *NADA*, 1956, **33**.

Garlake, P. S. 'Excavations at the seventeenth-century Portuguese site of Dambarare, Rhodesia', *Proceedings and transactions of the Rhodesia Scientific Association*, 1970, **54**, 1, 23–61.

Garlake, P. S. *Great Zimbabwe*. London, 1973.
Garlake, P. S. 'Rhodesian ruins – a preliminary assessment of their styles and chronology', *Journal of African History*, 1970, **11**, 4, 495–513.
Garlake, P. S. 'Seventeenth century Portuguese earthworks in Rhodesia', *South African Archaeological Bulletin*, 1967, **21**, 84, part 4, 157–70.
Garlake, P. S. 'The value of imported ceramics in the dating and interpretation of the Rhodesian iron age', *Journal of African History*, 1968, **9**, 1, 13–33.
Hall, R. N. and Neal, W. G. *The ancient ruins of Rhodesia*. London, 1902.
Holleman, J. F. 'Some "Shona" tribes of Southern Rhodesia', in Colson, E. and Gluckman, M., eds., *Seven tribes of British Central Africa*, pp. 354–95. Manchester, 1959.
Hoppe, F. *Portugiesisch-Ostafrika in der Zeit des Marques de Pombal*. Berlin, 1965.
Isaacman, A. F. *Mozambique: the Africanization of a European institution—the Zambezi prazos, 1750–1902*. Madison, 1972.
Krige, E. J. and J. D. *The realm of a rain-queen*. London, 1943.
Lestrade, G. P. 'Some notes on the ethnic history of the Vhavenda and their Rhodesian affinities', *South African Journal of Science*, 1927, **24**, 486–95.
Lloyd, E. M. 'Mbava', *NADA*, 1925, **3**, 62–4.
MacIver, D. R. *Mediaeval Rhodesia*. London, 1906.
Marodzi. 'The Barozwi', *NADA*, 1924, **2**, 88–91.
Melo e Castro, F. de. *Descripção dos Rios de Senna anno de 1750*. Goa, 1861.
Montez, C. *Descobrimento e Fundação de Lourenço Marques 1500–1800*. Lourenço Marques, 1948.
Montez, C., ed. 'Inventário do fundo do século XVIII', *Moçambique—Documentário Trimestral*, nos. 72–89. Lourenço Marques, 1952–7.
Mudenge, S. I. 'The Rozvi Empire and the Feira of Zumbo'. Ph.D. thesis, University of London, 1972.
Muhlanga, S. 'In the early days', *NADA*, 1926, **4**, 107–10.
Muhlanga, S. and Lloyd, E. 'Mbava and others', *NADA*, 1926, **4**, 91–3.
Newitt, M. D. D. *Portuguese settlement on the Zambesi*. London, 1973.
Pacheco, A. M. *Uma viagem de Tete a Zumbo*. Moçambique, 1883.
Posselt, F. W. T. *Fact and fiction*. Bulawayo, 1935.
Rita-Ferreira, A. *Agrupamento e caracterização étnica dos indígenas de Moçambique*. Lisbon, Junta de Investigações do Ultramar, 1958.
Robinson, K. R. 'A history of the Bikita district', *NADA*, 1957, **34**, 75–87.
Robinson, K. R. *Khami ruins*. Cambridge, 1959.
Robinson, K. R., Summers, R. and Whitty, A. *Zimbabwe excavations 1958*. Occasional Papers of the National Museums of Southern Rhodesia, no. 23A. 1961.
Schebesta, P. *Portugals Konquistamission in Sudost-Afrika*. Studia Instituti Missiologici Societatis Verbi Divini, no. 7. St Augustin, 1966.
Sebina, A. M. 'Makalaka', *African Studies*, 1947, **6**, 2, 82–94.
Sicard, H. von. *Ngoma Lungundu: Eine afrikanische Bundeslade*. Uppsala, Studia Ethnographica Upsaliensia, vol. v, 1952.
Sicard, H. von. 'The origin of some of the tribes in the Belingwe Reserve', *NADA*, 1948, **25**, 93–104; 1950, **27**, 7–19; 1951, **28**, 5–25; 1952, **29**, 43–64; 1953, **30**, 64–71; 1955, **32**, 77–92.

Sicard, H. von. 'Reiche und Königtum der Rozwi vom Ende des 17. bis zum Angang des 19. Jahrhunderts', in Haberland, E., Schuster, M. and Straube, H., eds., *Festschrift für Ad. E. Jensen*, II, 635–63. Munich, 1964.

Silva, A. da. *Mentalidade missiológica dos Jesuítas em Moçambique antes de 1759*. 2 vols. Lisbon, 1967.

Smith, A. K. 'The struggle for control of Southern Moçambique, 1720–1835'. Ph.D. thesis, UCLA, 1970.

Sousa, Francisco de, S.J. *Oriente Conquistado a Jesus Christo pelos Padres da Companhia de Jesus da provincia de Goa*. Lisbon, 1710. 2 vols.

Stayt, H. A. *The Bavenda*. London, 1931.

Sutherland-Harris, N. 'Trade and the Rozwi Mambo', in Gray, R. and Birmingham, D., eds., *Pre-colonial African trade*, pp. 243–64. London, 1970.

Theal, G. M. ed. *Records of south-eastern Africa*. Cape Town, 1898–1903. 9 vols.

Warmelo, N. J. van, ed. *Contributions towards Venda history, religion and tribal ritual*. Union of South Africa, Department of Native Affairs, Ethnological publications, vol. III. Pretoria, 1932. Reprinted with corrections, 1960.

Warmelo, N. J. van, ed. *The copper miners of Musina and the early history of the Zoutpansberg*. Union of South Africa, Department of Native Affairs, Ethnological publications, vol. VIII. Pretoria, 1940.

Welch, S. R. *Some unpublished manuscripts relating to the history of South and East Africa*. Pretoria, 1933.

South Africa

Alberti, L. *The Kaffirs of the south coast of Africa*, tr. W. Fehr as *Ludwig Alberti's account of the tribal life and customs of the Xhosa in 1807*. Cape Town, 1968.

Arbousset, T. and Daumas, F. *Narrative of an exploratory tour to the north-east of the colony of the Cape of Good Hope, 1846*, tr. J. Crombie-Brown. Reprint, Cape Town, 1968.

Bergh, O. and Schrijver, I. *Journals of the expedition of Olof Bergh and Isaq Schrijver*, [*1682–3; 1689*], ed. E. E. Mossop (Van Riebeeck Society, **12**). Cape Town, 1931.

Barrow, J. *An account of travels into the interior of South Africa*. London, 1801. 2 vols.

Barrow, J. *A voyage to Cochinchina...to which is annexed an account of a journey made in the years 1801 and 1802 to the residence of the chief of the Booshuana nation...* London, 1806.

Beyers, C. *Die Kaapse Patriotte, 1779–1791*. Johannesburg, 1930.

Bird, J. ed. *Annals of Natal, 1495–1845*. Pietermaritzburg, 1888. 2 vols.

Bleek, D. *The Naron*. Cambridge, 1928.

Bleek, W. H. I. 'Researches into the relations between the Hottentot and Kafir races', *Cape Monthly Magazine*, 1857, **1**, 4, 1, 199–208 and 289–96.

Boeseken, A. J. *Nederlandsche commissarissen aan de Kaap, 1657–1700*. The Hague, 1938.

Botha, C. G. *A brief guide to the various classes of documents in the Cape Archives, 1652–1806*. Cape Town, 1918.

Botha, C. G. ed. *Collectanea*. (Van Riebeeck Society, **5**.) Cape Town, 1924.

Botha, C. G. *Collected works*. Cape Town, 1962. 3 vols.

Boxer, C. R. *The Dutch seaborne empire 1600–1800*. London, 1965.

Boxer, C. R. *The tragic history of the sea, 1589–1662*. Cambridge, 1959.

Brink, F. C. and Rhenius, J. T. *The journals of Brink and Rhenius (1724; 1761–2)*, ed. E. E. Mossop. (Van Riebeeck Society, **28**.) Cape Town, 1947.

Brown, J. T. *Among the Bantu nomads*. London, 1926.

Brownlee, C. *Reminiscences of Kaffir life and history, 1896*. Lovedale, n.d.

Bryant, A. T. *A history of the Zulu and neighbouring tribes*. Cape Town, 1964.

Bryant, A. T. *Olden times in Zululand and Natal*. London, 1929.

Burchell, W. J. *Travels in the interior of South Africa, 1812*, ed. I. Schapera. London, 1953. 2 vols.

Buttner, J. D. *Accounts of the Cape and brief description of Natal...1716–1721*, ed. and tr. G. S. Nienaber and R. Raven-Hart. Cape Town, 1970.

Campbell, J. *Travels in South Africa undertaken at the request of the Mission Society, 1813*. London, 1815.

Campbell, J. *Travels in South Africa...being a narrative of a second journey, 1820*. London, 1822. 2 vols.

Casalis, E. *The Basutos*. London, 1861.

Chavonnes, M. P. de and Imhoff, Baron van. *The reports of De Chavonnes and his council, and of Van Imhoff, on the Cape*, introd. J. X. Merriman. (Van Riebeeck Society, **1**.) Cape Town, 1918.

Coetzee, C. G. *Die Kompanjie se besetting van Delagoabaai* (Archives Yearbook for South African History, pt. 2), pp. 167–276. Pretoria, 1948.

Cope, J. *King of the Hottentots*. London, 1967.

Davies, O. 'Excavations at Blackburn', *South African Archaeological Bulletin*, 1971, **26**, parts 3 and 4, nos. 103 and 104, 164–78.

Dornan, S. S. *Pygmies and bushmen of the Kalahari*. London, 1925.

Ellenberger, D. F. and MacGregor, J. C. *History of the Basuto; ancient and modern*. London, 1912.

Ellenberger, V. 'History of the Batlôkwa of Gaberones', *Bantu Studies*, 1939, **13**, 3, 165–98.

Elphick, R. H. 'The Cape Khoi and the first phase of South African race relations'. Ph.D. thesis, Yale University, 1972.

Engelbrecht, J. A. *The Korana*. Cape Town, 1936.

Forbes, V. S. *Pioneer travellers in South Africa*. Cape Town, 1965.

Fouché, L. *Die evolutie van die Trekboer*. Pretoria, 1909.

Fynn, H. G. *The diary of Henry Francis Fynn*, ed. J. Stuart and D. McK. Malcolm. Pietermaritzburg, 1950.

Gardiner, A. F. *A narrative of a journey to the Zoolu country*. London, 1836.

Godée-Molsbergen, E. C. *Reizen in Zuid-Afrika in de Hollandse Tijd*. (Linschoten Society.) The Hague, 1916–32. 4 vols.

Goodwin, A. J. H. 'Jan van Riebeeck and the Hottentots, 1652–1662', *S.A. Arch. Bull.*, 1952, **7**, 25, 2–53.

Goodwin, A. J. H. 'Commentary on "Jan Van Riebeeck and the Hottentots"', *S.A. Arch. Bull.*, 1952, **7**, 26, 86–91.

Goodwin, A. J. H. 'Metal working amongst early Hottentots', *S.A. Arch. Bull.*, 1956, **11**, 42, 46–51.

Guy, J. 'Cattlekeeping in Zululand', unpublished paper presented to the research group on cattle-keeping in Africa, School of Oriental and African Studies, London, 1970.

Hahn, T. *Tsuni-||Goam, the Supreme Being of the Khoi-khoi*. London, 1881.

Hammond-Tooke, W. D. 'Segmentation and fission in Cape Nguni political units', *Africa*, 1965, **35**, 3, 1965.

Harris, W. C. *Wild sports of Southern Africa*. London, 1852.

Heese, J. A. *Die herkoms van die Afrikaner*. Cape Town, 1971.

Hoernlé, A. W. 'The social organization of the Nama Hottentots of South West Africa', *American Anthropologist*, 1925, **27**, 1–24.

Humphreys, A. J. B. and Maggs, T. M. O'C. 'Further graves and cultural material from the banks of the Riet river', *S.A. Arch. Bull.*, 1970, **25**, 116–26.

Hunt, D. 'An account of the Bapedi', *Bantu Studies*, 1931, **5**, 4, 275–326.

Irle, J. *Die Herero*. Gütersloh, 1906.

Isaacs, N. *Travels and adventures in Eastern Africa, 1836*, ed. L. Herrman. (Van Riebeeck Society, **16–17**.) Cape Town, 1935–6. 2 vols.

Jeffreys, M. K., ed. *Kaapse plakkaatboek*. Cape Town, 1944. 6 vols.

Jensen, F. H. W. 'A note on the Bahurutse', *African Studies*, 1947, **7**.

Kay, S. *Travels and researches in Caffraria*. London, 1833.

Kock, V. de. *Those in bondage. An account of the life of the slave at the Cape in the days of the Dutch East India Company*. London, 1950.

Koeman, I. C. *Een Nieuwe ontdekking van Kaarten en Tekeningen van* R. *J. Gordon*. Overdruk int Tydschrift van het Koninklijk Nederlandsch Aardrijkskundig Genootskap, 1951, part 68, 4.

Kolbe, P. *The present state of the Cape of Good Hope: or a particular account of the several nations of the Hottentots...*, tr. G. Medley. London, 1738. 2 vols.

Krige, E. J. 'Note on the Phalaborwa and their Morula complex', *Bantu Studies*, 1937, **11**, 4, 357–66.

Krige, E. J. 'The place of the North-Eastern Transvaal Sotho in the South Bantu complex', *Africa*, 1938, **11**, 3, 265–93.

Krige, J. D. 'Traditional origins and tribal relationships of the Sotho of the Northern Transvaal', *Bantu Studies*, 1937, **11**, 4, 321–56.

Kropf, A. *Das Volk der Xosa-Kaffern im Ostlichen Sudafrika*. Berlin, 1889.

Kruger, F. 'Tlokwa traditions', *Bantu Studies*, 1937, **11**, 2, 85–115.

Language, F. J. 'Herkoms en Geskiedenis van die Tlhaping', *African Studies*, 1942, **1**, 1, 115–32.

Legassick, M. 'The frontier tradition in South African history', in *Collected seminar papers on the societies of southern Africa in the nineteenth and twentieth centuries*, **2**. University of London, Institute of Commonwealth Studies, 1970–1.

Legassick, M. 'The Griqua, the Tswana and the missionaries, 1780–1840'. Ph.D. thesis, UCLA, 1969.

Leibbrandt, H. C. V. ed. *Précis of the archives of the Cape of Good Hope*. Cape Town, 1896–1906. 17 vols.

Le Vaillant, F. *Travels into the interior parts of Africa by way of the Cape of Good Hope in the years 1780, 81, 82, 83, 84 and 85*. London, 1790. 2 vols.

Lichtenstein, H. *Travels in southern Africa in the years 1803, 1804, 1805 and 1806*. Reprint of the original translation from the German by Anne Plumptre. (Van Riebeeck Society, 10–11.) Cape Town, 1928–30.

Loeb, E. M. *In feudal Africa*. Publication no. 23 of the Indiana University Research Center in Anthropology, Folklore and Linguistics. Bloomington, 1962.

MacCalman, H. R. and Grobbelaar, B. J. 'Preliminary report on two stone-working Ovatjimba groups in the Northern Kaokaoveld of South West Africa', *Cimbebasia*, 1965, **13**.

McCrone, I. D. *Race attitudes in South Africa: historical, experimental and psychological studies*. Johannesburg, 1937.

Maggs, T. M. O'C. 'Bilobial dwellings: a persistent feature of southern Tswana settlements', in The South African Archaeological Society, Goodwin Series, 1, *The interpretation of evidence*, pp. 54–65. June 1972.

Maggs, T. M. O'C. 'Pastoral settlements on the Riet River', *S.A. Arch. Bull.* 1971, **26**, 37–63.

Matthews, Z. K. 'A short history of the Tshidi Barolong', *Fort Hare Papers*, 1945, **1**.

Maingard, L. F. 'Brikwa and the ethnic origins of the Batlhaping', *South African Journal of Science*, 1933, **30**, 597–621.

Maingard, L. F. 'The first contacts of the Dutch with the bushmen until the time of Simon van der Stel (1686)', *S.A.J.Sc.*, 1935, **32**, 479–87.

Maingard, L. F. 'The lost tribes of the Cape', *S.A.J.Sc.*, 1931, **28**.

Maingard, L. F. 'The origin of the word "Hottentot"', *Bantu Studies*, 1935, **9**, 63–7.

Maingard, L. F. 'Studies in Korana history, customs and language', *Bantu Studies*, 1932, **6**, 2, 103–62.

Marais, J. S. *The Cape coloured people, 1652–1937*. Johannesburg, 1962.

Marais, J. S. *Maynier and the first Boer Republics*. Cape Town, 1944.

Marks, S. 'Khoisan resistance to the Dutch in the seventeenth and eighteenth centuries', *Journal of African History*, 1972, **13**, 1, 55–80.

Marks, S. and Atmore, A. 'The problem of the Nguni: an examination of the ethnic and linguistic situation in South Africa before the Mfecane', in Dalby, D., ed., *Language and history in Africa*, pp. 120–30. London, 1970.

Mason, R. J. *The prehistory of the Transvaal*. Johannesburg, 1962.

Mason, R. J. 'Transvaal and Natal iron age settlement revealed by aerial photography and excavation', *African Studies*, 1968, **27**, 4, 167–180.

Mentzel, O. F. *A geographical and topographical description of the Cape of Good Hope (1787)*, tr. G. V. Marais and J. Hoge, rev. and ed. H. J. Mandelbrote. (Van Riebeeck Society, **2**, **6**, **25**.) Cape Town, 1921, 1924, 1944.

Merwe, P. J. van der. *Die noordwaartse beweging van die Boere voor die Groot Trek*. The Hague, 1937.

Merwe, P. J. van der. *Trek, studies oor die mobiliteit van die pioniersbevolking aan die Kaap*. Cape Town, 1945.

Merwe, P. J. van der. *Die Trekboer in die geskiedenis van die Kaap Kolonie*. Cape Town, 1938.

Merwe, D. F. van der and Schapera, I. *A comparative study of Kgalagadi, Kwena and other Sotho dialects*. (Communications of the School of African Studies, University of Cape Town, **9**.) 1943.

Monnig, H. O. 'The Baroka ba Nkwana', *African Studies*, 1963, **22**, 4, 170–5.

Moodie, D. Lists of official documents relating to native tribes (CO 6127), Cape Archives.

Moodie, D. *The record, or a series of official papers relating to the condition and treatment of the native tribes of South Africa 1838–1842* (photographically repr.). Amsterdam and Cape Town, 1960.

Native Affairs Department. Ethnological publications, vols. 5, 12–22, 26, 28–38, 40–4, 46, 49. Pretoria, 1935–63.

Nienaber, G. S. *Hottentots*. Pretoria, 1963.

Nienaber, G. S. 'The origin of the name "Hottentot"', *African Studies*, 1963, **22**, 2, 65–90.

Nienaber, G. S. 'Die vroegste verslae aangaande Hottentots', *African Studies*, 1956, **15**, 1, 29–35.

Neumark, S. D. *Economic influences on the South African frontier, 1652–1836*. Stanford, 1957.

Paravicini di Capelli, W. B. E. *Reize in de binnen landen van Zuid Afrika,... 1803...*, ed. W. J. de Kock. (Van Riebeeck Society, **46**.) Cape Town, 1965.

Paver, F. R. 'Trade and mining in the Pre-European Transvaal', *S.A. J. Sci.*, 1933, **30**, 603–11.

Paterson, W. *A narrative of four journeys into the country of the Hottentots and Caffraria...* London, 1789.

Raven-Hart, R. *Before van Riebeeck, callers at the Cape from 1488 to 1652*. Cape Town, 1967.

Raven-Hart, R. *Cape of Good Hope, 1652–1702*. Cape Town, 1971. **2** vols.

Reenen, D. G. van der. *Die Journaal van Dirk Gysbert van Reenen, 1803*, tr. into Eng., J. L. M. Franken and I. M. Murray, ed. W. Blommaert and J. A. Wiid. (Van Riebeeck Society, **18**.) Cape Town, 1937.

Robertson, H. M. '150 years of economic contact between Black and White', *South African Journal of Economics*, 1934, **2**, 4, 403–25; 1935, **3**, 1, 3–25.

Ross, R. 'Speculations on the origins of South African society'. Unpublished paper. Cambridge, 1972.

Saunders, C. C. 'Early knowledge of the Sotho', *Quarterly Bulletin of the South African Public Library*, 1966, **20**, 3, 60–70.

Schapera, I. *The Bantu-speaking people of South Africa*. London, 1937.

Schapera, I. ed. *The early Cape Hottentots, described in the writings of Olfert Dapper [1688], William Ten Rhyne [1686] and Johannes Gulielmus de Grevenbrock [1695]*. (Van Riebeeck Society, **14**.) Cape Town, 1933.

Schapera, I. *The ethnic composition of Tswana tribes*. London, 1952.

Schapera, I. *Government and politics in tribal societies*. London, 1956.

Schapera, I. *The Khoisan peoples of South Africa*. London, 1930.
Schapera, I. 'Notes on the history of the Kaa', *African Studies*, 1945, **4**, 3, 109–21.
Schapera, I. *A short history of the Ba-Kgatla-baga Kgafêla of Bechuanaland Protectorate*. (Communications of the School of African Studies, University of Cape Town.) 1942.
Schapera, I. 'A short history of the Bangwaketse', *African Studies*, **1**, 1, 1942, 1–26.
Schapera, I. 'The social structure of a Tswana Ward', *Bantu Studies*, 1935, **9**, 3, 203–24.
Schapera, I. and Merwe, D. F. van der. *Notes on the tribal groupings, history and customs of the Bakgalagadi*. Cape Town, 1945.
Scholtz, J. du P. *Taalhistoriese opstelle. Voorstudies tot in Geskiedenis van Afrikaans*. Pretoria, 1963.
Schoute-Vanneck, C. A. 'The Shell Middens on the Durban Bluff', *S.A. Arch. Bull.* 1958, **13**, 50, 43–54.
Seddon, J. D. 'Kurrichane: a late iron age site in the western Transvaal', *African Studies*, 1966, **25**, 4, 227–31.
Silberhauer, G. B. *Bushman survey*. Gaberones, 1965.
Smith, A. *The diary of Dr. Andrew Smith*, ed. P. R. Kirby. (Van Riebeeck Society, **20–1**.) Cape Town, 1939–40. 2 vols.
Soga, J. H. *The south eastern Bantu*. Johannesburg, 1930.
Sparrman, A. *A voyage to the Cape of Good Hope*, 1772–6. Dublin, 1785. 2 vols.
Spilhaus, M. W. *The first South Africans*. Cape Town, 1949.
Spilhaus, M. W. *South Africa in the making*. Cape Town, 1966.
Spoelstra, C. ed. *Bouwstoffen voor de Geschiedenis der Nederduitsch-Gereformeerde kerken in Zuid-Afrika*. Amsterdam and Cape Town, 1906–7. 2 vols.
Spohr, O. H. ed. *The Natal diaries of Dr W. H. I. Bleek, 1855–1858*. Tr. from German. Cape Town, 1965.
Stel, S. van der. *Simon van der Stel's journal of his expedition to Namaqualand, 1685–1686*, tr. and ed. from a Ms. in the library of Trinity College, Dublin by G. Waterhouse. Dublin, 1932. Supplement and corrigenda. Dublin, 1953.
Stow, G. W. 'Emigrant Kafirs in the Zuur-veld' and 'The intrusion of the stronger races'. Unpublished Mss, South African Public Library, n.d.
Stow, G. W. *The native races of South Africa*. London, 1905.
Sydow, W. 'The Pre-European pottery of south west Africa', *Cimbebasia*, memoir 1. Windhoek, 1967.
Stuart, J. Unpublished papers on the early history of Zululand, recorded interviews (early twentieth century). Killie Campbell Library, University of Natal, Durban. (These are now being prepared for publication by Professor Colin Webb and John Wright, University of Natal.)
Suid-Afrikaanse Argiefstukke. *Resoluties van die Politieke Raad*. Cape Town and Johannesburg, 1957–68. 6 vols.
Tas, A. *The diary of Adam Tas (1705–6)*, ed. L. Fouché. London, 1914.
Terry, E. *A voyage to East India...(1655)*. London, 1777.

Theal, G. M. ed. *Belangrijke historische dokumenten verzameld in de Kaap Kolonie en Elders*. Cape Town, 1896–1911. 3 vols.

Theal, G. M. *History and ethnography of South Africa before 1795*. London, 1907–10. 3 vols.

Thom, H. B. ed. *Journal of Jan van Riebeeck*. Cape Town and Amsterdam, 1952. 3 vols.

Thomas, E. M. *The harmless people*. London, 1959.

Thompson, G. *Travels and adventures in southern Africa*. London, 1827. 2 vols.

Thompson, L. M. ed. *African societies in southern Africa, historical studies*. London, 1969.

Thompson, L., Elphick, R. and Jarrick, I. *Southern Africa before 1900: a select bibliography of articles*. Stanford, 1970.

Thunberg, C. P. *Travels in Europe, Africa and Asia...between...1770 and 1779*. London, 1795. 4 vols.

Tobias, P. V. 'Physical anthropology and somatic origins of the Hottentots', *African Studies*, 1955, **14**, 1, 1–15.

Tobias, P. V. 'On the increasing stature of the Bushmen', *Anthropos*, 1962, **57**.

Tönjes, H. *Ovamboland*. Berlin, 1911.

Transvaal Native Affairs Department. *Short history of the native tribes of the Transvaal*. Pretoria, 1903.

Valkhoff, M. F. *Studies in Portuguese and Creole: with special reference to South Africa*. Johannesburg, 1966.

Vedder, H. ed. *The native tribes of south west Africa*. Cape Town, 1928.

Vedder, H. *South West Africa in early times*, tr. C. G. Hall. London, 1938.

Walt, A. J. H. van der, Wiid, J. A. and Geyer, A. L. eds. *Geskiedenis van Suid Afrika*. Cape Town, 1951. 2 vols.

Walton, J. *African village*. Pretoria, 1956.

Walton, J. 'Early Bafokeng settlement in South Africa', *African Studies*, 1956, **15**, 1, 37–43.

Walton, J. 'Early Ghoya settlement in the Orange Free State', *Researches of the National Museum, Bloemfontein*, memoir no. 2.

Wikar, H. J., Coetse Jansz, J. and Reemen, W. van. *The journal of Hendrik Jacob Wikar (1779)...and of Jacobus Coetsé Jansz (1760) and Willem van Reenen (1791)*, tr. A. W. van der Horst and E. E. Mossop, ed. E. E. Mossop. (Van Riebeeck Society, **15**.) Cape Town, 1935.

Wilson, M. 'The early history of the Transkei and Ciskei', *African Studies*, 1959, **18**, 1, 4, 167–79.

Wilson, M. and Thompson, L. eds. *The Oxford history of South Africa*, vol. 1. *South Africa to 1870*. Oxford, 1969.

Ziervogel, D. *A grammar of northern Transvaal Ndebele*. Pretoria, 1959.

Madagascar

Birkeli, E. *Marques de boeufs et traditions de race: document sur l'ethnographie de la côte occidentale de Madagascar*. Oslo Ethnografiske Museum, Bulletin no. 2. Oslo, 1926.

Chapus, G. S. and Ratsimba, E. trs. and eds. *Histoire des rois (Tantaran'ny Andriana)*. Tananarive, 1953–8. 4 vols.

Deschamps, H. *Histoire de Madagascar*. 2nd ed. Paris, 1961.

Deschamps, H. *Les pirates à Madagascar aux xviie et xviiie siècles*. Paris, 1949.

Drury, R. *Madagascar or Robert Drury's journal during fifteen years' captivity on that island*. 7th ed., ed. P. Oliver. London, 1890. Orig. ed. 1729.

Du Bois. *Les voyages faits par le sieur D.B. aux Illes Dauphine ou Madagascar, & Bourbon, ou Mascarene, és années 1669–1672*. Paris, 1674.

Fagereng, E. 'Histoire des Maroserana du Menabé', *Bulletin de l'Académie Malgache* (new series), 1947–8, **28**, 115–35.

Ferrand, G. *Les Musulmans à Madagascar et aux Îles Comores*. Paris, 1891–1902. 3 vols.

Ferrand, G. 'L'origine africaine des Malgaches', *Journal Asiatique*, 1908, **40**, 353–500.

Flacourt, E. de. *Histoire de la grande île de Madagascar*. 2nd ed. Paris, 1661.

Flacourt, E. de. *Relation de ce qui s'est passé en Ile de Madagascar depuis l'année 1642 jusqu'en 1660*. Paris, 1661.

Foury, B. *Maudave et la colonisation de Madagascar*. Paris, 1956.

Grandidier, Alfred et Guillaume, eds. *Collection des ouvrages anciens concernant Madagascar*. Paris, 1903–20. 9 vols.

Guillain, C. *Documents sur l'histoire, la géographie et le commerce de la partie occidentale de Madagascar*. Paris, 1845.

Kent, R. K. *Early kingdoms in Madagascar 1500–1700*. New York, 1970.

Mayeur, N. 'Journal de voyage au pays des Seclaves (1774)', *Bulletin de l'Académie Malgache*, 1912, **10**, 49–91.

Rusillon, H. *Un culte dynastique avec évocation des morts chez les Sakalaves de Madagascar: Le 'Tromba'*. Paris, 1912.

Valette, J. 'Madagascar vers 1750 d'après un manuscrit anonyme', *Bulletin de Madagascar*, 1964, **14**, 214, 211–58.

7. EASTERN AFRICA

Abdallah bin Hemedi al-Ajjemy. *The Kilindi*, ed. and tr. J. W. T. Allen and William Kimweri. Nairobi, 1963.

Abrahams, R. G. *The political organization of Unyamwezi*. Cambridge, 1967.

Almeida, F. I. de Lacerda e. *Travessia da África*. Lisbon, 1936.

Alpers, E. A. 'The French slave trade in East Africa (1721–1810)', *Cahiers d'études africaines*, 1970, **10**, 37, 80–124.

Alpers, E. A. *Ivory and slaves in East Central Africa*. London, 1975.

Axelson, E. *Portuguese in South-East Africa, 1600–1700*. Johannesburg, 1960.

Axelson, E. 'Portuguese settlement in the interior of south-east Africa in the seventeenth century', Congresso Internacional de História dos Descobrimentos, *Actas*, v, parte II, 1–17. Lisbon, 1961.

Berg, F. J. 'The Swahili community of Mombasa, 1500–1900', *Journal of African History*, 1968, **9**, 1, 13–33.

Boxer, C. R. 'Moçambique Island and the "Carreira da Índia"', *Studia*, 1961, **8**, 95–132.

Boxer, C. R. 'The Portuguese in the East, 1500–1800', in Livermore, H. V., ed., *Portugal and Brazil*, pp. 185–247. Oxford, 1953.

Boxer, C. R. and Azevedo, C. de. *Fort Jesus and the Portuguese in Mombasa, 1593–1729*. London, 1960.

Brock, B. 'The Nyiha of Mbozi', *Tanzania Notes and Records*, 1966, **65**, 1–30.

Césard, E. 'Le Muhaya', *Anthropos*, 1937, **32**, 32–57.

Charsley, S. R. *The princes of Nyakyusa*. Nairobi, 1969.

Chittick, H. N. 'A new look at the history of Pate', *Journal of African History*, 1969, **10**, 3, 375–91.

Cohen, D. W. 'The Chwezi cult', *Journal of African History*, 1968, **9**, 4, 651–57.

Cohen, D. W. *The historical tradition of Busoga: Mukama and Kintu*. Oxford, 1972.

Cohen, D. W. 'A survey of interlacustrine chronology', *Journal of African History*, 1970, **11**, 2, 177–201.

Cory, H. *Historia ya Wilaya ya Bukoba* (*History of Bukoba District*). Mwanza, 1958.

Cory, H. *The indigenous political system of the Sukuma and proposals for political reform*, East African Institute of Social Research, Nairobi, 1954.

Cory, H. *The Ntemi. Traditional rites of a Sukuma chief in Tanganyika*. London, 1951.

Crazzolara, J. P. *The Lwoo*. Verona, 1950–4. 3 vols.

Driberg, J. H. *The Lango. A Nilotic tribe of Uganda*. London, 1923.

Dunbar, A. R. *A history of Bunyoro-Kitara*. Oxford, 1965.

Ehret, C. *Ethiopians and East Africans: the problem of contacts*. Nairobi, 1974.

Ehret, C. *Southern Nilotic history: linguistic approaches to the study of the past*. Evanston, 1971.

Evans-Pritchard, E. E. *The divine kingship of the Shilluk of the Nilotic Sudan*. Cambridge, 1948.

Evans-Pritchard, E. E. *The political system of the Anuak of the Anglo-Egyptian Sudan*. International African Institute, London, 1940.

Fallers, L. A. *Bantu bureaucracy*. Cambridge, 1956.

Fallers, Margaret. *The eastern lacustrine Bantu*. International African Institute, London, 1960.

Feierman, S. *The Shambaa kingdom*. Madison, 1974.

Forbes-Munro, J. 'Migrations of the Bantu-speaking peoples of the eastern Kenya highlands: a reappraisal', *Journal of African History*, 1967, **8**, 1, 25–8.

Ford, J. and Hall, R. de Z. 'The history of Karagwe', *Tanganyika Notes and Records*, 1947, **24**, 3–27.

Fosbrooke, H. A. 'An administrative survey of the Masai social system', *Tanganyika Notes and Records*, 1948, **26**, 1–50.

Fosbrooke, H. A. 'The Masai age-system as a guide to tribal chronology', *African Studies*, 1956, **15**, 4, 188–204.

Freeman-Grenville, G. S. P. *The East African coast: select documents from the first to the earlier nineteenth century*. Oxford, 1962.

Gray, Sir John Milner. *History of Zanzibar from the middle ages to 1856*. London, 1962.

Gray, Sir John Milner. 'A journey by land from Tete to Kilwa in 1616', *Tanganyika Notes and Records*, 1948, **25**, 37–47.

Gray, Richard and Birmingham, D. eds. *Pre-colonial African trade*. London, 1970.

Gray, Robert F. 'The Mbugwe tribe: origin and development', *Tanganyika Notes and Records*, 1955, **38**, 39–50.

Gray, Robert F. *The Sonjo of Tanganyika*. Oxford, 1963.

Guillain, C. *Documents sur l'histoire, la géographie, et le commerce de l'Afrique Orientale*. Paris, 1856. 3 vols.

Gulliver, P. and Gulliver, P. H. *The central Nilo-Hamites*. International African Institute, London, 1953.

Gulliver, P. H. 'The Teso and the Karamojong cluster', *Uganda Journal*, 1956, **20**, 213–15.

Hamilton, R. A. 'The route of Gaspar Bocarro from Tete to Kilwa in 1616', *The Nyasaland Journal*, 1954, **7**, 2, 7–14.

Harding, J. R. 'Conus-shell disc-ornaments (*vibangwa*) in Africa', *Journal of the Royal Anthropological Institute*, 1960, **90**, 2, 52–66.

Hasani bin Ismail. *The Medicine Man: Swifa ya Nguvumali*, tr. and with an introduction by Peter Lienhardt. Oxford, 1968.

Heusch, L. de. *Le Rwanda et la civilisation interlacustre*. Brussels, 1966.

Huntingford, G. W. B. *The Nandi of Kenya*. London, 1953.

Huntingford, G. W. B. *The northern Nilo-Hamites*, International African Institute, London, 1953.

Huntingford, G. W. B. 'Remarks upon the history of the Nandi till 1850', *Journal of the East African and Uganda Natural History Society*, 1927, no. 28.

Huntingford, G. W. B. *The southern Nilo-Hamites*. International African Institute, London, 1953.

Isaacman, A. F. *Mozambique: the africanization of a european institution – the Zambezi prazos, 1750–1902*. Madison, 1972.

Jackson, K. 'An ethnohistorical study of the oral traditions of the Akamba of Kenya'. Ph.D. thesis, University of California, 1971.

Jacobs, A. 'A chronology of the pastoral Maasai', *Hadith*, 1968, **1**, 10–31.

Jellicoe, M. 'Praising the sun', *Transition*, 1967, **6**, 31, 27–31.

Kagwa, Apolo. *The kings of Buganda*, tr. and with an introduction by M. S. M. Kiwanuka. Nairobi, 1970. 1st ed. 1901.

Kalinga, O. 'The Ngonde kingdom'. Ph.D. thesis, University of London, 1974.

Katoke, I. K. *The making of the Karagwe kingdom*. Historical Association of Tanzania, paper no. 8. Nairobi, 1970.

Kidamala, Daudi, and Danielson, E. R. 'A brief history of the Waniramba people', *Tanganyika Notes and Records*, 1961, **56**, 67–78.

Kimambo, I. N. *A political history of the Pare of Tanzania*. Nairobi, 1969.

Kimambo, I. N. and Temu, A. J. eds. *A history of Tanzania*. Nairobi, 1969.

Lambert, H. E. *Kikuyu social and political institutions*. London, 1956.

Lambert, H. E. *Systems of land tenure in the Kikuyu land unit*, part 1, *History of the tribal occupation of the land.* Capetown, 1950.

Lawren, W. L. 'An historical analysis of the dissemination of Masai culture to five Bantu tribes, with special emphasis on the Kikuyu'. M.A. dissertation, University of California, 1968.

Lawren, W. L. 'Masai and Kikuyu: an historical analysis of cultural transmission', *Journal of African History*, 1968, **9**, 4, 571–83.

Lawrence, J. C. D. *The Iteso.* London, 1957.

Legassick, M. 'The Griqua, the Sotho-Tswana, and the missionaries, 1780–1840: the politics of a frontier zone'. Ph.D. thesis, University of California, 1969.

Lienhardt, P. 'The Mosque College of Lamu and its social background', *Tanganyika Notes and Records*, 1959, **53**, 228–42.

Martin, B. G. 'Notes on some members of the learned classes of Zanzibar and East Africa in the nineteenth century', *African Historical Studies*, 1971, **4**, 3, 525–45.

Mercer, P. 'Shilluk trade and politics from the mid-seventeenth century to 1861', *Journal of African History*, 1971, **12**, 3, 407–26.

Middleton, J. *The central tribes of the north-eastern Bantu.* International African Institute, London, 1965.

Morris, H. F. *A history of Ankole.* Nairobi, 1962.

Morris, H. F. 'The Kingdom of Mpororo', *Uganda Journal*, 1955, **19**, 204–7.

Morris, H. F. 'The making of Ankole', *Uganda Journal*, 1957, **21**, 1–15.

Muratori, C. *English-Bari-Lotuxo-Acoli vocabulary.* Okaru, 1948.

Muriuki, G. *A history of the Kikuyu 1500–1900* Nairobi, 1974.

National Archives of Tanzania, Dar es Salaam. District Books.

Newitt, M. D. D. *Portuguese settlement on the Zambesi.* London, 1973.

Nicholls, C. S. *The Swahili coast, politics, diplomacy and trade on the East African littoral 1798–1856.* London, 1971.

Ogot, Bethwell A. ed. *Aspects of the pre-colonial history of Kenya.* Nairobi, forthcoming.

Ogot, B. A. *History of the southern Luo*, vol. 1. Nairobi, 1967.

Ogot, B. A. 'Kingship and statelessness among the Nilotes', in Vansina, J., Mauny, R. and Thomas, L. V., eds. *The historian in tropical Africa*, pp. 284–302. London, 1964.

Ogot, B. A. and Kieran, J. A. *Zamani: a survey of East African history.* Nairobi, 1968.

Oliver, R. 'The traditional histories of Buganda, Bunyoro and Ankole', *Journal of the Royal Anthropological Institute*, 1955, **85**, 111–17.

Oliver, R. and Mathew, G. eds. *History of East Africa*, vol. 1. London, 1963.

Osogo, J. 'The historical traditions of the Wanga kingdom', *Hadith*, 1968, **1**, 32–46.

Osogo, J. *A history of the Baluyia.* Oxford, 1966.

Pachai, Bridglal, ed. *The early history of Malawi.* London, 1972.

Pagès, A. *Un royaume hamite au centre de l'Afrique.* Brussels, 1933.

Pearce, F. B. *Zanzibar, the island metropolis of eastern Africa.* London, 1920.

Phillipson, D. W. and Fagan, B. 'The date of the Ingombe Ilede burials', *Journal of African History*, 1969, **9**, 2, 199–204.
Price, T. 'Malawi rain-cults', in *Religion in Africa*. Edinburgh, 1964.
Price, T. 'More about the Maravi', *African Studies*, 1952, **11**, 75–9.
Prins, A. H. J. *Didemic Lamu: social stratification and spatial structure in a Muslim maritime town*. Groningen, 1971.
Rangeley, W. H. J. 'Bocarro's journey', *Nyasaland Journal*, 1954, **7**, 2, 15–23.
Ranger, T. O. and Kimambo, I. N. eds. *The historical study of African religions*. London, 1972.
Richards, A. I. ed. *East African chiefs*. London, 1959.
Robbins, C. 'Rwanda: a case study in religious assimilation'. Paper delivered at the Dar es Salaam–UCLA Conference on the Historical Study of African Religious Systems, University of Dar es Salaam, June 1970.
Roberts, A. ed. *Tanzania before 1900: seven area histories*. Nairobi, 1968.
Robinson, K. R. 'A preliminary report on the recent archaeology of Ngonde, Northern Malawi', *Journal of African History*, 1966, **7**, 2, 169–88.
Robinson, K. R. and Sandelowsky, B. 'The iron age of North Malawi: recent work', *Azania*, 1968, **3**, 107–46.
Roscoe, J. *The Baganda*. London, 1911.
Roscoe, J. *The Bakitara*. Cambridge, 1923.
Roscoe, J. *The Banyankole*. Cambridge, 1923.
Sassoon, Hamo. 'Engaruka: excavations during 1964', *Azania*, 1966, **1**, 79–99.
Schurhammer, G. 'Die Entdeckung des Njassa-Sees', *Stimmen der Zeit*, 1920, pp. 349–58.
Shorter, A. *Chiefship in western Tanzania: a political history of the Kimbu*. Oxford, 1972.
Southall, A. W. *Alur society: a study in processes and types of domination*. Cambridge, 1956.
Southall, A. W. 'Alur tradition and its historical significance', *Uganda Journal*, 1954, **18**, 137–65.
Southwold, M. *Bureaucracy and chiefship in Buganda: the development of appointive office in the history of Buganda*. East African Studies, no. 14. East African Institute of Social Research, Kampala, n.d.
Southwold, M. 'The history of a history: royal succession in Buganda', in Lewis, I. M., ed. *History and social anthropology*, pp. 127–51. London, 1968.
Strandes, J. *The Portuguese period in East Africa*, tr. J. F. Wallwork, ed. J. S. Kirkman. Nairobi, 1961.
Sutton, J. E. G. *The archaeology of the western highlands of Kenya*. Forthcoming.
Sutton, J. E. G. 'Iron age trade in Eastern Africa'. Paper presented to the Universities of East Africa Social Science Conference, Dar es Salaam, 27–31 December 1970.
Taylor, B. K. *The western lacustrine Bantu*. International African Institute, London, 1962.
Theal, G. M. *Records of South-Eastern Africa*. London, 1898–1903.
Thiel, P. H. van. 'Businza unter der Dynastie der Bahinda', *Anthropos*, 1911, **6**, 497–520.
Vansina, J. *L'évolution du royaume de Rwanda des origines à 1900*. Brussels, 1962.

Vansina, J. *Kingdoms of the Savanna*. Madison, 1966.
Vansina, J. *La légende du passé: traditions orales du Burundi*. Tervuren, 1972.
Walter, B. J. *Territorial expansion of the Nandi of Kenya, 1500–1900*. Papers in International Studies, African Series, no. 9. Ohio University, 1970.
Were, G. S. *A history of the Abaluyia of Western Kenya, c. 1500–1930*. Nairobi, 1967.
Were, G. S. *Western Kenya historical texts*. Nairobi, 1967.
Willis, R. 'Traditional history and social structure in Ufipa', *Africa*, 1964, **34**, 4, 340–51.
Wilson, G. *The constitution of Ngonde*. Rhodes-Livingstone Papers, no. 3. Livingstone, 1939.
Wilson, G. 'The Tatoga of Tanganyika', *Tanganyika Notes and Records*, 1952, **33**, 34–47; 1953, **34**, 35–56.
Wilson, M. *Communal rituals of the Nyakyusa*. London, 1958.
Wilson, M. *Peoples of the Nyasa-Tanganyika corridor*. Capetown, 1958.
Young, T. *Notes on the history of the Tumbuka-Kamanga peoples*. London, 1932.

8. ETHIOPIA AND THE HORN OF AFRICA, 1543–1820

Abir, M. *Ethiopia: the era of the princes*. London, 1968.
Almagià, R. 'Un mercante anconetano in Etiopia alla fine del secolo XVI', *Contributi alla storia della conoscenza dell'Etiopia*. Padua, 1941.
Almeida, M. de. *The history of High Ethiopia or Abassia*, eds. C. F. Beckingham and G. W. B. Huntingford. London, 1954.
Aregay, M. W. 'Southern Ethiopia and the Christian kingdom, 1508–1708'. Ph.D. thesis, University of London, 1971.
Asmiye Alaqa, Ato. 'Ye Galla tarik'. Unpublished manuscript in the National Library, Addis Ababa.
Barros, J. de and Couto, D. de. *Da Asia*. Paris, 1936.
Basset, R. 'Chronologie des rois de Harar 1637–83', *Journal asiatique*, March–April 1914.
Basset, R. 'Études sur l'histoire d'Éthiopie', *Journal asiatique*, 1881, ser. 7, **17** and **18**.
Beccari, C. *Rerum Aethiopicarum scriptores occidentales inediti a saeculo XVI ad XIX*. Rome, 1914.
Beccari, C. *Il Tigre del secolo XVII*. Rome, 1909.
Beckingham, C. F. and Huntingford, G. W. B. *The Prester John of the Indies*. Cambridge, 1961. 2 vols.
Beckingham, C. F. and Huntingford, G. W. B. *Some records of Ethiopia 1593–1646*. London, 1954.
Bruce, J. *Travels to discover the source of the Nile in the years 1768, 1769, 1770, 1771, 1772 and 1773*. Edinburgh, 1790. 5 vols.
Budge, E. A. W. *A history of Ethiopia, Nubia and Abyssinia*. London, 1928.
Cerulli, E. 'Documenti arabi per la storia dell'Etiopia', *Rendiconti della Reale Accademia dei Lincei*, 1931, ser. 6, **4**.

Cerulli, E. 'Gli emiri di Harar del secolo XVI alla conquista egiziana (1875)', *Rassegna di Studi Etiopici*, 1942, **2**.

Cerulli, E. 'La lingua e la storia di Harar', *Studi Etiopici*, vol. I. Rome, 1936.

Civezza, M. da. *Storia universale delle Missioni Francescane*. Florence, 1857–95.

Conti Rossini, C. 'L'autobiografia de Pawlos monaco abissino del secolo XVI', *Rendiconti della Reale Accademia dei Lincei*, 1918, ser. 5, **27**.

Conti Rossini, C. 'I Galla Raia', *Rivista di Studi Orientali*, 1919, **8**.

Conti Rossini, C. 'La guerra turco-abissina del 1578', *Oriente Moderno*, 1921–2, **1**; 1922–3, **2**.

Conti Rossini, C. *Storia d'Etiopia*. Vol. II of *Africa Italiana*. Milan, 1928.

Conti, Rossini, C. 'Due squarci inediti di cronaca etiopica', *Rendiconti della Reale Accademia dei Lincei*, 1893, ser. 5, **2**.

Conzelman, W. E. *Chronique de Galawdewos (Claudius) roi d'Ethiopie*. Bibliothèque de l'École des Hautes Études, Sciences philologiques et historiques, vol. 104. Paris, 1895.

Correa, G. *Lendas da India*. 4 vols. Lisbon, 1858–64.

Gallina, F. 'I Portughesi a Massawa nei secoli XVI e XVII', *Bolletino Società Geografica Italiana*, 1890, ser. III, **3**.

Guidi, I. ed. *Annales Iohannis I, Iyāsu I et Bakāffā*. Paris, 1903.

Guidi, I. ed. *Annales regum Iyāsu II et Iyo'as*. Paris, 1910.

Guidi, I. 'Di due frammenti relativi alla storia di Abissinia', *Rendiconti della Reale Accademia dei Lincei*, 1893, ser. 5, **2**.

Guidi, I. 'La Chiesa abissina', *Oriente Moderno*, 1922, **2**, 5.

Guidi, I. *Historia gentis Galla*. Paris, 1907.

Guillain, C. *Documents sur l'histoire, la géographie...de l'Afrique Orientale*. Paris, 1856. 3 vols.

Hamilton, A. *A new account of the East Indies*. Edinburgh, 1727.

Huntingford, G. W. B. tr. and ed. *The glorious victories of Amda Seyon king of Ethiopia*. Oxford, 1965.

Huntingford, G. W. B. *The land charters of northern Ethiopia*. Addis Ababa and Nairobi, 1965.

Jones, J. W. ed. *The travels of Ludovico di Varthema 1503–1508*. London, 1863.

Kamil Murad. 'Letters to Ethiopia from the Coptic patriarchs Yo'annas XVIII 1770–96 and Marqos VIII 1796–1809', *Bulletin de la Société d'Archéologie Copte*, **8**. Cairo, 1942.

Kammerer, A. *La Mer Rouge, l'Abyssinie et l'Arabie depuis l'Antiquité. Essai d'histoire et de géographie historique*, vols. II, III, part I and III, part 2. Cairo, 1935, 1947, 1949.

Kammerer, A. tr. *Le routier de Dom Joam de Castro. L'exploration de la Mer Rouge par les Portugais en 1541*. Paris, 1936.

Kolmodin, J. *Traditions de Tsazzega et Hazzega*. Uppsala, 1915.

Le Grand, J. ed. *Voyage historique d'Abyssinie du R. P. Jerome Lobo*. Paris, 1728.

Lewis, H. S. 'The origins of the Galla and Somali', *Journal of African History*, 1966, **7**.

Ludolphus, J. *A new history of Ethiopia*. London, 1864.

Ovington, J. *A voyage to Suratt in the year 1689*. London, 1929.

Paulitschke, P. *Harar*. Leipzig, 1888.

Peiser, F. E. *Der Gesandschaftsbericht des Hasan ben Ahmed al-Haimi*. Berlin, 1894.

Pereira, F. M. E. *Chronica de Susenyos, Rei de Ethiopia*. Lisbon, 1892–1900.

Perruchon, J. 'Notes pour l'histoire d'Éthiopie. Le règne de Galawdewos (Claudius) ou Asnaf-Sagad', *Revue sémitique*, 1894, **2**.

Perruchon, J. 'Notes pour l'histoire d'Éthiopie. Le règne de Yohannes (Ier), roi d'Éthiopie de 1667 à 1682', *Revue sémitique*, 1899, **7**.

Poncet, C. J. *A voyage to Aethiopia made in the year 1698, 1699 and 1700*. London, 1709. Hakluyt Society, London, 1949.

Purchas His Pilgrims. Hakluyt Society, Glasgow, 1905–7. 20 vols.

Roncière, C. de la. *La découverte de l'Afrique au moyen-âge. Cartographie et explorateurs*. Cairo, 1925–7. 3 vols.

Roque, J. de la. 'An account of the captivity of Sir Henry Middleton at Mokha by the Turks in the year 1612', *A voyage to Arabia Faelix...in the years 1708, 1709, 1710, 1711, 1712 and 1713*. London, 1732.

Saineano, M. *L'Abyssinie dans la seconde moitié du XVIe siècle ou le règne de Sartsa-Dengel (Malak-Sagad) (1563–1594), d'après les annales éthiopiennes inédites*. Leipzig, 1892.

Saint Aymour, C. de. *Histoire des relations de la France avec l'Abyssinie Chrétienne 1634–1706*. Paris, 1886.

Salt, H. *A voyage to Abyssinia etc. in the years 1809 and 1810*. London, 1814.

Sapeto, G. *Viaggio e missione cattolica fra i Mensa, i Bogos e gli Habab, con un cenno geografico e storico dell'Abissinia*. Rome, 1857.

Somigli di S. Detole, T. *Etiopia francescana nei documenti dei secoli XVII e XVIII*. Vols. I and II of *Biblioteca Bibliografica della Terra Santa e dell'Oriente francescana*, ser. 3. Florence, 1928–48.

Suriano, F. *Il Trattato di Terra Santa dell'oriente*. Milan, 1900.

Tamrat, T. *Church and state in Ethiopia 1270–1527*. Oxford, 1972.

Tellez, B. *A view of the universe, or a new collection of voyages. The travels of the Jesuits in Ethiopia*. London, 1710.

Thevenot. *The travels of Monsieur de Thevenot*. London, 1687.

Trimingham, J. S. *Islam in Ethiopia*. London, 1965.

al-Umarī b. Faḍl Allāh. *Masālik el abṣār fi mamalik el amṣār*. Paris, 1927.

Wansleben, J. M. *A brief account of the rebellions and bloodshed occasioned by the anti-Christian practices of the Jesuits and other popish emissaries in the Empire of Ethiopia*. London, 1679.

Weld Blondel, H. ed. *Royal chronicles of Abyssinia*. Cambridge, 1922.

Whiteway, R. S. *The Portuguese expedition to Abyssinia in 1541–1543, as narrated by Castanhoso with some contemporary letters, the short account of Bermudes, and certain extracts from Correa*. London, 1902.

Wiet, G. 'Les relations Egypte-Abyssinie sous les sultans Mamlouks', *Bulletin de la Société d'Archéologie Copte*, 1938, **4**.

9. AFRICA IN EUROPE AND THE AMERICAS

Aptheker, H. *American Negro slave revolts*. New York, 1943.

Aptheker, H. ed. *A documentary history of the Negro people in the United States*. New York, 1951.

Asiegbu, J. *Slavery and the politics of liberation*. Edinburgh, 1970.

Banton, M. *Race relations*. London, 1967.

Barker, J. A. 'British attitudes to the Negro in the seventeenth and eighteenth centuries'. Ph.D. thesis, University of London, 1972.

Bastide, R. *Les Amériques Noires: les civilisations africaines dans le nouveau monde*. Paris, 1967.

Beltran, G. *La población Negra de Mexico, 1519–1810*. Mexico, 1946.

Benoit, P. J. *Voyage à Surinam*. Brussels, 1839 and Amsterdam, 1967.

Bontemps, A. ed. *Great slave narratives*. Boston, 1969.

Boxer, C. R. *The golden age of Brazil*. Berkeley, 1962.

Boxer, C. R. *Race relations in the Portuguese colonial empire*. Oxford, 1963.

Braithwaite, E. *The development of Creole society in Jamaica, 1770–1820*. Oxford, 1972.

Catterall, H. T. ed. *Judicial cases concerning Negro slavery*. Washington, 1926–7. 4 vols.

Cavignac, J. *Jean Pellet, commerciant de gros, 1694–1772: contribution à l'étude du négoce Bordelais au XVIIIe siècle*. Paris, 1967.

Césaire, A. *Toussaint l'Ouverture*. Paris, 1961.

Chaunu, H. and P. *Séville et l'Atlantique*, vol. III. Paris, 1955.

Clarkson, T. *The history of the abolition of the African slave-trade*. London, 1808. 2 vols.

Coornaert, E. L. 'European economic institutions and the new world', *Cambridge Economic History of Europe*, vol. IV. London, 1964.

Curtin, P. *The Atlantic slave trade: a census*. Madison, 1969.

Curtin, P. *The image of Africa: British ideas and action 1780–1830*. Madison, 1964.

Dark, P. J. *Bush Negro art*. London, 1954.

Davis, D. *The problem of slavery in western culture*. Cornell, 1968.

Debien, G. *Les Colons de St. Domingue et la révolution*. Dakar, 1953.

Debien, G. *Plantations et esclaves à Saint-Domingue*. Dakar, 1962.

Dundes, A. 'African tales among the North American Indians', *Southern Folklore Quarterly*, 1965, **29**, and Bobbs-Merrill Black Studies Reprint.

Dykes, E. B. *The Negro in English romantic thought*. Washington, 1942.

Eaden, J. ed. *The memoirs of Père Labat*. London, 1970. 2 vols.

Eduardo, O. da Costa. *The Negro in Northern Brazil*. Washington, 1966.

Elkins, S. M. *Slavery, a problem in American institutional and intellectual life*. Chicago, 1959.

Edwards, B. *The history of the British colonies in the West Indies*. London, 1801–7. 3 vols.

Fisher, M. *Negro slave songs in the United States*. New York, 1953.

Franklin, J. H. *From slavery to freedom*. New York, 1947.

Freyre, G. *The masters and the slaves*. Tr. New York, 1956.

Genovese, E. D. *The political economy of slavery*. New York, 1961.

Genovese, E. D. *The world the slaveholders made*. London, 1970.
Goveia, E. V. *Slave society in the British Leeward islands at the end of the eighteenth century*. New Haven, 1965.
Goveia, E. V. *A study on the historiography of the British West Indies to the end of the nineteenth century*. Mexico, 1956.
Grant, D. *The unfortunate slave*. Oxford, 1968.
Grieve, A. McK. *The last years of the English slave trade*. London, 1941. Reprint, 1968.
Harris, M. *Patterns of race in the Americas*. New York, 1964.
Hecht, J. J. *The domestic servant class in eighteenth century England*. London, 1956.
Henriques, F. *Family and colour in Jamaica*. London, 1953.
Herskovits, M. J. *The myth of the Negro past*. New York, 1941.
Herskovits, M. J. *The New World Negro*. Bloomington, 1966.
Hoetinck, H. *Caribbean race relations*. Tr. London, 1971.
Hughes, L. and Bontemps, A. eds. *Book of Negro folklore*. New York, 1958.
James, C. L. R. *The Black Jacobins: Toussaint l'Ouverture and the San Domingo revolution*. Revised ed. New York, 1962.
Jameson, R. P. *Montesquieu et l'esclavage*. Paris, 1911.
Johnston, Sir Harry. *The Negro in the New World*. London, 1910.
Jones, E. *Othello's countrymen, the African in English renaissance drama*. London, 1965.
Jordan, W. D. *White over black*. Chapel Hill, 1968.
Kent, R. K. 'Palmares: an African state in Brazil', *Journal of African History*, 1965, **6**, 2, 161–75.
Klein, H. *Slavery in the Americas: a comparative study of Cuba and Virginia*. Chicago, 1967.
Le Blanc, Vincent. *Les voyages fameux*... L. Coulon, ed. Paris, 1649. English tr., London, 1660.
Le Clerc, L. 'La politique de Club Massiac', *Annales Historiques de la Révolution Française*, 1933, vol. x; 1937, vol. xiv.
Le Page, R. B. ed. *Creole language studies*. London, 1960.
Ligon, R. *A true and exact history of the island of Barbados*. 1657.
Little, K. *Negroes in Britain, a study of racial relations in English society*. London, 1948.
Lokke, C. L. *France and the colonial question, 1763–1801*. New York, 1932.
Long, E. *The history of Jamaica*. 1774. Reprint, London, 1970.
McCloy, S. T. *The Negro in the French West Indies*. Lexington, 1966.
McCullough, N. V. *The Negro in English literature*. Bristol, 1962.
MacInnes, C. M. ed. *Bristol and its adjoining counties*. Bristol, 1955.
Martin, G. *Histoire de l'esclavage dans les colonies françaises*. Paris, 1948.
Masefield, G. B. 'Crops and livestock', *Cambridge Economic History of Europe*. vol. iv. London, 1964.
Mason, P. *Prospero's magic: some thoughts on class and race*. Oxford, 1962.
Mauro, F. *Le Portugal et l'Atlantique au XVIIe siècle, 1570–1670*. Paris, 1960.
Miller, E. ed. *The Negro in America: a bibliography*. Revised ed. Cambridge, Mass., 1970.
Montejo, E. *The autobiography of a runaway slave*. New York, 1968.

Moret, M. *Aspects de la société marchande de Séville au début du XVIIe siècle.* Paris, 1967.

Nichols, H. *Many thousands gone, the ex-slaves' account of their bondage and freedom.* Leiden, 1963.

Ortiz, A. D. 'La esclavitud en Espanha durante la edad moderna', in Vinas y Mey, C., ed. *Estudios de historia social de Espanha.* Madrid, 1952.

Ortiz, F. *Hampa Afro-Cubana: los Negros esclavos.* Havana, 1916.

Pares, R. *A West India fortune.* London, 1950.

Pares, R. *Yankees and Creoles.* London, 1956.

Patterson, O. *The sociology of slavery, an analysis of the origins, development and structure of Negro slave society in Jamaica.* London, 1967.

Pierson, D. *Negroes in Brazil: a study of race contact at Bahia.* Urbana, 1967.

Pike, R. *Enterprise and adventure: The Genoese in Seville and the opening of the New World.* Ithaca, 1966.

Pope-Hennessy, J. *Sins of the fathers, a study of the Atlantic slave traders, 1441–1807.* London, 1967.

Ragatz, L. *The fall of the planter class in the British Caribbean.* London, 1928.

Rens, L. L. *The historical and social background of Surinam Negro-English.* Amsterdam, 1953.

Rodrigues, J. H. *Brazil and Africa.* Tr. Berkeley, 1965.

Rogers, J. A. *Sex and race.* New York, 1940. 2 vols.

Rogers, J. A. *World's great men of colour.* New York, 1947 and London, 1972. 2 vols.

Rogers, J. A. *100 amazing facts about the Negro.* New York, 1934.

Saco, J. A. *Historia de la esclavitud de la raza Africana en el Nuevo Mundo.* Havana, 1938. 2 vols.

Scobie, E. *Black Britannia: a history of Blacks in Britain.* Chicago, 1972.

Seeber, E. D. *Anti-slavery opinion in France during the second half of the eighteenth century.* Baltimore, 1937.

Tannenbaum, F. *Slave and citizen.* New York, 1947.

Thorpe, E. *Negro historians in the United States.* Baton Rouge, 1958.

Turner, L. D. *Africanisms in the Gullah dialect.* Chicago, 1949.

University of Edinburgh, Centre of African Studies. *The transatlantic slave trade from West Africa.* Edinburgh, 1965.

Walvin, J. *Black and white: the Negro and English society, 1555–1945.* London, 1973.

Walvin, J. *The Black presence: a documentary history of the Negro in England.* London, 1971.

Westergaard, W. *The Danish West Indies under Company rule, 1671–1751.* New York, 1917.

Williams, E. *British historians and the West Indies.* London, 1966.

Williams, E. *Capitalism and slavery.* Chapel Hill, 1944.

Williams, G. *History of the Liverpool privateers, with an account of the Liverpool slave trade.* 1897.

Winks, R. *The Blacks in Canada.* Montreal, 1971.

Work, M. *Bibliography of the Negro in Africa and America.* New York, 1928.

Wyndham, H. A. *The Atlantic and emancipation.* Oxford, 1937.

Wyndham, H. A. *The Atlantic and slavery.* Oxford, 1935.

INDEX

Page numbers in italic indicate substantive references

Abankeseso 297
Abbai r. 557, 562
'Abbāsi 40, 51
'Abbasids 58, 148; descent 137
Abbo, M. with Mohammadou, E. 131n., 626
'Abd al-Jalīl 73
'Abd al-Karīm (Wadai) 58, 63, 133, 137, 140
'Abdallāb clan, 'Abdallābī 42, 43, 49, 53, 57, 625
'Abdallāh (Bagirmi) 63, 132–3
'Abdallāh I al-Quraynātī al-Qāsimī: *see* 'Abdallāh Jammā'
'Abdallāh III ('Abdallābī) 48
'Abdallāh IV ('Abdallābī) 48, 49
Abdallah bin Hemedi al-Ajjemy 510 and n., 643
'Abdallāh b. Yasin 200
'Abdallāh Jammā' 41, *42ff.*, 52
'Abd al-Qādir, Shaykh (Mandara) 131
'Abd al-Qādir (Bagirmi) 77
'Abd al-Qādir I (Funj) 44
'Abd al-Qādir II (Funj) 43
'Abd al-Qādir al-Wālī (Bagirmi) 134
'Abd al-Qādir b. Ḥammadi (Futa Toro) 209, *212–14*, 215, 216
'Abd al-Raḥmān al-Rashīd, sultan (Darfur) 9, 51, 52
'Abd al-Raḥmān Kâhya al-Qāzdughlī 32, 33
Abdel Rahman el Nasri 626
'Abdulai Bademba (Futa Jalon) 210
'Abdullāh b. 'Abd al-Jalīl (Koyam) 112
Abdullay Boru 138
Abeche 139
Abesim 313
Abgal 554
'abīd (Morocco), *'abīd al-Bukhārī* 149–50
abiiru (Rwanda) 477
Abiodun, *alafin*, 229, 232, 242, 250, 251
Abir, M. 570n.
Abiye (Shoa) 567
Aboh 255, 257
Abomey 230, 232, *233ff.*, 243, 245
Abora 307
Abraham, A. 293n.
Abraham, D. P. 391n., 398n., 638
Abrem 299
Abubakar Sano (Gambia) 286
Abū Bakr (Mandara) 130
Abu Dilayq 52
Abu'l-Dhahab: *see* Muḥammad Bey Abu'l-Dhabab
Abū Likaylik (Funj) 45, 46, 49
Abu'l-Nūr Muḥammad Pasha 27
abuna 548, 551, 568, 575
Abun-Nasr, J. M. 630
Aburi 311
Aby lagoon 313
Accra 235, 300, 302, 309, 310, 311–12, 319, 321
Acholi 473, 486, 491
Acre 34, 35
Ada 309, 319
adai festival 318
Adal 537, 538, 539–40, 541, 543, 546, 550, 552, 555, 576
Adamawa 110, 111, 132
Adandé, A. 636
Adandozan 242–3
Adangbe 300, 309, 310, 617; Adangbe in Eweland 310, 320
Adansi 297, 299, 303, 314
Adar 125
Aden 550
Adesi (*see also* Guan) 297, 299, 619
'Adlān I (Funj) 43
'Adlān II (Funj) 46, 49
'Adlān (regent) 47, 48, 49
'Adlān walad Ṣubāḥi 46
Adoimara Danakil 554, 555
Adrar of the Iforas 168
Aflao 310
Afranj Aḥmad 29–30
African Association: *see* Association for Promoting the Discovery of the Interior Parts of Africa
Afrikaner 446
'afrit 85
Afro-American culture 612
'Afro' music 614
Afro-Portuguese: *see* Luso-African
Afuno 78
Agabba 125
Agades 76, 82, 83, 86, 128, 129; Chronicle 124, 125, 626
Agaja Trudo 9, 236–7, 239, 320
Agaw 546, 548, 557, 558, 571
Agballa 271
age-sets 74, 259, 484, 491, 495, 540

agha 145
Aghrezeur 126
Ag-Madol, *amenukal* 168
Ag-Moru 169
Agni 313, 314
Agona clan 298; state 301, 302
Agonglo 248
Agriculture
as basis of economy 179, 283, 372, 388, 508; with pastoralism 7
cereal 21, 233
interference with 75–6
introduction of 1
labour: free black 452; serf 210, 372; slave 86, 98, 143, 181, 274; in Cape 448, 458; in Europe 582–3; in Americas 593, 603, 616
mixed farming 247, 425, 460, 464
shift towards 84, 111, 328, 499, 552, 562
yam 253, 275
Agyensam 300
Ahaggar 98
Ahanta 297, 307, 308
Ahensen 303
Aḥmad (Fezzan) 129
Aḥmad, Shaykh (Mombasa) 528, 529
Aḥmad al-Ṭayyib b. al-Bashīr 56
Aḥmad Bābā 78, 159
Aḥmad Bey the Bosniak 27, 28
Aḥmad b. al-Ḥajj Abū ʻAlī 624
Aḥmad b. Idrīs al-Fāsī 57
Aḥmad b. Saʻīd al-Busaʻidi 533
Aḥmad Bukar (Darfur) 139
Aḥmade, *imam* 574
Aḥmadi Gaye 215
Aḥmad Karamanli 119
Aḥmad Pasha (Egypt, 16th c.) 18
Aḥmad Pasha al-Jazzār 37
Aḥmad Pasha the Albanian 27
Aḥmad walad ʻAli, shaykh 46
Aḥmadi Issata, *almamy* 215–16
Aḥmadi Pate 215
Aḥmad Köprülü 29
Aïr 66, 75, 86, 94, 112, 115, 117, 123, 125
Aja people, states 223, 229, 233, 234, 236, 243, 320, 592, 612, 616, 618, 619
Ajagbo, *alafin* 229
Ajase Ipo (= Porto Novo) 230, 250
Ajayi, J. F. A. and Crowder, M. 6n., 90n., 628
ajele 231
ʻAjīb al-Kāfūta, *al-Mānjilak* 42, 44, 52, 53, 54, 55, 57
ʻAjīb IV, Shaykh 48, 56
Akan 10, 144, 182, 223, *296ff.*, 321, 612, 617, 618, 619, 635
forest 182, 184, 188–9; northern (Brong) 315; southern 315
ʻAkani' 297, 299, 300, 303
Akele-Guzay 563, 567
Akindélé, A. and Aguessy, C. 636
Akinjogbin, I. A. 90n., 223n., 246n., 633
Akintoye, S. A. 229n.
akomfo 298
Akpa 270, 272
Akron 301, 306, 319
Akunakuna (Ekoi) 272
Akure 227, 228
Akwamu 8, 235, 296, 300, *301ff.*, 303, 305, 309, 310, 311, 312, 318–19, 320, 322–3
Akwamuhene 302, 303, 305, 311, 323; Asante commander 303
Akwapim 8, 300, 305, 309, 311, 316, 322–3
Akyem 296, 297–9, 300, 304, 305, 306, 311, 312, 313, 315, 316, 319, 322–3; Abuakwa 299, 311; Kotoku 312
alafin 118, 229ff., 241–2, 251
Alagoa, E. J. 256n., 635
Alawi: *see* Ba-Alawi
ʻAlawid dynasty 148, 156, 629–30
Alays 44
Albert, Lake 472, 488
Alberti, L. 437 and n., 639
Albreda 219
Alcáçova, Diogo de 395 and n.
ʻAlcance' (? = Adansi) 300
Alcazar, battle 147
alcohol (*see also* arrack, brandy, gin, rum) 248, 291, 348, 371, 400, 401, 445
Alego 485
Aleppo 15
Alexandre, P. 632
Alexandria 23, 37, 122
Alfaya 210
Algiers 22, 104, 119, 145
Algeria (modern) 145; (Regency) 66, 88, 144, *145ff.*
ʻAlī (chief of Awlād ʻUmar) 180
ʻAlī, *mansa* 192
ʻAlī, *ras* 573, 574
ʻAlī (Tunisia) 119
ʻAlī al-Tlimsānī, *qāʼid* 155
ʻAlī Bey, *shaykh al-balad* 32
ʻAlī Bey al-Faqārī 26
ʻAlī Bey, *Bulut kapan* 32, 33–5
ʻAlī b. al-Ḥajj Dunama, *mai* 131
ʻAlī b. Dāwūd 552
ʻAlī b. ʻUmar, *mai* 67, 78, 80, 87, 94, 95, 101, 103, 107, 112, 116, 122, 123–4, 135
ʻAlī Gaji, *mai* 134
Aligaz, *ras* 574
ʻAlī Kawrī 212
ʻālim 45, 53
ʻAlī Pasha 25

'Alī Shandora 151, 222
Alkalawa 117
Allada 229, 230, *233ff.*, 236–7, *243ff.*, 247, 249, 252, 259–60, 319, 321, 589, 594
almamy (Bondu) 215; (Futa Jalon) 208, 209, 210; (Futa Toro) 204, 209, 212
Almeida (Jesuit, Ethiopia) 647, 648
Almeida, Francisco d' (viceroy) 439
Almeida, Francisco José de Lacerda e 521n., 638
Almoravids 65, 167, 199, 216
Aloma, *mai* Idris 8, 67, 121, 136, 154, 626; conquests and tribute 81, 95–6; fighting and raids 62, 63, 65, 68, 105, 111, 113, 115, 123, 126–7, 129–30, 132; opening of roads 84, 86; Islam 92, 93, 94, 99, 102, 133
alpai 494n.
Alpers, E. A. 506n., 529n., 532n., 642
Alur 486, 488–9, 643
Alvarez, F. 646
Alvaro I 334
Alvaro II 331ff.
Alvaro III 336, 337, 355
'Alwa 40
amadzlozi 427
Amakiri dynasty 265, 269
amanto 303, 304, 316
amanyanabo 266, 268, 271
'Amāra Dūnqas 41, 52
'Amāra II Abū Sikaykīn 42
Amarar Beja 44
Amat 235
Ambasel 574
ambergris 90
Ambriz 343, 359
Ambuila 339, 340, 341, 342
Ambun (= Bambun, Mbuun) 365–6
Ambundu: *see* Kimbundu
Amed Ber (battle) 574
amenukal 168, 170
American crops (*see also* cassava, maize, *etc.*) 8, 11, 328, 382, 622
American Indians 602, 605, 621, 622
America, North 3, 99, 591, 593, 597, 599, 600, 602, 603, 607, 620, 621
America, Spanish 592, 593, 594–5, 598, 602, 609, 617, 619, 650
Americas, the 250, 260, 296, 321, 338, 582, 591, 596, 602, 619, 621
Amhara 10, 544, 547, 556, 557, 558, 559, 560, 563, 566–7, 570, 572, 573, 576
amharization, amharized elements 557, 559, 565, 566, 569, 572, 577
'āmil 20
amīn 20, 155ff.
al-Amīn, *askiya* 166
al-Amīn b. Sīdī al-Fāḍil 201
al-Amīn walad Musmārr, Shaykh 46, 47, 49
amīr al-mu'minīn 116, 154
amīr al-Ḥājj 22
amīr Miṣr 30, 35
Amis des noirs 600
Ammehayes 560
Amo, William 588 and n., 589
Amsaka 71
Amsterdam 595
amulets 247, 287
Anago 232
'Anaj 41
Anania, G. L. 627
Anansi (Anancy) 618
Anatolia 23
Andalusians 152
Andes 602
Andoni 258, 265, 266, 269
Andrade, A. A. de 404n., 640
Andriamanely, 461, 462
Andriana dynasty 467, 468
Andrianampoinimerina 468
Andriandahifotsy 462, 463, 466
Anfilla 543
Angareb r. 569
Angoche 390, 517, 518, 522, 523
Angola 2, 4, 325n., 333, 335, 361, 376, 424, 579, 592, 594, 612, 618, 637, 638
  Dutch 338, 339
  modern 423
  slave trade 259–60, 344, 346–8, 351, 593
  white colony 321, 322, 334, 350, 356, 383
'Angolas' (slaves) 615, 616, 617
Angot 557
Anguiano, M. de 633
'ankoses' 431
Anlo 310, 319
Anokye, *okomfo* 303–4
Anomabo 320, 321
Ansa Kwao 319
Ansa Sasraku 302, 305
Antanosy 467
Anteimoro culture 467
anthropology 628, 633, 634, 635, 640, 643, 644
Antigua 611
Antioquia mines 592
Antongil 467
Antonine movement 342
Antonio of Crato 583
Antonio I (Kongo) 340, 341
Antonio Manuel ne Vunda 332
Anuak 486, 487, 488
Anville, J. B. B. d' 306
Anyi: *see* Agni

Aowin 296, 297, 312, 313, 315, 320
'Aperme' 279
Appolonia 313
Aptheker, H. 651
Aqīt family 158, 159
Arabia 86, 563, 575
Arabic chronices 623; language 111, 197
Arabs 1, 11, 40, 582, 592; in East Africa 505, 506, 513, 314; in Ethiopia 556, 563; merchants 83, 458, 541; nomads 157; Omani 467; tribes 15, 146, 458
Aragon 582
Arawan 171
Arbaji 41, 46, 47, 49
Arbo 249
archaeology 283n., 394, 401, 404, 409, 411, 413, 418, 422, 428, 430, 433n., 540, 627–8, 635, 636, 641–2, 645
archers, bows and arrows 2, 70, 72, 301, 323, 395
archives 623, 624, 628, 630, 631, 633, 635, 637, 640, 641, 642, 649
Arcin, A. 632
Ardener, E. 327n., 638
ardo 163, 198
'Ardra' slaves 616
Aregay, Merid Wolde 647
Argentina 602
Arguin 221, 222
Argyle, W. J. 239n., 636
Arhin, K. 634, 635
Arho salt plains 543, 554
Ari II, *ngola* 358
Ari Kiluanji, *ngola* 354, 357
arimo 358
Arkiko 550, 567, 575
arma 142–3, 155–7, 161, 168, 170
Armenian traders 551
armour 73–4, 79
Arnett, E. J. 109n.
Aro (oracle) 255, 258; (town) 270, 271, 273; (traders) 270ff.
Arochuku 270, 271
Aro Ndizuogu 271
arrack 443
Arquivo Histórico Ultramarino 405n., 642
Arquivo Nacional da Torre do Tombo 642
Arquivos de Angola 637
artillery 50, 72, 358, 362, 399, 463, 544
artisans 98, 149, 160, 284, 367, 604–5
Asaimara Danakil 554
Asal, Lake 554
Asante 6, 9, 10, 144, 184, 195, *302–5*, 312, 313, 320, 322, 631, 632
Asante Akyem 313, 323
Asantehene 304, 312, 315, 316, 317
Asantemanso 303
Asebu 299, 306, 308, 309, 310, 589
Asere clan 314
Asfa-Wasen 561, 575
Ashrāf 38
Asian imports 527
Asimini 271
askiya 137, 154, 158, 161, 163, 168, 174, 191
Asmiye, Ato 541n., 648
Assab 541
Assin 297, 299–300, 306, 315
Assini 313, 320
Association for Promoting the Discovery of the Interior Parts of Africa (African Association) 82n., 178n., 601
Astley, T. 580
Aswan 14, 17, 38, 40
Asyut 22, 57
Atakpa (Creek Town, New Town, Duke Town) 267
Atakpame 315
Atbara r. 40, 43, 54
Atkins, J. 246n.
Atkinson, R. 473n.
Atkinson, W. C. 582n.
Attaqua 443, 453; Attaqua's Kloof 454
Austrian (trading co.) 408
'Awaḍ al-Karīm Abū Sinn, Shaykh 47
Awbek b. Ashfagu 200
Awjila 82, 86, 121
Awka oracle 255, 271
Awlād Muḥammad (Fezzan) 95, 128, 129
Awlād Sulaymān (Arab nomads) 74, 102
Awlād 'Umar (Brakna) 179, 180
Awlil 201
Awole, *alafin* 250, 251
Awsa oasis (Ethiopia) 541, 552, 554
Awsenba, *amenukal* 168
Axelson, E. 388n., 640, 642
Axelson, S. 332n., 638
Axim 320, 321
Ayalon, D. 623
Ayi Kuma Teiko 312
Ayiwaso 300, 310
Ayūba Sulaymān Dyallo 220
Ayyubids 14
Azande 8, 10, 325
Azawad 170
'Azebān 19, 24, 27, 30, 31, 32
Azebo 557, 560, 575
Azevedo, W. d' 635
Azezo 571
al-Azhar mosque 14, 22, 39, 54, 95, 107, 110
Azna 116

Ba market 234
Ba-Alawi 554
Babanango mts. 430

Babba Zaki 73
Babwa 327
Badagry 246, 250
Bādī I Sīd al-Qūm 43, 56
Bādī II Abū Daqan 44
Bādī III al-Aḥmar 44, 55
Bādī IV Abū Shulūkh 45, 46, 56
Bādī VI 47
Bādī (regent) 46, 48
Bādī walad Rajab 47
Badibu 218, 280
Bafing r. 207, 217
Baga 276, 293, 603
Bagamoyo 509, 534
Baghayogho brothers 198
Baghdad 14, 53, 107
Bagirmi 58, 61, 63, 69, 77, 81, 92, 94, 96, 99, 100, 101, 103, 106, 107, 108, 109, 111, 129, 130, *132ff.*, 137, 141
Baher-Meder 538, 544, 546, 557, 563, 566, 568, 575
Bahia 250, 593, 616, 618
Bahr al-'Arab 95
Bahr al-Ghazal 486, 487
Bahri (monk) 647
bahr-negash 538, 544, 545, 546, 567
Bai Farma 278
Bailundu 362
Bainuk 276, 281, 290
Bakary (Bambara) 176–7, 192–3
Bakkā'iyya 170
Bakongo: *see* Kongo
Bakosse island 221
Balaba 282
Balante 276, 281, 290–1
Bali 538
balopwe 377
Balowoka 505, 513–14, 515
Baltimore 605
Bamako 183
Bamba, Duke of 332
Bambala (Madagascar) 460, 464, 465
Bambara 163, 164, *171ff.*, 182, 185, 186, 192, 209, 220, 631, 632
Bambuk 206, 216, 219, 221, 285, 286, 317
Bambun: *see* Ambun
Bamileke 326
Bamum 326
banana 8, 327, 364, 372, 494
Banda 313, 314
Bandama r. 295, 313
Bandia clan 325
Bandiagara 166; mts 185
Bandundu 363
Bangassou 325
Bangura 293
Banks, J. 601
Bani r. 171, 184
Banian traders 524, 525
Banmana 174
Bantaji 134
Bantam 440 and n.
Banton, M. 649
'Bantu' slaves 616, 618
Bantu-speaking peoples 325, 327, 469, 482, 483, 494, 531, 639, 641
Banū Daymān 200
Banu'l-Kanz 40
banyamai 402
Baqqāra 51
Bara (Gambia) 218
Bara (Kordofan) 51
Bara state (Madagascar) 461, 462, 467
Barābra 17
Baraguyu 498, 506
baraka 54, 200, 201
Barama N'golo 174, 175, 176
Baraytuma Galla 540, 543, 547, 554, 560
Barbados 591, 611, 617
Barber, F. 585
Barbot, J. 204n.
Barcelona 583
Bari 486, 490–1
Bariba 190, 196, 207, 230
bark-cloth 7
Barker, J. A. 590n., 648
Barneveld (ship) 463, 466
Barradas (Jesuit) 647
barrafula cloth, 284, 285
Barrakunda 216, 286
Barreto, Francisco 2, 385–6, 389, 393
Barreto, Manuel (Jesuit) 390n., 392, 393, 522, 523n.
Barros, João de 581, 646
Barrow, J. 417n., 639
Barry, B. 633
Barsbāy (Sultan) 26
Barter, Edward 308
Barth, H. 86, 90, 325n., 627
Barwe 393
Başbakanlık Arşivi, Istanbul 623
Bashee r. 434
Bashilo r. 572
baskets 329, 381
basorun 241
Bassa 276
Bassari (Gambia) 281, 291
Basset, R. 632, 646
Basters 445
Bastide, R. 618n., 650
Basuo (Nembe) 256
Batavia 445, 551
Bate 183
Bathily 217

Batrān, ʻAbd al-ʻAzīz 632
Battell, A. 637
battle-axes 395
Bauer, R. and A. 608n.
Baule 314
Baviaans r. 456
Bawa, *sarkin* Gobir 76, 90, 117, 125
bayʻa 115, 155, 200
Bayão, Sisnando Dias 392, 393, 397
Bayyūmiyya 39
Bazin, J. 632
Beach, D. 391n.
'Beachrangers' 440, 441
beads 386, 411, 433, 437; akori 299; copper 382, 417; coral 229; glass 417, 514; gold 401; imported 181, 348, 381, 382, 400, 401, 409, 410, 439, 443; iron 417; local 325; precious 298; red Indian Ocean 436; Venetian 525
beans 229, 233, 364, 368
Beatrix Kimpa Vita 342
Beccari, C. (ed.) 646
Beckford, G. L. 604n.
Beckingham, C. F. and Huntingford, G. W. B. 646, 647
Begemder 547, 557, 559, 572, 573
Begho 184, 188, 297, 313
Beja 40, 44
Bekaffa 565, 569
Bekwai 303
Belbelec 112, 125
Beledugu 175, 176, 179
Belesa 574
Belew 550
Belle 276, 279
Bello, Sultan Muḥammad 94, 272
Bemba 380, 637
Bena (Susu) 281
Bena (Tanzania) 508
Benadir 541, 550, 553
Bende (Tanzania) 500
Bende fair 271, 273
Benefali 176
Benezet, A. 600
Benghazi 82, 86, 89, 141
Bengo r. 334, 357
Benguela colony 350n., 358, 361, 377; plateau 350, 352, 357, 359–60
Benin 4, 6, *226ff.*, 230, 234, 236, 240, 243, *248ff.*, 252, 254, 255, 257, 259, 268, 318, 321
Ben Messaib 96n.
Benue 134, 253
Berabish 171
Berbera 553
Berberistan (Lower Nubia) 17
Berbers 72, 147, 148, 150
Berbice 609
bere 231
Berg, F. J. 642
Berg r. 422, 443
Bergdama 417n., 422, 424
Betsileo 467
Betsimisaraka 466, 467
Beutler, A. F., Ensign 435 and n. 437, 454
Beyers, C. 641
Beyla 183
beylerbeyi 19, 147
bey, beylicate 19, *24–5*, 29, 31, 145–6
Bhila, H. K. 641
Biafada 276, 281, 287, 291, 603
Biebuyck, D. 373n.
Biafra, Bight 260, 269, 272–3, 275, 307, 325, 616, 617
Bidderi 95, 109, 137
Bihé 360–1, 383
Bijago 276, 291
bilād al-makzin 147
bilād al-sibā 120, 147, 148
bilād al-Sūdān 51
Bilma 73, 86, 127, 128
Bina 162
Binawa 84, 107
bindígà 71
Bindugu 171, 174
Bini 223: *see also* Benin
Bintang creek 290
Birkeli, E. 640
Birmingham, D. 350n., 351n., 352n., 362n., 376, 638
Birwa 410
Bisa traders 11, 379, 513, 521, 533
bishops 331, 337
Bisina lake 486
bisserin (= *imām*) 286
Bissau 290, 296, 589
Biton Kulibali (Mameri) 175, 176, 177, 184, 192, 193, 631
Bivar, A. D. and Shinnie, P. L. 627
biwi 521
Bizamo 561
Blackburn Ridge 428
Black Caribs 621
Black Volta 187, 197, 314, 317, 322
Blanc, Vincent le 581
Bleek, W. H. I. 640
Bletterman, E. 440n.
Blondel, H. Weld 575n.
Blue Nile 40, 41, 54
Boa Amponsem, *Denkyirahene* 298, 303
Boahen, Adu 315n
'Bobangi' peoples 348, 363
Bobo 182, 184

Bocarro, António 389 and n., 519
Bocarro, Gaspar 524, 526–7
Boeseken, A. J. 641
Bohannan P. and Dalton G. 366n., 368n.
Boina Bay 458, 460; State 462, 467
Bokkeveld 453
'Bolaudi' (?Swaziland) 409
Bole 313
Bolewa 116
Bolivia 602
Boma 343
Boma-Sakata 363, 365
Bombay 408, 564
Bondu 178, 205–6, 213, 215, 219, 220, 633
Bonduka 217, 218
Bonduku 184, 313ff., 631
Boni 612
Bonny 256, 257, 258, 260, 263, 269, 273
Bono 302
Bono-Mansu 184, 185, 297, 314, 317
bontan cloth 284, 285, 316
Bontemps, A. (ed.) 650
Bontinck, F. (ed.) 341n.
booty 69, 70, 80, 91
Bopolu 293
Borana 540, 547, 560
Borbor Fante 306
Bordeaux 596, 600
Borgu 104, 190, 196, 281, 632
bori 59, 104
Borku 127
Bornu 10, 58ff., 62, 65, 66, *67ff.*, 78, 81, 86, 87, 90, 91, 94, 99, 100, 101, 102, 106, 107, 111, 120, 126, 128, 129, 136, 137, 140, 626
Boro r. 95
'Bosjesmans-Hottentotten' 452–3
Bosman, W. 233n., 306n.
Botswana 410, 411, 412, 418
Bouchaud, J. 638
Boukar Adji (= Bukar al-ḥājj), *mai* 131
Boulègue, J. 633
'Bouques' 460
Boussouma 186
Boutillier, J. C. 632
Boxer, C. R. 357n., 592n., 617n., 641
Bradbury, R. E. and Lloyd, P. C. 634
braffo 305–6
Braithwaite, E. 613n.
brak 203, 204
Brakna Moors 151, 179, 200, 203, 212, 222
brandy 382, 439, 594
Brásio, A. 340n., 352n., 355n., 637
brass 229, 311, 317, 348, 410, 437
Brass Ijo: *see* Nembe
Brava 533, 550
Bravmann, R. A. 298n.
Brazil
  Afro-Indians 622
  alcohol 347, 357
  Dutch in 243, 347
  free blacks and mulattoes 605
  forces from 338, 354
  gold 319, 593, 594
  persecuted groups 357
  plantations and mines 351, 357, 592, 593, 603, 605, 608–
  profitability of slave production 601
  racial situation 591, 609
  relations with Portugal 593
  rice production 603
  size of African population 602, 650
  slaves: categories 616; language 613; origins 463, 594, 618; manumission 620; *quilombos* 611; revolts 609, 616; syncretism 613
  sugar plantations 3, 594
  tobacco 250, 347, 357, 594
Brazilian banks 358; plantation interests 357; sources 637
Brazilians, Luso-Brazilians 319, 340, 347, 593
Brenner, L. 78n., 84n.
Brer Rabbit 615
Bretuo clan 303
Breutz, P. L. 639
brick 92
bride-wealth 382
Briqua (Tlhaping) 416 and n.
Brissot 600
Bristol 596, 599
British: in Cape 458; in Caribbean 601; ships 436, 439; traders 424, 551, 564, 596; *see also* English
Brock, Beverly 512n.
Broecke, P. van den 636
Broglie 600
broker kingdoms 354, 356, 358, 383; *see also* trade
Brong 188, 313, 315
Brown, W. A. 632
Browne, W. G. 52, 625–6
Bruce, James 41 and n., 44, 49, 557, 625, 647
Brüe, André 217, 219, 220
Bryant, A. T. 428 and n., 429, 430, 639
Bryce, James 399
Bubba 200
Būbū Mālik Sī 206
Bucquoy 463, 466n.
Budduma people 98, 101, 105, *113*
Buddu 472, 481
Buffalo r. 434
Buganda 7, 8, 9, 472, 473–4, *478ff.*, 485–6, 507, 643, 644

Bugerere 472
Bughe 510
Bugungu 472
Buha 500, 507, 645
Buhaya 645
Buhweju 472, 475–6
Buipe 631
Bukar, *alfa* 165
Bukar (Mandara) 130
'Bukkameale' 346
Bulala 68, 69, 73, 74, 78, 91, 126–7
Bulaq 23
Bullom 276, 278, 279, 280, 293
Bultu 85
Buluba 500
Bulut kapan 32
Buna 184, 187, 314, 317, 631, 632
bundu 280
Bungonde 511
Bunyoro 472ff., 480, 481, 500, 644
bur 285
burba 204
Burchell, W. J. 418 and n.
Burckhardt, J. L. 22n., 49, 50, 54, 55 and n., 57, 625
Bure 181, 216, 285, 317
burgama 92
burguram 92
burghers 441, 445ff., 450–1
burial 87, 93
Burton, R. 243n.
Buruli 472
Burundi 469, 500, 644
Busa'idi dynasty 507, 509, 525, 532, 534, 536
Bushman r. 434, 435, 455
'Bushmen' 452–3, 454
'Bush Negroes' 611, 612, 618
Bushong 368
Busoga 473, 481, *485ff.*, 644
Butana 42, 46, 52, 55
Butua 385, 393ff.
Buys, Coenraad de 457
Buzimba 476
Buzinza 472, 500, 645

cabildos 614
Cabinda 343, 344, 349, 350, 359
caboceers 299, 307, 308
Cacheu 280, 290, 296
Caconda 362
Cadiz 583
Cadornega A. de O. 355, 356n., 637
Caetano Pereira family 521
Cahill 178n.
Cairo 15, 17–19, 21, 22, 23, 24, 33, 62, 79, 94, 95, 96, 110, 118, 133, 623
Calabar r. 258
Caledon r. 442
caliph 154, 156
Callet, Fr. 640
Calonne-Beaufaict, A. de 638
Caltanisetta, Fra Luca da 341n., 636
Camara e Coutinho, L. G. da 532n.
Camdebo 454
camel nomads 51, 111
camels 22, 50, 69, 72, 86, 89, 113, 127, 128
Cameroun 4, 252, 259, 275, 325, 638
Campbell, J. 413 and n., 418 and n.
candomble 618
cannibalism 352
canoes and boats 23, 41, 72, 82, 113, 160, 252, 253, 290, 295, 363, 367, 381, 466; making and selling 253, 256, 259, 308; trade 275, 460
  trade canoes 256, 261
  war canoes 261, 291
Canoe Houses 261, 264, 269, 295
Cape, Cape Colony 393, 408, 415, 416, 418, 422, 424, 427, 435, 436, 437, *439ff.*, 457, 465, 540; Cape Archives 409n., 440n., 443n., 452, 453n., 641; Cape Coloureds 445; Cape Malays 448; Capemen 441–2; Cape Patriot movement 447; Cape Town 357, 417, 436, 444, 446, 450
Cape Blanc 221
Cape Coast, Cape Coast Castle 297, 320, 321, 593
Cape Delgado 518, 526, 528
Cape Mesurado 278
Cape Mount 278, 279, 293, 295
Cape Palmas 276, 278
Cape St Catherine 348
Cape Three Points 308
Cape Verde, peninsula 204, 579
Cape Verde Islands 284, 617
capital accumulation 264; investment 7, 13, 286, 358, 385, 595, 649; credit 264, 596
capitalism (European) 578, 583, 585, *592ff.*, 598, 603, 615, 622
'Captain of the Gates' 386
'Captain Pepple' 270
capitania 616
Capuchins (Italian) 338, *341ff.*, 352, 354, 580, 630
caravans 49, 86, 87, 98, 102, 125, 126, 285, 322, 336, 337, 343, 357, 362, 370, 373, 374, 380, 410, 550, 553, 555, 562, 563
  caravan routes and centres 22, 36, 41, 43, 66, 189, 191, 195, 507; tolls 123, 168
Caribbean 3, 320, 463, 526, 594, 596, 601, 602, 607, 613, 614, 620

Caribs 621
carpenters 604
carpets 386
Carré, J.-M. 624
Carson, P. 633
Cartagena 592, 609, 617
Carteret, G. 151n.
Carvalho, H. D. de 371n., 638
Casamance 280, 290, 603
'Casanga' 290
cassava 8, 11, 328, 364, 368, 372, 379, 382
castes 142, 283, 284, 289, 292, 317, 468, 478
Castries, H. de 70n., 151n., 630
Catalonia 582
Cathedral of São Salvador 332
Catholics in Ethiopia 538, 544, 548, 549, 564, 591, 598, 613, 614, 646
Caton-Thompson, G. 404 and n., 641
Cattle 7, 8, 163, 198, 218, 233, 318, 329, 381, 382, 385, 393, 400, 411, 413, 422–3, 428, 433, 439, 449, 453, 460, 462, 464, 496, 561, 603; cattle nomads and pastoralists 106–7, 207, 287–9, 422; cattle raiding 363, 433, 453–4, 455; cattle trade 91, 329, 409, 417, 435, 436, 437, 438, 439, 443, 456, 496
Caulker family 295
cavalry 2, 7, 45, 72–3, 229, 239, 242, 313, 325, 358, 559, 571
Cavazzi, G. A. 354 and n., 580, 636
Cavignac, J. 649
Cele 430
census, Dahomey 239
Central Africa 325ff., 615
Central Records Office, Khartoum 625
ceramics, imported 386, 394, 480, 514
Cerulli, E. 647
Chad region 65, 69, 86, 98, 111, 113, 127, 325n.
Chaga 495, 497, 510
Chainouqua 442, 443, 451
Chakossi 189, 194
Chalumna 434
Chamatowa 'the conqueror' 522
Chamboneau, L. M. de 203n.
changamire 384, 394–5, 398ff., 405, 408; dynasty 398, 403, 406
Chapus, G. S. and Ratsimba E. 468n., 640
Charsley, S. R. 644
Chassebeuf, C.-F. (Volney) 624
Chaunu, H. and P. 649
chawa 545, 547, 548, 559, 562, 564, 566
Chelga 43
Chenier, M. 630
Cheshme 34
Chewa, 512, 517, 520, 521, 645
Chicoa 390
chikanga 392
Chikulamayembe lineage 513
chikunda 397, 521
Childs, G. M. 360n., 362n., 638
Chile 621
Chilga 550
China 465
Chobona 425
Chokwe 368, 369; forest 374
Chombe 390
Chonyi 535
Christian Ethiopia 537ff.; kingdoms in Sudan 53, 57; priests in Ethiopia 538ff., 558, 564, 577; in Kongo 332–3, 341, 391, 565; in Sohio 337; slaves 88, 145
Christianity in Kongo 331–2; messianic 342
Christians: in Egypt 38; in North Africa 65, 66, 104, 119, 120, 147
Chronicles: Arabic 623, 628, 629; Agades 626; Ethiopian 646; Funj 624; Gonja 631; Kano 626; Senegal 632; Walata 631; *Ta'rīkhs* 629, 630–1; Turkish 623
chuanga 389, 397
chuano 388
Church, Dutch Reformed 446, 450; Ethiopian 558ff., 575ff.; Kongo 331
Churchill, A. and J. 204n., 580
Chwa I 474–5
'cimarrones' 610
'Cimbeba' 423
Circassians 14, 19, 25, 26, 582
Cissoko, S. M. 282n., 631, 635
civet 596
clan 233, 484
Clapperton, H. 90, 272n.
Clarkson, T. 598
Cleveland family 295
clientship 289, 300, 414, 419, 420, 457, 464, 470, 535, 568; client states 312
cloth, cotton 86, 87, 229, 233, 283, 285, 286, 324, 388, 400–1, 460; Asian 22, 371, 379, 533, 554; imported 7, 23, 87, 146, 217, 324, 339, 348, 350–1, 382, 386, 388, 390, 391, 410, 481; local 7, 86, 87, 90, 91, 181, 229, 233, 251, 283, 286, 299, 317, 325, 381, 388, 554; palm fibre 344, 346, 349, 355, 364, 367
clothes 91, 284, 348, 382, 508
Club Massaic 600
coastal influences (East African) 503, 505, 507, 509
Cochoqua 442, 443, 451
Cockpit Country 612
Coelho, L. A. 285n.

coffee 21, 22, 36, 550, 551, 597
Cohen, D. W. 486n., 644
Cohen, Ronald 628
Coillard, F. 638
collaborators and allies 4, 443–4, 608
colocasia 364
Columbia 602
colonial economy 5, 275, 595
colonos 397
Combe, E. 624
'comey' 266
commando 453, 454, 456
commerce: *see* trade
Comoro Is. 467, 533
compradors 250, 295, 308
Conceição, Fr. Antonio da 8, 394–5, 395n., 397, 640
concubines, concubinage 99, 107, 445
Condorcet 600
Congo basin 8, 325n., 612, 618; lower 325, 328ff.
Congo r. 328, 329
Conjour (= Goundiourou) 217–18
Connah, G. 628
conquistador 392
Constantine 87
conversion: to Christianity 561, 571, 610; to Islam 85, 103–4, 114, 124, 132, 134, 551, 552, 560, 576
Conzelman, W. E. 646
coopers 604
copper
  crosses 371, 377
  mines 335, 340, 344, 371, 374, 378, 384, 409, 424
  ornaments 345, 382, 401, 434
  trade: external 4, 345–6, 349, 359, 408, 439, 443; internal 7, 91, 344–5, 364, 371, 374, 379, 433, 436–7
coral 22, 88
'Coromantee language' 612; *see also* Twi
'Coromantine' slaves 617
Correa, Gaspar 646
Correia, Bras 333
Correia, Silva 637
corsairs 88, 119, 120, 145
Corubal r. 280, 281
Cory, H. 643
cotton 7, 21, 160, 233, 249, 286, 599, 600, 603, 604; *see also* cloth
Coufo r. 236
Courlanders 296
Coutinho, Souza 358 and n.
Couto Lupi, Eduardo do 522, 523n.
cowries 76, 90, 226, 239, 248, 250, 319, 514
crafts 62, 91, 233, 234, 246, 279, 283, 289, 308, 333, 367, 401, 517, 619
Crawford, O. G. S. 625, 626
Crazzolara, J. P. 643
Creole 613, 614, 615, 618, 650
Cromme r. 454
Creek Town 258, 259, 267
crop complex 327
Cross r. 252, 256, 257, 260, 262, 267, 269, 273; Ibo 258
Cuba 601, 603, 613, 618, 650
Cogoano, Ottobah 585
Cultru, P. 291n.
cults: ancestral 9, 159, 239, 267, 286, 388, 460, 465, 478, 523; fertility 185; harvest 301; M'bona, 522–3; millenarian 452; Mwari 9, 403, 638; oracle 270, 403; 'pagan' 356; rain-making 388; totem 286; war 301; water spirits 257, 266, 268
cult slaves 274
Curação 592, 595, 611, 620
currency 345, 365, 367; bars 220, 284; beads 364, 375; copper wire bracelets 376; cotton cloth 284, 286; cowries 76, 90, 226, 239, 248, 250, 319, 364; crusados 386, 400, 436; inflation 339, 344; krakra 318–19; manila 364; minted silver 85; mithqal 101; *nzimbu* 332, 334, 339, 364; palm fibre cloth 344, 355; shell 344
Curtin, P. D. 3n., 351n., 580n., 632, 633, 648, 649; and Vansina, J. 273n.
curva 386, 390, 391
Cushitic-speaking peoples 496, 498–9, 540, 543ff., 645
customs (duties) 23, 43, 82, 91, 213, 221, 270, 296, 364, 529–30, 564
'customs' 240, 248
Cwama 435
Cyrenaica 119

Daaku, K. Y. 308 and n., 633
Dabarki 548
Daboya 188
Dadog 499
dady 465, 466
dagga 417, 436, 439, 445
Dagomba 187ff., 189, 194, 196, 314, 322, 631
Dahomey 4, 6, 9, 223, 229, *232ff.*, 242–3 252, 265, 315, 590, 619, 636
Daisy Kulibali 179, 180–1
Dala'iyya 148–9
Dalby, D. 428n., 635
Dalzel, A. 590, 634
Dama 422–3; Berg Dama 422
Damagaram 116
Damara (Herero) 422

Damasak 74
Damascus 15, 33, 34
Dambarare 388, 393, 396, 641
damel 202, 213
Damietta 23
al-Damir 54, 55, 56
dammūr 50
Damot 537, 546, 558, 561–2, 566, 567, 570, 571, 572
Dampierre, E. de 325n.
Dan 276
Dan, Père 630
Danakil 540, 541, 543, 553, *554*, 576; Dankali coast 541, 543
Danāqla 50
Daneel, M. L. 638
Dande r. and valley (Angola) 334, 339, 357
Dande (Mozambique) 386, 405
Danes 300, 320
Danger Point 442
Dan Guddi, *sarki* 76
Dan Marina 95, 116, 118, 135
Dan Masanih 116, 118, 135
Danso 286
Dapper, O. 580, 636
Darb al-Arba'īn 22
dardai 126
Dar es Salaam 509
Darfur 9, 22f., *50ff.*, 55, 57, 63, 81, 89, 95, 97, 101, 103, 111, 136, 139–40, 624, 625
Dār Ja'al 49
Darkoh, M. B. K. 310n.
Darod 541, 553
Dar Tama 140
Dassa 238
dates 86, 129; date palms 86
Dau 406
Daura 115
Davies, K. G. 347n.
Davies, O. 428n.
Davis D. 585n., 651
Davis, John: *see* Yakuba
Dawint 572
Dawit III 564
Dāwūd, *askiya* (independent Songhai) 166
Dāwūd, *askiya* ('the great') 165
Dāwūd (Kebbi) 115
Dāwūd (Tunjur) 138
De 276, 279
Debe 430
Debien, G. 649
defterdār 52
Degha 322
Dehérain, H. 624
Delcourt, A. 631
dejazmaches 573
Dekle 212
Dekuru 176
Delagoa Bay *408ff.*, 410, 427, 429, 430, 431, 432–3, 436, 458, 465
Delgado, R. 340n., 358n., 638
Dembya 546, 548, 557
Demerara 609
Dendi 158, 159, 165, 190, 192; people 190, 191, 196
Denham, D. 127, 131; and Clapperton, H. 272n.
Denianke 202, 204, 205, 211, 212, 214, 632
Denkyira 297, 299, 303, 305, 306, 309, 313, 315, 316, 320
Denkyirahene 298, 303
Derricourt, R. 433n., 642
Desbrosses, 462 and n., 464
Deschamps, H. 463n., 640
Dey 145
al-Dhababī 'the golden' 151
Dhlodhlo 399, 401, 404
dhows 460
Dhu'l-Faqār Bey 30
Dia 198, 217
Diafarabe 198
Diagné, P. 283n., 633
Dial Diop (= Serin Ndakaru) 204
Diamme 282
Diaobe 198
Diara 163, 179, 180, 217
Diara dynasty 163, 164, 177, 193
Dias 2
Dias, L. F. de Carvalho 395n., 399n., 640
diaspora 50
diatigi 181
Diawara 179, 180
Dibarwa 538
Difaqane 415, 417, 429; see also *Mfecane*
Digo 535
Dijil Somali 553
Dike, K. O. 252n., 633
dikko 163
Dikwa 132
Dimbanyika 406
dinars 148
Dinder 43
Dinka 486, 487
Diola 276, 281, 284, 290–1, 603
Diop, A. B. 633
Dir Somali 541, 553
di-songo 179
distilleries 324
distortion 5, 6, 7, 274
Dithakong 412, 416, 417, 418
Divan 19, 145
diwal 208
Djougou 189, 190
Djuka 612

Dlamini-Ngwane 432, 433; *see also* Mbo-Dlamini
Dodoth 486
Doe 509
Dogbagri 234, 235, 237–8
Dogon 185
dokpwegan 239
Domaa 303, 313
Doman 442, 444
Dombo, *changamire* 8, 393, 394ff., 405, 406
Dominican missionaries 332–3, 386, 393, 394, 400, 515
Dongola 40, 43, 44, 52, 57
Donso, *serin* 286
Dorha (= 'Klaas') 443
Dos Santos, J. 386 and n., 393n., 515, 642
Douglas, M. 366n., and Kaberry, P. 262n.
Drakensberg mts 406, 425, 529, 431–2
Drakenstein 446
drosdty 456
Driberg, J. H. 643
Drury, Robert 463 and n., 464 and n., 641
Duala 325
Dubayna Arabs 563
Du Bois 462n.
Duhaga I 476
Duke Town 267
Dukodonu 235
Dulo 569
Dulugu, *naba* 196
Dunama b. 'Alī, *mai* 96
Dunbar, A. R. 644
Dupuis, J. 323n.
Duruma 535
Dutch: and Portuguese 221, 305, 591, 593; at Allada 244; at Arguin 221, 222; at Cape 357, 416, 424, 437, 438, *439ff.*; at Delagoa Bay 408, 465; at Luanda 338, 339, 354; at Mozambique 519; at Portendick 222; gold trade 321, 595; in Caribbean 591, 592, 594, 609, 650; in Europe 284, 345, 584, 588, 594, 595, 648; in Kongo 336–7, 339, 340, 345; ivory trade 346, 347; on Gold Coast 305, 306, 309, 310, 321; ships 325–6, 436, 463; slave trade 4, 243, 321, 347, 351, 589, 594; sources 250, 300, 425, 427, 465, 533, 636; traders, trading companies 146, 219, 249, 259, 299, 300, 325–6, 359, 408, 551, 564, 597
duumvirate (Egypt) 36–9
Duysters, L. 373n.
dwarfs 87, 99
dyahilaaku 198
Dyakaba 207, 208, 217
Dyakanke 207, *217*, 218, 219, 220, 282 285, 286, 633
Dyalonke 207, 210, 280, 281, 283, 285, 292
dyeing 62, 289
dyewood 295, 336, 340, 596
Dykes, E. B. 648
dyula: *see* traders: Dyula
Dzata 406, 407
Dzivaguru 388

East African Coast 460, 524–5, *527–9*, 553, 578
East India Company: English 34, 440; Dutch 438, 440, 447, 449–51, 458
East Indies 599
eastern Africa 10 *469ff.*, 601, 610, 618, 642ff.
eastern Nigeria 252ff.
Eastern Nigritic languages 327–8
ebi 223, 245
ecological warfare 75, 134, 126
economic specialisation 91, 252–3, 257, 283, 345, 349, 364, 367, 384, 401, 604
economy: *see* capital accumulation; credit; enclave; export licences; finance; industry; investment; luxury goods; markets; middlemen; price control; production; trade
Ecuador 621
Ede 231
Eden, Richard 579
Edo 240
education 93, 337–8; *see also* Islam: centres of learning, education
Edwards, P. 228n., 607n.
Efik 9, 253, 254, 256, 258–9, 260, 268, 270, 271
Efiom Ekpo (Creek Town) 267
Efut 267
Egba 229, 231
Egbado 229, 231–2, 251
Egharevba 634
egwa 262
Egyira 296
Egypt 2, 14ff., 57, 127, 551, 563, 623; Egyptian goods 50
Ehengbuda, *oba* 227, 241
Ehret, C. 484n., 495n., 498n., 499n., 645
ekine 263
Ekiti 226, 227, 229, 231
Ekoi 254, 257, 258, 264, 272
ekpe 9, *264–5*, 268, 272, 280
elehin-odo 232
elephants 346, 380, 506, 507, 521; elephant tails 349
El Fasher 52
Elgon (Mt) 482, 484, 493, 494

elimani (Mālik Sī) 205–6
Ellenberger, D. F. and MacGregor, J. C. 413, 639
Elmina 235, 297, 305, 592
El Obeid 49, 57
Elphick, R. H. 420n., 425n., 439n., 451n., 640, 641
Ema lineage 267
enclave (export/import) 275
Encyclopaedia of Islam 624, 626
Engaruka 645
England 584, 595, 597, 598, 599
English: competition 359, 362, 408; forts and factories 238, 320, 617; merchants 146, 220, 243, 249, 320, 343, 347, 440–1, 592; mulattoes 295; ships 336, 362, 408; sources 463, 580, 633; supporters 220, 309; trading companies 219, 320, 617
Enkoje 359
epidemics 3, 24, 48, 104, 118–19; *see also* plague; smallpox
Equiano, Olaudah 228n., 272, 586, 606–7 and n., 634
Eritrea 41
escrivão 356
Esien Ekpe Oku 264
Essequibo 609
estates (social) 194, 195; *see also* stratification (social)
Estermann 638
Ethiopia 2, 3, 10, 43, 45, 49, 57, *537ff.*, 557, 578, 579, 645ff.
Ethiopian escarpment 469
etsu 118
eunuchs 51, 87, 89, *100–1*, 133, 141
Europe and Africa 578ff.; investment in 595
European: aggression and invasion 2, 110, 145–7; consuls and agents 121, 219, 291; factories 144, 183, 184 (*see also* forts); firearms 146; goods 50, 220, 231, 245, 268, 275, 319, 336, 371, 554; growth 3; ideas and ideology 3; naval expeditions 145, 146; sources 580, 628, 629, 633–4; traders 11, 146–7, 183, 202, 207, 210, 211, 220, 228, 239, 243–6, 249, 259–60, 263, 308ff., 580 (*see also* Dutch; English; French; Portuguese, *etc.*)
Europeans in South Africa 458
Eva 445
evangelization 546, 547, 602
Evliya Çelebi 623–4, 627
Ewe, Eweland 300, 301, 309, 310, 314, 319, 320, 612, 617
Ewostatewos order 555, 570
exploitation 261, 595, 606, 620
export licences 88
Eyamba I 264
ezomo 241

factions 14, 17, 28, 30–2, 33–4, 47, 161, 329; religious (Ethiopia) 549, 555–6, 570–1
factories 246, 551
Fadoku 174
Fagitta 571
fā'iḍ 20
Falaba 292
Falasha 544, 546, 548
Faleme r. 206
Fali 85
Famaghan 184
famines 3, 24, 29, 93, 97, 117, 118, 123, 140, 160, 166, 170, 204, 342, 352, 429
fandroana 468
Fante 235, 297, 299, 301, *305ff.*, 315, 320; Confederacy 307
Faqāriyya 20, 25–8, 30, 31
al-faqīh, fakī, fuqahā' 55 and n., 159, 198, 201
Far East 15, 552
Faria e Sousa, Manuel de 431
faring Kabu 281, 282, 292
farma 178
Fasil 571, 572
Fasiladas 549, 550, 551, 555ff., 563
Fāṭima 54
Fatimids 14
Fati-Morukpe 194
Fazughli 43, 548, 567
Feierman, S. 510n., 644
Felner, R. J. de Lima 637, 646
Felou rapids 219
Fernandes, Valentim 292n.
Fernandes (Central Africa) 393n.
Fernandez (Ethiopia) 648
Feroge people 95
ferries 339
fetish: *see* cults
Fetu 299, 305, 308, 309
Feyiase (battle) 305
Fez 62, 137, 148, 152, 156, 159
Fezzan 66, 82, 86, 87, 89, 95, 101, 102, 120 127, *128*, 141
Field, M. J. 318n., 634
Fielding, J. 585
Figuerido, Luis 399
Filamanka 279
finance 80, 596
Fipa 643
Firdu 287
firearms: adoption and use 147, 149, 195, 399, 456; artillery 72, 309, 362, 399; Cape Dutch 453, 457; importance and

firearms (*cont.*)
limitations 2, 22n., 64, 66, 70–1, 79–80, 183, 185, 301, 323, 390, 424, 442, 462–3, 563; Moroccan 65; Portuguese 383, 385, 389, 395; trade and importation 5, 22, 23, 70, 72, 87, 88, 89, 122, 135, 139, 143, 146, 183, 217, 220, 222, 302, 348, 359, 400, 465, 467, 468, 563, 568, 575; Turkish, Turco-Egyptian 50, 71; *see also* musketeers; fusileers
firewood 91, 231
Fish r. 435, 436, 455; *see also* Great Fish r.; Little Fish r.
Fish-eagle, people of 398
fishing, fish-trade 113, 233, 257, 258, 300, 328, 329, 363, 368, 378, 379, 381, 416, 428, 430, 460, 464
al-Fishtālī, 'Abd al-'Azīz 154n., 629
Flacourt, E. de 461n., 462, 640, 641
Florida 622
Fogny 290
Fokeng 413, 418
Folayan, Kola 232n., 635
folle 540
fonio 283
food prohibitions 492
foodstuffs: trade 63, 86, 91, 129, 161, 168, 181, 210, 221, 233, 234, 257, 319, 327, 359, 373, 384, 388, 402, 597, 603; supply 36, 63, 129, 140, 160, 282, 357
Forde, Daryll 487n.; and Kaberry, P. M. 317n.
Fort Dauphin 462
Fort Jesus 528, 530, 532, 645
forts: Angola 334, 352, 358, 359; Benguela 361, 362; Cape 442–3; Guinea coast 3, 246, 301, 302, 307, 319, 321, 580; Kongo 337, 343; Mombasa 528, 530; Mozambique 386, 519; Senegambia 219, 220, 296; upper Guinea 296
Fortune, G. 638
Franciscan missionaries 564
Françoine (renegade) 152
Franklin, J. H. 650
Freeman-Grenville, G. S. P. 532n.
Freetown 79, 95, 140, 296
French, France
Africans in France 584, 586, 587; in French West Indies 591
anti-slavery movement 600
consulates 104
emancipation 601
Huguenots 446
in Egypt 39, 110
invasion rumour (Cape) 443
Madagascar and Mascarene Islands 463, 467, 526, 641
Senegambia 203, 213
ships 336, 362, 408, 436, 439
sources 152, 250, 580, 624, 648
trade 23, 181, 200, 211, 219–22, 243, 244, 321, 343, 347, 359, 551, 564, 592, 596–7
Fresnel, M. 629
Freyre, G. 617n., 650
frontier wars (Cape) 455
Fugumba 208, 209, 210
Fuladu 287
Fuladugu 175, 178, 180, 184
Fulakoro 176
fulakunda 287
Fulani 10, 63, *105ff.*, 199, 216; Bagirmi 132–3, 137; Bambara 175, 177, 182; Bondu 206, 214; Bornu 75, 79, 80, 85, 113, 123; Futa Jalon 183, 207, 208, 209, 219; Futa Toro 7, 207, 208, 219; Hausaland 62, 73, 95; Kwararafa 135; Mandara 131; Massina 160, 162; upper Guinea 283, 285, 287, 294; Walo 203
Funj 17, *40ff.*, 50, 52, 53, 55, 57, 99, 108, 140, 547, 548, 550, 551, 563, 567, 624, 625
Funj Chronicle 41, 45, 49, 624
fuqahā': see *al-faqīh*
Fūr 25n., 45
Furley collection (Ghana) 320n., 321n., 594n.
furs 410, 414, 417, 419
fusileers (Ethiopian) 559, 566, 570, 571
Futa Jalon 183, 198, 206, *207ff.*, 219, 281, 285, 289, 292, 293, 603, 632
Futa Toro 152, 179, 198, 200, 202, 204, 206, 207, *211ff.*, 217, 218, 219, 632–3
Futas, the 144, 208

Ga 235, 300, 309, 310, 311, 318, 617
Gabon 344, 638
gada 540
Gadiaga 205–6, 217
Gago (Gao) 151
Gaha, *basorun* 241–2
Galadyo Tabāra 205
Galagansa 500
Galam 152, 205, 211, 219, 220
Galawdewos, king of kings 537–9, 543, 555
Galilee 34
Galla 10, 496n., 531, 533, 537, 538, *543–4*, 552–5, 557, 558, 559, 560–2, *564ff.*, 566, 569ff., *576*, 645, 647–8
Galla, amharized 565, 566, 569, 572
Galla (Unyamwezi) 503 and n., 546
Gallabat 550
Galligna (language) 569
Gallinas 279

Galvão, Manuel 396
Gambaga 195; scarp 187
Gambia 181, 216, 217, 218, 276, 280, 296, 580, 583, 617, 631, 633
Gamitto 638
Gamtoos r. 438, 454, 455
Ganda 479–81; *see also* Buganda
Gandowentshaba 435
Ganum, A. 154n.
Gao 151, 154, 166, 170, 186, 630
Garcia II 8, 338–41
Garlake, P. S. 641
Gash r. 43
Gaskeru 107, 112–13, 125
Gatsi Rusere, *mwene mutapa* 386, 388–90, 518
gau 243
Gaya 190
Gaza 32
Gbande 278
Gbanya 187–8, 194
Gbouele 238
Gcaleka 436
Geba r. (= Corubal r.) 280
Gebru 575, 576
'Gedingooma' (? = Guidioume) 180
Geel, Georges de 338
genealogy 26, 40, 51, 53, 411, 425, 430, 625, 642
Genoa 121
Genoese favourite, Tunis 104
Genovese, E. D. 651
Georgia 88, 89
Germany, Germans 345, 424, 446, 580, 599
Gezira 40, 44, 46, 49, 51, 53, 57
Gezo 243
Ghadames 59, 81, 82, 86, 87, 101, 103, 104, 126, 128, 129, 158
Ghana (ancient) 167; (modern) 635
gharama 199
Ghat 128
Ghulāmallāh b. 'Ā'id 52
Gibe 547, 561–2
gin 7
giraffe 122
Giriama 531, 535
Gisaka 472, 477
glassware 87, 386, 480
Goa, Goans 396, 521, 525, 529, 533, 544; viceroy at 396, 642
goats 325, 327, 332
Gobir 62, 76, 110, 117, 125
Godée-Molsbergen, E. C., 454n., 641
Gogo 491, 498, 508
Gogosa 442
Gojjam 555, 557, 558, 559, 560, 562, 564, 571
Gola 276, 279, 280
Golbéry, S. M. X. de 631
gold: Brazilian 319; coinage 148; exactions 157, 160; export 3, 5, 87, 144, 219, 296, 300, 320, 521, 528, 552, 589, 592, 595, 597; internal trade 50, 160, 161, 182, 184, 189, 202, 285, 297, 302, 313, 386, 396, 400, 521, 546; local use 7, 298, 318, 337, 388, 401, 404; loot 148; mining and sources 313, 317, 384, 385, 388, 389, 393, 397, 398, 400, 517, 520, 580, 593, 603; trans-Saharan trade 144, 150, 181, 216, 217, 221; tribute 81, 154, 155, 561; gold work 288, 388, 401
'gold' (=copper) 335, 339–40, 417n.
Gold Coast 4, 184, 222, 223, 233, 236, *296ff.*, 307, 580, 589, 593, 595, 603, 612, 617
Gombe 627
Gomes, Fr. Antonio (Jesuit) 388n., 394
Gona 435
Gonapamuhanya 513
Gondar 43, 557, 558, 564, 565, 566, 568, 570, 571, 572, 573, 574, 575, 576, 646, 647
Gonja 62, 89, 187–8, 189, 194, 196, 314, 322, 631, 632
Gonnema 443, 452
Goody, J. 632, 634
Gorachouqua 442, 451
'Goree' 440
Goringhaikona 441–2
Goringhaiqua 451
goromondo 395
Gorowa 499
Goshu 572
Goundiourou 218
Gouritz r. 454
Gouro 276, 283
government 18, 19–21, 44, 83, 226ff., 418, 466, 539, 544, 545, 546, 559, 566; bureaucracy 316, 317, 373, 377, 479; foreign relations 63–4, 121–2, 135, 331, 551, 589; police 64, 621; revenue 20–1, 80, 82–3, 88, 546, 554; *see also* military; monopoly; state; taxes
Gqunukwebe 434, 456
Graaff Reinet 450, 454, 456, 457, 458
Graça, J. R. 373n., 374, 638
Gragn, *imām* Aḥmad 537, 539, 541, 543, 544, 552
Graham, J. D. 248n
grain 21, 23, 86, 233, 325, 332, 381, 409, 417, 420, 445; *see also* maize; millet, *etc.*
grain beer 382
Grain Coast 294
Grand Cess r. 278

grandees (Egypt) 18, 23, 25, 30–1, 35–6
Grandidier, A. and G. 460n., 461n., 465n., 466n., 641
Gravelotte 410
Gray, R. and Birmingham, D. 409n., 645
Great Akani 298
Great Assin 299
Great Benin 226, 227
Great Brak r. 455
Great Camp (Bornu) 74, 75
Greater Antilles 605, 609
Great Fish r. 425, 438, 452, 456
Great Lakes region 469
Great Moghul 551
Great Popo 235, 237, 243, 244–5
Great Zimbabwe 13, 394, 398, 403, 404, 461, 641
Greece, Greek: merchants 551; legends 579
greegrees: *see* amulets
Greenberg, J. H. 327n.
Gregoire, Abbé 600
Grieve, A. McK. 588n.
Grigriqua 451, 452
griots 202–3, 283
Griqua 416, 458, 522
groundnuts 11, 364
Grumania 189
Guadeloupe 601
Guan 297, 298, 300, 303, 306–7, 311, 316, 322, 617; language 188, 306
Gudru 559, 562
guelwar 282
Guemu 179, 180, 193
Guerreiro, Fr. Fernão 579
Gugsa, *ras* 574, 575–6
Guidi, I. 559n., 570n., 646, 647
Guidioume 180
Guillain, C. 541n., 640
Guinea (Republic) 197
Guinea-Bissau 290, 603
Guinea Coast 2, *223ff.*, 594–5, 603, 612
'Guinea' slaves 616
gum 22, 23, 50, 200, 202, *221*, 596
gumsu 107
Gur 619
Gurma, Gurmantche 189, 190
Guruhuswa (= Gunuvutwa = Butua) 394
Guy, J. 433n.
Guyana 602, 609, 611, 612, 618, 619, 622
Gwali 434, 436
Gwaranga 134
Gwari 98
Gyaman 313–14
Gyamanhene 314
Gyaasewahene 317
gypsies 357
Ha 500
Hab 424
Haberland, E., Schuster, M. and Straube, H. 403n.
Ḥabesh 17, 26, 27
Hadejia 627
Hadhramaut 554
Hādī 200–1, 203
Hagan, G. P. 317n.
Haha 154
Hahn, T. 640
Haile-Maryam 576
Haiti 613, 618
ḥajj caravan 22, 96; routes 121; *see also* Pilgrimage
ḥākim 120, 161
Hakluyt, R. 579, 580
Halfaya 42, 53
Hall, R. N. and Neal, W. G. 401n., 404n., 641
Hallett, R. 157n., 221n.
Halpularen 206
Ḥamad Abū Dunāna 52, 54
Ḥamad al-Naḥlān 55
Ḥamad b. Muḥammad al-Majdhūb (*al-Kabīr*) 54, 56
Hamaj 46, 47, 49, 563
Hamasien 563, 567
Hamburg 597
Ḥamdūn b. Dunama, *mai* 96
Hamet, I. 632
Ḥamid b. 'Umar 54
Hamitic hypothesis 139
Ḥammadi Amina I 163
Ḥammadi Amina II 164, 198
Hanang, Mt 506
Hancumqua 425, 436
Handeni 509
Hango clan 512
Hannibal, Ibrahim 584 and n.
Hanotaux, G. 624
Harar 541, 552, 553, 555, 560, 576
harem 100, 101, 104
Harinck, G. 433n., 434n., 639
Hārūn, *askiya* 166
Ḥasan Bey al-Faqārī 27
Ḥasan b. Aḥmad 529
Ḥasan Pasha, Jezā'irlī Ghāzī 37, 38, 39
Ḥasan walad Ḥassūna 53, 55, 71
Ḥasan, Y. F. 625
Hāshim al-Musabbaʿāwī 51
Hashimite family 34
Ḥassān 151, 199–202, 205, 212
Hatsa 499
Haupt, C. A. 454n.
Hausa States 61, 62, 65, 81, 106, *114ff.*; markets 326; traders 190

Hausaland 7, 12, 63, 78, 79, 86, 89, 90, 94, 97, 101, 102, 112, 125, 129, 134, 188, 189, 198, 247, 324, 626–7
Haveaux, G. L. 369n.
Hawiya Somali 541
Hawwāra tribe 17, 33, 34, 35
Haya 500, 515
Ḥaydarzāde Muḥammad Pasha 26
Hedges, D. 432n.
heemraden 450
Heese, J. A. 450n.
Hehe 508
Hejaz 33, 56, 99, 101, 122
Hembapu 424
Hemmy, O. L. 465 and n.
Henga 512
Henshaw Town 267
Herero 422–3
Herry 8, 440–2, 444
Herskovits, M. J. 636, 650
Hessequa 442, 451
Heusch, L. de 644
Hex r. 454
Heyling, Peter 550
hides and skins 22, 87, 160, 207, 221, 285, 287, 361, 384, 410, 414, 417, 419, 494, 596
highway robbery, kidnapping 36, 85, 124, 574
hijra (re-enactment) 61
hi-koi 165
Hilālī 51
Hill, R. L. 626
Hillelson, S. 55n., 625
Hima/Tutsi 470, 477, 500
ḥimāyāt 28, 29
Himba 423
Hintsati 435
hippopotamus hide whips 113
Hiskett, M. 90n., 627
Hispaniola 597, 603
Hispano-Portuguese monarchy 592
Hlengwe 410
Hlubi 431–2
Ho 310
Hodh 170
Hoengeiqua 435
Hoernlé, A. W. 640
Hoetinck, H. 592n., 620n., 651
Hofrat en Nahas 7
Hogben, S. J. and Kirk-Greene, A. H. M. 628
Hoho 436
Holo 356, 376
Holt, P. M. 623, 624, 626
Hombori 166
Honduras 621
honey 381, 420
Hopen, C. E. 628
Hoppe, F. 640
horn 504–5
Horn, the 10, 537, 540–1, 550, 552, 576, 645–6
Hornemann, F. 82 and n., 110n., 125
horses: absence of 402; export 50; gifts 124; import 7, 9, 73, 87, 123, 127; military use, cavalry 7, 64, 72–3, 74, 75, 76, 134, 149, 189, 242, 424, 543; prestige use 355; raids for 453; trade and exchange 55, 87, 89, 90, 118, 134, 206; trappings 284
Horton, R. 262n., 635
Hottentots 425, 444, 578
Hottentots Holland r. 442, 443
Houdas, O. 150n., 152n., 154n.; and Delafosse, M. 152n.
Houghton, Maj. 221
'House' organization 256, 259, 260ff.
Hova 463, 467, 468
Huambo 360, 362
hubūs 59
Huffon 235, 237, 238
Hughes, L. and Bontemps, A. 615n.
Hughes, V. 601
Huguenots 446
Huising, Henning 447
Hulet Ledet 570, 573
Huma: *see* Hima/Tutsi
Humām b. Yūsuf, Shaykh 33
humanitarians 586, 598–9
Humbe 401
Hume, D. 588
Hungu 376
hunters, hunter-gatherers 327, 328, 413, 415, 416, 420, 431, 454, 492, 495, 499, 501, 503, 508, 510, 527; ivory 325, 346, 419, 438, 451, 507, 509, 513
Huntingford, G. W. B. 487n., 643
Hunwick, J. 628
ḥurma 198
Hurutshe 412, 415
Ḥusayn Bey b. 'Alī (Tunis) 65, 96, 119, 122
Ḥusayn Bey Kishkish 33, 34
Husaynid dynasty 96, 104
Ḥusayniyya suburb 39
Hutu 477

Iberia 581, 592
Ibibio 223, 253ff., 257ff., 265, 270, 273
Ibn al-Mukhtār 630
Ibn Baṭṭūṭa 170
Ibn Fartuwa, Aḥmad 67, 69ff., 70n., 74, 77 84, 85n., 91, 92, 93, 121, 124, 141, 662
Ibn Iyās 623

Ibo, Iboland 10, 223, 252ff., 256, *257ff.*, 265, 273, 614, 617
Ibrāhīm, Sultan 26
Ibrāhīm (b. Aloma) 93
Ibrāhīm al-Būlād b. Jābir 54, 55
Ibrāhīma Sambeghu (= Karamokho Alfa) 208
Ibrāhīm Bey (Faqāriyya) 29, 30
Ibrāhīm Bey (*mamlūk*) 35
Ibrāhīm Kâhya 31, 32, 33
Ibrāhīm Pasha (al-Maqtūl) 24
Ibrāhīm Pasha (Grand Vizier) 18
Ibrāhīm Ṣidayq 625
Ibrāhīm Sori (= Sori Maudo) 209, 210
Ibrāhīm Zaki 108
Ibrim 17, 22
ichege 575
Idah 253
Ida Oranyan 230–1
Idaw Balhasan 201
ideas and ideologies 3, 12, 91, 136, 239, 289, 338, 403, 578ff., 619; *see also* cults; religion; Islam
Idoma 254
Idrīs, regent 47, 48, 49
Idrīs (Sa'dābī ruler) 49
Idrīs Aloma: *see* Aloma
'Idrishu of the fair skin' (= Idrīs Aloma) 68
Idrīs Katagarmabe, *mai* 68
Idrīs Muḥammad al-Arbāb, Shaykh 43, 53
Ifat 560
Ife 229, 230, 238, 251
Ifonyin 232
al-Ifrānī 151 and n., 152n., 154n., 629
Ifrīqiya 145
Igala 254, 272–3
Igana 231
Igara 475
igba iwa 231
Igbomina 229
Igede people 235
Igelefe 237, 238, 247
Iguana cult 266
Igulwibi 506
Igwebe, R. O. 255n.
Igweke Ala 271
Ijanna 232, 242, 252
Ijebu 226, 230, 251, 252
Ijesha 229, 231, 618
Ijo 228, 249, 252ff., 257, 265, 268
Ikot Akpa-Atakk 272
Ikot Ekpene 258, 273
Ikot Etunko 258
Ikoyi 231
Ilamba 506n.
ilari 231
Ilaro 232
Ilesa 229
iltizām 20, 23, 33
Imagsharen Tuareg 168
Imaliza 505
imām 92, 108, 112, 133, 154, 193, 196, 198, 200, 202, 212, 286, 533, 534, 538, 551
imāmuna 200
Imbangala 351, 353, 355, 360, 374, 637, 638
Imerina: *see* Merina
Imhoff, Commissioner van 447
Imo r. 258
Īnāl 18
incense 546
India 15, 408, 551, 564, 642; India Office 440n.
Indian goods 22, 50, 371, 379, 408, 527, 554
Indian Ocean 384, 436, 465, 528, 530, 533, 541, 551; trade 407, 458, 463, 527, 553
indigo 202, 294, 547, 603
Indonesia 448
induna 427
industrial revolution 596, 601
industry, manufacturing 358, 596, 604
inflation 21, 23, 339
Ingombe Ilede 516
Inhambane 407, 408, 409, 419
inkosis 427
Innarya 547, 561–2, 564
Inqua: *see* Hancunqua
insignia of office, regalia 229, 268, 318, 366; bell of state 355; bracelet of sinews 370, 377; conus shell disc 504–5; cowhide belt 372; crown (Ethiopian) 567; divination calabashes 231; drums 136–7, 140, 388, 473; ghost horns 504–5; head-dress 505; palanquin 315; robe of honour 37, 129; *siwa* horn 506; staff of office 444; state sword 298, 304; stool 298, 301, 304, 612; turban 513; umbrella 315
Intarahna, battle 47
Intelligence Reports (Nigerian Government) 258n., 274n., 634
intelligence service 9, 314, 403, 612
interlacustrine kingdoms 7, 10, 470ff., 500, 644
intermarriage 40, 119, 126, 157, 219, 295, 357, 416, 435, 445, 493, 498, 545, 550, 559, 583, 587, 591
International African Institute 634
invasion and conquest 2, 18, 23, 48, 113, 142, 145–6, 148, 515–17, 522, 538
Inyaka 432
ipantia 494n.
iqṭā' 19
Iramba 498, 499, 506

Irangi 498
Iraqw 499
Irdāb, *amīn* 44
Irle, J. 640
iron: implements and weapons 229, 345, 382, 417, 424; imports 275, 284, 345, 348, 439; internal trade 7, 327, 381, 382, 417, 436, 443, 494, 496, 512; mining 409, 411, 413, 423; tribute 318, 381; work 233, 253, 257, 275, 311, 384, 401, 416, 500, 504; workers 283, 284, 410, 431
Iron Age (southern Africa) 411, 413–14, 419, 428, 437, 642
iron bar currency 220
irrigation 42, 55, 290, 381, 468, 492
Iru 477
Isaacman, A. F. 641, 645
Isanga 506
Isaq Somali 541
Isenga 506
Ishan 227
Isḥāq (Darfur) 51
Isḥāq, *askiya* 158, 165
al-Isḥāqī 623
Isichei, E. 254n.
Islam 1, 2, 9, 12, 14, 43, 61, 63, 64, 65, 67, 76–7, 92–3, 118, 128, 140, 142, 187, 190, 191ff., 202–3, 286, 293, 467, 502; centres of learning 12, 50, 52, 53, 55, 65, 112, 160, 183, 191, 207, 211, 217, 287; education 54, 55; expansion *52ff.*, 58, 118, 218, 222, 292, 632; holy men 53, 54; law, courts 38, 42, 69, 80, 82, 92, 102, 198, 210, 214; orders 39, 53, 54–5, 56, 110; prophecy 109–10; reform movements 57, 110, 131, 137–8, 142; revolution 92, 137, 144, 576; *see also* jihad; Muslims; Pilgrimage; Ramadan
Ismā'īl, *askiya* 167
Ismā'īl (Funj) 46
Ismā'īl Bey 33, 35, 36, 38
Ismā'īl Bey (son of Īwāẓ) 30
Ismā'īl b. 'Abdallāh 57
Ismā'īl b. Jābir 55
Ismā'īliyya 57
Ismā'īl Kāmil Pasha 48, 49, 50, 55
Isna 22
Istanbul 19, 23, 25, 26, 27, 31, 81, 89, 101, 118, 121, 122, 145, 147, 623
Iswangala Kamanga 505
Iswangala Mwanisenga 505
Italy, Italians 550, 551, 583, 593
itéma 'míse 504
'itq 103
Itsekiri 223, 226, 249, 252, 254, 259, 274
Ivondro 467
ivory trade: exports 5, 589, 597; central Sudan and Darfur 22–3, 87; East Africa 378–9, 481, 503, 505, 506, 507, 509, 513–14, 516–17, 519, 521, 524, 528, 531–2, 533, 536, 592; Loango, Kongo, Angola 4, 336, 347, 349, 355, 359; southern Africa 384, 401, 407, 410, 419, 431–2, 438; local 229, 361, 417
Ivory Coast 183, 189, 197, 202, 296, 312, 314
Īwāẓ Bey 30
Iwillimidden Tuareg 107, 168, 169–71
Iwo 231
iyase 240, 241
Iyerhiomo 227
Iyasu I 8, 558ff., 567
Iyasu II 566, 567, 568
Iyoas 568–70
Izard, M. 632

Ja'al, Ja'aliyyūn 40, 47, 49, 137
Jaarsveld, A. van 455–6
al-Jabartī, 'Abd al-Raḥmān b. Ḥasan 32n., 36, 37n., 39, 623
Jackson, J. G. 150n., 151n., 630
Jackson, K. A. 497n., 644
Jacobs, A. 643
Jadin, L. 342n., 637
Jaffa 35
Jaga 334, 350, 366, 515; mercenaries 335, 355n.
'Jaga' 355, 360
Jager Afrikaner 452
jāhiliyya 198
Jakin 237, 244
Jakpa 188
jallāba 22
Jamaica 609, 611, 614, 617, 618, 619, 621
James, Preston 605n.
James Island 219
Jameson, R. P. 649
jangali 107, 164
Jānim 18
Janissaries 19, 23, 24, 27, 29, 31, 32, 119, 145, 550
Janjero 561
al-Jarmiyu 61, 108–9, 128, 137
Java (eastern Africa) 521
Jawdār: *see* Judār
Jebel Marra 50, 51, 52
Jebel Moya 44
Jebel Saqadi 44
Jedda 34, 552
Jefferson, President 600
Jenne 160ff., 166, 174, 178, 182, 184, 186, 192, 197, 630, 631
Jenne-were 161–2, 166

Jerma 167, 190
Jeronimo Chingulia (Yūsuf b. Ḥasan) 529
Jesuits: archives 386n., 390n., 394n.; missionaries 337, 338, 352, 392, 394, 396, 398, 458, 538, 544, 548–9, 550, 555, 564, 579–80, 646, 647
Jews 334, 357
Jezā'irlī Ghāzī Ḥasan Pasha: *see* Ḥasan Pasha
Jibrīl b. 'Umar 110
Jie 486
jihad 102, 158, 205; Fulani 62, 65, 67, 73, 77, 102–3, 108, *110*, 117, 196, 627; Futas 110, 183, 202, 281, 289, 292, 632; Massina 198; Zawāyā 199ff., 202, 205, 632
Jiji 500
Jimara 281, 287
jish 150
jizya 68, 77, 82, 83
Jobson, R. 216, 217 and n., 218, 631
John III 582
John IV 593
'John Africa' 270
'John Canoe' 614
Johnson, Samuel 598
Johnson, Rev. S. 230 and n., 634
Johnston, Sir H. 650
Jones, E. 579n., 648
Jones, G. I. 635
Jordan, W. D. 651
Josephine (Bonaparte) 601
Journal of Negro History 650
Juaben 303
Juba 543, 553
Jūdār (Jawdār) Pasha 152–4, 158, 163, 165
Juhayna tribe 40
Jukun (= Kwararafa) 129, 134, 135, 253, 272–3
Julien, C.-A. 629, 630
Junju 480, 481
justice 5, 120, 294, 374

Kaabine, *alfa* 183
Kaarta 176, 179, 180–1, 193, 213
Kabara 169
Kabes, John 308
Kabesterra 299
Kabu 218, 281–2, 284, 286, 289, 633
Kabundami III 475–6
Kaditshwena 412
kaffāra 103
'kaffirs' 460
kafu 182, 183
Kafuku 505
Kaguru 508
Kagwa, Apolo 643
Kahama 507
Kahaya ka Murari 475
Kahaya Rutindangyezi 475
Kairouan 65
Kakongo 344, 349
Kala 171, 174, 192
Kalabari 257, 258, 260, 262, 263, 266, 269
Kaladian Kulibali 175
Kalahari 384, 405, 414, *419ff.*
Kalanga 405
Kalck, P. 638
Kalenjin peoples, language 10, 484, 491, 492, 494
Kalinga, O. 515n., 645
kalonga 516, 517, 518, 520
Kalukembe 361
Kalundwe 374, 377, 378, 380
Kamalu 258
Kamara clan 278, 279
Kamba 11, 497, 507, 509, 535, 644
Kamil, M. 570n.
Kammerer, A. 647
Kana 232
al-Kānamī, Muḥammad al-Amīn 67, 78, 79, 96, 100, 103, 111, 132, 627
Kananiya 81
kanapumba 373
kanda la Pazi 509
Kane, O. 632
Kanem 58, 63, 68, 69, 70, 74, 81, 98, 102, 111, 129, 131, 132, 140; Kanem-Bornu 94, 126
Kanembu people 69, 111, 132
Kanemi hostel 94
Kanga 507
Kango, *naba* 185
Kaniok 374, 378
Kankan 183
Kano 58, 59, 62, 63, 65, 68, 71, 74, 76, 78, 80, 83, 89, 92, 107, 114, 115, 117, 133, 134, 135, 188
Kano Chronicle 59, 116, 626
Kanongesha 376
Kanta 166
Kantora 281, 285
Kanuba Gnuma 177
Kanuri 60, 68, 71, *79*, 83, 95, 106, 111, 113, 127, 132, 627, 628; language 79
Kaokaoveld 422–4
kapsiro 494
Karagwe 472, 473, 500, 507, 644
Karamanli dynasty 81, 89, 129
karāmāt 54
karamokho 197
Karamokho Alfa 208–10
Karanga 390, 402
Kariba, Lake 516

Kariega r. 436
Karimojong 486–7; Karimojong-Teso peoples, languages 473, 486ff., 495
Karkuj (battle) 43
Karra Haymanot 570, 571
Karroo 419
Karugire, S. R. 476n., 644
Kasai 363ff., 370ff.
Kasanje 348, *355ff.*, 360, 371, 374, 376, 383
kasanje 355
Kashemereh 141
kāshif 17
Kasongo 376, 378, 380
Kassanga 276, 281, 290
Katagum 85, 115, 627
Kateregga, *kabaka* 9, 478–9
Katoke, I. K. 644
Katsina, Katsinawa 62, 63, 73, 76, 78, 83, 89, 95, 101, 115, 117, 118, 126, 133, 135, 188
Katanga 7
Katonga r. 472
Kauma 535
Kaur 285, 286
Kavirondo gulf 482–3, 486
Kawar 66, 73, 86, 87, 112
kaya 531
kayl 85
Kayor 202, 204, 213
Kayra 50, 51, 57, 624
Kazembe 380
kazembe 378, *mwata kazembe* 379–80, 521
Kea, R. A. 302n.
Kebbi 114, 117, 125, 166
Kei r. 425, 434, 435, 436, 437
Keiskamma r. 435
Keita clan 182
Kenga 107
Kent, R. K. 462n., 463n., 612n., 640
kente cloth 324
Kenya 469, 482, 486, 487, 489–90, 491, 495, 516, 528, 530, 540, 645
Kenya, Mt 495, 497
Kenya Land Commission 643
Kerawa 130
Kereyu 540
Kerken, G. van der 638
Kerimba Islands 526, 533
Keta 320
Kete Krachi 314, 322
Ketshe 434
Ketu 229, 230, 233, 238
Kgabo 414
Kgalagadi 414, 415
Kgatla 410–11, 412
Kgatleng 415
al-Khaimī, Ḥasan 551, 555, 647
Khā'ir Bey 15, 17–18
Khalīl Bey 33, 34
Khalīl Pasha 30
Khami 401, 404
Khamiesberg 451
Khamīs walad Janqal, Shaykh 45
al-Khanqa, battle 24
kharāj 82
Khartoum 47
Khashm al-Bahr 46
Khasso 175, 178, 179, 181, 213
Khatmiyya order 57
Khoi 416, 418, 420 and n., 424, 425, 434, 435, 438, *439ff.*, 640, 641
Khoi war 442
Khoisan 413, 415, 420n., 439, 578, 638, 640
Khunwana 415
khuṭba 156
Kibamanduka (= Pazi Kilama) 509
Kibinda Ilunga 370
Kifle-Iyasu 571, 572, 575
Kikonja 378
Kikuyu 493–4, 495, 643, 644
Kilama, *pazi* 509
Kilimanjaro 495, 510
Kilindi dynasty 510–11, 535
Kilindini 534
kilolo 373, 377
Kiluanji, *ngola* 360
Kilwa 520, 524, 525, 526, 527, *529*, 530, *531*, 532, 533, 534, 535, 536; Kisiwani 535–6; Kivinje 534
Kimambo, I. N. 644; and Temu, A. 644
Kimbangu clan 341
Kimbu 503–4, 644
Kimbugwe 478
Kimbundu (Ambundu, Mbundu) 350 and n., 352, 354, 355, 360, 366, 637; language 613
kimpaku ('sorcerer') 338
Kimpanzu clan 341
Kimulaza clan 341
Kimweri ye Nyumbai 511
Kinga 645
Kingolo 360
king of kings 537ff.
kings, puppet 46, 393, 571ff., 576
kingship, chieftaincy: Accra 312; Aja 240, 241–3, 245; Benin 255; Bonny 257 265, 268; Igala 255; Interlacustrine 470; Janjero 561; Kongo 331; Kuba 328; Kwararafa 64, 135; Loango 349; Luba-Lunda 370, 377; Luo 482, 489; Malinke 290; Muslim 64; Mutapa 386; Nri 255; Shilluk 488; Teke 365;

kingship, chieftaincy (*cont.*)
Tumbuka 515; Ufipa 501; Unyamwezi 503
divine 64, 135, 377, 561
succession to 240, 241, 339, 402, 434, 466, 474, 475, 503
territorial 501
'king's servants' 245
Kingui 176
Kinshasa 332, 343
kinship 4, 5, 8, 11, 411, 457
Kinyashi, *simba mwene* 511
Kipsigis 493
Kirkman, J. 645
Kisama 352
Kishkish: *see* Ḥusayn Bey Kishkish
Kisonko Masai 491
Kissi 276, 279, 291, 293
kiswa 22
Kitagwenda 476
Kitui 497
kitunga (= *itéma 'míse*) 504
Kiwanuka, M. S. M. 644
Kiziba 472
Klerksdorp 411, 415
Knights of St John 119
Kobe Zaghawa 138, 140
Koekemoer, Daniel 453n.
Koelle, S. W. 95n., 627
Kofi (Cuffee) 612
kohl 90
Kohler, O. 640
Kok, Adam 451
Kokofu 303
Kokoli 276, 281, 293
kola 7, 63, 89, 161, 182, 187, *189*, 195, 217, 231, 294, 302, 364
Kolbe, P. 445
Koli Tenguella 204–5
Komati r. 431
Kombo 284
Komenda 299, 305, 306, 308, 309, 310
Konde Birama 183, 209
Kondo 293
Kondoa 498–9
Kong 175, 183–4, 631
Kongo kingdom 3, 6, 246, 329ff., 345, 353, 368, 369, 376, 383, 578, 579, 589, 638
Koni people 410, 431
Koniagui 281, 291
Koniakary 181
Konkomba 188
Konny, John 308–9
Konongo 503
Kony people 494
Konyan 278
Korana 415–16, 417, 451, 458
Koranko 283, 292, 293
Kordofan 23n., 44, 45, 46, 47, 49, 50, 51, 57, 110, 141
koringo 282
Kormantse 320, 619
koronogbo 263
Koshea 300
Kotoko (Bornu) 72, 113
Kotokoli 189, 190, 632
Koup 454
Koya (= Quoja) 278, 279
Koyam 59, 72, 74, 83, 92, 105, *111ff.*, 118 123, 124–5
Kpelle 278, 280, 283, 294
Kpengla 238, 239, 247, 250
kple 301
kposu 243
kra kra currency 318–19
Krige, E. and J. 639
Krim 279
Krobo 309, 319
Kropf, A. 639
Kru 276, 278, 279, 295
Kuba 328, 363, 364, *366ff.*, 382, 637
Kubayh 22
Kuburi 92
Küchük Muḥammad 29, 31
Kufra 127
Kuiseb r. 422, 424
Kukiya 165
Kuku 490
Kulango 187, 313
Kulibali clan 174ff., 193
kuloglu 119
Kumasi 189, 303, 304, 312, 316, 318
Kumasihene 316, 317
Kumbari, *sarki* 71, 83
Kumdumye, *naba* 186
Kunjara 50
Kunta 12, 170, 171, 178, 632
Kupela 190
Kurata Shuwa 111
Kusassi 187
Kusi Obodum 315, 316
Kusseri 81
Kutu 509
Kutukrunku 299
Kwa (Ekoi) 258
Kwa fishermen 313
Kwa languages 276, 279
Kwadjo (Cudjoe) 612
Kwahu 296, 300, 314, 315, 319
Kwa Ibo r. 272
Kwa Kwa (= Quaqua) coast 294
Kwaman 302, 313, 314
Kwane 435

Kwango r. 328, 343, 350, 356, 365, 368, 369, 371, 374
Kwanyama 423
Kwanza r. 350, 352, 354, 359
Kwararafa 64, 70, 76, 80, 81, 101, 116, 117, 124, 129, *134ff.*, 253, 272
Kwena 411, 412, *413ff.*, 417, 418
Kwia, Kwiate 279
Kyabaggu 480
Kyamutwara 472
Kyebambe II 476, 481
Kyerepong 311, 322
Kyungu 511, 514
kyungu 514

Labadi 312
Labat, J. B. 176n., 217n., 218n., 530, 631
labour: wage 308; white 449, 620; *see also* slave
la Courbe, Sieur de 291n.
Ladoku 301, 302, 310 312
Lafayette 600
Lagos 226
laḥma 199, 200
Laikipiak Masai 492
'Lala' Nguni (= 'Tsonga-Nguni') 429, 430, 437
Lama marshes 236, 239
lamanes 202
Lamba 378
Lambert, H. E. 643
Lamu 506n., 534
Lam'ul, La'ul 41, 45
land grants 2–3, 19, 42, 45, 56, 112, 141, 334–5, 392, 449; 'fiefs' 19, 82, 84; grievances 442
landdrost 445, 450, 453
Landouma people 210
Lange, D. 627
Lange r. valley 453, 454
Langeberg 416
Lango 489
language: adoption and assimilation 111, 188, 217, 218, 263, 316, 328, 464; dialects 281, 297, 306; diversity 139, 473; evidence 327n., 365, 469, 628, 635, 640, 645, 648, 651; expansion 9, 79, 313, 378, 475, 482, 487, 488–9, 490, 497, 619; *lingua franca*, language of commerce 215, 231, 270, 299, 444, 613; retention 111, 263
  in Central Africa 327, 363, 364, 368; Gold Coast 297, 306; Madagascar 460; southern Africa 422, 425, 428, 444; upper Guinea 276, 297; Volta basin 184
  see also under separate languages
Langworthy, H. W. 645
La Palma, W. de 320n.
La Rochefoucauld 600
Laroui, A. 630
Lasta 557, 558, 566, 567, 572, 574, 575, 576
Late 310, 311, 321
Latham, A. J. H. 268n.
Latin America 592, 621, 622
Latoyo, *gbonka* 242
La'ul: *see* Lam'ul
Lavers, J. 58n.
Law, R. C. C. 223n.
Lawal, *mbang* 134
Lawrence, J. C. D. 643
lead 505
leather 229; goods 90; workers 62, 283, 284, 285; *see also* hides and skins
Lebeuf, A. M.-D. and J. B. 628
Lebna-Dengel 537, 547
Lebombo mts 429, 431–2
Lebou 204
Le Clerc, L. 649
Legassick, M. 412n., 457n., 522n., 639
Le Grand, M. 541n.
Le Herissé, A. 636
Leibbrandt, H. C. V. 443n., 453n., 641
Lele 363, 364, 366–7
Lemba 341
Leo Africanus 134, 579, 627, 637
Leonard, A. G. 634
Le Page, R. B. 651
Lepanto, battle 65
Lesotho 411, 413, 432
Lestrade, G. P. 406n.
Lévi-Provençal, E. 629
Levtzion, N. 632
Lewis, H. S. 541n.
Lewis, I. M. 327n.
Leynaud, E. 632
Leyti, O. N'D. 633
Liban Galla 557, 559, 561
Liberia 183, 278
Libolo 352
Libya (modern) 65, 119
Lichtenstein, H. 447 and n.
Lienhardt, P. 534n.
Liesbeck r. 441
Likaylik: *see* Abū Likaylik
Lilima 401
Limba 276, 278
Limpopo r. 384, 385, 403, 405, 641
Lindeque, Barend 456
lingua franca: *see* language
Linnaeus, Carl 601
Liptako 190
Lisbon 332, 333, 385, 582, 592, 594
literacy 1, 93, 457, 537

Little, K. 649
Little Fish r. 434
Little Karroo 450
Little Popo 235, 244, 302, 310
Liverpool 596, 599
Livingstone, D. 638
Livro das Monções 532n., 533n.
Lloyd, E. M. 394n.
Loango 4, 329, *344ff.*, 359, 362, 383, 638
Loango bay 344
Lobato, A. 640
Lobi 187, 317
Lobo, Jerome 541n., 648
Loeb, E. M. 640
Lofa r. 293
Logon 100, 111
Lok 584
Loko 276, 278, 279
Lokwe lagoon 231
Loma 278, 280
Lomami r. 378, 380
Lombard, J. 632
Long, Edward 591 and n.
Los islands 278
Lotuko 486, 490–1
Louisiana 618
Lovale people 377
Lovedu 406–7, 409–10, 639
Low, V. N. 627
'loyal' Khoi 444
Lozi *380ff.*, 637
Lualaba r. 368, 371, 376, 377, 378
Luanda 3, 332, 333, 337, 338, 348, 350, 353, 357, 361, 362, 371, 593, 612, 637
Luanda Island 334, 340
Luangwa r. 397, 469, 513, 521
Luapula r. 378, 379, 380, 382
Luba *377ff.*, 380, 500, 501, 511, 512, 638
luba (Galla) 540
Lucas, S. A. 377n.
Luena 369, 377
Lugbara 490
Luguru 508
lukano 370, 377
Lukelele 509
lukonkeshia 370, 373
Lulami 167
Lulu mts 410, 412
'lūlū' (Funj) 45
Lulua 368, 378
Lunda 10, 355, 361, 363, 366, 368, *369ff.*, 378–9, 383, 500, 513, 637, 638
lundu 517, 518, 520, 522–4
Luo 11, 470, *482ff.*, 485, 489, 494, 644; language 473
Luso-Africans 219, 331, 343, 374, 641
Luso-Brazilians 347
Luyia 483, 644
lwembes 514
Ly, A. 631
Lyangalile 501
Lydenburg 411

MacCalman, H. R. and Grobbelaar, B. J. 423n.
McCloy, S. T. 650
McCullough, N. V. 648
MacIver, D. R. 402 and n., 641
MacMichael, H. A. 624–5
Mabudu 432
mabvudzi 403
Macequece 396, 405
Machakos 497
Machinga 526
machira cloth 388
Macuana 517, 523, 524–5, 528
Madagascar 8, 385, 448, *458ff.*, 640, 641, 642
'Madagascars', slaves 612
Madeira, Diogo Simões 389, 390
Madi language 473, 490
Madi Makia (= Muḥammad al-Makkīyī) 130
Madoc, Laurence 151n.
Mafia Island 466
mafouk 349
Magaliesberg-Pilansberg dist. 414
maganga 460
Maggs, T. M. O'C. 414n., 418n., 419n., 642
Maghembe 511
al-Maghīlī, Muḥammad 82, 83, 170
Maghrib 14, 22, 53, 104, 119, *145ff.*, 325, 629; products 217
Maghrib al-Adnā ('Near West') 65, 66, *118ff.*, 129
Magumi 126
Magyar, L. 638
Mahajamba Bay 458, 460
Mahamat el-Kap, el-Kab 136
Mahdi 61; Mahdia 50
Mahi 236, 237, 238, 248, 619
maḥlab 50
maḥmal 22
Maḥmūd (Mali) 182
Maḥmūd al-'Arakī 53
Maḥmūd b. Abī Bakr, *amīn* 156
Maḥmud b. Zarqūn 154, 165
maḥram 122, 626
Mahungwe, battle 395–6, 399; kingdom 402
mai 61, 66, 67, 90, 95, 99, 107, 108, 111, 112, 121, 129, 131, 133
Mainga, Mutumba 381n., 637
maize 8, 11, 233, 328, 364, 368, 372, 382, 384, 429, 494, 527
Majādhīb 54, 55

al-Majdhūb, Muḥammad al-Kabīr 54; Majdhūbiyya order 55
Majerteyn 541, 554
Majorca 582
Majunga 467
Makaba II 415
Maka Jiba 206
Makanga 522
makhzin 149, 629
Makia 130
makoko 345, 365
Makonde 526, 645
Makonde plateau 527
Makono 183
Makua 523, 524, 525, 526, 527; Makua-Lomwe peoples 517, 519, 520, 522–3, 645
Malagasy 360
Malaguetta coast 294 pepper; 294
māl al-kharāj 20
malaria 409
Malawi 380, 469, 516
Malawi, Lake 379, 469, 507, 511, 512, 520, 525, 527, 645
Malay (language) 444, 460
Malemba 344, 349
Mali empire 64, 160, 163, 167, 174, 182, 191, 218, 280, 281, 282
malik al-umarā' 17
Mālik Sī 205–6
Maliki school 53
Malindi 460, 516, 528–9, 541
Malinke 142, 163, 174, 182, 197, 206, 217, 218, 276, 280, 283, 287, 289, 290, 633
mallamari 113
maloango 348, 349
Mamadu Konte 286
Mamari: *see* Biton Kulibali
Māmāy Bey 26
mambo 9, 394, 402, 406
'Mambari' 362
Mamfe 316, 322
Mami, *qā'id* 158
Mamluks 14ff., 50, 623; *mamlūk* 33; 'neo-Mamluks' 17
Mampon 303; *Mamponhene* 304
Mamprusi 187, 189, 190, 195, 196, 631
Mamvu 327
Mandara 58, 80, 83, 87, 100, 106, 111, 112, *129ff.*, 133, 626
Mande 144, 175, 187, 189, 276, 280, 281, 294, 324, 603, 615, 619
Mandenyi 278
Mandīl, S. D. 625
Mane (Mossi) 186
Mane clan (Kabu) 282
Mang'anja 517, 523, 642
Manganja da Costa 523
Mangbetu 8, 327
Mango (Grumania) 189
Mangoky r. 464
Mani 278, 279, 283, 293, 295
Maninka-Mori 197
Mankessim 306, 307
mankralo 310
mansa 191
Mansa Felupe 290
mansa Kabu 281
Manso, Paiva 637
Mansong 178, 180, 186, 193
Mansour, Chefik 623
an-Manṣūr 115, *146ff.*, 152, 629
Manṣūr, pasha of Timbuktu (1695–6) 159
Manṣūr, pasha of Timbuktu (1716–19) 157, 166
Mantoux, P. 596n.
mantse 310, 312; stool 301
Mantaub 566ff.
Manyika 391–2, 393, 394, 396, 400, 401, 405, 408
Maqdūm 52
al-Maqtūl ('the Slain') 24
marabout, maraboutism 53, 146–7, 170, 191, 195, 211, 286, 293
Maracci, G. (Jesuit) 394n.
Maradi 77
Marakwet 493
Maramuca 392, 397
Maranhão 603
Maravi 390, 458, 516, 518, 519, 521, 522, 524–5
Mareb watercourse 563, 567
Marees, P. de 580
Mariano, Luigi 458, 460 and n., 461n., 464, 465
marīsa 55
Marj Dabiq, battle 15
Marka 161, 181, 197, 217
markets and fairs 65, 114, 234, 257, 270–1, 325, 344, 353, 355–6, 364, 367, 396, 400, 405, 553; economy 11, 13, 344, 384, 525–6; revenue 7, 65; supervision 64, 355, 356; world market 5, 514, 527
Marodzi 639
Marks, S. 420n., 428n., 439n., 639, 641; and Atmore, A. 428n.
marombe 388
maroons 610, 611, 613
Maroserana dynasties 461ff., 642
Marovoay 465
Marrakesh 148–9, 151, 154, 156, 159
marriage alliances 84, 138, 338, 461, 561, 567, 576

Martin, B. G. 529n., 628
Martin, P. M. 346n., 638
Martinique 601
Marty, P. 176n., 207n., 628, 632
Martyr, Peter 579
Marwa, 131
Marx, K. 593 and n.
Maryam-Barya 571
Masai 10, 491ff., 494, 508, 643; *see also* Kisonko; Laikipiak; Samburu; Wuasinkishu
Masamba 475
Masapa 386, 389
Mascarene Islands 407, 467, 526
Mashau 407
Mashonaland 392
Mashra' al-Raml 149–50
Mashwe 416
Mason, M. 90n.
Mason, P. 649
Mason, R. J. 411 and n., 642
mason-drano ('eyes of water') 465
masons 604
Massa 176
Massalagem 460
Massangano 354, 357
Massasi (Beledugu) 176, 179, 180
Massawa 17, 26, 550, 551, 563–4, 567
Massenya (Bagirmi) 98
Massina 160, *162–3*, 166, 177, 178, 198, 206, 632
Matadi 341
'Mataman' 423
Matamba 8, 353, *354ff.*, 366
Matendere 404
Matopos 403
Matras, Consul 156
mats 231
Matuzianhe 389, 390
Mauritania (modern) 221, 222
Mauritius 601
Mauro, F. 649
maurusa 523, 524
Mavura, *mwene mutapa* 391–2, 393
Mawanda 479, 480
Mawlāy 'Abdallāh 150
Mawlāy 'Abd al-Malik b. Zaydān 156
Mawlāy Aḥmad al-Manṣūr: *see* al-Manṣūr
Mawlāy al-'Abbās 156
Mawlāy al-Rashīd: *see* al-Rashīd
Mawlāy Ismā'īl 146–7, 149–52
Maynier, H. C. 456
Mayombe 328
Mazoe 397
Mazrui dynasty 535, 536
Mbala 363, 369
Mbalu 434
Mbande Hill 514
Mbanderu 422
mbang 97
Mbange 435
Mbegha 510
Mbo-Dlamini Nguni 429, 430, 431
Mbogho 510
Mbomu basin 10
M'Bona cult 522–3
Mbugu 496, 510
Mbugwe 499
Mbulu 498–9, 645
Mbuun: *see* Ambun
Mdange 436
Mecca, Medina, holy cities of the Hejaz 14, 21, 26, 33, 52, 53, 56, 57, 90, 93, 94, 96, 97, 100, 104, 106, 107, 122, 137
Mecha Galla 547, 557, 559, 561–2, 565, 567, 571, 572
Mediterranean 86, 88, 118, 145, 222, 578
Medley, G. 445n.
Meek, C. K. 628
Meerhoff, P. van 445
Meḥmed IV, sultan 26
Meḥmed, grand vizier 29
mehu 238, 243
Meillassoux, C. 632
Meknes 149
Melakori r. 293
Mel languages 276, 278, 279
Melo e Castro, Francisco de 404 and n., 640
Menabe 462ff.
Mende 279, 280, 293, 294
Mendez, Afonso 549, 647
Mendonça, João Furtado de 334
Meneses, S. de 391–2
Menwe 412
Menz 560; Menzian dynasty 554, 567, 575
Merca 554
'merchant princes' 308, 320
Merina kingdom 468, 640
Meru 497
Merwe, P. J. van der 641
mestizos *357*, 521
metal goods 23, 371, 382; industries, 329, 416, 417, 425, 429, 437; *see also* brass; copper; gold; iron
métis 219
Mexico 602, 610, 617, 622
Mfecane (Zulu wars) 429, 430, 432, 433 524; *see also Difaqane*
mfumu 377
Mhlatuze r. 430
mhondoro cult 403
Middleburg 411, 413
middleman 5, 307, 354, 524, 531

Miji Kenda ('Nine Tribes') 531, 533, 535
migan 238, 243
migrations: Central Africa 328, 352, 365, 366, 369, 378; central Sudan 58–9, 61, 62–3, 106, 117; eastern Africa 470, 482, 483, 496–7, 499, 501, 503, 511–12, 527, 531, 534; Ethiopia and the Horn 539, 543, 547, 553; Guinea 231–2, 233–4, 255, 261–2, 313; Nilotic Sudan 40; southern Africa 398, 408, 425, 430, 432, 446
Mika'el Suhul 568, 569, 570, 571, 572
Milansi 501, 506
Milansi III Ntaseka 501
military: apprenticeship, training 9, 17, 139, 236, 351, 353, 475–6; aristocracy 547; development 64, 68, 314, 353, 373, 539; discipline 396, 399, 462; guards 545, 556, 565, 566, 673; innovations 433; militia 545, 559; organization 19, 453, 454, 546, 547, 559, 612; mutiny 24–5; penetration 114; private armies 545, 573; tribal units 548
milk 201, 287
milk 56, 112
Miller, J. C. 351n., 370n., 637, 638
millet 50, 86, 217, 233, 301, 328, 372, 388, 428, 500, 503
Milo r. 183
'Mina' slaves 616
Minas 544, 545
Minas Gerais 603, 616, 618
Mindouli 344–5
minerals 7, 335, 389, 603; *see also* copper; gold; iron; salt
mining 603, 605, 621
Mira 138
Mirabeau 600
mirrors 87, 90
misonkho 397
missanga 375
missionaries 358, 564, 601; *see also* Dominicans; Capuchins, Jesuits, *etc.*
missionary sources 458, 579, 580, 581, 633, 636, 640
Mixonga 521
Mkpokk 272
Mlowoka 513
mobility 58, 114, 131, 543, 604
Moçâmedes 350n.
Mocha 550, 551
Modibo Bakr Traore 192
Mogadishu 469, 541, 550, 554
Mogador 147
mogho-naba 186, 196
Mogopa 414
Mohamma Kisoki 115
Mohammadou, E. 131n.
Mohammed Seghir 628
Mohammed Sheriff 178n.
Mohube 410
Mokgosi 415, 416
Mola clan 189
molasses 597
Molemane 415
Molepolole 414, 415
Moleta 415
Molopo r. 415
'Molua' (= Lunda) 376
Mombasa 509, *528–9*, 530, *531ff.*, 642, 645; Mombasa-Mvita 534
Monclaro (Jesuit) 388
Mondari 490
mondyo 161
Mongala 415
Mongo 328, 363, 365, 366, 368, 638
'Monmouth' House 271
Mono r. 236, 310
Monod, Th., Mota, A. T. da, Mauny, R. 292n.
monopoly: African states and rulers 7, 146, 331, 348, 350, 361, 374, 375, 380, 386, 397, 400, 413, 419, 432–3, 437–8, 480–1; Banian 525; Dutch 441, 446; French 221, 222; Portuguese 336–7, 346, 519; sale of 88
Montejo, E. 650
Monteil, Ch. 632
Monteil, V. 632
Montesquieu 600
Montez, C. 640
Moodie, D. 442n., 641
Moore, F. 631
Moore, W. A. 227n.
Moors (Mauritania) 203, 211, 212, 216, 217, 221; 'Moors' 161, 178, 181, 460; (Portugal) 582
moradores 357
mori 286
morikunda 286
Morocco: Arab sources 629; conquest of Sudan 2, 65, 66, 115, 120, 129, 137, 142, 192, 631; Europeans 119, 144, 629; ruler 97; trade 22, 90, 181, 188, 216; warriors 220
Moroto, Mt 486
Morton-Williams, P. 232n.
Morwamotse I 410
mosques 92, 112, 141, 193, 287
'Mosquito' Indians 621
Mossi *185*, 187, 195–6, 207, 632; Mossi-Dagomba 182, *184ff.*, 187, 197

Mossop, E. E. 416n.
Mossul 343
Mossuril 519, 520
Motsele 414
Mouëtte, Sieur G. 630
moyo ndizvo 398
Mozambique 386, 448, 460, 466, 516, 525, 581, 612; channel 461, 463; coast 525; Island 391, 517, 519, 523, 524, 525, 526, 538; modern 469
'Mozungullos' 531–2
Mpinda 337
Mpondo 431, 433, 434
Mpondomise 433, 434
Mpororo 475, 476
mrima coast 506, 509, 530, 534
Mshihwi 511
M'telegwa 404
al-Mubārak, Muḥammad 124, 125
'Mubires' (= Vili) 344
Mudaito tribe 554
mudd 85
Mudenge, S. I. 638, 641
Muhlanga, S. 638
mugabe, mugave: see *ngabe*
Mugodo 407
Muḥammad, *askiya* al-Ḥājj 165, 192
Muḥammad (= 'Abd al-Qādir) 77n.
Muḥammad, *mansa* 192
Muḥammad Pasha 24
Muḥammad 'Abdullāh 74
Muḥammad Abū Likaylik: *see* Abū Likaylik
Muḥammad al-Amīn, *mbang* al-Ḥājj 96, 97, 100, 101, 133, 134
Muḥammad al-Amīn al-Kānamī: *see* al-Kānamī
Muḥammad 'Alī Pasha 20, 48, 121, 576
Muḥammad al-Makkīyī 130
Muḥammad al-Mubārak: *see* al-Mubārak
Muḥammad al-Nāsir 128
Muḥammad al-Wālī 109
Muḥammad al-Yadālī 199
Muḥammad Bey Abu'l-Dhahab 33, 34, 35
Muḥammad Bey al-Faqārī 27
Muḥammad Bey Khusraw 52
Muḥammad Bey the Circassian 30
Muḥammad b. 'Abd al-Karīm al-Sammānī 56
Muḥammad b. al-Ḥājj Ḥamdūn, *mai* 80, 96
Muḥammad b. Ḍayfallah: *see* Wad Ḍayfallah
Muḥammad b. Ibrāhīm Gāssā 541
Muḥammad b. Muḥammad 95
Muḥammad b. Muṣṭafā 96
Muḥammad b. Rajab 48
Muḥammad Faḍl 52
Muḥammad Gao 165
Muḥammad Ibrāhīm Abū Salīm 624
Muḥammad Joda 140
Muḥammad Kai 116
Muḥammad Kurra 51, 52
Muḥammad Sharīf 75, 90
Muḥammad Tayrāb, Sultan 9, 51
Muḥammad 'Uthmān al-Mīrghanī 56–7
Muḥammad walad 'Adlān 48, 57
Muḥammad walad Nimr 49
Muḥammad Yaji 59
Muḥammad Zaki 73, 76, 77
mujaddid 133
Mujaji 407
mukhrijāt 20–1
Mukombwe, *mwene mutapa* 395, 396
mulattoes 219, *295*, 308, 583, 587, 591, 602, 605, 618, 620, 621
multazim 20
Munīr al-Dīn 201
mupeto 390
muqaddam 171
al-Muqurra 40
Murād IV 26
Murād Bey 35, 36
Muratori, C. 491n.
Murdock, G. P. 327n.
Muriuki, G. 644
Murzuq 59, 81, 82, 90, 125, 128
Mūsā, *mansa* 205
Mūsā Pasha 25
Musabba'at clan 45, 47, 50, 51
Musā'id 49
Musallim, *maqdūm* 52
Muscat 533
Musgo 99
Mushī' al-Dīn 200
music and dance 229, 255, 263, 388, 613, 619, 650
musketeers and fusileers: in Central Africa 340, 348, 355; in central Sudan 70, 87; in Ethiopia (fusileers) 559, 566, 570, 571; in Guinea 189, 195, 302, 323; in Madagascar 463; in southern Africa 399, 444; Moroccan 2, 65, 182; Portuguese 391, 392, 395; Turkish 70
Muslim clerics and scribes 105, 107–9, 112, 115, 118, 130, 133, 136, 316
Muslims: in Egypt and North Africa 14, 578; in Ethiopia 537–9, 540–1, 544, 551, 552ff., 560, 572, 647; in Sudan 102, 113, 144; *see also* Islam
Mussorongo 343
Muṣṭafā (Koyam) 112
Muṣṭafā Kâhya al-Qāzdughlī 29
Muṣṭafā Pasha (viceroy *c.* 1615) 25
Muṣṭafā Pasha (viceroy 1660) 28
musumba 371, 375, 378, 380

Musuubo 485
Mutapa kingdom 6, *384ff.*, 398, 401; *see also* *mwene mutapa*
Mutebi 478, 479
Mutui, P. 495n.
Muyinga dynasty 508
Muzafar dynasty 541
Muzura, *kalonga* 390, 517, 518
Mwamlima 511
Mwari cult 9, 403, 638
mwata kazembe 379–80, 521
mwata yamvo (= *mwant yav*) *370ff.*, 376, 379
mwene mutapa 2, *385ff.*, 402, 405, 406, 422, 519, 578, 579, 581, 638; drum 388, 465
Mwera 526
mwine ntanda 377
Mya 506
Myburg, A. C. 639
'Mygrygas' 428

naba 185
Nabahani dynasty, Pate 530, 532, 535
Nachtigal, G. 79, 132n., 625, 627
Nafana 313, 322
Nagmaal 450
Nago (= Yoruba) 618
nā'ib 550, 563, 567, 568, 575
nakomse 185
Nalerigu 195
Nalu 276, 291, 293
nam 185
Nama 417n., 422, 424, 436, 442, 444, 452
Namaqualand 422
Namib desert 420
Nandi 493, 494; Nandian group 493, 494
Nango 510, 511
Nantes 596
Napoleon 31, 52, 110, 601, 623
naqīb al-Ashrāf 38
Nāṣir, son of Bādī IV 46
Nāṣir (brother of regent Rajab) 47, 56
Nāṣir, regent, son of 'Ajīb 55
Nāṣir, son of Shaykh al-Amīn 48
Nāṣir al-Dīn (Awbek b. Ashfaga) 200–2, 205, 206, 632
Natal 408, 410, 427, 428, 429, 430, 458, 642
National Archives, Tanzania 643
Native Affairs Department 639, 640
natron 23, 90, 91
Na'ūm Shuqayr 625
Naweji I 374
nayiri 195
Ndabarasa 476
Ndebele 395, 398, 399, 417, 431, 639
ndem, oku ndem 268, 308
Ndembu 352, 376
N'Diaye Sall 203
Ndlambe 436, 456
Ndokki 258
Ndombe 360, 361
Ndonde 526
Ndongo 6, 260, 351, 352, 353, 355, 357, 367
Ndoori 476
Ndorwa 477
Ndulu 360
Ndwandwe 432, 433
Neal, W. G. 401n., 641
Near East 14, 88, 527
Necker 598
negrero, slave trader 589
négrier, slave trader 589
Nembe (= Brass Ijo) 254, 256, 257, 262, 274
nerwande 403
Netia 485
New Calabar: *see* Kalabari
New England 605
Newitt, M. D. D. 641, 645
Newman, T. M. 283n.
New Town (Creek Town, Duke Town) 267, 268
New York 605
ngabe 504
Ngalangi 360
Nganguela 355
Ngasargamu 85, 92, 107, 109, 115, 124, 131, 132, 135
Ngassa: *see* Ongamo
Ngbandi language 327
Ngindo 526
ngola 2, 350n., 351
ngola a kiluanje 351
N'golo Diara 177, 179, 186, 193
ngoma drum 388
Ngona 406
Ngonde 511, 512, 514, 515, 644, 645
Ngoni 508, 515, 527
Ngouma 84
Ngoyo 344, 345, 349
Ngqika 436, 457
Ngulu 506, 510
Nguni 8, 385, *425ff.*, 433, 458, 639, 642
Ngwaketse 412, *414–15*
Ngwane 432
Ngwato 412, 414, *415*
Niamey 167
Niamina 179
Nia N'golo 174, 176
Niani (Mali) 182
Niani (Gambia) 218, 280, 285; Niani Maron 285
Niari r. 345

Nichols, H. 650
Nicolaisen, J. 628, 632
Nienaber, G. S. 641
Niger r. 152, 160, 171, 257, 630, 632
Niger bend 62, 152, 166, 324
Niger delta 226, 252, 594
Niger, inland delta 162
Niguse 560
Nike 271
Nikki 191
Nile 14, 23, 51, 53, 486
Nilotic languages 469, 643, 645
Nimr 49
Nimrāb 49
Niṣf Ḥarām 33
Niṣf Sa'd 34
Niumi (Gambia) 280, 282
Njimi 68
Nkansi 501
Nkhamanga 512
Nkoranza 314, 316
Nkore 470, 472–6, 644
Nogomo, *mwene mutapa* 389
Nokaneng 416
nokena 83
nomads 17, 40, 41, 48, 51, 58, 75, 84, 86, 97, *105ff.*, 113, 120, 128, 167, 552
Norris, H. T. 199n., 632
Norris, R. 590
North Africa 12, 23, 51, 64, 65, 66, 76, 82, 88, 91, 96, 99, 111, 161, 578, 628; merchants 72, 85, 89
North-Central Africa 10, 325–7
Northrup, S. 608n.
Notwane r. 414
Nova Scotia 602
Novo Redondo 359, 362
Nri Ibo 255, 271
Nsawkaw 314
Nsundi 328
Nsuta 303, 312
Ntare IV 474, 475
Ntare VI, *mukama* 500
Ntatatkwa 500–1
ntemi 503, *504*, 508, 644
ntemi ngboja: see *ngabe*
Ntinde, 434, 435, 436
Ntungwa Nguni 429, 430
Nuba 44, 45, 487
Nubia, Nubians 17, 40, 52, 136; Lower Nubia 17, 52
Nuer 486, 487, 488
Nūḥ, *askiya* 165–6
Nūl 45
Numu caste 317
Nuñez r. 603
Nungwa 312, 319
Nupe 62, 64, 71, 89, 90, 112, 118, 230, 242, 247, 249, 251
Nūr b. Mujāhid 539, 541
Nyaghse, *na* 187
Nyaka 431
Nyakumbiru, *mwene mutapa* 396
Nyakyusa 512, 514, 515, 644, 645
Nyambo Kapararidze, *mwene mutapa* 390–1, 392, 393
Nyamwezi 11, 363, 498, 500, 503–4, 644 644
Nyanaoase 300, 302, 311
nyancho 282, 287
Nyandarua (Aberdare) mts 495
Nyang'ori 493
Nyangwila 506
Nyanza 482–4, 485, 494
Nyarwa 475
Nyaturu 499
Nyazina 503
Nyiha 501, 511
Nyika 531
Nyisamba 503–4, 506
Nyitumba 504, 505–6
Nyoro 472–6; *see also* Bunyoro
Nzega 507
Nzhelele valley 406
Nzima 297, 313, 588
nzimbu shells 332, 339, 340
Nzimiro, F. I. 255n.
Nzinga 8, *353ff.*
Nzoia r. 485
Nzowa 511

oba 4, 223, 240, 249, 250
Obanosa, *oba* 228
'Obeah' 614
Obia 256
Obiri Yeboa 303, 304, 305
obong 268
Obutong (= Old Town) 267
ochre 494
Odienne 183
odwira festival 318
Oedasoa 443
O'Fahey, R. S. 9n.
Offin 297
Ofori Dua 311
Ofori Panyin 311
Ofusuhene Apenteng 299
Ogaden 553
Ogba oracle 271
Ogbanika 271
Ogboni 241–2
Ogidiga 254
Ogio 256
Ogoja 257

Ogot, B. A. 483n, 484n., 489n., 644
Ogowe r. 346
Ogun r. 230
ojaq 145
Ojigi, *alafin* 229–30, 232, 242
Okai Koi 300
Okango 332
Okposi 271
Okrika 254, 269
Old Cairo 21
Old Calabar 258, 264, 268, 272
Old Oyo 250
Old Town 267
'Old Whydah' 237–8
Olifants r. 422, 454
Olimi III 576, 481
Oliver, R. 644
olpul 494
olu of Warri 227, 240; of Ilaro 232
Oman 507, 526, 532, 533, 536, 551, 553; Omani Arabs 469, 530, 532
Omdurman 56
Ondo 226
Ondonga 423
Ongamo (= Ngassa) 495
oni 230
Onilahy r. 462
onisare 232
Onisile, *alafin* 229
Onitsha 255, 257, 271, 273, 274
Onyili-ora 271
Oorlams 416
Opoku Ware 312, 313, 314, 315, 317, 323, 324
oppression 36–7, 39, 604ff.
Orange Free State 411, 413, 418, 642
Orange r. 416, 419, 422, 424, 425, 436, 451, 458, 641
Oranmiyan 223
Ormans 151–2, 211, 220
Oromo (= Galla) 539ff.; *see also* Galla
Ortiz, F. 650
Osei Bonsu 323
Osei Kwadwo 9, 315, 316–17
Osei Kwame 323
Osei Tutu 303, 304, 305, 313
Osogbo 229
Osogo, J. 644
ostrich feathers 22, 87, 221
ostrich eggs, 401; shell beads 420; pendants 382
Osu 310, 312
Oti r. 188
Ottoman Empire 2, *14ff.*, 34, 37, 52, 65, 66, 81, 119, 120, 145, 147, 538, 541, 544, 546, 550, 551, 563, 623, 624, 647; practice and organization 18, 19; conquest of Egypt 137, 623
Otutu shrine 303, 305
Ould Dede, Muḥammad (? = Waldid) 109
Ovambo 422, *423–4*, 638
Ovimbundu 350, 351, 355, 357, *359ff.*, 376, 638
Owerri 254, 257, 271, 273
Owerri Daba 271
Owo 226, 228
Owu 229, 251
oxen, pack 90; riding 402
Oyo 6, 90, 223, *229ff.*, 234, 236, 237, 238, 240, 241, 247, 250ff.
Oyoko clan 303, 304
Oyo Mesi 241–2
Ozanne, P. 283n., 635
Özdemir Pasha 17
Ozuzu 255

Pachai, B. 642, 644, 645
Pachana 281
Padhola 485
padroado 331
Paez, Pero (Jesuit) 548–9, 647, 648
Pageard, R. 632
Pai (Swaziland) 431
Paiva Manso: *see* Manso
'palace chiefs' 240
palm products 229, 233, 253, 276, 346, 364, 599
Palmares 611, 612 and n.
Palmer, H. R. 68n., 70n., 73n., 75n., 76n., 83n., 90n., 91n., 108n., 109n., 110n., 121n., 126n., 135n., 138n., 627
Palo 435–6, 438
Paluo 472
Panama 602, 617
Pangani r. 506, 509, 510
Panjim 642
Pâques, V. 632
Parakou 191
Paraotte (= Phalaborwa) 409
Pare 494, 496, 497, 500, 644
Pares, R. 649
Park, Mungo 178 and n., 180 and n., 181 and n., 186, 193 and n., 212, 213 and n., 214n., 215 and n., 216 and n., 296, 601, 631
Parry, A., 584n.
Partridge, C. 634
pasha: Algeria 145, 147; Timbuktu *154ff.*, 161–2, 163, 167, 168–9, 170; Tripoli 95
pashalık of Timbuktu 142, 148, 152ff.
pastoralism 7, 41–2, 51, 98, 106, 113, 207, 413, 416, 419, 420, 429, 451, 457, 461, 464, 483, 492, 510, 540, 547, 552, 562, 563, 567

Pate 530, 532, 533, 536
Patterson, J. R. 627, 651
Patterson, O. 607n.
Paul V, Pope 332, 355
Paulitschke, P. 647
Pawlos (monk) 646
pawning 88
pazi 510
Pearce, F. B. 506n.
pearls 22
Pearson, J. D. 624, 626
Pedi 408, 410, 412
Pedro II (Kongo) 336
Pedro IV (Kongo) 341–2
Pehla 432
Peiser, F. E. 647
Peki 310
Pellow, T. 630
Pemba island 505, 530, 536
Pende 354, 363, 366, 369, 375
Penn, A. E. D. 625
Penn, W. 600
pennisetum 283
Pepel 276, 281, 291
pepper 5, 231, 249
Pereira A. B. Bragnança 519n.
Pereira, F. M. E. 646
Pereira do Lago, B. M. 404 and n.
Perekule dynasty 265, 266, 269
Peres, Damião 285n.
Peresuo 256
perfumes 87, 90
periodical literature 624, 625, 635
peri ogbo 263
Pernambuco 594, 612
Perron, A. 626
Perruchon, J. 646
Persia 15, 564; Persian Gulf 532
Person, Y. 183, 280n., 632, 633
Peru 602
Pétion 600
Phalaborwa 407, 409–10
Pheto 413
Philadelphia 605
Philip II (Spain) 65
Phiri clan 516, 519, 520
Phodzo 523
Phoka 512
Phuti 432
Pike, R. 649
Pilansberg 413
Pilgrimage (Muslim) 12, 14, 19, *21–2*, 37, 51, 54, *57*, 61, 63, 65, 70, 78, 82, 93, 94, 97, 98, 100, 103, 110, 121, 128, 129, 130, 133, 191, 551; hostel 94, 99; commander of Pilgrimage 22, 25, 26, 27, 32, 33, 37
Pindiga 134
Pinto de Miranda, A. 405
Piquetberg 453
pirates and corsairs 120, 465, 469, 630
pitso 417
plague 39, 118–19, 340; *see also* epidemics
plantations 246, 358, 536, 590, 592, 604, 608, 620, 621
Plettenberg, Governor van 455
Plumptre, Anne 447n.
poço dos negros 582
Pogge, P. 371n., 638
Pokot 487, 493, 494
Polane 432
Polanyi, K. 636
poles, export 460
Pombal, Marquis 398
pombeiros 336, 343, 354, 355, 357
Poncet, C. 647
Pongola r. 425, 431, 432
poor whites 620, 621
Popo 233, 235, 236, 238, 242, 614
population 3, 4, 8, 22, 59–60, 91, 233, 256, 258, 273, 292, 303, 326, 351, 360, 363, 364, 366, 368, 384, 404, 411, 414, 415, 419, 429, 445, 448, 468, 497, 527, 574, 602ff.,
poro 280, 295
Porte, the 119, 145; *see also* Ottoman Empire
Portendick 201, 222
porters 1, 339, 340, 358, 603
Port Loko 278
Porto, Silva 638
Porto Bello 592
Porto Novo 90, 230, 231, 237, 250, 252
Portugal: and abolition 601; defeat 147, 148; intelligence reports 533; slaves in 582–3, 648; trade in Europe 592
Portuguese: in Central Africa 4, 246, 328, 329, 331, 333, 348, 350, 353, 356, 376, 383; in eastern Africa 469, 516, 517, 518, 527ff., 534, 535; in Ethiopia 538, 544, 549, 556; in Guinea and Cape Verde Islands 221, 259, 284, 296, 305, 319; in Red Sea and Indian Ocean 15, 21, 550, 551; in South America 347, 607, 615; in southern Africa 391, 397, 407; language 356, 444; sources 202, 280, 256, 290, 404, 423, 427, 428, 437, 470, 526, 579, 581, 637, 640; traders and mulattoes 219, 295, 336, 337, 340, 361, 389–90, 391, 439
Pory, John 579
Posselt, F. W. 638
Potosi mines 592
pottery 253, 257, 259, 283, 300, 311, 317, 329, 364, 382, 384, 401, 420, 428, 430

poultry 233
Pra r. 297, 312; Pra-Offin confluence 297, 303
Prampram 312
prazos 358, 392, 397–8, 641; *prazo* holders 392, 398, 457, 520, 645
'presents' 122
Prester John 578
Pretoria 409, 410
price control 29
Priestley, M. and Wilks I. 635
Prietze, R. 83n., 95n.
Principe 336
Prins, A. H. J. 534n.
prize money 88
production 5, 286, 295, 401, 417; *see also* agriculture; crafts, *etc.*
Prosser, G. 610
protection money 28
Prutky, Remedio 647
Puerto Rico 620
Pulana 431
Pungu a Ndongo 358, 360
Purchas S. 515, 579, 580
pygmy 327

qāḍī 92, 115, 133, 154, 158, 164, 192, 197, 198, 200, 218, 551
Qādiriyya 53, 56, 170, 171, 198
qā'id 152, 154, 155, 158, 161–2, 168, 170
Qānṣawh al-Ghawrī 15
Qānṣawh Bey 26
Qānūn-nāme 18, 20, 37
Qarri 41
qaṣaba 150, 155, 158
al-Qaṣar al-Kabīr battle; *see* Alcazar
Qāsimiyya 20, *26–8*, 30, 31, 33, 35
Qayla 556
Qayṭās Bey 30
Qāzdughliyya 20, 29, 31, 32, 33
Qerlos, *abuna* 575
qibat 555; *qibatoch* 556, 558, 565
Qibla 151, 200
qottu 552
Quakers 599
Qua Qua Coast 294
'Quashee' 607, 610
Quebec 602, 621
Quelimane 391, 519
Quenum, M. 234n.
quilombos 611
Quoja (Koya) 278, 279
Quraysh 26, 136
Qusayr 21, 57
Qwabe 430
Qwara 566, 568, 569, 570, 571

Rabai 535
Rabaratavokoka 461
Rābiḥ 113
racism, racial antagonism 5, 450, 587–8, 589, 590ff., 607, 648, 657
al-Radaniyya, battle 17
raffia 7, 249, 259, 369, 371, 374, 382; *see also* cloth; palm-fibre
Rahad 43
Rahanweyn Somali 543
Raheita 543
Rahesaf 463
al-Rahmaniyya, battle 37
raids 86, 107, 113, 115, 117, 123, 124–5, 168–9, 176, 438, 449, 452, 463, 466, 467, 488, 510, 528, 538, 541, 543, 553
rainfall 384, 385, 388, 419, 429, 433, 449, 456, 553
rainmaking 407, 427, 488–9, 490, 508
Rajab, regent 47, 51
Ralambo 468
Ramabulana 406
Ramadan 76, 77
Ramaḍān Bey 81
Rançon, A. 206n.
Randles, W. G. L. 638
Ranger, T. O. 403n.; Ranger, T. O. and Kimambo, I. 523n., 642
ransom 88, 104, 390
Rarabe 436
Ra's al-Fīl (= Qallabat) 46
ras bitweded 565, 570–1, 572, 573
al-Rashīd, Mawlāy 148–9, 156
Ratelband, K. 337n.
Ratsimilaho 467
Rattray, R. S. 628, 634
Ravahiny, Queen 467
Raynal, Abbé 600
Redinha, J. 638
Red Nation (Nama) 424
Red Sea, 15, 17, 21, 57, 538, 549, *550ff.*, 563, 647; trade *550ff.*, 563
Red Sea Hills 57
refugees 50, 137, 365, 534
Reindorf, C. 311, 634
religion, animist: Central Africa 338, 342, 356, 370, 371; Ethiopia 562, 577; Madagascar 467; New World 613, 618, 619; southern Africa 385, 395, 398, 404, 427; Sudan 104, 136, 159, 167, 171, 184, 193, 198, 211; savanna 187, 190, 194, 202
religion, snycretic 9, 338, 613–14
religious controversy, Ethiopia 549, *555ff.*, 558, *569ff.*, 573, 575
religious orders, Ethiopia 555, 558, 565, 570ff.

renegades (Christian) 87, 100, 145, 152, 154
repatriation 296
resident (at court) 354, 355, 362
resistance 4, 126, 158, 163–4, 195–6, 226, 290–1, 294, 301, 315, 336, 353–4, 378, 399, 439–40, 443, 528, 533, 610
reth 487, 488
Reubeni, David 41, 49, 52, 625
Réunion 601
revolts 18, 23, 24, 27, 29, 34, 39, 44, 94, 103, 128, 143, 161–2, 166, 294, 315, 340–1, 354, 391, 397, 530, 549, 556, 558, 568, 570, 571, 598, 609ff., 616
Rezende 391 and n.
rhinoceros 99
ri'āsa 30, 33
Ribe 535
rice 210, 283, 290, 292, 295, 445, 460, 468, 530, 603
Richardson, J. 98 and n.
Richer, A. 631
Riḍwān Bey al-Faqārī 25–7, 34
Riḍwān Kâhya al-Julfī 31
van Riebeeck, J. 441, 424n.
Van Riebeeck Society 641
Rift Valley 492, 494
rimaibe 210, 294
Rimfa 82
Rio de la Plata 592
riropenga 403
Ritchie, C. I. A. 203n., 632
Rivara, J. H. da Cunha 395n.
Riversdale 442
Rivières du Sud 183, 218
Rivier Zonder End 442
rizaq jayshiyya, rizaq aḥbāsiyya 19–20
roads 84–5, 141
Robbins, C. 478n.
Roberts, A. D. 500n., 510n., 512n., 644, 645
Robespierre 600
Robinson, D., Curtin, P. D., Johnson, J. 632
Robinson, K. R., 404n., 638, 641
Rodney, W., 5, 275n., 347n., 618n., 632, 633
Roemer, R. F. 319n.
Rogers, Joel 649
Rogers (family) 295
Roggeveld 454
Roka 410
Rolong 412, 415, 418
Roma, Francesco da 636
Rome 332
Roodezand 446
Roscoe, J. 643
Rosetta 23, 37, 122
Ross, R. 445n., 450n.
Rossini, C. Conti 646, 647, 648
Rouch, J. 631
Rougerie, G. 314n.
Rovuma r. 527
Royal African Company 220, 308, 320, 589, 593, 617
royal residence 52, 401, 404; *see also musumba*
royal treasure 465
Rozvi 7, 8, 9, 395, 398–408, 462, 466, 520, 638, 641
Rratlou 415
Rubāṭ 42, 43
Rudolf, Lake 486, 492
Rufiji r. 506
Rugujira 476
Ruhinda 500, 515
Rujumbura 475
Rukwa, Lake 500, 503, 506
rum, 319, 347, 354, 382, 594
rumāt, al-rumāt 152, 155
runde 210
Ruregeya 477
Rusillon, H. 640
Russia 34, 35, 88, 584
Rustenburg/Marico district 411, 413
Rusuubi 500
Ruvu r. 509
Rwanda 9, 469, 472, 473, 474, 475, *476–7*, 500, 644
Rwebishengye 476
Ryangombe 9, 478
Ryder, A. 228n., 633

Sá, Salvador Correia de 339, 340n., 354
Sabaluqa gorge 40
Sabarkusa, battle 572
Sabbaboye 211
Sabe 229, 230, 233
Sabi r. 394, 407
Sabiny: *see* Sebei
Sabun, 'Abd al-Karīm 63, 66, 67, 69, 72, 74, 75, 77, 81, 85, 89, 92, 99, 121, 141
sachiteve 386
Saco, J. A. 650
sacrifice, 248, 286
Sa'd (Ja'alī ruler) 47, 49
Sa'dāb clan 49
Sade, Marquis de 606
al-Sā'dī 154n., 161, 174, 175, 192, 197, 198, 205, 630–1
Sadia 460, 462, 465
Sa'did dynasty 148, 629
Safavid dynasty 15, 26
Sagali chiefdoms 504, 507
Sagara (= Nyitumba) 504, 645
Sahara 67, 82, 98, 105, 110, 118, 578

Sahel 114, 168
Ṣaḥīḥ (of al-Bukhārī) 149
Sahle Sellassie 576
Sa'īd b. Aḥmad 533
Sa'īd b. Ibrāhīm Sori 210
Saifawa 58, 62, 94, 629
St Anthony 342
St Augustine Bay 462, 463
St Domingue 526, 597, 598, 602, 609, 610, 611, 618, 650
St Ewostatewos (order) 555, 570
St John r. 283
St Joseph, fort 219–20, 221
St Louis 181, 203, 221
St Lucia 601
St Paul r. 283
Saint-Père, J. H. B. 632
St Vincent 621
St Vincent de Paul 104
Sakalava 8, 9, 385, *462*, 464, 468, 640, 641
Sakalava r. 464
sake cloth 284, 285
Salaga 190, 314
Sālāmat Shuwa 111
sal-ammoniac 23
Sale 146
Ṣāliḥ Bey 33, 34
al-Salihiyya, battle 35
Salisbury archives 638
salt, salt trade: 7, 86, 91, 113, 126, 144, 168, 181, 202, 216, 217, 229, 231, 257, 259, 285, 339, 344, 346, 355, 359, 374, 376, 379, 382, 384, 509, 512; salt mines, salt pans, salt working 98, 113, 154, 233, 252, 308, 361, 378, 543, 554, 563, 594
Salt, H. 541n.
saltpetre 23, 146
Salum 280, 281, 283, 285, 290
Sama (Kabu) 281, 287
Samba Lam 205
'Sambo' 607, 610
Samburu Masai 491, 492, 495
Sammāniyya 56
Samo 185
San 420 and n., 423, 424, 439, 443, 452, 640
Sana 174
Sancho, Ignatius 585
Sandawe 499
Sande 280
Sane clans 282
Sanga 378
Sangi 496
Sangu 508
Sanhaja 167, 199
Sankarani r. 209
Sankong 293
Sankuru 364
Sansanding 181, 217
Sansanne-Mango 189, 190, 194
Sanūsīya 128
Sanyati r. 392
São Salvador (Kongo) 331, 332, 337, 338, 341
São Sebastião 519
São Tomé 259, 329, 331, 333, 334, 336
Sapi 278, 279, 282
al-Ṣaqlī 158
Sara people, Sara-Majingai 132
Saramaka 612
Sarkin Gobir 72, 125
Sarkin Kano 73
Sarkin Nupe 90
Sarwa 415
Sassoon, H. 645
satigi, silatigi 152, 205, 206, 211
Saulspoort 413
Saunders, C. C. 641
savanna belt 10, 64
Say (Lower Nubia) 17
Say (on Niger) 190
Sayf b. Sulṭān 553
Sayyid Aḥmad al-Badawī 24
Sayyid Sa'īd b. Sulṭān 509, 533
Sayyidunā 200
Scandinavia 589, 597; *see also* Danes
Scarcies r. 278, 293
Schapera, I. 418, 639, 640
Schebesta, P. 640
Schechter, R. 377n.
Schmidt, P. 645
Schoffeleers, M. 523n., 624, 625
Schofield, J. F. 401n., 428 and n.
Scholtz, J. du P. 444n, 641
Schurhammer, G. 517n.
scientific exploration 296, 601
Scobie, E. 649
'sea' power 480
Sebei (Sabiny) 494
Sebina, A. M. 638
'secret societies' 241, 259, *263ff*., 279
sedentary population 40, 50
Sedi 208
Sefwi 296, 297, 312, 313
Sega Gaye 215
Sega Lijoch 556
Segu 160, 164, 175, 177, 180, 184, 185, 186, 193, 217
Seguela 183
sekiapu 263
Sekondi 320
Seku Wattara 184
Sela 362
Selīm I 14, 17, 38, 623
Semakokiro 480

Semhar plain 550
Seminoles 622
semitic language 552
semiticized elements (Ethiopia) 546, 547, 548, 559, 570, 574, 576
Sempi ward 310
Sena 386, 389, 390, 393, 397, 399, 519; battle 385
Senegal, hinterland 12; lower 63, 152, 203, 221; middle 152, 217, 219, 220, 221; upper 216, 603; valley 179, 199, 200, 211, 596, 631
Senegambia 110, 144, 181, *216ff.*, 289, 589, 603, 631, 633
senna 22, 23, 81
Sennar 22, 41, 45, 46, 49, 51, 57, 99, 547–8, 563, 564, 567
Senufo 182, 183, 184, 197
Seoke 415
Serer 276, 281, 283, 289, 633
serfs 289, 323, 372, 478, 582, 586
Seri 208
serin (= *bisserin*) 286
Serin Donso 286
Serin Ndakaru (= Dial Diop) 204
Serse-Dingil *545ff.*, 558, 559, 560, 561
sertanejo ('backwoodsmen') 361–2
servants, Khoi 452, 456; in Europe 584ff.
service: carrier, labour, military, roadwork 340, 358, 392
Setlagodi 416
Setlagole r. 415
settlement, resettlement: of nomads 106, 138, 548, 552, 559–60, 562; white 435, 439ff., 445; colonies 593; African in Madagascar 458
Seville 583, 592
Seychelles 601
Shā'a Maka 174
Shādhiliyya 54
Shafi'i school 53
Shāh Ismā'īl 15
Shāhsuwāroghlū Ghāzī Muḥammad Pasha 27, 28
Shai 310
Shaka Zulu 399, 415, 428, 430, 432, 639
Shambaa 510, 644
Shango 614
Shangwe 394, 402
Sharī'a 53, 69, 80, 82–3, 92–3, 102, 198, 210, 214; courts 38, 42
Sharif 42, 53, 90, 95, 115, 128, 137, 138, 157, 554; Sharifian dynasty 148, 150, 154, 156; *see also Ashrāf*
Sharīf (sultan of Wadai) 97
Sharp, Granville 586
al-Shāṭir Buṣaylī 'Abd al-Jalīl 45n., 624
Shaw, Stanford J. 623
shaykh 146; *shaykh al-balad* 30, 31, 36, 38
Shāyqiyya 23n., 44, 50, 72, 563
Shayṭān Ibrāhīm Pasha 28
shea butter 318, 381
Shebele r. 543
sheep, shepherds, 107, 422, 436, 441, 452, 454
Shekhu Aḥmadu Lobo 178, *198*
shells (sea) 382; *see also* cowries; *nzimbu*
Shendi *49*, 54, 57, 137
Sherbro 278, 279
Shibayka, Makkī (Mekki Shibeika) 624
shields 70, 71, 72, 89, 465
Shilluk 11, 41, 44, 54, 486, 489
Shinduru 490
Shinje 355, 366, 376
Shinqit 149, 201
Shirazi 528–9, 534
Shire r. 517–18, 520, 523
Shoa 539, 544, 553, 554, 555, 557, 560, 562, 567, 573, 575, 576, 577
Shona *394ff.*, 398, 406, 409
Shorter, A. 503n., 506n., 644
Shoshong hills 415
Shukriyya nomads 47
Shungwaya 513
Shurbubba 200, 202
Shuwa Arabs 63, 105, *111*
Shyaam 368
Sibotu, *na* 187
Sicard, H. von 403n., 638
Sidama peoples 10, 546, 561, 562
Sidama plateau 561
Sīdī Aḥmad 126
Sīdī al-Mukhtār al-Kabīr 170, 171, 632
Sidibe, B. K. 282n., 287n., 635
Sīdī Muḥammad 147, 150
Sīdī Ṣiddīq al-Kuntawī 170
Sīdī 'Umar 170
Sierra Leone 95, 209, 221, 273, 278, 279, 283, 292, 296, 586, 601–2, 617; peninsula 278
Sihanaka peoples 466
Si'ile Kristos 549
Sikhomo 433
Silberhauer, G. B. 640
silks 87, 90, 324, 355, 386, 388
Silva, A. da 640
silver 85, 388, 417n., 592
simba mwene ('lion-king') 511
Simbeya 511
Simien 544, 546, 548, 557, 575
Sinai Desert 15
Sinān Pasha 23
Singida 498–9, 645
Singo 406

sīpahīs 24
Sira Bo 179
Sire Sawa Lamu, *satigi* 211
Sisibe 206
'Skeleton Coast' 422
Skins: *see* hides and skins
Slatin, Rudolf von 625
Slave Coast 593, 617
slave: emancipation 103–4; labour 3, 520, 602ff.; -owning 97; -raiding 22, 58, 65, 86, 101–2, 113, 131–2, 134, 149, 244, 247, 248, 251, 260, 269, 290, 291, 294, 318, 319, 322, 325, 343, 355, 357, 363, 372, 374, 378, 383, 466; as spoils of war 69, 77, 143, 181, 220, 374; revolts 103
slavery 651; in America 590ff.; in Europe 581ff., 583, 584, 589; chattel slavery 581, 585, 589, 590
slaves: agricultural and domestic 5, 7, 86, 94, 95, 98, 99, 105, 143, 167, 181, 210, 246, 274, 291, 292, 293, 298, 322, 323, 358, 372, 381, 448, 581, 603; as craftsmen 98; as porters, miners, salt workers, canoemen 98, 261, 264, 592, 603; as soldiers and officials 9, 44, 55, 72, 74, 87, 98, 99, 100, 144, 149, 157, 177, 181, 185, 202, 231, 353, 397, 400, 545, 556, 566; as tribute and gifts 81, 107, 122, 141, 154, 231, 376; as wealth 218; freed, 'free blacks' 104, 545, 582–3, 584–5, 586, 591, 605, 610ff., 620, 621; importance 59, 105, 261; incorporation 97ff., 105, 289, 293, 372; luxury 99; Muslim 448; runaway 103, 357, 452, 454, 456, 606, 610ff.; status and condition 102–3, 214, 289, 293, 452, 584–5, 606; stereotypes 607, 615ff.; white 88, 104–5, 620
slave trade 1, 3, 4
  Egypt and eastern Sudan 22, 23, 50
  central Sudan 63, 64, 87, 100, 101, 113
  western Sudan and Senegambia 181, 202, 207, 209, 216, 217
  Guinea 243, 247, 259, 261ff., 285, 299, 318
  Central Africa 325, 329, 339, 346, 351–2, 353, 354, 361, 374–5
  Madagascar 463, 465
  eastern Africa 467, 468, 525, 533, 536
  Ethiopia 546
  Atlantic 3, 90, 99, 143, 144, 210, *260ff.*, 290, 293, 318–19, 346, 350, 351, 377, 383, 524, 582, 594ff., 649
  Indian Ocean 3, 407, 460, 465, 467
  Saharan 99, 150, 272, 292
slave trade: abolition and emancipation 88, 296, 586, 597ff., 601, 609–10
slave villages 44, 55, 99, 290, 291
smallpox 102, 315, 453
Smeathman (botanist) 296
Smith, A. 404n., 433n., 641
Smith, Abdullahi 628
Smith, M. G. 628
Smith, P. 633
Smith, R. S. 634
smiths 32, 259, 271, 284, 333, 345, 604; *see also* copper, iron
'smuggling' 343, 362
Sneeuwbergen 425, 454
So 62, 68, 75, 113
soapstone carving 401
Sobo 259
soda 88
Sofala, 386, 407, 409, 527, 531
Soga, J. H. 639
Soh, Siré Abbas 214n., 632
Sohantye 192
Sohio 336, *337ff.*, 340
Sokoto 61
solategi 280
Solima Dyalonke 208, 209
Somali 540, *541ff.*, 552, 553; Somalia (modern) 553
Somerville 417
Somigli di S. Detole, T. 647
Son Bawa ('the Desirer of a Slave') 59
So N'gafata 74
Songhay empire 62, 64, 65, 66, 78, 114–15, 117, 120, 129, 137, 142, 154, 158, 159, 160, 165, 174, 182, 185, 191, 192, 196, 631; independent 165, 190, 192
Songo (Central Africa) 355, 361
Songo (East Africa) 507
Soninke 142, 174, 197, 205, 217, 286
Sonjo 492
Sonko clan 282
Sonni 'Alī 165, 185, 192
sorghum 364
Sori Maudo: *see* Ibrāhīm Sori
Soriya 210
Soso 244
Sost Ledet 570, 571, 573, 575
Sotho 8, 406, 407, 409, *410ff.*, 417, 429, 431, 639; Sotho-Tswana peoples 410ff. 639
Soubise 585
sources: consular 628–9, 630; linguistic evidence 71; oral tradition, evidence 625, 627, 629, 631, 632, 634, 635, 637, 638–9, 640, 642–3
Sousa, Francisco de (Jesuit) 396 and n.
South, the (of mainland North America) 591, 600, 610, 611, 620
South Carolina 615, 617

Southall, A. W., 643
southern Africa 8, *384ff.*
South-West Africa *419ff.*
Southwold, M. 643
Souza, Dona Ana de (= Nzinga) 353
Souza, João Correia de 335
Spain, Spaniards 53, 65, 119, 148, 154, 221, 338, 581, 589, 591, 592, 594, 611, 648
Spaniard, anon 70
Sparrman, A. 444n.
spears 149, 395
spices 21, 36; 'spice merchant' 53
spoils of war: *see* booty
Starrenburg, W. A. 453n.
state formation and building: cattle basis 7–8, 411; centralization 6, 11, 61–2, 143, 192, 357, 402, 514–15, 523, 559, 561, 562, 576, 612; consolidation 58–9, 91, 114, 188, 247, 312, 470, 567; decline 4, 10, 337, 383, 554–5, 557–8, 569, 576; expansion, territory and population 302, 312, 368, 462, 524; external influences 116, 139, 292, 311, 360, 473, 500, 522; Islam 93, 116, 194, 197, 208, 576; nomads and hunters 105ff., 113, 570; territory 226, 501; trade 62, 91, 269, 276, 383, 419, 526
stateless peoples 7, 182–4, 189, 195, 197, 276, 383, 420, 472, 482, 484, 488, 526
Stavenisse 428, 430
Stayt, H. A. 639
Stel, S. and W. A. van der 445, 446, 448, 453n.
Stellenbosch 445, 446, 450, 452, 453, 454
Stenning, D. J. 628
Stewart, C. C. 630
stockades 74, 424
Stone Age peoples (southern Africa) 419, 420, 422, 423
stone buildings 401, 409, 460, 642; stone-walled villages 411, 413
Storms r. 442
story-telling 615, 618
stratification (social) 38, 223, 268, 276ff., 289, 290, 292, 318, 417, 458, 477; *see also* estates
'strong names' 232
Stow, G. W. 431 and n., 640
Strandes, J. 642
Stuart, J. 639
students 32, 95, 97, 112, 589
Suakin 17, 26, 50, 55, 57, 551, 563, 567
Suba 40, 41
Sudan: eastern 12, 22, 28, *40ff.*, 51, 52, 57, 624, 626; southern 469, 486; west and central 6, 12, 14, 22, *148ff.*, 153ff., 578, 629, 938
Sudan Notes and Records 625
'Sudanese' slaves 616
Suez 21, 23
Sufi 52, 53, 54, 110, 147
sugar 3, 21, 146, 357, 364, 526, 594–5, 547, 599, 603, 604, 606
Ṣughayyirūn 54, 56
Suid-Afrikaanse Argiefstukke 641
Suku 354, 369, 376
Sukuma 503–4, 505, 507, 515
Sulaymān, *askiya* 165, 166
Sulaymān (Bagirmi) 109
Sulaymān (pasha of Timbuktu) 155, 159
Sulaymān Bal 211, 212, 214
Sulaymān Solong 51, 139
Sule Ndyaye, *satigi* 206
Sule Ndyaye II 212
Süleymān 'the Magnificent' 18
Sulima 292
Suma, M. T. Petti 625
Sumbwa 500, 503
sun symbol 505–6
sunbul 50
Sundays r. 425, 434
Sundiata 182, 282
sungura 618
Sunna 92
Sunsan 176
Supet, *ol-oiboni* 492
Surat 408, 533
Suret-Canale, J. 632
Surinam 592, 609, 611
Sus 151
Susenyos, king of kings 43, *147ff.*, 555, 559, 563
Susu 207, 276, 280, 281, 283, 287, 289, 292–3, 294
Sutoko 285
Sutton, J. 645
Swahili language, speakers 469, 505, 506, 509, 514, *528–9*, 530, 532, 534, 535, 536
Swakop r. 422, 424
swana mulopwe 373
swana mulunda 370
Swarteberg 454
Swazi 404, 639; Swaziland 431, 432
Sweden 595
Swellendam 438, 450, 452, 454, 456
swords 22, 55, 87, 90, 121, 122, 301
Syria 14, 15, 23, 34, 35

Ṭabaqāt of Wad Ḍayfallāh 53, 625
Taba zika Mambo 404
Table mt 441
Tabora 507
Tadhkirat al-Nisyān 152 and n., 156n., 160n., 162, 169n., 177, 184, 631

Tadmekket 168–9
Tado 233, 234
Tafilelt 148, 151
Tafo 303, 304
Tafsiru Boggal 212
Tagant 170
Taghaza 167
al-Ṭāhir b. Ibrāhīm 109
Ṭāhir b. al-Nāsir 128
taifa (corsair captains' guild) 145; ('tribes', Mombasa) 535
Taita 496, 497–8, 645
Tāj al-Dīn Muḥammad al-Bahārī, 'the spice-merchant' 53
Tajura, Tadjoura 543, 554–5
Taka 548
al-Taka 43
Takārīr, Takārna (sing. Takrūrī) 57; *see also* Takrur
Takaté 127
Takrur (= Sudan) 156, 169; ancient 199, 204
Tallensi 187
Tama 72, 75
Tambounkane 220
Tana, Lake 546, 557
Tananarive 467, 468
Tanga 536
Tanganyika, Lake 377, 469, 500, 511
Tannenbaum, F. 651
Tano r. 313
Tanta 24, 34
Tantara 468
Tanzania 379, 469, 480, 482, 491, *494ff.*, 503, 527, 530, 640, 645
Taodeni 170, 171
Taqali 44, 55
ta'rīkh 152, 171, 629; *al-Fattāsh* 152n., 159n., 218 and n., 630; *al-Sūdān* 154n., 164n., 167, 174n., 175, 197n., 198n., 204, 205n., 630
ṭarīqa 12
tarjama 629
Tarka r. 456
al-Taras, battle 47
Tatoga: *see* Dadog
Tau 415
Taung 415
Taungs 415
Tauxier, L. 632
Tavhatsindi dynasty 406
tawahdo 555–6
tawba 200
taxes 7, 20, 36, 44, 55, 56, 81, 82, 88, 107, 108, 112, 120, 125, 150, 164, 231, 240, 281, 287, 296, 339, 341, 348, 386, 531, 547, 563, 656
Tchad, Republic 127
Tebandeke 479
technology 1, 4, 5, 8, 9, 11, 91, 275, 333, 367, 596, 604, 605, 622; military 2, 143–4
'Teesee' 213
Tegbesu 238, 243, 247
Teke 345, 346, 348, 364, 637
Tekeze r. 557, 559, 566, 568, 572, 574, 575
Tekla-Giyorgis 572, 573
Tekla-Haymanot (son of Iyasu) 564, 565
Tekla-Haymanot (son of Yohannes Agaw) 571, 572
Tekla-Haymanot order 555–6, 558, 565, 570, 572, 575
Tekto (= *ton-tigi*) 176
Tekyiman 313, 316
Tekyimanhene 316
Tema 312
Tembe 408, 432
Tembien 571
Temne 276, 278, 279, 293
Temple, O. 628
Tenda 210, 276, 281, 291
Tengrella 183
Terik (Nyang'ori) 493
Terrasse, H. 630
Teshie 320
Teso 486
Tete (Zambezi) 379, 386, 389, 390, 396, 405, 516, 521, 524
Tete Ahene Akwa 312
Tetela 328
Tewoflos 565
Tezifon 244
Thabazimbi 413
Theal, G. M. 386n., 389n., 391n., 393n., 523, 640, 641, 642
Thekiso 412, 413
Thelatha Taifa ('Three Tribes') 534, 535
Thembu 434, 437
Thenashara Taifa ('Twelve Tribes') 534
Thomas, E. M. 640
Thomas, L. V. 290n.
Thompson, L. 411n., 412n., 428n., 433n., 434n., 639
Thulare 410
Thurayya: *see* Tireya
Tibesti 98, 102, 126, 127
Tienga 190
Tigre 538 and n., 544, 545, 546, 548, 557, 563, 566, 568, 570, 571, 573, 575, 576, 577
Tihama coast 550
Tijāniyya 214
Tikar 326
Tilho, J. 628

al-Tilimsānī al-Maghribī 53
Tillabery 165
timar 20
timber 5, 349, 597
Timbo 208, 209, 210
Timbuktu 66, 79, 91, 142, 151, 152ff., *158ff.*, 161–2, 167, 168, 176, 188, 198, 626, 630
tin 408, 409, 411
Tingimaro 460
Tiramang Traore 282
Tireya (Thurayya) 139
Tisa Taifa ('Nine Tribes') 534–5
Tjimba 423
Tjiponda 424
Tlemcen 53, 96
Tlhabane 413
Tlhaping 412, *415ff.*, 418, 451
Tlokwa 410
tobacco, smoking 55, 98, 181, 243, 250, 319, 347, 348, 354, 357, 364, 368, 371, 374, 382, 402, 417, 420, 439, 440, 443, 451, 454, 494, 594, 603
Togo 189, 190
Togo Hills 310
Togu 433ff.
Togwa dynasty 394, 398, 401, 402, 403
tobusu 238
Tokot 487
Tokple 236
Tomagra 126, 128
tolls 123, 168, 189, 212, 247, 300, 313, 374
Tombo 166
Tomistas: *see* São Tomé
ton *174ff.*, 193; *ton-dyon* 175, 176–7, 193; *ton-tigi* 174–5, 177
Tondibi, battle 2, 6, 152, 161
Tonga (plateau) 380, 381
Tonga (lower Zambezi) 390, 393
Tongwe 500
Ton-Mansa 177
Tönjes, H. 640
Topkapı Sarayı Arşivi 623
Topotha 487
Torodbe 202, 205, 206, 207, 211, 212, 214, 215, 216
Touba 183
Toussaint l'Ouverture 610
town chiefs 240
towns, cities 42, 47, 49, 91, 115–16, 134, 325, 371, 527–8, 628
trade: and political development 11, 62, *84ff.*, 144, 168, 218–19, 239, 240, 245, 249, 265, 271, 272, 337, 342, 348–9, 354, 369, 370, 384, 400–1, 419, 463ff., 552, 553, 554; coastwise 460, 464; entrepôt 21, 276, 561; external 1, 3, 21, 62, 86, 242, 251, 525, 564; exports 2, 23, 345, 563; imports 22, 23, 87, 345, 371, 375, 376, 382, 385, 386–7; Indian Ocean 527–8; internal 6, 22 89–91, 222, 345, 382, 384, 494, 509; internationalization 596–7; luxury 87, 91, 122; networks 11, 181, 207, 216, 259, 270–3, 346, 363, 371, 384, 409, 423, 436, 480, 497, 506, 530; routes 15, 21–3, 43, 49–50, 62, 66, 127, 129, 176, 181, 195–6, 247, 280, 297, 302, 343, 361, 367, 374, 399, 405, 408, 436, 524, 527, 562, 567; stagnation (Red Sea) 531, 552, 554, 563; trans-Saharan 122, 123, 125–6, 144, 181, 216, 221; war 235; with Europeans 218ff., 223ff., 280, 307, 335, 439, 634
traders and merchants: Arab 83, 541, 551, 553; Dyula 11, 12, 144, 161, 175, 185, 197, 217, 283, 285–6, 294, 317, 632; external 7, 11, 551; Hausa 190, 195; Indian 396, 467, 524, 551, 553; Muslim 193, 250, 386, 390, 517, 549, 551, 576 (*see also* Dyula, Hausa, Indian); Timbuktu 157, 158, 160
trading association 229
trading companies (European) 219, 408, 438, 439
Traill, A. 420n.
trans-continental route 12, 57, 64, 66
transhumance 42, 287, 441
Transorangia 522, 641
transport 1, 66, 90, 105, 126, 346, 448; communications (internal) 6, 10–11, 64, 131, 239, 436
trans-Saharan routes 66, 85, 121, 125, 129, 141, 148, 188, 252
Transvaal 409, 410, 411, 412, 413, 418, 431, 642
trans-Volta Akwamu 309, 312, 320
Trarza Moors 151, 200–1, 212, 222
travel literature 579, 580, 624, 625, 627, 631, 636–7, 638
trekboers 449, 453, 454, 457
Trevor-Davies, R. 591 and n.
triangular trade 593, 596, 597
tribute: Central Africa 340, 346, 372, 374, 377, 379; central Sudan 66, 77, 80, 81, 90, 101, 115, 135, 141; eastern Africa 473, 496, 509, 518; eastern Sudan 42, 44, 46, 48; Ethiopia 561, 568, 573, 575; Fezzan 129; Guinea 227, 231, 232, 281, 298, 300, 301, 302, 312, 318; Portuguese 390, 401 (*see also curva*); southern Africa 399, 402, 414; western Sudan 154, 161, 163, 169

tribute-convoy 19, 23, 372
Trimingham, J. S. 71n., 191n., 647, 648
Trinidad 618
Tripoli 22, 66, 70, 81, 82, 87, 89, 95, 97, 100, 101, 102, 103–4, 119, 188; Arabs 128
Tripolitania (regency) 66, 88, 89, 104–5, 128, 129
tromba 465, 466
Truter 417
tse-tse fly 163, 273, 385, 409
Tshawe 434, 435
Tshiwo 435
Tshwenyane 412
Tsibiri 117
Tsimanatona 462
Tsimanongarivo 462, 464
Tsiribihina r. 460, 464
Tsonga 11, 408, 410, 429, 430
Tsumeb 424
Tswana 385, 402, 405, *410ff.*, 427, 436, 437, 457, 639
Tuareg 64, 69, 78, 80, 89, 98, 99, 101, 105, 107, 108, 110, 112–13, *123ff.*, 135, 160, 163, 164, 167ff., 628, 631
Tuat 125, 126, 170
tubenan 203
Tubu 64, 69, 74, 78, 86, 91, 105, 125, *126ff.*
tubungu 373
Tugela r. 429, 430
Tugo 488
Tugulu (Uticulo) 523
Tuken 493, 494
Tukolor 203, 204–5, 221, 283, 285
tukwata 373, 374
ṭulabā' 202
Tulama 557, 559, 560, 567, 572
ṭulba 24
Tuli 430
Tully, R. 96n., 119n., 120n., 628
Ṭūmān Bāy 15, 17
tumbare 395–6, 402
Tumbuka language 512–13; people 512, 513, 514, 515, 644; Tumbukaland 505, 513, 515
Tunis 22, 65, 81, 86, 87, 89, 96, 104, 119; bey 88
Tunisia (modern) 65; (regency) 66, 88, 104, 145
Tunjur 63, 136
tunka 205–6
tunny fisheries 88
al-Tūnusī, Muḥammad b. 'Umar 79, 89, 103 and n., 141, 625, 626, 627
Tura 127, 129
Turaki Kuka Tunku 83
Turco-Egyptian conquest 11, 48, 49, 50, 57
Turkana 486, 487
Turkey, Turks 530, 538, 550, 556–7 (*see also* Ottoman Empire)
Turkish sources 623; chronicles 623
Tuscany 23, 122
Tutsi 477, 501
Twa dynasty 501, 506
Twi language 189, 297, 313, 612, 619
Twifo 296, 297, 320
tyeddo 202, 204

Ubena 508, 512
Ubiqua 443
Ubisa 511
Ubungu 504
Uburu 271
Udo, R. K. 268n., 274n.
Ufipa 500–1, 506, 511
ufok 259
Ugalla 507
Uganda (modern) 469, 483, 487; Uganda-Kenya border 486
Ughoton 249
Ugogo 506, 508, 511
Ugweno 496
Uhehe 506, 508, 511
Ukambani 497, 498
Ukimbu 498, 503, 504, 506, 508, 511, 644
Ukonongo 503
Ukwu, I. U. 271n.
'ulamā' 20, 21, 37, 39, 45, 149, 157, 158, 160, 168, 169, 191–2, 193, 197, 206, 207, 208, 209, 212, 218
'ulamā' al-sū' (venal clerics) 108
'Umar, al-ḥājj 200, 214
'Umar, *mai* 78, 86, 94, 128, 133
'Umar, Shaykh (Bornu) 81
'Umar b. 'Abdullāh (Koyam) 107, 112
'Umar b. Maḥmūd Aqīt 158, 159
'Umar b. 'Uthmān 92, 107–8
Umayyad pedigree (spurious) 53
Umhlanga rocks 428
umnumzane 427
Umonoha 255, 271
Umuahia 254
Umvoti r. 430
umwàantándi: see *ngabe*
Umzimkulu r. 430
Umzimvubu 427, 428, 431, 433, 436
underdevelopment 6, 275–6
undi 512, 517, 520–1
United States of America 601, 613, 614, 615, 618, 620, 622, 649, 650
Unsa III 45
Unyamwezi 503, 504, 506, 507, 514, 575
Unyanyembe 506, 507

Upare 510
Upper Egypt 17, 23, 26, 27, 28, 31, 32, 33, 34, 35, 36, 37, 57
Upper Guinea Coast 144, 183, 207, 218, 222, 223, 269, 276, 579, 592, 603, 617, 618, 619
'Uqbah b. Nāfi 106
Urhobo people 228
Uruan 258
Urvoy, Y. 105 and n., 124n.
Usagara 506, 508
Usambara 510, 511
Usanga 402, 407, 408
Usere 271
Usukuma 505, 645
Usumbwa 503, 505
Usuman dan Fodio 61, 66, 69, 72, 77, 83, 94, 108, 109, 110, 117, 132
Ute (Owo) 228
Uteve 386, 392, 407, 408
'Uthmān, *mansa* 192
'Uthmān, Pasha 122
'Uthmān, *qāḍī* 201, 203
'Uthmān Bey 31
'Uthmān b. Kaday 41
'Uthmān Pasha al-Ṣādiq 33
Uticulo 523
Utondwe 530
Uways Pasha 23
Uyo 258, 273
Uyui 507
uzama 240
Uzaramo 509–10
Uzdamir Pasha 538
Uzuakoli 271, 273

Vaal r. 413, 417
Vai, 278, 279, 280, 294
Vail, L. 644, 645
Valencia 582
Valkhoff, M. 444n.
Vambe (= Va-Mbo) 431
Vansina, J. 273n., 328n., 364n., 366n., 368n., 373n., 637, 638, 644
Vasconcellos, L. M. de 352
va-shambadzi 379, 397–8, 400
Vatican archives 582n.
Vazimba 464, 467, 468
Vedder, H. 639
veldkornets 450
veldkos 454
Veloso 393n.
Vellut, J.-L. 356n., 369n., 374n., 637, 638
Venda peoples 405–6, 408, 409, 410, 639
Venezuela 594, 602
Venice 23, 121
Vera Cruz 592
Verhulpen, E. 638
Vertua, J. C. 386n.
Victoria Falls 405
Victoria, Lake 470, 472, 480ff., 644
Vili (Mubires) 344, 348, 349, 357
Villiers, C. C. de and Pama, C. 445n.
Vinza 500
Virginia 610, 618
vizier 85, 88, 123, 200, 563
Volney (Chassebeuf, C.-F.) 624
Volta r. 296, 301, 311, 314, 319, 322; basin 187–9, 194, 632
Voltaic languages, speakers 184ff., 632
Voodoo 614, 618
Vugha 511

Wa 187, 195
Wadai, Wadawa 51, 58, 63, 66, 67, 69, 74, 75, 79, 81, 85, 89, 91, 94, 100, 101, 103, 108, 111, 115, 121, 122, 127, 129, 133, *136ff.*
Wad 'Ajīb 41
Wadajo 566, 567, 569
Wad Ḍayfallāh 53, 625
Wade, A. 633
Wadla 572
Wag 557, 566, 572, 574
Wagadugu 186, 196
'Wagalla' 496
Wagera 546, 548, 557
Wahhābī revival 110
Wahiguya 185
Walata Chronicle 170, 176 and n., 631
Walde-Gabri'el 572, 574, 575
Walde Giyorgis (= Bekaffa) 565
Walde-Li'ul 567ff.
Walde-Sellassie 575
Waldid 108–9, 115, 133, 137
Wald Qib 570n.
al-wālī 133
Wali of Wuli 282
Wallo Galla 557, 560, 567, 568, 569, 571, 572, 573, 574
walls (town) 75, 134, 325
Walo 152, 203
Walqayt 548, 578
Walvin, J. 585n., 649
Wand Bewasen 572
Wanga 485
Wankie 405
Wankit r. 572
waqf 19, 56, 57, 59, 112
Wara 137, 138, 141
war chiefs, captains 174, 178, 182, 185, 279
wards (Efik): *see* Houses
Warena 566–7, 571
Warga, *naba* 186

Warmelo, N. J. van 639, 640
Wansbrough, J., 629
Warri 226, 227–8, 256
Wasangarani 190
Wasen-Seged 573, 575
Wassa 296, 297, 315, 320
Wasulu 175, 183, 209
Waterberg 413
Wattara 183, 184, 189
Waveren 454
wax 88, 295, 460, 589, 596
weapons 69, 70, 80, 494; *see also* archers; firearms; shields
weaving 62, 98, 234, 285, 286, 324, 384, 401, 450; *see also* cloth
Webb, C. 433n.
Wegbaja 9, 234, 235–6
weights and measures 64, 84, 141
Welch, S. R. 396n.
wells 202
Weme 236, 237
Weme r. 229, 230, 238
Wenchi 313
Were, G. S. 644
West Atlantic languages 276, 282
West-Central Africa 612, 636ff.
Westergaard, W. 650
western desert 27, 28
West India Company (Dutch) 321, 594, 595
West Indies 347, 584, 585, 586, 593, 596, 598, 612, 649, 650; British 599, 609, 614; French 606
Westphal, E. O. J. 420n.
wheat 21, 446, 447, 448
White Nile 487
White Volta 187
Whydah 233, 234, 235, 236, 237, *243ff.*, 247, 249, 252, 301, 319, 321, 393
Wiet, Gaston 623
Wikangulu 503
Wikar, H. J. 614n.
Wilks, Ivor 6n., 8n., 317n., 632, 635
Williams, E. 649
Willis, R. G. 500n., 643
Wilson, Anne 380n., 638
Wilson, Monica 411n., 639, 640, 641; Wilson, Godfrey and Monica 644
Windus, John 630
Windward Coast 294
wine 326, 355, 446, 447, 594
Wing, J. van 638
Winks, R. 650
Winneba 301, 306
Winyi II 473
Winyi III 475, 476
wire bangles 381
Wissmann, H. von 638
Woeke M. H. O. 456
Woina-Dega, battle 537
Wolof 200, 201, *202ff.*, 212, 221, 283, 284, 603, 632
women 7, 38, 319, 372
women soldiers 236, 315
wood carving, woodwork 257, 259, 283, 612
woollen goods 23
Worodugu 182
writing-paper 22
Wuasinkishu Masai 485, 491, 493, 494
Wukari 134
Wuli (Gambia) 280, 282, 285
wulomo 300, 312
Wurrio 134
Wyndham 584
Wyndham, H. A. 587n.

Xhosa 408, 418, 425, *433ff.*, 451, *454ff.*

Ya'arubi dynasty 532
Yadega, *naba* 186
Yaiyu 108
Yaka 354, 369, 376
Yaka-Suku 363
Yako 186
Yakuba (John Davis) 140
Yala r. 485
Yalunka (= Dyalonke) 281
yams 253, 257, 275, 301, 313, 317, 364
Yanzi-Ambun 363
Yao 11, 379, 380, 513, 520, 521, *524ff.*, 527, 533, 645
Ya'qob 547
Yarse 196
Yatenga 185, 186
Yau Yamba, *basorun* 242
Yedseram r. 68
Yeji 314
Yejju 557, 560, 567, 569, 571, 572, 573, 574, 575, 576
Yekunno-Amlak, House of 569
Yemen 15, 17, 24, 50, 52, 546, 550, 551, 555
Yendi 188
Yendi-Dabari 187
yevogan 238
Yishaq, *bahr-negash* 538, 544, 545, 546
Yo r. 68, 74
Yohannes (Ethiopia) 550, 551, 555ff.
Yohannes Agaw 571
Yoruba, Yorubaland 90, 103, 118, 223, 250, 251, 255, 615, 618, 619; language 613
Yosab, *abuna* 575
Yostos 565
Yūsuf As'ad Dāghir 626
Yūsuf b. Ḥasan 529, 530

Za 238
Zaberma: *see* Jerma
Za-Dingil 547
Zaghawa 138, 140
Ẓāhir al-ʿUmar, Shaykh 34, 35
Zaïre 325n., 327, 363, 369, 380, 638
zakāt 82, 200, 201, 202; *zakāt al-fiṭr* 83
Zamana Mesafent ('era of the princes') 571ff.
Zambezi 2, 325, 362, 376, 379, 384, 389, 405, 407, 458, 469, 515, 516, 517, 518, 523, 524, 527, 637; upper Zambezi 377ff.
Zambezia 517–19, 521, 524, 526, 581; Zambezian interior 385
Zambia (modern) 8, 325n., 369, 376, 379, 390, 511, 516, 637
Zamfara 62, 117, 125
Zande: *see* Azande
Zanzibar 509, 529, 534, 536; town 534
Zaramo 509
Zaria 74, 78, 116, 135
Zawāyā nomads 12, 199, 200–2, 211, 216
zāwiya (pl. *zawāyā*) 126, 147, 170
Zayla 141
al-Zayyānī 150 and n., 151n., 630
Zeila 541, 553
Zeltner, J. C. 72n., 626
Zigua 511
Zimba 389, 515, 516, 517, 522, 524, 527, 531
Zimbabwe: *see* Great Zimbabwe
Zinza 500
Zizi 431–2; Zizi-Bhele 431–2
Zombre, *naba* 186
Zou r. 238
Zoutpansberg mts. 406, 408
Zulu, Zululand 430, 431, 432, 639
Zumbo 343, 376, 379, 397, 399, 400, 401, 405
Zuurveld 434, 455–6

DUE DATE